PENGUIN BOOKS

REAGAN

Bob Spitz is the award-winning author of the biographies *Dearie: The Remarkable Life of Julia Child* and *The Beatles*, both *New York Times* bestsellers, as well as six other nonfiction books and a screenplay. He has represented Bruce Springsteen and Elton John in several capacities. His articles appear regularly in magazines and newspapers including *The New York Times Magazine* and *The Washington Post* among others.

* * *

Praise for *Reagan*

FINALIST FOR THE *LOS ANGELES TIMES*
BOOK PRIZE IN BIOGRAPHY

NAMED ONE OF THE TOP 10 BOOKS OF 2018
BY *PUBLISHERS WEEKLY*

"No biographer has dug as deeply or with such verve into the making of Reagan the star. . . . Energetic and engaging."   —*The Washington Post*

"*Reagan: An American Journey* is a handsome, handy introduction to the twentieth century's last hero."   —*The Wall Street Journal*

"Bob Spitz, whose previous biographical subjects include Bob Dylan, Julia Child, and The Beatles, has written a solid, sweeping narration of Reagan's life, sympathetic but not sycophantic."   —*USA Today*

"This comprehensive examination of America's fortieth president represents presidential biography at its best. Noted biographer Bob Spitz (previous subjects have included The Beatles and Julia Child) researches like a historian, writes like a novelist, does the hard work of providing ample and intelligent context, and remains able to take an evenhanded approach to his subject."   —*Christian Science Monitor* (10 Best Books of October)

"Publication of Bob Spitz's massive biography of Ronald Reagan couldn't have been more timely. . . . A significant marker against which to measure our current politics and political leadership." —*Los Angeles Times*

"A significant contribution to the Reagan literature."
—*The National Review*

"This is a book admirers and critics of Reagan will enjoy. The roots of the conservative movement that gave life to both the party and Trumpism can be found here, and on an even broader level Reagan's life story is a story of America and all its promise." —*Dallas Morning News*

"A balanced, comprehensive view of Reagan and his legacy . . . Spitz manages to evoke Reagan's heyday in the 1980s with compelling clarity—and to suggest how the Gipper's legacy continues to shape twenty-first-century politics. . . . One marvels at the telling details that Spitz manages to get in."
—*Christian Science Monitor*

"If you find yourself longing for the golden age of the Republican Party, brush up on the humble story and folksy charm of our previous celebrity president, whose legacy—for better and worse—still animates politics today."
—*Vulture*

"Bob Spitz's nearly eight-hundred-page book paints a spectacular, sometimes thorny portrait of President Ronald Reagan, the man who is credited with ending the Cold War (and appointing the first woman to the Supreme Court, Sandra Day O'Connor) while, as Spitz writes, struggling to show empathy for victims of AIDS and Americans with great financial burdens."
—*O, The Oprah Magazine*

"Readers of all political stripes will find much to enjoy in this evenhanded intelligently written biography of our fortieth president." —*People*

"This captivating and evenhanded biography of America's first celebrity president, Ronald Reagan, reads like a novel but doesn't skimp on the scholarship. . . . Impressive research, including numerous interviews with a wide array of Reagan cohorts, from 1930s movie star Olivia de Havilland to national security adviser Robert 'Bud' McFarlane, undergirds the exceptional writing. Spitz synthesizes other scholars' analyses, the firsthand memoirs of key players, original press coverage, and archival holdings. Readers need not be Reagan fans or Republicans to enjoy this outstanding biography."   —*Publishers Weekly* (starred review)

"The strictly chronological approach is easy to track, and because the author is such a skilled stylist, the narrative flows smoothly. The major strength of this version is Spitz's consistently diligent effort to provide context beyond just his main subject. . . . Spitz also skillfully portrays numerous supporting characters, especially Reagan wives Jane Wyman and Nancy Davis. A solid entry in the realm of presidential biography."   —*Kirkus Reviews*

"This is the book so many of us have been waiting for: an epic life of one of the most significant presidents in the history of the Republic. In Bob Spitz's graceful and absorbing narrative, Ronald Reagan emerges in all his complexity and charm, a warm yet enigmatic man who did so much to shape the way we live now."

—Jon Meacham, #1 *New York Times* bestselling presidential
historian, Pulitzer Prize winner, and author
of *The Soul of America*

"Bob Spitz's *Reagan* is a masterfully written and well-researched biography of America's fortieth president. All the crescendos and diminuendos of Reagan's vibrant Hollywood and political careers are judiciously investigated. Truly engrossing and monumental!"

—Douglas Brinkley, professor of history at Rice University
and editor of *The Reagan Diaries*

REAGAN

$=$ AN AMERICAN JOURNEY $=$

BOB SPITZ

PENGUIN BOOKS

PENGUIN BOOKS
An imprint of Penguin Random House LLC
penguinrandomhouse.com

First published in the United States of America by Penguin Press,
an imprint of Penguin Random House LLC, 2018
Published in Penguin Books 2019

ISBN 9780143110590 (paperback)

THE LIBRARY OF CONGRESS HAS CATALOGED THE HARDCOVER EDITION AS FOLLOWS:
Names: Spitz, Bob, author.
Title: Reagan : an American journey / Bob Spitz.
Description: New York, New York : Penguin Press, [2018]
Identifiers: LCCN 2018019603 (print) | LCCN 2018025882 (ebook) |
ISBN 9780525560272 (ebook) | ISBN 9781594205316 (hardcover)
Subjects: LCSH: Reagan, Ronald. | Presidents—United States—Biography. |
Governors—California—Biography. | Motion picture actors and
actresses—United States—Biography. | BISAC: BIOGRAPHY & AUTOBIOGRAPHY /
Presidents & Heads of State. | POLITICAL SCIENCE / Government / Executive
Branch. | HISTORY / United States / 20th Century.
Classification: LCC E877 (ebook) | LCC E877 .S75 2018 (print) |
DDC 973.927092 [B] —dc23
LC record available at https://lccn.loc.gov/2018019603

Printed in the United States of America
1   3   5   7   9   10   8   6   4   2

Designed by Gretchen Achilles

To
Barbara Aikman
for her wisdom and generosity
and
Becky Aikman
for the same—and everything else

If the single man plant himself indomitably on his instincts, and there abide, the huge world will come round to him.

—RALPH WALDO EMERSON

If you have a bat in your hand, you have a chance to change the story line.

—REGGIE JACKSON

CONTENTS

PROLOGUE 1

PART 1

DUTCH

PART 2

RONNIE

PART 3

GOVERNOR

PART 4

MR. PRESIDENT

REAGAN

PROLOGUE

Ronald Reagan had lost his way.

Identical corridors splayed through the Hotel Last Frontier like spokes on a wheel, and none of them seemed to lead to the Ramona Room. One spoke led off to the Gay '90s Bar, where the Kirby Stone Four were setting up for their midnight-to-dawn gig. Another cut through the 21 Club Casino, whose rows of ravenous slot machines were clacking away like castanets. The hall to the left emptied into the Carillo Room, a tony watering hole for the after-show crowds, and past that to the Chuck Wagon, its wood-paneled pub. A fifth spoke descended to a subterranean passage known to hotel guests as the Marine Room, offering underwater glimpses into the deep end of the pool. The Ramona Room, for all Ronald Reagan knew, might have been located on Mars.

He stood at the hub, deciding which way to turn, like a piece on a game board. The wrong move would make him late for his own opening night.

The Last Frontier had pulled out all the stops for its Ronald Reagan showcase. The hotel's nightclub was known for its top-flight entertainers, but rarely attracted Hollywood stars. Most actors steered clear of Las Vegas engagements, fearing its seamy aura would tarnish their fame. But Reagan, whose own aura of late had dimmed, had little choice.

He was forty-three and experiencing what he referred to as "some rough sledding," a Hollywood euphemism for a career on the skids. His contract at Warner Bros., where he'd been a studio stalwart since 1936, had ended in a whimper of lowly scripts and lower box-office receipts. Freed to work for any studio, he hadn't fared much better. He made, in his words, "a couple of turkeys"—*Tropic Zone*, an unimaginative action yarn, at Paramount, even though he "knew the script was hopeless," followed by *Law and Order* at Universal, based on a stale, B-western formula. Since then, he'd rejected every dismal script, setting off a six-month drought. It was the longest layoff of his professional career.

Throughout that career, Ronald Reagan had been a reliable if unspectacular movie star, with a body of solid roles to his credit. Pictures like *Knute Rockne, All-American* and *Kings Row* had elevated him from feature player to marquee prominence. His agent, Lew Wasserman, was a powerhouse, the *capo di tutti capi*, with the clout to keep Reagan gainfully employed. In 1947, Reagan had been elected president of the Screen Actors Guild, a position that bestowed prestige even as the parts failed to measure up. And his new wife, Nancy Davis, ten years his junior, attractive and smart, was what Hollywood called a comer. Together, they spent nights dancing at the Mocambo and Ciro's or in their booth at Chasen's, breaking bread with the Dick Powells or the Jack Bennys or the Bill Holdens—Hollywood royalty. On the surface, Ronald Reagan was similarly enthroned.

But in the film business, the surface was usually make-believe. Reagan was still handsome, still virile, still radiantly charming, but he was too old now to play the lead in a romance or action flick, he didn't sing or dance well enough to do musicals, and he wasn't the subtle kind of actor who might get parts in more nuanced fare. So at the moment, the Reagans were in a real crunch.

Money was tight. Having gone for a while without getting his standard $75,000-per-movie fee, Reagan had been dipping into savings to cover his myriad necessities. There was child support to his ex-wife, Jane Wyman, and a new, unexpected baby, Patti, his first with Nancy. He was paying off two homes—a new hideaway in Pacific Palisades and a 350-acre ranch, Yearling Row, in the Malibu Hills—that together required three mortgages. The ranch, in particular, was a financial black hole: $15,000 in new pumps to make the water potable, veterinary care for fifty steer that had contracted pink eye, unanticipated fees to ranch hands. And taxes. *Taxes!* They were enough to send Ronald Reagan's blood pressure soaring. The federal government had him in a chokehold. He had made a serious tax miscalculation that plunged him into debt to Uncle Sam. During World War II, when Reagan served in an Army Air Force stateside unit, he took advantage of a serviceman's right to defer taxes until after the war. Reagan had heard that servicemen after World War I had been forgiven their tax debts, and he gambled on a similar gift the second time around. Gambled—and lost, bumping him into a predatory tax bracket that left him $18,000 in the hole. To make matters worse, in addition to his screen layoff, there had been a freak accident—a broken leg sustained in a charity softball game—that sidelined him for another long stretch, as hospital fees in the five figures piled up.

"I'm living from guest shot to guest shot on television, and an occasional personal appearance," he complained to a friend who had recently thrown him a bone of a role: to narrate a public service film for North American Rockwell, the military manufacturing behemoth, that would pay him scale, around $240.

Money was so tight that he shopped a radio series based on the hijinks "of a Hollywood couple, an Actor and Actress who go into ranching," but no one bit. Then came the biggest blow. Just before Christmas, Reagan accepted a part in a picture called *Prisoner of War* to begin filming at MGM in the spring. But the script, about American captives during the Korean War, was a feeble piece of work designed to take advantage of recent headlines. When Reagan accepted it without so much as a hiccup, Lew Wasserman palmed his client off on a second-string colleague, more or less scuttling their longtime relationship.

Reagan's new agent, Art Park, scrambled to come up with something lucrative. Broadway beckoned, but Reagan was adamantly opposed to moving to New York. Television, still in its infancy, had become a viable option, where an actor of Reagan's particular stature would feel right at home. He had nothing against TV; some of his best friends wound up there. But a *series* . . . just didn't feel right. He was convinced that after two or three years playing the same one-dimensional role—say, a masked man with an Indian sidekick or a father who knew best—it would be difficult for producers to see him as anything else.

When Art Park proposed doing a Vegas nightclub act, Reagan didn't immediately reject it. Yes, it was preposterous, well beneath his standards, but the money Park mentioned was too good to dismiss. Reagan could make as much in two weeks as he could over several months on a picture. And it was easy work. Over the years, as a popular emcee on the mashed-potato circuit—a backdrop that included meetings, rallies, and charitable benefits—he'd introduced hundreds of acts with humorous patter. He was a natural at it. That was all that would be expected of him in Las Vegas.

Billed as "Ronald Reagan Presents," he'd introduce four or five acts each night—a couple of singing groups, a comic, a dancer, whomever the hotel had booked—tell a few jokes, maybe join in a skit with the featured act, nothing he'd be uncomfortable with.

Reagan thought it over. It didn't demean his dignity, it wasn't humiliating work. In essence, he saw himself "as sort of an impresario," like Ted Mack or his old friend Louella Parsons, in whose traveling review he once appeared. That experience, in 1939, had been pretty much of a hoot. "Louella Parsons and Her Stars" crisscrossed the country, playing to packed houses everywhere they landed. He loved cavorting in the skits with Joy Hodges and Susan Hayward; it's where he fell in love with Jane Wyman, another member of the Parsons cast. With the right material, he'd feel at ease.

Reagan's agency, MCA, had deep roots in Las Vegas. Its beginnings in show business, booking talent into nightclubs and ballrooms, gave the agency the kind of primacy that packed Vegas showrooms with its clients. MCA had relationships with every hotel in town. All it took was a phone call to book the Ronald Reagan Show.

The El Rancho was the obvious choice. It was the first resort on the Strip and boasted the largest casino in Nevada, where no less than Howard Hughes was a regular at the blackjack tables. Its lounge, the Round-Up Room, was a Vegas institution, whose recent lineup of headliners included Buddy Hackett, Vic Damone, Nat King Cole, Hoagy Carmichael, and Joe E. Lewis. If one's reputation was determined by the company one kept, Ronald Reagan had nothing to fear.

The deal was negotiated in a matter of minutes, and fell apart in almost as little time. The El Rancho's owner, Beldon Katleman, insisted the show run over the Christmas holiday, which was a deal breaker as far as Reagan was concerned. Christmas with the family was sacrosanct and unfit for Las Vegas. The coup de grâce, however, was the headliner, Lili St. Cyr, one of America's premier strippers, "who left almost nothing to the imagination when she stepped dripping wet out of her onstage bubble bath." Reagan was having none of it, and directed his agent to cancel the deal.

Within minutes, another offer materialized at the Last Frontier, just down the Strip. The Last Frontier held more promise than its name. The hotel was part of a vast resort complex just off US-91, the Last Frontier

Village, one of those kitschy tourist attractions designed to resemble an abandoned ghost town from the Gold Rush days. Guests could visit the Old Trading Post or head over to the stables, with its collection of antique stagecoaches, or ride the bumper cars. The Shooting Gallery boasted a $100,000 collection of guns and pistols. There was a museum of mechanical pianos, and a miniature train traveled around the entire grounds. After a day's sightseeing and with the kids tucked in bed, adults gathered in the hotel's casino and showroom, where a who's who of entertainers played to sellout crowds—Xavier Cugat & His Latin-American Orchestra, Dorothy Lamour, Señor Wences, Zsa Zsa Gabor, Howard Keel, Abbe Lane, and the Liberace/Phil Foster Show. In August, the legendary Dorsey brothers, Tommy and Jimmy, were reunited onstage after twenty years of leading competing bands. The only hitch came when Dorothy Dandridge, the first black actress nominated for an Academy Award for Best Actress, performed. As a condition of her residency, she was warned not to go anywhere near the swimming pool, which was still strictly segregated. When she hinted she might "stick her toe in the water," the pool was suddenly "under construction" and closed to everyone for the duration. Had Ronald Reagan known about the treatment of Dandridge, he might have balked, but that little tidbit had been carefully concealed.

MCA wanted him focused on the showcase, certain he would be scrutinized by tastemakers for future work. It was a demanding routine—two shows a night, three on Saturday, each running a little over an hour and a half—showbiz lite, placing it somewhere just north of vaudeville. He would top-line a bill featuring four frothy acts: the Continentals, a veteran male quartet that mixed barber-shop songs, soft-shoe, and knockabout schtick; the Blackburn Twins, with Evelyn Ward, a glamorous Broadway showgirl and mother of future pop star David Cassidy; the Honey Brothers, a trio of dancing acrobats; and the Last Frontier Dancers, nicknamed the Adorabelles, who high-kicked their way through a chorus line, dressed in skimpy peekaboo costumes.

It was a fast-moving show, with a number of tricky entrances and well-timed choreography, all the more difficult for a nightclub novice who, according to critics, was "no singer or dancer and could scarcely qualify as a comedian."

Ronald Reagan had worked hard to nail down his part. In January, he and the Continentals had set up shop on a Hollywood soundstage, rehearsing bits in sessions that often lasted four hours or more. Nancy sat quietly in a corner of the room, sipping ice water and scribbling notes on a legal pad. "She was a great audience for him," said comedy writer John Bradford, "because she laughed at every one of his jokes." At the outset, Reagan "was rough as a cob," but he "was a fast study [who] must have worked hard at home in the evenings," honing his part after those grueling workouts. "By the end of the first week, he was moving like the rest of us," recalled Ben Cruz, a member of the group. In early February, they tried out the act at the Statler Hotel in downtown Los Angeles, spending a week polishing the routines in front of an audience, at the end of which they were good to go.

Las Vegas, however, presented a different set of circumstances. The audiences were larger—the Ramona Room was a hearty 600-seat theater—and more discerning; they could just as easily wander up the Strip to the Thunderbird, where the Four Aces were appearing, or over to the Sahara for Kathryn Grayson and the Sonja Henie ice show; the Desert Inn's marquee advertised Jackie Miles, billed somewhat extravagantly as "America's Leading Night Club Entertainer and Comedian," while Tallulah Bankhead cavorted at the Sands "in a flimsy, see-through dress that shocked even Las Vegas." The competition was fierce. Ronald Reagan had to be on top of his game.

Not wanting to cut things close, he and Nancy had arrived in Vegas a few days early. The surroundings were still pretty foreign to him. Reagan wasn't a gambler or much of a drinker. He and Nancy kept to themselves and spent their days lounging by the pool with their noses in books. Still, he managed to make a few waves.

Reagan was still smarting from his Hollywood woes and had expressed as much in an interview with Bob Thomas, who covered the movie business for the Associated Press. In particular, he resented the decline of the studio system, forcing bona fide stars—like himself—to freelance in other media. "This business was built on the basis of offering the public stars they could see nowhere else," he argued. If John Q. Public can encounter you in places like the legitimate stage or on TV or in Las Vegas, he "will certainly think twice before paying to see a movie with a star he has seen so often" elsewhere.

Reagan also lit into what he called the "benefit bureaucrats," who put the squeeze on actors to appear for free at charity functions, especially tele-thons, where "the net return comes to something like a nickel a head." He'd done a slew of them himself to no real effect, and it disturbed him to see screen idols like Clark Gable and Jimmy Stewart herded across a stage, while only the producers of the events profited from their appearance.

But Reagan knew the score. Only a year earlier, he'd told a group of Kiwanis, "If you didn't sing or dance in the Hollywood of my day, you wound up as an after-dinner speaker."

Bob Thomas knew he could count on Ronald Reagan to provide some juice for his column, comments that strayed beyond simply promoting the Vegas opening. In Hollywood, Reagan had always been a columnist's dream source. He was eminently approachable, an actor who didn't shy from the press or buckle to the dictates of studio publicists. Thomas had often relied on him for quotes that were thoughtful, even somewhat flammable, as did those irrepressible yentas Louella Parsons and Hedda Hopper. This issue of actors working for free was a case in point. It was a persistent plaint in Reagan's repertoire of workforce grievances. Publicity for the Vegas debut offered another forum in which to air his opinion.

R onald Reagan had never shrunk from expressing himself about the kinds of contentious issues that other actors went out of their way to avoid. He'd never been shy about speaking out, taking a stand. As a fresh-man in college, he happily allowed himself to be recruited to lead a student strike by upperclassmen. After school, his honeyed Midwestern voice drew listeners from five states to his nightly radio broadcasts of Cubs games and variety shows. And in Hollywood, he was elected by a broad consensus of his peers to head the preeminent Screen Actors Guild in a highly unusual perch for such a relatively modest screen star. He won the gratitude of his fellow actors for his efforts to wrest professional respect from tyrannical studio bosses and ease labor unrest and, more controversially, to fight against communist influence infiltrating the ranks. It was this latter concern—the spread of communism, of "Russian aggression aimed at world conquest"—that impelled Ronald Reagan to engage in public dialogue that extended well beyond standard union issues and to speak before Congress in an effort to root out radicals and extremists.

Along the way, he'd formed strong opinions he felt necessary to convey—about government, the economy, a moral malaise, taxes. Above all he could communicate. He was eloquent, plainspoken, convincing. President of the Screen Actors Guild was arguably Ronald Reagan's star turn.

But now Reagan was no longer SAG head, and his acting career seemed to be slipping away. Reagan knew the movie business was changing, the spotlight moving to younger stars like James Dean, Paul Newman, and Marlon Brando. Television was siphoning audiences away. Roles for plain-vanilla actors like Reagan were drying up; there were fewer opportunities, no guarantees for continual work. It was high time to rethink his career.

What he felt most passionate about was speaking out on issues that he believed in. He'd formed strong opinions he felt obliged to share. Politics? Friends teased him incessantly about a future on the political stage. He had a knack for politics, qualities that were perfectly suited to it, but he seemed to be getting further and further away from them. Here he was in Las Vegas of all places, introducing the Honey Brothers and the Adorabelles and giving an interview about a fairly minor issue concerning actors and freelancing. Was this all there was for him? He had a facility for something so much more than what he was doing right now. He wanted—needed—to be on a bigger stage.

Interestingly, another MCA agent, Taft Schreiber, had just floated the framework of a new kind of project. There was interest from BBD&O, the New York advertising giant, for an actor such as Ronald Reagan to serve as program supervisor for a new TV series—a dramatic anthology—that already had a sponsor in place: General Electric. There would be limited acting involved. Reagan would introduce each show as its host and occasionally function as a producer, and he could have first dibs on choice parts if he wanted.

At first, it didn't resonate. Ronald Reagan was a hardcore skeptic where television was concerned. Even though this new medium was taking America by storm, "everyone of stature in Hollywood," he maintained, "was delicately holding their noses about it." His "personal interest in television was nil."

Still, there were incentives. Reagan would get equity, a small percentage of royalties that could add, over time, to a generous salary. He'd have creative input, help select scripts—and court his Hollywood friends. The show was already attracting major stars; Cary Grant, Bill Holden, even Jane Wyman had already performed, and Reagan's old pals Bob Hope and Jack Benny were slated for the new season. Plus, it was a family affair—produced by none other than Revue Studios, a wholly owned subsidiary of MCA, two entities Reagan was familiar with. Taft Schreiber dangled an even more delectable carrot: GE wanted its new host to spend a quarter of his time offscreen, touring the plants in its corporate empire, speaking to assembly-line employees. He'd be a traveling ambassador, exchanging ideas with regular folks.

He'd been thinking it over, weighing the pros and cons. The new places it might take him. The things he'd learn. It was an odd way to jump into public life, backed by corporate money to express a point of view, certainly not a traditional route, but it intrigued him. Instead of, say, running for the city council or state legislature, and instead of getting bogged down in the nuts and bolts of minor political issues, this might be a way to gain prominence and hone his political views. All of this was on his mind when he finally found his way to the Ramona Room and took the stage.

R onald Reagan was a pro, a natural the moment the spotlights hit him. He clicked right into his onstage role, the affable, aw-shucks charmer who drew audiences in by his presence alone. People *liked* the Ronald Reagan they encountered, the all-American image he presented. They felt they could relate to him as someone like themselves—not flashy, not glib, not in a Fred Astaire kind of way—just a man of the people, which is what he gave them that night in spades.

Reagan's only nod to fashion was the streamlined, pocketless, black gabardine tuxedo he'd designed himself for the occasion. When the Continentals introduced him twenty minutes into their spot, the Ramona Room buzzed. He looked stunning as he ambled into view. He was tan, trim, suave, glowing: a movie star. He commanded the stage. The Continentals had lukewarmed up the crowd, singing corny old chestnuts like "Donkey Serenade" and "Flight of the Bumble Bee" accompanied by sound effects, but Reagan turned up the heat with a rat-a-tat attack of self-deprecating jokes.

He opened with one of those a-funny-thing-happened-on-my-way-to-Las-Vegas bits, claiming that he was magically transformed from Hollywood typecasting as a briefcase-wielding house-husband into "a joy-boy." In fact, his stodgy screen image was so ingrained, he said, that his last leading lady, a woman older than he, called him "father." Seamlessly, he lapsed into a joke-filled routine that required a playful Irish brogue.

Later in the show, after dispatching the Blackburn Twins and the Adorabelles, he returned for another workout with the Continentals, this time sporting a straw hat and cane. Reagan sat on a makeshift chair formed by the legs of two group members pretending to shave his cheeks while singing the barber-shop quartet mainstay "Sweet Adeline." This was followed by a beer-garden skit in which he wore a Pabst Blue Ribbon apron with the legend "Vos vils du haben?" scrawled across it, danced and sang, and murdered the German language to howls of laughter. The evening ended with the star standing solo, center stage, sans props, delivering a meditation called "The Definition of an Actor," by Irvin S. Cobb, noting how actors weren't quite like doctors or lawyers, they didn't do regular work, but they still left the world a better place.

Leaving the world a better place. Was he doing enough to leave the world a better place? He'd been mulling that over for the past couple of years, how he could do something about all the issues—the everyday battles confronting hardworking Americans—that had been gnawing at him. It wasn't too late to start doing something about it. He'd made a name for himself in a superficial business, but it gave him the kind of visibility that could wield influence beyond stage and screen. His mother always told him how important it was to help others, to put the needs of those who were disadvantaged ahead of one's own. Once, when he was in high school, she hosted a Women's Missionary Society meeting whose topic was "The Large World—My Neighborhood." Didn't that just about say it all?

Las Vegas, he knew, wasn't the answer. The nightclub act did relatively decent business—good enough to prompt an offer for a return engagement—and was well received by the critics, for the most part. But the experience left Ronald Reagan unfulfilled. He made only $5,500 a week, not the windfall he expected. And the city itself was a strange place to work, even more of a fantasyland than Hollywood, if that was possible.

After the shows, when most performers hit the casino or checked out an act at a neighboring hotel, Ron and Nancy went back to their room, where they spent the time reading, talking, and thinking about the future. "The nightclub life was not for us," she recalled.

This gave him time to think about broader issues. Reagan had become disillusioned with the direction the country was taking. The newspapers he combed through each morning were full of stories that disturbed his sense of right and wrong: the federal budget was seriously out of balance, forcing postponement of the tax reductions President Dwight D. Eisenhower had promised; Nikita Khrushchev was saber rattling; the Supreme Court had heard a case, *Brown v. Board of Education*, that threatened to upend how Americans sent their children to school; the Communists had stepped up their aggression in Southeast Asia; and taxes were keeping Reagan himself trapped in an 87 percent bracket.

Where did he figure into "The Large World—My Neighborhood"? Not too long ago, he'd been clearer about it. As a lifetime Roosevelt Democrat, he'd embraced the New Deal coalition, especially FDR's efforts to encourage labor union growth and his promise to reduce the size of the federal government and cut the budget. He loved Roosevelt's view that common people can have a vision that included all social classes for the good of the country. All of that had made perfect sense. Reagan had even supported the election of Harry Truman, whom he admired. But, lately, he'd become disillusioned with the Democratic Party and its penchant toward "encroaching government control." Reagan deplored "the problems of centralizing power in Washington," which he felt took inalienable rights and freedoms away from citizens such as himself. To him, it seemed the party's liberal faction also went to great lengths to defend the shady Hollywood clique that had romanticized and dabbled in communism.

All this served to redirect Ronald Reagan's political antennae. He'd become more agitated in the past few years, more impatient with the country's direction, more clear-cut in his feelings about right and wrong. When it came right down to it, he'd been gravitating toward a conservative philosophy, siding with Republicans on issues concerning the economy and the spread of Soviet influence, military strength and smaller government, law enforcement and tax reform. His closest friends—Dick Powell, Bill Holden, and Bob Cummings—were steadfast Republicans who had tirelessly drawn him to their side. And he'd gone for Ike in 1952, the first time he'd ever voted for a Republican candidate.

Ronald Reagan spent the rest of his Las Vegas engagement turning everything over in his mind—how a nightclub career didn't suit him and his movie career was very possibly over, how his new wife and new daughter gave him the kind of emotional anchor he'd never had before, how he might transition to a smaller screen where his ideas and opinions would have more of an impact (and help dig him out of debt), how his convictions and talent for airing them gave him entrée onto an entirely different stage.

These things were all starting to coalesce as Reagan returned each night to his hotel room, making his way through the mazy corridor of the Last Frontier.

Yes, Ronald Reagan had lost his way—but he thought he had found the path back.

PART 1

DUTCH

CHAPTER ONE

AN IDEAL PLACE

*"It is worthwhile for anyone to have behind him a few
generations of honest hardworking ancestry."*

—JOHN P. MARQUAND

More than any one person or principle, it was a place, or at least
the idea of a place, that formed the bedrock of Ronald Reagan's
character. Even well into his eighties, he could still summon up a
movie's worth of memories that cast a resonant glow on his Midwest upbringing: the seemingly boundless cornfields studded with grain elevators
jutting into the stratosphere; the daily caravan of boxcars rumbling over
miles of newly laid track, carrying staples through the heartland; the seduc-
tive and moody Rock River, whose treacherous crosscurrents challenged
him as a teenage lifeguard; the modest wood-framed family homes surrounded by white picket fences; the scenic prairie roads he hitchhiked,
from Dixon to Kewanee, Danville, Rock Island, and Davenport. "My
hometown was a small town, and everybody knew everyone else," he recalled near the end of his life. In his case "hometown" was a composite of
his best recollections of the whistle-stops the Reagan family made as they
migrated fitfully across Illinois and Iowa, from Tampico to Galesburg to
Monmouth to Dixon.

Ronald Reagan clung to a story of his Midwestern childhood that he
described as "one of those rare Huck Finn-Tom Sawyer idylls." In fact, Ronald Reagan's upbringing owed more to the moodier, crisis-filled sagas of, say,
Willa Cather or Upton Sinclair than to Mark Twain. Granted, there are

many heartwarming chapters to his family history, but they are interrupted by long passages of strife and great hardship.

Ronald Reagan had little to go on when it came to his ancestry, the sketchy Reagan lineage that stretched back to nineteenth-century Ireland and Scotland. In a 1987 letter to Hollywood friends, he said, "I've never known anything about my father's family," lamenting the gaps in his family history.

His great-grandfather, Michael Reagan, with his wife, Catherine, and their three children—Thomas, John, and Margaret—stepped off the cargo ship *Joseph Gilchrist* in lower Manhattan in 1857. Others in the sickly, penniless O'Regan* family held on in Doolis, a mud-gash of an Irish village— just twelve sod-and-stone huts—west of Ballyporeen below the Galtee Mountains. But Doolis held no future for Michael, the "bright and ambitious" potato farmer's son, one of the few local men able to read and write. London was his first gateway to opportunity. When he turned twenty-two, Michael made a beeline for the British capital, where he landed in an Irish ghetto in the Peckham district.

He wasn't alone in his quest. Throughout the 1850s and 1860s, thousands of refugees from the widening Irish potato famine squeezed into Victorian London, relegated to a warren of overrun slums. North Peckham was particularly squalid, marked by high unemployment, rampant crime, raw sewage, and the inevitable cholera outbreaks that swept through the neighborhood, ravaging the population. Michael O'Regan, who took shelter in a boardinghouse with twelve fellow Irishmen at 24 Benley Street, proved luckier than many of his mates. He found steady work in a soap factory, earning enough to save a few shillings each payday.

A year after Michael settled in London, he met Catherine Mulcahy, a "gardener's laborer" six years his senior, who lived in a boardinghouse directly across the street. Catherine was an iron-willed woman, escaping her own sorry circumstances. Her three uncles were notorious scoundrels, overly familiar with the inside of Irish jails. Two brothers had earned their stripes by teaming up in a pub brawl that ended with a death, while the third brother, James, a notorious game poacher, was arrested for an act of "barbarity and atrocity" in which he ripped the wool off the backs of living

* The original spelling of the family name.

sheep. Leaving home—an extraordinary step for a young Irish woman—gave Catherine a new purchase on life. On May 15, 1852, she gave birth to her first son, Thomas, and five months later, on October 31, Michael O'Regan and Catherine Mulcahy made it official, marrying at St. George the Martyr, a Catholic church in Southwark. Michael signed the marriage certificate "Reagan" instead of O'Regan, an act that forever altered the family name; Catherine merely scrawled an X on the space provided.

Despite gainful employment and a roof over their heads, the Reagans were eager for a change. Soapmaking was a hard business with long hours and repulsive conditions. In filthy, unventilated sheds, chandlers (as they were called) rendered chunks of slaughtered pigs for fat, then cooked the lard with lye in cauldrons over a sweltering fire before pouring the slime into trays to harden.

From the moment they touched land in New York City—"the Golden Doorway"—the new world's promise was evident. Waves of new arrivals, mostly from Europe—the displaced, the desperate, the hopeful—swept through the portals at Castle Garden, a sandstone fort in what is now Battery Park, America's first immigrant-processing depot. A registration office, a medical examination facility, a currency exchange, guidance counselors, all synced to manage the human flow. Somehow, the Reagan family avoided the scam artists that prowled the docks, selling phony railroad and boat tickets to unsuspecting aliens. They ignored the "runners" speaking in Gaelic who conned Irish immigrants into renting Manhattan's vermin-infested hellholes at egregious rates. City living wasn't for them; they'd had their fill of it in London. The Reagans came from country stock and decided to push their way inland, where cheap land awaited those who understood its soil.

Michael and Catherine, Ronald Reagan's great-grandparents, along with their children and Michael's two older brothers, John and Nicholas, set out by train for the unspoiled Midwest—the Iowa Territory—only days after arriving in America. They had read promotional circulars from banks, railroads, and farm-equipment companies lauding generous land grants and peerless weather. "For richness of soil; for beauty of appearance; and for pleasantness of climate, it surpasses any portion of the United States," one read. The Midwest was where their destiny awaited them. The Reagans, dreamers of big dreams, pushed west into the American frontier, toward the Mississippi River. Packed into the bowels of an overstuffed train, the family traveled overland from New York to Chicago, where they most likely transferred to one of the local lines of the Illinois Central that snaked off to the edges of the frontier. Chicago to Dixon to Galena to Savanna.

Their destination, Fair Haven, Illinois, was far off the beaten track. In most cases, newcomers to America who headed into the heartland had someone—a relative or family contact—waiting to help get them on their feet. Instant shelter was needed on arrival, some means of finding food and other forms of sustenance. There is no record of how the Reagans established their first home. It is reasonable to assume Michael and his two older brothers banded together, using whatever skills they'd learned in Doolis in order to erect suitable shelter. You could cobble together a sod-and-stone cottage no matter where you set down, but that's where all comparisons to Ireland ended.

Whoever named Fair Haven must have seen it only in the spring. The settlement, if one could call it that, was bleak, desolate, dispiriting in its isolation, a flat prairie outpost in the northwest corner of the state. As the early settlers discovered, the prairie was deceiving—there was nothing to distinguish it across the entire horizon, no hills, no trees, no contour of any kind. It was flat—flat and barren. You could gaze off for twenty miles in any direction and not detect so much as a shadow. Which isn't to say the area didn't have its charm. April through June, there were few places more inviting—clear, crisp air; perpetual sunshine; and a landscape that was nature's masterpiece. But the summer months were brutally hot, racked by fierce, pounding thunderstorms, tornadoes, and flash flooding, and the winters . . . the winters made settlers feel they were being tested by their faith. Long months, short days, temperatures often in single digits, and wild snowstorms made life a brutal battle against the elements. When Michael Reagan arrived in early December 1857, there was little to recommend this godforsaken terrain.

Still, he would learn soon enough that the farmland was incomparable. What blessed the prairie was the luxury of its soil. Only a few hard miles from the Mississippi River, the land conferred the richest river bottom imaginable, black gold. There were already a sizable number of immigrant farmers in the county, drawn there by the generous yield. And game was plentiful, with deer, buffalo, grouse, and prairie chickens roaming wild.

Michael took advantage of the Preemption Act of 1841, which allowed settlers such as the Reagans to claim a substantial parcel of federal land for a fair-minded sum—about $1.25 an acre, payable within a year of making application—so long as they lived on it for five years and improved it. These weren't squatters, but tenacious pioneers who intended to stay and contribute. The government saw it as a way to develop the frontier; Michael Reagan saw it as a good deal. He claimed a small tract—Section 21—in the southern part of Fair Haven, near a post office and a makeshift school. His brothers took adjoining plots, Sections 22 and 23.

By 1858, Fair Haven was a village on the rise. There was enough of a growing population in surrounding Carroll County to support a sawmill, a distillery, and several churches. But for the most part, the families were dependent on their own resolve. They built small, rudimentary log cabins and forged the utensils necessary to cultivate crops: a moldboard plow to scour the tough June grass, a drag and a grain cradle, sharp axes, wedges— all handmade except for a scythe.

Frontier life was hard work—hard and debilitating. There were so many critical necessities: not only a house but a barn, a team of horses, and enough seed to sow the fields, plus a little to put away each month toward the price of a newfangled McCormick reaper. And just as many setbacks: drought, deadly heat waves, grasshopper plagues, locusts. The prairie contributed its own challenges, chief among them the ornery, shoulder-high grass, whose gnarled roots reached "clear to hell," according to the farmers, and put up more of a struggle than a team of mules. European transplants like Michael Reagan, who worked the fields with rickety wooden plows, felt bullied, terrorized by the soil. Many settlers without the fortitude to tough it out pulled up stakes and moved to more forgiving climes. Michael was luckier—or more capable—than most. By the time the 1860 census was registered, his property was valued at $1,120 and his personal wealth at around $150. By 1870 the combined worth had soared to $3,850—not bad for a man who had begun his new-world dreams with little more than the shirt on his back. He and his brothers shared sixteen acres of arable land, which over the years returned an ample yield. In nearby Savanna, the so-called emporium for all of Carroll County, the Reagans joined farmers within a thirty-mile radius who swapped crops for provisions, often on credit—"buy and pay after harvest" was the rule—giving them the breathing room to bridge the growing seasons.

Michael and Catherine were prudent and practical. Not idealists, not gamblers, not wishful thinkers, they understood the reality of the prairie, its exacting demands. Like their neighbors, they lived modestly, raising a few dozen chickens to complement a string of milk cows, and planting little more than what they needed to get by: corn, wheat, vegetables, and soybeans. The land was good to them, and they put everything they had back into the land while raising children, five in all, and sending them to school.

But farm life was punishing. Up before dawn, still at it after dusk, they worked constantly, and there were no guarantees. It was a never-ending struggle to keep a farm above water. Farmers' children who spent their youths performing a litany of routine chores grew restless and often took the first road out. Moving to town was, for them, a liberation. Among the five children of Michael Reagan and Catherine Mulcahy Reagan, only William, the youngest boy, remained at home, where he died from tuberculosis at the age of twenty-two. Thomas, the eldest son, moved to Savanna and found work as a car repairman for the Chicago, Milwaukee, and St. Paul Railroad. John, Ronald Reagan's grandfather, moved to nearby Fulton, Illinois, a riverboat boomtown on the eastern banks of the Mississippi, where he married a local woman, Jennie Cusick, and went to work at one of the Third Street grain elevators opposite the railroad. Margaret, known as Maggie, and her sister Mary also wound up in Fulton, where in the spring of 1886 they opened a store on the corner of Base and Cherry streets, selling exquisite "millinery and fancy dry goods."

Having broken free of the farm, Michael Reagan's offspring prospered, but their lives would be marred by tragic blows.

Thomas, who had a wife and three children, enjoyed running skiffs on the river. On July 4, 1889, he and six of his fellow CM&StP workers celebrated the holiday by sailing to one of the outer islands for a little bacchanal. While rowing back to town, lighthearted and tipsy, according to a newspaper account, "the party began skylarking and rocked the boat so that it was half full of water." Thomas, positioned at one of the oars, tried to rein in the horseplay, but thirty yards from shore they capsized. A nearby skiff raced to the scene, pulling the struggling men to safety, but Thomas, a nonswimmer, and two others drowned.

Six months later, Maggie kept an evening appointment to visit one of her customers, forgetting to blow out one of the table lamps in the store. While she was out, the lamp exploded, "setting fire to a pile of velvet and untrimmed hats." Fortunately, O. G. Baldwin, the owner of a dry-goods emporium around the corner, was passing by. He was able to throw "a few pails of water" on the fire before it spread from store to store. But the damage was done; most of the stock was destroyed. If there was a silver lining to the mishap, it was Maggie's portentous introduction to O. G. Baldwin, who would become her husband. For the time being, however, the fire put the Reagan sisters out of business.

Oddly enough, John Reagan, the young son who hated farmwork, didn't shrink from the rigors of the Fulton grain elevator. The daily grind inside those rank, sweaty silos was subhuman—and dangerous. The job was rife with tales of stevedores getting caught in the flow of grain or coal and, in one brief and terrible moment, disappearing under tons of spill-off. John managed to avoid such a fate.

John's bad luck stemmed from fragile health. From the outset, Jennie, a frail, withdrawn woman, struggled with fatigue and infirmity. Nevertheless, she was eager to begin a family. But the birth of each new child left her worn to a shadow. After the couple's first two children arrived, John moved the family to a more favorable location, building a two-story shingled house that sat atop a gentle rise on Seventh Avenue so that Jennie would be within shouting distance of their doctor, Henry Kennedy, who lived just down the hill. In 1883, the third of their four children, John Edward (known as Jack), was born: Ronald Reagan's father.

Two years later, after the youngest, Annie, arrived, Jennie's condition deteriorated. She developed a chronic cough and began losing weight. Her symptoms took "an unfavorable change" around Thanksgiving 1886, when her breathing grew labored and the wrenching night sweats began. The symptoms consuming her were all too evident: tuberculosis, "a fatal disease." She lasted another two weeks.

Somehow, John Reagan managed to care for four children, two boys and two girls, the youngest of whom was only nineteen months old. There is every indication he tried his best to cope with the situation and that he had plenty of help. His two sisters lived a short distance away, as did his mother, who moved in with her daughters after the death of Michael in March 1884.

But it was an uphill battle. Soon after Jennie passed, tiny Annie contracted whooping cough, which damaged her auditory nerves, leading to the permanent loss of hearing and speech. Although for some time John maintained a balance between the frenetic demands of work and his needy household, it took a toll on his health. He came home from long spells in the grain elevator feeling exhausted and running a fever. Days off with bed rest failed to improve his condition. The work-related stress brought on bouts of nausea, wild swings of temperature, and the sweats. By mid-1888, reports that John was seriously ill, even "failing," circulated in Fulton, and by Christmas the worst was acknowledged. No one needed Dr. Kennedy to confirm that John's symptoms mirrored those of his wife: the fatal grip of tuberculosis had taken hold.

Jack Reagan, Ronald's father, was only five years old when he watched his father grapple with the inescapable. It was a solemn New Year's in 1889, as his father lay wasted, eyes sunken and cheeks emaciated, gasping for breath and coughing up blood until his heart finally gave out. His death on January 10 had repercussions into the next generation. As an obituary in the Fulton newspaper lamented, "John Reagan, aged thirty-four years, seven months and ten days . . . leaves four children under ten years of age."

The family, what was left of it, was thrown into flux. Jack and his siblings moved in for a while with his aunts and grandmother, three strong-willed and resourceful women. Soon, Jack was the only child living at home. An older sister, Katie, moved out when Aunt Mary married; little Annie was placed in a state institution for the deaf and dumb; and Will, now a sulky, diffident teenager, packed in school to work in the grain elevator.

While his aunts worked long hours at their recently rebuilt millinery shop, Jack spent plenty of time on his own. Fulton was a kind of riverside Dodge City, intoxicating to a boy his age. Bootlegging, smuggling, and prostitution were part of its gritty underbelly. Situated on a channel called the Narrows, named for its position at the most tapered part of the river, Fulton was an early key crossroads of the upper Mississippi River Valley. Commercial cargo of all types, especially lumber, made its way downriver from Wisconsin and Minnesota, then was loaded onto one of the railroads that scissored through town. The Chicago Northwestern, the Burlington Northern, and the CB&Q (Chicago, Burlington & Quincy) merged their lines in Fulton. Such a busy Midwestern hub became a magnet for undesirables. "Those riverboat crews were tough characters," says a longtime resident who resented the riffraff. Taverns along the banks serviced the men from the steamships and logging boats that tied up on the docks.

Those establishments would have a significant impact on Jack Reagan's adolescence.

Aunt Maggie, by that time, was on Jack's case. Her marriage to O. G. Baldwin in 1894 provided an opportunity for a change of scenery. In 1896, Orson G. Baldwin, one of Fulton's most prominent merchants and local legislators, decided to close his emporium and move inland, across the Mississippi to Bennett, Iowa. Jack, who had just turned thirteen, was coming with them.

To Jack, Bennett was a punishment, in the middle of nowhere, little more than a train stop created by the railroads, halfway between Clinton and Cedar Rapids, a scattering of houses on a grid of muddy, unpaved streets. Why O. G. Baldwin chose to drag a new wife and ward to this scrubby outpost was anyone's guess. Perhaps he saw it as a timely opportunity to capitalize on frontier expansion. The eastern corridor of Iowa, from Davenport down to Burlington, was growing at a terrific rate. A wily tradesman such as O. G. might have recognized an opening. Or perhaps he wanted to get away from the sprawl. Bennett had no river, no scoundrels, no tavern culture.

One can only imagine Jack Reagan's sense of displacement. To a thirteen-year-old with a high-spirited streak, Bennett was lifeless, the heartland without an identifiable heartbeat. From its depot, one could take in the whole depressing square: a few general stores, a small hotel, a stockyard with several butchers, a barbershop, and a pool hall. The majority of families who settled there were stolid German Lutherans, not the Irish who had shaped Jack's world. He soon made it clear that he was no scholar, and by the sixth grade he dropped out of school, leaving him free to help clerk in the family store located in the new bank building at Third and Main, and to play baseball.

Since the end of the Civil War, baseball had become grouted in the

American mosaic and was already considered "the national pastime." Every town in the country, no matter its size or location, refashioned a grassy patch into a makeshift baseball diamond, where kids of all ages played the game. Jack found his footing on the local Bennett ballfield, playing right field for the Junior Tigers and acting as their manager. Jaunty and gangly in his navy-blue team jacket and pinstriped cap, Jack took the field for each week's games with lively dispatch, an unconventional teenager who stood out from his teammates with a cheeky hairstyle parted down the middle. The sparkle in his eye was impossible to miss. If anyone wondered how Ronald Reagan grew to love the sport, his enthusiasm for it can be traced directly to his father.

Jack's job clerking at Baldwin's Dry-Goods was mundane at best, though it did put fifty cents a week in his pocket, enough to finance a ticket to the wrestling matches—or for a drink from one of the three kegs of beer smuggled weekly into the bone-dry town. But there was no future in his uncle's store. By 1901, it was hardly turning a respectable profit, and after only five years in business, and with several dry-goods stores opening within a few blocks, the Baldwins decided to close up shop. Jack was eighteen. He opened a lunch counter for a while, but after a few weeks of scant foot traffic, he packed up and returned to Fulton on his own, taking a clerk's job at the J. W. Broadhead store.

Broadhead's, in the middle of town, was a "quite well-respected" Fulton institution. A grand brick structure on the corner of Fourth Street and Tenth Avenue, it was the forerunner of the modern department store, several floors comprised of individual departments—men's and women's clothing, shoes, a boutique for hats, bolts of the most soignée fabric imported from Chicago, housewares, and notions, such as candles, umbrellas, perfume, and sewing supplies.

Jack found his calling on Broadhead's mezzanine level in the smart women's shoe department, overlooking men's furnishings, where he developed a flair for fitting the female foot. He harnessed the powers of his genial nature, his gift of gab, and his intuitive salesmanship into a profession that would occupy him for the next twenty-five years. He was well-suited for the job. Jack cut a "tall, swarthy, muscular, and handsome" figure, stalking the mezzanine floor like a panther. And he was single. Especially on snowy days, when Broadhead's tended to draw capacity crowds, Fulton women stood in line, angling for Jack's attention. "You could hear his name called right across the store," says a woman whose grandmother recalled having her eye on Jack and an occasional foot in his hand.

But Jack had his own eye on a pretty, auburn-haired clerk who worked part time on the first floor. Nelle (pronounced "Nellie") Wilson had recently moved to town from North Clyde, Illinois, a desolate stretch of farmland on the outskirts of the county. She was a delicate wisp of a girl, only seventeen when Jack first spotted her, agreeably self-possessed considering her fractured upbringing, with a high forehead, ghostly pale-blue eyes, and alabaster-white skin.

Like Jack, Nelle descended from a long line of immigrants who had reckoned with their share of trouble, her forebears an amalgam of adventurous, some might say shiftless, men and flinty, Bible-fearing womenfolk. Her grandfather John Wilson, a burly Scotsman, migrated to Canada in the early nineteenth century, eventually drifting south across the border before winding up in North Clyde. There, in 1841, he married Jane Blue and staked a claim to farmland within a short ride of where Michael Reagan's family lived, in northern Illinois. But farming was too prosaic for such a restless adventurer. Just weeks after his eighth child was born, John Wilson took off with his brother and Jane's father, Donald, to join the gold rush frenzy in California.

The responsibilities of running farm and family were left to the resilient, hard-shelled Jane Wilson, who shepherded her children through the ardors of prairie life. Because she was so isolated from the nearest town, there was no end to the pressing imperatives: feed the children, tend the crops, slaughter the chickens or hogs, shoe the horses, sew and mend the clothes, handle the washing and ironing, sell off any of the harvest not used for subsistence. Raise the kids. For a woman on her own in what was still essentially frontier, Jane proved a more than able matriarch. Three years later, when John returned from the west without so much as a nugget to his name, he found the farm humming along.

But Jane had her own setbacks to contend with. Her brothers—Daniel, Alexander, and Charles, great-uncles of Ronald Reagan—along with a cousin and his friend, set off on a similar quest for gold that ended in disaster when they were caught in a terrible snowstorm and resorted to eating the flesh of those who had died. Only Daniel Blue returned alive.

Jane Wilson, devastated, retreated "in the teachings of the Christ life." With two brothers dead and an impetuous husband to contend with, religion proved a genuine comfort. "The Bible became her constant companion," its sacraments governing every phase of her life. She handed down a legacy of strong faith to her children, all of whom followed her lead except Thomas, Nelle's father and Ronald Reagan's grandfather.

Thomas Wilson shared his own father's wanderlust. He was a dapper, well-dressed man "with a flamboyant mustache and a goatee" who, by all accounts, "radiated an air of self-confidence." When he was twenty-seven, Thomas married a thirty-five-year-old domestic named Mary Ann Elsey, staking out a farm life in North Clyde, near his parents. The Wilsons bore seven children in quick succession, the youngest of whom, Nelle Clyde Wilson, born in 1883, would become Ronald Reagan's mother.

Life in that part of the state was still a primitive affair—miles from the closest town, open to the elements. "How those people survived out in the middle of nowhere . . ." mused a Fulton historian, "it took a lot of guts." Perhaps more guts than Thomas Wilson could muster. When Nelle was five, Thomas abandoned the family. He simply rode off one morning, leaving his wife and seven children to fend for themselves on that hardscrabble farm. The Wilson children were pressed to take over the full-time farming duties, tending the fields, baling the hay, and milking the cows. They worked that inhospitable land until their knuckles were raw, only breaking on Sunday, when they would travel by horse and wagon to the Methodist Episcopal Church, a few miles off, for religious services.

Nelle, being the youngest, was often spared the harshest chores. When she was old enough, she churned the butter with her three older sisters, leaving plenty of time for her mother's readings from Dickson's *New Indexed Bible,* which never left Mary Wilson's side. She felt that the parables in it contained everything her children needed to instruct them in their young lives, as did Nelle, who inherited the Bible after her mother's death, and her son Ronald, who was sworn in as president on it almost a hundred years later. Leaning heavily on that Bible, Mary did all she could to maintain the pretense of a normal family life; in time, no one made much of the fact that Thomas Wilson was no longer part of it.

All of that changed in the early spring of 1894, when Nelle's grandmother Jane, who was now seventy-seven, complained of pain and took to her bed. It was clear that Jane's illness was terminal, and she went immediately about settling her affairs. One unfinished piece of business, reported vividly in a local newspaper, was a "deep-seated yearning . . . to see once more for the last time her son, Thomas, gone so long." His brother, John, found Thomas living in La Crosse, an unplowed enclave in the southwest corner of the state, and persuaded him to honor his mother's last wish.

He had been gone almost six years without so much as a word or a contribution toward the family's welfare, and he returned with no explanation offered. To the children, he was a virtual stranger. Yet, upon his return, Thomas gravitated back into the family in an abstracted, melancholy way. He was noticeably restless, distant, unsure of his role. Mary had displaced him as head of the household, her reliance on the Bible too formidable, making it impossible to stand up to her moral authority.

One thing was for certain, Thomas's farming days were over. Whatever his affairs those six years in La Crosse, he'd lost all of his natural affinity for the land. It was a disconnect so profound that, after bumping around North Clyde for eight months, he felt compelled to sell what was left of the farm and move the family to a less isolated place.

At first sight, Fulton seemed like a natural choice. It was a town that had grown steadily over the years since the Reagans settled there. Coming from the country, the Wilsons surely marveled at the string of shops lining the newly electrified Fourth Street, beginning with J. W. Broadhead, its commercial centerpiece, and beyond that, Utz the butcher, whose icehouse in the rear held mammoth blocks cut from the Mississippi to be used for refrigeration all year round. There was also a redbrick grocery store stocked with every conceivable staple, and the imposing Fulton Bank. Across the street was the Reagan sisters' millinery shop, a soft-drink parlor, a confectionery, a newsstand, and the Union Hotel. Here, at last, community seemed possible. Further on, there was an opera house that featured vaudeville acts, a skating rink, and a baseball diamond in Pleasure Park, where the town's young men, including Jack Reagan, played. And there was a profusion of churches, most notably the Christian Church on Eleventh Avenue, which became a vital influence on Nelle's character.

In Fulton, it was impossible to avoid the Mississippi and everything that was brought with it. A tidal swell of opportunity arrived on its banks, pumping hard cash into the general economy. Businesses rose up and thrived from the constant river traffic; just across the water, in Clinton, Iowa, stood millionaires' mansions, visible to all. But Fulton also bore the brunt of the river's powers. Swimmers were unable to resist jumping in for a dip, despite the ever-changing currents that were known to sweep bathers under. "A lot of capable people drowned there every year," recalls a Fulton resident, "even off the designated swimming hole just south of town." Skiffs, like the one that held Thomas Reagan, capsized regularly in the strong currents. His sister Mary's first husband also drowned in the Mississippi. And roughnecks passing through often brought with them drunken tavern fights, horse-and-carriage accidents, and an upsurge of burglaries.

All in all, it was an unlikely town for an ex–dirt farmer and his Bible-clutching wife. Nevertheless, the family moved into a white clapboard house on the northwest side of town.

For Nelle Wilson, the move was heaven-sent. As a thirteen-year-old with an enthusiasm for poetry, she was drawn to the social life that Fulton had to offer—a real school, a library teeming with books, the camaraderie of other children her age, and above all the churches. No longer restricted to the farm and its chores, Nelle cultivated a circle of friends and a growing interest in her new community. She remained tightly bound to the family, but the center of her life shifted somewhat from home to church, where she immersed herself in its various charitable endeavors, a practice that became a lifelong pursuit. Years later, her son, Ronald, would say that "she was a natural, practical do-gooder, but never self-serving, always with humility."

Helping people was something Nelle Wilson did without asking; helping herself was another matter. Nelle was bright, but she regarded her own schooling as an unnecessary extravagance when she could work to help support the family. As soon as she turned fifteen, she dropped out and took a job in the wrapping department of the Mississippi Valley Stove Company.

Did the Wilsons need the money? It's hard to say. The sale of the farm gave them a tidy cushion; the oldest children had married and moved on. But Thomas was idle, and relations between Nelle's parents were tense in the house. For all intents and purposes, Thomas and Mary's marriage lay in ruins. Though they lived together under the same roof, Mary, "toothless and wizened," had begun referring to herself as a widow. Perhaps Nelle needed to distance herself from the fray.

In 1902, to her great delight, Nelle moved jobs from the stove works, which lay in the farthest reaches of Fulton, to the J. W. Broadhead store owned by the same family, just a few blocks from home. For Nelle, the timing couldn't have been more auspicious. Within months of her transfer, stores like Macy's in New York, Filene's in Boston, Nordstrom in Seattle, Dayton's in Minneapolis, and J. C. Penney in Kemmerer, Wyoming, opened their retail outlets, expanding the concept of dry goods into the modern department store. Broadhead's had already undergone an expansion earlier that year, hiring a wave of new young clerks, one of whom—the wily shoe salesman—lost no time moving in on the slight, auburn-haired salesgirl.

It is difficult to imagine a more unlikely couple than Jack Reagan and Nelle Wilson. The dapper, raffish Jack was a character "known for his copious blarney" who had already "developed an early thirst for corn whiskey." Yet there was no defense against his infectious charm. And once committed, Nelle never looked back. For Jack, the family-oriented Nelle augured potential for a rooted, stable life after years of shuttling between relatives. He must have also recognized in Nelle a woman much like her mother who could roll with the punches.

The religious innocent and the vivacious man-about-town—the only meaningful thing they seemed to have in common was that they both had known deep and unsettling grief. Sometime before Nelle arrived at Broadhead's, her mother, Mary, died suddenly, leaving Nelle alone at home with the task of caring for her father. Jack, orphaned as a child, lost his sister, twenty-two-year-old Katie, in 1901. She had been working at the Fulton Steam Laundry when she suffered "an attack of lung fever and [was] sent home from work." What seemed like nothing more than a nagging ailment ultimately stretched on for months, until Katie's death in November from pneumonia. A year and a half later, Annie Reagan, who had been sickly for some time, died at the age of eighteen. Such loss was a powerful unifier. Jack and Nelle, both emotionally adrift, took solace in each other's company.

Not everyone viewed their relationship favorably. Nelle's father, Thomas Wilson, it was said, "disapproved of Jack Reagan." Thomas was protective of his youngest daughter and depended on her. And perhaps he recognized Jack's wild streak, one spitfire to another.

It is not known whether Thomas Wilson gradually came around or if the young couple decided to marry without his blessing, but at their wedding—on the evening of Tuesday, November 8, 1904—it was Nelle's uncle, Alex Wilson, who gave the bride away, not her father. Most likely Thomas did not attend.

In any case, he would have disapproved of the venue. The couple got married not at the Wilson family church but at Immaculate Conception, the Catholic facility on Twelfth Street, which the Reagans attended. In Fulton, it was rare that Protestants and Catholics intermarried; as late as the 1950s it was still considered unseemly. The pastor considered the union "a mixed marriage," and the church prohibited them from marrying at the altar, bumping the ceremony from the main sanctuary to the parsonage next door.

To save money, the newlyweds moved into the little house on Twelfth Avenue with Jack's grandmother Catherine, now living on her own. Jack and Nelle took over the spare bedroom in the back. The arrangement was convenient for everyone—for a while. Catherine, whose health was failing, was grateful to have family to help around the house. Nelle couldn't have been more attentive. She doted on Jack's grandmother and pitched in with his aunts at Palace Millinery, settling into her new life. But Jack Reagan was a young man on the move. Only twenty-two, he always had one eye on the door. "He was a restless man, burning with ambition"—a description offered fifty years later by his son, Ronald, but just as fitting in 1904. Sixteen months after his wedding to Nelle, Jack seized an opportunity to work as "senior salesman in the clothing and shoe department" of a new business. It meant relocating, uprooting Nelle, and leaving their families behind. A half hour's ride southwest on the CB&Q was the rural farm town of Tampico, Illinois—an ideal place, Jack and Nelle thought, to begin a family.

CHAPTER TWO

"A LITTLE BIT OF A DUTCHMAN"

"Sons are the anchors of a mother's life."

—SOPHOCLES, *Phaedra*

T ampico looked more like frozen tundra when Jack and Nelle Reagan first laid eyes on it. They arrived in February 1906, in the middle of a brutal cold snap, with miles of farmland buried under a thick crust of snow. The wintry landscape, silvery and bucolic, could have been the very model for a Currier and Ives postcard. The town itself was another story.

A visitor might have felt he'd stumbled onto the set of a low-budget Hollywood western. Main Street, the only commercial thoroughfare, was nothing more than an unpaved rutted lane, owing to an uneasy alliance of horse wagons and automobiles. A single block of two-story brick buildings lined either side of the street. There were sidewalks of a sort, but to reach them one had to wade through ankle-deep muck and scale an inclined plank. The stores were limited to basic essential services: a few groceries, a bank, a barbershop, two pharmacies, a general store, a hotel. Otherwise, most of the businesses that drove the economy—the stockyards, Simpson's lumberyard, Legg's poultry house, the feed mill, and the grain elevators— lay, literally, off the beaten path. Almost all of the fifteen hundred residents were scattered across farms. As the birthplace of a president, Tampico wasn't much to whistle at. In fact, you could whistle "Dixie"—maybe just the first few lines—and be through town before you hit the second verse.

Jack and Nelle had rented a modest second-story flat at 111 Main Street, empty since the local pub owner vacated the building after Tampico residents voted the town dry. Modest but comfortable, it consisted of five rooms at the top of a narrow flight of stairs, with a pair of windows facing the opera house across the street. A nice-sized front parlor led to the dining room, and a screened-in porch overlooked the alley, where the couple could sleep once the weather cooperated. In the meantime, they placed their bed in the corner of a gloomy interior room illuminated only by an overhead skylight. The makeshift toilets lay out back near the water pump and were reached via "a treacherous-looking stairway from the dining room"; the kitchen sink sufficed in lieu of a tub. Nevertheless, the apartment was certainly large enough for two young adults starting their lives together.

Jack started work at a salary of forty dollars a month. Between rent, food, and clothing they would just about get by. They managed to stretch their budget by living above the shops. It wasn't ideal; hauling endless buckets of water and coal up those stairs took a physical toll, especially for the delicately built Nelle, and it was noisy, with traffic pulling in and out all day long. Still, as newcomers, the Reagans didn't feel so isolated and weren't in need of a car to do their everyday shopping. For Jack, the commute to the H. C. Pitney Variety Store was barely a two-minute walk up the street, at the corner of Main and Market. At first, Jack flourished. He became the proverbial big fish in a small town, "an extremely popular man . . . with more gloss" than the local denizens. "Everybody liked Jack," says a woman familiar with his position in town. "He was smooth, a real charmer, with a great laugh and ready yarn."

And H. C. Pitney's was the perfect forum for Jack's brand of amiable soft-shoe. It offered him a larger profile than he'd had at Broadhead's, as a master salesman with the chance to work the whole store. He'd ply his specialty in the shoe department and then work the other aisles, chalking up a pant-leg hem or outfitting a toddler for a church social. In 1906 and for a steady stretch of years, Pitney's did great business clothing most of Tampico's citizens. "What You Buy We Stand By" was the store's well-known motto. In addition to his position as clothes manager, Jack was also the store's buyer, which meant long train trips between Tampico and Chicago, where most of their merchandising originated.

Jack hopscotched between Tampico and Chicago in a well-worn seat on the CB&Q. It was a punishing journey that meant four or five transfers and could take up to five hours for the 125-mile trip. Many regulars who traveled that route soothed themselves with a bottle of whiskey, especially on the return leg from Chicago, where liquor was plentiful. During the trip, there might be any number of businessmen who passed out and missed their stop.

Jack Reagan was no exception. Alcohol was in his blood. His family, dating back to the O'Regans in Ireland, were earnest drinkers, a distinction that extended all the way through their line. Thomas, Michael . . . "the whole family drank—*a lot*," says a person familiar with the Reagan ancestry. Jack's father, John, had a reputation for being "a two-fisted drinker," but it was his brother Will who grappled hardest with the bottle. Will Reagan drank badly—the kind of fall-down-drunk drinking that attracted attention, the wrong kind of attention, in an unforgiving town. It was a taste he passed on to his younger brother, Jack.

Jack drank with gusto, but not without restraint. There is strong evidence that he could go cold turkey for long spells—or maybe just periods when he didn't drink to excess. But Jack Reagan was a binge drinker. He'd go on a weekend bender now and then and eventually stumble home roaring drunk. In April 1907, a year after the Reagans arrived, Tampico tightened restrictions on alcohol. Jack had to have heard the complaints from customers at work about how Tampico men were being corrupted by liquor, how the saloons only reinforced the problem, how the children were at risk. Saloonkeepers, scarce though they were, had run afoul of the Tampico chapter of the Women's Christian Temperance Union. A local Law and Order League was formed to tackle the issue, and a week later legislation was passed ending all liquor licensing in town. People like Jack Reagan were forced to drink secretly—or elsewhere. In Jack's case, that meant Chicago—not in Tampico, where he'd have to face Nelle—but during buying trips, real or otherwise, which occurred with more frequency beginning that spring.

Nelle wasn't blind when it came to Jack's drinking—she could smell it on him when he returned from Chicago—but more often than not she turned a blind eye. As long as he stayed sober at home, she kept it to herself. It was only when his brother Will showed up, bottles in hand, that things got messy. He was always ready to share a bottle with his brother—and Jack was always ready to oblige. Nelle dreaded these dissolute family reunions. Will Reagan was a surly drunk, abusive and foul-mouthed, who had caused a lot of havoc dating back to Fulton, where Nelle had angled to keep the brothers apart. Will, in her mind, was a terrible influence on Jack, and it is believed that she encouraged the move to Tampico in order to put some distance between the two men. It was bad enough that Will worked with roughnecks in the grain elevator, where that kind of behavior was generally accepted. But Nelle was having none of it.

In 1906, Will Reagan and alcohol seemed like the only two burdens on what was otherwise a relatively happy marriage. Money was always an issue, but there were plenty of affordable pleasures to be had. Since arriving in Tampico, Jack and Nelle had managed to assimilate into the social fabric of the community. They were welcomed into the cast of local players who staged amateur productions at the Burden Opera House. Nelle loved the theater. She had a natural talent for it, and in Tampico it blossomed. She acted with intensity and gave dramatic recitations—short readings with moralistic overtones delivered in the footlights downstage. She regularly shared billing with Jack, who often appeared onstage in blackface. Their grandson Ron later referred to them as "the Lunt-Fontanne of the northern Illinois farm set," as apt a handle as any to describe them.

There were also Chautauquas, community assemblies held under a tent in a field near town with inspirational speakers, entertainers, educators, and musicians. And revival meetings, most notably those featuring Billy Sunday, the ex–National League outfielder cum barnstorming evangelist who worked the so-called Kerosene Circuit—the small towns not yet electrified—in western Illinois. Sunday was a dynamic and inspired performer, and his sermons offered pious Midwesterners new ways of coping with their daily problems. He opposed dancing, reading novels, playing cards, the teaching of evolution, and, most vehemently, alcohol, encouraging his followers to "get on the water wagon," a message that no doubt resonated with Nelle. "Whiskey is all right in its place," he'd holler, high-kicking across the stage, "but its place . . . is . . . *hell!*"

Tampicans heard him loud and clear. After Sunday's revival at the nearby Prophetstown Tabernacle in June 1906, during which he reformed twelve converts from Tampico, the town welcomed fellow reformer Dr. L. W. Munhall's tabernacle, which raised another hundred for its penitent flock.

Weekends in Tampico were especially festive affairs. The town converged on Main Street every Saturday night. "It is an interesting sight," a visitor observed, "to see the more than 100 rigs or teams and vehicles tied up to the hitching cable running through the posts." Whole families off the farms poured onto the street and sidewalk, strolling arm-in-arm. Windows were lit up, doors thrown open, refreshments offered to one and all.

The Reagans could observe the developments from their front windows. Still in their early twenties, Jack and Nelle were game to mingle, and they swept downstairs to join the crowd as soon as it gathered. With Jack's arm clamped tenderly around Nelle's waist, they were familiar figures at the Saturday soirees, and "it was often after midnight before they got back home."

Their carefree lifestyle got derailed somewhat when their first child, a son, was born on September 26, 1908. He became the third boy in the family tree to bear the name John Reagan, although to distinguish between father and son his parents decided to call him by his middle name, Neil, an alliteration of Nelle. Later, there would be some wrangling over which church would lay claim to the baby, but there was never any doubt that his initial baptism would take place in the theater. "My first appearance on the stage was when I was about three or four months old," he recalled, when Nelle cast him opposite her as a dying baby in the Tampico Players production of *The Dust of the Earth.*

With Jack gone much of the time, on the road buying merchandise or managing the store, Nelle was often alone with Neil. She made the most of that time, reading to her son from Scripture or taking him on errands along Main Street and beyond. In the spring, when the weather cooperated, they would rock for hours in front of the open window, where "Nelle would count the endless line of farmers with their wagons of corn, oats, or wheat waiting to unload at the Boyer Brothers' elevator."

Nelle was accommodated. Life in Tampico was relatively comfortable, even gracious when compared with her childhood on the farm. Jack had a good job, a job with potential, and they had a healthy young son. But something was missing. By early 1910, Nelle had found it in the Christian Church, and became active in its affairs.

The Disciples of Christ, as the sect was known, believed that a true, devout Christian dealt directly with the day-to-day issues in this world. "Living the gospel"—the idea of *social gospel*—was a strong part of the Disciples' doctrine. Unlike the Methodists and others in the mainstream, they incorporated poetry and played music in their services and extolled missionary work, encouraging congregants to serve those in need—not only the poor, but anyone who had fallen from grace. The spirit of unity and inclusiveness appealed to Nelle's sense of generosity, to say nothing of the church's militant stance against alcohol.

Jack resented the rift that divided their home along a religious Mason-Dixon Line. Nelle had "tried very hard to bring herself to join the Catholic Church when she and Jack were married," Neil recalled years later, but she ultimately rejected it. Over time, it created issues over which church would prevail. As a prerequisite for a church wedding, Jack had promised the pastor who married them that he would raise his children as Catholics. Whether he forgot to inform Nelle, as he later insisted, or simply reneged is a matter of speculation. But a tug of war over Neil's faith—and the widening family schism—persisted. Nelle wouldn't be deterred. On Easter Sunday in 1910, she underwent baptism by total immersion, sealing her membership in the Christian Church of Tampico.

How this weighed on their marriage is a matter of conjecture. Jack's persistent drinking was a growing problem, and suspicions arose about other women. This breach of religious unity presented yet another source of conflict. Whatever the case, the landscape shifted again when, shortly after her baptism, Nelle became pregnant with her second child.

It snowed viciously all Sunday evening, February 5, 1911, in what the *Tampico Tornado* called "one of the worst blizzards" to hit the region in years. "The snow was ten inches to a foot and drifted badly, making the highways nearly impassable." Strong winds had blown across miles of open prairie, burying Main Street. No traffic could get into or out of town.

For two people in particular this was a hell of a time for a storm. Nelle Reagan had gone into labor early that morning, and her doctor, Harry

Terry, was stranded elsewhere, presumably on a house call. Nelle was not having an easy time of delivery. Her pelvic muscles had weakened alarmingly during labor, and the baby wasn't moving properly. Her contractions were excruciating, so much so that "Jack feared for her life." Three-year-old Neil was shipped off to a neighbor's care, while Mrs. Roy Rasine and Mrs. John Daly, two "midwives with a hardiness of pioneer dedication," struggled to stabilize the delivery.

Nelle's labor stretched on well into the next morning. Finally, around 3:00 a.m., Dr. Terry stumbled into the flat bleary-eyed and half frozen. When the baby finally appeared at 4:16 a.m., its feet came first through the birth canal, compressing the umbilical cord and requiring the doctor to pick up the pace in order not to deprive the newborn of oxygen. It was a touch-and-go process that took serious skill.

The baby, another boy, weighing in at just over ten pounds, was fine, but Dr. Terry informed Nelle it would be her last child. Her pelvic muscles had stretched during the birth and would no longer support the uterus. So be it; this baby was a gift. All along, she had planned to call him Donald, after her great-grandfather, but her sister, Jenny, had beaten her to it with her own son. Instead, Nelle named the child Ronald with Wilson, her maiden name: Ronald Wilson Reagan.

There is a famous anecdote—probably apocryphal—that has Jack bending admiringly over his new screaming son and uttering an opinion that branded the boy forever: "For such a little bit of a Dutchman, he makes a hell of a lot of noise, doesn't he?" *Dutch*—he would be Dutch from now on because of the incident. It was a good story, but many years later, in a handwritten letter to the *Holland Herald*, Ronald Reagan explained that the name Dutch "evidently came about because of a hairstyle for children— a Dutch Bob"—that was given to him when he was "three or four years old." He wrote, "My father started calling me Dutch, and an older brother kept it alive."

But in February 1911, it was a grudging effort for Neil to call him anything at all, much less "brother." The older Reagan boy had been promised a baby sister. Nelle was certain of it from the moment she became pregnant. So Neil felt shaken and betrayed when the neighbor he had been staying with told him, "Now you can go home and see your baby brother." In fact, for two days he downright refused to go into the bedroom where his mother and brother were recuperating. "I didn't want any part of a brother," he recalled.

It became perfectly clear to everyone, especially Neil, that Ronald was destined to be Nelle's boy, while Neil was cast in Jack's long shadow. Ronald had his mother's tender features and serene, somewhat subdued temperament. There were echoes of her straight brow and strong jaw and two rosy dimples. His thick mop of hair was courtesy of Jack.

When Jack Reagan agreed to manage the H. C. Pitney store in Tampico, he thought he was on his way. At least that's the way it had been presented. After years of clerking for his aunt and uncle and apprenticing at Broadhead's, he was finally calling the shots. But H.C. had him on a relatively short leash. There were other outlets in the boss's retail empire, such as it was, that remained off-limits to Jack. He was Pitney's man in Tampico, and even though that took Jack to Chicago and Clinton, Iowa, a manufacturing hub, the stakes were too small for his burning ambition. Yes, Jack "loved shoes," as his son later noted, but he wanted something more substantial for himself, something solid, with no one looking over his shoulder or telling him what to do. He was always searching for an opportunity that would give him the independence he craved.

One option he considered was a complete change of scenery. In early October 1909, Jack had jumped at the chance to score a valuable piece of property in a government land lottery under the homesteading act. It seemed like a long shot, with so many applicants registered for the raffle, but—wouldn't you know it!—Jack won a 160-acre farm in Aberdeen, South Dakota. He immediately jumped on a Burlington overnight train headed north to check on this windfall. But the dream fell apart soon after he arrived. The property, he discovered, was remote and isolated. Aside from the wayward location, one thing crystallized: he was a shoe man. Farming, he reasoned, wasn't part of his makeup, he had none of the skills, no feel for the land. Grudgingly, he stuck it out for a week or two before returning the land and heading home.

Nelle kept Jack on solid ground. She spent her days largely in service to her sons, with any time left over cooking and sewing or ironing the spotless white shirts Jack wore to work. Time to herself was a rare commodity. In those odd spare moments, Nelle would drift to the back of the flat and commiserate with her neighbor, Daisy Seymour, through the common window of their adjoining back porches. Daisy's son Fred was a few months older than Ronald. Whenever possible the two young mothers bent toward the wall and discussed "looking forward to God's plan for a better world . . . and setting a good example for [their boys] to follow." When one woman needed to do some shopping, she would pass her son through the window for some free neighborly babysitting.

Like Jack, Nelle was restless, too. Their apartment was unsuitable for her needs. "Upstairs flats were not very desirable in those days," noted a Tampico historian. They absorbed considerable street noise, particularly from the backfire of cars that had multiplied since the Reagans moved to town. The stairs were hard on the bones and treacherous when it came to children. And winter made that trip to the outhouse an ugly affair.

Once the spring thaw took hold in 1911, Nelle leaned on Jack to find a better home in which to raise the boys, someplace where Neil and Ronald would flourish. She envisioned "a nice, white bungalow with modern plumbing, grass lawn, and spacious playground for the children." By May, Jack found their place—the old Burden House on Glassburn Street, just south of the town depot and right around the corner from Pitney's. It was everything Nelle had asked for. It had a white picket fence, no steep stairs, an indoor toilet whose flush shook the walls, and an adorable front porch. Right across the street was a manicured town park featuring a Civil War cannon mounted on wooden standards and a seventeen-foot obelisk inscribed with names of local men who had died serving their country—the perfect playground for two rambunctious boys. The one drawback was the railroad, whose tracks ran adjacent to the property by a grain elevator.

One morning, when Ronald was two and a half years old, these elements conspired to give Nelle a terrible fright. From the porch she contentedly watched the boys playing in the park. No one paid much attention to the idle coal car parked on the tracks, just across the street. "We spent a few minutes in the park," Neil recalled, "and I took [Ronald] by the hand, and we got down on our hands and knees and crawled under the train." An ice wagon had pulled up on the other side of the tracks, an oasis in summer for Tampico kids. "They'd give you a piece of ice that you could suck, and we thought it was like candy," according to Ronald.

Nelle didn't see them make it safely across; she saw only their little legs disappearing under the train chassis. While the boys were still at the ice wagon, the train chugged to life "with a hissing burst of steam" and Nelle let out a scream that rivaled its shrill whistle. Neil could hear her from the other side of the tracks and decided to let her cool off rather than to go home and face the music. "So we went down and played in the sand until the train pulled out, probably an hour or so later."

More than seventy years later Ronald recalled how Nelle gave them a reminder never to repeat that stunt—"physically, a reminder."

Whereas Jack only went through the motions. He'd growl and threaten, then strip off his belt as a preview of the whipping to come, but he was all bluster. Jack had enough on his plate without cuffing his boys. The store kept him busy, but he had a hand in a number of other pots. He practiced rescue drills routinely with Tampico's volunteer fire department, helped manage the local softball team, devoted hours to the local chapter of the Knights of Columbus, and became active in the town's Businessman's Association.

There was also his brother Will to contend with. Will's life had come dangerously off the rails. In the spring of 1912, he had been jilted by a Fulton woman and drank himself into such a stupor that the local paper reported that he was "seriously ill . . . unable to leave his room" for ten days. There followed a series of brawls and unprovoked attacks on colleagues, and a drunk-and-disorderly charge in nearby Sterling that earned Will time in Whiteside County Jail. A reporter noted that "he has not appeared to be just right," which was code for "off his rocker." Jack eventually committed his brother to a sanatorium for a stretch and later had him officially declared "mentally deranged."

Jack also argued openly about politics, a pet topic. Tampico was an overwhelmingly Republican stronghold, with Jack an impassioned Democratic voice in the wilderness. Nothing made him more animated than castigating President Taft and his conservative cronies for wrenching the Republican Party to the right. There were also exposés in the newspaper that fed Jack's sense of injustice, such as the Triangle Shirtwaist Factory fire in New York City, which underscored the issue of dangerous working conditions for the poor, and a coup in Honduras custom tailored to an American tycoon's interests.

Growing up in Illinois, Ronald Reagan would always hear some form of political talk in the house. Jack Reagan was devoted to the kinds of social causes that would one day be construed as entitlements: relief for the working poor, trust-busting, child labor laws, a fair minimum wage, regulation of communications conglomerates, a graduated income tax.

Nelle's own views supported her husband's when it came to giving the downtrodden a leg up. Since her conversion by the Disciples of Christ in 1910, she burned with charitable devotion, convinced that generosity and good works were God's greatest gifts. She set aside parts of every day to perform some public-spirited deed, whether it was visiting someone in town who was suffering from an illness or reassuring people in desperate straits with words of hope and encouragement.

The church also offered her escape from the gnawing problems at home. Jack was growing frustrated with a career in stasis. Pitney's sales were solid and steady, but they weren't growing, and Jack saw no room for advancement. His forty dollars a month had been sufficient for two people, but now they were four. These days, he was always strapped for cash, always just making the wages stretch. As ever, Jack tried to put a good face on things, but he was restless.

Occasionally, that provoked blithe bouts of extravagance such as the purchase of a Ford Model T in June 1913. "It was on old touring car," Ronald remembered vividly more than seventy years later. Jack had talked H. C. Pitney into lending him enough cash for the car. There were more cars in Tampico than Main Street could handle—and a legion of horses unwilling to cede precious ground. Driving could be a hair-raising experience. On the afternoon of December 14, while Jack was driving the family to Rock Falls for a Sunday outing to visit Nelle's sister, not far from Tampico, the "steering gear . . . failed to work properly and the car suddenly shot to one side of the road and turned completely over in a ditch." Nelle and Neil were thrown wide of the car, but the roof was bashed in, pinning Jack and Ronald underneath. There was just enough air between the seat and the roof for Ronald to breathe—a circumstance that triggered a lifelong struggle with claustrophobia. Jack eventually wriggled free, but it took several men from a nearby house to rescue Ronald, still in swaddling clothes, by pulling him through a rear window.

There were hardships and near-catastrophes for the family, but also amusement. Both boys had fond memories of their parents' acting endeavors. Nelle and Jack starred in a succession of shows at the Burden Opera

House, and by 1913 they were minor celebrities among the towns west of the Rock River. On April 19, several hundred people from as far off as Yorktown thronged the theater to catch their star turns in *A Woman's Honor*, a four-act piece that featured "intense dramatic action, thrilling climaxes, uproarious comedy, and a story of absorbing romantic interest." A reviewer praising Nelle's performances in two roles, as Olive and Sally, said, "A pin dropped could not be heard in the entire house." Later that year, on Thanksgiving night, the couple brought down the house in *Millie the Quadroon*, a five-act tearjerker by Lizzie May Elwyn, in which Nelle played three roles. One can only imagine the spectacle when Millie mused about the life of Gyp, her slave, and Jack bounded onstage in blackface. "Well, yo' see, missus, I nebber was anything else. I know de whip was dreffel. Golly," he moaned, massaging his backside, "I feel de smart now."

Show business: it was in the family.

For the Reagans, Tampico seemed to have it all—small-town community spirit, a stable economy, strong moral values, a place to call home. But to Jack it was the sticks. He had bigger dreams, and by 1914 they prevailed. He'd been casting around for a better job, looking as always for something with a higher profile, something more financially rewarding. If Tampico couldn't accommodate his ambition, then the answer might lie in an urban area. To an Illinois native that could mean only one thing. So in January 1915, a few days after New Year's, the Reagans packed up and drove east.

They were heading to the big city. They were bound for Chicago.

CHAPTER THREE

"THE HAPPIEST TIMES
OF MY LIFE"

*"Poverty is a soft pedal upon all branches of human
activity, not excepting the spiritual."*

—H. L. MENCKEN

Over the next six years, the Reagan family would repeatedly be on the move—haphazard migrations from town to town that were not always well planned and purposeful. "We moved to wherever my father's ambition took him," Ronald recalled, but more often it was a matter of outracing the bill collector.

The Reagan family pulled into Chicago at the beginning of 1915, filled with optimism. The city churned with energy drawn from a vastly diverse populace on the make and an infrastructure racing to accommodate it. Evidence was visible everywhere on the skyline; since the turn of the century, Chicago had been transformed by an array of palazzo-style structures—the Rand McNally Building, Peoples Gas, the Unity Building, the Railway Exchange, and the Continental Illinois bank—symbols of growing prosperity. A few years earlier, a network of trains began operating on an elevated track above the streets. Trolleys clattered up and down the avenues. It was all here, in a sprawling twenty-six-by-fourteen-mile stretch—ironworks, garment manufacturing, commercial printing, broadcasting, transportation, meatpacking, chewing gum, and crime, plenty of crime. Chicago, wrote Nelson Algren, was "a city that was to forge out of steel and blood-red neon its own particular wilderness."

What a contrast from tiny Tampico. To a four-year-old who'd never been farther than the Rock River, Chicago was an eyeful, "a congested urban world of gaslit sidewalks and streets alive with people," 2,185,000 strong pressed shoulder to shoulder. Ronald Reagan might not have been old enough to fathom the life of the city, but it stuck in his pores. From the outset, he was struck by its energy. Not more than two weeks after landing there, he came down with bronchial pneumonia, a strain so powerful it almost killed him. Shortly after that, his brother, Neil, fell off the back of a horse-drawn beer truck, which promptly ran over his leg.

Early one evening, soon afterward, the boys ran off. Jack and Nelle had left their sons home alone, which eventually triggered their fears. Neil—or Moon, as he was nicknamed—blew out the gas on the kitchen stove and grabbed his brother (now invariably called Dutch) by the hand, and they took off across the Midway to search for their parents. Night descended and the dark shadows morphed into spiders and bogeymen. Moon and Dutch soon realized they were lost, at which point their bravado turned to tears. Somewhat miraculously, Jack swooped in to rescue them, but they weren't off the hook. They'd blown out the gas in the apartment, but hadn't turned it off, so when Jack and Nelle returned they realized the place was about ready to blow. "I got a larruping for that," Dutch recalled. And a new set of rules. Thereafter, the boys were restricted to the streets around the hard-scrabble South Side, on the edge of the University of Chicago campus, where their father had rented a cold-water flat.

Modern upscale department stores were a natural stepping-stone, and Jack had seemingly stepped into the toniest. In July 1914, the local Tampico paper reported that he had "accepted a good position in the retail shoe department of Marshall Fields & Co." Its opulent building filled with luxurious merchandise in the Loop of downtown Chicago was a far cry from H. C. Pitney's. But by the time Jack got to Chicago that job had disappeared. Instead, he wound up working at the Fair Store, a discount emporium billing itself as "the store of the people . . . the market place for the Thrifty." A discount outlet didn't have the cachet of Marshall Fields, or its salary.

At the Fair Store, Jack felt like a drone, working long, ten-hour days for next to nothing, hardly enough to make ends meet. The bulk of his pay went toward the rent, with little left over for anything that wasn't absolutely essential. "We were poor, and I mean poor," Moon recalled. To save money, Nelle made all of Moon's clothes, which were eventually handed down to Dutch. Just feeding the family took creativity. Every Saturday morning, the boys were given a dime and sent off to the meat market on Cottage Grove Avenue. The money covered the cost of a scraggly soup bone. Moon also asked the butcher for liver for their cat. "We didn't have a cat," he admitted years later, "but our big meal on Sunday was always fried liver," organ meat usually headed for the bin. "We ate on the soup bone the rest of the week." Nelle would roast it, then boil up a watery beef stock, adding table scraps like potatoes and carrots, even oatmeal on occasion, to make the broth stretch as long as possible.

Despite the appreciable hardship, Jack always came up with enough to keep himself in drink. He was drinking more openly here—and with more abandon. Not yet officially a "toddlin' town," Chicago had saloons on practically every corner—especially in the Reagans' predominantly Irish neighborhood—so Jack never lacked for opportunity, despite the wave of temperance sweeping the country. On Saturday afternoon he would start early, sending the boys out to fetch buckets full of "backdoor beer," brew bought cheaply from unlicensed joints run sotto voce—or "speak-easy"— by the mob. When he drank, he'd go until he couldn't see straight. Inevitably, he'd make a spectacle of himself, becoming rowdy, stumbling, falling down—or worse. "There were times," Moon remembered, "when he didn't open the screen door, he just walked through it."

The boys were finally old enough to understand that their father's drinking was a problem. They could see how it caused tension between their parents. Little Dutch certainly knew the score. "I can remember overhearing my father, after one of those [binges], say to my mother, 'If you ever smell a drop on my breath, lock me in the bedroom if you have to. Don't let me get out, because there is no way that I can stop.'" But Nelle was no match for Jack's frequent lapses. When he staggered home drunk, she flew straight into safeguarding mode, circling mother-bear arms around her young sons. "She always tried to protect us," Moon said.

Nelle was careful to give the boys some perspective about Jack's alcoholism. "She told us that we must not turn against our father for that," Dutch recalled, "that it was a sickness he could not help, and that we should try to be of help to him in this at all times."

Other times, help was beyond everyone's control, no more so than in December 1915, when Jack's behavior cost him his job. The Fair Store must have run out of patience with his repeated "coffee breaks," his overexuberant exchanges with customers, his mounting unreliability, all the familiar warning signs.

With or without a job, Chicago was too expensive for a shoe salesman's family. Nelle had tried to compensate by taking in needlework on a freelance basis, but even with that it didn't provide nearly enough. So the Reagans packed up and moved on. Again.

Jack caught on with a department store in Galesburg, about two hundred miles southwest of Chicago. Founded as a college town, Galesburg had the kind of amenities that coalesce around campuses. There was a music conservatory whose house bands gave concerts on the town square, regular parades that were all well attended. Acts like W. C. Fields and Harry Houdini appeared at the opera house, where the Marx Brothers were given their nicknames during a backstage poker game. Chautauquas flourished a few miles off at Lake George, with its own natatorium. There was even a resident poet—Carl Sandburg, known around town as Charlie—who had grown up across from the railyards and gave frequent readings.

Because Galesburg sat at the crossroads of the Burlington and Northern, the CB&Q, and the Santa Fe, most of its populace descended from Swedish, Italian, and Irish immigrants who had come to work on the railroads in the mid-1800s and stayed on. In the sixty years since, they had parlayed their hands-on expertise into the construction of homes, one of which Jack rented on North Kellogg Street, in a new subdivision practically at the end of the city limits.

For five-year-old Dutch, Galesburg was a lovely, manageable town, unlike Chicago. It had a big-city feel but a quaint, sleepy nature. There were any number of thriving factories, like Western Tool Works, Polter's Disk, and Frost Manufacturing, which made boilers for the locomotives, but their expansion was limited by town boss Omer N. Custer, a benevolent autocrat who feared that runaway growth would destroy Galesburg's character. In the summer, Dutch could watch the two semipro baseball teams in the Illinois-Missouri League square off in Lincoln Park. In all likelihood, he got a chance to see the Galesburg Boosters' ace pitcher, future Hall of Famer Grover Cleveland Alexander, whom he would portray in 1952 in his final film for Warner Bros. No doubt he was taken on a tour of Old Main, a red-brick building with a cream-colored cupola on the campus of Knox College, where Abe Lincoln had debated Stephen Douglas in 1858.

Dutch could come and go as he pleased here. Trolling through the weedy empty lot directly across the street, with its barrier of poplar trees, he'd forage for jungle treasures, like grass snakes. He learned how to ride a bicycle outside his house, wobbling over the street's bumpy bricks produced by the same local Puritan plant that shored up the brand-new Panama Canal.

Jack also used the bike, which he rode to work each day at the O. T. Johnson store in the center of town. Known as the Big Store by nearly everyone in the state, O. T. Johnson's was a commercial showpiece—two massive buildings that took up an entire city block and catered to a genteel clientele from as far off as Peoria and the Quad Cities. It had a bookstore, bakery, flower boutique, camera shop, and soda fountain, as well as a fine-dining restaurant on the ground floor that offered French service.

Jack felt right at home in the Big Store's massive shoe department. It had an imposing display wall that ran the length of the floor, stacked with thousands of cardboard boxes. From nine to five it was Jack's little fiefdom and a wonderful companion piece to the house he was renting, number 1219, on the corner of North Kellogg and Fremont. Overall the house was quite comfortable, if modest compared with the nearby Victorian mansions on Quality Hill. It had a wide front parlor cordoned off by oak-and-glass pocket doors, and behind it a dining room and kitchen with built-in pine cupboards. Upstairs were three ample bedrooms and a dormered attic that looked out over a silver maple shading the front lawn.

D utch's five-year-old mind was brimming with curiosity. At night, after the supper dishes were put away and only the soft glow of lamplight filtered through the parlor, Dutch and Moon would curl up on the couch, one boy on either side of Nelle, as she read to them from books they'd borrowed from the library. This was Dutch's favorite activity of the day. It didn't matter that he couldn't make sense of the letters on the page, it was the learning process that so intrigued him. He hung on the words, following along as Nelle ran her finger under each one. In time, he began to decipher the hieroglyphics. By the summer of 1916, Dutch was claiming that he knew how to read.

Jack was a serious skeptic. One balmy July night in 1916, watching his young son stretched out on the floor all but wrapping himself in the pages of the *Galesburg Evening Mail*, he asked Dutch what he was doing.

"Reading."

Jack decided to play along. "Well, read me something," he said, swallowing a chuckle.

Dutch folded back the front page, squinted at one of the long columns, and began delivering an account of an act of sabotage at a munitions depot on an island in New York harbor.

Jack was stunned. Nelle drifted in the room to see what all the commotion was about, which provoked a hasty repeat performance. Soon, she flew off across the street to roust their neighbors, the McGowans and the Tennerys, to come over and hear Dutch read.

Now there was no stopping him. Dutch combed the paper every day, proudly reading aloud. He was especially drawn to graphic accounts about the progress of Allied troops in Europe. For over a year, much of the world had been at war—a war that was about to reshape the map in ways no one could have foreseen. In 1916, there was no sentiment in insular Galesburg to join hostilities that were viewed as alien to American interests. The largely Republican townsfolk, including the newspapers, were vehemently opposed, supporting Woodrow Wilson's efforts to keep the United States neutral.

Jack, a diehard Democrat, was on the fence. Like most Irish Catholics, he was adamantly opposed to aiding the United Kingdom, which persistently denied independence to Ireland. But his convictions got the better of him. He was a humanitarian first and therefore leaned toward intervention as a means of saving lives and ending the monstrous slaughter that had already claimed over two million casualties. When, in April 1917, President Woodrow Wilson finally declared war on Germany, Jack was one of the first men in line at the local recruiting office. It was a valiant, if futile, act of patriotism; there was little chance he'd be allowed to enlist. He was thirty-three that spring, two years beyond the age limit set by the Selective Service. He was out of shape and the family's sole supporter.

Instead, Jack remained behind in Galesburg as the younger men in town hoisted duffel bags onto crowded troop transports leaving from the depot en route to Chicago. It was the scene of numerous teary farewells. Many afternoons, after Moon was done at school, Nelle would walk the boys to the railyards—a distance of more than two miles—to cheer on troop trains passing through town and hand the doughboys good-luck coins through open windows. Nelle did her part as well, helping the Red Cross to distribute care packages among the men.

That September, when Dutch was six, he started first grade at the Silas Willard School, a block from his house. The classes were huge because the rooms were enormous; often there were sixty-five children in a class. Because there was no lunchroom, Dutch walked home at noon, usually joining his father for what they called "the dinner meal."

He took to school with unbridled enthusiasm. Unlike his classmates, who were struggling to read simple phrases, Dutch was already racing ahead by plowing through books. "I could pick up something to read and memorize it fairly quickly," he recalled, "a lucky trait that made schoolwork easy for me but sometimes annoyed my brother, who didn't have the same ability."

Siblings, especially brothers, are naturally competitive, and things can get tense when a younger boy begins to outshine his big brother. Moon was no exception. Not particularly the brightest student, he bristled when Dutch called attention to himself by reciting a poem by heart or reading aloud to his parents. There were other times when Moon watched his younger brother sitting all by himself, playing contentedly with a cherished collection of lead soldiers, shutting him out.

Resentment boiled over one day after school, when the boys were messing around across the street in the vacant lot. They had the area—their fort—"booby-trapped for adults, [with] caves [they had dug] covered over with boxes" to foil anyone who trespassed on their turf. Eventually, they decided to build a campfire. "I got the ax out of the garage," Moon recalled, "and [Dutch] would hold the [logs] while I cut them." The second the ax made contact with the wood, Dutch would let go of his end so that the piece flew up, hitting Moon in the face. The older boy had had enough.

"After three or four times like this, I let him have it in the head with the ax." Fortunately, the blade caught bone, sparing any critical damage, but there was enough blood to satisfy Moon.

But beyond the sibling rivalry, there was a kinship regarding the tensions at home. Relations were unusually fraught between Jack and Nelle. "Sometimes," Dutch recalled, "my father suddenly disappeared and didn't come home for days, and sometimes when he did return, my brother and I would hear some pretty fiery arguments through the walls of our house." Occasionally, when things boiled over, Nelle would bundle up the boys and take them to her sister's house until everyone's emotions calmed down.

During this time, Galesburg seesawed in its official policy toward alcohol; one year the city was wet, the next dry, which made casual drinking difficult—but not that difficult. A barfly like Jack would always find a way. Paydays were the worst, when Jack would inevitably take his earnings to the nearest bar. Nelle did her best to run interference. She even petitioned the payroll department at O. T. Johnson's to give Jack's paycheck directly to her, but they refused. His drinking put the family in a familiar financial squeeze.

Dutch remembered hearing his father promise Nelle that better days were just ahead. But if so, the family wouldn't be enjoying them in Galesburg. By the summer of 1917, the drinking had caught up with Jack again, and as a result he was fired from his job at the Big Store.

After struggling to make a few payments on the rent, Jack and Nelle grew desperate, and in January 1918, under cover of night, they packed their belongings and hopped a train heading west.

Monmouth was the first town they came to and was as good a place as any to start over: smaller than Galesburg, larger than Tampico, with a booming wartime economy and lush surrounding farmland that produced a wealth of corn that made livestock fat. The local hogs especially thrived, giving Monmouth bragging rights as the biggest bacon-processing center in the country. In order to plow the cornfields, James H. Pattee invented a new, revolutionary machine—a cultivator named after "the Swedish nightingale" Jenny Lind—which begat three factories that employed half the town. All of which meant there was a prosperous downtown anchored by a department store. With a shoe department.

For a while, everything went fine. The Reagans managed to rent a house at 218 South Seventh Street in a neighborhood called the College Addition. Jack indeed got a job at the store, E. B. Colwell, selling shoes in the basement. And the boys were enrolled at Central School, just a few blocks away.

Dutch's teacher, Mabel Lukens, made a big production of introducing him—the new boy—to the rest of the second-grade class. He was escorted in after the other kids were already seated, causing several students to make note of how he carried himself, so self-assuredly, "with his jaw set, as though somebody was going to take a poke at him and he was ready for the punches." That was all it took to convey the impression that Dutch was "stuck up or something." Gertrude Romine, who sat a few rows in front of him, remembered how half a dozen classmates waited after school and "chased him all the way home, up onto his porch." Nelle intervened to save Dutch's skin, giving the young posse "a red-hot lecture." Eventually, Dutch managed to win them over, and life again fell into a comfortable routine.

Dutch had a frankly appealing soft side. Neighbors remembered seeing him rescue a nest of birds that had fallen out of a tree on the campus of Monmouth College. But he was also an incorrigible scamp. As a member of the Knot Hole Gang, there was never any question who would lead the pack sneaking in, under the fence, to the college football games.

But, as usual, extenuating circumstances intervened. In the fall of 1918, an influenza outbreak cut a swath of devastation from Europe to the Pacific islands. In less than three months, more than twenty-five million people died from the flu. And by early November, it had arrived in Monmouth.

Every precaution was taken. The city ordered its schools closed. A student Army Training Corps set up emergency facilities on the college campus, and face masks were distributed to anyone who asked. Thankfully, Monmouth and the neighboring towns were largely spared the flu's impact, but not the Reagan household.

Nelle came down with all the dreaded symptoms—a scorching fever, the telltale scarlet flush, an inability to move off the couch. There was never any doubt as to what it all meant. "The house grew so quiet," Dutch recalled. He took up sentry at the front window to watch for Dr. Lawrence, who lived around the corner, to arrive and examine his mother. "When he came down, Jack went outside with him and I waited with a lurking terror for him to come back and say, 'She's going to be all right.'" But the doctor wasn't optimistic; Nelle wasn't out of the woods, and Dutch went to sleep, as he recalled, "with a weight dragging at the pit of my stomach."

It was touch-and-go for days. Jack dragged himself to church to pray and to light altar candles for Nelle's recovery. Dutch brooded obsessively. He didn't put much stock in idol worship, and was less sure about Dr. Lawrence's advice to "keep [Nelle] stuffed to the gills with old green cheese, the moldier the better." (No one called it penicillin for another ten years.) Not even the armistice and its furious all-night celebration were enough to allay the family's worst fears. Finally, though, the fever and night sweats had run their course, and Nelle began to respond. Jack doubled down: "She's going to be all right."

But her upturn was the beginning of their downfall in Monmouth. The onerous medical bills bore heavily on Jack, who dealt with the pressure the only way he knew how. There was really no way for him to avoid the bars—the 100 block of South Street was crawling with them. Respectable ladies wouldn't walk on that side of the street, but the bars were on Jack's route home from work. Easy for him to make a brief pit stop. Before long, the drinking had reclaimed him. How long before they cost Jack his job?

A letter arrived in the nick of time from his old boss, H. C. Pitney. Pitney was losing his eyesight, and he wanted Jack to consider returning to Tampico. He offered an irresistible profit-sharing incentive. Tampico—a step backward—wasn't what Jack had envisioned for himself, but he must have seen there was little time left for him at Colwell's in Monmouth. Maybe he was better off being a big fish in a small pond again.

Soon enough, the *Fulton Journal-News* broke the story that on August 25, 1919, Mr. John E. Reagan and family had moved back to Tampico, where Mr. Reagan, formerly of Broadhead's et al., would once again "take charge of H. C. Pitney's large store." The *Tampico Tornado* ran a corresponding piece, announcing that no less than "a graduate of the American School of Practipedics" would be returning as the shoe authority in town.

Both papers made it sound like a grand homecoming. But Jack was disgruntled from the start. Pitney's illustrious "shoe department" was barely a cubbyhole in the store; the styles hadn't changed since he'd last managed the place. He knew there was no future in this job, and his restlessness set in immediately.

His family, on the other hand, settled right in. They occupied a spacious apartment above Pitney's store, across the street from their former flat. Moon found a posse his own age to run with, and Nelle burrowed deeper into her beloved Christian Church. Dutch fell in love with Tampico, later calling the move there "the most fortunate shift in my life." He set out on a deliberate exploration of every delight and diversion the town had to offer. "There were woods and mysteries, life and death among the small creatures, hunting and fishing." He learned how to swim—a pastime that would gratify him for the rest of his life—frequenting two local sources: a clear-water creek just north of town where the county ditches merged, and the Hennepin Canal, which he reached by walking along the cinder path that hugged the railroad tracks. Like Moon, Dutch found his own crowd, palling around with a few boys he knew from school—a third-grader named Vern "Newt" Dennison, Gordon Glassburn, and Harold Winchell, whom everyone called Monkey. According to Newt Dennison's account, they played tag across the pens of the city stockyards, smoked corn-silk cigarettes, and had food fights with fruit salvaged from garbage cans behind the Main Street shops.

Although Dutch could read better than most classmates at Tampico Grade School, his progress was stunted by the school's limitations. The building, nothing more than a four-room steepled box, did not have adequate space, so classes were combined—third- and fourth-grade students shared one teacher, Miss Nellie Darby. Providing schoolbooks was the responsibility of each pupil. Dutch was reading well beyond the fourth-grade level, and in an effort to remain stimulated, he resorted to borrowing books from a library stack displayed in a glass case at the front of the room—titles such as "The Sermon on the Mount," *King Solomon and the Ants* by John Greenleaf Whittier, a biography of Alfred the Great, and *History of the United Netherlands*. For a curious student such as Dutch, it was catch-as-catch-can. And he was a quick study. Classmates were impressed by his "photographic memory for dates," and his mastery of the curvy Palmer Method handwriting.

Home life was more of a challenge. After school, most boys his age, sons of farmers, were expected home straightaway to attend to a litany of chores. Dutch invariably returned to an empty house. His father was either minding the store or away on one of his buying trips, and his mother was burdened with obligations at church. To say she was an "active" member would be an understatement. Since returning to Tampico, Nelle assumed a variety of administrative duties at the Christian Church, which in 1919 had no pastor and few volunteers. She wrote most of its bulletins, handled mailings, prepared Sunday services, oversaw charitable programs, and took on virtually any outstanding task. A well-informed source reported that "Nelle ran the . . . church almost single-handed" and fanned speculation that she often preached. The woman who began life as a freethinker was a deacon now.

Nor was her ministry confined to four walls. Nelle often took her faith on the road, giving scores of religious and spiritual recitations "in tragic tones, [in which she] wept . . . and poured out poetry by the yard." Dutch referred to her as "the dean of dramatic recitals for the countryside," not without a touch of irony. For him, Nelle's devotion signified countless afternoons spent mostly on his own.

It took his neighbors, the Greenmans, to come to his rescue. They were an unfussy, elderly couple whom Dutch called Aunt Emma and Uncle Jim, and they ran a jewelry business in a shop adjacent to Pitney's. He would come to spend most weekday afternoons at the Greenmans', curled up in their old oak rocking chair with a plate of homemade cookies and hot chocolate. It was a strange environment for an eight-year-old boy, with a parlor that both fascinated and repelled him. Fifty years later he could still envision the "horsehair-stuffed gargoyles of furniture, its shawls and antimacassars, globes of glass over birds and flowers, books and strange odors." Occasionally he would wander into the jewelry shop, filled with similarly kooky relics, a parallel universe to explore and contemplate. Dutch endeared himself so much to the couple that they gave him a weekly ten-cent allowance. But their contribution to his welfare was far greater, helping to fill an emotional absence.

His father was only growing more distracted, and restless. He would never have come back to Tampico if it hadn't been for the profit-sharing scheme, but its yield hadn't panned out as expected. With H.C. unable to assist him on the floor, Jack was more or less on his own, working long days without much to see for it.

Almost from the outset, he wanted out. According to Tampico historian Paul Nicely, "Immediately they tried to sell the store because Pitney was sick and Jack Reagan didn't want to live here." They put out feelers through 1919 and into the next year, without generating much interest. The only prospective buyer died during negotiations. Truth be told, there was little opportunity for growth in Tampico. No one wanted a stagnant business.

In the meantime, the Reagans made the most of their time in town. The cost of living there was reasonable. For once, their bills were paid without too much personal sacrifice. There was no chance of Jack's getting fired, no bars within walking distance. On the face of it, life in Tampico was agreeable, as agreeable as the picture-postcard vistas that framed the town, the verdant farmland that stretched on forever under brilliant blue skies. Snapshots of that time remained vivid in Ronald Reagan's memory— the Sunday picnics along the Hennepin Canal, horse-and-buggy rides across pristine fields, flickering silent-movie nights in the town square under firefly-filled skies, riding seesaw on the enormous iron cannon in Railroad Park, those July Fourth all-day celebrations featuring chicken roasts followed by fireworks and square dancing, and ice skating on a makeshift rink filled by a firehose that Jack Reagan manned. Dutch credited such days for providing "the happiest times of my life."

A childhood in Tampico was a refuge from the complexities of the wider postwar world. Life in this remote pocket of the Midwest changed hardly at all. There, boys were isolated from the influence of radio, the rampaging stock market, and the hedonism of Jazz Age America. They weren't affected by the sweeping changes reshaping the country, such as the new leisure class and the reduction of the workweek to forty-eight hours. None of it touched the lives of the farm community, where everyone, from generation to generation, worked from dawn to dusk seven days a week—but worked contentedly, with a shared sense of worth.

Dutch would have been happy had this simple, unpretentious lifestyle been his fate, to grow up in sleepy Tampico among these good people— *idyllic*, as it would always remain in his perception. He must have been heartbroken when, in the fall of 1920, Jack came home from work practically levitating, jubilant, with news he couldn't wait to relay. H. C. Pitney had finally conceded Jack's point that there was no future for retail growth in Tampico. Such opportunity abounded in larger towns, with diverse economies and booming populations. Pitney proposed that the two of them open a shoe store in a place that fit the criteria. They were moving again, twenty-five miles north, to Dixon, Illinois.

CHAPTER FOUR

READY TO SHINE

"In love of home, the love of country has its rise."
—CHARLES DICKENS

For Dutch, Dixon was everything his father had promised—a small town masquerading in big-city clothing. It was a thriving town with a population just under the ten thousand mark and an abundance of solid industry. Held up against Chicago, however, its small-town traits were clear—a whistle-stop on the Illinois Central line, God-fearing, conservative, a handmaiden to the mighty Rock River, which cleaved a swath through the center of town. Dixon wasn't a country crossroads, nor was it a Windy City in all the respects that nickname implied—no crime, no Al Capone, no Democratic political machine, no el. Dixon prided itself on its downhome, esoteric character and frontier past.

The story of the town's namesake, John Dixon, was practically scripture. He had come from New York in an ox-pulled wagon with his wife and children in 1820, venturing into what was Indian territory—the Potawatomi to the east, the Winnebago to the north, and the Sauk and Black Hawk to the west. It was fertile prairie, some of the most gorgeous river-valley land this side of the Mississippi. The Indians had farmed it for 150 years. For a white man, settling there took enormous courage. Though the tribes tolerated outsiders, there was only fragile peace. In the spring, the Indians traditionally ferried travelers and their draft animals across the Rock River—which they called the Sinnissippi, meaning "rocky bottom"—shuttling them back over in the fall. Any competitor was burned down and driven off—that is, until Joseph Ogee, a French Canadian married to a Potawatomi princess, got into the game. He constructed a rival ferry service at the river's narrows, just south of Grand Detour, in 1828. John Dixon bought it from him two years later, adding a tavern and a log cabin that doubled as a trading post and inn, thus establishing a legitimate settlement, which people began calling Dixon's Ferry.

Dixon gained the Indians' trust by learning their language, giving them credit, and respecting their traditions. And the trust was mutual. In return, the Potawatomi gave Dixon the job of collecting their debts and paying off their creditors. Later, in the fall of 1852, General Winfield Scott charged him with distributing fifty thousand meals of grain and beef to the Sauk and Winnebago, whose hunting grounds had been decimated by federal troops.

Dixon rubbed elbows with generals and presidents alike. Martin Van Buren commissioned him to move the state land office to his town; Zachary Taylor consulted Dixon during the Black Hawk War; Jefferson Davis oversaw the building of Fort Dixon on the north bank of the river; and, when the Republican Party was formed in Bloomington-Normal in 1858, the principal speaker before Abraham Lincoln took the lectern was the ubiquitous John Dixon. In fact, a young Captain Lincoln spent forty-five days with the Sangamon County volunteer militia in Dixon and, according to John Dixon's books, still owes money for supplies he bought on credit.

But Dixon was a vision as well as a visionary. He had a mane of fine-spun silver hair that flowed in waves below his shoulders, earning him the nickname Father John. And his accomplishments were epic. He built dams and bridges across the Rock River, brought the railroad—not one but two major lines that crisscrossed just south of town; you could get on a train in Dixon and end up in Texas, Florida, or California—plotted a business district along the river, set up a local government, and established schools, banks, and a hospital, all feats designed to speed progress. By the end of the Civil War, his efforts had paid off by way of a vast immigration that fortified the town's future. People poured into Dixon from across the Erie Canal and the Great Lakes, and down the Rock River. The town grew exponentially—not quite as large as nearby Aurora or DeKalb, but by the turn of the century Dixon was a budding industrial center, with businesses drunk on the lavish hydropower.

It had a thriving industrial center: the Anglo-Swiss Condensed Milk

Factory (which became Borden's in 1903) was producing milk products and caramels in a section of town called Swissville; Reynolds Wire hit it big supplying metal screen for the U.S. Army camps in World War I; and the Medusa Portland Cement Company plumbed the rich limestone deposits along the river and produced foundations for commercial buildings in Chicago. And there were shoe companies galore—Watson Plummer, Freeman, Brown, and Red Wing—as well as the Grand Detour Plow Company, an offshoot of an outfit started a few miles up the road by a man named John Deere, who invented the iron-faced plow in 1837. Local entrepreneurs made their fortune off the river. There were flour mills, sawmills, mills that converted flax into burlap used for bags that shipped almost every conceivable commercial product

By the time the Reagans moved to Dixon, the downtown had pushed out from the riverbanks to an area that extended a half mile in every direction. "Main Street is the climax of civilization," Sinclair Lewis wrote (ironically) in 1920, and Dixon could boast a superb specimen—Galena Avenue—which ran the length of the city, north and south. The courthouse, built in 1901, was the focal point of town, a stately limestone structure stretching an entire square block. Three years later, the O. B. Dodge Library, with its stone-faced turret, opened with a collection of more than two thousand volumes a few blocks from the Dixon Theater, where for the general admission of one dollar the nightly bill featured six vaudeville acts and a silent movie accompanied by a seven-piece orchestra.

The first landmark that caught any newcomer's eye, however, was the wooden "Welcome to Dixon" victory arch that spanned Galena Avenue between the courthouse and the post office. The sign was erected in May 1919 to honor the local veterans and commemorate the site where an ecstatic celebration took place the day the War to End All Wars concluded. All the bells in the churches of Lee County sounded as fifteen thousand strong turned out to greet companies of returning troops from Camp Grant. Dutch Reagan knew the details by heart. He walked through that arch almost immediately upon arriving in Dixon, gazing at the legend inscribed on its base:

A Grateful People Pause In Their Welcome
To The Victorious Living To Pay Silent Tribute To The Illustrious Dead.

For the Reagans, Dixon was a huge upgrade in many respects. The rented house they moved into on South Hennepin Avenue was a handsome white clapboard structure with a covered front porch, built in 1891 on a parcel of land once owned by John Dixon himself. It was more than comfortable by neighborhood standards. It had a large parlor with a fireplace, which Nelle designated "for special occasions only," sealing it off with a bifold pocket door; and upstairs were three bedrooms and a closet-sized bathroom with a claw-foot tub. Dutch and Moon assumed they'd each get their own bedroom, but Nelle had other plans. "She'd never had a guest room before," says a present-day caretaker. "So she laid claim to the front bedroom, with the best view and the most light, that looked out toward the street." Dutch and Moon discovered they were going to share, and not only a room, but a bed as well. On humid Midwestern summer nights, when body heat turned the space into a sticky steam bath, the arrangement was less than ideal. Neither brother liked the setup. But come winter, with those frigid winds blowing through the single-pane glass window, all was forgiven.

Behind the house, just off Galena Avenue, was a dilapidated barn with a hayloft, where the boys could play, and adjacent to it a small patch of ground appropriated by Nelle, an avid gardener with plenty of farming in her genes, for growing tomatoes and broccoli.

Dutch was fascinated with the wildlife that drifted into the neighborhood, a virtual menagerie of muskrat, possum, and rabbit, the latter of which he kept in wire cages in the garage. "He went through this period where he was going to become a great trapper," Moon recalled. He'd "hunt" muskrat along the hillsides that rose above the river, chasing his shadow more often than not. Otherwise, Dutch kept pretty much to himself. He was a quiet boy compared with his brother, more introspective, comfortable to be by himself.

Both Dutch and Moon attended South Central Grammar School, about a five-minute walk down Hennepin Avenue. It was a basic elementary school, but uncompromising. "The teachers didn't allow any nonsense or backtalk," says Esther Haack, a classmate of Dutch's. "We paid attention and were quiet. No speaking unless you were spoken to." Dutch, a fifth-grader, was your average B student. He loved to read and write but showed little effort when it came to other subjects. Part of the inertia can be attributed to his eyesight. Dutch was severely nearsighted. He could see—shapes, but not much more. In later years he would reminisce unflinchingly about this boyhood burden he called a handicap. "I simply thought that the whole world was made up of colored blobs that became distinct when I got closer, and I was sure it appeared the same way to everyone else." In class, he could never see the blackboard, even from the front row. And he seldom played sports. Baseball was out of the question; he couldn't hit the broad side of a barn or field a pop-up, much less a grounder. Basketball?—not if he was expected to catch it. He was incapable of anything that required hand-to-eye coordination. The school playground, for Dutch, was a no-man's-land, recess a stressful ordeal. He was embarrassed at always being taken last when teams were choosing sides. It never occurred to him that wearing glasses might correct his vision; he only assumed that he wasn't as coordinated as other boys. All told, it caused him "a lot of heartache."

The only game that gave him any solace was football. There was little likelihood of his hauling in a pass, but tackling an opponent wasn't a problem. He was small but strong. As long as he played defense, he could hold his own.

This led to after-school pickup games on the empty lot at the side of the Reagans' house. The O'Malley brothers would come across the street and play a Hennepin Avenue version of two-on-two with Moon and Dutch. Of course, the sides were usually stacked—Moon and George O'Malley against the two younger boys, who inevitably got creamed in the pileups. If the score was too lopsided, Moon and George would entertain themselves by tricking Dutch. They knew he squinched his eyes shut when carrying the ball. Ed O'Malley recalled how the two older boys would pretend to fall back as Dutch charged blindly ahead. Just as he was about to break open, they'd nudge him with a hip, sending him flying into a large bush or the side of the barn. It was always good for a laugh.

Dutch was a pretty good sport about it. He smiled his way through such monkey business, doing his best to maintain the peace. To that extent, friends considered him "something of a goody-goody," but he had a latent rogue nature that every so often steered him onto dicey terrain.

One Halloween, he and Ed O'Malley joined their two older brothers in giving the rite of shivaree—the Midwestern version of the French *charivari*, by which newlyweds were hazed on their wedding night—to Joe Vail, a bridegroom who would later become the mayor of Dixon. The four boys made off with an old baby buggy, which Dutch tossed onto the Vails' porch. He was in the midst of making a clean getaway when Vail, a big man lying in wait, took off after the boy. "[Dutch] was the slowest one [of us]," recalled Ed. Vail was just about to grab him, "when my older brother cut in between them . . . and Dutch got away."

He wasn't as lucky that July Fourth, when Moon goaded him into setting off a handful of torpedoes—a type of illegal fireworks that exploded on impact—from atop a stoplight in the middle of the Galena Avenue Bridge. Dutch was still clinging triumphantly to the pole when a police car pulled up and asked him what was going on. No doubt Dutch cast a guileful eye at his brother, whose approval he sorely craved, before blurting out: "Twinkle twinkle little star / Who the hell do you think you are?" It was as reckless and cheeky as it was uncharacteristic, and while it was meant to impress Moon, the policeman wasn't buying. He hustled Dutch into the backseat of his car and sped off. At the station house, the police chief, J. D. Van Bibber, intervened and, as a favor, called Jack, with whom he played cards. Some favor. It cost Jack $14.75 to pay his son's fine, a small fortune considering his meager salary.

For the most part, Dutch was a model boy. He respected his parents—whom he and Moon always called Nelle and Jack rather than Mom and Dad—and did all his chores on time and without complaint. His primary job was to empty the drip tray beneath the clunky oak icebox in the kitchen. "If you neglect to do that and it overflows onto my floor," Nelle warned him, "your work just got bigger. You'll have to clean up the spill, and while you're at it the entire floor." He was also responsible for putting a cardboard sign in the window to signal the iceman whenever they needed a delivery. Occasionally, he was recruited to help Jack at the Fashion Boot Shop. Dutch said he "found it boring," but that might have been an excuse for avoiding the still in the store's basement where Moon helped his father brew Prohibition beer. Otherwise, Dutch's time was mostly his own. He and Ed O'Malley joined the Boy Scouts together and sat through double features at the Saturday matinee in the front row of the Family Theater.

But mostly he read. The library was a few blocks down Hennepin Avenue; Dutch had a library card from the time he was ten and was a fixture there most evenings, camped out on the window seat in the turret by the front door. "The library was really my house of magic," he acknowledged. But there were snags. The stacks were closed, which meant he had to ask the librarian, Mrs. Elizabeth Camp, for any book he wanted, and if she didn't think it was an appropriate title, she would refuse to get it. What's more, he could check out only one book at a time. If he was lucky, Nelle would borrow something he could read as well, but there were only a couple of days when women were allowed in the library (and even then, they had to remain in a section by the fireplace known as the Ladies Reading Alcove, which was off-limits to men). So Dutch often read an entire book in the library before heading home with another title under his arm.

His reading was eclectic (he called it "undisciplined"). Dutch devoured books about birds and local wildlife, paging repeatedly through the incomparable Audubon color plates. Nelle gave him a copy of Gilbert Parker's *Northern Lights*, a collection of stories about the Hudson Bay Company's trappers and their pursuit of white wolves in the Saskatchewan Valley, which he "read over and over, imagining [himself] with the wolves in the wild." He plowed through the Rover Boys series, featuring a trio of mischievous brothers at a military boarding school; the Horatio Alger books about the dreamy-eyed rags-to-riches paths of boys not unlike himself; Burt Standish's Frank Merriwell stories, immortalizing the all-American Yale athlete who solved mysteries and righted wrongs. "Then I discovered Edgar Rice Burroughs," he recalled, "and not only all the Tarzan stories, but his science-fiction *John Carter Warlord of Mars* and all the other John Carter books." Nothing was off Dutch's reading radar—Zane Grey, Mark Twain, the Sherlock Holmes mysteries, Alexandre Dumas, the kind of derring-do adventures that mesmerized teenage boys. Even poetry: he read and reread Nelle's Robert W. Service collection, memorizing "The Shooting of Dan McGraw" and "The Cremation of Sam McGee," both of which he'd recite in bed later in life to help him fall asleep.

No book had more of an impact on Dutch than a turn-of-the-century spiritual bestseller, *That Printer of Udell's* by Harold Bell Wright. Nelle had given a copy to him in the spring of 1922, no doubt to prick his interest in the church and its mission through the exploits of a character very much like her son. It was an allegorical tale, loaded with messages of faith and redemption, but its real pull was the novel's opening scene, the depiction of a wretched family dynamic: the book's hero, Dick Faulkner, a young

Midwesterner, experiences his long-suffering mother's grim death while his drunken father, passed out cold, lies snoring in a corner.

Earlier that winter, on his way home one evening, Dutch had encountered Jack "spread out as if he were crucified," on the front porch. "He was drunk, dead to the world," Dutch remembered, snoring exactly like Dick Faulkner's father. Dutch's initial reaction was darkly ambivalent. If he just stepped over his father and went inside, he figured, the situation would eventually resolve itself. Ignore it, "pretend he wasn't there," and it would go away. That's how he'd dealt with Jack's benders in the past.

But not this time. As the reality of what happened began to sink in, Dutch grew more conflicted. This was his father whom he loved dearly, the man whose infectious happy-go-lucky spirit imbued every good thing in his life. A man of principle, dedicated to his family. Jack's litany of faults couldn't wipe that out. And Dutch was no longer the innocent child always protected from the truth. He was eleven years old, old enough to accept responsibility in situations such as this one. Dutch claimed that he grabbed a fistful of Jack's coat, dragged him inside the house, and got him to bed.

This dramatic rescue is most likely apocryphal—he was hardly able to drag his comatose father into the front hall, carry him up a narrow, L-shaped flight of stairs, undress him, and put him to bed. The way Dutch chose to remember this event owes plenty to William James's adage that truth *happens* to an idea. In this case, it might have been more of a symbolic expression. Dutch, wanting to rescue his father, imagined himself as a lifesaver, a role he would play many times over the years.

That Printer of Udell's had a powerful impact, not just because of the parallels it drew to Jack but through its positions on charity and the church. "I was struck by the hero in the book," Dutch said, "and the good things that he did." The criticism voiced by the hero, Dick Faulkner—that "people follow the church and not Christ; they become church members, but not Christians"—stayed with him. There is little doubt that Dutch was exhilarated by its argument about practicing what is preached—what the book called "practical Christianity."

It also gave him plenty of ethical morsels to chew on. Dick Faulkner, a printer's assistant, becomes an activist for the needy, a role that arises from an epidemic of homelessness, but he divides such people into "two classes . . . the deserving and the undeserving." The undeserving, he maintains, benefit from social-welfare policies that "encourage the idle in their idleness" to the detriment of those more deserving of a helping hand. To help the undeserving, Dick says, demeans those in real difficulty. Rather than encourage "the shiftless and idle" in their freeloading, he proposes offering assistance only to those willing to work—"the test of work," he labels it. Of course, once people are self-sufficient, they go off the dole. It is impossible to read the book now without relating its essential values with positions Ronald Reagan took later in public life.

Dutch later said *That Printer of Udell's* had a strong impression on his spiritual development. "I found a role model in that traveling printer," he wrote to the book's author's daughter-in-law more than sixty years later. After finishing the book, he told Nelle, "I'd like to be like him," like Dick Faulkner. The feeling lingered for a few days, building inside Dutch, until he finally announced: "I want to declare my faith and be baptized." Was this a youthful caprice? Nelle couldn't be sure at first. He wasn't even twelve years old, and she firmly believed "you had to be ready to make the decision." For that very reason the pastor of her church usually refused to baptize children. But Dutch convinced Nelle and the pastor that the time was right. Moon decided that he would participate in his brother's ritual as well, but his apostasy was sure to cause fireworks at home. In fact, his friend George O'Malley recalled encountering the boys a short time before the service and being warned, "Shh, we're going to get baptized—don't let Jack know." Nevertheless, both Reagan brothers were baptized at the First Christian Church on June 21, 1922.

Her sons' commitment to their faith was deeply satisfying to Nelle. Her involvement with the church had become stronger than ever in Dixon, and more profound. She was immediately elected to its inner sisterhood, the C. C. Circle, a group of women dedicated to bringing the good works of the church to the wider community. And she was a missionary—a true missionary—for its values. She even became president of the Women's Missionary Society and taught the True Blue Class as part of the church's Sunday Bible school program. The more the church asked, the more she'd take on. She gave readings, sang in the choir—often as the soloist—trained religious teachers, led prayer services, wrote and performed in church plays, staged charity events, represented the church at state conventions, striving, always striving, to aid those in need. Moon recalled how "she sandbagged merchants for clothes and food that she then distributed on the east side," where Dixon's neediest lived. Cenie Straw, a neighbor, marveled at Nelle's bottomless energy, how when she finished with her duties at church, she would slip away with a basket of apples or cookies and head across the street to visit at the county jail. "She would take her Bible and go read to the prisoners." And her generosity didn't end with readings. Typically, prisoners were released late in the day, when there was a greater temptation for encountering trouble. "So she would often invite them to come and spend the night in her guest room, give them a hot meal, and make sure that they got a good foot into the right path." The next morning, Nelle helped them clean up so they could look for work.

On Thursdays, she took her ministry to the Dixon sanatorium, where she distributed gifts and entertained tuberculosis patients. And if time permitted, she detoured to the Dixon Home for the Feeble-Minded to visit Jack's brother Will, who was confined there with "alcoholic psychosis."

Faith and charity upstaged her passion for performing—but not by much. "Performing, I think, was her first love," Dutch recalled. She acted any chance she got in any part, big or small, that came her way. "Whether it was low comedy or high drama, Nelle really threw herself into a part."

There was plenty of opportunity to act in Dixon. The church staged morality plays, several of which Nelle wrote herself. In a temperance one-act she scripted for the church, a particularly resonant line—"I love you, Daddy, except when you have that old bottle"—sounded like a personal appeal. Other plays were less preachy: "George Had a Grouch with His Sisters," "Cornelia Pickle, Plaintiff," "The Shepherd's Christmas," "The Italian Story of the Rose," every other week seemed to feature her in another role. When the American Legion staged its 500-person "Pageant of Abraham Lincoln," Nelle starred as the president's mother, Nancy Hanks.

Much of her standard repertoire took the form of readings. Frequently, she would get up at a meeting or public gathering and deliver a recitation from memory in the form of a parable or poem that took on themes of courage, integrity, and principle. "How the Artist Forgot Four Colors" and "On the Other Train" were among Nelle's narratives. On Sunday afternoons she was a fixture on the upper level in the library, standing by the railing that overlooked the main floor, for one of the public readings that showcased her sentiments.

"My mother inveigled me into learning a few things, and she'd take me with her sometimes," Dutch recalled. "She'd have me do humorous things, and I learned what a kick it was to make people laugh." As early as the summer of 1920, only nine years old, he delivered two recitations as warm-ups before his mother's appearance: a tearjerker of a poem called "About Mother" and an allegory, "The Sad Dollar and the Glad Dollar."

One of their joint efforts was a lighthearted church play of Nelle's about the dangers of family fighting, set in a community not unlike Dixon, where everyone knew everyone else's business and gossip was harsh. Dutch was roped into playing the aggrieved father, sporting a cast on his arm, the result of a well-placed thwack by his wife.

Another of her routines was an old vaudeville monologue entitled "Lavinsky at the Wedding," popularized by a Polish-Yiddish comic named Julian Rose. Nelle did all the voices—the disgruntled guest, the intruding Irishman, the rabbi (Dutch remembered him as "the minister"), the pushing and shoving around the crowded buffet table—delivering punch lines with a stand-up's timing. Nelle's delivery of the Irish policeman declaring "I'm cleaning out the Jew wedding" never failed to get a laugh.

"I think that's where I got the bug [to perform]," Dutch said—the applause, the way a performance connected with the audience. At the outset, Nelle had to twist his arm, but as time wore on Dutch eagerly joined her onstage, whether at church, at the library, in a hospital ward, or at one of the local theaters.

Dutch had replaced Jack as Nelle's favorite co-star. Jack was too busy trying to make a go of it at the Fashion Boot Shop. He still sold shoes, but now he saw himself as something more, a foot specialist, or "*practipedist*," as the store's ads ordained him. He had completed a Dr. Scholl's correspondence course to justify that title. "I remember my father studying at night," Dutch said, "about every bone in the foot and . . . he must have been a damn good student at it, because people would come in for shoes that had something wrong, some deformity and . . . he was always able to equip them with an arch support and fit their shoes and correct what was wrong."

Other times, however, Jack fell back on his innate charm. A classmate of Dutch's remembered sitting through a string of disastrous shoe fittings with her aunt, when finally Jack threw up his hands and said, "Mrs. Wallace, it just isn't the time of year for your size." He had a way about him that delighted customers. He might tell them, "Jesus walked barefoot, but then, he didn't have to deal with our Illinois winters, now did he?" Or: "I'm glad you chose that pair, they can walk to church and dance a jig on the way home." But he was also savvy when it came to business. He was "the first salesman in Dixon to X-ray people's feet," which gave his customers a sense they were in the hands of a healer. And Dutch recalled how H. C. Pitney relied on Jack to canvass the state for stores that were going belly-up and to buy up their shoe stock at auction. "He'd buy them for pennies. Good lord, he could sell some of them for twenty-five cents and make a profit."

Jack was well liked, but a livable wage remained elusive. Competition was fierce; Geisenheimer's, a department store next to the Fashion Boot Shop, also sold shoes. Despite the financial struggles, though, and even in the grip of Prohibition, Jack was always able to manage a bottle.

Jack's carousing and the family's ensuing money woes meant that Nelle had to be creative just to feed her family. Her specialty in this regard was a dish she called "oatmeal meat"—a thick patty consisting mainly of cereal flavored with only enough hamburger to disguise its blandness, buried in gravy made from the residue left clinging to the hamburger pot.

The rent on the Hennepin Avenue house ate up the majority of Jack's salary. Nelle also insisted on tithing, giving 10 percent of everything they made to the Christian Church. Her monthly mantra—"Don't worry, the Lord will provide"—was righteous in spirit, but it didn't pay the bills. Dutch offered to contribute what he could. In a hutch behind the barn, Dutch and Moon raised rabbits and pigeons, and on Saturday mornings Moon went door-to-door in the neighborhood, peddling squab and rabbit meat.

Moving to a cheaper rental was inevitable. In the spring of 1923, the Reagans packed up again for a move across the Rock River, to the north side of Dixon, where housing was more available—and more affordable. The boys were distraught. They'd loved the Hennepin Avenue place, with the big side yard and the O'Malley brothers nearby. Jack took a lease on a smaller house some distance from downtown, on West Everett Street, an unprepossessing block of working-class families. There was no front porch, no parlor to speak of, no guest room, and only the stingiest slip of a yard.

Jack tried to put a good face on it. "No need to put up curtains here," he advised Nelle. "We won't be staying that long."

Dutch tried to embrace his father's optimism. He made the best of the move, and soon after their arrival he scouted the new neighborhood, taking stock of what it had to offer. There were a few grocery stores, a confectionery, a barber shop and pharmacy, but not much else in the way of conveniences. On sultry summer evenings residents pulled chairs outside to avoid the oppressive heat and to chat with neighbors. Saturday nights everyone headed downtown, where businesses stayed open late to accommodate the social do-si-do. In the dappled light of the store windows, Dixonians took care of their weekend shopping, then congregated on the porches and benches beneath the low-slung awnings, catching up on local gossip. Occasionally, Dutch joined his parents among the congenial horde; otherwise he rambled around the backyard for hours by himself, staring pensively over the tree line, where the brooding Rock River loomed in the distance. "The whole street was up on a bluff," he recalled. "And right out the back door the bluff sloped down to the high-school playing field." He would matriculate there in a few years, as soon as he was old enough. Moon was scheduled to start there in the fall, but when it came to it, he flat-out refused to attend. He remained enrolled at South Central High. It was the first time he and Dutch would be separated like that. They began to grow apart in other ways as well. Moon now ran with a rough bunch from the south side of Dixon that hung out in Red Vaile's pool hall, an unsavory little basement dive a few doors up from the Fashion Boot Shop. And there was an element of cruelty now in the way he treated Dutch, something in his manner that hadn't been there before, a harder edge. It was easy to pick on a boy he viewed as "quiet" and thoughtful, a boy who couldn't see two feet in front of him. He knew when Dutch had his "down moments," but refused to comfort him with a kind word. He saw Dutch "as a scared kid burying his snuffling tear-streaked face in Nelle's apron" and developed a talent for locking in on the younger brother's insecurities with a well-placed dig that further reduced him to tears. Years later Moon would say, "We didn't have what you would call great companionship." Their palling-around days were over.

Dutch's faulty eyesight continued to dog him in every phase of his life—in the classroom, on the playing field, in his engagement with the world around him. What he couldn't see traumatized him throughout his adolescence and made him skittish, occasionally insular. Neither of his parents seemingly paid enough attention to notice. Perhaps his awkwardness seemed more like a lack of coordination, something he'd grow out of or learn to compensate for. Nothing tested Dutch more severely or caused more frustration than his inability to see things clearly.

An idle gesture changed everything. In the spring of 1924, Jack and Nelle took the boys on one of their frequent Sunday outings, an afternoon drive meandering through the Rock River Valley countryside. "Nelle had left her eye-glasses in the back seat," Dutch recalled. As they edged out of Dixon into the dense prairie, he reached over and, out of curiosity, slipped them on.

It was as though someone had flipped a switch and he could suddenly see. Colors came at him from every direction. And distinct forms, not the ghostly images he'd struggled to make out for years. There was a billboard he could read and cows grazing in the field. He shrieked with delight. For a boy of thirteen, it was an epiphany. "I'd discovered a world I didn't know existed before."

The next day, Dutch went with Nelle to see Dr. George McGraham, an optometrist located on the next block from Jack's shop. The diagnosis was extreme myopia. Dutch was nearsighted—nothing corrective lenses couldn't remedy. He would be wearing glasses from now on, a pair of thick black frames. Embarrassing, yes, but they did the trick. He took a lot of heat at first—kids on the block calling him "four eyes"—but he could see. It was a life-changing experience.

After years imprisoned by the shadows, Dutch was ready to shine.

CHAPTER FIVE

"EVERYONE'S HERO"

"Throw out the lifeline, throw out the lifeline,
Someone is sinking today."

—EDWARD SMITH UFFORD

Dutch's life shifted into a new and promising phase. His North Side neighborhood was filled with children his age who went to the same school and church. He'd replaced Moon by making his own set of friends—Harold Marks, Herb Glessner, and Dick McNichol, along with his old pal Ed O'Malley. And he began to fill out, no longer the scrawny four-eyed fumbler of Hennepin Avenue but an amiable, starkly handsome young man.

He volunteered much of his spare time at the Christian Church, where he taught a Sunday school class across the hall from his mother and was an active member in the K.K.K., the acronym—which mortified Jack—stood for the Klean Kids Klub. The YMCA became his after-school hangout. He joined its swim team, and the Boys Band, in which Moon shouldered a tuba. Lacking any discernible musical skill, Dutch functioned as the marching band's drum major, a position coveted for its spiffy uniform—a blue-and-crimson cape thrown over white duck pants and a towering beaked hat, with a baton patched together from a brass-bed leg and its crown.

He would start pumping his arm to set the band in motion as it followed him in the syncopated "hippodrome strut" along a parade path. That was always the plan, and it was effective—when it worked. During a memorable Memorial Day celebration in 1923, Dutch recalled how, in the nearby town of Amboy, he was assigned to lead his team behind the parade marshal's horse. They ran through the standard set of patriotic anthems—"Under the Double Eagle," "The Stars and Stripes Forever," and "Semper Fidelis." At a certain point, the marshal made an unexpected U-turn along Main Street and rode back along the marchers to make sure everyone was in their proper places. Dutch, ever the standard-bearer, kept pace at the front of the pack, pumping that arm, pumping, pumping, never missing a beat. Unbeknownst to him, however, the marshal led the band off-route, on a detour down a cross street. It was some time before Dutch realized he was high-stepping along on his own. Rather than continuing on alone or quitting in defeat, he sprinted across several streets and backyards cutting through a block of houses, tuning his antennae to the distant ripple of melody, until he located the wayward troupe and fell back in step at the front of the procession, as though nothing had happened. It was a scene adapted years later for an Andy Hardy movie.

Movies became a passion. Dutch and his buddies went two or three times a week, whenever they could scrape together their dimes for tickets. The Dixon Theater on Galena Avenue, just north of the arch, was a grand old palace, with a monster three-keyboard Barton organ whose deep-pitched drone accompanying the silent films sounded celestial when it resonated through that cavernous space. Ed Worley's brother Bill played that organ, which allowed him to occasionally sneak in friends—and friends of friends—for free. "They changed the movies often," recalls a classmate of Dutch's. You could count on seeing a new short, a serial, and a two-reel feature almost every other day. The theater drew a lively but well-mannered audience, especially on matinee day, when a throng of kids filed in past L. G. Rorer, the procrustean owner, who stood sentry in the lobby to root out candy, popcorn, or soda pop, which were forbidden in the theater.

Dutch cultivated a new set of heroes. In addition to the Rover Boys, Frank Merriwell, and John Carter, he now included Tom Mix and William S. Hart, two of the cinema's foremost cowboy stars; swashbuckler Douglas Fairbanks; Wallace Beery; Laurel and Hardy; and wonderdog Rin Tin Tin. His role models were the men on white horses who knew right from wrong.

Jack Reagan forbade his sons from seeing a reissue of *Birth of a Nation* when it came to Dixon in 1925. "It deals with the Ku Klux Klan against the colored folks," Jack declaimed, "and I'll be damned if anyone in this family will go see it." Having been discriminated against himself for being Catholic, he fulminated against any group that degraded people for their race or beliefs. "There was no more grievous sin at our household than a racial slur or other evidence of religious or racial intolerance," Dutch would say. While barnstorming as a traveling salesman, Jack refused to stay at a hotel that barred Jews from its premises. And he was more than familiar with the Klan's brand of prejudice. One of its klaverns operated out of Grand Detour and made its presence felt in Dixon, where they had burned a cross on the courthouse lawn.

Even though he wasn't an educated man, Jack Reagan was forceful and articulate when it came to questions of fairness. His politics reflected his idealism. He expressed his views daily, with Dutch listening intently at his elbow, on any number of compelling social issues and maintained that it was the duty of the government to help people personally and have their interests at heart. It was easy for a man who could barely afford to eat liver or subsisted on "oatmeal meat" to lash out against the rapacious banking and railroad magnates whose fortunes influenced most legislation. He spoke often about reapportioning the immense wealth hoarded by the iron barons in Galena in order to bolster the living conditions of the people whose land they were mining and whose water they were polluting.

Unabashedly liberal and a Democrat, Jack wasn't afraid to take positions that were detested by most people in town. Dixon was conservative—"ultra-*ultra*-conservative," according to local historian Greg Langan—and solidly Republican. Only one time since Lincoln was elected did the town not support a Republican for president, and that was in 1912, for the Bull Moose candidate, Teddy Roosevelt. The powerful Shaw family, which controlled the only newspaper in Dixon, made sure, through editorials and the slant of its coverage, that the world its readers read about tilted strongly to the right.

It didn't matter to Jack Reagan what anyone else thought. He had his viewpoint and he was sticking to it. Dixon Democrats tended to keep their heads down and mouths shut. Jack "was probably the most outspoken of them," Dutch recalled, "never missing a chance to speak up for the working man." It was a matter of duty to your fellow man. This all made sense to Dutch. He respected his father's views, especially as they paralleled the principles he was taught in church. *Let us not be weary in well doing. Be kindly affectioned one to another with brotherly love. God loveth a cheerful giver.* He knew that William S. Hart had opened his ranch "for the benefit of the American Public of every race and creed." And while some of his schoolmates bullied Dutch as a result of Jack's politics, he clung even closer to his father's ideals.

Dutch Reagan was a reflection of both his parents—parroting his father's politics, admiring his independence, resembling him in appearance if not in spirit, while practicing his mother's faith, applying scripture, appearing in her inspirational skits. But as he entered high school in 1924, Dutch drifted toward forming his own identity and distinguishing himself in areas that veered from his parents' paths.

He was athletic, an aptitude that surprised practically everyone, including himself. He started for the Whiffle Poofs, the YMCA's intramural basketball team, ran track—although according to Ed O'Malley, "he was very slow of foot"—and played outfield on the North Central baseball squad. But deep down, he "worshipped football more than anything else in the world." Moon starred on the high school team, and Dutch deep down still worshipped him, too. Joining his brother on the playing field became a singular goal, but following tryouts in his freshman year, Dutch was cut on the last day of practice. Too lightweight, at 108 pounds, to do much damage, too short, too weak—maybe next year, he was told. In 1925, thanks to a new division created for players of smaller stature, Dutch, now a heftier 120, won a key spot and was elected captain.

In time, swimming became equally important. He was good at it, some said blessed. He had broad shoulders—a swimmer's shoulders—and long arms. One could tell from watching the way he knifed through the water that he swam effortlessly, not with the herky-jerky body motion that typified most teenagers. His stroke was smooth, *efficient*—not a lot of splash upon contact. He was a natural, like Johnny Weissmuller, who'd won the 100- and 400-meter freestyle gold medals that summer in the 1924 Olympics. American kids everywhere were influenced by Weissmuller's coup to take swimming more seriously, and Dutch was no exception.

And he was strong. He added muscle to those broad shoulders, working out afternoons at the big YMCA pool. Crawl, backstroke, butterfly, Dutch switched among strokes as fluidly as some switched radio stations. And when the spirit moved him, he would spring high off the diving board, grab on to the overhead bar, and swing like a trapeze artist over the pool to execute a neat backflip into the water.

His performance in school was less impressive. Ed O'Malley remembered Dutch as being "a better than ordinary student," but that was a faithful buddy's assessment. His Dixon High School teacher Freya Lazier described him as "just an average student." Dutch did just enough work to get by. It wasn't that he wasn't bright. He had an unusual talent: total recall for dates and facts; he could read over a page of text and recite it verbatim. But he was preoccupied by extracurricular activities and, most of all, by a young woman who had hijacked his attention.

Dutch had first noticed Margaret Cleaver at the First Christian Church, when her father, Ben, settled in as the congregation's new pastor. The family had arrived in Dixon after a stint in Canton, their ninth ministry in an eighteen-year circuit that took them through small communities dotting the Missouri and Illinois countryside. Margaret was easy to spot. "She was very pretty," recalls Esther Haack, a classmate at North Side High. "We all tried making ourselves up like her." She was an attractive, fresh-faced brunette with lively button-brown eyes and an easy smile framed by a mop of wavy hair. Margaret's most distinguishing trait, however, was an easygoing disposition. She was polite, friendly, and smart, maybe the smartest girl in Dutch's class. Her name first started appearing in the newspaper early in 1924, entertaining as a soloist at church meetings and acting in plays, often opposite Nelle Reagan in the cast. Dutch eventually got into the act, appearing in the church's 1924 Christmas program with his mother and Margaret in an inspirational piece called "The King's Birthday."

Dutch was smitten with Margaret. He had no trouble finding an excuse to be around her—they were together at school, at church, at the Y, onstage—but she was quite popular with everyone in their circle, including several young men. Dick McNichol, the captain of the football team, already had his eye on her, but Dutch had an ace up his sleeve: McNichol was a "mere Methodist," according to Dutch, whereas he was a Disciple, a bona fide member of Margaret's father's congregation.

Dutch made his affections known, giving her a pet name—Mugs—and escorting her home from school whenever possible. "They'd walk along the street, holding hands," a classmate recalls, Mugs's books tucked snugly under Dutch's free arm. Most days they'd stop off at Fulfs' Confectionery, the local hangout on North Galena Avenue, a Dixon institution, where soda jerks served up malteds, phosphates, and Cokes in tall frosted glasses. Dutch especially liked Fulfs' because of its dual character—it was a place where he could socialize with Mugs, but it also had an annex where they sold sporting goods. He'd often leave Mugs talking to her best friend, Dorothy Bovey, and steal away for a few minutes to run his hands over a dimpled football or to swing one of the shiny baseball bats showcased in a rack. Fulfs' gave Dutch an opportunity to ply the Dixon social scene.

The summers presented fewer occasions. For several years, Nelle had taken her boys to the Chautauquas in Assembly Park on the north side of town. The Chautauquas were the most popular events in Dixon. Large crowds of people either rented or pitched tents, and many stayed on the grounds for weeks on end. There was a big tabernacle with a dais that seated as many as five hundred people, and for several weeks, usually in August, it featured a revolving lineup of figures: educational and inspirational speakers, marching bands, opera soloists, monologists, storytellers, comedians, preachers, politicians, faith healers, and suffragettes.

Religion was an underlying current of the Chautauqua experience. Dutch heard the festival's flamboyant star, William Jennings Bryan, deliver his famous "The Prince of Peace" oratory, arguing that Christian theology was the basis for morality, and that morality was the foundation for peace and equality. Another yearly stalwart, Russell Conwell, stirred up the crowd with a fiery sermon exhorting the town's young men to get rich, "for money is power and power ought to be in the hands of good people." And a succession of temperance advocates rose to make their case.

In the summer of 1925, when he was fourteen, Dutch took his first real job, with a local construction contractor. It was an eye-opening experience, involving everything that went into building a house: digging the foundation, framing the structure, pouring concrete, laying flooring, putting in plumbing, shingling the roof, painting, the works. Dutch worked strenuous, ten-hour days for a miserable thirty-five cents an hour. At the end of the season, however, he had two hundred dollars to show for his effort—a nice nest egg for his first bank account.

Sometime between his thirteenth and fourteenth years, Dutch decided he wanted to go to college. It was a pipe dream for a boy of his background. Most Dixon students who graduated from high school went straight to work. Looking back years later, Dutch would observe that "in the 1920s, fewer than seven percent of high school graduates in America went to college," and, if anything, that's an exaggeration. The odds were stacked against him. But he had watched how hard his father struggled to make ends meet as a shopkeeper and desired a different fate. What's more, Dutch's personal hero, Garland Waggoner, the former captain of North Side High's football team, was a freshman at a school called Eureka, not too far from Dixon. College, he thought, was the key—but an expensive key. Jack was all for it, as long as Dutch realized he couldn't count on his father for financial help.

He'd never make it earning thirty-five cents an hour. In his spare time, Dutch caddied at the local country club, and according to boyhood friend Bill Thompson, "Dutch and his brother were roustabouts" for the Ringling Bros. circus, "carrying water to the elephants and following the parade path" when its train cars pulled into the vacant lot on West Seventh Street in Dementtown each year. Every little bit helped; still, at this rate he'd be woefully short.

In 1926 Dutch learned about a job opening on the Rock River, a lifeguard, paying eighteen dollars a week plus all the hamburgers and root beer he could pack away, a respectable salary that would give him enough to contribute to the family and still save toward his college fund.

He might have had an easy time landing the job had it been at the YMCA pool, in a controlled environment. But the post was at Lowell Park—a thicket of hilly woodland about three miles from downtown Dixon, with hiking paths and a generous picnic area adjacent to a crescent of man-made sandy beach at a bend of the river. The land had been purchased in 1860 by Charles Russell Lowell, a businessman who was killed during the Civil War, and was given to the city by his daughter, Carlotta, in 1906. A group of town fathers helped clean it up and build a watering stall for horses and a bathhouse. Townspeople flocked to it. It was peaceful there and bucolic, with a beautiful view, a fine place to escape from the hustle of town. The crowds would start drifting into the park at ten in the morning, picnic along the water, and wouldn't disperse until well after dark.

"Lowell Park was a great place to go," says historian Greg Langan, "but not the safest of swimming holes." The currents of the Rock River were a lot swifter than most people realized. Supply boats routinely capsized. The water was murky and polluted with industrial waste from Rockford and other places upstream. All of which is why a lifeguard was necessary.

Hiring one was the responsibility of the park's concessionaires, Ed and Ruth Graybill, a high-minded couple who oversaw the picnic and beach area. Dutch felt he had an inside track. The Graybills had lived a few blocks north of his old Hennepin Avenue house, and he used to wave to them on his way to and from the library. He knew Ruth Graybill from church. And he'd even been invited into their place a few times to listen to a baseball game on the radio.

Ed Graybill wasn't convinced. When Dutch presented himself as a candidate, Ed saw a fifteen-year-old boy with a very slight physique and wondered how someone like that could save a person twice his size and weight. "You're pretty young, my lad," he said. "I'll have to talk to your father."

Jack wasn't at all hesitant. "Give the boy a chance," he told Ed. Remarkably, Dutch got the job.

It might have been more than Dutch bargained for at the outset. His responsibilities began at eight each morning, when he reported for duty at the Graybills' home, where he picked up their old Dodge truck and began a round of deliveries to prepare for the day. The first stop he made was at Beier's Bakery on Hennepin Avenue for dozens of just-baked buns, then farther along the block to Hartzell & Hartzell, the butchers, for a mountain of hamburger, and finally over to the icehouse, where he helped load a three-hundred-pound block, which he'd later break into three sections for the soda-pop coolers. Once he got all that squared away, he'd change into his suit, a skintight one-piece tank with "lifeguard" stenciled across the front, and swim the area from rope line to rope line to get a sense of that day's current. By the time the park officially opened, Dutch would already be tired.

That boy had stamina, though. He was on duty at the beach for twelve hours each day, seven days a week, from June through August, perched atop a wooden lifeguard chair that looked out over the water. "Dutch was no-nonsense," remembers a frequent bather at the park. "He was as handsome as they come in his bathing trunks, and he smiled at everyone. But you couldn't chat him up or distract him while he was on duty." He had to keep his eyes peeled on a wide stretch of the landscape, where as many as several hundred people were in motion at all times—swimming, diving, splashing, engaged in all sorts of horseplay, in his words: "a mob of water-seeking humans intent on giving the beach guard something to worry about." There were plenty of distractions to test his mettle: a wooden raft with a low diving board and slide, an anchored "tipping disk" that swiveled much like a mechanical bull and challenged swimmers to hang on for dear life, a chain of slippery moss-ridden barrels that bobbed as floating boundaries for swimmers, and girls. Dutch was a magnet for gushing teen-age beauties who mooned over his studly appeal.

Dutch had grown substantially in just a few short months. "He was the perfect specimen of an athlete," recalled Bill Thompson, a neighborhood friend who often described himself as Dutch's little brother. He was "tall, willowy, muscular, brown, good-looking. The girls were always flocking around him." And Dutch knew it.

The girls were a perk—and often a peril. More times than he could count, Dutch would see a swimmer flailing in what he knew was dangerous water and bolt off into the river . . . only to "rescue" a young woman too eager to snuggle in his grip. Many a Lowell Park habitué saw the drama for what it was. "I had a friend who nearly drowned herself trying to get him to save her," said one. Dutch was never amused, not under those conditions. There was too much at stake, and the responsibility weighed on him. "At the first hint of trouble, Dutch would be in the water, moving like a torpedo," said Thompson. Many years later, he could close his eyes and envision how Dutch would "look over his glasses to see who was out there in the water, and if somebody went down . . . he'd just throw off the glasses and take off." He'd hit the water running, and with a few powerful strokes he'd be upon the hapless struggler, just the two of them thrashing about in the current until he could bring his quarry under control. On those occasions when he had to perform such a rescue, the situation was risky and demanded courage. As Dutch himself recalled to a reporter: "The drowning person invariably is panic stricken," a condition that made everything doubly dangerous.

There were plenty of genuine rescues in the six years Dutch patrolled the beach. Fred Moore, who was ten at the time, recalled how he was about fifty feet from shore when the current grabbed him and he started gulping for air. "I sank under the water and thought: 'So this is what it's like to die,'" he said. "But then I felt an arm wrap around me, and the next thing I knew my head was out of the water. Within seconds Dutch had me back on shore . . . and was squeezing the water out of me."

Another beachcomber saw Dutch rescue a four-year-old girl who had wandered too far from shore. "One second he was on a raft, and the next he was pulling the girl out of the water." Afterward, everyone on the beach applauded.

One weekend, a local man named Bert Whitcombe, who was attempting to mount the high diving board, slipped off the ladder and sustained a serious head injury as he tumbled to the platform. "He was unconscious when he struck the water and soon sank beneath the surface," according to a newspaper account. "Beach guard Dutch Reagan . . . hurried to his rescue and dragged the unconscious body to the shore," after which CPR was performed and lucky Mr. Whitcombe was whisked off to a local doctor's office.

Occasionally, things took a scarier turn—like the time Dutch thought *he* wasn't going to make it. One night, under a gibbous moon, a blind man visiting the park had waded into the water by himself. "He started for a float guided by a friend's calls, but the river current pulled him away," Dutch recounted. It was a mismatch from the get-go. "He was a big fellow— outweighed me by sixty pounds or so—and he was thrashing badly." By the time Dutch reached him the guy was in full crisis mode, and in the struggle that ensued it seemed they might both go under. That was always a lifeguard's worst nightmare. A man struggling for air took on enormous strength in the throes of drowning. Sometimes it meant Dutch taking a drastic measure, like a stranglehold from behind, even on occasion "a right cross to the jaw." In this particular instance, he was resourceful, needing only to rely on tried-and-true water-safety technique. Ultimately, he defused the situation to a point where the two men could eventually float into shore.

Forty years later, during an event in San Francisco, James Benton Parsons, the country's first African American federal judge, was swapping stories with California's newly elected governor, Ronald Reagan, about their experiences as Boy Scouts in Illinois. Benton recalled an outing with his troop to the McCormick Farm, a camp on the Rock River, where he decided to try out for his badge in swimming. "I had to be pulled out," he admitted to the governor. "What was your name?" the governor demanded. "Were you Jimmy?" McCormick nodded. The governor roared with laughter. "I was the one who pulled you out."

Legend has it he made seventy-seven such rescues, although the number could certainly be held up to scrutiny. His exploits repeatedly garnered headlines in the *Dixon Evening Telegraph*. "Dutch Reagan Has Made Fine Mark As Guard—Dixon Youth Has Made 71 Rescues at Lowell Park Beach" and "James Raider Pulled from the Jaws of Death." But lifeguarding wasn't just a succession of daring rescues. "When the beach was not busy, he taught kids to swim," recalled Ruth Graybill. "And if he was in a jovial mood, he'd start walking like a chimp and give us a little entertainment." Dutch would perform graceful swan dives off the springboard, arcing high out over the river, arms spread like an eagle in mid-flight, or sing standing up in the bow of a canoe—both exercises part feat, part performance. His swimming stroke was beautiful, elegant—built for speed. In the summer of 1928, Dutch set a record in the annual Labor Day race across the river and back with a time of two minutes eleven seconds, finishing just strokes ahead of his cousin Donald Hunt.

Over time, Dutch developed quite a reputation in Dixon. "He was everyone's hero," a schoolmate recalled. "All the young teachers would go see him whenever he was in a play," said Esther Barton. You could detect a swoon in the audience when Dutch made an entrance onstage." At school, as Esther Haack noted, "every girl talked about how good-looking he was and felt special around him." Dutch had come to carry himself with a sense of purpose and distinction that belied his seventeen years. It seemed to come naturally—an innate inclination to do good, not unlike his mother's. But was it something else? Was some of the public facade Dutch's way of protecting himself from the painful realities of his family? A saintly mother too wrapped up in her good works, an alcoholic father who withheld the emotional guidance a son needs to thrive, a sharp-tongued brother whose constant put-downs knocked him off balance. Dutch certainly didn't learn intimacy within his family. Whatever insecurities he might have fostered, he kept them walled off from his parents, brother, outsiders—maybe even himself. He didn't share his thoughts and feelings with anyone. He was popular and admired but had no close friends.

If there was an exception it was Margaret Cleaver. There was no doubt as to how he felt about her. "Me—I was in love!" he wrote some years later about his first and mightiest teenage crush. Margaret—Mugs—was more reticent. "Love" might not have been her response, had she been asked.

She was a serious girl, the daughter of a sober-minded minister, not one to swish-and-sashay around the lifeguard's chair at Lowell Park. She rarely if ever went to the park when Dutch was on duty; it just wasn't her scene.

There were other reasons to keep her emotional distance. Mugs was appalled by Jack Reagan—more than appalled, offended. Her father, Ben Cleaver, was violently opposed to the drinking of alcohol. He had no tolerance for anyone who indulged, and he made his feelings known freely from the pulpit and in private. If you were his daughter, this issue was especially acute. Drinking wasn't only out of the question, it was repugnant in others, period.

Dutch never spoke about Jack's alcoholism, certainly not to Margaret. It was a family secret, always something he dreaded dealing with. But at some point, Jack had gone on a bender and she heard about it. "Somebody," Dutch said, "had given her a very vivid account of his behavior." Dutch tried to explain that his father's drinking was a sickness beyond his control. He used all of Nelle's logic and sensitivity to describe Jack's longtime weakness, which only seemed to upset Margaret more. It didn't make any sense to her, no matter how Dutch put a spin on it. She wanted no part of it, and he could feel her distancing herself from him.

This pall over Mugs and Dutch's relationship caused him no small degree of heartache. Margaret meant the world to him; he'd convinced himself she would eventually be his wife. "I thought I was going to lose her," he admitted. He was so shaken by her resistance that he vowed "to disown" Jack if Mugs broke things off with him.

There is no record of how the two resolved the conflict, but it seems reasonable to believe that her father, the hardest of hard-core temperance advocates, might have helped his daughter come to terms with her boyfriend and his family. For all his fixed beliefs, Ben Cleaver was a reasonable man. He was extremely fond of Dutch, offering him advice and guidance that would influence Ronald Reagan for the rest of his life, regarding tolerance, pacifism, charity, and the brotherhood of man. To be sure, they had their disagreements—Reverend Cleaver was irreconcilable when it came to dancing and stood firmly opposed to movies being shown on Sundays—but on matters of faith and morality the two men formed a great bond. Helen Cleaver, Margaret's sister, thought that Ben Cleaver was as close to a father figure as Dutch ever had. He stepped in on matters of spiritual growth where Jack was either inadequate or unavailable. Jack wasn't big on fatherly advice; he had little to say about preparing for the future. Expressing needs and emotions wasn't part of his makeup. All that was left to Ben Cleaver. The importance of going to college was often a topic of discussion. He even taught Dutch how to drive. More than likely, he counseled Margaret that Jack and Dutch should be judged separately, as individuals, that she recognize Dutch's higher, nobler ideals, that his spiritual values were beyond reproach.

If Mugs still had any doubts, they were expunged during the final two years of high school.

Throughout 1927 and 1928, Dutch and Mugs were inseparable. They were the leaders of their class, the golden couple. For the Indian Ritual at the Junior and Senior Powwow—a vaunted dinner-dance at the Colonial Inn in Grand Detour—they starred as Heap Big Chief and Cloud Shadows. They anchored their high school's Dramatic Society soirée, with Dutch as its president, and appeared opposite each other in a number of productions: Walter Hackett's adventure yarn *Captain Applejack,* in which Dutch played both a pirate and the pirate's aristocratic descendant; *The Pipe of Peace*; and Philip Barry's urbane comedy *You and I.* They spearheaded myriad programs for the church's Christian Endeavor Society, singing, delivering recitations, giving readings, writing skits. They attended the senior banquet together, the football banquet, the prom. Mugs was secretary of the Girl's Hi-Y, Dutch vice president of the Boy's. Dutch was elected president of the student body, while Mugs was senior class president. And they worked hand in hand on the high school yearbook, *The Dixonian,* which Dutch, as art director, designed as if it were a series of filmstrips.

Friends laid even money that a Cleaver-Reagan wedding was inevitable after graduation in 1928. High school sweethearts with as much going for them as Dutch and Mugs often married early in Dixon. But with his senior year well under way, Dutch was too busy to think that far ahead. With all his extracurricular activities, including team sports and church, there was plenty of work to keep up with at school. Dutch was a talented writer, and he was encouraged by his most influential teacher, Bernard Frazer, who was not only the principal but also taught literature, English, and social studies, and served as the drama coach in his spare time. "Everybody was a little scared of him," Esther Haack admits. But Dutch liked Frazer best of all his teachers, and it was in English IV he was most inspired, though he wasn't much when it came to spelling and grammar. Frazer overlooked those shortcomings and encouraged him to concentrate instead on the more creative aspects of writing. That gave Dutch the leeway to stretch a bit with essays, to tap into his imagination and sense of humor.

It was as if a valve had been opened and words began to flow. Dutch Reagan had the storyteller's gift. He wrote with energy and fervor; on sheet after sheet of lined notebook paper, he sketched out lifelike yarns in a strong, legible, streamlined hand. In a very early essay entitled *Nov. 11 1918*, he envisioned a troop of soldiers "of the 77th" camped out in a machine-gun nest reminiscing in "an amiable free for all" about things that fascinated Dutch: the supernatural, football, women, and religion. *Yale Comes Through* retooled one of Dutch's beloved Frank Merriwell adventures in which two college seniors foil a plot to empty canisters of poisonous gas into the ventilation system of the U.S. Treasury building. The writing, for the most part, was lively and artfully evoked, except for the occasional purple prose, such as: "My heart suddenly cross-blocked my liver, and my adam's apple drop-kicked a tonsil."

Bernard Frazer urged him on, steering him to narrative forms such as essay and opinion. Under the heading "School Spirit," Dutch wrote, "Service is the only road to loyalty, for 'As ye sow, so shall ye reap.' That is why the freshman who goes out for football, who stands up and takes his turn, makes a good student. After he has been battered and bruised for two years, he has had a love and loyalty born in him that is as true as the temper of a fine steel blade."

Writing—the process of organizing his thoughts in a coherent form—became a crucial resource in Dutch's development. Years later, colleagues in every phase of his life would recall the radio announcer, the president of the Screen Actors Guild, the governor of California, and the president of the United States immersed in his own private world with just a yellow tablet and fountain pen, undisturbed by his surroundings, writing umpteen drafts of speeches, radio broadcasts, and letters in longhand, even at times when others were hired to do his bidding.

He also loved acting. Nelle had ignited that fire in Dutch, but his enthusiasm was more secular than hers. He relied on Bernard Frazer to fan the flames of this exciting new passion for him. Frazer formed an after-school drama club, emphasizing the motivation of character—the "why, why, why," as he put it. To heighten student interest, he ditched the fusty old melodramas that were standard high school fodder, instead staging plays based on recent Broadway hits. Being onstage felt right to Dutch. He became relaxed and uninhibited. He found it comfortable "to get under the skin" of a character, easy to be someone else for a while. And he was a quick study. "Ronald was good," Frazer said. "He fit into almost any kind of role you put him into. Wisecracking, hat-over-the-ear, cigarette-in-the-mouth reporter—he could do that as well as any sentimental scenes." The knack evolved into a craft. "He never forgot his lines or his actions. When he got on the stage, he *was* the character."

Dutch talked incessantly about acting and movies, with an idea of perhaps pursuing that calling when he graduated from high school. Movies continued to captivate him. He never missed an opportunity to take in a new feature, and his excitement only built in 1927 upon the news that soon audiences would be able to actually hear the actors speak. In the meantime, he was content to mimic the radio.

Radio came to Dixon in 1923. Dutch claimed he got an early taste of radio magic one Sunday afternoon when a local character named Howard Hall tuned in to KDKA—the country's first commercially licensed station, broadcasting from East Pittsburgh in Pennsylvania—on a homemade crystal set he'd cobbled together on his porch. "We walked all around, and he had this aerial and had to have headphones to hear, trying to see if he could bring something in. And down by the river it was coming," Dutch recalled. "'This is KDKA of the Westinghouse and Manufacturing Company. . . .'" *Pittsburgh*—halfway across the country! Everyone passed around headphones to hear the faint strains of an orchestra playing. "Well, I tell you that was as big a miracle as anything that could ever possibly occur. We were all agog." With patience, he learned, you might even pull in an inning or two of a Pittsburgh Pirates baseball game.

By 1926, the radio phenomenon had swept the country. More reliable tube sets replaced crystals, and in Dixon, you could hear clear nightly broadcasts from any of the top Chicago stations—WGN, WMAQ, or WLS. The Reagans didn't have a radio; it was a luxury they couldn't afford. But whenever possible, at a friend's or neighbor's, Dutch listened to Cubs games and shows such as *Amos 'n' Andy*, which were all the rage. He and his friend Gladys Shippert would tune in to WOC from Davenport, Iowa, which struck a series of chimes to mark the break between programs. Dutch would imitate them incessantly. "To hear the chimes from WOC," Gladys recalled, "we sometimes had to put a pillow over Ronald's face to keep him quiet for a little while."

Dutch's potential seemed enormous. He was handsome, unnaturally so, and a local hero to boot, with the class valedictorian on his arm, a winning personality, a clear grasp of right and wrong, and a deep, abiding faith. "Life is one grand sweet song, so start the music" read the tagline under Dutch's yearbook picture (while misidentifying him as *Donald* Reagan). But shortly before graduation the melody hit a sour note.

The April 3, 1928, edition of the *Dixon Evening Telegraph* announced that Jack Reagan "severed his connection with the partnership operating the Fashion Boot Shop," a polite gloss on the reality that he'd been fired yet again. Dutch always maintained that the shoe store was an early casualty of the Depression and that Jack had gone down with the ship, so to speak. But the newspaper article clearly stated that "the business has enjoyed a thriving growth" since opening its doors in 1920 and that H. C. Pitney "will continue to conduct the store."

The Reagans, who were poor, now became poorer precisely at the time Dutch was focusing on college. His goal was slipping further from his grasp. There was no money for it. Moon had known that a year earlier, when he defied his mother's wishes and scrapped college for a good-paying job—$125 a month working at the Medusa Portland Cement Company, a local institution that employed hundreds of Dixon men. Going to college was a waste of time, he told Dutch.

A *waste of time*. Moon's cynicism cut him to the bone. College wasn't just a dream for Dutch, it was a way out of his disadvantaged background. A guy like Moon might flourish in a traditional work situation. He had a way about him that would be easily suited to a blue-collar job and the camaraderie that went with working with guys' guys. He had an attractive blend of his father's cheeky bonhomie and his mother's vanity. But Dutch had loftier ambitions. He wanted to make more of a mark in the world.

Jack was no help. He wasn't working, but he was busy—busy canvassing for the Democrat Al Smith in the upcoming 1928 presidential election. Nelle was distracted as well. In addition to her ongoing civic missions, she had taken to writing inspirational poetry, reams of epic verse, which was regularly published in the local newspaper, and she had taken on the presidency of the school PTA.

One can only imagine Dutch's feelings as his girlfriend prepared to live out the dream he had once planned on for himself. She was following both her older sisters to Eureka College, a small Disciples church–affiliated institution about sixty miles to the west. The school had taken on "an almost mystical allure" for Dutch because his boyhood idol, Garland Waggoner, had been a standout football player there. Helping Mugs pack provided some distraction but little comfort.

He volunteered to drive Mugs to Eureka a few days before the semester began. At the beginning of September 1928, they piled her belongings into her father's car and set off from Dixon, taking the scenic road along Route 52 that followed the railroad tracks to Peru and cut through seamless miles of lush farmland. He must have considered the possibility that once he and Margaret said their goodbyes he might lose her as well. They had assured each other that nothing would change, and perhaps they both believed it. But Dutch couldn't have been optimistic. He'd be returning to Dixon without a job, without much money, without prospects. What kind of a future could he expect?

All that was rattling around as they turned into East College Avenue, the main artery that ran through Eureka's campus. Dutch took one look at the picture-postcard quad and was thunderstruck. "It was even lovelier than I'd imagined it would be," he recalled. The tableau said *college*: five ivy-covered Georgian brick buildings surrounded by acres of rolling hills. Fresh-faced young students were meandering along the paths that connected the classrooms to the few outlying dorms.

It was a beautiful, crisp day, and Dutch stood by the car, open-mouthed, taking it all in, as Margaret began to unload her luggage. The school that was rightfully his, the girl that was rightfully his, the future that was rightfully his . . . all right in front of him.

He made up his mind at that instant: he was never going back. He would simply have to find a way.

CHAPTER SIX

"LIVING THE GOSPEL"

"Eureka! I have found it!"

—ARCHIMEDES

T here was no limit to Ronald Reagan's Eureka moment. He had hit the mother lode, as far as he was concerned—a gorgeous campus, a school whose intimate size seemed poised to embrace him, a legacy of church and sports, and Margaret Cleaver. He knew it from the outset when he staked his claim.

Eureka's heritage appealed both to Dutch's deep-rooted faith and his liberal principles. The school was chartered on February 6, 1855, Dutch's birthday, by a band of abolitionists determined to combine the pursuit of higher education with their spiritual values. Its precepts were scholarly but tethered to the Christian Church, whose congregants received generous grants to study for the ministry. The Bible was the essential textbook, Christian doctrine its academic bedrock. "Religious values shall be found in all courses of study," its catalog stated. "The development of religious attitudes . . . is essential."

Faith—but coupled with a streak of progressive Christianity that placed great emphasis on social reform. The first generation that established Eureka College opposed slavery on a moral and intellectual level. Their sons formed Company G of the 17th Illinois Volunteer Infantry on a spring day in April 1861 beneath a Dutch elm—henceforth the Recruiting Elm—in the middle of campus and fought in the Civil War. The second generation championed the women's suffrage movement. And their offspring, a generation before Dutch enrolled, struck out to effect social change. "Living the gospel," they called it. *Social gospel*. To be true Christians meant doing something about the problems that were here and now.

Living the gospel. It was already in Dutch's blood. Nelle had raised him to practice his faith by striving to alleviate poverty, denouncing segregation, welcoming immigrants, elevating abysmal labor conditions, and opposing war. Eureka College's activism no doubt would have seemed familiar and right to the young man. Alva Wilmot Taylor, who taught at Eureka in the first decade of the twentieth century, produced students who went on to establish the Southern Tenant Farmers Union and organize black and white sharecroppers in the delta of Arkansas. In 1915, the college sponsored a chapel service featuring Irwin St. John Tucker, who spoke on behalf of the Intercollegiate Socialist Society; at the end of his talk nearly a third of the campus signed up to start its own chapter. Pastor Fred Helfer, the campus's spiritual mentor, was a robust Christian Socialist. Eureka was a hotbed of progressive activism.

Dutch was desperate to enroll. Grades weren't an issue. All that was required was a high school diploma. The stumbling block was money. Standing in the registration line, he did a quick calculation: tuition was $180, room and board another $270, plus a $5 enrollment fee. He had a grand total of $400 in his savings account from his lifeguarding proceeds— not enough to cover basic costs. Another $35 was needed for meals, books, and unforeseen expenses. He'd never make it.

The registrar sent him into the dean's office to plead his case. Dutch wasn't alone. Many hopeful freshmen came from poor rural families and struggled to raise even the meager Eureka tuition. A college education was their only hope of improving their futures and avoiding a life of physical labor. But it meant receiving outside aid, often charity. Eureka's own finances teetered on collapse. Enrollment had shrunk to 187 students. The college was in constant debt, with barely enough money to meet its payroll, often paying its bills with produce from a farm that functioned as its endowment. Faculty often had to brave long dry stretches before salaries were paid.

Samuel Glen Harrod, who was in charge of admissions, was a three-hundred-pound bear of a man but was a notoriously soft touch. Time and again, he scraped together whatever spare resources he could muster to help disadvantaged students fund an education. This year, however, was unusually fraught. Many more students were squeezed financially. The Great Crash was a year away, but farms across the Midwest were in the grip of an economic malaise, and their sons and daughters descended on Sam Harrod's office in greater numbers, soliciting aid.

Dutch knew he had to argue his worth. He sat down and talked to Dean Harrod about his background in Dixon—teaching Sunday school, saving lives at Lowell Park, living the gospel. Reverend Cleaver, a formidable influence, was offered as a reference. Dutch knew the college had a football team—though not a very good one—and offered his services. He dropped the name of their last notable star, fullback Garland Waggoner, his personal hero, and mentioned that he'd like to follow in his cleats. Harrod must have been impressed, because he immediately sent Dutch to speak with Ralph McKinzie, Eureka's football coach and campus legend.

McKinzie was a tougher sell. He didn't fall for Dutch's "inflated tales" of his football prowess. Coach Mac had scouted all the local high school phenoms and knew Dutch wasn't one of them. His gridiron legacy in the 1928 Dixon yearbook—"Dutch Reagan took care of his tackle berth in a creditable manner"—said it all. But at six feet and 160 pounds the boy had the right size, with those swimmer's shoulders, and Eureka was in desperate need of big bodies. They'd gone the past year without winning a single game—through the whole season the football team scored a total of two points. And 1928 would be another "rebuilding" season; they'd take anyone able to compete.

Financial assistance was cobbled together that very afternoon. Sam Harrod came up with something he called a Needy Student Grant—half of the $180 tuition—"created on the fly" in his office. The $270 board would be deferred until later in the next semester. In the meantime, Dutch could share an apartment for $2.50 a week above a commercial building in downtown Eureka with another freshman, Samuel Rode, shaving another $125 or so off his account. There was also a package of work deferments, which included jobs waiting tables, washing dishes in the women's dormitory, raking leaves, and working at the school's steam plant. Taken together, this gave Dutch the wherewithal to enroll, along with some breathing room— not much, but enough to get by. He'd not be returning to Dixon.

College—Dutch was going to college, the first in his family to make the leap. It was a personal victory. He'd dreamed about making a better life for himself. He'd worked hard and saved every cent he could. Now he was on his way: a freshman at Eureka College.

D utch got swept right into the spirit of things. His class was the first to have an organized orientation, and the program was a humdinger. The guest of honor was the oldest living alumnus of the college, Benjamin Johnson Radford Jr., a member of the Class of 1867 and one of the boys of Company G. An actual Civil War veteran who had known Abraham Lincoln. Dutch made it a point to introduce himself to Radford out by the fabled Recruiting Elm, which still stood in the middle of campus. Afterward, he took part in the Ivy Ceremony, a Eureka tradition for all incoming students. The west face of Burgess Hall—the main building on campus—was covered in ivy taken from the grave of Alexander Campbell, one of the co-founders of the Christian Church. The class of 1900 had planted it and created the ritual that took place each fall, when incoming freshmen are given a sprig from the wall to drop into a community basket, thus investing themselves in Eureka for the next four years. When they graduated, their diplomas would contain another sprig, the symbolic significance being that ivy can be planted anywhere, and graduates with the skills, abilities, and talent can now plant themselves anywhere. Although no one would be so bold as to think in the White House.

What Dutch would remember most about it was the feverish political climate. Much of the conversation that dominated his first day at Eureka—September 20, 1928—concerned the hurricane that had swept through Puerto Rico and South Florida, killing 2,500 migrant workers when the levees at Lake Okeechobee broke. There was plenty of grousing about President Herbert Hoover's focus on the fate of the sugar crop and factories in the area. What about God's children? The doctrine of moral sense? The attention paid to developments on the world stage was a revelation to Dutch. The atmosphere was highly charged, passionate. It galvanized him.

His course load, on the other hand, wasn't that demanding: English lit, French I, rhetoric, history. Most electives he chose were in the combined major of economics and sociology, started only that year and headed by

Archibald Charles Gray, who taught all of its classes. Among Eureka's free-spirited faculty, A. C. Gray stood out as its freest and most spirited. He had studied at Yale with Reinhold Niebuhr and came to Eureka as a professor of Bible studies. Gray, in his travels, had witnessed the demoralizing effects of greed and industrialization on the American worker and felt the system needed a top-down overhaul. *Social reform . . . social justice*—they were favorite topics that Gray propounded. A former student recalled those opinionated lectures and said, "He couldn't stand the rampant capitalism of the 1890s, the robber baron control of the railroads, Rockefeller's monopoly of oil." Over time, he pressed Eureka's administration to devote more attention to the evolving study of economics and sociology, convincing them in 1927 to create the department that he would spearhead.

"Daddy" Gray's courses were a popular draw: he was a dynamic lecturer—some considered him a firebrand—and famously generous when it came to grades. Even so, Dutch got C's early on in his economics classes. Studying wasn't exactly his primary concern. He got D's in a religion lecture called "The Time of Christ" and in a gut course on romantic literature. Instead he gravitated to extracurricular activities. Two weeks into the first semester he joined the school's weekly newspaper, writing unsigned pieces for *The Pegasus* about sports and breezy observations on the goings-on around campus. He pledged a fraternity—Tau Kappa Epsilon—and haunted the TKE house, where nightly pinochle games among the "fraters," as they called one another, stretched well into the morning and Monopoly games lasted all week. And, of course, there was Margaret Cleaver.

Dutch saw Mugs whenever he could. Despite the fact that she had come to Eureka primarily to study, there was still plenty of time to socialize. There were mixers in Pritchard Gymnasium, ice-cream socials on the lawn, and movies at the Jewel Theater a few blocks away. Mugs pledged Delta Zeta sorority, which met in the parlor of a women's dormitory, where couples sought dark corners and swayed to the music, occasionally sneaking a kiss or two. And on warm nights they participated in a Eureka tradition known as kegging. According to a fellow student of Dutch's, "The practice might be compared with entertaining a girl in the rear seat of a parked car, but since we had no cars we used the woods." One routinely saw couples strolling along College Avenue with a blanket and picnic basket in tow, heading toward the cemetery on the far edge of campus. The baskets, however, were strictly a ruse. "A dormitory housemother would make a sandwich and thermos of coffee to legitimize the pretense," but the chief purpose was some serious necking. Kegging couples would angle for a headstone large enough to throw "a sizable pool of shadow," providing cover from prying eyes. Dutch and Mugs liked to think their romantic trysts were private, but in eerie moonlit moments, one of the TKE fraters might give out the fraternity whistle, prompting echoes of recognition throughout the cemetery.

Kegging was an innocent kind of hanky-panky just this side of improper. Eureka advocated strict standards of conduct that weighed more on the women, who were repeatedly admonished about decorum. There was a dress code: skirts had to be long enough to ensure that the calf wasn't exposed, and slips were mandatory under sundresses. A rigid nightly curfew prevailed. Miss Lydia Wampler, the dean of women, "took a head count of the girls in the dormitory before and after each dance." She also made it a point to speak to everyone as they returned from an outing, leaning in close to determine if there was anything untoward on a student's breath.

Dutch also found time to pursue his other true love: football. Coach Mac took a hard look at the recruits and determined that Dutch was not as advertised—certainly no Garland Waggoner. He was "slow afoot, average in size, and lacking in many techniques." Then, of course, there was the nearsightedness to consider. Glasses were out of the question on the playing field, which meant that Dutch couldn't see a 200-pound nose tackle, let alone a spiraling football. It was hard to envision him making a contribution to the squad. Still, he had a "good attitude" and there was all that enthusiasm to consider. In the end, Mac couldn't afford to be choosy. He needed to field a team of twenty-seven players, with Dutch the twenty-seventh—and last—student to apply. Process of elimination: he'd take Reagan, but he wasn't happy about it.

Ralph McKinzie was a difficult man to please. He was what the Reagan biographer Edmund Morris called "an austere, flinty little Okie . . . [who] betrayed the effects of being tackled too often." But to the Eureka faithful he was "revered and loved," as close to a god that the Church would sanction. As a Eureka student, he had lettered in every sport throughout all four years of his college career and was elected as halfback to the Midwest All-Time Football Team. In one legendary basketball game against Bradley,

Mac scored all fifty-two of Eureka's points, prompting the newspaper headline "McKinzie Beats Bradley 52–0." He had heart, but so did Dutch, who was determined to prove to his coach that he deserved to play.

During team drills and practices, Dutch was fodder, a glorified tackling dummy. It was clear that he wasn't going to play. "Dutch—I put him at end on the fifth string," Coach Mac recalled, which was football code for riding the bench. He wasn't even given one of the maroon-and-gold team uniforms: he wore a white practice jersey even during games. Week after week, Dutch sat and stewed. And watched. The way Eureka played against other schools—miserably, always miserably—it seemed senseless, if not cruel, not to give him a shot, especially if one of his teammates needed a blow. The games were exhausting affairs. There was no platooning involved. "You played offense," a teammate described, "and when the other team got the ball, you played defense." Dutch could have stepped in for a quarter or two, but he was his own worst enemy. "I told everyone who would listen that the coach didn't like me," he said.

Reagan was quickly shining in other arenas, however. Within two months on Eureka's campus, according to an observer, he "was already known as a good speaker." He expressed himself regularly in *Pegasus* columns, and sharper opinions and insight were reserved for bull sessions at the TKE house, where politics was often debated. There, Dutch was in his element. Jack had indoctrinated him in liberal ideology, and he found plenty to rail against in this Republican milieu.

Dutch soon developed a reputation as a debater. He never let his emotions get the best of him—never raised his voice, gestured wildly, or pounded the table. He wasn't hotheaded, even when he stood his ground in fiery debates against the upperclassmen in the house, brothers who were already involved in the political rumblings on campus. And from the time classes started in 1928, those rumblings had been building. Eureka's board of trustees was scrambling to manage runaway debt. As the board assessed it, the problem stemmed from overreach. The college offered courses in twenty-eight majors, a luxury for such a small, impoverished school. Rumors had been circulating all semester that certain departments would be scaled back, and several eliminated, along with a number of professors, at the whim of Bert Wilson, the college's authoritarian president.

Wilson was already a much-despised figure on campus. "Domineering" and "driven by a stern fundamentalism," he had persisted for years in outlawing dancing, a form of entertainment that he found personally objectionable. He was so dead-set against it that, a year earlier, when students attended an American Legion dance in town, he had them confined to campus afterward and subtracted grade points from their records.

Relations deteriorated further when word got around that the board of trustees, which met in October 1928, had ratified Wilson's austerity program. Art and home economics were to be dropped entirely from the curriculum, with no recompense for the juniors and seniors already majoring in those programs. Football and basketball were on the bubble. Students, predictably, were up in arms. The TKE fraternity president, Leslie Pierce, felt that the student body had been sold out and began to organize opposition to Wilson's cutbacks. Pierce didn't trust the present student government. He knew that two years earlier Bert Wilson had reformed that organization in order to limit its power. At Les Pierce's bidding, a secretive organization was formed—a student government within the student government—called the Committee of 21. It was without portfolio but its members had plenty of influence—the leaders of fraternities, sororities, and sports teams from every class.

A pivotal moment occurred on November 16, 1928, when the trustees agreed to further cost-cutting by reducing the remaining departments to eight, combining related subjects such as English and rhetoric, and mathematics and physics. This triggered an initiative by the Committee of 21 to circulate a petition calling for Bert Wilson's resignation. It took less than a week of canvassing to collect 143 signatures, enough to present it to the school's trustees.

"Ronald W. Reagan" was scrawled clearly across the document, along with every other member of Tau Kappa Epsilon. Whether Dutch was part of the volunteers collecting signatures is unknown, but he was certainly an activist for Wilson's demise. He felt the board was "cutting out the heart of the college." On November 23, when it became apparent the board intended to ignore the petition, a committee was formed to explore the possibility of a student strike, with Dutch representing the freshman class.

This was no slapdash action. The students were organized. They met off campus, in both a local bank and at the courthouse, and hired a University of Chicago Law School attorney, Frances Ridgeley, whose father was the state's attorney for Woodford County and a Eureka alumnus. Both Ridgeleys, father and daughter, had political clout, while the school relied on advice from a small-town lawyer. "The board was outgunned in terms of legal representation," says Junius Rodriguez, a current Eureka professor and historian. "The students came at them with everything in their arsenal."

But President Wilson fired back. On November 23, *The Pegasus* reported that he had intimated to the board that the college might be better suited elsewhere—perhaps in a larger, more diversified city like Springfield. "Eureka was too small a town to provide jobs for students," he said. There was no daily newspaper to furnish the publicity a college needs. The day of rural towns was over; people were abandoning them in favor of metropolitan areas.

Many of the town's leading lights sat on Eureka's alumni committee and the board. In one fell swoop, Wilson had managed to turn them against him. The next day, Bert Wilson resigned.

It was an empty gesture. The following Tuesday, November 27, with the entire student body crammed into the stadium for the afternoon football face-off against rival Illinois College, word started circulating that Wilson's resignation wasn't accepted. The trustees had met throughout the day and not only given the president a vote of confidence, but considered reprisals against certain students and faculty responsible for the attack against him. Dutch recalled looking up at the bleachers from his spot on the bench and seeing everyone hidden behind a copy of *The Pegasus*. "A few copies even showed up on the bench."

That sealed it. The students were due to leave for Thanksgiving holiday after the game, but those plans were abruptly postponed. The agitation on campus was undeniable. An emergency summit would take place later that night. Dutch, who was set to depart for Dixon with Mugs and Sam Rode, his roommate, headed to the TKE house to await further word.

The sign came just before midnight. Members of the Committee of 21 arranged to have an old college bell toll for fifteen minutes straight, a ferocious sound that cut through the night and could be heard for miles in every direction. Students emptied out of the dorms, many still in their pajamas. Faculty came running from their homes. Within minutes, the chapel was jammed—more than two hundred people sat shoulder to shoulder.

The chapel was a campus touchstone. Sunday services and mandatory convocations were held there, but it doubled as a common room that had been used for years by a literary society. It had high, dark wood-beamed ceilings and a propellerlike chandelier whose glass sconces threw beams of soft light across the clustered student conclave. That night, everyone knew what they were there for. The word "strike" buzzed in all corners of the room. Emotions ran high; the chapel fairly percolated with nervous anticipation while the leadership huddled to one side, drafting the prospective resolution.

Restive voices cut through the hall. It was well after midnight, pushing toward one. To calm the situation, the leaders drafted George Gunn, a music professor who had joined the rally, to sing a medley of old Negro spirituals. It was that kind of surreal atmosphere.

The holdup, on the other hand, was anything but dreamy. The student leaders struggled with how best to deliver the strike resolution they had written. Somebody had to address the crowd in a persuasive enough manner for the students to adopt it by acclamation. But—who? The seniors were graduating; they wouldn't be effective. It had to be someone who was a dynamic speaker and could captivate the crowd, but also someone perceived as having plenty at stake. A freshman, perhaps, with four years ahead of him.

Finally, Leslie Pierce brought the meeting to order, offering reports from the minutes of the trustees' meeting. The news wasn't favorable, as expected; none of their complaints had been given consideration. A procession of student speakers followed in his wake. Then came the moment everyone had been waiting for: Dutch ambled up onto a stage, clutching the resolution. The crowd grew hushed. As he looked across the hall he could make out many familiar faces, among them Dean Harrod, his journalism teacher Professor Wiggins, and A. C. Gray, all of whom had sided with the students. "I'd been told that I should sell the idea so there'd be no doubt of the outcome," Dutch recalled. Drawing on experience from acting in his mother's morality plays in Dixon, he mixed old-fashioned preaching with a generous dash of stage presence to deliver the motion that would rock the audience:

> We the students of Eureka College, on the twenty-eighth day of November 1928, declare an immediate strike pending the acceptance of President Wilson's resignation by the board of trustees.

The spectators had waited until 1:45 a.m. to hear those words. Now, according to Dutch, "they came to their feet with a roar," ratifying the strike by unanimous approval. The room resonated with peals of thunderous applause. He recalled the reaction as "heady wine," and he drank it in. Howard Short, who was the senior class president, must have felt exonerated. "We put Reagan on because he was the biggest mouth of the freshman class," he recalled. "He was a cocky s.o.b., a loud talker." And also, Short knew, effective. Dutch knew how to sell an idea.

It was a triumphant moment. And the triumph—something he took as a personal triumph—was a revelation. He was exhilarated. He'd discovered the power of performance, how his words could spark action. It was a defining moment in Ronald Reagan's life. As the students straggled back to dorms just after two in the morning, he came to terms with the realization that the poor boy from Dixon, the modest scholar, the fifth-string athlete, the cocky SOB, was blessed with a talent.

That Thanksgiving weekend delivered further revelations. Dutch arrived home, back in Dixon, to a rash of heavy storms and a family in the throes of transition. Jack was still out of work, and Moon's job had changed. His monthly $125 salary at the Medusa Portland Cement Company had been keeping the Reagans afloat, but casework evaporated. His new position paid a pittance. There was barely enough to keep the family fed and warm. And Jack was back on the prowl, sneaking out at night to indulge his craving for bootlegger booze, filling Nelle with resentment and despair. "Neighbors and relatives suggested she get a divorce," a friend recalled, "but this was absolutely against her beliefs." As dark as things had grown, she and Jack had kept their marriage together. He didn't repeat the sins of men in previous generations of Nelle's family who abandoned home when wanderlust struck. And she was determined to continue as a family, however fractured. But there was a streak of tension that ran through the house, which Dutch did his best to avoid.

When the Cleavers invited him to attend a play with them in Rockford, he jumped at the chance. There was a touring-company production of *Journey's End*, the sensational R. C. Sherriff antiwar drama that had thrilled London audiences and was set to open on Broadway months later in New York. This was a first for Dutch. Up to now, the sum total of his theater experience was church skits and amateur school productions. He had never seen a professional play. He was overwhelmed by the performances, the way the actors used silence as well as words to convey emotion, how they modulated their voices and moved their bodies as instruments of storytelling. "In some strange way," he recalled, "I was also on stage." Margaret had already joined Eureka's Dramatic Club. Now Dutch was eager to get involved.

But when they returned to school following the holiday break, the drama on campus took precedence over the arts. The Eureka students were effectively on strike. Academics had ground to a halt. Sympathetic professors who faced empty classrooms marked everyone present.

A committee of student leaders was busy negotiating with the trustees and alumni for a resolution to end the strike. The sticking point was President Bert Wilson's tenure. The students refused to entertain any outcome that left him in place; the board opposed dismissing him under pressure. They were willing to accept Wilson's resignation so long as the same fate befell several administration and faculty members sympathetic to the strike (including Sam Harrod, Dutch's financial benefactor), as well as its ringleaders.

In the end, the students prevailed and Bert Wilson resigned, although the number of departments at Eureka was greatly reduced and the school remained on the verge of insolvency. Everything else went on as before.

For Dutch, the memory of the strike would always be bathed in a golden glow. He was recused from the nitty-gritty, the long hours of arduous negotiations that ultimately deposed a school president. He let others do the complex work of bringing the dispute to an end. Instead, he concentrated on the spirit of the strike, on increased campus morale and solidarity. For him, the highlight would always be that night in the chapel, that moment in front of the student body when he discovered what it felt like to be at the

front of a just cause, and to be heard and acclaimed. Once the spring semester began, Dutch beat a path to the Dramatic Club, where a new young
teacher, Ellen Marie Johnson, was making her name as someone who knew
how to teach the fundamentals of stagecraft with contemporary flair. Up
until her arrival, the club's productions were fusty retreads of Victorian-era
melodramas or Gilbert and Sullivan light opera. But Miss Johnson edged
into vaudeville and farce.

She immediately recruited Dutch for *The Brat*, a domestic comedy with
a role that seemed almost too close to home. He played an alcoholic, the
dissolute son of a well-to-do family who is reformed by a witty street urchin
who charms him into marriage. For a novice actor experimenting with
character, there was plenty of personal history for Dutch to draw on. A
rousing dance number served to lighten the mood.

That play was like catnip to Dutch. He'd gotten a taste of the spotlight
during the strike, but this was a completely different type of performance.
The rush he felt from acting was visceral. The opportunity to get under the
skin of a character, to put his own stamp on it, to hear the feedback and
the applause—there was nothing like it. He was sold from the moment the
curtain went up.

If the Dramatic Club helped carry him through the rest of the semester,
his academic pursuits certainly didn't. Dutch's grades were a mix of C's and
D's. He barely maintained a grade-point average high enough to remain
eligible to play sports. Not that he seemed any closer to playing on the
football team. Coach seemed even less inclined to start him in his sophomore year, and Dutch was convinced it was personal. "I'd tolerated Mac
McKinzie's lack of appreciation for my gridiron skills long enough," he decided. It was humiliating. What's more, he was broke. Freshman year had
effectively wiped out his savings. The ordeal of raising enough money to
return to college seemed insurmountable. He wasn't even certain he wanted
to go back.

Things weren't much rosier in Dixon. The best one could say of the
Reagan family was that they were coexisting, holding things together. Jack
had a part-time job at the sanatorium where his brother Will had died, and
Nelle was working downtown as a seamstress at the Marilyn Shop, for $14
a week. All warmth had gone out of their marriage. Dutch's return to his
old job on the lifeguard chair in Lowell Park provided an escape as much as

it did a wage. It was liberating to be out of the family crucible during daylight hours. At the water's edge, elevated above the crowd, he was a local hero again. When he wasn't in action, he relaxed in the shade, arguing politics with his boss, Ed Graybill, whom his wife described as a "strong Republican."

That summer isolated Dutch from the big decisions in his life. But when the park closed down at the end of August, his irresolution about college was stronger than ever. His financial situation was pitiful. He'd made only $200, not enough to cover his share of tuition. It didn't seem worth the effort to go begging again. An old high school buddy who worked as a rodman for a local surveyor confided that he was quitting his job and suggested that Dutch step into the vacancy. It seemed like a reasonable solution. He could earn some real money for a change, contribute to the family. As extra incentive, the surveyor made him "an offer too good to refuse." If he worked for a year, his boss would help him get a full-ride athletic scholarship to his alma mater, the University of Wisconsin.

That sealed it. His days at Eureka were over. It meant a separation from Mugs, whom he loved more than ever, but they could spend weekends and holidays together. And acting would just have to wait. Perhaps his presence might help stabilize things at home. In any case, he had made up his mind. The road crew he joined was involved in some work around Lowell Park, but the work was wholly dependent on the weather. As it happened, Dutch's first day on the job was rained out, owing to a typical fall Midwestern rainstorm. To pass the time, he decided to accompany Mugs, whose parents were driving her back to college. He could help move her into the dorm, then stop in to see old friends, if only to provide some closure.

Once he hit campus his heart started to beat fast. The place felt like home. The grounds looked lovely. The TKE house beckoned. He even paid a visit to the fieldhouse, where Coach Mac was finalizing plans for the new football season while complaining that the team would be a couple of men short. Dutch felt his defenses breaking down.

Before he knew what was happening, Mac was on the phone to Dean Harrod, arranging for another Needy Student Scholarship, along with part-time work to help cover expenses. The rest of Dutch's tuition could be deferred until after graduation, and he could board at the TKE house.

Dutch called his mother and gave her the news, along with a sweetener:

he'd also arranged a football scholarship for Moon, who could take over Dutch's old job waiting tables at the TKE house.

Moon recalled how he scoffed at the offer and made light of it the next day, when he recounted the story to Mr. Kennedy, his boss at the cement plant. An hour or two later, Kennedy sent his secretary to see Moon, along with a paycheck and a reproach: "Mr. Kennedy says if you're not smart enough to take the good thing your brother has fixed up for you, you're not smart enough to work for him." Moon stopped at the bank to cash the check, then went home to pack his bags.

Dutch moved right into the TKE house. "It was about three-quarters of a mile from campus," according to a professor, "way out in the boonies surrounded by pasture." Twenty-three brothers slept stacked in bunk beds in the uninsulated third-floor attic. "If it was twenty below outside," a neighbor noted, "it was twenty below upstairs. You put on a sweatsuit, wool cap and stockings, and went to bed." Dutch spent most of the evenings in the second-floor study with his bunkmate, Elmer Fisher, cracking the books—or at least making a show of it—in an effort to maintain an acceptable scholastic average. Otherwise, he gravitated to the cemetery, where he and Mugs renewed their "stargazing" on a blanket sprawled across one of the plots.

Dutch cruised through his sophomore year with few ripples. His academic performance remained mediocre at best. Easy as the coursework was, it was hard for Dutch. He had no gift for French, *pas du tout*; despite being tutored by Mugs, who spoke it beautifully, the best he could pull was a D. Religion was also a slog, as was American lit. Daddy Gray's econ courses, while fascinating, required a good deal of analytical thinking, and Dutch wasn't wired that way. For one thing, it meant plowing through chapter after chapter of a tedious textbook and digging into details. Moon, who shared some of the same econ classes, recalled how "Ronald very seldom cracked a book." Instead, when it came time for a test, he spent "a quick hour" flipping through the pages and relied instead on his photographic memory. Daddy Gray wasn't fooled one bit, but it exasperated him. He grumbled about Dutch's lack of applying himself to coursework, complaining, "And yet I have to give him a grade."

Dutch was too caught up with sports and acting to focus on schoolwork. Football occupied most of his attention. Mostly he continued to warm the bench while his brother blossomed into the Golden Tornadoes' star.

Halfway through the season, Dutch got the nod to replace an injured team-mate at right end and performed in a game without embarrassing himself. And during a scrimmage, he stood out for a brutal hit on a more experienced man Mac had pitted against him. Gradually he wore Coach down, working his way into the starting lineup.

Secretly, Mac admired Dutch's determination, the way he hung in there, biding his time. He was "a good plugger," in Mac's eyes, and "a pretty good leader" on and off the field. He brought a sense of camaraderie to the locker room. Mac appreciated how Dutch "used to take an old broom from the locker room and pretend it was a microphone and 'announce' the game play-by-play afterward." The photographic memory helped: "Never forgot a play either!"

Sportscasting—he was an aficionado. If he had a favorite pastime it was imitating announcers. "He'd sit in front of a radio and listen to sports-casters by the hour," Moon recalled. There was a boxy Westinghouse Radi-ola on the second floor of the TKE house, which pulled in games from across the state and beyond. Dutch parked himself in front of it night after night, dialing in broadcasts of Michigan and Ohio State games. There was Red Grange, the "Galloping Ghost" of Illinois, Knute Rockne at Notre Dame. On the weekends, he listened to Chicago Cardinals and Bears games. Maybe a Jack Dempsey or Joe Louis bout. It was the sportscasters who intrigued him most, with their colorful phraseology, a language all their own. This was a dialect that Dutch could master.

When football went on hiatus, the Reagan brothers doubled as the college's sole basketball cheerleaders. Dressed in matching white sweaters and khakis, Dutch and Moon patrolled the home-crowd sideline, drumming up pep with a half dozen wacky chants.

> O, we'll whoop 'em up for Eureka, Eureka,
> Eu Re,
> We'll whoop 'em up for Eureka,
> A jolly bunch are we

When their voices gave out, they performed "the Skyrocket." "They ran down the floor," recalled a spectator, "they lit a fuse—'SISSS . . . ,' jumped in the air, 'BOOM' and landed—'BAH.' EUREKA!"

When basketball season ended, Dutch joined Eureka's swim team. In fact, he *was* the swim team.

There had never been a great deal of interest in competitive swimming. It was never considered a major sport, certainly not in the same league as football, not even tennis, but the landscape began to gradually change after the 1928 Summer Olympics. The Games, held in Amsterdam that year, were broadcast for the very first time, and Americans sat around their radios in parlors and kitchens, listening as Johnny Weissmuller put on an aquatics show, winning two gold medals with his incredible skill. That was all Dutch needed to get a "team" going on campus, even though the resources for it were slim. No one else tried out, and even if they had, it would have been difficult for more than one person at a time to train. There was a pool below Pritchard Gym, but it wasn't conducive to competition—five feet at the deepest end and only twenty-five feet long. Dutch made the most of it, knifing through the water and doing flip turns to simulate regulation-sized lanes. He was already in top shape from lapping across the Rock River all summer, giving him an edge against schools with more accomplished programs.

In the 1929–30 season, Dutch swam for Eureka against other colleges in the Little 19 Conference—much larger schools for the most part, such as Bradley, Illinois Wesleyan, Millikin, Springfield, and Northern Illinois. He wasn't a giant-killer, not yet, pulling down respectable fourth-place finishes in two events in the spring meet at Saint Victor, but there was plenty of upside to his effort, which became evident the following year, when he placed first in the state meets, setting a record of fifty-one seconds in the 100-yard freestyle.

Otherwise, Dutch devoted the spring semester to sharpening his acting skills. There was a warm-up show, *The Dover Road*, which was staged for the Mononk Women's Club. Then Miss Johnson entered her untested Eureka Players troupe in the Annual Theater Tournament held each April at Northwestern University. This was considered a big-time event, drawing colleges, as well as audiences and critics, from across the Midwest. Most participants had theater departments that rivaled a professional stock company. Was little, nearly bankrupt Eureka up to the challenge? The play they took on was *Aria da Capo*, a blank-verse one-act by Edna St. Vincent Millay that dealt with human greed, moral decay, and the futility of war. Dutch led the cast as a Greek shepherd opposite his football teammate Bud Cole, with Mugs in a supporting role as a flighty socialite.

By all accounts, there was real power in Dutch's performance, his deft alternation between low comedy and barbed sarcasm, his stage presence. The Eureka Players were awarded the third-place trophy, and Dutch was named one of the six best actors in the tournament. It was quite an honor, considering his meager experience on the stage, and it intensified the pull toward acting.

But to what end? "In those days, in the middle of Illinois," he acknowledged, "you didn't run around and say, 'I want to be an actor.'" It was preposterous. "They'd throw a net over you."

CHAPTER SEVEN

"THE DISAPPEARANCE OF MARGARET"

"Love knows nothing of order."

—ST. JEROME

D utch wasn't acting when it came to courting Margaret Cleaver. He was as committed to her as he had ever been, and throughout the school year of 1929–1930 the two were rarely apart.

They took advantage of the intimacy that a small, cozy campus provided, walking to classes together, huddling close over lunch, running lines of plays they were rehearsing, kegging any chance they got. In March, they were inducted side by side into Alpha Epsilon Sigma, Eureka's exclusive drama society, and coordinated their outfits with its somber black and blue pledge colors. On weekends, they snuggled in seats at the Jewel Theater, a late convert to talkies, where they delighted in the Marx Brothers in *The Cocoanuts*, Ronald Colman in *Bulldog Drummond*, and Gary Cooper in *The Virginian*.

They were a golden couple, in demand for a profusion of social engagements—the Tau Kappa Epsilon dinner-dance at the Jefferson Hotel, the annual TKE Halloween getaway at Camp Lantz on the Mackinaw River, Delta Zeta's Harvest Moon dance, the Christmas party at Professor Jones's home, the TKE New Year's bash just before winter break. Every week seemed to spin them into another gala affair. If there was any downside, it wasn't yet evident. Even their differences complemented—Mugs's quiet intensity, Dutch's big personality; Mugs's intellect, Dutch's intuitive nature; Mugs's stoicism, Dutch's exuberance. If there was a strain, it was in the way they viewed their futures. Mugs had a plan mapped out. After college, there was a student-teacher position awaiting her in Cropsey, Illinois. Dutch, on the other hand, was undecided. Reverend Cleaver had often talked to him about a role in the ministry. He had all the right qualities: leadership, compassion, unshakable faith—*character*. But college had awakened Dutch's curiosity. There were other opportunities beyond the conventional, beyond Dixon. What about sportscasting—and acting? It seemed like a wildly attractive alternative to a more traditional profession. He'd never considered going that route, but now he was keeping an open mind, especially after Dutch's bravura performance at Northwestern, when the director of its School of Speech, Garret Leverton, took him aside and suggested he give strong consideration to an acting career.

All this talk might have served to unsettle Mugs, who as a minister's daughter took a dim view of the bohemian lifestyle. Actors were gadabouts. They had shaky prospects for success. And Dutch already walked a fine line. "He was an indifferent student," Mugs recalled, "although I always knew he was a leader."

Their dream had been to teach—Mugs instructing an elementary school class, Dutch running the phys-ed department. But somewhere along the way, for Dutch, that dream's luster had dimmed. He'd taken a good, hard look at Coach McKinzie and "wanted more than he had." He acknowledged, "I was afraid. . . . I might end up an athletic teacher at some small school, raising little football heroes." Not that it would have been a bad choice—"for some people." But it wasn't acting.

Dutch and Mugs could still make it work. Dutch was so certain of it that he decided to seal their relationship by "hanging" his fraternity pin on her, a gesture tantamount to an engagement, especially for a young man who couldn't afford a ring.

He did the deed one evening that spring in the backseat of Dean Harrod's green Buick. Dutch and Mugs were on a double date with Harrod's daughter, Mary Eleanor, and her boyfriend, Harry Marshall, a TKE frater. As they were returning to campus, Dutch got up his nerve. It wasn't just the pin, but a proper marriage proposal.

If it took Mugs by surprise, she didn't flinch. Presumably, she had made up her mind about Dutch long before that evening. She never undertook any important decision without the approval of her parents, and she knew all along they would give it their blessing. Her father regarded Dutch like a son; from the outset, he was practically a member of their family. And she loved Dutch. Without any hesitation, she accepted his pin to cries of congratulations from the front seat.

How the news was greeted back in Dixon by Dutch's parents was another matter. Jack and Nelle's marriage was a shambles. They'd long maintained separate bedrooms, and by the spring of 1930 they were living separate lives. Jack hardly spent a night at home anymore. In January, he'd gotten a job with the Red Wing Shoe Company as a traveling salesman, operating out of Springfield. It was a godsend; they were practically broke. The $260 monthly salary was more than enough to get by on. But the demands of the job kept Jack pretty much on the road, where there was unfettered access to alcohol and worse. Rumors persisted of another woman—women. And these excesses siphoned off a chunk of his paycheck before any of it found a way back home.

By the time Dutch got home from school for the summer, his parents had moved to a new, more affordable place—not even a house, just two rooms they sublet—at 226 Lincoln Way, still on the north side of town. There were few amenities, not even a kitchen. Whatever food Nelle prepared was cooked on a bedroom hot plate, but even that was hardly put to use. Helen Kennedy, who lived in the house just behind them, remembered how her grandmother made extra portions of her own dinner so that Nelle and Jack would enjoy a hot meal once in a while. Their front door had a panel of sliding screens. "Nelle would open the top screen," she recalled, "and we would hand the food through."

Dutch went back to work at Lowell Park, but instead of saving for next year's tuition, most of his pay went to helping out at home. Dixon, like most of the Midwest, was hit hard by the Depression. The city was ravaged by unemployment, and according to an article in the *Dixon Evening Telegraph*, "near starvation stalked the community." Transients begged on the streets. More than 350 families were officially destitute, with five times that number seeking relief—groceries, clothing, and coal—from the Dixon Welfare Association and the American Legion. Newman's Garage offered bread and coffee to the jobless who queued up each morning. A Community

Kitchen, supported by donations from citizens, opened a soup kitchen in a building behind the Dixon Theater. And a Paul Rader Pantry of Plenty, backed by nineteen local churches and patriotic organizations, was launched at Assembly Park, where ten huge steam-pressure cookers were used to can huge quantities of food for distribution to the needy.

Jack and Nelle put up a good front. Friends and neighbors recalled that they were "always well dressed," with two sons in college and a roof over their heads. All around them the devastation left its mark. Dixon was surrounded by farming country, which was reeling from years of plunging crop prices. During 1931, foreclosures hit an all-time high, with almost four thousand American families thrown off farms by the government. The John Deere Company announced the closing of six plants. The Reynolds Wire factory, a pillar of Dixon's economic strength, was laying off one production line after another.

Eureka College was in even worse shape, its financial situation dire. To make ends meet for the coming year, an emergency "Eureka Plan" was initiated, requiring every student to pitch in by taking over routine services at the library and cafeteria as well as helping out at the heating plant and doing heavy maintenance around the grounds. They would also have to put in time at the farm that endowed the school, which meant milking the cows and harvesting crops whose proceeds covered faculty salaries.

Dutch pledged to do his share, and with help from a Disciples of Christ loan he was able to register for his junior year. Many of his classmates found similar ways to return, determined to continue their education despite the ongoing hardship. The first week in September 1930 the campus was buzzing with energy that signaled the start of another school year. Everyone was primed and ready to go except for one significant absence: Margaret Cleaver.

According to most accounts, Margaret, a straight-A student, found the coursework unchallenging and opted to take a semester or two at the University of Illinois at Urbana-Champaign. It seemed an odd choice for a gifted young woman who was also the president of her class. "If you were going to do a semester away," says a Eureka professor, "you don't just go down the road to U. of I." There was Northwestern or the University of

Chicago, with arguably more challenging curricula, or even nearby Drake, its religious orientation more suited to someone with Margaret's background. And financial considerations. With three daughters in college it was difficult for the Cleavers to bear up under such an expense. Like Dutch, Margaret required that a sizable portion of her tuition be covered by a Eureka scholarship.

Were the courses at the University of Illinois that much superior? There is a transcript in Margaret's file at Eureka, allegedly from the University of Illinois, indicating that she took Intermediate French, Intro to Comparative Literature, American Lit., Geology 1, the History of Education, Rhetoric, and Educational Psychology—all courses that were offered at Eureka. It would seem superfluous, if profligate, to take them at the U. of I. And odd, given that her new fiancé was back at Eureka.

In fact, she didn't. The University of Illinois has no record of Margaret Cleaver's ever attending the school. Its chief archivist exhausted every possible avenue in search of her records—the morgue files, the student files, and the university's microfilm collection of transcripts—without finding any trace of her. "There is no matriculation record that she ever enrolled at the University of Illinois," he says. "The transcript, if accurate, must originate from some other institution." In any case, for a six-month period— from September 1930 to the spring of 1931—her whereabouts are unexplained, a period referred to by a Eureka College official as "the disappearance of Margaret."

Where was she if she wasn't at the U. of I.? It is possible that during the height of the Depression the Cleavers were unable to afford the remainder of her tuition. Margaret could have been kept home in Dixon for a semester until there was enough money to resume her education. But there are other explanations. While searching for answers in Eureka's voluminous archives, a college official speculated that "she could have gone away to have a child—or an abortion." There was a nearby facility called the Baby Fold in Bloomington-Normal, a town halfway between Eureka and Urbana-Champaign, that was noted for "taking on and finding homes for adopted babies from sorority girls from Northwestern and some of the smaller Illinois schools." Was a dummy transcript placed in her Eureka file to preserve her reputation? It remains a possibility.

Margaret's reappearance at Eureka for the spring semester in 1931 also invites speculation. No longer was she residing with other students in the dormitory, where she had lived the first two years, but in a house a few hundred yards off campus, with her parents. In the interim marking Margaret's "disappearance," Ben Hill Cleaver relinquished his congregation in Dixon to become pastor of the Eureka Christian Church, a much smaller parish firmly rooted in the social gospel. The hastily arranged move created an impression that the Cleavers wanted to keep a closer grip on their daughter.

Another clue in the mystery was a postscript on Margaret's college transcript noting that she took General Zoology in the summer of 1932, a month *after* her graduation from Eureka. Had she taken this "for fun," as a current college official speculates, or was it rather "as a make-up course and . . . condition of being allowed to [graduate] with her class"? It seems likely that if Margaret had taken a semester off she might be several credits short at the end of four years.

Whatever the reason, Mugs returned to pursue a regular load of classes at Eureka, where she and Dutch were a couple for the remainder of their college careers.

By his junior year, Dutch was a hugely popular student on campus, even if scholarship continued to elude him. He was a BMOC, no longer the "cocky SOB." whose motormouth had inflamed the strike with bombast and swagger, but more of an all-around guy, whom classmates remembered for his affability and unselfishness. Image as well as charm impressed. He had a way of presenting himself that was natural but alluring: an easy smile, a silvery voice, arresting pale-blue eyes. He had lost the physical awkwardness that trailed his adolescence. He stood, solid and muscular, inching past six feet tall, with "absurdly handsome" well-set features that retained their boyishness while suggesting virility. His face had what a casting director might call "character," dominated by a good jaw and luminous complexion. An affectation he'd adopted—smoking a Yachtsman-style pipe—lent an airbrushed intellect to an otherwise unbookish bent.

Dutch's grades junior year were dismal; he eked out two B-minuses to go with an array of C's and D's. Even so, the mediocre grades weren't the only story. A trove of his writing exists from that period, revealing an enlightened, imaginative thinker. When he dealt with interests close to his heart—as he did in an essay entitled "This Younger Generation," which received a worthy ninety-six (although he might have earned a perfect hundred had the professor not marked the paper "late")—he demonstrated a breezy, unlabored style, wry and engaging commentary, and a note of authenticity. Another example—"Sweet Young Things," about "the fair, and sometimes not so fair sex"—earned a respectable ninety (also "late"). Dutch could express himself eloquently. But he was too distracted, often too lazy, as shown on many of his compositions by the many misspellings, scratched-out phrases, and doodles, lots of doodles.

Football loomed too large. By his junior year, Dutch figured into the starting lineup with regularity. Coach Mac didn't mince words: "He was *no* star"—simple as that. He wasn't big enough, strong enough, fast enough, or selfish enough to reach that level. But what Dutch had was spirit. He was a team player. And when pressed, Mac had to admit "he was a pretty good leader, strong in cooperation, self-discipline, self-sacrifice and determination."

His senior year, one remarkable football play that involved Ronald Reagan occurred *off* the field. In October, the Golden Tornadoes traveled north for an away game against archrival Elmhurst College. It was a decisive point in the season. "Elmhurst hadn't lost a game, and we hadn't lost a game," recalled Franklin Burghardt, the team's center. In the minds of most players, the trip promised to be a lark. It meant an overnight stay at a hotel.

Not this time. It didn't turn out as planned. The Eureka team was an anomaly. It was integrated—Burghardt was one of two current black players on the squad—as early as 1921. (By comparison, the University of Illinois did not integrate its football team until 1943.) And the Midwest was a hotbed of racial prejudice. According to a Eureka student from Dutch's class, "There were many towns in Southern Illinois where segregation was as bad as it was in the South." In fact, many of the Golden Tornadoes were from Kewanee, where the local paper routinely printed ads that stated "Klansman, Klanswomen, Kiddies and Friends—Kome to Kiwanee Kounty," and promoted events boasting the "Largest and Highest Fiery Cross." Closer to Eureka, Pekin—a town that produced Everett Dirksen—had a noted Klan community well into the 1970s.

None of this was taken into account when the team bus pulled into a hotel in downtown LaSalle, halfway between Eureka and Elmhurst. Coach McKinzie went inside to make arrangements, while the team waited on board. After what seemed like a ridiculous amount of time had passed, Dutch went into the lobby to see what the problem was. The problem was Burgie and Jim Rattan—"your two colored boys," as the hotel manager put it. They weren't setting foot inside. Nor, he said, would any other hotel in town take them. Everyone else—every white player—was welcome.

Mac's solution was for the team to sleep on the bus, but Dutch interceded. "Mac, if you do that, it will be worse for [Burgie and Jim]," he said. Instead, he suggested Coach tell the players that there wasn't enough room in the hotel for everyone, that they'd have to split up. Dixon was only thirty miles away—if it was all right with Mac, he'd take a cab there with Burghardt and Rattan. They'd be welcome to stay overnight at his home. That way, no one would be the wiser.

It was a noble and altogether sincere gesture—although sleeping on the bus in the hotel parking lot might have made a more provocative point. In any case, it didn't fool Burghardt or Rattan. Burgie knew the score before Dutch ever left the bus. He'd experienced discrimination for as long as he could remember, especially throughout the Midwest. "You never knew when you were going to walk in the door of a restaurant and the man would say, 'We can't serve you here,'" he said. Dutch knew it, too. Even on the playing field, he acknowledged, black players "took an awful lot of abuse."

History never mentions whether Moon took part in the incident. The older Reagan brother seems to have disappeared from the football squad's archives, as well as Dutch's account of his later years at Eureka. There is little doubt that Neil Reagan remained at the college. He was an A student, an active brother in the TKE fraternity, and a tuba player in the college marching band. "On campus, he was a legendary character much like Jack," a friend recalled. In only one instance does Dutch allude to encountering Moon at school. It had to do with a Golden Tornadoes contest in Springfield in the fall of 1931. After the game, which Eureka lost, they decided to pay a surprise visit to Jack, who had left Red Wing Shoes for a job managing a shoe store in East Springfield. It seemed like the perfect position for their father and triggered memories of his various tenures in Tampico, Galesburg, Monmouth, and Dixon. They couldn't wait to see him in all his glory, crouched over a chorus line of customers' feet, with his cocky smile and marvelous gift of gab. But when they arrived, instead of seeing him in the deluxe emporium Jack had described, they found him bumping around a deserted, squalid excuse for a shoe store, a "hole-in-the-wall," as Dutch recalled it, "with garish orange paper ads plastered over the windows in front and one cheap bench." The scene must have broken their hearts.

This was the end of the line for Jack. He'd burned bridges at shoe stores across Illinois. He'd run out of money, out of luck. His marriage had hit a wall. Despite his pitiful circumstances, he still managed to put a good face on things. Coach McKinzie recalled how the boys brought Jack back to join the team for dinner at a dormitory where they were staying outside Springfield. You'd never have known Jack's pitiful situation from the way he commandeered the spotlight. "A gifted storyteller," he held court all night. By Mac's account, "he started telling stories when they sat down and was still talking when the boys walked him down to the door."

Jack couldn't talk his way around his lousy luck. In December, with the family reunited on Christmas Eve, he suffered another setback. The Reagans had downsized again—to a tiny second-floor apartment on Monroe Street, back on Dixon's South Side. Everyone had gathered in the small parlor, the family's grim circumstances evident in the sad attempt at Christmas cheer. There was no money for a tree. In a pinch, Nelle had arranged a few homemade decorations across part of a coffee table as a stand-in for a tree. As Dutch remembered it, "Moon and I were headed out on dates when a special delivery [letter] arrived for Jack." A last-minute gift? He'd been holding out hope for a year-end bonus. Instead, the envelope contained a single blue sheet. "Well, that's a hell of a Christmas present," he said. "I've been laid off."

This new blow to the family's fortunes made a powerful impression on Ronald Reagan at a crucial moment in his life. With graduation only six months away, his father's latest dismissal impressed upon Dutch the need to create his own future. He was now old enough to understand the dysfunctional dynamics of the life his parents had made. His father was too unreliable to hold a job; they'd moved five times in ten years. Stronger than any lesson Dutch learned in college was the knowledge that he needed to cultivate the qualities essential to creating a rewarding life: steady personal habits and clear-eyed focus on success. Charm was fine if it was applied to getting ahead. He determined that his life couldn't be the life that his parents led. He loved them, but Dutch needed to escape from this grinding cycle. He couldn't spend his life eking out a bare existence, stumbling from one lame opportunity to the next. He had to forge a different future for himself, something more meaningful—and stable. After he finished his education, he couldn't look back.

CHAPTER EIGHT

"A PEOPLE-PLEASER"

*"There is always one moment in childhood when
the door opens and lets the future in."*

—GRAHAM GREENE, *The Power and the Glory*

J ust days before clearing out of the TKE house in May 1932, Ronald Reagan made a declaration to the other departing brothers. "If I'm not making $5,000 a year in five years," he said, "I'll consider these years here wasted."

It was an extravagant sum in the heart of the Depression. In 1932, more than thirteen million Americans remained out of work, a shocking 25 percent of the labor force, up from 3 percent in 1929 and less than 8 percent in 1930. No one had ever experienced anything like this. Farms were being foreclosed on at a rate of 20,000 per month. More than 5,500 banks had already closed. Herbert Hoover continued his administration's tone-deaf policy of not directly intervening in the economy. "We cannot squander ourselves into prosperity," he declared. Worse than his sins of omission were his sins of commission, including his move against the Bonus Army—43,000 marchers, World War I veterans and their families, many now unemployed, who squatted in Washington, D.C., demanding payment in cash of promised service "bonuses." On July 28, Hoover sent federal troops, led by General Douglas MacArthur, to run them off their campsites, burning their shelters and belongings in the process. It was an outrage, an American black eye, certainly in the partisan Reagan household.

The Reagans were already caught up in the drama of the forthcoming election. That June the Democrats had nominated Franklin D. Roosevelt, and Jack canvassed for Democratic support in Dixon. The *Dixon Evening Telegraph* was solidly behind Hoover, as were almost all Jack's friends and neighbors—even Moon. Roosevelt's victory was greeted with joy in the Reagan home, even if his "new deal for the American people" wouldn't come soon enough to help Dutch's employment prospects.

Dutch needed a job. Since graduation, he had been biding his time on the lifeguard chair at Lowell Park, but it was strictly a summer position. He discussed his situation with a visitor he'd befriended, a Kansas City businessman named Sid Altschuler, whose two daughters had taken swimming lessons from Dutch. In years past, Altschuler had promised to help him find work when he was ready. But when Dutch laid out his plans to become a radio broadcaster, Altschuler balked.

"Well, you've picked a line in which I have no connections," he said. All he could offer was advice—knock on doors, take any entry-level job, "take your chances on moving up," don't get discouraged, all the usual tips from empty-handed benefactors.

In the meantime, Jack had heard about an opening at the Dixon branch of Montgomery Ward, a job in the company's sporting goods section. It paid $12.50 a week, not bad for a rookie in the current economy, but it entailed a full six-day shift that included Saturday nights with a couple of random weekday nights thrown into the mix. It would have to suffice until something better came along. Dutch felt compelled to contribute to the family pot. Moon was headed back to Eureka. It seemed like the least Dutch could do, a son's obligation. He agreed with a heavy heart to sit for the department-store interview. "Believe you me," he told Mugs's friend Dorothy Bovey, "I am never going to be satisfied with a $12.50 a week job." His old high school mentor, Bernard Frazer, encountered him sometime toward the end of that summer and recalled a boy whose spirit was filled with dejection. "Aren't you going to have a shot at communications, the field in which you have so much talent?" Frazer wondered. But Dutch seemed resigned to his fate.

By a stroke of luck, George Joyce, a Dixon high school basketball star, was up for the same job. It came down to the two of them, and Joyce won out. Even though it came as "quite a blow," there was no shame in rejection for Dutch. Quite the opposite: it provided him with the excuse and freedom to look for other work—the kind of work he'd dreamed of for himself.

The next day, he swung into action. Moon was heading back to Eureka for the start of his senior year. Dutch went with him, ostensibly to spend a few hours with Mugs, who was preparing to leave for her teaching assignment, and to sort out the strategy for his coming job search. He had decided that his best chances of breaking into broadcasting lay in Chicago, the Midwestern media mecca; a Eureka grad attending medical school there would give him a bed for a few nights. Every national network had an affiliate there, and a number of independents. He'd knock on doors, the way Sid Altschuler recommended. After an inauspicious farewell with Margaret, Ronald Reagan hit the road.

Not many doors would open in Chicago. The effects of the Depression were starkly visible. Droves of the downtrodden and desperate wandered aimlessly in the streets. Factories were shuttered, their smokestacks eerily idle across the horizon. Long lines snaked down sidewalks outside soup kitchens. It was a humbling scene.

Yet Dutch pressed on, clutching a page torn out from the city telephone directory and using it to make the rounds. In a two-day span he hit the CBS affiliate WBBM; the Tribune Company's WGN; WLS, which broadcast the wildly popular *National Barn Dance*; WJBT; WCFL; WENR; WSBC—on and on. In every place, he couldn't get past the front desk no matter how much he laid on the charm. The only ripple in the sea of futility came at his visit to the Merchandise Mart, where NBC's WMAQ was quartered. The station's program director refused to see Dutch, but a sympathetic assistant offered a piece of advice. He was going about this job hunt the wrong way, she told him. Chicago was the big leagues. If you wanted to break into radio, you started in the minors—out in the sticks, at one of the smaller stations. "You'll find someone who will take you on and give you experience; then you can come [back] to Chicago."

The trip back to Dixon was more humbling than ever. Dutch hitchhiked the hundred miles, with long waits between rides, intermittent rain, and creepy characters behind the wheels. Returning home without a job was a crushing disappointment. There was nothing in Dixon for him, and Mugs had been cool when discussing their future. She had made it clear they shouldn't marry without financial stability—not just a job, but a responsible job, which she couldn't envision in radio. Dutch must have also mentioned acting as a possibility, because Margaret later said, "Hollywood was never my cup of tea."

Discouraged but not defeated, he asked Jack to borrow the car in order to return to Eureka, though that was never his destination. "This is the one time I deceived my father," Dutch later admitted. Instead, he drove south and west along Route 34. His plan had been to tour the backroads, visiting farm-town radio stations to inquire about work, but first he stopped in Kewanee to visit friends. Five Eureka buddies lived there—Udell "Lump" Watts, Bill Jenkins, and George Kleist, former football teammates, along with Fred Mursener and Elmer Fisher.

No evidence exists as to whether Dutch tried his luck at WKEI in Kewanee, but he soon obtained another position in town. Kewanee might have been small potatoes as a media market, slightly smaller than Dixon, but it had a vibrant newspaper in the *Star Courier*, with a circulation upward of thirteen thousand. In those days, when the locals wanted news in the afternoon and evenings, they would walk up to the *Star Courier* plant on Tremont Street, where big sheets of newsprint were hung on a wire in the window. Baseball scores, however, were a different matter. They came through on the AP wire service at night, after the last edition had already published. To satisfy his readers' interest, Phil Adler, the *Star Courier's* publisher, hired Dutch to walk out on the paper's second-floor balcony with a small megaphone and announce the scores to Cubs fans standing in the street. It wasn't broadcasting, exactly, but it was a start.

No sooner had he landed at the *Star Courier* than he began pestering Phil Adler about helping him to move on. Adler had influential contacts across all of Iowa. Before coming to Kewanee, he had run the *Daily Iowan* in Iowa City, and his father, E.P., oversaw the *Daily Times* in Davenport. Of more use, perhaps, was one of Phil Adler's closest friends, a man named Dave Palmer, whom he'd grown up with in Davenport and who was the heir to Palmer Broadcasting, where he acted as business manager at its flagship radio station, WOC, and hosted a show, *Dave's Barn*, featuring a twelve-piece band. After much cajoling, Dutch persuaded Adler to call Dave Palmer on his behalf. As Lloyd Schermer, Adler's son-in-law, describes the exchange, Phil said, "I have this young guy here who you might be interested in for the radio station." Dave Palmer agreed to meet him.

D
avenport must have seemed strangely familiar to Ronald Reagan as he crossed the bridge from Illinois into Iowa. The city was more than three times the size of Dixon, but it lay at a confluence of rivers—the Rock and the Mississippi—with a skyline that mimicked his much cozier hometown. It was part of the so-called Tri-Cities, along with neighboring Rock Island and East Moline. The mighty John Deere Company was headquartered to the north, in Moline, but Davenport's industrial muscle designated it the metropolitan center. "It was about as strong a blue-collar town as there was in America," says James Leach, a former U.S. congressman from the area. Alcoa opened the largest aluminum rolling plant in the Riverdale suburb, and a local entrepreneur named Judge French founded a company there that built undercarriages and wheels for virtually every railroad car in the country.

For news and entertainment, Davenport tuned in to WOC, at 1420 on the radio dial. Dutch had listened to the station with regularity growing up. Its 5,000-watt signal served as a beacon across the heartland: "Where the West begins and in the state where the tall corn grows." WOC's owner, a wily character named Bartlett Joshua Palmer—Dave Palmer's father—claimed, with typical excess, that it "held the world's record for long-distance transmission . . . heard in Stockholm, Paris, Rome, and Manila."

B. J. Palmer was one of the most prominent men in Davenport. He ran a printing press, a dance hall, a roller rink, an insane asylum, several restaurants, and a private garden—A Little Bit O'Heaven—featuring Greek statues, a Buddhist shrine, a Japanese temple gate, and alligators, real alligators, that snapped around the heels of visitors who paid to gape at the grounds. His broadcasting empire stretched across the Midwest, but his primary business was the Palmer School of Chiropractic, a private college dedicated to the alternative therapy—invented by Daniel David Palmer, B.J.'s father—that relies on the manipulation of the spine.

Mainstream physicians shunned chiropractic, calling it nonsense, even a "scientific cult." But its popularity had spread from Davenport throughout the Midwest and beyond. Allegedly, D. D. Palmer had stumbled on the procedure while making a deposit at the Davenport Bank & Trust. D.D. routinely used the side entrance of the cathedral-like building, where a platoon of shoeshine men was stationed by the door. His bootblack on that fateful day complained about nagging hearing loss caused by an accident. "I bent over," he explained, "and as I was picking something up my head hit the back of a boot." D.D. ordered him to turn around, grabbed the nape of the man's neck, and gave it a yank. His hearing returned, and chiropractic was born.

Like Rumpelstiltskin, B.J. spun the story into gold. He was a promoter at heart, an extraordinary raconteur, who traveled the country lecturing on alternatives to surgery and drugs. He was a fast-moving, tightly wound, theatrical man. He glorified something he called "*Innate*," a spirit power that guided him to every important decision in his life, including what to eat as well as how to remodel his home, which had a "world famous" collection of spines. "Innate" was the "internal natural intelligence," he claimed, "which knows when to sneeze, blow your nose, urinate, or defecate, blink your eyes, how to heal a cut or mend a fractured bone," among other things. "Innate" directed him to sleep with his head toward the north pole so the earth's currents would flow through him unimpeded, just as "Innate" led him to attach the radio station's ground wires to the city water main, which emptied into the Mississippi River, thus providing an "antenna" that flowed to the outer world. No matter, "Innate" in the guise of WOC gave B. J. Palmer a pipeline to sell chiropractic. By 1924, there were 25,000 chiropractors practicing in the United States, and by 1930 it was the largest alternative healing profession in the country.

When Dutch first noticed that WOC (whose call letters stood for World of Chiropractic) was connected to B.J.'s college remains unknown. It would have been hard for him to miss the portrait of Krishna discharging waves of enlightenment above the entrance on the fourth floor or the pithy aphorisms scrawled across its walls or the network of loudspeakers blasting announcements to the classrooms below. The broadcasting studio control room was a sight to behold, with teak-log furniture, a brass birdcage on a pedestal, and beams from which taxidermied animal parts—B.J.'s hunting trophies—dangled. Across the hall, in a larger studio, stood a white lacquered Chickering piano and, seemingly sleeping underneath it, a Saint Bernard—Big Ben, the beloved family pet, which B.J. had stuffed after its untimely demise and placed there for posterity.

Almost as strange as Big Ben was the awesome figure who emerged to greet Dutch. Peter MacArthur, WOC's crusty longtime announcer, who doubled as the station's program director, dragged himself down the hall with the help of two canes. MacArthur was a tall, imposing Scot whose once-strapping body was racked with crippling arthritis. After brief introductions, MacArthur explained that Dutch was too late. "Don't ye listen to the radio?" he asked in a "Scottish burr you could cut with a knife." Apparently, WOC had waged a lengthy on-air campaign to hire a new announcer; a few days earlier, the position was filled.

Dutch was crestfallen. Fuming at his lousy timing, he turned on his heels and pressed the call button for the elevator. "How the hell do you get to be a sports announcer if you can't ever get a job at a radio station?" he muttered under his breath.

"Hold up, you big bastard!" Dutch turned to find MacArthur bearing down on him. "What was that you said about sports announcing?" Dutch explained his ultimate broadcasting goal—and the seemingly elusive breakthrough job necessary to attain it. "Come with me," MacArthur said, leading him into the studio.

To Dutch, the room must have looked like the Great Oz's hideout, with its heavy blue drapes and wall of electronic gizmos. MacArthur stood him in front of a microphone boom and, without fuss, no rehearsal, instructed him to begin describing an imaginary football game when he saw the red light go on. "Make me *see* it," he said. "I'll be in another room listening."

Other prospects might have been daunted by such an assignment, but not Ronald Reagan. He'd been improvising games for as long as he could remember; it came as second nature to him. Drawing on his senior year on the Eureka football squad, he launched into a vivid play-by-play of the game against Western State University, climaxing in a breathless game-winning last-second touchdown. As soon as the hero crossed the goal line, MacArthur reappeared and told Dutch to come back on Saturday. On October 1, 1932, Reagan would be announcing the Iowa–Bradley game. He'd earn five dollars for the afternoon, with a promise that if he clicked on the air, more games would follow.

It was the breakthrough he'd been hoping for.

Dutch called the game with confidence, filling the halftime break with an insider's grasp of x's and o's and an explanation of each coach's strategy. Afterward, MacArthur delivered on his promise. The remaining three games now belonged to Dutch, along with a five-dollar-a-week raise plus bus fare to and from Dixon. And he was good at this job: in Davenport, after Iowa's final game against Minnesota, the *Democrat and Leader* reviewed Dutch's performance, calling him "a grand footballer and letter man." It went on to say, "His crisp account of the muddy struggle sounded like a carefully written story . . . and his quick tongue seemed to be as fast as the plays."

The end of the season ended Dutch's engagement with the radio station—for the time being. Pete MacArthur assured him that if he hung on, they'd call him as soon as something opened up. Dutch went back to Dixon to wait for the phone to ring. The first week in January, it did: he was offered a full-time announcer's job with WOC, spinning records and reading commercials. He'd start February 10, at a hundred dollars a month.

The new year was off to a promising start. Ronald Reagan was finally on his way—out of Dixon and inching west.

West—and west again, from Davenport to Des Moines, where the Palmers owned a new sister station, WHO. In May 1933, Dutch and Peter MacArthur were transferred to the new facility, with an enormous 50,000-watt transmitter capable of reaching not quite Stockholm, but the westernmost parts of America. The three months he spent in Davenport were filled with change—for the Reagans and the country in general. Dutch's salary gave the family a small financial cushion. A hundred dollars wasn't exactly a windfall, but it was enough to get by: a room in the Vale Apartments came cheap; a meal ticket at the Palmer college cafeteria was $3.65 a week; a few dollars went to the Strong Foundation to pay off his Eureka loan; Jack and Nelle got a sizable chunk; and, of course, the tithing—ten dollars, which he sent to needy Moon as a hedge against his college costs.

At WOC, Reagan performed any odd job assigned to the lowest staff member on the totem pole—sportscasting, spinning records, reading commercials, announcing local events. He read hope into the presidency of

Franklin Roosevelt, who had taken office only a month or so earlier but was already reversing the country's downward spiral. At the time of FDR's inauguration, on March 3, 1933, less than a month into Dutch's residency, 25 percent of Americans were still out of work, the stock market had plunged 85 percent from its high in 1929, businesses were running out of cash, and bank depositors who remained invested were losing their life's savings. The day afterward, on March 4, the president declared a national bank holiday, closing all banks to prevent the further collapse of the country's financial system.

In Dixon, where Dutch had gone to listen to the inauguration, effects of the edict were already being felt. You could read the optimism on people's faces. The downtown business district, long deserted, began churning again with life. One of the city's favorite sons, Charles Walgreen, the drugstore magnate, personally guaranteed all the deposits and mortgages for the Dixon National Bank. Jack Reagan, especially, benefited from the transition of power. Thanks to a patronage wave that swept the few local Democrats into government jobs, Jack landed a position that would bring him steady work. In May 1933, Harry Hopkins, FDR's federal relief administrator, created the Federal Emergency Relief Act to provide direct relief, job training, and work for the unemployed. Jack became supervisor of the Dixon office, a storefront at the corner of Hennepin Avenue and River Street. It was an instant magnet for hordes of Lee County men and women blindsided by the Depression, those whose lives had been overshadowed by poverty and hopelessness.

"That place was always crowded with long lines of people," says Esther Haack, Dutch's former classmate who spent long days bent over census logs as a clerk at the FERA headquarters. "People would come in with requisitions for food and wait to see Jack, who had a private office in the back." They never knew which Jack would emerge. "He could be feisty—or very nice," says Haack. It was no secret that he drank his lunch at the Stables, a side street bar behind City Hall, and co-workers often had to cover for him. "There were times he wasn't quite steady. He could get grumpy from drink or be very funny, when he'd do a little soft-shoe, tell jokes, chat you up." When things got out of hand, which they occasionally did, one of the staff would mobilize Neil Reagan, who had a desk out front with the other social workers.

When Eureka's semester ended that May, Moon assumed he'd rejoin the production line at the cement company, where he'd still worked during summer breaks. But the plant closed its doors a few months earlier. Jack shoehorned his son into a FERA job, which enabled him to earn his keep while looking after his father, although Moon shared some of Jack's traits.

Dutch was now twenty-two, earning a measure of respect and security in far-off Des Moines at WHO. In short order he had made a name for himself in late April announcing the Drake University Relays, the country's foremost track-and-field event, in front of eighteen thousand spectators at the college's horseshoe stadium. Dutch knew next to nothing about track, but crammed for the broadcast, studying past Relays and former record holders, as well as the histories of this year's participants. Shortly afterward, he was offered a job as WHO's chief sportscaster, a position that doubled his old salary.

He immediately signed a lease for a second-floor suite of rooms in a once-grand apartment building overlooking the Mississippi, then called Mugs to give her the news. If he thought it would seal the deal for an impending marriage, he was greatly mistaken. Their separation had given her some perspective on their relationship. All this talk about radio and big-city life and . . . and *Hollywood*, which he'd mentioned boldly as a possible destination in his excitement. He "was afraid to say [he] wanted to be a movie actor" outright, but it was clear to Mugs, who could read between the lines. "His ambitions sort of crystallized" was how she interpreted it—"after radio, Hollywood." It unnerved her, made her doubt his objectivity. "He had an inability to distinguish between fact and fancy," she told Edmund Morris in a 1988 interview. Flirting with the movie business especially put her off. "I didn't want to bring up my children in Hollywood."

If Mugs's lack of enthusiasm didn't worry him, her own news did. She was leaving the country in June, sailing to Europe with her sister, Helen. Leaving—for how long? She was vague about the trip's duration, vaguer still where it left them. In any case, it would give them some time to find themselves. He was shocked. They'd been a couple going on seven years, Mugs and Dutch, indivisible. They were *engaged*. He'd never envisioned his life without Margaret Cleaver. The separation cast a pall over his news.

To stanch his disappointment, he threw himself into his job. There was plenty for him to do at WHO. Beyond the Drake Relays and Big Ten college sports, he announced lead-ins to programs that aired on the station, syndicated shows such as the hugely popular *National Barn Dance* on Saturday evenings and nightly broadcasts of *Amos 'n' Andy*, which originated as a fifteen-minute serial, as well as *Fibber McGee and Molly*, Fred Allen's *Linit Bath Club Revue*, *Lum and Abner*, the Ameche brothers (Don and Jim), and *The Great Gildersleeve*, all fed by NBC to affiliates like WHO. Occasionally he subbed for newscasters. For a time, he also narrated *Iowa News Flashes*, a short reel of local interest stories "unabashedly swiped from *The Register* and *Tribune*" and shown in movie houses across the state. Although well liked by the producer, he was fired from that task for being unable—or unwilling—to follow the script.

Scripts were anathema to an overimaginative sportscaster. Dutch relied on his spontaneity when broadcasting games, especially when there was a live-action glitch, such as occurred when he was covering the Drake Relays. "All day long, I'd been telling the audience that the quarter mile was going to be the greatest event." But between heats, the president of Drake University showed up to say a few promotional words and wound up talking ad nauseam, while Dutch sat watching the quarter-mile race go by. "I couldn't tell the audience it was all over," he recalled, "so [as soon as the school official left] I said, 'We're *just in time* for the event I've been telling you about!'" He knew it lasted a mere forty-eight seconds, so he took out his watch and re-created the entire event from memory, with all the tension and excitement, bringing in the top three athletes in proper sequence. As for the absence of crowd noise, "I explained that it was because the audience was stunned by the sheer drama."

Dutch was mastering his trade, and his reputation was growing. He was on the air in some capacity several hours each day, with a daytime audience that blanketed the entire Midwest and nighttime listeners "from coast to coast, border to border, and then some," as their station ID boasted. "This is Dutch Reagan" was a familiar refrain, a velvety voice that fairly purred. Purred—but still needed fine-tuning. Peter MacArthur bristled at Dutch's Midwestern dialect that mispronounced words such as "rut beer" and "ruf" for roof. "I stumbled over my words," Dutch acknowledged, "and had a delivery as wooden as prairie oak." Myrtle Williams, who had just become the station's new program director, recalled, "[Peter would] sit at home and listen to the radio, and I can still hear him bawling Dutch out when he'd mispronounce a word or say something wrong."

But Dutch was a comer and MacArthur knew it. In no time, he had him headlining the *Teaberry Sports Review*, a popular roundup of the day's highlights that aired at 5:25 p.m. and again at 10:10 p.m. Reagan really blossomed that summer of 1933, when baseball season got under way. It fell to Dutch to broadcast the Chicago Cubs and White Sox games—quite a feat, given that he'd never set foot inside either of their stadiums, much less seen a professional game. In fact, he wouldn't be a presence in either team's press box. He re-created the games from data translated into Morse code and transmitted over the telegraph wire via Western Union's Paragraph One service—a pitch-by-pitch account of the game that was available to anyone who paid a small fee. A WHO engineer would pass him the ticker-tape report "through a slit in the soundproof wall between studio and control room," which read as a series of hieroglyphics—"S1C" for "strike one called" or "B2 LOOS" for "ball two, low and outside"—which Dutch would then spin into a breathless narrative. "Close to him was a turntable with a crowd applause record," recalled Van Donohoo, a Drake student who worked at WHO, "the volume of which was manipulated by Dutch with a foot pedal."

Re-creations were the way most listeners got the game. Only a few stations in cities with major-league teams broadcast live from the ballpark. In fact, many owners of Eastern teams forbade any accounts of games, convinced that newspapers and radio threatened attendance. The Yankees, Dodgers, and Giants, for instance, had an agreement until 1939 locking baseball broadcasts out of New York. In those cities, embargoes were circumvented by "bootleggers" who observed games from rooftops with binoculars and phoned in results, or bleacher bums who wrote game summaries on slips of paper and dropped them through the stands to runners. Chicago led the way to modernization, where both Wrigleys, William and Philip, were the most passionate pro-radio forces in the sport. The chewing-gum magnates recognized the value of two hours of free advertising for their product and fought against repeated attempts to ban broadcasts.

Even so, re-creations ruled the airwaves. Pat Flanagan, a former ad exec at WOC who had moved to WBBM in Chicago, is generally credited with inventing the form, although the Washington Senators authorized play-by-play from wire reports as early as 1925. But practitioners like Gordon McLendon refined it as an art. His dramatic accounts from a studio in Dallas were said to be "far better than the real thing created from the ballpark." Imagination was the key. If you could create an entertaining narrative from bits of data and convey it to the listeners in an exciting way, you could turn a slow hopper to the shortstop into a dramatic backhanded grab in the dirt. It left room for a tremendous amount of interpretation—stretching the truth—to keep an audience on the edge of its seat. An announcer could *not* invent a base hit, but that hit could be turned into a screaming line drive through the infield; a routine two-hop grounder at third could become a diving catch with a rifle shot to first base. It was entirely up to the man behind the mic.

Dutch got the hang of it in no time, with some early coaching from Pat Flanagan. It brought together his love of sports with his acting bona fides. He'd studied the live-action Chicago sportscasters, like Hal Totten on WMAQ and WGN's Bob Elson and Quin Ryan, who delivered patter such as "This Tiger fielder, Fothergill, has a neck as wide as a chimney . . . [and] runs as though he were pulling a sleigh," or "Kamm flies out to left field—Hunnefield rolls to short and is thrown out at first—and two men die on the sacks." Dutch imitated their jazzy lingo, mixing in a healthy dollop of Grantland Rice, whose verbal acrobatics in the Paramount newsreels had dazzled him since he was a kid.

He re-created dozens of games that first summer, becoming "the voice of Chicago baseball" throughout the prairie states. It was a punishing apprenticeship; he was often on the air, live, six days a week. The Cubs drew a devoted, even rabid, audience of hard-core fans. They had won the National League pennant in 1932 and finished a respectable third in 1933, so Dutch had plenty of good baseball to work with.

As much as he enjoyed the work, it exhausted him—all that talking, talking, talking. The re-creations demanded that he rattle on nonstop, often for two to three hours at a clip. "He had to ad-lib enormously when he did the play-by-play," recalled Jack Shelley, a popular WHO reporter. The toll it took was significant, so much so that WBBM's Pat Flanagan claimed to lose four to nine pounds during an average broadcast. Dutch didn't exhibit that kind of physical wear-and-tear. But after signing off at the end of a workday, he'd have given it everything he had.

Because there was no such thing as night games in 1933, Dutch found plenty of time to relax. He had cultivated a circle of friends from among a class of journalism students at the local college, Drake. Besides Hubert "Pee Wee" Johnson, who served as Dutch's field spotter at football games, there was Will Scott and his brother Walt, Glen Claussen, Leroy Austin, Ed Morley, and Walt Roddy, men who would appear in Ronald Reagan's life off and on for decades. They would gather several times a week at the Moonlight Inn, a bar on Seventy-third Street and University Avenue in Windsor Heights, whose rundown charm was its dirt floors and spiked beer—a highly illegal low-alcohol concoction in which the bottle's long neck was laced generously with grain alcohol then flipped upside down so the two could mix. According to Dutch, who wasn't much of a drinker, "It'd almost blow your nose off." The gang would cram into one of the booths in the back room to watch couples slow-dance to records, and after two or three doctored beers, all bets were off. "We sang midwestern fight songs around the piano," Glen Claussen told author Garry Wills—barn burners like "On Wisconsin" and "Baby Won't You Please Come Home." They'd let it rip, singing "what we called harmony" until Cy Griffiths, who owned the place, grew apoplectic, ordering them to keep it down—or else.

Occasionally, Myrtle Williams and Pete MacArthur would join them, and toward the end of summer Moon Reagan appeared.

Dutch was still covering for his older brother, whose life had achieved a certain stasis in Dixon. Moon had applied to Northwestern, to study law, and was awaiting word on his application. In the meantime, Dutch had bought a car, a flashy metallic-brown 1934 Nash Lafayette convertible, from Margaret's brother-in-law, and asked Moon if he would drive it from Dixon to Des Moines. "Plan to spend two or three days out here," Dutch told him, "see the station and meet the guys." The day after Moon arrived in Iowa he got roped into auditioning for an announcer's spot on a new show, Deep Rock Oil's *Scoreboard of the Air*, and won the job. It paid only five dollars a week, not nearly enough to get by on, but Peter MacArthur agreed to subsidize it with freelance assignments designed to give Moon a livable wage.

The Reagan brothers were together again. There were crucial differences between the two men, some residual jealousy, and much competitive jostling, but once again, when Dutch was newly settled in a place and had earned a measure of respect, he found a way to bring his brother along.

After a few days living together in Dutch's flat in Des Moines, Moon was moved to WOC, in Davenport. Perhaps it was providential. Dutch was establishing his own routine, independent of his brother. It was that summer of 1933 that he developed his lifelong love of horseback riding. At Myrtle Williams's invitation, he and two buddies—Murray Goodman and Don Reid—spent free afternoons riding the trails on the old military grounds at Fort Des Moines, taking the cavalry horses out for exercise. Dutch had been on a horse before—during his summers lifeguarding, a Danish immigrant who ran the lodge in Lowell Park owned a big gray nag and let him ride it on the beach—but it was nothing like this. These were *horses*, thoroughbreds, not "old plugs," as Myrtle Williams warmly described them. They'd been groomed. They looked like what Tom Mix rode in all the serials that had dazzled Dutch as a boy. And when the cavalry horses weren't available, he rode with Dave Palmer, who had two show horses, King Cole and Copper Flash, on a farm on Credit Island in the Mississippi River. "All he ever wanted to talk about was horses," said Rich Kennelley, a noted Des Moines gambler who encountered Dutch in clubs. It was then, Dutch said, "I began to dream of owning a ranch."

When he wasn't in the saddle that summer, Dutch took to the water in "a huge pool the size of a football field and end zones" at Camp Dodge, an old military installation that was open to the public. Often, he'd combine the two, following a ride with a refreshing dip—posing actually, beguiling the goggle-eyed bathers who knew him from the radio. In a few short months, Dutch had become a local celebrity in Des Moines. He was dashing and, word had it, gallant. People were already gossiping about his heroism early that fall, during an incident outside his apartment. Around eleven p.m. on a Sunday night in September 1933, he'd heard a ruckus on the street. Someone could be overheard saying, "Take anything I got, but let me go." Dutch shot out of bed and squinted out his second-floor window. "Right there in the light of the streetlight was this gal with a suitcase by her side, standing there with her hands in the air," he recalled, "and a man standing there with a gun." The gal was a twenty-year-old nursing student named Melba Lohmann, who had just arrived at the bus station and was on her way to Broadlawns General Hospital, across the street from Dutch's flat. Not willing to be shot for the three dollars in her purse, she handed it to the mugger, along with her suitcase.

What to do? Thinking fast, Dutch slid open his night-table drawer and grabbed an unloaded handgun, a Walther PPK .380 pistol that he had bought as soon as he'd moved in. Pointing it at the action in the street below, he shouted in his best basso profundo: "Leave her alone or I'll shoot you right between the shoulders!" Any self-respecting mugger would have checked the source of the threat to gauge its merits, but this one simply dropped his stash and ran. A few minutes later, wearing house slippers, pajamas, and a robe, Dutch emerged and chaperoned the shaken nursing student to the door of the hospital.

After his brush with violence, Dutch decided to move. He'd had his eye on an apartment, a fixer-upper "in a fine old home on the east side of Fourth Street . . . once a wealthy neighborhood of stately homes" but now considered "threadbare." The ground-floor flat itself was a remnant of days gone by, featuring a large entrance hall carved out of what had originally served as a sitting room and butler's pantry with "heavy dark varnished woodwork" throughout. It was a step up from his former digs and quite spacious for a bachelor, which might have prompted him to take in a roommate. In any case, he decided to share it with Art Mann, an assistant coach at Drake. He could have swung the rent by himself—he was doing well financially. He was still contributing a third of his paycheck to his parents and tithing, but there was enough left over to fund a jolly social life. With Margaret Cleaver out of the picture in Europe for a while, he had begun squiring young women around town, nothing intimate or romantic, not wanting to torpedo his longtime relationship. He still intended to marry Mugs, but in the meantime he began seeing Mildred Brown, whom he met riding one afternoon at Fort Des Moines. The attraction was easy to understand. She was "quite the most glamorous-looking girl he had ever known," exceptionally tall and statuesque, a free spirit, and an equestrian to boot. She was from Monmouth, of all places, where her mother had worked in Colwell's Department Store, across the aisle from where Jack sold shoes; if that wasn't coincidence enough, her cousin happened to be his old Dixon playmate Gertrude Romine.

There was plenty for them to do in Des Moines. Movies galore—all the new releases played in a city lousy with theaters: *She Done Him Wrong, Dinner at Eight, 42nd Street, Duck Soup*, and the enormous, literally enormous, crowd-pleaser *King Kong*. They had their pick of pictures now considered classics and went to as many openings as they could manage. In the evenings, they met for dinner at the chichi Fort Des Moines Hotel, across the street from WHO, or at the Hotel Kirkwood, managed by Paul McGinn, Dutch's swimming partner at Camp Dodge.

Things turned more serious for them early in 1934, after Dutch got a Dear John letter from Mugs. She'd met another man, a foreign-service officer, aboard a cruise ship in Europe, and they were engaged. *Engaged!* Dutch had to read the letter again to absorb it. They planned to *marry*. He was "shattered."

Mildred wasn't Mugs, but she was a suitable stand-in. They got on famously, and Dutch liked her family, particularly her father, who enjoyed talking football with WHO's chief sportscaster. Things might have gone further between them, but Mildred made it clear she didn't intend to marry anyone other than a Catholic, effectively shutting the door on Dutch.

He shook it off by throwing himself even more deeply into work. His plate was overflowing at the station in 1935, with sportscasts as well as more straight-ahead work: interviews with celebrity evangelist Aimee Semple McPherson, cowboy crooner Gene Autry, Hollywood star Leslie Howard, and boxer Max Baer, who accidentally knocked out WHO's mailroom clerk while demonstrating his championship form.

Even that didn't compare with the punch of the '35 Drake Relays, which Dutch called live from the college's Memorial Stadium press box. The competition was world-caliber, the action tense and thrilling. There were the usual photo-finish dashes and relays, the nerve-racking marathons and decathlons. But the highlights were provided by an Ohio State sophomore named Jesse Owens, who set a record in the 100-yard dash minutes before being called to participate in the broad jump. Before he'd even caught his breath, Owens raced down the gravel runway and soared an improbable twenty-six feet in the air—a record that was instantly shattered when officials noticed he took off nine inches before the starting board, which was yet another eight inches wide.

That summer, Dutch broadcast 160 baseball games, refining his bravura patter with the benefit of an actual sponsor, General Mills, intent on targeting mothers and children to buy Wheaties, their "breakfast of champions." Bent over the black-and-silver microphone, a brown fedora tipped rakishly over a brow, unlit pipe in hand, he lit into vivid replays of Sox and Cubs games, oblivious to the claque of faithful fans who collected in front of WHO's glass partition to watch him perform. The White Sox tanked early in the season, headed for a dismal fifth-place finish, but the Cubs won an astounding hundred games and the National League pennant. Dutch had a colorful cast of characters to work with: the power-hitting second baseman Billy Herman; "assistant manager" Gabby Hartnett, one of the greatest catchers in baseball history; and Charlie "Jolly Cholly" Grimm, the team's banjo-playing manager; as well as opposing greats such as Lou Gehrig, Mel Ott, Lefty Gomez, Carl Hubbell, and Jimmie Foxx.

The most memorable moment came in the middle of the season. It was a story Ronald Reagan would recount—often fantastically, and with different players involved—for the rest of his life. It was the ninth inning of a scoreless game between the Cubs and the St. Louis Cardinals. The great Dizzy Dean was on the mound for the Cards, and the batter was Augie Galan—though in some accounts it was Billy Jurges. Harold Norem, Reagan's control-booth engineer, whom he affectionately called Curly, slipped him a note that said *The wire has gone dead.* For the next six minutes, without a peep from Western Union, Dutch had the batter foul off balls, while he invented action in and around the field—a kid in the stands snagging a souvenir, a near-miss at the foul pole, the manager coming to the mound to check on his pitcher—anything he could think of to kill time. He couldn't admit the glitch in the studio transmission; it would have destroyed the illusion he'd worked so hard to create. When the teletype finally clicked back into gear, he learned the batter had flied out on the first pitch.

Four years into the job, Ronald Reagan had hit his stride. He made a comfortable living; he was a well-known radio personality, a local celebrity. A wall-sized photo of Dutch hovering over the WHO microphone hung behind the bar at the Moonlight Inn. His much-sought-after presence as a speaker at civic functions and events reflected his gift to deliver an entertaining off-the-cuff address in a throaty vibrato that would serve him for the rest of his life. When a *Sporting News* poll rated the best baseball announcers in America, Dutch's name was fourth on the list, ahead of future legend Red Barber. The *Des Moines Dispatch* summed up his achievement in various columns. An early post noted: "To millions of sports fans in at least seven or eight midwestern states, the voice of Dutch Reagan is a daily source of baseball dope." Another, in 1936, praised his studly man-about-town image: "He is over six feet tall with the proverbial Greek-god physique: broad-shouldered, slim-waisted and a face that would make Venus look twice before running to her man Zeus!"

His charms were not lost on the young women of Des Moines. For a while, he dated Lou Mauget, an attractive clerk in WHO's accounting department, and Ann McGuire, who sang in a musical revue, and model Gretchen Schnelle. His attraction to Jeanne Tesdell, a hazel-eyed Drake senior, seemed to be different, deeper. She was tall and sophisticated, and another accomplished equestrian, who sat a horse with particular poise—and a knockout. According to one of Dutch's friends, "She was one of the best-looking gals in town." For almost all of 1936, Dutch and Jeanne were Des Moines's "it" couple. He seemed to have found a replacement for Margaret Cleaver.

But as they saw each other more frequently, Jeanne began to feel that something important was missing. Dutch was personable, a wonderful storyteller, and a perfect gentleman. But the more they went out, the more she sensed she played second fiddle to his ambition. "I always had the feeling that I was with him but he wasn't with me," she said. At Club Belvedere, where they often took in the floor show, a change came over him. He shifted into celebrity mode, playing to the room. Jeanne couldn't help noticing how "he was always looking over his shoulder, scanning the crowd." He was too much of "a people-pleaser" for her tastes.

Was there more beneath the surface of this glad-handing careerist? If there was, he wasn't revealing it to her. Ultimately she decided there was no future in that kind of "bittersweet" relationship, and she broke things off with Dutch.

Neil Reagan fared better. Soon after he began working at WOC, he fell hard for a soft-spoken Drake coed named Bessie Hoffman and, two weeks after meeting her, proposed. News of their impending marriage unsettled Dutch, who viewed it as happening "way too fast," even for his impetuous brother. It seems unlikely, however, that Dutch discussed his disapproval with Moon; the Reagan brothers avoided such intimacy. Nor did he rise to object during the ceremony. He might have been more disturbed by his father's appearance. There was little evidence of the old Jack Reagan in the man who sat next to him in the church pew that day. The last vestiges of the cocky Irish leprechaun, the "practical joker," had been dispatched by a recent heart attack, which left Jack withered and unsteady. His left arm dangled at an unnatural angle, its nerves damaged irreparably; his face, once ruddy, looked ashen. Dutch realized that his father's working days were over.

In any event, the groom, his brother, and his father avoided any argument, including a political one, which was a challenge considering the circumstances. It was an election year in 1936, and while Roosevelt was enormously popular, not everyone was an FDR flagbearer. In the Reagan family, Moon stood alone as a fierce opponent to the New Deal's magic formulas. It was a lonely position against rabid believers of the Democratic ethos like Jack and Dutch. "We used to have some great go-arounds," Moon recalled. Moon believed "the Democratic party was going to make a welfare state out of the country," and he wasn't afraid to say so. In fact, he relished saying it if only to see the fur fly.

Jack no longer had the energy to engage, but Dutch unfailingly took the bait. He had his own doubts about long-term relief, though he had confidence that the New Deal would stabilize the economy. And he idolized Roosevelt. He'd actually seen his hero on FDR's swing through Des Moines, when the president's limousine passed under the station's windows and Dutch grinned and waved back at the familiar figure "with his cigarette and his head held high." On the radio, he couldn't hide his enthusiasm for the president, putting in a few good words for him wherever possible. Off the air, he'd mastered an admiring impression of FDR, which he performed for friends and colleagues any chance he got.

One co-worker who wasn't that amused was H. R. "Hal" Gross, a highly-regarded journalist who had joined WHO's staff in 1935. Gross, who would go on to become a thirteen-term congressman from Iowa's Third District, hosted the enormously popular *Tomorrow's News Tonight*, sponsored by Kentucky Club and introduced nightly by Dutch Reagan. The two pros clicked beautifully on the air, but once the studio's red light went off, politics often intervened, and they would go at it like snapping dogs. Gross was a fiscal penny-pincher (later he would be the only member of Congress to vote against funding the eternal flame at JFK's gravesite, calling it a waste of money), someone one admirer termed "a classic small-picture conservative . . . whose life was about embarrassing liberals." Dutch staunchly defended the liberal cause.

Politics had become a staple of Dutch's daily diet, but baseball was still his main fare. To prepare for the 1936 season, Dutch persuaded his station chief, Joe Maland, to send him to the Cubs spring-training facility on Catalina Island, twenty miles off the California coast. The trip would expand his familiarity with the team, Dutch argued, but deep down he knew it was nothing but a boondoggle—the chance to get away at the company's expense, to see what the West Coast looked like, spend several weeks in the sun, and maybe pick up a few extra dollars writing freelance articles for the newspapers back home. He'd never been west of Iowa. It would be a new experience, a way to expand his horizons.

CHAPTER NINE

"ANOTHER ROBERT TAYLOR"

"Nothing endures but change."

—HERACLITUS

I f nothing else, the train trip out west was an eye-opener.

Dutch joined the Cubs on the Santa Fe Special, a caravan of wood-and-brass-appointed Pullman cars, in Kansas City, where it stopped to pick up Charlie Grimm and other team members from the Plains states. The three-day excursion had an anything-goes atmosphere. There was no escape from the all-day dominoes, dice, and card games, and the epic drinking jags. Rookies were victims of regular practical jokes. Veterans were notorious for planting items in rookies' berths—enormous iron train wheels or crates of garlic, or furry creatures smuggled on board especially for the occasion, or giving an unsuspecting player a hotfoot, or worse. Shortstop Woody English made an art of lighting a newspaper while someone was reading it. "His escape is made during the smoldering state," Dutch recounted in a column he wrote, "and he is innocently dozing when the reader finds himself possessed of a flaming torch."

For Dutch, the scenery whizzing by the picture-frame window was another kind of education. It offered a snapshot of America he'd only read about in books. Nebraska first: mile after mile of treeless prairie pimpled with herds of cattle grazing on its vast grassy carpet. In Wyoming and Utah, he got his first look at the massive snow-capped Rocky Mountains, where streams gouged into the gnarled rockface raced down the dramatic slopes like skiers on a doomsday run. No humanity anywhere in sight—

nothing, just dense coverage of juniper and ponderosa pine. Then suddenly, out of nowhere, Ogden, and beyond it Salt Lake City nestled in the décolletage of mountains and canyons. There was a lot of beautiful country out there.

When the train finally pulled into Central Station in Los Angeles, Dutch stepped off into a plume of midsummer heat. There was much to love about the balmy weather after months in the frigid Midwestern tundra. The air was refreshing, even savory, with its distinctive notes of flora and sea salt. You could actually feel your skin awaken, as if it had emerged out of a deep freeze. The dry climate, the clear blue sky, the radiant sunshine were tonics that went straight to the soul of a weary traveler. Dutch had come prepared. His valise was stocked with an appropriate wardrobe: linen suits, a white sport coat, white bucks, a pair of swim trunks.

The entourage was whisked off to the port a few blocks away, where they boarded the SS *Catalina*, a converted Great Lakes cruiser, for a two-hour trip to the island. It was anything but a pleasure cruise. The team veterans knew what was in store: this annual voyage across the choppy San Pedro Channel was a nonstop roller-coaster ride that left even the most able-bodied ballplayers doubled over the railing, gasping and vomiting. Legendary catcher and future Hall of Famer Gabby Hartnett was usually the first player each spring to throw up.

But Catalina was worth the grief. It was an island gem, with a picture-postcard harbor, a country club and world-class golf course, tennis courts, a bird sanctuary, a dance hall, a 1,200-seat theater, resort hotels, and a baseball stadium framed with fragrant eucalyptus trees. A number of public figures kept homes in the hills, among them Zane Grey, Betty Grable, and a sixteen-year-old military wife named Norma Jeane Dougherty, who later became Marilyn Monroe. The Wrigleys had bought the island sight unseen in 1919 and developed it into an exclusive travel destination. Once they shook off the seasickness, the Cubs loved Catalina. The weather was semitropical; the players got the same royal treatment as glamorous celebrities. And for three weeks, they could unwind, really unwind. But once they took the field, the Cubs—as well as their media retinue—got down to business.

Dutch had his daily routine. He arrived at Wrigley Field early each morning to claim a prime spot between the first-base line and the grandstand for a bird's-eye view of the action. Because he was reporting for the

Des Moines Dispatch as well as WHO, he spread out across several chairs. This didn't sit well with the old-school beat reporters, who bore grudges against the new wave of radio interlopers. One evening, shortly after his arrival, Jimmy Corcoran of the *Chicago American* sought Dutch out at the White Cap, a local bar, and exchanged words, words Dutch didn't like. A lot of "Oh *yeah?*" and "Sez *who?*" passed between the two. Jimmy the Cork eventually threw a punch, but Dutch saw it coming and ducked, deflecting it squarely into the stomach of the *Chicago Tribune's* Ed Burns. Such were the burdens of a spring-training rookie.

Perhaps Corcoran resented seeing WHO's sportscaster taking batting practice with the Cubs. Dutch had never fully shaken off the dreams of playing ball, even if the ball wasn't his beloved pigskin. Charlie Grimm allowed Dutch to occasionally suit up for an afternoon workout, with batting instruction from first baseman Phil Cavarretta. At twenty-five, Dutch still had the form and physical dexterity, even though Cavy decried his "slow bat." He couldn't hit the broad side of a barn or field a pop-up without his glasses.

Dutch adored his spring-training getaway and was quick to reenlist for duty in 1937. The terms were the same: he sacrificed paid vacation in exchange for the three-week excursion, and the *Dispatch* picked up his option for a series of articles. This year, however, he had an ulterior motive.

In January, Dutch had spent some time chatting with members of Al Clauser and His Oklahoma Outlaws during a live broadcast of the Saturday-night *National Barn Dance*. The Outlaws were a popular act throughout the Midwest and regulars on WHO. Now they were moving on. They had been signed to appear in *Rootin' Tootin' Rhythm*, a Gene Autry movie shooting at Republic Studios in Hollywood.

Dutch had never lost the acting bug. He had the talent and the looks, and he certainly had the desire. His four years on the radio had given him a taste. Announcing, after all, was a form of acting. He entertained an audience six days a week; it earned him local stardom. Movies seemed like the next logical step. A Des Moines theater owner had even broached the subject of an audition, alerting him to a screen test being offered in town. Now the Outlaws had rekindled his interest. Like him, they were headed west and told him to visit if the opportunity arose.

Hollywood. Surely he could play hooky from spring training for a day or two.

It was pouring when the Santa Fe Special arrived in L.A., so he told the Cubs he'd meet them later that night in Catalina. Instead, he hopped a trolley that took him over the Cahuenga Pass into the San Fernando Valley, where Republic Studios was situated among pepper trees at the foot of the Hollywood Hills.

Republic was originally Mack Sennett's studio but had evolved into a low-budget factory, churning out a slate of mostly cowboy films—good cowboy films, better than the major picture companies were making. Republic's biggest star was John Wayne, who had made his mark in a series known as *The Three Mesquiteers* and even sang in an early feature or two. Tom Mix, Lash LaRue, and Roy Rogers were also on the lot. In 1937, by the time Dutch arrived, the studio's rising star was Gene Autry, "the singing cowboy," with his newly minted sidekicks, the Oklahoma Outlaws.

Good to their word, the Outlaws welcomed Dutch as a guest on the set. Because of the weather, they were shooting indoors that day, giving him a chance to see how movies were made. It was an eye-opening experience—not at all like being onstage, where you had to know your lines cold and the action never stopped. There was really very little discipline involved in moviemaking. It employed a different kind of acting technique that relied on image more than ability. Dutch had a sense of his own appeal, and he knew he could act. "You know, just from watching, it sure looks interesting making pictures," he told Gene Autry. "I think I might like to get into that business." Republic's casting director offered to hear him read through a script sometime after spring training was over, but Dutch sensed the man's lack of enthusiasm and shrugged it off.

It was still on his mind that evening as he made his way back to the port. Movie acting seemed like a lark. Was there a place in Hollywood for him? It was an intriguing idea.

As luck would have it, he was stranded in L.A. Lousy weather made it impossible for boats and seaplanes to make the trip to Catalina, and Dutch was forced to spend the night in town. He checked into the Biltmore Hotel, downtown on Fifth Street, where it happened that a friend was in residence. He had met Joy Hodges at WHO, where she had started out at the age of twelve as part of the singing Blue Bird Twins (although there were three of them) on a nightly program called *Singing Coeds*. She had hit the big time in her teens, as a big-band singer and, later, an actress in

Hollywood. During a radio interview they did in 1936 to promote her debut film appearance in RKO's *Follow the Fleet*, Dutch asked her, "Well, Miss Hodges, how does it feel to be a movie star?," to which she replied, "Well, Mr. Reagan, you may know some day." They hit it off immediately. There was an attraction that might have developed into romance had Joy not left town soon afterward for Los Angeles as the singer in Carol Lofner's swing band. When Dutch reunited with her in 1937, she was in the midst of a three-year engagement fronting Jimmy Grier's orchestra at the Biltmore Bowl, the hotel's posh nightclub.

The Bowl was a scene-making place for Hollywood movie and radio people, an elegant room that hosted the Academy Awards in 1935 when *It Happened One Night* won Best Picture, and featured the talents of the most important musicians working in L.A. The Dorseys had played gigs there, as had Artie Shaw, Louis Armstrong, and Lena Horne, although the black stars were denied rooms upstairs and quartered instead at the Dunbar Hotel in South Central.

Dutch sat through Joy's opening set, then sent a note backstage asking her to join him for dinner. Hodges was an attractive, doe-eyed brunette who had managed to retain much of her Midwestern charm. Their reunion proved delightful. He delivered the requisite Des Moines gossip before tip-toeing toward his hidden agenda. He spoke glowingly about his day trip to Republic Studios and thought, if the time allowed, he might like to visit one of the majors, like Paramount or MGM. Joy offered to help arrange it for him, but she could tell he was dithering about; there was something else on his mind. Finally he spit it out. "He admitted he wanted a movie test," she recalled.

She sat back in her seat and stared at him for a moment. "Stand up and remove your glasses," she said. Dutch obeyed, prompting another staring spell. He was "*very handsome*," she thought, as physically appealing as the current crop of male movie stars. If an audition was what he wanted, she was determined to help—on one condition. "Promise you will never put those glasses on again."

The next morning, a Saturday, Hodges called her agent, Bill Meiklejohn, who ran a boutique talent agency that fed the studio pipeline. As a favor, he saw Dutch right away. The two men chatted across a desk for a few minutes—Meiklejohn giving the young man a good once-over while Dutch inflated his acting experience—before the agent picked up the phone. "Max," he said into the receiver, "I have another Robert Taylor sitting in my office."

Max Arnow, Warner Bros.' casting director, was used to such hype, but Meiklejohn had a good nose for talent. He'd "discovered" Robert Taylor, Ray Milland, Betty Grable, and a young contract player named Jane Wyman. And the studio had a dilemma. It was slated to begin shooting a B-feature called *The Inside Story* and were in desperate need of a leading man. It had originally been cast with a contract player named Ross Alexander, whose easy and charming style made him a natural for the part. But Alexander was anything but easygoing and had a messy personal life; in fact, he had committed suicide a few days earlier. Arnow was charged with finding a suitable replacement who could step in right away. Maybe Bill Meiklejohn had what he was looking for. In any case, he agreed to give him a once-over.

Within hours Dutch and Meiklejohn were driving into Burbank, past the sign at the corner of Cahuenga and Barham Boulevards emblazoned with the Warner Bros. logo and the studio motto: "Combining Good Citizenship with Good Picture-Making." (In 1944, during the violent union strikes, screenwriter Julius Epstein would suggest changing it to "Combining Good Citizenship with Good Marksmanship.") The lot itself was "rural and charming," according to Olivia de Havilland, one of Warner Bros.' leading contract players. "The buildings were low and influenced by the Mexican adobe style. There were lawns and flower beds, which were watered regularly—and a tennis court. The soundstages were very well kept. A river ran along one side of the lot, with mountains on the other side. Everything was well-thought-out and beautifully maintained."

Max Arnow, a tightly wound man who was all eyebrows and cheekbones, was waiting for Dutch and Bill Meiklejohn in the casting office on the north side of the lot, a stone's throw beyond Marion Davies's bungalow. For fifteen minutes, Meiklejohn and Arnow walked around him discussing his attributes as if he were a new car and they were kicking its wheels. "It was the quickest decision on testing I ever made in my life," Arnow recalled. Evidently, Dutch's voice closed the deal; there was something in the timbre that appealed to the casting chief—its resemblance to Ross Alexander's was downright spooky, "a nice resonant voice"—and he arranged a screen test for later that week. To prepare for it, Dutch was given a short scene from Holiday, the Philip Barry play that Warner was considering (it ended up being made by Columbia Pictures in 1938), for a read-through they'd film when he returned. It seemed like typecasting, Arnow thought; the part was for a character named Johnny Case, a clean-cut guy from the Midwest. "You don't have to memorize it," Arnow told him. "You can just read the thing." In the meantime, Meiklejohn hedged his bets by taking Dutch for an interview at Paramount Pictures, but the two walked out when the studio kept them waiting.

All day Sunday, he and Joy Hodges ran lines from Holiday, working on delivery and nuance. On Monday, it was back to reality. Dutch arrived in Catalina to resume his spring-training duties. Cubs management wasn't happy about his absence. Charlie Grimm let him know in not so many words that he was shirking his responsibility to the team. That evening, as he cut through the lobby of the Hotel Avalon on his way to meet friends, he noticed two faces he had seen on the screen. "Warner Brothers sent Anita Louise, their blonde ingénue, and me, their brunette ingénue, to Catalina Island on a picture-layout assignment for movie magazines and other publications," recalls Olivia de Havilland. They were barely out of their teens and were chaperoned by Scotty Welbourne, one of the studio's resident photographers. "As we descended into the lobby, a sports announcer presented himself, and we chatted for a few minutes." She could tell that Dutch Reagan was fascinated by moviemaking, but he gave no indication as to his upcoming screen test.

Almost immediately, he was due back in Los Angeles. That Tuesday, he took the boat to the city and roared off to Burbank in time for his late-morning appointment. This time, he was directed to the studio makeup department for a little powder and color to help counter the harsh lights before heading over to one of the standing sets where a movie had just finished production. Nick Grinde, an important action director from the silent-film era, was waiting for him, along with Joseph Patrick MacDonald, his silver-haired cameraman, another veteran of the silent era who was generally acknowledged to be one of Jack Warner's favorite technicians. Dutch's lack of experience in front of a camera was evident, but he relaxed after he met his co-star. The studio had arranged for him to test opposite one of its up-and-coming contract players, June Travis, a twenty-year-old green-eyed brunette, whose father, Harry Grabiner, happened to be the vice president and general manager of the Chicago White Sox. She and Dutch had plenty in common—both native Illinoisans, versatile athletes (she was an Olympic-caliber swimmer and "considered one of the best female hockey players in the country"), and spring-training veterans, Travis hopscotching between the studio and the Sox camp in nearby Pasadena.

The two actors rehearsed for a few minutes, then dove into a scene in which the protagonist, played by Dutch, explains to his fiancée's sister how he plans to retire after "making a bundle" before he turns thirty. It was filled with snappy repartee that Dutch handled easily and with relative charm. Max Arnow, who watched from the wings, was stunned by the would-be actor's facility. "He didn't refer to the script once," Arnow recalled. "He was letter-perfect and played the scene like it should have been played." Everyone seemed satisfied after two takes, and they wrapped before noon.

Before he left the lot, Max Arnow informed him that Jack Warner, the studio chief, probably wouldn't see the screen test before Tuesday night at the earliest. They'd let him know sometime on Wednesday how it panned out, so it would behoove everyone if he'd stick around until then. This news presented Dutch with a problem. He'd be on a train heading back east with the Cubs on Tuesday, no two ways about it. If it meant losing out on a movie career, so be it.

His job at WHO in Des Moines was a sure thing. For a once-poverty-stricken young man making $350 a month in the edgy world of late-Depression America, movies were pie in the sky. It would have been crazy to risk his job for that. Still, on the train ride home, he fought the sinking feeling that he might have torpedoed the opportunity of a lifetime.

Two days later, a telegram arrived for him at WHO.

WARNERS OFFERS CONTRACT SEVEN YEARS STOP ONE YEAR OPTION STOP STARTING $200 A WEEK STOP WHAT SHALL I DO MEIKLEJOHN*

Dutch didn't hesitate before answering.

SIGN BEFORE THEY CHANGE THEIR MINDS DUTCH REAGAN

* Max Arnow insists the contract was for $175 a week.

D utch remained in Des Moines, broadcasting Cubs games, through the middle of May 1937. He had plenty to do to prepare for his departure. There were loose ends he needed to wrap up, people to say goodbye to—his brother and sister-in-law in Davenport, his parents in Dixon, and all the friends he'd made in Iowa. He treated himself to a bespoke white sport coat and navy-blue slacks hand-sewn by a local tailor, which he swore off wearing until he reached Hollywood. He also performed a personal makeover, parting his wavy hair on the right instead of in the middle, as was suggested to him by a Warner Bros. hairdresser.

Try as he might to look the part, he was still a little reticent. "Somehow I can't see any Robert Taylor in me," he wrote to a friend back in Illinois, "but who the h—l am I to argue with them."

On May 19, his colleagues at the station threw him a farewell party that was broadcast on WHO. It was a measure of Dutch's esteem and how far he'd come that guests included the mayor of Des Moines, the parks commissioner, the state treasurer of Iowa, and the president of WHO, who presented him with a leather traveling bag. Before they signed off, an emotional Dutch thanked his listeners and everyone who contributed to his success, then took a moment to pay tribute to his mentor, Peter MacArthur, who was unable to be there, as his arthritis had rendered him an invalid.

Two days later, on Saturday, May 22, he packed his belongings into the trunk of his Nash convertible for the three-day drive west.

PART 2

RONNIE

CHAPTER TEN

LETTING DUTCH GO

*"The idea of a star being born is bushwa. A star is created carefully
and cold-bloodily, built up from nothing, from nobody. Age,
beauty, talent, least of all talent, has nothing to do with it. We
could make silk purses out of sow's ears."*

—LOUIS B. MAYER

On May 22, 1937, Ronald Reagan steered the Nash convertible across the Des Moines city line "with every intention in the world of taking things easy." There was no rush getting to California; his contract called for a June 1 arrival. For a change of scenery, he decided to head west across Nebraska, Wyoming, and Utah, then veer south through Nevada and the Mojave Desert before coasting into Los Angeles. It was an ambitious itinerary, five or six days driving on hardscrabble roads, but once he left Iowa, Dutch got antsy. The pull of Hollywood was too great. To make time, he drove a punishing 650 miles the first day. The next day he pushed another 600 miles, from Cheyenne, Wyoming, to Nephi, Utah, a whistle-stop on the Old Mormon Road. Neither leg, however, was as onerous as crossing the desert in an open-air car; it was "one awful ride," as he described it, delivering him to his destination sunburned and grimy. Nevertheless, he reported to Warner Bros. the next morning, several days earlier than he was expected.

The drive out to Burbank from Hollywood was a welcome respite from the cross-country ordeal. Once he crossed the gray-green chaparral hills into the San Fernando Valley, the sweeping vista flushed gold and pink, creating a rich, daydreamy glow. Across the Valley, through hazy sunlight, he could make out the Santa Susana Mountains, which lent the stretch of flatland some scale, a sense of greatness fortified by nature. There was a patchy evolution to what had once been open farmland and citrus groves— little ranches encircled by a snowballing suburbia carved up into small, distinct towns. Burbank was the largest, by far. By 1937, it had already been built out, owing to three movie studios—Warner, Universal, and Columbia—and Lockheed Aircraft, which was building twin-engine planes at a phenomenal clip.

The city's growth spurt was a recent development. As late as 1928, when Warner Bros. moved from Hollywood to Burbank, most days you could have fired a cannon in the vicinity and not endangered a life. The land surrounding the studio lot was nothing but open field, site of occasional location filming. In fact, *Birth of a Nation* had been made just outside the gates on a tract called the Providencia Ranch, now known as Forest Lawn Memorial Park.

Warner Bros. had grown, too. Until 1927 it had been a Poverty Row studio, one of the struggling independent picture companies clustered along a desolate stretch of Hollywood. The Warner brothers—Harry, Sam, Albert, and Jack—were arrivistes of a sort, the sons of Jewish immigrants who sought to escape a life of poverty through show business. They had operated nickelodeons and were later film exhibitors before deciding to venture into production. Harry and Jack had always wanted their own movie studio. In 1920, they purchased Beesemyer Farm, a former bean field at the corner of Gordon Street and Bronson Avenue, on which they built a barnlike interior stage with an exterior stage out back, the first home of Warner Brothers Pictures.

At the beginning, it was tough going. The brothers went deeply into debt trying to finance a slate of commercially shaky movies while paying off the mortgage for their new venture. In fact, they teetered on the brink of insolvency until 1923, when an unlikely movie star saved them. Rin Tin Tin was a scruffy German shepherd that had been rescued from a World War I battlefield by an American soldier. The dog's debut, in a Warner Bros. picture, *Where the North Begins*, was an instant box-office smash and lifeline for the studio. Over the course of twenty-seven movies, Rin Tin Tin rescued scores of characters in distress but none as desperate as the Warner brothers.

Then, in 1927, another godsend materialized, also unlikely—a Jewish cantor's son named Jack Robin (played by the inimitable Al Jolson), whose actual voice in *The Jazz Singer* ushered in the era of talkies. The movie wasn't the first to use sound. That distinction went to a sound-*synchronized* picture called *Don Juan*, which had premiered at the Egyptian Theater in L.A. the year before. But Warner Bros. took the concept to the masses by wiring theaters for sound to project the actors' voices—the brainchild of Sam Warner, who died the day before the movie opened.

It had been a risky venture. The Warners pumped everything they had into the technology. Millions of dollars were invested in wiring those theaters, most of it borrowed from a number of sober-minded banks. The brothers were well aware of the downside: if the bet didn't pay off, the lenders would take the studio.

Of course, *The Jazz Singer* changed motion-picture history. It touched off the sound era, which the Warners rightly believed would be "without a doubt the biggest stride since the birth of the industry." It launched Warner Bros. Pictures into the forefront of moviemaking and gave the studio a financial safety net. Practically overnight, its stock soared from $9 a share to $132.

Suddenly the Warners had money, more money than they'd ever dreamed of, and the ambition to compete as a Hollywood moviemaking force. But to leapfrog from Poverty Row to the major leagues—alongside Paramount, RKO, MGM, and Universal—required a bold move. Harry Warner had one up his sleeve. He acquired the mighty First National Pictures, which flourished on the legacy of beloved stars Charlie Chaplin and Mary Pickford. In addition to the massive First National catalog and its chain of theaters, Warner coveted its real-estate assets, most prominently the studio lot spread across a prime seventy-eight-acre chunk of Burbank.

From that day forth, Warner Bros. beckoned like a beacon on the horizon. You could see its distinctive First National water tower from miles around; it was Dutch's point of reference as he approached the studio. That tower was a landmark to many, but it also served as a symbol of accomplishment to the ever-striving Warner brothers, who, as historian Neal Gabler wrote, "regarded themselves as outsiders and underdogs."

No one regarded himself as more of an outsider or underdog than Ronald Reagan—and he was probably right. Every weekend, people in places like Dixon and Davenport and Des Moines flocked to theaters, where for ten cents they could lose themselves in the deeds of the scoundrels, heroes, and lovers that flickered across the screen. That someone from Dutch's background could envision himself up there took an incredible leap of imagination and invention, or at least the ability to ignore the improbability of it and plow ahead. He had only his natural poise to see him through, his gift for concealing any insecurities.

He was out of his element—*that* he knew for sure. As he drove onto the Warner Bros. lot the morning of June 1, he worried that he'd made a colossal mistake. He'd been hired to *act*, something he hadn't done since college, five years earlier, and to *act* opposite giants such as James Cagney, Errol Flynn, Bette Davis, and Paul Muni. One scene and they'd realize what an impostor he was. This became clearer while watching his screen test with Max Arnow soon after he arrived. Everything was wrong with it: the way he looked on film, the way he sounded, his delivery, his awkward gestures. By the time the test had run through the projector, he was already planning his escape back to Iowa.

Arnow tried to ease his mind, but not before raking over his appearance. Actors were required to wear their own clothes, but Dutch's newly purchased white sport coat would have to go. "The shoulders are too big—they make your head look too small," Arnow told him. He had the wardrobe department recut the jacket, altering the shoulder lines to make Dutch more proportional. And Perc Westmore, the studio's legendary makeup artist, performed a subtle makeover on his face.

His name also became an issue. Dutch Reagan sounded too pedestrian to the studio press agents. It didn't roll off the tongue. They needed a name that would look good on a marquee. There were plenty of examples: Archibald Leach read better as Cary Grant, and Lucille LeSueur as Joan Crawford. Even June Travis was a name that had been chosen out of the telephone directory. "Dutch Reagan" was a nonstarter. It had to be changed, no doubt about it. But—to what? After much back and forth, Dutch proposed a radical solution: his actual name. "How about Ronald . . . Ronald Reagan?"

From that day on, "Dutch" was officially retired. Everyone in Hollywood would know him as Ronnie.

Fortunately, he had someone by his side for moral support—George Ward, an associate at the Meiklejohn Agency, was designated as his agent and knew the ropes. Warner Bros., Ward explained, was basically a sweatshop. Contract players, who were required to punch a clock, reported at five-thirty in the morning and were expected to work from nine until six, but often much later—six days a week, no exceptions. "The pace was incredible," James Cagney wrote in his autobiography. "At times we started at nine in the morning and worked straight through to the next morning." Competition for roles was fierce due to the large number of actors on the roster, so Ronnie was advised not to get impatient; it would take time, perhaps several weeks, even as many as six months, until they found something suitable to cast him in.

No sooner were the words out of Ward's mouth than Ronnie was thrust into his first assignment, in the ill-fated movie *The Inside Story*, which had been slated to roll with Ross Alexander. He would be taking over the role, and it was tailor-made—a muckraking radio announcer at a small-town station. Warner had actually made this picture three years earlier as *Hi, Nellie*, with Paul Muni. This was more than a common occurrence. About half of these low-budget features were retreads. To save the cost of underwriting an original screenplay, the studio put new wheels on it, gave it a fresh coat of paint, and changed the name. They sometimes recycled the same picture four or five times. No one minded as long as it had fresh faces and a new title. The result wasn't an important feature; it was known around the industry affectionately as a B.

In the 1930s, as talking pictures exploded, a trip to the local movie house constituted a full night's entertainment. Theater owners ran an entire program, with a cartoon, a short, a newsreel, a serial, and two feature films. The B was the bottom half of a double bill, averaging a little over an hour in length, as opposed to the A, which ran about an hour and a half and top-lined the studio's box-office stars. With a Warner Bros. movie, that meant you saw the likes of Jimmy Cagney and Edward G. Robinson in an

A. The B's had smaller budgets and shorter shooting schedules—about three weeks, tops—allowing studios to introduce and test out a fledgling actor like Ronald Reagan to determine whether there was enough raw talent there to bump him up to the A's as a leading man.

The Inside Story was a B, no doubt about it. The cast was filled with new or run-of-the-mill contract players and was produced by Bryan Foy, who headed the Warner Bros. B unit. Foy started out as a director on the lot and had already made forty-five films by the time Ronald Reagan came aboard. His job was to produce twenty-six features a year at a total cost of $5 million. He was a taskmaster, not only because he had to rush dozens of movies through production, but also because he had production boss Jack Warner breathing down his neck. And Warner was a notorious fire-breather. It would be an understatement to say they had a rocky relationship. Warner fired Foy dozens of times, initially in 1928 for taking a short subject called *The Lights of New York* and extending it into the first all-talking feature, against the Warner brothers' strict orders at a time when they happened to be out of town. When the movie, a $100,000 investment, brought in $2 million, Foy was retained and given a raise and the reins of the B unit.

Now he was charged with steering Ronald Reagan through the process. This wasn't as easy as it sounded. Ronnie had no filmmaking experience whatsoever. Because working on a soundstage was completely different from acting in front of an audience, his first few efforts on the set unmasked him as stiff and awkward. And the camera was unforgiving. He had to learn to move properly and to deliver his lines while conveying *personality*. It helped that the studio had a dialogue coach on the payroll, but a profusion of little miscues are evident in his first movie.

The Inside Story, eventually retitled *Love Is on the Air*, was not exactly a work of art, but not embarrassing, either. It was, as one critic assessed it, "an undemanding broth of light comedy and even lighter romance," exactly what was required of a B picture. The *Hollywood Reporter* singled out Ronnie as "a natural, giving one of the best first performances Hollywood has offered in many a day," but the *New York Times* ignored him completely in its review of the movie, saying it "makes no pretensions to class and even less to credibility." There weren't a lot of expectations riding on it. No careers were going to be launched—or destroyed—as a result. Ronnie simply blended into the picture without making waves. In any case, Jack Warner, the production chief, was satisfied with the work. He watched the film's dailies each night after it had wrapped and decided there was something interesting in his new talent acquisition—at least interesting enough to give him another shot.

Ronnie immediately segued into *Sergeant Murphy*, opposite a horse, in a soapy B picture that cast him as a cavalryman. Coincidentally, the role was another instance of typecasting. During his spare time in Des Moines, he'd enrolled in the Citizens' Military Training Program, which was more or less a reserve candidacy in the Fourteenth Cavalry Regiment based at the local fort. It was less a desire to enlist than an opportunity to ride the Army horses for free, but it contributed familiarity and know-how to his second movie.

Before shooting began, as a favor to Jack Warner, he reported to Stage 6 to put in an uncredited appearance in the finale of *Hollywood Hotel*, a low-key Busby Berkeley musical based on the *Louella Parsons* radio series of the same name, playing a broadcaster. Ronnie's performance in it was inconsequential, but it lifted him into the orbit of the mighty gossip columnist, who had a role as a talent impresario.

L ouella Parsons stood practically alone as the missionary who introduced the gossip column to American readers. Her earliest years were spent barnstorming the Midwest, writing chatty news articles, movie reviews, and screenplays. Two short-lived marriages interrupted her career. By 1918, at the relatively late age of thirty-seven, she had moved to Manhattan, bringing her new form of whisper journalism to the *New York Morning Telegraph*, where she was noticed and snatched away by William Randolph Hearst. It was Hearst, the father of tabloid journalism, who turned Parsons's gimlet eye toward Hollywood and groomed her as a syndicated columnist for his Universal News Service.

Once installed in L.A., she began churning out daily columns for Hearst's *Los Angeles Examiner*, which were syndicated to six hundred newspapers with a readership of over twenty million, and soon added a Campbell's Soup–sponsored daily radio show, which shamelessly promoted stars and their latest releases. She cultivated contacts and amassed the kind of power—and fear—in the film industry otherwise possessed only by the mightiest of moguls. Parsons, it was said, could make or break a career with one swipe of her acid-tipped pen. She did it unmercifully and with impunity, mixing bedroom chatter and innuendo, even smear tactics when it suited her purposes, to elevate movie stars to a new level of public fascination.

Hollywood gossip might have helped promote films, but in the process it created a whole new set of problems. Divorces and scandals once confined to studio lots were now ripe for picking. If Parsons decided to break a story counter to a company's best interests, there was nothing much that could be done about it. So the studios, which saw her as both benefactor and threat, courted her, kowtowed to her, offered her exclusives, put her in films, anything she wanted in exchange for favorable press.

Louella Parsons immediately took a shine to Ronald Reagan. It would have pleased his new boss to think she saw promise in the young actor's ability. Warner understood the impact someone such as Parsons could have on Reagan's career. But, in fact, her interest in him was personal. As luck would have it, Louella Parsons was from Dixon, Illinois. She'd graduated from the old South Side High School, where Ronnie—Dutch—had begun his education, and she, too, had escaped the confines of Dixon through books borrowed from its public library.

Ronnie left the *Hollywood Hotel* set in a swoon. Out of water, but a fish swimming in the right direction, upstream. He'd encountered a galaxy of stars: Dick Powell, Ted Healy, Frances Langford, Benny Goodman, Fred Waring, Louella Parsons. He spotted the Lane sisters, Rosemary and Priscilla, in the cast and waved hello. They'd made their singing debut on his show at WHO, and he felt comforted by their presence. Afterward, he had lunch in the studio commissary in the company of more stars: Joan Blondell, Sterling Holloway, Errol Flynn, Anita Louise, and Edward Everett Horton, who grabbed his hand and welcomed him aboard. "Dick Powell . . . wished me luck," he recalled. *Dick Powell!* He'd come a long way in just a few short weeks.

Buoyed by the prospect of steady employment, he moved into the Hollywood Plaza Hotel, a ten-story "skyscraper" surrounded by a dense grove of date palms at the intersection of Hollywood Boulevard and Vine Street. It was "a hotel for film people," not four-star or grand like the Hollywood

Hotel at the west end of the block, "but comfortable, utilitarian, with a small lobby." The Plaza's greatest advantage was its prime location. It was the crossroads of Hollywood. He could walk to the Egyptian Theater, "an architectural crazy house of Chinese, Greek and Egyptian design," a few steps away, or shop at the Broadway, with its fabulous Tea Room. The Brown Derby, where Louella Parsons held court, was situated in the middle of the block, next to a miniature golf course, and Simon's, the iconic drive-in restaurant with carhops on roller skates, was on the corner. Across the street stood the Hollywood Recreation Center, a sprawling entertainment complex, which later functioned as the home of ABC Radio, and just down the street was Wallichs Music City, whose upstairs space became the birthplace of Capitol Records.

A sea of humanity flowed just outside his door. The once-sleepy boulevard was full of car traffic at all hours, and a trolley barreled down the middle of the street. And electricity of all kinds, the bright lights were literally dazzling. "Lights, millions of them," Reagan wrote to an audience back in Iowa, "their variegated colors giving out a brilliance of myriad Christmas trees." An infestation of sightseers never seemed to sleep. Prostitutes worked the shadows. "I was in a new world," Reagan acknowledged.

Thankfully, he had company. Hours after he moved into the Plaza, a whole Des Moines crew turned up on his doorstep—Pee Wee Johnson, Will Scott, Tommy Thompson, and a WHO vocalist, Ed Morely, all of whom had followed him west. They had dinner at the Brown Derby, then went to the Palomar, a glitzy dance hall, where, as Reagan recalled, "the manager introduced us to some girls" and they took over the microphone on the bandstand, singing "several Iowa songs."

He reveled in being Dutch again for a while. Being greeted as Ron or Ronnie at the studio sounded foreign to him. No one, not even his parents, had ever used that name, and it took some getting used to, letting Dutch go. He struggled to maintain an ordinary existence by going horseback riding in Griffith Park with Joy Hodges and bodysurfing off the Santa Monica pier. A date with June Travis sidestepped the café-society scene in favor of a county fair. Friends and he congregated at Barney's Beanery, a West Hollywood diner, instead of the high-toned haunts frequented by stars. But it wasn't easy to shake off the demands of his new job. The studio publicity machinery set to work to promote its young star, sending him to red-carpet premieres, having him emcee events, and staging photo shoots with his glamorous co-stars.

These activities were no guarantee of job security. Warner had signed Ronald Reagan to a seven-year contract, which seemed like an eternity on the surface of it. Most employees could relax with such a long-term deal. In the movie business, however, the salient details were buried in fine print. "When the newspapers announce that 'So-and-so has been signed to a long-term contract,'" Reagan explained, "it means that they are tied up for from three to six months definitely and up to seven years on a 'maybe' basis." Contract players signed an agreement that amounted to little more than servitude. "The studio had the option to abandon the contract at the end of each six-month period," says Olivia de Havilland, "whereas the actor had no such exit clause. The studio also had the right to lay an actor off without pay for three months each year." What's more, if an actor refused to play a role he or she had been assigned, the studio could suspend the actor's contract or add to the end of it the period of time it took another performer to complete the role. In essence, a seven-year contract could expire in six months or run . . . forever.

"It was like a fiefdom," says film professor Alan Spiegel. "If you obeyed the kings, you would reap financial glory. The studio would protect you. If you had eccentricities in drinking or drugs or sex or women, they would cover all that up and take care of you. But they *owned* you."

Ronnie had sweated out his first option period. Warner Bros. was notorious for chewing up and spitting out young actors after the initial six-month stretch. Many just didn't measure up, while others either proved difficult to work with or couldn't handle the pressure.

After making three movies, Ronald Reagan had no idea where he stood. He'd had two choice roles in B's to make his bones, and another, in an A picture called *Submarine D-1*, with Pat O'Brien, where his performance wound up on the cutting-room floor. The *New York Daily News* reported that he "has poise, a voice, and a face that the camera loves," but that might not be enough star power to convince the higher-ups.

His fate rested entirely with Jack Warner. The youngest of the four brothers, he was the studio's production chief, responsible for all filming, an enigmatic tyrant. He was "crude, vulgar, shallow, flaky, contrary and galling . . . loud and self-conscious," a tough and unpredictable autocrat when it came to contracts and performers. "He disliked actors and showed it," recalls de Havilland, who described Warner Bros. as "a prison" and Jack Warner as "the warden of the prison."

Reagan had seen Warner only from afar; he hadn't yet met him personally and therefore had no idea of the man's opinion of him or if his contract would be extended. Even though he was penciled in for two more features, there was no indication from the executive suite whether he would stick around to make them. On October 2, 1937, the day after *Love Is on the Air* was finally released nationally, Bill Meiklejohn called with the verdict. "MY OPTION'S BEEN TAKEN UP," Ronnie exulted. "While I haven't been in Hollywood six months yet, they've already notified me that they intend to keep me for the next six months period."

He was also getting a raise to $250 a week, with a guarantee of sixteen weeks' work. It was enough, at last, to make good on a promise. When he'd called home in May to say he was moving out to Los Angeles, he vowed to bring his parents west as soon as his finances permitted. He wanted to have Jack and Nelle close by to keep an eye on them. Jack's health had deteriorated, and they were barely getting by. A change of scenery would do them a world of good. With some creative budgeting, Ronnie sent them money for a train ticket and rented them a small ground-floor apartment in West Hollywood, convenient to shopping, that looked out on a flower garden.

It was time for Ronnie to balance work and family. He dug in assiduously at the studio, but the dutiful son made time to go to a Disciples church with his mother and to take walks with Jack, who shuffled wearily around the new neighborhood. The gang of Iowa friends that he saw regularly folded seamlessly into the new family structure, meeting for dinners that Nelle would prepare and following the meal with a trip to the movies. Hollywood was starting to feel like home.

The work was constant. Ronnie appeared in eight movies released in 1938, playing opposite Humphrey Bogart (*Swing Your Lady*), Dick Powell and Pat O'Brien (*Cowboy from Brooklyn*), James Cagney (*Boy Meets Girl*), and Susan Hayward (*Girls on Probation*). They were mostly B pictures and mostly forgettable, but they gave him solid credentials as a member of the Warner Bros. family. He was known for being a "dependable guy, never late, hung-over or difficult to work with." He learned his lines as well as everybody else's, a trusty college skill that earned the directors' respect. He polished his technique, refining his delivery, striking a balance between the blustery, quick-talking *rat-a-tat* tempo that was a Warner Bros. trademark and a more serviceable relaxed style that could land him in tough-guy roles as well as romantic leads. He projected a likable, all-American screen image useful to the studio.

Warner Bros. was the urban studio, the studio of charismatic stars who weren't patently handsome or glamorous. Cagney, Robinson, Bette Davis, Paul Muni, Joan Blondell, Humphrey Bogart: ferocious actors—but mugs. Errol Flynn, the studio's one dashing heartthrob, would have been more comfortable at 20th Century Fox, whose head, Darryl Zanuck, loved men with dark looks and mustaches. Nor did Warner's stars look like their MGM counterparts. MGM epitomized glamour: Clark Gable, Greta Garbo. Robert Taylor, MGM's top leading man, was known as "the man with the perfect profile," a beautiful statue. If an actor had looks and charm, MGM was the studio of choice.

Warner Bros. didn't try to compete with MGM. "Their actors portrayed the lowlifes," says Neal Gabler. "They spoke to a different constituency. They were the studio of the little guy, the underdog." No other picture company would have ended a movie like *The Public Enemy*, with Cagney all trussed up. Or subscribed to the philosophy of *I Am a Fugitive from a Chain Gang*: "How do you live?" "I steal." The big number at the end of Busby Berkeley's *42nd Street* is "The Forgotten Man." That forgotten man was Warner Bros.' audience.

How did Ronald Reagan fit into this scenario? In theory, he might have been at the wrong studio. His all-American looks, his wholesale affability, his aw-shucks nature would have been more at home at MGM. Its Andy Hardy movies were sentimental comedies celebrating an idealized—Midwestern—American life. He would have stood out in *Dinner at Eight*, *The Thin Man*, *Boys Town*, and *Goodbye, Mr. Chips*. At Warner Bros., his choices were narrower—darker.

But the boss liked him. Jack Warner saw something in his young contract player that fit into his concept of a Warner Bros. star. Ronald Reagan had an impact on the screen, that *je ne sais quoi*. It was impossible to put a finger on it, but Warner knew it when he saw it. From the outset, Ronnie was never without work. Through 1938 and 1939, he moved continuously from production to production, working with James Cagney, Dick Powell, Ann Sheridan, Ralph Bellamy, Pat O'Brien, and Wayne Morris. He was handed the starring role in an action-adventure series, playing Brass Bancroft, a Secret Service agent, based on the memoirs of former G-man William H. Moran. Those movies might not have been critical gems—critics referred to them as "uninspired" and "obvious . . . cheap action melodrama"—but they were popular, filling Saturday matinees with teenage boys.

The early Ronald Reagan films were a hodgepodge of threadbare plots woven together for production-line simplicity. Some, such as *Brother Rat* and *Going Places*, were loosely based on plays. Others, such as *Girls on Probation* and *Naughty but Nice*, were pedestrian B features saddled with mediocre screenplays. All of them quickly sank into obscurity.

Reagan wasn't being offered the juicy parts. "I learned that progress, career-wise, could be made only by getting into the A-pictures," he complained, and at the moment, they weren't being offered to him. Even so, he was thrust into the star-making machinery that contributed to building his stature. For the premiere of Warner's 1938 blockbuster *Jezebel*, starring Henry Fonda and Bette Davis, the studio enlisted him to escort "sweater girl" Lana Turner to the red-carpet gala at Grauman's Egyptian, after which it put out a photo spread of the two hinting at a romance. Of course, it was nothing more than a stunt. Publicity departments often manufactured relationships between their contract players, hoping to receive national newspaper and fan-magazine coverage. The flirtation with Lana Turner was pure Hollywood make-believe. Neither star had much interest in the other.

But the arrangement had its benefits. "Press agents were constantly trying to pair me with my leading ladies and new starlets," Ronnie recalled—and he wasn't bashful about taking them up on the offer. He enjoyed brief dalliances with actresses Margaret Lindsay and Susan Hayward, both of whom co-starred with him in 1939. His relationship with twenty-four-year-old Ila Rhodes developed into something more serious. They'd met while filming *Secret Service of the Air*, the first Brass Bancroft potboiler, and followed each other into *Dark Victory*, with bit parts opposite Bette Davis. Finding themselves together again in *Hell's Kitchen* spurred "lunch-break trysts and weekends together" that blossomed into a full-blown romance. Rhodes would claim she dated Ronnie throughout 1938 and "became engaged—with a ring on my finger." If that was the case, they kept it under wraps. There was no fan-magazine gossip, no active studio promotion; in fact, Warner Bros. might have downplayed the relationship as the studio lost interest in Rhodes's career and put its weight behind Ronnie's. In any case, after "eight or nine months," Rhodes said, he "grew distant, withdrew a little," which signaled to her the engagement was over.

Rhodes assumed the studio put an end to their affair. She might have read the tea leaves correctly, but she overlooked the obvious. Another co-star had taken her place.

CHAPTER ELEVEN

"BUTTON NOSE"

"You might as well back down, because I'm gonna get you."

—JANE WYMAN TO RONALD REAGAN, *Brother Rat and a Baby* (1940)

It would take a secret agent no less gifted than Brass Bancroft to uncover the truth about Jane Wyman's past. Her birthdate was given variously as either January 4 or 5, 1914, or January 28, 1917, depending on whether her name was Sarah Jane Mayfield or Sarah Jane Fulks. By the time she met Ronald Reagan, she had also been known as Jane Durrell, was rumored to be the daughter of French chanteuse LaJerne Pechelle, and had either been married once or twice, depending on whether her first husband, Eugene or Ernest Wyman or Weymann, was actually her stepfather or even existed. The Jane Wyman who, in 1936, became a member of the Warner Bros. stock company—the self-described cocky, loud, platinum-blonde chorus girl—was largely a figment of her own invention.

By the time Jane Wyman ascended to the screen, she was already an inveterate chameleon, leaving many to wonder who she really was. This much is indisputable: She was born Sarah Jane Mayfield in St. Joseph, Missouri, on January 5, 1917. When she was four years old, her parents, Manning Mayfield and Gladys Hope Christian, split, father heading to San Francisco and mother moving to Cleveland. Sarah Jane was handed off to neighbors. Richard and Emma Fulks, middle-aged empty-nesters, raised her as their own daughter. Like Ronald Reagan, she received a Midwest upbringing in a scenic river town founded by a fur trader, and she lived there as Sarah Jane Fulks, although she was never legally adopted. She was "crippled" by shyness and "grew up with hurt and bewilderment." And like Ronald Reagan, her childhood was shaped by an imperfect father figure, in her case Richard Fulks, an unsparing disciplinarian whom Sarah Jane detested and was unable to please.

Early in adolescence, Sarah Jane persuaded them to enroll her at the Edward A. Prinz Dancing Academy, a longtime St. Joseph's institution, where she blossomed from an introvert into a dancer whose talents were hard to ignore, especially for her foster mother, Emma. From the moment Sarah Jane strode onto the dance floor, angled her body into a well-formed plié, and launched into a routine, Emma's head swam with possibilities. Watching her daughter blossom also touched off a personal catharsis. When her husband died, in March 1928, Emma decided it was high time to escape St. Joseph, and Sarah Jane would be her ticket out. They packed up and headed straight to Hollywood, where Emma brought Sarah Jane around for auditions at every studio in town. But there were no takers. No matter how adorable and precocious Sarah Jane was, there were few parts for dancing twelve-year-olds claiming to be twenty.

In the meantime, Sarah Jane finished school in Los Angeles and apparently got married, though she refused to confirm or deny it for the rest of her life. Rumor had it that she had married a fellow high school student at the age of sixteen and separated from him after only a month. Eugene Wyman was the name most often bandied about by gossip columnists. A certificate was filed with the California Department of Welfare Services attesting to the marriage of Jane Fulks, daughter of Richard D. and Emma Reise Fulks, to Ernest Eugene Wyman on April 8, 1933. The bride listed her age as nineteen, though she had just turned sixteen.

It took another two years before a divorce became final. In the interim, Jane—she had left the name Sarah behind in Missouri—bumped around Los Angeles, waitressing in a coffee shop, modeling, and operating a switchboard. She later boasted that she'd gone back to school at the University of Missouri, that she'd done serious theater in St. Louis, and sang on radio shows throughout the country, none of which was true. Acting remained her ultimate goal. In an effort to attract attention, she bleached her hair Jean Harlow–blonde and plucked her eyebrows to a fare-thee-well. "Before I became a blonde, I had tried everything to get a start as an actress but no one in Hollywood gave me a tumble," she said. Her break came in 1935 courtesy of LeRoy Prinz, the son of her hometown dance instructor. He had become a noted Hollywood choreographer and was preparing elaborate routines for Leo McCarey's latest musical extravaganza, *The Kid from Spain*, on the Samuel Goldwyn lot. Thanks to Prinz's largesse, Jane won a part in the chorus line, alongside leggy Betty Grable, Paulette Goddard, and Lucille Ball.

Like most young dancers in Hollywood, Jane worked sporadically and lived hand-to-mouth. Her movie roles were bit parts, few and far between, and fraught with the kinds of casting-couch auditions that hardened her toward powerful, demanding men. "I had had enough of being manipulated and exploited by men for the wrong reasons," she would recall. She was also tired of the hard knocks, the constant struggle. Embracing her independence, she haunted the nightclubs, dance halls, and parties that drew the fast Hollywood crowd. At five feet five, with a short, turned-up nose and enormous eyes offset by exquisitely angled cheekbones, she was as striking as any of the town's other aspiring starlets. She became a fixture at hot spots like the Trocadero and the Cocoanut Grove, "a girl on the make," as Louella Parsons called her, invariably on the arm of an older man.

One such escort was Myron Futterman, who represented everything that was missing from Jane's life. He was mature, successful, and a gentleman, with courtly Southern charm and paternal instincts. A manufacturer of upscale children's clothes, he wore impeccably tailored suits and drove a late-model sedan. Futterman, at thirty-five, seventeen years older than Jane, was confident, outgoing, and thrillingly attentive. With her self-esteem at an all-time low, Jane threw herself into the relationship.

In May 1936, after a string of bit parts, Warner Bros. offered her the chance to become one of its vaunted contract players. This was a stunning break, though for most of a year the studio tucked her away, unbilled, in clunkers like *Smart Blonde*, *Slim*, *Public Wedding*, and *Ready, Willing and Able*. She was cast as the "wise-cracking chorus girl" or "dumb bunny" or "floozie" in a series of forgettable B's. While struggling to establish her identity as an actress, Wyman yielded to the promise of security that Myron Futterman represented and married him in New Orleans on June 29, 1937. The marriage quickly soured. He had a serious jealous streak, accusing her of flirting whenever they went out, and compared her unfavorably, ceaselessly, with a wife from a previous marriage. When she pressed him to begin a family, he refused. He showed little interest in Jane's movie career; in fact, he seemed to resent it. Three months later, she'd had enough. They separated and she filed for divorce. At this point, she already had her eye on Ronald Reagan.

Ronald Reagan arrived at Warner Bros. the same month Jane Wyman married Myron Futterman. It seems unlikely that they were formally introduced, but there is no doubt they were aware of each other, if only as "family members" of the studio. Legend has it that she was walking into the commissary for lunch and passed him on the steps, a tall, strapping Adonis, quintessentially Midwestern. "That's for me!" she supposedly told herself. The attraction was instant.

Friends might have dismissed it as another one of Jane's infatuations, of which there were a sizable number. But those closest to her knew otherwise. "Ronnie was the dream of true, perfect manhood personified that this little girl had always held in her heart through thick and thin," recalled William Demarest, one of her longtime confidants, who later portrayed grouchy Uncle Charley on TV's My Three Sons. Despite the failure of two short-lived marriages, she was still searching for her white knight. Ronald Reagan had the right credentials. He was secure, charismatic, understanding, and outwardly wholesome. "She was the aggressor," Demarest said, "the intent pursuer from the start." In the past, Jane had jumped in too quickly, pushed too hard, acted too vulnerable, demanded too much. She'd be more cautious this time. Besides, she was married.

Work also kept them apart. Each maintained a furious pace on different sections of the lot, and their paths never crossed until late in 1938, when both were assigned to Brother Rat. By then, Jane had been in twenty-four movies, Ronnie ten.

For both of them, Brother Rat was a giant step up. It was adapted from a hit Broadway play and developed primarily to showcase a cast of newcomers—Warner Bros.' fresh-faced young stock company. A rich lode of talent was on the verge of breaking out—Wayne Morris, Jane Bryan, Priscilla Lane, Eddie Albert, Johnnie Davis, and, of course, Ronald Reagan and Jane Wyman. In the story, three Virginia Military Institute cadets—or "brother rats," as they called themselves—are facing graduation and decide to take a weekend off to visit girlfriends. Naturally, hijinks and moral dilemmas ensue to ensure a slippery, frenetic pace.

Early in production Ronnie and Jane were ordered to report to Warner's Portrait Gallery—the room above the makeup department where photo shoots for ad campaigns, head shots, and pinups of starlets took place. Jane, impatient and high-strung, didn't like to be kept waiting and bristled at a delay in their scheduled appointment. In one recounting of this episode, Jane offered her first impression of Ronnie as being calm, cool, and imperturbable. "It's just a mistake," he told her. "It's no one's fault. No one would inconvenience us on purpose." To Jane, this was a display of incredible inner strength.

Ronald Reagan was still struggling to control what he called "leadingladyitis," an ailment he claimed he'd been afflicted with since college. The symptoms were unmistakable: a passing touch, an errant stare, a fatal kiss from a co-star—any one of those during the course of a scene could drive a young man to yearning and, worse, romance. He'd suffered it at Eureka and had even stepped out on Margaret Cleaver with his love interest in *The Brat* while Mugs was on sabbatical during her junior year. It hit him again with June Travis after their duet on *Love Is on the Air*. And so it was again: on the set of *Brother Rat*, he asked Jane Wyman out on a date.

By the time *Brother Rat* swung into production, the Reagan-Wyman romance was in full bloom. "Everyone could see that Janie and Ronnie had fallen in love," said Priscilla Lane, featured in the film as Wyman's college roommate. Wayne Morris also picked up on the intrigue. "You got the feeling those two couldn't wait to get to the love scenes."

There were more dates to restaurants and nightclubs, but with "hands held under the table" and an arm's-length distance between them when they got up to dance. Jane wasn't yet divorced from Myron Futterman, and a new relationship might compromise the proceedings. When Ronnie introduced Jane to his parents, nothing was said of her situation. Nelle, had she known, would never have approved.

Friends and cast members rooted for them, but not everyone did. "I just couldn't see [Jane] matched up with Ronnie Reagan," admitted Alex Gottlieb, who would go on to produce films featuring both of them, "but she wanted the semblance of propriety." They seemed to be on different trajectories to Gottlieb, who felt Ronnie's plain-vanilla B-picture appeal would

be a drag on Jane's path to stardom. "She had real fire," recalls Olivia de
Havilland. "Ronnie wasn't cut from that kind of cloth, and I worried he
would get burned by what she gave off." Jack Warner was also skeptical. He
eagerly encouraged romances between his actors, but for publicity and
make-believe, not for real. Real-life romance threatened to interfere with
their work.

None of their objections mattered once Louella Parsons got wind of the
Reagan-Wyman liaison. Parsons fed off such goings-on. Innuendo was catnip to her, but outright romance was a gold mine. She mined it for all it was
worth in her column. It was hard to believe that readers would crave gossip
about two relatively unheralded B actors, but she wrote as though they were
Gable and Lombard.

Her relentless promotion of Jane and Ronnie continued when they were
cast together later that year in *Brother Rat and a Baby*, a treacly sequel starring the same troupe of young actors. To some it seemed like Ronnie's heart
was no longer in the courtship, adrift from the fissionable chemistry so
obvious on their previous set. Perhaps her marriage-mindedness got too
real for him once her divorce from Myron Futterman was finalized, on December 5, 1938. On *Brother Rat*, Ronnie had nicknamed her "Button Nose,"
as an endearment. This time around, observers noticed that that nickname
had been downgraded to "good scout."

Reagan might simply have been distracted. Politics was claiming more
and more of his attention. Even in Hollywood, the darkening world situation was an unavoidable concern.

While *Brother Rat and a Baby* edged into production in late 1939, Germany invaded Poland, plunging Europe into war. Would the crisis give FDR
the impetus to run for an unprecedented third term? Would he, should he,
involve America in the conflict? As a loyal Democrat and avowed pacifist,
Reagan was consumed by the drama. He pored through the newspapers
each day, arming himself with an arsenal of facts to justify his political
opinions. "Ronnie always had a cause," said Leon Ames. "And he loved to
talk." He was a font of knowledge and information offered generously,
whether requested or not. Some considered him a know-it-all, a nuisance.
He held fellow actors captive during the long stretches of downtime on the
set. "This time appeared to represent a splendid opportunity for serious social discourse," recalled Larry Williams, "a chance to express his animated

views on an infinite variety of subjects to us." Williams, who worked on five movies with Ronnie, acknowledged that the novelty soon wore out its welcome. The worst that could befall you as an actor during camera setups and rehearsals, he said, was to have Ronald Reagan sit down next to you, push on a pair of oversized glasses, spread out a sheaf of notes, and launch into one of Professor Reagan's rambling discourses from which there was no escape. "When we were released around noontime to walk over to the studio commissary, the thing got to be to see who could come in last—or at any rate behind Ronnie." It gave them a chance to scope out where he'd be sitting so as to eat undisturbed, "in amiable but total silence."

If in general his colleagues were far from appreciative, Reagan did have a small, eager band of political sparring partners. Jane Bryan's boyfriend, a retailer named Justin Dart, looked forward to going head-to-head with Ronnie. Dart was from the opposite end of the political spectrum. His expertise lay in economics, and his conservative approach to all things financial began to chip away at Ronnie's New Deal resolve. Theirs was the kind of heated give-and-take that Ronald Reagan thrived on; Justin Dart provided it for the next forty years.

Ronnie also went at it with Dick Powell. They'd already appeared in a number of movies together and enjoyed a casual friendship, occasionally playing golf and double-dating. Powell was one of the few actors—and even fewer Hollywood Republicans—who regularly engaged him in political debate. "Arguing politics drew them together," June Allyson, Powell's wife, wrote in her autobiography. The two men's views were light-years apart. Powell hewed vehemently to the Republican Party line and spent countless hours attempting to convert Ronnie, warning him about the manipulation of left-wing radicals. It was futile. "I was a loyal New Deal Democrat," Ronald Reagan recalled. "I always believed that all of this left-wing talk was Republican propaganda."

Ronnie could always count on Jack when in need of support. His father might have lost a step or two as a result of the stroke, but he continued to be a liberal firebrand. Politics was the one issue that never failed to invigorate. If anything, the move to California gave Jack Reagan a prominent soapbox. In Los Angeles, unlike Dixon, he was surrounded by Democrats who were willing to listen to his fiery rhetoric, and who gave support to a president who was worshipped unconditionally.

Ronnie had moved out of the hotel in Hollywood to a snug cottage on a lovely palm-lined street just north of Sunset Boulevard, within proximity to his parents. The day was rare that he didn't visit. He'd stop by their place on his way home from the studio to fill them in on his work on the set as well as to keep tabs on his fan mail. Since *Brother Rat*'s release, the requests for autographed photos had swelled. Rather than handling the chore of responding to them himself, he created a job for Jack, who bemoaned his inability to do meaningful work. As a result, Jack made weekly trips to Warner Bros. where he interacted with the mail department and drew a steady if nominal paycheck.

Frequently, Ronnie would bring Jane Wyman along on his visits, which might have been a miscalculation. She had never come to terms with being abandoned by her own parents, and Reagan's closeness to his generated complicated emotions. "Ronnie had this wonderful relationship with his mother," Wyman said. "I sensed it. I wanted to have a part of it."

Marriage would seal the deal, but Ronnie was in no hurry to make the commitment. The former husbands, the unquenchable thirst for nightlife, the impulsiveness, the unrelenting drive, the *neediness* conspired to keep him at bay. For all the body heat he generated, Ronald Reagan was basically a down-to-earth man. Some friends questioned whether they were suited for each other. "She was so experienced, hard-boiled, intense, and passionate," observed an intimate of Jane's, who thought Ronnie "was so pragmatic . . . rather a square . . . a little earthbound" for her. Even Louella Parsons found Jane "so nervous and tense" compared with "steady, solid, decent young Ronnie." Leaping into marriage seemed loaded with risk.

Jane claimed he eventually gave in, proposing on the set of *Brother Rat and a Baby*. In fact, evidence points to a different scenario. Their relationship had reached an intractable impasse. Jane couldn't stand it any longer, at which point she performed the ultimate act of desperation. As principal photography on the movie concluded, the Hollywood trades announced on October 4, 1939, that she had suffered the recurrence of an old "stomach disorder" and was hospitalized. It was the kind of vague press release that studios put out about stars to conceal a more serious disorder, like a breakdown—or worse. Years later, Nancy Reagan disclosed that Jane threatened to kill herself if Ronnie didn't marry her—and followed through by taking a stash of pills and leaving a suicide note to explain. At the hospital, she refused to see him. This tactic had the desired effect. The next day, he returned and demanded entry to her room. By the time he left, they were officially engaged.

W arner Bros. press-managed the marriage announcement. Louella Parsons was given the scoop, but she put off revealing it for another few months until her own plans were finalized. She had talked Warner Bros. into underwriting a traveling variety show—*Hollywood Stars of 1940 on Parade*—which would feature six of the studio's most promising contract players in a series of skits, and was designed as a starring vehicle for Parsons. There was plenty of groundwork yet to be laid—whittling down the cast, writing a script, booking an itinerary that would take them across the country. In the interim, she dropped hints in her column that "two of Hollywood's very nicest young people" were heading to the altar. The studio had already put out word that Ronnie had been "wooing the blonde Miss Wyman" and had given her a fifty-two-carat amethyst ring, leaving little doubt as to who Parsons's mystery couple might be.

In any case, Jane and Ronnie's presence would give her show the requisite sparkle. They were announced for the cast, along with actresses Susan Hayward, June Preisser, and Arleen Whelan. Joy Hodges was also recruited to provide musical relief. The focal point, however, was Louella's column, which would be "dictated" by her and "filed" live each night from a Teletype machine that was rolled onstage. Of course, it was so much hokum; the Teletype was a nonfunctioning prop, as was the telephone she used to "interview" Charlie Chaplin and Claudette Colbert. Her coup de théâtre would be the revelation that the two lovebirds, Jane Wyman and Ronald Reagan, were engaged.

Parsons took the show to Santa Barbara for a tryout, then moved the company to San Francisco, where subtle tensions surfaced among the cast. Jane's sonar picked up vibrations between Ronnie and Susan Hayward during a corny skit they mugged their way through, flinging her into a jealous funk. The discord didn't help the company's performance, which local critics found overly long and lackluster. It took everything Ronnie could muster to pacify Jane. He showered her with attention, teaching her his Eureka College songs, which they sang in harmony on buses transporting them to the theaters. On the trip east, during a terrifying plane ride—Ronnie's first—in which they were forced down in a blinding snowstorm, he comforted a distraught Jane Wyman, despite his own deepening dread, a dread that kept him off airplanes for the next twenty-seven years.

Once Jane's insecurity was neutralized, the show hit its stride. On Ronnie's first visit east, in Pittsburgh, Philadelphia, and New York, the actors played to sold-out audiences and were mobbed at the stage doors for autographs and photos. Ronnie found his footing as the troupe's amiable emcee, playing straight man to his various co-stars. His facility onstage seemed effortless, his charm infectious. He had a real gift for connecting with an audience that proved more potent in person than on a movie screen. He was obviously more comfortable playing himself than burrowing into the inner lives of fictional characters. Too often, he disappeared in a picture, unable to capture sustained emotions. He couldn't convey the necessary temperament that superior acting required. It was an entirely different story onstage, where he communicated an affability that was honest, and appreciated.

As 1939 drew to a close, the *Hollywood Stars* revue rolled into Washington, D.C., and Ronald Reagan got his first look at the nation's capital. To Ronnie's starry eye, Washington was still a city that symbolized the spirit of American democracy and national identity. He could feel it emanate from the rock-solid landmarks that set off the skyline—the awe-inspiring monuments to his boyhood heroes George Washington and Abraham Lincoln, and the White House itself, venerable home of his idol, Franklin D. Roosevelt.

Politics was very much on his mind. The papers had been full of reports that week about Finland's "stout resistance" to an attempted Soviet invasion and how Russian planes had dropped leaflets urging the Finns to rebel against their leaders "and join your Russian friends." During interviews with the Washington dailies that had been set up to publicize the show, Finland and politics-politics-politics was all Ronnie could talk about. "He did not always pick his spots to expound on such knowledge," Joy Hodges recalled. Louella Parsons seethed as he frittered away her moment in the spotlight.

Being in Washington captivated Ronnie. In between six days of shows at the Capitol Theater, with Jane and Joy in tow, he headed to Mount Vernon, to visit George Washington's homestead. "He was eager to absorb as much as possible about the history," Hodges recalled. He seemed particularly fascinated by Washington's rolltop desk. It was a magnificent piece—a *bureau à cylinder*–style console of mahogany and pine with maple inlay. Ronnie stood in front of it for an inordinate amount of time, "practically salivating over it." Jane also took note and decided to surprise him with a replica for a wedding gift.

The big day was drawing close. The tour officially ended on January 14, 1940, with the ceremony set for January 26. After an exhausting four-day train ride back to Los Angeles, there was little time left to finalize arrangements. No sooner had they set foot back in town than Warner Bros. seizing the chance to make hay of the marriage, slapped Ronnie and Jane into a paper-thin movie, announcing that "they'll be husband and wife for the first time in . . . *Angel from Texas*." Warner was doing them no favors. The vehicle was a tired, old warhorse—George S. Kaufman's 1925 Broadway farce *The Butter and Egg Man*—dusted off and re-saddled for the fourth time by the studio. (It had been made as *The Tenderfoot* in 1932, *Hello, Sweetheart* in 1935, and again as *Dance Charlie Dance* in 1937.) Most of the cast of *Brother Rat* was reassembled in the hope of making it a familiar, more audience-friendly movie, but nothing could salvage it.

In the meantime, the wedding came together with stunning swiftness. Louella Parsons stage-managed the affair, ensuring she'd have access to all the behind-the-scenes details. She even maneuvered her husband into giving the bride away and arranged for a gala reception following the ceremony at her house. Otherwise Jane and Ronnie opted to keep the chapel service small. Only their immediate families and a few close friends were invited to attend the rites at the Wee Kirk o' the Heather Church in Glendale, where Bill Cook, one of Ronnie's Drake College pals, stood in as best man. Jane, in a pale-blue satin gown and matching sable muff and hat borrowed from the studio's wardrobe department, stole the show, as expected. She was "beautiful beyond dreams," according to a guest—and visibly assured, optimistic, radiant. There was no trace of the awful insecurity or desperation that had plagued her earlier, no residue from the two hasty marriages that were over practically before they'd begun. "Third time's a charm," her appearance seemed to convey as she stood for pictures next to her dashing husband. They looked every inch the movie stars destined for a happy ending.

"Theirs is the perfect marriage," Louella Parsons gushed in print the next day. Not everyone saw it that way. "I hope my Ronald has made the right choice," worried Nelle Reagan in a letter to a Dixon friend. "I was in hopes he would fall in love with some sweet girl who is not in the movies."

No such luck, not in Hollywood, where the girl always gets her man.

CHAPTER TWELVE

"WHERE'S . . . WHERE'S THE REST OF ME?"

"Talk about a dream, try to make it real."

—BRUCE SPRINGSTEEN, "Badlands"

The movie business was a disconcerting dance. Every picture seemed to take Ronald Reagan one step forward followed by two steps back. His admirers saw the advances as part of a progression, moves up a ladder, that eventually led to stardom. Others, like Hal Wallis, who ran the Warner Bros. production line, felt that Reagan "was not an actor of depth or intensity," and was more suited to trivial adventure yarns and light romantic comedies. Each time Reagan edged close to prestige, as he did with fifth billing in *Dark Victory* opposite Bette Davis and Humphrey Bogart, he followed with a clunker, reprising Brass Bancroft or playing off the Dead End Kids. Rightly or wrongly, he'd been typecast as a lightweight. Even the relative acclaim that greeted *Brother Rat* hadn't been enough to raise his status. An actor's success was measured by the strength of upcoming projects on his schedule. "When you were struggling for recognition they only put you in the B's," recalls Olivia de Havilland. "As soon as you made an impact in one or two, the scripts they offered got measurably better, which meant you'd graduated to the A list. If you registered there, you had it made." De Havilland says that Ronnie "generated so much good will by his affability that everyone wanted him to make an impression in an important film." But good will didn't count in the Warner Bros. executive suite. When he and

Jane returned from their Palm Springs honeymoon, the studio played them up as "romantic young marrieds," but stuck them in a pair of inconsequential retreads—him in *Murder in the Air*, her in *Flight Angels*, and both in *Tugboat Annie Sails Again*. Ronnie determined to take matters into his own hands. He always felt that the right dramatic story would deliver a breakthrough role and that it might ultimately fall to him to track one down. From the moment he joined the Warner Bros. roster, he began waging an intense, unfaltering campaign to convince Bryan Foy that the saga of football hero Knute Rockne was worth a major feature. Foy never responded one way or the other, but shortly before his wedding Ronnie spotted an announcement in *Variety* that Warner Bros. was putting *The Life of Knute Rockne* into production, with Pat O'Brien in the title role.

Reagan felt he'd been had, but he also sensed an opportunity. There was a plum part for him in that story, not the title role of the Notre Dame coach, but that of George Gipp, the legendary all-American halfback who died of a throat infection at the age of twenty-five just days after leading the Fighting Irish to a win over Northwestern. Rockne used the apocryphal story of Gipp, with his deathbed line—"win just one for the Gipper"—to fire up his team in an improbable victory against Army in 1928. Ronnie knew that playing Gipp could steal the show. Never mind that George Gipp was a reprobate who drank, smoked, hustled pool, rarely practiced with the team, bet on Notre Dame games, and was expelled from the university for misconduct. In the movie version, he'd be a saint.

Unfortunately, Hal Wallis wanted no part of Ronald Reagan. In truth, he wasn't thrilled about Pat O'Brien, either. Casting the picture had proved nothing but a headache. Wallis always envisioned Spencer Tracy in the role of Rockne, but Tracy was under contract to MGM, which refused all entreaties to loan him out. James Cagney had been the studio's second choice, but the good fathers of Notre Dame balked. Cagney, the studio's spokesman argued, portrayed too many roles of "the gangster type," which would cast a pall over St. Knute, to say nothing of its opposition to Cagney's support of "the Loyalist Cause" in Spain. Pat O'Brien was a perfectly inoffensive substitute, which Warner Bros. reluctantly agreed to support, pretty certain "we could get those double chins off and knock ten or fifteen years off his looks."

Ronald Reagan was a harder sell. He'd never been on Wallis's radar. For

Gipp, Wallis had already rejected John Wayne, Robert Cummings, Robert Young, and William Holden, all certified stars, but not his idea of football players. Scripts were out to Dennis Morgan and Donald Woods, both beefier, more rugged specimens. A plea to Bryan Foy landed Ronnie in Wallis's office. This time, he came prepared with props—college photos of him in uniform as a Eureka College Golden Tornado. Grudgingly, Wallis agreed to shoot a test.

He needed no further convincing after screening clips of Ronnie, Morgan, and Woods, each competing in a scrimmage scene with O'Brien. It was clear from the outset that Ronald Reagan was a much more plausible football player, and he had Gipp down cold.

Winning the role was a turning point for Ronnie. And other things were falling into place, too. As of April 11, 1940, the day *Knute Rockne, All-American* began production on location at Loyola University, he was comfortably resettled into Jane's spacious apartment with a view of Los Angeles practically to the ocean. His brother, Neil, had moved to the city, and true to form, Ronnie got him work, bit parts in *Tugboat Annie Sails Again* and an Edward G. Robinson vehicle called *Destroyer*. In addition, Ronnie's Warner Bros. contract was being renegotiated, this time with more muscle. Only a month earlier, he had been notified that Bill Meiklejohn's agency had been absorbed into MCA—the powerful Music Corporation of America—which meant he would henceforth be represented by Lew Wasserman, a twenty-seven-year-old power broker whose furtive, low-key manner, it was said, was similar to a panther's that purred before it struck.

Being a client of MCA signaled a huge step forward. The agency had changed the way entertainment business was conducted. It already represented more than half of the big bands in the country, using tactics that some viewed as unethical. A pact with the American Federation of Musicians' union boss, James Petrillo, prevented competing agencies from obtaining licenses to operate, giving MCA a virtual monopoly of the business. The agency also received a pass to sidestep union rules prohibiting it from acting as both agent and radio production company—an obvious conflict of interest—thus allowing MCA to package a program from top to bottom with only its clients for as much as 30 percent of the profit. Rumors of mob influence were rife.

By 1937, MCA had spread its tentacles to motion pictures and landed

Bette Davis, just nominated for her second Best Actress Oscar, as its first nonmusical client. Her stamp of approval touched off a wave of movie-star signings that included Joan Crawford, John Garfield, Betty Grable, Errol Flynn, Barbara Stanwyck, and Jane Wyman. The agency pushed to get bigger fast. By signing up the most important names in Hollywood, it could put the same squeeze on studios that it had on ballroom owners. To strengthen its roster, MCA began raiding smaller agencies or, like Meiklejohn's, gobbling them up whole. Within eight years MCA represented practically a third of all Hollywood stars, including directors and producers, and had earned the nickname "the Octopus."

The agency's power delivered immediately for the Reagans. Jane, who was earning a pitiful $500 a week in trifles like *Gambling on the High Seas* and *Honeymoon for Three*, won a new three-year contract, with guarantees of $1,500 a week, escalating to $2,500. Ronnie's was an even better deal. On August 25, 1940, based on favorable word of mouth from *Knute Rockne* previews, Wasserman renegotiated a contract that would bring him $2,750 a week. For the newlyweds, it was a king's ransom.

Warner Bros. was betting on Ronnie's brightening luster. A week after seeing the finished print of *Knute Rockne*, they sent him the script for *Santa Fe Trail*. The movie, a Civil War adventure, had been conceived as a vehicle for its indisputable superstar, Errol Flynn. From his debut as the title character in *Captain Blood* in 1935, Flynn had emerged as an overnight sensation. Young, virile, and dashing, he gave off the kind of electricity few actors could match on the screen. He was a great physical presence, what critics call a "camera actor." In scene after scene, the camera loved him, as much for his charisma as his ability to wear costumes. How many male actors could strut around in tights, as Flynn did, in *The Adventures of Robin Hood*, and not get laughed off the screen? When he made his entrance in that movie with a deer slung over his shoulder, knocking people out of the way, the effect was hypnotic. It was impossible for the audience to take its eyes off the man. Ronnie considered him "a magnificent piece of machinery." Such flash came with a prodigious ego. Flynn was notoriously difficult—and arrogant. He refused to eat lunch with his fellow actors in the Green Room of the commissary, insisting on a seat at Jack Warner's table in an adjacent private dining room. He often holed up in his cushy bungalow on the lot, draining its well-stocked bar. His drinking binges and incessant lateness drove Warner crazy. During the filming of *The Adventures of Don Juan*, for example, Flynn grabbed co-star Robert Douglas and said, "On Saturday, let's go out on my boat"—and neither man showed up on the set until the following Wednesday. His misbehavior created enormous headaches for the studio, but none of that mattered, because Flynn's movies were blockbusters. Putting Ronald Reagan in *Santa Fe Trail* as a follow-up to *Rockne* was a calculated tactic. It would enhance his career to play opposite Flynn.

It also paired Ronnie with a first-class director in Michael Curtiz. One of Jack Warner's trophy European imports, the Hungarian had distinguished himself in the silent era with his deft, expressive camera work. He was a master of montage and loved chiaroscuro, most expertly demonstrated in his silent spectacle *Noah's Ark*. Some critics considered his direction of *The Charge of the Light Brigade* a masterpiece of action photography. "He loved motion and exciting scenes," says the film professor Alan Spiegel, "everything except developing the emotional life of a character." Later, during the filming of *Casablanca*, Curtiz made that sentiment perfectly clear. "Who cares about character?" he announced between scenes. "I make it go so fast nobody notices."

Actors were not Curtiz's cup of tea. "He was a bully," says de Havilland, who worked with Curtiz in four previous pictures before being cast in *Santa Fe Trail*. "He was rude, caustic, abusive, and we all dreaded working with him. Besides, he had no regard for actors or their craft." His battles with actors were legendary. Though he worked with Bette Davis in five Warner Bros. films, he dismissed her as a "goddamned nothing, no-good sexless son of a bitch." And he butted heads consistently with Errol Flynn. They had already made seven pictures together, including *Robin Hood* and *The Prince and the Pauper*. It didn't help matters that Flynn was married to Lili Damita, Curtiz's ex-wife.

To add to the volatility on the set of *Santa Fe Trail*, the script was a mess. It was a story about John Brown that couldn't make its mind up about slavery. Early on, Brown's abolitionist crusade is portrayed as just, but later he's presented as a demented fanatic and assassin who has to be destroyed. Van Heflin, who plays an abolitionist, is inexplicably the villain in the piece. And the central friendship between General J. E. B. Stuart, played by Flynn, and George Armstrong Custer, a dashing Ronnie sans the traditional

Custer beard and mustache, is more than a bit preposterous, considering the two men never met and were adversaries in the Civil War. The casting had itself ignited controversy. John Wayne initially agreed to play Custer, but he backed out after reading the script. Soon afterward, the studio announced that Wayne Morris, a highly regarded member of its stock company, had assumed the role. Once the *Knute Rockne* previews were seen, however, Morris was summarily replaced by Ronnie, which sowed little goodwill on the set. No one, least of all Errol Flynn, was happy.

"Flynn saw Ronnie as a threat," de Havilland recalls. "They were both strapping, incredibly handsome men, but one was the star and the other was gaining ground on him." She describes a publicity photo shoot that was scheduled between scenes, in which Flynn's Confederate troops were to be lined up around him. "Ronnie was centered behind and above him in the second row," de Havilland says. "Flynn noticed the placement and huddled with the director, who saw to it that the area was leveled. When the company was called together again for the actual shooting of the picture, Ronnie [noted] the change right away and quietly and inconspicuously began shifting the earth with his feet, forming a mound. Seconds before the photo was taken, he mounted that small knoll, his head rising above Mr. Flynn's."

Most of the scenes for the movie were shot on location at the Warner Ranch, a rural 2,300-acre spread of rolling hills and oak trees in Calabasas, where Harry Warner raised thoroughbreds and where the studio had constructed western sets and a facsimile Mexican town. *The Adventures of Robin Hood* and *The Charge of the Light Brigade* had done principal photography there. *Juarez*, with Paul Muni and Bette Davis, had just finished production.

From the outset, problems arose with Flynn. According to de Havilland, "Flynn repeatedly showed up hours late for outdoor night shooting, prolonging our work until sunrise." The actors joined forces to register a formal complaint with the company's union representative, Ronald Reagan, who was reluctant to take on the star. "Ronnie asked me to speak to Flynn on his behalf, figuring Flynn would not respect him. And he was right. Plus, there was too much rivalry. So the dirty work was left to me."

It was a rare instance of Ronnie backing down from a position he relished and took seriously. From 1938 through the summer of 1940, he'd acted as the designated union monitor on each picture he made, not only advocating on behalf of his fellow actors but promoting the Screen Actors Guild itself, an outfit he considered "a damned noble organization" that was instrumental in adjusting the balance of power in Hollywood at a time when actors had no rights.

Before SAG's formation in 1933, most movie actors toiled in conditions not unlike workers on a sweatshop assembly line. Not the stars, the actors whose marquee value gave them leverage, but the segment known industrywide as "day players," the almost 90 percent of the acting community who earned fifteen dollars for one day's work, which is about all they worked each week, if they were lucky. "There was a caste system at the studios," says de Havilland. Actors of her stature were protected by contracts, which limited the number of hours they worked and guaranteed livable salaries. Most, however, were on their own and subject to the whim of the owners. Freelance actors hired for a movie were on call twenty-four hours a day, seven days a week, often for weeks on end, but only got paid for the few hours they worked. There was no overtime, no compensation for late nights or travel. And they could be terminated at any time, without reason or means of relief.

The owners rule was all-powerful—despotic. At a meeting of the producers' association in early 1933, Louis B. Mayer and his head of production, Irving Thalberg, suggested "non-raiding" agreements between the studios to force actors to remain where they were. Only producer B. P. Schulberg spoke out against it, saying, "You know we had a war to solve that. It was called the Civil War and it freed the slaves."

The first shots were fired in March 1933, when the studios, feeling the pinch of the Depression, notified all actors making more than fifty dollars a week that they'd be taking a 50 percent pay cut. Actors earning less would be docked 25 percent. Without any recourse, the actors caved in. They'd attempted to organize before and were blacklisted for their efforts. This time, a cell of six actors met in secret at the home of Kenneth and Alden Gay Thomson to sow the seeds of a self-governing union. Papers of incorporation for the Screen Actors Guild were filed on June 30, 1933.

Studios threatened all kinds of repercussions, but the biggest stars rushed to the rescue. James Cagney, Cary Grant, Harpo Marx, Walter Pidgeon, Dick Powell, Joan Crawford, Boris Karloff, and half a dozen others signed their names to the guild charter, providing the actors with a wall of invincibility. "We were all from different studios and hadn't ever *met* each other," de Havilland recalls. "This brought us together in a powerful way." That exclusive star-studded committee had a snowball effect; by the end of the year, most of the industry superstars had pledged.

Still, the studios refused to surrender. It took another four years, and the threat of a strike, before they agreed to a union shop. But as of 1937, all actors were required to join SAG, a stipulation that at first bugged new Warner Bros. employee Ronald Reagan. He resented being forced to join a union and paying its quarterly dues of $7.50. It took an elderly silent-film actress named Helen Broderick to set him straight. He recalled how "she nailed me in a corner of the commissary . . . after I made a crack about having to join a union, and gave me an hour's lecture on the facts of life." He'd never realized the degree to which the studios had exploited its day players, the deplorable working conditions imposed on its ranks before collective bargaining took hold. Jack also helped to bring him around. His father was a flag bearer for workingmen's rights. But by the time he met Jane Wyman, Ronald Reagan's conversion was complete.

Jane Wyman was an active member of the Screen Actors Guild, "a good, solid board member," as she was recalled, "a hard worker, but not a leader." As far as leaders went, Jane told her fellow board members as early as 1938 that she "knew a guy who really had a lot on the ball," an actor she was dating named Ronald Reagan, who would be a valuable addition to their group. In fact, the way she introduced him—"I want you to meet the man who will one day be president of the Screen Actors Guild, and you're going to be delighted"—struck Jack Dales, the board's executive secretary, as a bit much. Nonetheless, Ronnie made an impression. Later, Dales would acknowledge, "Jane Wyman wasn't wrong. From the very start . . . one knew that he was in the presence of a fairly extraordinary man in terms of his ability to negotiate and to deal with union terms." Ronnie was a very quick study. His oratorical ability, coupled with strong social and political convictions—that attracted immediate attention. "Actors much better known and obviously more successful," Dales said, "accorded Ronnie tremendous respect from the beginning."

Again and again, he was nominated to be the guild's monitor—the actors' rep—on the sets of his films. He didn't mind standing up to management and had a way of airing grievances that didn't alienate them. According to an observer, "He seemed to enjoy the challenge."

Ronnie was settling into his skin. For the first time since he arrived in Hollywood, he was being taken seriously. He was married to an actress of great promise, his movies were garnering critical notice, and he was routinely being mentioned for projects earmarked for A-list stars. In a 1940 year-end wrap-up, *Variety* named him Warner Bros.' top contract player, which followed on the heels of a Louella Parsons announcement that "the whole country is getting Reagan conscious." The right movie, he knew, could catapult him onto the same plane as Pat O'Brien and Dick Powell, maybe even Errol Flynn. For a man who'd come west three years earlier with next to nothing, the view was promising indeed.

The year 1941 began and ended with a bang, with tremors reverberating from pole to pole.

Four days after celebrating the new year, Jane gave birth to a five-and-a-half-pound girl they named Maureen Elizabeth. According to Ronnie, Jane had begun campaigning for a baby practically from the day they were married. "I wanted one, too," he said to a reporter, "but I used all my male logic to persuade her that every young couple ought to wait a year. She agreed I was right as usual and she was wrong. So we had a baby."

Convinced it was going to be a boy, they printed up a humorous military birth announcement for "General Ronald Reagan Jr.," a play on Ronnie's upcoming role in *Flight Patrol* (released as *International Squadron*). Jane made no bones about her initial disappointment. "I wanted a boy," she admitted in a sulky postpartum moment. But she recovered quickly, and they both doted on their daughter, Maureen.

For a while, the Reagans fashioned a nursery in a vacant apartment adjoining their own, but they outgrew it almost from the outset. The apartment simply wasn't conducive to raising a child. Within weeks, they purchased a lovely plot of land on a secluded side street high in the hills above Sunset Boulevard. They would build from scratch. But—what? Not a palatial Hollywood "manse," as the trades called sprawling movie-star estates.

Not one of the gaudy Spanish-style villas or Norman chateaus that begged for envy in exclusive Beverly Hills. It had to be tasteful, a place where they could entertain but still be comfortable, livable, *modest*, something that reflected their current status. Ronnie, a stickler for budgets, was determined to economize. "We don't want to go out on a limb," he cautioned his wife.

Keeping house plans modest seemed like an impossible task. Their social circle—the Dick Powells and Jack Bennys—lived like pashas, with screening rooms and cabanas overlooking Mediterranean tiled pools. Stars were tempted to live up to their fairy-tale existences, but the Reagans struggled to stay low-key. That meant keeping things under control. For several months they pored over and rejected plans that made no sense, financial or otherwise. One night, while Nelle and Jack babysat Maureen, Ronnie and Jane slipped out to the movies and saw *This Thing Called Love*, a lowbrow comedy with Rosalind Russell and Melvyn Douglas. The couple in the film had little chemistry, but Jane couldn't take her eyes off their house. The layout was *exactly* what she wanted. "Next morning, we dashed over to Columbia [Pictures] and got the plans," she recalled. The house itself was a fairly middle-class affair: seven sun-washed rooms that included an open living room–den configuration, featuring built-in bookshelves on either side of a brick fireplace, three bedrooms, dressing areas for each of the movie stars, and a shaded flagstone patio fronting a breathtaking sweep of lawn with plantings that afforded plenty of privacy. Scaling back and counting pennies as they compromised, revised plans, then revised again, the house came in at an affordable $15,000. With a twenty-year government-backed mortgage, their monthly payment was a manageable $125.

Now more than ever, they swore to a budget. Ronnie continued to shoulder his parents' living expenses and Jane had gone overboard furnishing the house. Fortunately, however, neither was a spendthrift. Their impoverished childhoods remained a strong part of who they were, making them conscious of every dollar they spent. They pledged to adhere to strict allowances: no more than twenty-five dollars each per week.

Their finances took on more significance as the months passed and their respective careers suffered a series of setbacks. Jane had gotten side-tracked by "putting wifehood and motherhood first," while overseeing the house construction. Even though she'd gone swiftly back to work, the studio stuck her in a series of slapdash B's—*Honeymoon for Three*, *Bad Men of Missouri*, *The Body Disappears*, and *You're in the Army Now*. "I was twenty-seven years old, had been in films for nine years, and felt like a total beginner," she complained. Ronnie's career slid in the same sorry direction. After the promise of *Knute Rockne*, a superficial film like *International Squadron* did him no favors, nor did *The Bad Man* or the silly, slender *Million Dollar Baby*.

And the quality of the parts coming their way increasingly seemed like the least of their worries. America was on the verge of war. Western Europe had fallen into Nazi hands with horrifying swiftness. Hungary and Romania had joined the Axis. Japan was on the move. Up to now, America had remained assiduously neutral, but that was about to change. On October 29, 1940, FDR, poised for an unprecedented third term in office, ordered the first peacetime military draft in U.S. history. Defying widespread isolationist sentiment, in March 1941 Congress authorized FDR's Lend-Lease program to aid England, which was a virtual declaration of war against Germany.

In its way, Hollywood had already been at war for several years. Jewish studio chiefs and writers had mobilized in early 1936 to assess how best to respond to Nazi Germany's mounting anti-Semitism. The consensus among executives was to keep their heads down. "I don't think Hollywood should deal with anything but entertainment," declared Paramount Pictures founder Adolph Zukor. "To make films of political significance is a mistake." The writers, on the other hand, were ready to roll out the heavy artillery: scripts laced with snarling Nazi villains. It was a standoff.

No one side could make a move without the approval of a man named Joseph Breen, who reigned over the Production Code Administration—the form of moralistic self-censorship that the studios had adopted in 1934. Breen read every script before it went into production and adjudicated what would and would not be tolerated on the screen; anything he personally found unsuitable or intolerable could close down a picture. Unfortunately, Breen often deemed a misdirected wink to be salacious—and he was a raging anti-Semite. In a letter to a friend, he wrote that he worked with "people whose daily morals would not be tolerated in the toilet of a pest house. . . . Ninety-five percent of these folks are Jews of Eastern European lineage. They are, probably, the scum of the scum of the earth." Breen saw nothing objectionable in Adolf Hitler's mistreatment of Jews, and he warned the studios not to overtly criticize Nazi Germany.

By 1939, Warner Bros. had had enough. The studio's Berlin rep, Joe Kauffman, had been beaten to death by Nazi thugs. According to Jack Warner, "There are high school kids with swastikas on their sleeves a few crummy blocks from our studio." He had already caved in to Breen's demand that *The Life of Emile Zola* not mention that Captain Dreyfus was a Jew. No more. In 1939, Warner Bros. defied the Production Code and released *Confessions of a Nazi Spy*. It opened the floodgates, and pictures like *The Great Dictator, Night Train to Munich, Sergeant York,* and *Foreign Correspondent* followed in its wake.

Actors were eager to do their parts. In late 1938, fifty-six stars, along with the Warners, formed the Committee of 56, calling for a boycott of all German products until that country stopped persecuting Jews and minorities. Fredric March pleaded for ambulances for Spain; Joan Crawford denounced the invasion of Ethiopia. Some of the biggest names in Hollywood committed to movies that enabled them "to combine entertainment and larger implications that 'point up' social aspects and encourage awareness."

As immersed as he was in current events, the closest Ronald Reagan came to supporting the cause directly was his role as a brash American fighter pilot who joins the RAF in *International Squadron*. His wake-up call came on February 9, 1941, when an envelope arrived with his induction notice. As an officer in the cavalry reserves, which he'd joined back in Iowa, Ronnie's name was on the draft board's radar. He was thirty years old, in great physical shape. Of course, he was severely nearsighted and he had dependents; in the event of war, there was no chance he'd see action. Still, Jack Warner wasn't taking any chances with his prize asset. A rough cut of *International Squadron* reinforced Warner's notion that Ronnie might have real star appeal. Warner petitioned the Army for a deferment, which gave the studio time to develop his career.

Warner Bros. owned a property that might well be a suitable star vehicle for Reagan. In 1940, it had acquired the rights to *Kings Row*, a florid bestseller by Henry Bellamann, for $35,000, seven times what it had offered for *Gone with the Wind*. The book had all the components for a ripsnorter—a dark and complex coming-of-age story that explored love, friendship, treachery, sadism, homosexuality, and scandal in a rural Midwestern town. Those same elements posed a number of problems. "As far as the plot is concerned, the material in *Kings Row* is for the most part either censurable or too gruesome and depressing to be used," Wolfgang Reinhardt, the film's associate producer, wrote in a memo to Hal Wallis. "The hero finding out that his girl has been carrying on incestuous relations with her father, a sadistic doctor who amputates legs and disfigures people willfully, a host of moronic or otherwise mentally diseased characters, the background of a lunatic asylum, people dying from cancer, suicides . . ." He went on, raising a litany of objections.

They'd surely give Good Joe Breen a stroke. Even before a script was finalized, Breen notified Warner Bros. that his Production Code office would ban any attempt to make a film of *Kings Row*. "Any suggestion of sex, madness, syphilis, illegal operations, incest, sadism, all must go," Breen insisted. "If this picture is made . . . decent people everywhere will condemn you and Hollywood." Conditions he set for reversing his decision—slicing out every aspect of the book's central core—would have turned it into an Andy Hardy movie. Over time, Breen used the Production Code to reject four drafts of the script. Warner Bros. persisted, hiring director Sam Wood, who had recently scored a hit with *Kitty Foyle* at RKO, then whittled down a wish list of male and female megastars to four or five viable contract players. After Hal Wallis viewed the dailies for *International Squadron*, he cast Ronnie as Drake McHugh, the gadabout sidekick—and unrequited love interest—to both male and female protagonists. Billed as the studio's lead picture for 1941, *Kings Row* promised to be the opportunity Reagan had yearned for.

Before production got the go-ahead from Jack Warner, the studio sent Ronnie and Jane to several cities along the East Coast as part of a promotional "Bad Men" tour—he for *The Bad Man* in general release, she for the upcoming *Bad Men of Missouri*. While they were away, on May 18, Jack Reagan suffered another heart attack in the early hours of the morning. Nelle called for an ambulance, then dialed Neil, who rushed over with his wife, Bess, from a few blocks away. Jack was unconscious when they arrived; they could tell his condition was critical. Over the next half hour, Jack's breathing began to labor. The wait for the ambulance was agonizing.

Little did they realize that Los Angeles ambulances were in the midst of a nasty turf battle that divvied up the city into exclusive districts. The ambulance Nelle called was dispatched from a nearby Beverly Hills hospital. "It got to the end of the district and realized the address was further on and turned around and went back, but didn't notify anyone," Ronald Reagan recalled. "So my mother, my brother and his wife waited there while my father died for an ambulance that was never coming." He had lived a hearty life, not an easy one, cursed by a condition beyond his control. Jack Reagan was fifty-seven years old.

At the funeral service, on May 21, 1941, Ronnie was surprised by the way he processed his grief. Thoughts of the past, of his father, loving but unreliable, mingled with thoughts of the present, of Jack's last days, seeking to compensate for his persistent misconduct. At the end, all the reckless spunk had gone out of him, replaced by something softer, sober, more spiritual. Ronnie felt it intensely as he stood in the chapel during the funeral of the loving but unsteady man who had turned his childhood into an odyssey of disorder and insecurity. "All of a sudden a wave of warmth came over me and it was almost as if he was telling me he was just fine," he recalled. "It was just so pronounced that I just had to believe something approaching the psychic had happened to me."

Ronnie took comfort that summer in his work on *Kings Row*. The picture finally went into production in mid-July 1941, with high expectations. Yes, the story was a loopy hodgepodge, especially after the script was disemboweled by the censors, but there was plenty that worked to Ronnie's advantage.

Jack Warner spared no expense to ensure the success of his pet project. The cast he'd assembled was first-rate. For the male lead, Parris Mitchell, they'd signed Robert Cummings, star of the 1939 hit *Three Smart Girls Grow Up* and already in rehearsal for two pictures at Universal: *It Started with Eve* opposite Deanna Durbin and Alfred Hitchcock's *Saboteur*. The love interest would be played by salty "Oomph Girl" Ann Sheridan, an audience favorite with whom Ronnie had co-starred in *Angels Wash Their*

Faces and who was announced for the eagerly awaited release *The Man Who Came to Dinner.* The supporting cast was packed with some of Hollywood's finest actors: Judith Anderson, Maria Ouspenskaya, Charles Coburn, Broadway stage trouper Betty Field, and the incomparable character actor Claude Rains.

Ronnie remembered the production for its "long, hard schedule" and a demanding role that "kind of wrung me out." An unforeseen treat was his opportunity to talk politics between takes with director Sam Wood and Bob Cummings. They would sit for hours, earnestly discussing the European war and the country's responsibility to the beleaguered Allies. Wood was a Republican and devoted isolationist. In the years that followed, he'd emerge as president of the Motion Picture Alliance for the Preservation of American Ideals, an organization of high-profile Hollywood conservatives whose manifesto declared: "In our special field of motion pictures, we resent the growing impression that this industry is made up of, and dominated by, Communists, radicals, and crackpots." Much of that feeling was expressed on the set of *Kings Row.* Provoked by Ronnie's liberal views, Wood more than held his own in their often fiery exchanges, while Cummings fanned the flames with his conservative asides.

Ronnie struggled to put that same heat into his performance. The movie's characters brimmed with Freudian tics and neuroses. As *Daily Variety* noted, "Most of the leading characters are mad." Drake McHugh, Reagan's character, was a deeply conflicted man. Unfortunately, Ronnie didn't have the technique to do the part justice; it was beyond him as an actor. He grappled awkwardly with sustained emotions. But he had enough intelligence and common sense to relate well to the camera, to play the affable best friend to a more competent actor. And he had the right mentor in Sam Wood, who was an actor's director.

Despite the insuperable demands of the role, Ronnie found his footing, so to speak, in a pivotal scene near the end of the movie in which Drake, having lost his inheritance and the chance to marry a doctor's daughter, endures an accident that crushes the lower part of his body. In an act of rank sadism, the spiteful, perverse doctor amputates both of his legs, a deed the book intends as symbolic castration. Ronnie's character awakes from the operation to utter perhaps the most memorable line of his movie career—"Where's . . . where's the rest of me?"

The scene unnerved Reagan. It was so extreme, so remote from any real experience he knew or could imagine, and yet he had to dig deeper and summon real emotion. "I felt I had neither the experience nor the talent to fake it," he recalled. "I simply had to find out how it really felt."

Where's the rest of me? Those five words weighed on him. He rehearsed them repeatedly, turned them inside out, discussed them with friends, consulted disabled patients. "At night I would wake up staring at the ceiling and automatically mutter the line before I went back to sleep," he said. As the day approached to shoot the scene, he was no closer to understanding it and recalled being panicked. It was too far out of his comfort zone.

His ordeal deepened when he arrived on the set. To present as a credible amputee, he had to lower his torso from the waist down through a hole that had been cut into a mattress, then lie back in bed, immobile. Nothing happens quickly on a movie set. Once they got him positioned, lights had to be moved, the camera angled properly, cables taped down, chalk marks scratched out for the actors, a sound check run. It took about an hour, while Ronnie lay there, sinking—and *sinking*—into the part. "Gradually, the affair began to terrify me," he said. His latent claustrophobia kicked in. "In some weird way, I felt something horrible had happened to my body." He broke into a sweat. Beneath the boyish good looks and L.A. tan, real fear appeared in creases around his mouth.

When they were ready to shoot the scene, Sam Wood positioned himself close by the bed. Ronald Reagan has given conflicting accounts of the action in two memoirs. In the earlier version, he begged for a rehearsal, which Wood ignored and just shot the scene cold. Later, in a postpresidential autobiography, Ronnie took it upon himself to whisper to the director, "No rehearsal—just shoot it." Whatever the case, what mattered was on the screen. When the impact of the accident finally sank in, a sick horror gripped him. His eyes rolled in their sockets, and his face froze in a rictus of despair.

"*Where's . . . where's the rest of me?*"

The line sent a charge through the Warner Bros. executive suite. When Jack Warner saw the dailies, he felt their impact was strong enough to deliver the breakthrough he'd envisioned for Ronald Reagan. Within hours, he called Lew Wasserman and opened negotiations for a new seven-year contract that would practically double the actor's salary. Warner also decided to get his money's worth while he could, ordering Ronnie to report to the set of a new film, *Juke Girl*, only three days after he'd wrapped *Kings Row*.

It was a grind making back-to-back features. He became a fixture on the lot for months on end, six days a week, often fourteen hours a day. "I began to feel like a shut-in invalid," he grumbled, "nursed by publicity." He spent the rest of the summer on the studio treadmill: filming and giving interviews. But rumblings about his performance cast a giddy effect on the workload. He could tell himself it was in the service of his career, or because he was irreplaceable, or because the older stars like Cagney and Muni were making way for contemporary, more embraceable faces. Whatever the reason, he accepted each new assignment confident the effort would put him over the top.

In fact, he'd gone as far as it would take him.

CHAPTER THIRTEEN

IN THE ARMY NOW

"I have done the state some service, and they know 't."

—WILLIAM SHAKESPEARE

No one ever mistook the Dixon Theater for Grauman's Egyptian. The solid, unprepossessing building just a block or two south of the Rock River was wedged between retail establishments near the foot of Galena Avenue. Except on weekends, when kids flocked to matinees and parents took a well-earned evening out, the sidewalk outside the doors was mostly deserted. But early on a Monday evening in September 1941 it pulsed with all the pomp and excitement of a red-carpet extravaganza. Feverish crowds swarmed the street adjacent to the box office and klieg lights sent crisscrossed beams high into the dusky sky. Police struggled to surround the limos that pulled up to the curb, escorting the occupants inside. It seemed like the whole city was aware of the occasion, but if anyone still needed an explanation, they could find it splashed across the neon marquee.

WORLD PREMIERE TONIGHT
—*International Squadron*—
STARRING DIXON'S OWN RONALD "DUTCH" REAGAN

The screening put the finishing touch on a two-day homecoming he shared with Louella Parsons, the highlights of which included the dedication of a new children's hospital ward, a parade through town, several receptions, and a rally near the lifeguard's chair at Lowell Park. They'd brought along a celebrated entourage from Hollywood—Bob Hope, George Montgomery, comedian Joe E. Brown, Jerry Colonna, and Ann Rutherford, familiar to all as Andy Hardy's girlfriend in the beloved MGM series. But Ronald Reagan—*Dutch*—was the main attraction. It had been only a few years since he'd left Dixon, and plenty of locals had personal connections to him as a rambunctious neighborhood boy, an enterprising schoolmate, or the heroic lad who'd pulled seventy-seven people from the merciless Rock. Now he was back, a bona fide movie star, but as the marquee stated: one of their own.

As the lights went down inside the theater, Ronnie had to swallow a few emotional gulps. It wasn't all that long ago he'd watched countless movies from a seat in the balcony, fantasizing about being up on that very same screen. He was more than lucky—he was blessed. The stark reality of it hit him hard that evening, sitting among his Dixon and Hollywood peers.

He wished Jane could have been there to share it with him. A minor medical issue had forced her to remain behind in Los Angeles, so he'd taken Nelle along in her place. It was his mother's first real outing since Jack's death and an opportunity for her to reconnect with old friends. She'd hardly left her son's side since *The City of Los Angeles* chugged into the Chicago & Northwestern depot two days earlier. When they each stepped out onto a makeshift platform to address the welcoming crowd, Nelle received an equally genuine cheer.

But the trip was only a respite from Ronnie's creeping discontent. The feedback from *International Squadron* and *Kings Row* had been so promising, but the films that followed were dreadful, prompting anxiety and not a little resentment. An item Warner Bros. spun off to the trades announced his casting in a starring role in *Casablanca*, with Ann Sheridan. Only a rumor, as it turned out. What had he and Ann Sheridan done to deserve *Juke Girl*? It was a dark, tortured little melodrama—a poor man's *The Grapes of Wrath*—but without that movie's gorgeous script or performances. It wasn't a terrible picture, but it was forgettable. And the working conditions had bordered on punishment. "We shot night exteriors [from six p.m.] until sunup for thirty-eight nights," Ronnie remembered, most of them on location in central California farmland, where the night air felt more like Finland than Fresno.

Afterward, he was slotted into *Desperate Journey*, an overheated Errol Flynn vehicle, classic B-movie hokum that might have been an installment in the *Brass Bancroft* series. It was "an action melodrama of the wildest stripe," one critic noted, full of slangy one-liners and wild-goose chases. It was impossible to take seriously. Ronnie drew passable notices for his performance as Johnny Hammond, a brash, irreverent, implausibly brave fighter pilot, but he was again playing second fiddle to a brasher, more irreverent, braver Errol Flynn.

The assignments he was getting vexed Ronnie. It was difficult to determine what the studio had in mind for him. He'd shared star billing with Errol Flynn, but what did it matter if the movie stank? He was being passed over for pictures like *Casablanca* and *Now, Voyager*. Maybe he shouldn't have said yes to every script put in front of him. Bill Meiklejohn recalled that "he did more or less what the studio asked him to do" without exercising much critical judgment. Perhaps if he had declined a few of the lamer scripts, as Bogart, Cagney, and Flynn had done, he might have found himself in a better negotiating position—or at least in better movies. He was still putting finishing touches on *Desperate Journey* and wrestling with his frustrations on December 7, 1941, when the Japanese bombed Pearl Harbor.

N ow America was finally at war. Reagan would most likely see it from a distance. He'd be thirty-one in another two months, just about the top age limit set by the Selective Service. He had a dependent child, as well as being the sole supporter of his mother. If nothing else, his eyesight remained disqualifying. Besides, Jack Warner had secured another deferment for him, keeping him off the active duty rolls until April 9, 1942. But the War Department made it clear that Ronnie's name was on a priority list and would be called whenever his name reached the top. Studios were hemorrhaging male stars who rushed to enlist in the weeks immediately following Pearl Harbor. Jimmy Stewart was already gone, along with Clark Gable. Warner was determined to keep Ronnie working for as long as possible. To be on the safe side, Warner had his general counsel, Roy Obringer, petition the U.S. Army on March 28, explaining the studio's "tremendous investment" in its current production and requesting an extension on Ronnie's deferment so that he could complete "the patriotic film" *Desperate Journey*.

Someone must have slipped the Army a copy of the script, because on April 2, they sent Warner a telegram denying his request due to a "shortage of available officers." They expected "2nd Lt. Ronald Wilson Reagan" to report for duty at Fort Mason, California, no later than April 19, 1942.

Jane didn't take the news well. She was enjoying a late-afternoon visit with Claudette Colbert when Ronnie arrived home and blurted out the details of his orders. "She was furious with him," Colbert told Edmund Morris. "She said he'd gone behind her back to sign up," stranding her at home to take care of Maureen at a time when she'd planned to relaunch her career. And that wasn't all. Jane also knew that, patriotism aside, Warner Bros. stood by a strict policy to suspend actors' salaries the same day they went off to war. His Army pay amounted to a measly $250 a month. How did he expect they'd make payments on their new home, raise a child, and maintain a Hollywood standard of living on only her income?

And there was the cost of supporting Nelle, with the house rental and weekly allowance. Ronnie dashed off a memo to Jack Warner's office, suggesting that his mother be put on the studio payroll at a cost of $75 a week to answer his fan mail and take care of other minor details. Warner didn't even draft a personal response. He simply scrawled "We can't set a precedent" across Ronnie's request and had it returned. It took several additional pleas until Warner relented, agreeing to take Ronnie's note for an interest-free loan of $3,900 repayable upon his return to work, against which the studio would send Nelle $75 a week for a year.

There were still fourteen days of work left on *Desperate Journey*, requiring the production to shuffle the schedule in order to complete Ronnie's scenes. "Long shots and shots of my back were saved for a double after I was gone," he recalled.

There were plenty of other loose ends to wrap up, including the final details on his new contract that would be in force—but on suspension—while he served in the military. *Kings Row* was set for release after he left for Fort Mason, but there was no reason to worry about publicizing the movie. There was a war on. He was in the Army now.

After a nine-hour train trip from Los Angeles to a fog-bound San Francisco, Ronnie flagged a taxi to take him the last few miles to Fort Mason. Just past Russian Hill, the cab headed toward the corner where Franklin intersected Bay Street, plunging down the hilly landscape as though on a final hair-raising roller-coaster drop. Looking down from the road, Ronnie could see the chalky ramparts of the fort stretched out like a mirage over the Pacific Ocean. Wedged between Fisherman's Wharf on the northern rim of San Francisco Bay and the Marina District to the south, the fort was an enormous compound of forty-nine buildings situated on a headland close to water level.

Fort Mason served as the principal logistical and transport hub for U.S. military operations in the Pacific. No other port aside from New York harbor had a more vital strategic function. In the eighty years since the government had seized the site for use as coastal defense, an extensive sprawl of warehouses, batteries, and tunnels had been added to shore up its fortification.

It took Ronnie hours to locate his commanding officer, Colonel Philip T. Booker, a no-nonsense military lifer with a ramrod-straight bearing and clipped way of delivering orders. Booker was specific and to the point. Ronnie was to act as a liaison officer, directing a company of ROTC cadets who were in the process of loading convoys of troops headed to Australia. Two days earlier, the last U.S. forces holding on to the Bataan Peninsula in the Philippines had surrendered to the Japanese, necessitating a build-up of American strength to protect its forces in the southern Pacific.

It was tedious work. Long days were occupied greasing the wheels of a lumbering bureaucracy—cataloging orders, assigning itineraries, sorting baggage and food requisitions, shuffling paper. Ronnie preferred to keep a low profile, but as the only celebrity on the base he was roped into performing in several military sideshows—as the centerpiece in a Sunday-newspaper spread in full dress uniform, at a Hollywood rally to launch the USO program, in bond drives, at charity benefits, at several dinners with high-ranking officers, and, worst of all, at a squirmy screening at the post-theater of *Kings Row*, his first opportunity to see the final print, in which he was introduced from the audience and prodded to speak. He grew "tired of being used as a showpiece."

A remedy arrived just in time. In late May 1942, after only five weeks at Fort Mason, Lieutenant Reagan was notified that he was being reassigned—transferred out of the cavalry into an Air Corps unit. How ironic—he a man who refused to fly. There was no telling where he would wind up. One could only imagine the outposts where wartime efforts were churning around the clock—places like Kearney, Nebraska; Spartanburg, South Carolina; Paris, Texas; Neosho, Missouri; Camp Breckinridge in the extreme western part of Kentucky; Camp Blanding in Florida, described as "a playground for . . . the most stylish group of alligators this side of the Congo." When his assignment came through, it was all he could do not to burst out laughing. He was being sent to . . . Hollywood. His orders were to report to 4151 Prospect Avenue, the old Vitagraph Studios in East Hollywood that the Warner brothers had purchased in 1925 when they gambled their future on talking pictures.

Since 1940, Hollywood had been doing its part in the U.S. military's propaganda efforts. All of the major studios had been commissioned to make short training films for the Army Signal Corps. Disney had made a number of aircraft identification films. Warner Bros. was responsible for producing a slew of military shorts, including 1940's *March On, Marines*, *Meet the Fleet*, *Service with the Colors*, and *Wings of Steel*. The next year, the studio doubled down, producing *Here Comes the Cavalry*, *Soldiers in White*, and The *Tanks Are Coming*.

Now that America was at war, each branch of the military reassessed how it was perceived by the public and how best to attract new recruits.

The Air Corps had its own particular image problem. After a long, enervating battle to free itself from Army control, the Air Corps was determined to assert its autonomy through a vigorous public-relations effort. By coincidence, in 1941 Jack Warner wrote to Lieutenant General Henry "Hap" Arnold, chief of the U.S. Army Air Corps, to gauge the possibility of making a feature based on the life of William "Billy" Mitchell, the charismatic World War I flying ace who was court-martialed for insubordination. The project was eventually shelved; however, in Warner, Arnold had found the perfect partner for his autonomy message.

Later that year, the studio put itself in service to the Air Corps by making a short recruiting film, *Winning Your Wings*, narrated by Jimmy Stewart. The pitch it made was so effective that Arnold later claimed it helped attract more than a million cadets. Still, he and Warner knew there was more work to be done.

The two men met in Arnold's Washington office on March 8, 1942, at which time Warner, toting a sheaf of carefully typed notes, floated the idea of producing and distributing Air Corps short subjects and feature films.

"After the war is won," he emphasized, "we want to be sure that the American people will realize that it was the Air Corps that was responsible for achieving victory." Warner proposed forming an Air Corps film-production unit under his supervision, utilizing the greatest talent Hollywood had to offer. In return, he expected to be commissioned as a "high ranking" Air Corps officer to ensure "people will know we really mean business and will be much more willing to cooperate." The upshot was the formation of the First Motion Picture Unit—known as FMPU—under the guardianship of Lieutenant Colonel Jack Warner, Public Relations Division, Army Air Corps.

Owen Crump, one of Warner's short-subject producers, now an Air Force colonel, was holding down the Vitagraph post when the division got under way. The old studio donated by his boss was "virtually in shambles," he recalled, "and with no equipment for filmmaking." Nothing was available from the regular military supply. Warner finally sent over "three old cameras and film for training" inexperienced camera crews. However, the immediate problem wasn't moviemaking; it was hospitality. Recruits, from technicians and craftsmen to writers and actors, were pouring in without essential facilities. Only the officers were allowed to go home at night, which left most of the company stranded at the studio. According to Crump, "We had to have cots so men could sleep on the soundstages . . . a mess to feed them." They borrowed beds, installed showers. Crump felt increasingly overwhelmed.

On June 8, 1942, a knock on the office door signaled unexpected relief. "I looked up and Ronald Reagan was standing there, and he had on cavalry boots," Crump recalled.

"Sir, I'm reporting," Ronnie announced.

Crump waved him inside and immediately promoted him to personnel officer, largely dumping the housing responsibilities into Ronnie's hands. There were three hundred men under his care stationed at Vitagraph, nearly four hundred a month later. Reagan was also given the job of expanding the production ranks. "My first assignment was to recruit technicians and artists from the movie business," he recalled. Those eligible for the draft were off-limits. His conscripts were drawn from the pool of leftovers—men deemed either physically unfit or exempt from military duty but willing to serve. There were plenty to choose from; in early 1942 "less than three percent of Hollywood was in the service." But getting top-tier talent took some arm-twisting. "I was offering majors' insignias to half-million-dollar-a-year movie directors."

The First Motion Picture Unit was officially activated on July 1, 1942. By this time, the regiment had outgrown the shabby Vitagraph quarters and was moved across town to the fully operational Hal Roach Studios in Culver City, where production on its first film, *Learn and Live*, was under way. At the same time, work had begun at the Las Vegas Gunnery School on *The Rear Gunner*, another recruiting effort. Ronnie and Burgess Meredith co-starred as a wayward youth from Kansas and his Air Corps mentor who gives him a chance to blossom into an expert marksman, eventually winning the Distinguished Service Medal. It was twenty-six minutes of pure Hollywood corn, and young men took it to heart, in some cases rushing from theaters directly to local recruitment centers.

Once enlistment quotas increased, the FMPU turned its attention to instructional films, believing that movies offered the most efficient methods to teach raw recruits. One of the earliest efforts in this vein, released in the spring of 1943, was *Recognition of the Japanese Zero Fighter*, in which Ronnie played a hotshot pilot who must learn—the hard way, by accidentally shooting at the wrong plane—to distinguish between American P-40 Warhawk aircraft and Japanese Zero aircraft.

Reagan's work as adjutant and personnel officer kept him busy with administrative duties, but he also narrated a number of films. *Cadet Classification*, made in early 1943, illustrated the process whereby cadets in flight training are selected for positions as pilots, navigators, or bombardiers. In *Behind the Line of Duty*, chronicling the heroic exploits of Captain Hewitt T. Wheless, Ronnie's narration was paired with President Roosevelt's to explain how to conduct a successful mission. *The Fight for the Sky* followed bombing raids from the English coast into northern Germany, and featured Ronnie's prediction that "when we start heading over Berlin and Tokyo it's really going to be a picnic." Another film, *Westward Is Bataan*, was noteworthy for its graphic depictions of American servicemen wounded or killed in the Pacific. The gain was to convince audiences that drastic action was essential to ending the war soon. In a voice-over, Ronnie warned viewers that Japan was "prepared to lose ten million in its war with America." As the scene cut away to a Japanese woman cradling a receptacle containing the ashes of her son, he said, "We don't raise our boys to be gods in little white boxes."

On February 23, 1943, Jack Warner arranged leave from the FMPU for Ronnie so that he could appear in *This Is the Army*, a joint venture of the War Department and Warner Bros. that was to begin filming in Burbank. Warner Bros. had purchased the rights to two Irving Berlin musicals, his 1917 soldier revue, *Yip, Yip, Yaphank*, and the 1942 Broadway stage sensation *This Is the Army*, which had helped to raise $10 million for war relief. The screenplay was a mash-up of the two shows, and George Murphy and Ronald Reagan were cast as father and son, both producers of Army spectacles but a war and a generation apart. Directed by Michael Curtiz and loaded with seventeen heart-stirring patriotic songs, including Kate Smith's legendary rendition of "God Bless America," the movie built to a grand finale that featured a platoon of soldiers high-stepping like Rockettes out of the theater and off to war. "All this," as *Variety* wrote in typical breathy excess, "is morale in capital letters. It's democracy in action to the hilt. It's showmanship and patriotism combined to a super-duper Yankee Doodle degree."

In between all the showmanship and patriotism, there were long stretches of mundane administrative duties—the paperwork involved with staffing thirteen hundred soldiers, the endless housekeeping, personnel requests, facility maintenance. And training—roll call each morning, calisthenics, drills, marching. There was plenty of downtime confined to the fort. To stem the boredom, Ronnie played on the post basketball team and read. He combed through four or five daily newspapers, studying the progress of the war, struggling to understand and make sense of the flow of events. He had always been curious about the world at large, more curious than a lot of his fellow actors. He wasn't a deep thinker, but his thinking was deeply felt, personal. What animated him the most was how the news of the world affected everyday people.

It was during this period that Reagan began reading a publication that would have an outsize and enduring influence on his thinking. It is unclear who first put a copy of *Reader's Digest* in Ronald Reagan's hands, but he began reading each monthly issue from cover to cover while on duty at Fort Roach. He loved the magazine's breadbasket offerings—homespun stories, can-do tales, inspirational pieces, condensed articles of topical interest, all aimed squarely at the American heartland. The magazine offered just what he needed on any given subject—not a fact-riddled academic thesis, but the broad strokes, enough information to provide a good overview, allowing him to decide where he came down on an issue. Sixty years later, his private files—those that had accompanied him through every phase of his career—would contain reams of clippings from *Reader's Digest*, all dog-eared and underlined, reflecting ideas he'd co-opted, positions he'd agreed with, homilies he'd used in various speeches.

He'd pounce on each issue as soon as it hit the fort PX and practically memorize the new batch of articles, regurgitating them for anyone who would listen. He sounded off on anything that had captured his attention—FDR, whom he still revered, the $109 billion federal budget, the lack of a decent American diet, a new miracle drug called penicillin, various state laws requiring students to salute the flag, the volcano Paricutin that erupted in Mexico. No subject was outside his expertise. He could do twenty minutes without coming up for air on the war, the economy, religion, foreign policy, the military, socialized medicine, or the dwindling rights of screen actors. Enlisted men had difficulty escaping the nonstop chatter. He'd corral them at various points in the fort and launch into the topic du jour, much like Plato lecturing students in the Agora. Screenwriter Irving Wallace, who was stationed at Fort Roach, often found himself a captive of these ongoing monologues, recalling Ronnie as "a lovable scatterbrain," but basically a "man who parrots things—shallow and affable." And he regaled Jane when he was home on leave, sitting for hours over the morning papers, then holding forth about the stories he found interesting, giving each his own interpretive slant. "All he talks about morning, noon, and night is world affairs," she told Robert Cummings. She could never get a word in edgewise. More than one mutual friend suspected that his constant sermonizing put a crimp in their relationship. "Ronnie," Jane reportedly told Ann Sheridan, "was such a talker, he made speeches in his sleep."

The war, which had sidelined many actors, actually gave the careers of Ronald Reagan and Jane Wyman an unforeseen boost. Fan magazines like *Photoplay*, *Motion Picture*, and *Modern Screen* featured spread after spread of the Reagans as the ideal wartime couple, Ronnie pictured in uniform as "the perfect American officer who had gone to war"—*gone to war!*—"despite the responsibility of a wife and daughter"; Jane by his side, the supportive wife, the woman left behind, who kept the home fires burning while holding down a job of her own. "My Soldier, by Jane Wyman" appeared in January 1943, followed by "You're Mrs. Ronald Reagan," and similar mawkish items. Warner Bros. sent out publicity shots of Jane writing letters to her soldier as if Ronnie were stationed somewhere overseas. His leave was documented in excruciating detail. Practically every fan knew he always said "So long, Button Nose" when getting ready to leave for duty. The public couldn't get enough.

A t home, the reception was mixed.
Resentful of Ronnie for stranding her in the house and furious with Warner Bros. for spoon-feeding her syrupy scripts, Jane treated his homestays with a frosty detachment. It aggravated her to put a good face on the situation. She was trying to juggle raising Maureen and pursuing a precarious acting career. Edward G. Robinson recalled, "I always felt it was most patient and steady of her to take all those undemanding, silly roles they handed her." One after the other—*My Favorite Spy, Footlight Serenade, The Animal Kingdom, Crime by Night, Make Your Own Bed, The Doughgirls.* She grumbled about the roles to Louella Parsons, "asking why, why wouldn't someone give her a real chance."

In truth, she was lucky to be working at all. All Hollywood studios had scaled back production during the war years. Most B pictures were eliminated altogether, making competition for leading roles in the A's much keener. Raw film stock was being rationed, creative crews and craftsmen diverted to the military. Equipment was redistributed for defense purposes.

To spell time between pictures, Jane joined the Hollywood Victory Committee, a loose organization of screen and stage performers not engaged in military service who contributed to the war effort by entertaining troops, boosting morale, and raising money through various bond drives. She could sing, and she entertained regularly at the Hollywood Canteen, a club for servicemen on their way overseas. And she waited, holding out hope that a choice movie role would come her way.

The WAC officer wife she played in *Princess O'Rourke* toward the end of 1943 was not such a role. The picture was an absurdly labored, lightweight fable that spotlighted Olivia de Havilland in the title role. Still, a poignant restaurant scene allowed Jane to show something more than the usual flaky comic turn, and the consequences of that scene redirected her career.

Someone slipped a workprint of the film to Charles Brackett, a producer on the Paramount lot who was preparing *The Lost Weekend* for Billy Wilder to direct. It was a serious drama about the horrors of alcohol addiction that most studios were loath to tackle. Jane wasn't the obvious choice to play the woman who stands faithfully by a lover, Ray Milland, with a lethal drinking problem, but Brackett saw something in her that conveyed exactly the quality he was looking for. Jack Warner was more than happy to lend her out. There was nothing for Jane in the works at Warner Bros. Besides, he was convinced "that drunk film," as he referred to *The Lost Weekend*, was box-office poison. He knew the liquor industry had offered Paramount $5 million to bury the picture. It'd probably never see the light of day.

Other opinions were more admiring. In fact, *all* other opinions, once the film opened in early December 1945. The *New York Times*' formidable critic Bosley Crowther, a hard-to-please, snappish iconoclast, led the adoring press, declaring, "*The Lost Weekend* is truly a chef d'oeuvre of motion-picture art." He lauded the movie for being "shatteringly realistic" and singled out Jane Wyman's "quiet authority."

The movie upended the industry's appraisal of her. Jane Wyman could act—not just act as she'd done in the Warner Bros. comedies, but . . . *act*. She had what Stanwyck had and Davis and de Havilland and Hepburn had. *The Lost Weekend* had succeeded in outing her as an actress. "It changed my whole life," she later admitted.

Only Jack Warner didn't grasp her potential. He, alone among fellow moguls, still saw Jane as a blond, feisty, wisecracking comedienne more suited to pedestrian fare. Which is why he was willing to lend her out once again, this time to MGM, for another picture trailing built-in difficulties.

Ronald Reagan spent much of 1944 as the narrator of the FMPU's Special Film Project 152 series, a succession of bomb-run simulation films shown to pilots as a kind of visualization of what they should expect to see when flying tactical missions over Japan. Once these raids were devised as an endgame strategy, the FMPU's creative staff moved quickly. A team of movie special-effects men who had been drafted into the unit built a replica of Tokyo on a Fort Roach soundstage that was sealed off to visitors by a phalanx of MPs. "Above this they rigged a crane and camera mount and could photograph the miniature," Ronnie recalled, "giving the effect on the screen of movies taken from a plane traveling at any prescribed height and speed." The films were then airlifted to bomber bases in the Pacific to update pilots on visuals and targets.

Ronald Reagan might have never left California during the war, but his military service projected him to America as a war hero. He appeared constantly in uniform, wearing wings, in color layouts for recruiting efforts, and at events around the country on a bond-selling tour. On the screen, audiences repeatedly saw his character confront the enemy and display courage under fire. It was difficult to equate his war experience with that of, say, Jimmy Stewart, who flew actual combat missions, or Clark Gable, who was with a bomber squadron overseas. But there were patriotic optics to exploit, rooted in a genuine effort to do his part—and he made the most of them. As a Reagan historian noted, "No twentieth-century president, with the exception of Dwight D. Eisenhower, had been seen in uniform by more people."

CHAPTER FOURTEEN

"A DANGEROUS MAN"

*"An actor is not a person apart from life, but a citizen who
should participate actively in his government."*

—EDWARD G. ROBINSON, 1947

When he was discharged, on December 9, 1945, having been promoted to the venerable rank of captain, Ronald Reagan was eager to pick up where he'd left off. He hung up the uniform, had his contract reinstated, and made quick for the sanctum of Hollywood. Ronnie knew that readjustment was inevitable. He'd been away for four years, and there were no guarantees, but he'd left on a high note. He still had the same square-jawed features, the same good-guy demeanor, the all-American movie-star image. Warner Bros. was up and running at peak production. It was cranking out films.

He looked the same—but Hollywood didn't.

In the four years since America entered World War II, Hollywood had undergone a top-to-bottom makeover. Studios reorganized their vast operations to reflect the retrenchment in the number and cost of movies they were making. It was no longer feasible to churn out sixty pictures a year. Audiences' tastes had changed, and the studios were scrambling to keep pace. Darryl F. Zanuck was one of the first to see the handwriting on the wall. He recognized that servicemen who had been stationed overseas were "coming back with new thoughts, new ideas, and new hungers." Their attitudes and perceptions had changed, and as a result audiences were more sophisticated, perhaps more cynical. "We've got to start making movies that entertain but at the same time match the new climate of the times. Vital, thinking men's blockbusters, big-theme films."

Those kinds of movies required actors with nuance—they were no longer all good or all bad. To that end, a cluster of new stars had emerged like Gregory Peck, William Holden, Robert Mitchum, Cornel Wilde, and Zachary Scott—rugged, flawed, rough around the moral edges. Humphrey Bogart, who used to play a bad guy, now played a good guy—or, at least, a better guy—with elements of darkness. Tyrone Power, once strictly a paragon of swashbucklers, sought to portray tormented characters searching for meaningful experience. Modern heroes could be haunted, self-interested, or even corrupt. Ronald Reagan's relatively bland, one-dimensional persona—the idealistic, likable best friend—felt dated in this new atmosphere.

It didn't help Ronnie's career that he was no longer protected by the old studio system that slotted him into six or eight quickie films a year. As Otto Friedrich noted in *City of Nets*, "the sprightly little movies of the 1930s, the B-pictures, the cheap westerns and detective stories, would never again support the Hollywood studios." The Brass Bancrofts and Tugboat Annies and Dead End Kids were the past. Studios, in 1946, were releasing *Notorious*, *Duel in the Sun*, *To Each His Own*, *The Postman Always Rings Twice*, and *The Best Years of Our Lives*. Even Jane Wyman had elevated her game.

The structure of the business worked against Ronnie as well. In August 1943, Olivia de Havilland sued Warner Bros., arguing that her seven-year contract—suspended six times by the studio, each suspension adding months to the term—violated an archaic California law that forbade binding someone to an employer beyond seven years as being tantamount to slavery. When the court ruled in her favor a year later, the entire studio system came undone. Suddenly, every contract player who had put in his seven *calendar* years became a free agent. Actors could now move from studio to studio, from picture to picture, renegotiating their deals as the situation demanded. High-profile movie stars rejoiced that the business no longer resembled high-security feudal plantations where they toiled in servitude.

But the studio system had been helpful for some actors—those who weren't skilled enough or aggressive enough or in great enough demand. At Warner Bros., it was those actors who suffered most after the war as the studio prepared to release more emotionally complex films like *Rhapsody in Blue*, *Mildred Pierce*, *Night and Day*, *Of Human Bondage*, and *Deception*.

Ronnie found himself sitting on the sidelines from his Air Force discharge on December 9, 1945, through the end of the year. "Just relax until we find a good property for you," Jack Warner advised him, but it was clear that scripts weren't coming Ronnie's way. Even so, there was no reason for panic. He remained a popular face for moviegoing audiences—ranked sixth among male Hollywood stars. And he had a new, long-term contract that guaranteed him $3,500 a week for forty-three weeks a year, whether he was working or not, a nice little nest egg.

Relax, as Warner had said. It wasn't such a bad idea.

The war had forced him to recalibrate his career, and there were personal issues that required attention as well. On March 18, 1945, just months before Japan surrendered, Jane and Ronnie sent out a communiqué from the adjutant's office of the FMPU announcing the birth of their son Michael Edward. In fact, they adopted the infant boy, who was twelve hours old when he was given to them by his birth mother, Irene Flaugher, a Kentucky farm girl. Speculation was rife as to why they chose to adopt. "Sources," which usually meant Hollywood gossip mills, intimated that either Jane was no longer able to conceive or that she was too busy with her flourishing career to risk another year's hiatus from the screen. Whatever the case, the Reagans explained that there were too many orphans in need of loving homes and they felt it was important "to add from the outside to our family."

For a while, Ronnie puttered around their new house, building a sidewalk and laying flagstone for a patio. Soon, however, he grew bored and lonely. Jane was away on location at Lake Arrowhead in the San Bernardino Mountains filming *The Yearling*, based on the Pulitzer Prize–winning Marjorie Kinnan Rawlings novel. With the children in tow, it was the perfect place for Ronnie to "laze around and take time to figure things out" until Warner Bros. came calling.

In September 1945, with the summer crowds departed, Lake Arrowhead was blissfully serene. MGM had rented the Reagans a cottage at the edge of the lake, so close to the water that runabouts were needed to take Jane to and from the set. From the front porch, they could see co-star Gregory

Peck's house with its long dock jutting over the shoals. In the evenings, the Reagans and the Pecks would often carry food back and forth, sharing dinners and doting on each other's kids. Occasionally, June Lockhart, another cast member, would join them, and afterward, with the kids tucked in bed, the actors retired to the porch, talking over the day's work and gossiping, while a choir of cicadas communed in the trees.

The time away from Los Angeles was leisurely, even therapeutic, but for Ronnie it proved a mixed blessing. His wife was kept busy from dawn to dusk, working on the kind of important, star-making vehicle he'd been hungering for, while nothing much was stirring on his end. He passed most of the days building a two-foot-long replica of the SS *America*, an ocean liner converted to troop transport during the war, taking long walks around the lake, tooling a rented speedboat from shore to shore, and tending the kids. When Jane returned from the set, she was still in character, spent, oblivious to Ronnie. It irked him how "she would come through the door, thinking about her part, and not even notice I was in the room." He felt neglected. It was galling enough being out of work. Jane's behavior only served to rub it in his face.

Late in 1945, Warner Bros. finally came through with the promised "good property," attaching him to *Stallion Road*, a big-budget Technicolor feature that was the cornerstone of the studio's upcoming slate. A first-draft script by no less than William Faulkner was developed from Stephen Longstreet's bestselling novel. It was a story dear to Ronnie's heart—a western about horse ranching, allowing him to do his own riding and giving him plenty of screen time to gambol across the gorgeous mountain meadows of the Sierra Madre Range. To top it off, he was co-starring with Humphrey Bogart and Lauren Bacall, the hottest properties on the Warner lot. What a comeback this would be for him! The picture was scheduled to begin shooting in March 1946. In the meantime, Ronnie shuttled between Lake Arrowhead and Hollywood, where broader issues for the industry were heating up.

The world might have been racked by war from 1940 to 1945, but it had been a period of relative peace for the Hollywood studios. The American Federation of Labor had given Franklin Roosevelt its pledge that there would be no slowdowns or strikes for the duration of the war. The union had been good for its word, but now that the war was over all bets were off.

What seemed at first like standard union-management horse-trading would in fact prove to be the beginning of Reagan's involvement over the next five years in what would become the most divisive issue in the history of Hollywood—the role of communists in the shaping of the movies and public life, and the frenzy to stamp it out. This marked a radical switch from an era when talking politics was a harmless sport at social events to a climate in which there was an ongoing toxic debate that could destroy lives and careers.

Trouble was brewing from an unexpected source: a jurisdictional dispute involving two competing local unions representing the craftsmen whose work was critical to every phase of moviemaking. Since before the turn of the twentieth century, these craftsmen had been represented by the International Alliance of Theatrical and Stage Employees, known by its acronym, IATSE. A couple of Chicago mobsters—Willie Bioff and George Browne—took control of the union in 1934 and set about bilking the studios out of hundreds of thousands of dollars through threats and intimidation. When they were convicted of extortion and went to jail in 1941, control passed into the hands of Roy M. Brewer, a union strongman who sought to preserve IATSE's dominance as Hollywood's main labor organization.

In 1941, Herbert Sorrell, who ran the painters' guild, began building an independent alternative to IATSE, establishing locals to unite the unorganized trades—film technicians, carpenters, cartoonists, and machinists, among others—into the Conference of Studio Unions (CSU). By 1945, it had enrolled nearly ten thousand members, a serious challenge to IATSE's control, setting the stage for an inevitable confrontation. When interior decorators sought to decamp from IATSE to the CSU in January 1946, they were refused recognition by the producer's association—and promptly went on strike.

Ronnie read about the walkout from his Lake Arrowhead retreat. The action was confined to the Warner Bros. lot, where strikers had overturned cars at the Olive Street gates. The destructive demonstration wasn't the kind he subscribed to, but he sympathized. "What I heard and read in the papers placed me on the side of the strikers," he recalled. He was a union man. He believed strongly in the right of workers "to refuse to work for just grievances." He favored cooperation and compromise, but if all else failed and it meant striking for an honorable cause, then so be it.

At first, it didn't trouble Ronald Reagan that opponents had smeared the CSU's Sorrell by spreading rumors that he was a Communist. Everyone knew CSU supported and was supported by a number of progressive and Popular Front organizations. But communist? Ronnie was convinced that label was flung around anytime a right-winger wanted to impugn a liberal cause. His brother, Neil, the family Republican, who had drifted by now into an advertising career, was always warning him that such-and-such was a "commie front." Moon would "bring up the names of people who were 'bad actors'"—wink-wink—and "Ronald would immediately rear up on his hind heels" and fire back: "Oh, you're coming out with the Communist story." They'd gone head-to-head on this topic so often it was like an Abbott and Costello routine.

Reagan was a "hemophiliac liberal," as he put it, who attached his name to every left-leaning organization whose goals ostensibly were peace, disarmament, and equality. According to FBI files, Ronald Reagan joined the Hollywood Democratic Committee, the Committee for a Democratic Far Eastern Policy, the United World Federalists, the International Rescue and Relief Committee, and the American Veterans Committee. He wrote articles denouncing Gerald L. K. Smith, the firebrand clergyman and right-wing political organizer, and others he referred to as "home-grown fascists." He joined with internationalists advocating a ban on the atomic bomb and signed a petition protesting U.S. support for Chiang Kai-shek against Mao Tse-tung. Later, in hindsight, he would say, "I was not sharp about Communism."

Forty-five years later, Howard Fast, the noted writer and avowed Communist, told Edmund Morris that Ronald Reagan made serious inquiries about joining the party early in his career, and he might have, too, had Eddie Albert, his *Brother Rat* co-star, not succeeded in talking him out of it. Party leaders, according to Fast, didn't trust Ronnie's political philosophy—probably recognizing him more as an idealist disposed to "helping the dispossessed, the unemployed, and the homeless" than as a disciple of Lenin or Marx. In any case, it appears that he flirted with the party's issue-oriented politics and progressive causes that were treated with indifference by a majority of Americans.

That all began to change when the CSU strike began in early 1946. Across America labor had set off an explosion of work stoppages seen as crippling essential industries. Since the end of the war, an astounding 4,600 strikes had occurred, with hundreds more threatened. Hollywood was no stranger to this phenomenon. Unable to achieve fair terms suitable to its rank and file, the CSU expanded its action on behalf of the decorators and launched an industry-wide action aimed at all major movie companies. It was a long, drawn-out, ugly affair, with studios and their IATSE allies employing scabs, thugs, a private police force, and fire departments to thwart picket lines and break the strike.

IATSE launched an all-out publicity assault demonizing the CSU union as a Communist tool. Roy Brewer sent letters to prominent actors and producers intimating that if they didn't declare themselves loyal to IATSE and against the CSU, "then that person was *ipso facto* an agent of un-Americanism, an enemy of IATSE, and a likely candidate for boycott by the film projectionist members."

The war had touched off a wave of patriotism across the country that cast suspicion and slapped a badge of un-Americanism on anyone who thought differently or dared to buck the status quo. Progressives, antifascists, and liberal activists found themselves at risk of being called communists, the bogeymen du jour. As conservative national interest groups would have it, communists were out to infiltrate all phases of democratic society in an effort to subvert the government. Alleged communists became a lightning rod for the anger and resentment of anyone who had lost family in the war, suffered economic setbacks, or felt differently about freedoms and religion. Tarnishing the reputation of adversaries by merely insinuating they were communist was a tactic that touched raw nerves. When Roy Brewer circulated a document that celebrated "the sturdy Americanism of IATSE in contrast to the alien nature and beliefs of its opponents," the battle lines were drawn.

Two of the CSU's leading proponents had been the Screen Actors Guild and an organization called the Hollywood Independent Citizens Committee of the Arts, Sciences, and Professions (HICCASP). Founded in early 1946 as an offshoot of the Hollywood Democratic Committee, HICCASP counted among its 3,300 members—"3,300 professional exhibitionists," as *Time* labeled them—the cream of Hollywood liberal society, not just its top-tier actors like Humphrey Bogart, Gregory Peck, Orson Welles, and Olivia de Havilland, but "everybody who was anybody": writers, directors, and serious-minded luminaries who lent their names, such as Linus Pauling, Albert Einstein, Harold Ickes, and Max Weber. James Roosevelt, FDR's son, served as the group's national director.

Ronald Reagan became a member in 1944, lured by the group's hard work in promoting President Roosevelt's reelection. At the time, he seemed unaware of the strong voice that radicals, communists, and fellow travelers exercised on the committee's executive council, a fact not lost on a contingent of genteel country-club liberals who resigned in protest. Like many who remained, he was attracted to the group's strong political and social agendas—supporting the United Nations and universal disarmament, denouncing colonialism, and advocating stronger price controls, unemployment compensation, a minimum wage, federal aid for education, and improved housing and health care. "Many actors were caught up in HICCASP's policies," recalls Olivia de Havilland, who acted as the board's vice chairman and helped generate widespread industry support. "Actors empathize—that's their talent, empathizing with the role they play, which they couldn't do without that gift. And they have a tendency to empathize with the maltreated, the underdogs, and different types of people."

Such empathy for "an institution he [thought] was humanitarian" was Ronald Reagan's motivating force. In the summer of 1946, when asked to fill a vacancy on HICCASP's executive council, he jumped at the chance, saying he "felt honored" to serve in a more prominent capacity.

His enthusiasm was short-lived. At his first council meeting, on July 2, 1946, a brouhaha erupted over whether HICCASP was "controlled by the left" that further separated the remaining moderates from the radicals. *Life* had recently published an excerpt of Arthur Schlesinger Jr.'s *The Vital Center*, in which he singled out HICCASP as a Communist front. When George Pepper, the executive director of HICCASP, asked the council to respond, Jimmy Roosevelt suggested they compose a statement repudiating communism. A flurry of epithets were directed at him: "fascist" . . . "capitalist scum" . . . "witch-hunter" . . . "Red-baiter." Several dissidents staged a stormy walkout.

Olivia de Havilland announced that she wouldn't remain a member of the group without a suitable declaration. She was "sick and tired," she said, of the way the communist sympathizers "manipulated" the meetings. "Whenever a motion was proposed that their opponents objected to, somebody rose and said, 'Why not table this so we can get on with other business. It can be introduced later.' If it was brought up again, Dalton Trumbo, a brilliant man, got up and spoke absolute nonsense to delay the vote, like Jimmy Stewart in *Mr. Smith Goes to Washington*." Similar motions were tabled repeatedly, prolonging meetings well past eleven o'clock, when members on early call the next morning got up, one by one, and left. "At which point, the radicals untabled the motion and passed it, one-two-three." As far as de Havilland was concerned, the tactic outed them as "a bunch of communists." She'd be damned if they were going to get away with that type of stonewalling any longer, which is why she backed Jimmy Roosevelt's suggestion. Over loud, angry protests, he appointed a committee to draw up a statement they could present to the membership for debate. Reagan thought it was a reasonable idea. He believed it was worth distinguishing liberalism from communism. De Havilland recalls that "Ronnie got up and volunteered to write it," a deed that touched off a vicious reaction from screenwriter John Howard Lawson, "who accused him of being a stooge of the Hollywood aristocracy."

Afterward, Dore Schary, who ran RKO's motion-picture production arm, invited Ronnie to join a renegade faction of HICCASP for a strategy session at Olivia de Havilland's apartment on Shoreham Drive. De Havilland appreciated Ronnie's willingness to stick his neck out for the group. "He was very effective with people—*very* effective," she recalls. "And he was willing to take the responsibility, which put him in a precarious position." It also pleased her that he had separated himself from the radical element. "We were all so suspicious of each other," she says. "At the time, in that atmosphere, you never really knew who was or wasn't a communist, and I just thought he might be one." When he walked into her place with the anticommunist bloc, she broke into a grin and admitted as much to him. "That's funny," he shot back, "because I thought *you* might be one."

The Screen Actors Guild was enmeshed in talks to help resolve the various labor strikes, which forced the actor's union to take a stand. In February 1946, Ronnie was chosen as a temporary SAG board member, replacing actor Rex Ingram (and in March again for Boris Karloff), spin-ning him center stage in these messy affairs.

It was a tense, difficult period. SAG worried that a strike would force actors to choose sides: either to walk out in sympathy or cross the picket lines. The IATSE–CSU fracas was especially thorny. "It's a war to the fin-ish," Roy Brewer declared, ruling out any possibility of labor peace in Hol-lywood. A wider strike was only a matter of time—SAG, under its contract with producers, had a legal obligation to order its members to work. On the other hand, all unions were in effect a brotherhood and bound to support one another. When the CSU had threatened a strike in early 1946, the guild sided with the producers, who promised to keep the studios "open at all costs." But an all-out showdown was another story.

Ronnie was full of misgivings about the situation. He had his hands full with *Stallion Road*, which was about to start production by the beginning of April. The movie, in essence his long-awaited comeback, had become an afterthought for Warner Bros. A week before the cameras were scheduled to roll, Bogart and Bacall dropped out over Jack Warner's refusal to assign Mike Curtiz to direct. "We'll have to use a B team," he told producer Alex Gottlieb. In the ensuing scramble to launch on time, Gottlieb swapped in Zachary Scott and Alexis Smith, both capable actors but without the star-power of their predecessors. He wasn't any happier about Ronald Reagan, whose presence he considered comparable to "a mannequin in a store win-dow with a built-in smile." And the Faulkner script was gone, too—too literary. The studio downgraded the movie to reflect the changes. The bud-get was slashed and Technicolor was scrapped in favor of black-and-white photography, the kiss of death in postwar Hollywood.

This turn of events was "a blow" to Ronnie, who admitted he'd been "looking for a free ride" on the Bogart-Bacall locomotive. Now he was part of a slow-moving boxcar. Still, it was a horse story, which meant plenty of outdoor work and riding, which he especially looked forward to. The movie filmed on location in Hidden Valley, an equestrian ranch community in the Santa Monica Mountains, about forty miles northwest of Los Angeles. Jane had just returned from Florida, where retakes for *The Yearling* were shot, and was spun right into *Cheyenne*, a Warner Bros. western, without a day off to catch her breath. By the time they got home at night, husband

and wife had barely time enough to eat a light supper and kiss the kids before collapsing into bed.

Whatever little downtime there was, Ronnie devoted it to union affairs. He was having second thoughts about his relationship with HICCASP. Neil Reagan badgered him ceaselessly about its communist leanings. He was like a broken record: "Get out of that thing," he implored his brother. "There are people in [HICCASP] who can cause you real trouble." Moon claimed he was "doing little things for the FBI" that included hiding in the bushes outside HICCASP meetings and taking down the license plate numbers of people who attended, certain the members were "more than suspect . . . not exactly American."

But the drumbeat of accusations about communism in HICCASP and CSU began to harden Ronnie's views against them—and against communism in general. All the vitriol from friends like Robert Montgomery, his brother, and the Red-baiting press was having an effect. Reagan concluded that "this little rump group of unions . . . had been infiltrated and taken over by the communists." It was easy to believe the CSU strike "was a plot to get economic control of the picture business," that the AFL-CIO was the root cause of all labor unrest, and that Communists were subverting Hollywood to spur revolution.

Later that summer he proposed a written doctrine that HICCASP could use to separate itself from the Popular Front, more or less sidestepping the issue. The statement, as he composed it, said that HICCASP "has no affiliation with any political party or organization, Republican, Democratic, Communist, Socialist or other. Its policies are determined solely by the majority will of its membership." Olivia de Havilland, for one, "thought it didn't go far enough." She pushed for a total renunciation of communism, without much support. The council finally approved another version, but neither faction, the liberals nor the radical left, was satisfied, and ultimately the resolution was rejected. A few days later Jimmy Roosevelt and de Havilland resigned in disgust. "Ronnie hung in for another couple months," de Havilland recalls, but his good-faith efforts went for naught. There was nothing left to hang in for. The organization had lost its way. "Very shortly," as he recalled, "HICCASP gave its last groan and expired."

It was a sorry affair—but a learning experience. Prior to this, he "shared the orthodox liberal view that communists—if there really were any—were liberals who were temporarily off track" and posed no threat to the greater good. Now he was convinced otherwise. The episode, he said, made him consider the possibility of not only a communist infiltration but an "attempted takeover of Hollywood."

I n late September 1946, Ronnie started filming *Night Unto Night,* a gloomy melodrama that Warner Bros. developed as a showcase to debut the darkly exquisite Swedish actress Viveca Lindfors. Just four days into production the CSU strike erupted, and actors had to cross picket lines to get to work. This presented a real problem for Ronald Reagan. A week earlier, he'd been elected vice president of the Screen Actors Guild, whose sympathies should have obliged it to support the protesters. But a secret deal had been struck between IATSE's Roy Brewer and high-level industry leaders to force the CSU out of the studios. Ronnie persuaded SAG's board to throw in with management as well. He had bought into the argument that CSU was too compromised and not representing the best interests of guild membership.

By September 24, twelve hundred of the CSU's carpenters and painters had been summarily fired. Outside the gates of Warner Bros. which had dismissed more craftsmen than any other studio, the CSU's Herb Sorrell addressed the pickets. "There may be men hurt, there may be men killed before this is over," he screamed through a megaphone, "but we're in no mood to be pushed around any more!"

It was the spark that ignited the firestorm. Sorrell's remarks touched off a wave of violence that was as ferocious as depicted in any Hollywood gangster film. Both sides contributed to the mayhem. On October 5, according to a CSU account, "Warner Bros. turned high-pressure fire hoses on peaceful pickets in front of the studio gate . . . [and] continued the assault with tear gas." Five days later, known as Bloody Monday, "certain IATSE heads recruited non-Warner workers to smash a picket line . . . armed with chains, clubs, battery cables and other weapons." As *Time* reported, the CSU's demonstrators "scattered tacks in the path of movie stars' automobiles, threw coffee in the faces of picket-line crossers, [and] stoned busloads of rival AF of L workers convoyed through their jeering, milling ranks."

Windshields were smashed, cars overturned. Ronnie later claimed that "a bus used to take extras through the picket lines was bombed and burned out just a few minutes before [he] was scheduled to board it." In any case, each day he rode a bus driven by Teamsters through the barriers, ignoring the advice of Warner Bros. security guards that he should lie down in order to avoid the rocks and Coke bottles launched toward the windows.

Those missiles turned out to be the least of his worries. On September 24, while shooting a scene on location at Point Mugu beach, Reagan was summoned to the phone at a nearby gas station. A voice on the other end of the line delivered an unmistakable threat. "A squad was ready to take care of me and fix my face," Reagan recalled, "so that I would never be in pictures again."

Fix his face. That could only mean one thing: acid. There were rumors that goons had a batch of it ready. Warner Bros. wasn't going to take any chances. A studio cop was instructed to "take Reagan home and stay on patrol all night." The studio also issued him a Smith & Wesson revolver and ammunition.

The craziness was taking its toll. There was turmoil in the streets, on the set, at union meetings, in Hollywood hangouts—and inevitably at home. Jane wasn't thrilled with having a gun in the house. She was naturally "high-strung," as Hedda Hopper pointed out. Now threats of violence and . . . *a gun*, which lay prominently on their bedside table. It unnerved her, especially when she woke up in the middle of the night to find Ronnie sitting up, holding the weapon, having imagined a noise somewhere in the vicinity. To say nothing of his ranting and raving about unions and communists. They seemed to imperil, for Reagan, everything he cherished: the movies, American values, his personal safety. Jane thought he was home in body but not spirit, consumed by the guild's affairs, with a phone glued to his ear or his nose in the pages of ongoing negotiations. It was all starting to get to her.

Bob Cummings sensed something was amiss. During the shooting of *Princess O'Rourke*, he'd mentioned Ronnie's impressive "grasp of politics" and drew a blustery stare from Jane. "Politics!" she hissed. "He gives me a pain in the ass. That's all he talks about. If you had to sit and listen to him like I do . . ." She shook her head, unable to finish. Jane was rarely that candid. Despite the frustration with Ronnie, public criticism was off-limits.

But occasionally a potshot slipped out. One of their friends recalled a party that fall when "Ronnie lectured everybody in the room about Communism, and Jane whispered to a friend, 'I'm so bored with him, I'll either kill him or kill myself.'"

As the strike wore on, Ronnie became convinced that Herb Sorrell and the CSU were controlled by Communists. On October 18, Reagan repeated that opinion in a speech to the film technicians of Local 683, who were supporting the CSU pickets, ultimately changing their minds. His next target was the Screen Actors Guild. Any official policy, however, had to be voted on by referendum, which meant putting it before the entire guild.

That opportunity came on October 30, 1946. A special mass-membership meeting was called to explain the strike at the Hollywood Legion Stadium, a six-thousand-seat concrete arena on the city's west side that was outfitted for boxing and wrestling matches. Close to four thousand actors and "interested parties" funneled into the facility on a gorgeous fall night, passing through a gauntlet of eerily silent CSU pickets handing out literature. The place was packed with the kinds of A-listers you'd see at the Oscars ceremony: Kate Hepburn, Bogie, Ingrid Bergman, Edward G. Robinson, Marlene Dietrich, Frank Sinatra, every movie star from June Allyson to Vera Zorina.

Ronnie delivered the keynote address. He'd put a lot of thought and effort into it. There are reams of yellow-lined notebook pages in the archives of the Screen Actors Guild that document his speech, neatly hand-written paragraphs crammed with comprehensive ideas that are simply conceived, almost colloquial in their delivery. He clearly wrote it straight out of his head. There are very few revisions. He knew what he wanted to say, and he said it in a way that would speak to such a fractious yet homogenous crowd without alienating any of the thin-skinned factions. The speech had substance; he referenced labor reform going back to the birth of the studio system as a way of comparing previous actions to the present strike. Everything steered the discussion toward his ultimate objective.

Standing inside the boxing ring, flanked by other board members—Robert Montgomery, George Murphy, and Edward Arnold—he "made the pitch to the membership that we'd learned it was a phony strike," he recalled, convinced that CSU was infiltrated by communists, "and therefore our recommendation . . . was [that] we honor our contract with the producers and that we go to work."

The reception he received was anything but cozy. Plenty of actors supported the strike. Katharine Hepburn and Edward G. Robinson—"the liberal opposition"—spoke in favor of SAG's remaining neutral, protesting the board's proposal. As they finished, a general racket broke out, and a squad of so-called bodyguards—bulked-up stuntmen moonlighting for their union—came "down the aisle slapping bicycle chains against the chairs" in an attempt to restore order. It was a thinly disguised exercise in intimidation. In the end, however, the guild members voted 2,748 to 509 not to honor the picket lines.

According to George H. Dunne, a Jesuit priest and Hollywood labor expert, "If the actors and actresses had simply refused to cross the picket line, the strike would have been settled in twenty-four hours." They held the power; the studios couldn't make pictures without them. Now that card was off the table.

Even without the actors' support the strike dragged on, but Ronnie made clear where his sympathies lay. "I am no longer neutral," he declared in a subsequent address to a veterans' group. "The CSU . . . does not want settlement of the strike. It stands to gain by continued disorder and disruption in Hollywood."

It was a key pivot in his outlook away from a purely liberal mind-set to a more centrist, even conservative-leaning stance. He continued to refer to himself as a New Deal Democrat, more out of nostalgia for FDR than as a party-line stalwart. And he still "thought government, not private companies, should own our big public utilities." The same went for public housing—the "government should build it," he argued. It was the *extreme* liberal sector that rankled him. He considered them "fellow travelers." He had concluded that communists had infiltrated and corrupted every group he'd been involved with—the Hollywood Democratic Committee, HICCASP, the American Veterans Committee, CSU. For all he knew, SAG was crawling with them.

If there was one irritant that now stirred his blood and arguably blurred his vision, it was the influence of communism. He believed that "America faced no more insidious or evil threat" and that the movie business was especially vulnerable. "Joseph Stalin," he said, "had set out to make Hollywood an instrument of propaganda for his program of Soviet expansionism aimed at communizing the world." Liberal sympathizers—as opposed to "well-meaning liberals (like me)," he determined—were playing right into his hands. They had to be stopped. The good guys (like him) had to root out the culprits and "protect the people who were innocent." This became his mantra—his mission. It rattled George Dunne, who upgraded it to an obsession after a meeting about the strike. He believed that Ronnie, "interpreting everything in terms of the Communist threat," had a mind-set that made him "a dangerous man."

Most friends in the business were willing to cut him some slack, so long as the acting never got too far away from him. He needed to strike a happy balance. But with all that had transpired, he was no longer content to soldier on, playing charming men-about-town or sidekicks. Acting alone didn't sustain him. He'd had a taste of engagement with something larger.

Ronald Reagan had found a more meaningful outlet for that charm.

CHAPTER FIFTEEN

TROUBLE IN PARADISE

*"The chief internal enemies of any state are those public officials
who betray the trust imposed upon them by the people."*

—DALTON TRUMBO

During the spring of 1947 Ronnie took a decisive step.

As soon as *Night Unto Night* finished shooting, at the end of 1946, he was offered a plum role in *The Treasure of the Sierra Madre*, directed by his pal John Huston. He and Huston had bonded over their mutual interests in horse breeding, and their wives—Jane and Evelyn Keyes—were friendly. In fact, the Reagans had recently bought a ranch they named *Yearling Row* (a mash-up of *The Yearling* and *Kings Row*) in Northridge, within walking distance of the Hustons' farm. Ronnie was convinced *Sierra Madre* would be a smash. It had a crackling good script with Bogie in the lead role and a director whose artistic vision inspired an actor's best work. And it would be shot on location in the state of Durango with street scenes in, of all places, Tampico, Mexico. *Tampico!* Could there be a more auspicious sign?

Jack Warner wouldn't hear of it. The part wasn't big enough, he insisted. Ronnie would be "nuts" to take what amounted to a supporting role when the studio continued to groom him as a leading man. Especially now, when it was trying to resuscitate his career. There was too much on the line. Besides, Warner wanted him to step into *The Voice of the Turtle*, a key picture for the studio, which was to begin shooting at the same time as *Sierra Madre*, the second week in February. Cary Grant and Tyrone Power had already turned *Turtle* down, Dana Andrews, too, and the producer, Irving Rapper, lobbied hard for Bob Cummings, to no avail. Jack Warner's fallback position: it was to be a star vehicle for Ronald Reagan.

Ronnie was in a bind. He "fussed around trying to get out of it," but knew he'd tried Warner's patience with all the "extracurricular activity"— the HICCASP and Screen Actors Guild business—that intruded on his career. As a one-time favor, the studio had held up production on *Night Unto Night* while Ronnie led a guild delegation to the AF of L convention in Chicago, hoping to get some kind of clarification about the strike. He was also in the midst of renegotiating SAG's contract with producers. All things considered, Warner wasn't pleased. The studio had put a lot of promotional effort into relaunching Ronnie as a movie star following his hiatus in the service. How galling that he seemed to have greater visibility on the speech-making circuit than with theater audiences. What's more, Warner had just seen a finished print of *Night Unto Night* and hated it, so much so that he ordered it shelved indefinitely.

Against his better judgment, Ronnie accepted the assignment in *The Voice of the Turtle*. It was a more-than-adequate enterprise. The script was adapted from John Van Druten's genial wartime play that had opened on Broadway in 1943 and was still running in 1947. But Ronnie's part—a charming soldier with a glib repartee—offered no challenge; it wasn't meaty, like the role of Curtin in *Sierra Madre* that eventually went to Tim Holt. That movie had Oscars written all over it.*

Complicating these developments was Jane Wyman's good fortune: she had been nominated for an Academy Award as Best Actress for *The Yearling*. Ronnie was thrilled for her, nevertheless it hit a nerve. He was desperate for the sort of role that Jane now got, one that allowed him to do serious work and to stretch. Even though there had never been competition between them, a shifting could be felt. *The Yearling* was a smash hit; it was the top-grossing movie of 1947. Ronnie's career seemed headed in a different direction. *Stallion Road* languished in postproduction; he had no pictures in release to Jane's two. He wasn't out of work, but the work was lame. And Jane's latest assignment was a starring role in *Magic Town* opposite Jimmy

* *The Treasure of the Sierra Madre* won three Academy Awards: Best Director and Best Adapted Screenplay (both to John Huston), and Best Supporting Actor (to Walter Huston, the director's father).

Stewart. Jimmy Stewart was box-office gold—like Humphrey Bogart. And John Huston. It didn't help that the Reagans worked in a notoriously cruel town. The Hollywood gossip mills were already trolling for muck. One rag, *Screen Album*, insinuated that "marriage mourners are wondering if Ronnie's role in *Stallion Road* will prevent his becoming Mr. Wyman."

Closer to home, he had more to sustain him. Just after New Year's they learned Jane was pregnant again. They made no secret of the fact they wanted a boy—Jane was telling friends to expect Ronald Reagan Jr. She was excited, felt great physically, and looked forward to extending the family. There were other reasons to be optimistic. The pregnancy would give her some precious time off and hopefully rescue Ronnie from all the union squabbles—and from himself. He was still working at the studio all day and on guild business to all hours of the night. Maybe this, she thought, would change things.

No such luck.

On March 10, 1947, three days before the Academy Awards ceremony, the board of the Screen Actors Guild met in a hastily called session to resolve a thorny jurisdictional problem. Because of a newly enacted resolution that prohibited members with production interests from serving on the board, Robert Montgomery, its president, announced his resignation, along with Jimmy Cagney, Dick Powell, Franchot Tone, Harpo Marx, and John Garfield. Replacement officers were pressed into immediate service, along with a vote to name Montgomery's successor. George Murphy and Gene Kelly were nominated from the floor. At the last minute, as paper ballots were being handed out, Gene Kelly rose and placed Ronnie's name in contention. Ronnie, as it happened, was conspicuously absent. He was attending a gathering of the American Veterans Committee, a group that linked veterans to potential employers, unaware that a consequential summit was taking place. When the vote was tabulated, the outcome was decisive.

Bill Holden called later that night with the results. Ronald Reagan had been elected president of the Screen Actors Guild. The news delighted Ronnie. Whatever burden SAG had caused him, whatever turmoil in its ranks, deep down he loved the politics. He was as proud of the role he had played in the guild's evolution as of any movie he had ever made. There was still much to be done about negotiating a new, stronger contract with producers and navigating a wealth of complex labor problems—leveraging the influence he could bring to bear on those issues.

There were other advantages, namely the added visibility it would give him in Hollywood, the kind of visibility he didn't have in pictures. This wasn't a supporting role. The Screen Actors Guild represented every movie actor in Hollywood; their lives and welfare depended on its heft, and he felt an obligation to defend their rights. It was a position of considerable stature.

Skeptics wondered whether he was up to the job. Many actors knew Ronnie only as a likable but lightweight guy, "not the two-fisted fighter we needed for the position." Hedda Hopper voiced their concern when Robert Montgomery reported Ronnie's promotion. "He's as green as grass!" she squawked. "What does he know?" According to one version of the encounter, Montgomery grinned knowingly and said, "Have you ever heard him talk?" In a few weeks even Hopper had changed her tune. "I was never more wrong," she admitted after watching him in action.

At home, Jane was much less enthralled. She was four months pregnant, with two young children on her hands, publicity for *The Yearling* to do, and an absentee husband. "Let's face it," said a friendly industry insider, "he neglected Jane."

Three nights later, on March 14, 1947, the spotlight was all Jane's. With Ronnie on her arm, she strode into the Shrine Auditorium in front of 6,700 colleagues to celebrate the Academy Awards. Her Best Actress nomination was a very big deal. After making fifty-two mostly forgettable movies in fourteen years, she'd demonstrated her versatility in a role of the highest caliber. From now on, producers would not be able to peg her as the ingénue, a ditzy blonde or a gum-snapping, "glamorous little cookie." She lost the Oscar to Olivia de Havilland in *To Each His Own*, but it didn't matter. The nomination had given her a new status. She'd become an *actress*.

No acting was necessary on June 17, an unusually balmy L.A. evening. Jane left a studio premiere at the Carthay Circle Theatre and found her husband on the steps outside, hunched over and gasping for air.

Tremendous coughing came in waves, the pain was excruciating. "I was sure someone in the crowd had stabbed me in the chest," Ronnie recalled. It was all he could do to struggle home to bed.

Jane, six months pregnant, flew into nurse mode the next morning when his temperature spiked to 102. He was so weak she had him taken by ambulance to Cedars of Lebanon Hospital, the medical fortress on Fountain Avenue that tended to the Hollywood elite. His condition was diagnosed as a rare strain of viral pneumonia. The doctors offered no guarantees he'd even pull through. Ronnie was due on the set of a film that morning, and Jane could hear over the phone that the studio suspected malingering. He'd been conscripted into a picture called *That Hagen Girl* that every instinct advised him to reject. The Hagen girl in question was Shirley Temple, who up to this point had been the most beloved—and adorable—child star in the world. A child no more, she was nineteen and intent on making the leap to more mature, adult movies. Jack Warner was intent on giving her that chance. For too many years he seethed while moppets like Temple, Judy Garland, and Mickey Rooney made bundles of money for MGM and Fox. But *That Hagen Girl* was terrible, and nobody knew it better than Ronald Reagan. The premise was preposterous, a convoluted soap opera about an illegitimate small-town schoolgirl who falls in love with a returning war hero who, as it turns out, may also be her father. The relationship was downright creepy. Ronnie was twice Shirley Temple's age and felt ridiculous with her in his arms. He explained this to Jack Warner, to no avail.

Warner reminded him of how he had tried to wriggle out of *The Voice of the Turtle*, and it was now turning into an all-out hit. Jack pressed hard: he knew what fared best on the screen, Shirley Temple was cherished by audiences, and Ronnie's career could use the kind of boost she would give it. Besides, it would be inadvisable for him to drop out with a baby due in four months. Grudgingly, Ronnie agreed to do the picture.

Production began on June 4, 1947. Twelve days later, Ronnie appeared in a scene in which young Miss Hagen attempts to drown herself in a lake. Who better than Dutch to perform the rescue? Ronnie insisted on doing the stunt himself, jumping off the pier of a river location, which had to be shot six or seven times. The water was cold, the weather muggy. The director ordered up an artificial rainstorm.

Reagan came down with pneumonia soon afterward. Jane kept a vigil at the foot of Ronnie's hospital bed. His temperature hit 104, bringing chills and sweats. He lapsed in and out of consciousness and suffered hallucinations, including one with Humphrey Bogart in a supporting role. He was fighting for his life. Doctors prepared the family for the worst.

Jane was a wreck. Her nerves were shot. And she sensed that something was physically wrong with her. On the morning of June 26, she went into premature labor and was rushed to Queen of Angels Hospital, a few blocks from where Ronnie lay bedridden. According to a press release issued later that day, Jane gave birth to a tiny girl who was "given a good chance of survival." That was so much Hollywood hokum. In reality, it was touch-and-go. By evening, the baby went into cardiac arrest and died a short time later.

Only when Ronnie was safely out of danger was he given the news. "He tossed and fretted in his hospital bed," despondent that he'd been unable to support Jane. He was too frail to get up, having lost seventeen pounds. Six days later, when he was eventually released, they named the baby Christine and had her cremated.

Jane was inconsolable. She became melancholy, withdrawn. It didn't help matters when Ronnie went back to work on *That Hagen Girl* and resumed duties at the Screen Actors Guild. "When they were together at Yearling Row," according to Hedda Hopper, "life at the Reagan ménage became icily polite." He "tried to coax Jane out," Hopper claimed. They'd always enjoyed going dancing, but even then, at a supper club or at Chasen's for dinner, it usually resulted in bouts of despair, and he'd end up having to take her home early.

"Work is the only answer for her," producer Jerry Wald, a friend, observed. He'd sent Jane the script for *Johnny Belinda*, his big-budget follow-up to *Mildred Pierce*, and persuaded Jack Warner to give her the starring role. She'd play a deaf mute, which meant getting into character—days, weeks, *months*, spent plugging her ears with wax to block out sound. It became an obsession with her, though it did little to help a struggling marriage.

Throughout the summer of 1947, Ronnie and Jane kept busy with their separate pursuits. They rarely overlapped in each other's company. "It was hi, how are things going, coming in, going out, passing in the hall," Hopper recalled. As June Allyson noted, "They just seemed to pass each other headed in different directions."

Ronnie had his hands full with SAG's role in the growing public alarm about Communism. In 1944, Representative John Rankin of Mississippi had announced an investigation into "the greatest hotbed of subversive activities in the United States"—by which he meant Hollywood—pledging to expose "one of the most dangerous plots ever instigated for the overthrow of the government."

The House Un-American Activities Committee—whose acronym, HUAC, sent chills down the spines of politically active filmmakers—launched an anticommunist crusade that terrorized the community for almost a decade. Were there radicals and communists in Hollywood? You could throw a stone and hit one at any studio. But as Ronald Reagan later pointed out to a skeptical columnist, "I'm not in favor of outlawing any political party. If we ban the Communists . . . we set a precedent. Tomorrow it may be the Democratic or the Republican Party that gets the ax."

That sentiment was upright and magnanimous—on its surface. Time and again, in public and in private, Reagan had condemned the practice of Red-baiting as unpatriotic, but he also despised communism, and increasingly sought to undermine its tenets.

He was in the right place. The presidency of the Screen Actors Guild gave him the soapbox from which to launch an anticommunism campaign, and a faction of his membership was ready to ride sidekick. There had always been a predominantly conservative element at the top of the guild. Robert Montgomery, Adolphe Menjou, Dick Powell, Robert Taylor, and George Murphy, among others, were determined to oust the liberal influence that they said corrupted Hollywood and was a threat to American ideals. They belonged as well to the Motion Picture Alliance, a breakaway watchdog group, whose members included Gary Cooper, Ginger Rogers, John Wayne, Ward Bond, Charles Coburn, and ZaSu Pitts. The MPA's charter made no bones about its ultimate goal. "In our special field of motion pictures, we resent the growing impression that this industry is made up of, and dominated by, Communists, radicals and crackpots," it stated.

"We pledge to fight, with our organized command, any effort of any group or individual, to divert the loyalty of the screen from the free America that gave it birth." The MPA set its sights on suspected sympathizers— "*subversives*," as it labeled them. The era of Red-baiting in Hollywood had begun in earnest.

The Screen Actors Guild became a hotbed of infighting. On September 12, 1947, at a routine SAG board meeting, a proposal was raised that would require all SAG members to sign a loyalty oath. Ronnie felt it was self-defeating, "inasmuch as there would be no reason Communists would not sign it since it would give them a screen against any person who failed to sign such an oath." Instead, he proposed making the oath voluntary. It was passed after little debate.

Reagan signed an affidavit that very night, along with five other officers of the guild. Only Anne Revere, its treasurer, refused "for principle." Later, she recalled being unsettled by Ronnie's response to a question from the floor about dealing with HUAC, should they be called to testify. "You know, anybody that's got a problem," he said, "all they have to do is come talk to us." The reply was greeted by an uneasy silence, until Revere raised her hand and said, "I have a problem; what's your suggestion?"

"It's so simple," Ronnie responded. "All you've got to do is just name a couple of names that have already been named."

Just name a couple of names. It was a glib suggestion for a serious ethical problem that was roiling Hollywood. HUAC was demanding that people turn in the names of anyone they suspected of disloyalty or engaging in subversive activities. So-called friendly witnesses, many from the Motion Picture Alliance for the Preservation of American Ideals, came forward to volunteer the names of colleagues with alleged Communist affiliations. Robert Taylor, Richard Arlen, Leo McCarey, Adolphe Menjou, and others fingered fellow actors, directors, and producers they had worked with. Jack Warner divulged the name of every liberal, left-winger, or union member who worked for him, all of whom he labeled "Communist."

The SAG loyalty oaths were a knee-jerk reaction to a government inquisition that was tightening its grip. FBI agents had long leaned on industry informants to supply the bureau with names of people expressing anti-American sentiment. Walt Disney, for one, routinely shared information about people he considered "Commie sons-of-bitches" with the FBI and with representatives of HUAC. Records show that Ronald Reagan did as well, making contact with the FBI as early as September 17, 1941, and later cooperating, with Jane, in April 1947, when he was recruited as Source T-10, naming "at least six SAG members whom they suspected of being Communists." Nor would it be the last time.* In fact, Parnell Thomas, a New Jersey congressman heading HUAC, claimed that, thanks to the Motion Picture Alliance, "hundreds of very prominent film capital people have been named as Communists to us." Since 1944, congressional investigators had been rooting through FBI files, compiling long lists of suspected communists in the movie business. Suspicion fell on anyone who "had openly worked for causes ranging from the Roosevelt reelection campaigns to international anti-fascism to organizing and supporting labor activity."

In the fall of 1947, the hammer came down. In what could be viewed in hindsight as a pivotal, if blockheaded, act, the Producers Guild volunteered its "full cooperation" with the HUAC Mafiosi, thus touching off a witch hunt that called Hollywood leftists to account for their beliefs. Pink subpoenas were issued to scores of the film community, demanding they appear before the House Un-American Activities Committee in Washington. *The Hollywood Reporter* and *Variety* published the names of more than forty people who had been called, a majority of them screenwriters or screenwriter-directors whose work was considered full of communist propaganda. Another list identified "the conservative eminences" who were invited to testify as friendly witnesses to the communist threat: Jack Warner, Louis B. Mayer, Walt Disney, Robert Montgomery, Adolphe Menjou, George Murphy, Gary Cooper, Robert Taylor, and Ginger Rogers's mother, Lela.

An additional friendly witness received his subpoena on September 25. Ronald Reagan was happy to receive it. He was eager to speak his piece.

H is domestic affairs were deteriorating. Jane had withdrawn into the character of Belinda McDonald, the tormented deaf-mute living in isolation and shame on remote Cape Breton, a coastal province of Nova Scotia. She had tapped into her own miserable childhood to convey her

---

* FBI files reveal that Source T-10, on February 10, 1948, named five names belonging to a "clique . . . who invariably followed the Communist line" at SAG meetings.

character's inner life. The subplot, in which she struggles to keep from losing her baby, cut close to the bone. The work was intense and all-consuming, and it reverberated at home.

Ronnie hoped things would lighten up for her when the company went on location to Mendocino, an old logging community about two hundred miles north of San Francisco. The director Jean Negulesco was famous for his location photography and for getting good work from difficult actresses, most recently Geraldine Fitzgerald in *Three Strangers* and Ida Lupino in *Deep Valley*. Jane would be in good hands. But the work took its toll. "When she would come in the door [after a day's shooting]," Ronnie said, "I could just tell by the way she came in . . . bad day."

He decided to accompany Jane to the set, making an eighteen-hour drive along the California coastline. Jane was locked into her role, not particularly receptive to his chatter. After a day spent bumping around the set, Ronnie packed up and returned to Los Angeles. No doubt the situation made him feel out of place. The village was sleepy, a primitive old campsite; accommodations for the actors were makeshift at best. There was no place in town for them to unwind, which drew cast and crew unusually close together. "We felt so isolated, yet oddly at peace," Jane recalled. They mingled for hours by a cedar lake near their cabins, watching the mist form over the water and the mountains vanish as twilight fell. "In the evenings we made our own fun, formed a community sing among our company—hymns and folk songs."

Jean Negulesco helped fan the camaraderie, organizing outings to nearby Russian Gulch. Hours were set aside for late-afternoon swims. Meals were mostly taken together. The actors created their own world in Mendocino, discovering a refuge from the toxic political atmosphere they'd left behind.

The poignant subject of the movie and the inspirational locale encouraged them to talk to one another about their lives and their work in ways that were strikingly personal, even confessional. Jane found she was able to express herself without the magpie sermonizing and run-on minutiae that animated so much of Ronnie's ambition. More and more, she was drawn to her philosophical, deeply spiritual co-star, Lew Ayres. She'd become extremely fond of the man who initially considered her nothing more than a "hey-hey blonde ingénue" and unequipped, certainly lacking the depth, to deliver the powerful performance the role required.

Ayres was something of an enigma in Hollywood. He'd attracted attention as the confused and remorseful young soldier in *All Quiet on the Western Front*, before finding stardom as the eponymous lead in the *Dr. Kildare* series. A combination of offbeat qualities set him apart from his Hollywood counterparts. He was a quiet, pensive man and longtime vegetarian, who prayed every day and was guided by deep religious convictions, especially those opposing cruelty toward mankind. An accomplished musician, he sat in with renowned orchestras and played on some jazz recordings. But his career had been turned upside down. He'd been a conscientious objector during World War II, causing an uproar with sweeping repercussions, including a front-page drubbing in the *Hollywood Reporter*. The Army Medical Corps deployed him as a chaplain's assistant to the front lines in the South Pacific, where, under constant fire, he administered medical assistance and prayer to men wounded and dying. He returned home a hero.

Jane couldn't avoid contrasting the two men. She admired Ayres's soulfulness, his quiet independence and common touch. He was compassionate. He was easy to talk to. Ronnie, on the other hand, was in his own world, leading the guild, fighting communists, testifying in Washington, informing for the FBI. Neglecting his family. They rarely shared intimate talks. It wasn't what she had envisioned in a marriage.

It helped her to be around Lew Ayres. They took long walks, discussing their work on *Johnny Belinda*, talking over their lives. A relationship developed—"platonic—yes, but it was intense," according to a studio publicist—and it set in motion a reevaluation of her marriage.

Ronnie sensed something was up. The Hollywood film community was notoriously gossipy, with a robust grapevine, and word flitted around pretty freely about Jane's new Mendocino infatuation. Reliable or not, it was impossible for Ronnie to ignore, and he spent as much time as possible visiting Jane on the set.

Between SAG business and the upcoming HUAC hearings, however, he had little free time. By his account, he "was spending five nights a week at the guild," leading the arrangements for a new ten-year labor pact with motion-picture producers. Negotiations stretched on for five punishing months.

On April 21, 1947, Jack Warner, in a screed facilitated by the *Hollywood Reporter*, called for an "All Out Fight on Commies" who had infiltrated moviemaking. Then, on May 15, he appeared as a friendly witness before the investigative committee in Washington, D.C. Without being asked to name names, he voluntarily blurted out sixteen writers his studio employed who were "injecting Communist stuff" into screenplays.* Most of his accusations were laughable at best, inaccurate at worst. His announcement that Warner Bros. would be happy to organize a "pest removal fund" to get rid of the "ideological termites" was typical blather. Even so, it gave the committee the extra ammunition it needed to accuse nineteen Hollywood men as being agents of subversion and called on them to appear as witnesses— "unfriendly witnesses," as the *Hollywood Reporter* dubbed them.

The hearings opened on October 20, 1947, amid the kind of spectacle that Cecil B. DeMille would have envied. The Old House Office Building was full to bursting; a breathless horde elbowed its way into the second floor Caucus Room. The media trucked in a bank of newsreel cameras, heavy broadcast equipment, a full battalion of technicians and engineers, and a national press corps of close to one hundred. Film crews lit the scene with klieg lights. It was a star-studded event. The revolving cast for the weeklong session included everyone from Louis B. Mayer and Walt Disney to Gary Cooper and Robert Taylor to a group who supported the writers and called itself the Committee for the First Amendment, which included Danny Kaye, Bogie and Bacall, Gene Kelly, June Havoc, and John Huston. Ronald Reagan was to appear on the final day, but he was upstaged, for the most part, by his colleagues, many of whom couldn't wait to turn on the Nineteen.

Adolphe Menjou, an outspoken opponent of any federally funded social program who famously declared, "Scratch a do-gooder like Hepburn, and they'll yell 'Pravda,'" behaved like a diva during his appearance. *Time* noted how he "sauntered jauntily up to the witness stand," bowed and smiled to

---

* Warner named Guy Endore, Howard Koch, Ring Lardner Jr., Emmet Lavery, Alvah Bessie, Gordon Kahn, John Howard Lawson, Albert Maltz, Robert Rossen, Irwin Shaw, Dalton Trumbo, John Wexley, Julius and Philip Epstein, Sheridan Gibney, and Clifford Odets.

applauding fans, then rattled off names faster than an auctioneer at Sotheby's. Robert Taylor suggested the government round up his communist colleagues and "send them back to Russia or some other unpleasant place." Louis B. Mayer fingered directors Edward Dmytryk and Adrian Scott and writers Dalton Trumbo, Lester Cole, and Donald Ogden Stewart, all of whom were known for their first-rate work at MGM. Robert Montgomery and George Murphy, in subsequent mealy-mouth performances, gave just enough credence to support the innuendo.

To his credit, Ronald Reagan referred to a "small group within the Screen Actors Guild which . . . has been suspected of more or less following the tactics that we associate with the Communist Party," but admitted he had no concrete evidence they were, in fact, party members. He named no names. When it came to a question about communist infiltration of the Screen Writers Guild—namely, the Nineteen slated as unfriendly witnesses—Ronnie rejected it as "hearsay."

On the whole, Reagan's testimony was bloodless, a dodge. The former lifeguard artfully treaded water. He knew how to avoid being pulled under by the treacherous current. By his account, the accused writers were nothing more than "strange creatures crawling from under the make-believe rocks." They would have to sink or swim on their own accord. He met with committee counsel prior to his appearance to determine what they expected of him and how much leeway he'd be given on the stand to express his views. As president of SAG he intended to promote the guild as a democratic bulwark able to "fight against the inroads of any ideology," while putting in a few words to praise the beleaguered film industry.

Then Hollywood went into damage control. After ten of the nineteen "unfriendly witnesses" refused to answer HUAC's questions and were cited for contempt, the producers beat Congress to the punch by blacklisting them.* The studio bosses delivered the coup de grâce. On December 3, 1947, in a show of extraordinary unity, they met in a suite at the Waldorf-Astoria in New York to hammer out a joint statement, a portion of which "deplor[ed] the action of the ten Hollywood men who were cited for contempt" by Congress and pledged to "forthwith discharge or suspend" them

---

* The Hollywood Ten were Alvah Bessie, Herbert Biberman, Lester Cole, Edward Dmytryk, Ring Lardner Jr., John Howard Lawson, Albert Maltz, Samuel Ornitz, Adrian Scott, and Dalton Trumbo.

without pay. There'd be no work for these creatures anywhere in the movie business. At no time did it mention the word "blacklist," although that's what it was. MGM's general manager, Eddie Mannix, insisted to a worried screenwriter that no such list existed, but assured him "that when I get back to the studio, I'll have your name taken off it."

As Garry Wills noted, "The purging of suspected Communists was a preemptive move on Hollywood's part to keep the government away." In effect, "running them out of the business—for the good of the business." No government oversight would be necessary.

Ronnie apparently saw nothing wrong in this, or if he did, he kept it to himself. After returning from the Washington hearings, he proposed and helped to pass a SAG resolution mandating that every board member sign an affidavit avowing "that he is not a member of the Communist Party nor affiliated with such a party." This effectively locked out any of the Ten or their compatriots from serving in the guild's executive ranks.

Ronnie didn't figure into the greater struggle. The Screen Actors Guild, he told actress Gale Sondergaard, was staunchly opposed to any secret blacklist. On the other hand, SAG wasn't about to force any studio to hire an actor who "so offended public opinion that he has made himself unsaleable at the box office." No, he wanted no part of that business. He had his own battle to fight.

W hen Ronnie returned to Los Angles in early November, Jane ambushed him coming up the walk, demanding a divorce and insisting that he vacate the premises. He was "blindsided," he told Hedda Hopper shortly afterward. "I suppose there had been warning signs," he said in retrospect, but the fact was he'd been too damned distracted. Jane's order, coming without warning as it did, seemed unconvincing. Only two months earlier they'd been expecting another baby. And they'd agreed to star in a movie together—a film version of Norman Krasna's romantic farce, *John Loves Mary*, that was still running on Broadway to sold-out houses. The way Ronnie saw it, they had so much going for them. There had to be a way to patch things up. In the end, he got Jane to sleep on her decision—to talk through their difficulties with him on the chance they could save their marriage.

To Jane, however, talking *was* the problem. His incessant chatter infuriated her. Day and night, it never stopped. During a recent evening out with Viveca Lindfors and Don Siegel, when Ronnie launched into a typical run-on dialogue, she sputtered, "Hey, 'diarrhea of the mouth,' shut up! Maybe we can get a word in edgewise." The man was unable to give it a rest. "Ronnie talked all the time," a friend agreed. He was the authority on everything under the sun: sports, horses, politics, Reds—you name it, he'd launch into a long-winded lecture. June Allyson remembered Jane telling her, "Don't ask Ronnie what time it is because he will tell you how a watch is made."

They tried holding the marriage together, but couldn't get a strong enough grip. A reporter observed them having dinner at Le Papillon and felt an unmistakable chill emanating from their booth. "They weren't laughing at all, and their few smiles were pretty wooden," she said. "Once or twice Ronnie went into long dissertations, and I gathered from Jane's expression that she was pretty uninterested in what he was saying." A few nights later they had a blow-up outside the Beverly Club, a favorite show-business haunt. While he was helping her into the car, Jane was overheard shouting, "I got along without you before, and I certainly can get along without you now."

The next day she made good on her threat. There were some final retakes scheduled for *Johnny Belinda* in a soundstage on the Warner Bros. lot. After the last scene wrapped, Jane announced that she was heading to New York—alone. She needed to get away and think things over. The studio covered for her to avoid starting rumors. It issued a press release claiming she was visiting a girlfriend who'd just had a baby. That might have been the end of it, except that Harrison Carroll, the *Herald-Express*'s East Coast gossip columnist, spotted her alone in Manhattan and wheedled an interview that broke as news. "There's no use in lying," Jane told him. "I am not the happiest girl in the world." She implied her marriage to Ronnie was on the rocks, although optimally they'd try to "avoid a separation." But to Joy Hodges, with whom she spent an evening during that trip, Jane came clean. "We're through," she confessed. "We're finished. And it's all my fault."

The news took Hollywood by surprise. In a town where marriage was the shakiest of propositions, the Reagan-Wyman union had seemed like a solid bet. An eight-year stretch was considered practically eternal. It was almost as though the film community had a stake in its success. Friends like the Powells and the Hustons were disheartened by the news, but no one took it as badly as Ronnie. He was back in Eureka, Illinois, back as Dutch, for the weekend, visiting his old coach Ralph McKinzie and anointing the Pumpkin Festival queen, when the story broke in the local Illinois papers. It hit him, people said, "like a ton of bricks."

When he returned home, Hedda Hopper and Louella Parsons circled like a pair of vultures. Louella, his longtime advocate, picked at him first. No match for her meddling, Ronnie poured out his heart, unmindful that the seal of the confessional didn't apply. Indiscreetly, he admitted that Jane had told him she still loved him but was no longer *in love* with him. That distinction seemed beyond his grasp. Even so, he was willing to give her plenty of space, hoping it would reignite a flame. "Right now, Jane needs very much to have a fling," he said. "And I intend to let her have it. She is sick and nervous and not herself." Hedda Hopper piled on in a subsequent *Modern Screen* column that aired the couple's private affairs.

The holidays that season were a dismal affair. Together, Jane and Ronnie celebrated Christmas with the kids and discussed a reconciliation, but Jane took off again soon afterward. At a New Year's party in Beverly Hills, Ronnie showed up stag, but sulked through most of the festivities, coming undone when the clock eventually struck twelve and every couple around him fell into each other's arms. Pat Neal, who was brought in to replace Jane in *John Loves Mary*, saw him stumble outside, supported by an older woman, where, oblivious to watchful eyes, he wept on her shoulder.

The new year brought no hopeful outlook. The Reagans made a few abortive stabs to get back together, with little progress. Jane was overheard telling friends, "I'm in a situation a lot of women are in. I don't know whether it is better for the children's sakes to hold an empty marriage together, or to start afresh and hope for future happiness."

Toward the end of January 1948, Ronnie moved into the Garden of Allah, a legendary celebrity residential hotel on Sunset Strip that had, at one time or another, given refuge to Buster Keaton, the Marx Brothers, and Bogie and Flynn, as well as F. Scott Fitzgerald, Igor Stravinsky, and Ronnie's boyhood idol Edgar Rice Burroughs. There was plenty of work to keep him occupied. *John Loves Mary* was finally under way, and he agreed to segue into *The Girl from Jones Beach*, another frothy comedy, as soon as it ended.

But Jane wasn't waiting around for the credits. In early February, she had her lawyer get Ronnie's signature on a separation document, a preamble to an inevitable decree. Five days later, she flew to Las Vegas in order to set up the required residence for an eventual divorce. Then Jane experienced a sudden change of heart. Without explanation, she headed back to Los Angeles, more uncertain than ever of what to do. Throughout the spring, the couple oscillated between blame and forgiveness, rejection and reconciliation. Friends tried everything—pleading, commiserating, sweet-talking—in an effort to keep them together. Richard Carlson and his wife staged an intervention with other actors at their home in the Hills. Dana Andrews recalled that it was Ronnie who eventually sabotaged the affair. "[He] started talking and talking and talking . . . just holding forth." Before he finished, Jane stalked out, saying, "I came here hoping that you had changed, but you haven't. You're still the same loudmouth. I might as well go home."

They had been through these scenes before, but this one was different. Days passed, then weeks, without any further contact between them. On July 28, 1948, Jane filed suit in Superior Court. She appeared before Judge Thurmond Clarke, testifying that Ronnie spent "too much time in film colony politics." She felt left out, she said, "because my ideas weren't considered important." In the end, none of that mattered. The verdict rested on her argument that "there was nothing in common between us," and she was granted an uncontested divorce that gave her custody of Maureen and Michael.

Divorce. "Such a thing was so far from even being imagined by me," Ronnie later admitted. He had a more conventional outlook, the product of Midwestern expectations, but in Hollywood such conventions were for the other side of the camera, not real life.

CHAPTER SIXTEEN

THE BLUE PERIOD

"Alas, how love can trifle with itself!"

—WILLIAM SHAKESPEARE

D ivorce knocked Ronald Reagan flat. He mourned, he grieved, as if a death had occurred. Errol Flynn encountered him on the lot soon afterward, ever the inappropriate guest at the wake. "Be happy, old sport," Flynn told him with swashbuckling esprit. "Think of the parties, think of the *girls*. Do what I do."

What Flynn did was anathema to Ronnie. He was in no shape to date a woman, much less . . . no, he couldn't even go there. He wanted to be left alone. The gossip columnists took to labeling him "one of Hollywood's most eligible bachelors," but the only thing he felt eligible for was counseling. He found it impossible to conceal his hangdog gloom. Eddie Bracken, his co-star in *The Girl from Jones Beach*, typed him as "a lonely guy" who craved nothing more than honest companionship. In the months that followed, Ronnie avoided the Hollywood social scene and especially the spotlight. He clung to the set all week long. Otherwise, he drifted out to the Northridge ranch, where he had three horses that required his attention, or stayed holed up in the Garden of Allah, "often in its bar, talking politics by the hour."

Politics had become a more confusing discipline for him. Ronnie still identified as a liberal Democrat—he'd signed on as co-chairman of the 1948 "Hollywood for Harry Truman" reelection committee—but a disillusionment with the federal bureaucracy was tugging him steadily to the right. He was furious with a snafu over his taxes that began during World War II. He had read that veterans of the First World War had been forgiven their tax assessments for the years they had served, and he had withheld his wartime payments assuming that the same amnesty would apply to him when the war was over. But no such amnesty was offered, and he was now in a financial bind as a result. He cursed the government every time he wrote a quarterly check to pay off the debt. Reagan wasn't a stingy man; he continued to pay a tithe to the church throughout his life. But that was his choice, not a burden imposed by a government bureaucracy. For someone who'd grown up with his family scraping for every extra penny, having the government's hand in his pocket rankled, even though his pockets were now full beyond his boyhood imagination. Reagan wasn't the first or the last person to feel a greater resentment of taxes as he had greater means to protect.

Robert Montgomery and George Murphy—both former presidents of SAG whom he greatly respected—stoked his discontent. They blamed the Democrats for excessive taxes and for creating and expanding government agencies, taking money from their pockets to fund social programs that Montgomery and Murphy felt were best left to private enterprise. To them, this reeked of socialism, and Ronnie couldn't help but agree. They also saw eye to eye when it came to opposing government regulation of the movie business. "The Justice Department issued a series of decrees that the studios could either make pictures or operate theaters—they couldn't do both," he lamented, so studios like Warner Bros. were forced to divest their theater-chain holdings to comply with antitrust laws. Ronnie abhorred any further interference. He remained a staunch anticommunist and an FBI informant whose conversations with agents helped to shift his positions. The divisive Hollywood politics, the disruption in his chosen industry, the upheaval of the divorce—all contributed to a restlessness that pushed him to reevaluate his longtime ideals.

He struggled with his political identity, unable to reconcile his current thinking with his lifelong beliefs. His father's New Deal principles were so deeply ingrained. His own convictions—as a staunch Social Security advocate and self-proclaimed "rabid union man"—were at odds with these new buttoned-down stirrings.

Just then a new union squabble gave him a new sense of purpose. The labor peace was only months old when the gods of entertainment sent a lightning bolt into the proceedings. It was called television. Old movies were turning up on TV, filling up hours of broadcasting time without the necessity of having newly produced shows. The new medium was ushering in a revolution, and the potential for new revenue streams put men like Jack Warner and Louis B. Mayer into a trance. Studios realized they could recoup some of the income they'd lost to the theater divestiture by giving their movies a second life on the small screen. No one begrudged them this new revenue stream so long as everyone involved participated. "The actors feel they should get a reasonable portion of the additional revenue," Ronnie argued in a July 1948 newspaper column. The producers, unsurprisingly, disagreed. They claimed the right to use their films for any purpose they desired. The actors were their well-paid *employees*. There was no reason to cut them in.

As president of the Screen Actors Guild, it was Ronnie's job to step into the ring against management in an effort to negotiate a compromise. It was a good distraction from the stress of the divorce. He sensed this was an issue that would have tremendous consequences. "Everyone said [the studios would] be crazy to sell their movies to a competing medium," he wrote, but they never foresaw the pending financial windfall. Both screens, large and small, had found a way to not only coexist, but to feed off each other. And television was only in its infancy, its potential untapped. Its impact was going to be enormous—incalculable. If the actors didn't take a stand now, they would be left out of the equation.

The studios stalled, delaying a confrontation. It wasn't in their interest to reach an extra-royalty agreement with the actors' union, and they sensed there would be no end to actors' tapping into their profits. They certainly didn't want to go up against Ronald Reagan—not again, not after the last bitter go-round. Jack Warner knew what to do. Ronnie's next assignment, Warner announced, would be *The Hasty Heart*. In England.

If it ever occurred to Ronnie that he was being strategically sent into exile, he never said so. His objection to the project was purely artistic. The movie was another Broadway retread, another pawky melodrama, another "breezy, amiable"—inconsequential—"piece of escapist filmfare" that would do nothing to advance his reputation. Postwar audiences, he believed, "wanted adventure and excitement," the kind of pictures John Wayne and Gary Cooper were making. Ronnie saw his future in action-packed, out-doorsy shoot-'em-ups, depicting a time, he mused wistfully, "when our blue-eyed cavalry stayed on a wartime footing against the plains and desert Indians." It was an old refrain, and Jack Warner had heard him sing it too many times.

He wanted Ronnie in England—yes, to get him out of his hair, but there were other factors that figured in. The studio altruists felt that Ronnie was "on the verge of emotional collapse" and that a change of scenery would do him good. And the bookkeepers needed his assistance to over-come a financial issue. With so many films being made overseas, Great Britain had imposed a requirement that box-office receipts earned in the country remain there to fund new productions. If *The Hasty Heart* shot at a London facility, Warner Bros. could pay for it with the frozen funds. Jack Warner explained this to Ronnie and said he'd consider it a personal favor.

What about *That Hagan Girl*? Ronnie reminded Warner. That had been a favor, too. And *John Loves Mary*?—he'd made that one, as well, against his better instincts. There were half a dozen others he could add to the favor list. Warner proposed a trade-off. He suggested that after making *The Hasty Heart*, Ronnie could find a project that suited him, and the studio would do its part to accommodate him.

A few weeks later, he sent Warner a story called *Ghost Mountain*, by Alan Le May. It was a morality play about a Confederate cavalry detach-ment and its heroic failed attempt to plant its flag atop a mountain in California. A post–Civil War western, the kind of picture Ronnie longed to make. Warner dragged his feet. The story line, as he read it, was lumber-ing and banal. And it was expensive—$35,000 to acquire the rights. As a result, the deal between the two stalled, and Ronnie sulked around the lot, implying he was in no condition to work. When it became clear he needed incentive to go abroad, Warner pulled the trigger. His hatchet man, Steve Trilling, called Ronnie with the news. "We've bought it," he reported. Ron-nie, delighted, upheld his end of the bargain. On November 20, 1948, at two in the morning, in high spirits and low-visibility fog, he set sail from Halifax, Nova Scotia, on the *Britannic*, his first trip out of North America.

The fog was thick in war-torn London, an opaque miasma mixed with soft-coal smoke that lodged in the lungs like a fur ball. Even from his aerie in the über-posh Savoy Hotel, the ravages of conflict were readily visible. Whole sections of neighborhoods were reduced to rubble, rows of houses gap-toothed and cordoned off to traffic. He thought he'd seen it all in the Fort Roach footage, but this was devastation up close and personal. In a moment of naïveté, he was overheard asking Richard Todd, his British co-star, "What's rationing?"

During the two weeks before production began, he could gauge the deprivation for himself in a country he described as "dismal wilderness." Every commodity was in short supply—fuel, food, medicine, tobacco, grain. Pubs were even thinning their beer with water. Newspapers were full of stories speculating that the new Marshall Plan might generate relief, but Ronnie dismissed it as "overgenerous." To him, it was another example of governmental excess, forcing American taxpayers to pay for rebuilding Europe.

Of course, *The Hasty Heart* company lacked nothing. The Savoy imported luxuries the destitute British masses only dreamed about, and Warner Bros. ensured every other comfort imaginable. A chauffeur-driven Rolls-Royce limo was put at the actors' disposal, they dined on pheasant under glass, and a dozen steaks were sent over from the 21 Club in New York. The studio strove to make amends for the dismal conditions at Elmstree, a series of bone-chilling soundstages an hour's drive from London, where the production set up shop for the next three months. The facility, only recently abandoned by the War Office storage depot, was a nearly deserted outpost during the winter of 1949. It was a thoroughly disagreeable work environment.

Ronald Reagan made the best of it. The work wasn't that demanding, and his director, Vincent Sherman, ran a fairly tight ship. Reagan was already familiar with co-star Patricia Neal from their recent *John Loves Mary* outing. Neal was just twenty-two, with statuesque Tennessean beauty and a charm she had cultivated in the same Northwestern drama program Ronnie had established himself in fifteen years earlier. In London, they kept each other company on weekends, and shared adjoining suites at the Savoy, where they were frequent dinner companions. There were, however, limits to their intimacy. Studio publicists hoped to spark an off-screen romance, but neither of the stars' hearts was in it. "Although I was a young, pretty girl," Neal recalled, somewhat incredulously, "he never made a pass at me." Ronnie was "in a depressed state," according to an eyewitness in London.

Instead, he spent most of his evenings doing what he loved most—talking politics at the Savoy's art deco bar. He was fascinated by the British appetite for politics and world affairs. London published an astounding eight daily newspapers. Over cocktails, he and Vincent Sherman regularly went at it. Sherman knew Ronnie by his reputation on the Warner lot as "a walking encyclopedia" who could "expound on almost anything." In London, he didn't disappoint. The Soviet Union was a favorite whipping boy. Bertrand Russell had touched off a public firestorm by suggesting that the West should deal with Russia "while we have the atomic bomb and they have not." Ronnie didn't agree, but he didn't go out of his way to disagree, either. But he had plenty to say about socialism. The British system of government confounded him—a "womb-to-tomb utopian benevolence," he called it. Ronald Reagan was not a man given to abstract thought. Socialism versus capitalism, for him, was obvious, a black-and-white issue. "I saw firsthand how the welfare state sapped incentive to work from many people in a wonderful and dynamic country," he said. Socialism, in his view, was an obvious stepping-stone to communism, and he vowed to prevent its possible migration to America.

Vincent Sherman, "a liberal, left-wing Democrat," took the nightly polemics in stride, but he couldn't help detecting that Ronnie, whom he'd long known to share his political views, had made a "move toward the right." There was a stridency to his opinions. Any challenge to its precepts struck a blow against liberty. Even Richard Todd, who stayed out of the fray, was impressed by the power of Ronnie's faith in the system. "I have never met an American," Todd concluded years later, "who so profoundly believed in the greatness of his nation." At the time, he wondered how Ronnie could possibly channel all that conviction.

R onald Reagan had more than a vague idea. He found that politics captivated him. His position as president of the Screen Actors Guild gave him just enough of a taste. He loved the strategizing, the intrigue, and the challenge, using the powers of persuasion, fighting for something he really believed in. Apparently, he was good at it, too. His popularity with the membership had earned him reelection to the post. It was a function for which he seemed better equipped than for acting. He demonstrated a real aptitude for expressing the will of his constituents. All his life he'd been unafraid of the spotlight. He wasn't afraid to stand up, to speak out—to speak his mind—and to lead. Perhaps acting was only the warm-up to a larger role in the public sector. Admittedly, he was ambitious and he harbored dreams. In an unguarded moment, he confided to Pat Neal that he wanted to be "President of the United States."

But as he sailed back to the States on March 24, 1949, the only thing on Ronald Reagan's mind was resurrecting his career. While he was overseas, *Night After Night* had opened to less than enthusiastic notices. *The New York Times*, in a particularly scathing review, said, "The Warner Brothers went to the bottom of the well" in their effort to bring the film to the screen, and castigated Ronnie "who," the paper said, "wears a fixed troubled look and moves about stiffly as a scientist who can do with some mental and physical therapy himself." He'd always known that picture was a loser. But it came on the heels of *The Voice of the Turtle* and the lingering stench of *That Hagan Girl*. He was in a tailspin.

Fortunately, there was *Ghost Mountain*. But as the *Queen Mary* docked in New York, Ronnie learned from an announcement in *Variety* that Errol Flynn had been signed to star, not him. He felt blindsided—and betrayed. Jack Warner had promised him that picture—*promised*. Ronnie had brought it to the studio! A jolt of rage and adrenaline got the best of him, and before anyone could say "Call Lew Wasserman!" he dashed off a telegram to Warner feigning disbelief in the *Variety* story, knowing Warner couldn't have gypped him out of the role "when I've always been good and done everything you've asked."

Worse, the studio blamed the role reversal on him. How could it entrust him with such a prominent part after the string of duds he'd been in? *Those were your duds!* he wanted to scream. *You put me in them!* The studio also denied promising him a starring role in any property he brought in. It was clear Ronald Reagan's star had faded at Warner. "He was not clicking at the box-office," the studio explained, "and the company was a little cold on him." There were three years remaining on his studio contract. One could only imagine how Warner Bros. would fill out the term.

Other factors contributed to his distress. Jane Wyman had been nominated for an Academy Award for her performance in *Johnny Belinda*, and she was pegged as the favorite. The scuttlebutt was she'd asked Lew Ayres to escort her to the ceremony. Ronnie would have gladly skipped the event, but as president of the Screen Actors Guild he was expected to attend. In any case, he decided not to take a date. He'd been seeing writer Doris Lilly on and off since the divorce, but realized that if it was going to be Jane's night, he'd be wise to keep a low profile. Under no circumstances, however, would he put in an appearance at Jack Warner's post-Oscars bash at the Mocambo. That was also Jane's turf, and anyway he remained furious at Jack.

In the meantime, Ronnie had Lew Wasserman renegotiate his studio contract to extricate him from Jack Warner's oppressive stranglehold. There was little resistance on management's part. It had gone about as far as it could with him, taken him as high as he was going to climb. At thirty-eight years old, he was no longer in his prime; he'd never emerged as an A-list star. To retain him as a contract player, the studio offered him a deal worth $75,000 for one picture a year for three years, basically half of what he was guaranteed previously. In exchange, he got his independence; he was free to make pictures for other studios as well.

It was a calculated gamble on Ronnie's part. He'd no longer be assured a six-figure yearly income—he was banking on his appeal to land deals elsewhere. But with thirty-nine pictures to his credit, none of them a game changer, it was debatable whether there would be any takers. Incredibly, it paid off. Only one week later, he noted, "Lew added a five-year, five-picture deal at Universal," worth $350,000. It would net him a very cushy nest egg, more than he was making at Warner Bros. What he never mentioned—or might not have understood at the time—was that Wasserman's agency, MCA, was busily buying up shares in Universal Pictures, which it planned to take over as soon as the agency gained a majority share of the company. Negotiating for MCA clients at a company owned by MCA—it made for a sticky situation further down the road.

Ronnie was thrilled. Financial security was a huge relief. "I didn't exactly know how to be a bachelor all over again," he wrote, but he had always been a quick study. He moved out of the Garden of Allah into his old bachelor pad on Londonderry Terrace above Sunset Strip and proceeded to hit the town. Chasen's, Ciro's, the Cocoanut Grove, and Slapsy Maxie's became part of his regular circuit. "He loved to go out and be seen at all the nightclubs," recalled Doris Lilly. "He also loved the comedians, so we'd go to hear George Jessel and Sophie Tucker." He began to spread his wings. Hollywood served up a feast of gorgeous young women eager to socialize with eligible movie stars. Ronnie wasn't in Errol Flynn's league—he wasn't a swinger by any stretch of the imagination—but he began to play the field with great enthusiasm. There was a revolving cast of young, blond, outdoorsy, all-American beauties—his frisky "cocker spaniels," he called them. A twenty-three-year-old knockout named Betty Bligh, who was purported to have "the best figure in Hollywood," took him home to her parents for Sunday dinners. In New York, where he maintained an apartment at the Sherry-Netherland, he saw quite a bit of Betty Underwood, a twenty-one-year-old Powers model who found him "charming and delightful and very romantic," and Monica Lewis, an MGM starlet, who became a steady crush. Actresses Ruth Roman, Adele Jergens, Ann Sothern, and a relative newcomer to the screen—big-band vocalist Doris Day—provided regular company. "There was a little place on La Cienega that had a small band and a small dance floor where he often took me," Day recalled. But there were other, more intimate rendezvous, and eventually all the carousing started catching up with him. His nightclub bills had gotten out of hand—$750 a month, by his own estimate—and his retinue of women was spinning out of control. Many years later, he admitted "to sleeping with so many girls that the morning came when he did not know who one of them was."

On Sunday, June 20, 1949, Ronnie's carousing was brought to a violent stop. He'd agreed to appear in the Movie Star World Series, a charity baseball game between leading men and comedians at Wrigley Field in L.A. to raise money for the City of Hope. On the day itself, Ronnie planned to skip the event. He was scheduled to begin shooting his first Universal feature, a thriller with Ida Lupino, the next morning and decided to take the day off to recharge. But a chance encounter with Eddie Bracken, his co-star of *The Girl from Jones Beach* and the ball game's organizer, shamed him into keeping the date. "We put him up to bat first, so that he could go home early,"

Bracken recalled. Taking a few warm-up swings, showing his old Dixon High form, Ronnie stepped in to face a star-studded battery—Bob Hope on the mound with Ward Bond behind the plate. Hope lobbed the kind of softballs he used in his routines, so Ronnie had no trouble making contact. He hit the first pitch he saw to Bracken at short and legged it out down the first-base line, hoping to beat the throw. Before he reached the bag, he went into a slide, then grabbed his right leg high on the thigh as he writhed on the ground. At first glance, it seemed he had strained a ligament, but X-rays at Santa Monica Hospital revealed a multiple fracture—the bone was shattered in six different places, requiring a traction cast and bed confinement. He'd be out of action for six to eight weeks.

From a bed with a view of the Pacific Ocean, Ronnie could envision his acting career washing out to sea. Just as the support structure of a Warner Bros. contract could no longer protect him financially, his relationships with women, after all this time, could no longer sustain him emotionally. As he lay bedridden, contemplating the future, he faced a kind of existential crisis. He was thirty-eight years old and felt every day of it, bone-weary, his body aching in places he'd never identified before. Creases had begun to appear at the corners of his eyes and around his mouth—faint, but plain enough to age him. He no longer met the requirements for the strapping young star featured in a studio's beefcake photos. The playboy roles lay slightly out of his reach. There were younger, hunkier actors waiting in the wings to eclipse him—Jeffrey Hunter, Marlon Brando, and James Dean, among a crowded field. His desirability quotient in Hollywood rated highest at the Screen Actors Guild or the Friars Club, where the membership was graying. By the fall of 1949, when he struggled gingerly to get back to his feet, Ronald Reagan's mood was fairly bleak.

And sometime just after that, Nancy Davis phoned him.

CHAPTER SEVENTEEN

"NANCY
(WITH THE LAUGHING FACE)"

"Henceforth, I ask not good fortune, I myself am good fortune."

—WALT WHITMAN

According to family legend, Nancy Davis was born on July 6, 1921, two days after her scheduled due date. A prospective actress, she was poised to make her entrance punctually on the fourth, so the story went, but her mother, a rabid New York Yankees fan, somehow—inexplicably and beyond all medical science—delayed the birth in order to watch the Bombers whip the Philadelphia Athletics, 6–4 and 14–4, in a doubleheader in the Bronx. *And the next day*, too, when they beat the A's again. Luckily for Edith Luckett the Yanks had a day off on the sixth, otherwise she might have delivered her daughter during the seventh-inning stretch.

Luckett, Nancy Davis's mother, had been center stage since she was twelve, at the dawn of the new century, when she made her debut in a play at Washington's Columbia Theater. A fearless competitor and gifted self-promoter, she hit the road at the age of sixteen and never looked back. By 1905, Luckett was appearing with a succession of top-notch touring companies, alongside Chauncey Olcott, the celebrated Irish tenor, and Broadway wunderkind George M. Cohan, whose musical revues—*Broadway Jones* and *The Fortune Hunter*—played to packed houses in every major city between New York, Chicago, and Miami. One of Luckett's earliest notices praised her "beauty, wit, and talent," and the presence of "remarkable cleverness." Glamour as well as grace impressed. She had soft, delicate features, a creamy complexion framed by straight blond bangs, with dazzling cornflower-blue eyes. A Southern, sugarcoated drawl conveyed culture and refinement.

But they were stage props. "Edie had the foulest mouth in the world," a friend told a biographer, "and she told the dirtiest, filthiest jokes you ever heard in your life." Another person described her as an outrageous character, unfiltered, "exuberantly unshockable." The ladylike, antebellum facade was pure self-invention. Fellow actors who gravitated to her during the run of a play were entertained by the evocative details of her classy background—the idyllic childhood on a Virginia plantation, a prestigious ancestry with roots on the *Mayflower*, education in the finest private boarding schools, aristocratic parents whose generosity left her wanting for nothing. Mark Twain couldn't have concocted a more fanciful tale.

As Twain might have said, Edith Luckett was born with a tin spoon in her mouth—the youngest of nine children, in a hardscrabble section of Washington, D.C., known as Swampoodle for its fetid, heavily rutted streets. The "plantation," so to speak, was a series of scrubby, cramped tenements near the railroad tracks—the wrong side of the tracks—where her father, Charles, worked as a shipping clerk for Adams Express and her mother, Sarah, ran a squalid boardinghouse. Private education wasn't even a pipe dream to the scrum of neighborhood children. Very few local families sent their girls to school, but those like Edith who gained the opportunity attended whatever public facility had a spare desk available.

Edith never graduated. By the time she turned sixteen, she was appearing steadily on provincial stages, inching her way toward Broadway. In 1910, Alla Nazimova, the theater world's reigning superstar, provided Luckett with her break by casting her in a production of *Drifting* at New York's 39th Street Theatre. It was there, in the city, that she acquired the nickname Lucky, though her luck lasted only until the end of the play's run. Three years later, she gravitated to Pittsfield, Massachusetts, performing as a member of the popular Parke Stock Company, managed by local impresario William Parke. While seguing from production to production at the

Capitol Theater, she met the feckless but handsome scion of an old New England family, who fell for this rather earthy twenty-eight-year-old actress six years his senior.

Kenneth Robbins was a pale, sandy-haired, well-built young man—soft-spoken and polite to a fault. He'd led a fairly sheltered and pampered life, "kind of a mama's boy," according to a relative's account, "sweet and charming," but lacking any worldly experience. He had only recently weaned himself from the ancestral nest, and Edith served as his first serious relationship. In Pittsfield, where an actor was regarded with about as much respect as a stray dog, the Luckett-Robbins liaison was a *scandale*. Theatergoers craned their necks to see young Robbins seated front and center nightly in the Capitol audience, staring moon-eyed as the leading lady swept across the stage.

His mother, Anne "Nanee" Ayres Robbins, was a steely New England matriarch, someone not to be trifled with, especially by an actress with her sights set on Nanee's son, her only child destined to carry on the family name. Her firm, upper class, Episcopalian ethos hardly sanctioned such an inauspicious match. But Kenneth saw in Edith much of the same spunk and tenacity embodied by his mother, and this mama's boy found comfort in that.

Despite the family's disapproval, the romance flourished. Nanee Robbins, to her credit, overcame her prejudice and allowed Edith to gradually win her admiration. On June 27, 1916, Edith and Ken drove north to Burlington, Vermont, and got married quietly in a simple ceremony in a Congregational church.

If only married life had progressed as smoothly. Edith vowed to quit the stage in order to commit herself wholeheartedly to a wifely routine. Preposterous though it sounded to anyone who knew her, she attempted to take on a traditional role. Ken's parents contributed a farmhouse in the Berkshires. It wasn't long, however, before Edith got antsy. Her foulmouthed, chain-smoking, and lusty nature didn't play well in New England. Besides, she missed the theater. Obligingly, Nazimova came to her rescue. She was about to star in a new Broadway play, *'Ception Shoals* at the Princess Theatre, and offered Edith a part in the cast. Persuading Ken to move took little effort, and by the first week in 1917 they were in New York City, where Edith jumped right into rehearsals and Ken took a job selling automobile insurance.

The play, which opened on January 10, lasted only thirty-seven performances, the marriage not much longer. The Robbinses remained together, but in name only. Edith went on the road with a touring company of 'Ception Shoals, and in April, following the U.S. declaration of war against Germany, Ken enlisted in the Army and shipped out overseas. When he returned two years later, the couple made an effort to rekindle their relationship. Again, Edith abandoned her acting career to play the compliant wife, and they set up home on Amity Street in Flushing, a middle-class neighborhood in the borough of Queens. Not long afterward Edith became pregnant.

New York City, Ken argued, was no place to raise a child. He was miserable in his job. He insisted they move back to Pittsfield, where a tidy inheritance awaited along with plenty of family support, but Edith wasn't about to revisit that scenario. At thirty-three, playing the happy homemaker was about as absurd an image as she could imagine for herself. Acting was her life's blood; it was impossible to pretend otherwise any longer. Pittsfield, in any case, was out of the question.

That was all Ken needed to hear. He decamped to his mother's house, leaving Edith Luckett to fend for herself through the last stages of her pregnancy. When she gave birth to a baby girl, on July 6, 1921, "their relationship was so tenuous," Nancy Reagan later wrote, "that Kenneth Robbins wasn't even at the hospital."

The birth certificate recorded her name as Anne Frances Robbins, but her mother never called her anything but Nancy. She was an adaptable, well-behaved baby, Edith Luckett recalled. Nevertheless, it was a challenge raising the child in a cramped New York apartment, with auditions and the burdens of a show-business life. Ken drifted in and out of the city, but by 1922 the couple had divorced. Though the great Nazimova served as Nancy's godmother, it was purely ceremonial. In the two years since 'Ception Shoals had closed, Nazimova had taken Hollywood by storm in a series of silent blockbusters. Edith was left to juggle new motherhood on her own.

She and Nancy became a familiar duo on the demanding theater circuit. They went everywhere together, day and night—to casting calls, talent showcases, agency conferences, rehearsals, even parties. Colleen Moore, the silent-screen star, was taken aback when she encountered Edith at a First National studio party "carrying a tiny baby in her arms."

In 1922, a touring company offered Edith a steady income. But it meant endless travel, living out of a suitcase, and because regional theater rotated plays on a weekly basis—sometimes twice weekly—the demands on actors were extraordinary: the incessant memorizing of new lines, afternoon rehearsals, and nightly performances. Taking a baby along was out of the question.

Edith had little recourse but to leave two-year-old Nancy with her older sister, Virginia, and her brother-in-law in Bethesda, Maryland. The Galbraiths lived on a quiet street in a small but handsome Dutch colonial with a proper front porch and enough frontage for a pair of shade trees that fanned out across the lawn. The house itself was somewhat less expansive. There were only two bedrooms—one for Nancy's aunt and uncle, the other for her cousin, Charlotte, who was five—so a sleeping nook was created on the upstairs porch. There was no hardship. Nancy was made welcome and felt the embrace of a normal family life.

Every once in a while, Edith would show up. She'd blow into Bethesda between dates in Atlanta or Dallas or St. Paul or Cincinnati, each of which she made sound like a glamorous resort, her stories of road life recited like fairy tales. Her vivacious personality and stagy delivery varnished each anecdote with layers of high-toned exotica. The descriptions held Nancy in thrall. She especially enjoyed hearing about backstage hijinks with a recurring cast of character actors. One in particular, a natural performer with a supple, gravelly voice named Spencer Tracy, Edith had befriended and trusted as a confidant. There were others just as exceptional in her inner circle—Walter Huston, ZaSu Pitts, Louis Calhern, and Don Ameche. She made their lives sound thrilling and rewarding, but in truth it was a constant struggle, living on a scant sixty dollars a month, often in fleabag hotels, waiting for the next gig to turn up. Still, within two years she had performed in a mixed bag of forty-two plays—drawing-room comedies, Greek tragedies, Grand Guignol, Shakespeare, farce, whatever came her way. "It was hard, brain-tormenting, bone-breaking work, but gratifying," recalled Pat O'Brien, another young actor who frequently crossed paths with Edith.

The real payoff for Nancy came those times when Edith landed a part in a legitimate play on Broadway, when the Galbraiths took Nancy and Charlotte on the train to see her act. Nancy would stay with her mother for the length of the run in a one-room residential hotel on West Forty-ninth Street. From there, they walked to the theater each night, hand in hand, the lights of Broadway dazzling and magical to a wide-eyed four-year-old. Nancy sat through those productions over and over, watching her mother transform herself, escaping into the fantasy of stagecraft, rushing into Edith's arms after the curtain came down, watching, fascinated, while she removed her makeup. "I quickly came to love the special feel and the musty smell of backstage," Nancy recalled. But just as quickly the show would close, and Edith would pack and be on a train out of town—by herself.

Inevitably, Nancy's mother's absence was devastating. But despite the heartache, Nancy's world remained deceptively calm. The Galbraiths treated her "with great love," like a second daughter. They provided every comfort within their modest means, and beyond. In 1925, they enrolled her in the first kindergarten class ever offered at Sidwell Friends, the tony Washington private school attended by children of ambassadors, senators, Supreme Court justices, and princes, along with such White House elite as Theodore Roosevelt's son Archibald. In the summer, Nancy and Charlotte swam at a local pool or, if they were lucky, were invited to a country club by one of their classmates' well-to-do parents. Occasionally, Nancy's father and Nanee Robbins would visit, though she was careful never to mention seeing them to her mother.

In the summer of 1927, Edith accepted a job with a touring company in England, and while headed overseas on the SS *New York* she fell into a shipboard romance with a married doctor. Loyal Davis was on his way to London to deliver a paper on neurology to a conference of physicians at the National Hospital. A thirty-one-year-old specialist from Chicago, he was a tall, robust man with a sonorous baritone fleeing a marriage as broken as Edith's. He and his wife had begun living apart just prior to his departure.

Edith Luckett lost no time moving in on him. Loyal Davis represented everything she was missing in her life—status, stability, and the promise of security. Other than his marital setback, he appeared to lead a charmed life. There was a distinctive aura about him, from his impeccable, aristocratic appearance to a litany of sharp, uncompromising judgments delivered nonstop throughout their dinner conversation. To Edith, they sounded clever and intellectual—like the ruminations of a Eugene O'Neill monologist. She shadowed him through the rest of the crossing. An entry in her journal, written while at sea, mentions the "doctor she wanted to marry."

In 1928, while co-starring opposite Spencer Tracy in *Baby Cyclone* at Chicago's Blackstone Theatre, Edith revived her romance with Loyal Davis. He was recently divorced and hopscotching between Northwestern University, where he held an assistant professorship, and a practice at the luxurious new Passavant Memorial Hospital, which fronted onto Lake Michigan. By June, when Edith segued into *Elmer the Great*, a baseball comedy by Ring Lardner and starring Walter Huston, Dr. Davis decided to propose.

They chose not to wait to marry until a lavish celebration could be arranged, opting for a private wedding with a judge during the run of *Elmer the Great* in New York. According to Nancy, "Uncle Walter stood up with my mother and father when they were secretly married in New York in October." Then, when the show moved to Chicago, they made it official on May 21, 1929, in a chapel service at the Fourth Presbyterian Church, with Nancy serving as her mother's bridesmaid. Both the bride and the groom gave their ages as thirty-three, although Edith was pushing forty-one. Not that Dr. Davis complained about a disparity in their ages. "My professional and personal life became calm and happy," he explained.

For Nancy, it was everything she could hope for. In one fell swoop, she got rolled into a family, with her mother at home on a full-time basis. But there were growing pains. The newlyweds, unaccustomed to caring for an eight-year-old, got precious little time to acclimate themselves to married life, while Nancy struggled with adapting to her uncompromising stepfather. "He seemed formal and distant," she recalled, "and at first I resented having to share my mother with him." Even friends found Loyal Davis a hard person to warm up to. "He was an austere, forbidding man, tight-assed and straitlaced," said Lester Weinrott, a family intimate. He was intolerant of those he deemed intellectually inferior, but also of blacks, Catholics, and especially Jews. At the hospital no one dared challenge his authoritarian conceits. With Nancy, he was an imposing, "rock-hard disciplinarian," insisting on her fealty, strict punctuality, and deference to his high-handed opinions. She called him Dr. Loyal out of respect, chewed each bite of food thirty-two times, as he'd instructed, and accepted his view that "men were to be the leaders and women to follow."

But if he was "gruff on the outside," as Nancy pointed out, he was also generous and kind. In 1929, in the midst of the Great Depression, Loyal Davis provided handsomely for Nancy. He sent her to the University School for Girls, a private institution, and later to Girls Latin, one of the most exclusive and prestigious private schools in the Midwest. At night, they spent long hours discussing issues he deemed worthy for her edification, and later, when he adjourned to his study to write poetry, a private guilty pleasure, verses in progress were often slipped underneath her bedroom door. On weekends, she accompanied him on his rounds at the hospital—sometimes even into surgery—where he introduced her as his daughter to colleagues and patients alike. Friends recall her gazing up at him with unconcealed awe, the same way she would, years hence, at Ronald Reagan. In no time she grew to adore her new father.

Dr. Loyal brought structure to Nancy's adolescence, but Edith—Edith provided the excitement. Her risqué personality seemed more outrageous than ever, her language saltier, her jokes cruder. She'd sworn off her former heady itinerant life in order to give marriage and motherhood her full attention, but that didn't mean shunning show business altogether. As anyone observing Edith's transition might have predicted, you could take the actress out of the theater, but never the theater out of the actress. Some big names on the entertainment circuit regularly dropped by the Davis's East Lake Shore Drive apartment. Nazimova showed up first with her lover Glesca Marshall while she was appearing locally in A Month in the Country. Spencer Tracy, chaperoned by Katharine Hepburn, came to visit "so often," Nancy recalled, "that he practically became a member of the family"—and often to dry out under Loyal's care; Walter Huston and his wife, Nan, moved in while they were starring in Dodsworth; Helen Hayes was a regular, as was Colleen Moore, Mary Martin, and Lillian Gish; Carol Channing brought Eartha Kitt. "Jimmy Cagney was always there," Edith recalled. The star light burned brightly in that fourteenth-floor duplex.

In October 1932, just after Nancy's eleventh birthday, Edith went back to work—not on the road in a theatrical stock company, but in radio, the explosive new medium that had just begun broadcasting serials and soap operas. NBC, in Chicago, was blazing new trails in radio production—in fact, it was that very company's outpost in the Merchandise Mart that had attracted Dutch Reagan on his early job-seeking odyssey. Edith became a mainstay of the company's evolving lineup, first doubling as a socialite mother and a Negro maid on *Betty and Bob*, before eventually moving on to roles in *Ma Perkins*, *Broadway Cinderella*, *Stepmother*, and *Amos 'n' Andy*.

Edith's work heightened Nancy's interest in show business. Every Saturday and Sunday afternoon, she and a friend, Jane Wescott, rode the el to a downtown movie theater where they thumbed fan magazines and sat through endless double features. "She liked Bing Crosby," Wescott recalled. When Jane revealed the name of her current heartthrob, Nancy shrugged indifference. "I don't know what you see in Ronald Reagan."

The family's apartment listing read "Luckett—Davis," but Nancy was neither. Being Anne Frances Robbins made her feel like an outsider. Every place she went, every social situation, necessitated an explanation of who she was and how she fit in. She no longer felt like a Robbins. The minimal contact she had with her father only served to emphasize his irrelevance to her. Loyal Davis had effectively taken over that role. Though Nancy didn't call him Dad, he was every bit the father figure whose guidance she sought, whom she respected, who supported her financially and emotionally. "In my mind, he is my father," she insisted. "I have no father except Loyal Davis."

She yearned to make it official. Davis was unwilling to adopt her legally while Ken Robbins and his mother, Nanee, remained vital presences in Nancy's life. But at seventeen, after she reached legal age, Nancy took the initiative. She consulted Orville Taylor, an attorney who lived in the same apartment building, about the steps necessary for filing papers, and she set the wheels in motion. In the spring of 1938, the wheels began to spin. She flew east, asking her father to meet her in New York at the city's most famous rendezvous spot—under the lobby clock in the Biltmore Hotel. It is unlikely he suspected the purpose of the get-together; otherwise he might not have brought along his mother, who never missed a chance to visit with her granddaughter. Instead of the anticipated happy reunion, the encounter was all business. Nancy produced the adoption papers and asked for her father's consent, and, as she recalled it, "they agreed reluctantly." The adoption was granted on April 20, 1938, with an additional rider attached to the court order: Anne Frances Robbins would henceforth be known officially as Nancy Davis.

Not long afterward, she got to see her new name blazoned as she'd always fantasized it: above the title in George S. Kaufman's *First Lady*, her senior class play. In her autobiography she wrote, "I don't recall much about the story." That's hard to imagine. She played the president's wife.

Like most families who lived on East Lake Shore Drive, the Davises were socially ambitious. They courted people with prominent pedigrees, traded on their movie-star friendships, moved in elite civic circles, and vacationed at the most exclusive resorts, but their real efforts went into grooming Nancy for a proper upper-crust life. As a debutante, her debut at the posh Casino Club was splashed across Chicago's society pages. She joined the class of 1943 at Smith College, one of the tony Seven Sisters schools, where girls from fancy backgrounds prepared for more of the same. For a while, she dated a Princeton student whose parents were friends with Edith and Loyal, and on June 24, 1944, she became engaged, albeit briefly, to James Platt White Jr., an Amherst grad from a well-to-do East Coast family. But Nancy's true affections lay elsewhere.

Nancy had chosen drama as her college major and participated in several of the school's productions. She had loftier goals in mind. Intent on paying her dues, she interned with summer-stock outfits in Massachusetts and Wisconsin that provided scant opportunity to appear onstage. But poor critiques and the lack of encouragement didn't deter her. After graduating in 1943, she bided her time as a salesgirl at Marshall Field before family connections finally opened a door. Thanks to Edith's intervention, ZaSu Pitts offered Nancy a walk-on in *Ramshackle Inn*, which had opened in New York earlier in the year and was now touring to cities around the country. No sooner had she shaken free of its three-month run than a better opportunity arose, again as a favor from a family friend. Mary Martin, a longtime patient of Loyal Davis's, was rehearsing *Lute Song*, a new Broadway musical that gave Yul Brynner his breakout performance. There was a small part—a Chinese handmaiden—that suited Nancy's nascent talents.

Three weeks into rehearsal, however, the director disagreed. John House-man found Nancy's acting skills "awkward and amateurish" for a top-drawer Broadway production. "I suggested to the producer that she was not physi-cally convincing," recalled Houseman, who had been hired after Nancy joined the cast. He was told to take it up with Mary Martin. In all fair-ness, he'd have fared better asking her to replace Yul Brynner. Fire Nancy Davis?—not a chance, the star argued. Her bad back took precedence, and she wasn't about to alienate her precious doctor by sacking his daughter.

Following two additional short-lived stints in road companies with ZaSu Pitts, Nancy turned to another of her parents' friends to facilitate a difficult leap from stage to screen. Spencer Tracy happened to be in New York on his way to shoot a film in London. For years, Tracy had plugged away in second-rate stock companies alongside Edith Luckett, banking on an even-tual break. Now, in 1944, he was MGM's most important male star, having won back-to-back Oscars for *Captains Courageous* and *Boys Town*. A mea-sure of that success he owed to Loyal Davis, who nursed Tracy through harrowing alcoholic binges. As a matter of payback he took Nancy to din-ner, during which he promised to help get her a Hollywood screen test. In the meantime, he gave her phone number to his buddy Clark Gable, who dated her fairly steadily for several months.

It was a fabulous time for her to be in New York. The war was over. The mood throughout the city was upbeat, euphoric. Swells of humanity flowed up one side of Times Square and down the other, genial and giddy. Several times daily, carloads of servicemen emptied out of trains at Pennsylvania Station, their return a poignant reminder that the future was a precious gift. Cars honked their horns in acclamation. In the West Forties, the the-ater was experiencing an unprecedented burst of riches, with twenty-four smash hits lighting up Broadway. Nancy could walk down the street past the neon glare of marquees heralding *Carousel*, *Oklahoma!*, *The Glass Me-nagerie*, *On the Town*, *I Remember Mama*, and *The Hasty Heart*, whose film version would later star Ronald Reagan. The latest hits were being sung in jam-packed cabarets and clubs—"Straighten Up and Fly Right," "Senti-mental Journey," "Twilight Time," "You Always Hurt the One You Love," and a particular favorite, "Nancy (with the Laughing Face)."

New York had an invigorating effect on Nancy. Since graduating from Smith, she had morphed from a chubby schoolgirl into a slim, fashionable, pretty young woman with an intelligent face and a coquettish smile. And there were many familiar faces to smile at in New York City. Walter and Nan Huston—Uncle Walter and Aunt Nan—lived around the corner from her flat at the Barbizon Hotel for Women. On Spencer Tracy's advice, she'd struck up a friendship with Katharine Hepburn, who lived a few blocks farther south. "I also had dinner a lot with Lillian and Dorothy [Gish]," she recalled, "and then we'd go to a movie."

Her social life stretched beyond the circle of glamorous family friends. A posse of suitable men, not all of them young and many of them homosexual, took her out on the town on a regular basis—producers, assistant directors, publishers, actors. She became a fixture at all the city's showbiz hot spots—the Stork Club, 21, El Morocco, the Colony, Sardi's, parties at the Waldorf Towers. There were plenty of dates, but nothing that clicked. "I had no serious romances," she allowed.

No romances—and little or no work. There were few callbacks from her endless loop of Broadway auditions, no serious offers. In early 1948, a friend booked her into a limited-run revival of *The Little Foxes* at the Shubert Lafayette in Detroit, but that was it as far as stage work went. She kicked around New York for the rest of the year, appearing in, as a magazine column noted, "feature roles on the Kraft Television Theater and the Lucky Strike dramatic series," but calling them feature roles was stretching it. There were a few lines here and there, a walk-on or two, nothing more substantial than what actors call window dressing. "I wasn't setting show business on fire," she acknowledged.

Her career seemed ripe for a serious reassessment. Four years in New York offered little to show toward the kind of theatrical success Nancy Davis had dreamed of. Despite the smattering of breaks, famous family intermediaries who went to bat for her, a series of first-rate drama classes, and the concentrated effort she'd made, the outlook for a Broadway breakthrough was dismal. As 1949 began, a good New Year's resolution might have been to consider another line of work.

But then, on January 2, Nancy got a call from her agent, informing her that "someone from Metro" had seen one of her television appearances and suggested she fly out to Los Angeles for a screen test at the studio. Who that "someone" might be wasn't a mystery. On and off, she had dated Benny Thau, MGM's collegial vice president, who not only oversaw casting but was said to have initiated the practice of the casting couch. Though he was short, portly, balding, and, at fifty-one, old enough to be her father, Nancy found Thau an enthusiastic and supportive companion. No doubt his influence in Hollywood lent his countenance an attractive glow. In any case, his most important male star, Spencer Tracy, went to work on Dore Schary, Metro's head of production. "The girl knows how to look like she's really thinking when she's onstage," Tracy told him.

As they soon discovered, however, it would take more than an intellectual expression to turn Nancy Davis into a star. Despite an embarrassment of riches invested in the test, there was no heat on the screen. Tracy had talked his pal George Cukor into shooting the audition, a favor comparable with an author having F. Scott Fitzgerald edit his manuscript. Cukor was one of Hollywood's A-list directors—MGM's top director—the man who drew remarkable performances from his female actors in *Little Women*, *Dinner at Eight*, *The Women*, *Camille*, *The Philadelphia Story*, and *Gaslight*. The scene he chose for Nancy was from *East Side, West Side*, a high-priority studio project scheduled to shoot later that year. He even recruited hunky Howard Keel to read opposite her. It still didn't add up to much. Cukor knew what a star looked like when he saw one. After watching a print of the finished test, "he told the studio Nancy had no talent."

In most cases, if a tastemaker of George Cukor's esteem delivered such a verdict, the star-making machinery would have ground to a halt. Not this time. Thau and Tracy had the power to veto the director's opinion, and they exercised it. They convinced Schary that signing her would eventually pay off, and he acquiesced.

On March 2, 1949, MGM announced that the studio had given a seven-year contract to Nancy Davis at a starting salary of $300 a week. She was twenty-eight years old (dropped down to a more marketable twenty-six on the official document). One of her professional goals was snagging an eligible bachelor from among Hollywood's leading men. Six months later, Ronald Reagan separated himself from the pack.

CHAPTER EIGHTEEN

"RONNIE'S FINEST HOUR"

"Untwisting all the chains that tie,
The hidden soul of harmony."

—JOHN MILTON

The "How Ronnie Met Nancy" story has gone through many rewrites over the years. In an early draft by a Hollywood historian, a hard-charging Nancy Davis asked Dore Schary to introduce her to Ronald Reagan, preferably in an intimate setting, preferably at Schary's Brentwood estate, where she could take the measure of this desirable single man. She knew all about his recent divorce, his wounded heart. In a later version, Schary's wife, Miriam, claims she extended an invitation to both parties. The Scharys' daughter, Jill, distinctly recalled the pleasant but otherwise unexceptional dinner at their home in early October 1949. "There was a lot of political talk and some arguments. Nancy listened to [Ronnie] attentively . . . and she kept smiling at him in agreement."

According to Nancy Reagan, it never happened. With unwavering certainty, she insisted their introduction was triggered by an article in the October 28, 1949, edition of the *Hollywood Reporter*. In a move to out as communist sympathizers the co-signers of a Supreme Court amicus curiae brief filed on behalf of Dalton Trumbo and John Howard Lawson, the far-right-leaning trade paper published all 208 names, one of which was Nancy Davis. Seeing it included there, in black-and-white, unnerved Nancy, who'd never signed the brief. "I knew my name did not belong on that list," she protested.

The next morning, on the set of *East Side, West Side*, a melodrama in which she had been cast to fill a small supporting role vacated abruptly by Mary Astor, Nancy cornered her director, Mervyn LeRoy, and asked him how to correct the mistake. LeRoy had the studio arrange for a retraction in a Louella Parsons column, in which the gossip doyenne declared Nancy "100 percent American," while fingering another Nancy Davis—the wife of agent Jerry Davis—as an actress who supported "leftist theater" and "Henry Wallace's politics." This still wasn't enough to satisfy Nancy, so LeRoy volunteered to call the SAG president. A callback from Ronnie to solve her dilemma prompted a dinner date, which, according to Nancy's version of the encounter, sparked instant romance: if "not exactly love at first sight . . . it was pretty close."

Her version is dramatic and satisfying, and Ronnie repeated it in his various autobiographies. But no matter how well they told it, or how often, that didn't make it true.

When Nancy climbed into Ronnie's swank green Cadillac for their first date, on November 15, 1949, they'd already met at two previously arranged fix-ups. There is little doubt that they'd dined together at Dore Schary's home in mid-October; too many of the participants recalled specific details about the evening. ("She was sitting opposite him at the table." "I don't recall his saying much to Nancy.") And sometime after that, later in the same month, another Hollywood couple—Phyllis Lawton, head of the talent department at Paramount, and George Seaton, a screenwriter and actor who originated the role of the Lone Ranger on radio—repeated the gesture. "Phyllis told me they invited Ronnie to dinner to meet Nancy," recalls Olivia de Havilland. "They thought he was deeply affected by the divorce, in need of companionship—and they knew her." From all indications, it was another successful get-together, according to de Havilland's memory. "Phyllis talked to me the night after they had Ronnie and Nancy over, and they felt they had made a match." And somewhere in between those dinners, Nancy had called Ronnie at the SAG offices and "indicated her willingness and desire to run for the Board" at the guild's annual election in November. It was as good a ruse as any to signal her interest in him.

In all likelihood, Nancy had been running a shadow campaign to land

Ronald Reagan as a lover long before she slid into the front seat of his car. He remained at the top of her "hot prospect" list. She had been trying for some time to meet someone who was more stable and marriage-minded than the other men in her life. Her affair with Benny Thau had certainly helped to jump-start her career, but it wasn't headed anywhere serious. Already past the age of fifty, Thau polished his reputation as a confirmed bachelor, and Loyal Davis had voiced his strong disapproval, probably because Thau was a Jew. Nancy's other relationship, with actor Robert Walker, faced different obstacles that were equally as discouraging. The thirty-year-old, perennially boyish actor's life was a mess. His ten-year marriage to Jennifer Jones had recently fallen apart, as had a five-month marriage to John Ford's daughter, Barbara. Not long before he began dating Nancy, Walker was jailed for drunk driving and confined for a period to the Menninger Clinic in Kansas, where he was treated for "a psychiatric disorder" that was code for acute alcoholism. There is no written record of Loyal Davis's opinion of Walker, but it wouldn't be hard to imagine his distaste. Even Nancy, to whom marriage was the highest priority, knew better than to pin her hopes on a prospect like Robert Walker.

She was having plenty of trouble finding the right man. At twenty-eight, without a marriage—or two—under her belt, she was approaching old-maid status in a town like Hollywood. Nancy was not a fabled beauty on the order of Ava Gardner or Rita Hayworth. But she was a handsome woman— "attractive," in Benny Thau's estimation, "but not beautiful." The impression she gave was that of a woman on the make. "Maybe it was because she was so ambitious," Ann Sothern, a recent co-star of hers, surmised. Nancy's routine table-hopping in the MGM commissary was considered déclassé, too aggressive for a minor contract player. You might be a personal friend of Spencer Tracy's, Walter Huston's, and Clark Gable's, but studio policy demanded a certain social formality, especially in the commissary, where stars were segregated from the proletariat. Most actors were wary of women who came on too strong, but Ronald Reagan, in his rather vulnerable state, was the perfect candidate for Nancy's forward approach.

When he arrived to pick her up, she was dressed in a sedate black sheath dress with a white collar that emphasized her figure without giving too much away. Ronnie was still leaning heavily on a pair of canes, a holdover from his charity-baseball-game injury. He insisted that "bells didn't ring or skyrockets explode," but there was an instant attraction. Mutual, Nancy admitted, thinking, "He looks as good in person as he does on the screen."

Ironically, they headed to La Rue, the upscale French restaurant on Sunset Boulevard owned by Billy Wilkerson, the ultra-right-wing publisher of the *Hollywood Reporter* responsible for the "Nancy Davis" mess. There, seated in one of the tacky gold leather banquettes, Ronnie suggested that if she wanted to resolve the business with her name she should subscribe to the time-honored Hollywood practice and simply change it to something else. Nancy wouldn't hear of it. It had taken her years to become Nancy Davis; there was no way she was giving it up. There had to be something Ronnie could do to help.

After dinner, they rode farther down the Strip and caught the midnight show at Ciro's, where Sophie Tucker was in residence. This was one of Ronnie's mainstays on the dating circuit, the same place he'd taken Doris Lilly and Monica Lewis. But with Nancy it was different. There was enchantment in hearing each other laugh at La Tucker, discovering they shared the same sense of humor. They drank copious amounts of champagne. When the comedienne segued from stand-up to song, lapsing into *"If I had my life to live over / I'd still fall in love with you,"* Ronnie struggled to his feet and half-danced, half-stumbled to the music, holding Nancy, who felt just right, in his arms.

Nancy was drawn to his easy conversation. She saw his legendary effusiveness as exuberance, enjoyed how he shifted from discussing his love of ranching to his work for the Screen Actors Guild to his infatuation with Civil War history to his interest in wine. Where these digressions might have sent Jane Wyman running for an exit, Nancy found them enchanting. "I loved to listen to him talk," she later admitted. "I loved his sense of humor. I saw it clearly that very first night. He was everything that I wanted."

Ronnie wasn't as certain. For the first time in his life, he was playing the field, and the field, he discovered, was very fertile ground. Nancy Davis was a fine occasional date, but there was an ample stream of fine dates in the Ronald Reagan queue. His uncharacteristic conduct warranted a caution about conspicuous consumption. An extraordinary editorial in the May 1950 edition of *Silver Screen* posited, "Never thought we'd come right out and call Ronnie Reagan a 'wolf,' but leave us face it. Suddenly every glamour gal considers him a super-sexy escort for an evening." For a man needing two canes for support, he had no trouble legging it around town. There were pictures of him in practically every local paper and fan magazine—at the Mocambo or Ciro's or the Cocoanut Grove or the Trocadero or King's or Slapsy Maxie's—with a different starlet on his arm. In between the outings, there were other, more intimate liaisons. Piper Laurie, the eighteen-year-old co-star of *Louisa*, Ronnie's first film at Universal, lost her virginity on their first and only date. (He was twenty-one years her senior.) His relationship with ingénue Jacqueline Park ended abruptly after she informed him she was pregnant by him. There is no record available documenting whether she gave birth to a child. And a romance with actress Christine Larson, a ravishingly beautiful young woman, sparked an outright proposal and an engagement gift.

Nancy Davis had become a regular presence in his life; she'd been introduced to Neil and Nelle (as had Christine Larson); spent weekends with Ronnie's children, Maureen and Michael, on a new 290-acre ranch he'd recently bought in Malibu Canyon; had joined the board of the Screen Actors Guild; occupied his booth at Chasen's. Photos of them together began popping up often in gossip columns and magazines. Hedda Hopper reported that "Ronnie Reagan is a happy man these days. . . . It's very obvious that he's in love with Nancy Davis." Even Neil Reagan had taken notice. "Looks like this one's got her hooks in him," Moon observed. Ronnie's social life seemed to be closing in around him. He admitted as much to colleagues at the studio. He needed to get a grip on things, he said, before they got too out of hand.

Or his hand got forced.

One evening in February 1952, while having dinner at Chasen's, Nancy dropped a bombshell: she was pregnant. He was caught off guard, staggered. This wasn't a woman to be easily dismissed, sent packing, like Jacqueline Park. But—marriage? He'd been ducking the issue with her for some time. And there was Christine Larson to deal with. Their so-called engagement flew under the Hollywood radar. Neither Hedda nor Louella had gotten wind of it yet. He'd given Christine a diamond wristwatch to pledge his troth, not a ring, which would have been difficult to explain. He'd have to wriggle free of that situation. In any case, time had run out on Ronald Reagan's amorous exploits. It had been three and a half years since his marriage to Jane Wyman ended. Marrying Nancy Davis now seemed—appropriate. Not exactly the way he had planned things, but—appropriate. They shared a lot of interests, his kids liked her well enough, and she was compliant beyond any expectation, seconding every proposal he put forward at the SAG board meetings, staring raptly at him, nodding agreement at each of his innumerable opinions. Now she was pregnant. Marriage began seeming less like something appropriate and more like a fait accompli.

Once Ronnie agreed, they moved swiftly to lock in his commitment. On February 20, 1951, he called Loyal Davis and Edith Luckett at their winter home in Scottsdale, Arizona, to formally request their daughter's hand in marriage. On February 21, Louella Parsons's column appeared below the headline "Davis Reagan Nuptials Set." Six days later, MGM issued a press release announcing the couple's wedding, which would occur on Tuesday, March 4, at "some small church in Southern California."

There was one blessing they still required. For the past five years, Ronnie had religiously consulted astrologer Carroll Righter, the self-styled "guru to the stars," whose weekly horoscopes guided the careers of Clark Gable, Bette Davis, Lauren Bacall, Marlene Dietrich, Lana Turner, Ann Sothern, Bob Cummings, and Susan Hayward. Arlene Dahl, another acolyte, revealed that "Carroll was helpful in choosing dates [on which to hold important meetings] for Ronnie when he was president of SAG," among other essential matters. According to an associate of Righter's, even the Reagan-Wyman divorce date was charted to assure that the heavens smiled favorably on the lawsuit. Nancy understood that astrology offered a key to Ronnie's affections. Shortly after their first date, she showed up at one of the invitation-only monthly gatherings at Carroll Righter's mansion and became an instant convert. She tapped into all kinds of gainful wisdom—that "Aquarians are capable of love, but their version is somewhat impersonal." More aptly, "Aquarian men are often slow to get married." Now they sought the astrologer's sanction that their wedding plans were aligned with the stars.

The wedding itself was more down-to-earth. They chose an innocuous, out-of-the-way chapel in the Valley—the Little Brown Church, associated with the Disciples of Christ. Ronnie dreaded a typical Hollywood affair attended by studio suits and especially the press. It had hounded him mercilessly since his divorce from Jane Wyman, souring him to public scrutiny. This time around he mandated that things be kept low-key. As a result, Nancy missed out on wearing the kind of wedding gown she'd always dreamed of, substituting an off-the-rack gray wool suit with white collar and cuffs that she found at I. Magnin, with a flowered, veiled hat and a strand of pearls her parents had given her at her debutante party. "We didn't invite anybody," Nancy recalled, "no press, no family, no fuss." Aside from the preacher who officiated, the only witnesses were Bill Holden and his wife, Ardis (known on the screen as Brenda Marshall), who threw them a private party afterward at their home in Toluca Lake.

The post-wedding plan was to spend a few days at the Mission Inn in Riverside before driving to Phoenix for some extended downtime at the Arizona Biltmore, where they'd visit with Edith and Loyal, who lived just next door. The newlyweds had plenty of time on their hands. After a string of forgettable movies that included *Night into Morning*, *It's a Big Country*, *Shadow in the Sky*, and *Talk About a Stranger*, Nancy had been notified in November 1951 that her option at Metro would not be picked up in March, when it came up for renewal.

Ronnie's movie career was spiraling along a similar trajectory. His relationship with Warner Bros. had deteriorated steadily, beginning with an ill-considered interview he'd given to Bob Thomas of the Associated Press in January 1950. Smarting from losing *Ghost Mountain* to Errol Flynn, Ronnie complained that the parts the studio gave him were beyond awful. "I could telephone my lines in and it wouldn't make any difference," he said. After reading that comment, Jack Warner went ballistic. He dashed off a letter to Ronnie suggesting that if this was indicative of his attitude toward the studio, perhaps they should go their separate ways. "I would greatly appreciate your sending me a letter cancelling our mutual contract obligations with respect to the two remaining pictures you are about to do with this company," Warner wrote. Once he cooled down, Warner put the letter in a drawer rather than a mailbox; instead, he dispatched his hatchet man, Roy Obringer, to read Ronnie the riot act. As a result, more grievances filtered back to Warner. It rankled Ronnie that he played in Richard Todd's shadow in *The Hasty Heart*; he was blamed for *That Hagen Girl* tanking at the box office; no one from the studio visited him during the six weeks he lay in the hospital with a broken leg; and "he was being double-crossed in not getting *Ghost Mountain*." He also felt that his high-profile post at SAG put a target on his chest, though no studio official would admit as much. If Ronnie's pictures had fared better, the squabble might have blown over. But *Storm Warning*, about a small-town Ku Klux Klan skirmish, proved a box-office disappointment, and no less a critic than Bosley Crowther called Ronnie's performance "pat and pedestrian." The reviews weren't much better for *She's Working Her Way Through College*, a threadbare musical showcasing Virginia Mayo that floundered and quietly sank from view. An actor could carp all he liked if his movies made money, but Jack Warner had just about run out of patience with his fading star.

Things weren't much rosier for Ronnie at Universal. *Louisa* garnered decent reviews but only did what studios called so-so business. In *Bedtime for Bonzo*, a puerile comedy made in late 1950, he played second fiddle to a capricious, scene-stealing chimp who had been rescued from the Jungle-land in Thousand Oaks, and was killed in a fire the night the picture premiered. Two subsequent scripts offered to Ronnie—*Fine Day* and *Just Across the Street*—were rejected for not meeting his standards.

Both studios were having second thoughts in the weeks following New Year's in 1952. On January 15, Universal decided to cut its losses and reduce its contractual obligation with Ronnie to three films from the original five. And on January 28, following the last scene shot for *The Winning Team*—a film about baseball great Grover Cleveland Alexander, Ronald Reagan's forty-second movie for Warner Bros.—the studio allowed his contract to lapse and he left the lot for the last time. Lew Wasserman managed to attach him to a few freelance assignments at Paramount, but those efforts— *The Last Outpost* and *Hong Kong*—failed to win audiences over. He had one more shot at Paramount. *Tropic Zone*, a convoluted adventure with Rhonda Fleming set on a banana plantation in Central America, was set to begin shooting a week following the honeymoon. On the whole, it didn't have much going for it. "I knew the script was hopeless," Ronnie recalled. It gave off a solid B-picture vibe. Otherwise, the outlook for meaningful work was slim for the forty-one-year-old actor.

Money was becoming an issue. Ronnie had just one picture left on his Universal contract, which would net him $41,000, slightly more than half of his former Warner Bros. rate. He and Nancy planned to spend $42,000 on a lovely three-bedroom cottage in Pacific Palisades alone. With a baby on the way, they wanted a reasonably priced home, somewhere outside the Hollywood rat race. Pacific Palisades was an up-and-coming neighborhood west of Santa Monica that mixed rusticity with charm. The dozy streets saw little L.A. traffic; the ocean lay just over a rise. "It was almost like living in the country," Nancy said. A country populated by actors. Jerry Lewis lived down the street, and Arlene Dahl, Fernando Lamas, Joseph Cotten, and Gregory Peck were scattered nearby in the woodsy environs. The cost of the house wouldn't wipe them out, but it was difficult keeping pace with so many expenses. A hefty mortgage remained on the Malibu spread, and Nelle Reagan's upkeep was modest but not insignificant. Ronnie's thoroughbred enterprise—more expensive hobby than moneymaking venture—demanded a constant investment. There were also his payments to the IRS against the taxes he'd deferred during the war. Debt was consuming Ronald Reagan. For the time being, he couldn't afford to buy furnishings for their living room. It was time to consider alternatives to making movies.

For the past couple of years, Ronnie had made the rounds of the after-dinner lecture circuit. He was a sought-after speaker for civic groups and at colleges, where his unfettered opinions on such issues as the spread of communism, excessive taxation, and governmental bloat drew an enthusiastic reception. He'd also published dozens of politically charged editorials in ideological journals of the left and the right. He'd honed his delivery on the radio and on the screen, and his SAG presidency had provided influential muscle, giving him the opportunity to express his views with authority. These were rewarding forums he continued to explore, but they were by no means lucrative enough to sustain his lifestyle.

Television remained a viable possibility, but so far Ronnie had resisted its pull. In 1952, serious film stars still considered TV a place where second-rate talents and has-beens plied their skills. But the landscape was changing—and fast. According to the 1950 census, five million U.S. homes now had a television, creating unprecedented demand for content. Ronnie had long claimed of TV that "everyone of stature in Hollywood was delicately holding their noses about it," but that wasn't in fact always the case. Top-tier actors like Dick Powell, Ida Lupino, David Niven, and Charles

Boyer were appearing regularly on *Four Star Playhouse*, a dramatic anthology series on the CBS network. Lucille Ball starred in her own weekly show. Ronald Colman, Joan Fontaine, and Gloria Swanson turned up in segments on the small screen. Television was becoming a force to be reckoned with.

By virtue of his presidency in the Screen Actors Guild, Ronnie became more than a bystander in TV's emergence. Actors were his primary constituency, no matter where they did their work. Midway through 1952, however, the union had no jurisdiction over actors on TV. If SAG intended to serve its members and continue protecting them in all provinces of the entertainment world, he knew some accommodation had to be made concerning the new medium.

Despite his good intentions, TV lay well out of SAG's reach. The major movie studios, fearing television would siphon off their audience, refused to allow small-screen production on their lots. As a result, TV production was strictly an East Coast phenomenon controlled by broadcasting networks and advertising agencies. Logistics aside, the guild's main obstacle to concentrating its power had less to do with the actors themselves than with the individual shows they were featured in. A majority of television was broadcast live in 1952, and SAG admitted it had no jurisdiction in that area. The guild claimed control only over *filmed* TV shows and theatrical movies that were later televised. But other unions were being organized that sought to preempt SAG's authority in the new medium, and a battle royal ensued.

Heated meetings went on "for seven months twice a day, five days a week," Reagan recalled. As he saw it, the bedrock of actors' inalienable rights was at stake. The guild's jurisdiction had to be preserved in order to protect actors from being exploited by television producers, and a pay scale had to be established to determine residuals in the event of reruns. If the producers reaped huge profits from reruns, he argued, the actors needed to receive a fair share.

Ronnie and his SAG colleagues came under attack from every quarter—from the American Association of Radio Artists (AFRA), which for years had represented radio artists, many of whom had gravitated to TV; renegade unions looking to cash in; disgruntled actors caught in the middle; aggrieved broadcasters reluctant to cede control; even government agencies trying to influence the negotiations. Ronnie saw communist conspirators lurking in the shadows. "The same group that had pestered us in the CSU mess was back in uniform," he concluded, "ready to lead an assault from the rear on the guild board." Negotiations that seemed resolved one day broke down the next in a huff of accusations and name-calling. The wear-and-tear took its toll. Ronnie commuted between L.A. and New York by train, rather than flying, which he dreaded—four endless days on the Super Chief, anchored to his seat as a result of the crutches he continued to depend on. And his career continued to suffer because of ongoing distractions of his SAG duties and wrathful studio bosses, who regarded him as their foe.

Two years later, when the smoke had cleared, he seemed to think that the personal costs had been worth it. The guild had emerged stronger from the hostilities by solidifying its grip on all performers in the motion-picture field, whether their films appeared in theaters or on television. Moreover, an agreement governing residuals for actors had been won—not the windfall he wanted, but a foot in the door. A jubilant Reagan wrote, "It was a victory even more complete than we had hoped."

But the victory spun off a new headache for Ronald Reagan. MCA, his own agent, announced its intention to get into the television production business.

This wasn't just a headache—it was a full-blown migraine. It went against everything the Screen Actors Guild stood for.

SAG's bylaws strictly prohibited agents from engaging in theatrical film production without a waiver from the guild. The rule, instituted in 1939, protected actors against an agency's representing them in negotiations with the agency's own production company—in other words, being an actor's agent *and* his employer, clearly a conflict of interest. The rule was drawn up not least with MCA in mind. The agency had become such an all-powerful force, perhaps the *most* powerful force in Hollywood, and its nickname, "the Octopus," because it had "tentacles reaching out to all phases and grasping everything in show business," continued to inflame. Studio bosses such as Jack Warner complained loudly—if futilely—that movie companies were at MCA's mercy when it came to putting pictures into production. If the agency represented the star of a film, it often insisted that an MCA writer or director or one of its lesser-known clients be hired as well; otherwise the star might decide at the last minute to walk—or "get sick" a day or two before shooting began, or demand that the studio contract be renegotiated.

Keeping agencies out of the production business served to maintain the balance of power. An agency could apply for a waiver to the rule—a waiver SAG granted infrequently and only on a one-time basis and only after scrupulous deliberation. But MCA was requesting a *blanket waiver*; the agency wanted the guild to officially bless it as a full-blown producer of television fare—MCA would be a talent agency *and* a television production company known as Revue Productions—without giving other agencies the same sweeping right.

The request by MCA was extraordinary. Jack Dales, SAG's phlegmatic executive secretary and longtime Reagan sidekick, remembered the board's reaction at the time the issue was first raised. "Well, of course, that was a shocking thought," he said. "MCA had come on strong, saying, 'We'll guarantee to make lots of filmed television if you can work it out with us,'" the implication being that they'd bring television production back to Hollywood. This was tantalizing. Moviemaking was steadily on the decline—felt nowhere more profoundly than in the Reagan household—and dangling new production was like catnip to the board. There were plenty of actors in the guild's membership in desperate need of a good-paying job, and here was MCA saying it had jobs to dispense. Ronald Reagan thought the proposal made good sense.

If the agency could overcome a few sticky issues, there might be a way to swing such a deal, but the guild proposed a few guidelines: in the event of an MCA production "they could not charge their own clients any commission; [and] if they ever put their client in a picture made by them, he had to get the highest salary he'd ever gotten in any picture in his life." On the surface, the deal appeased many in the SAG hierarchy, but beneath it, in the murky depths, it laid out a veritable minefield for Ronald Reagan.

The waiver request put him, an MCA client, in the awkward position of standing up for the interests of his members in dealing with MCA. In retrospect, it might have been wiser had he recused himself from the negotiations in order to avoid any appearance of favoritism. MCA's attorney in the negotiations, Laurence Beilenson, a former SAG lead counsel, had represented Ronnie in legal matters, including his divorce from Jane Wyman.

Jack Reagan

The Reagans: Will (left) and Jack (second from right) with two aunts and sister (unidentified boy at right), July 4, 1899, Fulton, Illinois

Main Street, Tampico, Illinois, c. 1900

Ronald Reagan's baby portrait, 1911

The Reagan family 1914.
Left to right: Jack, Moon,
Dutch, Nelle

The O.T. Johnson "Big Store" shoe department (Jack Reagan at right)

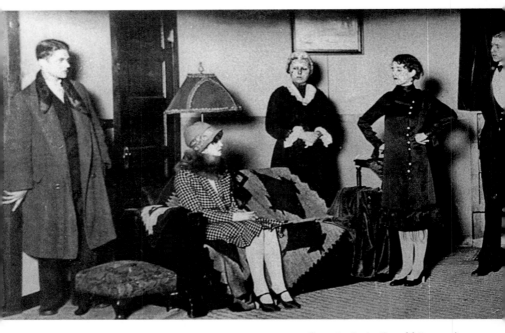

Captain Jack, *Ronald Reagan's senior class play, January 20–21, 1928 (Margaret Cleaver standing at right)*

Ronald Reagan, Eureka College football photo, 1930

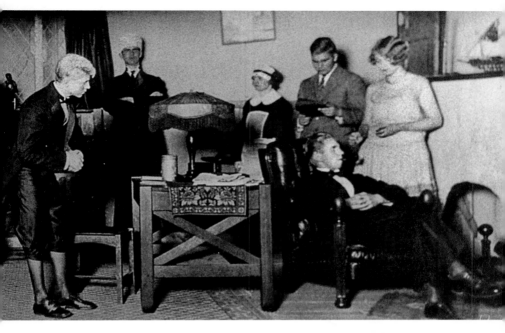

Moon and Dutch, Eureka College cheerleaders, 1930

The Eureka College swim team, 1929

Dutch, Lowell Park

*Dutch on the air, WOC,
Iowa, 1933*

Dutch Reagan WHO promotional postcard, c. 1935

Earliest Warner Bros.
headshot, 1937

Warner Bros. cheesecake
photo, early 1940s

Wedding day: Nelle,
Ronald, Jane, Jack,
January 26, 1940

The Gipper bites the dust. Left to right:
*Ronald Reagan, Donald Crisp, Ruth
Robinson, Pat O'Brien*

*Ronald Reagan and Nelle
Reagan, January 1941*

Staged photo: Ronald Reagan "leaves for military duty," 1942

The Reagan brothers lunching at the Brown Derby, Holly-wood, California, 1943–44

Left to right: *James Skelton and Herb Sorrell (Conference of Studio Unions), Ronald Reagan and Edward Arnold (Screen Actors Guild), Roy Tindall (C.S.U.), George Murphy and Gene Kelly (SAG) in telephone conference in which AFL officials denied issuing a clarification, which set off the film strike, October 26, 1946*

Captain Reagan, First Motion Picture Unit, 1943–44

Edith Luckett, 1914

Nancy Davis and her mother,
Edith Luckett, January 1932

The only known photo of Ann Frances Robbins (Nancy Davis) with her parents, Edith Luckett and Ken Robbins, 1921

Nancy Davis, Smith College photo for production of Make with the Maximum, *1943*

Ronald Reagan, Nancy Reagan, Louella Parsons, Doris Day, Hollywood 1951

Date night at Ciro's, Hollywood, early 1950s

*Ron and Nancy's
engagement photo,
January 1952*

*Ronald and Nancy
Reagan's wedding, with
Ardis and Bill Holden,
March 4, 1952*

Addressing workers at a General Electric plant, Danville, Illinois, October 1955

"Ronald Reagan Presents," Last Frontier Hotel, February 1954

Ron's christening. Left to right: *Ronald Reagan, Ron, Nancy Reagan, Edith Luckett, Nelle with Patti, Bess and Neil Reagan, Loyal Davis, 1958*

Now he sat across the table, quarterbacking for the other side. Beilenson insisted there was no impropriety, but many observers disagreed. His promise that by joining MCA he would "not take part in any negotiations with the guild" seemed to evaporate on impact. It didn't help matters that no records of private meetings held in July 1952 between the SAG board and MCA/Revue Productions were kept.

No records—and no opposing voices. The next thing anyone knew, on July 14, 1952, the SAG board announced that "an agreement was reached which permits MCA to enter and remain in the field of film television" so long as certain checks and balances were met. It was the blanket waiver the agency had sought, launching Revue Productions as a wholly owned entity. And it was exclusive, meaning other agencies like William Morris and General Artists were excluded from doing the same kind of business. According to a secret Justice Department memo, "The deal vaulted MCA to the head of the television agency with advantages that its competitors could never hope to equal." They couldn't possibly promise their clients that kind of TV exposure. MCA also extracted a special letter agreement stating that if the guild adopted "agency regulations in the future . . . which prohibited agents from engaging in television production, it would grant MCA a waiver," shielding it from such regulations.

To no one's surprise, Revue immediately began churning out TV shows—*Chevron Theatre*, *The Jack Benny Program*, *Biff Baker U.S.A.*, *The Adventures of Kit Carson*, *City Detective*, and *The Pepsi-Cola Playhouse*, and that was just for openers. And speculation began to heat up along the Hollywood grapevine that Ronald Reagan had received special dispensation for his part in the deal's approval, in the form of either a payment or a promise—perhaps a show of his own—from MCA or Lew Wasserman. He always denied there were payoffs of any kind. Still, eyebrows were raised at the end of July when Universal, which MCA controlled, reactivated his contract, with an offer to appear in *Law and Order*, a low-budget western. Those eyebrows shot further skyward at the news that his old rate of $75,000 was guaranteed. It wasn't so much that it was out of line; it was more that it was unheard-of, certainly for an actor with negligible box-office appeal. Was this a reward for his help in securing the Revue waiver? Later, Ronnie admitted to a federal grand jury investigating MCA, "I felt a little self-conscious about it" due to the possibility of a conflict of interest, but ultimately he saw only pragmatism in his actions. "I was all for anyone that could give employment," he maintained, dodging the issue with wide eyes.

In fairness, with MCA's production interests thus made viable, Ronald Reagan had been able to oversee for the Screen Actors Guild a revitalization that left it poised to capitalize on the breakaway television era. It yielded an infusion of new members, new opportunities for actors, new revenue streams, new strength. Jack Dales, who served on SAG's executive board for thirty years, would look back on this period marked by spasms of turmoil and growth and call it "Ronnie's finest hour." Dales attributed the success to Ronald Reagan's stamina, his ability to compartmentalize, "because we were balancing so many balls in the air, all at the same time." He could also tell that Ronnie's work leading the union was consuming him, that he was tapped out, ready to move on. There was a lot of hand-wringing over the nature of his identity. "What am I doing here?" he asked Dales after they'd settled the MCA business. "I'm not a professional labor leader. I'm an actor. I have other fields to conquer."

He'd held the top post of the Screen Actors Guild for six years, longer than any other person ever had. He'd seen it through the final chapter of Hollywood's heyday, through violent strikes, through expansion, through the end of the studio era, the anticommunist purge, and into the television age. His contributions would protect the guild's future.

Finally, on August 27, 1952, an article in *Variety* announced the inevitable: Ronald Reagan was stepping down as president of SAG at the end of his present term. No reason was given for his eventful decision, but those who knew him understood that he'd come to a crossroads.

His stature as a Hollywood movie star was sputtering to an end. He was forty-one and accustomed to a spotlight that was fading. It was time to decide what other fields were left to conquer—what to do with the rest of his life.

CHAPTER NINETEEN

MOVING FROM LEFT TO RIGHT

*"A fanatic is one who can't change his mind
and won't change the subject."*

—WINSTON CHURCHILL

Vegas wasn't the answer. Ronald Reagan suffered through the two-week stand of his uninspiring nightclub act at the Last Frontier, but the interval had given him time to think.

The last year and a half had felt like a watershed in every sense of the word—a body drained of its natural resource, and a juncture, a turning point. His dance card was suddenly empty. "His movie career was at a standstill," Nancy recalled. Picture offers still came in, but nothing considered respectable, nothing worth sacrificing his dignity for.

If Vegas wasn't enough of a jolt, new fatherhood made him take stock. Patti Reagan was born on October 21, 1952, eight weeks prematurely—difficult right out of the gate, a mode that would stalk them through her adolescence and beyond. She was "headstrong," a demanding baby, which cut into the couple's close-knit relationship and sowed resentment, whether conscious or not. This feeling trickled down to other key parties. "I felt rejected," Michael Reagan, who was eight at the time, admitted. "Dad and Nancy became a family unto themselves after Patti was born." Michael and Maureen felt shunted aside, like interlopers in the Reagan family picture.

Other concessions were made. Ronnie had sworn not to do commercials, but as 1953 wore on and the employment scenario became more precarious, he appeared in advertisements for Chesterfield cigarettes (a lifelong nonsmoker, he noted that "they painted in the cigarette in the ad") and Arrow shirts (which he never wore). There was even some talk about voice-over work.

A watershed with shifting currents. During 1953, a year in which Ronnie resolved to reject every feeble movie offer that came his way, he made exactly one picture, *Prisoner of War*, for a sum about half of his usual fee. Otherwise, he picked up pocket money making guest appearances on random TV shows. He turned up frequently on *The George Burns and Gracie Allen Show* and *The Milton Berle Show*, half-hour comedies that required little more of him than delivering a few straight-man lines, and in anthology dramas, like *Lux Video Theatre* and *The Revlon Mirror Theater*, all orchestrated by MCA. Following a featured role in an episode of *Medallion Theatre*, another of Revue Studios' ubiquitous TV productions, Taft Schreiber, now Lew Wasserman's chief lieutenant, had Ronnie screen-tested for a high-priority job.

Since 1949, General Electric had been sponsoring a half-hour program with bandleader Fred Waring on Sunday night at nine o'clock following *Toast of the Town*, a variety show hosted by Ed Sullivan, another MCA client. When the ratings for GE's show began to slip, the company, disinclined to give up that plum Sunday slot, began looking around for a replacement for Waring.

MCA rode in like the cavalry. It knew that nothing attracted viewers like Hollywood stars, despite the reluctance of big names to appear on TV. "MCA promised us that they would be able to break that barrier if we would go along with a plan they had," recalled Earl Dunckel, GE's advertising account supervisor. The strategy the agency laid out was simple: if GE agreed to replace Fred Waring with a dramatic anthology series—something along the lines of, say, *General Electric Theater*—MCA would paper it with its big-name clients. To test it out, beginning in July 1953, GE alternated weeks with Fred Waring and *General Electric Theater*, and MCA delivered the stars. That first year alone, Cary Grant, Ronald Colman, Van Johnson, William Holden, Joan Fontaine, Judy Garland, James Mason, and Jane Wyman appeared in the half-hour-long dramas. The show was an instant smash—gorgeous adaptations of short stories, novels, plays, or films performed live, without a safety net, by rotating casts of actors. By summer

1954, it was clear to all concerned that Fred Waring's services were no longer required.

General Electric Theater was scheduled to begin airing weekly on September 26, 1954, but the show's format still lacked a key element. It begged for a host, someone to introduce each week's drama, which would give the series a sense of continuity. Taft Schreiber proposed Ronald Reagan for the position, even though Ronnie had put his foot down about attaching himself to a full-time TV job. "I was always gun-shy of television," he acknowledged. Years later, long after the show was committed to legend, Ronnie spun the story that what ultimately sold him was an offer of "some personal appearance tours, in which for a number of weeks each year [he would] visit GE plants," acting as the company's goodwill ambassador. That hardly seemed like an irresistible perk. In the end, it really came down to money. He was just about tapped out, with nothing in the pipeline, and GE was offering him $125,000 a year, plus an open-ended expense account. He wasn't about to get that anywhere else, a detail his agent, Art Park, underscored in so many words. MCA turned up the pressure. "Not only would MCA have Reagan on *GE Theater*, but we also produced the show," Park explained. "So it was a very, very large commission for our company." If Ronnie didn't accept the role, if he rejected television out of hand, if his screen test wasn't an absolute knockout, it was unlikely that MCA would keep coming to his rescue.

The screen test was only part of GE's selection process. Whoever hosted the show had to be the *right* person, someone who not only looked good on camera but conveyed a personal outlook that corresponded to the company's underlying philosophy. As historian Rick Perlstein noted, "Few corporations were as obsessed as GE with the problem of corporate image—an image, it was at great pains to establish, of GE as a keystone institution of the American Way." Since the end of World War II, General Electric had been engaged in a stealth crusade to keep the power of organized labor in check. But unlike companies constantly at odds with its unions, GE utilized a novel approach, initiating informative programs designed to influence its employees—many of them blue-collar workers—not only to win them over on labor issues but also to enlist them as emissaries of the company, to have them, in effect, sell the company's image to the general public. It was an audacious strategy, and for the most part it worked.

Thanks to measures instigated by a revolutionary thinker named Lemuel Boulware, GE dispatched executives on regular outreach visits to all of its plants, speaking with plant managers as well as workers, constantly seeking feedback through focus groups, in order to gauge the most intimate attitudes and economic interests of its employees—the better to influence their politics. GE's conservative agenda was straightforward. It sought to ensure corporate well-being by turning people against government encroachment and regulatory interference, while neutralizing the union's effectiveness. Ronald Reagan chose to view it as a management-labor partnership.

Whoever hosted *General Electric Theater* would have to carry the company torch. "We had been very, very definite as to the kind of person we wanted," Earl Dunckel recalled, "good moral character, intelligent . . . a good, upright kind of person." Both Edward Arnold and Walter Pidgeon had been considered, but neither man apparently fit GE's criteria. Ronald Reagan "was accepted almost by accord." He was telegenic, with a down-home, folksy appeal—"as natural as anyone you would ever meet . . . a regular guy," Dunckel thought—and eager to take on the diplomatic role. Equally important, Dunckel noted, was Ronnie's choirboy image—he didn't come "with the reputation for the social ramble."

Like its biweekly predecessor, *General Electric Theater* hosted by Ronald Reagan was a success right out of the box. His first year, introducing thirty-seven episodes, the show jumped into the top ten in television ratings and continued to build a tremendous audience on the strength of its cast. Long-established movie stars sprang into the series—Joseph Cotten, Alan Ladd, Myrna Loy, James Stewart, Joan Crawford, Dick Powell, Henry Fonda, and Jack Benny, to name a few—but also fascinating newcomers like Natalie Wood, Lee Marvin, and James Dean, who appeared twice.

In the third episode, "The Long Way Round," shot live on a set at the old Republic Studios, Nancy starred as a wife so intent on helping her husband recover from a nervous breakdown that she nearly drives him over the edge. It was such a good script that Ronnie couldn't resist playing opposite her, an experiment they repeated occasionally over the years. The hosting duties required little preparation—a two-minute introduction that he memorized, along with a brief sign-off at the end of the show. There was plenty of time and incentive for him to act, an assignment he undertook four times a season. The parts were diverse, wonderfully atmospheric, pressure-free, and "hand-tailored for him," allowing him to project something richer than what he had done in the movies. The shows provided the perfect outlet for his small-screen talent, extending Ronald Reagan's acting days and serving as a bridge into a new media era.

In mid-September 1954, concurrent with the launch of *General Electric Theater*, Ronnie and Earl Dunckel left for their first two-week promotional swing of GE factory visits. They kicked it off at a plant in Schenectady, New York, on the campus of the company's vast, thirty-one-acre headquarters. It was a huge plant, comprising 240 buildings, in which twelve hundred workers made everything from steam turbines to waterwheel generators and the parts that went into them. In the giant maw of that facility, Ronnie couldn't help but feel the company's almighty power. The place churned with noisy productivity, which ground to complete silence as he made his way inside. It was as impressive an entrance as he'd ever made. Because many of the workers led the kind of blue-collar lives that often left them feeling marginalized and at times underprivileged, the appearance of a movie star in their midst delivered a prodigious jolt of morale. Ronnie seemed larger-than-life, even among those enormous turbines. Tall, impossibly good-looking, and serenely self-contained, he embodied the workers' very ideal of a big-screen hero come to life. It was as if the Gipper or Grover Cleveland Alexander or . . . *Brass Bancroft* . . . had stepped out of the frame, and the impact it made was galvanizing. It was something for the GE employees to take pride in. He was GE's personal Hollywood star—*their* star—who looked into the camera at the end of each week's show and paid them tribute by invoking the company motto, "Here at General Electric, progress is our most important product." Seeing him there, on their turf, they considered him one of their own.

Ronald Reagan didn't waste the opportunity. He spent four hours making his way around the mazy factory floor, stopping to talk with the workers and signing autographs. He didn't function as a celebrity on a pedestal. He worked that plant feverishly, making a real connection with those people, a personal connection, calling them by name and asking after their families. It was a Friday afternoon, with gorgeous fall weather enveloping upstate New York, leading to questions about how they would spend their weekend. He'd always find something pertinent with which to establish a rapport. Otherwise, he chatted about Hollywood because he knew how much people loved a peek behind the scenes. There was a set reservoir of stories he drew from—fond recollections about working with Flynn, Bogie, and those two chimps: Bonzo and Jack Warner. The ghost of Knute Rockne never failed to rear its head. But there was also a round of obligatory PR, perhaps a reflex left over from the Screen Actors Guild. "His main talk was in defense of Hollywood," Dunckel remembered, how "the divorce level in the nation-at-large was higher than the divorce rate in Hollywood." Ronnie lamented how actors were regarded as second-class citizens, how until recently, churches refused to bury actors in the same cemetery with their parishioners. He expressed an unflagging pride in his profession, a profession too easily misunderstood and maligned.

A lot of effort went into that performance, and it paid off: his audience loved it. And the type of performance that Ronald Reagan was making now was about to have an impact on his audience unlike anything he'd ever experienced before.

That Friday, after every last hand had been shaken and they were on their way to the hotel bar, Earl Dunckel got called to the phone. He was informed that Dr. Alexander Stoddard, the controversial Los Angeles school superintendent and scheduled dinner speaker at a convention of teachers at the Schenectady Armory, had suffered a heart attack. The person on the other end of the line asked, "Can Mr. Reagan speak to us Saturday night?"

It was out of the question. A major talk on education by his prize property meant writing a speech that required considerable research. They'd need to know what issues were of critical importance to the teachers, as well as how to address them. There was no time to prepare. They were committed to GE business through most of Saturday afternoon. Besides, education was an area outside of Ronald Reagan's expertise. Dunckel knew that if such a speech went badly, it would leave "a real black mark on [his] career," threatening the rest of the tour.

Ronnie, who happened to overhear the call, insisted that he take a shot at the speech. This was right up his alley, he argued. All those banquet groups and civic organizations he'd spoken to over the years had given him plenty of practice for just such a speech. In fact, he'd cobble one together in his room later that night. *Cobble together?* Dunckel was distraught. He did everything he could to talk Ronnie out of it, but it was useless. Ronnie was adamant and instructed Earl to accept the invitation.

Neither man expected to face the crowd that greeted them when they entered the Schenectady Armory at eight o'clock the next night. This wasn't a tidy conclave of educators. There were three or four thousand high school teachers packed into the hall, making as much racket as the turbine plant. Dunckel wasn't just nervous. "I was scared stiff," he admitted. When he realized Ronnie wasn't going to fall back on his Hollywood spiel, he imagined the worst: "I could see him falling dead on his face."

What he didn't take into account was Ronald Reagan's ability to speak extemporaneously on any topic he was passionate about. All actors have lines to say and the innate gift of delivery, whether they are playing a G-man, a sports hero, or even a president. But they didn't all have Ronnie's gift of *speaking his mind*, to aggregate facts and statistics from reliable sources, to create instant empathy on subjects as diverse as communism, overpopulation, taxes and, as luck would have it, areas of interest to teachers.

"He got up there and gave a speech on education that just dropped them in the aisles!" Earl Dunckel recalled. It was a heartfelt address that mixed the challenges of an overtaxed and underrated American public school system with a young, idealistic generation facing a communist threat. Granted, a lot of his comments were uninformed by any in-depth knowledge of the issues. He quoted sources like *Reader's Digest* and *Human Events*, a conservative political newspaper founded in 1944. In between, he touched on aspects of the good ol' days, when he was growing up in the Midwest, where teachers were as respected—and as feared—as the gods. That really brought those teachers to their feet. They were still standing and applauding ten minutes later, when Ronnie finally left the stage.

No one was more roused than Earl Dunckel. His job had been to shape Ronald Reagan into a glorified glad-hander, someone who could promote GE's image and raise company morale. But this guy, he realized, was made of something more. He had more "breadth and depth" than anyone expected. He had substance, he was a *communicator*. Ronnie had reached out to an audience he had nothing in common with, and the audience reached out to him in return. It was something to see, Dunckel reported back to his superiors, "an amazing tour de force."

And it didn't end in Schenectady.

That initial tour of plant visits hit GE's major East Coast facilities in Erie, Cleveland, Cincinnati, Boston, and Philadelphia. In every city the itinerary was the same. They started early—a 6:30 a.m. arrival on the red-eye special at a local train platform (Ronnie still refused to fly), where a GE factotum separated them from their luggage before whisking them straight off to the factory. As always, Ronnie would begin a slow, earnest trek circulating through the aisles, making contact with as many employees as time allowed. And, as always, the first few minutes had the awkwardness of a junior high school dance. The women came rushing up, fluttering around Ronnie with mash notes, autograph books, and lips eager to be kissed, while the men huddled against a wall, eyeing him with squinty suspicion. Often, they made a disparaging remark—"I'll bet he's a fag" or some similar insult. Ronnie pretended not to hear—a ruse he would perfect during his days in political office—but "he knew what was going on," according to Earl Dunckel. It was part of his performance. A seasoned actor knows you time your entrance to have the greatest effect, and Ronnie was waiting for the right moment. When it came—and it was at a point only he seemed to know—he made a move toward his cynical antagonists.

In the short time it took to introduce himself, the men's whole mood did a sharp about-face. Their shoulders came unglued, scowls disappeared, clenched fists reached out to shake Ronnie's hand, even to slap him affectionately on the back and elsewhere. "That's the way, Ron!" one of the men might say, before summoning buddies from a neighboring production line to join them. Whatever Ronnie said, whatever it was he did to break the ice—an inside joke, a self-deprecating remark, a reference to something one of the women had confided—it instantly cemented a rapport that allowed these men to drop their tough-guy armor. Earl Dunckel, watching the polished yet homespun actor work that crowd, decided "this guy was so charming, so nice" that "he could convince a skeptic of anything."

Plant tours that were supposed to take a few hours created havoc with their schedules. It began with fifteen-minute talks with plant and section managers before huddling with the hourly employees who manned the machinery. A conversation with, say, a drill-press operator would drag on and on, despite an effort by Dunckel to lead Ronnie away. And the operator would latch on and walk off right along with them, still chatting, keeping pace, picking up other workers as they made their way from station to station, so that pretty soon a crowd had formed in the aisle. Brief exchanges meant to take a few minutes or more would stretch into hours. Running to an office phone, Dunckel would frantically shuffle appointments, canceling dinners, rearranging train times, so that often they wouldn't get to their hotel until well past midnight.

Then, the next morning, they'd be up at dawn, ready to repeat the routine with unflagging enthusiasm.

"Boy," Dunckel recalled of the experience, "we walked our legs right down into stumps." Those concrete floors took their toll. And the handshakes—hundreds of handshakes every day—were crippling. The wear-and-tear on the body was tremendous. It was a test of physical endurance.

But it wasn't enough to tour the plants. As word of Ronnie's virtuosity spread, invitations for speeches began pouring in. Wherever he went, the question was the same: Would he speak to the Chamber of Commerce, the Lions, the Rotarians, the Elks, the Kiwanians, the California Fertilizer Association, the National Association of Manufacturers? GE sponsored husband-and-wife book clubs and coed bowling leagues. Could he put in an appearance and say a few words? How about an address to local hospital administrators? No opportunity was left unexploited. He said yes to everything. GE gave Ronald Reagan a platform. It gave him a chance to speak about issues he cared about, to get things off his chest.

It often started with a few humorous Hollywood anecdotes. And jokes—he had a slew of them ready for every occasion, set pieces that never failed to warm up an audience. A seasoned GE plant manager said, "He was the most inventive man with a dirty joke I've ever known," although he white-washed them in the retelling. But then the jokes gave way to economic and philosophical patter, and it might veer off to the right—how "the Communists had pretty much taken over the Screen Actors Guild, that they had taken over most of the unions involved with making films." Maybe your union. That struck a chord. So did his rant about taxes. "There can be no moral justification of the progressive tax," he said, tracing its origin to the Communist revolution. Ronnie groused about being in the ninety-first percentile. *The ninety-first percentile!* Imagine that. You worked like a dog, put every effort you had into your best work, and the government took the bulk of what you earned. It wasn't fair, he complained. Taxes were too high. He'd really get going, making his case, and the crowd would be listening hard, nodding its agreement.

He saw how the financial squeeze affected these people, hardworking people who needed to make every dollar count—people like his father, Jack—and he spoke directly to them. "I was seeing the same people that I grew up with in Dixon, Illinois," Ronald Reagan recalled. "I realized I was living in a tinsel factory. And this exposure brought me back." He had advice, meaningful advice, that he wanted, *needed*, to share. At stake, he maintained, was their very financial security, their seemingly uphill ability to make ends meet. The greatest impediment to that was the "ever-expanding federal government," a glutton that devoured resources and trampled on individual liberties.

To develop and support most of these positions, Ronald Reagan studied a virtual library of material that a consortium of GE's top executives funneled to its employees—corporate bulletins, books, and magazines specifically tailored to educate its workers and middle management while promoting the company's long-range point of view. An underlying free-market philosophy permeated the propaganda. There was a decided prejudice against ballooning government expenditures and deficit spending. Free enterprise needed to function unencumbered by intrusive federal programs and oppressive taxes. Once he might have disagreed with this view, but now it made perfect sense to Ronnie. He more than fell in line behind the corporate program; he believed it.

GE was determined not to take a partisan political stand, yet it needed to address what it deemed "external challenges." That meant supporting candidates in state, congressional, and presidential elections who were sympathetic to the company's interests; achieving an advantageous balance of power in negotiations with the unions; subduing the company's ideological competitors; and "spreading its influence beyond industry and finance." To those ends, it was crucial, as GE saw it, to reeducate its workers and their neighbors—to engage and indoctrinate them at the grassroots level the way the unions did it, so that the workforce would, in effect, influence the broader community by spreading GE's view of the country, as

well as promoting its products. It emphasized "the importance of recognizing each GE employee as a member of the community, with interests
broader than the narrow boundaries of his or her job." The secret weapon
would be the community-relations outreach. In Ronald Reagan GE had
found its mouthpiece, someone who was "out there, beating the bushes for
private enterprise."

The program worked like a charm. For one thing, *General Electric Theater* vaulted to the top of the prime-time ratings chart, with its genial host
a nationally recognized figure. His visibility on the show eclipsed his mid-
dling movie-star image, making him "one of the most recognized men in
the country." Each time an announcement of Ronald Reagan's forthcoming visit to a GE plant appeared in a local paper, requests for speeches
poured in. This gave GE's management the luxury to pick and choose
which venues would best serve its purposes. Often, GE scheduled a speech
at the weekly luncheon of a civic organization, then later the same night at
a function—perhaps a reception or a banquet—for another business or
community group. "His speech was always the same," recalled one of the
GE chaperones; "he had it polished to perfection."

Ronald Reagan's talking topics—chosen expressly by him, without cen-
sorship by GE—were nevertheless in sync with its wishes and hit his audience in exactly the places consistent with the company's objectives. When
he segued from the jokey, let's-get-acquainted portion of the program into
weightier realms, the meat of his speech, he'd remove any barriers between
him and his audience to demonstrate how their interests were the same. If
Hollywood was paralyzed by antitrust restrictions and government interference, then *any* government interference—of free enterprise or worship or
what we see on TV or read in books—was antithetical to the American
way of life. While actors were subjected to excessive tax rates, the average
citizen's pockets were being picked. "Thirty-four percent of your phone bill
is taxed, and twenty-seven percent of gas and oil use, and more than a
fourth of the automobile you drive is in direct and indirect taxes." He was
plagued by the same outrageous medical bills as everyone else and warned
against what he saw as the socialization of medicine. And the outrageous
cost of putting food on the table—no wonder when so much of farming was
regulated and controlled by the federal government. "Freedom," he liked to
remind his audience, "is never more than one generation from extinction."

Ronald Reagan struck the right notes with these listeners, who were muddling through the awkward transition from a wartime economy to the emerging modern world. The changes were coming so fast that they were difficult to absorb. Life in general was increasingly complex, more demanding, less rewarding. The traditional American values of the good ol' days—the values that were predominant in the Hollywood movies of the 1930s, the white picket fences and Andy Hardy innocence—seemed lost in the balance. "There appears to be a lessening of certain moral standards and certain principles of honesty and honor in our country," he lamented during an address to a business group, "even a lessening of patriotism." There was something in Ronald Reagan's voice and in his face that signaled to his audience that he understood.

Earl Dunckel, who watched every speech from the sidelines, marveled at the way Ronnie read the disposition of those audiences, how he shifted his remarks in midflight based on how they responded. The man's antennae, he thought, were "absolutely uncanny" and attuned to perceiving the slightest changes in the crowd's mood. In time, the Hollywood anecdotes stirred less of a reaction compared with the comments dealing with government regulation and the erosion of personal freedoms. People were dissatisfied with the way things were going in the country. They felt maligned and they wanted more bang for their buck. The working-class community was moving away from FDR's New Deal progressive policies to a more conservative outlook. They were moving from left to right, and so was Ronald Reagan.

His disillusionment with the Democratic Party wasn't an overnight phenomenon. It had begun soon after World War II ended, almost in sync with his diminishing movie-star status. Ronald Reagan refused to believe that an actor's popularity—*his* popularity—could slip so precipitously. Instead, he blamed it on the government's ham-fisted intrusion—antitrust restrictions that, in his view, were responsible for bringing down the studio system. Once studios felt the pinch, they lost the resources to offer him good stories and better parts. And, of course, elements of the press—"the kind that are addicted to yellow journalism, certain kinds of gossip columnists"—perpetrated "an invasion of our personal and private lives." The situation gnawed at him. It reflected the larger picture.

Even though Ronnie's fortunes dwindled, he somehow had more income taxes to pay. Every time he turned around, the government had its greedy hands in his pocket. This soured him toward the system, a system that he decided was becoming more intrusive. His feeling about it was disquieting, that "a slow invisible tide of socialism was engulfing America, held back only by a few brave businessmen." He was still on the warpath about the mounting communist threat, and about big government, but now a specific menace, crippling entitlements, grew in his mind. All those wasteful baby-fat programs! Even Social Security, an FDR centerpiece, rankled; in a speech delivered to insurance executives, he floated the idea of making it voluntary.

Ronald Reagan was balancing a Jekyll-and-Hyde existence. By day, he was the loyal New Deal Democrat, espousing strong unions, fair pricing, and adequate low-cost housing. It was as much a part of his makeup as his Midwestern charm. But come nightfall, when the sun retreated and the like-minded audiences rolled in, a crusading conservative emerged from the shadows.

Plenty of neighborly advice helped to influence his conversion. Since his marriage to Nancy and move to the Palisades, the Reagans had developed a new circle of Hollywood friends who were fiercely conservative Republicans. Robert Taylor, perhaps Ronnie's closest friend and a rabid anticommunist, had risen up the ranks in the right-wing Motion Picture Alliance for the Preservation of American Ideals, as had Robert Arthur, the producer, a frequent Saturday-night companion. Both men and their wives spent long evenings around the dinner table, where hearty helpings of politics were served with every course. Along with conservative proselytizers like George Murphy, Dick Powell, Edgar Bergen, and the irrepressible Neil Reagan, the diehard Republicans laid it on thick. Their arguments were convincing to a man whose faith in progressive New Deal policies was shaken.

Dana Andrews, who later followed in Ronnie's footsteps as the president of SAG, laid the change at the feet of Reagan's current employer. "It was the GE managers of those factories who changed his politics," Andrews asserted. "They groomed him—and they did a good job of it." Earl Dunckel, a self-styled "arch-conservative," made no bones about his own contribution. "I was drumbeating at him all the time," Dunckel recalled. "Whenever he tried to defend New Dealism, or what was passing for it at the time, we would have some rather spirited arguments." According to Dunckel, he had no trouble wearing Ronnie down. He struck at a particularly vulnerable Achilles' heel when they hashed over the union strikes at the movie studios in 1947. Dunckel seized on "the degree to which [Ronnie] was disillusioned" by the seeming communist involvement and went to work exploiting the doubt it had caused.

Ronald Reagan had supported Harry Truman in 1948 and made speeches on behalf of Hubert Humphrey, the Minneapolis mayor running for the Senate seat in Minnesota occupied by Joe Ball, a conservative who had actually crossed party lines to endorse Franklin D. Roosevelt. Then, in 1952, Ronnie did the same by voting for the Republican presidential candidate, Dwight D. Eisenhower. He had never cast a vote for a Republican before.

It was not without some serious hand-wringing. Ronnie thought some of the issues that the Democratic challenger, Adlai Stevenson, had campaigned on were "intelligent, honest and smacked of greatness." And he considered Ike's running mate the bogeyman. In a letter to Sam Harrod II, the son of Ronnie's old Eureka College benefactor, he warned that Richard Nixon was "a hand-picked errand boy with a pleasing façade and naught but emptiness behind. . . . He is *less than honest* and he is an ambitious opportunist completely undeserving of the high honor accorded him."

His disdain for Nixon came from experience. They had crossed paths on two occasions, and Ronnie never forgave Nixon's duplicitous shenanigans, especially in 1950, when Ronnie campaigned on behalf of Helen Gahagan Douglas, the wife of his acting pal Melvyn Douglas, who was running against Nixon for the open Senate seat in California. Ronnie admired Helen Douglas's accomplishments—organizing relief efforts for migrant workers during the Depression, establishing family farms in California's Central Valley as a hedge against giant agricultural interests, sounding early warnings to women of Hitler's impending rise, making impassioned pleas for peace in Congress after the bombings of Hiroshima and Nagasaki. Helen Douglas was a good woman who exhibited boundless energy and ingenuity to promote good causes. Nixon's only strategy against her was to go negative. He chose to smear her as a communist, which she was not, calling her "Pink right down to her underwear," as though she were an emissary from the Kremlin. "Don't Vote the Red Ticket, Vote the Red, White and Blue Ticket." He relied on a mixed bag of dirty tricks to win the election. The behavior reflected his role in the House Un-American Activities Committee putsch, when he joined the gallery of smug Red-hunters pointing accusatory fingers at Hollywood liberals. Ronnie wasn't taken in by Richard Milhous Nixon.

Not at first, anyway.

There was still much to admire about the new president Eisenhower, but GE kept Ronald Reagan too busy speaking to immerse himself in national politics. The intensity of his schedule picked up pace. Eight to sixteen weeks a year were spent on the road. A journalist figured that with the first few circuits under his belt that Ronnie had visited 135 GE plants in twenty-five states and had shaken hands with more than 200,000 of the company's employees. "We drove him to the utmost limits," explained Edward Langley, a GE press officer who accompanied him on several of the later tours. "We saturated him in Middle America."

The hosting duties at *General Electric Theater* took up no time at all. "I had television work down to an average of about one day a week," Ronnie said. That freed up stretches for the pursuit of more lucrative movies. The prospects were slim for a featured actor approaching fifty. The most he got offered were scraps thrown from studio cast-offs. *Tennessee's Partner,* a western he made in 1955 with John Payne and Rhonda Fleming, was the kind of ragged Saturday-afternoon matinee that played to raucous teenage boys, and 1957's *Hellcats of the Navy*, a low-budget "jingoistic potboiler" in which he co-starred with Nancy, died at the box office, and essentially spelled doom for his movie career. The drop-off in work befuddled Ronald Reagan. He saw himself in the mold of John Wayne, making wide-screen action epics, unable to grasp that his star had faded.

The important roles disappeared altogether. After *Hellcats of the Navy,* another movie offer wouldn't come Ronald Reagan's way until 1964. And by then, he was on to his next act.

CHAPTER TWENTY

AN "APPRENTICESHIP
FOR PUBLIC LIFE"

"You have not converted a man because you have silenced him."

—JOHN, *Viscount Morley of Blackburn*

More and more, wherever Ronald Reagan spoke, his remarks dug deep into the anxieties of the heartland. A litany of grievances just poured out of him: the wrongheaded goal of government-paid medicine, excessive Social Security contributions ("Social Security is coming to the end of the road"), an unnecessary $2.5 billion program to alleviate allegedly crowded schools, the myth of underpaid teachers ("The truth is, not one shred of evidence has been presented that federal aid of any kind is required"), the "farm mess" (he was opposed to government subsidies), the progressive tax ("We have received this progressive tax direct from Karl Marx, who designed it as the prime essential of a socialist state"), the national debt, and his favorite whipping boy, "encroaching controls," all those entitlement programs that "equalize the earnings of our people." As he pounded the lecterns in those smoke-filled banquet halls to punctuate each injustice, a rhythm built steadily, the timbre of his eloquent voice rose and swelled, jacking up the temperature of the crowds. "He had them in the palm of his hand all night," recalled Paul Wassmansdorf, a GE advertising manager. "Those people just loved him," observed William Frye, who produced many of the *General Electric Theater* segments. "He was unbelievable. He sounded as though he were running for something."

The prospect had certainly crossed his mind. From as far back as Illinois, the impulse to stand out and govern was in Ronald Reagan's DNA. In high school he'd been elected president of the student body, and at Eureka to the influential college senate. The SAG presidency bumped up the wattage exponentially, not only in the amplitude of power but also with the range of its authority, a range that affected economics, legislation—*people's lives*. Many of those people had benefited from his leadership, and a few of them suggested that he consider a larger stage.

As early as 1940, with the world on the brink of war, Dick Powell had tried persuading Ronald Reagan to run for Congress on the Republican ticket. The likelihood of that happening, at the time, was absurdly low. His flag was firmly planted in Democratic soil, and switching parties was unthinkable. It was a nonstarter in 1950 when someone put his name up as a candidate for mayor of Hollywood, an honorary position. That left a cheesy, tinsel aftertaste. Better offers were floated from time to time. Local Democrats had asked him to run for Congress in 1952. Not to be outdone, that same year, Holmes Tuttle, an influential Republican contributor and prominent L.A. businessman, proposed that Reagan seek a Senate seat. Ronnie was flattered—but not even tempted. The urge to act remained too strong; he believed that he still had a full slate of movies ahead of him. "I did not want to leave the entertainment world to go into politics," he said.

But signals persisted. Every time he ran into Bob Cummings, his former Warner Bros. co-star said, "Someday I'm going to vote for this fellow for president." And while it was nothing more than playful banter and Ronnie persisted in laughing it off, the sentiment never failed to resonate. Over drinks one night at Trader Vic's, Robert Stack told him, "You know, you really should think about doing something for this country one day." He loved having Jack Benny address him as "governor," or answering to "Mr. President" at guild meetings.

But nothing satisfied quite as much as the approbation showered on him at the speeches he made for General Electric. These were the kind of people who made America what it was, applauding issues he cared so passionately, perhaps even obsessively, about. They listened carefully to him, these kindred spirits, people whose circumstances were difficult and whose destinies were linked by the dictates of big government. What he said really touched these people. They felt his determination not only to understand their lives, but to help change them by changing legislation. And they, too, pressed Ronald Reagan to seek office. After every speech, there would be a cluster of admirers lying in wait by the door, urging him to run for . . . something, a position where he could put his talents to use in solving the country's ills. He insisted, unconvincingly to some, that he wasn't interested. Even fifty years later, he swore, "Never in my wildest dreams did I even consider seeking public office." But the drumbeat continued.

General Electric preferred to keep him on the road. The company's TV show was scoring huge with home audiences opposite a new, struggling NBC western called *Bonanza*, while its host and spokesman made great inroads spreading GE's policies and ideology to the provinces. It was essential that GE keep him visible, focused—and happy. He was compensated more than adequately, but to sweeten the deal, General Electric offered to outfit the Reagans' new home in the Upper Riviera section of Pacific Palisades with every electrical convenience known to man. The house, by its sheer size alone, gorged on power. It was a rambling, five-thousand-square-foot ranch at the top of San Onofre Drive, one of the highest points in the Palisades, with each room overlooking the ocean. Once GE's contractors got their hands on it, the place required its own three-thousand-pound switch box to handle the enormous output of current. They went to town installing an array of gadgets and contraptions: a heated swimming pool with underwater lights, a retractable roof over the central atrium, an intercom in every room, a state-of-the-art screening room with high-fidelity sound, an electric-eye security system, remote controls that opened and closed the drapes, elaborate colored mood lights on the dining room dimmers so that "everybody would look better," heat lamps in the bathrooms, an outdoor electric barbecue pit with a rotisserie, and numerous television sets scattered throughout. The pièce de résistance was the ultramodern kitchen that fairly gleamed with GE appliances—three refrigerators, two ovens, a dishwasher with built-in garbage disposal, a high-end washer and dryer, and a full range of what Ronnie referred to as "electrical servants," such as a toaster oven, a waffle iron, a skillet, and a vacuum cleaner from the company's Monogram housewares division in Louisville. "We found ourselves with more refrigerators, ovens, and fancy lights than we could use," Nancy groused. Ronnie sent the company a bill to the tune of $17,000 to cover the installation of an air-conditioned wine cellar and other upgrades.

When all was said and done, General Electric showcased 1669 San Onofre Drive as "The House of the Future," featuring it prominently in a series of three-minute commercials with "television's first all-electric family," in which Nancy and Patti occasionally appeared and Ronnie assured viewers that "when you live better electrically, you lead a richer, fuller, more satisfying life."

H is life was also filling out in ways that weren't solely electrical. In the summer of 1957, shortly before moving into the new house, Nancy became pregnant again. It was cause for as much anxiety as celebration. She'd withstood two miscarriages since Patti's birth, and Ronnie was panicked over the state of her health. Nothing discouraged Nancy, not even strict doctor's orders that she remain in bed, flat on her back, and take weekly hormone shots throughout the final three months of her pregnancy. They weren't taking any chances this time; from the outset a cesarean section was prescribed. Nancy was determined to have a boy, and have one she did—Ronald Prescott Reagan—on May 20, 1958.

Nancy's mother, Edith, flew in to assist with the baby, but her presence underscored a notable absence. Nelle Reagan, who had been bedside at the birth of each of her grandchildren, wasn't up to the burden this time around. It was obvious that Nelle was failing—for the past year she had suffered through a wave of memory lapses and related heart problems that all but sidelined her. "I have hardening of the arteries in my head—and it hurts to think," she complained early in 1954. The neurological disease, not yet known familiarly as Alzheimer's, had started to spread its crippling roots. She fought increasingly long spells of forgetfulness, her bright blue eyes struggling behind clouds of confusion. By the time of Ron's birth in 1958, her condition had deteriorated. "I am a shut in," she wrote, opening her heart to a friend back in Dixon. She was no longer allowed to drive and restricted by a wave of small strokes and their aftershocks, and the seeming solitary confinement crushed her aging spirit. A lifelong stoic, Nelle had fears that began to show through. But, as always, she found solace in her religious convictions. "I will be 74 years young this month of July, and am grateful to God, to have been spared this long life. Yet when each attac [sic] comes I whisper—'Please God, let it be now, take me home.'"

When Nancy was back on her feet, she arranged to have Nelle Reagan moved to a nursing home. Nancy didn't need a battery of doctors to tell her that Nelle needed round-the-clock care. Even at the time, Ronnie sensed an eerie familiarity in Nelle's condition. His father, Jack, had experienced memory loss in the years just prior to his death. At first, Ronnie attributed it to the effects of alcoholism, the age-old mantra "It'll rot your brain," and, of course, the cigarettes—Jack was what he called "a three-pack, one-match-a-day man." But Jack's and Nelle's symptoms foretold a darker story, that his parents' afflictions might have hereditary implications. Moon's power of recall was already a bit wobbly.

Ronnie adored his son Ron, whom he'd nicknamed Skipper. Nancy was smitten with her tiny new son, too. He was a beautiful baby, with his mother's voluptuous cheekbones and his father's strong jaw and penetrating eyes. According to a friend, Nancy "worshipped at the altar of little Ron"; she went overboard indulging him, perhaps to the exclusion of the other three kids. Michael Reagan, who visited on weekends, acknowledged, "I was a little jealous of him because he got the attention I wanted." And Patti certainly felt a chill. At first, she took a special interest in her little brother. But she was put off by all the cooing and aahing, by being forbidden from entering the young heir's nursery. Instead, she took to stealing in for a clandestine peek, tiptoeing to circumvent the intuitive intercom system. Patti lost the exclusivity of being the only child in the home. She was no longer the family's center of attention. But Patti didn't surrender her standing without a fight. She morphed from the perfect precocious daughter into a "sullen" child who stood her ground by acting out and going head-to-head against her mother. This attitude didn't sit well on San Onofre Drive. Nancy sanctioned no disrespect, especially with Ronnie away on the road much of the time. Patti was equally obstinate. The mother-daughter relationship would be rocky for years.

The situation with Michael was also tempestuous, but a different kind of tempestuous—bottled-up, subject to an extraordinary build-up of pressure. Mostly, he'd lived with his mother, Jane Wyman, but her unstable lifestyle and succession of boyfriends and marriages wreaked havoc on

Michael's adolescence, in which he was bounced from stepfather to stepfather, from boarding schools to military academies. The constant turmoil set the tone for what he described in retrospect as "a lifelong roller coaster ride." He was molested by a camp counselor at the age of eight, became a chronic bed wetter, set fire to the house, slapped Jane Wyman, contemplated suicide, and grappled with anger and depression. Later, he haunted dingy sex shops and trolled for sex with streetwalkers. Michael's greatest grievance was that he felt unloved. His mother had no time for him and left him feeling not only that he "couldn't seem to do anything right in her view" but that she didn't like him. Maureen, who had always served as an intermediary, now spent most months away at a boarding school in Tarrytown, New York. Without her, the friction between mother and son hit an incendiary pitch. When Michael turned fourteen, Jane Wyman had had about all she could take and, at the suggestion of a psychiatrist, shunted him off to his father's house, where "a family environment" presented a foreseeable antidote.

What at first seemed like a godsend to the boy devolved into a series of demoralizing revelations. Most upsetting was learning that Nancy's condition for allowing him to move in was that he board at school during the week and accompany Ronnie to the Malibu Hills ranch on weekends. On the few occasions when Michael stayed at San Onofre Drive, his sleeping arrangement was the living room couch. Nancy intimidated him, and his father was away much of the time, traveling for General Electric, forcing Michael to compete for his father's attention during the days he was home, a situation that only fed his resentment.

Reflecting on this disruptive time, Ronald Reagan wrote, "Although GE kept me on the road a lot, there were long stretches of my life during that period when my daily routine focused entirely on my family." Perhaps in the abstract, that is. His family life resembled a sequence of guest appearances. Every few weeks he turned up on San Onofre Drive, picking up the threads from where the last episode left off. Even then, he gave the children only passing attention. It was primarily through Nancy that Michael's and Patti's issues were raised, and then only as she chose to present them. He went on to describe his short bursts of home life in terms of time spent stealing away to the Malibu ranch, where he felt alive and able to relax. In Ronnie's world, "the kinship between man and animal you find on the back of a horse" was commensurate with, if not a substitute for, what the family offered.

In November 1959, Reagan was dragged back to another Screen Actors Guild mediation battle, this time with film and television producers over residual payments to actors for the rebroadcast of old movies and the establishment of a pension and welfare fund.

Howard Keel, the sitting SAG president, had abruptly resigned in the middle of negotiations, and "so everybody's mind turned to Ronald Reagan," Jack Dales recalled.

Nancy, fearing a vengeful backlash, urged him to turn the guild down. Still, it killed Ronald Reagan to let the studio bosses dictate the terms of how actors got paid. Someone had to push back against the machine. Wrestling with whether to accept the challenge, Ronnie called Lew Wasserman for advice. It seemed almost certain that Wasserman would counsel him to back off. Ronnie was convinced that serving as SAG's president had damaged his career—that Jack Warner never looked at him again without seeing the face of the opposition, someone trying to put the squeeze on him and the other moguls. Lew would see the wisdom in keeping a low profile. There was nothing to gain by angering the gods. Surprisingly, however, Wasserman pressed him to accept.

It never dawned on Ronnie that Wasserman's company, MCA/Revue Studios—a company in which Ronnie was a client and now indirectly worked for—had so much at stake in the negotiations. Or if he had understood the conflict, he never admitted it. Should the guild order a walkout or a strike, MCA stood to lose a fortune. In 1958, the company had shrewdly purchased the TV rights to Paramount Pictures' backlist of films and had already earned $60 million on that investment. How much, if any, of that would flow back to actors was up for grabs.

Ronald Reagan's election to fill the top post at SAG—his sixth term— was pro forma. His name was placed in nomination without opposition, requiring a simple voice vote in lieu of a ballot. But other voices began sounding a note of disenchantment. No sooner had Ronnie taken office than a conservative faction led by Hedda Hopper staged a smear campaign to favor the producers. And word circulated through the guild membership that the man spearheading their fight was a wolf in sheep's clothing. Didn't Ronnie's cozy situation with General Electric give him a controlling interest in its TV show? The way some actors saw it, there was a giant conflict. A committee was formed to investigate and sort things out. Its findings, published in the December 1959 issue of *Screen Actor*, SAG's in-house bulletin, offered a rebuttal in the form of an exoneration. Of Ronald Reagan, it said, "He has no ownership interest, percentage, participation or otherwise in the *General Electric Theater*, or any other picture or series. He is not the producer of the series and he has no voice in the selection or approval of the actors employed."

In fact, the opposite was true. Months earlier, when Ronnie's contract came up for renewal, in addition to a significant raise in salary, the company kicked in an astonishing benefit: 25 percent ownership in all *GE Theater* productions, not just those that he appeared in. The perk was an annuity—it would pay enormous dividends for years to come through the selling and rebroadcasting of episodes worldwide. It also compromised his position in the ongoing negotiations. He didn't see it that way, of course. He was an ethical man, and fiercely vigilant about his integrity; instinctively, he took a hard line in his official role as the actors' emissary. Also, the thought that management might be strong-arming his protégés put his back up. But he was compromised just the same. A conflict of interest did exist.

The producers, his ostensible adversaries, also dug in; they refused to negotiate on any movie made before 1960, arguing that the TV revenues kept the studios solvent. When the studios refused to even discuss a compromise, the SAG membership voted to strike on March 7, 1960.

Reagan knew which side of the picket line his bread was buttered on. Most of the B movies he made were pre-1960, but his status as a producer—a status with a much greater upside—lay ahead, not in the past. It behooved him to resolve the situation as quickly as possible to keep the financial pipelines flowing. To hasten things along, he proposed a deal he felt both sides could accept. The actors would forfeit their claims to residual payments for TV broadcasts of all movies made prior to 1960—"thousands and thousands of pictures," by Bob Hope's accounting. In return, a pension plan would be created and funded by the producers with a one-time contribution of $2.65 million, a relative pittance that covered only the pre-1960 pictures. Actors would be entitled to a 6 percent residual on sales of movies made after 1960 to TV, but only after the producers deducted their distribution costs, which were often front-loaded and padded, lessening the payout. It was a mediocre deal at best, heavily weighted in the producers' favor, but one the guild was likely to ratify. Only a tiny fraction of SAG's 13,403 members were stars who could afford to stay out of work. As the strike stretched into its sixth week, the majority, in debt and with cash running out, was desperate to reach a settlement. To no one's surprise, it was put to a vote and authorized on April 18, 1960.

The deal was a particularly difficult one to swallow for longtime established stars who had been working steadily since the introduction of sound—screen veterans like Johnny Weissmuller, whose thirty Tarzan and jungle films were shown "eighty million times," it was said—an exaggeration, but germane nonetheless—and now earned him nothing as a result of the deal. The same with Bob Hope, who had made forty-six movies prior to 1960 and felt he was "sold down the river" by Ronald Reagan. Mickey Rooney, who had been making movies from the age of four and considered it a "crime showing our pictures on TV without paying us residuals," aired his blunt disapproval to anyone who listened. Years later, broke and resentful, he attempted to sue to reclaim those rights.

"Ronald Reagan," Rooney concluded, "was only a pawn at the time the deal was made." Rooney didn't hold him responsible for the pitiful outcome. "I believe that he did what he thought best at the time."

On June 7, 1960, as soon as the ink was dry on SAG's agreement with the producers, Ronnie submitted his resignation as guild president in a letter to the board of directors. "I plan to change [my] status by becoming a producer with an interest in profits," he wrote, trusting it would put an end to questions about his motives.

His primary concern now was keeping things on track with his duties at GE. There was a general concern that *Bonanza* was gaining ground on *General Electric Theater*, putting pressure on the anthology to revitalize its format. The new arrangement gave Ronnie input on the show's scripts and actors, which bit heavily into his speaking schedule. He enjoyed his new producer status, but it was essential, he knew, to continue making speeches, staying connected to "the unwashed public," as he referred to his audience, with his ear to the ground. Other people and experiences might have shaped Ronnie's attitudes toward life in general, but nothing had the impact of those GE tours. His early political thoughts were little more than the fanciful speculations of an impressionable, perhaps even a naïve, young man on what he perceived as "the American dangers." The tours were where he finally understood his political inclinations—his tilt to more conservative positions—and developed a way to convincingly express them.

Occasionally, however, they collided with his sponsor's interests, precipitating what GE called "a customer relations problem." On May 4, 1960, during a speech to the company's regional directors at its Nela Park facility in Cleveland, Ohio, Ronald Reagan cited the Tennessee Valley Authority as an example of how a New Deal program becomes bloated beyond its original purpose, putting the squeeze for its upkeep on U.S. taxpayers. The way he saw it, the country would be better off if the government turned the TVA over to private developers—or shut it down. Unbeknownst to him, the TVA was a contractor for electrical equipment—the *apparatus*, in manufacturing parlance—built by GE. Worse, GE was in the process of bidding for a $50 million contract for the TVA's generators, turbines, and switch gear. It didn't help matters that the tone of his remarks became more and more strident. He chastised the TVA for being "unfairly competitive with private business."

Word filtered back that he'd sunk the deal. He hadn't—but certain mid-level bureaucrats at GE and their sidekicks in Congress were up in arms. They wanted him muzzled, thrashed, if not fired. He prepared for the worst. His reigning handler, an ex-FBI agent named George Dalen, manned the phones in their hotel suite, awaiting a "no clemency" call from GE's president, Ralph Cordiner. After a few days of silence, however, Ronnie decided to go on the offensive. He picked up the phone and called Cordiner, a man whose power was legendary.

"I understand you have a problem and it concerns me," Ronnie said.

Cordiner was unconcerned to the point of uninterest. "I am never going to have GE censor anything you say," he told him. If a client of the company wanted to take its business elsewhere—so be it. Ronnie was free to speak his own mind.

He'd heard a lot about Cordiner's largesse and insight, but Ronnie considered his attitude beyond benevolent. He offered to "delete all references to TVA and public power" in the future, to make Cordiner's job easier.

But he didn't—and it didn't. No sooner were the words out of his mouth than Ronnie blasted the TVA all over again, in a scathing interview with the *Los Angeles Mirror*'s conservative syndicated columnist Hal Humphrey, who had goaded him into remarks seen as "lambasting venal big business." No matter what Cordiner's position was, the GE suits had had enough. "On future speaking engagements," they declared, "Mr. Reagan will be accompanied by . . . a competent representative of the company who will take all necessary steps to insure that no further embarrassment on this subject" occurs.

Embarrassment. It was a stigma Ronald Reagan wanted to avoid at all costs. Up until now, he had been GE's celebrity pet pitchman. "The biggest problem we had was the occasional shopgirl who would bare her left breast and want him to autograph it," Earl Dunckel recalled. But expressing political opinions at odds with the company's, conservative or otherwise, veered into dangerous territory. It was of vital importance to Ronnie that nothing jeopardize this job. He enjoyed the work. It paid well—very well. The exposure he got from appearing on TV was perhaps even greater than what the movies had given him. A survey found he "had one of the most recognized names in the country." As far as visibility and influence went, the payoff to him was incalculable. Although he was on the road an ungodly amount of time, away from his home and family, working sixteen-hour days, all in all it was an outstanding gig.

B ut he was now fired up with a fervent ideology that was informing every aspect of his life. Conservative journals like *National Review, The Freeman,* and *Human Events* fed his growing prejudices against government bloat and excessive regulation. Traveling between appearances, he pored over books like John Flynn's rebuke of the New Deal, *The Road Ahead;* Lewis Haney's *How You Really Earn Your Living;* Wilhelm Röpke's *Economics of the Free Society;* and Henry Hazlitt's *Economics in One Lesson,* which advocated free trade and opposition to price controls, inflation, and government stimulus. This was Ronald Reagan's enlightenment, what he called his "postgraduate education in political science" and his "apprenticeship for public life."

It was primarily through the speeches Ronnie gave that word of his partisan conversion filtered to Republican operatives. The one-time New Dealer was an attractive addition to their ranks, especially in 1960, during a crucial election year. Initially, Ronald Reagan had been courted by Joseph Kennedy, whose son Jack was running for president against Richard Nixon. The elder Kennedy flew out to see him in Los Angeles to ask for his support, where Ronnie turned him down flat. Party affiliation aside—and that was a huge aside—he vehemently opposed JFK's beneficence, spending taxpayers' money to aid education ("the foot in the door to federal control"), unemployment insurance ("a prepaid vacation plan for freeloaders"), public housing, and especially his plan to provide government health insurance for the elderly. This last scheme particularly rankled. Ronnie's father-in-law, Loyal Davis, regarded Medicare as an initiative emanating from the loins of Joseph Stalin himself. At Dr. Davis's prompting, Ronnie volunteered his services to the plan's chief opponent, the American Medical Association, for whom he recorded an incendiary spoken-word LP, "Ronald Reagan Speaks Out Against Socialized Medicine," played at women's organizations and social gatherings across the country. On it, he warned listeners that a program like Medicare was the portal to a government takeover of "every area of freedom as we have known in this country."

No, he wouldn't be supporting John Kennedy in the forthcoming election. But—Richard Nixon? This was the scoundrel who did a hatchet job on Helen Gahagan Douglas in 1950, the man Ronnie regarded in his letter to Sam Harrod II as "less than honest and . . . an ambitious opportunist." It would be an enormous leap of faith to endorse him now. He explained his misgivings in a phone call to Ralph Cordiner, GE's president, who replied, "I think you may be wrong about Nixon." Reagan regarded Cordiner as a man with a strong code of honor. If he thought Ronnie should give Nixon another look, he would.

Ronald Reagan never explained his reevaluation of Richard Nixon other than to say, "He wasn't the villain I'd thought him to be." Perhaps it came down to a rationalization: Nixon was the lesser of two evils. Or maybe he detected a promising statesman. In any case, Ronnie supported the Republican ticket. In fact, he'd go it one better. He wrote to Nixon after the

Democratic convention, cautioning that Kennedy's acceptance speech was "a frightening call to arms." He assured Nixon that there was plenty in it to run against, notwithstanding JFK's "idea of the 'challenging new world,' one in which the Federal Gov't. will grow bigger & do more & and of course spend more." The prospect appalled Ronnie, who concluded: "Shouldn't someone tag Mr. Kennedy's 'bold new imaginative' program with its proper age? Under the tousled boyish haircut it is still old Karl Marx—first launched a century ago."

Ronnie left little doubt that he would cross the aisle as a Democrat for Nixon, but he warned the candidate that he "cannot support the ticket if it includes Rockefeller." New York governor Nelson Rockefeller was anathema to die-hard conservatives. He was a liberal Republican, and to true believers the only thing separating him from a liberal Democrat was "the difference between creeping socialism and galloping socialism." Ronnie proposed a better number-two man: Arizona senator Barry Goldwater. Goldwater was a friend of his mother-in-law, Edith Luckett; they were next-door neighbors in Biltmore Estates. Ronnie had devoured the senator's best-selling manifesto, *The Conscience of a Conservative*, cherry-picking lines from it to quote in his speeches.

Nixon had no plans to anoint Goldwater. He was sending Goldwater to campaign for him in the South, where the senator's stand against civil rights legislation would go far toward attracting longtime Democratic segregationists to the party. But Nixon now saw a strong ally in Ronald Reagan, and scrawled a note across the top of the letter, which he passed on to his campaign staff: "Use him as a speaker wherever possible. He used to be a liberal."

That should have come as no great revelation. No less a cultural bellwether than *Time* had pretty much called it in an earlier editorial. Admitting that the magazine had only ever viewed Ronald Reagan as a run-of-the-mill actor—"a pleasant young man in white ducks, whose deepest thought was reserved for the next dance"—it now offered a pithy new appraisal. "Once an outspoken Democrat," its reporter observed, "Reagan is now a staunch Republican [and] has developed into a remarkably active spokesman for conservatism."

To former activist colleagues, this was a stunning piece of news. Olivia de Havilland found it "outrageous that he went over to the other side" after all their hard work for New Deal causes. Dana Andrews concluded Ronnie had been brainwashed by the "rich Republicans" running General Electric, stranding him "on the wrong side of the fence politically." But conservatives had long seen this coming. William F. Buckley Jr., founder and editor of the *National Review*, had corresponded with Ronnie since the mid-1950s, parsing nuggets from his book *Up from Liberalism* as well as think pieces in the magazine. And his closest social friends—the *really* rich Republicans like publishing magnate Walter Annenberg, Alfred Bloomingdale, and industrialists Earle Jorgensen and William Wilson—knew how much his views corresponded with conservative causes they'd been promoting and underwriting actively for years.

Jack Kennedy's election pushed Ronnie across the threshold. The badly bungled Bay of Pigs invasion, the North Vietnamese army's incursion into Laos, and the erection of the Berlin Wall were very discouraging developments, comingled with what he viewed as domestic boondoggles: the establishment of a food-stamp program, the raising of the minimum wage to $1.15 an hour under the Fair Labor Standards Act, and the launch of the Peace Corps. The twin screws of "socialism" and "communism" began to tighten in his chest. And yet, despite what Reagan saw as obvious misfires, Kennedy's approval rating jumped to a mind-boggling 82 percent.

In response, Reagan struck out on a new tour of speeches. He doubled down on opposing Kennedy, attacking his New Frontier initiatives as lapses in judgment that could lead to social "slavery." Communists, he insisted, were still "infiltrating all phases of the government," just as they'd edged their way back into the motion-picture industry.

Taking on the administration was a natural course of action, but if his instincts were keen, his timing was unfortunate.

During the fall of 1961, a commission headed by the president's brother Attorney General Robert Kennedy began investigating MCA's exclusive position as both a talent agency and a television film producer. Convinced that MCA had breached antitrust laws, the Justice Department launched a federal grand jury to probe the possibility of a conspiracy between MCA and the Screen Actors Guild, focusing on the blanket waiver that SAG had granted Lew Wasserman to expand his empire in 1952.

That put Ronald Reagan in the direct line of fire. As guild president when the waiver was requested, he had ushered it through the approval process with unusual finesse. Were there any irregularities behind the deal? A source for the government fingered Ronnie as "a complete slave of MCA who would do their bidding on anything." There had to be some kind of quid pro quo, the source suggested, perhaps "some type of consideration" in the form of a promise for future work or an exchange of cash "between the top people in SAG and MCA." As a result, Ronnie was subpoenaed to testify on February 5, 1962.

Why, the government wanted to know, did the guild grant MCA a blanket waiver in opposition to its bylaws? And how did he later come to have part ownership in the TV shows he produced for MCA?

Ronald Reagan's testimony—a bravura two-hour burlesque of feints, dodges, and humbug—functioned as the rehearsal for a routine he perfected as governor and president. As John Fricano, the government's point man, ran through his questions, Ronnie played the naïf, a bumpkin actor who, golly-gee, wasn't sure of any specifics. While he could rattle off intricate sequences of plays that his Eureka football team ran twenty years earlier, the man who Earl Dunckel said could quote dates and places "like a computer," that "virtually everything that went into [his] mind stayed there," couldn't name a single producer the Screen Actors Guild negotiated with in the residual dispute just four years earlier. "My memory would be pretty dim, I would think," he hedged. "Maybe—I don't honestly know." He couldn't recall if he even participated in the negotiations between SAG and MCA. Nor could he supply the number of waivers granted to other talent agents subsequent to MCA's blanket waiver. (The answer, of course, was zero.) The evasions came one after the other. "My memory is a little hazy." "I'm a little dim on that." "I'll have to take your word." "You have me there." "I'm not sure." "I couldn't say." "I wouldn't be able to tell you." And dozens of times: "I don't recall" and "I don't know." An observer was quick to put a name to it—"selective amnesia," a strategy that confounded his inquisitor.

After the testimony had concluded, the Justice Department suspected a sweetheart deal, concluding it was "likely that Reagan had been given a promise of the role of host of GE Theater as consideration for keeping his actors in line"—in other words, delivering the guild's vote in favor of the blanket waiver. To determine if there was any financial payoff, the Antitrust Division subpoenaed Ronnie and Nancy's tax returns for 1952 through

1955, as well as those of the members of the Screen Actors Guild's executive board. Ultimately, no inconsistencies were discovered and no charges were filed, but reverberations from the investigation were felt in the executive suite of General Electric.

It was alarming having your company spokesman dragged before a federal grand jury. GE was buttressed by lucrative government contracts. It couldn't afford a sideshow that might threaten essential interests. The company was already fending off an indictment by the Justice Department for price fixing in the electrical industry. The fallout from an individual's alleged indiscretions—legitimate or not—would only serve to bring unnecessary scrutiny.

Ronnie's politics had also become increasingly controversial. In a new round of speeches, he presented himself as "an orthodox and patriotic American, drawing attention to a problem of government growth that would destroy the country if it wasn't corrected." He refused to put the brakes on his repeated attacks of the Kennedy administration. And he'd undertaken what some considered an odious job—as campaign chairman for Loyd Wright,* an extremist who advocated an offensive nuclear strike against the Soviet Union, in his bid for a California Senate seat against Thomas Kuchel. This was entirely too radical for a company like GE. By 1962, even the AFL-CIO, so receptive to Ronnie's achievements as SAG president, had branded him "a right-wing zealot."

General Electric began to take a good, hard look at Ronald Reagan.

I t didn't help that GE Theater's ratings had suffered a steep and steady slide. Since Bonanza's weak debut in 1959, the NBC western had picked up steam and, by 1961, not only outperformed but decimated its anthology rival. CBS, GE's network, "was deeply and justifiably disturbed by this development," particularly since GE Theater followed The Ed Sullivan Show, its Sunday-night tent pole. That nine p.m. time slot was valuable real estate; the network had a franchise to maintain.

"The time had come to make a decision," recalled Paul Wassmansdorf. In early March 1962, he attended an after-hours meeting in the company's

---

* Strangely, Wright had represented Jane Wyman in her divorce proceeding against Ronald Reagan.

New York headquarters with Gerald Phillippi, GE's president, and Stanley Smith, the marketing vice president, specifically to decide the show's fate. But going in, it was a fait accompli. The ratings had dipped so low that they "couldn't see a future in it." GE Theater had run its course. They decided to replace the show with another Revue series, GE True, hosted by Jack Webb. The tribunal delivered its verdict to Ronnie, who was traveling at the time, and offered him an alternative, Wassmansdorf said. "Would he consider being just a spokesman for General Electric?"

Ronnie heard it as a sop—that any speeches he made on the company's behalf from then on "would be sales pitches for GE products," free of political substance. It didn't suit him to hawk appliances such as "the new 1963 coffee pot" or to "peddle toasters." "I'm not interested anymore," he told them.

The show's cancellation disappointed and embittered him. He was convinced it had nothing to do with ratings. "The government is trying to control everything," he disclosed to his family over dinner. Someone high-placed in the administration, he'd heard, had written a letter to General Electric threatening to cancel its contracts unless GE got rid of him as a spokesman. He had a pretty good idea who it was. "Robert Kennedy is behind this attack on me."

This notion surfaced again months later, after Ronnie sought Lew Wasserman's assistance in resurrecting his acting career. A comeback wasn't that much of a pipe dream. The majority of his friends were still making pictures—William Holden, Spencer Tracy, Bette Davis, Gregory Peck. "Like any actor," he rationalized, "I keep thinking that the big picture is still ahead of me." But weeks passed without an offer for his services. The opportunities were sparse for a fifty-one-year-old actor. He appeared in a segment of the Wagon Train TV series while waiting for a movie. Otherwise the phone never rang.

By the summer, frustrated by the radio silence and desperate to work, he confronted Wasserman, who advised him to modify his options, perhaps by doing more television. This wasn't the response Ronnie expected. "You told me to wait for the right movie script," he argued. Lew should know: Ronnie had always done everything that was asked of him. It was finally time for the agent to come through. There was a bit part for him in an upcoming Don Siegel film at Universal; otherwise no one in Hollywood expressed an interest in hiring Ronald Reagan. In his most patronizing voice, Wasserman said, "You've been around this business long enough to know that I can't force someone on [a producer] if he doesn't want to use them."

Ronnie stormed out of the office. "I felt that I had been betrayed," he said, "and I guess Lew felt that he was doing what he had to do." But deep down, he suspected it had more to do with politics. Wasserman, long active in Democratic causes, made no secret that he was a staunch Kennedy advocate. The long arm of government, Ronnie thought, was reaching out to silence him. If that was its objective, it had another thing coming.

CHAPTER TWENTY-ONE

THE FRIENDS OF RONALD REAGAN

"Man is by nature a political animal."

—ARISTOTLE

Holmes Tuttle, the hard-charging Oklahoman who presided over the splashy Ford showroom bearing his name at the corner of La Brea Avenue and Beverly Boulevard in Los Angeles, could hardly keep his mind on the business of car sales. He had a full lot of gleaming new Galaxies, Thunderbirds, Falcon Futuras, and Sunliners that needed clearing to make way for the revolutionary new Mustang promised later in 1964, but all he could think about was presidential politics. As the western financial chairman for Barry Goldwater's campaign, Tuttle was scrambling to right a leaky ship. Republican support was lukewarm for the candidate whose pugnacious, profane talk had alienated party moderates. The fund-raising spigot had just about run dry. An immediate infusion of cash was essential for the ticket to remain competitive.

Tuttle resorted to a fail-safe charity ploy: throw a posh dinner with a celebrity speaker and lean on guests to write big checks. He and two friends—Henry Salvatori and Cy Rubel, like-minded conservative million-aire entrepreneurs—swung into action. They rented out the Cocoanut Grove nightclub in the Ambassador Hotel and dusted off their list of local donors. But what attraction could they rely on to draw the city's wealthiest angels? John Wayne was off filming on location. Robert Montgomery hosted an eponymous TV anthology necessitating his round-the-clock presence. "We didn't have anybody," Tuttle recalled, "so I called up Ron and asked if he wouldn't give a twenty-minute talk."

Twenty-minute talks were Ronald Reagan's stock-in-trade, but this speech—so momentous that it would be known forever as "the Speech"—was about to give his abstract views their fullest expression in an entirely new arena, one where they would be taken seriously.

And so would he.

The first few months of 1964 brought him to the realization that his acting career had run its course. His appearance in *The Killers*, a joint effort of Universal Pictures and Revue Productions, was foreshadowed by John F. Kennedy's assassination the day before filming started. It cast a pall on the Burbank soundstage, where vivacious co-star Angie Dickinson—rumored to have been one of JFK's girlfriends—delivered her lines through a palpable mask of grief. The script required Ronnie, miscast as a scowling, squint-eyed heavy, to slap Dickinson, slap her hard, which, according to her, "he *hated* doing." It ran counter to his personal values, an impression he no doubt conveyed to the audience. If the original version, a 1946 "film noir masterpiece," functioned as Burt Lancaster's crackerjack debut, this Don Siegel remake served as Ronald Reagan's swan song, underscored by its eventual release on a double bill with *The Private Lives of Adam and Eve*, a Mamie Van Doren sex farce.

Forced to scramble for work, Ronnie succumbed to a pitch by his brother, Neil, now an advertising executive with TV clients, to succeed "Old Ranger" Stanley Andrews as the host of *Death Valley Days*, a half-hour TV series based on legends of the American West produced by Gene Autry's Flying A Productions. Moon, an executive with the McCann-Erickson advertising agency, represented the show's sponsor, U.S. Borax, which had no trouble with Ronnie's stepping in as its new emcee. It mirrored his duties on *GE Theater*—introducing each week's episode and acting whenever a role suited him.

It wasn't a dream job. The show, which had been around in one form or another since 1930, wasn't much of a challenge, nor was it considered an artistic ideal. The scripts were fairly banal, the acting serviceable. Under the circumstances, it was a decent paycheck. And as Neil Reagan shrewdly concluded, "It kept him in the public eye for what I figured might be helpful if he ran for governor in a couple of years."

Ran for governor? It was the first anyone had raised that prospect. Politics was one stage Ronald Reagan hadn't performed on, other than the speeches he delivered as after-dinner entertainment. Holmes Tuttle had approached him a few years earlier about challenging moderate Thomas Kuchel for a U.S. Senate seat, a seat his old Hollywood pal George Murphy was now running for in the 1964 election. Murphy's emergence as a candidate might have whet Ronnie's appetite for a similar ambitious effort. Politics, Tuttle argued, was the next logical step.

Holmes Tuttle had known Ronald Reagan since the mid-1940s, when Hollywood stars like Greta Garbo and Marlene Dietrich frequented his dealership shopping for a car that suited their outsize personalities. Jane Wyman introduced the men during a routine visit, and as Tuttle recalled, "I sold him a Model A Ford." Admittedly, it wasn't love at first sight. Tuttle was a hard-core internationalist who "hated Roosevelt" and couldn't stand Ronnie's New Deal proclivities. "He was a Democrat then, and we used to argue." But both men saw something in each other that rose above their political interests. Holmes Tuttle was a master charmer, tall, charismatic, and debonair—"an oracle," according to socialite Betsy Bloomingdale.

What his charm couldn't do was counteract the low approval rating dogging owl-eyed Barry Goldwater, making him, in the words of one conservative activist, "a tremendous underdog." Goldwater's candidacy had been rocky from the start. He was an outspoken opponent of the New Deal's progressive legacy, and his nomination had caused a schism in the Republican Party, pitting a grassroots conservative upsurge in the South and West against the moderate wing of "Rockefeller Republicans" predominant in the northeast corridor. Goldwater had fought and won a bitter primary against Nelson Rockefeller, William Scranton, and Henry Cabot Lodge Jr. The process had branded him the darling of the ideological right, but he was unable to soften his image because of his penchant for harsh rhetoric, exemplified by his paraphrase of Cicero toward the end of his acceptance speech:

I remind you, that extremism in the defense of liberty is no vice. And let me remind you that moderation in the pursuit of justice is no virtue.

During the campaign, Goldwater's Achilles' heel had been his mouth. He talked tough and loose, off the cuff but on the record—which loyalists like Holmes Tuttle had come to regret. In one famous missive, Goldwater argued that the United States could "lob one into the men's room of the Kremlin." In another, he called on the administration to violate the Test Ban Treaty. Labeled an extremist and a radical, his "abrasive *Götterdämmerung* approach" scared off the moderates in his party, so much so that Rockefeller, Scranton, Lodge, Jacob Javits, and George Romney refused to campaign for him. Ike, the party's standard-bearer, disdained Barry Goldwater, but he advised reluctant Republican intimates, "You're going to hold your nose and vote for him."

It was left to the true believers—the tight-knit band of self-made California tycoons—to scrounge up support. An observer might wonder: What was in it for them? Certainly, money wasn't the motivating factor. Like Holmes Tuttle, who ran Ford dealerships scattered throughout the West, the others were wealthy beyond their dreams. Henry Salvatori built Western Geophysical into the world's largest contractor for offshore oil exploration; Cy Rubel retired in August 1964 as the chairman of Union Oil; and Justin Dart headed the Rexall Drug empire. None of them sought political appointment, federal funding, or patronage. They weren't ambitious that way. Except for the blustery, pugnacious Dart, they were humble men, "not Wall Street, not corporate types," as Salvatori liked to remind people, but "men who saw the importance of preserving free enterprise" and, just as important, thwarting the worldwide spread of communism. "They were worried about the direction of the country," says Robert Tuttle, who worked closely alongside his father and later served in the Reagan administration.

Conservatism had given their expressed interests a name. For years, they had pushed back in fits and starts against the indomitable liberal tide, decrying entitlement programs and what they considered diminished freedoms. They spoke of the Soviet Union in apocalyptic terms, distrusted the Eastern establishment, the encroachment of Big Government. In time, they realized there were others across the country who shared their views. The intensifying strength of labor unions and the civil rights movement brought like-minded ideologues out of the woodwork and energized an emerging cultural right that had been growing in number and influence since the end of World War II. Some of the more intellectual members of the movement started a publication that pulled these ideas together. In 1955, *National Review* sounded an assertive public voice for conservative ideas and policies and spoke directly to its homogeneous flock. (Henry Salvatori put up seed money for the magazine.) In its charter issue, editor William F. Buckley laid out the doctrine of modern conservatism as the willingness to "stand athwart history, yelling Stop, at a time when no one is inclined to do so, or to have much patience with those who so urge it." By 1960, the movement had its inspirational manifesto—*The Conscience of a Conservative*, actually written by Buckley's brother-in-law, L. Brent Bozell—as well as its national spear-carrier in Barry Goldwater.

But weeks before the election, his campaign floundered on life support. It had all gone downhill following the Republican convention, which Holmes Tuttle, among other party stalwarts, considered "a fiasco." Piling on, Lyndon Johnson's reelection team released a devastating TV commercial titled "Daisy," depicting images of an adorable little girl picking petals off a flower that dissolved into a nuclear bomb explosion; it never mentioned Goldwater by name, but its critique of him was implicit. The dinner at the Ambassador wouldn't alleviate the woes, but at one thousand dollars a plate it would at least underwrite a few ads to soften the blows going into the home stretch.

Ronald Reagan understood the significance of the speech he agreed to deliver. He had stumped vigorously for Goldwater throughout the late summer and early fall of 1964, and he witnessed the collective malaise. He'd heard about it as well from Neil, who had accompanied the candidate throughout the summer on a swing through the Midwest and the South as a Goldwater operative. The odds of a Republican victory were growing dimmer by the day. Goldwater needed some inspirational help—a speech like the one George Gipp had used to rally his football team back in 1928. Someone had to step up and make the case. At any rate, this speech "was more important than all the others," Ronnie admitted, perhaps the most important one he'd ever make.

Writing it wasn't going to present any problems. He'd given one or another version of it, by his count, "hundreds of times before," switching up issues and references as the situation dictated. The old standbys never changed: the burden of taxes, encroaching government, welfare spending, the threat of communism. He'd hit the same notes as a Democrat and now as a Republican, having officially changed his affiliation in 1962. The speech played across the political spectrum to those who harbored fears that something serious was wrong with America. This time around, he'd give those fears a good shot of juice with many apocryphal examples of waste and overreach he'd plucked from various sources. Congress, he'd reveal, was on the verge of seizing farms and taking over the country's agriculture program. Apparently, the United States bought a $2 million yacht for Haile Selassie, dress suits for Greek undertakers, and extra wives for Kenyan diplomats. He'd make the president's plan to build more public housing sound like government internment centers, and Johnson's War on Poverty like a euphemism to step up welfare.

A judge, he wrote, had called him about a young woman who had come before the court in a divorce action. "She had six children, was pregnant with the seventh," he claimed. "She wanted a divorce so that she could get an $80 raise. She is eligible for $330 a month in the aid to dependent children program," and realized there was more to be made as a single mother on the dole than from a husband who pulled in a measly $250 a month. Years later, in future retellings, the woman in this story would morph into a welfare queen from the wrong side of Chicago's tracks, and another time a scam artist from Watts—Ronnie knew a powerful allegory when he heard one. And he knew how to deliver it, with unforced sincerity and the right touch of irony.

In a nod to a one-time hero, he appropriated a line from Franklin D. Roosevelt's inauguration that he'd use in closing out his remarks: "You and I have a rendezvous with destiny." A *rendezvous with destiny*. It was irresistible, poetic, such a powerful sentiment. He'd make it sound like an apocalyptic call to arms, a goal of all right-thinking Americans to make critical choices, none more decisive than casting a meaningful vote for Barry Goldwater.

He wrote the speech out in longhand on a yellow notepad and, as an afterthought, scrawled a title across the top: "A Time for Choosing."

The speech was a revelation. The Cocoanut Grove was packed with eight hundred Los Angeles power brokers to whom Ronald Reagan was nothing but the usual Hollywood raconteur recruited at functions such as these to soften them up with a few gossipy movie anecdotes before asking for donations. They clearly weren't expecting to hear an actor deliver cogent ruminations on the health of the nation or express the kinds of views that echoed concerns they'd been discussing among themselves. For half an hour he electrified that crowd, prompting an eruption of applause followed by a standing ovation.

Henry Salvatori, a man known for being stingy with praise, was besotted. "It was the best speech ever made by anybody," he raved. Holmes Tuttle recalled how afterward he was besieged by well-wishers who congratulated him on his inspired choice of speaker and pledged to support the campaign with newfound enthusiasm. The evening was more than a resounding financial success, it was an eye-opener as far as the organizers were concerned. Barry Goldwater had been making the same points for months, achieving nowhere near the impact. "His philosophy was sound," Salvatori thought, "but he didn't articulate it moderately." Ronald Reagan knew how to *communicate*, he *connected* with his listeners. They needed to bottle his eloquence and put it to use.

They didn't waste any time. Later that night, while the busboys were methodically clearing the tables, Tuttle and Salvatori cornered Ronnie with a proposal. "We've got to get that speech on television," Tuttle said. The voters needed to hear *Ronald Reagan* express the party's position on key issues if the Republicans had any hope of salvaging the election. He and Salvatori would put up the money to buy a half hour of national airtime on NBC if Ronnie was willing to repeat his performance.

The Goldwater camp was less than thrilled. The candidate's advisers worried that the speech was too controversial and would confuse voters about where they stood on certain hot-button issues, in particular Social Security and the TVA. There were concerns, too, about being upstaged. Instead, they preferred to use the same time slot to rebroadcast a meeting between Goldwater and Dwight Eisenhower at the president's home in Gettysburg. But Ronnie pushed back. He knew the speech was more effective—"it had always gotten a good response," he recalled—and went ahead with it as planned.

"A Time for Choosing" was taped before an invited studio audience in Phoenix and shown in prime time on October 27, 1964. Patti Reagan, who sat next to her mother, was mesmerized by the experience. "I remember my father molding the crowd with his words," she recalled, "quieting them at moments, inciting them at others, pulling tears from them as a finale." He was candid and direct, at times charming, at times paternalistic, injecting a Midwestern folksiness, like Nelle onstage with her religious parables. His delivery was engaging, dynamic, supremely well modulated. He projected confidence. He had gravitas. Those who watched at home came to the same conclusion as the audience had at the Cocoanut Grove: Ronald Reagan was a far better conservative advocate and came across as more reasonable and statesmanlike than Barry Goldwater.

Judging by the feedback, it was the most successful performance he'd ever given—on any screen. The minute the broadcast ended, the Republican National Committee's phones lit up. Contributions poured in at an extraordinary clip from all over the country—in all, close to a million dollars by the end of the week, enough to erase the campaign's deficit. The reviews were in and they were unanimous: the speech—*the Speech*—had launched Ronald Reagan as a political star.

Holmes Tuttle watched it at a friend's house, surrounded by his family, the Reagans, and the Salvatoris. "When it was over," recalls Tuttle's son, Robert, "my dad turned to Henry Salvatori and said, 'The wrong candidate is running for president.'"

The country reached the same conclusion. The Republican Party suffered its sorriest defeat in forty years, with Barry Goldwater managing to carry only six states. In California, where GOP stalwarts had pitched in plenty to promote the conservative cause, Lyndon Johnson won by more than a million votes. Holmes Tuttle took an unsparing measure of the situation. "The delegation was at its lowest ebb," he realized. Party moderates—those who had supported Nelson Rockefeller—felt betrayed and bitter. Unrepentant conservatives called the moderates traitors for abandoning Goldwater. Everyone was pointing fingers and grumbling. If they wanted to recover, to unite the factions, it was time to start reordering priorities. "We didn't want that to be the demise of the Republican Party, so we thought the best way to start rebuilding was here in California."

There were several viable pursuits. One in particular stood out—an upcoming gubernatorial race in 1966. And bright spots: George Murphy had won a precious Senate seat in the midst of the Goldwater debacle, evidence that a Republican—a Republican *actor*, no less—could prevail in an otherwise hostile election cycle. The incumbent, Pat Brown, was a popular two-term governor, but still considered vulnerable, a notoriously lazy campaigner whose eight years in office were coming a cropper. Notable candidates were lining up to challenge Brown. The conservative patriarchs wanted their say.

Tuttle, Salvatori, and Rubel repaired to an office they'd rented in the Union Oil Building on Washington Boulevard to review their prospects. "We were defeated, but not bloody," Salvatori concluded. Enough of a groundswell remained to press their beliefs, but they'd learned their lesson: the next horse they backed had to be eloquent and charismatic as well as a unifier. Holmes Tuttle already had a talented recruit in mind. "Gentlemen," he said, "I think we've got a candidate right here. How about Ron?" He had all the qualities they were looking for, as well as the right temperament and name recognition. His political philosophy was sound, his fundamental principles beyond reproach. He'd done everything they'd asked of him—and more. They were selling hundreds of videocassettes of the Speech at close to fifty dollars apiece. Both moderates and conservatives kept calling to voice their admiration. Cy Rubel, a tough-minded pragmatist who more or less functioned as the group's leader, was sold. "Reagan is the man who can enunciate our principles to the people," he said. Henry Salvatori made it unanimous. Stating the obvious, he chimed in: "Why don't we run him for governor?"

The first week in January 1965, Tuttle and his wife, Virginia, visited the Reagans for a New Year's drink and, ultimately, to make the pitch. He said that Ronnie "might be the only Republican around who had a chance of beating [Pat] Brown and bringing the party back together." There wasn't any question of financial support; Tuttle and his associates would see to a strong fund-raising effort. "I told him I knew it would be a terrible sacrifice but that he was the man we wanted," Tuttle recalled.

Nancy Reagan wasn't at all happy. She thought she had married an actor and wasn't prepared to pursue a political life. Even so, she'd seen the writing on the wall. "I knew those people were going to come up to the house after that disastrous election," she said. "I knew it. And they did."

Ronnie, for his part, took it in stride. This wasn't the first time he'd been approached to run for office. In the past, he'd always been adamant: hands-on politics wasn't for him. He reiterated his old line of defense, that he had neither the ambition nor the desire to represent the party in that capacity, but he also acknowledged that circumstances had changed. He was fifty-four. His movie career was finished. The *Death Valley Days* job wouldn't last forever, and besides it had none of the prestige or range he'd explored while at General Electric. In any case, he agreed to think over the offer and continue discussing it with Tuttle and his colleagues.

Holmes Tuttle judged the response as an excuse to press on. He organized a meeting at one of his homes in Palm Springs to sound out the support of a handful of influential men—wealthy like-minded entrepreneurs who'd backed Barry Goldwater and were invested in furthering the conservative mission. They were a formidable group: men for whom power and privilege were second nature; men who saw politics as a way of protecting their interests; men who expected their opinions on issues to have an impact. So they put their money where their mouths were. It was an incestuous group. Most had known one another for a long time. They did business with one another. They'd often get together for cocktails or dinner parties; their wives were friendly. They considered themselves Los Angeles *society*, as opposed to the Hollywood showbiz crowd, whom they mostly shunned as riffraff. They made an exception, of course, for the Reagans, who were regular members of their crowd.

Aside from Cy Rubel and Henry Salvatori, this group of men included Leonard Firestone, president of the family tire company and an energetic philanthropist who'd served as chairman of the doomed Rockefeller campaign; Alfred Bloomingdale, co-founder of Diners Club and heir to the department store fortune, whose energy and charm made him an attractive figure on the New York–Los Angeles social circuit; Earle Jorgensen, a prominent steel magnate serving the aircraft industry, who sat on the board of half a dozen corporations and universities, yet was quick to stand on his head as a stunt at public gatherings; Jaquelin Hume, chairman of Basic

American Foods, the world's largest producer of dried onion and garlic; Leland Kaiser, an investment banker; Arch Monson Jr., the western director of Autocall, which specialized in fire protection equipment; and two Reagan intimates—his lawyer, William French Smith, and Taft Schreiber, his agent at MCA.

By the end of the meeting they had decided to make it official, calling themselves Friends of Ronald Reagan.

They still weren't sure he would run for governor. Holmes Tuttle made that clear from the outset. But they were committed to backing him should he agree. They wanted someone in Sacramento who stood for the basic premises that Ronald Reagan was espousing. His belief system was their belief system, and they felt comfortable with him, they knew him. He was, in a way, one of them—maybe not in the business community, not even remotely on an income level, but in spirit, definitely in spirit.

Tuttle was given the assignment of leaning on Ronnie and soliciting a company to manage a political campaign. In only one of these endeavors was he soon successful. Friends pointed him to the Spencer-Roberts firm— Stuart Spencer and Bill Roberts—a pair of ballsy Republican operatives from Southern California who had nearly stolen the 1964 primary for Nelson Rockefeller. Before that, they'd enjoyed a spectacular string of victories in forty congressional races. They were the most aggressive strategists in the game, Tuttle learned, not least from Goldwater's people, who had taken their lumps.

But Spencer and Roberts were even less willing than Ronnie to launch his campaign. "It was out of the blue," said Spencer of a Reagan candidacy. "We didn't even know the guy." They'd heard through the grapevine he was "a real right-winger," which, in their judgment, precluded any chance of success. There was also a rumor making the rounds that Ronnie was a member of the John Birch Society, which was too extreme for their tastes. "Birchers vilified people they didn't like and started rumors that were untrue," Spencer says. "That would have been a deal-breaker for us." Anyway, their firm was in preliminary discussions with the former San Francisco mayor George Christopher, who'd already thrown his hat into the gubernatorial ring. Christopher was a well-liked moderate Republican who was capable of giving Governor Brown a run for his money. For Spencer and Roberts's money, Christopher was the better bet.

Still, they agreed to meet Ronald Reagan, to sound him out and judge for themselves. In April 1965, they had an exploratory lunch conference with him, Neil Reagan, and a Friends of Ronald Reagan intermediary named Thaxton Hanson at the Cave de Roy, a private club just above Beverly Boulevard that was founded by actors, among them Paul Newman and Tony Curtis. The meeting was less a lunch than a grilling. Spencer and Roberts bombarded Ronnie with nonstop questions: "Why are you doing this?" "What do you believe?" "How well informed are you on the issues?" It went on for several hours. Eventually they felt comfortable enough to ask the clincher: "Are you a Bircher?" Ronnie laughed uneasily. "I don't think so," he responded. The answer was artfully ambiguous. He had been a speaker at a 1962 fund-raiser for John Rousselot, a Republican congressman, who held prominent posts in the John Birch Society. And later, privately, he told Bill Roberts that "it was unfair to label all Birchers as 'crazies.'" He agreed wholeheartedly with the organization's underlying premise—that communism was the source of all evil. But was he a Bircher? *I don't think so.* For now his answer had to suffice.

Spencer and Roberts left the meeting impressed with Ronald Reagan, but more undecided than ever. "This guy's solid, he's new, he's articulate, and he's got great name ID," they agreed. He was also, Bill Roberts found, "a person of great compassion" with "a tremendous sense of humor," all of which contributed to their rising interest. But they knew from doing research sampling that George Christopher would beat him when push came to shove. Spencer had also talked to George Murphy, who gave him enthusiastic feedback, but with reservations. Murphy raved about Ronnie's ideology and work habits. "But he doesn't have a grasp of politics," he said, "and he can be prone to mistakes." Spencer and Roberts had a decision to make. "We were two young guys who understood politics was a gamble," Spencer says. "Every time you go to the mat you roll the dice." Ronald Reagan, they felt, was a man with a future, a pretty good bet to put their money on. After weighing the odds, they looked at each other and said, "Let's do it. Let's roll the dice."

Even with Roberts and Spencer on board, Holmes Tuttle couldn't budge Ronnie one way or the other. He refused to either rule out a run or commit. Nancy's father, Loyal Davis, had strongly advised him against it, and the prospect in general was daunting. "I kept saying no and Holmes Tuttle and his group kept coming back and saying they wouldn't take no for an answer," Reagan recalled. "They kept insisting that I offered the only chance of victory and to bring the party back into something viable." If they were unable to wear him down, they at least managed to make a dent in his armor. He proposed that he spend six months on the road making speeches to ordinary Californians, to take their temperature, so to speak. It would allow him to gauge their impressions of him as a viable candidate. At the end of that time, he said, "I'll make the decision whether you're right or wrong. I think you are wrong about me being the candidate." And he really meant that—at the time. No matter, by December 31, 1965, he promised to give the Friends of Reagan his decision.

Stu Spencer told him that if anyone asked if he was running for governor, he should say he's *exploring* it. Spencer also warned him that they'd be monitoring his progress. "At the end of the year, if you're not cutting it," he said, "we're going to tell you and you'll have a decision to make." Meanwhile, he and Bill Roberts would start laying the groundwork for a run so that the necessary machinery would be in place if they all decided to go forward.

Ronald Reagan's noncommittal stance was driving the Friends of Reagan crazy, but Spencer and Roberts plowed ahead. By October 1965 they had begun to see the basis for a candidacy taking shape. Money was flowing into a Reagan campaign chest, people were beating their doors down to pitch in on early strategy, and the media was drumming up speculation in the press, all while Ronnie zigzagged up and down the California coast, speaking to every Rotary Club, Chamber of Commerce, Lion's Club, and United Way affiliate that would listen to another variation of the Speech. Observers at these functions noted that "his appearance is statuesque," even that "he was heroic," and above all that "he had done his homework." Audiences were charmed by his "homespun spiel . . . spiced with wisecracks" about despotic Big Government. Occasionally reports filtered back that his exploratory work was encouraging and, as promised, he would issue his decision by December 31. But he'd already made up his mind. "They're right," he told Nancy about a month before the deadline. "I think I do offer the best chance of winning."

Stuart Spencer recalls, "We said to ourselves very privately, 'This exploratory thing is all bullshit.' We knew better—he was running for governor."

CHAPTER TWENTY-TWO

THE CITIZEN POLITICIAN

*"Wait a minute! If I win this damn thing I'm out
of show business! I'm in politics!"*

—RONALD REAGAN

B y the time Ronald Reagan hit the campaign's "sawdust trail" in the spring of 1966, the landscape had shifted. He found he could no longer train his focus solely on burdensome taxation, reducing big government, and containing the spread of communism. Circumstances demanded that a candidate running for governor of California now weigh in on the various social outrages that were dividing the country. Like *campus unrest*. In late 1964, free-speech demonstrations at UC–Berkeley and elsewhere propelled him toward labeling them acts of "anarchy, with attempts to destroy the primary purpose of the university." *Sexual deviance.* "Orgies . . . so vile I can not describe it to you." *Drugs.* Marijuana and LSD alienated children from their parents, perhaps nowhere more obviously than on San Onofre Drive, where Patti Reagan's rebellion raged in full force. *Vietnam.* American troops "are being denied the right to try for victory in that war." *Civil rights.* He opposed as unconstitutional the Civil Rights Acts of 1964 and 1965, as well as the Voting Rights Act and California's Rumford Fair Housing Act, which prevented bias and discrimination in housing sales and rentals. *Racial unrest.* "Our city streets are jungle paths after dark," he declared after a second wave of violence struck in riot-torn Watts.

These topics, and others like them, had insinuated themselves as prime sources of discussion among the agitated electorate. Wherever Ronald

Reagan went, at rallies along the campaign trail, at cocktail parties and fund-raisers, even around dinner tables or in line at the bank, the conversation had shifted from sweeping generalities to specific hard-core "gut" issues and what to do about them. Public opinion was churning, and nowhere more tumultuously than in the middle- and working-class suburbs where traditional values had come under siege. His conservative views struck a chord with this dissatisfied constituency. Still, many of the questions being thrown, he found, were tricky to handle. He was still transitioning from one profession to the next, still learning, still making up his mind.

Stu Spencer and Bill Roberts felt some coaching was in order.

From the beginning, they'd stage-managed the campaign with precision and panache. The formal announcement, on January 4, 1966, was a televised half-hour special direct from the studio set of *Death Valley Days*, lit gorgeously and staged with bookcases and a crackling fire in the hearth behind Ronald Reagan. He and Nancy filled the frame like sweethearts in a locket. And when he looked into the camera, "tanned and meticulously groomed," and described himself as a "citizen politician"—a *citizen politician*—it played like a Jimmy Stewart outtake from *Mr. Smith Goes to Washington*.

Despite the makeup, the actor's rapport with the camera, and his crackerjack delivery, there were cracks in the facade. During the broadcast, he mistakenly announced that 15.1 percent of Californians were on welfare—it was actually 5.1. And according to a political analyst, "He was overanswering every question." There was also his myopic perspective. Most of his opinions, even his fundamental knowledge of politics, were developed by combing through *Reader's Digest* and newspaper articles. This didn't foster critical thinking. "On matters on which he had no background," according to journalist Lou Cannon, "Reagan tended to believe anything he read without considering the source." He didn't consider, for example, that *Reader's Digest* slanted its articles to a largely old-fashioned, conservative, *alarmist* audience. His handlers sought to broaden his approach.

"His understanding of how government operated in California was next to nothing," says Stu Spencer. To prepare Ronald Reagan for the scrutiny he'd face in the coming months, they hired Charles Conrad, a classic, old-time congressman from the San Fernando Valley who also happened to be a member of the Screen Actors Guild, to give him a crash tutorial in civics and parliamentary procedure. "Every Tuesday, for two or three months, Charlie would go out to the house and say, 'Ron, here's a bill. Here's what happens when you take it through the process.'"

Those sessions primed him on basic logistics, but he required a much deeper grasp of legislation. More—an acuity that demonstrated his unique stand on individual issues and how it affected the welfare of the state, as well as the common man. To that end, two clinical psychologists—Stanley Plog and Kenneth Holden, who ran the Behavior Sciences Corporation, a West Coast think tank—were delegated to lay out a soup-to-nuts political program rich in populist themes. They identified eleven broad issues—such as transportation, agriculture, water, and the budget—and bombarded the candidate with data, background information, and position papers on which he could put his own spin.

That spin, they recognized soon enough, was Ronald Reagan's greatest asset. His instincts and timing were impeccable. "He could read an audience as well as any man I'd ever met," says Stu Spencer, who chaperoned him to events early on. "His short little one-liners . . . his ability to ad-lib" turned what could have been a dry stump speech into contextual stand-up. Audiences loved him. Even though he'd been a glamorous Hollywood star, people identified with his folksy demeanor. "Joe Dokes running for office," as Bill Roberts put it. "[His] solutions to most problems," Spencer adds, "were always the same as the guy in the bar." He knew what *played*—and how to play it.

But dealing with the press was a whole other story. From the outset, Reagan's interaction with the media troubled Stu Spencer. He recalled, "He was not being taken seriously by the press. To them, he remained a grade-B actor." And worse. The day after his announcement, the *San Francisco Chronicle*, the house organ of Northern California, reported that Reagan represented "the right-wing conservatives of the Republican Party," leaving no doubt it meant members of the extremist John Birch Society. The situation called for hiring an intermediary—someone with press credentials who could vouch for Ronald Reagan's legitimacy and live with his belief system. "Wasn't an easy person to find," Spencer admitted. He worked the halls at the *Los Angeles Times*, the *San Francisco Examiner*, the *San Jose Mercury News*, the *Sacramento Bee*, even the *Orange County Register*—and was turned down by every person he approached. Bill Roberts remembered a guy who had been with Copley News in its Burbank bureau but had gone to Washington as the bureau chief. Franklyn "Lyn" Nofziger was a delightfully irreverent, perennially rumpled character with great wit—"some of it occasionally clean," according to Paul Haerle, a Reagan colleague—who could have been lifted right out of a Damon Runyon scenario. "He was gregarious, savvy, impulsive, ideologically to the right, tended to shoot from the hip, and drank too damn much," Spencer says. Plus, he had no respect for the government. "A perfect candidate for our press secretary."

Right off the bat, Nofziger turned him down—and, again, even after Spencer offered to double his salary. Taking yet another stab at it, they flew him out to Los Angeles to meet Ronald Reagan in order to see if they were simpatico. The two men had met before, at a reception near Columbus, Ohio, in the summer of 1965, but, at the time, as Nofziger recalled, "I was not sober." Now, however, it was love at first sight. "Lyn attached himself like an abalone to a rock," Spencer says. "You'd have to have used a crowbar to pry them apart."

With Nofziger on board, the primary campaign officially kicked into high gear in late February 1966. But at the outset there were hurdles to overcome.

Ronald Reagan's candidacy still sounded like the punch line to a joke. Why not Clark Gable, Cary Grant—or Lassie? Who would play the lieutenant governor? He "was looked upon as being a glamorous curiosity," said William French Smith, Reagan's lawyer, who later served as the head of his executive committee. Even the state party leaders didn't know him or pay him much heed. They'd seen the "A Time for Choosing" speech, but that was about it. Reagan had been a Republican for all of three years. But now what? Was he one of *them?*—or one of *them?* Batting lefty or righty? The label "political switch-hitter" was starting to stick.

The first order of business was introducing Ronald Reagan, the citizen politician, to people across the state—party leaders and voters alike. It meant a tour of every city, town, and rural community where he could address small groups, meet with local businessmen, pick up newspaper coverage, and leave, having made an impression that he was serious about the challenges of running the state. Money wasn't an issue. Ample funds flowed from the Friends of Reagan to keep him out on the hustings for as long as necessary. But the tour was slow getting off the ground. Reagan had never gotten over his fear of planes. "So he would take a train everywhere, or drive," Nofziger recalled. From the outset, they put in long miles on the road, traveling up, down, and across the state. California was just too big; it covered such a huge, sprawling amount of territory, and train travel limited them to towns directly on the lines. Eventually, the Kitchen Cabinet, the nickname given to the Reagan backers, intervened. If Ron intended to run for governor, they said, he'd have to fly. So they hired puddle jumpers at first. Then once he got his nerve back, they upgraded to the Turkey, a big, old lumbering DC-3, lent to the campaign by a San Joaquin Valley turkey rancher who used it to haul his flock to market. When it hit the runway at the end of a flight, everyone on board threw their heads back and gobbled.

At first, very few who came out to hear Ronald Reagan were for him. They knew his face, his movies, but they didn't know *him*. Most people in the places he visited knew his Republican opponent, George Christopher. He was well liked and respected, especially in the north where the party leaders were horrified by the prospect of anyone running against him. Even though Christopher was an old face on the scene and had twice been defeated in statewide campaigns, as a two-term mayor of San Francisco they'd all done business with him. They'd rubbed shoulders with him at the Union Club, stoked his coffers with contributions. So when Ronald Reagan turned up in their districts asking for support, they tended to disappear. They weren't about to transfer their hard-earned allegiance to an interloper, particularly not to a Hollywood interloper.

Sometimes, during visits in the north, his dilettantism was all too evident. At an outdoor event in Clear Lake, an agro-resort community north of Napa County, someone in the crowd asked him, "What are you going to do about the Eel River?" After a moment, Reagan responded, "Where's the Eel River?" Another voice shouted out, "You're standing on it!"

He was a hard sell in the north—and elsewhere. George Christopher, the northern favorite son who appealed to moderate Republicans in many Southern California enclaves, hammered away at what he claimed was Reagan's "complete and utter lack of qualifications." His objective was to force Ron on the defensive and, if possible, to tease out his reputed temper. And for a while, it worked. Lyn Nofziger noticed that "it irritated Reagan"

when Christopher attacked his inexperience. He resented "the feeling—
that this guy didn't know very much," and occasionally he'd lash out at his
critics.

A dogfight among Republican challengers was the last thing party leaders wanted. The 1964 election had riven its ranks, with Goldwater "fire-
breathers" on one side and Rockefeller moderates, sneered at as "liberals,"
on the other. The upshot triggered a bloodbath among down-ballot candidates, ceding most of the state to Democratic control. Now here it was all
over again, with Christopher representing the moderates and Reagan the
conservatives. A lack of unity threatened to sink their chances in 1966 as
well. To stem the divide, Gaylord Parkinson, the California GOP chairman, handed down the so-called Eleventh Commandment: "Thou shalt
not speak ill of any fellow Republican." It was actually conceived by deputies of the Reagan campaign who felt it would rein in Christopher from
attacking their horse. Each of the candidates even signed a statement
agreeing to abide by it.

"I will have no word of criticism for any Republican," Ronald Reagan
stated during an interview soon afterward. The Eleventh Commandment
prevailed.

Except when it didn't. The first real challenge to it came on March 7,
1966, when the candidates appeared together at the National Negro Republican Assembly in Santa Monica. It was a peculiar event. Few members
had remained loyal to the party after its 1964 presidential platform had
rejected the Civil Rights bill. Still, a smattering of black stalwarts clung to
the outfit in the hope they could work from the inside to influence the
party. It stood to reason that the issue would be raised that afternoon. Almost immediately, a black businessman named Ben Peery stood and put the
question to Ronald Reagan. "How are Negro Republicans going to encourage other Negroes to vote for you after your statement that you would not
have voted for the Civil Rights bill?" he asked.

It wasn't a gotcha question. Reagan had encountered it before and had
a standard response that, up to now, had always sufficed. He would have
voted for the bill, he said, if it weren't "a bad piece of legislation." *Bad*
meaning keyed to a particular race as opposed to *all* races. Christopher
pounced. He began needling Reagan, questioning his ethics. "Contrary to
my opponent," he allowed, "I would have voted for the bill if I had been in

Congress." In his rebuttal Christopher insinuated that those who opposed the bill were out of touch with, and had lost respect for, the black community.

Ronald Reagan was visibly smoldering. This was the last straw; his temper boiled over. He jumped up, interrupting his opponent. "I want to make a point of personal privilege," he said. "I *resent* the implication there is any bigotry in my nature. Don't *anyone* ever imply that I lack integrity. I will not stand silent and let anyone imply *that*—in this or any other group."

With that, he wadded up a piece of paper he was clutching, flipped it into the stunned audience, and stomped off the stage. "I'll get that son of a bitch," he hissed, elbowing his way through the crowd toward the exit. Lyn Nofziger and Stu Spencer tried shushing him as best they could as the press closed in. Carl Greenberg, a *Los Angeles Times* reporter, grabbed Spencer by the sleeve and said, "Did I hear 'motherfucker'?" It was all they could do to hustle Reagan into the car.

It was an unmitigated public relations disaster. Afterward, Nofziger headed straight to the Reagans' house, where Ron and Nancy were assessing the damage. "You've got to go back," Nofziger insisted. It was the only way to rescue the situation. The black caucus was holding a reception later that evening, at which time amends could be made. There was no argument from Ronald Reagan. Go back he did, explaining contritely that his anger wasn't directed at the delegates. He felt any insinuation about bigotry was unjust. "Frankly, I got mad," he explained. "There are just some things you can't take as a man."

That was enough to mollify the group. Anger at being defined by others was something they understood and respected. But the next morning the newspapers had a field day with the incident. It made headlines in all the major dailies, with a blistering cartoon on the editorial page of the *L.A. Times*. In a spoof of Reagan's recently released memoir, *Where's the Rest of Me?*, it depicted a caricature of him standing headless, with a caption that said, "*I'm looking for the rest of me . . .*"

It wasn't his last brush with the press—not even that week. On March 12, he addressed a lumber industry trade group, the Western Wood Products Association, at its annual meeting in San Francisco. Playing to their prejudice against tree huggers, he quipped, "If you've looked at a hundred thousand acres or so of trees—you know, a tree is a tree. How many more do you need to look at?" It got a good laugh and sustained applause from the crowd. Later, at the group's reception, someone approached him about the state's "over-attention" to Redwood National Park. "Look," Ronald Reagan responded, "it only needs to be a half mile on either side of the freeway. That's all the people look at." It sounded funny at the time, and as Tom Reed, who'd accompanied him, noted, "If it's a good line, he loves to recite it. Often." But it didn't sound funny in the papers the next morning.

Strategists suspected these incidents were killing his chances of attracting crossover voters, and that might very well have been the case. But they were resonating with Republicans. Even so, Stu Spencer panicked when Reagan announced his intention of taking more questions from his audience at events. "If I'm asking them for their vote, they've got a right to find out anything they want to know," he argued, a good point, though not reassuring. "They were scared to death that he would really foul up," Lyn Nofziger recalled. "He didn't really know a heck of a lot about state government."

As it turned out, he didn't have to. Conservative voters were more interested in issues that affected them personally. They felt the cost of providing for their families was becoming unbearable. Runaway taxes were strangling them. There was rising discontent over frivolous cost overruns on new roads and schools. Welfare, in their eyes, was out of control. Civil unrest scared the hell out of them. The hippies had no respect for their middle-class values. These were the issues Ronald Reagan began campaigning on, and his frustration reflected the voters' frustration. He called for a "moral crusade" to close what he called the "decency gap," phrases that struck a chord with people who felt alienated by shifts in the culture.

In Fresno, at the end of a speech, he digressed from the prepared text, launching a broadside on campus unrest that got an especially big reaction from the crowd. He fingered the "small minority of beatniks, radicals, and filthy speech advocates" responsible for protests—he called them "shameful things"—at the University of California. "And if that means kicking them out, kick 'em out!" he declared. Afterward, in the car out of town, Stu Spencer confronted him about going off-message. "What are you doing?" he asked. "Campus unrest isn't even a blip in our polling data." Reagan looked at him and winked. "It will be," he said, "when I get through."

Tom Reed concentrated on moving Reagan around the upper part of the state to challenge the standard voting patterns. "The general doctrine was that Christopher was going to carry San Francisco and the north, Reagan would carry the south, and the rest was a toss-up," he recalled. "So I began fixating on carrying northern California."

His efforts paid off. By late spring, the national press was reporting that straw polls showed a sizable lead for Ronald Reagan in the Republican primary, "especially," the *San Francisco Chronicle* noted, "in northern California." This was an entirely unexpected development. And it had far-reaching consequences. Pat Brown, the Democratic incumbent, was rooting for a Reagan victory, handing him a challenger he thought was eminently beatable. Let him sweep the north in the primary, Brown thought. It would give him a nice false sense of security. The north was a Democratic stronghold. Reagan's support there would evaporate in the general election.

Brown should have paid more attention to the massing storm clouds. The times, as the poet wrote, were indeed a-changin' among the California electorate. A migration was under way from the left to the right. Early in 1966, polls had shown George Christopher out front by seventeen points. As the race tightened, his lead was down to two points, with Pat Brown ten points behind both Republican candidates. And by Memorial Day, the tide had turned. The *New York Times* offered a prediction that "Ronald Reagan has an excellent chance to be the governor of the most populous state in the union."

With the election just eight days off and feeling the heat on his neck, Christopher all but abandoned the Eleventh Commandment. He flew to Eureka College in Illinois to stage a last-ditch broadcast on former Reagan turf, citing evidence that his opponent had once belonged to both Americans for Democratic Action and United World Federalists, allegedly Communist front organizations. "Did he jointly sponsor protest on U.S. atomic policies with the chairman of the Communist Party in Los Angeles?" he posited.

He did, of course, but it didn't make a bit of difference. The accusations fell on deaf ears. Voters weren't interested in Cold War rhetoric. Ronald Reagan had hijacked the conversation with a revolving loop of populist issues, taking swipes at outrageous taxes, migrants who abused the state welfare program "to loaf"—*to loaf*—and an old standby: the encroachment of rights. So what if he rejected the Fair Housing Act? He defended his position by turning the issue away from discrimination. "I have never believed that majority rule has the right to impose on an individual as to what he does with his property," he said. Observers who surveyed his audience saw people nodding their heads in collective agreement.

North, south, and everywhere in between, the people were with him. And on June 7, 1966, when the results of the primary election were tallied, the people had spoken. Ronald Reagan had 1,385,550 votes to 663,199 for George Christopher. It was as decisive a victory as the campaign could have hoped for, but still left many scratching their heads. No less an authority than the *New York Times* noted: California Republicans, "against all counsels of common sense, insisted upon nominating actor Ronald Reagan for governor." And it wasn't even close.

I f the legions of doubters and naysayers had learned one thing, it was not to underestimate Ronald Reagan. So many had made that mistake along the way only to recognize that his glossy surface camouflaged a gift for plain speech that stirred deep emotions. And while the primary seemed to have made this abundantly clear, Pat Brown missed the lesson. He dismissed his opponent as a Goldwater clone who lacked any experience in the political arena. His press secretary, Jack Burby, set the tone early on when he scrawled "'Bring him on' is our motto" across a memo to his boss.

Bring him on. The charge became a rallying cry for a motivated Democratic delegation and a candidate who prided himself as the People's Governor.

It was hard to take a cudgel to a man like Edmund "Pat" Brown. Even his adversaries in the legislature felt kindly toward him. "A sweet, nice, all-around lovely guy whose heart was in the right place" was how Anthony Beilenson, a longtime state assemblyman, described him. And Stu Spencer, who sought to vanquish him, considered the governor "not only a good man, but an outright joy when a few beers were involved." Brown was an old-time Irish pol who never forgot a name and insisted everyone he met forgo formalities and call him Pat. A burly, gregarious, roly-poly man with a wardrobe full of identical baggy suits, he'd built a strong state Democratic machine serviced by unshakable union support, and yet his administration operated on the bedrock of bipartisanship. "There was no ideological divide in Sacramento," says Kirk West, a Republican legislative aide who became the state's deputy finance director. No one considered it far off base when he described his politics as being "reasonable, rational and realistic."

Brown's first two terms as governor might have given him the illusion that the fulfillment of initiatives required nothing more than a wave of his wand. He was a dynamo when it came to enacting legislation. In swift succession he oversaw two fair-housing bills and had a fair-employment practice put into place. The construction of great water projects were begun, with a $1.75 billion bond issue to finance them. New prisons and mental facilities were established. He increased benefits for the unemployed, the blind, and the elderly, and was instrumental in building the mazy state freeway system. Even more impressive was his expansion of the state's higher-education structure into a gold standard for the rest of the country, adding three new university campuses and six state colleges. In all, he superintended a period of growth in California that inspired admiration from coast to coast.

"We respected him a great deal," said Stu Spencer, "but he'd had his day."

In fact, many thought the state suffered from "Brown fatigue." Feuding had broken out among his inner circle, stymieing the momentum that had propelled his two terms. And his string of advancements had come at a cost—the state was deeply in debt. To contain the likelihood of a tax increase, he instituted a system called "accrual accounting," which enabled him to spend fifteen months' worth of revenues for the twelve-month budget period—in effect borrowing three months' income from the following year. Voodoo economics.

In an ordinary election against a routine Republican challenger, Brown might have been targeted as vulnerable, but against Ronald Reagan, an actor without a whiff of experience—the prospect was unthinkable. Bob Monagan, the Republican minority leader of the State Assembly, took one look at the matchup and declared, "Well, we'll probably have Pat Brown again." Politically, Brown still functioned as a force of nature. He'd beaten strong contenders in previous statewide races—William Knowland, a U.S. senator considered a "political giant," whom he'd defeated by a million votes in 1958; and, four years later, former vice president Richard M. Nixon, whose thrashing by Brown prompted the concession-speech outburst: "You won't have Dick Nixon to kick around anymore." Tom Reed, chairman of the northern Reagan for Governor campaign, thought that "Brown was going to be a very difficult candidate."

Pat Brown went right at Ronald Reagan, portraying him as a dangerous extremist, a "front man" who "collaborated directly with a score of top leaders of the super-secret John Birch Society." He also accused Reagan of being a "radical rightest who condemns Social Security and other advances as Communist-inspired." Reagan and his supporters had heard it all before. They'd rejected a platform initiative at the state Republican convention that said, "We should condemn the John Birch Society; they have no place in the Republican Party." Instead, long before the campaign was launched, they'd worked out a response to elbow aside the controversy: "I'm not going to condemn them or repudiate them. Anyone who chooses to support me has bought my philosophy—I'm not buying theirs." It became a mantra that Ronald Reagan evoked time and again. As to the charge that he lacked experience, Bill Roberts recalled that it was dealt with by Reagan admitting he wasn't a politician at all—"he was a *citizen politician*." Audiences bought into that the moment they heard it. "Nowhere in the state constitution does it say to be Governor you have to be a professional politician, and I'm not," he insisted every time he addressed another crowd. Roberts scanned the faces of people who attended those events and imagined them thinking, "Yes, by God, this is the way the country was started, with citizens assuming a responsibility in government." The strategy was so successful, in fact, that it forced Pat Brown into the position of defending professional politicians, which only fed the public's skepticism.

To the operatives working the angles, this was a big mistake. "He was running against Reagan instead of on his own [merits]," says Tom Reed, who monitored each of the candidates' stump speeches. "And once Brown decided not to run as the guy who had created the university system and built the great roads and great water plan, and was just a guy campaigning against extremism, I knew he was done."

The challenge for Ronald Reagan was winning over disaffected liberal voters. California was traditionally a solid Democratic state. But the Spencer-Roberts office discovered a new phenomenon that later became known as the Reagan Democrats. The state was full of transplants from Texas and Oklahoma whose granddaddies had migrated to California in search of gold and oil and would turn over in their graves if a scion of theirs didn't vote Democratic. "Our research showed us that in anywhere from one to two election cycles they would get up in the morning and say, 'This isn't the Democratic Party I know,'" says Stu Spencer, "for any number of philosophical reasons." On issues like campus protest, racial unrest, spending, and taxes, Ronald Reagan's message was grabbing them. "We could see it developing in South Gate, Torrance, and some portions of Orange County, where there were deep pockets of blue-collar laborers. And we knew Pat Brown was going to have a hell of a time with them."

Bill Roberts also identified a segment of potential converts in the rapidly expanding Mexican-American community, where he calculated a solid 25 percent were unhappy with Pat Brown's policies and lack of meaningful Latino appointments. "Our battle cry was 'Ya Basta?'" Roberts recalled— Had enough? They slapped it on bumper stickers and plastered telephone poles along with windows of bodegas. Slowly but surely, a coalition was being built.

Another advantage was party unity. A codicil to the Eleventh Commandment stipulated that whoever lost the Republican primary would support the candidate, no strings attached. Whether that would come off as planned was anybody's guess, considering the barrage of toxic rhetoric that had been traded during the contest. But Holmes Tuttle and the Kitchen Cabinet had intervened on primary election night to salve wounds. "The minute it became obvious that Reagan was going to win, they went to the Christopher people, threw their arms around them, and asked them to join in the campaign," recalled William French Smith, who headed a new endeavor, the Campaign Executive Committee, composed almost equally of Christopher and Reagan staff.

The unity played effectively against the opposition. According to Bill Smith, "The Democrats did everything wrong after the primary." For one thing, they had campaigned exclusively against George Christopher, certain in their wisdom that he would emerge the victor. Then, finding Reagan in their crosshairs, they began firing potshots that landed wide of the mark.

The "right-wing extremist" label wasn't sticking. Nor was the charge about their opponent's lack of experience. But neither of those indictments compared with the blunder of using a bizarre TV ad to demonize Ronald Reagan. It was entitled Man vs. Actor and began innocently enough, with

Pat Brown speaking to an integrated classroom and discussing the success of former Democratic governors. Then, incautiously, he leaped off a cliff. "I'm running against an actor," he tells a young black female student, "and you know who shot Lincoln, don'tcha?" It was dumbfounding and tasteless, a complete misfire. Ronald Reagan, reflecting on it later, said, "I couldn't believe the stupidity of it." He was embarrassed for Pat Brown, as well as for his Hollywood brethren. Even the committed Democrats among them deserted the candidate after that remark.

Though nowhere near as disastrous, the Reagan campaign had its own advertising woes. Its thirty- and sixty-second television spots were frumpy, hackneyed, distressing to watch. The extras in the ads were superimposed from stock footage of a 1940s theater crowd. In the background of one scene, a 1938 Oldsmobile cruised by. It conveyed the message that "Ronald Reagan is your grandfather's candidate, not a man for the sixties," in the words of a senior staff member. Tom Reed delivered a more critical judgment. "It was amateur hour," he says. "We looked at the ads and said, 'This is a disaster.'" Responsibility fell to McCann-Erickson, the advertising agency that produced them. Unfortunately, McCann's executive in charge of the account was its vice president, Neil Reagan.

In a closed-door meeting, the Executive Committee determined that the ads were counterproductive and unusable. Someone had to tell Ronald Reagan. "I drew the short straw," Stu Spencer recalls. "I went to Ron and said, 'We've got to make a change.' He looked up at me and said, 'I only have one brother.' End of conversation."

In the end, they were forced to go around the Reagan brothers' backs. "We couldn't show that crap, so we bootlegged, we went outside," Spencer explains. They produced their own spots, splicing together clips from revival-type rallies featuring the candidate at his dynamic best, cutting in wildly cheering crowds made up of blacks, Asians, and young enthusiasts. They were a revelation compared with the McCann spots, which were still running as well.

Moon blew his stack. He raised hell with the Kitchen Cabinet and drew Nancy Reagan into the fray. The north and south factions began whining, pointing fingers at each other; a power struggle between them ensued, threatening to undo all the months of unity and steady progress. A last-minute appearance by Bobby Kennedy endorsing Pat Brown didn't help.

But, oddly, none of the static mattered. Ronald Reagan insulated himself from it. He kept his focus on the message. He insisted to reporters that he was "running scared," but remained confident, "both inwardly and outwardly." His popularity continued to increase on the stump, where his theme of commonsense government by citizens resonated, a fact confirmed by the polls. The margins in the south had always been sizable; now new indicators showed him edging ahead in the north. The campaign's managers had been confident for months. According to Stu Spencer, "We figured by the spring of 1966, the son-of-a-bitch was going to beat Pat Brown."

They just never figured by how much. On November 8, 1966, when the votes were tallied, the word "landslide" could be heard throughout the giddy election-night celebrations. Ronald Reagan had beaten Pat Brown by close to a million votes—3,742,913 to 2,749,174. He'd won fifty-five of the state's fifty-eight counties, carrying traditionally Democratic working-class and suburban precincts, along with strong pockets of Mexican-American communities.

In the Biltmore Bowl, the same room where thirty years earlier a gangly Ronald Reagan had come to plead his case for an acting audition, he appeared briefly to thank the throng of supporters who unfurled an enormous "Reagan for President" banner. He was fifty-five years old and had finally landed the biggest role of his career, as a leading man in an A-list part: Governor of California.

PART 3

GOVERNOR

CHAPTER TWENTY-THREE

"PRAIRIE FIRE"

"We must, I think, take Reaganism seriously. It will be
with us for a long time under one guise or another."

—JAMES Q. WILSON, 1967

R onald Reagan felt at home in the north—in San Francisco, which was a vital, sophisticated city. But Sacramento was another world altogether.

Situated in the lush, flat valley halfway between Lake Tahoe and San Francisco—the mountains and the bay—Sacramento lacked its own strong, distinct character. Chinese immigrants who settled there to build the railroads called it "Yee Fow," Second City, and that more or less summed up its ongoing identity crisis. It played a poky second fiddle to San Francisco's offbeat *allegro* pulse and "existed as a cowtown" to those snobs farther south. Sacramentans hated the endless comparisons. In fact, there was ample homegrown pride. "It was a very sleepy little town," says Ken Hall, who served for a time in the governor's cabinet. "Wonderful people, very community oriented." C. K. McClatchy, the local newspaper baron who presided over the *Bee*, christened it "Superior California"—more agricultural, more water sufficient, a more prosperous middle class. Its well-planned grid of tree-shaded streets provided a lovely symmetry to the ever-expanding urban sprawl, and the city was as handsome and stately as the rivers that framed it. And beyond those rivers, before the first of the foothills of the Sierra Nevadas, lay a broad swath of the fertile Central Valley, whose fields and orchards fed the nation. The state capitol was another great badge of honor, but because the legislature was a part-time institution, the legislators put in their minimal three-day workweeks, even leaving their suitcases packed to enable a speedy getaway.

News of Ronald Reagan's election as governor threw the city into a tailspin. "We were in shock," says Burnett Miller, Sacramento's one-time mayor. "He wasn't considered a serious politician, and we took pride in the legislators who did vital work here." Though there had been discontent with Pat Brown at the end, he'd been an open, approachable figure in town, "an affable down-to-earth guy" to whom Sacramento County had delivered a plurality in the election. He'd done a lot in his eight-year term to revitalize the city. "Ronald Reagan, on the other hand, provoked a lot of negative feelings," says local historian Dr. Steven Avella. The populace was largely Democratic and progressive, the unions strong and inevitably wary. "There was a lot of consternation, people were dazed and confused."

There was confusion in the new governor's camp as well. No sooner had Ronald Reagan taken the oath of office than he realized the burden he'd taken on. "Here we are—now what do we do?" he asked a young volunteer who'd accompanied him to Sacramento. Reality hit hard: he now represented the welfare of nearly twenty million Californians, and without a clue as to how to go about governing them. "I guess I thought more about winning the election than the job to follow," Reagan admitted later. "Those first days were very dreary, very dark. . . . It just seemed like every day that I came into the office, almost immediately there was someone standing in front of my desk saying, 'We've got a problem.'"

Pat Brown had been right about one thing: no one involved in the new administration had any experience or knew what to do. "We were not only amateurs," Lyn Nofziger quipped, "we were novice amateurs." Governor Reagan had chosen as his chief of staff a young lawyer from Los Angeles named Philip Battaglia who, when it came to state matters, was as green as he was. Bill Roberts and Stu Spencer, who proposed staff assignments, "specifically wanted people who were ordinary citizens, with no prior experience," and Phil Battaglia fit the bill.

A short, slight, pious Catholic with olive skin and piercing dark eyes, he was considered "the fair-haired boy" of the Kitchen Cabinet—though he had little hair and less of a reputation for fairness. The appeal was his credentials, which jibed with their financial interests. A partner at Flint and McKay, perhaps the most prestigious white-shoe law firm in Los Angeles, Battaglia moonlighted as president of the Junior Chamber of Commerce, where he distinguished himself as an intractable business wonk. As Southern California chairman of the Reagan for Governor campaign, he built an operation amassing influence and power. "He was a charming, personable guy who was very well organized and got things done," recalls Richard Quinn, whom everyone called Sandy. "On the other hand, he could be as tough and cruel as a situation required." His intensity rubbed some people the wrong way. From the outset, he alienated Tom Reed, his campaign counterpart in the north of the state, who saw himself as the governor's éminence grise. "There was constant jockeying for position," Quinn says. Reed, from day one, had his eye fixed on Reagan's running for the presidency and saw Battaglia as an obstacle in the path.

Phil Battaglia opened the office for business on Monday morning, January 9, 1967, after a four-day lavish inaugural celebration, while the Reagans acclimated themselves to their new surroundings. In late December they'd moved the family into the governor's mansion at Sixteenth Street and H Street, a rambling old 1870s gingerbread Victorian located in the center of town. Gomez and Morticia Addams would have felt right at home in it. Ronald Reagan took one look at the place and declared it "the most dreary, dismal place in the world." The house, with its high-ceilinged rooms and narrow halls, had been owned by Albert Gallatin, a hardware merchant who had deeded it to the city at the turn of the twentieth century. Governor George Pardee moved in in 1905, and little upkeep had been done since then. Nancy Reagan decried it as "a wooden firetrap" and "a tinderbox," which weren't exaggerations. The beams were riddled with dry rot. A series of ropes that could be hung out the windows on the second floor substituted for fire escapes. The hot water didn't work. And the location—on Highway 160 at the corner of Sixteenth Street, the main drag from San Francisco that led to Lake Tahoe and Reno—was a traffic nightmare. "It backs up on the American Legion Hall," Nancy Reagan explained, "where I swear there are vile orgies every night." Trucks pulling out of the gas station across the street ground gears in a cacophonous fugue that played around the clock. "Those damn trucks!" Reagan complained to staff. "I think they shift gears every time I begin falling asleep." As far as Nancy was concerned, the place was uninhabitable. The morning after her husband was sworn in, she called his aides and put her foot down: find another place for them to live.

Governor Reagan had more pressing problems. On November 28, 1966, just days after winning the election, Phil Battaglia, along with a small team of aides that included Caspar Weinberger, had attended a meeting at the capitol with Hale Champion, the state's outgoing director of finance. "Gentlemen," Champion said, "I want to introduce you to Roy Ball and Ed Beach;* they know everything that is going on here. I also want you to know that the state is broke. I'm going on a boat trip to San Diego. In fact, I'm leaving right now. The very best of luck to you." And without another word, he walked out the door.

Worse than broke—actually in serious debt. With all the new programs that Pat Brown had pushed through, few had questioned what money would pay for them. He'd balanced the budget through the current fiscal year by borrowing from future revenues. It was a scheme Charles Ponzi would have admired. A cursory examination of the state's books revealed that next year's spending would exceed income by $250 million, with a shortfall that might run as high as $700 million. Ronald Reagan would have to initiate a tax increase to cover the deficit. It was the worst piece of news an incoming governor could hear.

"I didn't realize it would be this bad," the new governor admitted at a press conference in early January at which he announced the state was in a dire financial crisis.

It was actually worse. The Medi-Cal program that assisted the needy was running on empty, and swelling welfare benefits were draining the fund's reserves. Even education, the biggest portion of the state's budget, was unable to meet the demands of a ballooning school-aged population. Hints that Californians might be charged tuition at state colleges and universities for the first time in history touched off strong protests that spread across campuses. The state was hemorrhaging cash.

"Here I was, the big conservative who talked of cutting the cost of government, cutting taxes, faced with the realization that there was no way out except to raise taxes," Reagan concluded. His new, young, untested administration, desperate, put out feelers for outside guidance. At the annual

* Department of Finance career executives for the State of California.

Republican governors' conference in Colorado Springs, the California delegation—Reagan, Battaglia, Reed, and Nofziger—huddled with Ohio governor James A. Rhodes, who laid out a formula that had rescued his state from insolvency. It was elementary, Rhodes told them: cut appropriations across the board by 10 percent, eliminate as many state workers as possible, and assemble a task force of businessmen to slash government expenses.

It sounded like a workable plan. No one stopped to consider that Ohio's problems might be different from California's. When Governor Reagan faced the television cameras on January 16, he was confident the Ohio template suited his purposes. "Any major business can tighten its belt by ten percent and still maintain the quality and quantity of its operation," he explained. "So can government . . . including the university and college systems." The way he saw it there was no alternative. "Our state has been looted and drained," he said, laying blame squarely on the Pat Brown era.

The bloodletting began almost immediately. Early that March, a caucus called the Businessman's Task Force recommended the elimination of 3,700 jobs in the mental health sector. "We can close hospitals and bring people home to their communities," the governor said. It looked good on paper, but it was poorly thought out. "The whole system came unglued," says Ken Hall, "and it blew up in our faces right away." The newspapers had a field day. In Napa, Auburn, San Bernardino, across the state, editorials lambasted the new administration. "What are you going to do with all these people?" "Governor, you have no facilities for them." "Their families don't want them back." To make matters worse, there had been no communication with the legislators who represented those areas, most of whom were Republicans. And Ronald Reagan was forced to admit, "The roof fell in on the whole thing."

Undeterred, the task force kept bulldozing through each department of the state government. Most government maintenance was postponed; any construction requiring new money was halted; updating the fleet of aging state-owned vehicles got deep-sixed; career state employees were laid off. The ax fell on one program after another.

The biggest victim of discretionary cuts was the state's precious university system. Since the end of World War II, successive budgets had lavished money on higher education without so much as a glance at the cost. It was the jewel in the crown, sacrosanct. But now a new reality prevailed. The governor, as the *San Francisco Chronicle* noted, "took his big stick to the entire University administration." "We would like to welcome the academic community into the cold world of reality with us," Ronald Reagan told the UC Regents in the weeks immediately after he took office. He was trimming the university's operating budget by $13 million and ordering the Regents to kick back some $21 million in federal fees generated by UC researchers. What's more, free tuition for California students, a long-standing and proud tradition, was most likely coming to an end. He proposed initiating a modest yearly $400 fee. The way UC students reacted, it might have been $40,000. On impact, all hell broke loose. Students at Berkeley planned a mass march on the Regents to protest even a nickel's worth of a levy, while a UC–Santa Barbara faction 2,500 strong descended on the state capitol in a noisy but civil confrontation with the governor.

"He was having horrific fights with the University of California leadership," Stu Spencer recalls. The Regents had enjoyed a lifetime of autonomy and were unwilling to kowtow to the disciplines of a budget, much less a governor they viewed as a meddler. "But he was determined to make them toe the line."

The skirmish cost UC president Clark Kerr his job. Protesters on the Berkeley campus were rounded up and prosecuted. The FBI and CIA mounted a covert campaign "to harass students, faculty and members of the Board of Regents." Throughout the honeymoon phase of the Reagan administration, the university fracas dominated the news. "It was a real mess," Spencer allowed in retrospect.

Tony Beilenson, the Los Angeles assemblyman, watched from the sidelines, bewildered by the governor's unfocused initiatives. "It seemed that every place he put his foot, it sunk deeper into political quicksand," he says. "There was no forward progress being made, no momentum. He kept changing his mind and had difficult dealings with his own Republican base. To many in the legislature, he seemed distracted."

Distracted put it mildly. Ronald Reagan was being pulled inside out.

Nine days after the election, Tom Reed called the new governor and said, "I want to come talk to you about the prairie fire." It was an expression Reagan had used often while campaigning in the state: "If we win this election, it will start a prairie fire across the country." The way he saw it, a conservative win in California was symbolic; it would resurrect the philosophy that got decimated by the Goldwater debacle of 1964. Now Reed nursed greater ambitions.

The day before meeting with the governor, Reed arrived at the Spencer-Roberts office to give the political strategists a heads-up. The prairie fire was spreading and too hot to contain. "I want you to start laying groundwork for a campaign for the presidency," he told them. As Reed remembers it, "Their jaws dropped."

"Kid," Stu Spencer sputtered, "what are you *talking* about?"

Reed was adamant that the only way to effectively hobble Lyndon Johnson's reelection bid in 1968 was to run Ronald Reagan against him. No one else measured up against LBJ—not George Romney, the current front-runner, or Nelson Rockefeller or Richard Nixon, all potential candidates. "Ron has the talent, firepower, and momentum to take it all the way," Reed argued. And preparations for it had to start immediately, he insisted. Spencer considered the prospect less than hopeless. "The guy hadn't been in office two weeks," he said. "He wasn't ready for 1968, much less the immediate job of being governor."

Nevertheless, machinery was set in motion to start collecting delegates for a '68 presidential bid. Reagan knew it was premature, but he was willing to let Reed put out feelers. There were power brokers who needed to be brought on board if a serious run was going to be launched. At a meeting in Pacific Palisades with the Reagans, Phil Battaglia, and Lyn Nofziger, Reed outlined his wish list—Texas Republican chairman Peter O'Donnell, who had orchestrated the election of John Tower, the first Republican senator in the state since the Civil War; Clifford White, a virtuoso delegate collector who'd masterminded the Goldwater nomination; and *National Review* publisher Bill Rusher. It would be better, they decided, to bypass the Kitchen Cabinet. "Those guys talk too much," Reed said. Many of them were already committed to Rockefeller and Nixon and would raise hell if Reagan intervened.

The whole plan seemed far-fetched. The governor ran it by his new legal affairs secretary, Edwin Meese, a short, firepluggish, thirty-five-year-old assistant district attorney from Alameda County who would go on to work for Ronald Reagan for much of his career. "I was opposed to it," Meese recalls fifty years later. "I felt the governor needed to pay attention to California. He had essentially just been elected, and I got the impression he was not emotionally committed to [a presidential run]."

That might have been the case, but obligations for it began mounting. Reagan agreed to do some barnstorming throughout the spring of 1967—to Nebraska, for a featured speech at the Young Republicans national convention; on to Montana, where a contingent of western governors met; and afterward in Wyoming, addressing a full slate of Republican governors. At each event, seeds for the presidency were laid, though ambivalently. Stu Spencer had come around on the question of running, but he found these efforts "half-assed" and counterproductive. "This is not being done right," he complained to Ronald Reagan. "You've got to be courting people, be more definite in your goals." Did he really intend to run for president? Spencer wanted an answer.

"The office seeks the man," Reagan responded. It was the kind of artful dodge he often turned to when push came to shove.

"That's bullshit!" Spencer countered. "If you want it, you've got to go get it." It infuriated him that a comer like Ronald Reagan was wasting a perfectly good opportunity.

He wasn't the only one. Word of these probes eventually leaked out to members of the Kitchen Cabinet, who were exasperated and extremely upset. After all they had contributed to the governorship, they resented being left out in the cold. On July 7, 1967, Holmes Tuttle and Taft Schreiber turned up at Reagan's home in Los Angeles and, according to Tom Reed, who ushered them in, threw a major tantrum. "They went wild," Reed recalls. Not only had they underwritten Ron's entire campaign while he was organizing a presidential run behind their backs, they'd bought him and Nancy a posh house in Sacramento to circumvent the dreaded Governor's Mansion. They were really frosted. "Ron, what are you doing?" they demanded.

"The office seeks the man," he recited.

The man, they insisted, needed to get his act together. If things continued going downhill in California, there would be no legacy to build a future on, much less a stepping-stone to the presidency. According to Ken Hall, "Those first months were replete with error after error after error. And the

mistakes were really gratuitous." Reagan's relationship with the state legislators, for instance, was practically nonexistent. He shunned any social interaction with them, and usually left the office by five p.m. each night,
avoiding the after-hours period when much of the constructive glad-
handing occurred. As far as Bob Monagan, the Republican leader of the
Assembly, was concerned, "He wasn't interested in the legislature at all."
Without its cooperation, it would be next to impossible to move the Reagan agenda forward.

Others acknowledged the same impasse. George Steffes, a young deputy
secretary, blamed the standoff on Lyn Nofziger. "He convinced Reagan
that he didn't need the legislature," Steffes says. "Lyn told him, 'We can go
directly to the people if they don't do what we want.' And Phil Battaglia
agreed. They thought all they needed for success was Ronald Reagan. It
was a huge mistake."

An even larger one than they realized. Before 1967, California had a
part-time legislature. The first year of its term lasted only through June; the
second year was even shorter and dedicated solely to the budget; the legislature took July and August off. As a result of the abbreviated sessions, the
legislators didn't bring their families to Sacramento. It was a lonely, isolating existence; they had nothing to do during those nights in the city, which
meant they went out to eat and drink. Together. Democrats and Republicans. Because of the socializing and the fact that assemblymen were permitted to run for the nomination in both parties—and often got elected by
both Democrats and Republicans—the legislature was proudly bipartisan.
"There were several Republican leaders in the Assembly who felt alienated
by the governor and simply went their own way to work with Democrats on
successful issues," recalls Tony Beilenson, who had a soft spot for many of
his Republican counterparts. Harnessing the legislature was key to governing the state. It behooved Ronald Reagan to cultivate a working relationship with them.

Turning the tide, however, was not a mission easily accomplished. Phil
Battaglia, embracing his new power as executive secretary—Ronald Reagan's chief of staff—had effectively isolated the governor from most spontaneous encounters, including any with lawmakers in the capitol. "Every
piece of legislation had to come through Phil," says Paul Haerle, the

administration's assistant appointments secretary. There wasn't an area of state government he didn't hold sway over. Battaglia personally filled important staff positions and made key judicial appointments independent of his boss. He issued official press releases attributed to Ronald Reagan and held court with local reporters, while forbidding others on his staff to speak with the press corps. "He operated as if he were the de facto governor," Haerle says.

Battaglia also began laying down roots in Washington, D.C., assuming a Reagan move there sometime in the future. He used his growing influence to sow friendships among congressmen and lobbyists, forging alliances that benefited his own ambitions. Throughout the early summer of 1967, Battaglia and his deputy, Sandy Quinn, shuttled on a state-owned jet between Sacramento and Washington so often that his absence from the governor's office sparked open resentment among the staff. It fell to Bill Clark, the cabinet secretary, to manage the state's business that languished as a result, further raising hackles and provoking chatter. "I tried to run everything by [Battaglia], whenever I could find him," Clark explained, but it was becoming increasingly difficult.

Clark worked hard to bring the governor up to speed on policy and raise his image with legislators. "I started setting up lunches based on issues and bringing in legislators on an issue-by-issue basis," Clark recalled. "He seemed to enjoy the give-and-take with them and began experiencing some real success, where none of us thought it possible." Clark's most important contribution was the mini-memo, a system tailored to simplify and summarize issues before the Assembly. Each memo was a single page broken into four brief sections: 1) the issue itself; 2) any relevant facts; 3) a brief discussion—pro and con; and 4) recommendations. The last thing Ronald Reagan wanted was to anguish over reams of policy. Issues, he felt, "should be played by ear." He preferred getting the facts in a nutshell, then making a gut decision. That way, he could dispense with numerous issues at a clip. Refinancing the state Medicaid deficit—kill it. Property tax relief—go for it. Welfare reform—ditto. Funding for the Coronado Bridge—let's table it. At cabinet meetings around the jumbo rectangular conference table, through a bilious cloud of cigarette smoke discharged by his hyperactive aides, the governor listened intently to discussion, even occasionally joining in himself. "Finally," he recalled, "when I've really heard enough that I know what my decision is, I'd interrupt and say, 'Well, here's what we're going to do,' boom, and tell them."

He liked it that way—cut-and-dried.

O ne bill that couldn't be as easily dealt with was the Therapeutic Abortion Act, which came before the legislature in April 1967. Before the 1973 *Roe v. Wade* decision, individual states had their own abortion laws, most of which prohibited the practice other than to save the life of a mother. "The word 'abortion' didn't even appear in newspapers," says Tony Beilenson, who first introduced the bill in 1963 and again in 1965. "It was called 'an illegal surgical procedure.' It wasn't a public issue; nobody talked about it." Beilenson was appalled by the epidemic of back-alley abortions performed by quacks, which criminalized women and often resulted in their mutilation and death. The law was "archaic, barbarous and hypocritical," he felt, and he vowed to "restore a degree of freedom of choice and of conscience to many thousands of women." As Beilenson proposed it, the bill would extend the right to an abortion to victims of rape and incest, and in situations where there was risk a child would be born with grave physical or mental defects. Only Colorado and North Carolina had enacted similar laws; California, he felt, needed to move with the times.

Hearings around the state indicated that public opinion was changing. Field polls revealed that upward of 70 percent of Californians, including 67 percent who were Catholic, favored modernizing the abortion laws. So did the Episcopal Church, the American Baptist Convention, and the Lutheran Church. The State Board of Health, the California Medical Association, and the Junior Chamber of Commerce were also on board, as well as most of the major state newspapers. The only serious opposition was the Catholic Church, which was dead set against any alteration to the law. Priests instructed their flocks from the pulpit to write their legislators demanding they vote against the bill. As an illustration, George Danielson, a state assemblyman on the Judiciary Committee, got three thousand letters—much of it hate mail—from his Catholic constituents, all obviously turned out by churches. On the other side, women's groups rallied to demand change. These ground forces facing off and politicizing the issue offered a preview of the nationwide controversy to come in the aftermath of *Roe*.

The governor's top aides and members of the Kitchen Cabinet were divided along religious lines. The Catholics—Phil Battaglia and Bill Clark—urged Ronald Reagan to oppose the bill, while Lyn Nofziger, a non-Catholic, lobbied for its support.

The governor was unable to reach a decision. "I had never given much thought to abortion prior to [this]," he admitted. Although he was a man of deep convictions, the issue rattled his moral certainty. "I suppose I did more soul-searching on that than anything I'd ever faced," he said. At a press conference on May 9, 1967, he told reporters, "This is not in my mind a clear cut issue," refusing to reveal any personal feelings. "He was really torn," Ed Meese recalls. "Basically, he was opposed to the idea of abortion, yet at the same time he realized it was a medical necessity if a woman's mental state or her health was affected." For weeks he continued to grapple with the issue. He felt that life began at conception, which both colored and clouded his judgment. Nancy Reagan suggested that her husband take it up with her father who could at least provide some medical perspective. Dr. Davis supported relaxing the abortion laws, but while Reagan respected, even revered, his father-in-law's opinions, this one failed to sway him one way or the other.

Early on in the process, Ronald Reagan indicated he would sign the bill if it was passed by the legislature and reached his office, but he was in no way bound by such a commitment. In fact, he let it be known that he'd be grateful if the bill got bottled up in committee. And the lobbying activity began to weigh heavily. The Spencer-Roberts organization's newest client was Francis Cardinal McIntyre, the archbishop of Los Angeles and a canny political actor. On his orders, priests were dispatched to Sacramento to bring pressure on legislators, and the governor himself was even called to account. Stu Spencer was to recall vividly a meeting he arranged in which His Eminence loomed menacingly over Ronald Reagan. "Young man," McIntyre intoned in a voice reserved for sermons, "are you thinking of running for the presidency? You realize I've got a lot of friends around the country."

Reagan was being badgered from all sides. Most of the arm-twisting was fairly benign, but not in every case. One young woman, the head of the local antiabortion movement, convinced him that "very rarely has rape ever been followed by pregnancy," that it was just an excuse for women to solicit abortions. She recited facts and figures to support her argument—how in the event of a rape, standard medical treatment ensured that "no pregnancy takes place." It was utter nonsense, yet it was enough for the governor to seek changes to the bill. Rape, he insisted, needed to be removed as a blanket condition to sanction abortion. And while they were at it, he wanted the clause on fetal deformity deleted. "I cannot justify morally," he announced, "taking of the unborn life simply on the supposition that it is going to be less than a perfect human being."

Grudgingly, Tony Beilenson amended the bill to satisfy these objections before it passed through the legislature with enough votes to override a possible veto—49 to 30, a rough mix of Democrats and Republicans—on June 14, 1967. Ronald Reagan signed it just as grudgingly. A lingering sense of guilt persisted. "It just finally came to my mind," he said, "that an abortion was the taking of a human life." He told Lou Cannon in a 1968 interview that "he never would have signed the bill if he had been more experienced as a governor." And twenty years later, as he was leaving the presidency, he mentioned it as his one chief regret "in all the years he was governor of California and president of the United States."

Other decisions followed, victories he could stitch together into a larger legislative framework. New judicial appointments were made based on merit by a professional commission, eliminating the practice of political cronyism. He authorized conjugal visits in California prisons. And—perhaps his greatest success—a hard-fought tax "reform" bill (in fact a tax *raise*) was passed in July, giving him an extra billion dollars toward reducing the budget deficit.

Little by little, Ronald Reagan was settling in—at the office and at home. He and Nancy had fled the Governor's Mansion for a twelve-room Tudor on a tree-lined street in a section of East Sacramento called the Fabulous Forties. The house was a gem, perfect for entertaining. Nancy furnished it with an exquisite mix of antiques and contemporary pieces donated by her wealthy Los Angeles friends in exchange for generous tax deductions. Joan Didion famously ridiculed the decor as "a stage set," but there were elements that gave it a homey, lived-in look. Mementos from their respective movie careers hung whimsically on the walls. Two dogs, Lady and Fuzzy, roamed the premises. There was a pool and cabana in a fenced-in backyard and a basement recreation room whose pool table was surrounded by the kind of toy train set one encountered in a museum. The Executive Residence, as it was branded, cost the Reagans a modest $1,250 a month in rent, which they paid regularly to the state, even after it was purchased for them by the Kitchen Cabinet.

Ronald Reagan loved the residence. It was his refuge. Almost without fail, he arrived home at six each evening, showered, then slipped into his pajamas for some precious downtime in front of the TV. Nightly news broadcasts were required viewing before tuning in to the favorites— *Mission: Impossible* and reruns of his old nemesis *Bonanza*. On weekends, when his beloved Rams played at home, father and son, "Skipper," suited up to watch the games.

Social functions were avoided whenever possible, especially those attended by his staff. "There was always a distance between the Governor and his staff," said Kathy Randall Davis, Reagan's private secretary. "No one could say they really knew the Reagans. After the working day, the blinds were drawn and a veil of privacy separated the Governor from his public life." In the early days of the administration, Ron and Nancy rarely went out unless there was a state function that demanded his attendance. Even at those affairs, Phil Battaglia often felt he had to step in to ease his boss's anxiety. It wasn't until September 1967, at an assemblyman's annual crab feed at the Sutter Club in Sacramento, that Ronald Reagan began to unwind. It took more than two martinis to do the trick, and with no help from his executive secretary. By that time, Phil Battaglia was gone.

Unfortunately, there was no easy way to get rid of Battaglia. Using the imperial "we," Tom Reed says, "We could not get Reagan to throw him out, because Reagan doesn't fire people." Moreover, the governor "had total trust in Phil," often referring to him as "my strong right arm," frustrating efforts to invite Reagan's support. Instead, a whisper campaign was mounted to discredit Battaglia's motives and impugn his competence. A handful of co-conspirators joined in from among the governor's staff—Lyn Nofziger, Paul Haerle, Gordon Luce, and Bill Clark—men who, Sandy Quinn said, "had presidentialitis, had their eyes on the White House." With Phil off in Washington much of the time, it was relatively easy for Reed to convince them Battaglia was "a self-promoting autocrat"—citing how only he was permitted to stand by the governor at press conferences, how he monopolized Ronald Reagan's time and schedule, how he supposedly demeaned Reagan in private, how he mastered "cutting out and annihilating those who were perceived as a threat," how he was positioning himself as de facto governor. Furthermore, he took heat for the administration's early problems dealing with the state legislature—"trying to ram things through . . . without putting together the necessary pieces to build up support for the program."

Reed never let up, calling Battaglia "power-mad" and "clinically crazy," a "young kid who suddenly found himself operating the levers and buttons and strings of a . . . governor." None of this, however, was enough to vanquish him from Sacramento. "So we figured out that we had to use the political embarrassment of that time to get rid of him," Reed says.

They'd out Phil Battaglia as a homosexual.

In 1967, being gay in politics was the kiss of death. Any gay person in government—whether a politician, a consultant, or the lowliest aide—remained in the closet, under constant fear of exposure and banishment. Stu Spencer, whose two business partners, Bill Roberts and Fred Haffner, were gay, says, "It was *evil* to be homosexual." According to a gay staff member of Ronald Reagan's administration, the rampant homophobia created an environment of "fairly high paranoia." It was easier to reveal that you suffered from cholera. LBJ declared homosexuality "a case of sickness and disease" in 1964, when his top administrative aide, Walter Jenkins, was arrested in a YMCA restroom on a morals charge and forced to resign.

Was Phil Battaglia homosexual? There was never any evidence that he was. He had been seemingly happily married to the same woman for over forty years, a family man in most traditional respects. If he engaged in same-sex relationships, he kept it to himself. But Reed and company assembled a dossier that was loaded with ambiguities. They formed a committee to investigate Battaglia and his alleged love interests—Sandy Quinn and Jack Kemp, the Buffalo Bills' star quarterback who was interning in the governor's office. "Clark and I were the ringleaders," says Reed. "Ed Gillen-waters* and Gordon Luce ran the intelligence network; Curtis Patrick was in charge of planting bugs; Art Van Court involved the cops; Nofziger and I wrote the report—we dealt in adjectives and wild claims—and to back us up we wanted the lawyers, Meese and Haerle, on board." There were nine who helped plot the coup. It was a bungle: the private investigator they sent to tail Battaglia lost him, the bugs planted in Phil's office never transmitted a word of evidence, and an attempt to gain access to Sandy Quinn's apart-ment proved futile. "We made the Keystone Cops look good," Lyn Nofziger reported.

It didn't matter. In lieu of evidence, they concocted a report stating what they *suspected*. "We knew in our minds, though no place else for sure, that there was hanky-panky," Nofziger said, "we just couldn't prove it." The crowning touch was the graphic description of an "orgy" at a Lake Tahoe cabin jointly owned by Phil Battaglia and Jack Kemp. A snoop was dis-patched to peek in the windows for a glimpse of male sexual escapades. Again, there was no indication of untoward behavior—even Reed ac-knowledges, "I don't think there was anything going on in Tahoe." But a list of the cabin's occupants—Battaglia, Kemp, Quinn, and two gay sons of a Republican state senator—was evidence enough, however circumstantial.

"It was *all* circumstantial," Bill Clark admitted.

But it read guilty, according to Stu Spencer—a twelve-page report of who was sleeping with whom, who was taking trips together, what hotel rooms they'd stayed in, who was paying the bills. "We knew we had to get it to Reagan," Tom Reed says, "so we made a plan." "It was decided that the Labor Day holiday was the time to see the governor about it," Ed Meese recalls. "He was down at the Hotel Del Coronado [on San Diego Bay], re-covering from prostate surgery." They all decided to go, all of the "coup plotters," as Tom Reed called them, to put up a united front. Holmes Tuttle was recruited for extra influence. Despite the solidarity, paranoia reigned. "Everybody was nervous," Ed Meese says. "We weren't sure how the gover-nor was going to take it." Any publicity would prove disastrous. They de-cided it was best to travel separately and meet in San Diego. Ed Meese

* Ed Gillenwaters was California's representative in Washington, D.C.; Gordon Luce was Reagan's business and transportation director; Art Van Court was his security chief; and Curtis Patrick was an aide in the governor's office.

laughs when he recalls the cloak-and-dagger scenario. "Bill Clark and I went down together on a PSA flight from Los Angeles," Meese recalls, "and as we walked down the aisle, all our guys were seated in different places on the same plane."

They rented separate cars and rendezvoused in the parking lot of the Del Coronado around three o'clock in the afternoon. Reed knocked on the governor's hotel door, with the others huddled closely behind him. Ron and Nancy, just in from the beach, were dressed in bathrobes over their swimsuits. Reagan took one look at the gang, grinned, and said, "Golly, are you quitting all at once?"

His smile disappeared when he read their report. "He was absolutely shocked," Ed Meese recalls. "He looked up and said, 'After all my time in Hollywood, I thought I'd be able to spot this sort of thing.'" Bill Clark recalled him looking up ashen-faced and saying, "My God, has government failed?" Each man heard exactly what he wanted to hear. The governor went around the room asking everyone individually if they were sure the information was correct and seeking advice on how to proceed. "This is not a Monday problem," Holmes Tuttle said. "This is now."

"Yes," he agreed. "Phil has to go." Nancy, seated quietly on the bed, seconded him. "She saw the potential vulnerability for the governor," says Ed Meese.

Tom Reed recalls the relief everyone felt. "We'd put all our chips on the table. The last thing we wanted was for him to say, 'You guys get together and work it out.' Politically, personally, we would have been dead. Instead his decision was clean, decisive."

Phil has to go.

Afterward, on their way out of town, most of them convened in the airport bar and got fall-down drunk, barely making it onto the plane.

Bill Clark prepared a letter of resignation, and the next morning, Saturday, August 25, 1967, Holmes Tuttle took it to Taft Schreiber's house in Los Angeles, where they knew Battaglia would be meeting to discuss personal business. It was over quickly; the aging car dealer didn't mince words. "Phil," Tuttle said, "when you leave here today, understand that you will no longer be working for the State of California or the governor." Not a word of the document mentioned homosexuality. In fact, Battaglia was at a loss to know why he was being dismissed. He was shell-shocked; tears came fast.

Immediately, Bill Clark replaced Battaglia as the executive secretary and conducted state business as though nothing had changed. The staff liked Clark and welcomed the change. "He was very different, not political at all, but savvy, and a gentleman," says George Steffes, the governor's legislative aide. It was imperative, the staff agreed, that no publicity leak out. Phil Battaglia, to his credit, played the good soldier to the end. At a press conference the following Monday, he announced, "This citizen politician has determined it is time to go back to citizen life." The last thing he or anyone wanted was to set off a torrent of sordid headlines. "Besides," Tom Reed continues to point out, "this was not a scandal. It was a good, old-fashioned struggle for power." L'Affaire Battaglia was strictly hush-hush.

Lyn Nofziger, ever the squeaky wheel, couldn't control himself. It was a secret waiting to burst forth. At a reception for the National Governors' Conference aboard the USS *Independence* off the Florida coast, Nofziger, who was reportedly drunk, laid out Battaglia's dismissal to three reporters— Paul Hope of the *Washington Evening Star*, David Broder of the *Washington Post*, and Karl Fleming of *Newsweek*. "Lyn decided he needed to tell the story his way and attempted to tell it off the record, but his judgment was impaired," Spencer says. Details were leaked to muckraker Drew Pearson, and within days the full story—"Gov. Ronald Reagan Faces First Acid Test; Homosexuals Discovered in His Office"—was splashed across papers nationwide.

Demanding a fuller explanation, reporters converged on the governor's office. At a hastily arranged press conference on October 31, 1967, Ronald Reagan, clearly annoyed, issued an unqualified denial that he "had harbored a homosexual ring in his own executive office," and assailed Drew Pearson as a liar. "I'm prepared to say that nothing like that ever happened," he insisted. Then, he turned abruptly to Nofziger, stationed at his side, and said, "Want to confirm it, Lyn?" A visibly agitated Nofziger raised his hand and said, "Confirmed."

Many in attendance knew it was an outright lie, and "were astonished" by Reagan's reaction. It seemed incredible to them that a man mentioned seriously as a 1968 Republican presidential hopeful would risk his credibility by making such a bald-faced denial. In a follow-up column, Drew Pearson suggested the issue wasn't so much the "homosexual scandal" as it was Ronald Reagan's "credibility gap." Even Bill Clark, the governor's new chief executive, admitted that this "hurt our relationship with everyone—the legislature and the press."

Intrigue and confusion extended to the state capitol, where door locks were changed and guards posted to protect against anyone rifling the files. Staff positions were hastily shuffled, rumors churned up fresh suspicions. In one episode that illustrates the paranoia, Bill Clark's young assistant, Michael Deaver, confessed to his boss that he, too, "had experimented" sexually and intended to resign so as not to drag the administration into further embarrassment. According to Ed Meese, "Mike's father had caught him with a boy when he was twelve years old, but he'd been 'cured' with psychiatric help." This disclosure failed to sink Deaver, who proved invaluable to Ronald Reagan for the next thirty years. But the governor remained wary. When Truman Capote visited the office six months later, Reagan suggested to his lieutenant governor, Robert Finch, "We ought to troll him up and down the hall to see if there is anybody else in here we should wash out."

T he so-called homosexual scandal began to fade, and Reagan was able to return to pressing forward on his agenda, including air-pollution regulation, clamping down on alleged welfare fraud, establishing a system of mediation in farm labor disputes, and introducing laws to crack down on pornography. And despite the false starts and flawed appointments, by the end of 1967 the Reagan administration had reached cruising altitude.

Ironically, the more fit Reagan seemed to be doing his current job, the greater the distractions pulling him away from it, as speculation about the 1968 presidential race continued to intrude. Newspapers across the country had begun making proclamations like "Ronald Reagan has a strong chance for the Republican Presidential nomination next year." Forecasters saw him "rapidly displacing Richard M. Nixon" as the party's strongest conservative candidate. Henchmen began working behind the scenes in earnest to tune up the Reagan engine.

The prairie fire was heating up.

CHAPTER TWENTY-FOUR

THE NON-CANDIDATE

"Cleave ever to the sunnier side of doubt."

—ALFRED, LORD TENNYSON

The ridge road from Monte Rio to the unmarked turnoff a half mile away was shrouded in shadows, making visibility difficult. Redwoods the size of respectable skyscrapers lined either side of the dark corridor functioning as the sole access in or out of the Bohemian Grove. Cars approaching the Grove's front gate found it a slow, arduous trek through dense virgin forest ringed by thousand-foot-high hills, but once inside the grounds, past the armed security shack, the journey ended in a sylvan retreat.

For one week each July, the Bohemian Grove provided refuge to top politicians, titans of industry, and assorted power brokers from across several continents. The lot was full of Maseratis, Ferraris, and Rolls-Royces slotted so closely together that the young valets entrusted to park them had to crawl out the windows in order to return to their posts. Stress, anxiety, and—most important—women were strictly prohibited. The first order of business for any man arriving there was to head directly to the redwood just beyond the gate and to urinate on it. In fact, urinating on trees was both a ritual and a standard practice throughout the stay for all Grove guests—alone, in groups, whatever configuration, wherever one pleases—prompting "sword fights" and occasional misfires.

Men at play. This is where the powerful came to unwind and interact. Even though one of the camp's stated rules was "Weaving Spiders Come

Not Here"—loosely translated as "Don't Do Business on the Premises"—deals were negotiated, pacts made, agreements brokered, alliances strengthened, often with far-reaching repercussions. Campers answered to names such as Scripps, Rockefeller, Cronkite, Kravis, Goldwater, Kluge, and Kissinger. Presidents from Herbert Hoover to Dwight Eisenhower used Julys at the Bohemian Grove to float their ideas and gauge support. And in 1967, that tradition carried on.

This was Ronald Reagan's first visit. He was the guest of George Murphy, his old Hollywood co-star and first-term U.S. senator from California. No doubt Reagan was impressed, as everyone is, with the enchanting surroundings. The Grove was a beautiful 2,600-acre encampment of mostly rustic terrain close to the Russian River. Dragonflies convened over a kidney-shaped lake, a gathering point at the base of a great lawn, and bullfrogs crooned in the leafy underbrush. An untrained visitor could get seriously lost wandering the network of wood-chip trails that led off to 119 secluded "camps." The cottages on each site, stretching back into the hillside, were mostly rickety redwood structures, with inscrutable names such as Monkey Block, Valhalla, Mandalay, Owl's Nest, and Woof.

George Murphy's cabin, Lost Angels, named in honor of the Los Angelenos in residence, sat high above the road, requiring roughly eighty-five steps straight up to reach it. Considered large as these places went, it was stocked with enough liquor to run a booming pub along with relevant supplies like cigars and Cheetos. Early on the afternoon of July 23, 1967, its elevated deck was thronged with Messrs. Murphy and Reagan and their respective entourages, about a dozen men dressed in matching camp attire—polo shirts, khaki shorts, and boat shoes—sitting in wide wicker chairs and chuckling at the nonstop repartee. Seated in the middle, holding court and dressed in the only blue serge suit within thirty miles, was the man of the hour: Richard Milhous Nixon.

This was no chance get-together. The following morning, Nixon was slated to deliver the lakeside keynote address. He would later write, "If I were to choose the speech that gave me the most pleasure and satisfaction in my political career, it would be my Lakeside Speech at the Bohemian Grove in July 1967," but it paled in importance to the get-together in progress. The seemingly nonchalant banter and raunchy jokes traded on Lost Angels' cozy deck were a smoke screen for the very substantive conversation that was scheduled to take place. Perhaps that is why many among the group were not club members and just visiting for the day, outside normal procedure at the Bohemian Grove.

The California presidential primary was still up for grabs. Ronald Reagan was being positioned as the state's favorite-son candidate, but in customary form he had refrained from throwing his hat in the ring—or anywhere else, for that matter. Tom Reed, who had been flogging the Reagan cause, was beyond frustrated with the governor's ambivalence. Reagan kept chanting the same tired mantra: "The office seeks the man." He was still on the fence.

Richard Nixon wasn't. But even in July 1967, Richard Nixon seemed like a long shot. Since his defeats by John F. Kennedy in 1960 and by Pat Brown in the 1962 gubernatorial election, he'd been languishing in political purgatory, unable to shake the loser image. What's more, a survey of potential candidates for 1968 gave Michigan governor George Romney front-runner status, even if by the slimmest of margins. Nelson Rockefeller also lurked in the shadows. Neither Republican moderate was a shoo-in in California, where conservatism was engaging the party, and Nixon smelled an opportunity. Intently, stealthily, he was threading his way toward the primary, "working every state committee meeting since 1966," according to a Nixon adviser. But Ronald Reagan was blocking his path. If Reagan stepped up and made a credible play for the nomination, he could clearly spell trouble for Nixon. Was Reagan in or out? Nixon sought an answer.

Ronald Reagan had nothing concrete to offer. He was still trying to read the tea leaves, trying to determine whether he had a fighting chance of success. Tom Reed and Lyn Nofziger had turned up the heat. Both die-hard conservatives, they pummeled the governor with flattery to convince him he was the key to victory in 1968. Not only were they fearful of Lyndon Johnson's reelection, they dreaded the Republican nomination falling to Romney or Rockefeller. "Romney was wooden," according to Reed. "And the folks in Iowa were never going to trust Rockefeller." Other contenders, by his estimation, were Pennsylvania governor William Scranton—"charming, but a lightweight"—and James Rhodes from Ohio, "a heavyweight, but close to being a Mafia don." Nobody, aside from Reagan, really "had it."

Richard Nixon was a horse of a different color. He was smart, crafty—and a statesman. As his lakeside speech the following morning would reveal, Nixon's grasp of foreign policy was "close to genius." And when it came to political strategizing, he made Machiavelli look like Ashley Wilkes.

He let Ronald Reagan monopolize conversation through a light lunch on the deck of Lost Angels. He laughed at Reagan's jokes, encouraged his Hollywood stories. But afterward, over orange juice laced with vodka, Nixon leaned in to lay out his cards. He wanted to make it official: he had every intention of seeking the Republican nomination, and he wanted Reagan's endorsement. George Murphy, their host, had already promised to back him. Reagan's stamp of approval would practically clinch things for Nixon.

Murphy might have been the veteran hoofer, but Ronald Reagan proceeded to tap dance. "Gee, fellas . . ." he hedged. A Nixon endorsement? How could he, with his own plans up in the air. As to whether he was in or out, he was somewhere . . . in between. He'd accepted a full schedule of speaking engagements over the next few months. Perhaps they would help him make up his mind. That was as far as he would go at present.

In the meantime, Nixon's lakeside speech put a new sheen on his image. He spoke eloquently and convincingly about Asia's booming economies as a counterweight to the spread of communism; the Soviet Union's strategic parity with the United States; the importance of expanding bilateral agreements with China and Russia as a way of testing peace. His careful analyses made good sense to the two hundred men seated around that lake whose fortunes depended on an enlightened worldview. "Nixon had a way of converting an entrenched skeptic into a believer," recalls an ex-skeptic who listened to the speech.

One attendee, at least, remained unconvinced: Ronald Reagan.

Ronald Reagan didn't share Nixon's views on Vietnam—a war in which American forces had lost their ten thousandth airplane by January 1968—and he said as much, every chance he got. He believed the United States had a vested interest in stopping the spread of communism in Southeast Asia and favored a fish-or-cut-bait strategy. Either we should make every effort to win the war or we should withdraw, he insisted. "I'd step up the war and get it over with." Later, he shot down Muhammad Ali's attempt to obtain a boxing license in California, saying, "Forget it. That draft-dodger will never fight in my state."* Nixon refused to commit himself on the war one way or the other. He seemed content enough with the country's present Vietnam policy. Reagan also advocated eliminating the peacetime draft in favor of a professional Army. His approach, on the surface, was more pugnacious than Nixon's, and thus took a toll on Reagan as the months wore on. It was clear that Reagan's ideas resonated with the very conservative segment of the population, but the rest of the country preferred a less strident candidate.

The first indication of the electorate's preference was revealed on March 11, 1968, as the results of the New Hampshire primary were tallied. Romney and Rockefeller had failed to catch fire, while Nixon racked up a decisive 79 percent of the Republican vote. Democrat Eugene McCarthy, an antiwar poet-senator from Minnesota who had the temerity to challenge the incumbent president from his own party, nearly defeated LBJ with a head-spinning showing. Reagan, whose name didn't appear on the ballot, received 362 write-in votes. The strong Democratic antiwar sentiment threw the entire campaign out of joint. Lyndon Johnson became instantly vulnerable. Four days later, Robert Kennedy entered the race.

Ronald Reagan despised Bobby Kennedy, and it would be fair to say the feeling was mutual. Animosity lingered from Kennedy's McClellan Committee investigation into the relationship between MCA and the Screen Actors Guild. Two weeks after the grand jury testimony, he had subpoenaed Reagan's tax returns and had them audited, just before General Electric canceled *GE Theater*. Ronald Reagan read the coincidence as: *Kennedy got me fired*. Their most recent confrontation, on May 15, 1967, was a heated debate about the Vietnam War on "Town Meeting of the World," a CBS-TV broadcast, in which Reagan reportedly "destroyed" his opponent. With Kennedy now jumping into the fray, it gave Reagan some extra incentive. "It's almost as if a big light went on: here is the chance to settle up with that son of a bitch once and for all," Tom Reed says. "It energized him by two megatons."

If that wasn't incentive enough, Reagan got a truckload of it on March 31,

* When Ali heard Reagan's comment, he responded, "At least he didn't call me a *nigger* draft-dodger."

two weeks after the New Hampshire primary. That evening, Lyndon Johnson preempted network TV shows to announce that he would not be seeking reelection as President of the United States. It stunned leaders in both parties and sent all potential candidates scrambling to reassess their chances.

"I thought ours were just about nil," says Reed. "Ron kept insisting he wasn't a candidate, but he encouraged us to explore the opportunity." Reed designed a brief tour to help the governor test the waters. It had kicked off on September 28, 1967, in Eureka, Illinois, where Reagan dedicated a library and addressed his alma mater. But the visit had a larger agenda. It was essentially an opportunity to meet Everett Dirksen, the Senate minority leader who hailed from Eureka, and to elicit a token of his support. "Dirksen was very diplomatic," Reed recalls. "He was primed for Ron to bring up the election, but Reagan never did." Instead, he entertained the senator with recaps of legendary Eureka football games. Finally, Dirksen blurted out, "Are you in this thing?" To which Reagan replied, "Well, I think the office seeks the man."

The next day Reagan flew to Columbia, South Carolina. Following a raucous rally at the airport, where he reminded the crowd, "I am not a candidate," Ronald Reagan addressed a packed house at a Republican fundraising event organized specifically to stoke Strom Thurmond's campaign chest. Thurmond held a fistful of important cards. Four years earlier, he'd switched political parties, from Democrat to Republican, and delivered South Carolina—Southern working-class *Democrats*—for Barry Goldwater. In fact, many experts saw Thurmond's conversion as the catalyst that turned the Deep South from blue to red. After the dinner portion of the evening, Thurmond and his sidekick Harry Dent escorted the governor, along with Tom Reed and Lyn Nofziger, to an anteroom of the banquet hall, where they got down to brass tacks. "Strom wanted to know if Ron was going to run," Reed recalls, "and Reagan kept dancing around the question. Nofziger and I were grinding our teeth." Finally, Thurmond asked him flat-out: "Do you intend to be a candidate?"

"Well, the office seeks the man."

Thurmond simply shook his head. "Young man," he said, "you'll be president someday—but not this year."

Reed and Nofziger were beginning to agree.

Through the spring of 1968, Ronald Reagan kept on the move, burnishing his star. More than half his time was devoted to appearances outside California—whistle-stops in Iowa, Kansas, Texas, Ohio, Illinois, New Mexico, and Arizona, where crowds were reminded that *he wasn't running for office*. The former actor insisted he was merely "crusading on behalf of Republican unity." As the *New York Times* observed, "He reserved his best acting talents for his current impersonation of a non-candidate for the Republican Presidential nomination."

For all intents and purposes, Reagan had "pulled the 'off' switch," as one supporter judged it. In the meantime, Reed and Nofziger kept the non-candidate busy speaking to any group or civic association that attracted Republican voters and helped broaden his appeal, with the occasional detour to Washington. On April 4, a small Reagan contingent flew there for a series of meetings with Republican leaders in the House of Representatives and a private audience with J. Edgar Hoover. As they deplaned at Dulles Airport, Lyn Nofziger and Ed Gillenwaters, the governor's liaison in D.C., delivered the grim news that Dr. Martin Luther King Jr. had been shot in Memphis. "He's dead," Gillenwaters announced.

Reagan was shocked and concerned. He knew what this meant for the country and especially for California, which had experienced its share of civil unrest. By noon the next day, rioting was starting to accelerate in Los Angeles and in black communities along the coast. Hoover informed him that the FBI was monitoring the situation and warned that Washington was set to blow. Against the advice of his handlers, Reagan decided not to cut the visit short. Instead, he delivered a speech at the Women's National Press Club and then attended an untimely meeting with black community leaders that was intended to soften his image as a hard-liner. Not surprisingly, he found his hosts in an embittered state. "The city's going up," a local police officer advised the Reagan entourage soon after they'd arrived. "You'd better get out of here."

On his way back to the Madison Hotel, waves of rioters could be seen streaming along the Mall. Stores were being looted. Sounds of gunfire echoed in the vicinity. Traffic had choked to a halt, trapping the governor's limousine in a knot of abandoned cars. "There's no sense sitting here, let's just walk," Reagan suggested. "It's only six blocks to the hotel." His security detail insisted he don a pair of dark sunglasses as a disguise. The ruse was predictably lame. Only half a block from the car, he was accosted by a black man in the process of liberating a television set from an appliance store. "Governor Reagan!" the man shouted, his face lighting up. Putting his booty down carefully on the sidewalk, he stretched out a hand. "Can I have your autograph?" The men accompanying Reagan swallowed grins as the governor scrawled his name across a stolen box, but the situation was no laughing matter. Fires had broken out in surrounding neighborhoods as convoys of National Guard units descended, attempting to restore order.

California fared better. When the governor returned home the following day, the streets were relatively unperturbed. Still, the tragedy of Dr. King's murder served to underscore the woeful state of the country's race relations that dogged Ronald Reagan throughout the remainder of his term. The man who was raised to be color-blind, who took his black college teammates home rather than subjecting them to discrimination, who proposed scholarships and loans to aid poor minority children, was confronting issues that tested his principles. For all his past open-mindedness, his views were now at odds with those of most black Americans. He denounced militant black leaders and viewed laws promoting fair housing, welfare, and civil rights as benefiting blacks disproportionately, and it put his relationship with black constituents on edge.

Their support, of course, had little effect on Reagan's prospects in the ensuing primaries—even though he hadn't officially declared. Voter turnout in the black communities was infinitesimal when it came to Republicans. In Wisconsin, a nearly all-white electorate gave him 11 percent of the primary vote, and he got twice that in Nebraska, both landslide victories for Richard Nixon. Massachusetts handed its contest to Nelson Rockefeller. A long-shot strategy for a Reagan nomination at the 1968 Republican convention emerged directly from these results. "Conservatives believed that if Nixon did not win on the first ballot, Rockefeller would put up a real fight on the second or third," says Ed Meese. By keeping himself out of the hostilities, Reagan could lie low as Nixon and Rockefeller pummeled each other. "If Nixon faltered and Ronald Reagan put himself into contention, he would be the successor for sure."

Other scenarios were being floated. Spiro Agnew, who had just been elected governor of Maryland, showed up in Sacramento to broker a deal. If Reagan was amenable, Agnew could arrange for him to be Rockefeller's running mate. Or they could switch up the billing, it didn't matter. "I want a Rockefeller-Reagan ticket either way," he said, "either Rockefeller-Reagan or Reagan-Rockefeller." The response to Agnew's offer drew an immediate thumbs-down. Ronald Reagan had no interest in the number-two spot—he'd already rejected a Nixon-Reagan combo when Dwight Eisenhower proposed it—and as for Rockefeller, their political philosophies stood miles apart.

In the meantime, Nixon continued to rack up impressive wins in the primaries. Even in California, on June 5, where Reagan ran unopposed as the favorite-son candidate, over 50 percent of Republicans failed to cast ballots for him. All eyes were on the Democratic contest, in which Robert Kennedy scored a decisive win over Eugene McCarthy. The jubilation was short-lived. That same night, on his way to celebrate with supporters in the ballroom of the Ambassador Hotel in Los Angeles, Kennedy was shot while passing through the kitchen. His death two days later shocked the nation and threw the election into disarray.

Ronald Reagan was visibly shaken. "It is a great tragedy," he wrote to his daughter Patti, "just as it was a great tragedy for his brother." Reagan admitted having an intimation about Bobby Kennedy's assassination: "Our friend in Washington [a euphemism for astrologer Jeane Dixon] told me that she foresaw a tragedy for him before the election." The actual murder, however, hit him hard. "I've been here in the office all day, and feeling almost sick most of the time," he reported to his daughter. "I saw him the day after Bobby was shot, and he was rattled, depressed," Tom Reed recalls. The violence horrified him. "You could see his attitude change overnight. He'd continue stumping with an eye on the nomination, but the fire was gone."

Barry Goldwater urged him to get behind Nixon, as did his benefactors, the Kitchen Cabinet, who had already sunk $366,000 into the Reagan effort; if he continued to hedge about his candidacy, they'd turn the spigots off, refusing to raise any more money in support. They were embarrassed by

Reagan's lack of commitment. Hoping to clear the air, William French Smith called a meeting at Reagan's Pacific Palisades home on June 9, but it devolved into a shouting match between Henry Salvatori, Taft Schreiber, and Justin Dart, the top contributors. Things were coming apart at the seams. As Tom Reed later wrote, "The Reagan machinery, still in place, was a headless juggernaut."

And out of steam. As Lou Cannon observed, Ronald Reagan had "raised bundles of money for the Republican Party and won many a conservative cheer, but he had barely dented Nixon's delegate count." On August 5, 1968, as the Republican convention convened in Miami Beach amid antiwar demonstrations thronging the streets, Reagan clung to his favorite-son status, even allowed his name to be put into contention, but much too late to have an impact. The delegate votes were out of his reach. Nixon closed the deal on the first ballot, and it fell to Ronald Reagan, at two in the morning on August 8, to mount the podium and move for a unanimous vote in support of Nixon.

As he descended the platform, a delegate from South Carolina echoed Strom Thurmond's prophecy: "Not this year, Ron, but sometime."

Sometime. The presidency had become more than just a pipe dream. The support for Reagan throughout the state delegations had been palpable, even among Nixon stalwarts. "He had their hearts," says Stu Spencer, "if not their votes." Had a floor fight developed, there was reason to believe he could have stolen the nomination on the third or fourth ballots. He'd raised his profile more than a few notches. But now, *like that*, it had come to an end.

The governor couldn't wait to get out of the spotlight. Six hours later, as dawn broke over the South Beach shoreline, he and Nancy boarded a cabin cruiser and sailed out into the Keys, as far as they could get from the political tidewaters. That night, he slept fourteen hours—and the next night, too. "It was the greatest relief I've ever known," he recalled. There was a lot to think about. One thing for sure, he "wasn't ready to be president."

Not in 1968. But . . . *sometime.*

CHAPTER TWENTY-FIVE

THE CONSERVATION
GOVERNOR

"Marvelous Truth, confront us, at every turn, in every guise."

—DENISE LEVERTOV

R onald Reagan's performance as a governor was now so polished that a prominent Democrat called him "the Batman of politics." He seemed immune to the routine setbacks and embarrassments that ordinarily brought anguish to people in public office. Much later, and for much the same reason, he was nicknamed the "Teflon President" by wry observers. In 1970, when he was reelected as the governor of California, the jury was still out on the substance of his performance in Sacramento, but with an eye trained on a higher office, he began building his political résumé—as quickly as possible.

From the lectern at his second inauguration, he prepared for the next step toward his ultimate goal by launching a crusade for welfare reform. The cause offered villains he could flog: dependents of the state who he said milked "programs that reward people for not working." A distinction was drawn between "the truly needy as opposed to the lazy unemployable" that to many read as the same thing. The "welfare monster," as he took to calling it, proved a potent tool to stoke populist resentment.

He also pledged to rid California's campuses of "troublemakers," a catch-all term for protesters that he had softened from his previous characterization of them as "criminal anarchists and latter-day Fascists." Since running for governor in 1966, he'd tapped into public sentiment critical of activities on college campuses not related specifically to education. Strikes and demonstrations were particular targets, although he seemed to have forgotten that he'd led similar student actions at Eureka College. As far as Reagan was concerned, his approach back then was respectful. He saw the Eureka protest as orderly, ministered by leaders who respected college tradition. These students were, by choice, a disruptive force. They were protesting issues outside of education—about war, race, and politics—and they took positions he didn't agree with, to say nothing of their appearance and behavior. His sense of propriety was offended by their shaggy hair, drug use, inflammatory language, and general attitude of disrespect.

"We are called materialistic," he complained during a newspaper interview in defense of his own generation. "But our materialism has made our children the biggest, tallest, most handsome, and intelligent generation of Americans yet." Why couldn't they appreciate what they'd been given? Why were they bucking the system that put them on top of the world?

As much as his bedrock political views, Ronald Reagan believed in the importance of old-fashioned good manners. What he saw as the ill-mannered behavior of these radicals pushed his buttons. And his own daughter's college experience didn't improve his opinion of the modern student mind-set. Patti Reagan had embarrassed him by dropping out of Northwestern University, where she befriended a radical black activist and became embroiled in a scandal known as "the hot pants incident." According to press reports, she and a roommate had tussled with a local black peddler selling shorts in her dorm, which precipitated his arrest—and front-page headlines. Afterward, she gravitated to Oxford and later USC, before dropping out for good. "I can't say we're surprised," her father commented, but her misadventures fed his contempt for campus hijinks. He promised to submit legislation that would "provide for the expulsion of students or the dismissal of teachers who interfere with the educational process, and strengthen the trespass laws to keep the troublemakers off the campus." There would be zero tolerance for agitators. His platform toward them could be summed up by the inscription on a plaque above the doorway to his office: "Observe the Rules or Get Out."

"In the sixties, on campus, Ronald Reagan was evil incarnate," says Tom Reed. "So, to turn the tables, we made students the villains." By 1969, though, the counterculture was no longer quite so anathema to mainstream America, and their peace-and-love sentiments triggered a change in public opinion. Hippies were no longer considered "cowardly little bums," as Governor Reagan had branded students demonstrating at UC–Santa Barbara a year earlier. Now many saw them as idealists, deserving their say. Nothing underscored that more than the events of May 4, 1970, when National Guardsmen swarmed the campus of Kent State in Ohio and opened fire on demonstrators, killing four students. A month earlier, at the onset of new protests roiling UC–Santa Barbara, Reagan had ordered them put down straightaway, saying, "If it takes a bloodbath, let's get it over with." At the time, it sounded rash; in light of Kent State, inhumane.

Reagan was "determined to get something done on welfare and education," says Ed Meese, "and nothing was going to stand in his way." In the spring of 1970, he learned he would have no choice. Verne Orr, the governor's director of finance, delivered a bombshell during a weekly cabinet meeting. In order to balance next year's budget, based on projections of funding for welfare and education, a tax increase was unavoidable. The idea horrified Reagan, and he immediately ordered the formation of two task forces with mandates to "reform and restructure" each program, top to bottom.

Precedence was given to welfare reform, which he decided was "our number one priority." He wanted people to be self-reliant—to exemplify that old myth of the lone cowboy of the West making his own way. Welfare was the great trough that freeloaders came to drink from—"able-bodied people from around the country who preferred a handout to a job." When Reagan first took office, in 1967, more than 750,000 people were dependent on Aid to Families with Dependent Children (AFDC), the state's bulky welfare machine; just after his reelection, in early 1971, the agency's rolls hit the 1.5 million mark. Unemployment was skyrocketing and families were desperate, nevertheless the rising caseload threatened the state's solvency. Legislators of both parties understood the need to rewrite the laws, and they set to work, often at loggerheads, drafting comprehensive bills.

"Reagan wasn't interested in the politics of it," according to a Republican member of his bipartisan task force. "He was totally substantive." And he had an active to-do list. He was adamant that any statute reaching his desk contain measures "increasing assistance to the truly needy," requiring those who were able to work to seek a job or job training, and implementing laws to "strengthen family responsibility," which loosely translated meant that children with adequate incomes contribute to the support of indigent parents and that absent fathers provide for their children. "There was also a law enforcement part," says George Steffes—"cracking down on lady welfare cheats."

Lady welfare cheats. Like one of the *Reader's Digest* anecdotal stories that he could easily wrap his head around, Ronald Reagan fixed on the concept of the welfare cheat, disregarding the fact that there wasn't much evidence that such a phenomenon existed. Nevertheless, it seemed real to him, and it played well. He claimed his staff "discovered thousands of people who were receiving welfare checks at the same time they were gainfully employed," that "one couple . . . earned more than one hundred thousand dollars a year between them." These were compelling stories, but they were unsubstantiated. It didn't matter. There was a great public resentment against welfare and the people who sought to exploit it. It was an easy idea to convey, even if it ignored the real complexities of the issue.

While his rhetoric was punitive, Reagan and his task force developed a policy that was more constructive than his words implied. Previously, he had vetoed provisions for childcare, job-training, and family-planning programs, all of which got added back into the final bill. Additionally, it included an automatic cost-of-living increase for welfare recipients in order to keep their benefits from eroding as a result of inflation. Weeks of intense negotiations later, a compromise bill was hammered out, and the California Welfare Reform Act of 1971 sailed through both houses of the state legislature.

The governor, usually a passive participant when it came to negotiations, had actively pitched in behind the scenes. "He was very hands-on," says George Steffes, who served on the task force. "When things looked hopeless, as they often did, when frustration set in, when talks got stalled, we went to both Reagan and Bob Moretti [the Democratic speaker of the Assembly] and said, 'This is not going to happen if you two don't get involved.'"

The governor had learned how to put his power to use in delicate legislative transactions. "He knew when to back off, when to compromise—and when to shut up," says Stu Spencer. And he preferred to work a small room.

He didn't need to address the Assembly from an elevated podium, his voice amplified like the Great Oz. A one-on-one meeting with an adversary or legislative holdout was found to be a much more effective approach. Reagan's movie-star presence provided him with every opportunity to win over undecided assemblymen in close-call situations. In casual meetings, he was witty, he told Hollywood stories, he rattled off a slew of off-color jokes. And he possessed subtle persuasive powers. He didn't push or shove or cajole. But his steadiness and charm combined to woo—and prevail—in much the same way they had throughout his SAG tenure. His staff learned that Reagan was their secret trump card, and they delighted in playing him to seal a difficult deal.

"Getting the governor together with legislators became a joy," says Ken Hall. "He did so well in convincing them he was right, regardless of what the problem was." Whenever he was needed to do some gentle arm-twisting, Bill Clark or Ed Meese dispatched an aide to the floor of the legislature in search of the sergeant at arms. "Tony, I've got to talk to Walt," they would say if, for example, their quarry was the state senator from Bakersfield. Tony would retrieve Walt, who would be escorted to a corner where the governor's aide stood in shadows, like a spy. "Walt, we need to have you talk to the governor." Invariably, Walt (or whomever was summoned) grew visibly agitated, swiveling his head in a one-eighty in case someone might have overheard. "*I can't talk to the governor,*" he'd practically wheeze while struggling to remain inconspicuous. "My guys will kill me if I do that!" The aide would offer reassurance. "Don't worry about it. Nobody will ever know. Just go to the bathroom. Tony will take care of it from there." If Walt complied, they'd hustle him out of the bathroom, shove him into the elevator, take him down to the basement garage, run him through rows of parked cars, and get him into the private elevator that emptied right outside the governor's study. Ronald Reagan would be standing there, waiting. "Walt!" he'd say. "It's great of you to come." Whereupon Walt would be ushered into the inner sanctum and emerge twenty minutes later, grinning and pledging fealty. "We'd slip Walt back onto the floor of the legislature," Ken Hall says, "where he'd inevitably be voting 'yes' on our bill."

As a rule the governor needed twenty-seven votes to get any bill through the Assembly, and the key to victory was snagging number twenty-six. "People loved to jump on board as the twenty-seventh vote in order to put a bill over the top," says George Steffes, "whereas no one wanted to be twenty-six." Twenty-six was the game-changer, the goat, and it was the staff's job to shepherd him into their corner and put the bell around his neck. Walt—or somebody like him—was always sought to be the twenty-sixth vote. "And never fail, we'd get him," Hall says, "over and over again."

Reagan's intercession with the legislature was never more important than on June 30, 1972, during a bitter struggle over the new state budget. The governor's staff had reached an impasse with the legislature and was now three days past the official deadline. The Democrats prepared to shut down government offices. The *Los Angeles Times* ran fat headlines castigating the governor. It was an embarrassing mess.

That night, Ken Hall and George Steffes remained late in the capitol, drafting yet another version of the budget. At two o'clock in the morning, it seemed they were making headway. According to Hall, "We thought we had a chance this time to get it through *if* the governor was around." He'd gone home at ten o'clock, and the lights had gone out in the executive mansion sometime around eleven; the Reagans were sound asleep. Hall and Steffes flipped a coin to see who would wake the governor.

Nancy answered the phone. She was not happy. Steffes apologized, but assured Ronald Reagan they were close to getting the budget through the Assembly. "If you could just come down and talk to one more legislator," he said, "I think we can solve everything tonight." Unfortunately, Ronald Reagan had taken a couple of sleeping pills and was feeling fairly out of it. "But get the guys together," he relented. "I'll be there as soon as possible."

About forty-five minutes later, the governor arrived at the office dressed in a turtleneck and slacks, looking every bit the actor who had come to play his part. "What are we doing?" he asked in a businesslike voice. "Let's get this show going."

It was the signal to execute the usual covert routine. Steffes and Hall singled out a legislator they felt was ripe and had the sergeant at arms hustle him into the bathroom and the elevator, through the parking lot, up the private elevator, and into the study with Ronald Reagan. "An hour later," Hall says, "we had the budget out."

Almost six years into the Reagan administration, even skeptics had to acknowledge that it was a well-run machine. Bill Bagley, the Assembly's most liberal Republican who had dismissed Ronald Reagan as incompetent and "a know-nothing," admitted years later, "The governor got plenty accomplished that changed my opinion of him." In addition to welfare reform, his office delivered the largest funding increase to public schools in the history of California, imposed tax controls on county governments, delivered property tax relief to the middle class, passed legislation mandating strong pollution controls on automobiles, enacted the California Coastal Commission, and halted construction of the Dos Rios Dam, which would have caused flooding in Round Valley, a seven-million-acre feed and the spiritual preserve of the Yuki tribe. In 1972 he signed bills that protected the California coastline from development and set aside thousands of acres of parklands for public use.

His attention was increasingly drawn to the outdoors. "Environmentalists rarely regarded Ronald Reagan as a man in their corner," says Kirk West, the governor's chief deputy comptroller, "but his accomplishments in that area were long—and historic." In the summer of 1972, a proposed highway over the Minarets, a gorgeous, pristine mountain range around the Sierra Nevadas, became a political issue. The project was championed by the powerful Central Valley agriculture industry, which lobbied for a year-round route as a way of transporting its products to the east. "Conservationists were absolutely appalled," West says. "It would have sliced right through sections of the majestic John Muir Trail. The impact on the environment would have been devastating."

Pressure was brought to rush the highway bill through the legislature. Central Valley farmers had contributed heavily to the governor's campaigns, and they called in favors, while petitioning their local assemblymen to demand quick approval. Ronald Reagan refused to be pushed. "He decided to see the Minarets for himself," says Ed Meese, "and so he took his cabinet on a horseback trip."

The outing blossomed into a full-blown extravaganza on June 27, 1972, as members of the media were invited along. As Meese recalls, only a few of them could ride. George Skelton, who covered the event for the *Los Angeles Times,* described the image of Ronald Reagan, late of *Cattle Queen of Montana,* "waving a white hat, on a tall horse . . . as staffers and reporters struggled to mount and hang on to some strange beast." Reagan's Keystone

Kavalry rode six miles straight up treacherous trails to a clearing just below the Minaret Summit, where the governor delivered an impassioned speech. His awe was palpable. "Because such a crossing would do irreparable harm to the wilderness beauty and wildlife of the area—and because we simply don't need another highway—we have vigorously opposed such a crossing," he said. He asked the legislature to close the Minarets Corridor permanently, guaranteeing that the John Muir Trail remained a 250-mile swath of inviolate wilderness between Yosemite and Mount Whitney.

Years later, offshore oil drilling, mining exploration, opening wilderness to development, and wholesale timber cutting became closely associated with Reagan initiatives. The environment wasn't high on his presidential agenda. But in the summer of 1972, the badge he wore as Conservation Governor was a shiny ornament of his legacy in California.

D uring 1973, the Reagan polish began to wear off. It was often the case with multiple-term governors that either malaise took hold and they wore out their welcome or they began to feel too confident and overreached. Ronald Reagan suffered a series of stumbles that touched on both extremes. He misread the public's ability to unravel his aggressive fiscal gambles and its willingness to indulge his deepening conservative views.

One of Reagan's vulnerabilities was his habit of aligning himself with the last person to give him advice. "As a result, he'd only get one side of an issue," says George Steffes. His work with the Tax Reduction Task Force brought this into sharp focus. The committee, which was charged with shaping an agenda for the remaining years of the Reagan administration, fell into the hands of a man named Lewis Uhler, a former John Birch Society stalwart with extremist views. Ed Meese, who was a law-school classmate, defended Uhler as "a very decent guy, a very strong conservative with a libertarian outlook," but his bona fides set off alarms. His political philosophy was a precursor to the Tea Party's populist rhetoric. "I am absolutely convinced," he argued in early 1971, "that legislators, if left to their own devices, will, in short order, put an end to the Republic in the name of improving it unless we, the people, take aggressive action, change the environment in which they operate, change the rules of the game."

An antitax zealot, Uhler hijacked the governor's ear. He convinced

Reagan to set an extraordinary precedent by calling a special election to approve a state constitutional amendment. Proposition 1, as they labeled it, was cooked up to restrict government spending through rigorous tax-rate limits, while reducing revenues and rolling back personal income taxes. As a sop to encourage voters, an immediate 20 percent credit on their state income tax was promised. In any event, the new law, if enacted, would make it next to impossible for the California legislature to raise taxes.

Reagan called it a "once-in-a-lifetime opportunity." He envisioned it rolling out in much the same way as his welfare-reform bill. But the public felt differently. There was no great groundswell for tax reform, and unforeseen obstacles stood in the way. The California Teachers Association, with its mighty lobbying muscle, saw the measure as a direct threat to education funding and went all-out to vanquish Prop 1. The League of Women Voters called it irresponsible. So did the state's Democrats, denouncing it as "an economic war on the interests of most of the people in California." The proposition ran to almost ten pages of wonkish complexity, and voters found it impossible to figure out whether the amendment would lower or raise spending. Even the governor pleaded ignorance. When asked whether he thought the average voter understood the proposition, he quipped, "No, and he shouldn't try. I don't, either."

The wisecrack didn't help to boost his interests. Nor did the prospect of a special election. As the bill's proponents discovered, when you hold a special election, only truly interested people turn out. In this case, the voters who streamed to the polls were the state employees unions and the people they could muster who were vigorously opposed. Despite Reagan's efforts to sell the initiative—and an outsize $1 million to back them, including a $110,000 loan guaranteed by the Kitchen Cabinet to collect the signatures necessary to get it on the ballot—Proposition 1 went down to a resounding defeat.

In the summer of 1973, Reagan ran into another wall of disapproval when he tried to hand off the state's welfare programs for the blind, aged, and disabled to the federal government, whose payments were considerably lower than California's. A protracted fight broke out along partisan lines that reflected poorly on the administration. When Democrats in the legislature introduced a bill to restore state assistance for the handicapped, Ronald Reagan persuaded Republican senators to block it. This didn't sit well with the electorate. Radical students and welfare cheats were fair game; the disadvantaged and handicapped: strictly off-limits. He had touched a nerve, and the blowback was dreadful. Welfare groups sued the state, accusing the governor of legislative overreach—and they won on appeal, giving encouragement to the Democrats sponsoring the bill.

Two black eyes within months dealt the Reagan administration a withering blow. The mood of the electorate was turning chilly. Polls showed a growing disenchantment with the governor. Californians found him personally likable but inattentive. Many thought he seemed bored with the job. His staff knew the score. To pass legislation, it was generally better not to burden the governor with too much of the messy process. An aide let slip a well-known office slogan: "Let's work everything out before it gets to Ronald Reagan." Even the papers started tucking into the appreciable ennui. The *Los Angeles Times*, in a front-page analysis, quoted an anonymous Republican strategist who said, "There is a definite sickness in the administration." This gave a fright to the Kitchen Cabinet, which had eyed the future with increasing enthusiasm. Its horse seemed to be stumbling on his warm-up track. Reagan needed to keep his eyes on the prize.

U nfortunately, he would be blindsided by a scandal he refused to take seriously until it was far too late.

No one dismissed the Watergate scandal with as much conviction as Ronald Reagan. When he first learned of the break-in at the headquarters of the Democratic National Committee on June 17, 1972, he was convinced it had nothing to do with Republicans, much less the Nixon White House. As the affair unfolded, Reagan turned a deaf ear to the increasingly incriminating evidence. "It's a partisan witch hunt," he told supporters at a rally in Atlanta. The president, he was certain, wasn't culpable; for proof, he pointed out that Richard Nixon *himself* had ordered the Justice Department to prosecute the burglars. That same week, on a swing through Washington, he praised Nixon and insisted that Watergate mattered only if Americans allowed liberals to let it matter. In a letter to Ben Cleaver, the father of his high school sweetheart, he wrote, "I can't say publicly but feel very deeply that we are witness to a lynching." Nixon, he felt, was "a truthful man." The Watergate burglars were overzealous, nothing more than "well-meaning individuals committed to the reelection of the President," their offense "no worse than double-parkers."

The results of the 1972 election only reinforced Reagan's stance. Nixon trounced George McGovern, his Democratic opponent, in the largest landslide in American presidential history, helping to return Republicans to Congress in record numbers. Despite evidence mounting that suggested Nixon's stealth hand in Watergate, loyalty weighed heavily on Ronald Reagan—loyalty to the party and loyalty to the president. Dr. Parkinson's Eleventh Commandment remained very much in force. He had no intention of budging off its objective. Even when Nixon admitted sanctioning a program of wiretaps and initiating illegal campaign tactics between 1969 and 1971, Reagan continued to defend his leader. He maintained that Watergate was "not criminal, just illegal," that all reporting about it was marred by prejudice and innuendo. "About ninety percent of everything said so far is unfounded rumor, accusations, and so forth," he insisted.

He took the same public stance in August 1973, when Vice President Spiro T. Agnew came under investigation for corruption charges involving kickbacks he'd taken while serving as the governor of Maryland. As embattled governors, both men shared a common enemy in campus radicals, whose protests Agnew famously dismissed as "the cacophony of seditious drivel emanating from the best-publicized clowns in our society." Over the years, Reagan and Agnew developed a mutual admiration society. "They'd become friends," Ed Meese says. "Ronald Reagan really liked Ted Agnew and was shocked and outraged by the allegations."

He might have been alone in that opinion. Few colleagues, Republican or otherwise, were willing to go on record defending the vice president. Ronald Reagan, however, piped right up. "I have known Ted Agnew to be an honest and honorable man," he declared in a high-profile interview in the *Washington Post*. "He, like any other citizen of high character, should be considered innocent until proven otherwise." It was a generous gesture to the one person most likely blocking his path to the 1976 Republican nomination. A vice president was the natural successor to any president, and party strategists assumed that Agnew would run at the top of the ticket, just as Nixon had after Eisenhower left office. According to an April 1973 Gallup poll, 35 percent of Republican voters named Agnew as their choice in 1976 (slightly ahead of runner-up Ronald Reagan). Agnew was already in the presidential pipeline, making speeches written by William Safire and Patrick Buchanan. He even had a shrewd campaign manager waiting in the wings—Nixon advocate John Sears, who would eventually serve at Reagan's side. "Should Mr. Agnew somehow succeed to the Presidency before 1976," the *New York Times* suggested, casting a gimlet eye on the Watergate imbroglio, "Mr. Reagan would be shut out; Mr. Agnew would be . . . invulnerable to challenge." "To conservatives," says Jeffrey Bell, at the time a young Republican operative, "Agnew was a phenomenon. He was whacking the liberals and had eclipsed Ronald Reagan on issues that mattered most to us. We had him targeted as our favorite in '76."

It was a short-lived flirtation. On October 10, 1973, after being formally indicted, Spiro Agnew resigned as vice president, opening the nomination to all comers. It also created an immediate job opportunity in the executive wing of the White House. Speculation was rife over whom Nixon would appoint to fill the vice-presidential post vacated by Agnew. The Twenty-fifth Amendment required that the candidate be confirmed by a majority vote of both houses of Congress, so to avoid a partisan fight the nominee had to be someone moderate, someone acceptable to both factions, someone beyond reproach. *Someone supremely inoffensive.* Holmes Tuttle and Justin Dart considered Ronald Reagan the perfect choice and put the squeeze on Nixon to name him.

Realistically, Reagan's prospects were slim. While the Twenty-fifth Amendment charges the president with nominating a new vice president, the Twelfth Amendment, which established the Electoral College, requires that the appointee "not be an inhabitant of the same state with themselves." Since both Nixon and Reagan were registered to vote in California, such a pairing might trigger a challenge. Even more foreboding was Nixon's opinion of Reagan. In a 1971 conversation with Henry Kissinger, he summed up Reagan as being "pretty shallow" and "a man of limited mental capacity," a view he'd expressed in different ways over the years. If nominated and confirmed, the former actor would be a heartbeat away, which Kissinger termed "inconceivable."

Nixon ultimately chose someone even more supremely inoffensive: the current House minority leader, a six-term congressman from the Fifth Congressional District of Michigan named Gerald Ford. If Nixon ultimately resigned and the vice president became the president, Ford would be the only person in the history of the country not to be elected to either post.

In Ronald Reagan's eyes, that would make Ford nothing more than a surrogate—"a caretaker."

In that case, the presidency would be up for grabs.

CHAPTER TWENTY-SIX

"A HORSE OF A DIFFERENT COLOR"

*"There is no more miserable human being than one
in whom nothing is habitual but indecision."*

—WILLIAM JAMES

Richard Nixon was taking a schoolyard beating.

By the spring of 1974, the Watergate scandal had evolved into a full-blown spectacle and began closing in on the Oval Office. There was no place left to hide. New and incriminating revelations appeared daily in the country's major newspapers, spelling disaster for the administration, which inched closer to collapse. In the House Judiciary Committee, impeachment was in the air. Fourteen months of Watergate-Watergate-Watergate proved too exhausting for the most battle-tested pols. Even high-ranking Republicans, once fierce defenders of the president, threw in their towels and took early vacations.

The last loyal soldier was Ronald Reagan. The way he saw it, the Watergate conspirators were "not criminals at heart" and the president was an innocent man, hounded by "a lynch mob." Reagan's standard response to any question about Nixon was: "Let's give him the benefit of the doubt." Resignation—a solution gaining steam in the press—never entered into Reagan's thinking. "The governor was firmly and publicly behind Nixon right up until the end," says Ed Meese, who not only shared his boss's view but set the tone for the rest of the governor's office. As late as May 1974,

Reagan's lieutenants believed that Nixon would tough it out through the end of his term. But either way, they were looking ahead.

The 1976 election lay squarely in their sights. But his candidacy would run against all trends. His age was an obstacle: he would turn sixty-five during the election cycle. Nobody that old had ever been elected president other than William Henry Harrison, who had dropped dead within a month. And age wasn't the only obstacle. There was Reagan's strident conservatism, which had sunk Barry Goldwater in 1964 (and, some argued, the Republican Party). Reagan had sold his agenda to satisfied Californians, but voters in the East and South weren't familiar with his accomplishments—or with him.

When Nixon appointed Gerald Ford to replace Spiro Agnew as vice president, Ford promised him that he would not seek the GOP nomination in 1976 and would support John Connally. That suited the Reagan camp's interests. Connally, they reasoned, wouldn't pose a challenge. He'd recently switched parties—from Democrat to Republican—and both sides still viewed him with suspicion. But if Nixon ultimately resigned and Ford became president, it would greatly complicate Reagan's situation. As the incumbent, Ford would have a formidable advantage.

Some in the governor's office urged him to run for California's open U.S. Senate seat instead. His opponent would be Alan Cranston, a liberal and the perpetrator of the Democratic Truth Squad that had stalked and pestered Reagan from campaign stop to campaign stop in 1970 and, in Reagan's supporters' eyes, deserved a good thrashing. Reagan could beat Cranston, *that* they were sure of, but he had no interest in joining a body ruled by committee. He was his own man, a leader, not a team player. He'd also ruled out a third term as governor. When asked about the possibility—and he was asked incessantly from 1970 on—he never wavered in his reply: "One term may not be enough, but two is plenty. If you can't accomplish what you set out to do after two terms, you'd better leave it for the next team."

Anyway, he now had his eyes on one prize.

His lieutenants were even more focused. Since early 1973, a core group of Reagan insiders met for breakfast once a week at the Sutter Club in Sacramento to discuss their boss's future. They were all fully committed, come what may—Lyn Nofziger, Ed Meese, Tom Reed, and Mike Deaver, along with Bob Walker, Reagan's Washington aide; Jim Lake, officially the assistant finance director and California's representative in D.C.; and Pete Hannaford, a senior assistant to the governor. Later, Holmes Tuttle and David Packard, chairman of Hewlett-Packard, would join in. For now, they called themselves the Nofziger Group, after its loudest and most vociferous participant. They were unified behind one man, even though their goals often varied. Lyn Nofziger was a broken record: Reagan for President in '76, no matter who else ran. Ed Meese wasn't so sure. "My feelings were that it would be a very tough campaign," he recalls. "Watergate would be a specter that would permeate everything." He felt Reagan might fare better in the public sector as a mouthpiece for conservative causes. The others lined up behind either Nofziger or Meese but were obliged by circumstances to take a wait-and-see approach.

On August 5, 1974, events forced their hands. A bombshell struck: the "smoking gun" tape was released, revealing that Richard Nixon had orchestrated the Watergate cover-up and ordered his men to obstruct the FBI's investigation. It sealed the president's fate: Nixon would either have to resign or be removed from office. Even Ronald Reagan finally had to acknowledge Nixon's culpability. "In view of the President's statement," he said in a hastily prepared press release, "I believe it is absolutely imperative that he go before Congress and make a full disclosure of all the information he has in this matter, answering any and all questions they may have." Privately, Reagan was disgusted. According to Pete Hannaford, "he felt a sense of disappointment that Nixon had let his country down, mixed with anger over what he felt was the hypocrisy of many Nixon-haters, who had finally run their quarry to ground."

The next night, August 6, the Nofziger Group (now calling themselves the National Political Group) was hosting a dinner at the Firehouse Restaurant in Sacramento for a much-anticipated guest. John Sears, a thirty-four-year-old powerhouse lawyer and veteran of the Nixon White House, had been summoned from his office in Washington to discuss the possibility of managing a Reagan presidential campaign. Sears's reputation as a legendary "delegate hunter" preceded him. He had cherry-picked the delegates for Nixon's triumphant 1968 campaign and was known to have racked up political chips from coast to coast. As Nixon's political adviser, Sears understood how to run an effective operation. He was known as a master strategist with almost superhuman drive. If Reagan decided to make a run, the sentiment was strong that John Sears was their man.

Unfortunately, the person who showed up at the Firehouse powwow bore no resemblance to the legend. On the flight from Washington to Sacramento, Sears had drunk heavily and was "fairly smashed" when he arrived. His "rather oracular dissertation" delivered at dinner amounted to "nothing but babble," according to Pete Hannaford, who spoke for the rest of the group when declaring the meeting "a terrible disappointment."

A good night's sleep made a world of difference. The next afternoon, at Reagan's home, Sears dazzled an audience that included the governor and his wife, Ed Meese, Mike Deaver, Jim Lake, and a handful of financial supporters—Holmes Tuttle, Justin Dart, and David Packard. He put on a clinic on organizing a campaign, explaining his methods of analyzing prospects and motivating a staff. "Reagan didn't say much," Sears recalls. He found it difficult to get a read on Reagan. The governor remained Sphinx-like, noncommittal, when it came to running in '76. But at one point, he asked to take a poll of those assembled on the likelihood of Nixon's fate. Going around the room, one by one, it was unanimous—the consensus was that Nixon would survive. Sears came last. "Nixon will be out one way or another by fall," he insisted. "He'll either have to resign or be impeached and convicted. Ford will be president. But he'll be the strangest kind of incumbent because nobody ever voted for him, so he won't come to the campaign with any personal constituency. That makes him vulnerable in the political sense. He won't have the power an incumbent normally has, so it makes it possible to run against him."

Sears didn't hold Ford in high esteem. He liked him personally, but didn't think he had the stuff to be president. "Nixon told me that he picked Ford because he thought Jerry would be confirmed [as vice president]," Sears says, "but that *nobody would want him to be president!*" Nixon wasn't discreet about his estimation of Ford. With wicked acidity, he asked Nelson Rockefeller, "Can you imagine Jerry Ford sitting in this chair?"

John Sears could, but he didn't think Ford would be sitting in it very long.

On Thursday, August 8, 1974, Ronald Reagan was still processing Sears's analysis as he was leaving the Executive Residence on Forty-fifth Street in Sacramento for his trip a few blocks north to the capitol. Ed Meese was with him, and as they passed the maid's room, a little television on the bookshelf stopped them dead in their tracks. Richard Nixon's countenance filled the screen, his face serene but solemn. "I have never been a quitter," he was saying. "To leave office before my term is completed is abhorrent to every instinct in my body. But I've decided to put the interests of America first. . . ."

Reagan and Meese cut glances at each other and edged into the room in time to hear Nixon say, "Therefore, I shall resign the presidency effective at noon tomorrow. Vice President Ford will be sworn in as president at that hour in this office."

The next day, at noon, the staff assembled in Governor Reagan's office to watch the startling events that marked the unprecedented transition. It was a sultry Sacramento afternoon, the thermometer edging into the nineties, prompting shirtsleeves to be rolled up and ties loosened. It was almost surreal watching Nixon board the presidential helicopter and, grinning bizarrely, throw a V-for-victory salute to the throng of well-wishers. "Everybody was in a state of shock," recalls Jeff Bell, then a young aide who had been recently brought in to help lay the groundwork for a possible campaign. Reagan, watching intently, was unsettled—but also outraged. "He didn't have any good feeling for Nixon's enemies," says Pete Hannaford, "whom he blamed for the whole Watergate mess." He bristled when Walter Cronkite said, "I think we ought to take Lysol and scrub out the Oval Office." Reagan's sympathies were with Jerry Ford, a man very much in the Reagan mold, a Midwesterner who had also worked his way through college washing dishes at a fraternity house and who had starred as center on the University of Michigan football team. Dutch Reagan had even broadcast a game he was in. "We've got to give this man a chance," the governor told the others. "It would be unfair to do otherwise."

A few minutes later, he read a statement from handwritten notes to a group of reporters gathered outside his office. "It is a tragedy for America that we have come to this," Reagan said, "but it does mean that the agony of many months has come to an end." In response to questions that Ford might tap him to be his vice president, he hedged, suggesting Barry Goldwater instead. But strong speculation remained in the wind. If the post was offered, he wouldn't know how to respond. Accepting it would certainly throw a curveball at his objectives. In one respect, if Ford was to be taken at his word that he would not run for reelection, it would practically assure Reagan of the nomination in '76. But if Ford decided he liked the job enough to secure his own term, it would be nearly impossible to mount a challenge. To fully gauge the implications of both outcomes, John Sears was summoned back to Sacramento for a meeting with the Nofziger Group. He instructed them to flatly refuse an offer of the vice presidency, fearing it would tie Ronald Reagan to a doomed administration. "Ford isn't up to the job," he recalls telling them. "Why go there if it doesn't fit our needs? And it doesn't matter if he ultimately decides to run. I don't think he can win an election, so I don't see much trouble in running against him."

Sears didn't anticipate that kind of offer from Ford, but a few days later the new president's counselor, Robert Hartmann, sounded out the governor on a list of men they were considering for vice president: U.S. ambassador to NATO Donald Rumsfeld, New York governor Nelson Rockefeller, and Republican National Committee chairman George H. W. Bush. Would Reagan be interested? He wasn't, but he told Hartmann halfheartedly that if the president appointed him he would faithfully serve.

Practically as soon as they hung up, Gerald Ford announced that he was appointing Nelson Rockefeller as his vice president, surprising few but angering many. Conservatives were particularly up in arms. They detested Rocky—a congressman from Maryland called him "the single most unacceptable nominee one might contemplate." Rockefeller was wealthy, he supported abortion rights, and he was from New York City, a place many conservatives viewed as the habitat of Satan.

Reagan didn't share the disapproval. "He liked Rockefeller," Meese says. "They teamed up at governors' conferences and found common ground on many policies." Though ideologically miles apart, they were both pragmatists, and in 1968 they had worked together, attempting to stop Nixon's nomination, and there had been talk of a Reagan-Rockefeller ticket to soften the conservative platform for the moderate Republican voter.

There were more consequential reasons to ⬚⬚⬚⬚⬚⬚ ⬚⬚⬚⬚ choice of a vice president. On September 8, 1⬚ ⬚⬚⬚⬚⬚⬚⬚ his presidency, he granted an unconditional ⬚⬚⬚⬚⬚⬚⬚⬚ ting off a furor on both sides of the aisle. ⬚⬚ ⬚⬚⬚⬚⬚⬚ cans wanted Nixon punished. Again, Ronald Reag⬚⬚ ⬚⬚⬚⬚⬚ "I support [Ford] in the pardon," he told reporters during ⬚⬚⬚⬚⬚⬚⬚⬚ in Louisville.

Ten days later, Ford offered amnesty to tens of thousands of V⬚⬚ era draft evaders and deserters who agreed to perform two years in publi⬚ service jobs. The backlash was swift. The American Conservative Union was especially vocal in the outrage, insisting that "Rockefeller and Ford are not conservatives." Reagan remained silent, but privately he fumed. "Those who fought and served were patriots," he maintained. "Those who refused to serve . . ." A disgusted head shake punctuated his scorn. He stopped short of calling them traitors, but his long face spoke volumes.

The economy also bedeviled Jerry Ford. This was where Ronald Reagan sought to put distance between himself and the president. The economy was in dire straits and getting worse in alarming ways. Double-digit inflation was soaring higher; interest rates approached 10 percent; unemployment was up, too. What's more, crude-oil prices had skyrocketed and gas prices had doubled at the pump, sparking a severe energy crisis. "The governor felt that the deficit and big-government activities of the Ford administration were on the wrong track," Ed Meese recalls. "And that put him off Ford more than anything else."

On October 8, 1974, during an address to a joint session of Congress on the economy, Ford displayed his brainstorm to help turn things around: a "WIN" (for "whip inflation now") button pinned to his lapel. Grinning broadly, he asked Americans to wear one proudly, joining the fight to boost his economic program. Distributing feel-good buttons with an innocuous slogan struck Reagan as silly, a public-relations gimmick. He expected more from Ford. Across the country, as he made speech after speech, Reagan sensed the administration was failing to grasp the acuteness of the crisis. All around him, during question-and-answer sessions, at receptions, in hotel lobbies, and on the street, he heard anguished laments from people struggling to make ends meet.

Still Reagan refused to signal that he was running. Supporters weren't

...er he was playing his cards close to the vest or simply hadn't yet
...his mind. In December 1975, as his second term was drawing to a
...e met for lunch with his Kitchen Cabinet and longtime staff at the
...Angeles Country Club, where the chief topic of conversation was his
...mediate future. The financial backers had invested heavily in the Rea-
...an brand, but their enthusiasm for a challenge to Gerald Ford was muted.
Henry Salvatori and David Packard were flat-out against it, and even
Holmes Tuttle expressed skepticism. "It would be ridiculous to run against
an incumbent," he told *Newsweek*. "But if Ford doesn't run, it would be a
horse of a different color." The last thing any of them wanted was a schism
in the Republican Party.

There was palpable relief, then, when Ronald Reagan laid out his program for 1975. He wanted to speak directly to voters by hitting the mashed-
potato circuit—and to make some serious money in the process. Mike
Deaver and Pete Hannaford planned to put him on the road via a public-
relations company they'd spearhead in Los Angeles. A schedule of lectures,
radio commentary, and newspaper columns promised to make Ronald Reagan a wealthy man, and keep him in the national spotlight. The plan would
afford him some much-needed breathing room. Two terms as governor of
California had taken its toll. "I think he was tired of the job," Lyn Nofziger
recalled, "tired of dealing with the petty personalities in the legislature,
tired of commuting to Los Angeles on most weekends so his wife could
socialize with her rich friends, tired of the small-town atmosphere of Sacramento." The unrelenting politics—and protests—the go-go schedule, the
tenacious press corps, the responsibility of a state's overall health and that
of its constituents weighed heavily on his psyche. He'd put all he had into
it. It made him wonder if he had what it took to be president. He revealed
reluctance, but only to his wife. Nancy made no secret she was "dying to
return to Los Angeles and a normal, private life." They'd bought a new,
688-acre ranch high in the Santa Ynez Mountains above Santa Barbara to
serve as an escape, their private sanctuary, when the speaking circuit or
even L.A. closed in and they needed to "think something out." They were
ready to leave Sacramento to the new governor, thirty-six-year-old Jerry
Brown, Reagan's polar opposite and the son of his predecessor.

On January 3, 1975, after the final day in the governor's office, Ron and
Nancy took off for their new retreat, which they dubbed Rancho del Cielo.

It was easy to become intoxicated by the grandeur of its landscape: gently sloped meadows carpeted with wildflowers that stretched across the horizon as far as the eye could see; crystal-clear streams trickling through the low-cut brush; clean, cool breezes that swept off the ocean and made the climate so delightful; a sky so blue and brilliant that one could lie in a chaise longue abutting the small adobe ranch house and stare up at it, transfixed, for hours on end. Ideally, he and Nancy would be "content to spend the rest of our lives that way."

In reality, they had a couple of days, at best.

The phones started ringing even before the ex-governor crossed the Sacramento County line. Well-wishers, businessmen dangling ventures, and the curious checked in. Among the most curious was President Gerald R. Ford, who came courting just a day into the retirement. Would the governor, he wanted to know, be interested in a Cabinet post? A few openings were coming up. One particular in Transportation had his name written all over it. Or perhaps an ambassadorship? Walter Annenberg was leaving his post at the Court of St. James. There was no finer place to spend a few years abroad. Fortunately, the president couldn't see Reagan's grin through the phone. "Hell, I can't afford to be an ambassador," he told Ford. But his mirth was directed at the president's cheek. Ford had heard the rumors about a Reagan run, knew his staff was assembling a campaign. This was an obvious scheme to neutralize him.

There was no reason to cozy up to Gerald Ford. John Sears advised Reagan against it. "You'd be joining a ship that's going down in a few months," Sears said. When the president addressed Congress and the nation on January 15, 1975, declaring "the state of the Union is not good," Reagan knew Sears was right. Disenchantment would attach itself to this administration. Besides, he had his hands full with all of the offers that his new business managers, Deaver & Hannaford, Inc., dished up.

The actor Efrem Zimbalist Jr. told Reagan about his work with a radio syndicator who hired him to do short programs about fascinating historical figures. "The producer thinks there is a market for a daily conservative commentary, and he thinks you'd be the perfect person to do it," Zimbalist said. The show was the brainchild of veteran broadcaster Harry O'Connor, who proposed a five-minute spot bracketed by commercials they'd sell to local businesses in various markets. O'Connor figured they could attract a good hundred stations. In fact, no sooner had he announced the program than 350 signed up. (The first two were no surprise: WOC in Davenport and WHO in Des Moines.) When CBS television learned of the interest, it offered a competing proposal: a weekly commentary opposite Eric Sevareid on the *CBS Evening News* with Walter Cronkite. A *national* audience—it was hard to beat. Mike Deaver pushed Reagan to consider it, but he demurred. "With radio, you don't outlive your welcome very quickly," he explained. "If people like what they hear, they'll want to hear you again tomorrow, whereas with television you run the risk of overexposing yourself." Anyway, Ronald Reagan was an old radioman at heart.

They taped the show, *Viewpoint*—fifteen episodes at a clip at Harry O'Connor's Hollywood recording studio on the eighth floor of the Taft Building on Vine Street. The space was crammed with an audience of famous friends—Art Linkletter, Jack Webb, and John Carradine, among others. Sally Cobb, who owned the Brown Derby next door, showed up with platters of smoked salmon and champagne.

Pete Hannaford had also met with Vic Krulak, a former Marine Corps general who ran Copley Press, a right-leaning newspaper syndicate based in La Jolla, whose publisher, James S. Copley, and many of his employees had reportedly spied on antiwar protesters for the FBI and cooperated covertly with the Central Intelligence Agency. Copley Press signed up a Reagan column that began appearing in early March 1975 in thirty-nine papers. Hannaford wrote most of the material based on pinpoint conservative themes, but Reagan contributed his share. "He had a restless mind," Hannaford says. "He did a lot of reading. And when he went on the road for his speaking tour, he'd come back with a stack of legal-sized yellow-ruled pages and say, 'There! Three weeks of radio spots!'"

The first few shows of *Viewpoint* hit all his favorite Republican issues—a federal bill to create a consumer protection agency (he was opposed to it), one to tie congressional paychecks to budget balancing (he favored it), the threat of worldwide communist domination, the gospel of free enterprise, and a guaranteed-income plan such as the Family Assistance Program, which he had helped to defeat during his governorship. He knew how to capture his audience's attention:

If you've had the experience of standing in the checkout line in the super-market next to a strapping young fella with a big basket of groceries who pays for them in food stamps, and you're worrying how long you'll be able to find the cash to feed your family, and you've paid your taxes, you've probably worried about the food stamp program and how it works.

Occasionally, in the flush of delivering a real zinger, he'd roll out an anecdote without checking the facts:

If you're not familiar with the term "boondoggle," consider the fact that our federal government recently underwrote the cost of a study dealing with Polish bisexual frogs. If that doesn't give you a hint, stand by, I'll be right back.

He had stockpiled this yarn almost a year earlier, when he read a column in the *Congressional Record* about a "scandal" exposed on the House floor by an outraged Idaho congressman. A little digging might have uncovered a newspaper article revealing there was no taxpayer funding involved and, in fact, the "boondoggle" was scientific research into "the lingering mysteries of genetic evolution" and how hybrids might lead to improving the efficiency of agriculture. But the broadcast drew the anticipated storm of indignation.

The radio shows and columns were good and useful, but it was the speeches, the public appearances, that truly invigorated Reagan. He'd do eight or ten a month, barnstorming into the provinces, connecting with working- and middle-class people who, for the most part, shared his conservative views. It harkened back to his General Electric plant talks, when he took the pulse of a disgruntled constituency. After a short opening statement, he would slip his notes into a jacket pocket and say, "Rather than a monologue, let's have a dialogue. Tell me what you're thinking."

For speeches to political groups, however, there was business to conduct. Conservatism was gaining strength within the Republican Party, and its advocates—many of them young activists, particularly in the South and Midwest—demanded to be heard. They'd been demoralized by the pasting Goldwater took in 1964, but Ronald Reagan restored their confidence.

They pinned their hopes on him; he was their voice. In a speech in February to the Conservative Political Action Conference in Washington, D.C., he did not disappoint. He repeated the thrust of one of his radio broadcasts, decrying how the $52 billion deficit written into President Ford's new budget proposal "abandoned his pledge of a balanced budget . . . made little more than four months ago," requiring "borrowing on a scale too colossal to comprehend." It was old-fashioned conservative religion repurposed to fire a salvo into the Oval Office. While he ducked questions about a '76 run, going after Ford reminded his audience that, should the president cater solely to the party's moderate wing, Reagan stood poised to protect their interests.

The gung-ho reaction of the CPAC audience raised talk of a possible third-party alternative built around conservative values. The concept had been advanced by the *National Review*'s publisher, William Rusher, who with a corps of true believers had been promoting a Ronald Reagan–George Wallace ticket to the Republican Party's disenchanted ranks. Wallace, the segregationist Democratic governor of Alabama, had enormous blue-collar appeal, especially among Southern whites. In the 1972 presidential primary, he had run strong in Southern states and parts of the West when his candidacy was derailed at a Laurel, Maryland, campaign stop by an attempted assassin's bullet that left him paralyzed from the waist down. Nevertheless, the attack failed to end his political ambitions. There were clear signals from Wallace aides that he eyed the 1976 election with reinvigorated determination. Strategists feared he would split the conservative vote, handing the election to a Democrat. A new Conservative Party challenge might upend the status quo and prevail. They pointed to James Buckley's shocking win in the 1970 New York senatorial election, running on the conservative ticket. He'd targeted Republicans who were alienated from the GOP's silk-stocking ranks and disenfranchised Democrats—blue-collar Catholics from the suburbs and rural districts—whose interests lay outside the two-party debate.

Could it work again, this time on a larger scale? Ronald Reagan wasn't so sure. He much preferred "a new and revitalized second party . . . making it unmistakably clear where we stand on all of the issues troubling the people." And running with George Wallace? He found many of the governor's far-right-wing views repugnant. Despite Wallace's conservative appeal, there was little crossover in their ideologies. Wallace practiced the politics of negativism, with little or no interest in foreign policy. "We're completely different on a lot of issues, especially economics," Reagan said. Alabama's finances were a mess, and the state ranked dead last in public education.

The Kitchen Cabinet was also dead set against a third-party run. Holmes Tuttle had admonished Reagan: "You're a Republican—and you're going to stay one."

Still, Bill Rusher attempted to convince him that a third-party run was in his best interests. "He'd come out and visit us every few months," recalls Pete Hannaford, "begging Reagan to throw his hat in the ring as an independent." The Republican Party was dead, Rusher insisted, decimated by Watergate and moderates. He even recruited Jesse Helms to exert a little pressure, along with hard-core conservatives on the Reagan staff led by Lyn Nofziger and Jeffrey Bell. "I thought the party was in such bad shape that we should consign the Republicans to the ash heap of history and start over, with Reagan," says Bell, who was stationed in Washington with Nofziger and John Sears.

Sears put a stop to such talk. He knew third parties, historically, were doomed to failure, and they would never win an election "if voters saw Reagan as a Republican version of George Wallace." His biggest ally was Nancy Reagan who, Sears said, "would never stand for it" and made herself perfectly clear on that point. Eventually, Sears had Reagan put it to Rusher unequivocally. "If I were to run for president," he told him, "I intend to do it as a Republican."

If I were to run. He refused to commit himself. The evasion grew tiresome to those such as Sears and Nofziger who were "unofficially" conducting a Reagan shadow campaign, and it scared off potential top-notch staff. "He's running," Mike Deaver insisted as early as 1973 to anyone who would listen, but no official statement came from the perennial non-candidate.

The only place this waffling registered as a facade was in the Oval Office, where Gerald Ford viewed Reagan as a serious threat. It was an unspoken fact that Ford was running. He hadn't officially declared, but throughout the spring of 1975 his administration began to gain traction, with public opinion gently swinging his way. That old promise he'd made not to run was meaningless—it wouldn't stick. He'd grown into the job, and it suited him. What's more, the urge to win a full presidential term on his own was too tempting to ignore. As a formality, he notified the Federal Election Commission, authorizing supporters to raise money on his behalf. An incumbent deserved his party's nomination. Illinois senator Charles Percy was making noise about a possible challenge, but Ford knew that if there was a challenge from within the party, it would come from Reagan.

Ronald Reagan posed a threat he took very seriously. Ford had tried buying him off in January with the bogus Cabinet post offer. Now, in late February, he dispatched Paul Haerle, Reagan's former appointments secretary, to persuade his old boss to back off. And by March, Ford's aides and colleagues, led by Pennsylvania senator Hugh Scott, began circulating a document on Capitol Hill that some were calling a "loyalty oath"—a pledge to support Gerald Ford and his vice-presidential running mate (no mention was made of Nelson Rockefeller) for the Republican nomination in 1976. Astonishingly, it worked. It was signed by 113 of 145 GOP congressmen and 31 of the party's 38 senators in three days.

One rebel who refused to sign was Nevada senator Paul Laxalt. Reagan and Laxalt practiced mutual admiration that stretched back to their days as governors of adjoining states with common interests. They'd joined forces on half a dozen different compatible states issues—and, as things shaped up, they were joining again. Laxalt teamed up with the old Nofziger Group, now relocated to Los Angeles (and calling itself the Madison Group, or M Group, after Reagan's hotel of choice in Washington) and devoting itself expressly to a Reagan for President movement. "John Sears proposed pitching Laxalt to head the exploratory committee," recalls Charlie Black, a young aide from North Carolina whom Sears had recruited to assist him. At first, Laxalt expressed reluctance, but Sears turned up the heat. "Paul was a respected senator, good-looking, presentable—he had credibility," Sears says. Above all, Sears didn't want Jesse Helms dominating their spotlight. Helms, an early Reagan presidential advocate, was a conservative firebrand whose strident, often racially charged rhetoric placed him "to the right of Genghis Khan." He was a rabid third-party crusader who opposed civil rights, feminism, gay rights, disability rights, affirmative action, abortion, and the National Endowment for the Arts. "That was too much damn baggage," Sears says in retrospect. Laxalt, though every bit a conservative, was more pragmatic when it came to hot-button issues. He knew how to navigate the delicate ideological landscape without alienating the Republican base. Laxalt agreed to be the campaign's front man, he said, if he had assurances that Reagan would actually run.

Sears guaranteed him that Reagan was in the race—and in it to win—but could not announce for financial reasons. Due to Federal Election Commission laws, a person could not ask anyone for so much as a nickel without declaring his candidacy within thirty days. If he did not formally declare, Reagan could continue profiting from his lucrative radio and newspaper venues without triggering the commission's provision allocating equal media access to candidates for public office. There was no way he'd agree to abandon an enterprise that was bringing in a cool $800,000 that year. Still, Sears explained, they needed to launch a campaign committee to raise money right away in order not to fall behind Jerry Ford and his supporters. But—how to do that without violating the election laws?

Sears and a volunteer lawyer named Lawrence Smith studied the FEC laws, which they felt were murky, and came up with a dodge. They would announce the formation of a Citizens for Reagan committee, with a codicil—a convoluted letter from Ronald Reagan to Paul Laxalt affirming that he hadn't yet made up his mind to seek the nomination and wasn't endorsing the committee, but if he did eventually run, this committee would represent him. It was a dubious ploy. Sears admits the letter did not reflect the intention of those who wrote the election laws, but if it worked they were in business. In fact, the only pushback came from members of the press who demanded to know under what authority they acted. "We told them we had *a legal opinion*," Sears recalls, "and they bought it. We didn't tell them that it was Smith's and my opinion, but what they didn't know wouldn't hurt them."

Citizens for Reagan officially opened its doors on July 15, 1975. Paul Laxalt made the announcement at a press conference in Washington, at which he assured those in attendance that Ronald Reagan, at this time, was *not* running for office. "The purpose of this committee," he said, "is to build an organization and raise the money necessary to conduct a viable and effective campaign once Governor Reagan decides to become an active candidate." He was cautious not to attack Jerry Ford or any of his policies. "There was nothing that Ford was particularly vulnerable about," says Sears, who wrote Laxalt's speech. "He's the commander in chief. If you criticized him you're seen as being anti-American. But hidden in our strategy was the perception that Ford wasn't up to the job." To that end, he instructed Laxalt to say, "It's not that we think President Ford is doing a bad job. It's that we think Ronald Reagan can do a better job."

In effect, they had thrown down the gauntlet. The announcement was a clear signal to the Ford camp that Ronald Reagan would challenge him for the Republican nomination in 1976. Both camps sensed a deepening fissure in the party between the moderate-liberal faction and the conservative-right wing. If that splintered their constituency, the election could very well slip to a Democrat.

On September 5, 1975, President Ford flew *Air Force One* to Sacramento, presumably to speak to the California legislature on the success of détente in the Middle East and the "truly alarming increase of violent crime throughout this country." Keen political observers saw it as an incursion onto Reagan turf as a way of asserting his influence. Ford warmed up, delivering a breakfast address to the local Chamber of Commerce, then walked a few blocks to the capitol, shaking hands with a small crowd that had gathered to cheer his arrival. As the clock struck ten, a tiny woman in a red gown and turban—later identified as Lynette "Squeaky" Fromme, one of the Charles Manson "family" disciples—drew a .45 Army Colt from a leg holster and aimed it at President Ford. By a stroke of luck the gun failed to discharge. As Fromme was led away by a Secret Service agent, she shouted, "This country is a mess! The man is not your president!"

Almost as if in defiance of fate, Ford traveled to New Hampshire six days later on behalf of Louis Wyman, a Republican running for Congress, and worked the rope lines, shaking hands and kissing babies, going straight from Reagan's stronghold to the scene of the first Republican presidential primary, five months away.

Ford drew encouragement from the crowds—and from the press that covered his barnstorming through the state. James Reston, reporting on the president's reception for the *New York Times*, observed, "The notion that Ronald Reagan can get the presidential nomination is patently ridiculous unless you suspect the Republicans of suicidal tendencies."

But Ford wasn't the only aspirant to take heart from New Hampshire. Not to be outflanked, Reagan swooped into the state on the heels of Ford's departure, also stumping for Louis Wyman. Aides described the scenes along the tour as "a lovefest" packed with crowds "who cheered themselves hoarse for Reagan," attracting commentary that seemed to countermand the *Times'* harsh appraisal. "The universal, high-octane contempt for all politicians somehow stops short of California's former governor," Mary Mc-Grory wrote in the *Washington Post*. "He is perceived as a man of common sense who understands common people, especially New Hampshire retirees who turn purple as they talk of 'all the money Congress voted itself before they sneaked off on vacation.'"

The trip to New Hampshire produced other favorable consequences for the Reagan team. While there, Sears and Jim Lake detoured through the provinces to get the lay of the land. One of their first stops included a visit with Meldrim Thomson, the state's popular governor, who had been encouraging Ronald Reagan to run for president. "He was a hard-right-wing guy, regarded as a wacko, who people called Crazy Mel, but he was determined that Reagan should be president, so he was *our* wacko," Lake says. Thomson offered them a primer on how to approach the state and supplied letters of introduction to other highly regarded Republican legislators. He also recommended that they talk to Hugh Gregg, the former governor and Rockefeller Republican, who seemed like an ideal candidate to serve as their state chairman.

Sears and Lake made a beeline to Nashua, where Gregg received them with suspicion. "He was a crusty guy, salt-of-the-earth, opinionated and out-spoken," Lake says, "but John and I both liked him." Gregg was as prominent in New Hampshire as its "Live Free or Die" license plates. He came from a family of inherited wealth, with business and banking interests, and ran a prosperous furniture-manufacturing operation in Canada. Sears knew Gregg from the '67 campaign with Nixon and also knew that the Ford campaign had courted him but made no concrete offer. Over a three-hour conversation and subsequent phone calls, Sears persuaded Gregg to accept the Reagan state chairmanship. "Once we got Gregg," Sears says, "the press, who had been looking at us as a right-wing trip going nowhere, turned around and started trying to figure out what was wrong with Gerald Ford."

The New Hampshire dominoes began to fall Reagan's way. With Mel

Thomson and Hugh Gregg aboard, Sears and Lake dropped in on William Loeb, the publisher of the *Manchester Union Leader*, the most influential newspaper in the state. "He was another very conservative, outspoken guy, an independent tough cuss," says Lake, "who immediately decided to back Ronald Reagan." Loeb was a key addition. He was a noted kingmaker with a powerful public apparatus who believed that Reagan conservatives, no matter how far they leaned to the right, had to come across as being entirely rational. He was also essential to John Sears's strategy. Loeb was perhaps the one local individual with the ability to keep Governor Mel Thomson in check. "His heart is in the right place," Sears told Loeb, "but he is a loose cannon who says and does stupid things." Sears knew nobody could control Thomson. He was the guy who had threatened to send the National Guard into Maine over a minor fishing dispute, and many tagged him as "a racist." Thomson had his heart set on being Reagan's state chairman, and when he discovered Hugh Gregg got the nod instead Sears knew "he was bound to go apeshit." As a precaution, he charged Loeb with keeping a lid on Thomson, and the publisher readily stepped up to the task.

All the right elements were falling into place, except for one. "I could not get Reagan to say he would run," Sears recalls. "He *wanted* to, I was sure of that. But I got the impression he didn't know *how*." He continued to trot out the old adages, such as "the office seeks the man" and "if it's the will of the people, it will be," which frustrated Sears no end. The press continued to hound him about Reagan's intention, to which he typically responded, "If it looks like a duck and it quacks like a duck—it's a duck." Tom Reed had warned Sears he'd never get Reagan to agree to run. Even when Jerry Ford announced his candidacy on July 8, 1975, Reagan remained noncommittal. Eventually, Sears came to realize that deep down his candidate was inherently an actor accustomed to taking direction. It was "out of order" to ask him whether he was running or not, Sears decided. The actor needed a director to call the shots.

"Finally, I took him aside," Sears recalls, "and said, 'We're going to announce in November.' I handed him the draft of a speech and said, 'Look it over, add to it, rehearse the hell out of it, because you'll be using it to declare you are in the race.' He didn't say no, so we went ahead."

Ronald Reagan was ready to hit his mark.

CHAPTER TWENTY-SEVEN

"MOMENTUM"

"It's been said that if you put Ford and me together
in a dark room you can't tell us apart philosophically.
Well, if you turn on the light, you can."

—RONALD REAGAN

By November 20, 1975, when Ronald Reagan announced his candidacy for the Republican nomination at the National Press Club in Washington, D.C., the battle lines had been pretty well drawn. No other party member had stepped up to challenge the sitting president. It boiled down to Ford and Reagan, head-to-head, or as former Texas governor John Connally predicted: "a horse race."

The favorite had not yet emerged. Both candidates presented pros and cons, but the outsider aspect carried an appreciable prejudice. Many in the party—many in Reagan's inner circle, in fact—were not inclined to bless the undertaking. Henry Salvatori, one of the original Kitchen Cabinet financiers and a Ford confederate, considered it heretical to go against the GOP's man in the White House. He was having none of it, and tried to sway others to decamp. The same was true of Leonard Firestone and David Packard, who, according to Ed Meese, "stomped out of a strategy meeting at the Reagans' home," never to return to the fold. (Packard later became finance chairman of the Ford campaign.) Other prominent politicians made their displeasure known. The night before Reagan's announcement, Charles Percy expressed regret that "his candidacy would lead to a crushing defeat for the Republican Party in 1976." But no one registered his disappointment as crisply as the recipient of a phone call Reagan made that same evening from his suite at the Madison Hotel.

As a matter of courtesy, he placed a call to the Oval Office to inform Gerald Ford of his imminent announcement. The president's response was brief and brusque. "Well, Governor, I'm very disappointed," he replied. "I'm sorry you're getting into this. Regardless of your good intentions, your bid is bound to be divisive." How can you challenge an incumbent president of your own party and *not* be divisive? Ford wondered. "It will take a lot of money, a lot of effort, and it will leave a lot of scars."

Ford already had enough scars on his presidential résumé. His wife, Betty, an independent-minded First Lady, had veered off the reservation in an August 1975 TV interview with *60 Minutes* by acknowledging her support for the Supreme Court's legalization of abortion, condoning experimentation with marijuana, and suggesting that premarital sex might go toward reducing the country's divorce rate. Although some found her candor refreshing, attacks were swift and nonpartisan, with religious leaders across the spectrum feeding the outcry. Ford refused to criticize his wife's views, and the damage was felt. Only weeks later, his administration plunged further into disarray when he replaced his secretary of defense, James Schlesinger, with Donald Rumsfeld and dismissed William Colby, the director of the Central Intelligence Agency, in favor of George H. W. Bush. Soon afterward, Rogers Morton, the secretary of commerce, announced his imminent resignation. If a Cabinet shuffle didn't signal internal chaos, on November 3, 1975, Vice President Nelson Rockefeller added his two cents by sending Ford a letter: "After much thought, I have decided further that I do not wish my name to enter into your consideration for the upcoming Republican Vice Presidential nominee."

Rockefeller's departure—perceived as a rift, but more like a banishment— offered a blessing in disguise. For months, he'd been regarded as a liability by Ford strategists, who sensed growing discontent with him from the conservative faction of the party. Had Rockefeller remained as a running mate, there was every indication their loyalties might shift to Ronald Reagan instead. Even the *New York Times* saw merit in Rockefeller's withdrawal, noting that "his presence had become detrimental to Mr. Ford's efforts to win the Republican Party nomination." Aides suggested that holding an "open convention" to resolve the matter of a vice president would appease all sectors of the party. Still, it portrayed the Ford administration as coming apart at the seams.

Going on defense, Ford enlisted Reagan's old gun for hire, Stu Spencer, to serve as political director of his campaign. Snatching Spencer away from the opposition was a strong move, inasmuch as Spencer had designed Ronald Reagan's gubernatorial playbook and felt he knew how to counter it. "Unfortunately," Spencer says, "I was walking into a rat's nest." Donald Rumsfeld was busy consolidating power, which was creating turmoil in the Ford ranks.

Spencer knew what he was up against. One scene summed it up. He had attended a Reagan speech outside Cleveland's City Hall with fifty thousand spectators spread across the mall. "I was sitting in front of the stage with Ohio governor Jim Rhodes and Art Model, who owned the Cleveland Browns. We could see Reagan resting at the back behind a drape, looking almost lost on that giant platform." When he was announced, Spencer recalls, Reagan got up and appeared to be dwarfed by his surroundings. "As he strode to the podium, he looked this big," Spencer says, holding his thumb and forefinger an inch apart. "But he flashed that great Hollywood smile, and started growing right before my eyes, and by the time he got to the microphone, *he'd become the president.*"

Image—it won elections. Jerry Ford exuded a "Mr. Nice Guy image," which played well on the surface. But there was plenty of show business in politics, and Stu Spencer had witnessed how Ronald Reagan used its gloss to his great advantage. *Newsweek* pointed to his crackerjack delivery and "Cinerama grin," and how "he plays Presidential politics as if it were a remake of *Mr. Smith Goes to Washington.*"

Reagan's appeal was immediately apparent. Early polls splashed cold water in the face of Ford's campaign. A Gallup poll in mid-October had given the president a lead of 58 percent to 36 percent, but the margin was shrinking by the day as ground forces mobilized. "Polls show the President to be vulnerable," a newsweekly reported. The first real test would come in the New Hampshire primary, on February 24, 1976, which would serve to determine how the candidates were popularly perceived, if not as a referendum on moderate-versus-conservative Republicanism. Republicans in the state leaned sharply to the right—the *Boston Globe* called New Hampshire "one of the most conservative states outside the South"—but they were skeptical of slick outsiders. Many felt they owed allegiance to a sitting president. Both camps recognized that New Hampshire was pivotal to their success. Among the Ford team, Stu Spencer says, "I was the only guy who knew that if we lost New Hampshire we were dead."

John Sears regarded the state as a rocket launch.

"New Hampshire would establish the momentum," he recalls. "Momentum, says Charlie Black, "was his knockout strategy, his vision of how the whole thing was going to work." It was simple: if you won in New Hampshire, then you've got the momentum to win in Florida, the second primary on the calendar, and if that happens and you have the momentum going into Illinois, "then Ford is out of the race." Momentum, Sears believed, was a force you couldn't stop. His motto was: Politics is motion. "You are never standing still, so if you're not moving forward"—that is, if you don't have the momentum—"look out, because the other guy is."

Momentum was established early. On Ronald Reagan's first visit to the state as an official candidate, Hugh Gregg had laid the groundwork for getting a grassroots organization firmly in place. The Ford people lagged seriously behind. Sears also gave thrust to his strategy by announcing the selection of town chairmen for the campaign in all 278 municipalities in New Hampshire—the first time that had ever been attempted. The news coverage that followed was plentiful and all positive.

Meanwhile, the candidate was creating his own good first impression. In Manchester, at a jam-packed town meeting—a forum Ronald Reagan relished for its casual, spontaneous nature, where he could field questions, be more facile interacting with the public, and come across as one of them—the reception verged on the idolatrous. He mixed his talking points with homespun anecdotes and aimed a few well-placed zingers at his establishment opponent. Watching from the wings, John Sears and Jim Lake delighted in Reagan's comfort level, the way he handled the crowd and their questions. "He was a natural, he loved this part of it," both men recall identically in separate interviews. Interacting with people was essential to humanizing him. If he kept this up for the next few months, they felt certain of putting New Hampshire in their win column.

tu Spencer wasn't buying it. He was very familiar with Ronald Reagan's outsize charm and saw it as a smoke screen for his lack of substance, among other vulnerabilities. Spencer also recognized that the president had to counterpunch—and fast. "I was scared to death of New Hampshire," he admits. "I knew Reagan was ready [as a candidate] and worried that he was a threat to Ford."

Spencer had a plan. He would turn a speech of Reagan's into political dynamite.

Back in October, a reporter for the *Chicago Tribune* had walked into Spencer's office with a copy of an article he'd written about the speech Reagan delivered to the Chicago Executives Club. It was called "Let the People Rule" and laid out a radical plan for decentralization, returning government programs like Medicaid, housing, education, and welfare to the states, while providing for a 23 percent income-tax cut. John Sears had ordered up the speech to budge Ronald Reagan off his standard script. "He was still harping on the woman who was a welfare cheat and the communist threat and taxes," Sears says. Those topics no longer had the same impact. Instead, he directed Jeffrey Bell to come up with something more than a critique of big government, something that showed "a vision of the future."

The Reagan campaign had issued a press release immediately afterward, containing a transcript of the speech along with an itemized list of programs marked for reversion. All told, it eliminated a whopping $90 billion at the federal level, putting more onus on the states. No one so much as raised an eyebrow at the time the speech was delivered. "The press treated the whole thing with a yawn," according to Pete Hannaford. But Stu Spencer read the details a month later and got what he called "that tickly feeling" telling him something was seriously wrong with the bill of particulars. "They didn't add up," he says, and he instructed an aide to "run the numbers."

Even Jeff Bell, the author of the speech, admits the arithmetic was out of whack. "It wasn't well-designed," he concedes years later. "There were too many uncertainties involved. I'd gotten a little ahead of myself, and that gave the Ford campaign a huge target to attack."

Stu Spencer was ready the next time Reagan appeared in New Hampshire. On January 12, 1976, with the primary just a month and a half away and a Gallup poll showing him dead even with Ford, Ronald Reagan barreled back into the state on a four-day visit, intending to stump from town to town. It was a frigid winter's morning when he landed at the airport in Manchester, where Spencer was lying in wait. "Earlier that day, every reporter who covered the campaign, both in Washington and New Hampshire, got a copy of the $90 billion speech at exactly the same time," Spencer recalls with uncontained glee. "The minute Reagan disembarked and held an impromptu press conference, they nailed his ass."

To say the candidate was blindsided would be an understatement. Bombarded by questions referring to *the speech . . . the speech . . . the speech,* he was momentarily at a loss to respond. *What speech were they talking about?* When it finally dawned on him, it was too late. Unprepared with answers, he stumbled trying to defend the details. When reporters asked, "You say you can save ninety billion dollars—*how?*," the proper answer would have been, "I'll get back to you on it." But Reagan attempted to rationalize the sums, which only made his calculations sound worse. By the time he arrived at his first campaign stop, the speech had blown a hole in his campaign balloon.

Geographically, New Hampshire poses problems for the best political candidates. Because there are few large cities and so many small towns, most campaigning is done on a stump basis, where you gather in a local living room or in front of a store hoping to attract a decent crowd, talk to people for two or three minutes, and then open the session up to their questions. Ronald Reagan loved that setting, and he normally thrived in such situations. But the $90 billion speech cramped his style.

"We spent four days talking about that damned ninety billion dollars," recalls Jim Lake, "and it undercut our momentum something fierce."

With a little help from Stu Spencer's staff, the transfer of federal programs like Medicaid and food stamps sounded to wary New Hampshirites like "throwing elderly people out in the snow." In the past Reagan had talked about making Social Security voluntary. Did he intend to cut off their Social Security? What did he mean, they wanted to know, by saving $2.7 billion for the cost of air traffic control or by putting $2 billion earmarked for military pensions on a contributory basis? Why did he seek to cut funds from a national treasure like the Coast Guard? An even more controversial element was the price of decentralization. New Hampshire had neither a state income tax nor a sales tax. "If you send these programs back to the states," people argued, "it will mean enacting new tax structures." These issues pursued him from town to town.

Eventually, Ronald Reagan threw his hands up in surrender. "I guess I made a mistake," he admitted.

It didn't matter. The speech continued to haunt him. The only way to neutralize it, his handlers decided, was to run him ragged, blanketing the state so that people got a chance to experience the Reagan magic. In one forty-eight-hour stretch alone, he appeared in twenty-two rural communities, holding "citizens' press conferences" in places like banks, schools, and grocery stores. No hand was too remote to shake, no Instamatic too bothersome to pose for. Reagan was determined to work the state as if he owned it. John Sears told him, "We win New Hampshire, it's all over."

The same might be true if he ran a close second. No one had to remind him of the results of the 1968 primary, when Eugene McCarthy lost to Lyndon Johnson, the incumbent, by a slim 6 percent, virtually forcing Johnson to withdraw from the race. If Reagan polled between 40 and 45 percent of the 1976 vote, it was said, he could claim a moral victory.

That outlook sounded reasonable as a strategy and, for the most part, seemed to be working. Toward the end of January, aides told Reagan privately that he was polling ahead of the president by as much as 8 percent. Gerald Ford was nowhere to be seen in New Hampshire, and his presidency generated little enthusiasm. Over the course of the next few weeks, momentum began swinging back Ronald Reagan's way. His constant presence contributed mightily to the shift, but his message also began to resonate with voters. Instead of sticking to general political topics like taxes and foreign policy, he pounded out populist themes that struck at simmering resentments. Abortion "on demand," he stated, was snowballing to indulge "the inconvenience of the unwed mother." He blasted subsidized housing projects in New York City, where "if you are a slum dweller you can get an apartment with 11-foot ceilings, with a 20-foot balcony, a swimming pool and gymnasium, laundry room and play room, and the rent begins at $113.20, and that includes utilities." And he trotted out his old standby, the welfare queen, dredging up a woman in Chicago he claimed "has 80 names,

30 addresses, 12 Social Security cards and is collecting veterans' benefits on four non-existing deceased husbands," netting her "tax-free cash income of over $150,000."

He based these anecdotes largely on stories he'd read in unverified accounts in small-town newspapers and crackpot magazines. It didn't matter that most of the facts and figures didn't check out. They stuck where it mattered: in the craw of hardworking taxpayers who felt cheated by so-called government entitlements. John Sears grew concerned that these yarns of Reagan's might come back to haunt him. "He devoted hours to reading letters that people wrote," Sears recalls, "and would pick some awful stuff out of them that found their way into his speeches." Once, off the cuff, Reagan announced there was more oil in Alaska than in Saudi Arabia. "Someone wrote that to him and he took it for fact." Another person wrote him that the best way to get rid of atomic waste was forming it into golf-ball-sized projectiles and launching them into the ocean. When Reagan ran it past Sears to get his reaction, his campaign manager suggested they "save that one for later."

No one would have raised an eyebrow had Ronald Reagan read the briefing books his staff had prepared. Sears had introduced the briefing-book model in the 1968 election—comprehensive analyses of every imaginable topic, written by political heavyweights William Safire, Richard Allen, Martin Anderson, Pat Buchanan, and Alan Greenspan, among others—so that Richard Nixon not only knew the issues inside and out, but had the answers at his fingertips to any question ever asked by a reporter. The books were indispensable tools in confrontations with the media, especially when trying to defend a complex proposal, but Sears couldn't persuade his candidate to read them. "Reagan wouldn't do the homework," says Jeff Bell, a contributor to the 1976 books. "He had a framework that enabled him to answer questions, even when he didn't know much about the details." Occasionally that backfired, but more often than not Ronald Reagan came through convincingly on the strength of his storytelling talent and charisma.

An issue he orchestrated to his advantage was the notion that the Panama Canal, governed by the United States, would be slipping out of American control when the treaty with Panama expired. Jesse Helms had brought it to his attention during a campaign swing in Charlotte, insisting "there are secret talks going on about giving away the Panama Canal." Reagan looked it up in *Human Events*, the ultraconservative publication he read every week, and found all the evidence he needed to confirm his suspicions that little good could come of returning the canal to Panama with its current leader, Omar Torrijos. He told audience after audience: "We bought it, we paid for it, it's ours—and we aren't going to give it away to some tinhorn dictator." The first time he used the line, in a speech to a retirement community in Sun City, Florida, "it brought the house down," says David Keene. "Reagan was so taken aback that he momentarily lost his place, but you could see the wheels turning. Here was an issue, relevant or not, that tapped into the public's frustration about our misguided foreign policy. The way in which he presented it fired up their patriotism."

Subsequently, in one of his radio addresses, Reagan indicted Ford's secretary of state, Henry Kissinger, as the architect of the secret canal giveaway and implied it would lead to Americans having "all their mail monitored" by Panama's intelligence agency. And, now in New Hampshire, he poured it on, complaining that "our government had maintained a mouselike silence. . . . I don't understand how the State Department can suggest we pay blackmail to this dictator, for blackmail is what it is."

A bortion, subsidized housing, welfare, the Panama Canal—these issues, substantive or not, galvanized Republican conservative audiences. And when Ronald Reagan presented them in his inimitable way, they took on a kind of righteous quality. No one could stir up sympathies with as much seeming integrity or sensitivity. On a stage or standing in a small-town living room, he was a dominant, commanding figure, handsome, larger-than-life, and as polished and persuasive a speaker as politics had ever encountered. Even at sixty-five, with crow's-feet tugging at the corners of his eyes and the hint of a crêpey chin below a well-chiseled jaw, he came across in person as glamorous and elegant, a tall, strapping man with dark, fashionably styled hair and a ruddy California tan. A personality, but also a flawless orator. The well-modulated delivery he employed to emphasize his viewpoints—a synthesis of tones learned from veteran radio announcers and Warner Bros. vocal coaches—infused his speeches with dramatic intensity. He could segue from earnest to comic to indignant to authoritative as seamlessly as major-league infielders executing a triple play. He knew which tone to use when, how to achieve the maximum effect, and when a hand gesture like the pounding of a fist, the jabbing of a finger, or the swiping at an imaginary tear put the finishing touch on an emphatic point. Most times, in front of a sizable audience or at rallies, he spoke using a packet of his trusty four-by-six index cards full of hieroglyphics that steered him through the topical maze, but on the stump in New Hampshire aides suggested he slide the cards into a jacket pocket and instead "speak from the heart." On those occasions, he'd glance around the intimate gatherings, from face to face—at folks who resembled the Midwesterners he'd grown up with—leaving people with the impression he spoke directly to them. An instant rapport was established. And word began to spread across the state that Ronald Reagan was a man of the people.

John Sears noted how this was getting through to voters and decided to increase the number of meet-and-greets as a way of differentiating his candidate from the imperial president. The pace was grueling—but suited to a man whose increasingly confident staff sensed he was headed toward victory. "I worked Reagan hard in New Hampshire," Sears says, "long, fourteen-hour days for two weeks at a time, after which he needed a break." Nancy Reagan, who guarded her husband's stamina as if it were as rare and fragile as a Fabergé egg, was dispatched by Sears to make her own campaign appearances. "We'd create an event for her," Jim Lake says. "That way, John could handle him as he wished when she wasn't around." Otherwise, she never interfered with Sears or his strategy. Her only input toward scheduling was dictated by her reliance on astrology. She advised Sears that some days might be more advantageous than others for Reagan. "If I told you which ones were good days, would that be helpful?" she wondered. Sears recalls that she would phone him every so often to say, "Wednesday is a good day." Not that it mattered to him in the overall scheme of things. "We were always doing things on Wednesdays," he says with a shrug. "So she couldn't complain—and neither could I."

There were still too many hurdles to overcome to worry about Ronald Reagan's horoscope. As the campaign approached its first genuine test, on February 24, 1976, Sears kept an eye trained on the Democratic caucuses that were playing out halfway across the country in Iowa. For all intents and purposes, the New Hampshire primary was regarded as the first real gauge of the national pulse, but a slate of Democratic hopefuls had edged into Iowa, expecting that its early-January caucuses might provide an indication of who would catch on.

Ted Kennedy, long seen as the "inevitable" nominee, had taken his name out of contention in 1974, throwing the Democratic race wide open. In the intervening months, other candidates started to surface, chief among them Arizona congressman Morris K. Udall; former governor Terry Sanford of North Carolina; former senator Fred Harris of Oklahoma; Sargent Shriver, Ted Kennedy's brother-in-law; Idaho senator Frank Church; Senator Lloyd Bentsen of Texas; and George Wallace, the far-right Democrat who had the fringe vote all to himself. Washington senator Henry "Scoop" Jackson, a recognized front-runner with strong foreign-policy experience and an enormous war chest, decided to skip the Iowa caucuses and New Hampshire primary, which John Sears considered a foolish call, and it was ultimately fatal. Eyeing a possible challenger in the general election, Sears watched the action with great interest to see who would emerge from a crowded field.

No one—not even a hardened oddsmaker like Sears—imagined a longer shot or a darker horse than the one-term former Georgia governor Jimmy Carter. Sears admits freely, "I'd never heard of him." Carter, an energetic and determined campaigner, had zeroed in on Iowa, where he'd been stockpiling local coverage and goodwill for the better part of two years. Iowans took to his warm, personable style—one reporter called it "a kind of soft-sell evangelism"—that cut across the ideological divide. "I want a government," he told audiences, "that is as good, and honest, and decent, and truthful, and fair, and competent, and idealistic, and compassionate, and as filled with love as are the American people." Especially after the sour taste of the Nixon era, it was a hard credo to refuse coming from Jimmy—*Jimmy*—which he encouraged everyone to call him, putting his candidacy on a first-name basis. Potential voters who weren't at home when he knocked on their doors often found a note wedged in a crack that said, "Just stopped by to say hello. Jimmy." On January 25, 1976, Carter had staged an upset, emerging with a clear-cut victory in Iowa.

And John Sears knew that gave the dark horse *momentum*.

Momentum seemed to be on Ronald Reagan's side. As January drew to a close, polls showed him edging past Ford in New Hampshire, which shifted attention to the next major primary in Florida, on March 9.* A decisive win on February 24 would put Florida in play, where sixty-six delegates to the convention were at stake.

But momentum was a fickle thing. With days to go, both candidates made a final push through New Hampshire to move the needle to their advantage. The Reagan strategy designed by Hugh Gregg was to work their man hard the last week, doubling back through Manchester, Concord, and Nashua, then send him on to campaign in Illinois (including a visit to Tampico) the last three days before the primary, allowing his volunteers to get out the vote. It sounded good as strategies went, but in practice it proved their eventual undoing.

Things started to unravel very quickly. The moment Reagan left the state, Ford swooped in. Until that time, his staff had employed the Rose Garden strategy: polling showed them that, on the stump, Ford wasn't connecting with voters; when he stayed in the White House, appearing presidential, his numbers shot up. But in the final days before the primary, the campaign decided to turn him loose. "There is power in the presidency," Stu Spencer recalls thinking, "and it was time to put it to use." One of the powers at his disposal was *Air Force One*. "You fly it in and people drag their kids and grandkids out to see it, no matter who they're supporting in the primary." When the president landed in Keene, New Hampshire, where the short runway could barely support the plane, it seemed like half the state turned out to see it. An added attraction featured a firsthand glimpse of *the President of the United States*. Almost immediately, Ford began making up the difference in percentage, as the Reagan numbers began leveling out. Statistically, the race was a toss-up.

Governor Mel Thomson provided another chink in the machinery. The campaign had done a pretty good job of isolating him from the press lest he do or say something outlandish that sabotaged its efforts. But during

---

* Massachusetts and Vermont held primaries on March 2, 1976, but neither Reagan nor Ford campaigned in either state.

Reagan's last visit to New Hampshire, the candidate announced, "I want Mel Thomson on board. He is my friend, he's been good to me, and this is his state." So against everyone's better instincts, Thomson rode the bus with Ronald Reagan as they cruised through Manchester and surrounding communities. During the tour, word filtered through the ranks that private polling showed Reagan winning the primary by ten or fifteen points. Lyn Nofziger, in another lapse of discretion, shared the information with Thomson, who immediately reported it to the press. "It was a complete disaster," says Jim Lake, who had been running the state campaign. "We lost the overwhelming surge of Reagan volunteers—they sat out the last push because the papers assured them we were going to win. And on top of everything else, Reagan was in Illinois, nowhere to be seen."

On Election Day, Ronald Reagan and the senior staff crammed into two suites of the Highway Hotel, a stately but ramshackle old warhorse in downtown Concord, to await the returns. A bucket of chilled bottles of Almadén Blanc de Blancs bubbly sat in a corner for the anticipated celebration only hours away. "Everyone was in high spirits," recalls Jim Lake. "Dick Wirthlin, our polling guru, had done overnight tracking that showed we were going to win." Even Reagan himself predicted victory, a practice he'd avoided in the past so as not to jinx his chances.

Once the polls closed, the count started coming in fast. By ten o'clock, with the small towns reporting, Ford clung to a slim lead, but it seesawed—a hundred votes here, a couple hundred there. Lake confronted John Sears sometime later and asked, "What's going on?" The unflappable campaign manager replied, "Not looking good. The data coming in from key precincts is way too close. There is no ten- or fifteen-point victory in what I'm seeing." Charlie Black, who had joined them in the suite, says, "We were still holding out hope until about midnight, at which point we were down by about two hundred votes, but by two in the morning, Ford's lead built to eight hundred or nine hundred votes, so we knew we had lost." The mood turned grim.

"And what is worse," Black says, "Ford now had the momentum."

That was an understatement. Reagan had been six points behind in Florida before the New Hampshire primary. Two days afterward, his standing plummeted another thirteen points. Sears cautioned the staff "to *act* like we're ahead," but it was a struggle. Even David Keene, who was running Florida and North Carolina for the campaign, took a look at the landscape and thought, "We could never come back."

Ronald Reagan had damaged his chances in Florida by earlier musing that Social Security might be better served if it was voluntary, not mandatory, or that its funds should be invested in the stock market in order to profit from "the industrial might of America." He never actually *advocated* those changes, but in a state where a third of its population were retirees who depended on Social Security for subsistence, it reverberated. And the Ford campaign fanned it like a fire. "They made Reagan sound like a radical," says Charlie Black. A poll conducted in January showed Ford beating Reagan in Florida by three-to-one among Republican voters, 37 percent of whom were over the age of sixty-five. Another poll gave Reagan higher points for "the personality a President ought to have," but personality, politicians thought, only won beauty contests. None of this boded well for the March 9 primary. Even Reagan's repeated attacks on his opponent's foreign policies, an area of primary interest to Floridians, failed to arouse. Jerry Ford crisscrossed the state in a show of presidential pomp, flaunting *Air Force One*, motorcades of shiny limousines, an army of Secret Service agents, and buses filled with press. Ronald Reagan couldn't compete.

Ford smelled blood and an early knockout. "Florida is really the key," he told reporters. "If we win and win very well in Florida, they ought to know they can't win."

In the end, it was only a TKO. Ford won the state with 53 percent of the vote to Reagan's 47, a much smaller margin than anyone had expected. "We came up like a skyrocket at the end," Reagan told supporters, putting his best spin on a decisive loss. But next up was North Carolina, where they were sure another loss was imminent. John Sears knew the score, but figured they could hold on until the Texas primary scheduled for the first week of May. Reagan had a sizable hold on Texas. A win there could shake things up, but Texas was six weeks off.

And the pressure was on him to exit the race. The Ford people orchestrated an all-out effort encouraging Republican governors, senators, and congressmen to urge Reagan's withdrawal. Across the country, in a series of interviews, they echoed a coordinated statement. "Governor Reagan's made his point. Now is the time to bow out." Reporters picked up the message at every campaign stop, demanding, "When are you calling it quits, Governor?" Even Nancy Reagan considered that the time was fast approaching when it might be wise for her husband to throw in the towel. North Carolina seemed like such a lost cause. She could see the toll it was taking on Ronnie.

Secretly, John Sears called Rogers Morton, who had recently taken over the Ford campaign, and agreed to meet with him in Washington on March 20, four days before the North Carolina primary, to discuss the possibility of a dignified exit strategy should things go the way of the projections. "I wanted to cut a deal," Sears says in retrospect, "so they'd quit asking us to get out of the race." But not quite yet. Reagan had polled 49 percent in New Hampshire and 47 percent in Florida, both respectable showings. They'd wait until Texas, Sears insisted. "You beat us in Texas and we'll get out."

Morton agreed and called off the attack chorus. He also knew that other factors might vanquish Reagan before he ever reached Texas. It was no secret that the fiercely competitive primaries had plunged the Reagan campaign into serious debt. Some reports put it at $250,000, but it was closer to $2 million. At one point, the campaign was in Los Angeles, set to fly back to a North Carolina event, but the plane, a jet they'd leased from United Airlines for $50,000 a week, was stranded on the runway filled with staff and reporters. Pete Hannaford nudged Mike Deaver. "Why aren't we taking off?" he wondered. Because, Deaver said, they first have to open the mail to see if there were enough donations to pay for the flight. It was that bad. John Sears knew; he hadn't taken a paycheck in months. Contributions had dried up to the point that almost everyone on staff was working off the payroll.

On March 23, 1976, the day of the North Carolina primary, Ronald Reagan flew to Wisconsin for several unscripted campaign appearances. There wasn't anything more he could do in the South. They'd worked their hearts out there. The county organizations had blanketed the state, and Jesse Helms rallied his troops. "It was hand-to-hand combat," says Charlie Black. "The Ford people thought they could put us out of the race there, so we gave it everything we had." But most aides sensed it was a lost cause. Sears gathered the melancholy staff and proposed scrapping the upcoming Wisconsin and Illinois primaries, both of which they were certain to lose. "Why don't we fly back to Los Angeles instead," he suggested, "regroup, and use whatever money is left to buy a half hour of network TV time to speak to the nation and raise funds." No one objected. "We were all pretty depressed," Pete Hannaford recalls. "North Carolina was going down the drain, there was no upside in sight. What did it matter?"

That night, Ronald Reagan prepared to speak in the ballroom of a hotel in La Crosse, Wisconsin. The engagement was a dinner for Ducks Unlimited, a nonprofit dedicated to the conservation of wetlands and waterfowl. When Hannaford asked him if there was something special he wanted inserted in his speech, Reagan grinned. "Pete, we have five hundred drunken duck hunters out front. I think all they want to hear is some jokes." It was a typical Reagan performance, in which he dragged out all the old standby material—and brought the house down. Sears and his aides watched numbly from the wings. Sometime toward the end of the speech, Frank Reynolds, the ABC-TV anchor, wandered over and joined them. "It's fifty-five to forty-five in North Carolina," he said. "I know," Sears replied glumly. "You don't understand," Reynolds told him, "*you* have the fifty-five."

Sears was dumbfounded. Only 2 percent of the vote was in, but it had legs, he figured. When 25 percent was in and the margin hadn't changed, he knew the count would hold. They'd practically ceded North Carolina and everything in its wake. But a North Carolina win changed the stakes. Suddenly, Sears recalls thinking, "we were back in the ballgame."

The midnight plane ride back to Los Angeles was a full-scale party. The bottles of champagne left over from New Hampshire were opened along with several tubs of vanilla ice cream. Ronald Reagan sat in a seat near the cockpit, quiet and contemplative. "It's too early," he thought, refusing to declare victory. He remembered jumping the gun in New Hampshire, when he thought the primary was in the bag, and he opted to hold back any celebration until North Carolina was confirmed. A little past midnight, when the plane was somewhere over the Rockies, the pilot came on the public-address system to report that Reagan had won North Carolina, 52–46.

"Okay, I win," Reagan acknowledged with a smile.

Finally, the governor got up and worked the aisle, shaking hands and accepting congratulations. His son Ron tossed him a football, which he one-handed, before flinging it back. An aide broke out in song. "Mike [Deaver] and Lyn [Nofziger] told me there was more booze consumed on that flight than on the whole rest of the campaign put together," says Charlie Black. Finally, he said, "we had a good solid win."

More than that, they had momentum.

R eagan rode that momentum into Texas on May 1, 1976, and won every precinct in the state, along with its ninety-six delegates. "This is a turning point," he exulted upon hearing the news. Sears immediately put him on a plane to Indiana, whose primary was three days off. They were eighteen points behind Jerry Ford in the polls there, but Sears was upbeat. "Because we won big in Texas, we would win the next one no matter where it was," he says.

Momentum.

The force at Ronald Reagan's back was palpable—and on full display when he flew into Indianapolis. "It was like Napoleon entering Paris," says Charlie Black. "Huge crowds turned out, more conservative people than in most of the Midwest, which was surprising, because we'd stayed out of the state until the last possible minute." The turnout had been masterminded by L. Keith Bulen, one of the virtuoso political bosses of his generation. Bulen claimed responsibility for Richard Lugar's rise to prominence, as well as most politicians elected to the state legislature and not a few mayors and governors. Even though every elected official in Indiana was for Ford, Bulen instructed the precinct captains to shut down their efforts. He had the state sewn up. He not only turned people out, he told them how to vote, and when the polls closed in Indiana, more of them had voted for Ronald Reagan than for Jerry Ford.

It was a miraculous, come-from-behind win. Reagan won primaries the same day in Alabama and Georgia. That made it five in a row. They were on a roll.

Momentum.

After a victory in Nebraska on May 11 and a loss in Gerald Ford's home state of Michigan, where thousands of Democrats had crossed party lines to vote for Reagan, he was the undisputed front-runner for the Republican nomination. "We're way ahead of where our projections were for this point," he boasted to record crowds at a Louisiana rally. Data revealed he had surged ahead of Ford in pledged delegates, 357–297, but the count was too fluid to trust. "I believe in my own heart that I can go to the convention with enough delegates to win on the first ballot."

It would be a startling, unprecedented upset, though not out of the question. Five weeks before the Republican convention in Kansas City, Ford's delegate count stood at 1,104 to Reagan's 1,090, with 65 still up for grabs. With 1,130 required for the nomination, the situation was "highly volatile." Both camps were worried about poaching—luring delegates already committed to switch sides. As James Baker, who ran the Ford delegate operation, summed up the strategy: "Acquire delegates, protect your delegates and steal other delegates." Ford had an arsenal of weapons at his disposal that leveraged the prestige of his office: White House visits, Cabinet and ambassador appointments, special honors, personal phone calls. On July 4, 1976, the American Bicentennial, he invited seven uncommitted delegates to be his guest aboard the USS *Nashville* to watch the tall ships sail into New York Harbor. He'd courted the thirty-vote Mississippi delegation, which went to the convention uncommitted, by inviting its chairman, Clarke Reed, to be his guest at a state dinner for Queen Elizabeth in the White House Rose Garden. As the *New York Times* noted, "The Ford campaign threw all the perks of the presidency it could at delegates."

John Sears needed his own surefire method to lure away moderate and liberal Ford delegates as well as any "undecideds" leaning Reagan's way. Delegate support, he feared, "was in danger of slipping away." Not all the delegates on Reagan's scorecard were 100 percent committed to him. He also knew that CBS-TV planned to broadcast a story on July 26 announcing that its latest poll showed Gerald Ford had the nomination wrapped up, effectively ending the Reagan candidacy. His delegates would scramble onto the Ford bandwagon, like rats deserting a sinking ship. Now Sears needed more than a conventional weapon—he needed a bomb to blast CBS out of the water—and when he hit on one it was a doozy. With two weeks left before the convention, he persuaded Ronald Reagan to name his vice-presidential running mate—something that had never been done by a candidate—a move certain to shake up the race. "You think it'll work?" Reagan asked him when the strategy was proposed. "It's as good a shot as we'll get," Sears replied.

But—who? Sears's first choice, Nelson Rockefeller, would have alienated too many Southern supporters. William Ruckelshaus, the former attorney general, seemed ideal, but wouldn't bring any delegates to the table. And former Illinois governor Richard Ogilvie, Sears concluded, "was too much of a stretch—it would have looked like I was selling the vice presidency to get delegates." They needed someone from a big northeastern state committed to Ford, whose presence on the ticket would pry delegates away. Sears called Charlie Black and said, "What do you know about this guy Schweiker from Pennsylvania?"

Richard Schweiker was a choice from left field. He was a two-term senator who had twice defeated popular Democratic opponents, but he was low-key, practically off the radar. Black told Sears that Schweiker was a Ford supporter, "a very liberal guy, but solid on right-to-life issues, gun control, busing, fine on defense issues, and likable, but most people don't think he's a heavyweight." He also had strong union ties—a 100 percent rating from the AFL-CIO—which would put a scare into hard-core conservatives, but Sears thought he could convince them that in a general election union members might be persuaded to cross party lines and vote Republican. After all, Ronald Reagan was a union man.

But would Reagan go for it? "He'd never heard of Dick Schweiker," Sears recalls.* "And unbeknownst to me, Nancy had already instructed Justin Dart to see if he could wangle a second spot for her husband on the Ford ticket if we lost the nomination." According to David Keene, Nancy Reagan was appalled when she met Dick Schweiker. She felt he "dressed like a Cleveland auto dealer," and she ordered Keene to instruct Schweiker on the necessity of overhauling his wardrobe. Ronald Reagan proved more open-minded. After six hours pacing the patio together in Pacific Palisades, Ronald Reagan found Schweiker "easy to like" and, as Paul Laxalt told him, "no kneejerk liberal." "On things where we disagree," Schweiker assured Reagan, "I'll make my case, and then I'll support your position." That was all Reagan needed to hear. "I've made a decision, Senator," he said, "and I'd like you to be my running mate."

Before it was announced, however, Sears directed the staff to call their conservative supporters across the country to brief them, heading off any

---

* This is not exactly true. They'd met once before, at a dinner party at Walter Annenberg's home.

backlash. Charlie Black personally visited Jesse Helms, who said, "Well, I won't be able to say anything positive about it, but I won't say anything that would hurt you, either." Black next put in a call to John Ashbrook, another staunch supporter, which didn't produce as sanguine an outcome. After a long silence, the Ohio congressman barked, "Tell Reagan I say 'Fuck you!'" and he hung up, never to return to the campaign. Schweiker's selection proved that divisive. David Keene found out just how much when he took Schweiker and his wife to meet the Mississippi and Alabama delegations at a venue on the border of those states. Wallace Stanfield, the Reagan co-chairman in Alabama, told them, "When I heard about it, I just assumed my doctor told me I had the clap." Keene had even less success with the Mississippi delegation. Clarke Reed admitted he "was so shaken by the decision that he was thinking of switching his allegiance to President Ford."

Perhaps the most critical call was the one Schweiker placed to Drew Lewis, his closest friend—some said they "were alter egos"—and Pennsylvania power broker, who headed the state's Ford campaign. Lewis had handpicked and controlled Pennsylvania's 103 delegates, which were committed to Gerald Ford, but Schweiker estimated he could pry fifteen or twenty away. Not so, he quickly found out. Lewis was staggered by the news that Schweiker had crossed over to Reagan—and crossed Lewis by doing so—and refused to release even a single delegate. In fact, immediately after hanging up, Lewis called the White House and personally assured Ford that he'd deliver Pennsylvania for him.

No matter how it stacked up, naming Schweiker was a gamble. Loyal conservatives "were stunned and outraged by the choice," many felt betrayed, and several backed away, including trusty Mel Thomson, who announced he could no longer think of nominating Ronald Reagan at the national convention. And John Connally, who had remained neutral throughout, promptly threw his support to Ford, saying, "Reagan has scuttled his own political principles."

No one—not delegates, opposition forces, or Reagan staff—knew how the addition of Dick Schweiker would eventually shake out. Everything—polls and strategies alike—had to be reassessed and recalculated. But Ronald Reagan was not conceding anything. The nomination remained a wide-open race, and he was heading to the Republican convention with a fifty-fifty chance.

The Democrats had already selected their nominee—a man who delighted in reminding people, "I'm not a lawyer. I'm not from Washington. I'm not a member of Congress. I've *never* been part of the national government." Jimmy Carter, the onetime peanut farmer, had risen from national political obscurity to vanquish all worthy challengers, men who were all of the above, men who couldn't compete with his inspirational catchphrases—how Americans needed "to bind our people together to work in harmony and love one another." When his audience members denounced "lazy" welfare recipients, Carter explained how many of them were mothers and children or the handicapped, all of whom warranted compassion and respect. His call for "a new mood in America" resonated within a party in need of inspiration and hope. One by one, he'd picked off Morris Udall, Henry Jackson, Fred Harris, Sargent Shriver, Birch Bayh, and George Wallace to emerge as the Democratic candidate for president.

On Monday, August 16, 1976, as the Republican convention was gaveled to order in Kansas City, Missouri, the question that echoed through the brand-new Kemper Arena was: Who was better positioned to beat Jimmy Carter—Gerald Ford or Ronald Reagan? The 63 percent of Republican delegates who considered themselves conservative believed Reagan alone could win in November by giving voters an unambiguous choice. The moderate wing of the party remained convinced that Ford was the more inclusive candidate—and the incumbent, no small consideration in a national race. There were ideological factors that also weighed. Ford supported passage of the Equal Rights Amendment, a law that would prohibit discrimination based on sex, while Reagan was opposed. And Reagan endorsed an amendment to the Constitution banning abortion outright, while Ford proposed leaving that decision to the individual states. The 4,515 delegates and alternates had a clear choice to make on where they stood and whom they stood with. But on day one of the convention, there was no consensus. Each side was still scrambling for delegates. Most observers believed that President Ford had enough support to win the nomination on the first ballot. The *Washington Post* put him ahead by seventy-two votes, with "119 delegates remaining uncommitted and others changing their minds daily." The *New York Times* found "Mr. Reagan about 100 votes short of the 1,130 majority he needs." Ford was closing in on the target, but the Reagan team remained confident that it could tip the scales in its candidate's favor.

John Sears had one last ploy. "We argued an amendment to the convention rules that called for Ford to announce a running mate before the first ballot," he recalls. It was an audacious gambit that some read as "a desperate-hours attempt to sandbag the President into naming a Veep who would alienate some delegates." In any case, it threw the convention into a state of anxiety, forcing a floor vote on the proposal, which became known as the 16-C Rule.

"We knew 16-C was our last best shot," says Charlie Black, who was on the floor of the convention hall throughout the evening of August 17. For four frenzied, tension-filled hours, each camp worked furiously, putting pressure on the delegations and their floor leaders to side with them on the procedural vote. The stakes were huge; the outcome prefigured the eventual nominee. Both candidates rolled out the heavy artillery. Ronald Reagan darted this way and that, shaking hands and answering questions. Pat Boone and Efrem Zimbalist Jr. flew in to help sway the vote for Ford. Wavering delegates got a phone call from the president, who trumped Boone and Zimbalist with Cary Grant.

As the voting neared, it looked to both sides that the thirty delegates from Mississippi would determine who won. Enormous pressure was brought on its chairman, Clarke Reed, who swung back and forth all evening long. "I'll be all right on 16-C," he assured aides for both candidates, his voice rasping and shrill. It was anyone's guess which way he would fall.

In the end, Mississippi had no bearing on the outcome. At 10:30 that night, Florida, which had abstained during the first roll-call vote, switched to "no" the second time around, dooming 16-C to oblivion. With that, John Sears called all the field leaders back to the command trailer parked outside the arena. "We knew it was over," says Charlie Black. "From there, everybody went back to our hotel and started drinking."

Reagan, still processing the shock that the nomination had eluded him, offered his own concession speech. With most of his staff and campaign workers gathered in the Alameda Plaza ballroom, their eyes red and glistening with tears, he assured them, "Nancy and I aren't going [to go] back, sit on a rocking chair and say that's all there is for us. We're going to stay in there, and you stay in there with me—the cause is still there."

The script for the next night, the last night of the convention, was already written before the festivities began. Ronald and Nancy Reagan, along with three of their children, had a quiet dinner in their suite at the hotel before heading to Kemper Arena for the crowning event. It was a solemn affair. The family knew the race had ended in defeat and that the rest of the evening would unspool as a humbling experience. Before departing, Reagan gathered them in the living room and extended an apology. "I'm sorry that you all have to see this," he said. Nancy, in tears, toasted her husband, and then clamped down on her emotions in order to soldier the family through.

When both candidates' names were placed in nomination, there was no Reagan operation on the floor of the convention hall. The final vote went as predicted. Just after midnight, West Virginia put Ford over the top on the first ballot, handing him 1,187 delegate votes to Reagan's 1,070. Ronald Reagan, watching from a secluded skybox, nodded his head and murmured to no one in particular, "I feel at peace with myself."

For months afterward, delegates from the 1976 convention would claim their votes went for Ford but their hearts were with Reagan. They cheered lustily and wept when Ford invited Reagan to the podium to call for party unity and bid his farewells. For Ronald Reagan, it offered little consolation. He was sixty-five, lapsing into the realm of elder statesmanship. He had already experienced the comedown of outliving his relevance in Hollywood. According to Pete Hannaford, who accompanied him from Kansas City back to Los Angeles, "He almost certainly believed that his political career, in terms of any future candidacy, was at an end."

CHAPTER TWENTY-EIGHT

THE FRONT-RUNNER

"Let's talk sense to the American people."

—ADLAI STEVENSON

I 'm at peace with the world," Ronald Reagan assured a group of reporters that had surrounded him outside his polling place in Pacific Palisades on Election Day, November 2, 1976.

He had about twelve hours left to savor his serenity before learning that Jimmy Carter, the improbable Georgian, had defeated Gerald Ford, turning the presidency back to the Democrats for at least four years. It was reasonable to question how much peace Reagan actually enjoyed, considering his gimlet-eyed worldview. For the past three months, since his loss in Kansas City, he'd been retracing old steps on the mashed-potato circuit, railing against various national-security policies that concerned him, including détente. The country's military's dwindling preparedness preoccupied him, as well as the possibility of U.S. talks with the Soviet Union on limiting strategic arms, which he felt jeopardized America's security. And the Panama Canal treaty still signaled nothing more to him than another indication to U.S. enemies of "America's longing to withdraw inward" and to "create a power vacuum in the Caribbean that Fidel Castro and the Soviet Union will seek to exploit."

At peace with the world—not by any stretch of the imagination.

He was struggling to figure out where he fit in the Republican political apparatus. His function in the foreseeable future, he said, was as party missionary, "courting conservatives who now call themselves Democrats and Independents." Reagan and most conservative Republican leaders viewed Southern and Sunbelt Democrats as ripe for the picking. There was an enormous shift to the right among middle- and working-class voters from that swath of states who tended to feel fed up with big government's heavy hand and with liberal policies like forced busing of schoolchildren, welfare, and the right to an abortion. Many had been Wallace supporters, others were former cabinet members of Democratic governors, and still others were law-enforcement officers who advocated for less outside influence in their precincts. Richard Nixon's Southern strategy in 1972 had brought a lot of those people across party lines, people who had never voted for a Republican before and found that doing so didn't pinch them. Ronald Reagan's candidacy in 1976 had pushed the migration rightward so rapidly that the traditional Republican Party of Harding and Eisenhower was actively redefining itself. Its core principles—its very essence—were in a serious state of flux. One unknown still to be determined was Ronald Reagan's role in shaping this crazy-quilt constituency he called "the New Majority."

Many GOP stalwarts had hoped he'd accept the vice presidency to run with Gerald Ford, but he'd scotched that option months before the convention—and, in point of fact, the job was never offered. In a way, it was a blessing in disguise. There was no evidence that his inclusion on the ticket would have tipped the election to Ford, and the wages of campaigning had taken their toll.

At a rally, during an early primary stump in Florida, Secret Service agents had tackled a man who had pointed a toy gun at the podium. Some weeks later, another close call on the campaign plane warned of the tenuousness of life. Ronald Reagan had been relaxing just before takeoff in Ohio, enjoying a soda and a handful of peanuts, which he tossed in the air and caught in his mouth with a carnival flourish. As the plane rolled down the runway for takeoff, Darrell Trent, the young aide who was sitting directly behind Reagan, saw him come up out of his seat, struggling to breathe. "He was turning blue," Trent recalls. "He couldn't talk." Nancy Reagan, sitting across the aisle, heard someone yell, "Heart attack! Give him oxygen." Mike Deaver, in the seat next to Nancy, leaped over her and wrapped his arms around Reagan from behind, dislodging a peanut that had caught in his throat.

"He was ready to get off that treadmill," says Jim Lake. "You could see it in his face. The guy was just plumb exhausted."

And so was his bank account. Ronald Reagan had been campaigning for almost two years, during which time his income flatlined. Suddenly, there were plenty of expenses to consider. The new ranch in Santa Barbara required considerable upkeep, as well as an addition to its tiny adobe house. And his son Ron's college tuition had to be factored in; he'd been accepted into the freshman class at Yale, whose price tag for tuition was a hefty $4,750. Legally, Reagan could have tapped into his surplus campaign funds. Under federal election laws, a candidate with a balance left over after a race was entitled to keep it for personal use. It seemed incredible that a campaign once scrounging for nickels had anything left in the till, but miraculously, due to a deluge of last-minute contributions, the ledger showed a $1.5 million surplus. But swapping it into his personal account seemed impolitic, if not downright shameless. Ronald Reagan earned his money the old-fashioned way. It was time for him to go back to work.

A newly resurrected Deaver and Hannaford cranked up the old pipeline of radio broadcasts and newspaper columns, then booked a full schedule of dates on the after-dinner speaking circuit. The New York Times reported, "His income from these activities is expected to gross considerably more than $500,000 next year."

A political action committee—Citizens for the Republic—was also created so that Reagan could solicit contributions and underwrite the campaigns of Republican candidates to Congress and handpicked state legislatures. To administer it, Lyn Nofziger was installed as the executive director, along with a steering committee of the country's most prominent conservative ideologues, including John Sears and Richard Schweiker. But as confidants went, it was critical to have Nofziger and Mike Deaver on board, protecting his interests.

Nofziger and Deaver: no two advisers were as close to Ronald and Nancy Reagan.

"Nobody planted the seeds of conservatism deeper or more fruitfully than Lyn Nofziger," says Stu Spencer. "He kept Reagan focused on issues that mattered most to the base and never took his eyes off the White House. He saw Reagan sitting in the Oval Office as early as 1965 and was determined to install him there, come hell or high water." It was Nofziger who came up with the idea for Citizens of the Republic as a way of keeping Ronald Reagan on the path to the presidency. He devised a series of Citizens-sponsored weekend seminars—"How to Be a Good Campaigner"—for volunteers in different cities around the country, with Reagan featured as the keynote speaker and primary draw, that ran for a two-year stretch, from 1977 to 1979. The turnout was nothing less than sensational. "Folks came away with a good grounding in campaigning," says Pete Hannaford, "and it became the framework for a volunteer organization for the 1980 presidential campaign."

Nofziger's chief asset as a political strategist was his relationship with the press. Reporters were his brethren and favorite drinking buddies. As a former journalist, he understood their job and the access they required to file stories. Their relationship was symbiotic—even at times too much so. "Lyn was someone, I suspect, who loved to spill the beans," says Ed Meese, which was as polite an understatement as anyone could offer. Jim Lake, who replaced Nofziger as the campaign's press secretary in 1976, put it in stronger terms: "He was a loose cannon, and it created trouble." Nancy Reagan led the charge to get rid of him on the stump. Again and again, she complained about Nofziger's irreverence. "Oh, I wish he wouldn't do that," she'd lament. And his chronically rumpled appearance annoyed her no end. "Nancy thought of Lyn as a coarse individual," says Ed Meese. "He didn't fit in with her Beautiful People aesthetic." According to an intimate, "He did not dress to impress," especially with the food-stained Mickey Mouse ties he sported at events. And Nancy found his sense of humor offensive. Most of all, Meese claims, she never forgave him for outing Phil Battaglia to the press in 1967. "He was not, in her estimation, properly disciplined."

Mike Deaver, on the other hand, was meticulous to a fault, and for that he was one of both Nancy and Ronald Reagan's most trusted confidants.

"From the very start, the three of us hit it off," Nancy wrote in her 1989 biography, My Turn. There was something about Mike's character that spoke to their individual sensibilities. Deaver was a self-described poor boy from Bakersfield, California, whose "parents had scrimped and studied price tags and saved to buy appliances on a monthly plan." Ronald Reagan's upbringing was remarkably similar. "In that respect, from the beginning I felt an identity with him," Deaver recalled. They shared stories about the hard times they had growing up, about how poor they had been, and about the rigors of pulling themselves up from their bootstraps. There was a kinship that developed through their hardscrabble experiences. "Mike was emotionally tied to Reagan," says Sheila Tate, later Nancy Reagan's press secretary. "They were like alter egos. They understood each other so well."

By the time Deaver joined Reagan's Sacramento administration in 1966 as an aide to Bill Clark, he'd managed to transcend the shortcomings of his youth—not as a glamorous movie star, like his boss, but by capitalizing on an ingratiating personality. He had razor-sharp instincts along with style, and he understood how to cater to the Reagans. "Mike had a great gift in that he could sense what made the two Reagans happy," says Pete Hannaford, who became Deaver's business partner between the campaigns. From the day Deaver was promoted to be the governor's executive secretary, he made a determined effort to help Ronald and Nancy find small comforts—to put them at ease—in a job and a city that often bewildered them. "He babysat their son Ron and took the boy places," George Steffes recalls, "and he knew just what to say—and when to say it—to defuse any tense situation involving the governor." Deaver later wrote of Ronald Reagan, "I had never known anyone so unable to deal with close personal conflict." He saw behind the governor's assured public leading-man image to where the Midwestern reticence still constrained him, and made an effort to distract him by talking about Hollywood and the movies. "I enjoyed listening when he got the urge to reminisce," Deaver recalled, and he helped cultivate that urge every time they were alone. He knew that if things went smoothly for Reagan—if he felt relaxed and confident and in control—he would be at his best, and Deaver went to extraordinary lengths to nurture that mood. "He was the first priority, even above myself or my family," Deaver acknowledged.

With Nancy, Deaver played the Bob Cummings role—the fey, gossipy friend she needed to unwind with and confide in. The image Deaver cultivated with her was what Lyn Nofziger described as "much more than a purse-carrier," more like a professional son—the son she'd always wanted who shared her interests and social life. He loved hearing about the glamorous escapades with her well-heeled Los Angeles crowd and her excursions into the couture salons of Beverly Hills. He took an interest in astrology. He was always able to cheer her up; he could make her laugh and take the chill off in frosty situations. According to an aide of Nancy Reagan's, he "had the personality and the ability to anticipate her needs," which were not limited to the intrusions of government and the press. "Deaver was a great piano player," George Steffes recalls, "and whenever there was a function at the Executive Mansion, Mike would burn through a repertoire of show tunes and standards." At smaller, more intimate soirees, Nancy might sidle up to the piano and croon a rendition of "Our Love Is Here to Stay" or "Just the Way You Look Tonight." She had a good voice, not powerful but polished, and Deaver knew just how to show it off.

In time, Deaver's involvement with Nancy Reagan took on a stealthier shade. "He was her eyes and ears," says John Sears, who kept Deaver in the dark when he preferred that certain strategies not be reported. Staffers referred to it as "the Mommy Watch," in which Deaver served as a conduit to Nancy on her husband's well-being and, conversely, interceded between her demands and the outside world. She could be difficult and intimidating. "One thing you learn," Lyn Nofziger pointed out, "there is no sense getting into an argument with Nancy Reagan. You can't win." As Mike Deaver acknowledged, she was "a tenacious opponent," intense and occasionally vindictive, and when push came to shove, she often enlisted Deaver in her efforts to shove. When appropriate, he gamely conspired with her to vanquish a foe with whom she had a grievance—or tried to talk her out of it. "Deaver knew how to deal with her," says Jim Kuhn, later a special assistant in the White House. "He had a way of keeping her calm that nobody else could—calmer than even Ronnie. She really trusted Mike Deaver . . . and she didn't trust that many people."

Now, in 1978, Lyn Nofziger and Mike Deaver were enlisted, in separate endeavors, to keep the Reagan brand attractive and visible. They were devoted to the core, unwavering in their love and dedication. Both men were convinced that his presidential appeal remained stronger than ever—and equally convinced that he was determined to run in 1980.

There had been hints. As early as two days after the 1976 Republican convention, Ronald Reagan confessed he "wouldn't rule out and wouldn't rule in" another bid for the presidency. He was no longer "the reluctant candidate" of previous campaigns and, he admitted, "I wanted to be president." He also approved the organization of a makeshift campaign committee for 1980. Paul Laxalt, Lyn Nofziger, Mike Deaver, Pete Hannaford, economic adviser Martin Anderson, John Sears, pollster Richard Wirthlin, and the deep-pocketed contributors—"we all kept in touch," says Ed Meese. "We were like a political reserve unit, ready to spring into action." Their forums were informal at first—get-togethers from time to time in Reagan's Pacific Palisades living room to discuss speech themes, messages, and the political process. Richard Allen, a senior fellow at the Hoover Institution and an adviser to the Nixon White House, was brought in to shore up foreign policy and national defense. "Reagan was less than well prepared on those issues," Allen recalls, "but he had good instincts."

Allen recommended taking Reagan on a series of foreign trips to gain some credibility, burnish his credentials, introduce him to world leaders, and bank a wealth of media coverage. They would be "look-and-listen visits," as Pete Hannaford dubbed them—Asia first, in April 1978, and then a European swing in November of that year. "We wanted to present Reagan as a statesman—and knowledgeable," Hannaford says.

As arrangements for the trip were made, Nancy Reagan decided to accept an invitation from the Iranian ambassador to visit Tehran at the request of Mohammad Reza Shah Pahlavi. It presented a ticklish situation. Criticism of the shah had been building all year. "It's not a good idea, politically or otherwise," Hannaford and Allen agreed, but there was no changing Nancy's mind. To circumvent a possible backlash, they mapped out an itinerary that featured a Tokyo audience with the American ambassador, Mike Mansfield; Taiwan, where crowds lined the streets waving American and Nationalist Chinese flags; and Hong Kong, for a flyover of the new territories; with media coverage in each, then a quick stopover in Tehran on the back end. "And as far as I know," Hannaford says, "not a word about the Iran trip ever made it into a newspaper."

The European trip was more productive. The key country was West Germany, where Reagan had never been and needed exposure. There was a long meeting with Chancellor Helmut Schmidt, followed by Helmut Kohl, head of the Christian Democratic Union and the country's future leader. Afterward, Reagan was taken to the Axel Springer House near the Reichstag, giving him a bird's-eye view over the Berlin Wall where, a few weeks earlier, a young man had attempted to vault the wall and was machine-gunned, his body left hanging as an object lesson. Reagan declined a closer look at the wall, but its forbidding mass left an indelible impression. Later, he recalled a graffiti scrawl spray-painted across a bullet-riddled patch of concrete: "Those beyond this wall live in a concentration camp." Richard Allen claimed Reagan turned to him and said, "You know, Dick, we've got to find a way to knock this thing down."

London was eminently more upbeat. Reagan had a visit scheduled to see Margaret Thatcher. He had met her in the spring of 1975, during a trip arranged by Justin Dart. She had just become the Conservative Party leader, with an office so small that when Winston Churchill III stopped in to say hello there was no room for him to sit down. "I liked her immediately," Reagan said, sensing by their mutual interests that they were destined to be political "soul mates." She was first and foremost a free-market economist and a bitter opponent of Soviet Communism—both attitudes that dovetailed with his beliefs. Pete Hannaford recalled their attraction as "two peas in a pod." He says, "They had been great admirers at a distance, but took to each other immediately and saw eye to eye on policy—instant chemistry." This time, she was on the verge of winning the big election and her focus was on the Soviet threat—the fact that the Russians had SS-20 missiles aimed at every capital in Western Europe. Her message sank in very clearly with Reagan, who grasped how desperately eager she seemed to solve, or at least neutralize, this problem, hopefully with American assistance.

The meeting with Thatcher reaffirmed a growing concern—more than a concern, an *anxiety*, a *dread*—of nuclear war. According to Martin Anderson, Reagan's domestic-policy adviser, "the challenge to diminish the threat of that war was always foremost on his mind." He was convinced that the economy could be fixed with American know-how, but nuclear annihilation was something else entirely. "A nuclear war couldn't be won by either side," Reagan observed. The only way to assure that? "It must never be fought."

Still, he was opposed to any treaty arising out of the ongoing Strategic Arms Limitation Talks—SALT II—between Jimmy Carter and the Soviet Union. In the SALT I negotiations, which led to the Anti-Ballistic Missile Treaty in May of 1972, neither side committed to reducing nuclear weapons. The agreement only tempered the pace of growth by freezing the number of strategic ballistic missiles at existing levels. SALT II sought to curtail the manufacture of strategic nuclear weapons by banning new missile programs. Reagan believed this was self-defeating. To him, arms limitation wasn't the same thing as arms *reduction*. As early as 1976, he said, "I've always liked the idea of START"—STrategic Arms Reduction Treaty—"instead of SALT." When he began preaching this vision of a world free of all nuclear missiles, even his closest advisers "just smiled" patronizingly. The existing policy at the time was the doctrine of Mutual Assured Destruction, abbreviated ironically—or not—as MAD, which spelled the annihilation of both attacker and defender; in other words, a standoff so long as no one pulled the trigger. Reagan thought that was completely insane. A nuclear Armageddon didn't suit his worldview, but neither did a treaty that refused to go far enough. It seemed futile to pursue SALT II, and he began expressing himself freely on that topic upon his return to the States.

At the end of 1978 and into early 1979, he began to turn up the heat on the Carter administration. The passage of the Panama Canal Treaty in April 1978 infuriated Ronald Reagan; U.S. foreign policy was nothing more than wishful thinking; arms-control negotiations seemed riddled with concessions to the Soviet Union; America's human-rights policy was limited to merely scolding dictators instead of standing up to authoritarianism; and South Africa—"whatever we may think of [its] internal policies"—provided mineral riches and a strategic position that should not be ignored. He also spoke passionately opposing California's proposed ban of smoking in public buildings and offices, where he said "owners would have to foot the cost for the No Smoking signs," and made his feelings known that he opposed "ballot measures . . . that advanced certain 'gay rights,'" feeling that "these tended to promote and advocate such an alternative lifestyle." Mandating air bags in automobiles didn't fare any better. "If any of us would like to install such a device in the family car, shouldn't that be our decision to make?" he asked rhetorically in a syndicated radio broadcast. Setting the record straight, he also made it clear that he opposed abortion—*period*—admitting that the Therapeutic Abortion Act was full of loopholes and his signing it as governor of California misguided. To be clear on where he stood, he stated categorically: "I believe interrupting a pregnancy means the taking of a human life."

"There were other serious problems," he said, reflecting on the issues of the day. "Unemployment, inflation, and interest rates were climbing, and it looked as if administration policies would lead the nation into a serious recession."

The time was fast approaching when he had to take more than a stand with the issues, and decide once and for all whether to challenge Jimmy Carter in 1980. He already knew Republican hopefuls were circling the wagons. Philip Crane was the first to throw his hat in the ring, announcing his candidacy on August 2, 1978. The conservative Illinois congressman was an avowed Reagan supporter in 1976, but he suspected age would eliminate the former governor from making a 1980 bid. Reagan would be seventy if and when he ascended to the Oval Office, and the age factor generated a constant drumbeat. If victorious, he'd become the oldest elected president in U.S. history. "Age should be the least consideration," he bristled in a 1978 interview. But journalists mentioned it every chance they got, and public opinion strongly suggested his age remained a sensitive issue. "People don't knock him as too conservative," explained a voter at a rally. "But they bring up his age." "Love Ronald Reagan, but I can't vote for a man who's going to be seventy years old when he's elected," a Republican responded when the subject of age arose. "I'm sorry, but he's waited too long." For what it was worth, Reagan insisted he felt "thirty-nine or younger"—a man at midlife who was in great physical shape, radiated megatons of energy, and maintained a schedule that would test men half his age. "Look, it's steady as a rock," he told a convention crowd, exhibiting an outstretched hand as evidence. "Last week I was busting my keester at the ranch splitting rails."

"The age issue is a cover," John Sears scoffed when it came up in early meetings. "It was ammunition for anyone interested in challenging him for the nomination—and for the press, which needed an issue—but meaningless in the long run. As long as he was in the public eye, scoring with voters, age wouldn't factor in a decision at all."

Throughout the first ten months of 1979, Reagan's scorched-earth schedule of speeches often crammed more than twenty-five appearances into fifteen days a month as he crisscrossed the country espousing conservative doctrine. His speaking schedule certainly seemed presidential. In addition to themes of cutting taxes and the despotism of big government, he took on SALT II, a stagnant job market, an energy crisis that had raised

the price of gasoline from sixty cents to a dollar a gallon, and soaring inflation. But more important to his agenda than even these issues was the
message he embraced as the centerpiece of every speech: "Family, Work,
Neighborhood, Peace, and Freedom." Those five themes became the tent
pole on which hung all the thinking and policy for the upcoming campaign. "They were the essence of Reagan's thinking, what took priority in
the country," says Richard Allen, who formulated the platform along with
Martin Anderson.

Family. Work. Neighborhood. Peace. Freedom.

Reagan used these catchwords—"just five short words," he said—to il-
lustrate the concept of a "community of shared values." *Values.* Family values. It was a phrase he began to turn to frequently, equating it with
responsibility, love of country, and basic beliefs. *Traditional* values imbued
him with a "new way of looking at things," he explained with unforced
sincerity. He vowed to dispense with the jargon of professors and bureaucrats in favor of a more straightforward approach that explained programs
and policies in terms of how they affected families and neighborhoods.
"This isn't a change in what we believe," he emphasized. "We are simply
putting our belief into understandable language." The message connected
with audiences as never before and left them with an impression of a man
whose values, *traditional* values, were very much like their own. It was a
quality they desperately wanted in a leader. This man seemed to have their
interests at heart, a way of mending their shattered illusions.

Family. Work. Neighborhood. Peace. Freedom.

The man had a vision, audiences concluded. And they urged him at
every opportunity to run for president.

As late as September 1979, "the acknowledged front-runner" for the
Republican nomination was not yet a candidate. Ronald Reagan was
still "giving the matter serious consideration," still telling audiences that "it
was up to the will of the people" and "the office seeks the man," even
though a fully staffed Reagan for President Committee was operating and
raising funds in its headquarters a few blocks from the Los Angeles airport.
There were also volunteer offices and fund-raisers in every major U.S. city.
A full team of advisers was already working overtime, writing policy papers

and briefing books. Even John Sears was back in his role as campaign manager, despite the fact that he was a controversial figure within the Reagan camp who had caused considerable discomfort with key staff and supporters. "In 1980, I don't think any of us wanted him to run the campaign," said Pete Hannaford, a feeling echoed by others. "And his judgment wasn't perfect." Paul Laxalt, the campaign committee chairman, was vehemently opposed, and so was Lyn Nofziger, who "thought [Sears] was arrogant" and blamed him for the losing effort in 1976. They aired a litany of complaints: he was imperious, secretive, pushy, inflexible. The drinking problem so pronounced in 1976 was less of a factor—Sears apparently had brought it under control—but it threatened to rear its ugly head. And no one seemed pleased with Sears's plan to draw Ronald Reagan politically toward the center. That said, he was brilliant as a strategist, everyone agreed—there was no one else in his league. "The smartest guy I've ever known in politics," Charlie Black says forty years later. Mike Deaver argued strongly for him, and so did Ed Meese, who acknowledges, "Sears gave Ronald Reagan an authenticity with the establishment that he wouldn't have had otherwise." And Nancy Reagan considered him "the wonder boy of 1976 and . . . the best man to lead us to victory in 1980."

Sears took the reins early in 1979, along with his chief operatives, Jim Lake and Black. But the trio that had been so coordinated, so cunning, so productive in 1976 seemed jinxed from the moment they launched the '80 campaign. "We couldn't get it together from day one," says Jim Lake. The main snag was a division of leadership. Sears needed to run the show, but felt undermined by the support staff already in place. They were mostly the longtime Reagan sidekicks from Los Angeles and Sacramento—the Westerners, as they referred to themselves—Lynn Nofziger, Marty Anderson, Mike Deaver, and Ed Meese. According to David Keene, "Sears had undisguised disdain for them." He assigned each man a specific title and function, which didn't meet with anyone's approval. It touched off a storm of bickering and backbiting that seeped into every corner of the campaign. "We were in a constant mess," Lake says in retrospect. "It was a nightmare."

Marty Anderson, the domestic policy adviser, was the first to pack up and leave. He felt Sears undercut his authority by establishing a covert research policy office in Washington, D.C., which ostensibly repudiated and compromised Marty's work. Nofziger, who never liked Sears, couldn't hold his tongue. He would tell anyone who would listen that "that fucking Sears is a disaster." And Sears could not abide a fool. When Sears had enough of Lyn's constant badmouthing, he pulled him off the job as deputy press officer and reassigned him to run the state offices in California and Texas—out of sight, out of mind. Sears admits, "Life was easier with him out of the picture," and entirely more tranquil when Nofziger eventually quit.

Deaver, however, was not so accommodating. Mike refused to accept an official title—any title. He felt justified by his own instincts and management skills, and besides, he'd been there from the beginning. Instead, he bounced from office to office, from assignment to assignment, often working at cross-purposes to Sears's strategies. "Deaver was territorial," says Charlie Black, "interfering with the schedule and reporting only to the Reagans." This infuriated Sears, who resented being sabotaged. He explained that he needed Deaver to cooperate, invoking a simplistic metaphor in an attempt to tame the man's ego. "It's like an orchestra at the Hollywood Bowl," he began. "I'm conducting and I need everyone to take a chair and play their instrument. We need to be in harmony. So I don't care what you do, what instrument you play, but you can't dabble. You've got to take a title—*be in charge of something*." Deaver flat-out refused. "I can't put up with this," Sears fumed to his lieutenants. "We can't win this way."

In mid-November, when Sears made noises about quitting the campaign, Jim Lake approached Ronald Reagan and pleaded with him to intervene in order to resolve the dispute. "Governor," he said, "you've got to step in. John Sears is indispensable." Earlier, during an episode when Deaver had threatened to quit, Lake offered the same testimonial about him. Never mind: this time, everyone agreed on the necessity of a meeting to iron things out before they deteriorated any further.

The showdown took place on Thanksgiving Day at the Reagans' home in Pacific Palisades. Deaver arrived first, not realizing that his adversaries had also been invited. He found it odd when Nancy ushered him into the guest bedroom, asking him to wait for a few minutes until they were ready to receive him. After sitting alone for twenty minutes, he burst angrily into the living room, where he found Sears, Lake, and Black talking heatedly to the Reagans. "What's going on?" he demanded.

Charlie Black had been in the middle of explaining to Reagan that the Deaver and Hannaford firm had been billing the campaign from $30,000 to $50,000 a month to lease his private space in their offices and handling his schedule, marking up their commission 18 percent. "Reagan didn't like it a damn bit," Black recalls, "and Nancy liked it even less." As gently as possible, Black explained that he knew Deaver had done wonderful work for them over the years, but his interference in Sears's strategies was counterproductive. "It'd be better if Mike left the campaign. He can still help from the outside, and maybe his firm can do some of the PR."

Reagan reminded Jim Lake that he'd once said *Mike* was indispensable. "I believed that when I said it," Lake agreed, "but if you have to make a choice, John is more indispensable than Mike. Without him, this campaign cannot move forward."

Reagan eased himself out of a chair, but Deaver laid a hand on his shoulder. "Governor," he said, plainly rattled, "you don't have to make that decision. I'm quitting."

"No, Mike, you can't quit," Reagan protested—but too late. Without another word, Deaver walked out the front door in grand exit fashion.

Ronald Reagan's face flushed with anger as his eyes found John Sears and bored lasers into him. "The best man here just left the room," he said, barely able to contain his wrath.

He was about to express himself in a more vehement way, when Mike Deaver reappeared at the front door. "I forgot that Carolyn dropped me off," he said sheepishly. "Can I borrow Nancy's station wagon to get home?"

It momentarily broke the tension, but when Deaver left for the second time, there was barely enough time to clear the air. Everyone shook hands, and Charlie Black hugged Nancy Reagan. "I'm sorry," he whispered in her ear. "There was no other way." Jim Lake says she understood. "She loved Mike—but she didn't try to stop it. Without John, she knew her husband had no chance of getting past New Hampshire."

The last person left on Sears's hit list was Ed Meese, who was teaching part-time at a law school in San Diego but had Ronald Reagan's ear. "Sears thought Meese was ineffectual," says Jeff Bell, "but opted to cut his losses while he was ahead of the game." Sears left Meese alone—for the time being. It was a fortunate outcome in the long run; Meese, for all his organizational quirks, was an authoritative conservative who functioned as a trusted, dependable sounding board for Reagan, as he would for the next fifteen years. With Anderson, Nofziger, and Deaver gone, Sears had regained enough control of the campaign; his orchestra, composed of loyalists who knew the score, was finally free to fine-tune the arrangements.

There were more vital concerns to worry about. By the end of October 1979, nine candidates had declared to challenge Jimmy Carter for the presidency, not one of which was Ronald Reagan, the acknowledged front-runner. Positioning him took on tactical importance. "If you are the front-runner and you announce too early," Sears understood, "you put a target on your back for everyone to take shots at. Then you've got no place to go but down. And if your poll numbers decline, you lose momentum." By holding Reagan out of the fray as long as possible, the ten contenders concentrated on attacking one another.

And there was plenty of dissing to go around. The Republican rivals were formidable politicians. Many of the key Reagan supporters, along with the Washington beat reporters, believed that John Connally posed the toughest competition. He had name recognition and a bulging corporate war chest. But Sears and his staff dismissed Connally as a windbag without much substance. Their Southern aide, a young go-getter named Lee Atwater, reported early on that Connally's rallies in the Carolinas were ineffective affairs. "He's like a Chinese lunch," Atwater quipped, "great going down, but two hours later you're hungry again." Howard Baker, on the other hand, was a respected and personable politician with a natural base within the GOP who Sears thought had the wind at his back. Baker's poll numbers were substantial. What's more, he wasn't the moderate that everyone assumed he was. His lifetime rating by the Conservative Union was eighty-eight, second only to Ronald Reagan's among the Oval Office seekers. The other candidates, as Bob Dole admitted, were "just out here waiting for lightning to strike." Phil Crane was too much of a right-winger to gain traction; Larry Pressler, the South Dakota senator, had no operation in place; John Anderson was seen as too liberal, and his argument in favor of a fifty-cents-per-gallon gasoline tax would sink him; and George Bush, the former director of Central Intelligence, had no foreseeable constituency.* They could hit the campaign trail and scrimmage for all Ronald Reagan cared.

The only candidate who might have produced serious jitters was too preoccupied playing golf in Rancho Mirage. In September 1978, Reagan arranged an informal lunch meeting there to gauge Gerald Ford's intentions about a possible rerun in 1980. Ford was cordial, considering their tempestuous history, but hardly forthcoming. The most he would concede was an ambiguous shrug. According to Pete Hannaford, "Reagan's impression was that Ford liked what he was doing and, at that moment at least, was inclined to stay out of the race."

Sizing up the opposition, Ronald Reagan looked to many like the man to beat. "We're the front-runner," Sears declared pugnaciously in October 1979. "The race can't start without us."

But the start time was fast approaching. There were drawbacks to waiting too long to announce—not acting interested enough in the job, seeming too confident, giving the rest of the players too much time in the spotlight without having to take punches. Ronald Reagan still hadn't admitted he was running—not to the press, not even to John Sears. "I didn't even bother asking him," Sears recalls. "I knew he'd never officially declare. So I just told him to be ready on November 13. We were announcing his candidacy in New York City."

New York—enemy territory. It was a solid Democratic stronghold with a political counterbalance in Nelson Rockefeller, Jacob Javits, and John Lindsay, whose inclinations leaned so far left that they were barely considered Republicans. Still, as Sears counseled Reagan, "The President of the United States is always at home in New York," and someone not wellknown to New Yorkers needed to "go there and lay claim to it." It also indicated the campaign's intention to compete in the Northeast and to convert Democratic centrists to a Ronald Reagan constituency. Many, including upstart California governor Jerry Brown, sensed a watershed, a shift

---

* The other Republicans running were perennial candidate Harold Stassen and Benjamin Fernandez, a Los Angeles businessman.

in the country's views. "There will be some kind of political realignment," Brown reasoned. "The nation is not governable without new ideas."

The announcement, which doubled as a $500-a-plate fund-raiser, rolled out in a ballroom at the New York Hilton. Ronald Reagan surrounded himself with friends, contributors, and family. It was the first time in ages his children had all gathered together. Aides had held their breath over who would actually show up. Maureen, Michael, and Ron were expected to attend, as all three had done for the 1975 announcement, but Patti's appearance was always up in the air. In 1975, she was a no-show; she just flat-out refused to cooperate. Heading into the 1979 event, her whereabouts were unknown. Her parents had no idea where their daughter was living. Nancy finally learned through an agent at MCA that Patti had taken up with Bernie Leadon, one of the guitarists for the Eagles, and was traveling with the band. She had also changed her name—dropping Reagan for the more anonymous Davis, her mother's maiden name—adding distance from her father's political identity. John Sears tracked Patti down on the road and, through an intermediary, persuaded her to support her father in New York.

Patti's appearance was out of character. "I disagreed with my father's politics across the board," she recalled. "I did *not* want him to be president, for every reason imaginable." Arriving in New York, she told her friend the singer Paul Simon, "It's like every political disagreement I have ever had with my parents is now going to be played out in front of the whole country." But she ultimately showed up to indulge her desire to be part of a family.

Her brother Ron also needed a gentle nudge. He was "estranged a bit," according to Sears. Like the politics of his sister, Ron's hewed decidedly to the left, which caused its share of friction in the family. What's more, he'd declared himself an atheist while still a teenager and made it a lifelong cause. And like his siblings, Ron was starved for attention from his parents.

Every politician was expected to parade his children before the public to demonstrate that he was a family man, but for Ronald Reagan this took some doing. His family wasn't a warm and fuzzy clan. For the Reagans, public life had always superseded private life. When the children were young, Ronnie and Nancy were taken up with travel, with work, with perpetual socializing, all of which advanced his career. Now that the children were entering adulthood, there wasn't much parent-child foundation to call upon. Patti was always cynical about her father and his conservative ideals; Ron wafted in and out of engagement with the family. The way they saw it, their father had rarely been there for the kids when they needed him. They never had his full attention. Now, when the situation was reversed, Patti and Ron didn't feel any urgency about making an effort. So it was reassuring when the family united to stage a Kodak moment.

"Good evening," Ronald Reagan said, welcoming the packed crowd in the Hilton ballroom with his usual Hollywood polish. He promptly got to the point. "I am here tonight to announce my intention to seek the Republican nomination for the President of the United States."

Once again borrowing Franklin D. Roosevelt's most storied phrase, Reagan reminded the audience three different times that America had "a rendezvous with destiny." He intended personally to keep that assignation, and there wasn't one person in the seats—or among the millions of viewers who watched a videotaped broadcast—who didn't believe he had the means to pull it off.

CHAPTER TWENTY-NINE

"BIG MO"

*"There is a sea-change coming in American politics. This will be
the most important election in this century."*

—JOHN CONNALLY

J ust days after Ronald Reagan's announcement, his campaign kicked
off a four-day, eleven-state pacesetting tour with a splash of good
news: a *New York Times*/CBS poll showed him decisively ahead, with
37 percent of Republicans favoring him to 15 percent for John Connally
and 13 percent for Howard Baker. On the stump, he trotted out all the
themes he'd struck for the past fifteen years: reduced federal spending, a
sizable tax cut, a stronger national military, downsizing the federal bureaucracy, and a return to good old American values. One other issue emerged
that no one could have anticipated: on November 4, 1979, a throng of Iranian students seized the U.S. embassy in Tehran and took fifty-two Americans hostage. The shah had been overthrown in a yearlong revolution,
and the new Iranian government, presided over by fundamentalist Islamist
clerics, refused to negotiate for the hostages' release. Jimmy Carter set the
negotiations on a path of no return when he announced, "The United
States will not yield to terrorism."

Reagan initially held off from criticizing President Carter on Iran, not
wanting to interfere with efforts to free the hostages. But by mid-January
1980, after the Soviet Union had invaded neighboring Afghanistan, Reagan reconsidered and went on the attack. Speaking to reporters in South
Carolina, he stated, "I cannot doubt that our failure to act decisively at the

time this happened provided the Russians with the final encouragement to invade Afghanistan."

The Iranian and Afghan situations generated ample campaign fodder, but Ronald Reagan had a crisis of his own to attend to. The first real test of the campaign was the Iowa caucuses on January 21, 1980. Iowa was still pretty much an anomaly. Until the 1976 election, when Jimmy Carter used the state to launch his presidential bid, the caucuses were seen as nothing more than a beauty contest, with all the national spotlight focused on New Hampshire. But Carter showed that Iowa could propel an unknown into the Oval Office, so in 1980 it loomed large on the political map as a harbinger of things to come.

Everyone assumed Reagan would carry the day in Iowa. He was polling there at roughly 50 percent, so John Sears elected to keep his candidate's presence in the state to a minimum. "We were going to win Iowa anyway," Jim Lake explains. "Why go to a place that doesn't count for anything in terms of delegates?" Ronald Reagan made a few appearances in the state, but conserved his energy for rallies in New Hampshire and Florida, states that really mattered.

George Bush, on the other hand, practically lived in Iowa. No one had given him much of a chance in the race. He had low visibility and notoriously awful political instincts. At large rallies with formal speeches, he came off stiff and uncomfortable. "He was awkward, with a thin voice," says Jim Leach, Bush's co-chair in Iowa. But he turned out to be great at what strategists call *retail campaigning*—shaking hands, speaking to small groups assembled in somebody's living room, asking for votes on a one-on-one basis. And he had secret weapons: Barbara Bush, whom Leach credits as being "in many ways more impressive than her husband"; and Roy B. Keppy, the most respected farmer in the state, who became an emissary for the Bush campaign.

Keppy spoke on Bush's behalf to the Corn Growers Association, the Soybean Growers Association, the Cattlemen's Association, and the Pork Producers. "It meant that many farmers who naturally would have voted for Reagan, voted for Bush," Leach recalls. And anyone who even intimated they might vote for George Bush was courted by his aides. Their name was put on an index card, they were called repeatedly, sent updates, and encouraged over and over to get out and vote. Bush himself would follow up, calling people and writing them personal notes. What Bush lacked in political instincts he made up for in pure enthusiasm.

"We could sense him coming on," recalls Charlie Black, who had assumed the role of Reagan's national political director. Still, Ronald Reagan maintained a comfortable lead in the polls, and his operatives directed his efforts elsewhere. Perhaps their biggest mistake was holding him out of the all-candidates Iowa debate sponsored by the League of Women Voters on January 19. "Why give those other guys a chance to gang up on Reagan in a forum where he could only respond to any of their remarks when his turn came fifteen minutes later?" John Sears says.

Unfortunately, his absence at the debate spoke volumes to the voters and enabled the other candidates to direct all their energies to savaging the front-runner. The backlash was swift and brutal. A *Des Moines Register* poll taken the day after the debate showed Reagan's numbers plummeting by half. Workers at a local Reagan campaign office in the southwestern corner of Iowa were beside themselves with exasperation. "You've pissed off everybody in the state!" they complained to anyone who would listen. "Most of us still thought that Reagan was going to pull it out and win the caucuses," says Jim Kuhn, at the time a regional aide to the campaign, but the playing field had certainly been releveled to an extent.

The evening of the caucuses, the Reagan brain trust—John Sears, Charlie Black, and Jim Lake—convened in a suite at the Fort Des Moines, a hotel where forty-five years earlier Dutch Reagan had socialized with friends. One of their regional assistants was monitoring the vote count, county by county, and reported in by phone every hour. "This is not looking good," he said around nine o'clock. By one in the morning it was all over. George Bush had won.

Reality set in immediately that Ronald Reagan was no longer the front-runner. To drive a stake through the heart of his campaign, Tom Pettit, NBC's political commentator, announced: "You have just witnessed the political obituary of Ronald Reagan." George Bush now had the momentum—or "Big Mo," as he was calling it.

Big Mo, indeed. Two days earlier, Ronald Reagan was ahead of Bush in New Hampshire by twenty-five points. The day after the Iowa caucuses, Reagan lagged twenty points behind him.

"We were really shocked," Charlie Black admits. "It never crossed our minds that we could lose Iowa."

Ronald Reagan managed to take it in stride; he had a long-range view of things and resolved not to let a setback throw him off his pace. Nancy, however, was frosted—she wanted answers. The Reagans had been campaigning in Illinois, where they reconnected with their team, and on the flight to New Hampshire, they—Nancy especially—grilled John Sears, Charlie Black, and Jim Lake. "In Iowa we got caught with our pants down," Sears admitted, accepting full blame. "But the big contest is New Hampshire, where we are solid as a rock. We're going to do a poll tonight, Governor, and it wouldn't surprise me if Bush is ahead. But if we get within five points of him in New Hampshire, we'll win in South Carolina and be back on track."

Sears had a trick up his sleeve. Later that afternoon, after everyone was squared away in a hotel near Andover, Massachusetts, he gathered Black and Lake and laid out the strategy. "This time," he said, "no let-up. We'll do the League of Women Voters debate, though Reagan won't get much traction from it. What we need is a one-on-one debate with Bush. I think we could kick his ass."

Charlie Black shook his head. "They are too smart for that. They're ahead right now." He was adamant. "There is no fucking way they are ever going to do it." Recounting the conversation forty years later, Black can barely suppress a grin. "It took us an hour to figure out how to pull it off."

Reagan had been invited by both the *Manchester Union Leader* and the *Concord Monitor* to participate in a series of debates. Instead, Jim Lake proposed a debate sponsored by the *Nashua Telegraph*. "It's in the more liberal part of the state near Massachusetts," he explained, "which is Bush country." The trick was persuading Hugh Gregg—Reagan's New Hampshire state chairman in 1976, now performing the same job for George Bush—to agree. "I can get him to go for it," Lake said. "I know the guy. I know how to play this."

That night, following a speech of Reagan's at St. Anselm College, just north of Manchester, Jim Lake stole into the college president's office and phoned Hugh Gregg. "Looks like you're on your way to the White House," he said. "We're twenty points behind and two weeks out—you guys seem poised to win this big. So what we really need to do is get all these other turkeys out of the race. They're just stirring up things and making it more difficult for you and us. If we can get this down to a two-man race coming out of New Hampshire, it'll be all over except for the two of us." He explained to Gregg how a two-man debate would demonstrate the strength at the top of the ticket, forcing the other candidates to drop out.

"A week later," Lake would recall, "the *Nashua Telegraph* has a front-page story—a debate they are sponsoring on February 20, 1980, a week before the primary. Just the two of us: Reagan and Bush! Sears and Lake couldn't believe it, but I knew Hugh Gregg like a book. He couldn't resist taking the bait."

Sears warned his lieutenants to expect an uproar. "The other candidates will never take this sitting down."

B ob Dole was the first one out of his seat. "This is preposterous!" he fumed after arriving in New Hampshire. "You guys are arrogant. Jerks! This is nothing but a corporate contribution to two candidates." To stress his point, he filed a grievance with the Federal Election Commission, claiming the *Telegraph* was not a neutral observer. After all, he argued, wasn't Hugh Gregg, George Bush's chairman, on the board of the paper? Howard Baker joined Dole's complaint: it wasn't fair for a newspaper to underwrite such an event.

The FEC agreed. A day later, one of the Reagan aides called Jim Lake to notify him that the *Nashua Telegraph* was pulling out of the debate. The FEC ruled that the paper wasn't permitted to pay for it. "Tell them *we'll* pay for it," Lake responded. The campaign had more than enough money in the budget allotted to New Hampshire. Because there were ceilings placed on what a campaign was allowed to spend in each state—and because New Hampshire was considered crucial to the race—the Reagan forces had been staying in a hotel just across the border in Massachusetts so that the expenditure wouldn't count against the New Hampshire filing ceilings. "Tell them *we'll* pay for it," Lake repeated. "We'll pay for the whole debate."

When George Bush heard the offer, he accepted it with pleasure. Sure—let Ronald Reagan pick up the check. "That became the biggest damn gift he could ever have given us," Lake says.

New Hampshire was Reagan's last stand. He stumped through the state on a brutal dusk-to-dawn schedule, often sixteen hours a day for two weeks at a clip before grabbing a rare day off to recharge. Side excursions to Florida, Georgia, South Carolina, and New Jersey were mixed in. "He was dog tired," says Charlie Black, "but even when we worked him to the bone we made sure he got eight hours' sleep." Up to now, Nancy had ruthlessly limited her husband's schedule to four-day outings in order to protect his health and stamina, while carving out hours for naps and downtime, but she made concessions in must-win New Hampshire. From now on, his only off days would be Sunday. And Sears dispatched Nancy on her own itinerary of appearances.

The Bushes, George and Barbara, were tearing through the state. Big Mo—it was all Bush could talk about. The minute he hit the tarmac in New Hampshire, with snow practically obscuring his arrival, he was beguiling the press with the wonders of Big Mo. But Big Mo wasn't his only secret weapon.

"Barbara Bush was a dynamo," Charlie Black says, "George's greatest asset. Everyone who met her couldn't help but like her." She was the yin to Nancy Reagan's yang. There were no designer dresses in her trousseau, she didn't travel with her hairdresser or diet religiously or factor in the astrological details. Barbara Bush smiled engagingly, *warmly*, in a crowd of housewives. She projected a homespun, down-to-earth image: outgoing, earthy, unvarnished—"fake pearls and real family," as one writer described her effect. New Hampshire women gravitated easily to Barbara Bush, especially when she shared cookie recipes and needlepoint patterns and family stories. "I think women like me because they don't think I'm competitive, just nice," she reflected years later. But insiders knew she was a warrior who could go nose-to-nose with Nancy Reagan. "On the face of it, she is so benign," says Sheila Tate, "but she can be ruthless, tough as nails."

Nancy Reagan sensed this and picked up her pace. She was determined not to be outmatched by a jolly, silver-haired, cookie-baking mercenary. She also took more of a role in the Reagan campaign machinery, keeping close tabs on the team as they marched through the state. As far as she or anyone could tell, they were making headway, chipping away at George

Bush's lead, which stood at 37 percent to 28 percent with two weeks to go. Everyone felt they could close the gap, but morale had hit an all-time low. The Reagan campaign was bleeding money; so far, under the extravagant direction of John Sears, it had spent "close to $12 million, two-thirds of the $18 million total they were allowed to spend throughout the entire primary campaign" under federal financing laws. A review of the books showed they were $600,000 in debt. Moreover, a serious rift had developed between members of Reagan's California staff and the Sears faction, which had walled itself off from the rest of the team. Nancy Reagan sensed it and tried to defuse the mounting tension. "Every night, when we returned to the hotel," she recalled, "I would go from one room to another meeting in corridors and corners with John and the others, trying everything I could think of to bring people together and smooth things over." But Sears had grown moody, inscrutable—Napoleonic, many thought. "He was never one to talk a lot," Jim Lake recalls, "and he would stew inside and process things internally."

Ronald Reagan was shielded from the in-fighting as much as possible.

But there was no avoiding it: John Sears seemed to have lost control of the campaign. "Things started to unravel fast," says Ed Meese. "There were real problems with John, who was unwilling to delegate authority, while using every opportunity to make many of us look bad." The two factions often operated at cross-purposes, causing one staff member to comment: "It's like a civil war in here." The disharmony went straight to the top. "Sears became impatient and irritable with Reagan," Jeff Bell recalls. "You could sense they'd become alienated from one another." And Reagan still carried a grudge over the firing of Mike Deaver. "The chemistry between [Reagan and Sears] wasn't good to begin with, and now it was worse," Nancy Reagan recalled. Something had to give.

Ed Meese suggested that Ronald Reagan consider bringing in an ally to stabilize the staff, someone with good management skills who would be on an equal footing with Sears the rest of the way through. Reagan agreed and asked Bill Clark, his former executive assistant in Sacramento, to step in and help, but Clark had taken on a judgeship that prohibited his absence from California. As an alternative, they turned to William Casey.

Casey was an unconventional character with an eclectic résumé. He'd come out of law school during the Depression and made his fortune developing practice books for lawyers on tax regulations. During World War II he ran the secret war in Europe for the Office of Strategic Services and became involved in the management of the company that became Capitol Broadcasting. He had run for Congress, developed issue papers for the Nixon White House, and become the first undersecretary of state for economic affairs. Later, Casey resurfaced as the chairman of the Securities and Exchange Commission. An ardent conservative, he'd bought an interest in *National Review* upon its debut in 1955 and contributed unselfishly to Republican causes. "He's a smart guy with good management experience," Meese assured Reagan, and they invited him to discuss joining the campaign.

Casey met with Reagan on February 15 at the Holiday Inn in Worcester, Massachusetts, where Reagan was speaking over the weekend. Without beating around the bush, Casey said he'd looked over the campaign's books and confronted a financial disaster in the making. They needed to cut staff by half and retrench or they'd be bankrupt within weeks. He'd be willing to come aboard and realign administrative operations, which would leave John Sears with more time to concentrate on political strategy. Reagan thought it all made good sense, and conveyed as much to Sears later that night in his suite.

Sears listened to the proposal that he share duties with Casey and agreed at least to think it over. If he had left well enough alone and gone back to his room, the outcome might have been different. Instead, he launched into a tirade about the state of the campaign that touched a raw nerve of Ronald Reagan's. The gloves came off, and a shouting match ensued that could be heard up and down the hotel corridor. At some point, Sears must have expressed his desire to get rid of Ed Meese, because occupants in adjoining rooms overheard Reagan scream: "You got Lyn Nofziger. You got Mike Deaver. *You're not getting Ed Meese!*" Nancy Reagan hid out in the bedroom through it all and grew fearful as the hostilities escalated. Toward three o'clock in the morning, her husband's emotions seemed set to boil over. "I was sure he was going to hit John," she recalled. Bursting into the living room, she refereed as best she could and said, "It's late. We've got another long day ahead of us. I think we should all get some sleep."

Before they went to bed, however, it was decided that an indelible line had been crossed. The campaign needed a fresh, more cooperative outlook.

John Sears would have to go.

A transition strategy came together fast. Bill Casey agreed to take over the entire campaign, as soon as Sears was out of the picture. The details, for the most part, were kept under wraps, but on a bus the night before the Nashua debate, Reagan summoned Charlie Black to sit with him. "I'm very upset with John," Reagan confided in a whisper. "If we make a change, can we count on you to stay?" Nancy Reagan asked Black and Jim Lake the same question during a flight to a one-day event in Chicago. Both of Sears's men dodged answering, insisting it was imperative for the Reagans to stay the course. "It's not a matter of whether or not you *like* John," Black explained. "Nobody else is equipped to make Ron the president."

It was too late for a reprieve. The decision was made to replace Sears on Tuesday, February 26, while New Hampshire voters were still at the polls. The timing for the dismissal was crucial. "If Reagan lost the New Hampshire primary, we'd blame it on Sears," explains Dick Allen, one of the architects of the coup. "If he won, Sears would be a page-two story." That way, Reagan could never be accused of being an ungrateful winner or a sore loser. Bill Casey had already arrived to take his place. But first things first: the Nashua debate.

John Sears had one strategy left in his arsenal. Earlier on the Friday night that he'd sparred with Ronald Reagan, he summoned Black and Lake to his hotel room and laid out a plan. "You know, we ought to let the other candidates in the debate," he said. "Call them and invite them to take part." His two cronies were speechless. The maneuver was certain to cause mayhem. Everyone knew George Bush was salivating to go head-to-head with Ronald Reagan. The Bush team, they knew, would feel sandbagged and fight this tooth and nail. "John had it in his head to do this from the beginning," Black insists, although Sears only smiles cryptically when asked to confirm. In any case, he instructed his men to call the others and say, "Reagan's had second thoughts, and it's not fair to exclude you." Only John Connally, who was campaigning in Minnesota, was unable to accept.

Jim Lake had a press release drawn up to announce the last-minute change. When he showed it to Nancy Reagan, there was immediate relief. "We *have* to do that. It's exactly *right*," she said. She waved at her husband, who was on the phone, and after getting his attention she pointed furiously to the sheet of paper in Lake's hand. "I don't know what you're selling," Reagan said after hanging up, "but my wife's buying." As it turned out, he was buying, too, feeling that inviting the other candidates was absolutely the fair thing to do.

Now, all they had to do was to convince George Bush.

It went without question that Bush was not buying. "You can't do this," his field manager, Bruce Rounds, objected, "otherwise we're going to cancel the debate." Jim Lake shook his head. "You can't," he replied. "We paid for it. We're paying for everything." The tickets were already sold out. The whole town was abuzz. At seven o'clock, exactly as scheduled, the high school auditorium would be packed.

George Bush wouldn't have it. "No way you're taking this away from me," he fumed. "I've earned this. You're not going to screw me." At his bidding, the *Nashua Telegraph* threatened to pull out. John Breen, the editor, insisted they'd agreed to a two-man debate. "That's what we advertised and what everybody's expecting," he said, indicating it was the only way the paper intended to let the event proceed. But Charlie Black kept filibustering until it was past six o'clock and the auditorium was already filling up, too late to pull the plug.

Meanwhile, Jim Lake picked Ronald Reagan up from the hotel in order to brief him on the debate. "Governor, there has been some controversy," he explained. "The Bush people are upset, the *Nashua Telegraph* threatened to pull out, so we're going into sort of a hostile environment."

"We're going to have the debate?" Reagan wondered.

"We haven't gotten Bush's agreement to take the other guys. Still, we're going ahead with it even though there's a question as to whether they'll permit it."

The scene at Nashua High School offered no comfort. Ronald Reagan was herded into a kindergarten room, where the other four candidates were sequestered in tiny tables and chairs with their feet splayed into the aisles, surrounded by their wives and Secret Service chaperones and reporters shouting questions. It was chaos, steamy. Bob Dole was livid. "That no-account! Those no good sons of bitches!" he bellowed, throwing in a few choicer words to describe George Bush and his men. Bush, for his part, was barricaded in a holding room down the hall. His campaign manager, Jim Baker, stood guard at the door, refusing to allow even Gordon Humphrey, the senator from New Hampshire, to appeal to Bush's better instincts. Humphrey made his pitch to Baker while standing in the hall, claiming it would look bad for the state if everyone wasn't included. "Aw, fuck you guys!" Baker said, and disappeared inside, slamming the door.

At five minutes to seven, a student knocked on the kindergarten door with a message from the stage. "Mr. Breen says that if Mr. Reagan isn't onstage in three minutes, he's going to forfeit the debate to George Bush."

Reagan stood up and addressed the room. "Let's all of us go up there. I'll make my case, and if they won't take all six of us we'll walk out."

Jim Lake grabbed him by the cuff. "Governor—no!" he said. "You *must* stay, no matter what happens." Gordon Humphrey agreed. "You stay up there and you win," he insisted. "You walk off, you lose—Bush wins." Lake chimed in, "Whatever happens, you are going to stay there. *You have to stay onstage!*"

"Got it," Reagan concurred, leading Bob Dole, Philip Crane, Howard Baker, and John Anderson through a maze of back stairs and corridors up to the auditorium.

When they walked in, the place was mobbed, buzzing with anticipation. The audience sensed that something was amiss. George Bush was already seated onstage, his jaw set in granite. He stared straight ahead, refusing to shake hands with, look at, or acknowledge either Ronald Reagan or the four other Republicans who stood in a soldierly line behind him.

Reagan stepped gamely to the lectern, leaning over the microphone. "I'd like to have a word . . ." he began.

John Breen, the moderator, interrupted him. "There is no time for this."

"I want to have a moment to explain why these gentlemen, who are all candidates, ought to at least have the opportunity to introduce themselves," Reagan persisted.

"If you don't stop, Governor, we're going to turn off the microphone!"

Ronald Reagan shot bolt upright, a wave of crimson tided into his face.

"Just a minute here. *Mr. Green*," he thundered, botching the moderator's name, "*I paid for this microphone!*"

It was a seminal moment in the campaign. The crowd went nuts, stomping and applauding. A chant went up: "Bring them chairs! Bring them chairs!" It took several minutes to restore order. Reagan must have known the line would play well. He'd heard Spencer Tracy deliver it, almost word for word, as a Republican presidential candidate in *State of the Union*. George Bush, who had sped around the state on high-octane Big Mo, now looked wilted, like he had nothing left in the tank. After the four also-rans departed and the two-man debate got under way, Bush seemed unnerved, stumbling through his answers.

Jim Lake, watching from the back of the hall, borrowed a piece of paper from NBC anchor John Chancellor, who was standing next to him. Across the top he scrawled a short message, then scooted down the aisle and through a door that led backstage. "Would you please give this to the governor," he instructed a Secret Service agent positioned in the wings.

George Bush was in the midst of a feeble explanation about the perils of Soviet appeasement when the note was delivered into Ronald Reagan's hands. Reagan's face remained frozen in the same stern gaze that accompanied Bush's rebuttal as he glanced down and read the message. "Governor, you're doing great," it said. "That was fantastic. But *you have to stay on the stage.*"

Reagan gave Bush another determined scowl, then he turned around to where Lake was standing and winked.

It was unanimous. Everyone agreed Ronald Reagan had won the debate the minute he took the stage with the four uninvited candidates. George Bush's intransigence was regarded as a serious blunder by which, as *Newsweek* reported, he "thoroughly embarrassed himself." "Looking back on it," said Jim Baker, Bush's campaign manager, "I wish we had met with the other candidates before the debate." Had Bush said, "Governor, you make a good case," and welcomed the others, he'd have been applauded for his generosity and a hearty debate would have ensued. As it turned out, he came off as petty and weak.

Three days later, New Hampshire agreed. Reagan "handily defeated" George Bush in the primary, with a 50 percent, come-from-behind victory. It was a stunning reversal of the Iowa outcome and a harbinger of what *Newsweek* called "the engine of his revival."

Before any celebration, there was housecleaning to tend to. Nancy Reagan opened the deliberations by saying, "We can't go on like this. It's now definite—all three must go. Power must be handed over to Bill Casey." When her husband suggested that Charlie Black and Jim Lake might be persuaded to stay on through the remainder of the primaries, she waved him off. "Let's not go over this again." Their dismissal was choreographed with pinpoint precision. Sears, Black, and Lake were called into the Reagans' suite in Andover just after lunch on primary day and presented with their resignation letters. Before Charlie Black even read it, he said, "Don't bother—I quit!"

Bill Casey was a brilliant but awkward, enigmatic creature, tall and hunched-over with robotic movements. When he didn't want to be understood or quoted, he mumbled to great effect. And he did this now, in a hastily-pulled-together press conference, sounding almost cryptic and playing with his tie while attempting to explain the changing of the guard. The press was poised for a couple of pithy quotes, but as Casey rambled on in something that sounded like Urdu, the journalists cut glances at one another, wondering if this was part of a joke. "They would ask him questions," Pete Hannaford recalls, "and he'd go mumble, mumble, mumble and say three of four clear words."

Nevertheless, Casey got right to work—sharply cutting the staff in Washington and Los Angeles and slashing the salaries of everyone who remained. Cost-cutting was his first priority. Even Nancy Reagan's hairdresser was temporarily sent back to Los Angeles.

The campaign was headed to South Carolina with practically no money in the bank. But Casey had access to East Coast money, and he brought in Charles Wick, a social friend of Nancy and Ronnie's with connections to West Coast money, and together they turned on the fund-raising spigots, gradually replenishing the reserves. Money was crucial to maintaining the positive energy, but so was Big Mo—and now Ronald Reagan had it.

Big Mo swept him through the South Carolina primary, where he knocked John Connally out of the race. And three days later, he pulled out decisive wins in Alabama, Florida, and Georgia, forcing Howard Baker and Bob Dole to withdraw. For all intents and purposes, the Republican primary was down to a four-man race: Ronald Reagan, George Bush, Phil Crane, and John Anderson, although the Ghost of Elections Past was rearing its head.

By mid-March 1980, there were serious rumblings that Gerald Ford was considering wading into the mix. GOP moderates expressed concern that Reagan's eventual nomination as a right-leaning conservative might augur a repeat performance of the Goldwater debacle in a national election. Ford, they recalled, had nearly beaten Jimmy Carter four years earlier, and recent Gallup polls showed Ford leading Reagan among all candidates prepared to take on the president, and that "Carter would lose to Ford but would win handily over Reagan."

Reagan doubted Ford would run, and he goaded his former opponent, saying he "should pack his long johns and come out here on the campaign trail with us." But the press fanned the flames of a Ford candidacy, and Nancy Reagan took it to heart. "She was a nervous wreck about it," recalls Jim Kuhn, who escorted her during appearances in Florida. "*It's going to happen!* He's coming in," she insisted, certain it would derail her Ronnie's path to the White House. Her fears crescendoed further when news filtered back that John Sears and Stu Spencer had been summoned to Ford's home in Rancho Mirage to discuss a possible run and that Tom Reed, Reagan's devoted former national committee chairman, had launched a Draft Ford committee with GOP backing.

Ford continued to toy with Reagan, still stung by the challenge in 1976. "Ford was dismissive of Reagan," Tom Reed says. "He told me, 'Reagan isn't fit to be president.'" But by the end of March, with time closing in for him to file in the California and Ohio primaries, Ford convened a meeting of supporters in Palm Springs, and, as Reed recalls, "all those guys who were red-hot for him early on were suddenly nowhere to be found. The few of us who showed up went around the table saying, 'If you want to run, we're with you—but you can't win.'" Ford couldn't argue with such hard-boiled facts. "Let's not do that," he told them, realizing he had waited too long. Instead, he went directly from that meeting, called a press conference, and announced that he reached the decision not to run.

Ford's withdrawal propelled Reagan into a decisive win in Illinois on March 18, where he beat native son John Anderson. And on March 25, he converted enough moderates to win in New York before sweeping all challengers in Wisconsin a week later.

By mid-May, Reagan's nomination seemed like a runaway certainty. No less a skeptical authority than the *Washington Post* published articles with titles like "Why Ronald Reagan Will Be the Next President." Convincing losses in Michigan and Pennsylvania sent Reagan's Big Mo into a skid, and primaries in California, Ohio, and New Jersey on June 3 still gave some cause for concern. But not much. And on May 30, Memorial Day, Bush called a press conference and dropped out of the race. A Reagan landslide was inevitable, he conceded, and he refused to be a spoiler at the Republican National Convention.

The Republican National Convention opened in Detroit's Joe Louis Arena on Monday, July 14, 1980. The Reagans arrived in town around noon. "Nancy and I were just flying by and thought we'd drop in to see what was going on," Reagan joked to a crowd of supporters at the airport before checking into a sixty-ninth-floor suite at the Plaza Hotel in the Renaissance Center, their hideaway, more or less, until the nomination was resolved on Thursday night. From the outset, aides calculated Reagan had enough committed delegates to deliver a victory on the first ballot, eliminating the chore of trolling for votes. It allowed him to concentrate entirely on the most outstanding task: choosing a running mate.

As early as July, at Bill Casey's suggestion, they'd assembled a list of twelve possible candidates and enlisted Ed Smotes, the deputy secretary of the treasury, to collect their income-tax data, to give them physical exams, and, most important, to vet them. One of the contenders, Cliff Wallace, an appellate judge from San Diego, discovered during his physical that he had a cancerous tumor and removed himself from consideration; Jack Kemp was viewed as too young and inexperienced; Jesse Helms was well-liked by diehard conservatives but not by anyone else; Howard Baker lacked strong conservative credentials; Richard Lugar got rejected out of hand; and Richard Thornburgh, the popular governor of Pennsylvania, announced that "Reagan's people have given him 'no indication' they even know who he is." "Ronald Reagan would have loved to run with Paul Laxalt," says Ed Meese, who oversaw the selection process. The governors had become good friends over the years, and Laxalt wanted the job—badly. But Stu Spencer, who'd returned as an adviser to the campaign, explained to Reagan that Laxalt "was the governor of a gaming state, where you don't get elected without doing business with the boys." The last thing the campaign needed was fielding questions about the mob. There was already plenty of smoke about Nancy's buddy Frank Sinatra, who had applied for a gaming license in Nevada using Reagan as a reference while under investigation for alleged Mafia connections.

The obvious choice—George Bush—got short shrift from Ronald Reagan, perplexing many on his campaign staff. Bush was young and energetic with a strong New England base, and his moderate constituency would balance the ticket, uniting factions of the Republican Party. Moreover, he'd run strong in the primaries. But Reagan had never forgiven Bush for coining the phrase "voodoo economics" to describe Reagan's free-market and supply-side policies. And the lingering image of Bush freezing up on stage at the Nashua debate left Reagan feeling that Bush had no backbone. "Doesn't matter," Stu Spencer advised Reagan on the flight to Detroit, "you're a pragmatic guy and you need him." But Reagan wasn't convinced. "He just didn't like him," Spencer says.

Reagan was intrigued by a rumor that had been floated by Henry Kissinger and Brent Scowcroft—a "dream ticket," they were calling it, with Ronald Reagan as president and Gerald Ford as vice president. It seemed ludicrous at first. A former president returning to the White House in a lesser capacity was unprecedented and frankly inconceivable. Besides, there was no love lost between Reagan and Ford, which stemmed from the 1976 primary. Ford attempted to nip the idea in the bud, telling the press that he had no intention of running with Reagan as late as two days before the convention. But the scheme persisted as a potential bonanza—and it picked up steam. "There were a sufficient number of people in high places within the party who wanted this," Ed Meese recalls, singling out moderates and "establishment people" who he says weren't convinced that

Ronald Reagan had the stuff to be president—or to win. "So the governor felt we ought to at least look into it as a possibility."

Not an hour after the Reagans settled into their hotel room, Ronald Reagan hit the elevator directly to Ford's suite on the seventieth floor of the Plaza in order to sound out the former president's intentions. In a 1999 interview, Ford recalled the meeting as an outright invitation. "Ron said that he and Nancy wanted me to be his running mate in 1980! I was overwhelmed and flattered. In deference to his request, I said I would think about it and talk to Betty."

The offer, according to Meese, was intended as nothing more than a polite gesture, and Reagan "was surprised when Ford in essence said that he would think about it." In any case, the response kicked the idea of the dream ticket into high gear. The *Detroit News*, among the many papers who endorsed the notion, declared, "The ideal Reagan running mate would be Gerald Ford."

Ford got a jump on producing an overall game plan. The next evening, he spent two hours with Henry Kissinger and Alan Greenspan, devising a strategy by which "the President would be the Chief Policymaker, but the Vice-President would be the Chief Operator." In effect, it would give Ford control over the National Security Council as well as the Office of Management and Budget, with Kissinger and Greenspan as his respective point men.

Their proposal was delivered to Meese the next morning. "It was a bad idea," Meese thought immediately. "It gave away a lot of the power of the presidency. If we accepted it, it would be a sign that Ronald Reagan wasn't up to the job, that he needed bolstering, which would sink him in the campaign." Others on the staff agreed—Deaver, Nofziger, and Allen were flat-out opposed—but felt that, in good faith, they should negotiate with Ford's team.

Meese wanted the particulars on structure and duties spelled out: how the two offices would operate, how policy would be handled with Congress, who would dictate foreign policy. He, Bill Casey, and pollster Dick Wirthlin met with Kissinger, Greenspan, and Jack Marsh, Ford's former counselor, on Wednesday morning to flesh out details. They went back and forth all day long until, by evening, some clarity emerged. When Lyn

Nofziger asked Reagan how things shook out, he responded, "Ford wants Kissinger as Secretary of State and Greenspan at Treasury." Dick Allen, who overheard the exchange, blurted out, "That is the craziest deal I ever heard of." Nancy Reagan was beside herself. "I thought the whole thing was ridiculous," she recalled. "It can't be done," she told Ronnie. "It would be a dual presidency. It just won't work."

Reagan, however, remained vaguely optimistic. All signals from the convention floor were that the delegates loved it. Two Republican headliners taking on Jimmy Carter—the ticket, to them, sounded thrilling, unbeatable. Discussions between the interested parties continued, and by nightfall, the press had gotten wind of them, splashing news of the potential partnership across the TV networks.

At roughly seven-thirty, Reagan awoke from a catnap and plopped down on a couch in front of three muted television sets. A few minutes later, one set, tuned in to Walter Cronkite's broadcast, caught his interest when Gerald Ford sat down opposite the CBS anchor. Reagan motioned for the sound to be turned up.

"If I go to Washington," Ford was saying, "and I'm not saying that I'm accepting, I have to go there with the belief that I would play a meaningful role, across the board, in the basic, crucial, tough decisions that have to be made in the four-year period."

"It's to be something like a co-presidency?" Cronkite asked Ford.

A co-presidency!

Reagan nearly fell over on the couch. "Get Kissinger on the phone," he insisted. "I want Ford's answer right now. This has gone too far."

It was time for both men to put their cards on the table. Reagan ordered Bill Casey upstairs to confront Ford, relaying a message that any understanding between them "had to be based on faith or understanding, it could not be a written compact." Meanwhile, the networks were reporting the ticket as a fait accompli. Reagan began to realize the nomination was running away with itself. Doesn't Ford "realize there is no way in the world I can accept?" he said aloud to himself. "What kind of presidential candidate would I be in the eyes of the world if I were to give in to such demands?" Yet with all his irresolution, negotiations pushed on.

Ford had modified his demands. He no longer insisted that Kissinger become the secretary of state—a nonstarter as far as Reagan was concerned—but he wanted to be chairman of the National Security Council and to have veto power over major Cabinet appointments.

"Governor," Meese reported back, "I don't think this is going any place." Reagan agreed, discouraged by the impasse. "Let's get this over with," he told Meese, "now."

At 11:13 that evening, during the traditional roll call of delegates, the state of Montana put Ronald Reagan over the top on the first ballot. Word began circulating almost immediately that the nominee would put in an appearance at the convention hall with his running mate, an unusual development considering that the grand entrance was typically reserved for the final night as icing on the cake. But Reagan knew expectations were strong that he would arrive with Gerald Ford in tow. "I ought to go over there tonight," he decided, "if only to calm things down."

A string of limousines was lined up in the garage of the hotel, preparing for the convoy to the Joe Louis Arena. "The television was on in the garage," recalls Jim Kuhn, who was coordinating the motorcade, "and all the talk was about Reagan choosing Ford." One of the Secret Service agents poked his head in to announce, "We have movement coming down from the sixty-ninth floor." No one knew who was on the elevator, except that it was not Ronald Reagan. "Whoever gets off that elevator is *not* Reagan's choice," Kuhn announced to the gaggle of drivers and auxiliary staff. The wait was excruciating, Kuhn recalled. "We waited and waited and *waited*—that elevator took a long time coming down." Finally, the chime sounded, as everyone in the garage cast a furtive eye on the opening doors to see who emerged. A collective gasp was audible at the sight of Betty and Gerald Ford. "Governor Reagan will be down next," Kuhn said, "and it's anyone's guess who will be with him."

George Bush was in the bar of the Pontchartrain Hotel, Bush headquarters, having cocktails with his press aide, Pete Teeley. They were commiserating over the news that, a few hours earlier, Reagan staffers confirmed Bush was no longer under consideration as a vice-presidential choice. It was a humiliating blow. Bush felt he had deserved more respect than an out-right dismissal. After all, he'd beaten Reagan handily in five major prima-ries, but word had it that Ford had been chosen. As they talked, Teeley glanced over Bush at a man entering the room, shouldering a TV camera. "We'd better get out of here or you'll find yourself on the news," Teeley warned. Bush refused to budge. He was still smarting from Reagan's obvi-ous rebuff and feeling too proud to duck and run. Teeley, however, per-sisted, persuading Bush to head back to his suite. He arrived there to a state of general commotion.

Ronald Reagan was on the phone.

The governor explained he was leaving soon for a late-night appearance at Joe Louis Arena. "George," he said, "I would like to go over there and tell them that I am recommending you for vice president." Bush was so taken aback he could barely get the word "yes" out of his mouth. "Could I ask you one thing," Reagan continued. "Do I have your permission to make an announcement that you support the platform across the board?" This had been another serious factor against selecting Bush as a running mate. He had campaigned in favor of the Equal Rights Amendment, a woman's right to abortion, and gun control, to say nothing about crowning Reagan as the houngan of voodoo economics. Ed Meese later joked that Bush had an exorcism that night. He agreed wholeheartedly to endorse the platform from top to bottom. He "was honored," he said, and "would work, work, work." In fact, he'd change clothes in a jiffy and head over to the conven-tion in time to walk in alongside the party's nominee.

When Ronald Reagan and George Bush entered Joe Louis Arena, they carried themselves with the easy intimacy of longtime partners. The two men seemed dynamic, dignified—a force to be reckoned with. Together, they were loaded with Big Mo.

CHAPTER THIRTY

"A REFERENDUM ON
UNHAPPINESS"

*"Politics is just like show business. You have a hell of an opening,
coast for a while and then have a hell of a close."*

—RONALD REAGAN

Jimmy Carter seemed eminently beatable. Saddled with high inflation, spiraling unemployment, a groaning energy crisis, and a hostage
situation (including a botched attempt at a rescue) that confounded
his diplomatic efforts while scaring and demoralizing the country, Carter
led an administration that many saw as inept. Ronald Reagan offered a
stark alternative, promising to slash taxes, streamline the federal government, and show belligerent nations who's boss. Voters took an immediate
shine to him. Coming out of the conventions in early August 1980, polls
showed Reagan with a significant lead.

The contrasts between Carter and Reagan were significant, and battle
lines were quickly drawn. Intercepting a secret memo from the Oval Office
aide Hamilton Jordan, *Time* learned that "Carter is expected to portray
Reagan as a Red-baiting, trigger-happy right-winger who would be dangerous in the White House." In an early campaign speech, Carter set the tone
by knocking Republicans as "men of narrow vision who are afraid of the
future and whose leaders are inclined to shoot from the hip." It was a veiled
reference to the B-actor and cowboy labels Reagan's opponents customarily
attached to him. In Carter's acceptance speech at the Democratic

convention, the veil came off. The Reagan vision, he insisted, is "a world of tinsel and make-believe . . . [in which] all problems have simple solutions. Simple—and wrong."

Reagan also came out swinging. The president had the target of incumbency on his back, inviting potshots to be taken at his floundering policies. Reagan accused Carter of "economic failures" that amounted to "an assault on the hopes and dreams of American families." The Middle East and the Soviet Union also provided ripe targets. "Because of the weak and confused leadership of Jimmy Carter, we are approaching a flashpoint with Soviet power now deployed in a manner which directly threatens Iran, the Persian Gulf and the Arabian Sea; with Soviet fleets and air bases emplaced along the sea lanes along which we and our allies and the entire free world depend." As always, Reagan used humor to great effect. In one of his stock jokes, he claimed that Jimmy Carter came to him in a dream and asked him why he wanted his job. "I told him I didn't want his job," Reagan quipped. "I want to be President."

But front-runners stumble, and Ronald Reagan took his share of pratfalls. In the seventeen days following the convention, he committed a string of substantive gaffes that dented his credibility. The first was a foreign policy blunder in which he announced his "intention to reestablish official government relations with Taiwan" that left the Chinese "hopping mad." The Chinese foreign minister immediately denounced the scheme as an act of "retrogression . . . [that] would be detrimental to world peace," forcing Reagan to backtrack and to claim he'd misspoken. Days later, in a speech before the Veterans of Foreign Wars, he called the Vietnam War "a noble cause," which rankled a good deal of the electorate. And in an address to Dallas evangelicals, he admitted he had "a great many questions about evolution," adding, "I think that recent discoveries down through the years pointed [to] great flaws in it."

These gaffes created serious questions about his competence and gave the press license to revisit previous statements, such as Reagan's wacky claim that plants and trees caused more pollution than automobiles or industry, and that "Alaska has larger oil reserves than Saudi Arabia." There was little love, too, for his opposition to the minimum wage, Medicare, and unemployment insurance, which he called "vacation money for the lazy." But it didn't stop there. On Labor Day, when Jimmy Carter kicked off his campaign in Tuscumbia, Alabama, Reagan told a Detroit crowd, "Now, I'm happy to be here, while he is opening his campaign down there in the city that gave birth to and is the parent body of the Ku Klux Klan." He could tell right away from the audience reaction that he'd grossly erred, trying to tie Carter to the Klan. Afterward, he admitted to aides, "I blew it."

Worse than that. "This was the first week after the convention, and he'd fucked up something fierce," says Stu Spencer, who was called in by Nancy Reagan to help stabilize the campaign. Spencer had been on the outs with the Reagans for his role advising Gerald Ford in the 1976 primary and especially for a cheeky ad he'd authored: "Governor Reagan couldn't start a war, but *President* Reagan could." That had stung, but given the moment, it was deemed prudent to let bygones be bygones. The most recent Gallup poll had shown that Carter had pulled even, sending shivers through the ranks. The Reagans had moved into Wexford, the former weekend retreat of Jackie and Jack Kennedy on Rattlesnake Mountain near Middleburg, Virginia. Shortly after Labor Day, in a moment of snowballing panic, they convened a summit of the top command.

Spencer, who arrived late at Wexford, saw immediately that the problem was disorganization. Bill Casey, the campaign manager aides referred to as "Spacey," and Ed Meese were out of their depth; they'd never run high-powered national campaigns and had no experience with the volume and pace of decisions that had to be made. Lyn Nofziger picked self-defeating fights with the press for its relentless coverage of Reagan's blunders. Bill Timmons, in charge of field operations, had no rapport with the candidate, and Mike Deaver, who did, was drinking heavily.

Spencer knew someone had to be around full-time to hand-hold the candidate, to coach him to stay on point and to keep him poised. He sensed that Reagan's confidence level was shaky. "The level of campaigning he was in now was much different than he was in before," Spencer says. "He was no longer talking to audiences at every [campaign] stop—he was talking to the whole nation. And everything he said would be scrutinized ten times more than ever before." It was time to dispense with the repackaged rhetoric of past campaigns.

First, Spencer reshuffled the staff. He brought in James Brady from John Connally's campaign, and James Baker III, who had been George Bush's adviser. He summoned Ken Khachigian, a Nixon-era speechwriter from

California, to work with Marty Anderson and Dick Allen, the resident policy wonks. There would be no more clumsy chain of command where crucial details got lost in the bureaucracy. From now on, all decisions would be made and speeches written on the campaign plane, a Boeing 727 nick-named *LeaderShip '80*, where the atmosphere was purposely kept light and extremely loose. "If we have an uptight ship, we're going to have an uptight candidate," Spencer reasoned. So, each time the plane took off, Nancy Reagan bowled an orange down the aisle, trying not to hit any of the seats, while the cabin cheered her on, and a tape of Willie Nelson singing "On the Road Again" boomed over the sound system. As soon as the plane leveled off, Nancy passed out chocolates to the press corps in the back, keeping them lighthearted—and away from her husband. Spencer noticed a change immediately. "From that day on, it was the tightest, best, and most fun campaign I was ever involved in," he says.

A strategy materialized from the noticeable shift among working-class voters. The unions had always been staunchly Democratic, yet the workers themselves, suffering under crushing inflation and unemployment, were inching to the right, disgruntled with the status quo. Plant closings in the industrial heartland gave the Reagan campaign rich, fertile electoral fields to plow. Speeches were scheduled in towns like Steubenville, Ohio; Lang-horne, Pennsylvania; West Allis, Wisconsin; Allen Park, Michigan—places where blue-collar workers had been hit hard and were primed for Reagan's fiery message, which blamed the president for their miserable circum-stances.

Jimmy Carter and Reagan continued running neck and neck through early September, dogged by John Anderson, the moderate Republican con-gressman from Illinois, who had entered the general election race as an independent and managed to poll a respectable 15 percent. Anderson wasn't anyone for Reagan to lose sleep over, but another factor was. Dick Wirthlin, Reagan's pollster, raised it early in the campaign. "We may have a surprise coming in October," he warned.

An *October surprise*.

Reagan's chief aides sensed progress was being made in negotiations to bring the Iranian hostages home. Rumors of a military operation to rescue the hostages also circulated. A good outcome was fine by Reagan. In fact, Dick Allen had been dispatched to the office of Zbigniew Brzezinski,

Carter's national security adviser, with the following message: "We have heard that a hostage rescue attempt is underway. We want you to know that if you try and fail, you will not be attacked by Ronald Reagan. And if you succeed, you will be applauded."

This was true as far as it went, but there was still dread that Carter would time the release to late October, when it would have the greatest impact on the election, and the campaign took steps to blunt the impact of such an event. Marty Anderson and Dick Allen announced the formation of an October Surprise Group, with the aim of getting the press to carry the charge. Howell Raines, the *New York Times'* correspondent on the Reagan beat, took the bait. On October 9, 1980, he published a story under the heading "Reagan Aides See Way to Defeat Any Surprise." With that, "*October surprise*" was injected into the race. If the surprise came to pass, at least the triumph would be clouded by the suggestion of possible hidden motives.

Some would accuse the Reagan team of darker efforts. For years afterward, rumors persisted that Bill Casey slipped away to Madrid in early April 1980 to conspire with Mehdi Karubi, an Iranian cleric, to hold the U.S. hostages past election day on the chance that if Reagan was elected, he could bring them home in triumph. Others allege the negotiations occurred in Paris and that George Bush was present, although he persistently denied there was any truth to such charges, and there is absolutely no evidence.

In any case, Reagan had hoped to confront Carter directly about his thus-far failed efforts during the first presidential debate, in Baltimore on September 21. But Carter refused to participate so long as John Anderson was included. Sensing that Anderson drew votes away from the president, Carter's advisers felt the audience for the debate would be diminished if he was a no-show, rather than appearing and giving Anderson's stature a nationwide boost.

Reagan knew it was a mistake. By backing off the Iowa debates nine months earlier, he'd brought a serious defeat on himself. He attempted to underscore Carter's absence by demanding an empty chair be placed on the debate stage, but his request was denied. Not that it mattered. The president's nonappearance was a self-inflicted wound. The next day, editors across the country published reviews singling out Jimmy Carter as "the only loser in the televised political debate," while praising the performances of Reagan and Anderson. Anderson probably helped himself the most, giving an American public to whom he was largely unknown a chance to hear him express his views. The upshot was that Anderson came across as "an articulate fellow" and Reagan as "polished."

But no one was satisfied. People, including the candidates' handlers, wanted to see the two front-runners in a televised debate. That tradition, begun in 1960, humanized the presidential nominees and helped voters to make up their minds about the candidates and their policies. Including John Anderson was a fine diplomatic gesture, but his chances of winning were nonexistent and his attendance would only cloud the bigger picture. The very next day, Carter's staff, in damage-control mode, pressed for a title-bout debate between their man and Ronald Reagan.

Would Reagan agree? The campaign staff was divided. In a suite at the Waldorf-Astoria in New York City, the top advisers went around the room arguing for and against. Bill Casey, Dick Wirthlin, and Bill Timmons were dead-set opposed. If it was earlier, so that if he came off poorly there would be enough time left to regroup and make up lost ground—maybe. But this late in the game? They couldn't justify it. Meese, Deaver, and Nofziger— the men who knew Reagan best—were in favor, knowing he could hold his own. Nancy Reagan, who listened to both sides from a seat off in the corner, had plenty of reservations. Earlier that morning, Ronnie told her, "I can beat that guy," but she wasn't convinced. She feared that any spontaneous remark had the potential to doom the campaign. Was it worth taking a risk? She thought not. Stu Spencer "listened to all the bullshit from everybody," then took the offer straight to Reagan. "There's no way you can run for president without debating." "We're going to do it, aren't we?" the governor said eagerly. "Hell, yes!" Spencer exclaimed. "It's part of the culture." He knew Reagan understood the drama of the debate and would have done his homework when the cameras rolled.

Spencer was much more concerned about the latest poll numbers. "The campaign had gone flat; we had a big weakness," he recalls. There was a nine-point deficit among female voters and independents. "We knew we could deliver the base, but the gender gap was nose-diving, big-time." Reagan's positions on social issues—abortion, the Equal Rights Amendment, school busing, gay rights, public-school prayer, and apartheid—put him at odds with women and young voters. According to Betty Heitman, co-chair of the Republican National Committee, "Jimmy Carter has been very effective in painting Governor Reagan as trigger-happy and a warmonger. Most women are scared to death if they think anyone would get us into war."

In order to get a better handle on the problem, Ray Stark, a big-ticket Hollywood producer who was friendly with the Reagans, arranged a lunch between Spencer and Gloria Steinem at Universal Studios. "I'm not into this feminist shit," Spencer protested to Stark. Grudgingly, at Stark's insistence, he kept the appointment and came away from it an instant convert. "She delineated all the things that were wrong with our campaign and, in an insightful and *very charming* way, gave me a good understanding why women weren't going for Ronald Reagan," Spencer recalls. "I drove straight over to his house in Pacific Palisades and told him, "We've got a problem.""

Reagan wasn't about to alter the positions on social issues he'd held fast to for thirty years, but the gender gap dismayed him. He was still going to refer to women as ladies, no matter how many times Spencer warned him that it put people off, but when it meant alienating women, he was all ears. "What's your solution?" he asked. On the drive over, Spencer had been tinkering with a radical idea. "What if you tell the American public that your first appointment to the Supreme Court will be a woman?" he proposed. "Would you have a problem with that?" Reagan thought it through. "Not if she's qualified," he eventually responded.

The rest of the staff was a harder sell. "It bothered the hell out of all the hard-right conservative guys, like Marty Anderson and Lyn Nofziger," Spencer says. "They just didn't feel women were qualified for those kinds of positions." No woman judge had infiltrated the Court's brotherhood, and the ideologues saw no reason to break with tradition. Aides argued against taking a public position on it, but on October 14, at a press conference in Los Angeles, Ronald Reagan announced he would name a woman "to one of the first Supreme Court vacancies in my administration."

The campaign saw an immediate uptick in women's support. But after a two-day bump, the numbers leveled off again. The national polls continued to seesaw, with the lead changing hands on almost a daily basis. Jimmy Carter hammered away at the image of Ronald Reagan as "dangerous" and "scary," a warmonger, an irrational hawk who would divide Americans "black from white, Jew from Christian, North from South, rural from urban" and was eager to "lead our country toward war." Reagan, for his part, stuck to the script, portraying his opponent as an inept president who had dropped the nation into an economic and strategic abyss. Taking no chances, the campaign spent $150,000 for a half hour of prime-time TV, giving Reagan the opportunity to represent himself as a man of strength, whose goal "first and foremost is the establishment of world peace." But twelve days before the election, the polls showed Reagan with what the Associated Press termed "a narrowing lead," ahead by a hair, maybe only 1 percent, maybe as much as 4. More worrisome, however: he was not pulling away. The Reagan high command knew it was the tendency of undecideds to vote for the incumbent at the last minute.

Thought turned back to a debate. Carter kept insisting a two-man confrontation was necessary, but Reagan never deigned to accept his invitation. "Let's see what the polls are," he hedged, "then we'll make our decision." At this late date, the president didn't believe it would ever come to pass. Finally, on October 23—only two weeks before the election—Reagan publicly agreed.

The debate was set for October 28 in Cleveland, before a national TV audience. The League of Women Voters—"the *ladies* of the League," as Reagan called them—excluded John Anderson, who had fallen below their threshold of 15 percent in the polls. Reagan was ready for it. He'd been well-prepped by Jim Baker, who had put a book together covering every potential issue and staged three days of rehearsals. The goal wasn't for Reagan to match Carter point for point, but to appear poised and easygoing, projecting a presidential image. Nevertheless, Baker was relentless in his policy research, as was his stand-in for Carter, a brash, young staff economist named David Stockman, who pricked Reagan's fury with his aggressive comebacks.

In his hotel room before the debate, Reagan appeared fairly relaxed. Stu Spencer and Mike Deaver showed up just after dinner with a magnum of red wine meant to liquidate any residual anxiety. After a glass or two, Reagan began loosening up, telling jokes, doing impressions. There was no apparent case of nerves, considering he was about to perform—*live! unscripted!*—in front of an estimated hundred million viewers. His days at *GE Theater* had taught him a thing or two about live TV. And as far as jitters went, "I've been on the same stage as John Wayne," he quipped to reporters who greeted him outside the Cleveland Convention Center.

The debate itself offered no new insights. The repartee, for the most part, was respectful and civilized. Carter attacked Reagan for his "extremely dangerous" attitude toward arms control, as well as his positions on Social Security, the minimum wage, the Equal Rights Amendment, and health insurance. Reagan went on the offensive concerning the economy and the hostage and energy crises, defining Carter's four-year term by "unkept promises" and "despair," two phrases he saw spray-painted on walls during a visit to the South Bronx. Neither candidate scored the elusive knockout, not even the glancing blow their supporters were looking for. If any one line resonated with viewers, it occurred near the end of the evening, when Reagan looked into the camera and prompted the audience to ask themselves, "Are you better off than you were four years ago?"

According to most polls, the candidates had fought to a draw. "We doubt that it swung a large block of the undecided vote one way or the other," the *Los Angeles Times* concluded, "but at least it gave us voters a good look at the two of them." And what they saw, according to random interviews, was a Reagan "genial, open," at times "very reassuring," and a Carter "intense almost to the point of grimness," but "more informed, a better debater, and more presidential."

With a week left to go in the campaign, it was anyone's race to win.

R onald Reagan gave it a last, explosive blast, conducting a whirlwind tour of appearances through Pennsylvania, Wisconsin, Michigan, and Ohio. Twelve cities in three days, sixteen events, four hotel rooms—it was all he could do to remember his name. The weekend before Election Day, a pattern of voting became clear. "We were tracking polls nightly," says Stu Spencer. "I could tell we were starting to take off." Bellwether districts indicated that undecided voters and blue-collar Democrats were gravitating to Ronald Reagan. Ed Meese recalls, "We were relatively confident based on reports that the governor was going to win."

During a Saturday-night stopover on November 1, Stu Spencer visited the Reagans' suite at Neil House in Columbus, Ohio. He delivered the news that a win on Tuesday was all but inevitable. Reagan, habitually superstitious, warned him, "I don't talk like that!" Spencer said, "Okay. *In case* you win you've got to think about a chief of staff. Word on the street is that you're going to pick Ed Meese."

In unison, Ron and Nancy sang out: "Oh *no, no, no, no.*" Spencer was instantly relieved. He liked Meese and credited him with defining and shaping Reagan's vision, but felt Meese would be "a disaster" as chief of staff. "He was so disorganized," Spencer says. "If anything went into Ed Meese's briefcase, you never saw it again." Dick Allen referred wryly to "the Meesecase—a briefcase without a bottom"—and echoed Spencer's verdict that Meese, while "a wonderful thinker, was incapable of managing an organization." His office was a famous clutter of paperwork that started in piles on the floor and billowed up over his desk like a tidal wave. Meese would serve an important function, but not as chief of staff. Spencer brought up Mike Deaver's name, albeit reluctantly. He knew Mike thought he deserved the job, but worried about the drinking issue. Lately, Deaver had been missing scheduled meetings, "sitting in his room," Spencer recalls, "drinking a fucking gallon of wine." Reagan emphatically put an end to that idea, saying, "No, Mike's a number-two guy."

Considering the way Reagan governed—somewhat casually, relying on advisers—he needed a strong chief. Spencer then threw Jim Baker's name into the hat. "But he's Bush's guy," Nancy interjected. Spencer argued it positioned Baker as an excellent go-between with a vice president. "Besides, Baker is well organized, intelligent, and not a political operative. He'll work for your agenda, not his or anybody else's."

Nancy was adamant that a chief of staff be someone who could effectively insulate and protect her husband. As a lawyer, Jim Baker could handle the custodial structure, and as a former Marine whose code was semper fidelis they could rely on his loyalty. He had never been in Reagan's sphere of vision, but the more Spencer talked, the more intriguing he became. It was significant that Reagan could divest his ego and choose someone outside his circle to be his chief of staff. Unlike insecure leaders who surround themselves with yes-men, blind loyalists, he was willing to put himself in the hands of the most competent person on the list, even one who had worked for a former rival, now his running mate, not fearful of being managed—in fact, welcoming it.

The next day, en route to Cincinnati, Baker was offered a seat on the campaign plane, where the Reagans had a chance to observe him. They liked what they saw. When they landed, Nancy prodded her husband to intercept Baker and discuss the job. Reagan went one step further and offered it to him.

Neil Reagan was predicting "a landslide." He was one of about forty guests who had gathered in the late afternoon on November 4, 1980, at Marion and Earle Jorgensen's mansion in Bel-Air while Ronald and Nancy toughed it out at home. It was an Election Day tradition to await results at the Jorgensens'. The longtime faithful were all in attendance. Holmes Tuttle, Henry Salvatori, Justin Dart, William French Smith, Jaq Hume, Bill Wilson, and Charlie Wick, members of the Kitchen Cabinet, were interspersed among old Hollywood stars like Jimmy Stewart and Robert Stack. Nancy's society friends, the Annenbergs and the Bloomingdales, flew in at the last minute. Even the Reagan children—all of them, a rare occurrence—were part of the expectant crowd. There were three television sets in the living room, each tuned to a different network, all drawing anxious eyes to their muted screens. The polls were about to close on the East Coast, and the room was on edge. Only Moon, an unapologetic optimist, bounced from guest to guest, saying, "It's a landslide; don't worry about it."

If his brother, Dutch, had been there, he might have hustled the seventy-two-year-old Moon aside and ordered him not to jinx the results, but the Reagans were uncharacteristically late to the Jorgensen party. It had been a demanding day. They'd gone to vote early that morning, snaking through the street outside their home, which had been blocked off to traffic by wooden barriers and a Secret Service checkpoint. Stopping briefly to answer reporters' questions about the chances of a Reagan victory, only Nancy offered, "Cautiously optimistic." Their polling place, a few blocks away, was shoulder-to-shoulder with media, awaiting the arrival of the man they'd been following for close to eleven months. Lawrence Welk, Vin Scully, and Sylvester Stallone, all of whom lived in the precinct, had already passed through the gauntlet, but they didn't command a fraction of the press of paparazzi that converged on the Reagans. By the time Ronald and Nancy voted and returned home, they longed to escape the bustle and steal a few hours of peace and quiet.

They were due at the Jorgensens' at four o'clock. In the meantime, it was impossible to even venture into the backyard amid the olive trees and jacaranda, what with all the helicopters swirling overhead and reporters hiding in the bushes. Ron took his beloved midafternoon nap and awoke in time to get ready for the party. Nancy recalled that she was in the tub when she heard a news report on the TV set in the bedroom. John Chancellor was calling the election for "Ronald Wilson Reagan of California, a sports announcer, a film actor, a governor of California." Not quite the landslide Moon predicted, but a solid win, and by a respectable 51 percent of the popular vote to go with forty-four states in the Electoral College.

By the time Ron and Nancy arrived at the party, his longtime friends and family weren't sure what to expect. He shambled inside wearing a sport coat and open-collared shirt, slightly embarrassed, brushing aside the deferential salutes and honorifics from his closest friends who suddenly became stiff and unnerved in his presence. He reassured Marion Jorgensen that she could still call him Ronnie, but she and everyone else knew differently. When he walked through the door it was in an entirely new role. The poor boy from Dixon, Illinois, was the President of the United States.

PART 4

MR. PRESIDENT

CHAPTER THIRTY-ONE

"THE O AND W"

"The governor of a state plays in the minor leagues. When
you're President, you're in the big leagues."

—THOMAS P. (TIP) O'NEILL

JANUARY 20, 1981

Inauguration days are extraordinary occasions.

The ritual, which Ronald Reagan called "nothing less than a miracle," is an essential tableau in the greatest long-running dramas in American history: the peaceful transfer of power from one leader to another. But on this particular Inauguration Day, the ceremony was fast becoming the back end of a twin bill whose main feature was playing out 7,239 miles away.

Rumors had built all week that the Iranian mullahs had reached an agreement with U.S. authorities to release the hostages. Carter administration officials had negotiated for days on end to untangle last-minute snags. The president had gone without sleep for forty-eight hours trying to bring the crisis to a peaceful close, resolved to make it his final act—hoping to greet the hostages at Andrews Air Force Base before turning over the reins of government. One minute it looked promising, the next there was another infuriating setback. Time was fast running out.

Carter wasn't grandstanding. Ronald Reagan had been looped in to all the developing details as befitted a president-elect; Warren Christopher, Carter's deputy secretary of state, briefed Dick Allen on a daily basis. Two days earlier, just before lunch, Allen arrived at Blair House, where the governor was staying, to deliver the latest update. Reagan was in the bedroom with Jim Baker and Jim Brady, watching an ABC broadcast about the latest developments involving the transfer of $8 billion in frozen funds from twelve American banks to an Iranian escrow account. Reagan pursed his lips and scowled at the TV. "Shitheels!" he muttered. Had he been president, the hostages would have been on American soil before even a cent had been handed over to those blackmailers. He feared a charade.

On the morning of January 20, when Reagan shared the traditional cup of tea with President Carter at the White House, word drifted in that the hostages were on buses heading to Tehran's Mehrabad Airport, where two Algerian jets sat idling, poised to fly them home. But after fourteen months of false starts, Americans monitoring the situation still weren't sure whether the Iranians were jerking them around.

The agonizing uncertainty had taken its toll on Carter. He was drained, emotionally and physically. All the vibrancy that had swept him into office—the familiar toothy grin and irrepressible smile—was imperceptible in the grim little man with pouchy eyes who clenched his hands during the hour-long exchange. He'd famously said that the country suffered from a *malaise*, and it seemed to be reflected in his physiognomy. As the two men slipped into a limousine that would take them to the Capitol, the difference between the two was striking. Reagan looked every bit the leading man—*dashing*, as a Hollywood publicist might have described him—tan and rosy-cheeked, in a formfitting cutaway club coat and pinstriped pants that accentuated his cowboy build.

The crowds clustered ten deep on Pennsylvania Avenue as their motorcade proceeded slowly along the route. "[Carter] said hardly a word to me," Reagan recalled. He knew not to press him, understanding the tremendous pressure of the previous days and months. It was a balmy, overcast morning. Washington had suffered through weeks of freezing weather, but now experienced an unexpected thaw that pushed the mercury toward sixty degrees. Some 32,000 spectators had poured into an area below the grandstand, angling to witness the historic event.

The scene of this inauguration was especially momentous. Since 1829, when Andrew Jackson took the oath of office only three years after the Dome was unveiled, the swearing-in had taken place on the steps of the

East Front of the Capitol. It was an austere location, not especially scenic. From the makeshift podium, the view looked over a phalanx of government buildings. Senator Mark Hatfield, who chaired the inaugural committee in 1981, suggested moving the ceremony to the West Front, which overlooked the expansive outstretched Mall that included the Washington, Lincoln, and Jefferson memorials and, just beyond the Potomac, Arlington National Cemetery.

The cemetery played a significant role in Reagan's prepared address. Preston Hotchkis, a California land developer and friend to Republican presidents, had sent him a story about Martin Treptow, a small-town barber–turned–American soldier who had died valiantly in combat during World War I. According to the anecdote, a diary was found on Treptow's body on whose flyleaf he had scrawled "My Pledge: America must win the war. Therefore I will work, I will save, I will sacrifice, I will endure, I will fight cheerfully and do my utmost as if the issue of the whole struggle depended on me alone." Reagan was moved by those words—it fit his notion of old-fashioned patriotism and Americans working hard for the good of all—and wanted them incorporated into the end of his speech. Ken Khachigian, who had been brought in to compose it, envisioned an ending that referenced all the monuments on the horizon.

"Since the last one was Arlington, he wanted me to say, 'Also buried out there is this young man,'" Khachigian recalls. The speechwriter was skeptical. He knew Reagan was prone to apocryphal stories, many of which were taken from the movies, so he did some research and found out that the existence of Treptow's diary was largely an invention, and that he was buried not in Arlington but in Bloomer, Wisconsin. Neither was a small nor insignificant detail. "Reagan refused to take it out," Khachigian says. "I told him, 'Governor, it will diminish your speech when it comes out that this is false.'" Reagan shook his head and said, "It's too good a story. Just take care of it." So the Treptow reference remained. So did another story, this one appropriated from *Marine Raiders*, a 1944 RKO war epic, in which a character played by Frank McHugh utters the line, "This can't be happening to us. We're *Americans*. What happened to us?" Reagan knew a good line when he heard one.

"I don't want a speech with a lot of flourish," Reagan instructed Khachigian, "no fake eloquence, no soaring rhetoric." He wanted a sort of tone poem that spoke directly to the American people. Reagan wrote most of it himself on a yellow legal pad during a flight from Washington to Los Angeles. Later, a number of influential people weighed in, appealing to their special interests. Vernon Jordan solicited a line or two that advocated intolerance to bigotry. Paul Laxalt voiced concern that "Ron might be softening his views, so make sure he sticks to the conservative position." To appease Laxalt, Khachigian added the line, "On these principles we will not compromise." In the end, Reagan polished the hardest edges off the speech, then transferred it to the four-by-six-inch index cards, the format with which he felt most comfortable.

Despite his ease in front of an audience, there were plenty of nerves. The entire world would be watching. Near the speaker's platform he could look into a VIP area where folks who held the gold parade tickets, such as Jimmy Stewart, Henry Kissinger, Johnny Carson, Frank Sinatra, and William F. Buckley Jr., were seated. It helped that his family was within eyesight. Nancy gazed at him adoringly, pinning his every move with her doe eyes. Beside her sat Patti, looking more like her father than she cared to admit. Maureen escorted Dennis Revell, her new fiancé. And Ron his new wife.

Ron had dropped out of Yale to dance with the Joffrey Ballet troupe, fanning rumors that he was gay, which he wasn't. On November 24, 1980, he had married Doria Palmieri, at a New York City courthouse without so much as telling his parents. But the newlyweds wouldn't have missed the inauguration. Nor would Michael Reagan, who had already begun cashing in on his father's renown. Michael, along with his wife and son, sat next to Neil and Bess Reagan, and behind them, Edith and Loyal Davis, Nancy's parents.

Former presidents, mainstays of inaugurations, were curiously absent. Gerald Ford stayed home to keep a golfing engagement, while Richard Nixon remained out of sight, the specter of Watergate still too fresh.

Ronald Reagan became the fortieth president almost before he knew what was happening. Chief Justice Warren Burger produced a Bible, and not just any Bible, but the crumbling and bandaged Reagan family heirloom that had belonged to his mother, Nelle, and her mother before that, and just like that, he was intoning, "I, Ronald Reagan, do solemnly swear . . ."

Inauspiciously, Frank Sinatra's seat had originally been placed right be-hind where Reagan would be standing. But when ceremony strategists pre-viewed the camera shots, they realized that Sinatra and Reagan would be sharing the frame throughout the swearing-in. So at the last minute, chairs were rearranged to move Sinatra out of the shot.

Auspiciously, as if on cue, a shaft of sunlight broke through dense clouds as the new president finished repeating the oath of office and stepped back to savor the heavenly sign. A squadron of fighter jets burst out of the clouds, serenaded by a twenty-one-gun salute. Before the new president pivoted to the microphone to deliver his address, Dick Allen squat-walked down the aisle and handed him a slip of paper. Reagan glanced at the message on Situation Room stationery—"Wheels up in Tehran"—and winked at Al-len. The hostages had passed through Iranian airspace. He slipped the pa-per into his pocket, choosing not to mention it yet, not wishing to steal Jimmy Carter's last bit of thunder.

The address was straightforward, homespun, and warmly received. True to his word, there was no soaring rhetoric, no memorable *ask not what your country can do for you.* He stuck to the basics—an economic recovery, a strong defense, and the intrusion of government in everyday lives. The showstopper was saved for the luncheon with congressional leaders in the Capitol's Statuary Hall directly following the inauguration. *President* Rea-gan pulled the slip of paper out of his pocket and announced, "And now, to conclude the toast, with thanks to almighty God, I have been given a tag line, the get-off line that everyone wants for the end of a toast or a speech or anything else." Pausing dramatically, he said, "Some thirty minutes ago, the planes bearing our prisoners left Iranian airspace and are now free of Iran." As the cheers died down, he raised his glass of California chardon-nay. "So we can all drink to this one—to all of us together, doing what we all know we can do to make this country what it should be, what it can be, what it always has been."

There was a final hitch: one woman remained in Tehran who wasn't at the embassy—Cynthia Dwyer refused to get on the plane until the Irani-ans returned her camera. Reagan, who still had control of Iranian assets, pulled Dick Allen aside and said, "You tell those bastards if Cynthia Dwyer isn't out of there, the deal is off." The ultimatum produced immediate re-sults; Dwyer and her camera were on the next plane out. The last thing the clerics wanted was to test Ronald Reagan. They'd heard the accusations that he was trigger-happy, as well as the jokes. Question: What is flat and glows in the dark? Answer: Tehran, the day after Reagan's inauguration.

As president, he already had a sense of the power he wielded, and he intended to let those Iranians know they were finished interfering in American interests. If push came to shove, he'd shove—he'd use force. The sooner terrorists got that message, the better off the country would be. He'd said as much in his inaugural address: "When action is required to preserve our national security, we will act." It was a warning that resonated in many international capitals, but especially in Tehran.

So far, his tough talk was just that—talk. But legislators in both parties wondered where it would lead. Politicians who had resented being held hostage to the ongoing antics in Iran appreciated Carter's efforts that had gone into resolving the crisis peacefully, but understood that Reagan might have shown no restraint. Understood—and slightly feared. And slightly welcomed. The power at Reagan's disposal was enormous; there was no telling how he intended to use it.

The day went by in a blur; the only highlight he clearly recalled was seeing the Dixon High School marching band fronted by its high-stepping drum major, his former role in that very unit. As he stood in front of the mirror adjusting his satin bowtie before setting out for the inaugural balls, the road he'd traveled began to unwind. He was a long way from Dixon, a long way from his wildest boyhood dreams. A grin played at the corners of his mouth, his eyes grew big, delighted, amused. He jumped in the air and did a neat pirouette, shouting: "I'm the President of the United States!"

The brand-new Reagan administration had pledged to hit the ground running, and a skeleton staff calling itself the Economic Policy Group convened, somewhat bleary-eyed, at 10:30 the next morning in the Cabinet Room, chaired by the new president. There were several noticeable cosmetic alterations. Portraits of Thomas Jefferson and Harry Truman that had hung prominently around the room had been replaced by those of Calvin Coolidge and Dwight Eisenhower to keep Abraham Lincoln company. The other major addition was a huge Waterford crystal jar filled with multicolored jelly beans that sat directly in front of Vice President George

Bush, who eyed it somewhat circumspectly. The candy was a favorite of Ronald Reagan's, he was practically addicted to it. "When you need some energy," he advised his protégés, "I expect to see the jar going around the room." Eager to please, everyone dutifully passed it around and popped a few jelly beans in their mouths.

The Reagan Cabinet was a patchwork of newcomers. Assembling it had been the first priority after the election, perhaps more critical for this president due to his preference for a hands-off management style—deferring to staff and appointees for the heavy lifting. "He made no pretense at being an expert in all things," says Robert "Bud" McFarlane, a National Security deputy, "but he had a solid intellect, a solid grasp of American values, a sense of right and wrong, a tolerance for risk." Reagan expected to make the big decisions while relying on input that spared him too many details. His staff reintroduced the mini-memo, a holdover from Sacramento, which reduced the research on any given major policy to a single page of four paragraphs: one explaining the issue, followed by a summary of the facts and background data, a brief discussion, and suggested options and recommendations. If things got too complex and beyond his grasp, he'd invariably postpone discussion by saying "I want to roundtable this with the fellas" or "Maybe we should sleep on this."

He'd taken a similar hands-off approach with Cabinet appointments. Ed Meese, the future counselor to the president, was awarded the job of sifting through and interviewing prospective appointees, and making recommendations. Martin Anderson and Dick Allen were also encouraged to weigh in. As president-elect, Reagan isolated himself from the initial selection process to avoid being importuned by people who had ulterior motives or wanted to push candidates on him. One such special-interest group was the Kitchen Cabinet, now expanded to eighteen conservative businessmen, who "had their own ideas," according to Meese. Another was Richard Nixon.

Two weeks after the election, the former president sent Ronald Reagan an eleven-page memo, expressly intended to influence appointments to top-level posts in his administration. Nixon was especially expansive about secretary of state. He knew that Henry Kissinger, his candidate of preference, would never pass muster, and he had an alternate suggestion or two up his sleeve. Rumors had been circulating that Caspar Weinberger was under consideration. "That'd be a big mistake," Nixon had warned Dick Allen earlier. Allen knew Nixon wanted someone at the State Department who would act as a conduit for him, someone he could manipulate. "I knew that Nixon was fishing for Al Haig," Allen says.

Alexander Haig Jr. had been White House chief of staff under Nixon and Ford, and he was an autocratic, somewhat controversial figure on the fringes of Watergate. As supreme allied commander of NATO forces, Haig had refused to meet Reagan during his 1978 visit to Europe. He had also threatened to run against Reagan for the 1980 Republican nomination, which won him no affection. Dick Allen knew Haig well as "a very bright, energetic, and *very* mercurial fellow, but a schemer with an agenda, and not a very good guy at heart." And his heart lay at the core of his personality. Haig had recently undergone open-heart surgery and emerged from it, some said, a different person. "Before, Al was unflappable," according to John Lehman, Haig's longtime colleague and Reagan's newly appointed secretary of the Navy. "He would rarely lose his temper, and he had a real sense of humor. But after the surgery, he had a short fuse, became less of a listener and more of a my-way-or-the-highway guy." Even Nixon had asked Dick Allen, "Is Haig's heart operation making him crazy?" Allen vehemently opposed seconding Nixon's recommendation, and told Reagan as much. But Nixon was undeterred. In his memo, he promoted Haig as someone who understood the policies involving not only Europe but also the Soviet Union, China, Japan, the Middle East, and Latin America. "Those who oppose him because they think he is 'soft' are either ignorant or stupid," Nixon wrote.

Ronald Reagan wasn't so sure. He'd met with Haig on two occasions and both times came away scratching his head. "The guy came out to see me [in California], and I didn't know what it was all about," he complained. Plus, Haig was known to be intransigent when it came to entertaining opposing viewpoints. Reagan had been flirting with offering the secretary of state job to Henry "Scoop" Jackson, a Democrat with serious foreign policy expertise, but Jackson was blackballed by the Kitchen Cabinet, which resented his liberal position on domestic issues, and Nixon dismissed him as "a partisan Democrat." George Shultz was another heavyweight under consideration—a seasoned statesman who'd served as secretary of labor, director of the Office of Management and Budget, and secretary of the treasury. But Richard Nixon considered Shultz a "candy-ass" and too political, and he told Reagan, "I do not believe that he has the depth of understanding of world issues generally and the Soviet Union in particular that is needed for this job."

Ed Meese worried about Haig's loyalty to the Reagan agenda. Haig made no secret that he harbored presidential ambitions, and he had a lust for power that set off alarms. But in the end, Nixon was "very persuasive," according to Meese, and Reagan concluded that since Haig was a military man used to obeying the chain of command it was worth the gamble to appoint him secretary of state.

The bet started to unravel right away. Two days before the inauguration, Haig personally brought Meese and Jim Baker a twenty-page memorandum he'd prepared, entitled "National Security Decision Directive 1," which, he said, required their immediate signatures. Baker, who was a fairly fast read, took one look at it and said, "Why, this memorandum means that *everything* in the field of foreign affairs falls within your sole jurisdiction." From what he could tell, Haig was attempting to co-opt the National Security Agency, the CIA, the Reconnaissance Office, and the Department of Defense for State. "We're not going to sign this."

Haig complained bitterly and threatened to resign. Eventually, he was mollified and made to reconsider, but as Dick Allen notes, "Haig sealed his fate with Meese and Baker that day."

Many appointments were faits accomplis. From the beginning, Ronald Reagan selected Caspar Weinberger—Cap the Knife, as he was known—to head the Department of Defense; William French Smith as attorney general; and Bill Casey as director of the Central Intelligence Agency. Loyalists were rare commodities in an administration. William Simon was the initial choice to be secretary of the treasury, a post he'd held in the Nixon Cabinet, but he'd demanded control of the administration's economic policy—chiefly the Council of Economic Advisers and the director of the Office of Management and Budget—and that was a deal breaker as far as Reagan was concerned. The idea that one person would be a czar was not Reagan's idea of a collegial group of advisers. As an alternative, Bill Casey suggested a burly, no-nonsense character named Donald Regan, the former chairman of Merrill Lynch. Meese didn't know anything about him, but Regan made an immediate impression. As Meese recalled, "He seemed to be a very forceful personality. And the fact that he'd been a lieutenant colonel in the Marine Corps didn't hurt."

The second-tier Cabinet posts were not as easily filled. Candidates had to be vetted to satisfy the Ethics in Government Act, and several couldn't pass the review. "A lot of fairly well-to-do people who didn't want their neighbors to know what they had in the bank were unwilling to fill out a financial disclosure," recalls Fred Fielding, a young Washington lawyer at the time whose job was to process their statements. "Other people didn't make it because of undisclosed marital issues, as well as a very well-known fellow who was gay and wanted to remain totally in the closet."

In the end, they approved another Marine, Ted Bell, as secretary of Education, and rewarded Richard Schweiker with Health and Human Services, Drew Lewis with Transportation, Raymond Donovan with Labor, and David Stockman with the directorship of the Office of Management and Budget. The Interior Department remained up for grabs. Several good legislators were passed over because Ronald Reagan promised Paul Laxalt he'd appoint somebody from the West. Laxalt urged them to consider Clifford Hansen, a longtime Wyoming senator with impeccable credentials, but Hansen refused to submit a financial disclosure. Instead, Joseph Coors, a new Kitchen Cabinet member, proposed Denver attorney James Watt, the head of the Mountain States Legal Foundation, an organization that had been fighting the federal government on behalf of free markets and free enterprise. Watt was a controversial choice. Environmentalists considered his nomination "disastrous" and criticized his unshakable advocacy of opening up wilderness areas to energy exploration and the private development of natural resources. He was also an evangelical Christian whose extremist religious views alienated people of other faiths. But Laxalt heartily approved of Watt, and the transition staff signed off on him.

The first morning after the inauguration, the president looked around the Cabinet Room at his new team, which had been sworn in earlier that morning. It was a collection of intense men—and one intense woman, Jeane Kirkpatrick, a conservative Democrat appointed ambassador to the United Nations. There was no orientation or grace period, as there had been for Reagan's staff in Sacramento, no White House tour to locate the closest restroom. It was right to business that first morning, with the economy and energy crisis at the top of the list. The president planned to address the nation on those issues on February 5, just sixteen days after taking office, and he wanted something concrete to relate. "Everyone was prepared," says Dick Allen, the National Security director. "We'd been at it for weeks; we were in business from day one."

At a lunch not long after the Cabinet meeting, Ronald Reagan ate sandwiches in the little anteroom across from his desk with the three men who would make the key administrative decisions and guide his daily affairs: Jim Baker, Ed Meese, and Mike Deaver. Instead of having an almighty chief of staff, as was customary, the president established an unusual division of power—the triumvirate, or "Troika," as it became known familiarly. Baker, as chief, set the president's schedule and ran the White House operation, including responsibilities with the legislature and the press; Meese, as counselor, functioned as the president's principal adviser on the policy side and worked directly with the Cabinet; and Deaver dealt with things that pertained personally to the president, which included scheduling, travel, and security, but nothing that involved policy.

"Reagan's genius was to make sure that Mike was at his side as facilitator, Ed was there philosophically, and Jim was pulling the strings," says Ken Duberstein, the president's point man in the House for legislative affairs. The plan was for the three of them to meet with President Reagan to review his schedule every morning at 9:00 and remain with him through the "Morning Summary" delivered by the national security adviser at 9:30. From that point on, one or more of them would be at the president's side throughout the day, monitoring his activity via a little box that sat on each of their desks and binged every time he moved. "It was smooth from the start," Ed Meese recalls. Each member of the Troika had his own niche, but they kept each other honest. "Really, they were always at loggerheads," says Fred Fielding, "but they needed each other, which guarded against one of them taking out the other one." Meese suspected Baker the pragmatist of trying to move Reagan to the center; Baker warily eyed Meese the conservative for his influence on the president; and both Meese and Baker recognized that Deaver, since moving to Washington, "got totally entranced by power," which obscured his judgment.

Their chemistry was in much better shape than was the Old Executive Office Building. During the Carter administration the walls had been painted over with GSA green paint and needed stripping to the original wood. The carpets and desks were tortured with cigarette burns. Chairs were missing arms; upholstery was worn through. The White House was little better. It was a building that kids and animals had lived in and hadn't been renovated in sixteen years. There was lead-pipe plumbing throughout. "The Roosevelt Room was a mess," recalls Peter McCoy, Nancy Reagan's chief of staff, who'd accompanied her on an early tour. "The Carters had Xerox machines in the hallway blowing black dust all over the walls." Jody Powell, Carter's press secretary, defended the former residents, saying, "It's not like we left chicken bones behind the couch," but the new occupants weren't taking any chances. "This place needs *everything*," Nancy Reagan exclaimed, hand over mouth. Ronald Reagan was offended by the shabby appearance of the place and instructed his staff to upgrade the White House, along with its extensive grounds. A makeover was ordered from top to bottom. The war cannons were restored to the Pennsylvania Avenue entrance, the anchors returned to the side that faced the White House. Nancy Reagan imported her Beverly Hills decorator, Ted Graber, to help refurbish the Central Hall, and he had the floors sanded and refinished, the mahogany doors stripped, and the parlor wallpapered. Historical antiques, under layers of dust, were rescued from storage. In the Oval Office, Reagan brought back the octagonal desk that John F. Kennedy had used, which was made out of the wood from a number of old battleships. A new rug with the presidential seal was installed. Two small plaques he'd received as governor—"The Buckaroo Stops Here" and "There's No Limit to How Far a Person Can Go If They Don't Care Who Gets the Credit"—got pride of place on a mantel. As far as personal etiquette went, he resolved never to be seen in the Oval Office in shirtsleeves, or without a jacket and tie.

Order . . . dignity . . . leadership—these were protocols he was determined to establish. They'd set the tone for the rest of his agenda. The White House staff began referring to him as the "O and W"—Oldest and Wisest—a measure of the respect earned by the example he set. The presidential proprieties were clearly articulated. "It was time to start implementing his policies," Meese says. "Immediately. No time to spare."

First things first: the economy. As Ronald Reagan would soon tell the nation, "The country is in the worst economic mess since the Great Depression." All things considered, it was hardly an exaggeration. In the past two years, back-to-back inflation, inflamed by the rising cost of fuel and food, was at the highest rate since World War II. As the president was fond of pointing out, "a quarter, a dime, and a penny—thirty-six cents—what the 1960 dollar is worth today." More than seven million Americans were unemployed. The prime bank rate on loans to business reached 21.5 percent. And the Dow Jones Industrial Average had declined in eight of the ten trading sessions since Reagan took office—not a good omen.

"We've got to get control of the budget," Reagan implored only minutes into the first cabinet meeting. "It's out of control." The deficit for fiscal 1981 was headed for a record $60 billion. The president was determined to pull the American economy back from the brink. He ordered a federal hiring freeze and tried to cater to businesses by suspending pending regulations such as the requirement that automakers install airbags in cars, energy performance standards in new buildings, and noise standards in the workplace. Otherwise, he had faith, he said, in the resilience of the marketplace, relying on it to "let the people flourish." But the nuts and bolts of recovery were beyond his analytic grasp, so he left the strategy for it in the hands of the young prodigy David Stockman, the thirty-four-year-old former Michigan congressman who was in charge of the Office of Management and Budget.

Stockman, another devout believer in the free-market economy, had a diagnosis for recovery, but it was controversial—and not entirely sound. His antidote was based on supply-side economics, a philosophy that contradicted long-held Keynesian doctrine that government spending could provide a "fiscal stimulus," pumping up demand for goods and services and triggering a virtuous circle. Supply-siders flatly disagreed. They claimed that increasing supply rather than demand served to curtail inflation, and the only way to do it was by slashing taxes and reducing government spending to allow the private sector the means to produce a rapid increase in the supply of goods and services. To quote one of its principal architects, Jude Wanniski, "A tax cut not only increases demand, but increases the incentive to produce. . . . With lower taxes, it is more attractive to invest and more attractive to work; demand is increased, but so is supply." Tax reduction, he argued, would quickly stimulate a vigorous economic expansion by bringing in a flood of new revenues.

But most mainstream economists expressed grave doubts. From Keynesian John Kenneth Galbraith to conservative Martin Feldstein, president of the National Bureau of Economic Research, the criticism was forceful. Nevertheless, Ronald Reagan adopted supply-side doctrine as the basis of his Program for Economic Recovery and proposed implementing it in a sober prime-time speech broadcast on February 18, 1981. His strategy would focus on several priorities: a massive reduction of taxes and discretionary spending, regulatory relief, the elimination of wasteful or outmoded government programs, a balanced budget by 1984, and increased defense spending.

The overall scope of the program was extraordinary. The president embraced a bill introduced by Republican congressmen Jack Kemp and William Roth that called for reductions of 10 percent in personal income taxes in each of the years 1981, 1982, and 1983. "This tax program is not designed to simply reduce the burden of tax on the people," Reagan told his Cabinet during a meeting on February 10. "It's designed to get the damn country moving again." To pay for it and to slow the growth of spending, Congress was directed to trim the federal budget by $41 billion, which would be accomplished by reducing federal employees' benefits; grants for education and social services, including the food-stamp program, the child-nutrition programs, the free-school-lunch program, unemployment insurance, college-education benefits, and welfare benefits; aid to the arts, humanities, and sciences; and the elimination of public-service jobs. Eighty-three federal programs were gutted, for starters. Stockman was still scrounging to make further cuts that would be necessary to hit the $41 billion mark. Only military spending earned a significant raise, a $28 billion increase for 1981 alone,* the largest in peacetime history.

The administration might have promoted it as the Program for Economic Recovery, but it was forever after referred to as Reaganomics. It mandated a sweeping restructuring of the U.S. government and the way it interacted with all Americans. No matter how one did the math, the numbers never quite added up. The goals were ambitious but unrealistic, as the outcome soon proved. The budget reductions were riddled with special revisions that provided for tax relief to the oil industry, savings-and-loan associations, and corporations in general. The military spending hike—and hike and *hike*—offset any cutbacks to social programs. And the 10 percent

---

* Military spending was projected at $169.5 billion through 1986.

Kemp-Roth tax breaks were cut in half to ward off an estimated shortfall in revenues. All told, analysts projected, the administration would incur an $82 million shortfall in 1982, which would probably double by 1984. Orwell's depressing forecast of the future might arrive right on schedule.

Ronald Reagan remained obstinately rosy about making ends meet, convinced that the program would eventually work as planned. But as journalist Lou Cannon pointed out, "the way that Reaganomics worked was by mirrors." Or as George Bush, now a supporter (in public, at least), had said: it was "voodoo economics."

And the policy reflected poorly on the president, who spent much of the so-called Reagan Revolution dodging a succession of financial landmines. As astronomical budget deficits piled up year after year, tax increases became necessary. Stock and bond prices took a significant hit. Too many concessions had to be made to keep the economy above water. As David Stockman later reassessed the situation, "We were not headed toward a brave new world, as I had thought in February. . . . Where we were headed was toward a fiscal catastrophe."

Nancy Reagan, a not-so-innocent bystander, became a victim of the backlash. She wasn't used to being subject to criticism; she had managed to sidestep the spotlight as the governor's wife. As the First Lady, however, and in a time of economic duress, she very soon came under fire.

"Virtually everything I did during that first year was misunderstood and ridiculed," she recalled.

As early as the inaugural, Americans perceived—rightly or wrongly—that Nancy Reagan was an imperious character. While average Americans struggled to get by, she surrounded herself with her millionaire Los Angeles friends who arrived in Washington in private planes and limousines like potentates at the court of Louis XIV. Much was made of her visits to the New York showrooms of top fashion couturiers like Bill Blass, James Galanos, and Adolfo, where she tried on $25,000 beaded gowns and $1,000 cocktail dresses that skimmed her size-four figure. She was photographed in a $25,000 Maximilian mink coat, wearing $480,000 diamond earrings. It was no secret that her Beverly Hills hairdresser, Julius Bengtsson, traveled everywhere with her, and on *Air Force One*, at the taxpayers' expense. Her personal manicurist arrived once a week from Los Angeles to touch up her nails. One of the hottest-selling postcards in Washington, D.C., was a depiction of the First Lady wearing an ermine cape and crown jewels above the caption "Queen Nancy."

"We had a huge image problem on our hands," says Sheila Tate, who arrived late during the transition as Nancy Reagan's press officer.

No matter what the intentions of the president's wife, they were often construed as self-indulgences. There was scorn when she announced the redecoration of the White House residence for $822,640 and a national uproar at her purchase of 220 place settings of gilt-edged Lenox china at $1,000 per place setting, despite her insistence that the cost would be covered entirely by private contributions. On the same day the government set new nutritional guidelines declaring that, to rein in the cost of school lunches, ketchup would henceforth be considered a vegetable, the White House announced that Nancy Reagan had spent $209,500 for another set of new china, this one for the residence, each piece hand-painted and monogrammed with her initials. The press began referring to the whole mess as "Chinagate."

Her reaction to the criticism of these extravagances was tone deaf and defensive. She seemed to have no understanding that the country was mired in a recession, or of the straits most of the public was in. She lacked her husband's skill with people. And she was awkward and condescending toward the press, which showed her no mercy. "She was a target for reporters," says Peter McCoy, her chief of staff. "Everyone had it in for her; they just beat her up." Even social friends, like Dan Rather and Tom Brokaw, came down hard on her for indiscretions, perceived or otherwise. Comedians routinely made her the punch lines of their jokes. The situation confounded the First Lady, who was easily bruised. "There are times when I look out the window and, if it's raining, I think, 'It must be my fault,'" she complained.

The president wasn't amused. He resented the treatment his wife was getting—"a bum rap," he called it—though he misread it as "a backhanded way of getting at" him. "Dammit," he fumed, reminiscing about the situation, "you want to pick on someone, pick on me, not her." The constant sniping at Nancy was beyond his ken. Nancy, in his eyes, could do no wrong. As his personal secretary, Helene von Damm, explained, "Ronald

Reagan didn't even seem to see the same person the rest of us saw." The staff, according to von Damm, regarded Nancy as "demanding" and "aloof." Mike Deaver agreed, acknowledging that "she is tougher on people than her husband is," thus enlarging her image "as the Invisible Hand, manipulating, ruthless in dealing not only with her husband's adversaries but with friends who let him down." The president, for all his aversion to conflict, defended her as best he could.

For the most part, Nancy kept him in the dark about the grief she was taking. He was busy enough dealing with the budget and missile defense and upheaval in Latin America and the Middle East. He was struggling to push through a bill currently stalled in the House that proposed enabling the U.S. to sell AWACS—airborne warning and control systems for military airplanes—to Saudi Arabia. Each night, when he returned to the residence, exhausted by the day's events, Nancy had dinner waiting on little TV trays so they could sit serenely on the couch, dressed in pj's, and watch their favorite shows, rather than bombarding him with personal complaints. Those she directed at Mike Deaver, whom she called at least a dozen times a day. Deaver absorbed the First Lady's emotional distress and helped to soften the blows. There was also a special phone line installed in the residence that didn't go through the White House switchboard, so Nancy could make late-night calls to confidants Betsy Bloomingdale or Jerry Zipkin, who listened patiently to her and offered soothing advice.

She gave them an earful about her persistent friction with the press and waded into administration gossip. In the Troika, Jim Baker and Mike Deaver had paired off against Ed Meese. They didn't want him out; they just wanted to make sure he wasn't in the main flow. It was no secret who Nancy Reagan's favorites were in that fight. And as for Al Haig, she considered him "Ronnie's biggest mistake," a half-cocked bomb thrower and a "power-hungry" despot.

There were others with the same opinion of Haig, but none who carried as much clout.

Haig's tenure in the Reagan administration had gotten off to a fairly rocky start. In an effort to consolidate his power, he'd squared off against the White House Troika, complaining to the president in a desk-pounding harangue as early as March 19, 1981, that Baker, Meese, Deaver, and even George Bush were encroaching on his turf. In his view, they were variously "the beasts" or "second-rate hambones," nothing more than the president's toadies. And his attitude toward the president carried the same patronizing whiff. "Al would come back from a White House meeting and be *so dismissive* of Reagan," recalls Bud McFarlane, who at the time served as Haig's national security counselor. Haig had exhibited similar contempt for his former boss, Gerald Ford, whom he considered unintelligent, according to Dick Allen. "And he considered Reagan even less smart than Ford."

It was one thing to feel that way in private, and quite another to express it within earshot of the staff. But Haig wasn't much of a diplomat in that regard. He'd returned from a Cabinet meeting on missile defense and stomped around the office complaining that the president hadn't understood a word about America's intermediate nuclear weapons in Europe. In late March 1981, when he learned that Vice President Bush was tagged to head a Foreign Crisis Management commission, Haig was convinced that Bush along with others in the administration were trying to usurp his authority. He stormed into the Oval Office and threatened to resign, again. "He was very upset and angry," Ronald Reagan recalled. "He pounded the table and seemed ready to explode."

Haig's rants convinced the president that his secretary of state was "utterly paranoid." There had been six or seven resignation threats in the first two months, all signed and ready to submit. Sensing an opportunity to undermine their adversary, Deaver and Baker leaked news of the spate of resignation threats to the press. The *New York Times* was eager to engage. "So the single voice the Reagan administration intended to speak to the world has been saying nothing more urgent than 'I quit,'" the paper editorialized. The *Gainesville Sun* put it much more starkly, saying, "The man is dangerous. Somebody better pay attention, because Haig is going to get a lot of people killed—a lot of people—for no good purpose at all."

Nothing drove that point home more clearly than an exchange during an Oval Office meeting of the National Security Council on March 19, 1981. It would lead to one of the gnarliest messes Reagan would oversee as president.

One of Haig's first priorities as secretary of state was the shifting landscape in Central America, where the Soviet Union was actively sponsoring so-called wars of liberation, supporting the Sandinistas in Nicaragua and the FALN in El Salvador.

President Reagan had made his intentions clear about the U.S.'s neighbors to the south. "We're going to turn Latin America into a beacon of freedom," he declared.

Haig interpreted that to mean: *by any means necessary.* It seemed to him that the spread of Soviet influence throughout Latin America flowed through Cuba, the hub in the supply chain arming guerrillas in El Salvador and Nicaragua; he saw it as the base for the Soviet Union in the Western Hemisphere. "Right after the inauguration, Al thought the president should take on Cuba," Bud McFarlane recalls. Haig approached McFarlane with a two-fisted proposal: "We should get a band of brothers from CIA and put together a strategy for toppling Castro." According to McFarlane, "Nobody thought that made any sense." Jim Baker and Ed Meese were especially opposed and confirmed in their opinion that Haig was trigger-happy and downright dangerous.

Their fears were magnified during the March 19 meeting, when Haig again raised the subject of an incursion into Cuba. At one point, he turned to the president and said, "Give me the word and I'll turn that island into a fucking parking lot." Reagan had said as much about Vietnam during a speech in October 1965—"We could pave the whole country and put parking stripes on it and still be home by Christmas"—but his attitude toward armed conflict had softened with age and with the recognition that any parking lot under his watch would be *his* parking lot. Haig's tantrum sucked all the air out of the room. Deaver told Lou Cannon, "It scared the shit out of me . . . [and] scared the shit out of Ronald Reagan."

The president was beginning to have doubts about Al Haig, but the situation was not easily reconciled. His secretary of state's insights and advice on global affairs proved sound, often sage, even as his temperament was manifestly less than stable. As an adviser to the president observed, of the two Al Haigs, "one is the smooth-talking diplomatic machine who represents this country most capably. The other is an angry man who becomes unraveled whenever his mandate is challenged." In a few short months, Haig had picked fights with half the White House team, accusing them of either misleading him or plotting his downfall. He even fingered the president for lying to him—"not only once, but twice," as he complained to Bill Clark, the deputy secretary of state.

Alexander Haig still had his admirers in the administration, people who could see past the arrogance and the self-conceit. Even Ronald Reagan, at this stage in the game, was willing to excuse his persistent oversteps. The president had bigger things to worry about. He was still shaping policy, still establishing the tone of his administration. Cynics could scoff at how disengaged he seemed, but he was enjoying enormous public support. Let the media poke fun at his one-page memos, the jelly beans, the TV-tray dinners. Most people could relate. In many ways, he was the first president that they saw on their own level. He wasn't erudite like Kennedy, wasn't a master manipulator of Congress like Johnson, wasn't a policy wonk like Nixon, not a micromanager like Carter. What he did, in these times of upheaval, was to make Americans comfortable. He gave people the impression that things were on the right track, that he had the country's best interests—*their* best interests—at heart. Despite some early road bumps, the Reagan presidency appeared to be running smoothly.

On March 30, 1981, that would change.

CHAPTER THIRTY-TWO

SURVIVAL OF THE FITTEST

"Honey, I forgot to duck."

—JACK DEMPSEY, SEPT. 23, 1926

MARCH 30, 1981

Ronald Reagan couldn't have been very pleased. He was scheduled for an after-lunch appearance in the main ballroom of the Washington Hilton to speak to the AFL-CIO's Building Construction Trades Department—four thousand labor officials who were likely to vote Democratic in any election. The day had gotten off to an ominous start. Each morning, before heading to the Oval Office, the president perused the daily papers over his cereal and coffee. The news being reported was not very favorable. Those damn House Democrats were holding up his tax cuts, endorsing them for one year instead of the three he wanted, and weighted only to the lower half of the income scale. National business bankruptcies had surged 63 percent in the first ten weeks of the year, due to high interest rates and a sluggish economy. Leaders of the nation's colleges and universities predicted that Reagan's cutbacks to student aid would drive working-class students to drop out of college. And the Soviets—leave it to the Soviets to ruin his day—had stepped up their intimidation of Solidarity, the Polish trade union organization.

The AFL-CIO wouldn't be getting one of his showstoppers—just the basic, boilerplate spiel: the economy is killing us, too many workers unemployed, taxes too high, budget out of control. Short and sweet, twenty-five minutes at the most, an olive branch to an otherwise unsympathetic group. "This was going to be a minor speech, so I didn't go," Ed Meese recalls. Jim Baker also opted out. Better to send Mike Deaver to chaperone an event that didn't carry much weight. Even Jim Brady, the press secretary, decided to send his number-two man, Larry Speakes, in his place—that is, until the last minute, when he sized up the sorry-looking B-squad accompanying the president and decided his presence was called for.

The weather was overcast and damp. Washington was suffering through the wettest March in ten years. A light drizzle had been falling all morning, but as the three-car motorcade known as the package pulled away from the White House, the skies delivered a temporary reprieve. At least there was no long travel involved. The Hilton was a ten-minute drive without traffic, which the police had cleared from the president's route.

The event came off pretty much as expected. Polite if unenthusiastic applause. Nothing new in the president's remarks. The only thing that got a rise out of the crowd was the opening joke—a trademark opening joke on this day, baseball's opening day—about the wife of a ballplayer instructing her husband in the art of diapering their baby. "Look, buster, you lay the diaper out like a diamond, you put second base on home plate, you put the baby's bottom on the pitcher's mound," etc. How it had anything to do with building construction was anyone's guess, but Reagan knew to lead with his best stuff.

In all likelihood he'd get a better reception from members of the media, who had amassed by the hotel's VIP entrance on T Street. They were seeking his reaction to a report about an American shot by hijackers holding an Indonesian jetliner in Bangkok. The crowd, about two hundred strong, pressed in along a red rope line, as Ronald Reagan emerged through the special door just north of the main entrance. The press jockeyed with the public for position as the president waved and eyed his limousine, which had backed up and parked at an angle to the curb to ensure a fast getaway. Intrepid reporters began barking out questions.

"Mr. President . . ." "Mr. President . . ."

As Mike Putzel, the Associated Press reporter, succeeded in capturing Reagan's attention, Mike Deaver decided to intervene. "I grabbed Jim Brady by the arm," he recalled, "and shoved him over to the press to take the question so that Reagan could move, without answering, into the limo."

Not to be upstaged by the AP, Judy Woodruff, NBC's pool reporter, enlisted Dave Prosperi, the assistant press secretary, to escort her to the front so that she could interrogate Brady, whose bulky frame was blocking for the president in his path to the car. As Deaver cut around behind the limousine in order to get into the opposite side, someone stepped forward with two outstretched arms extended over Deaver's shoulder.

The fluttery pops, like balloons bursting or a string of ladyfinger firecrackers, echoed in the air. *One . . . two . . . three . . .* Six pops in all.

Those in the crowd more familiar with the sound dropped into a protective crouch. One person who understood was Jerry Parr, the Secret Service agent in charge of the presidential detail. "I sort of knew what they were," he said of the pops, "and I'd been waiting for them all of my career, in a way."

"*What the hell's that?*" the president wondered aloud.

Without answering, Parr tackled Ronald Reagan, pushed him into the backseat of the limousine, and threw himself over the spread-eagled president, oblivious to the fact that Tim McCarthy, the Secret Service agent who had opened the right rear car door for them was lying on the ground with a bullet wound in the upper torso, or that Thomas Delahanty, a Washington police officer, had taken a shot in the neck and was sprawled on the pavement. Or that Rick Ahearn, the White House advance man, was kneeling over Jim Brady, holding a handkerchief to the press secretary's head where a gaping wound was spewing blood.

"Take off!" Parr shouted to the bewildered driver, who stomped on the gas pedal, swerving around a stalled police car, then sped up T Street turning left onto Connecticut Avenue toward the safety of the White House.

Ronald Reagan let out a muffled groan followed by an expletive. "Jerry," he begged the Secret Service agent, "get off, I think you've broken one of my ribs."

The pain that shot through the president's upper back was "excruciating"—he could barely breathe. "No matter how hard I tried to breathe, it seemed I was getting less and less air," he recalled. He struggled to sit up, noticing blood smeared across the palm of his hand. "You not only broke a rib, I think the rib punctured my lung," he complained.

Parr gave Ronald Reagan a cursory once-over and announced over walkie-talkie, "Rawhide"—the code name the Secret Service used to identify President Reagan—"is okay." But when he saw bright-red blood coming from Reagan's mouth, Parr changed his mind and instructed the driver to head for George Washington University Hospital, located only minutes from their position in the tunnel beneath Dupont Circle.

The scene outside the Hilton had erupted in chaos. People ran in every direction, dodging a cluster of police who were swarming through the crowd. There had been no more shots since the president left the scene, but a shaggy-haired young man standing next to the ABC-TV cameraman continued to pull the trigger on an empty gun. One of the spectators, Alfred Antenucci, jumped on the shooter, while two Secret Service agents dived into the fray and wrestled the weapon away. A pair of paramedics who happened to be at the hotel rushed to give medical assistance to the two wounded officers, but James Brady's condition was beyond their abilities.

The injured press secretary was facedown in a heap of blood while Rick Ahearn applied pressure to the side of his head. Ahearn's handkerchief was soaked through and practically useless. Dave Prosperi, who was darting back into the hotel, stopped to hand over a spare handkerchief. "Jim was in bad shape," Prosperi recalls, "moaning and writhing, while Rick tried to keep him still." Prosperi was determined to notify the White House of the shooting. In those days before cell phones, he was dependent on public phones, but the bank of five just inside the Hilton was occupied by hotel guests unaware of the scene outside. As one came free, Prosperi called the press office and demanded to talk to Larry Speakes.

"Larry, the president's been shot at and Jim's been hit," he said.

"Got it—thanks," Speakes replied and hung up.

The news raced through the White House, which instantly went into lockdown mode. But even as officials followed procedures long in place for just such an emergency, information about the president's condition remained unknown.

A little before 2:30 p.m., the white Princess phone sitting on the corner of a desk in the nurses' station of George Washington University Hospital began to ring. Wendy Koenig, the nurse on duty, was startled by its distinctive sound. That phone *never* rang. Well, hardly ever. It was a direct link to a signal board at the White House, and to date it had rung only once, when Amy Carter scraped her knee in a fall. Nurse Koenig answered it immediately and was told only: "The presidential motorcade is en route to your facility."

Three minutes later, the black limousine with an American flag flapping on the antenna pulled into the ER driveway facing Pennsylvania Avenue. An ER nurse rushed out to greet it and was awestruck when the President of the United States stepped out. "I'll walk in," Reagan had told Jerry Parr. Mike Deaver, who was in a car following behind, felt some relief to see the president on his feet. "Reagan had a habit—if he'd been sitting in a plane or car, or even on a podium—when he got up, he would cinch his pants up and then he'd button his coat," Deaver recalled. "And that's exactly what he did. He looked all right to me." He cut a strapping figure in the brand-new blue pinstriped suit he wore for the occasion, but his face was a giveaway. To the skilled eye—and there were several sets trained on him between ER personnel, Deaver, and Secret Service—it was a mask of extreme discomfort mixed with panic; the color had drained from his always-rosy face. "I was having trouble breathing," he recalled. "Then all of a sudden my knees turned rubbery." As he pushed through the sliding glass doors into the trauma bay, his eyes rolled upward, he went slack, and began to collapse to his knees. Parr and a paramedic grabbed the president under the arms and loaded him onto a gurney while the trauma staff converged, responding to the alert—*"Trauma team to the emergency room . . . stat!"*— that blared over loudspeakers.

"I feel so bad," Reagan moaned. He was gasping for air. Blood-tinged spittle formed at the corners of his mouth.

Nurses suspected he'd suffered a heart attack and wasted no time with small talk. Following time-honored protocol, they began cutting away his clothes, laying waste to that natty suit and monogrammed dress shirt. "You're ruining my suit!" the president protested. Within seconds, the whole ensemble lay in shredded scraps on the floor. Anyone within the vicinity of the scene would have gotten an eyeful: the President of the United States lying naked as a jaybird. "It was an unforgettable sight," says Robert Roubik, a nurse anesthetist who barreled in and jabbed an eighteen-gauge needle in an area around the elbow. He began an IV drip with a solution called

Lactated Ringer's, a glorified Gatorade. Simultaneously, Nurse Koenig attached a blood-pressure cuff to Reagan's upper left arm and listened for the response in her stethoscope.

"I can't hear anything," she yelled above the ruckus in the overcrowded room. A cacophony of voices had crescendoed to a near-deafening roar, making it difficult for the attendants to consult one another. "I can't get a systolic pressure." A second test provided the same result: nothing. She began to panic. Was the president arresting? In desperation, she stimulated an artery with the tips of her fingers, hoping to jump-start pressure. *Ah, there it was*: she detected a slight but definite throb, enough to let her know Reagan was probably just in shock. But—from what? His body appeared unblemished. There wasn't any sign that he'd been physically wounded. But the blood on his hand and at the corners of his lips were evidence that something more was amiss. Not a heart attack. The president was injured. They needed doctors—fast.

Nancy Reagan and her press officer, Sheila Tate, had been at a luncheon in Georgetown for the National Trust for Historic Preservation, one of those worthy civic organizations that First Ladies are inclined to support. She left the affair early, bothered by a feeling of anxiety she couldn't pinpoint. To avoid reporters, the two women returned to the White House via the back door and went their separate ways—Mrs. Reagan veering left to the residence and Tate taking a right toward the East Wing. As Tate arrived at her office the phone was ringing. Jennifer Hirshberg was calling from the *Washington Star*. "The police radio is saying there was a shooting at the Hilton," Hirshberg said. "Has the president been hurt?"

Tate hung up without answering and ran, nearly colliding with Nancy Reagan, who came charging down the hall from the opposite direction. One of the Secret Service agents had told her that there was a shooting at the Hilton, that Jim Brady had been hit, and that the president was on his way to GW Hospital. "Take me to the hospital," the First Lady demanded of her Secret Service detail. It wasn't necessary, the agents assured her. The president was fine; he hadn't been hit. "*I'm going to that hospital!* If you don't get me a car I'm going to walk." Her limo and follow car were still parked outside, and she was already climbing in while the agents conferred.

"It was completely quiet in the car," Tate recalls. "She held my hand but never said a word." They'd been given no information; nothing was being reported.

At the hospital, the two women pushed through the knot of reporters and onlookers that had amassed outside the emergency room doors. One of the Secret Service agents stationed at the entrance grabbed Nancy Reagan and headed toward the trauma bay. Mike Deaver came out to meet her.

"He's been hit," Deaver said.

T he trauma bay at George Washington University Hospital, unlike the ER, was state-of-the-art, a gleaming jewel box of medical devices. Ronald Reagan lay on a gurney with a sheet draped over him and a strap across his knees. To provide a higher concentration of oxygen, he was fitted with a breathing mask.

The first two doctors to arrive on the scene were senior resident Wesley Price and intern William O'Neill. According to Bob Roubik, who was handling the IV, "If you were to call Central Casting and said, 'Send me two guys who are really nice folks and look like they might be surgeons,' these are the two they would send." Neither of them was what nurses referred to as hotheads—the ego-driven yellers and screamers who preside over ERs like dictators. Still, as one nurse recalls, "That day, everyone's blood pressure and heart rates were elevated, not only because it was the president, but because he was so badly wounded."

"Can anybody tell me what happened?" Price requested of the room at large.

The question drew nothing but blank stares.

The president reiterated that he was having trouble breathing. Aside from that, there were no other symptoms that gave Dr. Price anything to go on. Price knew from Jerry Parr that Reagan suspected he'd punctured a lung in the limo, and in the course of examining the chest area and abdomen, the doctor noticed a paper-thin, jagged slit, like a buttonhole, over the left axilla, a few inches below the president's armpit and on a plane even with the nipple area.

"Look, Bill," Price said to his colleague, "there is a hole."

He was careful not to say "wound" or "gunshot" in front of the scrum of people in the trauma bay—people in green scrubs, white lab coats, blue coats that had "Hospital Security" stitched across the chest, Secret Service agents in black Hart Schaffner Marx suits, and well-tailored physicians from other parts of the hospital who'd turned up to take in the spectacle— maybe thirty-five or forty people in a space not much larger than a galley kitchen. "The amount of noise was unbelievable," says a nurse on duty. "It was absolutely nuts."

"Am I dying?" the president asked through his mask.

An attending intern answered, "No, you're going to be fine." But it was a dodge; the patient's condition looked serious.

"We're going to do some films," Wesley Price announced, as technicians rolled in a portable X-ray machine. "Everybody needs to leave."

As the audience filed out through the doors, Dr. Price pulled Jerry Parr aside and quietly said, "It looks like he's been shot."

Dick Allen, the national security adviser, had taken a rare twenty-minute break from anguishing over a pair of Soviet subs lurking closer than usual to the East Coast, and had gone swimming at the University Club, two blocks from the White House. As he prepared to do a flip-turn in one of the pool's lanes, a hand reached down and pulled him up by the hair. His driver, Joe Bullock, knelt by the gutter and softly told him, "Something terrible has happened. The President's been shot."

Allen dressed in the backseat of the car as it roared down East Executive Avenue and around the Ellipse. The driver had radioed ahead so the gate would be open, and as they entered the driveway it became necessary to jam on the brakes to avoid broadsiding a car belonging to Don Regan. Allen looked at its passengers and saw Ed Meese and Jim Baker staring back at him. He knew they were probably headed to a hospital and figured he'd have to help hold down the fort. The White House would no doubt be in an uproar. There were precautions—a crisis management plan—that needed to be activated. As national security adviser, he was in charge of its implementation.

After clearing the corridors of an overwrought young staff, Allen and Al Haig huddled in Jim Baker's office and decided it was time to contact the vice president. George Bush was en route to a political fund-raiser in Texas, aboard a DC-9 that lacked secure voice communications. All that Haig could say to Bush on an open line was, *"George, it's Al—turn around, turn around!"* The ground-to-air reception was awful. Haig, dressed in an open trenchcoat with the belts flapping loosely, strode back and forth in front of a desk, growing increasingly frustrated that he couldn't be heard. *"George . . . turn . . . around!"*

In the interests of national security and to prevent leaks to the media, Allen and Haig herded key administration personnel into the Situation Room, a windowless hi-tech conference room secured by a guard and cipher lock in the basement of the West Wing, where Security Council planning sessions were held. It was an exclusive group: Allen and Haig, along with Secretary of Defense Caspar Weinberger, Treasury Secretary Donald Regan, Transportation Secretary Drew Lewis, White House counsel Fred Fielding, domestic adviser Martin Anderson, CIA director Bill Casey, White House Director of Communications David Gergen, Attorney General William French Smith, Bush's chief of staff Admiral Daniel Murphy, and, for some unknown reason, John Brock, the secretary of agriculture, who, according to Dick Allen, "sat against the wall and didn't know what the hell was going on."

"Nobody in the Sit Room knew what was happening," Fielding says. "It was March thirtieth, just two months after the inauguration, most of which were spent getting our staffs together. So we were basically a bunch of strangers."

Even so, Fielding notes, "it was pretty civilized." The first order of business was securing the "football," the briefcase that never left the president's side, containing the nuclear code sequences in case of a belligerent attack. There was a duplicate in the military aide's office, and Haig ordered it delivered to the Sit Room at once. No one knew if the shooting was part of a greater conspiracy or whether the Soviets might take advantage of the situation to launch an attack. Those Russian nuclear subs off the East Coast created a few unnecessary jitters—"two minutes closer than normal," Cap Weinberger pointed out, meaning the time it would take for a Soviet missile to reach Washington. According to Dick Allen, "We determined it was eight minutes' flying time from a submerged ballistic missile launch to the

White House." As a result, Weinberger increased the alert for the Strategic Air Command, which would save precious minutes should the Air Force need to get bombers aloft.

There was also the question of succession. "At that point, we didn't know how bad the president was," Fred Fielding recalls. "Baker and Meese were at the hospital, but they didn't know much, either. So the attorney general and I were there to deal with the Twenty-fifth Amendment." The proviso was relatively new, ratified in 1967 to establish a procedure should the president die, resign, or be removed from office. It stated clearly that the vice president automatically inherited the presidency, as enacted when Nixon resigned and Ford succeeded him. The president, if he felt compelled to do so, could, on a temporary basis, transfer his authority to the vice president. A document was prepared so Reagan could do exactly that.

But the president was currently on an operating table. And at 3:25 p.m., George Bush's plane had landed in Austin to refuel for the trip back, making him due for arrival at Andrews Air Force Base at approximately 6:30. That left succession pretty much up in the air. But not to Al Haig. "The helm is right here," he announced, jabbing a finger at his own chest, "and that means right in this chair for now, constitutionally, till the Vice President gets here." Others in the Sit Room rolled their eyes and several responded accordingly: "Fuck you!"

It hadn't taken long for Dr. Wesley Price to determine that a bullet had lodged somewhere in the president's chest or abdomen. There was no evidence of an exit wound. Eventually, the chest X-rays revealed "blood in the pleural cavity and the bullet behind the heart." Dr. Joseph Giordano, who headed the trauma unit, wasn't encouraged by Reagan's symptoms. "The President's blood pressure was very low, and his pulse was barely detectable," he recalled. "He was seriously injured. I think he was close to dying." A decision was made to call in Ben Aaron, a seasoned cardiovascular surgeon. Doctors Aaron and Price, and David Gens, a surgical resident, sat for a while and discussed their options—"Where do we go from here? What's our next move?"—while an operating room they ordered was being prepared. In any case, they felt the president was stable enough to receive a visitor and asked that Nancy Reagan be brought into the trauma bay.

The extent of her anxiety was written on her face. She had been prepped in advance for what to expect—that her husband had a tube in his chest and was breathing through an oxygen mask—but the reality was markedly worse. "Ronnie looked pale and gray," she recalled. "Underneath the oxygen mask, his lips were caked with dried blood." She recoiled when she saw him, but if there had been any questions that his faculties were impaired, he dispelled them with typical élan. With an unsteady finger, he pushed up the oxygen mask as Nancy bent close and kissed his forehead.

"Honey," he whispered, "I forgot to duck."

Both the president and the First Lady inquired about the condition of others who had been hurt in the shooting. No one responded. "We either pretended we hadn't heard or didn't know," said an attending medic. But not more than ten feet away and separated only by a curtain, Jim Brady lay on a gurney, critically wounded.

CT scans of Brady's brain showed an ugly, large clot developing in the right frontal region, exacerbated by swelling, not good signs. To make matters worse, he appeared to have been shot by a bullet known as a Devastator, which contains a charge of toxic lead azide meant to explode on impact. There were chances that fragments lay elsewhere unobserved. The bullet had traveled through Brady's sinuses, an air passage that often led to infections, complicating his recovery should he survive. There was some talk of not operating at all—that Brady's chances were one in ten—but Arthur Kobrine, the surgeon assigned to the case, insisted, "We are *not* going to *fucking* let this man die." One medic on the team who glanced at Brady's monstrous wound recalls, "I went straight down to the doctor's urinal and stood there for five minutes, so uptight I was unable to pee."

As nurses rolled the president out of the trauma bay toward the OR, one of them confided to Nancy Reagan, "We don't think Mr. Brady's going to make it."

Fortunately, the president didn't hear. He was distracted by the sight of three familiar figures hovering tentatively in the hallway—the Troika: Baker, Meese, and Deaver. Reagan's face lit up as they stepped gingerly toward his cart. "Who's minding the store?" he asked and winked. They were relieved that he had his sense of humor. A good sign, considering the circumstances. But Ed Meese recalls, "He looked terrible, pale—white." The fact that Reagan was a seventy-year-old man wasn't far from anyone's mind. Certainly the surgeon, Ben Aaron, worried about the president's ability to withstand major chest surgery. The patient was in shock and bleeding internally, which compounded the doctor's concern. He wanted to operate and stop the bleeding. Reagan gave his immediate approval, as did Nancy. A battalion of doctors escorted the procession, led by "extremely aggressive" Secret Service agents, who screamed "Move out of the way!" at staff and patients on stretchers. "Get out of the way! *Move! Now!*" The route to the OR was nearly a city block away, obstacle-laden and circuitous, necessitating a detour down narrow hallways past the urology suites and through the recovery room, where open-mouthed patients gaped in astonishment as the president was wheeled by.

Meanwhile, the Troika took Nancy Reagan into a meditation room inside the chapel. "She was very much agitated," says Ed Meese "We all were. We needed to pray."

Right now, their heavenly entreaties for Jim Brady were more urgently needed. "Reports kept coming out that he was dead," Meese says, "and we knew that it wasn't true. But he was so close to death that we didn't want to say anything. By the time we said it, Jim might in fact have expired."

The media had botched its coverage of Brady. CBS was the first to report that he had died at the hospital. A scene in the White House press room compounded the error. Bill Plante, the ABC News correspondent, had observed Dave Prosperi nodding affirmatively while on a phone call nearby and misinterpreted it as corroboration that Brady was dead. The correspondent commandeered a cameraman and, moments later, announced it on the air. In the Sit Room, where officials were monitoring TV screens, Dick Allen asked for a moment of silent prayer. Meanwhile, someone else at ABC was on a phone line to the hospital, forcing an awkward retraction from its anchor, Frank Reynolds. "Let's get it nailed down, somebody!" Reynolds huffed, disgusted by the clumsy reporting.

But it wasn't just the fault of his crew. Howard Baker, the Senate Republican leader, corroborated Brady's death. And Dick Allen was infuriated by David Gergen's repeated exits from the Sit Room, certain that the communications director, whom he called Professor Leaky, was disclosing privileged information to the press. Haig suspected the same thing. He touched

Allen discreetly on the shoulder and said, "He's making a mess of this up-stairs." Haig's comment served to describe two culprits—Gergen, but also Larry Speakes, the assistant press secretary, who was manning the Communications Center in Jim Brady's absence.

During a hastily called press conference updating the unfolding action, a reporter had asked Speakes, "Who's running the government right now?"

"I cannot answer that question at this time," Speakes responded.

"This is very bad," said Dick Allen, who was watching the proceedings on a separate monitor. "We have to do something."

Haig agreed. "We've got to get him off. He's turning this into a god-damn disaster."

Allen and Haig pounded up the stairs from the basement and raced across the hall into the Press Room. It was a full house; every major outlet was represented. Speakes was already finished talking, but Haig bulled his way to the lectern. "I just want to touch on a few matters associated with today's tragedy," he began. Allen jumped on the dais next to Haig, con-cerned about the secretary of state's visible agitation. "He started to quiver," Allen recalls. "His elbows were shaking, his voice was cracking, and his face was flushed and perspiring. I literally thought he was going to collapse."

Once again, someone in the audience asked the key question: "Who is making the decisions for the government right now?"

Haig didn't miss a beat. "Constitutionally, gentlemen, you have the President, the Vice President, and the Secretary of State, in that order. . . . As of now, I am in control here, in the White House, pending return of the Vice President and in close touch with him."

I am in control here . . .

"What's this all about?" said Don Regan, watching on a monitor in the Sit Room. "Is he mad?" Regan, like most government officials, knew that the secretary of state wasn't in the line of succession.

"He's wrong," Weinberger said. "He doesn't have such authority."

I am in control here . . .

Dick Allen's eyes bugged out of his head. "I thought, 'Jesus, Mary, and Joseph!'" he recalls. "Should I tell him, 'That's not quite right,' and we get into a tussle on the facts in front of the press?" He glanced down at the first row of the press corps seated in front of him, where Bill Plante and Sam Donaldson were furiously scribbling notes. Better not, Allen decided.

Instead, they went back downstairs to the Sit Room. "And that's where the real fireworks started," Allen says.

Cap Weinberger very calmly announced that he had moved two hundred bomb crews at the Strategic Air Command from the shacks to the cockpits of the B-52s as a precaution.

"You've done—*what?*" Haig fumed. "I think we could have discussed it [first]."

"Until the Vice President actually arrives here," Weinberger said, "the command authority is what I have . . . and I have to make sure that it is essential that we do everything that seems proper."

Haig nearly lunged across the table at the secretary of defense. "You'd better read the Constitution, buddy," he shouted.

Weinberger was incredulous. "What?"

"You'd better read the Constitution," Haig repeated, this time chasing it with a sarcastic laugh.

There was no love lost between Haig and Weinberger. "They were not getting along well, almost from September of 1980," says Ed Meese. "Al was used to the highly charged turf battles from the Nixon days, and he resented anyone who had the president's ear." Meese and Weinberger grew tired of hearing Haig, time and again, refer to himself as the Vicar of Foreign Policy. "It was Al's personality—he just couldn't get into the spirit of cooperation, especially when it came to Cap."

Haig was wrong about who was in charge at the White House and wrong about the chain of control pertaining to the National Command Authority, which went from the president to the vice president to the secretary of defense. But Weinberger didn't bother giving Haig a brush-up lesson in constitutional law. Word had arrived that George Bush's plane was on its descent to Andrews Air Force Base, abrogating any talk about succession. The vice president's impending presence preempted any conversation about who was in control until Ronald Reagan was out of surgery.

The operating suite—OR 2—at George Washington University Hospital was a chilly, old-fashioned medical facility, outfitted in jade-green ceramic tile and lit by blinding overhead lamps. It was built as an amphitheater with Hollywood-style windows around the ceiling so that medical students could observe surgeries, and every seat was occupied by hospital personnel, Secret Service agents in green scrubs with guns, and the simply curious, a gaggle of hospital personnel rubbernecking for a good view of the star patient. As the president was transferred from the gurney onto the operating table, his eyes swept across the crowded room.

"Please tell me you're all Republicans," he said.

Dr. Giordano, a lifelong Democrat, responded, "Today, Mr. President, we are all Republicans."

It didn't take much sodium pentothal to put Ronald Reagan to sleep. He was under in seconds as doctors, led by Ben Aaron, began making incisions to perform an abdominal tap. Afterward, they opened the president's chest to examine the heart cavity and search for a bullet. Thankfully, the aorta was unharmed. While two doctors gently nudged the heart from side to side, Aaron probed the lung with his fingertips, feeling for metal fragments. After ten futile minutes, he considered abandoning the search, leaving the bullet inside rather than risking harm. A determining factor for continuing was the president's physical shape. "He didn't look much different from the days when he was a lifeguard," says a nurse stationed at the operating table. He was trim with "a physique like a thirty-year-old muscle builder." And his heart was strong. Aaron figured he could withstand the stressful procedure. It took another X-ray before the surgeon spotted the bullet in spongy lung tissue, lower than where his fingers had probed. Making a slight incision and squeezing carefully, he guided the bullet with a finger through the tissue until it dropped into his hand. No wonder it had eluded him: the .22-caliber bullet was flattened to the size of a dime.

Later, they would determine that the assassin's shot had glanced off the rear panel of the limousine and passed through the door frame's hinged narrow opening before hitting the president and ricocheting off his seventh rib. By the time it entered his body, it was more a razor-sharp disk than a projectile.

"I've got it!" Aaron announced to a greatly relieved team.

Even better, the bleeding from the wound had finally stopped. Aaron stitched closed an artery that had been nicked by the bullet. No other internal damage was evident in the process. The surgery was a success. The President of the United States was going to survive.

B ut for Jim Brady, survival was anything but certain. He lay prostrate in critical condition on an operating table in OR 4, just one door from the president's surgical theater, with several holes drilled into the side of his skull. Bullet fragments were strewn across the right side of his brain, where a massive clot had formed exerting dangerous pressure.

"We are not going to let this fucking guy die," Arthur Kobrine continued to declare repeatedly, as he and a team of surgeons explored the damage. But as they drained blood and tweezed out shrapnel from the patient's ravaged skull, a radio broadcasting over the OR's speakers reported that Brady was dead. "Those fuckers," Kobrine said. "What do they think we're operating on, a corpse?"

Kobrine and his team did all they could to save Jim Brady. Friends and family affectionately called him Bear, an animal that was hard to bring down. But after a long, laborious surgical procedure, the best they could give him was a fifty-fifty chance.

Later that night in the ICU, Dick Allen and his wife visited the comatose press secretary, whose bandaged head was so swollen it looked like a blood-encrusted basketball. Heartbroken, Allen picked up Brady's lifeless right hand and cupped it gently in his own, perhaps as a way of saying goodbye. He was completely shocked when Brady squeezed back—squeezed long and hard.

Dick Allen, a notoriously tough piece of work, started to weep.

A llen and his wife also looked in on the president, who lay in a recovery room on a respirator, still under the effects of anesthesia. He began to regain consciousness around 7:30 p.m. The intertracheal tube and the ventilator frightened him, as did the pair of tubes draining fluid from his chest. He experienced extreme discomfort as a result of the surgery. Morphine helped. As a result of the drug, he grew groggy, slipped in and out of consciousness. When he came to again, after a short nap, he attempted to speak, but was unable to squeeze out a sound. A nurse handed him a clipboard and marker.

"Am I alive?" he wrote.

He followed with a sheaf of witty rejoinders. "All in all, I'd rather be in Philly." "If I had this much attention in Hollywood, I would have stayed there." "Send me to LA where I can see the air I'm breathing." "I'd like to do this scene over again, starting at the hotel." "I feel like I've done a re-make of *Lost Weekend*." To a nurse who assisted in monitoring his blood pressure, he wrote, "Does Nancy know about us?"

At some point, he began to regain his sense of purpose.

"Was anyone else hurt?" he wrote on the clipboard.

Joanne Bell, the change nurse on duty in the recovery room, had been instructed by the Secret Service not to give him any information about the attack. She hedged, anguished, froze. How to respond? It became an ethical dilemma: nurses don't lie to patients. "Mr. President," she hemmed and hawed, "I've been so busy taking care of you I couldn't say." She draped a washcloth over his eyes. "Go to sleep. You need your rest."

He lifted the clipboard and scrawled another question.

"Did they get the guy?"

The D.C. police had a suspect in custody. A Texas Tech student ID card in the young man's wallet identified him as John W. Hinckley Jr., a twenty-five-year-old "deranged loner," as far as anyone could tell. His last known address was an apartment in Lubbock, but there was some kind of tie to Evergreen, Colorado. Hinckley had been tackled and disarmed at the scene of the shooting. There was little doubt that he'd been the gunman, although it was unknown to law enforcement at the time whether there were more individuals involved or some type of conspiracy. Hinckley wasn't saying. The only thing he admitted to was his recent arrival on a Grey-hound bus from California and the room he'd taken in the city at the Park Central Hotel. As far as other evidence went, there were several photos in his wallet of a young, attractive woman, photos torn from a magazine—"a friend of mine," Hinckley explained. In a matter of hours, FBI agents con-ducting an interrogation of the suspect learned that the so-called friend was actress Jodie Foster, whom Hinckley had been stalking while she at-tended Yale University, and that the assassination attempt on Ronald

Reagan was intended to somehow impress her. "Jodie," he had scrawled on hotel stationery an hour before leaving for the Hilton, "I'm asking you to please look into your heart and at least give me the chance with this historical deed to gain your respect and love."

The investigation turned up further evidence that Hinckley might have attempted to kill a president before. In October, he'd been arrested in Nashville on possession of handguns, just hours before Jimmy Carter was due in the city. Police surveillance had been on top of that event. In Washington, Hinckley managed to find his target.

The president suffered through a restless night. Too many uninvited visitors and medical voyeurs marched through the recovery room, distracting him from precious sleep. His lungs were congested with mucus, prompting painful bouts of coughing, and he was agitated. On several occasions he lashed out at his oxygen supply from the ventilator in what nurses called "bucking against the tube." His son Ron, who had visited earlier in the evening, encouraged him to think of the apparatus in terms of scuba gear. Understandably, the endotracheal tube was a more punishing experience. "Let the machine breathe for you," he was instructed, but it was difficult to master.

Around three in the morning, Ben Aaron came by on his rounds. He'd been pushed to the brink, seguing from the surgery on the president directly into another difficult operation that lasted well into the middle of the night, and his scrubs bore bloody evidence of the grind. Exhaustion showed on his face. While he reviewed Ronald Reagan's chart with a colleague, the doctor at his side nodded gravely in response and said, "This is it . . . this is it."

Alarmed, the president grabbed the clipboard and scribbled, "What do they mean, 'This is it'?"

A nurse offered reassurance: relax, the news was good. They'd decided to remove the breathing tube that had caused him discomfort. He'd feel better now, more able to rest. Once the tube was out, however, Reagan began to talk incessantly. There were questions about his assailant—"What was that guy's beef?" he wondered—about others who were wounded in the attack, about his condition, about Nancy's state of mind. At 4:30 a.m., Jo-anne Bell placed a washcloth over his eyes. "Mr. President," she said, "in the most polite way I can tell you, when I put this over your eyes it means I want you to shut up."

S mall chance of that. The president slept intermittently. His blood pressure was taken every half hour; pain medication was administered at intervals; doctors streamed in and out probing, prodding, checking his vital signs. "There were times during sleep when he had trouble breathing," recalls Bell, "and I would touch him on the shoulder and say, 'Take a deep breath.'"

With morning came welcome signs: color had returned to his face and his eyes were brighter, clearing the way for a move to the intensive care unit just after daybreak, on the floor above the recovery room. When the elevator doors opened and the president's cart rolled out, more than twenty District of Columbia policemen in full dress lined either side of the corridor, standing at attention and saluting.

Later that morning, when Mike Deaver, Jim Baker, and Ed Meese laid eyes on him, Ronald Reagan was gingerly walking up and down the corridor in his bathrobe, clearly in a great deal of pain. "He looked pale and was grimacing," Meese recalls, "so we helped him into bed before getting down to business."

Mike Deaver assured the president that he needn't worry about the White House. It was functioning like a well-oiled machine. "What makes you think I'd be happy to hear *that?*" he responded.

There was no day off for the President of the United States, not even after surviving an assassination attempt. The Troika brought legislation he needed to sign—a price-support bill that terminated $147 million in subsidies to the dairy industry—that couldn't wait. If it wasn't signed by midnight of March 31, the money flow would continue unabated. "It was the first—and key—component of our freeze on federal spending," says Ken Duberstein, who helped steer the bill through the House committee. "We also knew that having Reagan sign it at the hospital sent a signal to the rest of the world that he was still in charge." Wincing, the president took a pen and scrawled his name in shaky script across the last sheet of the document: Ronald W. Reagan—the only signature in his eight-year term that included the middle initial.

That was the extent of presidential business. Reagan's physical condition fluctuated for several days as he was beset by severe congestion and spikes of fever. Only immediate family members were permitted to visit. Somehow, Strom Thurmond managed to talk his way past Secret Service agents posted at the door to the president's room, which outraged Nancy Reagan and spurred her to station Max Friedersdorf, the administration's congressional-relations chief, at the hospital to identify and intercept trespassers.

It wasn't until April 6 that an outsider was granted access. Friedersdorf recognized the person right away as he barreled down the hall, "a great big burly bear of a man": Tip O'Neill, the Speaker of the House, the president's number-one political nemesis, and in Friedersdorf's eyes, "a very fearsome person." O'Neill strode into the hospital room, went straight to the bed, and planted a kiss on Ronald Reagan's forehead. Then the Speaker dropped to his knees and recited the Twenty-third Psalm. It was a surreal display of affection from this hard-bitten politico. "The Speaker was crying," Friedersdorf recalled. He sat by the bed and held the president's hand for a long time until taking his leave.

By all appearances, it would be some time before Ronald Reagan was able to leave as well. He appeared weak, disoriented as a result of sedatives, and hammered by his ordeal. And yet, only five days later, on April 11, 1981, the doctors cleared him for release. All things considered, it was an extraordinary recovery for a seventy-year-old man who had taken a bullet to the chest. He even circumvented hospital protocol, which required that all patients leave the facility by wheelchair to avoid a potential accident.

"I walked in," Ronald Reagan declared. "I'm walking out."

CHAPTER THIRTY-THREE

CRACKS IN THE FOUNDATION

"Popularity? It is glory's small change."

—VICTOR HUGO

A window opened.

Following the assassination attempt, Ronald Reagan's heroic return to the White House brought him a media honeymoon that sent his poll numbers soaring into the upper-70 percent range. Even reluctant Democrats began edging to his side. Making his first public appearance, on April 28, 1981, for a speech to a joint session of Congress, he was greeted by a standing ovation and an explosion of cheers and whistles that stretched on for three minutes. "That reception," he joked afterward, "was almost worth getting shot for." Seizing the opportunity, he launched into a pitch for a series of key issues that had, so far, thwarted his young administration, in particular tax reform and the sale of AWACS to Saudi Arabia.

Reagan's aides milked it for all it was worth. They designed a strategy that merged the president's ongoing recovery with the kind of workload that allowed him to make political strides to advance his pet policies. Instead of meetings and official functions, he spent his days lashed to the phone, running down call lists to legislators still balking at his proposals. He courted, cajoled, and sweet-talked the most malleable holdouts: moderate Republicans and conservative Democrats. These members of Congress found themselves unable to resist his personal appeals to support even bills that put them squarely in jeopardy with their constituents.

At the outset, his Economic Recovery Program seemed dead on arrival. Skeptics had lined up to offer doomsday scenarios. But the president sent his emissaries on a goodwill rampage through congressional hallways and stepped up his calling campaign. "In order to win in the House, we needed twenty-seven Democratic votes," says Ken Duberstein, the administration's political lobbyist on the Hill. On May 7, sixty-three of them joined the Republican bloc to approve Gramm-Latta, a compromise bill that preserved the heart of the program. Five days later the Senate approved its own version by a sweeping majority, giving life to Reaganomics. Both houses needed to thrash out a bill to reconcile their differences, but the administration was optimistic.

The AWACS presented a thornier issue. In the words of Dick Allen, whose job it was to sell them to the Saudis, "I'd been handed a steamin' turd." The Israelis were dead set against the sale, and the American Jewish community was up in arms. Their fearsome lobby, AIPAC, the most powerful lobby on Capitol Hill, had the House completely wired, which meant the bill had to be won in the Senate, where fifty-eight of its one hundred members had already signed a pledge to vote against it. Complicating matters, Congress had placed a 120-day time limit on the sale, and the clock had started running under Jimmy Carter. It might have been politically prudent to simply let the clock run out, but the president was determined to see the deal through. Saudi Arabia was America's best friend in the Arab world. Reagan had accepted the argument that Israel was in no danger from the AWACS; it was a defensive, not an offensive, system. What's more, he was advised by Allen that "the Saudis, who were notoriously incompetent, were never going to be able to operate those bloody airplanes."

An early loose poll of senators revealed that the administration was down by a count of 92–3. "Totally hopeless" was how a Reagan official sized it up. "We pulled out all the stops," Ed Meese recalls. Every lobbying tactic was dusted off and launched—inviting senators to the Oval Office for one-on-one conferences, doling out presidential cuff links and tie clips as perks, arranging weekend junkets to Camp David, and providing rides on *Air Force One*. The president hit the phones. "We went up real quick to thirty, forty votes," recalled Max Friedersdorf, who oversaw the operation. From there, they developed a hit list, which Reagan worked with virtuoso skill. Every potential crossover got his arm gently twisted. The president leveraged his support with Democratic senators in states he'd won, promising them that, come midterm elections, he wouldn't campaign against them. It was a veiled threat, but wildly effective. In one case, involving Howell Heflin, the Alabama Democrat, Reagan exploited the senator's deep-seated religious beliefs, "reminding Heflin that the Bible said Armageddon would begin in the Middle East and that Russians would be involved."

Often, Reagan worked as part of a tag team with Nancy. Eavesdropping on calls he made from the residence, she would suggest something to use as ammunition to help change a senator's vote. Before a call to Mark Andrews of North Dakota, she said, "Now, Ronnie, you remember, you went up to Bismarck and campaigned for him in a snowstorm. You remind him of that."

It was a challenging but productive process. Still, two days before the AWACS vote, the administration remained down by a dozen votes. And the negotiations turned bitter. AIPAC played the anti-Semitism card and threatened senators who were still on the fence that Jewish contributions to their campaigns would dry up. Its party line was: either you're with Israel or against Israel. Four rabbis appeared in Warren Rudman's office, warning him, a dutiful Jew, that if he voted in favor of the AWACS sale, he was abandoning his religion.

Reagan was furious. He publicly castigated Israel, saying, "It is not the business of other nations to make United States foreign policy." Then he went back on the phones, working them with a vengeance in a last-ditch effort to turn the tide. Every no vote or holdout got a call or two. Financial backers of the senators still opposed to the sale were recruited to exert their influence by withholding support. Dick Allen says, "It was my job to bring the hesitating [senators] up to the White House, one by one, to sit with the president so he could sway them." It went down to the wire. "Within two to three hours before the vote, we switched three votes that won it," Max Friedersdorf recalled. The final tally was 52–48. Reagan had risked valuable political capital in the name of regional stability for the Middle East and the strengthening of the U.S.-Saudi relationship. The wager had paid off.

Yes, a window had opened. The Democratic majority knew the force it was up against. As Jim Wright, the House majority leader, wrote about the president, "His philosophical approach is superficial, overly simplistic and one-dimensional. What he preaches is pure economic pap, glossed over with uplifting homilies and inspirational chatter. Yet so far the guy is making it work. Appalled by what seems to me a lack of depth, I stand in awe nevertheless of his political skill. I am not sure I have seen its equal." Or, as Speaker Tip O'Neill put it, "The President has become a hero. We can't argue with a man as popular as he is [right now]. I've been in politics a long time and I know when to fight and when not to fight."

The Democrats weren't prepared to put up their dukes—not yet, at least, not while the president remained sidelined with his wound. But in mid-May, the administration overreached, announcing plans for a reduction in Social Security benefits—as much as 31 percent for early retirees—and the gloves came off. For good reason, Social Security is called the third rail of American politics. The bill was defeated in the Senate by a vote of 96–0. The president pivoted to other, more winnable fights.

He had been told by Vice President Bush that Potter Stewart intended to step down from the Supreme Court at the end of the current term, which meant an opportunity to appoint a judge with a conservative outlook. The Troika had discussed a replacement with Reagan early in April 1981, and William French Smith, the attorney general, was charged with submitting qualified candidates for consideration. "The president primarily wanted an originalist, someone who would be faithful to the Constitution," Meese recalls. His and Smith's marching orders were to find some "Constitutionally-oriented" women. Reagan seemed intent on making good on the campaign promise dreamed up by Stu Spencer—to name the first woman to the Supreme Court.

Bill Smith's list of eight nominees included four women, two of whom—Amalya Kearse and Sandra Day O'Connor—were leading candidates. The Troika wasn't familiar with any of them. Republican hard-liners preferred two strong conservative jurists: Antonin Scalia and Robert Bork. They argued that this might be the president's only chance for an appointment, and it should be someone philosophically compatible with him. But naming a woman captivated him, and Sandra Day O'Connor was particularly appealing. She'd been a Stanford Law School classmate and onetime date of William Rehnquist, an associate justice. What's more, she came highly recommended. Nancy's father also knew O'Connor through mutual friends in Arizona, where she sat on the State Court of Appeals, and he urged his son-in-law to seriously consider appointing her.

The president liked O'Connor immediately. In their initial meeting, on the morning of July 1, it came to light that she was raised on a ranch, and that she had applied for a job at Gibson, Dunn, and Crutcher, a white-shoe California law firm whose policy was to hire women only as secretaries. Spurned, she returned home and practiced law in a small firm, ran for the state legislature, and advanced to the court. She had grit, and coming from the West was another plus.

The president pressed O'Connor to reveal where she stood on abortion. The question opened a Pandora's box to be sure, considering the strong emotions of the electorate. And the president's advisers were divided about whether it was appropriate to apply a single-issue litmus test to a judicial appointment. "A woman's so-called right to choose was a non-Constitutionalist's position," says Ed Meese, "and there was no question in our minds that *Roe v. Wade* was not a Constitutionally oriented decision." Clearly, pro-choice people disagreed with equal fervor. But Ronald Reagan felt he had been duped into signing the therapeutic abortion bill as governor of California and was determined to be out in front of the issue should the Court take it up. Should Sandra Day O'Connor become the nominee—*his* nominee—he felt he had a right to know her position in advance. The question was awkward, but her response was unambiguous. O'Connor was personally against abortion, she said, but a woman's right to choose was the law of the land—and as a judge, she defended the law. It was as simple as that.

If that discouraged Ronald Reagan, he never said. O'Connor's personal opposition to abortion might have been all that was required. Or perhaps he didn't understand that, should she become a Supreme Court justice, in matters relating to *Roe v. Wade* she would not allow her personal opinion to sway her decisions. In any event, he decided "she was a woman of great legal intellect, fairness, and integrity—the antithesis of an ideological judge, and just what I wanted on the court." However much antiabortion forces wanted to make the issue a litmus test, this choice would purposefully avoid it. Sandra Day O'Connor made a powerful impression. Never one to procrastinate when making a decision, Reagan announced that she was his choice on July 7, 1981, only a week after meeting her.

It was not that day's most significant development.

That morning, Drew Lewis, the transportation secretary, appeared in the Oval Office with sobering news. It looked as though the administration had exhausted all efforts to reach a salary compromise with the nation's air-traffic controllers. Their union—the Professional Air Traffic Controllers Organization, or PATCO—was threatening a strike.

PATCO had been one of the few unions to endorse the Reagan campaign in 1980, and the president felt beholden to it and its membership. What's more, he was a lifelong union man and respected workers' rights. But none of that factored in to the outrage he now felt. A strike? By PATCO? He'd never permit it, not on his watch. The air-traffic controllers were federal employees and, therefore, not permitted to strike. They'd taken an oath to that effect. He was holding them to it. "Dammit," he fumed at a morning Cabinet briefing, "the law is the law." He threw down the gauntlet: if the controllers went ahead and struck, he wanted them to know, "they have quit their jobs and will not be rehired."

As the president saw it, the government had been negotiating with PATCO in good faith. He understood the union's complaints—"too few people working unreasonable hours with obsolete equipment" and too demanding of a workload in a high-pressure job. Reagan had expressed as much in a letter to Robert Poli, PATCO's president, promising to deliver "the most modern equipment available and to adjust staff levels and work days." But Drew Lewis reported that air-traffic control was presently overstaffed and that the workers had rejected an FAA offer to reduce their workload by 6 percent, along with a $10 million investment in new equipment. When it came to a pay increase, the two sides were far apart: the FAA proposed $50 million, the union was demanding six times that amount.

Reagan was worried—not about the money as much as the repercussions of an unlawful strike. The union had threatened to walk out a few years earlier, and the government had caved in to its demands. The president was determined not to let that happen again, a variation on his position that "we do not negotiate with terrorists." "The foremost factor in the front of his mind," according to Ed Meese, "was that air-traffic controllers were guarding our skies." If they struck, he'd consider it "desertion in the face of duty." There were thousands, *tens of thousands*, of flights each day; not only passengers, but the American economy, depended on a smoothly running system. The president wasn't about to allow air traffic to grind to a halt or, as the *New York Times* put it, "have airplanes fall out of the sky."

In the meantime, his Supreme Court nominee was facing headwinds. Reagan had certainly expected Republicans to get behind his choice, but as soon as word circulated that it would be Sandra Day O'Connor, opposing voices, mostly from the right, rose in unison to condemn her. Two hard-liners, Senator Don Nickles and Representative Henry Hyde, launched the attack. They phoned the White House on July 6 to warn that "her appointment would cause a firestorm among Reagan supporters" and "trigger a nasty political protest." In short order, they were joined by Jesse Helms and Strom Thurmond, who expressed similar dismay in a call to Ed Meese. O'Connor's record on social issues, it seemed, flouted conservative sensibilities. In particular, they protested her vote in the Arizona legislature against reversing *Roe v. Wade*; her sponsorship of a family-planning act that critics misconstrued as a license for minors to get abortions without parental consent; her support for the Equal Rights Amendment; and her participation as keynote speaker for the International Women's Year conference, "the bête noire of pro-family advocates." It didn't help that Tip O'Neill hailed the president's appointment of O'Connor as "the best thing he's done since he was inaugurated."

Ultimately, the opponents to O'Connor's nomination relented and she was confirmed by a vote of 99–0. Political opposition was to be expected when it came to Supreme Court appointments. What was new here, however, was the conservative right's concerted effort to loop religious leaders into the resistance. Calls started pouring into the White House from evangelical theologians, officials of the United States Catholic Conference, and fundamentalists like the Reverend Jerry Falwell, who preached that "good Christians" needed to be up in arms about the nomination. *Good Christians* were what Falwell labeled the Moral Majority in conservative America. This definition angered no less a conservative than Barry Goldwater, who upon hearing it said, "Every good Christian ought to kick Falwell right in the ass."

This backlash set a new high-water mark for the reach of religion into politics. It also set the stage for other incursions to come. The president was already enmeshed in a skirmish about school prayer. In 1962 and 1963, the Supreme Court had declared that religious prayer in public schools violated First Amendment rights guaranteeing the separation of church and state. But Reagan believed that voluntary prayer in school was a basic right—that it had been "practiced and revered from the early days of the colonies"—and felt the Constitution bore that out, if it was interpreted properly. He announced his intention to propose a constitutional amendment to allow voluntary prayer in public schools, reversing twenty years of precedent. It reflected his effort, he said, to foster "faith in a Creator who alone has the power to bless America." The religious right, led by Jerry Falwell, agreed wholeheartedly and was pushing to make school prayer a national policy.

This was dangerous territory for a president. Religion was like quicksand; it sucked other, more pressing policy into the muck. But with this proposal, new terrain had opened up in American politics. Intentionally or not, Ronald Reagan had touched off an emotionally charged stampede, and ideologues were rushing in to stake their claims.

R eagan took it upon himself to give the Soviet Union a strong dose of another kind of religion. He was convinced that the Carter administration had ceded too much ground to the Communists. "Our strategic forces were growing obsolete," he concluded, "and nothing was being done to reduce the threat of a nuclear Armageddon that could destroy much of the world in less than a half hour's time."

The U.S. military establishment suffered from years of neglect. "There was a perception that the Russians saw us as a declining power, losing confidence, disarming, and accommodating," says John Lehman, Reagan's secretary of the Navy. The Navy, in particular, was in distress, with a third of its fleet unfit to set sail. "Morale was bad—every enlisted family in our Oceana squadron was eligible for food stamps, and the dope problem was very real. Our big carriers were obsolete. We were outflanked in nuclear might." The Air Force claimed to be in similar shape: it lost more fighter aircraft in accidents than were being produced, and its ballistic missiles were past their sell-by dates. Platforms were simply deteriorating with age. America had to rearm, Reagan insisted, to reassert itself militarily, to push back on the Soviets.

Détente, especially the Kissinger doctrine of fence-mending with the Soviet Union, had failed, in Reagan's estimation. He called it "a one-way street that the Soviet Union has used to pursue its aims." He strongly believed, as he said repeatedly, that it "would be of great benefit to the United States if we started a buildup." If the Russians pumped money into their military machinery, America had to see them and raise the stakes. An *arms race*—always a touchy proposition. In its favor, he had bipartisan cooperation. John Tower, the Republican chairman of the Senate Armed Services Committee, and his Democratic counterpart, Henry "Scoop" Jackson, were in perfect harmony when it came to national security. There was bipartisan support on the House side as well. When the president asked for a considerable hike in financial resources for the military, Congress responded with a hearty "yea." Despite a weak economy, on July 16, 1981, the House ratified a $136 billion military appropriation bill that had already been approved by the Senate, the single largest military authorization in history. There was plenty in the pot for new, powerful weaponry: Navy F-14 fighters, Trident submarine missiles, B-1 stealth bombers, M-1 tanks, and a stipend to underwrite the MX missile program—"enough," as one official put it, "to blow the fucking Russians to kingdom come and back."

And yet the risk of war had always troubled Ronald Reagan. In early April, while he was convalescing in the hospital, the president began writing a letter to the Soviet leader, Leonid Brezhnev, that sought to extend the hand of peace. "I wanted to let him know that we had a realistic view of what the Soviet Union was all about, but also wanted to send a signal to him that we were interested in reducing the threat of nuclear annihilation." It was a simple, straightforward appeal that basically said, "If we could sit down together like two rational individuals, we could dispense with hostilities and broker a lasting peace." Disarmament was a real possibility, he suggested, even a world without nuclear weapons.

The president's advisers were conflicted. Dick Allen, to whom the handwritten letter was given for analysis and editing, understood what had prompted the missive. "Reagan had looked into the jaws of death and thought, 'I've got a chance to do something important here.'" Allen thought the letter was a "brilliant stroke." But his colleague Al Haig called it "naïve"; Haig thought "it was crazy and would ruin foreign policy." No matter what, Allen decided, the letter had to be restructured, and he set about giving it a diplomatic polish. Reagan regarded the redraft like a child who receives a plaid vest for Christmas. "This isn't what I had written," he lamented, "but I suppose they are the experts."

Mike Deaver happened to be in the Oval Office at the time. "You know, Mr. President, those assholes have been running the Soviet business for the last forty years, and they haven't done a very good job of it," he said. "Why don't you just tell them to stick it and send the goddamn letter?" Reagan agreed with the instincts, but in the end, the State Department version found its way into Brezhnev's hands. According to Richard Perle, the assistant secretary of defense, the Soviet leader quickly dismissed it.

Brezhnev discovered he had misjudged the president. When Reagan launched the massive military expansion of the United States, the Soviets got the message. They viewed the U.S. buildup of armaments as the work of a madman prepared to push the button at the slightest provocation. In response, they stepped up production of their SS-20s, the medium-range nuclear missiles they'd scattered throughout Eastern Europe. Reagan answered by offsetting the SS-20s with a deployment of cruise and Pershing II missiles in Western Europe.

Thus began an ominous game of chess that neither side could win and that was creating a political backlash across Europe. Out of the American policy process emerged an alternative to the madness: if the Soviets dismantled their SS-20s, the Americans would agree to cancel deployment of their cruise missiles and Pershing IIs. This approach came to be known as the Zero Option. It was the brainchild of Assistant Defense Secretary Richard Perle. "Ronald Reagan loved it," Perle recalls. "It appealed to his view of eventually eliminating all nuclear weapons. He thought it shifted the burden to the Soviets. If they agreed to it, this was great for the U.S., and if they didn't agree, we had significantly improved our political position by proposing the elimination of these weapons, while placating the pacifists and peace marchers all over Europe." The State Department, however, was vehemently opposed. Haig viewed the Zero Option as "a frivolous propaganda exercise." He felt that nuclear weapons were "still the greatest guarantor of peace and stability." If the president pursued the Zero Option, he maintained, "it would be a mistake he would have to modify within the year."

Reagan refused to back away from the approach. At every meeting at which the Zero Option was discussed, Haig or one of his underlings pushed to modify the plan in order to give them more muscle in negotiations with the Soviets. "I remember one meeting in which Paul Nitze, our arms-control negotiator who was about to leave for a round of talks in Geneva, pleaded for authority to back off Zero Option," Perle recalls. "He was so frustrated. 'What am I going to say to Futsinski?'" he asked the president, referring to the Soviet negotiator.

Reagan replied, "You just tell him that you work for one tough son of a bitch."

Ronald Reagan was flexing his muscles. When PATCO members rejected the government's offers to resolve their salary and labor differences and announced a strike to begin on August 3, 1981, thirteen thousand controllers vowed to walk off the job. "They cannot fly this country's planes without us," the president of the union warned, "and they can't get us to do our jobs if we are in jail or facing excessive fines." He warned Transportation Secretary Drew Lewis, "If passengers are killed, it'll be your responsibility."

Reagan didn't blink. "I must tell those who failed to report for duty this morning, they are in violation of the law," he announced at a press conference in the Rose Garden, "and if they do not report for work within forty-eight hours they have forfeited their job and will be terminated." There would be no amnesty. A federal judge in Brooklyn backed him up by ordering PATCO to pay fines of $100,000 for each hour the union struck.

The administration was prepared with contingency plans. "The weekend before the strike a few of us met in Drew Lewis's kitchen to make arrangements," says Ed Meese. They hastily assembled scratch crews—a hybrid assortment of nonunion supervisors, military controllers mustered by the Pentagon, and a few hundred non-strikers—to handle air traffic at the nation's airports. The administration gambled that most of the controllers would come back to work. When it was apparent that that wouldn't be the case, the president was forced into the nuclear option: replacing the entire force. "I'm doing the right thing, aren't I?" he asked Fred Fielding, his legal adviser, before delivering the verdict. "You are, Mr. President," Fielding replied, "unless there's a crash in the first forty-eight hours." In that case, Ronald Reagan would be a one-term president. He fired the strikers, had the union decertified, and ordered training programs for up to six thousand new controllers.

It made a huge impression on the country at large. "He wanted people to see he couldn't be pushed around," Meese says. It sent a message to critics who called him soft or disengaged that his administration wasn't to be trifled with. Those who didn't meet their obligations would be dealt with accordingly. Reagan's toughness paid immediate dividends. A Gallup poll showed an across-the-board approval of his handling of the strike, 57 percent to 30 percent. As David Broder intoned in a *Washington Post* column, "The message is getting around: You don't mess with this guy."

Muammar el-Qaddafi, the Libyan dictator, apparently didn't get the message. On August 18, he sent two Soviet-made Su-22 fighter jets to shoot down American aircraft that were on maneuvers with the Sixth Fleet in the Gulf of Sidra, beyond his country's twelve-mile territorial limit. Qaddafi had been threatening such an act for months, and Jimmy Carter had canceled similar exercises in 1979 to avoid potential skirmishes with the Libyans, but Reagan was not so deterred. He considered Qaddafi "a madman" and had already closed the Libyan embassy in Washington. At a National Security Council meeting in the Oval Office, the rear admiral who had responsibility for the Sixth Fleet in the maneuvers sought to clarify the rules of engagement. "What about hot pursuit?" he wanted to know. "If they fire on us and we chase them and they fly back over Libyan territory, can we pursue?"

"You can follow them into their own damn hangars if necessary," the president responded.

It was almost a foregone conclusion that the Libyans would engage, and the Sixth Fleet had its orders. When Libyan aircraft made good on the threat, the American pilots didn't hesitate. Two F-14s from the USS *Nimitz* shot down the aircraft on first pass.

Dick Allen got the news just after eleven p.m. on August 20, long after the Reagans had gone to bed. It was always a difficult decision whether to wake the president. Everyone knew how Nancy felt—that her husband's rest took the highest priority—and understood they interfered with it at their own peril. In this case, it was up to Ed Meese, who treaded lightly where the First Lady was concerned. Meese knew the score: she had little love for him; she considered him too ideological, too disorganized, too in-decisive. She continually raised concerns about his judgment. Her opinion had lost him the chief of staff job to Jim Baker. Were the Libyan jets worth incurring her wrath? "Let's make sure we have all the details before we wake the president," Meese told Allen. When it came to Nancy Reagan, Ed Meese couldn't win. "He made a serious mistake," she recalled in a memoir, "when American Navy jets shot down two Libyan fighter planes, and Ed waited five-and-a-half hours before calling Ronnie to wake him up and tell him about it."

Had Meese called earlier, the outcome would have likely been the same, but he'd waited, and he took the heat for it. "Meese's decision not to notify Reagan immediately raised once again a question that has popped to the surface from time to time in the Reagan administration," the *Washington Post* reported. "Who is in command?"

Anyone working at the center of the administration knew the answer to that. The president had strongly exerted his authority any number of ways his first year in office. But there were cracks in the foundation. Several of his appointments in particular were coming under increasing fire.

None more than David Stockman, the budget director who had miscal-culated when it came to projecting the budget deficit for 1982, deliv-ering a major embarrassment to the president. It now appeared as if the country's budget would be below water to the tune of $100 billion or more. "The balanced budget is long gone," Stockman fretted. From his per-spective, the president's Economic Recovery Program—indeed all of Reaganomics—teetered on the verge of collapse. The numbers on which Stockman had based his bullish forecasts no longer added up, if they ever did. The economy was weak; the financial markets were in a swoon, more than nine million Americans were out of work. According to the

Washington Post, "Federal interest rates soared to nineteen percent, making it expensive to borrow money and tipping the country into recession." "A slight one," the president admitted.

The administration fought to downplay the bad economic news, when a bombshell hit: an article appeared in the December 1981 issue of *The Atlantic Monthly* entitled "The Education of David Stockman." Not just any article, it was a fifty-page indictment of Reaganomics written with the full cooperation of the budget director himself. In it, he admitted to making "snap judgments" about the likelihood of being able to "zero out," or close down, federal programs, which was essential to the 1982 budget. He detailed how Cabinet officials "fought, argued [and] pounded the table" to restore their budgets, as did greedy legislators who flooded Congress with amendments to bills that reinstated generous subsidies for their local industries. He trashed Ed Meese and Jim Baker. It was an indiscreet takedown—but it got worse. Stockman "cheerfully conceded that the administration's own budget numbers were constructed on shaky premises in a way that, fundamentally, did not add up." Then he delivered the coup de grâce: "None of us really understands what's going on with all these numbers."

None of us really understands . . .

The White House nerve center was apoplectic. "My friend," Jim Baker warned Stockman, "your ass is in a sling." There was a clamor for Stockman's immediate ouster. The Troika met with the president in the Oval Office to discuss the matter. "I urged the president to ask for Stockman's resignation," says Ed Meese. "Jim voted to give him another chance. If at least one of us recommended another chance, it took the president, who couldn't fire anybody, off the hook."

For now, Stockman remained. For now. But his days as budget director were obviously numbered, as his adversaries lay in wait until he tripped up again.

There were other heads in line for the chopping block. Dick Allen was the first casualty. He'd had a rough time of it as national security adviser, with Al Haig riding roughshod over him in areas of foreign policy and relatively no direct access to the president. Allen was a brilliant but abrasive man, with a big personality that often rubbed colleagues the wrong way. He regularly undercut Haig and disparaged Jim Baker. Another aggrieved co-worker was Mike Deaver who, according to Ed Meese and others, "had a lot of hostility toward Dick." Deaver set out to poison the well. He told Nancy Reagan that Allen was overloading the president with homework and keeping him from quality time with her. Once you had an adversary in the residence, the die was cast. "Because of Deaver's animosity and the disharmony among the aides in general, the president felt it was necessary to make a change," recalls Meese. But how? He couldn't bring himself to fire him. That just wasn't part of Ronald Reagan's makeup, to part ways with someone he knew and liked.

Deaver had an idea. He recalled that the day after the inauguration Allen had arranged an interview with *Shufu no Tomo*, a Japanese women's magazine, for Nancy Reagan. As it concluded, the reporter handed over a packet of press clippings she'd done with previous First Ladies, which Allen intercepted as a matter of protocol. "I went across to the West Executive Building," he recalls, "and shuffled through the clippings, which is when I discovered an envelope mixed in with one thousand dollars in it." Allen recognized the gesture right away: it was an honorarium, a sign of great gratitude by Japanese reporters in exchange for interviews—standard operating procedure. Still, to Americans it would seem like a bribe of some sort. Allen turned it over to his secretary, who locked the cash in a file cabinet and promptly forgot about it. Unfortunately, in the same cabinet were three Seiko watches that had been part of an exchange of gifts between Allen and a former Japanese colleague. Another traditional Asian gesture that could be misconstrued. An anonymous tip in September 1981 led to the discovery of these items, which triggered an FBI investigation. And although Allen was eventually cleared of wrongdoing, the president now had the lever he needed to ask for his national security adviser's resignation. In effect, Allen was railroaded out. "The money and watches were just an excuse," says Ed Meese. "The president felt Allen needed to go."

He felt the same about Al Haig, but it was much tougher to get rid of him. He needed his secretary of state's expertise. Haig was the only member of the Cabinet with any kind of foreign policy experience. And he *was* astute. "Al hasn't steered me wrong yet," the president was heard to remark. He appreciated that Haig confirmed his belief that "we had the Soviets on their knees." But it was so damn difficult to deal with Haig. The anger and tantrums! He fought constantly with Cap Weinberger, whom Haig despised as an "arch villain," and he belittled the Troika—"the three beasts," he called them—who he felt alienated him from the president. "There was hardly an issue that ever developed between myself and the president that was not victimized by an undercurrent of mischievous misinformation," Haig later claimed. And when it came to his contempt for Reagan, Haig had no filter. "He isn't a mean man," Haig confided to Bill Clark, his deputy secretary. "He's just stupid." During a heated exchange with the president over Latin America policy in a National Security Planning Group meeting, Haig blurted out: "We'll see who has the balls in this administration, Mr. President."

It was hard for Reagan to resist accepting one of Haig's routine letters of resignation. There had been half a dozen opportunities, as well as other provocations. The petty issues were almost too absurd—Haig's hissy fit at being subordinated to the Reagans in a G7 motorcade, or the secretary's complete meltdown when he was removed from a receiving line at the American embassy in Rome so that the president could have his wife standing next to him instead. "He festered on that," says Bud McFarlane. "It was evidence to him of a White House conspiracy." Other points of contention drew greater scrutiny. Haig continued to press his belief that there was an opportunity for the United States to stir up sufficient opposition in Cuba to unseat Castro—a scheme his own lieutenants disagreed with and was far from Reagan's agenda. And he advocated for a more vigorous covert operation in Latin America, which Reagan initially shied away from.

What ultimately sank Haig, however, were events unfolding in the Middle East. In the summer of 1981, the Israelis had launched a surprise preemptive attack in Iraq, destroying a nuclear reactor. Reagan was angry that Israeli prime minister Menachem Begin, whom he personally loathed, had left him in the dark. But Reagan was sympathetic to Israel's efforts to protect itself, especially in regard to hostilities in southern Lebanon and parts of Beirut, alarmingly close to the Israeli border, where the Palestine Liberation Organization, armed with a cache of Soviet-built long-range missiles, had hidden twenty thousand fighters among the Lebanese population. It was a powder keg on the verge of explosion.

Six months later, in February 1982, Haig warned the president that a war in the Middle East was imminent and that if the United States did not take certain high-profile initiatives Israel would ultimately find a pretext to invade Lebanon. In fact, both Begin and Ariel Sharon, Israel's minister of defense, had asked Haig's permission to approve an invasion, which Haig firmly rejected. Reagan had already dispatched Philip Habib, his foremost Foreign Service envoy, to broker an agreement between the Israelis and the Lebanese in an attempt to head off an invasion. "There was a clash between Phil's and Al's recommendations on what we ought to do," says Bud McFarlane. Habib felt that, barring a diplomatic solution, the United States should cut off all military supplies to Israel and support a UN resolution calling for Israel's immediate withdrawal from Lebanon; Haig subscribed to stepped-up pressure on the PLO. "The president leaned toward Habib's position, which Al took as a personal rebuke rather than just substantive policy judgment."

Reagan did not subscribe to the concept of *Eretz Yisrael*—the Greater Israel—and Begin's ambition to consolidate Israel to include all of the West Bank, part of Jordan, and parts of Lebanon and Syria. While Reagan felt Israel was not defensible with its current borders, the United States would not be a party to the country's expansion.

On June 6, 1982, while Ronald Reagan was in Europe on a ten-day tour, Israel pulled the trigger, sending eighty thousand troops into Lebanon to establish a so-called buffer zone while wiping out the PLO. Afterward, Haig sent detailed negotiating instructions to Philip Habib, who was in Lebanon, without first running them past the president. Reagan was outraged and considered firing his secretary of state immediately, but balked and instead issued a stern warning. "This mustn't happen again," he told Haig. "We just can't have a situation where you send messages on your own that are a matter for my decision."

Haig understood this from a military perspective; chain of command must never be breached. What he couldn't condone, however, was what he saw as "petty maneuvering" by the White House staff, what he'd later describe as "guerrilla warfare by a bunch of second-rate hambones"—the Troika—who interfered with his ability to conduct foreign policy. Their fingerprints, Haig felt, were on everything that crossed his desk. More often than not, they blocked his path to the president. "I simply can no longer operate in this atmosphere," he insisted.

Haig had prepared a "bill of particulars"—really just a list of complaints—along with a letter of resignation, but in a last-minute decision he produced only the list, which he handed to Reagan before leaving the Oval Office. He also made it clear that he expected the president to reduce the authority of his new national security adviser, Bill Clark. That cinched it. The following morning, the president decided to give Haig's job to George Shultz.

Shultz was a solid, unflappable choice. He had impeccable credentials: a former Marine with degrees from Princeton and MIT, dean of the University of Chicago, three high-level government posts—secretary of labor, director of the Office of Management and Budget, and secretary of treasury—and president of the Bechtel Corporation, an international engineering and construction firm that also spawned Cap Weinberger. But more important, Shultz was a pragmatist who'd survived the fierce turf battles of the Nixon administration. He placed responsibility above ideology. He knew how to effectively manage difficult personalities in highly charged situations. He could be courtly or combative, depending on the situation. He had a clear understanding of "the crucial give-and-take of politics" and swore by the Princeton motto, "In the Nation's Service." What a welcome change from the histrionics of Alexander Haig. When Shultz accepted the job, Ronald Reagan was gratified and relieved.

So were Mike Deaver and Jim Baker, both of whom recognized a fellow pragmatist when they saw one. Shultz's nature would provide them with an ally at State, and in return they gave the new secretary the kind of access to the president that Al Haig had only dreamed about. Baker scheduled weekly private lunches for Reagan and Shultz. And Deaver, as was his wont, squared things with the First Lady.

But not all was wine and roses in the White House. Cap Weinberger was no fan of George Shultz. There was bad blood stretching back from their days at Bechtel, where Shultz had treated Cap like the hired help. And they had drastically different views when it came to relations with the Soviets. In Weinberger's eyes, a pragmatist like Shultz would revive détente and wreak havoc on the Defense Department's military buildup. Weinberger also believed that Shultz was quick to put American troops on the ground as leverage in diplomatic efforts, whereas Cap wouldn't commit troops to any situation unless it meant fighting was required. Nor would he condone negotiating with the Soviets, whereas Shultz maintained a core belief that "we should push very hard to engage" them.

Their difference in philosophies collided over the crisis in Lebanon. No sooner had Shultz been confirmed as secretary of state than on August 1, 1982, Israeli troops—the IDF, the Israel Defense Forces—laid siege to Beirut. The president had operated under the impression left by Menachem Begin that a diplomatic solution was being negotiated to broker a cease-fire. In the days and weeks that followed, numerous cease-fires were reached and breached while solutions were sought for the PLO's safe evacuation from Lebanon. The remaining Palestinians—a civilian population—were relocated in refugee camps so that their safety could be assured. Meanwhile, the Arab world looked to the United States to get the IDF out of Beirut.

On September 14, 1982, Bashir Gemayel, the new president of Lebanon, was assassinated, complicating matters exponentially. The Israelis decided to enter Beirut on the premise of preventing a bloodbath. Three days later, on September 17, on Rosh Hashanah, the IDF stood by while Maronite Christian forces swept into the Sabra and Shatila refugee camps, massacring six hundred Palestinians—entire families, whose bodies were bulldozed over with rubble using Israeli equipment. It was a horrible atrocity that shocked the world. Phil Habib, the U.S. envoy, had been given assurances, and in turn had given his assurances, that people in the camps would be protected; the Israelis and the Phalangists had promised not to intervene. "The brutal fact is, we are partly responsible," George Shultz admitted. "We took the Israelis and Lebanese at their word."

"Ronald Reagan was just livid," Bud McFarlane recalls. "He was normally an emotionally controlled man, but not this time. He was enraged." The next morning, he assembled his top advisers in the Oval Office to discuss the American response. "Get Begin on the phone," he demanded before anyone had a chance to weigh in. "Mr. Prime Minister," he bristled, "I cannot condone, and I am *outraged* by, your use of force against these defenseless people." Begin started to come back to him, but Reagan cut him off. "You're not hearing me, Mr. Prime Minister." The conversation went back and forth in the same manner, while Begin grew frustrated with the exchange. "Mr. President," he said, "you are not hearing my argument." "No, *I am not*—and I don't intend to," Reagan said. "And if you don't stop right away, we're going to review our whole relationship with you." That took Begin's defenses down a notch, inasmuch as it was code—a code he understood—to mean the severing of key U.S. support, including military assistance.

The president strongly considered sending the Marines into Lebanon to guard against further hostilities. "If we show ourselves unable to respond to the situation, what can the Middle East parties expect of us in the Arab-Israeli peace process?" he argued. Shultz agreed. But Weinberger and the Pentagon were dubious. "Israel has gotten itself in a swamp, and we should leave it at that," Weinberger concluded. Reagan listened to advice from both his secretaries and decided to "go for broke." He intended to demand publicly that the Israelis and PLO withdraw from Beirut, at which point he would commit Americans to a multinational force (MNF) to protect the Lebanese and allow them to reassert their authority. To do less would dash any hopes for a peace initiative. While Shultz organized official support for the plan, Weinberger threw a monkey wrench into the process: the Defense Department, he said, would not commit American troops to an MNF until *all* foreign forces left Lebanon. That meant not only the Israelis and Palestinians but the Syrians and Iranians as well. It was an agreement Shultz knew was impossible to pull together. It didn't matter. Over Weinberger's objections, the president was determined that a U.S. Marine presence be part of any multinational force in Beirut, and he ordered a detachment to be deployed to Lebanon.

It was a bold decision whose consequences would reverberate far beyond the Middle East.

A presidency that had begun on such a note of optimism was becoming mired in foreign policy in a time of global turmoil. The Middle East posed increasingly vexing challenges; the State Department endeavored to avert a war between Argentina and Great Britain over the sovereignty of the Falkland Islands; officials monitored guerrilla warfare in El Salvador and Guatemala, while supporting their brutal governments and underwriting covert paramilitary activities dedicated to the forcible overthrow of the Nicaraguan government. Meanwhile, troubles at home proved difficult to navigate as well.

By the summer of 1982, the American economy was in a free fall. More people were out of work than at any time since the Depression. "The nation," as Tip O'Neill needlessly pointed out to Ronald Reagan, was "in a fiscal mess." Unemployment had risen to an all-time high of 10.8 percent, businesses and factories were closing, and the deficit was ballooning. There was as yet no federal budget for 1983. More than a dozen budgets submitted by the administration had been introduced and rejected by the House, at an impasse over income tax cuts and defense spending. Finally, in August, Congress ignored the administration's latest budget proposals and wrote one of its own. As a sop to the president, the bill preserved the 10 percent personal income tax cut in exchange for new and higher taxes on cigarettes, telephone calls, medical expenses, investment income, and sundry business gains. "I had to swallow hard to agree to any revenue increase," Reagan admitted to a national television audience. Defense spending took a substantial hit, as did the food-stamp program and pensions for retired federal employees. On August 19, when Congress approved the budget, Reagan tried his best to put a good face on it, spinning the increases as *tax reform*. But no one was fooled. *Human Events*, Reagan's conservative bible, reviled it as "the largest tax increase in history."

The president's confidence rating dropped precipitously from 56 percent to 39 percent. Less than half the country approved of the job he was doing in the White House. More eye-opening perhaps was a private poll showing his "rapid decline of support among blue-collar families." The honeymoon was over.

On August 20, 1982, as Ronald Reagan ordered a battalion of eight hundred Marines to land in Beirut and then left on a sixteen-day vacation to his ranch, he was handed a memo prepared by the White House director of the Office of Planning and Evaluation. "The President's image as a leader has declined considerably," it said. "There is little reason to hope that economic conditions will improve significantly in the near future. . . . If the 1982 midterm elections were held on June 1 instead of November 2, Republicans would lose 44 House seats, 5 Senate seats, and 10 governorships." The prognosis was bleak: "For these and many other reasons, it appears to many that the Reagan Administration may have commenced its demise."

A window closed.

CHAPTER THIRTY-FOUR

WAR AND PEACE

"In foreign relations, as in all other relations, a policy
has been formed only when commitments and power have
been brought into balance."

—WALTER LIPPMANN, 1943

Mr. President . . ." Mike Deaver piped up during a daily briefing in the Cabinet Room in mid-January 1982. "The headlines are indicating you don't have a foreign policy." A mortified silence fell over the room. It was one thing to raise such an inquiry in private, and another to air it in a room packed with key administration officials and a gallery full of backbenchers. Especially considering the presence of the newly installed national security chief, Bill Clark, attending his first briefing along with his staff.

Ronald Reagan had enlisted "the Judge," his old Sacramento sidekick, to take up the position following the departure of Dick Allen. The appointment had not gotten off to an auspicious start. Other than serving as Al Haig's principal deputy, Clark had little foreign policy experience. This was exposed during his confirmation hearings, when he had been unable to define either "détente" or "Third World," nor could he name the prime ministers of Zimbabwe or South Africa. Clark drew harsh critiques from veteran diplomats. Haig echoed some interrogators in the Senate when he said of Clark, "He doesn't know his ass from third base."

What Clark knew, however, was how to serve Ronald Reagan's best interests. He was familiar with the president's shortcomings and quite adept at playing to his strengths. From experience, Clark was an expert when it came to distilling pages of bureaucratese to the few essential paragraphs that allowed the president to grasp a dense policy. And nowhere was this more useful than with national security.

It pained Clark and his staff to hear Deaver challenge his boss's record. The president, especially, was taken aback. He stood there, tight-lipped, unsure how to respond. Deaver had overstepped. It wasn't appropriate to put the President of the United States on the spot. Bud McFarlane, who had joined Clark's office from a chain of distinguished posts in international affairs, couldn't contain himself. Breaking the uncomfortable silence, he said, "Mr. President, *of course* you have a foreign policy." All heads swiveled to get a better look at the newcomer, and a backbencher at that, who had the nerve to speak out. "It is founded upon sufficient strength to deter any attack on our country and the means to prevail if we get into a war. Secondly, the renewal of allied strength and collective security that really gives meaning to Article 5 of the NATO treaty.* Thirdly, a commitment to advancing the cause of peace in the Middle East. Fourthly, a policy that encourages private investment and can stimulate growth in Third World countries to advance a more stable world. And, lastly, a defense against terrorism, which is on the rise."

An interval elapsed when everyone held their collective breath. "I'll be damned," Deaver finally chimed in, "I think we just got a foreign policy."

It wasn't as simple as that, and it wasn't conducted in a way that compartmentalized initiatives as cleanly as McFarlane had described them. But following a relatively sleepy 1982 in which fewer than a dozen National Security Decision Directives were published, 1983 would demand a fully articulated foreign policy ready to kick into gear as crises across the globe tested Ronald Reagan's ability to meet them.

The midterm election loss hadn't been as bad as the Office of Planning and Evaluation predicted. Still, the Republican Party took a drubbing, losing twenty-six seats in the House of Representatives, while eking out a 54 to 46 margin in the Senate. Also of concern, as the *New York Times*

---

* Article 5 considers any attack on a member state an attack against them all.

reported, was that "Republicans sought to disassociate themselves from President Reagan's record, especially on budget reductions in social programs."

Reaganomics was certainly on the ropes, and that dilemma was infecting the administration at the outset of the third year. "What we are witnessing this January, is not the midpoint in the Reagan presidency, but its phaseout," David Broder observed in his January 12 *Washington Post* column. "'Reaganism,' it is becoming increasingly clear, was a one-year phenomenon, lasting from his nomination in the summer of 1980 to the passage of his first budget and tax bills in the summer of 1981. What has been occurring ever since is an accelerating retreat from Reaganism, a process in which he is more spectator than leader." Three days earlier, the *New York Times* published an editorial over the title "The Failing Presidency," declaring "Mr. Reagan's loss of authority only halfway through his term should alarm all Americans."

Not all. He still had a grip on his fundamentalist Christian base and sought to tighten it in light of an overall 35 percent approval rating. Heading to Orlando, Florida, on March 8, 1983, he decided to make his case in an address to the National Association of Evangelicals. Most of his remarks were directed at the evangelicals' core issues: the evils of abortion, the transgressions of those who provide birth control information to teenage girls without parental permission, and the redemptive power of prayer. But buried in the fiery text was an appeal for the salvation of the Soviet Union couched in terms the audience embraced. "There is sin and evil in the world," he began, his voice rising in preacherly indignation. "And we are enjoined by Scripture and the Lord Jesus to oppose it with all our might." Some reporters covering the speech wondered where the president was going. "Yes, let us pray for the salvation of all those who live in totalitarian darkness—pray that they will discover the job of knowing God." He was clearly referring to the Soviet Union, which he called "the focus of evil in the modern world." Reagan then made a bid for the audience to scrutinize nuclear freeze proposals, considering the rejection of them as "the temptation of pride," while insisting that the arms race was anything but "a giant misunderstanding." It was "the struggle between right and wrong and good and evil." The crowd jumped to its feet, cheering the president, as a band fanned passions by playing "Onward Christian Soldiers." It was a startling spectacle that harkened to the fiery Chautauquas delivered by William Jennings Bryan that had electrified the young Ronald Reagan in Dixon. The *Washington Post* echoed a preponderance of major media by saying, "No other presidential speech has ever so flagrantly allied the government with religion."

There was cause for concern. For the first time in history, the President of the United States was tailoring his initiatives to the interests of a specific religious audience. But there was also a personal moral belief that Ronald Reagan was grappling with. He was haunted by the concept of a nuclear apocalypse brought on by human error and determined to find an antidote to the madness. He had touched on this concern a month earlier, on February 11, 1983, during a lunch with the Joint Chiefs of Staff.

That day, a powerful snowstorm had shut down Washington, forcing the chiefs to be transported over from the Pentagon in a tracked vehicle like sardines in a can. Most of the agenda concerned the defense budget and the MX missile program, which had suffered a stinging defeat in Congress. The U.S. weapons system was in disarray, and the chiefs were consumed with updating the military foundation of U.S. deterrence. As Bud McFarlane, the lunch meeting's chairman, recalls, "It was pretty clear that the Soviets had not only gone past us where land-based ICBMs were concerned, but that our side of things had become vulnerable. Our missiles were stationary targets, and the Soviet Union had introduced mobile missiles." America desperately needed the same, which is why the Pentagon had proposed a program called Big Bird—the mobile flying-around of ICBMs—but Congress wasn't buying the idea. The joint chiefs needed an alternative plan.

McFarlane and his colleague John Poindexter, the military assistant to Bill Clark, had been exploring another option. Rather than continuing to press the offensive program, they'd put a small group together to examine the state of research and technology available for a potential *defensive* program.

A *defensive program*. It was unheard-of—a radical approach. McFarlane had primed the pump by calling friends in the aerospace industry at TRW, Hughes, Lockheed, and Boeing, and asking them a number of hypothetical questions: "What if we were to build a bubble over the United States, a shield that couldn't be penetrated—an *anti*ballistic missile system—deployed either in space or on the ground? Perhaps a series of missile systems that would shoot down an incoming missile. Is any of this feasible? Is the state of the art good enough?" They'd actually entertained this discussion before, in the 1960s, when Robert McNamara was the secretary of defense. At the time, a couple of ideas called Sentinel and Safeguard were floated, and limited deployment was made. But the consensus of the aerospace community was that it wouldn't work. However, in the interim the technology had changed—and so had their minds.

John Foster, who had been the undersecretary of defense for research, development, and engineering during the Johnson and Nixon administrations and was currently a physicist at TRW, told McFarlane that in the 1960s, when the subject came up, available technology could not support such a concept. "Our computers weren't good enough to calculate whether a ground-based intercept force could be launched in time to hit six thousand incoming Soviet warheads," Foster explained. "Also the propellants in our defending missiles weren't good enough, and our guidance systems weren't good enough. In the meantime, however, we've made enormous gains in all those areas, so while I'm not telling you we can build it today, investments will enable you to do it soon."

McFarlane knew that "investments" and "soon" were valuable assets. A certain amount of psychology was involved in nuclear strategy; it was part science and part politics. If the United States, with its superior technology, committed to such a defensive program, it would have a psychological effect on the Soviet Union. And if the Soviet military saw the Pentagon investing $26 billion in defensive systems, the enemy might conclude that eventually American physicists were going to figure something out. American rhetoric could claim to have the technology ready to launch, even though it was ten to fifteen years off, *if it worked*. But the point was to let the Soviet minister of defense know his country was being exposed as backward. "It was Samuelson economics 101," McFarlane says. "Competitive advantage. You stress what you do best." John Foster advised him to play that for all it was worth. "If you do," he said, "the Soviets are going to want to stop us, and they'll come our way on arms control."

Still, a defensive strategy was a 180-degree change. McFarlane knew it would be a hard sell where the joint chiefs were concerned. "They didn't like all the money that went into it," says Richard Perle. "The Air Force saw it as meaning fewer fighter planes. To the Navy, it meant fewer ships, to the Army fewer tanks." But John Poindexter had laid important groundwork. His ace in the hole was James D. Watkins, the chief of naval operations. "I knew Jim was a devout Roman Catholic," Poindexter says, "and had moral objections to mutual assured destruction." To him, that strategy was irrational. Utter madness! One day, a poor silo guard in Siberia might drop a wrench down a pipe and accidentally launch a missile attack. Watkins came to the February 11 lunch fully on board and willing to rally his fellow chiefs.

McFarlane and Poindexter had primed the president. "He was all over it," McFarlane recalls. "I knew that Reagan was scripturally grounded and tended to orient himself in Revelations and the possibility of Armageddon." He was already on record warning a California legislator, "Everything is in place for the battle of Armageddon and the second coming of Christ." And, as late as 1980, in a television interview, he said, "We may be the generation that sees Armageddon." As president, Armageddon appeared to him as a catastrophic nuclear explosion sufficient enough to destroy humankind.

As a primer, Reagan had met with an organization called High Frontier, underwritten by the Heritage Foundation and headed by General Daniel Graham, the former head of the Defense Intelligence Agency. Its purpose was to promote research for a space-based missile defense, but a working platform hadn't yet been developed. Several core members of the Kitchen Cabinet supported the strategy and urged the president to give it high priority. A White House working group made up of Ed Meese, Bill Clark, and Marty Anderson also met regularly to discuss the prospect of missile defense. Reagan was intrigued but cautious. So far there was nothing to support the scheme other than moral goodwill and wishful thinking. He was not convinced it was either technically feasible or affordable. Even so, General Graham's five-page article about High Frontier in the January 1983 edition of *Human Events* had rekindled the president's interest.

McFarlane and Poindexter bet that Reagan would get behind a defensive strategy. They gave him talking points and briefed him on their conversations with Jim Watkins, who would be prepared to back him and intercede with the joint chiefs. "And we think you should invite the chiefs to comment on the plausibility of beginning work on a very robust R&D program to move toward a defensive strategy."

At the appropriate time near the end of a two-hour lunch, Ronald Reagan triggered the discussion, and Watkins rose to his cue. "Mr. President," he said, "it is just immoral for us to believe we can somehow deter a conflict. We need to defend against an attack. We have an obligation. *You* have an obligation, as commander in chief, to protect the American people. As a moral proposition, wouldn't it be better to defend people rather than to avenge them?"

The idea took the chiefs completely by surprise. There were plenty of head-shakes at the conference table, most vociferously from Jack Vessey, the chairman of the Joint Chiefs of Staff. He leaned forward, looking down the row of his colleagues—Charles Gabriel from the Air Force, P. X. Kelley for the Marines—hoping that somebody would pipe up and call the bluff. No one, however, raised so much as a peep. "They were too polite—and shocked," McFarlane says. "They knew they were on eggshells."

"Well, Jim, I think you may be on to something here," the president said.

Vessey wasn't about to let this go unchallenged. "We've done this before, Mr. President, and we found that it wasn't a plausible scenario," he said.

"Well, I'm looking at what we've done the last two years, and it sure doesn't seem like we're getting anywhere," Reagan countered. "So I really wish you would all put your hearts into this. I think it's the right way to go."

Bill Clark had also rehearsed a line, which he delivered with unequivocal precision. "So, Mr. President, you'd like the chiefs to study this and come back with a recommendation to you for whether this might be a sound way to restore deterrence?"

"Absolutely!" Reagan responded. "Let's go!"

Not five minutes after Clark got back to his office, Jack Vessey rang him on the phone. "Bill, is he *serious?*"

"Yes, Jack," Clark responded, "he sure is."

"So you *really* want us to study converting to a defensive program from an offensive? You're *sure?*"

"*Yes!* And the sooner the better, Jack. You may have six weeks, but you don't have any longer than that."

Actually, less. The president was so excited about the prospect of this reorientation that he wanted to clue in the American public as soon as possible, in a nationally televised address laying out the whole revolutionary scenario. He called it MX Plus and began formulating his remarks: "We are going to embark on a program of research to come up with a defensive weapon that could make nuclear weapons obsolete." Well . . . that was getting a little ahead of things. "He kept talking about a global shield, which would prevent anything from coming through it," recalls John Poindexter. "That was, frankly, over the top, and in that respect he was a dreamer."

Still, Reagan persisted. The speech would be forthcoming. He sketched out an address on a yellow pad. "Let me share with you a vision of the future, which offers hope," he began. "What if free people could live secure in the knowledge that their security did not rest upon the threat of instant U.S. retaliation to deter a Soviet attack, that we could intercept and destroy strategic ballistic missiles before they reached our own soil or that of our allies?"

No one was told about the contents of the speech. It was written and revised entirely in secret. Neither the State Department nor the Pentagon was consulted or forewarned. "We kept everyone, even the joint chiefs, in the dark," recalls John Poindexter. The bureaucrats would stop it dead in its tracks. It was also essential to keep news of the speech from leaking to the press, where it was sure to ignite a firestorm of criticism before the president went on TV.

Cap Weinberger and Richard Perle were at a NATO conference in the Algarve in Portugal when they got wind of the defense speech. "It was the first we'd heard of it," Perle recalls. "We were horrified. It would have been devastating for Cap in his relationships with all these defense ministers." They wanted time to consult with the allies. Besides, the Defense Department had no faith in the strategy. Perle says, "We thought the whole idea was crazy." They got on the phone immediately, pleading for a postponement of the speech, or at least a delay in the announcement.

George Shultz agreed. The day after the joint chiefs lunch, Nancy

Reagan invited Shultz and his wife to an informal dinner at the White House residence. The Reagans had planned to spend a cozy weekend at the Camp David retreat, but the snowstorm had intensified overnight, closing roads in and out of Washington, making even helicopter transit impossible. Over cocktails, the president regaled Shultz with the vision: "How much better it would be, safer, more humane, if we could defend ourselves against nuclear weapons." Shultz thought it could "present huge, perhaps insuperable, problems." It was a nice thought, but basically a pipe dream. "We don't have the technology to say this," he insisted. "The initiative will not be seen as a peaceful gesture. It will be seen as destabilizing." Subsequently, aides advised him that "a speech like this by the president will unilaterally destroy the foundation of the Western alliance."

It was unusual for Shultz and Weinberger to be on the same side of the argument. In addition to their personal animosity, there was a natural institutional rivalry between State and Defense. In this case, however, they both urged the president to reconsider. But he wasn't to be swayed. Besides, he argued, the television time had already been reserved. "Write the speech *right here*," Reagan instructed Bud McFarlane. "And don't bureaucratize it; otherwise it will be defeated before it ever gets out of the crib." He wanted to make sure, as the *New York Times* reported, that "strategic experts within the administration were not given an opportunity to review the proposal before he made his speech."

McFarlane knew he needed more substance and support for the president than inspirational rhetoric. "We've got to get some science guys, credible folk, in the audience at the White House," he directed his staff. "Have them sitting there, watching the TV when the president speaks so they can react and respond to the predictable criticism." As instructed, they rounded up the usual suspects, including Edward Teller, the father of the hydrogen bomb, who'd been hustling Ronald Reagan about his own defensive program—Excalibur—whose satellites, he claimed, would revolve around the Earth and direct X-rays and laser beams toward any missile coming from the Soviet Union. This had been part of an ongoing discussion since 1967, when Governor Ronald Reagan attended a briefing on Teller's research for nuclear explosives at the Lawrence Livermore National Laboratory. Teller's scheme was purely theoretical—there wasn't any support for it from the scientific community—but he wanted $300 million to build a prototype, and the president was all ears. To some, it sounded all too reminiscent of the Inertia Projector, a gizmo that shot rockets out of the air employed by Secret Agent Brass Bancroft, one of Reagan's favorite movie roles, in the 1940 movie *Murder in the Air*.

The president's televised speech, delivered as planned on March 23, 1983, drew parallels to a different movie. Ted Kennedy immediately ridiculed it as "a reckless '*Star Wars*' scheme." *Star Wars!* The allusion was irresistible to critics, who persisted in using it, implying that the idea of a missile shield was nothing more than science-fiction fantasy. Reagan hated the *Star Wars* nickname, preferring Strategic Defense Initiative, or SDI, but it stuck. Tip O'Neill, barely able to contain his mockery, reached back even further in the science-fiction pantheon, deriding the president's "Buck Rogers style."

No one was more critical of President Reagan's speech than the Soviet Union, which denounced it as a clear violation of the Anti-Ballistic Missile Treaty signed by Richard Nixon in 1972. Article V, Section 1 of that document was specific: "Each party undertakes not to develop, test, or deploy ABM systems." The Russians saw it as "cosmic war technology that can give the other side a first-strike capability." The Kremlin's anxious response was indicative of the shifting sands of the Soviet economy. In the past, the logic of the arms-control establishment's opposition to ballistic missile defense was: We build a defense, the Soviets will simply build a greater offense. But the Soviets did not have that capacity anymore. Their economy was falling apart, and they were staggering under a military budget that was possibly as much as 40 percent of their GDP. And General Secretary Leonid Brezhnev, an intractable militarist, had died in November 1982, replaced by Yuri Andropov, the former chairman of the KGB, who liked western music and drank whiskey, not vodka. The Soviet Union worried that its internal problems, along with Reagan's missile defense program, were destabilizing the balance of power.

It was logical, not only to the Russians but also to many pundits, that the shift in U.S. strategy could be interpreted as a hostile act—the development of new, sophisticated weaponry meant to escalate the arms race and achieve strategic superiority. This was expressed to the president during an Oval Office interview with a pool of White House correspondents on March 29, 1983, when missile defense dominated the conversation. Ronald Reagan answered their queries with a stunning revelation. The president, he said, "could offer to give that same defensive weapon to [the Soviets] to prove that there was no longer any need for keeping their missiles." *He would give the Soviets the missile defense system.* Had they heard him correctly? They had, he assured them. And if the two sides had the same system, he might conceivably tell the Russians, "I am willing to do away with all my missiles. You do away with all of yours."

It was a loopy-sounding plan to anyone who had followed three decades of the Cold War. *A missile shield . . . sharing it with the Soviet Union . . .* No less an authority than George Shultz feared the president had fallen prey to a serious weakness: his tendency to accept "uncritically—even wishfully—advice that was sometimes amateurish and even irresponsible." Other foreign policy priorities were more grounded in reality, for better or for worse.

The peacekeeping detachment of twelve hundred U.S. Marines in Southern Lebanon was welcomed by no one—neither the thirty thousand Israeli soldiers nor the fifteen thousand Syrian troops in the country, and certainly not the Palestinian fighters who refused to withdraw from the country.

Ronald Reagan grew frustrated at the lack of progress. He'd accepted Al Haig's view that the United States could cultivate a "strategic consensus" in war-torn Lebanon through diplomatic efforts with Israel, Egypt, and Saudi Arabia. But that tactic proved futile, and the Syrians had further complicated matters thanks to a supply of surface-to-air missiles from the Soviet Union, and to their arming of their Shiite proxy force, Hezbollah. Syria agreed to leave Lebanon only after Israel withdrew, and Israel wasn't budging until the Syrians were gone. It was a classic standoff. Reagan had insisted that the United States was committed to "a Lebanese government of national unity, security for Israel's northern border and expulsion of the PLO from Lebanon," but as the months wore on, those goals seemed increasingly remote.

Violence began to pick up, sporadically at first. Five Marines were wounded on March 16, 1983, when a grenade was tossed at them from a second-story window. Then, on April 18, a delivery van commandeered by the Islamic Jihad Organization and packed with two thousand pounds of TNT drove up to the front door of the American embassy in the Beirut suburbs and detonated in a suicide attack that took the lives of sixty-three members of the diplomatic staff, seventeen of them Americans. Caspar

Weinberger argued for a withdrawal of the Marines, or at least their removal to ships offshore, but George Shultz won the argument for maintaining their presence. "It was intended as a show of moral support, but nothing more," says Bud McFarlane. All efforts went toward keeping the peace and overseeing a program called Fire and Maneuver, essentially the training of a Lebanese Armed Forces unit. For the time being, the Marines were bivouacked at the Beirut airport, right out in the open. They needed a more clearly defined mission, and they needed cover.

A t the same time, Central America was an area of rising concern. Since becoming president, Ronald Reagan had his eye on the region, and on El Salvador, Guatemala, and Nicaragua in particular, which were threatening to become a footprint for the Soviet Union in the Western Hemisphere. Al Haig argued that such subversion by a foreign power violated the essence of the Monroe Doctrine—which guaranteed the freedom and territorial integrity of any Western Hemisphere state—and threatened the ultimate security of the United States. In any case, Reagan, recognizing a chance to push back the spread of communism, was willing to entertain an aggressive policy in Central America.

Bill Casey, the CIA director, agreed. Allowing the Soviets to establish a base so close to the United States was not in the country's strategic interest. He considered this "the most important foreign policy problem confronting the nation." Casey was almost obsessive in his focus on Latin America. "Mr. President, we have an historic opportunity," he said. "We can do some serious damage to them."

At the outset, the president approached the situation with caution, but developments in Nicaragua captured his foreign policy team's attention. Nicaragua, as they saw it, was a country in play. In 1979, the Sandinista National Liberation Front had ousted the dictatorship of Anastasio Somoza Debayle. Jimmy Carter had supported the new government, the Sandinistas, to the tune of $99 million in aid, and for a while it seemed as though Nicaragua was in the budding stages of a rebirth. Its leaders nationalized property owned by the Somozas, enhanced working conditions, instituted free unionization for all workers, mandated equality for women, abolished the death penalty, and improved public services, including housing and education. But they also abolished the country's constitution, its presidency, and all its courts, and cracked down brutally on dissent. A junta had consolidated power in Managua and began moving the country decidedly to the left; all signs were that its goal was to turn Nicaragua into a state much like Cuba.

During a meeting of the National Security Council in November 1981, Reagan became intrigued by the exploits of a ragtag Nicaraguan rebel group known as the Contras, shorthand for counterrevolutionaries. The Contras were ostensibly a 500-man unit engaged in an operation to undermine the Sandinista regime of Daniel Ortega Saavedra, the junta leader, and to stanch the flow of weapons into the hands of Marxist guerrillas amassing just across the border in El Salvador. Ronald Reagan romanticized the Contras as "freedom fighters," describing them as "the moral equal of our Founding Fathers and the brave men and women of the French Resistance." They were also poorly trained, poorly equipped, and lacking a territorial foothold, relying on safe harbor in neighboring Honduras for conducting raids in and out of Nicaragua.

Reagan allocated $19 million to retrain the Contras in Honduras and launch covert guerrilla actions in Nicaragua in conjunction with the CIA and the U.S. military. Despite good intentions, he was walking a fine line between legitimate aid and outright misconduct. Congress had barred the administration by law from taking any actions "for the purpose of overthrowing the Government of Nicaragua." Several senators were already up in arms over what they saw as another Vietnam-type imbroglio. Battle lines were also drawn between administration officials divided over the policy: Baker, Deaver, Shultz, and Weinberger opposed expanding covert action, while the conservatives—Meese, Casey, Kirkpatrick, and Clark—were gung ho. Not that it mattered: the president was hooked. He considered the Sandinistas agents of a communist threat "at our doorstep," and, as proof, persisted in repeating a quote he attributed to Vladimir Lenin (although Lenin never said it): "First we will take Eastern Europe, then we will organize the hordes of Asia . . . then we will move on to Latin America; once we have Latin America we won't have to take the United States, the last bastion of capitalism, because it will fall into our outstretched hands like overripe fruit."

To reinforce the president's thinking, *Human Events* was hitting the situation hard, portraying Nicaragua as a rat's nest of communist infiltration and an incubator of revolution in other Latin American nations. "The Sandinista Government *Should* Be Overthrown," a front-page editorial espoused in March 1982. "Nicaragua is not yet Cuba . . . [but] if we fail to oust the present rulers fairly quickly, it is bound to become another strong, Soviet-controlled base, complete with a Russian combat brigade."

Reagan clipped the article and added it to a folder he kept in a personal file—a thick sheaf of moralistic stories from *Human Events* and *Reader's Digest*—that he referred to for inspiration and even outright guidance. The magazine's commentary on Nicaragua helped to shape his attitude about events in Latin America, although he drew the line at its suggestion that the United States should act "alone, if necessary" to overthrow the Sandinistas. Nevertheless, he believed, "If the Soviet Union can aid and abet subversion in our hemisphere, then the United States has a legal right and a moral duty to help resist it." He cited for his rationale the Truman Doctrine, which called for fighting the spread of communism through U.S. support to countries "resisting attempted subjugation by armed minorities or by outside pressures." But the situation in Nicaragua was different. Reagan wasn't asking Congress to support a government *resisting* attempted subjugation; he wanted support for the armed minorities who sought to *overthrow* a government that was officially recognized around the world, even by the United States.

"The CIA's assessment of what it would take to support and grow an insurgency in Nicaragua varied between $60 million and $100 million a year," says Bud McFarlane. That was a hard pill for Congress to swallow. Ronald Reagan sought to cast it as a separation-of-powers issue—that is, constitutionally the President of the United States is responsible for the *conduct* of foreign policy. The congressional response to that was, "Yes, but . . ."—the *but* being that the money comes from Congress. The United States wasn't at war with either Nicaragua or El Salvador. Was covert assistance in the national interest? Congress didn't think so, at least not to the extent of the president's request. Initially, Congress granted $40 million to fund Contra operations in Nicaragua, effectively saying, "You can have that for the balance of this year, but there isn't going to be any more after that."

An amendment to the House Appropriations Bill—and attached as a rider to the Defense Appropriations Act of 1983—limited U.S. government assistance to the Contras in Nicaragua. Known as the Boland Amendment, after its sponsor, Massachusetts representative Edward Boland, it put a severe crimp in the administration's Latin America policy. But it was madness, administration officials thought, to tell the Contras they had until the end of the year to receive financial support and then, after that, they were on their own. A loophole had to be found.

Washington was a vast net with no shortage of loopholes; it took nothing more than a little creativity to circumvent a statute. Every bill was subject to interpretation, and the Boland Amendment presented no great challenge. It said that no federal funds could be appropriated for the Contras, but said nothing about private funds or money from other sources. At least, that's the way aides close to the president read it. Proponents of the covert efforts might conceivably approach other countries, like Saudi Arabia, for contributions to the cause. The NSC had its own financial reserves that could be tapped into. On July 12, 1983, President Reagan signed a secret "Covert Funding on Nicaragua" initiative, which more or less freed up questionable sources of cash earmarked to "support and conduct covert activities including paramilitary activities designed to . . . facilitate the efforts by democratic Nicaraguan leaders to restore the original principles of political pluralism, non-alignment, a mixed economy and free elections to the Nicaraguan revolution." It was imparted to Contra leaders that they could expect enough funding and equipment to support a force of twelve thousand guerrillas.

This meant the CIA was no longer aiding what was supposedly the original objective with regard to the Contras—stemming the flow of arms trafficking to Marxist guerrillas. The United States was actively supporting plans to overthrow the Sandinista government.

As the summer of 1983 heated up, American efforts to resolve the foreign occupation in Lebanon by Israel and Syria grew increasingly desperate. The Marine unit stationed on the flatlands of the Beirut airport was taking sporadic fire from Muslim artillery located in the surrounding mountains. But there was no great hope in the White House, and certainly no great plan. The president sought to avoid any involvement that would put at risk his domestic agenda. In the vacuum, Bill Clark, his national security adviser, seemed to be making key foreign policy decisions on his own.

Without consulting the president or even the secretary of state, Clark sent his deputy, Bud McFarlane, on an independent mission to the Middle East in July 1983. "My assignment was to try to get the withdrawal of all foreign troops in Lebanon," McFarlane recalls. In Damascus, he attempted to negotiate a cease-fire, a cooling-off period before even the word "peace" could be mentioned. His meetings with Hafez al-Assad were as eye-opening as they were fruitless. "Can't we find some element of common ground?" McFarlane asked the Syrian despot. "No," Assad responded. "Israel has no right to be a state, and Lebanon is really part of Syria. We are maintaining order there and will continue to do that."

McFarlane, who was a deeply religious man, attempted to appeal to Assad on humanitarian principles. "People are dying—yours, Lebanon's, Israel's, the Palestinians'. Can you at least agree on the sanctity of human life to stop the shooting long enough to make a feasible negotiation?"

It was at that point McFarlane first encountered a hand motion that he would learn was common among Muslims. Assad knitted his fingers together and then fanned them outward in a cupping motion and looked up, to indicate that the situation was in Allah's hands—it was God's will. "There is no sanctity of a human life of an Israeli," Assad told him. "Even Lebanese are subordinates, and I will determine what is best for them."

Six weeks later, McFarlane had another meeting with Assad but could see he was getting nowhere. It was clear to McFarlane that he wasn't dealing with a rational, analytical person. Assad was intractable when it came to establishing any kind of peaceful resolution in Lebanon. "I needed some leverage vis-à-vis the Syrian forces deployed in the Beqaa Valley," McFarlane says, "so I asked the president to send the battleship New Jersey to the eastern Mediterranean, and he agreed." Perhaps, McFarlane thought, Assad's belief in Allah's will could be blunted by a show of strength. "If he saw the New Jersey was positioned to blow away the army that props him up and keeps him in office, he might adopt a more humanistic approach."

The encounter in Syria left McFarlane depleted. Two days earlier, on September 1, 1983, he learned that a Korean passenger plane, KAL 007, with 269 people aboard, had been shot down—perhaps mistakenly, perhaps not—by a Soviet fighter. The loss of life haunted McFarlane. On

September 3, after informing Assad of the *New Jersey*'s arrival, he flew to Cyprus, and went straight to his hotel to try to decompress. "But I couldn't sleep," he recalls. He got up at three in the morning and called his pastor, Jim Macdonell, at Saint Mark Presbyterian Church in Rockville, Maryland. It was Sunday morning in the States, he'd be preparing for services. "Jim, I'm out of gas here," McFarlane confessed. "I'm not getting anywhere in my efforts with Assad. So I'd appreciate it if you'd just weigh in and ask the congregation to pray."

"Sure," Macdonnell assured him.

Three hours later McFarlane got word that Assad had agreed to a cease-fire.

McFarlane's mission brought a measure of peace to the Middle East at the expense of a measure of war with George Shultz. While Shultz considered "the cease-fire in Lebanon a major achievement of our diplomacy," the secrecy of the negotiations—kept even from him, the secretary of state—coupled with other secret orders that had established maneuvers for a naval blockade off the coast of Nicaragua—stirred anger that he "was totally out of the decision loop." Foreign policy, as far as Shultz could tell, was being made and implemented by Bill Clark. If he needed more evidence of this, he only had to consult the latest issue of *Time*, with the cover story "Clark Takes Charge" and the accompanying article depicting him as the administration's lead dog on foreign policy. It was the last straw.

Shultz stormed into the Oval Office on July 25, 1983. "The process of managing foreign policy has gone completely off the track," he fumed. "You can conduct foreign policy out of the White House if you want to, but you don't need me under those circumstances." Shultz told the president that "if he wanted an errand boy, he should get somebody else." In fact, he said, "Bill Clark seems to want the job, because he is trying to run everything." And with that, Shultz offered his resignation.

Ronald Reagan hadn't seen that coming. He was taken aback by Shultz's offer to quit and rejected it emphatically. He'd already lost one secretary of state. Another casualty so soon after Haig's departure was unthinkable. It would send the message that his administration was unstable, and in any case, he considered Shultz an exceptional statesman. "I told him he had my confidence," Reagan noted in his diary, "and that it would be a disaster for all of us if he left." The president's reassurance was gratifying to Shultz, but by no means the end of the problem.

Nancy Reagan had her own view. She nursed a grudge against Bill Clark that went back some years. "He struck me as a user," she wrote in her memoir, My Turn. She felt that he misrepresented her husband's positions when it came to foreign affairs. She found him too conservative and too confrontational, and she feared his influence would help to paint her husband as a warmonger. "Bill brought tough national security and foreign policy issues to the president," says John Poindexter. "Nancy thought those areas were too controversial and would lower his popularity, so she developed a real dislike for Bill and blamed him for hijacking Reagan's interest."

George Shultz was her idea of a mensch, not only "a tough negotiator with enormous energy" but also warm and cuddly, "a big teddy bear." When she learned that Shultz threatened to resign, she hit the roof. She called Shultz and argued that Clark should be fired, then took her case to the president. She knew in advance it would be rejected out of hand. Judge Clark was Reagan's adviser as well as perhaps the only person in the White House he considered a real friend, and there was no way he'd agree to dismiss him.

Clark didn't have to worry. He soon decided he'd had enough, and his disenchantment touched off a major shake-up. James Watt, the confrontational secretary of the interior, had also run afoul of Nancy Reagan, who engineered Watt's swift sacking. That opened an escape hatch for Clark, a Westerner and an outdoorsman. He requested a reassignment to Interior, a move the president was only too happy to make. But who would replace Clark as the national security adviser? A scramble developed in the White House. Jim Baker and Mike Deaver hatched a scheme, a switcheroo: Baker would take over as the NSC adviser, with Baker's deputy, Richard Darman, joining him there, and Deaver would fill the vacancy as White House chief of staff. The president thought it was a fine idea, and his wife was on board. He'd announce it on October 14, just before leaving for Camp David, at the end of a busy week. Baker and Deaver had even prepared a press release to report their promotions.

That same afternoon, at a National Security Council meeting, Bill Clark passed a note to Ed Meese about the Baker-Deaver move. Meese was stunned. "It would be a complete disaster," he decided. Baker, he felt, was too much of a pragmatist; he would attempt to move Ronald Reagan too far to the center. It would send a signal to the Soviets that the United States was in compromise mode. Deaver—the White House gatekeeper and go-between with Nancy Reagan, to whom he gave prejudiced information—was an even bigger liability. Meese came to the conclusion that "Mike was intoxicated with power." He'd lost his way, lost touch with his sense of responsibility to the president and the party. Meese felt Deaver wasn't capable of handling substantive issues. Clark felt the same way, and he persuaded the president to delay his announcement, at least until after the weekend, when he came back from Camp David.

Reluctantly, Reagan agreed. When he returned to the Oval Office, he summoned Baker and Deaver. "I've had a lot of opposition to this from some of the boys," he told them. "I want to think about it over the weekend."

Deaver was crushed. "You don't have enough confidence in me to make me Chief of Staff!" he screamed, fighting back tears.

Meanwhile, Clark rallied the troops, herding Meese, Weinberger, Bill Casey, and Jeane Kirkpatrick into his office to mount a strategy. They were in unanimous agreement. "We decided these appointments couldn't go through," Ed Meese recalls. Bill Casey was the most vociferous. "How can you make the biggest leaker in Washington the head of national security?" Casey huffed.

Leaking had been a scourge in the Reagan administration. Too many diplomatic issues and internal debates conducted behind closed doors wound up as stories in the national press. Risky initiatives, some unacceptable to Congress, often demanded secrecy and the strict confidence of parties, but participants found it difficult to keep the details to themselves. Leaking stories to the press, insider information, was ammunition and capital—a way to stir up public opinion or to expose a rival, altering the balance of power. According to Al Haig, a victim of persistent leaks, "In the Reagan administration, they were not merely a problem, they were a way of life. Leaks constituted policy; they were the authentic voice of the government."

The whole mess infuriated Ronald Reagan. Classified information was leeching out of the White House—*his* White House—and it embarrassed him. What's more, it said something deplorable about the men he trusted.

It was contemptible, to say nothing of the fact that it was jeopardizing policy. On Monday evening, September 12, 1983, Reagan bristled when NBC's Chris Wallace reported that Bud McFarlane and other key NSC officials advocated offshore air strikes against Syrian forces in Lebanon. On September 14, Reagan opened the *Washington Post* to find an article detailing the administration's Lebanon strategy, which cited "White House officials" as its source. Someone close to him had planted that story. It infuriated him. Adding fuel to the fire, Bill Clark complained that the story, by mentioning Bud McFarlane by name, put his deputy's life in danger in the Middle East. "I want you to consider ordering the Attorney General of the United States to investigate this forthwith," he demanded.

Ed Meese agreed and drafted a paper authorizing the investigation. "The problem was, there was no smoking gun," he says. Clark pointed the finger at Jim Baker, but Meese says it was hard for the president to believe anything negative about Baker. Meese knew better. Meese was convinced that Baker had given the *Post* the drop on the Sandra Day O'Connor appointment in advance of the announcement as well as countless other "anonymous" scoops. On other occasions, Baker sent his deputies, Richard Darman and Margaret Tutwiler, to do the dirty work. "They were the two principal leakers," Meese says. He had firsthand evidence. "One Friday night, I was working late," he recalls. "No one knew I was in the White House. But around eight o'clock, I startled Darman as I encountered him leading [syndicated columnist] Bob Novak up the back stairs."

Attorney General William French Smith decided to administer polygraph tests to the president's inner circle. *Lie-detector tests!* An uproar ensued. Jim Baker, in particular, was furious. He barged in on the president's lunch with George Bush and George Shultz to insist that the investigation be dropped. Shultz leaped to Baker's defense. "I'll take the test—*once*," Shultz said, "and afterward you'll have my resignation."

Ronald Reagan hadn't calculated on such a fierce backlash. He immediately telephoned the attorney general and retracted the polygraph order, opting to "roundtable it" that afternoon at a legislative strategy meeting. But if he was expecting an orderly dialogue, he'd miscalculated. The staff who gathered was as factionalized as the Middle East. The Baker people and the Clark people squared off against each other, pointing fingers and hurtling accusations. A red-faced Clark stormed out in a fit of protest. It was as ugly a display as had occurred in the Reagan White House, and it managed to destabilize the president's trust. It marked the end of both Baker's and Clark's influence on matters of national security, and damaged their reputations with George Bush and George Shultz.

As a result, neither Baker nor Deaver got the new job he sought. Clark was relocated, some say "banished," to Interior, far from the White House power struggle.

Ronald Reagan deplored this type of disturbance, but the real fireworks were only beginning.

CHAPTER THIRTY-FIVE

URGENT FURY

"October of '83 was an incredible time."

—JOHN POINDEXTER

I n the fall of 1983, the administration's Middle East policy went up in flames.

In September, the president's top command continued to wage fierce policy battles over strategy in Lebanon. There was serious discord between State and Defense officials, and the Marines stationed there were caught in the middle. They'd been taking fire on a daily basis, despite the administration's insistence that they were neither in combat nor targets, and they had been warned not to be drawn into a combat role. That position was part of a dodgy legal shield. Had American troops been in an *official* combat situation, the president would have to invoke the War Powers Act of 1973, forcing him to withdraw the troops in sixty to ninety days unless both houses of Congress authorized their presence. Ronald Reagan wanted to avoid that at all costs, insisting repeatedly that it would send "extremely dangerous signals" to Syria and the Soviet Union. When the Marines began exchanging mortar fire with Druze combatants in the Shouf Mountains on September 19, the president's spokesman, Larry Speakes, told the White House press corps: "The shelling out of the mountains is not directed at U.S. troops or diplomats and for that reason, U.S. personnel are not in a situation of imminent hostilities."

Tell it to the Marines!

In fact, Bud McFarlane says, "they were sitting ducks." He was in a position to know, barricaded as he was in the American ambassador's residence in the foothills of the Shoufs, where a mortar had blasted a gaping hole in the courtyard. He cabled Washington straightaway, warning that "ammunition and morale are very low. . . . In short, tonight we could be in enemy lines." He felt the Syrians and their compatriots in the mountains were committing acts of savagery that could eventually threaten the Marines, and he hoped the president "would just fish or cut bait." It was time, McFarlane said, "to put the screws to Syria." No good would come of things "until the U.S. and the Arabs applied some sticks to Assad." But his advice fell on deaf ears. Cap Weinberger told the president that the Marines didn't sanction McFarlane's "sky-is-falling cable." To strengthen the Defense Department's case, Weinberger instructed the commandant of the Marine Corps, General P. X. Kelley, to brief a congressional committee. "There is not a significant danger at this time to our Marines," Kelley insisted, "no evidence that any of the rocket or artillery fire has been specifically directed against Marines."

The White House response only reinforced McFarlane's opinion that Weinberger was a fool. "He wasn't really well qualified to be the secretary of defense," McFarlane says in retrospect. Weinberger was adamant that U.S. troops not engage in any circumstance that might lead to a fight with Muslims, fearing the alienation of Saudi Arabia and damage to U.S. oil interests. The national security adviser, along with George Shultz, felt the Marines would advance American interests by deploying with the Lebanese Armed Forces, training the LAF to become an army worthy of its name. It was imperative that the American presence be viewed as trying to prevent terrorism and add stability, rather than as an invading army.

Shultz talked to Howard Baker, the Senate majority leader, about congressional support to broaden U.S. involvement in Lebanon. That meant an unavoidable encounter with the War Powers Act. President Reagan was coming around to that inevitability on his own time. "Are we going to let the Syrians and the Soviets take over?" he asked Shultz. "Are we just going to let it happen?"

This was a situation that Ronald Reagan hadn't bargained for. When it came to the nitty-gritty of Middle East politics, he'd brought to office principles but not great depth. He'd intended to dedicate his first term to domestic policy—getting the tax bill passed and coping with what was needed to turn double-digit inflation and unemployment around—and here he was being sucked into a Middle East quagmire, into two thousand years' worth of tribal infighting, territorial disputes, religious intolerance, instability, and crisis upon crisis, the particulars of which were ridiculously complex. The Druze, Shiite Muslims, Maronite Christians . . . It wasn't like the movies, where you could tell the good guys from the bad guys by the color of the hats they wore. He was determined to do the right thing, but there were no simple answers on his one-page briefing papers. He depended on his advisers to steer him along the right path, but the route was pockmarked with disagreement and indecision.

On September 28, 1983, the House authorized the deployment of Marines in Lebanon for an additional eighteen months. It was a true bipartisan agreement, which the Senate echoed a week later. Marine lives were steadily being lost in Beirut: three on August 29, two the last week in September, two more in early October. French troops were taking casualties as well. "We have to show the flag for those Marines," Reagan said, agonizing over the lost and trying to rationalize further American involvement. "Our problem is do we expand our mission to aid the Lebanese army with artillery and air support?" he pondered in his diary. "This could be seen as putting us in the war." The human cost haunted him. The father of a Marine who'd been killed in combat put it to him unequivocally: "Are we in Lebanon for any reason worth my son's life?"

Weinberger remained staunchly against the mission. He continued to press to have the Marines stationed in Beirut removed to battleships off the coast in the Mediterranean, but the president resisted. "Something's got to be done," Reagan determined. Cut bait? That wasn't his idea of a forceful strategy. A strong American presence, he believed, would persuade the Syrians to pull back and disengage. His orders were to stay the course.

The stress and uncertainty were unrelenting. The president needed a breather, and there happened to be one on his schedule. On October 21, 1983, he and Nancy, along with George Shultz, Don Regan, and former New Jersey senator Nicholas Brady, flew south for a weekend of recreation at the Augusta National Golf Club. Augusta was a world away from Washington. Reagan was looking forward to the peace and quiet.

Ronald Reagan didn't even scrounge a single good night's sleep. The phone awakened him at four o'clock on Saturday morning. Bud McFarlane, who accompanied the group to Georgia as part of the presidential support staff, had gotten word from George Bush in Washington that Maurice Bishop, the prime minister of Grenada, and four members of his cabinet had been executed in a violent coup two days earlier.

Grenada. The smallest independent nation in the Western Hemisphere had in fact been on the president's radar almost since he'd taken office. As early as March 1982, he'd established the Crisis Pre-Planning Group to "think ahead about potential hot spots," and the Caribbean sat near the top of the list. Normally, U.S. interests in Grenada would not be significant. According to a top-secret brief prepared by National Security Council researchers, "Grenada has no known natural resources, no important products, and is of negligible economic significance." But the CIA had good surveillance showing Cuban workers building a powerful radio station and expanding Grenada's tiny airport landing field with a 10,000-foot runway so that it could accommodate heavier aircraft. "Grenada doesn't even have an air force," the president observed in a speech a year later. "Who is it intended for?" It was a rhetorical question. "The Soviet-Cuban militarization of Grenada, in short, can only be seen as power projection into the region." The NSC insinuated that the Soviets' decision to move offshore in Grenada "could be a base for subversion," enabling them to launch attacks from Colombia, Venezuela, and elsewhere in South America. And Grenada was perilously close to the Panama Canal. More than half of American oil imports passed through the Caribbean. He'd be damned if he gave the Soviets another footprint in the West.

Reagan wasn't losing sleep over the demise of Maurice Bishop. He'd been cozying up to the USSR since seizing power in 1979, expressing his admiration for Fidel Castro and staging anti-American rallies. Local teenagers patrolled Grenada's streets with AK-47 semiautomatic rifles. Earlier in the month the president had authorized a covert plan to destabilize Bishop's government and the island's economy. But Bishop's replacement proved to be an even worse character, Hudson Austin, a hard-line Marxist ideologue who, upon taking over, issued a twenty-four-hour curfew, warning that anyone seen in public would be summarily shot.

*Jane Wyman and
Ronald Reagan in
a rare promotional
photo*

*Ronald Reagan
reading to Ron and
Patti, Christmas
1964*

Campaigning for governor,
Chinatown, San Francisco,
November 3, 1966

Ronald Reagan and
Pat Brown in a light
moment during the
campaign, 1966

Ronald Reagan campaign billboard, 1966

Victory celebration for governor, November 8, 1966

Ronald Reagan breakfast meeting with the staff in the governor's office. **Left to right:** *Philip Battaglia, Lyn Nofziger, Lt. Gov. Bob Finch, 1967*

The Governor's Mansion, Sacramento, 1967

Ronald Reagan swearing in as governor (private ceremony) with Ron looking on, January 1, 1967

Lampooning Reagan's meltdown at the National Negro
Republican Assembly, March 7, 1966

A typical ad for Reagan's
daily radio broadcast, 1966

Ron, Maureen, Michael,
Patti, Christmas 1974

The Reagan family. Left to right: *Patti, Nancy, Ronald Reagan, Michael, Maureen, Ron, outside Pacific Palisades home, 1976 campaign*

GOP primary debate, Nashua, New Hampshire: "I paid for this microphone, Mr. Green!" Left to right: *Ronald Reagan, John Anderson, Howard Baker, Bob Dole, Philip Crane; (seated) John Breen, George Bush*

Chaos outside the Washington Hilton after the assassination attempt. James Brady and police officer Thomas Delahanty lie wounded on the ground, March 30, 1981.

The Sit Room during the aftermath of the assassination attempt. **Left to right:** *Martin Anderson, Ed Meese, George Bush, Richard Allen, Larry Speakes, David Gergen, Al Haig, James Baker, Richard Darman, Richard S. Williamson, March 30, 1981*

Ronald Reagan in a customary pose, working on his trusty yellow tablet in the stateroom aboard Air Force One, *February 19, 1981*

Nancy Reagan's customary bowling of the orange down the aisle on LeaderShip *'80 on takeoff*

Evening meeting in the Sit Room to discuss Lebanon Marine barracks bombing with George Bush, George Shultz, Caspar Weinberger, and senior staff of National Security Planning Group, October 23, 1983

Bud McFarlane and George Shultz brief Ronald Reagan on the situation in Grenada, Eisenhower Cabin, Augusta Golf Course, October 22, 1983.

*Ronald Reagan and Prime Minister Margaret Thatcher during her visit to Camp David:
"I can do business with Gorbachev." December 22, 1984.*

*Ronald Reagan in Bud McFarlane's office with Contra leader Alfonso Calero and Oliver
North—the last time Ronald Reagan would smile about Contra aid, April 4, 1985*

ABOVE: *"Coats on, or coats off?" Ronald Reagan greets Mikhail Gorbachev outside Fleur d'Eau, Geneva Summit, November 19, 1985.* BELOW: *The famous "red couch photo" with Don Regan center stage, between Ronald Reagan and Mikhail Gorbachev, Geneva Summit, November 20, 1985*

"Queen Nancy"

The look on Ronald Reagan's face tells the entire story as he receives the Tower Commission Report from John Tower and Edmund Muskie, February 26, 1987.

Ronald Reagan takes a last look around the Oval Office (note the bare desk), January 20, 1989.

"Mr. Gorbachev, tear down this wall!" Ronald Reagan speech at Brandenburg Gate, Berlin, June 12, 1987

Ronald Reagan shows off his new haircut following brain surgery, September 1989.

A final farewell. Left to right: *Ron Reagan, Nancy Reagan, Michael Reagan, Patti Davis*

Dutch, Ronnie, Governor, Mr. President

The president, sitting in his pajamas in Augusta, listened to McFarlane's briefing and conversed by a secure line to Washington with Vice President Bush, who'd been monitoring the situation. There were roughly a thousand Americans presently in Grenada, including 650 students at St. George's University School of Medicine. "Their being there was a lucky break for us," Ed Meese admits, forty years later. In truth, the students were never in any danger, but they were as good an excuse as any for sending in the troops. The island was "in chaos," according to Bud McFarlane's report. Bill Casey concurred. "Hey, fuck, let's dump these bastards," he intoned. So with some prompting from Vice President Bush, Eugenia Charles, the prime minister of neighboring Dominica and the titular head of the Organization of Eastern Caribbean States, "requested" U.S. assistance in restoring order and stability to Grenada, providing the legal cover they'd need to launch such a mission.

"We certainly can't refuse the five sovereign countries that are concerned about their security in our hemisphere," Reagan said, somewhat disingenuously. As a precaution, he ordered a flotilla of Navy vessels headed toward Lebanon to detour to the Caribbean and asked McFarlane, who'd been his national security adviser for a grand total of four days, how long the Pentagon needed to prepare a mission to liberate the island and rescue the students. When he was told forty-eight hours, the president nodded and said, "Do it." But he insisted on strict secrecy. The last thing he needed was word leaking out, giving the Cubans time to prepare and retaliate. Fortunately, Jim Baker and David Gergen, the administration's two principal leakers, were sidetracked by attending the wedding of Bill Plante, the CBS White House correspondent. That, at least, gave the president a few hours' head start.

The weekend golf game presented its own set of security issues. The course itself was closed to the public for what was being jokingly referred to as the George Shultz Invitational. The president, dressed jauntily in a yellow sweater, had held his own on the front nine, but at 2:15 p.m., as the foursome approached the sixteenth hole, he was grabbed by Secret Service agents and then loaded headfirst into an armored limousine. A few minutes earlier, a blue Dodge pickup truck had crashed through the course's cyclone gate. Its driver, a local man named Charles Harris, raced into the pro shop and fired a gunshot into the floor before taking hostages, among them David Fischer, Ronald Reagan's personal assistant. The gunman demanded to speak to the president, which was out of the question. Such ultimatums were a weekly occurrence in Washington. The first such time was when a gunman who'd seized an abortion clinic threatened to kill the owner and several hostages unless the president appeared on TV, denouncing abortion. Reagan had vacillated that time, saying, "I don't want anything to happen to those people." "If you want to do it—fine," said his legal counsel, Fred Fielding. "We'll set aside fifteen minutes every Tuesday and Thursday and talk to the various groups that have demands." Reagan got the message. But this time was different. Dave Fischer was at his side all day long; he was practically a member of the family.

Reluctantly, Reagan tried several times to make contact by phone with the gunman. "This is the President of the United States. This is Ronald Reagan. I understand you want to talk to me."

His appeals were greeted by radio silence. Finally, however, the hostages were released and the assailant apprehended. Everyone was rattled by the incident; dinner would be a subdued affair. The Secret Service detail urged Reagan to return to Washington, but he refused, determined to salvage another day or so of relaxation. To get a jump-start, he and Nancy turned in early.

At 2:30 that morning, Ronald Reagan was roused once again by a call from Bud McFarlane.

"Mr. President, I have bad news," he began. In a voice filled with anguish, McFarlane informed the president that a yellow Mercedes truck filled with 2,500 pounds of dynamite had burst through the wrought-iron fence of the BLT—the Battalion Landing Team headquarters—at the Beirut airport in Lebanon, where more than three hundred U.S. Marines were barracked. The truck exploded on impact in the center of the building, causing the four-floor concrete structure to lift off its foundation and collapse on the sleeping Marines. The blast touched off an arsenal of ammunition and rockets stored in the BLT. Most likely hundreds of young Americans lay dead under the rubble. In a simultaneous suicide attack, another truck slammed into the barracks of a French paratroop regiment in the Ramlet al Baida area of West Beirut, two miles away, exploding and killing many of the 110 men sleeping there.

Ronald Reagan, along with George Shultz, in their pajamas and robes, rushed into the living room of the golf-course cottage, where McFarlane was engaged in gathering information from military sources. "The president was distraught," McFarlane recalls. "He tried to take in what I was telling him, but the horror of it was beyond any of our grasp."

"Who . . . who did it?" Reagan stammered. "How could this happen?"

"The indications are it's terrorists from the Beqaa Valley," McFarlane reported. "Bill Casey is already on the case." The only thing definite at this point was that casualties were going to be high. The dead and wounded were being airlifted by helicopter to the *Iwo Jima* and *El Paso*, amphibious assault and cargo ships in the Mediterranean, or flown to the British Royal Air Base in Cyprus. "We're going to know more, but we'd better go back to Washington immediately and begin to focus on this."

The president agreed. They'd go back as soon as the sun came up. But he insisted, "We cannot let this stand. We must engage with whoever did this, so get the guys together and come up with a plan."

The situation in Washington was chaotic. By the time the presidential party arrived in D.C. early Sunday morning, the American death toll had risen to 207 servicemen (it would climb to 239). The French loss was 58. The press wanted details—answers. Legislators, too. "Congress was in an uproar," Tip O'Neill recalled. How could this have happened? Who was responsible? So far, the facts were few and far between. The CIA was still gathering details about the bombing and its aftermath. Enough intelligence had already materialized to determine that it was "a well planned and professionally executed attack" most likely coordinated by "twelve persons who rapidly left the Iranian 'Special' Embassy in West Beirut . . . less than 15 minutes after the incident," ten of whom "have been identified as Syrian military officers." Security at the BLT was less than adequate. The truck had been waved through an army checkpoint without a search; it wove through a parking lot that was unattended before crashing through the building's main gates. "The sentry on guard could not get his weapon loaded in time to stop the truck . . . " a Marine corporal stationed in Lebanon reported, "because we're not allowed to have [a magazine] in our weapon."

"Remind me never to go away again," the president muttered to Cap Weinberger as he entered the Situation Room just after 9:00 a.m. Reports described him variously as looking "haggard" and "grief-stricken," but those words didn't do justice to the emotions churning inside him. He'd been raised by his mother to abhor human cruelty, and the horrid loss of life exceeded his worst imaginings. His vision coming to office was to guide the nation through its brighter moments. He wasn't naïve; he knew that the rolls of history listed innumerable tragedies. But his predilection for seeing more light than dark made it difficult for him to comprehend so much ugliness at once.

The agenda that morning was extremely complicated. Not only did the circumstances in Beirut beg for analysis and insight, the joint chiefs were well under way with plans for an invasion of Grenada. Operation Urgent Fury, as it was called, was scheduled to commence at dawn Tuesday and was already mired in logistical snags. Weinberger had been reluctant to endorse any kind of intervention, feeling there was not enough information for the military to act. Time was short; there was little coordination among the armed-service divisions. And the pre-landing intelligence was pathetic. "Grenada wasn't part of the Army map service," says Ed Meese, who sat in on the meeting, "so they had to rely on gas-station maps. In effect, they'd be improvising the entire invasion." A contingency plan was to drop a small band of Navy SEALs and Army Rangers into Grenada at midnight on Monday in order to get the lay of the land for a Tuesday campaign. The president would make a final go/no-go decision by five o'clock Monday night, at which point he'd review the situation and have the joint chiefs update the plans.

In the meantime, he ordered his team to begin taking measures to retaliate against the terrorists in Beirut. Francois Mitterrand warned him against such a venture. "There are Soviet officers in uniform twenty kilometers from Beirut," Mitterrand said. "Attack Syria, and you attack Moscow." But Reagan was undeterred. "I want you to be absolutely confident about who did this, where they trained, the evidence, the proof," he instructed Bill Casey. "I intend to go after them."

At 5:00 p.m. on Monday, October 24, 1983, Ronald Reagan issued the order that the invasion of Grenada would proceed. A strategy had been prepared over the weekend by the NSC's deputy director for

political-military affairs, Lieutenant-Colonel Oliver North, which the president approved. To comply with the War Powers Act, Reagan summoned
congressional leaders to the White House that night to inform them of his
plans. The briefing was a classic cloak-and-dagger affair. The leaders, knowing nothing of the president's motives, were each told to cancel his evening
plans and not even inform his wife of his whereabouts. They were picked
up individually in unmarked cars and driven to a garage in the basement of
the Executive Building, where a private elevator led directly to the residence. At eight o'clock, Tip O'Neill, Robert Byrd, Howard Baker, Jim
Wright, and Robert Michel arrived in the family quarters, and the president laid out the operation. "This is moving right now," he told them.
O'Neill, for one, had serious reservations. "They're invading Grenada so
people will forget what happened yesterday in Beirut," he thought, unaware
that the operation had been in the works for days.

"What does Mrs. Thatcher think about all this?" the Speaker asked.
Grenada was part of the British Commonwealth. Surely, the prime minister's opinion weighed heavily in the decision to launch.

"She doesn't know about it," the president responded awkwardly.

No sooner were the words out of his mouth than he was interrupted:
Margaret Thatcher was on the phone. She'd gotten wind of the operation—
and she was steamed. Ed Meese, who was sitting with the legislators, could
hear only Reagan's side of the conversation as he struggled to explain. "We
had to Margaret. . . . Yes, Margaret . . . no Margaret. . . . We *really* had to,
Margaret. . . . I'm sorry, Margaret. . . . I'm *really* sorry, Margaret. . . ." Several
times, she demanded "in the strongest language" that he call off the invasion, reminding him that "the United States has no business interfering in
[a British protectorate's] affairs." The fact of a request for help from the
eastern Caribbean states had no favorable effect on her. Thatcher remained
adamant that he cancel the invasion. It was as uncomfortable a conversation as the president ever had with her, and when he returned to his guests,
he wore an embarrassed grin. "That was tough," he announced.

With the congressional leaders, he faced an easier audience. The way
the meeting evolved they could do little more than listen. Naturally, the
Democrats were opposed to the operation, fearing it might be a rehearsal
for a future invasion of Nicaragua, but at this point there was nothing they
could do. "The decision had been made, orders had been given," Jim Wright

later reported. The landing of Navy SEALs was already under way. The president assured everyone he was taking full responsibility; none of them would be blamed if anything went wrong.

As the meeting drew to a close and the guests left the room, Tip O'Neill turned back to Ronald Reagan for a ceremonial handshake. "I'm not confident," he said, clasping both hands in his, "but God bless you, Mr. President. It's your war."

A s wars go, it was over before it had even begun.

The next morning, October 25, shortly before dawn, nineteen hundred Marines and Army Rangers were dropped onto the coastline of Grenada. Prowling the route to the capital in jeeps was a surreal experience, with only two paved roads serving the entire nation. Fairly quickly, the assault force gained control of the island's two airfields, including the 10,000-foot runway under construction at Point Salines. The students at the medical school were also evacuated. But the operation itself did not go down without a struggle. Two U.S. helicopters were shot down and American soldiers withstood "fierce house-to-house combat," taking heavy fire from Cuban "construction workers." When the fighting stopped and the insurgents were neutralized, nineteen Americans lay dead and more than a hundred were wounded.

The American public was stunned by news of the affair. Most people had never heard of Grenada, much less knew where it was. Why would the United States invade a tiny Caribbean nation? And only days following the tragedy in Lebanon? It was too much to comprehend all at once. In a speech, the president presented it as a vital national security measure, indicating he took action to forestall "another Iran or another Beirut." "I had no choice but to act strongly and decisively," he said, worried, as he was, that "a brutal gang of leftist thugs" were a strategic concern to the United States. Much was made of possible hostage-taking, what with 650 American medical students stranded in Grenada. They put a human face on the operation, providing justification.

Most members of Congress had been caught totally off guard, but at the outset of the operation, they reserved judgment, declining to criticize the president or publicly question the wisdom of the attack while American troops were in jeopardy. "I have no intent to get into any type of dialogue critical of my government at this time," Tip O'Neill announced to a conflicted legislature. For the most part, bipartisan leadership supported the operation, though there were strong misgivings among the opposition and even some Republicans who were still processing the Lebanon debacle. American lives were piling up. To anyone expressing doubts, Cap Weinberger was quick to remind them, "The price of freedom is high."

It was time to pay the piper.

At President Reagan's request, Bill Casey delivered unequivocal intelligence detailing exactly how the attack on the Marines in Lebanon was planned. "We had imagery of the Sheik Abdullah barracks, a mud-and-brick structure in the Beqaa Valley, near Baalbek, surrounded by sand," recalls John Poindexter, the deputy national security adviser. "It was a Hezbollah camp, and we could see from the overhead photos how they had been training." Oil drums were positioned across the perimeter of the camp, the geometry of which replicated a blueprint of the embassy in the suburbs. Beside the oil drums were tire tracks that indicated that a truck had been practicing high-speed turns.

On November 16, 1983, after viewing the surveillance, Ronald Reagan approved a retaliatory strike. From the outset, Cap Weinberger lobbied against it. Objecting "very vigorously" at a meeting with the joint chiefs in the Cabinet Room, he demanded of Bill Casey, "Can you guarantee to me there are no civilians in the Sheik Abdullah barracks?" Casey ignored the secretary of defense, displaying the evidence to the president, photograph by photograph. Weinberger continued to raise objections. As a matter of courtesy, Reagan polled those around the table, including George Shultz, Bud McFarlane, and George Bush. "All right, I've heard everyone's argument here," the president said. "We cannot let this stand. I want you to go ahead and launch, but do it as soon as possible."

The mission was to go off the next morning, before sunup, so that pilots, lifting off the aircraft carrier *Foch* in the Mediterranean, would not be flying into the sun. "Everything was teed up," Bud McFarlane recalls. "The

French were with us because they'd lost men—the Italians, too." Planes were already in the air. Suddenly, word came down through the chain of command: *Abort.*

How was this allowed to happen? It took McFarlane, who was "white-knuckled, livid," years to get to the bottom of it. As late as 2013, he discovered that Weinberger called the president the night of the mission. "But he didn't call through the White House switchboard," McFarlane recalls, "knowing they would have alerted me or Jim Baker." Instead, the call was placed to an office in the East Wing answered by the military aide who carries the football. As a result, it bypassed everyone in the chain of command. He reiterated his concern that any retaliation would kill innocent civilians. "And he persuaded the president to call off the mission."

"All right, Cap. If you think it's the right thing to do."

Instead, it was left to French warplanes to attack installations belonging to Shiite Muslim militiamen; Israeli jets took out the Sheik Abdullah barracks and nearby terrorist positions.

McFarlane couldn't contain his anger. The next morning, he told Ronald Reagan, "You approved this operation, and Cap decided not to carry it out. The credibility of the United States in Damascus just went to zero."

"Gosh, that's really disappointing," responded the president. "That's terrible. We should have blown the daylights out of them."

Weeks later, on December 3, another mission was launched to revenge the attack, but Poindexter says, "It was so poorly ordered that it was incredible. Somewhere between Weinberger and the task commander, the launch time was delayed." The Navy pilots had to quickly reroute and circle until new coordinates were delivered, allowing them to be picked up by Syrian radar. Now they *were* flying into the sun. An American A-6E was shot down and a pilot was captured. Later that day, eight Marines were killed by Syrian artillery fire.

The situation in Lebanon continued to deteriorate. Hopes of achieving a stable Lebanon had essentially collapsed. What's more, there was no central government left in the country; its political landscape had been ravaged by sectarian conflict and what amounted to civil war. The president insisted that America would not "turn tail and leave," but congressional support was eroding. Washington had what George Shultz referred to as "pullout fever," with Tip O'Neill leading the charge. "He may be ready to surrender, but I'm not," the president demanded. But by the beginning of 1984, the handwriting was on the wall. Even leading Republican legislators petitioned him to end the deployment.

The president grew increasingly frustrated. He railed against "second guessing" on Lebanon, saying it had "severely undermined our policy" there. In a last-ditch attempt to convince a wary American public that Lebanon was a worthy cause, he claimed in a special address, "We have information right now that they have marshaled a force, particularly of Iranians in Lebanon, that numbers up to 1,000, who are all willing to sacrifice their lives in a kamikaze attack." But nothing could win over skeptics. "Our policy wasn't working," he eventually admitted. "No one wanted to commit our troops to a full-scale war in the Middle East." On February 1, 1984, Reagan decided to evacuate the Marines to ships anchored in the Mediterranean. The last patrol pulled out on February 25, leaving the Lebanese to fend for themselves.

The Lebanon retreat dealt a severe blow to the administration's foreign policy prestige. "America is back—standing tall," the president had announced in his State of the Union address on January 25, 1984, but the reality didn't measure up. Continual stalemates in the Middle East and the lack of breakthroughs in Central America did little to burnish America's stature. A special commission appointed by the Defense Department examined the various actions and came to the conclusion that "a more vigorous and demanding approach to pursuing diplomatic alternatives" was needed. Ronald Reagan had always preached a gospel of renewed military strength, but actions spoke louder than words, and America's recent efforts had made a lot of noise to little effect. The president had read Moscow the riot act over the downing of the Korean airliner without extracting any real payback. He'd moved the battleship *New Jersey* into the Mediterranean as a warning to Syria, but failed to avenge the attack on the Marines. The invasion of tiny Grenada had served as one small demonstration of America's power, but no one argued for that mission's lasting importance.

The Soviet Union played a decisive role in every one of the conflicts. Relations with the Russians were at an all-time low. It was not enough to label the Soviet Union the Evil Empire without endeavoring to ratchet back its aggression by negotiating a reciprocal arms pact—to pursue, as the Defense Department report suggested, *diplomatic alternatives*. But in a televised speech to the nation on January 16, 1984, diplomacy was in short supply on Ronald

Reagan's agenda. Most of his remarks were directed at castigating the USSR for its warmongering and global overreach, but he refused to close diplomatic doors. "We don't refuse to talk when the Soviets call us imperialist aggressors and worse," he said, "or because they cling to the fantasy of a communist triumph over democracy." Despite all that, he expressed his intentions to pursue all diplomatic efforts to achieve peace, to find some common ground, perhaps even with his Soviet counterpart, Premier Yuri Andropov.

"Andropov," by George Shultz's assessment, "seemed to want something going." Shultz thought the premier "projected immense intelligence and energy." He'd even shared *Time*'s 1984 "Men of the Year" cover with Ronald Reagan—obstinate adversaries, but the world's last best hopes for peace. Unfortunately, Andropov hadn't been seen in public for almost half a year. Efforts were made to approach him through diplomatic channels, without the courtesy of a response. On February 10, 1984, the reason for his silence became clear. The Kremlin announced that Andropov was dead.

It was suggested by Jack Matlock, the NSC's Soviet specialist, that the president might want to attend Andropov's funeral in Moscow, signaling a willingness to engage with the next premier. Reagan had no such intention. "I don't want to honor that prick," he snapped. Bud McFarlane had advised the president "to stress in public your call for dialogue and your desire to reduce tensions and solve problems," but Reagan wouldn't be goaded into paying tribute to a Soviet leader who had continued to subvert democracy, interfere in the affairs of the Americas, and threaten the security of the United States.

Whoever succeeded Andropov, the Soviet Union promised to remain a keen and constant irritation, to say the least. Reagan devoted an inordinate portion of his presidency to the issues it presented. In just three years he had dealt with Soviet interference in Poland, Libya, Angola, Grenada, Nicaragua, and the Middle East, to say nothing of its ever-growing arsenal of weaponry. Reagan saw no escape from the situation.

Ronald Reagan loathed the Soviet Union and all it stood for, but if he intended to run for a second term, if he intended to make good on his litany of campaign promises that remained unaddressed, he'd have to find a way to tame his great Soviet nemesis.

CHAPTER THIRTY-SIX

"TEFLON MAN"

*"Government is like making sausages. Even if you like the end result,
it's best not to look too hard at the process."*

—OTTO VON BISMARCK

By January 1984, the presidential sweepstakes was already well under way. It seemed inevitable that Ronald Reagan would run for reelection, but the White House was uncharacteristically mum on the subject, minus even the usual leaks. The president's closest aides were kept in the dark when it came to his intentions. Reagan dodged the question every time it came up. "We'll see," was all he'd say. But the party faithful had been hard at work since the fall of 1982, plotting reelection strategy. The GOP enlisted Edward J. Rollins, a seasoned campaign gladiator, and his boy wonder, Lee Atwater, to set the table for another Reagan run. "No matter who we have running for president," Rollins said, "we cannot ignore the Democratic attacks that will start long before the campaign season begins in 1984."

There were enough issues for the Democrats to exploit. Reagan's Economic Recovery Program was still far from a triumph; unemployment remained stubbornly high. Reagan's failed effort to revamp Social Security was another target. As was *fairness*—a loose buzzword that encompassed everything from tax cuts for the rich to budget cuts for working women to new china for the White House. "No matter what we do in the interim, the public's sense that this administration is 'unfair' will linger," Rollins wrote.

In early 1983, Reagan's Gallup poll approval rating had reached a low of

35 percent, but since then it was making steady gains. Despite that, the GOP had its work cut out for it. There were three strong Democrats circling the nomination: John Glenn, Walter Mondale, and Edward Kennedy. Each possessed his own strengths: Glenn, the American hero; Mondale, labor's ardent champion; and Kennedy, the charismatic Senate workhorse, with his fabled heritage. Rollins and Atwater predicted that "Kennedy will cruise to the Democratic nomination in 1984," but Kennedy shocked supporters when he succumbed to his family's fears for his personal safety and withdrew in 1983. And John Glenn's glow faded fast. As the Democratic hopefuls headed to Iowa for the caucuses, Gary Hart, a rising star from Colorado, and Jesse Jackson were picking up steam.

The only person in Reagan's inner circle who was ambivalent was Nancy. "She was hesitant because of the assassination attempt," says Stu Spencer, the Reagans' longtime confidant. "She was petrified by it." And there was her general disdain for the Washington hothouse.

Nancy Reagan knew she hadn't gotten great reviews for her role as First Lady, and it rankled. There remained a perception of imperiousness to her manner, an iciness, that didn't play well at the president's side. Ronald Reagan's persona shouted Man of the People, someone who had the common touch. He was often photographed on his ranch, in a rumpled work shirt and blue jeans, mending fence posts and cutting sagebrush. He relished talking to his constituents—people whose situations were all too familiar from his humble Midwest upbringing. Nancy couldn't shake the label of the socialite who traveled in wealthy Beverly Hills circles and attended functions in thousand-dollar designer Adolfo, Galanos, or de la Renta dresses. She was clearly uncomfortable milling among the general public—it came through in her body language and icy smiles. The public perceived her as vain and ambitious—not at all like Jackie Kennedy, whose wealth and sophistication were tempered by her extreme vulnerability and grace; not like Lady Bird Johnson, who projected homespun warmth and traveled extensively to promote the American infrastructure; not like Pat Nixon, who undertook numerous solo goodwill missions in Africa and South America, while promoting volunteerism at home; not like Betty Ford, whose courage to voice support for the Equal Rights Amendment, a woman's right to choose, and gun control flew in the face of her husband's policies; and not like brainy Rosalynn Carter, a tireless public-policy crusader, advocate for mental-health issues, and champion of women's rights. "Everybody does it differently," Nancy insisted of the job, but the unflattering comparisons to former First Ladies persisted.

Nancy Reagan's official undertakings seemed to come up short. She'd originally focused on a foster-grandparents program but realized it couldn't sustain a viable image campaign. Her antidrug initiative—"Just Say No!"—was regarded as simplistic and naïve. According to her press secretary, "The staff didn't know how to get its hands around the issue." Without the appointment of a drug czar and official policies supporting drug-abuse issues, the program lacked muscle—and credibility. This backfired in terms of building the First Lady's image. Her reputation as a "tough interview" didn't win her media support; she often came across in print as a scold. Other stories appeared regularly detailing how she interfered in White House business and imposed her will on administration officials, creating tension among the staff.

At some point, the press got wind that Nancy Reagan relied on astrologers to predict the best dates to schedule her husband's obligations. In Sacramento, she'd relied on Jeane Dixon, a syndicated columnist with conservative roots, who fed the Reagans a diet of warmed-over prophecies, until she fell out of favor. Later, Merv Griffin, with whom Nancy Reagan regularly exchanged show-business gossip, introduced her to Joan Quigley, a noted San Francisco socialite and astrologer to the rich, who was a frequent guest on his TV variety show. Quigley became known as the "White House astrologer," charging $3,000 a month to read the Reagans' charts. On Quigley's advice, Nancy Reagan rearranged the dates and times of the president's events, occasionally canceling his trips, while carving out chunks of time from his agenda that were marked "stay home" or "be careful" or "no public exposure." The backlash contributed to more bad press.

Nancy Reagan was ready to call it a day. "I yearned for more family time, and more privacy," she acknowledged. She missed California and her circle of well-to-do friends, and she was more than a bit concerned about her husband's safety. How many John Hinckleys were out there on the stump, waiting to take a shot at the president? It unnerved her. More than anything, she loved her husband, and her private role as First Lady superseded anything she owed to the public. For Ronald Reagan, she was the perfect First Lady. She gazed at him adoringly, listened to his problems, served as a good sounding board, defended his private time, provided him with restful company during the evenings, and evaluated every situation with an eye on what was best for him, personally and politically.

They went back and forth about a second run for the presidency. Nancy expressed her misgivings, how she "was not crazy about it." But Reagan seemed determined; there was so much unfinished business he wanted to tackle. In his memoirs, he cited "cutting the deficit and balancing the budget," both of which had ballooned beyond all projections.* And he resented "polls showing the people have an image of [him] that [he] might recklessly lead the country to war." He'd already dropped hints in his State of the Union message: "We will finish our job." There wasn't much doubt that he'd run. Nancy consulted Joan Quigley, who told her that "he was a cinch to win the election." That helped to bring her around. Once they'd made up their minds, Quigley talked them out of announcing it to the public in December, a month, she said, whose "astral indications" were not promising. Instead, on January 29, 1984, without any prior indication about his decision to run one way or the other, Ronald Reagan delivered a television address from the Oval Office.

"It's been nearly three years since I first spoke to you from this room," he said, posed solemnly, hands folded, sitting behind his desk. "Tonight I'm here for a different reason. I've come to a difficult personal decision as to whether or not I should seek reelection."

By this time, anyone tuning in probably recalled Lyndon Johnson's speech sixteen years earlier, during which he withdrew his name from the presidential race in an almost similar setting. Reagan's countenance seemed to suggest the same outcome. A bit of acting from his Hollywood training kept him in character as he ran down a grocery list of his accomplishments— a reduction in inflation and unemployment, interest rates cut nearly in half, an overhaul of America's defense system, more homes being built, more cars being sold, the price of oil coming down. The economy was on the road to recovery, he insisted. When he declared that "America is back and standing tall," it seemed as though his work as president was finished. He continued building tension, not giving too much away, until delivering

---

* The federal deficit in fiscal year 1984 was estimated at $190 million.

the surprise twist at the end: "I am therefore announcing that I am a candidate and will seek reelection to the office I presently hold."

"He made good sport of it," the *New York Times* conceded. Checking the president's daily horoscope, the Paper of Record noted it was "a good time for an Aquarius to avoid a confrontation" but also "a good time for 'a memorable rendezvous.'" It would have cost Nancy Reagan the price of the paper for that advice had she not already retained Joan Quigley.

The '84 campaign, according to its de facto manager, Stu Spencer, had one overarching guideline: "Don't screw up." The polls, Spencer knew, were good to Ronald Reagan. More than half of the American public approved of his job performance, and voters felt some kind of affection for him, if not as their president then as a man. He invoked the traditional American values of family and community that were predominant in the movies of the 1930s—not the dark, gangster-laden Warner Brothers movies, many of which he'd starred in, but those made across town by MGM: the white-picket-fence America with archetypal American families. In a way, that dreamworld Ronald Reagan cherished and longed for might have been his most valuable asset. People of both parties identified with him, they were inspired by his optimism, felt he was honest and forthright, despite any specific missteps. He'd stood up to those PATCO bullies, which showed he had backbone, strength of character. It seemed, from his rhetoric, he was standing up to the Soviets. According to a *Washington Post–ABC News* poll, a third of registered voters approved of Ronald Reagan while disagreeing with his policies. Even to them, he appeared decisive—*presidential.*

Spencer assumed he had a lot to work with, but as he delved into his campaign research, he started to feel otherwise. The strategists assigned to the effort were unable to define a clear-cut agenda. "They don't have a goddamn thing in the pipeline," Spencer concluded. From what he determined, "the Reagan administration fired all its bullets very early and very successfully in the first two years—all their plans, all their priorities, all their programs." "There is nothing left," Dick Darman, Jim Baker's deputy, told him. "We've shot our load." The reelection committee desperately needed something to hang the election on, something specific, something important to Americans. Polls showed that much of the public feared the continual arms buildup, resisted any tinkering with Social Security and the tax code, were baffled by the Strategic Defense Initiative, and preferred to avoid hot-button issues like abortion and AIDS. The strategists weren't able to lead with policy, so they decided to abandon it altogether, opting instead to promote a much broader message: We're not turning back to the bad old days of the Carter-Mondale administration. "Reagan was *focused*—he was looking ahead. That was our strategy," Spencer recalls.

The Madison Avenue image brokers came up with a suitable feel-good theme. "This is America, Spring of 1984," a creative director from Della Famina, Travisano & Partners emoted to the ad agency "dream team" that was auditioning spots. "What do we see? Jobs are coming back. Housing is coming back. And for the first time in a long time, hope for the future is coming back." *Perfect!* They instantly put a name to the campaign: "Prouder, Stronger, Better." It was one of the most effective campaign spots ever created. Over soft, gold-toned, quintessentially American images—a paperboy on his bicycle, campers raising the Stars and Stripes, a farmer plowing his field—an announcer suggested, "It's morning in America." *Morning in America.* The symbolism was irresistible. At the conclusion a voice asked, "Why would we ever want to return to where we were, less than four short years ago?" A new day had dawned, a better day than before, and Ronald Reagan promised better days ahead. Let the Democrats cope with that.

The Democrats had enough to grapple with, determining their nominee to take on the president. The Iowa caucuses in mid-February hosted an eight-candidate field that included senators Alan Cranston, Ernest Hollings, and George McGovern, but former vice president Walter Mondale led the pack by more than a nose. He finished well ahead of all challengers, giving him enough confidence to boast, "I am ready to defeat Mr. Reagan." A week later, however, in the New Hampshire primary, Gary Hart challenged Mondale's claim, upsetting him by a two-to-one ratio.

Gary Hart gave Nancy Reagan pause. He was young and handsome— Kennedyesque—and his "New Ideas" message was "so broad and unspecific," newspapers said, "that voters interpreted it to suit themselves," giving him a flexible political appeal. It was conceivable to her that Hart's charisma could swing independents and undecideds to his side, especially after his campaign picked up steam in March 1984 by winning the Massachusetts, Florida, and Rhode Island primaries.

Ronald Reagan, however, was undeterred. He saw himself as maintaining a steady hand on the campaign throttle, with a willful detachment from the crucial decision-making process, but aides worried he wasn't as engaged as was necessary. Nancy Reagan picked up the slack, keeping the strategists on track and her husband on message. Yet she couldn't prevent his screwing up. On an appearance on *Good Morning America*, discussing the plight of the country's dispossessed, Reagan suggested that "the homeless, you might say, are homeless by choice." That certainly didn't play well with urban audiences. Later that summer, when doing a voice check before his weekly radio address, he joked, "My fellow Americans, I am pleased to tell you I just signed legislation which outlaws Russia forever. The bombing will begin in five minutes"—unaware that the microphone was live on the air. Incredibly, these gaffes failed to dent his momentum. Even more serious blunders survived critical blows.

His initial refusal to honor Martin Luther King Jr. with a national holiday, a fact that Jesse Jackson continued to hammer home, did little to endear him to a black constituency. The failure to acknowledge the AIDS epidemic alienated him from gays and others affected by the disease. James Watt, his insensitive secretary of the interior, was forced to resign for a wisecrack he made about appointments to a commission to study the leasing of federal lands to coal companies, in which he blithely remarked, "I appointed five members . . . I have a woman, a black, two Jews, and a cripple." The failed mission in Lebanon and the death of Marines was still hanging in the air, and in late April, revelations emerged that, on orders from the president, the CIA was secretly mining Nicaraguan harbors, which violated international law. Any one of these issues might have hobbled another sitting president, but not Ronald Reagan.

Reagan seemed invulnerable to anything but kryptonite. The *New York Times* anointed him "Teflon Man." In a rambling Sunday *Magazine* think piece by Steven Weisman, the paper concluded that the president's astonishing success hinged on the fact that "whether or not they agree with him and his policies, Americans *like* him." Despite his "untold public bloopers and . . . dozens of factual mistakes and misrepresentations," despite "the abortive mission in Beirut [that] cost 265 American lives," despite the "sharp escalation in United States military involvement in Central America," and despite "an extraordinary number of Mr. Reagan's political appointees who have come under fire, with many forced to resign because of ethical or legal conflicts . . . nothing sticks to him."

Teflon Man.

Teflon was a difficult protective coating to penetrate if you were running against Reagan.

The only real threat to the President's Teflon armor was a self-inflicted wound. The Nicaragua entanglement, which grew more complicated and mazier by the day, was increasingly displaying that very potential.

Ronald Reagan was unconditionally committed to supporting the Contras, his idea of "freedom fighters," in their effort to overthrow Nicaragua's leftist Sandinista government. "I've always thought it was a tragic error for President Kennedy to abandon the Cuban freedom fighters during the 1961 Bay of Pigs invasion," he wrote in his memoirs. It was a direct result of Kennedy's inaction, Reagan believed, that Cuba was a fully entrenched Soviet satellite. He didn't intend to make the same mistake on his watch. He had a chance to stop the spread of Soviet colonization in the Western Hemisphere, and he would.

Congress wasn't supporting him in this mission, nor was most of the American public, which feared that involvement in Central America would lead to another Vietnam. Only a mere 18 percent of the 37 percent who had even *heard* about Nicaragua endorsed the president's handling of the situation. Congress had effectively tied his hands. His only alternative was to resort to covert operations conducted by the CIA under Bill Casey's direction.

Because of the Boland Amendment, the 1984 appropriation for aid to the Contras was capped at $24 million, less than half of what the White House had requested. On May 22, 1984, the House of Representatives approved an additional $62 million in funds for an aid package to El Salvador, which had just staged its first democratic election, but voted overwhelmingly to cut off all aid to the Contras, even the $21 million already approved by the Senate. Even the Republicans deserted the president. Outrage over the mining of Nicaragua's harbor was too strong. It was a stinging defeat to the administration's initiatives, especially following the president's nationally televised plea for more Contra aid two weeks earlier. To make matters worse, another Boland Amendment was passed restricting the use of any funds appropriated for the intelligence community to be used in support of the Contras. Despite these roadblocks, Ronald Reagan remained determined to see the Contras succeed. He pulled aside Robert McFarlane and said, "Bud, I want you to do whatever you have to do to help these people keep body and soul together. Do everything you can."

Do everything you can. The directive was loaded with peril. Since the spring of 1984, Bill Casey and Bud McFarlane had been exploring alternative ways of getting money and weapons to the Contras. Normally, such ventures would go through the President's Foreign Intelligence Advisory Board, a body that met regularly and whose minutes were circulated to the appropriate congressional committees. But a smaller offshoot—the Intelligence Oversight Board—operated within the PFIAB when more sensitive situations demanded confidentiality. "The IOB concluded that the Boland Amendment didn't have any impact on the National Security Council staff because the NSC was not officially part of the intelligence community," says John Poindexter. "That allowed Bud and Ollie North to take over the operation supporting the Contras with *non*-appropriated funds."

The most likely place to obtain large sums of cash and weapons was from foreign allies—countries beholden to the United States for assisting them with financial aid, equipment, or armaments. Saudi Arabia, Israel, and South Africa nicely fit the bill. A week after the House vote, McFarlane had extracted a promise from Prince Bandar, the Saudi ambassador to the United States, for a million dollars a month to be placed in a Miami bank account belonging to the political director of the Nicaragua Democratic Force. In exchange for the money, the White House announced during the Memorial Day weekend, when most members of Congress were out of town, that it was shipping Air Force tankers to Saudi Arabia, along with an emergency sale of four hundred Stinger ground-to-air missiles and two hundred launchers—*emergency* in order to avoid a thirty-day mandatory delay in which Congress would have certainly rescinded the sale. The following Tuesday, during the president's morning security briefing, Bud McFarlane passed Reagan a note about the Saudi money for the Contras.

On the back, the president wrote, "Mum's the word," and slid it back to McFarlane.

The president didn't have to worry about spilling the beans. Two days later, on June 1, 1984, he left for a ten-day trip to Europe, which included the annual G7 economic summit in London followed by a visit to Ballyporeen, his ancestral village in Ireland. It was there, 150 years earlier, that Michael O'Regan made plans to better his circumstances, moving to London and finally to the United States. No one had to remind Ronald Reagan that for immigrants America was the land of unlimited opportunity. He underscored that theme on June 6, the fortieth anniversary of D-Day, when he stood on Pointe du Hoc, the cliff overlooking Utah Beach in northwest France, where, choked up and close to tears, he described American soldiers who gave their lives there as "champions who helped free a continent."

He saw the Contras in the same spectral light. Upon his return to Washington, their plight once more rode the top of the agenda as he continued to explore alternative ways to aid them with funds and military support. A National Security Council meeting on June 25 was devoted almost entirely to Contra aid. In an extraordinary two-hour session, eighteen of the administration's highest-ranking officials weighed in on the subject. Talk focused on soliciting money from U.S. allies, which few in attendance knew was already in the works. George Shultz, for one, expressed skepticism. "Going to third countries is very likely illegal," he counseled. Cap Weinberger, who disagreed, implied that any outside funding would not be officially earmarked for the anti-Sandinista program. "It is merely helping the anti-Sandinistas obtain the money from other sources." McFarlane knew they were walking a fine line. "I certainly hope none of this discussion will be made public in any way," he said. The president seconded McFarlane's concern. "If such a story gets out, we'll all be hanging by our thumbs in front of the White House until we find out who did it."

Walter Mondale surely longed to host such an event.

The first week in June, following primaries in California and New Jersey, Mondale had captured the 1,967 delegates necessary to sew up the Democratic nomination. Gary Hart, who slipped after a scandal and ran a close second, vowed to wage a convention fight, but most observers saw the outcome as incontrovertible. The presidential race was a classic match-up: Mondale versus Reagan, liberal Democrat versus conservative Republican. Their differences were perfectly clear. The American public had a choice.

Mondale enjoyed visibility as Jimmy Carter's former vice president with a solid labor endorsement. But his challenge to Ronald Reagan was an uphill slog. From the outset, the polls showed the president with an eight-point lead, and Las Vegas oddsmakers gave him a four-to-one edge. Statistics lined up to support the numbers. The economy was now robust, inflation had plummeted to an all-decade low, and unemployment had fallen from double digits to 7.4 percent. The president's approval rating was a vigorous 65 percent. "Reagan only has himself to beat now," a pollster observed, and even Mondale's supporters tended to agree.

Mondale needed to pull a rabbit out of a hat, and it just so happened he had a big one in reserve. Sidestepping a traditional running mate, he unveiled someone he considered "an exciting choice," Representative Geraldine Ferraro. A *woman*. It was the one constituency that continued to give Ronald Reagan trouble. "Questions about Social Security, education, abortion, public housing are bound to take on a special quality when a woman addresses them," Roger Rosenblatt wrote in an editorial in *Time*. No one knew what the effect of a woman national candidate would be on the female vote—or the male vote, for that matter.

There was excitement, but laced with anxiety. If Mondale hadn't broken the glass ceiling of American politics, he'd at least put a pretty good crack in it. His choice was bold, unprecedented—historic. The female factor gave his stagnant candidacy a lift out of the gate. In the days immediately after the convention, Mondale, who had been sixteen points behind Ronald Reagan, pulled even. But polls revealed that only 22 percent of women were excited about Ferraro's selection, and in any event the election was not a referendum on women in politics. An age-old political philosophy held that people vote for the president, not the vice president. The race came down to the two candidates at the top of the ticket.

"Reagan is detached from reality," Mondale argued, soft on civil rights, arms control, women's rights, and the environment. But the criticism fell on deaf ears. Nothing—not Reaganomics, not Star Wars, not the deficit, not policy gaffes, not napping in high-level meetings—stuck to the Teflon president. Several incidents should have tarnished his bulletproof image. In March, William Buckley, an American diplomat, was kidnapped in Lebanon and later exposed as the CIA station chief. On September 20, 1984, twenty-three people were killed when a suicide bomber detonated a truck full of explosives outside the new American embassy in Beirut, and ten days later four CIA operatives died in a plane crash in El Salvador. These were clear foreign policy embarrassments. But no matter how much hay the Democrats made of it, voters failed to hold Ronald Reagan accountable.

Two debates were staged. The first one, held in Louisville, Kentucky, on October 7, a date chosen by astrologer Joan Quigley, was an unmitigated disaster for the president. He seemed indecisive, fuzzy-headed, often losing himself in the midst of an answer. After a particularly hard-hitting challenge from Walter Mondale, Reagan mumbled, "I'm all confused now. . . ." Afterward, he admitted, "I flattened out," and he blamed it on "too many hours poring over briefing books, and in skull sessions and mock debates preparing for the encounter." Stu Spencer, however, had joined the president at Camp David the weekend before the debate and observed that Reagan never opened the briefing books. "We spent eight hours watching old movies," Spencer recalls, "most of them his movies. The next day, the books were still sitting here. He didn't do his homework." Spencer told Lou Cannon, "He was just plain lazy in preparing, and he knew it."

Spencer walked out of the debate with the president, who was reeling from the lopsided exchange. "God, I was awful," he groaned. Mondale was coming down the ramp behind them, and from where they stood he appeared "twenty feet high." "I *killed* him," Mondale exulted. "I *killed* him."

Nancy Reagan was furious. In her estimation "that debate was a nightmare," and she vented her spleen at Mike Deaver. "What have you done to my husband?" she cried. Deaver had always handled these situations with aplomb. He was the facilitator, he made sure the president was at ease and prepared. He had the magic touch. But in the days leading up to the debate—in the entire campaign, for that matter—Deaver was nowhere to be found. Later, he admitted to Stu Spencer, "I was sitting in my room drinking." Deaver's alcoholism had taken root. "He was trying to combat it in his own way," says his wife, Carolyn, but it was undermining his effectiveness with the First Family. "His body was worn down, it was hard for him to find the energy to keep up." The president depended on Deaver to orchestrate the daily grind, and the paces Nancy Reagan put him through were grueling. "I could always tell when he was on his way home," Carolyn Deaver recalls. "The White House operator would call and say, 'Mrs. Reagan would like to speak to Mike.' But he was in transit. She would call again as soon as he got home, and again in the evening. And again, and again. She had to churn through her day with him every day."

Deaver pulled himself together enough to prepare for the second crucial debate, and he had plenty of help. This time, Stu Spencer and Paul Laxalt were recruited to restore the president's confidence. They eliminated the briefing books in favor of one-page memos, deciding to "let Reagan be Reagan." Richard Nixon gave him a pep talk. And the election team brought in a media coach, Roger Ailes, whose reputation as "Dr. Feelgood" was the perfect elixir for a candidate whose spirits had taken a hit. Ailes was primarily concerned with postdebate criticism that focused on Ronald Reagan's intellectual acuity, the fact that he might be too old and disengaged. A headline in the *Wall Street Journal* put it bluntly: "New Questions in Race: Is Oldest U.S. President Now Showing His Age?" Ailes reviewed the age issue with Reagan, reminding him that "for the last ten days you've been pounded that you're too old for the job." He could count on it being a factor in the next debate. The president assured Ailes, "I can handle it." In fact, he had a comeback he'd tried out on Mike Deaver a few days earlier. The opportunity to use it came midway through the next and final debate with Mondale, in Kansas City on October 21.

For the first thirty minutes, Mondale relentlessly attacked Reagan's handling of foreign policy in Central America, Eastern Europe, the Middle East, and the Soviet Union, demanding to know, "Who's in charge? Who's handling these matters?" One of the moderators, Henry Trewhitt, the diplomacy correspondent for the *Baltimore Sun*, saw it as an opening to segue into the age issue, casting it in terms of national security. "I recall," Trewhitt said, "that President Kennedy had to go on for days on end with very little sleep during the Cuban missile crisis. Is there any doubt in your mind that you would be able to function in such circumstances?"

This was the question the president had been waiting for—and he pounced. "Not at all, Mr. Trewhitt," he said matter-of-factly, "and I want you to know that I will also not make age an issue of this campaign. I am not going to exploit, for political purposes, my opponent's youth and inexperience."

It was vintage Ronald Reagan and the crowd loved it. No matter what the previous exchanges had revealed or the doubts they raised about the president's ability to effectively govern, Reagan's quip deftly swept them aside. The cleverness, the *performance*, was what the audience in Kansas City and those watching at home wanted from their popular president. Here, at last, was their Great Communicator, who warmed their hearts with his ability to deliver a great line. Mondale grinned at the witty rejoinder, but knew he'd been upstaged. More than that. He later admitted, "I knew he had gotten me there. That was really the end of my campaign that night."

Mondale read the tea leaves correctly. Three days following the debate, a *New York Times*–CBS poll indicated the margin had widened considerably. It revealed that "among probable voters fifty-three percent favored Reagan and thirty-five percent favored Mondale," with 12 percent of registered voters still undecided. On November 6, 1984, Ronald Reagan swept to reelection in perhaps the greatest landslide in American political history, carrying forty-nine states to Mondale's one, his home state of Minnesota, as well as the District of Columbia.

To Reagan, the outcome had endowed him with a mandate to press his agenda for the next four years. Nancy Reagan agreed, telling Mike Deaver on election eve that they had "taken enough and swallowed enough." Echoing her friend Frank Sinatra, she declared, "From now on we're going to do it our way."

CHAPTER THIRTY-SEVEN

"LET REAGAN BE REAGAN"

"I sit here all day trying to persuade people to do the things they
ought to have sense enough to do without my persuading them."

—HARRY S. TRUMAN

O n the same day Ronald Reagan was racking up his resounding election victory, a National Security Council deputy, Lt. Col. Oliver North, held a secret meeting on the third floor of the Old Executive Office Building across the street from the White House, where he coordinated a full-service undercover operation known as Project Democracy. North's guest was an unnamed Contra operative who requested help for a plan to "borrow" a jet from Honduras, paint it with Sandinista markings, and use it to attack Sandinista installations. Such covert operations had been under way since December 1981, when Reagan signed the presidential finding approving aid for the Nicaraguan rebel force. CIA chief Bill Casey, along with NSC staff, interpreted the directive to their own satisfaction in order to underwrite guerrilla warfare in Nicaragua, concealing it from Congress. In explaining such activities to the president, Casey remained purposely vague, often mumbling unintelligibly, as he was prone to do when he preferred to conceal the details of secret foreign-policy arrangements. And he knew that in Ronald Reagan, he had a listener who, consciously or not, would tune them out.

The Contra situation began to unravel almost as soon as the election returns were in, and it would snowball across Reagan's second term, overshadowing domestic achievements, Soviet peace initiatives, and arms-control triumphs, while shredding his credibility. Part of the damage stemmed from the fact that he was ill-served by some of his most trusted advisers.

The Troika in particular had functioned well beyond anyone's expectations through the first four years. All in all, it had effectively run the nerve center of the U.S. government. Jim Baker, Mike Deaver, and Ed Meese managed to strike a balance of duties that, while competitive and frequently at cross-purposes, kept the Oval Office humming and the president on track. They'd observed Reagan's dictum "There is plenty of work for everybody," adhering to their own policy of mutually assured destruction— that is, recognizing that any attempt to sabotage one of them would doom them all. They protected the president from rapacious influence peddlers (and from himself). But the constant pressure had taken a toll. "These were tough jobs," Mike Deaver recalled, "and we all had to get out of there."

Jim Baker got high marks as chief of staff, but he was burned out and felt underappreciated. Nancy Reagan viewed him warily. Fingering him early as "an ambitious man," she said, "I always felt that his main interest was Jim Baker." And his persistent press leaks drove her to distraction. It was obvious to White House staff that Baker wanted out—but not that far out. Though he'd flirted with becoming commissioner of baseball, another, less stressful job in the administration was more suited to his purposes. A Cabinet post was at the top of his list.

Mike Deaver, the Reagans' loyal retainer, set his sights elsewhere. Since moving to Washington, he'd caught a case of what Nancy Reagan called "Potomac fever," whose symptoms were exacerbated by power and money. "The power intoxicated him," Ed Meese says. Deaver was a working stiff in a league of men worth many millions of dollars, which frustrated him no end. For all his talent in handling the president of the United States and his wife, for all his control of the daily schedule, for all his skill and influence as the White House facilitator, Mike Deaver was barely eking out enough money to cover his living expenses. He'd shown considerable flair for public relations in his early efforts with Pete Hannaford and nimble interplay with the Washington press corps. If he parlayed that into a lobbying job, the payoff would be tremendous, but it would take some doing to extricate himself from the Reagans' grip.

Ed Meese was already in the wind. Eight months earlier, when William French Smith resigned from the Justice Department to return to private practice, Reagan nominated Meese to take over as attorney general, the job the faithful counselor had always coveted. The appointment, however, had been held up ever since, pinned down by embarrassing revelations about Meese's personal finances. Reports surfaced that Meese had obtained a low-cost mortgage from a savings-and-loan bank whose officers he'd helped obtain government jobs, along with a long-term loan from his accountant. Adding insult to injury, someone in the General Services Administration accused him of accepting gold cuff links during a fact-finding trip to Korea. As a result, the Senate had held up his confirmation while an independent council debated whether there were grounds to indict him.

In any case, it was clear that the palace guard was breaking up.

Donald Regan was also on the fence. As secretary of the treasury, he'd launched the overhaul of the tax code while continuing to wrestle with the massive federal deficit. He'd kept his own counsel throughout the first term, managing the department with sovereign command, much as he did at Merrill Lynch, where he'd served from 1946 to 1980, lastly as its CEO. Regan was acknowledged to be a tough sonofabitch and ambitious. He was bored at Treasury; as he put it, "finding the same problems—third world debt, trips to the economic summit, the IMF. Who the hell needs this stuff." He was looking for a more prestigious job with greater influence that brought him to the inner sanctum of the Oval Office.

"You know what's wrong with you, Baker?" he asked the beleaguered chief of staff during a meeting days after the election. "You're tired. You're fed up. You want to get out but you don't know how. We ought to swap jobs." They'd each get what they wanted—Baker his precious Cabinet post, Regan the ultimate White House appointment.

Deaver helped sell the plan to Nancy Reagan, whose imprimatur was necessary on any high-level appointment affecting her husband. As much as she frowned on Jim Baker, she recognized his value as an effective administrator. He was politically astute, knew how to delegate, and was fundamentally loyal, leaks notwithstanding. And he coordinated with Deaver, who conveyed her wishes. But Deaver convinced her that Baker was definitely leaving and it was in her best interests to approve a replacement who would counsel the president in much the same way. He assured her that Don

Regan was "a bright man and a strong manager," someone they could all get along with. To Nancy Reagan a decisive man like Regan seemed like a logical alternative. On the surface, he had no personal agenda. He was mature, sophisticated, polished, fabulously rich, and successful in his own right—a man, in many respects, like her Beverly Hills friends.

It was an ill-fated choice.

Don Regan's management style was legendary, if not notorious, on Wall Street, where he had often bragged, "I don't get ulcers—I give them." A former battalion commander in the U.S. Marine Corps, he was used to barking out orders and having them obeyed. It had been that way at Merrill Lynch, the international brokerage he was said to have presided over with despotic insensitivity, some said as "an absolute dictator." With Regan as Ronald Reagan's chief of staff and with the Troika dismantled, there would be no challenge to his authority. There was no need for consensus policy. He alone would determine what was best for the president. And he intended to seal off the Oval Office from quotidian traffic, running it as he saw fit. Everything—*everything*—would come through him.

Even before the appointment was announced, Regan was signaling his independence. In a revealing bull session in the Oval Office, minutes before facing the press as the new chief of staff, he surveyed the room's occupants with an appraising gaze. Baker, Meese, and Deaver had joined the president to salute Regan's appointment with a show of unified support.

"Mr. President," Regan said, "you might as well realize it. I got something these other guys haven't got. Jim Baker's got some of it. Meese doesn't have it, maybe never will. And Deaver will try to get it."

"What's that?" the president asked, arching a curious eyebrow.

"I've got 'fuck you' money," Regan said. It was true; he had a $40 million blind trust he registered per the Office of Government Ethics. "Anytime I want, I'm gone."

But he'd never tangled with Nancy Reagan before.

The First Lady was laying the groundwork to secure her husband's legacy. She had her own ideas about the kinds of big, consequential accomplishments that would follow him into history. "More than anything," Stu Spencer recalls, "she wanted him recognized as a man of peace." The image that trailed Reagan as he'd entered the presidency—that he was dangerously confrontational, a warmonger, "a trigger-happy cowboy"—galled her. And during the first term, his hard-line stance with respect to the Soviets, the tough talk, the massive military buildup, hadn't done much to alter the image. As she saw it, he had a great opportunity in the second term to change the course of history by improving relations with the Soviet Union. "Improving U.S.–Soviet relations became Nancy Reagan's special cause," according to Lou Cannon. "Although few thought of her as a peaceful force, she became a force for peace within the White House."

No less a strategist than Richard Nixon agreed. As he'd done prior to Reagan's first inauguration, the former president produced a memo—this one a five-page effort entitled "A New Approach for the Second Term," which laid out his vision for an effective agenda. "The President has already won his place in history as the leader . . . who restored the American people's faith in themselves," Nixon affirmed. "He can become the preeminent post–World War II foreign policy leader by establishing a new, less dangerous relationship with the Soviet Union."

But where to begin? Reagan had made no real headway with Brezhnev or Andropov. Their successor, Konstantin Chernenko, presented an opening by agreeing to resume nuclear-arms-control talks between the two countries. Soon after the election he sent a letter to the U.S. president: "We propose that the Soviet Union and the United States of America enter into new negotiations with the objective of reaching mutually acceptable agreements on the whole range of questions concerning nuclear and space weapons." A follow-up letter a month later called for "the elimination of all nuclear weapons and of 'strike weapons' in space," an indication that the Strategic Defense Initiative alarmed the Soviets. So be it. If all went according to schedule, George Shultz and Foreign Minister Andrei Gromyko would meet in Geneva on January 7, 1985, the first step toward determining how to reach these objectives.

It was a first step into the unknown. No one knew how serious the Soviets were or what the substance of their ideas were. Despite a storehouse of American intelligence, no one could decipher the Russian mind. And Chernenko was mysteriously indisposed. American officials understood that the Soviet premier was gravely ill with emphysema, signaling the possibility of another untimely transition of power. They were already combing pictures of Politburo meetings trying to determine a likely successor.

The odds-on favorite was Heydar Aliyev, a longtime KGB hardliner and leader of Azerbaijan. But Shultz told the president that the Kremlin's number-two man, Mikhail Gorbachev, a protégé of Andropov, was "the man to watch." Unlike some Moscow hardliners who argued the Marxist-Leninist line, Gorbachev had risen through the Interior Ministry at the Republic level and took a less insular approach to Soviet doctrine. He was less reactionary. At fifty-four, he was younger by decades than his predecessors, and the first high Soviet party official to be college-educated. What's more, he was well traveled. He'd engaged with Helmut Kohl in Germany and Canada's Pierre Trudeau. During a visit to London in December 1984, Margaret Thatcher came away impressed with what she'd heard. "I like Mr. Gorbachev," she said afterward. "We can do business together."

She reiterated this opinion to Reagan over the 1984 Christmas holiday, during a private, off-the-record meeting at Laurel, his cabin at Camp David. Mrs. Thatcher was eager to see the president. She wanted to make her feelings known about his Star Wars strategy, which she had learned about only through the encounter with Gorbachev a few weeks earlier. Why hadn't she been briefed on this? Why hadn't Reagan confided in her? "He knew what she was coming for," says Bud McFarlane, who joined them in front of the fireplace in the rustic living room, "so he was prepared."

Thatcher wasn't hesitant or circumspect. Moments after alighting from a helicopter, she launched into a full-on condemnation of SDI. "Look here, Ron." She enunciated each word sharply, "I'm alarmed that you have apparently put at risk your commitment to the strategy that NATO has developed and relied on for forty years." She was referring to Flexible Response, a program in place since the Kennedy administration that mandated a seamless transition from conventional to nuclear weapons in Europe to deter or prevail against Soviet aggression. "Point one: you seem to be separating the United States from Europe. Secondly, you're making it appear that the United States may have in mind establishing the ability to launch a first strike—to be the aggressor, to not wait to ride out an attack because you have a bubble over the United States, or so you expect. Thirdly, it won't work. It's technologically beyond reach. And, lastly, you're wasting money on this that would be better spent on improving the strength of the NATO forces."

She had done her homework, some of which had come through the Soviets, but she was also speculating and overreaching to gain whatever information the president was willing to share on the subject. Despite her tenacity, he wasn't about to give Thatcher anything that divulged where the technology stood. If Gorbachev and the Soviets were intimidated about SDI, then the strategy was already working, whether the mechanics ever would or not. All Reagan could do was attempt to reassure her while acknowledging the risk and exorbitant cost of the program—a five-year commitment of $26 billion for starters. "But with regard to separating us from Europe," he pledged, "count on it, Margaret, we will never do that. And, similarly, under my leadership, we'll never launch a first strike or undertake aggression as a moral proposition."

He was gracious to a fault, laying on the charm. "She wasn't buying it," McFarlane recalls. "She wanted some earnest commitment." Her dander was up. "What is this special relationship we're supposed to have?" she huffed. "Come on, Ron! I'm embarrassed, and I want to see some evidence that you and I are joined at the hip on this."

Thatcher wasn't entirely satisfied by the president's response and left in a state that McFarlane called "gruntled," not at all pleased, but she was at least willing to paper over their differences, for now. However, Ronald Reagan was concerned with her unhappiness. To mollify her, he dispatched McFarlane to London close on her heels to do some fence-mending, basically repeating the same feeble pledges that were made at Camp David. As he was leaving Number 10 Downing Street, McFarlane delivered a parting gift. "Prime Minister, I'm authorized by the president to say that he believes there ought to be as much as $300 million a year in contracting to British firms on the SDI program."

Later that spring, during the much-publicized appropriation cycle that involved funding for SDI, not a word of complaint emerged out of London. A few months later, at a reception in Bonn, Mrs. Thatcher drew McFarlane into a corner and said, "About that dustup we had—I've been thinking about it, and I can find a way, given the president's assurances, that we can be supportive of this."

The president was committed to the Strategic Defense Initiative as the cornerstone of his goal for peace. He'd been rereading the Book of Revelation, especially the concept of Armageddon, and worried that at this point in history the state of weaponry might hold the potential for a catastrophic explosion sufficient to destroy humankind. "This could happen now," he warned an aide. There was plenty of such inflammatory enlightenment in his old fallback reference *Human Events*, which he read religiously, annotated in the margins, and filed away for further reference. "When he read something in *Human Events*, he believed it," Don Regan confirmed, even though the factual basis for the magazine's positions was often threadbare at best. *Human Events* had helped to convince him that Social Security was an outright failure. It preached that the Sandinista government should be overthrown and that the Contras were great patriots, and it advocated for the Strategic Defense Initiative, which it believed would work and would guarantee America's future.

It "horrified" the president's top men that he embraced such pabulum. More than one White House official asked Don Regan, "How the fuck can you get that magazine away from him?" Although he tried, Regan wasn't able to stop the subscription. "The damn thing came to the family quarters," he said. Stu Spencer ordered Mike Deaver to hide it, but to little good. The magazine was Ronald Reagan's bedrock reading, more than a guilty pleasure, often isolating him from a broader, more informed perspective on key issues. The president was guided by instinct, Regan noted, developing his gut feelings about issues culled from articles he read and letters ordinary people sent him in the mail, and "once they were ingrained in the brain of Ronald Reagan, they stayed there and hell wouldn't eradicate these things when he had the basic belief."

When it came to SDI, he was convinced beyond doubt it would work. In his mind, he envisioned a space shield against these missiles and, by God, he was going to provide the American people with that shield, despite considerable misgivings from scientists and engineers. *This is what the President of the United States does for his people*, he thought. He intended to *make it happen*. Nothing would crown his second term more than if he gave the country such a new sweeping sense of security.

Whether this instinctual decision-making was managed or contained well enough by his advisers remains open to question. But they had learned that the path of least resistance to maintaining the president's overwhelming popularity was to "let Reagan be Reagan." The rallying cry of the 1984 presidential campaign had carried into his second administration.

Let Reagan be Reagan. Occasionally, it would have been better if advisers had intervened. There were times they were frustrated when he stood for what he thought, against prevailing political and public sentiment, in favor of what he regarded as just and right, whether people agreed with him or not, heedless of the potential fallout. Advisers as influential as the secretary of state deemed Reagan's "stubborn determination and willingness to do what he considered to be right" both an advantage and a disadvantage in setting policy.

He dug in even deeper when he'd given his word. In a calamitous example of Ronald Reagan's resolve, he accepted an invitation from Chancellor Helmut Kohl to commemorate the fortieth anniversary of V-E Day, which would include visiting a military cemetery in Germany where "a handclasp over the graves of the fallen" would be a testament to the two countries' reconciliation and friendship. Implicit in the details: the visit was payback. Kohl was facing tough regional elections, and the president agreed to help his cause in return for the chancellor's support in 1983 for situating new U.S. Pershing II missile installations in Europe. The visit dovetailed with the upcoming G7 economic summit in Bonn.

In January, *Der Spiegel* reported that Reagan's agenda might include a visit to Dachau, the site of the former Nazi concentration camp in Bavaria. The White House quickly scratched Dachau. "You know, he's a cheerful politician," an aide told a reporter. "He does not like to grovel in a grisly scene like Dachau." But the suggestion that he go there was enough to prick old wounds. For many Americans—those who lost loved ones and those who had fought—the horrors of World War II were still too fresh and painful. The visit to Germany alone was controversial enough.

In late February 1985, Mike Deaver led an advance team to Germany in order to survey alternative sites for the president's trip. The state visit in May would effectively serve as Deaver's swan song. He was fed up with the punishing government grind, and his alcoholism had spun out of control. "I had to get out of there," he admitted. "I was a sick guy." He had informed the Reagans that he would be leaving the White House for good in June, and overseeing a glamorous European swing that included stops in Spain, France, and Portugal would usher him out the door in style. But Deaver's due diligence fell woefully short and planted a lamentably wrong step in his stride across the threshold.

Among the prospective sites under consideration was Kolmeshöhe cemetery, in the quaint town of Bitburg near the Luxembourg border. A U.S. airbase was located on the outskirts of the town, and every year since 1959 American and French officials had joined German locals in a wreath-laying ceremony at the cemetery. It was a lovely tradition, Deaver thought, that would dignify the solemnity of the occasion. "It was very picturesque," he recalled. "A beautiful little spot." He didn't spend much time at the site. There was a fresh blanket of snow on the ground, and the gravestones were mostly covered. But he was assured by German authorities that there was nothing there that would embarrass the president.

For the most part, the trip's schedule would fall into place around various political events and meetings, including an address to the European Parliament in Strasbourg. The president's main concern at the time was jump-starting the arms-control negotiations with the Soviets, slated to begin in Geneva on March 12, 1985.

Early that morning in the hours before dawn, Reagan was awakened by a call from Bud McFarlane, which never augured well. McFarlane bore news that Konstantin Chernenko was dead, the third Soviet premier to die since the president had taken office. It was disruptive, but not obviously consequential. The Soviet hard line hadn't budged an inch in the past twenty years. The Americans knew, more or less, what to expect no matter who sat in the Kremlin. Chernenko's successor was announced within hours. Shultz had predicted correctly—it was Mikhail Gorbachev.

The president had no intention of attending Chernenko's funeral. He sent Vice President Bush instead, along with a letter to Gorbachev extending an invitation. "You can be assured of my personal commitment to working with you and the rest of the Soviet leadership in serious negotiations," it said. "In that spirit I would like you to visit me in Washington at your earliest convenient opportunity."

It was a coincidence that Gorbachev took office on the day that Soviet and U.S. negotiators resumed arms-control talks. Both sides continued the time-honored pas de deux. But a breakthrough, of sorts, arrived in a Gorbachev response. On March 24, he wrote the president that he had "a positive attitude to the idea you expressed about holding a personal meeting between us."

That was a game-changer.

If Margaret Thatcher could do business with this man, perhaps Ronald Reagan could as well. But on that same day, Major Arthur Nicholson Jr., an American Army officer stationed in Germany, was shot by a Soviet sentry in East Germany, reminding the president just how fragile the Cold War relationship was. If he needed further proof, it came in an intelligence report that revealed that the Soviets prevented the administering of first aid to the wounded soldier, resulting in his bleeding to death. Was Gorbachev the kind of man who condoned such barbarous acts of cruelty? Thatcher might have cozied to his ingratiating smile, but clearer heads accepted Andrei Gromyko's warning that Gorbachev's nice smile "has iron teeth."

With the Soviet Union in uncertain transition, the president doubled down on American security interests. Throughout the early spring of 1985, he pressed for a new $1.5 billion appropriation to build twenty-one MX missiles, those ferocious long-range mastodons. A similar bill had been defeated in 1982, but a renewed lobbying effort gave the administration hope. This time, as a result of the full-court press, Congress bestowed its blessing, upping the ante in the ongoing arms-control negotiations in Geneva. MX missiles could carry up to ten warheads, and in theory represented a major leap forward in missile performance. The reality never quite squared with the theory, but they worried the Soviets greatly, so they were good bargaining chips and gave the negotiators leverage.

With the appropriations bill in the win column, the president decided to push his luck to persuade Congress to resume funding for the Contras in Nicaragua, which the legislature had cut off in 1984. "The Contra funding is like the MX spending," Reagan rationalized during a National Security Planning Group meeting on Central America. "It is what will keep the pressure on Nicaragua." The request he made was for $14 million window-dressed as *humanitarian aid*, but those operating behind the scenes knew it was earmarked to arm the rebels in their fight against the Sandinistas. In fact, third-party contributions to the Contras had amounted to more than $24.5 million since appropriated funds had stopped, but more—much more—was needed to keep the operation intact. At the rate things were going, the well would soon run dry. Oliver North, who was coordinating the operation with National Security director Bud McFarlane, recommended an additional $15 million to $20 million to maintain the Contras' momentum.

The president agreed to do what he could. On April 15, 1985, he addressed a fund-raiser to benefit the Nicaraguan Refugee Fund. He was in his element as the after-dinner speaker, trading barbs with his old sidekick Bob Hope. After the usual jokey exchange, Reagan came right to the point. "We cannot have the United States walk away from one of the greatest moral challenges in postwar history. . . . We will fight on. . . . We will win this struggle for peace. *Viva Nicaragua Libra!*"

Viva Nicaragua Libra!

News broke the same week that the president's trip to Germany included his laying a wreath at the cemetery in Bitburg. "Who's buried in Bitburg?" the White House correspondent for *Newsday* asked Larry Speakes. The press officer threw up his hands; he had no relevant information. But others did. Elie Wiesel, the esteemed Holocaust survivor and human rights advocate, was aghast at the news, and the American Legion announced it was "terribly disappointed."

Two days later, word leaked out that forty-nine members of the Waffen SS, the elite Nazi military unit responsible for brutal war crimes, were among the soldiers buried in Bitburg. The goodwill excursion devolved into a crisis. Would the president really agree to visit graves containing soldiers involved in atrocities against Americans? Most had belonged to the Second SS Panzer Division—Hitler's elite regiment known as *Das Reich*—which had massacred civilian families in France. One of them, Otto Beugel, had been awarded the Cross of Gold for having killed ten Americans in combat. The Waffen SS crimes detailed at the Nuremberg trials were all too fresh in the public's mind.

The visit created a public-relations nightmare. Once the press got wind of it, there was no letup. "Get off this—don't go," Don Regan advised the president. But Reagan remained adamant. "I've promised," he replied, his eyes doleful. He'd given Helmut Kohl his word. "We were hoping that Kohl would reconsider," says Jim Kuhn, Reagan's second-term executive assistant, "but the chancellor was intractable." Kohl sent Reagan a "Dear Ron" letter that said canceling the visit would have a serious psychological effect on the way Germans viewed Americans. He laid it on thick, going so far as to claim that Soviet propaganda was driving this agenda. Canceling the trip would be a political catastrophe for him.

Reagan was between a rock and a hard place. "He sure as hell wanted this to go away," Kuhn recalls, "but backing down was never an option. In fact, the outcry may have strengthened his resolve to go."

Mike Deaver flew to Germany in an attempt to salvage what he could of the visit. Efforts were made to find an alternative site to the Bitburg cemetery, but Kohl wouldn't hear of it. Instead, Deaver, trying to soften the edge, decided to add a concentration camp visit to the schedule, either at Dachau or Bergen-Belsen. This only drew more rebukes from congressional leaders, veterans, Jews, and especially Elie Wiesel. On April 19, in a nationally televised ceremony broadcast from the Roosevelt Room of the White House organized to award Wiesel the Congressional Gold Medal, the fragile honoree stopped the proceedings cold when he chastened Reagan directly. "That place, Mr. President, is not your place. Your place is with the victims of the SS."

The outcry was taking its toll. As Bud McFarlane described it to his counterpart in Germany, "The drumbeat of criticism gathers momentum with every hour here." Pressure was coming from all quarters to do something different, something decisive, about the Bitburg visit. George Shultz told the president, "Bitburg is a disaster . . . hitting the most sensitive people at the most sensitive time." The Senate voted 82–0 against the president's going; the House followed suit, 390–26. The Israelis were strongly opposed. Margaret Thatcher condemned the event as "deeply offensive and insulting to the memory of the victims." In an ABC News poll, 52 percent of respondents urged Ronald Reagan to cancel the trip. But Richard Nixon advised him to stay the course, arguing that the visit would only strengthen U.S.-German relations. Henry Kissinger chipped in with his endorsement. Every day brought a new, conflicting opinion. The press was reporting it like a soap opera. They were "really sucking blood," Reagan fumed in a diary entry, "and finding every person of Jewish faith they can who will denounce me." It only reinforced his determination. "Well, d—n their hides.

I think it is morally right to go & I'm going." His back was up. He resolved not to cancel the trip "no matter how much the bastards"—the Holocaust survivors and war veterans—"scream."

But the controversy was swamping the presidential agenda. Ten days later, on April 29, Reagan placed a call to Helmut Kohl, ostensibly to wheedle the chancellor into letting him off the hook. It was a long, impassioned conversation that ran on for almost twenty minutes. The president suggested an alternative to Bitburg—Festung Ehrenbreitstein, the shrine at Koblenz. "It's a memorial to your soldiers," he said. "It honors your four or five million war dead." Kohl wouldn't hear of it. "But, Helmut," he pleaded, "you and I will be there together." That made no difference to Kohl. He'd put himself on the line about Bitburg. All of Germany was watching. If Reagan changed the itinerary, Kohl said, he would lose face. It would cause his government to fall.

Jim Kuhn entered the Oval Office moments after the president's phone line went dead. "He was just sitting there. His head was bent, his eyes were downcast," Kuhn recalls. "I asked him whether we were going to Bitburg. He looked up and barely muttered, 'Yeah.'"

The only thing now was to make the best of it. Nancy Reagan was furious with Kohl and with Mike Deaver for not handling damage control. Deaver had always made things like this go away—or at least smoothed them over to her satisfaction. But this time—perhaps his last duty as the Reagans' consigliere—he hadn't come through. "I'm trying to do my damnedest to make the best of a very difficult situation," he implored her. "Let me get on with it, please." It wasn't enough to assuage her fears; she decided to take things into her own hands. Panicked that something dreadful might come of the Bitburg trip, the First Lady turned to astrologer Joan Quigley for advice. Charts were drawn up of the various events, requiring that their times be shuffled or rescheduled to satisfy the astrologer's concern that certain indicators put the president "in starry danger zones." Deaver was ordered to coordinate with Quigley so her advice could be implemented. When he protested, Mrs. Reagan let him have it. "We're talking about my husband's life," she shouted.

The day of the Bitburg event brought no relief. "She was a nervous Nellie that morning," says Jim Kuhn. "She was really agitated: 'Ronnie is not *touching* the wreath! He's definitely not placing it!'" On Quigley's say-so, the wreath-laying was moved from the morning to the afternoon, their departure from Bonn delayed two separate times when the astrologer determined it was dangerous for the president to be airborne. In the hotel beforehand, Nancy Reagan came apart, her husband standing by, seemingly at a loss. "She was near-hysterical," recalls Kuhn, who had never seen her like this before. Kuhn picked up the phone and ordered the White House operator who monitored the line to send Mike Deaver straight to the suite. No more than thirty seconds later, Deaver walked into the room, made a beeline for Nancy Reagan, and wrapped her in a bear hug, with the president watching from a corner. "He held her for a long minute or two," Kuhn says. "Neither of them exchanged a single word." Finally, Deaver let go of her, patted her on the back, and simply walked out the door. She was fine, exorcised, ready to go.

Deaver, too, had received comfort from an unexpected source. Days before the Bitburg ceremony, he took a blind call from retired General Matthew Ridgway, the ninety-year-old World War II hero, who, in a heroic gesture, offered to accompany the president to the grave site and lay the wreath. For symmetry, Kohl volunteered the services of Luftwaffe ace General Johannes Steinhoff. The presence of both aging soldiers took some of the sting out of the occasion.

In fact, the day, for the most part, passed without incident. Reagan acquitted himself well with a moving speech against the imposing backdrop of Bergen-Belsen. There were protests and demonstrations, but they were restrained. The streets along the presidential route to the Bitburg cemetery were lined with Jewish protesters who stood shoulder-to-shoulder with tender-faced Germans, many waving American flags. Lost in the rhetoric of postwar reconciliation was evidence that the healing process was already taking root. The wreath-laying ceremony was a superficial exercise. It took all of eight minutes. Reagan and Kohl made their way silently along the brick walkway around the graves, solemn eyes drawn down, expressionless, neither man acknowledging the crowd or ever touching the wreath. Aides said the president was deeply affected by the surroundings, haunted by recollections of the concentration camp footage he'd viewed at Fort Roach in 1945. "I promise you, we will never forget," he told a small audience in a ceremony afterward at the Bitburg Air Base.

Ronald Reagan had taken a beating while the affair unspooled, committing the prestige of the presidency to a relatively minor state function. At the end of the day, it caused unwelcome distractions and unnecessary embarrassments. The failure to allay its emotional impact was compounded by the president's stubbornness, his unwillingness to back away from a promise once he'd given his word. But in the days following the Bitburg visit, his popularity stabilized. The way he'd handled himself in Germany—his presidential gestalt, the common touch—provided an image of dignified leadership that many Americans placed above substance.

Instead, the blame for the Bitburg controversy was laid off on the president's staff. They had dealt with it haphazardly. There was no oversight, none of the collective coordination that had given the first term its ballast. One man, Don Regan, was now calling the shots, and he had mismanaged the situation right out of the box. He isolated the president from opposing viewpoints. He sparred with the press. He hadn't been straight with Jewish leaders who'd sought his help in reaching a fair solution. Nor had he mollified congressional leaders who had called seeking to voice their concerns. The new chief of staff's inability to control the political fallout had cost Ronald Reagan heavily.

Regan had no real experience in day-to-day administration. He constantly flashed his credentials as a Wall Street manager, but he hadn't been a *hands-on* manager. His role at the brokerage had been dictatorial. On Wall Street, he hadn't roundtabled issues with the fellas, hadn't built consensus or cultivated opposing viewpoints, as Ronald Reagan encouraged. He issued orders and demanded results. Those were the ground rules Don Regan established as he revamped the business of the Oval Office. He insisted on compliance. He demanded loyalty—"loyalty up, and loyalty down," as he put it. He didn't like being disagreed with—or contradicted. To solidify his authority, he enlisted the help of four aides—David Chew, Al Kingon, Tom Dawson, and Dennis Thomas, yes-men referred to throughout the White House as the Mice. "They were the court jesters," Ed Meese says.

Regan had the staff on edge, and the tension extended right up the chain of command. He'd already read the riot act to National Security Adviser Bud McFarlane for telephoning the president directly when Chernenko died and again when Major Nicholson was shot. As a result, McFarlane told George Shultz he intended to resign, citing his inability to work with Regan and his henchman, Pat Buchanan, the new White House communications director. Other officials became similarly disgruntled. Accustomed to having access to the president, they found him suddenly unapproachable, insulated from his longtime advisers, the Oval Office off-limits. The White House became Don Regan's bailiwick, and throughout the spring of 1985 he broadened his command over it.

B ut there were meatier, more exigent problems. During the president's state visit to Germany, Congress had dealt the administration a foreign-policy blow, cutting off all aid to the Contras, humanitarian or otherwise. And his tax-reform bill dangled by a thread. A summit with Gorbachev was on again, off again. SALT II remained a strategic hot potato. The administration was having trouble implementing its agenda.

Nixon had warned of this. "A President in his second term, even after a landslide, has a much briefer honeymoon and a less effective mandate than after his first election," he wrote to Reagan. He needed to somehow set new and inspiring goals rather than cling to the policies of the past.

But first the administration had to reckon with a dark act of terrorism. On June 14, 1985, gunmen, members of Hezbollah and Islamic Jihad, hijacked TWA flight 847, en route from Athens to Rome, and held 153 passengers hostage, 104 of them Americans. One of them, a Navy diver named Robert Stethem, was shot in the head and dumped onto the tarmac in Beirut. The terrorists demanded the release of 766 Shiite Muslims held "for security offenses" from Israeli custody, threatening to shoot another hostage every five minutes and to blow up the plane if it came under attack. Israel was willing to swap its prisoners in exchange for the hostages *if the United States made such a request*, but the concept was loaded with pitfalls. "This of course means that we—not they—would be violating our policy of not negotiating with terrorists," Reagan concluded. A trade for American hostages put Americans at risk anywhere in the world. He refused to set that kind of precedent, ignoring Cap Weinberger's and George Bush's advice to make the swap. He resorted to diplomacy instead.

It took seventeen days to finally secure the release of the hostages, and involved such characters as Nabih Berri, the commander of the Amal militia, and Syrian president Hafez al-Assad, an acknowledged sponsor of

Middle East terrorism. Negotiations were strained and often murky. It was never certain who was in control of the hostage situation or had the authority to make decisions.

The president was determined not to let this develop into a fiasco like the Iranian hostage crisis six years earlier. The hijacking was already a spectacle. Much of the crisis had played out on television, with a rapt audience following each new development. The major networks and CNN had camera crews on the ground, capturing the whole tension-packed affair live, day after day—the pilot of the hijacked plane who leaned out the cockpit window with a gun to his head while being interviewed, the hijackers who screamed their threats, the hostages as they were released one by one. The whole world was watching. Public outrage built with each new episode.

The media circus made U.S. efforts to deal with the crisis much more difficult. The president was under pressure to make some kind of a deal. For the longest time, the coverage made it seem as though negotiations were going nowhere. Television demanded action and resolution. Where was Delta Force? Or those crack-shot Israeli commandos? Reagan had spent one of the evenings at Camp David watching *First Blood Part II*. Where was Rambo? Negotiators were working with every available resource behind the scenes, involving the diplomatic branches of as many as six different countries, until a deal was agreed to. The hostages were freed, and several weeks later, Israel released some seven hundred Shia prisoners, though it claimed there was no quid pro quo.

The president was satisfied with the results. It wasn't pretty, but no further lives had been lost in the process and no agreements had jeopardized U.S. policy. But another hostage crisis was already under way, one that would mar the Reagan administration's final three years and deal a blow to the president's legacy. Another seven Americans kidnapped by extremist groups were still being held hostage elsewhere in Beirut, among them William Buckley, the CIA station chief; David Jacobsen of the American University in Lebanon; Terry Anderson, the Middle East bureau chief for the Associated Press; and a missionary, Reverend Benjamin Weir. Ronald Reagan made it clear to Bud McFarlane that he intended to secure their release at all costs. "Let's get them out. Do whatever you have to."

CHAPTER THIRTY-EIGHT

INTO THE ABYSS

"I claim not to have controlled events, but confess
plainly that events have controlled me."

—ABRAHAM LINCOLN

I n July 1985, Nancy Reagan's worst fear came true.

During the president's annual physical in March, doctors found traces of blood in his stool and two small polyps on his intestinal wall that, out of an abundance of caution, they decided to remove. It was a routine procedure, during which a colonoscopy was performed, which is when the situation took an ominous turn. A large tumor the size of a baby's finger was discovered that couldn't be easily dismissed or removed. The official designation was "precancerous," a nebulous term whose meaning ranged anywhere from benign to malignant. No matter. The patient was the President of the United States. Nobody was taking any chances.

The First Lady was "beside herself." She'd spent four years fretting about her husband's safety, from the attempted assassination in 1981 and Anwar Sadat's murder later that same year. "If she could, she'd have placed him in a protective bubble," says Sheila Tate. Nancy Reagan was at her happiest when she had the president to herself in the residence. Barring that, she'd taken every precaution possible, from shuffling his schedules on the advice of her astrologer to having trucks filled with sand placed at the entrances to the White House, heat-seeking devices on *Air Force One*, and armed SWAT teams escorting the presidential motorcade. The assassination attempt continued to haunt her. Safety became an obsession—not only

Ronald Reagan's safety, but the family's in general. Weeks earlier, when her son, Ron, dismissed his Secret Service detail as an unnecessary bother, Nancy wound up on a screaming, sobbing phone call with him, pleading for its reinstatement.

The initial operation had been postponed one time on the advice of Joan Quigley. There was no such allowance this time. The president had already been admitted to Bethesda Naval Hospital, and the doctors were recommending immediate surgery. Ideally, the First Lady wanted them to hold off until she could reach "My Friend," as she referred to Quigley. The astrologer needed to "clear" the date. Reagan himself put a stop to this. He was already prepped and ready to go. He wanted to get the procedure over and done with. His brother, Neil, had undergone an operation for cancer of the colon and gall bladder not even a week earlier. If this business ran in the family there was no time to waste in treating it.

The First Lady launched into protective mode. She insisted that the White House had to manage the media. There would be no pictures of the president in his hospital room trussed up in tubes or wires, nothing that showed him the least bit indisposed. "He can't be seen this way," she ordered White House photographers. "We don't want people to know it's this bad." And she laid down the law to Larry Speakes: "no mention of the words *cancer* or *malignant*." There was already news enough to alarm the public. The president was undergoing major surgery . . . he'd be under anesthesia . . . a seventy-four-year-old man. It was essential that they put the best spin on it.

The surgery was scheduled for 11:00 a.m. on Saturday, July 13. A half hour beforehand, the president signed two identical documents—one to the president pro tempore of the Senate (Strom Thurmond), one to the Speaker of the House (Tip O'Neill)—authorizing Vice President George Bush to "discharge powers and duties in my stead commencing with the administration of anesthesia." It was the first official transfer from a president to his vice president in the nation's history. It wasn't in effect that long. The operation itself was over three hours later. The polyp was not cancerous, and Ronald Reagan pronounced himself "fit as a fiddle." By seven o'clock that same evening, he had signed orders reclaiming all presidential powers.

Nancy Reagan wasn't happy about the transfer, and she was less than thrilled by the president's prescribed recovery. He needed rest, she insisted, casting the evil eye at the White House staff that slipped in and out of his room carrying briefs and papers. Don Regan kept him posted on the ongoing budget battle and the legislative agenda. There was good news: the Soviet Union had agreed to a Gorbachev-Reagan summit in Geneva on November 19 and 20. The president would finally get his face-to-face with a Soviet premier. And the hostages. "Any word on the hostages?" It was the first question Ronald Reagan asked; he was preoccupied with their return. The two men spent considerable time—"longer than I would have thought wise," Regan recalled—discussing the situation. The president was frosted that U.S. citizens were being held by common criminals and that foreign governments were possibly involved. Bud McFarlane, the national security adviser, had some relevant news, but Nancy Reagan had barred him from the premises.

In fact, McFarlane had information for the president that was sensational and time-sensitive. On July 3, 1985, he'd been visited by David Kimche, an old intelligence friend who had been deputy director of the Mossad and was currently director general of the Israeli Foreign Ministry. The Mossad, Kimche revealed, had identified "a moderate faction in various Iranian legislative branches that, if nurtured over time, could form an opposition to Ayatollah Khomeini." They could become powerful allies if . . . if . . . the right pieces fell into place. There were a lot of moving parts in the offing, with mysterious characters moving them. It went without saying that such an operation was dangerous and risky. "No one is going to put their lives on the line," Kimche told McFarlane, "unless you've got some skin in the game. The Iranians' offer to demonstrate their bona fides is to release hostages. But they are not going to spend that chit unless the United States provides them with weapons that could make a difference in a war with Iraq."

McFarlane's head was spinning. This could be the breakthrough he and the president were looking for. But *Iranians? Weapons? The Mossad?* McFarlane remembers thinking: "It's fraught."

He expressed as much to Kimche. "David, you've got to have a lot of confidence in these interlocutors we're talking about. Do they really have current standing to build on? Are these people qualified to broaden a political opposition, or are they just frustrated military officers?" Kimche shrugged and shook his head. "I really don't know," he admitted.

Kimche's vague response worried McFarlane, but he knew the president would be intrigued. He needed to run this by him as soon as possible.

For three days—three very unsettling days—Nancy Reagan refused to let McFarlane into Reagan's room. Don Regan made the case that national security was involved, but she wouldn't hear of it. The president needed his rest. Regan eventually smuggled an envelope from Bud McFarlane into the president, outlining the discussion with David Kimche. The next morning, July 18, Nancy relented and McFarlane finally got his audience. "It could be a breakthrough on getting our seven kidnap victims back," an optimistic Reagan wrote in his diary that night.

McFarlane says he simply presented the facts, emphasizing that the Israelis believed the intermediaries were legitimate. The Iranian faction would show its goodwill by releasing William Buckley and perhaps others if . . . *if* . . . in return, the Americans shipped a small quantity of TOW missiles, state-of-the-art antitank weapons, to Iran. Ronald Reagan's eyes were as big as saucers. "Gosh, that would be great!" the president said, obviously focused on only the human dimension of the details. McFarlane made sure to outline the risks, including some pertinent history and the vulnerability of such an exchange. "But I could tell it went in one ear and out the other," McFarlane recalls. "He drilled down exclusively on getting the hostages back."

In retrospect, McFarlane believes he should have waited until Reagan was out of the hospital and in a less emotional state. The geopolitics, he says, were lost in the details. But it wasn't the job of the national security adviser to protect the president from himself. All he really owed Reagan was accurate, up-to-date intelligence. He didn't realize at the time that his boss was about to take a step that would be politically cataclysmic. In any case, the president wasn't oblivious. "We have to be very careful here," he acknowledged. Reagan knew enough to convey he was "unwilling to allow the United States to supply arms directly to Iran." That would amount to trading arms for hostages, which violated U.S. policy. But "it did not seem unreasonable" to the president "that Iranian moderates . . . would ask for weapons in order to strengthen their position." He "was all for letting the

Israelis do anything they wanted." If they had possession of TOWs and took it upon themselves to ship them to Iran . . . well, there was a lot to be said for such an operation. Reagan admitted, "I didn't have to think thirty seconds about saying yes to their proposal." His instruction to McFarlane was: "Yes, go ahead. Open it up."

O pen it up—as in Pandora's box. Ronald Reagan had no idea what he was unleashing. For him, there was no intent to negotiate directly with kidnappers. He saw it as being all aboveboard. "He was dealing with an *agent* who might have *influence* with the kidnappers," as Don Regan suggested. Reagan likened the Israelis to "Jafsie"—the anonymous go-between conscripted by Charles Lindbergh to make contact with his son's kidnappers in 1932. The chief of staff wasn't sure whether it was "naïve thinking" or "good statecraft." In the end, he decided it was nothing more than "rug dealing"—that is, if the rugs you were dealing looked like bazookas on steroids.

Two weeks later, on August 6, 1985, the top command attempted to sharpen its focus. President Reagan, still in pajamas and under his wife's eagle-eyed care, arranged a White House meeting upstairs in the residence to discuss the operation with Don Regan, Bud McFarlane, George Bush, Bill Casey, George Shultz, and Caspar Weinberger. All of them had heard bits and pieces of the caper, but Reagan asked McFarlane to lay out the details, including reasons why he thought it should be pursued. It wasn't just the hostages. A strategic partnership with Iran might provide a block on the Soviet Union's securing a direct path to the Indian Ocean's warm water. It was also seen as a deterrent to Hezbollah. But it always led back to the return of the hostages. When McFarlane finished, the president canvassed the room. "Tell me everything," he said, "whatever you feel." Shultz was aghast. "This is almost too absurd to comment on," he'd written on a directive. He dismissed it to Reagan as "a very bad idea." Shultz could read between the lines. It was "the arms-for-hostages business, and we shouldn't do it," he said. That was mild, compared with Weinberger's reaction. "Cap was livid," McFarlane recalls, "just violently opposed." The two secretaries rarely agreed on any foreign policy. If either of them opposed an initiative, the president usually edged away from it; with two of them opposed, he'd run. But the hostages gnawed at him. He'd met with a few of their family members, and their misery stuck with him. Now he listened to everyone's opinions and said, "Okay, thanks. I'll let you know."

It didn't take him long to sift through the variables. He called Bud McFarlane the following weekend. "You know that thing we were talking about?" he said elliptically. "I want to take the next step." McFarlane understood the president's intent. It meant exchanging TOW missiles for hostages. "You are authorized to tell the intermediaries to get back to their Iranian contact."

"Mr. President," McFarlane said, "you know Cap and George are against this."

Reagan stood his ground. "I've thought about that, but I believe we ought to explore it to see if we get results."

The operation's intermediary was Manucher Ghorbanifar, a supremely shady character. A former agent of Savak, the Shah of Iran's secret police, and a partner in Star Line Shipping, a joint Iranian-Israeli firm that moved oil between the two countries, he had lived in exile since the Iranian revolution, operating as an international arms merchant under different identities. His Portuguese passport was issued to Ismael Pereira, his Greek passport to Nikolaos Kralis, and his Iranian passport to Ja'far Suzani. As a result of two polygraphs administered by the CIA, the agency slapped a Fabricator Notice on Ghorbanifar, warning that he "should be regarded as an intelligence fabricator and a nuisance." No less an agency official than Bill Casey corroborated the verdict in blunt terms: "Ghorbanifar is a con artist," he stated conclusively. This was the intermediary the NSC entrusted to broker the exchange of TOW missiles for hostages.

Oliver North had dredged up Ghorbanifar as part of "contingency plans for extracting hostages . . . from Lebanon." In early September 1985, North had traveled to Europe on his own sham passport, issued in the name of William P. Goode, to arrange transport for the freed hostages and to bridge a relationship with Israeli arms merchants and Adnan Khashoggi, a Saudi wheeler-dealer often referred to as the richest man in the world. Initially, McFarlane authorized the Israelis to send a shipment of mortar shells to Iran that Ghorbanifar demanded as a show of good faith. Afterward, the ante was upped to the TOWs.

The Israelis worried John Poindexter. "You were never quite sure what their motivations were," he says. "With Ghorbanifar as a middleman, it doubled my apprehension." But the president was relatively sanguine. "We had great respect for Israel's intelligence abilities relating to matters in the Middle East," he said, "and, as a result, we gave their assertions a great deal of credence." Meanwhile, David Kimche had given Ghorbanifar his blessing, which was good enough for Bud McFarlane.

The situation became even murkier when the Israelis delivered ninety-six TOWs to Iranian agents at Mehrabad, an international airport on the outskirts of Tehran—and no hostages were released. Apparently, the shipment of missiles was intercepted by the Iranian Revolutionary Guard as opposed to the moderate faction for whom they were intended. Ghorbanifar was indignant when pressed. Because the faction he represented got nothing, it owed nothing in return. His contacts, he claimed, wanted all five hundred TOW missiles up front before delivering the hostages. "Do you want the Iranians to send an arm and a leg of Buckley as an advance?"*

The U.S. operatives were already in so deep that they had little choice but to proceed. McFarlane reportedly told the president, "We might as well go ahead and do the whole thing and see what comes of it." Disappointed but determined, Reagan gave the plan his approval. On September 14, 1985, the Israelis loaded crates containing 408 TOW missiles with all identifying marks sanded off onto an unmarked jet, which flew to Tabriz, in the northwest of Iran, where, this time, the moderates collected them. But the terms of the deal were then changed.

"It looks as though we've been deceived," David Kimche told McFarlane. "The dealers can't deliver all the hostages. We can expect only one." It was up to McFarlane which person would be released. He chose William Buckley, whom the CIA was eager to have freed, but was told by Ghorbanifar that Buckley was too ill to travel. The next day, Reverend Benjamin Weir, who had been held the longest, was released outside the old, bombed-out U.S. embassy building in Beirut.

One hostage for five hundred TOWs. And a new demand from the

---

* It is likely that Ghorbanifar knew that William Buckley had already died in captivity when he made this threat.

Iranians delivered by Weir—the release of seventeen Shia prisoners held in Kuwait. "Though they do not want to harm anyone," he reported, "they will go so far as to proceed to execute the six hostages if their demand is not met."

While these events were unfolding, Ronald Reagan was in seclusion at Rancho del Cielo, his mountaintop aerie above Santa Barbara. On August 4, 1985, he'd returned to Bethesda Naval Hospital, where doctors biopsied a sore that had developed on the right side of his nose. Once again, Nancy Reagan sought to stage-manage the details. At her insistence, hospital officials were ordered to send the tissue sample to the laboratory under an assumed name, and if the result revealed a malignancy it was not to be announced. In fact, the biopsy indicated that the president had a mild form of skin cancer, basal cell carcinoma, though a press release dictated by the First Lady avoided any mention of the diagnosis, saying only that her husband was in excellent health.

None of this sat well with Don Regan, who urged her to be candid about the president's condition. He'd returned to the White House with a Band-Aid on his nose, a beacon to the intrusive press corps. To quell their curiosity, the First Lady instructed Larry Speakes to say, "He had a pimple on his nose which he picked at and irritated." In any case, Speakes was to deny that a biopsy had been performed. He was to call it "an irritation of the skin." Regan knew that if she kept up the deception, the press would eventually uncover the truth and it would backfire on the president.

But Don Regan wasn't calling the shots. Nancy Reagan was, as she made very clear to him. "Don was already on the First Lady's shit list," Sheila Tate recalls. During the president's first confinement to the hospital, the chief of staff and the vice president had requisitioned a helicopter for their daily visits, which had put Nancy Reagan's nose out of joint. "That seemed wrong to me," she wrote in her memoir. Her reaction at the time was exponentially stronger. She felt Regan was overstepping, just as she felt he'd taken liberties by enlisting a Secret Service detail for his own safety, a perk never previously awarded the position. A story appeared in the next day's edition of the *Washington Post* insinuating that the chief of staff was comporting himself more like a "prime minister." There was nothing dubious about its anonymous source. According to a White House aide, "It came directly from [Nancy Reagan's] Chief of Staff to the reporter."

There was no love lost between the First Lady and her husband's chief of staff, but for a time they maintained a kind of wary coexistence. But they were both strong-willed, controlling figures used to running the show, and neither was inclined to share authority. Nancy didn't want any backtalk from Regan. And he was fed up with her incessant phone calls and constant meddling. He told Sheila Tate that "he intended to bring in 'some socialite lady' to intercept Nancy Reagan's phone calls." None of this boded well. Both adversaries angled to influence and safeguard the president, but only one person was married to him.

As Ronald Reagan tried to keep his focus on the hostages and his upcoming summit with Mikhail Gorbachev, he found himself dodging increasing criticism of U.S. policy toward South Africa. The Reagan administration had always maintained a position of neutrality on the issue of racial segregation in South Africa, threatening to veto any legislation imposing sanctions on the country. At the president's direction, Jeane Kirkpatrick oversaw vetoes of United Nations Security Council resolutions condemning apartheid. Pat Buchanan, a fierce defender of the regime of Prime Minister Pieter Willem Botha, helped cement the president's viewpoint by sending him a constant flow of right-wing propaganda justifying Pretoria's government and condemning antiapartheid protests. As congressional support for sanctions began gaining steam, the president, in an interview with a Washington radio news director on August 24—the same day that South Africa arrested twenty-seven opposition leaders calling for Nelson Mandela's release from prison—declared that South Africa had "eliminated the segregation that we once had in our own country, the type of thing where hotels and restaurants and places of entertainment and so forth were segregated—that has all been eliminated." It demonstrated a stunning misunderstanding of a country where blacks were still denied voting rights and the use of most public facilities. Thomas Dawson, the executive assistant to Don Regan, seemed to sum up the White House attitude by saying that as far as South Africa went, "I couldn't care less." But on September 10, sensing rebuke by the Senate, including many Republicans, the president abruptly reversed course by signing executive orders banning future loans to South Africa as well as equipment to the country's military.

This reversal occurred at a moment when the administration was facing criticism from the right that he was losing sight of his core principles, or at least failing to follow through on them effectively. Even the *Washington Times* had published a stinging editorial—"Fish or Cut Bait, Mr. President"—questioning Reagan's commitment to conservative ideals and his seeming inability to strike back at terrorists. The sense of internal fighting and disorganization was not helping matters. Just then a new act of terrorism occurred that distracted from the institutional crises.

On October 7, 1985, an Italian cruise ship, the *Achille Lauro*, was hijacked in the eastern Mediterranean, off the coast of Alexandria, Egypt, by a faction of Palestinian extremists. Among the 755 passengers on board, 72 were American citizens, but at the time of the hijacking, all but 80 of the ship's passengers had disembarked in Alexandria to visit Cairo and tour the pyramids. That left only 19 Americans and 61 other passengers on board. The ship was prohibited from docking, to avoid a repeat of the TWA hijacking in which hostages were removed from a vessel and secreted away in a hostile environment.

The NSC planned to launch an immediate rescue mission. "We had the JSOC [the Joint Special Operations Command] standing by," says John Poindexter, who was monitoring the situation as it unfolded. A Special Forces squad deployed to Akrotiri, a British air force base on Cyprus, and prepared to take over the ship, when the *Achille Lauro* began to move north toward Tartus in Syria, where the hijackers presumed they would get asylum.

Under pressure from American diplomats, Syria and Lebanon refused to let the *Achille Lauro* dock. Instead, it sailed to Port Said, on the Mediterranean side of the Suez Canal. The ship's captain reported that everyone on board was in good shape, but this was said with a Kalashnikov machine gun at his head. The four hijackers had already killed one passenger, a sixty-nine-year-old wheelchair-bound American named Leon Klinghoffer. His body had been dumped overboard.

Egypt agreed that if the hijackers surrendered, they would be granted safe passage out of the country in the custody of the PLO. Unaware that anyone had been killed, the Egyptians, Italians, and British agreed, over objections of the United States, which "advised strongly against the release of the terrorists or any concessions to them."

Later, when all the details were in, President Reagan said as much in a personal phone call placed to Egyptian president Hosni Mubarak. He made it clear that he expected Egypt to extradite the hijackers to the United States, where they would be tried for killing Leon Klinghoffer. "They aren't here anymore," Mubarak explained. "I've already let them go."

The Americans knew differently. "We had a guy—a spy, an agent—in Mubarak's office," Bud McFarlane recalls. The NSA had also made an intercept of a phone call made by Mubarak, in which it was clear that the hijackers were still in Egypt and were on their way to an air base known as Al Maza, on the outskirts of Cairo, planning to get on a plane to Tunis. Oliver North had similar intelligence from an Israeli defense attaché named Uri Simhoni, who told North that he knew which plane the hijackers, along with terrorist mastermind Mohammed Abbas, were departing on, and that his agents in Egypt could get the plane's tail number before it took off. Any action for engagement, however, had to be authorized by the president. In the interim, the U.S. Navy aircraft carrier *Saratoga*, with two F-14 Tomcat fighters, moved into position in the Mediterranean.

Poindexter relayed the intelligence to Bud McFarlane, who was in Illinois with the president, where he was scheduled to address workers on tax reform at a Sara Lee plant in Deerfield. "You may be in a situation where that aircraft goes airborne," McFarlane told Reagan. "If the plane fails to acknowledge or comply with normal emergency signals sent by the Sixth Fleet, what do you suggest we do?" The president didn't hesitate. "Do all the aerial maneuvers possible to demonstrate our firmness," he replied. "If they still don't respond, you can bring it down." A few minutes later, Poindexter called with an update. Israeli agents, using only a flashlight, had gotten the plane's tail number just before Egyptair flight 2483 had taken off. In any case, the plane was in the air. Reagan remained unmoved: "The order stands."

The plan issued to the *Saratoga* was to send the Tomcats up with all lights out and no radio communication, to intercept the plane, and to force it to land at Sigonella, the NATO air base in Sicily, where the terrorists would be removed and flown to the United States. George Shultz worried about the Italian reaction. Diplomacy required him to notify the proper authorities in Italy, but the NSA objected, fearing leaks. The president agreed. "I don't want to give them a chance to say no," he said. "I'll apologize afterward."

Later, when Italian authorities refused permission for the plane to land, he changed his mind and decided to call Italian prime minister Bettino Craxi. "But we couldn't get through to him," Poindexter recalls. Michael Ledeen, an NSA Middle East consultant who was in the Situation Room, called one of Craxi's aides and browbeat him into divulging that the prime minister was off with his mistress, which is where Reagan eventually got through to him to brief him on the mission. Reluctantly, Craxi agreed to let the plane land, but only after Reagan promised that the hijackers would be prosecuted in Italy.

It took some time for the F-14s to locate Egyptair 2483. They intercepted several other planes before they found the right one, in the air off Crete. Creeping up on either side of the jet, they positioned themselves on the end of each wing and behind the tail, switched on their lights, then identified themselves to the pilot of the jet. "You are to follow us and land immediately at Sigonella," they instructed him, using an international frequency reserved for skirmishes.

Less than an hour later, the plane was on the ground at Sigonella. American troops surrounded the jet, only to find themselves in turn surrounded by Italian soldiers, rifles drawn. It was an armed standoff. The U.S. squad was told it had no right to use the base for anything other than NATO activities. Cap Weinberger was on the phone to Carl Steiner, the Navy colonel in charge of the force in Sicily. "Can you get the terrorists off and onto one of our planes?" Weinberger asked. Steiner replied, "Well, Mr. Secretary, I can do that, but I will have to shoot my way through a line of *carabinieri*." It wasn't until Prime Minister Craxi weighed in that the hijackers and their PLO escorts were handcuffed and led away.

The president was ecstatic with the results of the mission. It had come off exactly as planned, a pinpoint operation with no leaks, no casualties, and no American hostages being held. As a senior White House aide pointed out, it was "a God-sent opportunity" and helped to alter the impression of many Americans that their government was "virtually helpless in the face of terrorism." Ronald Reagan resolved to capitalize on the outcome. At a hastily arranged press conference the next afternoon, he trumpeted the capture of the hijackers, offering "a message to terrorists everywhere: 'You can run, but you can't hide,'" the motto of one of his boyhood heroes, boxer Joe Louis. Newspapers in France and Egypt condemned Reagan as "the cowboy," eager to pull the trigger in dangerous situations. Italians were furious at his "reckless trespass" on their soil.* But it played well at home. Reagan's approval ratings rose from the mid-50s to almost 70 percent, literally overnight. Across America, Republicans and Democrats alike celebrated an inspirational victory considered "a major turning point in the hostage era."

The only person not rejoicing in the aftermath was Bud McFarlane, who was tying up loose ends on the intelligence side. Throughout the week of October 14, he sat stone-faced in front of his television set as a succession of political "grandstanders," as he called them, made the rounds of the morning talk shows, heaping praise on the president and his operatives in the affair. One particular exchange brought McFarlane out of his chair. "The president's done a great job," boasted Dave Durenberger, the Republican senator from Minnesota. "Fortunately, we had an agent in Mubarak's office."

We had an agent in Mubarak's office.

McFarlane couldn't believe his ears. The CIA had shared that detail with a delegation of senators, but made it clear the information was top secret and especially sensitive. McFarlane knew the outcome of Durenberger's "outrageous" blunder. "That guy in Mubarak's office is *dead*," he told himself at the time. His suspicion was confirmed. "Our agent in Egypt was never heard from again."

The *Achille Lauro* affair kept the glare off the transfer of arms to Iran. The Middle East operation proceeded apace with more weapons sales to grease the wheels. Throughout the fall, Oliver North, now running the show, negotiated with Manucher Ghorbanifar on another secret transaction, which would send a total of 120 sophisticated HAWK antiaircraft

---

* As a result of protests in Italy, Bettino Craxi's government fell, and he resigned on October 17, 1985.

missiles to Iran in exchange for more hostages—one French and five Americans. North was also overseeing the covert supply of military aid to the Contras in Honduras and Nicaragua.

North, at Bill Casey's insistence, enlisted a consultant to run the supply chains, a master of covert operations—Richard V. Secord, a veteran of the CIA's secret war in Laos, one-time chief adviser to the shah's air force in Iran, and latterly something of an arms merchant himself. Subsequently, Secord was dealing in Iranian government contracts, working in tandem with the CIA. He was perfectly positioned to buy weapons for the Contras— antiaircraft missiles from China, ammunition from Romania, and plastic explosives from Portugal. He'd also directed a shipment of AK-47 rifles from Poland to a Honduran port. And he was marking up his commission at a 30 percent profit. North also looped in Duane "Dewey" Clarridge, the CIA's head of European covert operations, who had access to clandestine diplomatic and transportation channels.

Oliver North kept a close grip on U.S. operations in Nicaragua via a covert operations group known as the Restricted Interagency Group, or RIG, basically three highly placed administration officials who issued orders to support the Nicaraguan resistance to the ambassadors of Costa Rica, El Salvador, and Honduras. Wealthy Republicans such as Joseph Coors, Ross Perot, Nelson Bunker Hunt, and Barbara Newington had already donated hundreds of thousand of dollars to the cause, diverted to a Swiss bank account controlled by North in the name of Lake Resources. By October 1985, the account bulged with almost $2 million in contributions.

In the meantime, Ronald Reagan was focused on his upcoming summit with Mikhail Gorbachev. There hadn't been significant face-to-face dialogue between the two heads of state in more than six years. This summit seemed to promise a breakthrough—"without grand expectations," as Gorbachev predicted, but meaningful, perhaps even a turning point in U.S.-Soviet relations. On October 24, 1985, Reagan addressed the General Assembly of the United Nations, declaring, "When Mr. Gorbachev and I meet in Geneva next month, I look to a fresh start in the relationship of our two nations." The president had reason for qualified optimism. The rhetoric already coming out of the Kremlin was encouraging, and his top aides delivered an upbeat analysis. Gorbachev, they told him, was "from a distinctly different mold" than that of his predecessors; he wasn't a rock-hard ideologue. "In Gorbachev, we were clearly dealing with a new kind of man," George Shultz concluded, "one ready to make radical changes but not ready to bring the Soviet Union in real parity—in terms of missiles and warheads—with us." The stumbling block was the SDI program—Star Wars—which tormented Gorbachev. "Was it science fiction, a trick to make the Soviet Union more forthcoming, or merely a crude attempt to lull us in order to carry out the mad enterprise—the creation of a shield which would allow a first strike without fear of retaliation?" He didn't know. And Reagan didn't know how much leeway he had in his endeavor to negotiate with this man. "What is Gorbachev made of?" he wondered. "What are the influences that have shaped his life? Let's find out everything we can about his family."

In an effort to size up his Soviet counterpart, Reagan sent George Shultz and Bud McFarlane to Moscow for an intimate meeting with Gorbachev in his private office on November 4, 1985. The Americans found the new premier in "a feisty mood." He went on the attack from the moment they were seated, and sought to demonstrate how well informed he was about the U.S. and its political system, but he wasn't shrill or dogmatic, and all in all the diplomats were encouraged.

Some of Gorbachev's information was wildly inaccurate. "I am familiar with the U.S. economy and it is strong," he said, "but of course it relies totally on your aerospace industry." Shultz couldn't help but chuckle at the misconception. McFarlane said, "To give the general secretary an idea about the role of aerospace, if we closed all the factories in our country this year it would only affect about six percent of the GDP." A disbelieving Gorbachev nearly came out of his seat. "This *cannot* be true," he said. "I am informed—this is just false." But they could see that he was agitated. "We knew then that the Soviet intelligence system was not informing their leadership about the true extent of our economy and military industrial complex," McFarlane recalls. "And two weeks later, in Geneva, it was clear that Gorbachev had taken the KGB to task about the productivity of the United States in nondefense areas."

But Gorbachev remained unmoved in his conviction about SDI. "SDI obviously hit a raw nerve," Shultz observed. He let the U.S. delegation know in no uncertain terms that they could expect no slack from him when it came to discussing missile reduction and arms treaties. "The Soviet

Union will only compromise on the condition that there is no militarization of space," Gorbachev stated. Otherwise, he said, nothing would come of the negotiation. "If you want superiority through your SDI, we will not help you. . . . We will not reduce our offensive missiles. We will engage in a buildup that will break your shield."

Afterward, Shultz called his boss in the White House. "Gorbachev," he reported, "wasn't going to be a pushover." The SDI ultimatum was going to be a sticking point, and he had reinforced his deep commitment to Communism as an ideology." Still, Gorbachev seemed receptive to reducing nuclear weapons. It was substantially more encouraging than when Jimmy Carter sent his secretary of state, Cyrus Vance, to Moscow with a message that the president wanted to reduce nuclear weapons, and the Soviets laughed him out of the room. There was an outside chance that Gorbachev would move the needle toward disarmament, but Shultz wondered aloud if the most they could hope to expect from the Soviet premier in Geneva was an agreement to hold another summit.

That wasn't all right by Nancy Reagan. She urged her husband to push beyond just making nice with the Russians. She told him, "Thanks to what you've done in your first term, you are in a position to get something accomplished, but it has to be more than 'peace in our time.' It has to be something that will last beyond your term in office." She was emphatic about this throughout 1984, and even more so in 1985 as Geneva grew near. Taking Bud McFarlane aside during a dinner-and-movie night in the residence, she said, "I want you to tell Ronnie he has an opportunity here—he has an *obligation*—to engage and to listen. He has a chance to make history here. He's got to get a treaty. Make sure he understands that." It was safe to say that he did.

CHAPTER THIRTY-NINE

"A FRESH START"

"We have it in our power to begin the world over again."

—THOMAS PAINE (*Often Quoted by Ronald Reagan*)

Ronald Reagan was noticeably edgy about his meeting with Mikhail Gorbachev. On the night flight to Geneva on November 16, 1985, the president sat alone in the front compartment of *Air Force One*, somber and untalkative, buried in briefings, his shirt clinging limply to his broad shoulders. He was oblivious to the festive stir at the back of the plane, where his wife "bounced around, joking with the staff and the press, her mood uncharacteristically *loose*."

The summit was Nancy Reagan's prize success. For more than a year, she had relentlessly pressed her husband to meet with the Soviets. Margaret Thatcher's Camp David appraisal of Gorbachev had teed it up for the First Lady. This man was a leader very much like the president, she thought, compassionate, a visionary, who had the potential to transcend the rigid Soviet bureaucracy and be a different kind of leader. He'd already demonstrated his willingness to compromise by announcing a reduction of SS-20 missiles fixed on European targets. Now the Reagans were headed to Geneva with world peace the ultimate pursuit. *World peace*—it would seal Ronald Reagan's legacy. Nancy Reagan couldn't have been more excited.

The entourage had in fact left Washington on a discouraging note. The day they took off, the *Washington Post* and the *New York Times* published a letter from Cap Weinberger to the president urging him to renounce the SALT II treaty, signed by Carter and Brezhnev in 1979, and not to give ground on SDI. The disclosure shattered the administration's carefully cultivated image of unity. On the surface, it seemed as though the letter was leaked to deliberately sabotage the summit. Insiders suspected the hand of Bill Casey, who argued vehemently against any efforts to improve relations with the Soviets. A few suspected the leak came from Weinberger himself, as revenge for not being invited to attend the summit. He'd been excluded to give George Shultz a free hand in negotiating the variables of a jampacked agenda—covering trade, bilateral relations, human rights, and regional disagreements—inasmuch as diplomacy traditionally leads with State, not Defense. Moreover, the president had stressed the importance of presenting an image to the Soviets devoid of any trace of hostility or muscle-flexing. "Goodwill without illusion" was his mantra. In any case, Weinberger's letter cast an awkward pall over the U.S. delegation, which had spent months preparing for the meetings.

And no one had prepared more than Ronald Reagan. He had been working for months to get on top of the summit's talking points. He had no illusions about his lack of Soviet expertise. Aside from his long-held convictions about the USSR's corrupt communist doctrine, he knew relatively little about the nation's mode of governance, its weapons, or its capabilities. "I want to know things that count," he told his aides. "What are their strengths and weaknesses? What are their vulnerabilities, economically as well as politically? Find out all you can about the relationship between the Party and the military." He knew he'd have to dust off his skills as a negotiator. "Go back and put together a précis on Soviet negotiating style," he requested of his intelligence team, "both in terms of grand strategy and human terms." He wanted to absorb and understand these topics in order to have the confidence to engage with and negotiate the larger issues.

Between the spring of 1985 and the following November, Donald Fortier, a deputy national security adviser, prepared twelve tutorials for Reagan in answer to his request. Each contained no more than a dozen pages—bigpicture topics that covered modern Soviet history, the KGB and the military, the country's economy, its resources, and Gorbachev's roots and strengths. Reagan devoured them with great enthusiasm. He annotated their margins, dog-eared the pages, and made copies for George Bush, Ed Meese, Don Regan, and Jim Baker. He also held regular meetings with Suzanne Massie, an authority on Russian culture. The president delighted in sharing the information he'd gleaned—about the Soviet Union's agricultural challenges, its vulnerability to seasonal change and how a drought could take food off the table countrywide; how it had an A-plus aerospace team; how its wealth of metals allowed it to do extravagant things, such as build an entire submarine out of titanium that could emit tones at the bottom of the Mariana Trench. This gluttony for Sovietology made Cap Weinberger and Richard Perle nervous as cats. They worried that once the president got to Geneva he would give away the store. The policy issues were only part of his goal. "I want to get to know this guy," Reagan said, referring to Gorbachev. "We're going to have to deal with him for a long time, and it's important I get to know him." He was convinced that if he could sit down, look Gorbachev in the eye, and talk to him, the larger issues would fall into place. Geneva, as he saw it, was a place "to make a fresh start."

The president took two free days to unwind. He and Nancy settled into the Maison de Saussure, an eighteenth-century lakeside château borrowed from Prince Karim Aga Khan IV, the Swiss-born imam of Shia Muslims and a mainstay on the *Forbes* list of wealthiest men in the world. The setting was magnificent, with a mazy sweep of formal grounds and a distant view of the snow-capped Alps. The couple took long strolls in the garden, acclimating themselves to the six-hour time change, and reviewed details for the four-day event. Nancy had Joan Quigley prepare Gorbachev's horoscope before they left Washington. And Reagan took time out to feed the goldfish there, as per a note left for him by the Aga Khan's young son, Hussein. (Apparently not well enough, as one of them died while he was there.)

On Tuesday morning, November 19, 1985, the president was ready to go. He paced impatiently before leaving the château. "Are you ready, Dad?" asked his son Ron, who was in Geneva on assignment for *Playboy*. "Absolutely," the president responded. In the motorcade on the way to the summit, he remained silent, lost in thought.

It was an overcast morning, unseasonably cold. Bitter winds had swept across the city, sending local residents cowering indoors. The weather didn't stop the crush of international press. More than three thousand journalists converged on the scene, held back by double rows of baton-wielding Swiss police. A horde of TV crews jockeyed for position. The summit itself was held at the Villa Fleur d'Eau, an elegant Georgian stone mansion that overlooked a picturesque expanse of Lac Léman. Nancy Reagan had signed off on the location, attracted by its intimate pool house with a fireplace on the fringe of the grounds, where she encouraged her husband to buttonhole Mikhail Gorbachev for a one-on-one talk.

Reagan arrived a few minutes early for the scheduled 10:00 a.m. start. Word circulated among those gathered that the Russian delegation was ten minutes out. Standing in the ornate foyer, the president eyeballed his appearance in the mirrored wall panels and waved over his valet, Eddie Serrano. "Eddie, can I have my coat and scarf?" Jim Kuhn, Reagan's personal assistant, felt an internal alarm. "We were very photo-conscious," Kuhn recalls. He had glanced outside moments earlier at the vast sea of press from around the world poised on risers in front of the entrance to capture the ceremonial greeting. "Reagan looked outstanding," Kuhn recalls. "He had on a finely tailored blue suit; he was perfectly groomed. He looked very much like an aging movie star." But, Kuhn thought, if the fifty-four-year-old Gorbachev gets out of his car without a coat on, looking spry, the seventy-four-year-old Reagan all bundled up was going to get killed in the footage.

"Mr. President, I'm not so sure you're going to need that coat and scarf," he said. "You don't know what Gorbachev's doing. He may not have his coat on." George Shultz, standing nearby, looked at the young assistant as if he were crazy. "It's not an issue," the secretary of state growled, not disguising his displeasure. The Russians were now five minutes out, but Kuhn kept working on the president, who was in a serious frame of mind and didn't want to be bothered. "Jim, it's okay," he said, slipping into a nubby woolen overcoat. "Look," Kuhn persisted, "nobody has any idea what's going on with these coats, but if Gorbachev gets out of his car with just his business suit on . . ." Reagan had heard enough. "All right, Jim, *goddammit,* have it your way," he said, ripping off the coat and scarf and throwing them at Kuhn. "*There!* Is that what you want? Are you satisfied now?"

Kuhn merely smiled. "Now," he said reassuringly, "you're ready to go."

Sirens could be heard in the distance, signaling the arrival of the Gorbachev motorcade. The president moved outside to the front steps of the villa, flanked by Don Regan, George Shultz, and Bud McFarlane. Moments later an armored black ZIL limousine pulled up to the door, its windows darkened. Reagan shuffled down the few steps, as Mikhail Gorbachev emerged, all bundled up, in an overcoat buttoned to his ears, a scarf muffered around his neck, and a dowdy black fedora. As he shook hands with Ronald Reagan, he pointed inquisitively at the president's chest, as if to say, *Where's your coat?* As the two men stood side by side, their ages seemed magically reversed. Walking into the building, Reagan took Gorbachev by the elbow to help him up the stairs and guide him inside. It was a gesture that did not go unnoticed, either by the press or the Russian premier. For the rest of the summit, before each event, Gorbachev leaned in to ask an aide, "Will it be coats on or coats off?"

After handshakes and a marathon photo op, the two leaders were scheduled to speak privately, with just their interpreters present, for twenty minutes in a small salon. "Here we are," Ronald Reagan said, as they settled into armchairs positioned in front of a fireplace. "Between us, we could come up with things that could bring peace for years to come." It was a good opening, if a bit wide-eyed, as their conversation soon devolved into a back-and-forth of confrontational rhetoric, braced by ideological bickering over the usual talking points, including human rights abuses and the arms race. To Gorbachev, it sounded like "the No. 1 Communist and the No. 1 imperialist trying to out-argue each other." But they both felt good to get the points off their chests, sensing an underlying rapport they could explore later on.

There was something about the other that each man admired. Reagan sensed in Gorbachev "an intelligent man and a good listener." There "was warmth in his face." While he stood his ground on Communist Party policy, he was someone the president felt he could negotiate with. Meanwhile, Gorbachev sensed Reagan's "desire [that] they understand each other." Despite their adversarial positions and their irreconcilable differences, Reagan, too, "was a man you could do business with."

Their introductory meeting stretched well past its twenty-minute limit. Don Regan and Bud McFarlane paced in front of the salon door, checking their watches and shaking their heads—when their boss was unscripted, he had a tendency to go off the reservation. They had briefed him well. He'd be on point for twenty minutes, but after that it was anyone's guess. McFarlane suggested that Jim Kuhn rescue the president. "I'm not walking into that room," Kuhn protested. "What do you think?" Regan wondered. Kuhn backed away from him. "I don't think anything. Leave them alone." At the forty-minute mark, Regan told Kuhn, "We're too far behind schedule. You've got to go in and get him." Kuhn demurred. "I don't think the president would want that," he said. The chief of staff and national security adviser continued their pacing and head-shaking. Finally, McFarlane ordered Kuhn to ask George Shultz what to do. Shultz was in an adjoining room, holding court with his Russian counterpart, Eduard Scheverdnadze, the Soviet foreign minister. Kuhn crept in and interrupted the conference. "The meeting's gone way over schedule," Kuhn said. "McFarlane and Regan think it needs to end. They want your input. What do you think?"

Shultz rose from his seat, his face flushed with anger. Ignoring Scheverdnadze, he laced into Kuhn, saying, "If you're that stupid to walk into that room, then you don't deserve the job you have." McFarlane suggested sending in a note. "Are you crazy?" Shultz bellowed. "This is our guy."

Sixty-four minutes after the meeting began, the two leaders finally emerged from the room, smiling to show their encouragement. Each had laid his cards on the table, but acknowledged that they were opening hands. "This guy is different," Reagan told his delegation during a debriefing over lunch at the Villa Palmetto, a mansion next to the Reagans' where the staff was quartered. "We are able to talk; there is a chemistry we developed." The American officials told the president that he had "done good," and they meant it. McFarlane noticed how radiant Reagan was. "You'd have thought he had just gotten an Oscar," he says.

The good news was temporarily suspended by McFarlane's disclosure before lunch was served that eighty HAWK missiles were being sent by Israel to Iran in exchange for hostages. This was the first the president had heard of the operation. He was razor-focused on the summit agenda and was having trouble absorbing what McFarlane was telling him. What's more, the details were complicated—Regan, listening to the conversation, described them as "bizarre"—and difficult to follow. The missiles were being disguised as oil-drilling equipment to evade customs inspections and were siphoned off the Israeli stockpile, which the United States agreed to replenish. If all went according to plan, the exchange would take place two days hence at a secret rendezvous in Portugal.

The president nodded mechanically throughout the conversation; it was clear he had other things on his mind. "Well, let's see what happens" was his distracted response. As soon as McFarlane was finished, Reagan launched back into the debriefing of his and Gorbachev's exchange. "He's really head-up over the Strategic Defense Initiative," the president reported to no one's surprise. Right off the bat, Gorbachev tried to disabuse him of illusions that SDI could bankrupt the Soviet Union. "Make no mistake," the general secretary had warned him, "we can match you whatever you do."

Gorbachev continued this line in the afternoon session. He grew animated as he gave a penetrating criticism of SDI, leaning right across the conference table. "Mr. President, you *cannot* do this!" he exclaimed, striking the table sharply with the side of his hand. "You are taking the war to the heavens." He argued that SDI was forcing both countries into a new, more dangerous arms race. Reagan had anticipated this line of attack and was ready for it . . . with a stunner. "This is something you and I have an obligation to do," he said, "and because we do, once the system has been technically perfected, I fully intend to open our laboratories and to share the technology with you."

He intended to give the Soviets the Star Wars technology.

Gorbachev wasn't buying it. "Mr. President," he scoffed, "you don't understand me. You are spending enormous amounts of money you ought to be devoting to education, health care, and housing."

"Well, we're going to have to find a way to do that, too," he replied in a lighthearted manner.

Again they went back and forth—Gorbachev presenting fiery, passionate critiques of SDI, Reagan rebutting him lightly, almost tenderly, as if he were a consoling pastor of the Beverly Hills Church. Gorbachev took a long moment to collect himself before fixing a steely eye on the president. "We should ban introduction of all space weapons," he said. "Ban them! Ban all space weapons!" They had reached an impasse. After this last go-round, Gorbachev slouched in his seat. "Well, I disagree with everything you've said," he conceded, "but I will reconsider."

He'd reconsider. McFarlane and Shultz exchanged incredulous glances. McFarlane thought, "*Wow!* This is the turning point of history right here."

Ronald Reagan could sense they needed a breather. "How about taking a walk?" he asked Gorbachev.

"*Da*," the general secretary replied. "Maybe fresh air will bring fresh ideas."

This was no spur-of-the-moment thought. The president had concocted it with his wife and Bud McFarlane before they arrived in Geneva. It would give Reagan a chance to take a reading of Mikhail Gorbachev and perhaps to connect with him in a more intimate way, without any interference from their handlers. The pool house at the end of the garden walkway had been staged for just such an opportunity. Logs blazed in the fireplace, the dimpled surface of the silver-blue lake shimmering in the window. The president knew how to break the ice when they settled there. Earlier, he'd overheard Georgy Arbatov, the Soviet foreign policy adviser, take a swipe at his acting career. Now he implored Gorbachev to "tell Mr. Arbitov that I did some good pictures and not just grade-B movies." Gorbachev smiled and said, "I know. I saw you in one where you played the man without legs." *Kings Row*, Reagan's personal favorite.

Gorbachev later acknowledged this helped to break the tension, but soon enough they were at odds again. The president had brought with him a nine-point proposal for arms control that would be raised in the next phase of their negotiations. It was a list of guidelines that the Soviets could browse through, but not choose from, he said; the package was offered on an all-or-nothing basis. Gorbachev read carefully through a Russian translation and rejected it out of hand. Sandwiched between the proposals to reduce nuclear arms by 50 percent and an agreement on intermediate range missiles in Europe was a provision that allowed the United States to proceed with its space-based defense program.

In the course of this exchange, the president let go a doozy. A lifelong Edgar Rice Burroughs fan, he told the Soviet premier that he was certain the U.S. and the USSR would cooperate if Earth was threatened by an invasion from outer space. Gorbachev politely ignored the comment. Discouraged, he shook his head. He could see that he wasn't going to move Reagan off SDI.

The two men put on their coats and went back outside. They'd decided that their attendance at an afternoon plenary session was pointless and that it would be better to catch up on some rest. Pausing in the parking lot while their staffs regrouped, Reagan invited Gorbachev to another summit, this time in Washington. Without hesitation, Gorbachev accepted—and extended the same offer to Reagan: "I invite you to come to the Soviet Union." "I accept," the president said. Neither had consulted their advisers on the matter, but it was a done deal. If nothing else came of the Geneva summit, this was no small thing.

The evenings were devoted to entertainment. Protocol demanded that a dinner thrown the first evening by the Soviets at their Geneva mission would be reciprocated the next night at the Maison de Saussure with the Americans as hosts. On both occasions, the president was at his toastmaster's best, mixing Hollywood stories with jokes that got lost in the translation. Nevertheless, his charm wasn't lost on the Soviet premier, whose "eyes shone" at Reagan's accounts of showbiz elbow-rubbing with Jimmy Stewart and John Wayne.

It was Nancy Reagan who suffered through the events. She found the Russian mission cold, the food distasteful, and the conversation hijacked by Gorbachev's wife, whose loquacious nature unsettled her. "My fundamental impression of Raisa Gorbachev was that she never stopped talking," Nancy complained. "Or lecturing, to be more accurate." The First Lady was accustomed to holding up her end of superficial chitchat with diplomatic spouses—"our husbands, our children, being in the limelight," their supportive roles. Raisa Gorbachev was no such animal. "We have things of substance to discuss," she said earlier over tea. "She was very sharp-tongued," according to an administration official, "insulting at times, short, and curt." She was an educated woman, a professor of Marxist-Leninist theory, and was particularly eloquent when it came to the fundamentals of Soviet policy. Nancy Reagan didn't want to hear it. "Who does that dame think she is?" Don Regan overheard her say after their initial social engagement.

Don Regan was his own protocol liability. The final evening in Geneva, the summit's major players repaired to a salon to review the text of a joint communiqué they'd issue at the conclusion of the negotiations. They were still working on wording about reducing strategic arms by half—the only substantive agreement to come out of the meetings—so that it was agreeable to both sides. In the interim, champagne was passed and the two leaders toasted peace. When the terms of the communiqué were finally approved, the pool photographer from *U.S. News & World Report* was ushered in to record the official handshake. Ronald Reagan and Mikhail

Gorbachev, seated on a lipstick-red couch, edged closer to each other and smiled genuinely, aware that the ensuing photo would appear the next day in newspapers around the globe. As etiquette required, their aides stepped away, but Don Regan, who was standing behind the couch, didn't budge. Instead, he planted his elbows on the cushions between the two leaders and leaned in for the shot. "He just couldn't resist," a disbelieving observer recalls. "Everyone in the delegation kept asking, 'What the hell is Regan doing in that photo?'" But it was too late; he'd literally stepped in it, big-time.

Regan was already on the First Lady's "Least Wanted" list for any number of transgressions. She'd never forgiven him for building an ostentatious patio outside his office in the West Wing and parading himself grandiosely as the administration's "chief operating officer." Keeping his Secret Service detail was another blot on his record, as was his bringing into the administration Pat Buchanan, whose strident right-wing politics she loathed, and his animosity toward Bud McFarlane, of whom she was particularly fond. And there was the interview Regan gave to the *Washington Post* before leaving for Geneva, in which he suggested that details of the negotiations would be too difficult for women to grasp. "They're not going to understand throw-weights or what is happening in Afghanistan," he said. But planting himself in the photo with her husband and Gorbachev completely infuriated her. "How dare he upstage Ronnie's triumph?" she was heard to exclaim. She had already warned Regan to "keep a low profile," insinuating that "people are talking" about his imperious behavior. This latest overstep put the idea in her head that Don Regan should look for other employment.

If nothing else, the Geneva summit came off to the world as a public-relations success. The negotiations didn't yield much in terms of policy breakthroughs. Sure, the two leaders had developed some personal chemistry, but the talks had failed to solve the very complex issues that fueled the arms race. As Gorbachev was quick to reflect, "Both sides are going to have to do an awful lot of work." Reagan agreed. "We remain far apart on a number of issues," he said, addressing a joint session of Congress the night he returned home. But Americans sensed that the winds of change were blowing. Popular opinion of the president's performance in Geneva was strongly positive. An overnight CBS News poll indicated an 83 percent approval of his handling of the negotiations.

Only Larry Speakes had his doubts. The acting press secretary worried that the eloquent Gorbachev might have upstaged Reagan as the more committed peacemaker, and for insurance, Speakes fabricated two quotes that he attributed to Reagan in a conversation with the Soviet chief— "There is much that divides us, but I believe the world breathes easier because we are talking together," and "Our differences are serious, but so is our commitment to improving understanding." This wasn't the first time Speakes put words into the president's mouth. "Larry often made up quotes," Jim Kuhn recalls, "touching up and enhancing them. We were on to him, but couldn't get him to stop."

Ronald Reagan emerged from Geneva enormously encouraged by his personal connection to Gorbachev. Certainly, Mikhail Gorbachev was dynamic, charismatic, and more open-minded than his predecessors were. And, yes, he was forward-thinking, someone who preferred peace over the insanity of mutually assured destruction. "If I could ever get him alone and work on him," Reagan reckoned, "I think I could bring him around." But it was something that Gorbachev had let drop during their personal talks at the boathouse that Reagan deemed more profound than any of the other signals that Gorbachev gave off. Gorbachev let it be known that, "on some level," he believed in God. *A Communist leader believed in God.*

Regardless of the level, with God in the mix, Ronald Reagan was convinced there was hope for peace.

In the meantime, on no level was there any sign of hope in the Middle East. As soon as the president returned to Washington, he learned that upon delivery of the eighty HAWK missiles to Iran, not a single American hostage had been released.

The whole operation was a fiasco. McFarlane had originally issued orders that no weapons were to be exchanged before hostages were released. Convinced that Manucher Ghorbanifar was a con artist, McFarlane wasn't taking any chances. But with the national security adviser preoccupied with negotiations in Geneva, the undertaking was left in the hands of his deputy, Oliver North, who directed the Israelis to go ahead and ship the HAWKs without any assurance of recompense. Meanwhile, the plane carrying the missiles was denied landing rights by Portuguese officials, who were confused that the plane's manifest for medical supplies differed from the crew's explanation that it carried oil-drilling parts. North flew to Lisbon under the alias John Copp to plead the case, but the cargo transport had already returned to Tel Aviv. Desperate, North went rogue. He appealed for help to his old buddy Dewey Clarridge, now the CIA's European operations director. Clarridge agreed to let North use the CIA's sham St. Lucia Airways and arranged with Turkey for clearances for a "humanitarian" flight to Iran. On Monday, November 25, 1985, the plane landed in Tehran and the missiles were delivered.

As McFarlane suspected, Ghorbanifar reneged on the deal. "The missiles arrived, and they were the wrong missile!" he protested. They were obsolete, technically unable to shoot down high-altitude targets.* What's more, they bore Israeli markings, including the Star of David, which was repugnant to the Iranians.

Yes, the operation was a fiasco—and that wasn't the worst of it. To pull off the weapons transfer, Oliver North had enlisted the assistance of master-of-stealth Richard Secord. Secord's job in the HAWK missile transfer was to procure the weapons. Secord had worked in the foreign sales of weaponry in the Pentagon, and he knew where to go to get the job done. Ollie North had persuaded an Israeli arms merchant to deposit $1 million into North's Lake Resources slush-fund account to cover expenses, but Secord had managed to bring the deal in for only $150,000. That left a cool $850,000 profit—which North diverted to the Contra operation.

This rechanneling of funds would later prove disastrous and give name to the Iran-Contra scandal. In the meantime, however, there was hell to pay elsewhere. By enlisting help from the CIA, through his dealings with Dewey Clarridge, North had in all probability breached the Hughes-Ryan Amendment, a 1974 federal law requiring the president to inform a congressional committee before the agency initiates a covert operation. "This

* Actually, Ghorbanifar had requested the wrong missile.

is criminal!" North was told by John McMahon, deputy director of the CIA, who was livid when he learned of the agency's involvement. He insisted his aides produce a proper presidential finding, which would authorize the action and send it to the proper congressional committee. "And I want it retroactive to cover that flight."

The turmoil and disappointment only seemed to increase Ronald Reagan's determination to get the hostages back, whatever the cost. The president was particularly anguished over a letter he'd received from four Americans held captive in Iran. "We know of your distaste for bargaining with terrorists," it said, "but do you know the consequences your continued refusal will have for us? It is in your power to have us home for Christmas. Will you have mercy on us and our families and do so?" *Christmas . . . mercy . . . families*—the letter hit all the right notes that played on the president's heartstrings. "This thing is really eating away at Reagan, and he's driving me nuts about it," North complained to an associate. "He wants them out by Christmas."

It was unlikely that Reagan was driving Oliver North nuts. As far as official records reveal, Ronald Reagan and Oliver North had virtually no direct interaction. Still, the order to bring the hostages home had come down the chain of command, and no doubt North felt the pressure to get something done. He was on a mission, his own mission, inspired by his sense of patriotism and a gung-ho desire to succeed at all costs.

That desire was slowly draining from his boss, Bud McFarlane. McFarlane had been under siege since replacing Bill Clark as national security adviser in October 1983. The pace of crises was unmercifully demanding, but it was the politics, the unrelenting politics, that was wearing him down. In the tug-of-war for control of territory between State and Defense, McFarlane was a one-man demilitarized zone. He'd been caught so often in the Shultz-Weinberger cross fire that he'd actually beseeched the president to choose between the two.

Shortly before the inauguration in January 1985, McFarlane found himself sitting alone with the president in the forward cabin of *Air Force One*. They were returning to Washington from an appearance in California and McFarlane sensed an opening. Treading cautiously, he said, "I think the tension between George and Cap undermines the pace at which you can achieve your goals. At any rate, you'd be better off if you changed one or the other." He knew that Shultz had recently made the same argument, offering to resign and ceding State to Weinberger, claiming it would give the president the policy he was comfortable with. "Unless you choose to do that," McFarlane agreed, "you're going to have to endure meeting after meeting with them and be the arbiter."

A reflective mood came over the president. He sat silently for a while, mulling the situation, before saying, "If I fired George and Cap became dominant, I'd get bad policy recommendations.* And if I kept George, I'd have to fire Cap, and I don't want to do that. He's my friend. So you'll have to act as the arbiter for me. Bring me their opposing views, and I'll make a decision. But I'm not going to fire either one of them." Case closed.

It had worked for a while. McFarlane cha-cha'd gingerly between the two Cabinet officers, neither of whom was a graceful dance partner—Shultz, who treated him contemptuously, and Weinberger, who McFarlane felt was unqualified. There was a lot of stepping on toes in the process, and McFarlane, although fleet of foot on the dance floor, didn't always have the steps. The same went for McFarlane's interactions with Don Regan. From the outset, the domineering chief of staff conspired to blunt the National Security head's authority. It had been a constant struggle for McFarlane to get past Regan's blockades at the president's door. Judge Clark, McFarlane's predecessor, established that the national security adviser would have direct access to the president. Jim Baker had honored the arrangement both with Clark and when McFarlane took over. But Don Regan made it clear that McFarlane reported to him. It was infuriating that a man with no real foreign policy experience and few ideas about national security could interpose himself between the president and his trusted adviser. Regan began offering comments in the morning security briefings, often interrupting McFarlane to press his opinion. And when McFarlane prepared to address a congressional committee to advocate for funds for the MX missile, Regan dismissed him, saying, "I'll go—they don't want to hear from you."

The issue, of course, was control. Regan had made it abundantly clear. "You get it into your thick head that *you* work for *me*," Regan had

---

* Reagan told the NSC's Soviet expert Jack Matlock, "Cap wants to be Secretary of State but he'd be a disaster."

instructed McFarlane, stabbing a finger at him. "I don't want to hear anything more from you."

That tack might have worked on Merrill Lynch underlings, but McFarlane wasn't cowed. "I don't work for you; I work for the president," he said.

"The hell you do! And everything you do comes through me or you'll be out of here. *Got that?*"

"All right," McFarlane responded calmly. "I'll be out of the office by the end of the day."

Don Regan eventually backed down, but soon after returning from the Geneva summit, he rolled out a new offensive. If he couldn't dispose of McFarlane by intimidation, he'd do it with innuendos and allegations. Meg Greenfield, the editorial page director of the *Washington Post*, warned McFarlane that the chief of staff was "putting out stories" about him. According to a "source," which she later named as Regan, McFarlane was reputed to be having affairs with two women—his press assistant, Karna Small, and NBC News White House reporter Andrea Mitchell. The rumors had even been planted anonymously in *Parade*, the Sunday newspaper supplement. Naturally, Regan denied any involvement. "Well, let's leave it at that you're not involved," McFarlane told him during an edgy lunch in Santa Barbara, "but please stop it."

No such luck. Reports of McFarlane's alleged exploits continued to leach out of Don Regan's office. The chief's Mice nicknamed McFarlane "Loverboy," their focus sharpened by Regan to undermine McFarlane's authority. Tensions built steadily between the two ex-Marines and permeated the White House. After a year of this, it was clear to McFarlane that Regan was determined to get rid of him, and if not, then to eviscerate his authority in the Oval Office. McFarlane conceded that he was no longer up to the fight. He was an unusual combination of case-hardened Marine and tender soul, a man who took every setback to heart, who brooded, who was consumed with self-doubt, who seethed with frustration, though outwardly he seemed unflappable, stoic. "He's the most complex man you will ever meet," a former Reagan official recalled. Another official recalled that "he broke down and sobbed more than once in his final weeks at the White House." Several times while recalling those days for this book, he stopped to choke back tears. For a Vietnam vet who had never been wounded in battle, who had faced down Hafez al-Assad and bloodthirsty Iranian clerics, the pitched fight with Don Regan was taking its toll.

A final showdown came in the fall of 1985, during deliberations over a five-year plan to balance the budget through deficit reduction. Cutting the size of government was one of Ronald Reagan's key objectives, the tent pole of his presidential campaigns, and he put his weight behind a scheme hatched by two Republican senators, Phil Gramm and Warren Rudman, and a Democrat, Fritz Hollings. The bill, known as Gramm-Rudman-Hollings, legislated automatic across-the-board budget cuts in each of the five years, regardless of the impact they would have on government programs. Senate Republicans had stuck their necks out to support the cuts, risking the anger of their elderly constituents by voting to slash Social Security cost-of-living adjustments (COLAs) and other popular entitlement programs.

Gramm-Rudman-Hollings, while appealing to conservatives, was loaded with political obstacles. Cuts across the board *meant* cuts across the board—an astonishing $50 billion hacked dispassionately from the budget—which did not spare even defense spending. The measure earmarked an automatic cut of $10 billion for the Pentagon. If the president sought to continue the military buildup and SDI, it practically required him to come up with new taxes to finance them. "*Never!*" Ronald Reagan bellowed in response. "When Mondale said what our country needs is a tax bill, I said, 'There'll never be a tax bill as long as I'm President of the United States.'" He'd meant it then, and he was doubling-down now. At the last minute, though, the president took Social Security cuts off the table as being too painful for public consumption and vulnerable to Democratic retaliation. Military spending was also untouchable. He'd basically stripped the bill of its belt-tightening guts and left the Republican coalition that had backed it hanging out to dry heading into midterm elections.

Initially, Don Regan had used his bully pulpit to sell the president on Gramm-Rudman-Hollings (before he understood that it jeopardized the administration's defense program). At a morning White House staff meeting in the Roosevelt Room, Regan announced to those attending that there would be unilateral support for the bill. Bud McFarlane sensed reckless haste and sought to put the brakes on. "I think we need to discuss this," he said, interrupting Regan. McFarlane "knew the president didn't understand the risks, probably didn't grasp the specifics of the bill." He told Regan that the president needed to know the choices involved.

The chief of staff threw an all-out tantrum, pounding on the table and firing off expletives. "*No!*" he screamed, flying into a rage. "No such choices!" It was a startling spectacle, and those watching it cut open-mouthed glances at one another. Bud McFarlane decided he'd had enough.

On November 26, McFarlane flew out to California, knowing the president would be at the ranch for Thanksgiving. He'd already written a letter of resignation and dropped it off with a military adjutant. Once before, Ronald Reagan had refused to accept McFarlane's resignation, but this time would be different. McFarlane had an ace he intended to play. When the two men met in a Los Angeles hotel suite on December 2, McFarlane said, "I need some more time with my family"—the magic phrase he knew the president wouldn't dispute. "It was a cop-out," McFarlane admits in retrospect, "but unassailable. Family was the one thing Ronald Reagan placed above service to country."

Still, the president seemed troubled by the situation. "Bud," he said, "I have never had at any time in my life someone who is indispensable to me. I'd like you to reconsider, but . . ."

McFarlane took him off the hook. "Mr. President," he said, "the time has come."

Most accounts of the meeting contend that McFarlane recommended his deputy, John Poindexter, as his successor, but he maintains the president never asked. Had he done so, McFarlane says he might have named Undersecretary of State Lawrence Eagleburger or Navy secretary John Lehman. Poindexter, whom he admired as a solid naval officer, had no real experience serving with civilians. The job required that the national security adviser engage with those who have an influence on policy, specifically the U.S. Congress and the press. Poindexter, he knew, was dismissive of both bodies, an attitude not uncommon among military officers. The political process offended him.

In McFarlane's estimation, John Poindexter was not the right man for the job. He was a classic number-two man, much like Mike Deaver, who must have recognized a fellow traveler when he saw one. When Deaver got wind of Poindexter's imminent appointment, he rushed to a pay phone and called Nancy Reagan. "It's a big mistake," he warned the First Lady. "He's too weak to mediate between Defense and State."

Mrs. Reagan understood the stakes. The second term was off to a rocky start. Aside from the Geneva summit, the White House appeared to be in disarray, its policies neither well defined nor well served. She'd admired Bud McFarlane, felt he'd given the president honest, often difficult advice. John Poindexter, as far as she knew, was a blank slate. Would he have the president's back? She had no clue. "I think it's too late," she told Deaver. "It's already settled."

CHAPTER FORTY

"SO FAR DOWN THE ROAD"

"Into the darkness they go, the wise and the lovely. Crowned
With lilies and with laurel they go; but I am not resigned."

—EDNA ST. VINCENT MILLAY

O n the morning of December 5, 1985, the day after his appointment, Admiral John Poindexter, the fourth national security adviser in Ronald Reagan's presidency, visited the Oval Office for the first time in his new official capacity to deliver the finding required by the CIA that gave retroactive approval to the transfer of TOW missiles to Iran.

It was an extraordinary document. It clearly laid out the arms-for-hostages arrangement and instructed CIA Director Bill Casey not to brief Congress on it. In a separate memorandum, Casey advised Reagan to sign it, and sign it the president did, giving it nothing more than a cursory glance and saying nothing. "He understood what it laid out," Poindexter insists. "He thought it was no big deal to sign the finding; if necessary, we could clarify it later." If the new national security adviser had misgivings about it, he kept them to himself, but his subsequent actions spoke volumes. Rather than circulating copies of the finding to the usual selection of key Cabinet officers and depositing it in the NSC archives, as one normally would, he put the original in the safe of his counsel, Paul Thompson, and left it at that. Later, Poindexter admitted that he realized the document could cause "significant political embarrassment" to the president. At the time, he decided, "anyone who wanted to see it could come to my office and I'd show it to them."

With the finding authorizing the operation properly signed, events began to unfold at a breakneck pace. Oliver North, sensing an ally in the new national security adviser, sent Poindexter a long, rambling message making the case for keeping the Iran operation alive. It laid out a new, bigger, and more fantastic arms sale to trigger the release of more hostages. The United States would send Iran a mind-boggling 3,300 TOWs and 50 HAWK missiles, but in staggered increments, each shipment eliciting the release of one hostage. When all was said and done, they'd have one French and five American hostages to show for the swap. "We all agree that there is a high degree of risk in pursuing the course we have started," North wrote, "but we are now so far down the road that stopping what has been started could have even more serious repercussions." To jack up the stakes, he mentioned the likelihood of additional hostage seizures, hostage executions, and "a renewed wave of Islamic terrorism."

Poindexter was sold. He sent North flying off to New York to gauge the Israelis' interest in continuing as intermediaries, and from there on to London to make arrangement for the missile sale with his trusty supporting cast: Secord, Kimche, Ghorbanifar, and the financiers. All that was holding things up was the president's approval.

A powwow to discuss the situation was convened in the Reagans' White House residence on Saturday, December 7, 1985, with nearly all the president's principal advisers in attendance. Only George Bush was absent, in Philadelphia to attend the Army–Navy football game, though some observed that this provided him with cover in case any blowback threatened his presidential ambitions. The rest—Shultz, Weinberger, Regan, McFarlane, and John McMahon (sitting in for Bill Casey, who was in New York for treatment for prostate cancer)—lounged on sofas and chairs grouped in the front of the grand Palladian window at the west end of the main hallway. The president, dressed for the weekend in a western pearl-button shirt and jodhpurs, was perched atop a camel saddle and rocked back and forth, distracted, as Rex, a frisky King Charles spaniel that Nancy had adopted only a day earlier, darted about.

McFarlane, returning informally only days after his resignation, laid out

North's scheme in great detail. Shultz and Weinberger, in another rare show of unity, expressed vehement opposition, arguing that it betrayed U.S. policies against negotiating with terrorists and would only encourage more hostage-taking. Weinberger pulled no punches. "I think this is a terrible idea," he said, before spending a half hour explaining to the president that such an arms deal violated the U.S. embargo against selling weapons to Iran. And the operation raised any number of other legal issues. Don Regan and John McMahon agreed. Reagan was undaunted. "Look," he said, "if I've got a child kidnapped for ransom, I don't believe in paying ransom. But if I suddenly discover there's somebody else who might be able to get that child back from the kidnapper and knows a way to get it back, yes, I'd reward that individual." A missile exchange was one way of doing that. He was adamant that "no stone be left unturned," reducing the arms transfer to "Israel selling some weapons to Iran." He certainly didn't intend to disengage. "The American people will never forgive me if I fail to get the hostages out over this legal question."

Rather than belaboring the pros and cons, it was suggested that McFarlane join Oliver North in London to discuss all the options with Manucher Ghorbanifar and the Israelis and report back to the president. McFarlane, who was already regretting his resignation, was only too happy to get back into the game. And he had never met Ghorbanifar, who seemed to be holding the crucial cards. The president opted to think it over.

He concluded the meeting by saying, "It's a risky operation. But I couldn't forgive myself if we don't keep trying. If it should ever become public, I think I can defend it, but it will be like trying to describe how many angels can dance on the head of a pin."

It was a rare occasion when Ronald Reagan rejected the advice of his most trusted advisers—especially the secretaries of State and Defense—but this was an instance when his heart led him to make a murky choice. Those who knew him well chalked it up to his eternal optimism and unwillingness to retreat. Aides knew he tended to deal in sweeping principles. He didn't have a great grasp of the technical aspects of policy. As an official pointed out, "He didn't know the difference between a ballistic and a cruise missile." But he knew what he felt: the safety of the hostages trumped legal niceties. Still, no final decision was rendered that day. The plan called for some due diligence, and Shultz, Weinberger, and Regan left the residence feeling that the operation would effectively be shut down. Caspar Weinberger recalled telling his deputy, "The baby has been strangled in its cradle."

O thers heard the baby crying for its bottle. At a meeting in London, on December 9, McFarlane witnessed a fired-up Oliver North actively pursuing a third arms deal with Ghorbanifar, Dick Secord, and the Israelis. The encounter, at a posh safe house in the West End, revealed a troupe of players eager to engage. McFarlane was stunned at their collegial complicity, especially at the appearance of Manucher Ghorbanifar, who wasn't at all the kind of diplomat he'd expected. "If you had to cast somebody as a shrewd, rather brutal, husky child of criminals, this was Ghorbanifar," McFarlane recalls. "He was nothing but a self-interested arms merchant." McFarlane's antennae were already twitching. A few months earlier he'd been approached by Michael Ledeen, the Middle East consultant, who told him Ghorbanifar was asking for Phoenix heat-seeking air-to-air missiles, the United States' most technologically sophisticated weaponry in the naval inventory. "Mike, you cannot be serious!" McFarlane bristled. "This is a system we don't even sell to our allies." McFarlane sensed they were being taken to the cleaners, but it wasn't until meeting Ghorbanifar that he realized the extent of the full scrub. The guy was never going to deliver what he'd promised.

It was time to cut bait. "The President has decided this is not developing in the direction we had anticipated," McFarlane told Ghorbanifar. "The opportunity for nurturing a successor to the Ayatollah is not evident, so the President has approved closing down the operation." Ghorbanifar flew into a predictable rage. He hurled a volley of accusations at the Americans, accused them of cheating Iran, not dealing in good faith. "The hell with the hostages! Let the Hezbollah kill them!"

McFarlane had heard enough. "Go pound sand!" he told him, and strode out of the room.

The next morning, Ronald Reagan got a full report from his former national security adviser. The deal wouldn't bear fruit, McFarlane warned the president, explaining that there was no real definable opposition cell in

Iran worthy of support to either push out or succeed the ayatollah. As far as he could tell, all real dissent had been effectively eradicated by the Revolutionary Guard. Every decent family in Iran had lost a father, a brother, a husband. And then there was Ghorbanifar, "a borderline moron, one of the most despicable characters [McFarlane] had ever met." Despite all this, McFarlane could tell his message wasn't getting through. "The president's gut sentiment on this was totally different," he says. "He would have liked to have seen the government of Iran overthrown, but it was the hostages that still moved him, not the geopolitics of it." Nevertheless, McFarlane advised the president that he had shut down the operation. Reagan was visibly chagrined. "I wish we could have found a way to keep it going," he said.

That wish would lead the president further into trouble.

O liver North was already cooking up a plan. He began working the weapons angle with John Poindexter, who was disposed to keep the operation going. They decided to simplify the process by eliminating Israel from the picture and dealing directly with the Iranians. Without a middleman, they could show a tidy profit—which could be used to underwrite Project Democracy, North's covert Contra operation. The overall plan was baldly illegal, putting the United States in a direct deal with Iran, but if they worked it using freelancers instead of the CIA or the Defense Department, it would eliminate, so they thought, a good deal of the risk.

A parallel scenario was unfolding that interfaced with the North-Poindexter scheme. On January 2, 1986, Amiram Nir, Israel's expert on terrorism, explained to North and Poindexter that Israel's government was prepared to release Shiite prisoners with the understanding it would encourage Hezbollah to free the American hostages. He had already discussed the plan in London with Ghorbanifar, who suggested that shipping four thousand TOWs to Iran would certainly grease the wheels and go a long way toward aiding "Ollie's boys in Central America." Nir, knowing North and Poindexter were keen to divert money to the Contras, mentioned the use of profits from the TOWs for "other cooperative activities." Israel, for that matter, also stood to profit. By shipping its arsenal of outdated TOWs to Iran, Israel would get theirs replenished with the U.S.'s latest, more technologically advanced version of the missiles. It was a win-win-win-win situation, if they all ignored the law. America got its hostages, Iran got its missiles, Israel got a weapons upgrade, and the Contras got financial support.

The president bought it. On January 6, after idly perusing a draft of the proposal, he signed a new finding that permitted the sale of weapons to Iran without notifying Congress. He wasn't particularly troubled by the legal consequences—Ed Meese assured him he had "inherent powers as commander in chief" and that if he signed a finding it was legal. Nor was the president troubled by Ghorbanifar's involvement, despite the thumbs-down review Bud McFarlane had given him. As John Poindexter later pointed out, "Sometimes you have to deal with pretty rotten characters." Bill Casey assured the president that Ghorbanifar was essential to freeing the hostages.

It was Casey, more than anyone, who persuaded Ronald Reagan to pursue the initiative. At a National Security Council meeting in the Oval Office the following day, the ailing CIA director led the charge, explaining that the hostages would be released in late February if all went according to plan. Shultz and Weinberger continued to rail against the sale of arms to Iran, unaware that the president had already signed the finding authorizing it. In fact, they'd been purposely kept in the dark. "Casey believes that Cap will continue to create roadblocks until he is told by you that the President wants this to move NOW and that Cap will have to make it work," North wrote to Poindexter on January 15. Two days later, Casey reported that Weinberger had called him to say that "his people have looked it over and signed off on the project," but this would have been news to Weinberger, who never made such a statement, much less signed off on it. In any case, once the president was told that Cap was on board, he signed another new finding along with a memorandum prepared by Oliver North that set the arms-for-hostages deal in motion. Though the president never bothered to read the memorandum,* there was no question he knew what he was doing. The finding ordered Cap Weinberger to release 3,504 TOW missiles to the CIA on January 17. In his diary entry later that night, Ronald Reagan wrote: "Involves selling TOW anti-tank missiles to Iran. I gave the go ahead." About the hostages, he'd written earlier: "We sit quietly by & never reveal how we got them back."

---

* John Poindexter signed it for him: "RR per JMP."

The president was an ardent believer in coincidence and had noted as serendipitous the two events planned for January 28, 1986. His sixth State of the Union address was scheduled for eight o'clock that evening, during which he planned to talk up his tax reform program and to congratulate the nation on its overall good health. And because of two previous weather-related postponements of NASA's latest shuttle launch, the *Challenger* was set to lift off sometime just after 11:30 that morning. At last word it was all-systems-go.

Two major events, two presidential priorities.

Ronald Reagan was particularly interested in the shuttle's mission inasmuch as it marked the flight of the first private citizen into space—Christa McAuliffe, a thirty-seven-year-old high school teacher from New Hampshire. It was the kind of heroic story he could relate to. He'd juggled his schedule to fit in a visit to the Kennedy Space Center in Cape Canaveral to coincide with the liftoff. However, he'd caved in to aides who oversaw a last-minute rewrite of his speech that required rehearsal, and the trip was scratched.

The State of the Union address was roiled in dispute. At the congressional leadership meeting that morning, Tip O'Neill took Reagan to task for painting a misleadingly rosy picture of the unemployment rate that he intended to promote later that evening. O'Neill was especially peeved at the president's claim that Americans on the unemployment rolls were content with their circumstances. "Those people out there can get jobs if they really want to," Reagan argued. He cited a situation he believed to be endemic, in which "the fellow on welfare" looking for work makes a series of job-seeking calls, but when he is finally offered work "he hangs up."

"Don't give me that crap!" the Speaker bellowed. O'Neill, a passionate advocate for the poor, was beside himself. This was the same kind of fictitious anecdote the president used when talking about the black woman in Chicago living high on the hog from welfare checks she collected under various names. "The guy in Youngstown, Ohio, who's been laid off at the steel mill and has to make his mortgage payments—don't tell me he doesn't want to work. Those stories may work on your rich friends, but they don't work on the rest of us. I'm sick and tired of your attitude, Mr. President."

Alan Simpson, the senator from Wyoming, tried intervening to calm things down, but O'Neill was unbowed. "I'm sorry," he said, "but I just can't sit here and listen to him talk like that."

Tip O'Neill and Ronald Reagan came at the issue from radically different perspectives. O'Neill was sympathetic to people who struggled as a group. While Reagan was sympathetic to struggling people as individuals, it didn't extend to seeing the wisdom in providing practical assistance. From his childhood, he knew well what it was to be poor, but his own up-from-the-bootstraps story had left him with disdain for those who couldn't manage the same feat. His attitude was: "This is America, land of plenty!" A handsome, charming, white, and educated but self-made man, he didn't see the impediments that others viewed as being insurmountable. As far as he was concerned, America provided boundless opportunity and people were responsible for their own fates. That perspective infused all of his views about domestic policy.

The you'll-do-fine-on-your-own attitude also colored the growing AIDS crisis, which the Reagan administration regarded with apparent indifference. The president's staff wanted him to say something in the State of the Union about the sexually transmitted virus that was decimating the nation's gay community. As many as 12,500 deaths had been credited to AIDS in 1985, with projections ranging into the hundreds of thousands over the next few years, but so far the administration's response to the epidemic was nonexistent. According to the White House physician John Hutton, Reagan thought of AIDS as though "it was measles and would go away." Rock Hudson's death in October had jolted him awake, but the White House still avoided the crisis as if it were, well, the plague. The president's speechwriters thought he needed to acknowledge the disease, and to do it in a forum like the State of the Union address, where it would have the greatest impact.

Would he say the word "AIDS"?—that was the question being debated right up until the deadline. It was a delicate topic in 1986, when a large part of America refused to legitimize homosexuality. In the end, Reagan decided he would direct the country's surgeon general, Dr. C. Everett Koop, to launch a national study of the disease, but there were provisos. The Republican base had to be satisfied. No mention would be made of prevention through sex education or the use of condoms.

Just before noon, the president was briefing Larry Speakes on the details of the speech when Pat Buchanan burst through the Oval Office door.

"Sir," he cried, "the *Challenger* just blew up!"

The news stunned Ronald Reagan. "Oh, no!" he sighed, covering his face with a hand.

Jim Kuhn, his assistant, ushered the president, Don Regan, and Pat Buchanan into the small study adjoining the Oval Office, where a television was already tuned to a news report. "We watched that footage play over and over without anyone saying a word," Kuhn recalls. There it was, in living color: the *Challenger* lifting off flawlessly and rising with grace for a minute before erupting in a ball of flame. "Reagan seemed unable to make sense of it in his head, as if it were a movie he couldn't follow." The death of Christa McAuliffe touched him personally. Months earlier, he'd made the announcement that she had won the coveted seat on the flight, and her involvement in the disaster, he said, "added proximity to the tragedy—made it seem even closer and sadder to me."

Once the immediate shock wore off, the staff underwent plans to postpone the evening's State of the Union address. Instead, the president went on TV to offer some consoling words to the country, which had witnessed the catastrophe and was traumatized with collective grief. Relying on a script hastily cobbled together by a then relatively unknown speechwriter, Peggy Noonan, he appeared grim-faced, even a bit lost.

"Ladies and gentlemen," he began haltingly, "I had planned to speak to you tonight on the State of the Union, but the events of earlier today have led me to change those plans." He explained his own shock and regret before singling out the entire flight crew by name. "We've grown used to wonders in this century. It's hard to dazzle us. But for twenty-five years, the United States space program has been doing just that. We've grown used to the idea of space, and perhaps we forget that we've only just begun. We're still pioneers. They, the members of the *Challenger* crew, were pioneers."

He paused to collect himself, overcome by emotion. "I want to say something to the schoolchildren of America who were watching the live coverage of the shuttle's takeoff," he said. "I know it is hard to understand, but sometimes painful things like this happen. It's all part of the process of exploration and discovery. It's all part of taking a chance and expanding man's horizons. The future doesn't belong to the fainthearted. It belongs to the brave. The *Challenger* crew was pulling us into the future, and we'll continue to follow them."

He ended with a dramatic flourish.

"The crew of the space shuttle *Challenger* honored us by the manner in which they lived their lives. We will never forget them, nor the last time we saw them, this morning, as they prepared for their journey and waved goodbye and 'slipped the surly bonds of earth to touch the face of God.'"

The quote was from the poem "High Flight" by John Gillespie Magee, a nineteen-year-old Canadian Air Force pilot who died in an inflight collision and had written those words on the back of an envelope that eventually reached his parents. The president was already familiar with the verse. In some recollections, he said it was emblazoned on a plaque outside the grade school of his daughter Patti. Other times, he insisted it was carried through World War II by a pilot in the U.S. Marine Corps—his old Hollywood buddy, Tyrone Power. Either way, the speech touched the TV audience as few had in American history. Appreciative phone calls and mail poured into the White House, exceeding any such outpouring in the past.

One viewer watching at home recounted being overcome by the president's words. "As I listened to him, I had a tear in my eye and a lump in my throat," Tip O'Neill later admitted. He considered Ronald Reagan "the best public speaker I've ever seen," and that included Franklin Roosevelt and John Kennedy. Still, O'Neill refused to credit the president for anything much more than a magnetic stage presence. "He lacked most of the management skills that a president needs," the Speaker reflected. "But let me give him his due: he would have made a hell of a king."

"Magisterial" is a word that could have been applied to Ronald Reagan's popularity with the general public. People identified with him as they might an understanding, big-hearted uncle. They focused not so much on what he said about policy and more on his reassuring demeanor. During the *Challenger* speech, he used all his actorly skills: the way he cocked his head ever so slightly to the side while maintaining perfect eye contact with the camera; the brief catch in his delivery as he appeared to be collecting his thoughts; his voice, soft but resolute; his comfort with the camera and, therefore, with the audience on the other side of it. He conjured everyone's ideal memory of being read to as a child.

This is what the public wanted most in their president. For those on the wrong side of his domestic policy decisions, such as letting the Organ Donor Registry lapse and all but ignoring the AIDS crisis, the rhetoric might ring hollow. But they were a distinct minority. In the wake of the *Challenger* remarks, his approval rating climbed to an unheard-of 74 percent.

When the president finally delivered his State of the Union address on February 4, 1986, not a word was mentioned about the AIDS epidemic. The next day, facing fresh criticism for that absence, he addressed an audience of employees from the Department of Health and Human Services, telling them, "One of our highest public-health priorities is going to continue to be finding a cure for AIDS." Later that same day, his new budget proposal called for deep cuts in AIDS research. His conservative base was opposed to candid talk about the disease and specific methods that spoke to its prevention. He also had to contend with remarks such as this statement by Pat Buchanan in a newspaper column: "The poor homosexuals. They have declared war on nature, and now nature is exacting an awful retribution."

Just days after the State of the Union address, the administration faced another test of its values when the Philippines prepared for a historic election amid a crisis of corruption.

Most U.S. officials thought the Reagan administration should back away from the ruling regime, but the president's judgment was colored by his personal feelings for Ferdinand Marcos. The Philippine head of state had ruled the country since 1965, his tenure branded by self-dealing and violence. Historically, elections challenging his presidency were "marked by considerable fraud," to put it gently. In 1983, Marcos had ordered the assassination of a key rival, Benigno Aquino Jr., who was shot as he stepped off a plane from the United States. Nevertheless, Marcos was considered a frontline American ally, and as the president noted, the Philippines were a pillar "of great importance to the United States, anchoring our huge military stations there, Clark Air Base and the Subic Bay naval base," for which the United States paid an annual $180 million stipend. Reagan considered Marcos a friend, an anticommunist partner. They'd established personal warmth and a rapport during meetings at the White House; Nancy Reagan and Imelda Marcos shared a country-club mentality and bonded over clothes. But political winds in the Philippines had shifted. Public outrage was steadily building against Marcos.

To reassert his command, Marcos called a snap election, hoping to get himself reelected before anyone could mount a serious challenge. Several rivals announced their candidacy, but the strongest opponent to emerge was Corazon Aquino, a political neophyte and widow of the assassinated opposition leader. She announced that if she won, she would put Marcos on trial for the murder of her husband. The prospect troubled Ronald Reagan. He was further alarmed by a conversation with *New York Times* managing editor Abe Rosenthal, who had interviewed Aquino and told the president over dinner that she was "a dazed, vacant woman . . . an empty-headed housewife [with] no positions."

Events quickly deteriorated. Aquino's populist candidacy caught fire with Filipinos, despite the fact that she was denied any access to the state-run media, which was controlled exclusively by Marcos confederates. Word filtered back to Reagan through U.S. State Department channels that "the Marcos people were considering abducting Mrs. Aquino." Still, he refused to take a stand against Ferdinand Marcos. The president had been disgusted by the way the United States had abandoned the Shah of Iran, and he vowed not to repeat the mistake with Marcos. Yet he was caught between a rock and a hard place. If Marcos won the election by fraudulent means, Congress promised to cut off American assistance to the Philippines. And on February 4, 1986, when more than a million Filipinos turned out in Manila to show support for Aquino, it was clear that she stood a strong chance of unseating Marcos.

Everything depended on a free and honest election, which was highly unlikely, considering what was at stake for the Marcos regime. There were already indications of widespread intimidation, vote-buying, and violence. "The Philippine elections are looking more and more like the kind of elections they have in the Kremlin," said Alan Cranston, who chaired a Senate committee established to track the process. In an attempt to contain the situation, Reagan sent a delegation of observers to the Philippines to monitor the election and report irregularities.

On February 8, before the vote count was official, Marcos declared himself the winner. Nevertheless, "a very disturbing pattern" of widespread cheating and fraud was reported by Senator Richard Lugar, who headed the president's fact-finding group. The Philippine government was rigging the tally, Lugar found; ballots were being destroyed, returns falsified. One Marcos critic was chased and killed by six masked gunmen in the town square of San Jose de Buenavista; the bodies of ten opposition leaders were found in the Quirino Province. A day or two later, Reagan was told that Aquino had won more than 70 percent of the vote, yet on February 15, the Philippine National Assembly formally announced that Ferdinand Marcos had been elected to a new six-year term. "I am the President," he gloated victoriously.

Despite evidence to the contrary, Reagan declared during a contentious news conference that the United States was remaining neutral. His ambassador to the Philippines, Stephen Bosworth, cabled that "the election has effectively cost Ferdinand Marcos his remaining political legitimacy and credibility," but the president remained unwilling to accept that view. According to George Shultz, "Ronald Reagan still had no intention of abandoning Marcos, nor could he conceive of Marcos's departure from office." It didn't help matters that Don Regan had already served notice that even if Marcos won fraudulently, "if it's a duly elected government and so certified, you'd have to do business with it."

Marcos flat-out refused to step down, but the people of the Philippines had other designs. On February 23, 1986, Aquino supporters mobilized in the streets of Manila as government troops prepared to confront them. It was a tense standoff that eventually culminated in the army's refusal to fire its weapons. "The Marcos era has ended," Philip Habib, Reagan's special emissary, notified the president. George Shultz agreed: "He's had it." It was time to move on.

At Reagan's behest, the White House sent a message to Marcos offering him and Imelda sanctuary in the United States. On February 25, they fled Malacañang Palace to Clark Air Base and were airlifted to Guam, with an entourage of eighty-nine aides, suitcases and crates bulging with jewelry and gold bars, and $7 million in cash looted from the Philippine treasury.* Later, it was determined that perhaps as much as $10 billion had been

---

* Kitty Kelley reported that Nancy Reagan received "an emerald necklace worth $60,000 from Imelda Marcos (Kelley, *Nancy Reagan*, p. 445).

siphoned off by the Marcoses and stashed in secret offshore shell companies and bank accounts in places ranging from Hong Kong to Aruba. Documents showed they owned copper mines in the Philippines, land in Corpus Christi, Texas, and office buildings in New York City. "What we have here is an international mass burglary achieved through classic political skimming," said Representative Jim Leach, a ranking member of the House Foreign Affairs subcommittee investigating Marcos's hidden wealth.

The Reagan administration, on February 6, had given safe passage to another dictator, Haiti's Jean-Claude "Baby Doc" Duvalier, flying him, his wife, his children, and twenty of his relatives on a U.S. Air Force plane from Port-au-Prince to asylum in France, where they lived lavishly, having stashed $400 million—the spoils of an impoverished nation—in foreign banks.

While the evacuations of Marcos and Duvalier were hastened to avoid civil war and bloodshed in their respective countries, they signaled a shift in U.S. policy that propping up authoritarian governments opposed to communism could not be taken for granted. "The Reagan administration deserves credit," Newsday asserted in an editorial, asking: "Is it possible that the U.S. government has finally learned how to shed its ties with repressive governments?"

There might have been a mixed assortment of answers to that question had the public been aware of the plans being drawn in the third-floor office of the Old Executive Office Building, where Oliver North was stepping up efforts to find secret funding for the Contra war in Nicaragua.

O nly hours after Marcos had fled the Philippines, Ronald Reagan approached Congress for $100 million in Defense Department funds for renewal of military aid to the Contras. He presented the legislators with a stark choice. "If the Sandinistas are allowed to consolidate their hold on Nicaragua, we'll have a home away from home for Muammar Qaddafi, Arafat and the Ayatollah," he argued. "If we don't want the map of Central America covered in a sea of red, eventually lapping at our own borders, we must act now."

The White House turned up the heat on congressional leaders who continued to oppose the policy. Republican Henry Hyde led the charge in the House, Red-baiting his colleagues across the aisle. Wyoming representative Dick Cheney did his share, too. Democrats, fearing "another Vietnam," complained that administration officials and their congressional allies were stooping to slur tactics to impugn their patriotism. In response to the criticism, the president softened the allegations, suggesting that Democratic naysayers were "inadvertently" supporting Communists. But Pat Buchanan, his director of communications, was characteristically more candid. In an op-ed piece published in the *Washington Post,* he said, "With the vote on Contra aid, the Democratic party will reveal whether it stands with Ronald Reagan and the resistance, or Daniel Ortega and the communists."

Up until now, bipartisanship had always been more or less a mainstay of the Congress. "Republicans and Democrats went to dinner with each other," recalls Ken Duberstein; "their families socialized. Tip O'Neill's poker games were full of Republicans. We understood each other and wanted to govern." But the tradition of cooperation and teamwork—the show of respect for different opinions—was eroding, due in large part to a growing ideological divide. The civil voice of opposition gave way to hardline rhetoric. If you disapproved of prayer in school, you were godless; if you supported abortion, you sanctioned killing. *If you refused aid to the Contras you were unpatriotic.* In one-on-one encounters, Ronald Reagan was a master of smoothing over rough edges, but during his administration the political polarization became more acute. The shift happened in degrees, masked in part because the president himself covered such partisanship with his trademark warmth.

The president did what he could to maintain harmony, but the Contra issue pushed him into the fray. He applied gentle arm-twisting to holdouts on his aid policy, phoning legislators who resisted, sometimes two or three times a day. He even appeared on television, showing a map of Central America bathed in red and urging Americans to pressure their congressmen to support him. Public opinion, however, was downright cool. Few people perceived a Sandinista threat to their lives, nor were they concerned about Nicaragua. As a result, there was no collective outcry when, on March 20, the House ultimately rejected the $100 million Contra aid package.

The president took it personally. "H—l of a way to run a country," he wrote in his diary that night. In his view, it was "a dark day for freedom."

After the vote was in—and before the dark day was out—he was back in the huddle with his National Security Planning Group staff to hatch an alternate Latin America strategy. He was determined to liberate Nicaragua, which he considered to be in the grip of "an outlaw regime" more harmful than those in the Philippines and Haiti. He often cited Jeane Kirkpatrick's argument that authoritarian right-wing regimes were not as detrimental to American interests as totalitarian communist ones. "A second Libya," he called the Nicaraguan peril, "right on the doorstep of the United States."

As if to underscore the threat of "a second Libya," Muammar Qaddafi steered his country straight into a violent confrontation with the United States.

The president had reached his limit of tolerance for the erratic Qaddafi. He was worse than a nuisance. Evidence of the Libyan dictator's support of terrorism was overwhelming. In 1984 alone, the State Department identified fifteen terrorist incidents traced directly to Libya, including the mining of the Red Sea and a failed attempt to assassinate Egyptian president Hosni Mubarak. And there was strong evidence that Libya was behind the December 1985 terrorist attacks at El Al ticket counters in the Rome and Vienna airports, in which twenty people, including five Americans, were killed. In response, on January 7, 1986, Reagan issued an executive order severing diplomatic ties with Libya. Privately, he told John Poindexter, "The next time we have an incident, a smoking gun that we can pin on Qaddafi, I want to respond."

He didn't have long to wait. Soon after the diplomatic rift was announced, Qaddafi vowed publicly to attack any vessel that sailed within 150 miles of shore—his so-called Line of Death—in the Gulf of Sidra, on Libya's northern coast. This was a clear violation of international navigation laws, which defined territorial waters as extending only twelve miles beyond a country's coast. Qaddafi defied anyone to challenge his edict, knowing that the American Navy routinely patrolled the gulf. "We are ready to die for it," he announced in March, promising to send suicide squads to strike U.S. targets should American naval vessels cross his 150-mile line.

In an effort to reassert the right of navigation, Ronald Reagan scheduled a naval maneuver in the Gulf of Sidra for later in March and ordered the Sixth Fleet into the area just in case. The Sixth Fleet was no small show of force—it comprised three aircraft carriers with 240 warplanes, twenty warships, and several nuclear-powered submarines. Its presence promised to goad Qaddafi's air force into an aggressive response. As early as 1981, Libyan boats had fired on U.S. aircraft flying over the gulf, and intelligence pointed to another imminent attack. As expected, on March 24, Libya launched two SA-5 missiles against U.S. planes. Navy pilots responded by knocking out the radar installation that had guided the missiles. Seventy-two Libyans were killed without a single U.S. casualty. The next day, Qaddafi sent messages to his embassies in Berlin, Paris, Rome, and Madrid to plan a series of terrorist attacks "causing maximum casualties to U.S. citizens and other Western people."

More than ever, Ronald Reagan was determined to subdue the man he called "the crackpot in Tripoli."* He'd already sanctioned a strategy of disinformation—"a little psychological warfare," George Shultz called it—designed to keep Qaddafi off balance in his own country. But some harder evidence was needed to justify stronger measures.

Qaddafi delivered on cue. On April 5, 1986, the president was awakened by John Poindexter, who informed him that a bomb at La Belle discotheque in West Berlin had killed a U.S. soldier and wounded 155 people, about a third of whom were American servicemen. "We have unmistakable proof that Libya is responsible," Poindexter told him. U.S. intelligence had intercepted Libyan mail claiming that the bombing had been carried out successfully "without leaving clues." It was the smoking gun the president had sought.

Reagan ordered an immediate military action, signing a National Security Division Directive the next day. "We have five specific targets in mind," he wrote in his diary—the Tripoli air base, the Benghazi naval base, a terrorist training camp, Qaddafi's desert encampment, and his command headquarters. But leaks about the operation prompted two postponements. And U.S. allies still had to pledge their support. France and Spain refused to allow American jets to fly through their airspace, but Margaret Thatcher granted permission to launch eighteen U.S. F-111s from bases in

* A few days later, Reagan referred to Qaddafi as "the mad dog of the Middle East."

Mildenhall, England; another fifteen jets were to take off from aircraft carriers in the Mediterranean.

The president was determined to keep the mission a secret. To throw the press off the scent, he pretended to keep a scheduled visit to the annual Paul Laxalt lamb fry. "We let the White House staff and the Secret Service get dressed in black tie, thinking they were going to that event," recalls Jim Kuhn. "The motorcade was lined up, our advance guys stood by, the press was ready to cover it." At the eleventh hour, Pat Buchanan was given Reagan's address to the nation to write rather than letting any details leak out through the usual team of speechwriters.

On the evening of April 14, under cover of darkness, the squadron pounded its targets in Libya: "the headquarters, terrorist facilities and military assets that support Muammar Qaddafi's subversive activities," as the president reported in a televised address. Qaddafi's home, the Bab al-Azizia compound in the desert, was among the buildings hit in the raid by a missile that had gone astray. Two of his young sons were injured when bombs blew out the walls of their living quarters, and an adopted infant daughter was killed, though the dictator escaped unharmed. A longstanding executive order forbade the United States from assassinating foreign heads of state, so Qaddafi himself had not been targeted. "If he had been killed," Poindexter admits, "it would have been fine by us." Reagan secretly hoped the Libyan leader had been in one of the targeted locations. During a reflective moment in the Oval Office, he confided to Jim Kuhn, "The one that missed had Qaddafi's name on it."

No matter—the mission, which lasted a total of eleven minutes, sent an unqualified military and public-relations message. It effectively isolated Qaddafi on the international stage, while bathing the president in a triumphant light. His prime-time televised address only hours after the operation presented a strong, uncompromising leader, in command, explaining how once the United States had exhausted all diplomatic options with Libya, he had resorted to force to curb Qaddafi's reckless behavior. "He counted on America to be passive," Reagan said with unsparing tenacity. "He counted wrong." The president's standing, measured by overnight opinion polls, soared to new heights. Seventy-five percent of Americans supported his handling of the raid.

But he'd made one mistake. He had agreed to trade arms for hostages.

CHAPTER FORTY-ONE

"BACK ON THE ROLLER COASTER"

*"In time of war, the truth is so precious, it must
be attended by a bodyguard of lies."*

—WINSTON CHURCHILL

In the wake of the Libya operation, the president's team brought new
energy to the exasperating Iran initiative. In early May 1986, Ronald
Reagan approved a secret mission to send Bud McFarlane to Tehran,
ostensibly to rendezvous with Ali Akbar Hashemi Rafsanjani, the speaker
of Iran's parliament, and Mohammed Ali Khamenei, the country's president. Word had been passed by Manucher Ghorbanifar that these officials,
alleged pragmatists, were willing to entertain the reestablishment of
relations—or, at least, open a dialogue—with the United States. Inasmuch
as there had been no communication between the countries since the Iranian revolution in 1979, any interaction, however modest, had the potential to affect the political dynamic of the Middle East.

In fact, political dialogue was only a pretext for the trip. The primary
objective was the release of American hostages. As an incentive, the plane
carrying McFarlane and Oliver North contained a pallet of HAWK missile
parts the Iranians had requested. Eleven more pallets of HAWK parts,
along with sophisticated radar equipment, were loaded on a second plane,
idling on the ground in Israel. Once the hostages were safely freed, and *only*
then, would McFarlane order the second plane into the air.

The whole operation was not only illegal but dangerous. The American diplomats had no idea whether they'd be welcomed—or detained and held hostages themselves. It was always possible they were walking into a trap. Another member of their delegation was Amiram Nir, Israel's chief terrorism adviser, disguised as an American, which increased the risk significantly. They were all traveling on fake Irish passports and carried suicide pills should the operation go awry. As their plane touched down in Tehran, they noted a banner strung across the airport terminal, featuring an image of the Ayatollah with one of his favorite sayings: "America Cannot Do a Damn Thing."

McFarlane insists he was focused on diplomacy. "I was convinced that a meaningful dialogue could nurture an effective opposition to the clerics in Iran," he says. He says he was oblivious to a parallel scheme North was running that would divert a considerable surplus from the Iranian missile deal to finance the Contra operation in Nicaragua. It was a classic bait and switch. The Iranians were prepared to pay an inflated price for the 236 HAWK parts, which would give Project Democracy an $8.6 million profit. Ghorbanifar would turn a cool $9.5 million for himself. The problem was, no one could deliver on the deal.

The Iranians had no control over the hostages, who were in Lebanon in the hands of Hezbollah. The clerics hardly seemed interested in opening up ties to the West; Rafsanjani and Khamenei never appeared. What's more, new terms were introduced: the Iranians demanded that before any hostages could be released, Israel had to withdraw from the Golan Heights and release fifteen Lebanese prisoners who had been convicted of a series of bomb attacks and were being held in a Kuwait jail. "They're just stringing us along," a disgusted McFarlane told North. "Let's pack up and go."

Ronald Reagan was duly discouraged. "It was a heartbreaking disappointment for all of us," he noted in his diary. But then, on July 25, Father Lawrence Jenco was freed in the Beqaa Valley in Eastern Lebanon after eighteen months in captivity and handed over to U.S. officials in Syria. As a result, the president was advised by Bill Casey and John Poindexter to deliver the eleven pallets of HAWK parts, still on the plane in Tel Aviv, to Iran as a gesture of goodwill. Inexplicably, he signed off on it, despite the fact that the Iranians had failed to honor an agreement on four separate occasions. "It gives us hope the rest of the plan will take place," Reagan wrote in his diary. Yet the president acknowledged the uncertainty of it by saying, "Back on the rollercoaster."

A few days later, Reagan faced a minor health scare. "I've been passing blood in my urine since last night," he wrote on July 28, 1986. His doctor suspected that it was simply an inflamed prostate, but the president was unnerved. He feared he was "falling apart." He was under enormous stress. The White House was in the throes of "a kind of low-level guerrilla warfare" between the conservatives and the pragmatists. They were divided about sanctions on South Africa and conventional weapons reductions with the Soviets. The intelligence agencies seemed to be operating independently of any oversight, often withholding or even distorting information. Bill Casey and John Poindexter pushed their own dark agendas. The chief of staff played personnel off one another, sowing an environment of dissention and discontent.

George Shultz, for one, had had enough. On August 5, he submitted his third letter of resignation. Again the president refused it, but he got the message.

While he was in Santa Barbara on a long-overdue vacation in late August, Reagan planned to address the disorganization, but events intruded. On August 30, 1986, he learned through the State Department that Nicholas Daniloff, the Moscow correspondent for *U.S. News & World Report*, had been arrested on charges of spying. Aides informed Reagan that Daniloff had been set up. Someone had handed him an envelope containing classified papers, and the minute it was in his hands the KGB swooped in and apprehended him. It was a clear case of retaliation. A week earlier, the FBI had caught Gennadi Zakharov, a Soviet attaché to the United Nations, at a subway stop in Queens, New York, red-handed in the act of exchanging cash for classified documents. It was a cut-and-dried case of espionage, which had embarrassed the Soviet Union.

Reagan by his own account was "mad as hell." "We catch a spy as we have this time and the Soviets grab an American—*any* American and frame him so they can demand a trade of prisoners," he said. He immediately cabled Mikhail Gorbachev. "I can give you my personal assurance that Mr. Daniloff has no connections whatever with the U.S. government. If you have been informed otherwise, you have been misinformed."

Gorbachev promptly rejected the president's message, announcing publicly that Daniloff was "a spy who was caught in the act." He offered an immediate trade of the two detainees. The president refused to sanction it. That would be caving in to the bogus Cold War gambit. Then a new twist: it emerged that Daniloff *had* been compromised by the CIA. He'd never been on the agency's payroll, but he'd occasionally passed on sensitive material to various American officials in Moscow. This changed the dynamic. Suddenly, Reagan was satisfied with a one-for-one trade, and on September 29, 1986, Daniloff and Zakharov were released simultaneously to their respective embassies. Reagan was criticized by the right-leaning media for, in essence, swapping a spy for a hostage. He consoled himself that he'd gotten the better end of the deal by securing the freedom of several Soviet dissidents, thrown into the exchange at the last minute. "In the final analysis," he believed, "we stood our ground and the Soviets blinked."

The Soviets remained upset about the matter—they felt as though American authorities had fudged the facts and were "treating them as less than a superpower." Eduard Shevardnadze stormed into the White House on September 19 to express Russia's displeasure, carrying with him a letter from Mikhail Gorbachev to Ronald Reagan. It was six pages long, mostly a condemnation of the way the U.S. handled the Zakharov–Daniloff business, accusing the United States of using it to incite a "massive, hostile campaign" against the Soviet Union. There was also a rehash of the various proposals they'd discussed in Geneva concerning medium-range missiles in Europe and nuclear testing. "There has been no movement on these issues," Gorbachev protested. "They will lead nowhere unless you and I intervene personally. I have an idea, Mr. President, that in the very near future and setting aside all other matters, we have a quick one-on-one meeting, let us say in Iceland or London, maybe just for one day, to engage in a strictly confidential, private and frank discussion."

Reykjavik or London—two NATO capitals. It seemed out of character coming from a Soviet leader. Reagan accepted without hesitation. "I opt for Iceland," he wrote in his diary that night. Iceland was out of the major-media glare and free of interference from the Thatcher government.

Reagan was delighted by the prospect of a second summit. It played to his belief that if he could just talk to the Soviet leader face-to-face, man-to-man, they could resolve their basic differences. But before he could give his full attention to it, he had to deal with another matter that would have a lasting impact on his legacy: the composition of the Supreme Court.

He had already made quite a significant impact on the ideological balance of the federal court system and thus on the national legal agenda. He'd quietly and consistently appointed seventy-eight appeals court judges and 290 district court judges, determined to seat justices who "interpret the laws, not make them." In the wake of Warren Burger's resignation as chief justice in June 1986, Ronald Reagan got his chance to make his most meaningful maneuver to date. On Ed Meese's advice, the president nominated William Rehnquist to replace Burger as chief justice. In Meese's view, "Rehnquist would reshape the Court in a more *constitutional* manner," meaning as per the framers' original intentions as opposed to thinking of the Constitution as an evolving or *"living" document*. As an associate justice for fifteen years, Rehnquist had faithfully advanced the conservative viewpoint. He'd voted against laws extending the minimum wage; defended state-sanctioned prayer in public schools; supported warrantless searches; voted against school desegregation and the establishment of legalized abortion; argued against affirmative action and sex discrimination; and held that capital punishment was constitutionally permissible.

When Rehnquist was eventually confirmed as chief justice on September 17, the president filled the vacancy his promotion created by appointing Antonin Scalia as associate justice. Scalia had been in consideration in 1981, when Potter Stewart retired, but he was passed over in favor of Sandra Day O'Connor. As a consolation prize, Reagan appointed him to an influential seat on the U.S. Court of Appeals in Washington, D.C. Scalia's legal philosophies were, if anything, to the right of Ronald Reagan's political philosophy. Scalia assailed what he called the "Imperial Judiciary" for deciding issues it had no business deciding—"social judgments that ought better be left to the democratic process." As a practicing Catholic, he was especially vocal in his opposition to abortion and laws protecting the rights of homosexuals. There was a great hue and cry against his nomination from critics on the left. Nevertheless, Scalia was regarded as one of the smartest legal minds on an American bench, a sharp-tongued wit, and a frequent dinner guest of Republicans and Democrats alike. On September 26, he was confirmed by unanimous vote.

With that neatly tucked away, the president gave his full attention to the upcoming summit in Reykjavik. This time around, there were no briefing books, no practice sessions or tutorials, little formal preparation. The whole thing had come up so suddenly. And Reagan had been otherwise engaged—on the road campaigning for Republican candidates in the midterm elections, which was only three weeks off. "Not having a lot of time to prepare was of no concern to him," recalls John Poindexter. Reagan had an agenda—to rid the world of nuclear weapons, especially the intermediate-range missiles in Europe—but there was no alternative strategy covering anything else Gorbachev might propose.

The president seemed distracted in the few briefings staged to bring him up-to-date. He resisted being stage-managed. He was more interested in the negotiation process, his power of persuasion. He felt he could wing it with Gorbachev and get his points across. Down to the wire, his handlers were concerned about his readiness. At a final meeting before leaving for Reykjavik, they felt the president had trouble following John Poindexter's rundown of the various positions taken by the two superpowers. On the other hand, they observed, he was emotionally up for the confrontation. His mood said it all. "He was awfully excited."

On October 5, just days before the summit, the national security team was hit with an ominous distraction. White House officials were informed that a C-123K cargo plane belonging to Southern Air Transport had been shot down by a Sandinista patrol in the jungles of Nicaragua. What was the extent of American involvement? As far as anyone in the White House knew, none. But the phone wires began burning between Bob Dutton, Oliver North's Project Democracy airlift coordinator, and Joe Fernandez, the CIA station chief in Costa Rica. "Situation requires we do necessary damage control."

How much damage no one realized until the next day, when Sandinistas revealed they'd captured the plane's pilot, Eugene Hasenfus, a Wisconsin resident and veteran of Air America, the CIA airline used in the Vietnam War. Southern Air Transport was another CIA contrivance, a cover used in covert operations. Moreover, it became apparent the plane shot down was loaded with Contra supplies: rifles, grenade launchers, jungle knives, machine guns, ammunition, combat gear, and medicine.

American officials were quick to deny American involvement. George Shultz insisted that, as far as he was aware, the plane "had no connection with the U.S. government at all." *As far as he was aware.* But there were others working in the Old Executive Office Building who knew the airlift of supplies was one of Oliver North's operations, and there were Americans involved from Washington, D.C., to Jinotega.

The president wasn't briefed until three days later, when John Poindexter laid out the still-sketchy details. "We don't know exactly who [is responsible]," he said disingenuously. "But I think you should be careful about denying any U.S. role."

Later that day, Hasenfus appeared on TV in a news conference staged by the Nicaraguan government in Managua. He readily admitted that the supply flights to the Contras were supervised by the CIA. It was a well-known fact throughout Washington that the CIA was forbidden by Congress to deliver arms to the rebels, and when the press asked Reagan if his administration had any link to the flight, he responded categorically, "Absolutely none." Assistant Secretary of State Elliot Abrams echoed his denial. "That would be illegal," he said during an interview with Robert Novak on CNN. "It is not in any sense a U.S. operation." But savvy observers knew—this was another fine mess you got us into, Ollie.

It was time for Oliver North to start covering his tracks. Later that month, Bill Casey turned up the heat. "This whole thing is coming unraveled," he warned North. There was too much collateral evidence—the Swiss bank accounts held by Lake Resources, the ledgers containing the financial transactions for Project Democracy and payments to Contra leaders, the incriminating PROFs and memos that outlined the diversion of funds. "Get rid of things," Casey told him. "Clean things up."

Ronald Reagan was only too happy to bolt for Reykjavik. Joan Quigley had signed off on the trip. October 14 yielded only favorable signs. But while the stars might have been aligned, not all the ducks were in a row.

The American delegation was relatively small. Cap Weinberger had remained behind in Washington; the chairman of the joint chiefs sent an Army general instead. Gorbachev hadn't advanced a specific agenda he wished to pursue. But watching the arrival of the Soviet premier on TV from an apartment in Reykjavik, the Americans saw that he was accompanied by a much larger staff. His principal military strategist, Marshal Sergei Akhromeyev, a sophisticated man with extensive arms-control experience, was at his side. And both men carried bulging briefcases. Perhaps the rumors that the Soviets would arrive with a blitz of proposals were true. Were they gearing up to discuss key nuclear issues? Reagan scowled at the image of his Soviet rival. "When you stop trying to take over the world," he snarled at the screen, "then maybe we can do some business."

The grimace was gone on Saturday morning, October 11, 1986, when a smiling Ronald Reagan approached the clunky Russian sedan carrying Mikhail Gorbachev to their opening negotiating session. The weather was unkind—raw and piercing—but Gorbachev had learned his lesson in Geneva; he emerged from the car in a well-tailored suit: no overcoat, no scarf, no fedora. Following a cordial handshake and photo op, the two leaders disappeared into Hofdi House, a rather bleak, boxy structure—the former residence of the British ambassador, who had sold it back to Iceland, claiming the place was haunted—perched on a barren edge of the Atlantic Ocean. As far as anyone could tell, the only spectral presence was the ghost of the unresolved Geneva summit, which both world leaders were hoping to dispel.

Reagan and Gorbachev met alone for an hour. The exchange, according to Gorbachev, seemed disorganized, the president confused. He consulted note cards, shuffling them, looking for answers to Gorbachev's arguments, thrown off that they didn't seem to follow any script. When they were joined by their chief stewards, Shultz and Shevardnadze, Gorbachev suddenly became animated. Later he would say, "We believe the world wanted bold decisions," and he now had a few he was eager to advance—sweeping proposals on strategic and intermediate-range arms, and nuclear testing. His approach was threefold: (1) a 50 percent reduction in the strategic offensive weapons of the Soviet Union and the United States; (2) the complete elimination of Soviet and U.S. medium-range missiles in Europe; and (3) a pledge not to withdraw from the Anti-Ballistic Missile Treaty for ten years, during which time the testing of all space-based elements of antiballistic missile defenses would be prohibited. Jack Matlock, who took notes in the meeting, scrawled: "Gorbachev indicated that . . . the mutual ultimate aim was total elimination of nuclear weapons."

"This is the best Soviet proposal we have received in twenty-five years," said Paul Nitze, the special adviser to the president, during the lunchtime debriefing in the SCIF,* a bubble room that was acoustically isolated to prevent eavesdropping. Others in the delegation were similarly enthusiastic—surprised, even astonished. Gorbachev had come a long way toward meeting the Americans in their own objectives. There was optimism that some historic agreement might be reached over the weekend. Reagan was more subdued. "He's got a lot of proposals," the president said, "but I'm afraid he's going after SDI." If they were going to do business, SDI was untouchable.

Gorbachev was more persistent when they reconvened after lunch. He wanted some commitment from his American counterpart, specific answers to his proposals. The president was cautiously approving, but he insisted on going forward with research on SDI. "The American people," he said, "should not be left defenseless." Again he repeated his intention to share SDI with the Soviet Union. Listening to this, Gorbachev was unable to conceal his cynicism. "If you will not share oil-drilling equipment or even milk-processing facilities, I do not believe you will share SDI. Sharing SDI would provoke a second American revolution!"

At dinner that evening in the embassy residence, John Poindexter produced a proposal from Cap Weinberger that the secretary of defense had given him some months earlier. It was a straightforward plan to do away with all land-based ICBM missiles and to continue with research on SDI. Reagan supported it wholeheartedly, so did George Shultz. They immediately ordered their senior people to work on drafting a counterproposal based on Weinberger's strategy. "We didn't have a lot of space for the staff," Poindexter recalls, "so they found a big plywood board and laid it over the bathtub in the upstairs head, and spent all night crouched there working on it."

The U.S. proposal wasn't as dramatic as doing away with all nuclear

* Special Compartmented Intelligence Facility

weapons, but it was a step in the right direction. Their Soviet counterparts were intrigued. At two in the morning the American strategists woke George Shultz. The Russians were agreeable to across-the-board cuts, they said, but there was dissention within their ranks. A joint U.S.-Soviet team met from 3:00 a.m. to 6:30 a.m. in an effort to hammer out a mutual agreement. In the end, the language both sides came up with would commit the superpowers to destroy more than four thousand missiles and twenty thousand nuclear warheads.

Sunday morning, having studied the joint agreement, both Reagan and Gorbachev expressed their disappointment. The president thought it fell short on INF, the Intermediate-range Nuclear Forces accord that limited Soviet missiles in Asia. The Soviet general secretary expected a more definitive response to issues in the ABM Treaty. And he was adamant about curtailing SDI. Gorbachev was more than disappointed—he was exasperated, resentful. "We've accomplished nothing," he said, throwing up his hands.

"Are we going to leave with nothing?" the president asked him.

"Yes," Gorbachev said. "Let's go home."

Cooler heads prevailed, and the leaders agreed to a final, midafternoon meeting. Gorbachev, taking Reagan's commitment to SDI under consideration, suggested an addition to the ABM Treaty for the Americans to discuss among themselves: "The testing in space of all space components of anti-ballistic missile defense is prohibited, except research and testing conducted in laboratories." It was a compromise. The treaty enabled the United States to continue SDI research for a period of ten years, but not to deploy the system in space.

Reagan took his team back to the bubble room to discuss Gorbachev's proposal. He went around the table, asking for advice. George Shultz and Paul Nitze urged him to take it. Richard Perle was the sole dissenting voice. "If you accept this proposal," he warned, "it will mean the end of the SDI program." The president listened to the conflicting opinions and posed his own argument: "If we agree to this, won't we be doing it just so we can go home with an agreement?" In the end, he decided to reject Gorbachev's proposal.

As the U.S. team headed back to the negotiating table, Reagan pulled his chief of staff aside. "Don," he said, sotto voce, "this is taking too long." He wanted to leave later in the afternoon, as scheduled. He'd spoken to Nancy earlier and promised her he'd be home for a late dinner. Regan informed him that both sides felt they were close to a breakthrough. It might be worthwhile to continue for an extra day. "Oh, shit!" the president said. "Nancy would kill me."

She was already steamed about Raisa Gorbachev's presence in Iceland. Wives had not been invited to the summit, but Mrs. Gorbachev showed up on her husband's arm. When a reporter asked her about Nancy Reagan's absence, the Soviet First Lady blithely answered, "Perhaps she has something else to do. Or maybe she isn't feeling well." To add insult to injury, Raisa Gorbachev carried out a full schedule of public-relations appearances throughout the weekend that got plenty of TV coverage.

No, Nancy wouldn't be happy if the summit stretched on. The president made it clear—no more extensions. He intended to wrap up negotiations by the end of Sunday and be in Washington in time for dinner.

But at 5:30 p.m. Gorbachev was clinging to limitations on the deployment of SDI. "You can conduct laboratory research," he argued. "And after ten years, we can completely eliminate all strategic weapons." The way he described it made it so tempting.

The elimination of all nuclear weapons by 1996. They were so close . . . so close.

"Let's do it!" George Shultz interjected.

The president shook his head. "I have promised the American people that I would not give up on SDI," he said. "I can't confine work to the laboratory. I can't give in." The matter of deployment remained the only sticking point, a question of one word. That was all. He asked Gorbachev to drop it from the agreement as a favor to him—and to world peace.

"If I let go on the testing of space weapons, I couldn't return to Moscow," Gorbachev countered. "But if we could agree to ban research in space, I'd sign in two minutes." He delivered an ultimatum. "It's 'laboratory' or goodbye."

So close . . . and yet so far apart. A gloomy silence fell over the meeting as their positions hardened, solidified. It was obvious the negotiations had collapsed. Both men knew they had given ground but had taken things as far as possible. They stood up and gathered their papers. Without another word they walked out of the room.

Anticipation was high that the leaders would make a joint statement to the press gathered expectantly outside the front door in the dark, but the president refused. "*No* statement!" he bristled at his assistant, Jim Kuhn, unable to mask his anger. His face was grim; inside he was seething. He pushed through the throng of diplomats crowding the entrance, avoiding eye contact with Gorbachev, who was beside him.

"I don't know what else I could have done," the Soviet leader said.

Without turning his head, Reagan said, "You could have said yes."

Gorbachev shook his head contemptuously. "We won't be seeing each other again," he said.

The president followed George Shultz into a waiting limousine. As the door closed, one word escaped: "Goddammit!"

D espite the crushing diplomatic failure, the delegation rolled out its biggest guns to rewrite the event and to put a positive spin on it. The party line would be that Ronald Reagan had refused to sell America short; in the process, he'd stood up to the Soviets. John Poindexter briefed the press on *Air Force One*. He implied that it was never the intention of the president to negotiate a nuclear weapons ban, that he had wanted to focus on issues that could be agreed upon later. George Shultz delivered the same summary to the *New York Times*, the *Washington Post*, and the *Wall Street Journal*. The three networks were serviced by Pat Buchanan, Ken Adelman, and Paul Nitze. Even Henry Kissinger pitched in to do his part. "When one side suddenly springs a major plan on the other and expects it to be negotiated in thirty-six hours, that's preposterous and outrageous," he told Tom Brokaw on *NBC Nightly News*. It was a highly polished group effort, and the polls reflected it had done its job. A *Wall Street Journal*/NBC News poll indicated Americans supported the president's performance, with a 71 percent favorable rating. No one seemed to realize that a stride toward world peace had been sacrificed to the whim of a space shield, still in its early development stages, that scientific and military establishments believed wouldn't be deployable for another ten years—if ever.

While the country seemed willing to give Ronald Reagan a pass on Reykjavik, the support wasn't enough to alter the midterm elections. He attempted to convince campaign crowds on the stump that the Strategic Defense Initiative was essential to national security and would stimulate the economy, "opening the door to a new technological age," but voters couldn't grasp its importance, or how SDI related to them. On November 4, 1986, control of the Senate changed hands, giving the Democrats a 55–45 edge. They now controlled both houses of Congress, which put the president in a weak position to pass legislation that remained on his to-do list.

The administration could spin that, too. The president would forge new alliances, he would sow bipartisan support, his popularity would carry him nicely through the next two years, the Soviets would come around, the economy had momentum—the spin doctors were in full-throttle mode. But the same day, another story appeared under the headlines that announced the election returns: "Iran Says McFarlane and 4 Others Went to Tehran on a Secret Trip." That was a story no doctor could spin.

CHAPTER FORTY-TWO

SNAKEBIT

"Every advantage in the past is judged in the light of the final issue."

—DEMOSTHENES

The story actually broke on November 3, 1986, in *Al-Shiraa*, a pro-Syrian Arabic magazine in Lebanon. It laid out the startling details of Bud McFarlane's secret visit to Tehran in May. On November 4, picking up the narrative, Ali Akbar Hashemi Rafsanjani addressed Iran's parliament, highlighting the extent of weaponry that accompanied the Americans. He revealed their fake Irish passports and said the envoys brought a Bible, signed by President Reagan, and a cake, a chocolate cake decorated with a key that symbolized the key to American–Iranian friendship. Magnanimously, he left out the pair of gift-wrapped .357 pistols that were confiscated by the notorious Revolutionary Guard.

Reagan aides expected the story would be eclipsed by the midterm election results and more encouraging news from the day before—that an American hostage, David Jacobsen, had been released and was on his way home. John Poindexter assured his NSC staff that any uproar would fizzle out in a few days. But as George Shultz predicted, "this snake never died." Its venom had leached out in a series of well-timed leaks citing an array of "intelligence sources." By November 6, both the *Washington Post* and the *Los Angeles Times* carried colorful accounts of the Iranian arms initiative. A follow-up report revealed that the initiative had been going on for a year.

The Reagan administration was flat-out snakebit.

It was critical they circle the wagons and perform some hasty damage control, explaining away the arms shipment and preventing further revelations from tying it to the Oval Office. A day earlier, when the president was asked by reporters to confirm McFarlane's visit, he had tersely responded, "No comment." But aides knew that would never suffice. There were already cracks in the rickety facade. Rumors circulated that George Shultz opposed the arms deal. During a Rose Garden ceremony honoring David Jacobsen, the president insisted that everyone in his Cabinet supported his policies. "And Secretary Shultz supports the policy, and so does Cap Weinberger?" a reporter persisted. "Yes," Reagan assured him. But the opposite was true. Shultz and Weinberger were infuriated that they knew nothing about four arms shipments. They'd been purposely kept out of the loop, and were only now, in the face of a snowballing scandal, being asked to pledge allegiance to the ludicrous scheme. "This has all the feel of Watergate," Shultz thought.

George Bush reached much the same conclusion. By Sunday, November 9, he was carefully distancing himself from the evolving scandal. In a conversation over drinks with the secretary of state, he professed his ignorance of the arms transfer in exchange for hostages. Shultz, irritated by this sudden backpedaling, reminded Bush of a meeting in which the deal was proposed and that Bush had made no objection, in contrast to Shultz's and Weinberger's own opposition. Later, the vice president would claim, "We were not in the loop." To Bud McFarlane, that was particularly galling. "The hell he wasn't. He was up to his eyebrows in it. He supported it all the way."

The administration needed a concerted strategy in order to address the mounting congressional and media outcry. On Monday, November 10, the president convened a National Security Planning Group meeting in the Situation Room that featured a star-studded cast: Vice President Bush, Attorney General Meese, Chief of Staff Regan, Secretary of State Shultz, Secretary of Defense Weinberger, CIA Director Casey, and National Security Adviser Poindexter.

"We must say something because I'm being held out to dry," Reagan complained, according to notes that were taken by an NSC deputy. "A basic statement has to come out. [We] have not dealt directly with terrorists, don't know who they are. This is a long-range Iranian policy. No further speculation or answers so as not to endanger hostages. We won't pay any money or give anything to terrorists."

It was Poindexter who had advised the president that it was more strategic to say less about what they were doing and more about what they weren't doing, and told him it was essential to convey that their main objective had been a "long-term strategic relationship" with Iran.

Ed Meese offered a dodgy legal rationale. Referring to the sale of TOW missiles for hostages, he said, "We didn't sell them; Israel did."

"We have not dealt directly with terrorists, no bargaining, no ransom," Reagan insisted. "We don't talk TOWs, don't talk specifics, avoid specifics."

Shultz took issue with the president's analysis. "It is ransom," he objected.

Reagan did not want to hear it and made his annoyance known. Glaring at the secretary of state, he said, "I would appreciate people saying you support the president's policy."

"I support you, Mr. President," Shultz replied. "I'm more concerned about the policy."

Despite the misgivings, an official statement was hammered out,* and on November 12, the president parroted it ably, attempting to convince congressional leaders that he'd complied with U.S. policy. "We have not negotiated with terrorists. We have not broken any laws. It was a covert operation . . . designed to advance our strategic interests in the Middle East." He gave them just enough information to support his claim, but it was obvious from the follow-up remarks of Robert Byrd and Bob Dole that they didn't believe a word of it. Dole called the operation "inept," while Byrd termed it "a major foreign relations blunder." In any case, leaders on the Senate Intelligence Committee demanded full disclosure and made it clear that they intended to launch investigations into all aspects of the affair. Subpoenas were already being discussed.

The president refused to cave in to the legal threat. He was convinced the lives of too many people hung in the balance—the hostages, of course, but also operatives working undercover in the Middle East. Peter Wallison, the White House counsel, had been in a meeting with Oliver North, who warned, "There'd be heads on stakes in Tehran if we acknowledged these transactions were going on." Wallison concluded that this claim was "a completely made-up story that would manipulate the President." Sure

---

* The statement said: "Our policy of not making concessions to terrorists remains intact."

enough, North's "pungent language" had its effect. John Poindexter subsequently advised Reagan that, for the safety of all concerned, it was prudent to withhold information.

The following night, on October 13, the president decided to make his case to the nation. He was very cautious about how much to disclose. In an unusually somber address from his desk in the Oval Office, he said:

> The charge has been made that the United States has shipped weapons to Iran as ransom payments for the release of American hostages in Lebanon, and that the United States undercut its allies and secretly violated American policy against trafficking with terrorists. Those charges are utterly false.
>
> The United States has not made concessions to those who hold our people captive in Lebanon, and we will not. The United States has not swapped boatloads or planeloads of American weapons for the return of American hostages, and we will not.

He did admit to "the transfer of small amounts of defensive weapons" to Iran, but said that "these modest deliveries, taken together, could easily fit into a small single cargo plane." The president knew this was an outright lie—the two thousand TOWs, eighteen HAWKs, and assorted HAWK parts had necessitated eight cargo planes to transport them. And even as he said it, his narrative was unraveling. The press sensed it was getting "less than the full story." Information was already slipping out from unsourced administration officials that "the arms may have included surface-to-air missiles, antitank weapons, and spare parts" and that "some of the weapons may have been sent by Israel," a fact the president chose not to mention. Another "senior official" disclosed that "the Iran operation was approved by Reagan in a directive signed in January."

Press skepticism was the least of his problems. Richard Nixon, watching at his home, felt an uncomfortable tug of déjà vu. "Get the message out," he counseled Pat Buchanan. "Admit you made a mistake—you tried something and it turned out badly. But don't cover it up." His views were shared by many members of the American public, long-faithful supporters of the president, who felt they were being deceived. An ABC News poll taken immediately after the speech found that 72 percent of respondents disapproved of the president's policy of shipping arms to Iran to improve relations, while 56 percent believed he'd swapped arms for hostages.

As the staff started to scramble, Ronald Reagan was oddly passive. His team put together an all-out public-relations campaign to salvage the situation, but it only seemed to make matters worse. Bud McFarlane discussed his trip to Tehran with Ted Koppel on *Nightline* supposedly to come clean, only to deny bringing a Bible, a cake, or pistols. John Poindexter appeared on *Meet the Press* in a futile effort to convince viewers that the Iran initiative was in the nation's best interest, implying more arms sales were to come. And George Shultz, under a ferocious interrogation by Leslie Stahl on *Face the Nation*, did nothing but dodge her questions about the trading of arms for hostages, an operation that, of course, he vehemently opposed. Nevertheless, Stahl pressed him on whether there would be any more arms shipments to Iran. "I would certainly say, as far as I'm concerned, no," the secretary responded, throwing down the gauntlet. That might have gotten him off with only minor bruising. But when she persisted, asking him if he had the authority to speak for the administration, Shultz shook his head forlornly and answered, "No."

Shultz's acknowledgment was considered an embarrassment by White House officials. His public ending of arms sales put them in a bind, evidence of his increasing disloyalty. George Bush, when asked to comment, called the secretary's remarks "inappropriate." Don Regan was vastly more disapproving. "I don't know what's gotten into George," Regan chafed. "If he doesn't like it, he should quit." But Regan had plunged into even hotter water than Shultz thanks to an unguarded interview he'd given to the *New York Times*. Defending himself against criticism that the chief of staff had failed to adequately serve the president in a series of stumbles, Regan said, "Some of us are like a shovel brigade that follow a parade down Main Street cleaning up. We took Reykjavik and turned what was really a sour situation into something that turned out pretty well. Who was it that took this [Libyan] disinformation thing and managed to turn it? Who was it who took on this loss in the Senate and pointed out a few facts and managed to pull that? I don't say that we'll be able to do it four times in a row. But here we go again, and we're trying."

If Nancy Reagan had her way, both Shultz and Regan would have been fired posthaste. Neither man seemed to be protecting her husband from a tidal wave of political damage. Bill Casey, who cited Shultz's "public pout-ing" and failure to support the Iran initiative as breaches of trust, peti-tioned the president to replace the secretary of state with either Paul Laxalt or Jeane Kirkpatrick. The disenchantment found its way into national news reports. But the president swore, "I'm not firing anybody."

He was still convinced of the merit of the policy and still convinced he could use his powers of persuasion to talk his way out of the crisis and sal-vage the situation. But another, more convulsive crisis was billowing on the horizon, and he would need every last dependable advocate to keep it from demolishing his presidency.

R onald Reagan had always relied on his ability to communicate with any type of audience, friend or foe, and draw people surely into his confidence. He'd employed this talent, this gift, his entire adult life— during the Eureka College campus strike when, as he recalled, "for the first time in my life, I felt my words reach out and grab an audience"; as a silken-voiced announcer on Iowa radio stations; opposite the world's most glamor-ous stars on movie and television screens; across the negotiating table as president of the Screen Actors Guild; in front of hostile cross-examiners of the House Un-American Activities Committee; convincing workers in General Electric's plants that a fading movie star had their best interests at heart; persuading people who had never voted for a Republican, much less a conservative, to support him as governor and president. He had never failed to get his message across, and so now he decided he could speak un-scripted and convincingly to his greatest adversary—the White House press corps—in order to explain away the Iran controversy. It was a disaster.

The press conference was scheduled for November 19, 1986, a date cho-sen by the chief of staff after receiving word that the First Lady's "friend" in San Francisco had signed off on it as being favorable to the president. Ev-eryone knew what was riding on this event and pulled together to help. John Poindexter had supplied Reagan with a seventeen-page chronology of the Iran initiative, albeit one that was inaccurate and incomplete, to pre-pare and guide him through the ordeal. There was a run-through on No-vember 17, at which his staff peppered him with likely questions, the most difficult questions they could think of, so he could formulate credible answers well in advance. The run-through left the staff badly shaken. It "was about as bad as I'd ever seen it," recalled Peter Wallison, the White House counsel. The president was confused, error-prone. "He seemed to know nothing about what had happened. . . . We couldn't imagine how he was going to go into a full-scale press conference the next evening when he was so ill-prepared." A second run-through the next day was somewhat better, but by no means was it Ronald Reagan at the top of his game. Still, he remained confident that he would rise to the occasion, and he decided to go ahead as scheduled.

His discomfort was obvious to the press. The president was defensive from the outset. He seemed poorly informed and lacking the trademark Reagan charm. Grasping a lectern in the East Room, a formal reception hall on the ground floor of the Executive Mansion, he attempted to justify his decision to sell arms to Iran, and in doing so, he jumbled the facts, often contradicting previous comments he'd made. Only a week earlier he'd assured the country that he "did not, repeat, did not, trade weapons or anything else for hostages." Now he changed his story, admitting—inadvertently—that an exchange had been made. He asserted that Iranians had ceased kidnapping Americans, failing to mention that three more Americans had been taken hostage as recently as September by jihadists associated with Iran. He seemed to be unaware that Iran's military was training and financing terrorist groups in Lebanon, that its clerics were indoctrinating Islamic radicals. The biggest faux pas, however, was the president's answer to a CNN reporter who asked if the United States dealt with Israel in supplying weapons to Iran. "We, as I say, have had nothing to do with other countries or their shipment of arms or doing what they're doing," Reagan said. This left reporters scratching their heads, as most of their papers had already published articles verifying Israel's involvement, and his chief of staff was on record saying that the U.S. government had condoned an Israeli weapons shipment to Iran before the release of Benjamin Weir.

Reviews of the president's comments were unsparing. The *New York Times* said, "The conflict of pretension and fact was so preposterous," the focus "distinctly Reaganesque: a determined effort to believe in fairy tales." The *Los Angeles Times* upgraded the charge of fairy tales to lies.

Even the staff wondered if Reagan was losing his ability to cope, let alone to grasp basic details, in a complex situation with so many legal and moral considerations to weigh. In the wake of the dreadful press conference, staff members tried to follow up with a swirl of activity on their own, but the president seemed absent. He listened, but he didn't seize control.

No one was more aghast at the president's performance than George Shultz. Shultz had warned him beforehand to come clean, that he had been "deceived and lied to" by the CIA and the NSC staff. "You must not continue to say we made no deals for hostages." Now he saw that his admonishments had been futile. Shultz recognized right away that "many of the President's statements were factually wrong." And he found incredible Reagan's insistence that "what we did was right, and we're going to continue on this path."

Shultz visited the president in the residence the following evening and engaged in "a long, tough discussion, not the kind of discussion I ever thought I would have with the President of the United States." He attempted to set Reagan straight on the myriad falsehoods disseminated in the press conference and warned him that Bill Casey was preparing to lie in his testimony before the congressional intelligence committees by swearing no one in the government had knowledge of the 1985 HAWK shipment to Iran beforehand. Shultz and Reagan went at it for an hour, "hot and heavy," but the secretary's appeals were mostly in vain. According to Don Regan, who monitored the conversation, "The President seemed puzzled" by the litany of complaints. "He refused to recognize that there was a problem," Shultz would recall. The secretary of state left the meeting more frustrated—and alarmed—than before.

Casey's testimony on November 21, 1986, was an exercise in obfuscation. He and John Poindexter conflated their accounts, using cover stories that the CIA had been asked by the NSC staff to transport oil-drilling equipment to Iran and was unaware "until later on" that the cargo contained missiles. Casey lied about the U.S. role in the HAWK shipment, and Poindexter did the same about the president's involvement, claiming that when Reagan found out that HAWKs were involved, he persuaded Iran to return them to Israel. Both deceptions were patently transparent. When Shultz related the testimony to Abe Sofaer, the State Department's legal adviser replied, "The President is in the hands of people who are lying."

The stories were growing more tortured and incredible. With the president seemingly disengaged, steadier heads in the Oval Office strained for the truth. An agitated Don Regan believed that North and Poindexter were fudging facts, and he pushed for accuracy. He charged Ed Meese with "getting his arms around the Iranian initiative" in an effort to "make sure we have a coherent and accurate narrative." Over the weekend, while the president relaxed at Camp David, watching old movies, Meese began a fact-finding inquiry, conducting interviews with Bill Casey, George Shultz, and Bud McFarlane.

On Saturday morning, November 22, Meese sent a team to the NSC offices to examine relevant documents. But Oliver North had been tipped off to the investigators' arrival by John Poindexter and had spent all day Friday and Saturday morning hosting a "shredding party." Assisted by his deputy, Robert Earl, and his secretary, Fawn Hall, North fed two feet of documents into a shredder and altered other memos and correspondence pertaining to the operation, taking great care to destroy the five memoranda outlining the plan to divert Iranian arms profit to the Contras. During the long and haphazard process, North read aloud a page from his notebook—"R.R. directed operation to proceed"—before feeding it into the shredder. Other documents were hastily edited and retyped to omit incriminating evidence. It never occurred to North that Fawn Hall's files still contained the original versions.

North had already left when the investigators arrived at his third-floor suite in the Old Executive Office Building. Their search was facilitated by Bob Earl, who handed over a cherry-picked selection of documents contained in six accordion files. Brad Reynolds, an assistant district attorney, and John Richardson, Meese's intelligence chief, sifted through what was left of North's archives. Ostensibly, they were looking for evidence of the HAWK shipments and whether there had been an arms-for-hostages deal. As the search wore on with little progress, Reynolds noticed a manila folder that seemed out of place. It contained a long memo—"Release of American Hostages in Beirut"—from North to Poindexter, outlining the May 1986 sale of weapons and HAWK parts. He started turning the pages . . . slowly . . . then more slowly.

"Holy Jesus! Look at this," he exclaimed, targeting two paragraphs he bid Richardson to read:

$2 million will be used to purchase replacement TOWs for the original 508 sold by Israel to Iran for the release of Benjamin Weir. This is the only way that we have found to meet our commitment to replenish these stocks.

The residual funds from this transaction are allocated as follows: $12 million will be used to purchase critically needed supplies for the Nicaraguan Democratic Resistance forces. . . .

The two men couldn't believe their eyes. A diversion of funds to the Contras. It was a clear violation of American law.

At two o'clock that afternoon, Reynolds and Richardson met Meese for lunch at the Old Ebbitt Grill on Fifteenth Street, near the White House. Minutes after they sat down, an uneasy Reynolds blurted out the news of their discovery. Meese's shoulders collapsed against the back of his chair. "Oh, shit!" he groaned. He remembers thinking: Iran and the Contras joined at the hip—this just took a big problem and turned it into a gigantic problem, even to the point of threatening the presidency. "It was like putting gasoline on a smoldering fire."

A more vigilant attorney general might have rushed to the phone and ordered the FBI to seal North's office. Meese made no such request, nor did he realize it gave North the opportunity to return to the scene and continue the shredding of documents, which he did throughout the remainder of the day until nearly dawn on Sunday.

Meese needed to inform the president before the details leaked and the press got wind of it, but first he intended to interrogate Oliver North. The two men met the next afternoon, November 23, after North had returned from church. The "wily renegade," as *Time* referred to him, launched into a carefully planned cover story, and Meese didn't interrupt, allowing North to dig his own hole. "He said nothing about the diversion of funds," Meese recalls. "It was all gobbledygook—carrying out the exchange of weapons because the people before him had fouled it up." North lied about his knowledge of the cargo, then he lied again about the excess funds. He insisted the whole thing was an Israeli operation. "Finally," Meese says, "I showed him the incriminating memo—and he blanched. At that point, he totally confessed, he laid out the whole scenario."

Meese's chief concern was whether or not the president knew. North refused to answer specifically. The closest he came to acknowledging White House collusion was admitting he reported through John Poindexter. Did Poindexter tell the president about the diversion of funds? Forty years later he insists he did not. "In theory, I knew the president would agree," Poindexter says. "But I also knew that it would be too controversial if it became public, and I wanted him to have plausible deniability. I was the one who gave Ollie the go-ahead. By withholding the details from the president, I wanted him to be in the position to deny that he had approved it."

The president was about to get an earful. Monday morning, first thing, Meese charged into the Oval Office. He was "sitting on a nuclear bomb," as his deputy, Brad Reynolds, described it. If the truth about the diversion leaked, the consequences would be catastrophic. Don Regan was the first to get the news about the diversion of funds. "The phrase," he recounted, "made my blood run cold." He felt "horror, horror, horror," believing the money had been skimmed from the U.S. Treasury. "We're facing a problem here that looks much like Watergate," he thought. But Meese's details were sparse. Reagan's time was short. Zulu chief Mangosuthu Gatsha Buthelezi was waiting outside to see him, and a foreign dignitary was never kept waiting. Meese had just enough time to reveal "the headline version": he'd "uncovered a terrible mess" concerning the arms transaction. He'd explain in full later that afternoon, when the president had more time to listen.

In the meantime, Meese confronted John Poindexter outside the Situation Room about whether he knew of North's clandestine affairs. "Yes, I did," the admiral admitted, "but it was consistent with the president's wishes and nothing about it was illegal." When Meese asked if anyone else in the White House knew about it, Poindexter answered, "No."

Nothing further was said of it in the afternoon National Security Planning Group meeting. The president, Shultz noticed, "was in a steamy, angry mood." He was incensed that the press had broken stories about the exchange of weapons for hostages and blamed the publicity for the failure to get more released. "We are right!" he insisted, pounding the table with his fist. "We had to take the opportunity! And we were successful! History will never forgive us if we don't do this! And no one is to talk about it!"

Afterward, around 4:30 p.m., Meese and Regan reappeared in the Oval Office and elaborated in detail about the Nicaragua connection, including what Meese had learned from Poindexter. The president, Meese recalls, was "absolutely shocked." He said, "We've got to get this out as quickly as possible so there is no sense we're trying to cover it up." Regan proposed that congressional leaders and the press be informed in the morning that laws had been broken. But it was crystal clear that the perpetrators had to be fired. "North and Poindexter would have to go."

For the longest time, Ronald Reagan said nothing. Don Regan had seen this before: the president was trying to process the facts. "His fault was he didn't manage details," Regan said. He didn't ask enough questions. And worse: the chief of staff observed how, from time to time, the president's mind wandered, that perhaps he was slipping.* Reagan had shared this worry with his wife, and was worried the effect this latest revelation could have. It was clear that Reagan was shaken, but Regan couldn't seem to formulate a response. He suggested that the president pack up for the day and retire to the residence. As to the fate of Poindexter and North, Reagan said he wanted to sleep on it.

But he didn't sleep well. He recognized what Meese's investigation had uncovered: "a smoking gun," something that violated U.S. law and could be laid on the doorstep of his office. Crestfallen, he tried to come to terms with it later that night. Sitting at his desk, bent over his diary, he worked over the day's troubling revelations. Many of the details continued to elude him. Still not acknowledging that Americans were running the operation, he wrote, "On one of the arms shipments the Iranians paid Israel a higher purchase price than we were getting. The Israelis put the difference in a secret bank account." *The Israelis*—he'd convinced himself they'd managed the whole deal. Of his own advisers, he expressed a reservoir of dismay. "North didn't tell me about this. Worst of all John Poindexter found out about it & didn't tell me."

In the morning, he concluded that Don Regan was right and gave him the order to fire John Poindexter. The imperturbable national security adviser was calmly enjoying breakfast and unrepentant upon hearing the

---

* Biographer Edmund Morris interviewed Reagan four days before and wrote that "he did not speak with much clarity" (*Dutch*, p. 607). The next night, as well, he recorded in his diary that the Israelis "past [sic] the balance in a Swiss account belonging to the Contras" (RR, diary entry, Nov. 25, 1986).

news, but he had already prepared a letter of resignation, which he handed to the president at the regular morning briefing. Reagan interpreted it as a gesture of honor—"In the old Navy tradition he accepted the responsibility as Captain of the ship," he noted, perhaps not considering that it was he, the president, who captained the ship. He continued to trust that Poindexter was "a fine naval officer" who was innocent of wrongdoing, and he regretted losing such a trusted adviser. North, who was regarded as a "detailee" and not officially a member of the administration, would be sent back to the Marine Corps. But the president refused to badmouth the charismatic intelligence deputy, convinced he'd gotten a raw deal.

"He thought North had done his best and had gotten mixed up in a thing that was beyond his skills," according to Peter Wallison, who personally believed North was "a liar" and "a fantasist." Not so, according to the president. "He is a national hero," Reagan told *Time*'s White House correspondent in an interview later that day, a conclusion that confounded many of his staff.

The day itself dredged up a cornucopia of alibis and apologies. At 10:00 a.m., the president met with the Cabinet to fill its members in on the latest developments. Afterward, the joint leadership of the Congress was summoned for a similar report. The grand finale, however, was scheduled for noon, when full disclosure would be dropped in the lap of the press. That was an event Reagan sorely dreaded. He was still blaming the press for the collapse of negotiations with Iran on recovering the American hostages. Their report of the scandal was "irresponsible," he declared. "They were like a circle of sharks."

The circle closed in around the president as he recounted an abbreviated version of the facts, emphasizing the dismissals of Poindexter and North. His most forthcoming comment on the Contra disclosure was: "I was not fully informed." It underwhelmed; the press wasn't about to be placated. The diversion of funds was a bombshell. They wanted answers. Reagan didn't intend to accommodate. He appeared unrepentant, strangely defiant in the face of such damning news. And he had a prior commitment—his annual lunch with the Supreme Court—which gave him an excuse to run off. After the briefest exchange, he left Ed Meese to mop up the press corps' questions.

As he turned to leave, a reporter called out: "Did you make a mistake in sending arms to Tehran, sir?"

"No," the president answered testily, "and I'm not taking any more questions."

Now that that was over, he'd be out of the media glare for a while. The next morning he was scheduled to fly to Santa Barbara, where he'd spend a long holiday weekend at the ranch with extended family.

It was November 26. There was little to give thanks for.

New polls were published on December 1, 1986, showing a drastic plunge in the president's approval rating—from 67 to 41 percent. A 26 percent drop—a modern-day record. A *Wall Street Journal*/NBC News poll revealed that a meager 28 percent of the public approved of his handling of foreign policy. And the president's private pollster, Dick Wirthlin, reported that 60 percent of the American people felt he was not telling the truth, which confused them because they liked him personally. "The administration is in disarray," Vice President Bush acknowledged in his diary, and most knowledgeable onlookers agreed. "Your Presidency, sir, is teetering," Senator Daniel Patrick Moynihan warned in a response to Reagan's weekly radio address. "Reagan has surrounded himself with second-rate minds," echoed an editorial in the *Philadelphia Daily News*. Bob Dole urged recalling Congress for an inquiry into the mess. *Time* wondered how Oliver North, "a furtive 43-year-old member of the NSC staff . . . had arranged the Contra scam without the knowledge of the State Department, the CIA, the Joint Chiefs of Staff, the White House Chief of Staff or anyone in authority" and concluded, "this disaster throws a pitiless light on the way the President does his job, confirming the worst fears of both his friends and his critics."

The Reagan administration seemed to be bleeding out.

Every major newspaper and weekly newsmagazine had, by now, done its homework, and the facts came pouring out—all the seamy names and details: David Kimche, Amiram Nir, Manucher Ghorbanifar, Richard Secord, Dewey Clarridge, Contra leader Adolfo Calero, a list of the weapons exchanged, the shipments, the planes involved and their flight routes, the money that changed hands, the Lake Resources bank account in Zurich. *Oliver North!* All of it was churned over in account after account, article after article.

The Israelis publicly denied setting a price for the missiles and any links to the Swiss bank. Covert payments to the Contras—$2 million by Texas billionaire Ross Perot and $10 million by the Sultan of Brunei—were unearthed. The *New York Times* reported that "the first flight to El Salvador [to supply the Nicaraguan rebels] had to jettison $50,000 worth of cargo over the countryside and nearly crash-landed," and was followed by "a dozen secret arms drops." Failed ransom attempts were disclosed, including a swap of $2 million and three hundred Lebanese Shiite prisoners for hostages in May 1986. It seemed that ships laden with weapons parts left under cover of darkness from ports in Sicily. Documents were shredded in the NSC offices. And Oliver North became a cause célèbre. His exploits had a James Bond touch to them that made for good copy. He was cast as a dashing roué, his outsize personality and career splashed across newspapers around the country.

"Washington is awash with rumor, intrigue, and treachery," Senator Moynihan cautioned the president on November 29. "I tell you it is deeply dangerous." The White House had to take action—and fast—to stanch the damage.

The president announced that if the Justice Department recommended it, he welcomed the appointment of a special prosecutor to investigate the Iranian arms deals and the funneling of funds to the Contras. In the meantime, a special independent review board would be impaneled to arrive at a complete and accurate account of what had transpired. Former Republican senator John Tower was Don Regan's choice to head this group, balancing it out with a Democrat, Ed Muskie, and Brent Scowcroft, who had been Gerald Ford's national security adviser.

No matter what they concluded, however, their judgment would never be as severe as the one being formulated in the White House residence. Nancy Reagan was on the warpath. Her husband was being castigated for the entire Iran-Contra fiasco, and she wanted to spread the blame around to more deserving candidates. Her laser focus trained on Don Regan. She had never liked the blustery chief of staff, never thought he put her husband first. He hogged the spotlight, blocked access to the president, and talked too damn much. The "shovel brigade" comment really set her off. "If that's how Don saw his job," she fumed, "what kind of loyalty could Ronnie expect from him on other issues?" Obviously, she thought, he had a hidden agenda. She wanted Regan out of the picture. "I can't deal with that man anymore," she complained to the president, urging him to make a change at the top. At the time, the president ignored her appeals. "He genuinely liked Don Regan," Jim Kuhn says. "They were very much alike, a couple of old-school Irishmen, and Reagan could relate to him. He felt comfortable with him in the Oval Office. There was a strong camaraderie." With all that was going on, Don's presence was a soothing factor. None of that carried much weight with the First Lady, who knew best when it came to her husband's welfare. Don Regan had to go, she decided. It was time to turn up the heat.

Coincidentally—perhaps too coincidentally—on December 2, Mitch Daniels, the president's assistant for political affairs, "privately polled large numbers of Republican Party officials and told Regan that without exception they thought he should resign." Stories were planted in the press quoting anonymous sources that Regan was considering leaving or there might soon be a change in leadership. "She was behind it all," says Jim Kuhn. Her sentiment was spreading through Congress. Utah senator Orrin Hatch called for Regan's resignation, as did Richard Lugar. George Bush tended to agree and conveyed that opinion to Nancy Reagan, although he refused to share that sentiment with the president. It was left to the First Lady, who began laying the groundwork for a defenestration.

She enlisted two old allies, Stu Spencer and Mike Deaver, to spearhead her efforts to oust the chief of staff. And just in case they didn't provide enough firepower, on December 4 she invited the former secretary of state William Rogers and the former Democratic Party chairman Robert Strauss to the residence to discuss Regan's fate with the president. Strauss's assessment was particularly brutal. "You have a serious Hill problem—Don Regan has no allies on the Hill," he said. "And you have a serious media problem—Don Regan has no friends there. You have got to get a fresh face in that job." Strauss expressed an opinion that the crisis was being poorly managed by Regan, but the more he poured it on, the more Ronald Reagan dug in his heels. "Don Regan has been loyal to me," he argued. "I am not going to throw him to the wolves." The First Lady was unhappy with the outcome, but she was undeterred. And she was just warming up.

Regan felt her hot breath on his neck, but he had other issues to deal with. There was a job to fill at NSC now that Poindexter had vacated the office—the fourth national intelligence adviser to leave in a span of six years. Regan was instrumental in convincing Frank Carlucci, a man who'd already served three presidents with distinction, to accept the job, a first-class appointment lauded by both houses of Congress. But he wasn't able to persuade the president to admit publicly that he had made a mistake by trading arms for hostages and to take responsibility for it, a concession that aides felt would go a long way toward reassuring the nation and taking the edge off the uproar. The president continued being battered in the press. His credibility and integrity were at stake. His popularity was in freefall, and the White House staff was taking it hard. "Staff morale was very low," Peter Wallison recalls. "We were in terrible shape . . . working twenty-hour days under very difficult circumstances." The chief of staff was trying to hold it all together, but he was human. "He was getting wound tighter and tighter."

The expanding congressional investigations added to his worries. The truth was a problem to be solved. It was no longer feasible to sentimentalize it using the hostages as human shields. Too many half-truths were leaching out, uncontainable. On December 1, Bud McFarlane had testified before the Senate Select Intelligence Committee in a closed-door six-hour session, and had contradicted the White House's assurance that the president had not approved Israel's shipment of arms to Iran. McFarlane also let slip that Reagan decided at that time against notifying Congress, as was his legal duty. Oliver North and John Poindexter followed him days later, throwing the White House version into further confusion. To each question the committee asked, both men consistently invoked the Fifth Amendment: "On the advice of counsel, I respectfully and regretfully decline to answer the questions based on my constitutional rights." They refused to incriminate themselves, which only served to undermine the president's credibility. It also contradicted Reagan's assurance that his aides would come clean.

"I don't think there is another person in America who wants to tell this story as much as I do," North announced, making it clear he was holding out for immunity.

The Senate committee concluded that the White House had been taken in by North and Poindexter, but it could not render a clean bill of health for the president without their testimony. If they received immunity, the committee could probably close the book on the investigation and clear the president, and granting immunity to the guilty before the full scope of the crime was clear was politically fraught. What a mess.

Bill Casey was scheduled to testify the next afternoon, December 15. The occupants of the Oval Office were holding their breath. All covert operations in Iran and Nicaragua had gone through the CIA. Casey was the linchpin that kept all the moving parts operating. As late as three days earlier, he was still negotiating to trade arms for hostages, offering to deliver more TOWs to Iran and promising to pressure Kuwait to release terrorists in its prisons. Casey had originally told the Senate Intelligence Committee that he had no prior knowledge of diversion of funds to the Contras, but now he was headed back for a more rigorous grilling. The senators saw his fingerprints all over the operation and were giving him an opportunity to set the record straight. But as he was preparing to leave for Capitol Hill, Casey collapsed in his office, suffering a powerful seizure that rendered him incapacitated. Don Regan took Casey's place on the witness stand and gave a credible accounting of what the president knew and when he knew it, contradicting McFarlane's testimony and shoring up Ronald Reagan's defenses.

Nancy Reagan still wasn't satisfied. Not only did she want Regan removed from the scene, she turned her animosity on Bill Casey as well. The seizure stemmed from previously diagnosed brain cancer. In her eyes, a sick Casey was just as much of a threat as a healthy Casey. She was convinced that he "was deeply involved in the Iran-Contra affair" and that his brain cancer had affected his judgment, imperiling her husband's presidency. Politically, he remained a liability. "He's hurting Ronnie," she told Don Regan. The way she saw it, the job fell to the chief of staff to immediately find someone to replace Casey at the CIA. Regan told her that such an action was "unwise as well as inhumane," given that the man was critically ill, most likely dying. Regan knew "it was obvious that Casey would not continue as Director, but the question of common decency remained." Doctors were in the process of trying to save his life by operating on a cancerous tumor. Besides, Regan insisted, the president wouldn't want it, not now, not like this. Despite his objections, she bombarded Regan with phone calls—her direct line to the Oval Office, "WH 1," blinked with increasing regularity—demanding Casey's dismissal, each one ignored, each instance of being ignored another blot on her Regan scorecard.

The president was beleaguered by her persistent carping. She wouldn't let up: fire Regan, fire Casey. Wash your hands of Poindexter and North. Listen to Mike Deaver and Stu Spencer. Listen to *me*! "Nancy made it clear to us, the White House staff, that we had to get him thinking along those very lines," recalls Jim Kuhn, who spent all day at the president's side. "'You need to start working on Ronnie,' she told me. 'I want you to do that.'"

Kuhn broached it gently with his boss in mid-December. "All these stories about Don won't go away, will they?" he prompted during a quiet moment in the Oval Office.

"No, they won't," Reagan answered reluctantly. "But I've been very pleased with him as chief; he's worked hard for me. Still . . . that *photo*."

Photo? The president admitted the photo of Regan squeezing himself into the frame with Gorbachev in Geneva still rankled. Kuhn suspected that the First Lady continued to make a case about it—and that, finally, she was having some impact. The president seemed "in a daze . . . tentative and deferential."

The next weekend, just before the Christmas vacation, the tension between the couple came to a head. Nancy started in on her husband again during their weekend getaway to Camp David: fire Regan, replace Casey. Jim Kuhn removed himself to a desk in the pantry to get away from the bickering. "Then there was an explosion," Kuhn says. "I heard Reagan scream at her—'Get off my goddamn back!' It was so loud, the whole cabin shook." In her memoir, Nancy Reagan dismissed the scream as fiction, but forty years later, as Kuhn recounts the episode, his face betrays undeniable truth. The man who idolizes both the Reagans is hesitant about sharing a confidence he was privy to and shudders visibly as he recalls the scene. "I'd never heard him yell like that. It scared the hell out of me."

She was not about to be deflected from her objective of cleaning house of the turncoats and slackers by an outburst. In this time of crisis, she intended to speak up, to hold nothing back. During a Christmas party at Walter Annenberg's in Palm Springs, the First Lady cornered Cap Weinberger. She expressed her "disgust" with Poindexter and North. "They should be court-martialed," she said. She aired views on other issues as well that dogged the administration—the independent counsel charged with unraveling the facts of the Iran-Contra case, the question of offering immunity to renegade aides, the upcoming State of the Union address, and, of course, Don Regan, Don Regan, Don Regan. She had no intention of letting up on him. The president, on the other hand, retreated when it came to shoptalk. Throughout the vacation he seemed withdrawn. George Shultz, who joined him on the golf course, said, he "just didn't seem ready to engage."

No doubt the crisis had taken a lot out of him. There is a time every enterprise needs to do serious self-examination and to regroup, and for the Reagan administration this was it. Things had broken down. The administration's troubles ran much deeper than anyone imagined. If it was going to rescue the remainder of the president's second term and fulfill the goal to pass meaningful legislation, the New Year—1987—had to set a new course. There were too many loose ends, too many loose cannons, too many loose lips sinking ships. It was time to tighten the steering on this ship. The question was whether the president had the wherewithal to do it.

CHAPTER FORTY-THREE

RECLAIMING THE SPOTLIGHT

"Our moulting season, like that of the fowls,
must be a crisis in our lives."

—HENRY DAVID THOREAU, WALDEN

T he first thing on 1987's agenda was getting the president's story
straight. He was due to appear before the Tower Commission later
in January, and it was essential that he be well prepared. Don Regan and Peter Wallison were enlisted to help stimulate his memory "about
what he knew and what he did" so that he would face his inquisitors in
command of the facts. In a diary entry for Sunday, January 3, 1987, Ronald
Reagan furnished his usual, sunny outlook: "Put together some sequence of
events on the Iran affair by comparing our memories."

If only it had gone that smoothly.

The three men convened in the residence after the Sunday football
games, in front of the same fan-shaped Palladian window where the top
brass had met months earlier to debate the Iran initiative. Wallison hoped
the president's memory would provide a clear picture of events, but his expectations were dashed from the outset. Reagan had no recollection of approving the Israeli shipment of TOWs to Iran in August 1985. He could not
remember meeting with Shultz, Weinberger, Casey, and Regan about it,
nor could he recall saying he did not want to ship weapons if the United
States didn't know who it was dealing with. His memory of McFarlane's
briefing about the HAWK missile shipment at the Geneva summit was

similarly vague. Regan, who was at that briefing, recounted it in detail for the president's benefit, right down to a vivid description of the room, but it did nothing to jog his memory. When Wallison asked about the decision not to inform Congress about the shipment of weapons, there was no recollection of it.

"Do you remember Bud or John Poindexter ever telling you anything about the Contras?" Regan wondered.

"No," the president responded.

"Well, that's the story you've got to tell."

Reagan's lack of memory was alarming—and encouraging. Could the mind of the President of the United States be that cloudy, that confused? What did that say about his ability to govern? Then again, if he couldn't remember issuing orders to sell the weapons, as he claimed, then perhaps that was evidence that he wasn't directly involved, that others had run the various operations behind his back and the responsibility lay with them, not the president. It was a precarious strategy to base one's testimony on, but it was a strategy nonetheless.

As evidenced by his wispy diary entry, the president wasn't getting all worked up about it. He was more concerned about an upcoming surgery on January 5 to remove an obstruction from his prostate and the wear and tear it would have on his seventy-six-year-old body. He grew more unsettled after a spinal prep that left him with "total numbness from the waist to [his] toes"—a sensation that must have dredged up his postoperative shock in *Kings Row*. Nancy Reagan intended to see he got plenty of downtime to heal after returning to the White House, and she issued orders that nothing be scheduled for her husband for a period of six weeks, to prevent any setbacks. At the very least, she wanted him to avoid any public activity for the remainder of the month, based on the advice of astrologer Joan Quigley, who "told her that January was a bad month for the President." That meant no appearances, no speeches, no press conferences, no travel, no unnecessary meetings—no exceptions.

This ran counter to the agenda Don Regan had set for the president. In an effort to show the country that Ronald Reagan was still able-bodied, still in charge, not "an old man hiding behind his desk in the White House . . . for fear of what this Iran-Contra thing would show," Regan had set up an active schedule of appearances in order for the president to high-light forthcoming policy initiatives—the line-item veto, Star Wars, a possible INF treaty with the Soviets.

"Absolutely nothing doing," the First Lady told the chief of staff. "He isn't going to move."

That edict was, more or less, a declaration of war. Nancy Reagan made it clear that she ran the show; Don Regan wasn't about to let her usurp his duties and dictate the Oval Office schedule. In the meantime, she continued to badger him about replacing Bill Casey. The ailing CIA director was partially paralyzed, was incapable of coherent speech, and trembled uncontrollably. The president was waiting for the proper time to ask Casey to step aside, but the First Lady wanted Regan to expedite the process. She called his office repeatedly throughout January—about Casey, but also about a multitude of other things that irked her about the administration. "She had CNN on all day long in the residence," says Jim Kuhn, "and when she heard something or saw footage she didn't like, she'd call. 'Why is Ronnie saying *this*? Why isn't Ronnie saying *that*?' All the time—she called *all the time*." Eventually, the subject of her calls turned to policy in the upcoming State of the Union address, things she wanted to be taken out of the speech—references to abortion and Iran. That's where the chief of staff drew the line. He took it up with the president.

"Look, this is wrong," Regan told him. "Your wife's interfering in the schedule. And I don't think you should be sitting still, Mr. President."

Ronald Reagan assured his chief of staff that he'd rein in his wife to the extent that he could, but it was no easy matter.

And she had new targets now, Pat Buchanan and Larry Speakes. Buchanan was too much of a hard-liner for her taste, dragging her husband too far to the right with his inflammatory positions on the Contras, the Tower Board, South Africa policy, and abortion. If he intended to launch a bid for the presidency in 1988, as insiders were hinting, she was not about to let him do it from the Oval Office. Buchanan asked to be named ambassador to NATO, but that was a nonstarter—he was too provocative, too much of an agitator. With his power at the White House sluicing away, Buchanan announced he would be leaving as communications director in February.

Larry Speakes would follow him out the door. His job had been in jeopardy since July 1986, when an incident on board *Marine One*, the presidential helicopter, sealed his fate. The president and First Lady had been staying at the Rockefeller estate in Sleepy Hollow, along the Hudson River in New York, in preparation for an appearance at the 100th anniversary of the Statue of Liberty. On the fifteen-minute flight to New York City, the Reagans were engrossed in the morning newspapers. Nancy read one of the president's quotes aloud from an article in the *New York Times*. Refolding the paper, she said, "I don't remember you talking to the press last night." Her husband squinched up his face. "Hell, I never said that." While this scene was unfolding, Jim Kuhn leaned back to where Speakes was sitting and whispered, "You've got to knock this stuff off."

Speakes and his deputy, Mark Weinberg, were known to "polish up"—that is, enhance, revise, or even make up quotes to showcase the president in a more distinctive light. They'd ginned up a humdinger after the Geneva summit in an effort to brighten an otherwise lackluster result. "We were in the back of the car," Weinberg recalls, "and came up with: 'The world breathes easier because we have met.'" Before the ink was even dry, Speakes was at a lectern, saying, "The President told Gorbachev . . ." Until the incident in the helicopter, the practice went pretty much undetected. Now it was clear that Speakes would have to find another job.

E veryone was tense about the president's appearance before the Tower Commission. So much was riding on what he remembered about his involvement in the Iran-Contra affair. According to George Shultz, "The President had completely buffaloed himself, truly believing that he had not traded arms for hostages." What would Reagan say when he was under oath? He'd refrained from speaking publicly about it, in part so as not to accidentally contradict or incriminate himself, but also to place himself above the fray. But on January 26 he was called to account. In a secret session, he stumbled over details and was inconsistent in his answers to the panel's questions. Eventually, he admitted that he'd authorized the arms shipments from Israel to Iran in August 1985, as Bud McFarlane had already testified, and that he'd agreed to restore Israel's stock of weapons.

Little did anyone know that Reagan had gotten his hands on a copy of McFarlane's testimony and had used it to refresh his memory. Afterward, his stupefied advisers reconnoitered to walk the president through a reconstruction of events, in effect coaching him to say he was "surprised to learn that the Israelis had shipped the arms," and that once he was informed, his only recourse was to relent: "Well, what's done is done." If he relied on McFarlane's testimony, it would shake out that he *hadn't* authorized the arms shipment in advance, necessitating a second appearance before the Tower Commission so he could set the record straight.

In the meantime, on January 29 the Senate Select Committee issued its official report on the investigation into the Iran-Contra affair. It reached a damning verdict, calling the operation an irrefutable arms-for-hostages deal and concluding that President Reagan had approved all aspects of it. What's more, it revealed that the NSC had provided top-secret military intelligence to the Iranian government and that CIA operatives controlled secret bank accounts in Switzerland and the Cayman Islands for the purpose of supporting the Contras. The report traced a tangled web of deceit that Reagan administration officials had woven: how McFarlane had lied to a Senate committee about the role of Manucher Ghorbanifar; how North told CIA officials that the president had signed a finding that never existed; that Poindexter and Casey lied to Shultz about ending the Iran operation; that Casey masked the CIA's involvement to avoid having to report to Congress; and that U.S. officials lied about the cargoes the various planes were carrying.

The Senate report threw more suspicion on Bud McFarlane's part in the affair. As a result, the Tower Commission summoned him to testify for an unprecedented third time. It was daunting to McFarlane, a proud, honor-bound Marine, that he should now have to confess he'd taken part in a cover-up and had lied under oath. He'd given the board his word that the NSC hadn't solicited foreign contributions for the Contras, but he could no longer stand by that account. He felt alone, abandoned. The president could have exonerated him during his State of the Union address, in an ideal world could have admitted his own role and taken responsibility. But Reagan had ducked the issue, saying only that it was time for the country to put the unpleasantness behind it. That hurt McFarlane in a deep and personal way.

McFarlane grew despondent. He didn't know how he could bring himself to recant his testimony, especially in front of John Tower and Brent

Scowcroft, both of whom he considered mentors. The night before he was scheduled to appear, he drifted into a dark place, brooding about the mess he was in. He was exhausted, empty; he had nothing left in him. Letters were written—to his lawyer and members of the House and Senate Intelligence committees, confessing to concealing the foreign contributions. The contents of a third letter, to his wife, Jonny, have never been revealed. But after he wrote it, McFarlane propped it against his briefcase, where she was sure to find it, then gulped down more than twenty Valium pills, washing them down with wine. Then he crawled into bed, expecting to die.

The next day, February 10, while McFarlane lay recuperating in the hospital, the Tower Commission disclosed that there were additional matters it intended to discuss with the president. The board's investigators had come across documents that revealed meetings Oliver North had had in Germany with Iranian officials in October 1986, at which time he shared top-secret U.S. intelligence concerning the position of Iraqi forces. The board also had data that tied the NSC to Contra aid. Furthermore, there were transcripts of conversations North had with the Iranians in which he claimed "he had walked in the woods with the President of the United States at Camp David, and they had talked about how admirable the Iranian Revolution was." Even more fantastic, North boasted that Reagan expressed great admiration for Ayatollah Khomeini.

Ronald Reagan was furious when North's comments were shared with him. "That's just bullshit," he said, spitting out a word that aides had never before heard come out of his mouth. "Never happened."

No one believed for a moment that it had. North had never been at Camp David, nor was he ever alone with the president, as White House records confirmed. He'd most likely uttered this nonsense in an attempt to butter up the Iranians, hoping to get the hostages released. Nevertheless, wild statements such as these, which North had made as a representative of the United States, had the potential to backfire later. The more Reagan learned, the angrier he got. It finally dawned on the president that North wasn't the American hero he thought he was.

But by the time of Reagan's second go-round with the Tower Commission in the Oval Office, on February 11, the focus was on whether he'd authorized the August arms shipment in advance. This time he was more prepared—too prepared, in fact. He opened his desk drawer and slipped out an aide-mémoire that Don Regan and Peter Wallison had drafted and began reading from the portion that described his surprise at learning of the shipment. Unintentionally, he also read aloud their instructions to him—"You might want to go back over the question for the Tower Board"—raising the panel's suspicion that the president's testimony was canned.

The confusion was making Ronald Reagan look incompetent—and worse. Was he out of touch with what was going on under his nose? Was he losing his faculties? Not only did he seem at sea when it came to details and events, but the conflicting accounts, the constant flip-flopping, were destroying his credibility. His distressing behavior during the testimony had been leaked to the press and was inflicting real damage on his image.

Don Regan heard "a chorus building up—'he's a do-nothing president'—and it was feeding on itself." For the first time Washington scuttlebutt raised the prospect of impeachment. "Whether Mr. Reagan leaves the White House," the *New York Times* speculated, "may hinge on whether the President accepts the advice of those urging him to become more aggressive once the [Tower] report is released."

Regan was pushing harder than ever to put the president back into circulation. It had been weeks since he'd been seen in public, and three months since he'd held a press conference. There was a desperate need to accommodate the press and to restore the public's confidence. This was the moment, Regan explained to Nancy in a phone call on February 8. She continued to waver: Ronnie still wasn't well enough. "We can't have him talking to himself in the West Wing," Regan persisted. "It looks like we're shielding him."

"Okay," she said, "have your damn press conference."

"You bet I will," he said, and slammed down the receiver.

A few minutes later, after he had collected himself, Regan appeared in the door frame of Jim Kuhn's office across the hall. "I've done a very bad thing," he muttered to the president's assistant. "I just hung up on Nancy Reagan." Kuhn could tell from Regan's hangdog appearance that he knew his days as chief of staff were numbered. Hanging up on the First Lady was an unpardonable offense. (In case anyone doubted that, her office leaked the details of the phone slamming to the *Washington Post* and NBC News.) So was the ongoing clamor that he had engineered the president's embarrassing performance in front of the Tower Commission. But there was a greater wave of disapprobation amassing against him.

A draft of the Commission's conclusions was delivered personally to the president on February 25. It left no doubt about what had transpired: Reagan had traded guns for hostages. But it credited his "obsession with the release of the hostages [as] the driving force behind the continuation of the Iran arms sales." It also found, as John Tower emphasized in a follow-up press conference, that "the President clearly did not understand the nature of this operation, who was involved and what was happening." Blame was placed on his "detached style, in which considerable authority was delegated to subordinates" and allowed the Iran-Contra business to "move forward without adequate scrutiny or supervision." But its harshest criticism fell on Don Regan. "He especially should have ensured that plans were made for handling any public disclosure of the initiative. He must bear primary responsibility for the chaos that descended upon the White House when such disclosure did occur."

He must bear primary responsibility. Those words were enough for the president to finally accept the inevitable fate of his chief of staff.

Nancy Reagan had already been reviewing possible candidates to replace Don Regan. A number of names had been bandied about: Labor Secretary William Brock; Charles Price, ambassador to Great Britain; Drew Lewis, now chairman of the Union Pacific Corp.; and longtime stalwart Paul Laxalt, the First Lady's top choice. Laxalt wanted nothing to do with it. He was all too familiar with the president's managerial style from their days as governors of neighboring states. "I'm a delegator," Reagan had told Laxalt at the time. In the interim, Laxalt had come to understand that "he delegated everything out and didn't know what the hell was going on in the basement." No, the new chief had to be someone who could stand up to that kind of disengagement and bring some order to the Oval Office—a Washington insider who had stature on the Hill. There was one obvious person who fit that description, a consensus candidate: Howard Baker.

Senate majority leader until 1985 and now in private practice, Baker was respected in Washington on both sides of the aisle. He asked tough questions—none more famous than the one he'd asked during the Watergate hearings: "What did the president know, and when did he know it?" And he cast tough votes—none tougher than his support of the Panama Canal Treaty, which had effectively eliminated him as Ronald Reagan's vice presidential running mate in 1980.

Baker's initial instinct was to decline the chief's job. He enjoyed his current work and was making real money for a change, "over a million dollars" last year, he told an aide. If in 1988 he decided to run for president, a job he'd always coveted, it would be unwise to have the detritus of Iran-Contra soiling his résumé. Still, on February 28, as a courtesy to the Reagans, he agreed to fly from his vacation home in Florida to discuss the position. During the flight, he grew certain that he'd decline it, but as he arrived at the diplomatic entrance on the south grounds of the White House, a gate that the press did not monitor, the power of the presidency washed over him.

"What am I doing here?" he facetiously asked Jim Kuhn, who met him at the entrance.

"Senator, he needs you," Kuhn answered. Baker just grinned in response. Upstairs, in the residence, when he saw the president standing by himself in front of the Palladian window, all his defenses slipped away.

"Howard," the president said, shaking Baker's hand, "we've got a bad situation on our hands here, and I need you to be my Chief of Staff."

Without a moment's hesitation, Baker said, "All right."

Paul Laxalt, who was also there, suggested that the president invite Don Regan to join them so that a peaceful transfer of power could be arranged.

"No, George has got that in place," Reagan said.

He dreaded any confrontation of the sort, especially with Regan. To head off the possibility, he'd delegated George Bush to deliver the bad news the next day so he wouldn't have to face his chief of staff.

Laxalt knew it would leak before then and said, "There's no way you're going to hold this [until then]. If you don't tell Don, you're going to have a hell of a problem."

He was right. CNN had the story within the hour. Frank Carlucci, the new national security adviser, listened to the report and headed straight into Regan's office. Regan was stunned—and furious. Two days earlier, on February 26, George Bush had assured him he would have until March 2 to prepare for a gradual, face-saving exit.* Anything less would impugn his years of service. "I deserve better treatment than that," he'd told the president himself. But, this—this was a slap in the face. He sat down at his desk and scratched out a one-sentence letter of resignation, then grabbed his hat and coat and left in a huff. He never returned.

By every account, the Tower Commission report left the president "badly shaken." But at least he felt a corner had been turned. One thing was certain: the culture of the White House needed an overhaul, starting at the top. Paul Laxalt warned that Reagan "can't delegate freely" anymore. "For the first time in his political career he has to develop a hands-on approach." Howard Baker's debut as the new chief of staff brought a measure of confidence, a boost to morale. He had assured Reagan on his first day in office "that you are the President and I am not." That was a step in the right direction. So was Baker's announcement that there would be no wholesale housecleaning. The only change at the outset was to discharge Regan's Mice, who had complained to Baker's aides that the president was "inattentive and inept. . . . He was lazy; he wasn't interested in the job." In their place, Baker installed Ken Duberstein as his deputy chief of staff (primarily to deal with Nancy Reagan) and a young Tennessee protégé, Arthur Boggess Culvahouse, whom everyone called A.B., charging him to "find out everything there is to know" about Iran-Contra, but to give "special emphasis to the diversion of funds," because that held the potential to create enormous problems. "You don't want to be the only White House counsel to have your client convicted in an impeachment trial in the U.S. Senate."

Culvahouse briefly talked to the president. From what he could tell, many details revealed in the Tower Commission report clashed with what Reagan thought he knew. "He was still resisting the notion that he had traded arms for hostages," Culvahouse says, "and we had to disabuse him of that." Baker, who was standing by, said, "You told me you did not know about the diversion of funds. I want you to repeat it for A.B." A bit

---

* When Bush told the president that Regan agreed to leave, he wrote in his diary: "My prayers have really been answered." (RR, diary entry, Feb. 26, 1987.)

awkwardly, the president said, "There wasn't supposed to be any extra money." All three men exchanged satisfied nods.

"We need a communications strategy, Mr. President," Baker said, "to start to deal with the loss of trust."

A speech. He had to address the nation, make a full confession, admit to the American people he traded arms for hostages. But even while such a speech was being drafted, the president was reluctant to take the rap. "He kept arguing that the arms went to people who had *influence* over the hostage takers," says A. B. Culvahouse, "not to the hostage takers themselves. I assured him the facts revealed otherwise, but he still had a tough time admitting it." Stu Spencer was recruited to sort this out with Reagan, but found him foggier than ever on the facts of the case. Spencer needed help to make the president understand his role in the mess, to accept the reality of what had been done and his obligation to be held accountable for it. It was the only way he could put the controversy behind him.

On February 27, 1987, Spencer summoned John Tower to the White House, which was a dicey proposition. Assisting the president on his response to the Tower Report only a day after it had been issued could be considered, at the very least, a conflict of interest. To avoid notice, Spencer says, "We snuck Tower in through Treasury, underneath the Oval Office, and directly up to the residence, where the Reagans were waiting."

It was anything but a pleasure-filled reunion of old friends. "Poor Tower got so emotional when he arrived," Spencer recalls. "He'd always been a big Reagan supporter, and now this." He laid it on the line to the president in no uncertain terms about the board's findings. "What you're saying is not consistent with what the public believes. Just buckle down, take the heat. It's not going to destroy your presidency." It was pretty brutal. Afterward, Reagan stood and thanked Tower for his service to the country. "It was too much for John," Spencer says. "He fell apart, he started crying."

The president was convinced by Tower to speak honestly to the public, to accept his complicity in Iran-Contra, and to acknowledge that it had been wrongheaded from the start. On March 4, he made good on his decision. In a twelve-minute televised address, he said, "A few months ago, I told the American people that I did not trade arms for hostages. My heart and my best intentions still tell me that's true, but the facts and evidence tell me it is not." He danced around an apology, but never quite delivered it. Activities were undertaken *without my knowledge*. There were *secret bank accounts and diverted funds*. The fault lay with *some who served me*. It happened *on my watch*, but *I am still the one who must answer.* "I asked so many questions about the hostages' welfare that I didn't ask enough about the specifics of the Iran plan."

To many watching, it sounded as though the president hadn't paid attention to what was going on right under his nose. Part of the lingering problem was his reluctance to condemn the operation. "I think he privately still holds to his initial conviction—that the policy was well worth it," Paul Laxalt summarized. Still, the reviews of Reagan's speech were mostly favorable. Overnight polls showed a slight boost in his overall approval rating, which had suffered a serious downturn since the scandal erupted. And the press, for the most part, gave him a passing grade. "The President did what he had to," the *Washington Post* allowed; "he admitted plenty, and he pledged to redeem the damage in his final two years in office." *Newsweek*, however, reported that one-third of its poll respondents "say Reagan should consider resigning."

But even as he determined to move on, to refocus the nation's attention on long-delayed policy such as an arms treaty with the Soviet Union and the veto of an $88 billion highway construction bill—the drumbeat of Iran-Contra continued.

For the next six months, the drama played to rapt audiences on television and the front pages of the nation's newspapers. Congressional hearings and the ongoing investigation by the special prosecutor, Lawrence Walsh, provided a bounty of startling revelations that kept Americans glued to the saga in a way that competed with their infatuation with *Dallas*. The president had told Oliver North that his story would make a good movie someday, and NBC News anchor Tom Brokaw seemed to agree. "The most popular soap opera on television this week is the Iran-Contra inquiry," he said, "starring Lt. Co. Oliver North." Oliver North's secretary, Fawn Hall, described how she stuffed incriminating intelligence documents in the back of her blouse and into her boots before walking undetected past White House security. It was revealed that, on a day the president was at Camp David, North and Richard Secord chaperoned three Iranians, one of whom was Rafsanjani's nephew, through a midnight tour of the White House. And that Elliot Abrams, an assistant secretary of state, had accidentally transposed two digits of a bank account deposit so that a $10 million donation from the Sultan of Brunei intended for the Contras wound up in the personal account of a shipping company owner, who promptly withdrew it.

John Poindexter and Oliver North were given immunity to testify, and when they did, all sorts of secret dealings came pouring out. Poindexter, defiant and proud, admitted destroying the original finding that the president had signed on November 21, 1986, which had confirmed the arms-for-hostages deal.* And North . . . North stole the show. Turning up in full battle dress, dripping medals that included the Purple Heart, he kept the audience transfixed with his bravado-filled tales of secret flights and payoffs, all in the name of patriotism and advancing the president's agenda. In between the mythmaking, he admitted providing false statements to Congress about the NSC's role in aiding the Contras, shredding classified documents, and misusing government funds.

A cavalcade of rogues was implicated in the aftermath—CIA station chiefs, intelligence analysts, a Texas dowager heiress, a beer magnate, gunrunners, Arab princes and potentates. Witnesses began pointing fingers at one another, and after Bill Casey died of a brain tumor on May 6, 1987, their fingers were redirected at him with impunity. The paper trail detailing the diversion of funds had been scrubbed clean, so facts and lies were mixed liberally. The exaggerations and outright fabrications got so ridiculous that two files on A. B. Culvahouse's desk were labeled "Oliver North Is a Liar" and "John Poindexter Is a Liar." Wyoming congressman Dick Cheney lobbied Culvahouse for pardons for both men. "He said it was a witch hunt, that these guys thought they were doing the right thing, the Boland Amendment was unconstitutional—a usurpation of the president's powers—and that political activity was being criminalized."

The only pardon being considered was for Bud McFarlane. The president was very sympathetic. McFarlane was a favorite of his—in the words of one aide, "*very much* beloved." He had a conscience; he'd tried to kill himself. Ronald Reagan thought he deserved to be let off the hook. But

---

* He told this author, "I destroyed it by burning. I have no regrets." (Email, Sept. 8, 2017)

aides convinced him that pardoning McFarlane would be akin to throwing Poindexter and North under the bus. And despite all the trouble they'd caused for the president, he still had great affection for them as well. While he was struggling with how to work out a solution, McFarlane sent word that pardoning him would be a mistake. He didn't want a pardon and wouldn't accept it if one was granted.

In fact, the first person from the Reagan administration to be indicted for wrongdoing had nothing to do with Iran-Contra. On March 18, 1987, the day of the president's first press conference in almost half a year, that distinction went to Mike Deaver, the former deputy chief of staff. Deaver had left his $72,000 White House job to start his own company and parlayed it into a multimillion-dollar lobbying concern. Along the way he'd allegedly sidestepped federal laws on influence peddling—time limits on when former top government officials were allowed to trade on their access and to cultivate business with agencies that once employed them. To make matters worse, the indictment charged that in appearances before a congressional subcommittee and the grand jury, Deaver had lied five times about his lobbying work.

The First Lady sensed that Deaver "went off track" and was heading toward real trouble. Like everyone else in Washington, she had seen Deaver's picture on the March 3, 1986 cover of *Time*, perched ostentatiously in the back of a Lincoln Town Car, talking on a cell phone, an unheard of futuristic toy, with the Capitol Dome in the background. The subtitle of the story was "Influence Peddling in Washington," which did not bode well from Nancy Reagan's point of view. She and Deaver still spoke regularly, and she warned him in no uncertain terms, "Mike, you've made a big mistake and I think you're going to regret it." But the warning came too late.

It galled Deaver that he was only *accused* of lying but portrayed as a miscreant, while Oliver North *admitted* he'd lied and earned rock-star status. A pardon from the president might have put the matter to rest, but Deaver never expected one. The most that Reagan was prepared to offer came in a statement to the press: "Mike Deaver has been our friend for twenty years. We wish him well."*

---

* In 1987, Deaver was convicted of three counts of perjury, fined $100,000, and given a three-year suspended prison sentence.

Ed Meese was also in hot water for ongoing alleged ethical violations. The Office of Government Ethics had already concluded in 1985 that Meese had violated conflict-of-interest rules in helping his friend E. Robert Wallach obtain a noncompetitive government contract for the Wedtech Corporation. Now, in 1987, an independent prosecutor was investigating Meese's effort to help Wallach secure government backing for an oil pipeline from Iraq to Jordan.

Morale in the Justice Department had hit rock bottom, the lowest it had been, a Justice appointee facetiously noted, "probably since the founding of the republic." High-placed officials threatened to quit over Meese's conduct. Deputy Attorney General Arnold Burns and Assistant Attorney General William Weld actually met with the president and vice president to complain that the attorney general had created an atmosphere that made it impossible for them to continue. Reagan listened (although he nodded off during Weld's presentation), but was unmoved. Meese had insisted he had done nothing wrong, and the president took him at his word. "I still have confidence in Ed Meese," he told the two men. "I hope you won't leave, but if you do there will be no hard feelings." (In March 1988, Burns and Weld resigned from Justice. Wallach would later be convicted in a scandal involving defense contracts. Meese was charged with complicity in an influence-peddling scheme, prompting his resignation, but the independent prosecutor decided against prosecuting him.)

Throughout the spring and summer of 1987, these embarrassments, especially the Iran-Contra investigation, drew attention away from the president's initiatives. Progress on an INF treaty that would eliminate all intermediate- and short-range missiles in Europe generated little public excitement. Reagan's long-overdue acknowledgment that "AIDS affects all of us," in a major AIDS speech on May 31, drew boos from the audience, which had expected much more from him at this late date. Reagan even had a hard time focusing the nation on good news about the economy. Individual income taxes were considerably lower, the stock market had experienced a record run-up, and interest rates and unemployment were down. The view was hardly bleak. But most front pages across the country kept their focus on the nonstop scandals and what they said about the president's disengagement as head of state.

It was time for him to reclaim the spotlight, and he set out to do so on a nine-day European tour in early June. He zeroed in on an address he'd agreed to give in Berlin to celebrate the city's 750th birthday. Jack Kennedy's *Ich bin ein Berliner* speech was still fresh in everyone's mind, and Reagan intended to use that as a benchmark, but significantly raise the stakes. On June 11, 1987, a crowd estimated at twenty thousand assembled in front of the Brandenburg Gate, just a hundred yards from the Berlin Wall. From where the president stood he could peer into the East, where an armed sentry stood at a brick security post. Two panes of bulletproof glass shielded Reagan in case the guard or anyone else got any ideas. There had been hope that his words would carry into the Communist sector, but East German police prohibited people from being within earshot of the loudspeakers.

"I come here today because wherever I go, whatever I do," Reagan began, "*Ich hab' noch einen Koffer in Berlin*." This line from a popular old German song translates as "I still have a suitcase in Berlin." Endearing, though no match for JFK's barnburner. But Reagan still had an ace up his sleeve. Later in the speech, following the introduction of an initiative to make Berlin the aviation hub of Central Europe, the president launched into a broadside questioning the sincerity of the Soviet Union's desire for peace. "There is one sign the Soviets can make that would be unmistakable, that would advance dramatically the cause of freedom and peace," Reagan said, his face flushed, his conviction palpable. Raising his voice a few decibels, he proclaimed, "Secretary Gorbachev, if you seek peace—if you seek prosperity for the Soviet Union and Eastern Europe—if you seek liberalization: come here, to this gate. Mr. Gorbachev, open this gate. *Mr. Gorbachev, tear down this wall.*"

The crowd went nuts. It was the line they'd been waiting to hear, a line that gave voice to the captivity of their city from the mouth of the President of the United States. So simple, and so effective. So Reaganesque. The line played repeatedly on television sets around the globe.

Mr. Gorbachev, tear down this wall.

Ronald Reagan drew strength and satisfaction from the worldwide reaction to his words. But back in Washington, D.C., the mood quickly dimmed again. Throughout the rest of June and most of July, the Iran-Contra hearings continued to dominate attention in the nation's capital, and its glare cast a collateral pall over the White House and its occupants. The testimony implicating Oliver North and his accomplices was piling up;

witnesses accused him outright of being both a thief and a compulsive liar. And it was reflecting on Ronald Reagan. The president tried to make light of it, quipping, "I think the spotlight has been growing so dim in recent days that when you get a mile and a half from the Potomac River, there are an awful lot of people who have gone back to their favorite television shows."

If they had, however, it was out of disgust. Polls showed that only 42 percent of the public approved of his handling of the job, the lowest rating of his entire presidency. More than 50 percent thought he was lying to them. The New York Times reported that the hearings were taking a personal toll on the president. "More than ever he is showing signs of his 76 years, so much so that his memory lapses and rambling discourse are no longer a source of friendly jokes, but one of concern, friends say." He'd always had trouble with putting names to faces. But "at a recent news conference, for instance, the President was unable to remember the name of the United Nations Security Council." And he'd referred to his secretary of state as "General Secretary Shultz." It didn't help that his new defense for avoiding reporters' questions at an event was cupping a hand to his ear and shaking his head, pretending he couldn't hear.

Howard Baker had been forewarned about the president's "recent detachment and vagueness and . . . about whether the president was fully functioning." Baker's former chief of staff, Jim Cannon, reported that Reagan was "failing—fast," and that "members of his staff had been signing his initials on policy papers." But after close personal observation, Baker found the opposite was true—that, in his estimation, the president was in complete control of his faculties.

His leadership abilities were put to the test over the opportunity to fill another vacancy at the Supreme Court. On June 28, 1987, Justice Lewis Powell notified the White House that he intended to retire after serving fifteen years on the bench. Powell was seventy-nine, a Nixon appointee who had undermined conservative causes by casting deciding votes in favor of abortion, affirmative action, and separation of church and state "regardless of his own personal views about the case." Reagan intended to appoint a judge who would impart a stronger conservative footing and rebalance the court in a shift to the right—"toward the Constitution," as Ed Meese emphasized. In fact, a candidate was already at the top of the list.

On July 1, Reagan announced he was nominating Robert Bork, a former Yale law professor and judge on the U.S. Court of Appeals for the District of Columbia. It touched off a firestorm that seized the front pages from Iran-Contra. Bork's writings from the appeals court bench were viewed by many as strident and ideological. The president insisted, "He is widely regarded as the most prominent and intellectually powerful advocate of judicial restraint in the country," but an outcry was heard almost as soon as the words were out of Reagan's mouth.

Ted Kennedy led the charge to dispatch the Bork nomination. In a denunciation issued immediately on the floor of the Senate, he declared, "Robert Bork's America is a land in which women would be forced into back alley abortions, blacks would sit at segregated lunch counters, rogue police could break down citizens' doors in midnight raids, school children could not be taught about evolution, writers and artists could be censored at the whim of government, and the doors of the federal courts would be shut on the fingers of millions of citizens for whom the judiciary is—and is often the only—protector of the individual rights that are the heart of democracy." No justice, Kennedy said, "was better than this injustice." Benjamin Hooks, the executive director of the NAACP, trailed Kennedy's blast, saying, "We will fight it all the way—until hell freezes over, and then we'll skate across on the ice."

The fight against Bork began to escalate. No one challenged his legal qualifications. The *New York Times* editorial board wrote, "Robert Bork is a lawyer and judge of formidable intellect. His wit and charm made him a hit with Yale law students of all philosophical persuasions." But his judicial philosophy alarmed centrists and liberals who vowed to fight—and defeat—his confirmation.

It was an extraordinary conflict. Only rarely—in fact, only once, during the Depression—had a justice been rejected for his political beliefs. Conventional wisdom held that a Supreme Court nomination was above politics. But the Reagan administration had set the table for battle with Antonin Scalia's appointment in 1986. Scalia's adherence to "strict constructionism," or "originalism"—interpreting law according to values explicitly expressed by the framers of the Constitution—left all other decision making up to legislatures. In other words, a state law prohibiting the use of contraceptives, which the Supreme Court had struck down in 1965 (a decision Bork criticized), would not be heard by a bench with originalists in the majority. The same was true of *Roe v. Wade* and *Brown v. Board of Education*. Democrats vowed not to seat another ideologue on the Court.

The president was determined to stand by Bork. He had been a leading contender when Sandra Day O'Connor was picked and a leading contender when Antonin Scalia was picked. "I've passed over Bob Bork twice," Reagan said. "This time, he's my nominee, and we're going to make sure he's confirmed."

It wasn't as easy as that. The confirmation process became a political knife fight. Joe Biden, an early Bork supporter, had second thoughts this time around. Howell Heflin, a senator from Alabama, led an exodus of Southern Democrats, which churned up doubt in some "squishy Republicans," including Oregon senator Robert Packwood, a confirmed "no" vote. And Robert Bork wasn't helping himself. He came off as brusque, pompous, and ungracious in person, and he handled himself poorly as a witness in front of the Senate Judicial Committee.

After polling key officials on the Hill on October 1, aides advised the president that the confirmation was a lost cause and that it would be best if Judge Bork withdrew. Reagan demurred. "He thought it was Bob Bork's decision," A. B. Culvahouse recalls. "If Bork wanted a vote, he'd support him." However, Howard Baker and Ken Duberstein met with the president and Bork on October 9 to report that the votes were not there. The Judiciary Committee had voted against recommending the judge to the full Senate. Robert Bork was not going to be confirmed.

"What do you want to do?" Duberstein asked him.

Bork's eyes narrowed, he leaned forward in his chair. "I want to line them all up and make them vote," he said, to everyone's dismay.

On October 23, 1987, the roll-call vote wasn't even close: forty-two for, fifty-eight against. It was official: he was the first person to be "borked." He would not be the last.

Ed Meese immediately proposed they nominate Douglas Ginsburg to fill the empty Court seat. Ginsburg was a former Harvard Law professor, a vigorous conservative, more conservative than Bork, and young—only forty-one years old. Howard Baker pushed hard for Anthony Kennedy, a more mainstream conservative who had been close to the Reagan administration in Sacramento. He was a perfectly acceptable candidate with a number of close Democrats for friends. However, two factors tipped the scale in Ginsburg's favor: his young age increased expectations that he'd serve longer on the Court; and his brief experience as a judge meant there would be less writing—a grand total of thirteen appeals-court decisions—for opponents to pick apart and criticize. Timing was another consideration. It was important to put Bork's defeat quickly behind them by nominating a worthy replacement. Meese assured everyone that it wasn't necessary to delay Ginsburg's nomination by performing a thorough scrub. He'd already gone through an FBI background check as an appeals judge. "I know him well," Meese said, "and he's as clean as a hound's tooth."

"Okay," the president said, "let's go ahead and nominate him."

They might have given that hound's mouth a more thorough examination. In no time, Right to Life supporters expressed outrage at news that Ginsburg's wife, an obstetrician, had performed abortions. She'd also lied about winning a beauty pageant. And on November 5, Nina Totenberg, NPR's legal affairs correspondent, dropped a bombshell, reporting that Ginsburg had smoked marijuana socially while teaching at Harvard. Ginsburg admitted he'd smoked pot "on a few occasions." "I don't see any reason why I should withdraw his name," the president mused. But White House aides looking into the allegation found "he not only smoked a lot, but he had actually formed a little cooperative to buy pot." What kind of example does this set, with the "Just Say No to Drugs" campaign? they wondered.

Ken Duberstein called Ginsburg and said, "You're going to withdraw your nomination tomorrow. I'll draft a statement for you to read."

Howard Baker and A. B. Culvahouse delivered the news to the president. He looked up from his desk and said, "I should go with Tony Kennedy, right?"

There wasn't much choice. Kennedy was the last name on his list. This time, the nominee got a thorough scrub. "A.B. and I interviewed him on a Sunday at the Justice Department," Duberstein recalls, "and asked him all these mean, nasty, invasive personal questions." Kennedy assured them it would be a "very boring Sunday morning," and he didn't disappoint. On February 2, 1988, the Senate confirmed him 97–0 in a rare bipartisan effort.

But it was the last cooperative moment of its kind. With less than a year left in the Reagan era, "the Democrats," Howard Baker told the president, "are in no mood to send you out of office on a high note."

CHAPTER FORTY-FOUR

THE LONG GOODBYE

"All finite things reveal infinitude."

—THEODORE ROETHKE

Neither, it seemed, was the economy, which delivered a series of seismic shocks.

The stock market had been driven up to hallucinatory heights, "powered by consumer spending and fueled by debt." The country was living beyond its means. America's level of private and business debt approached a gargantuan $8 trillion, twice the country's gross national product. Consumer borrowing was out of control. Dozens of savings-and-loan associations had filed for bankruptcy. The economy was on a collision course with recession.

Anticipating such a possibility, the Dow Jones Industrial Average suffered a nasty fall of almost two hundred points between late August and mid-September 1987, and U.S. bond prices dropped 30 percent, prompting economist John Kenneth Galbraith to warn of "a very, very nasty run on the dollar and also a nasty collapse of the stock market." Within weeks, the worst-case scenario happened. On October 19, the Dow plunged 508 points, a spectacular collapse, obliterating an astounding 22.6 percent of its value in a single day—double the loss in 1929 that touched off the Great Depression. The president assured investors that "the underlying economy remains strong," unwittingly quoting Herbert Hoover almost word for word. President Reagan also called the crash "just a correction," which did little to restore public confidence. Nor did it comfort the thousands of investors wiped out by margin calls in the liquidation. Ten days later stocks declined another 8 percent before the market began to stabilize, but the "correction" had exposed a cicatrix of economic fault lines.

Most economists recommended a tax increase mixed with regulatory reforms to trim the budget deficit, but on both fronts Reagan continued to resist. He abhorred governmental red tape almost as much as he loathed taxes. "His trust," as Lou Cannon noted, "was in the magic of the marketplace." According to the president, the deficit was Congress's burden to bear. "I have great confidence in the future," he reiterated. But his morning-in-America optimism was no longer enough to give him a pass. As the Dow continued to seesaw, the president was forced into action. "I will meet with the bipartisan leadership of Congress to arrange a procedure for deficit reduction," he promised in a press conference on October 22. Reluctantly, he conceded, "I'm putting everything on the table with the exception of Social Security." Did that mean he'd consider new tax increases? The president remained vague. "They'll find out when I sit down there," was all he'd allow.

As a close friend revealed, "I promise you, the stock market is the last thing on his mind right now."

At that moment, Nancy Reagan's health was dominating his thoughts. On October 5, during her annual mammogram at Bethesda Naval Hospital, doctors had detected a suspicious lesion—possibly a malignant tumor—in her left breast. A biopsy revealed that it was cancerous, but noninvasive; it had not spread to other areas of the breast or to nearby lymph nodes. Doctors recommended she consider a lumpectomy, in which only the tumor and some surrounding tissue would be removed; otherwise it meant undergoing a radical mastectomy, a more drastic procedure in which the entire breast and underlying muscle are extracted. According to one of her physicians, "She went against all medical advice in deciding to have her entire left breast removed and the underarm lymph nodes." He described it as the most aggressive option, like "taking a shotgun to kill a fly." Doctors at the Mayo Clinic delivered a similar opinion. But the First Lady had made up her mind. "A lumpectomy seemed too inconclusive," she said, and required follow-up radiation treatment. "I couldn't possibly lead the kind of life I lead, and keep the schedule that I do, having radiation or chemotherapy." A mastectomy was "the best way to get it all over with."

"Ronnie wept," she said, when he learned of her diagnosis, but understood there was no further malignancy. Based on all indications, the cancer had been contained, "making her prospects for a full recovery virtually certain."

That was more than could be said for the administration. More tremors rumbled through the White House during the fall of 1987.

Rumors were rife that Howard Baker, whose arrival as chief of staff had done much to stabilize the administration, was "all but certain to leave his job before next year is up." "Very soon after Howard took the job, I could see him pulling back and looking for a way out," a close associate recalls. If the whispers were true and Baker did in fact step down, aides feared the president would lose his dependable keel.

Other exits were not viewed as entirely unfavorable. In early November, Caspar Weinberger announced his resignation as secretary of defense. His wife, Jane, was ill, which directed his priorities elsewhere, but truth be told Weinberger had been marginalized in recent key policy initiatives, none more consequential than the Reykjavik agreement to limit intermediate-range missiles in Europe, which he continued to oppose and lobbied to overturn. He also advocated a thinly disguised twist on Star Wars—the development and deployment of satellites armed with interceptor missiles in order to defend U.S. interests against Soviet attacks in space. He had virtually no support on Capitol Hill for his Defense budget. His mantra, "Never compromise," no longer felt in step with the moment; only hardcore conservatives continued to hew that line. Pat Buchanan, for one, remained a voice in that wilderness. "The spirit of compromise is in the air," he remarked with distaste. "The theme is, 'Let's go up and compromise one for the Gipper.'" But pragmatists and most mainstream Republicans ignored such commentary.

Weinberger's departure would help to spur progress toward a more meaningful strategic arms-reduction treaty—or START—with the Soviet Union. With his naysaying out of the president's ear, George Shultz had a mandate to pursue further negotiations. Shultz was also tasked to close a deal for a Reagan-Gorbachev summit in Washington, as the two leaders had proposed during their talks in Reykjavik. Summit fever was running high. To stimulate it, in the spirit of glasnost, the Soviets advanced several landmark reforms: allowing the refuseniks—mostly Russian Jews—to emigrate if they chose to do so, agreeing to sign an INF treaty, and revealing that they were pulling out of Afghanistan as soon as was humanly possible. There was also talk of reforms in some of the Warsaw Pact countries. Shultz felt that "a profound, historic shift was under way" and that the Soviet Union was "turning a corner." To top it off, Gorbachev, for no apparent reason, dropped his insistence on limiting SDI development as a prerequisite to signing the INF treaty.

"Gorbachev just blinked," Shultz reported to the president, who thought there was now no limit to agreements they might reach. Had Gorbachev finally surrendered to the inevitability of SDI? Not in any passive sense. Gorbachev had been assured by his top scientists that "SDI was not realistic from the technical point of view. It looked frightening initially, but it wouldn't work." It was "more dream than threat." Let the Americans waste their resources, he reasoned. There was other turf on which he'd stand his ground.

The Soviet leader arrived in Washington on December 7, 1987, in an effort to produce a substantive arms-reduction agreement, a meaningful first step toward ending the Cold War. The INF treaty, Gorbachev said, would "set the whole process in motion." But he was concerned with reports of a congressional backlash. A group of conservative senators, including Jesse Helms, Malcolm Wallop, and Dan Quayle, had already announced their opposition to the treaty. They feared it would lead to a denuclearized Europe, leaving the West vulnerable to conventional Soviet forces, and they intended to amend it—and amend it *and amend it*—whatever it took to dilute and ultimately scuttle its chances of passing. Even Bob Dole, usually a productive partner in the Senate, accused the president of "stuffing this treaty down the throats of the allies."

The hard-line conservatives were harsher in their criticism. The head of the Conservative Caucus, a right-wing public policy organization, derided Reagan as "nothing more than a useful idiot for Soviet propaganda." And

George Will accused him of accelerating America's "intellectual disarmament" and effectively losing the Cold War.

Reagan basically ignored the opposition. He planned to sign the treaty in a televised ceremony with Gorbachev soon after the general secretary set foot in the White House—just after lunch, at 1:45 p.m., a time set by Joan Quigley. The president was eager to make an impression. He'd already arranged for Gorbachev's flight path to take him low and slow over Southern California so he could see endless private houses with backyard swimming pools, "perhaps with a second car or a boat in the driveway." "These are the houses of the working people," he wanted to tell Gorbachev. Reagan had always harbored a secret wish to fly the Soviet premier through American suburbs, showing off its factories and parking lots jammed with the workers' gleaming late-model cars as a contrast to the Soviet way of life. Americans had been doing this to Soviets at least since Nixon showed off the American model kitchen in the so-called Kitchen Debate. But this was the sentimental MGM ideal of America. Gorbachev knew enough not to be taken in by that image. When the president, during their initial discussion, brandished it in his argument against Soviet human rights abuses, Gorbachev replied to him much as Khrushchev had replied to Nixon: "What about your people who sleep in the streets and all your unemployed?" He also rebuked Reagan about "a proposal then current in Washington to build a fence along the Mexican border," which he said "was as bad as anything the Soviets had ever done." He was well informed about the United States and especially its cultural idiosyncrasies; he wasn't about to let its president reprimand him—and he pushed back. "I'm not on trial here," he snapped unapologetically. "I'm not a defendant and you're not a judge to judge me."

Gorbachev proved his mettle in the Cabinet Room immediately following the treaty ceremony, during an interlude when the president was still basking in the glow of the treaty and not focused on what his guest was saying. Members of both delegations crowded into the cramped space, expecting to hear informal remarks from the leaders on their objectives for the summit. Reading from prepared notes, Gorbachev enumerated a list of items for discussion, including chemical weapons and troop reductions. He found it incomprehensible that the Soviets were actively destroying chemical weapons while the United States seemed to be replenishing its reserves.

He also took issue with the president's favorite Russian aphorism, *doveryai no proveryai*—"trust but verify"—at a time when the United States continued to propose verification of only state facilities. "That would include all the Soviet Union's, but not all of the U.S.'s," he complained.

The president appeared flustered. Without prepared talking points, he didn't know how to respond to the specific issues Gorbachev had raised, ceding the microphone to George Shultz to offer a spontaneous rebuttal.

Before that, however, the president delivered a lame joke. "An American scholar, on his way to the airport before a flight to the Soviet Union, got into a conversation with his cabdriver, a young man who said that he was still finishing his education. The scholar asked, 'When you finish your schooling, what do you want to do?' The young man answered, 'I haven't decided yet.' After arriving at the airport in Moscow, the scholar hailed a cab. His cabdriver, again, was a young man, who happened to mention he was still getting his education. The scholar, who spoke Russian, asked, 'When you finish your schooling, what do you want to be? What do you want to do?' The young man answered, 'They haven't told me yet.' That's the difference between our systems."

Instead of the usual chuckles, the punch line was greeted in silence. A flush of embarrassment tided into Gorbachev's face. The situation had called for a more statesmanlike response, and Reagan had failed to meet the moment. "I was disturbed and disappointed," Shultz recalled, telling the president later, "That was terrible."

"We can't let this happen again," Howard Baker agreed.

There'd be no more big meetings in the Cabinet Room. From now on, they'd confine the president to smaller get-togethers in the intimacy of the Oval Office, where he'd be prepared in advance and the agenda could be controlled.

Gorbachev meant business. He was determined to go the INF treaty one better by "entering a new phase, a phase of reducing strategic offensive arms." He proposed a 50 percent reduction in strategic arms and expressed his desire to sign an agreement as they had the day before. There were disagreements about linking it to SDI, as there had been in Reykjavik, but Gorbachev brushed them aside. Earlier that morning, when Reagan assured him the United States was going forward with research and development in the interests of eventually deploying SDI, Gorbachev cavalierly said, "Mr. President, do what you think you have to do. And if in the end you think you have a system you want to deploy, go ahead and deploy. Who am I to tell you what to do? . . . We are moving in another direction."

Anything more substantial would most likely be negotiated next year in Moscow, where Reagan had agreed to continue their talks. In the remaining time in Washington, Gorbachev expressed his desire to "meet American people outside the official events." In a large respect, he viewed himself as the Soviet Union's emissary, "sending out good vibes," as he assured a contingent of U.S. senators. But so far, much to his consternation, he had been isolated from the general public for security reasons.

On December 10, he broke with the script. There had been a breakfast at the Soviet embassy with George Bush, who was actively campaigning for a 1988 presidential bid. Running late, the two men headed to an appointment at the White House to meet with a group of America's top business leaders. As their motorcade inched along Connecticut Avenue, Gorbachev stared out the window, intrigued by the lunchtime crowd waving at them. At the corner of L Street, he shouted, "Stop the car!" and leaped out before his panicked security detail could intervene. Grinning broadly, he reached out to shake hands with people who converged around him, stunned and delighted by his presence. Others leaned out windows and hung over balconies. To each well-wisher, he said, "World peace."

It was a brilliant public-relations maneuver. Reagan now had competition as the Great Communicator, as the *Christian Science Monitor* acknowledged in a pithy front-page headline. The Soviet premier— referred to affectionately by his American fan base as "Gorby"—had done some serious image-building during his five-day visit, displacing the legacy of his stone-faced, shoe-banging predecessors. *Time* even named him its "Man of the Year." Most members of the business community at the White House joined the Gorby lovefest. Only one holdout claimed he was still suspicious of Gorbachev and hoped Americans were not overly eager to deal with him. "In the art of deal making," said real-estate developer Donald Trump, "you should not want to make the deal too much." It was only after the Russian told Trump that he loved Trump Tower and invited him to build a hotel in Moscow that the New York real-estate magnate changed his tune.

Gorbachev turned out to be a man of his word. On February 8, 1988, he announced the withdrawal of 115,000 Soviet troops from Afghanistan, promising that the last would be out by the summer of 1989 (sooner if Reagan agreed to stop financing the Afghan mujahideen rebels, which the president refused to do). And Gorbachev began to speak more positively about democracy and capitalism. This was astonishing. Gorbachev's turn of the Soviet system toward openness—glasnost—and reform—perestroika—were the first real signs of change after decades of repression and stagnation. For openers, he legalized small-scale private enterprise and promoted free discussion within the Communist Party. He'd also instituted term limits, as well as secret ballots for legislative and party posts. Reagan had famously called Russia the Evil Empire, but he was having second thoughts. "Yes," he stressed, "it was an evil empire," but the nickname pertained to the old Soviet model of Communism. He read *Perestroika*, Gorbachev's manifesto for restructuring the Soviet system, and declared it "an epitaph: Capitalism had triumphed over Communism." That might have been an overly broad evaluation, but the manifesto certainly supported his belief that "the forces of Communism were in retreat."

The rollback hadn't spread to Nicaragua. The Sandinistas remained firmly entrenched in their control of the government. And despite the existential damage of Iran-Contra, President Reagan was still committed to undermining them. He pressed Congress for more aid to the Contras to the tune of $270 million. "This is not the time to reverse progress," he implored. When Congress balked, the request was reduced to $43 million and later to $36.2 million, until it was finally defeated outright, a clear rebuke to the White House. "True humanitarian aid," House leaders instructed the president, "would not include weapons and ammunition." Nor would the CIA be involved any longer in supplying *any* aid to the Contras.

The cutoff of U.S. aid forced the Contras to reconsider their prospects for continuing the fight against a much more powerful foe. On March 21, 1988, they met with Sandinista leaders and signed a cease-fire agreement that effectively ended a decade of internal strife. Both sides worried, however, that U.S. operatives would undermine the truce, as they had done in the past. "We are afraid that the field commanders are under a lot of pressure from Washington," a Sandinista official said. But the two sides seemed determined to honor the peace. To support it, the U.S. House and Senate passed a bipartisan $48 million nonmilitary aid package to cover the Contras' expenses.

Only a week earlier, a federal grand jury investigating the Iran-Contra affair had returned a twenty-three-count indictment of Oliver North, John Poindexter, and two other key participants, Richard Secord and Albert Hakim, on charges of obstruction of justice, conspiracy, wire fraud, and theft of government property. If found guilty, each of the defendants faced decades of prison time, setting up speculation as to whether the president would pardon them. Poindexter had testified that he was the highest-ranking administration official to approve the diversion of funds to the Contras and decided not to inform the president, affording him deniability in the end.

"I have no knowledge of anything that was broken," Reagan said again during a press conference at the White House, with Israeli prime minister Yitzhak Shamir at his side. "From all the investigation and everything else, we don't know where that money came from and we don't know who had it and we don't know where it went." That would have been disingenuous enough had a reporter not confronted him with a follow-up about Bud McFarlane's guilty plea to four misdemeanor counts of withholding information from Congress. "He just pleaded guilty to not telling Congress everything it wanted to know. I've done that myself." The president knew the comment was a mistake the moment it was out of his mouth. Without delay, he turned and fled with Shamir, but not before whispering to his guest, "Oh, boy. Just for that careless remark . . . they'll go wild about Reagan wants to lie to Congress or something." Unfortunately for the president, the whisper was picked up by a microphone, giving reporters the kicker to their stories.

As America's sorry relationship with the Contras limped to an end, the president shifted his attention from Nicaragua to Panama, where another sorry relationship, with an even more flawed U.S. client, military dictator Manuel Noriega, was reaching its endgame. Noriega had been one of the CIA's most valuable intelligence sources in Latin America, but he was a brutal despot, and his personal fortune stemmed from drug trafficking and money laundering. According to John Poindexter, "Panama had been helpful in support of the Contras, and the CIA had been using Noriega in sensitive operations." But he'd been warned: his defiant criminality was becoming an embarrassment. And he was weird. He had a voodoo room in his residence that showcased dolls with pins sticking in them, and a bowl containing slips of paper denoting names on a "hit list"—Ronald Reagan, Bill Casey, George Bush, Poindexter. On February 4, 1988, the Justice Department indicted Noriega on drug trafficking and racketeering charges. Two months later, President Reagan froze all assets of the Panamanian government, tightening the squeeze on its obstreperous leader.

Negotiations with Noriega stretched on for four months. He promised to resign, reneged, demanded a payoff to leave, then withdrew it, enjoying his success in "screw[ing] around with the gringo," as he put it, and manipulating the political system. Reagan promised that the United States would not use military force to push Noriega out of power, but the dictator's persistent arrogance made it tempting. If not for George Bush, the Panamanian leader would have been long gone. Noriega's ties to Bush during his tenure as CIA chief had the potential to compromise his presidential campaign. An indictment, especially, might disclose sensitive transactions. Bush was dead-set against pursuing any arrangement to oust Noriega, insisting "we should sit back and analyze the situation for a couple of weeks." Or more: at least until after the election. "If we back away," George Shultz argued, "we leave this guy in charge of a whole country and with all his drug affiliations and Cuban support."

The president agreed to "roundtable it with the guys." On May 16, 1988, in a meeting in the Oval Office, he listened to the arguments. Shultz and Colin Powell, the new national security adviser, urged making a deal with Noriega to leave Panama in exchange for dropping the indictment. Money was involved, a golden parachute, so to speak, but it was a small price to pay for ridding Panama of Noriega. Jim Baker, Bush's surrogate, argued vehemently against the deal, warning Reagan that such an agreement would be "as big a problem for him as 'Irangate.'" Baker and Bush enlisted Republican congressional leaders to shore up their opposition by mounting a strong campaign against Noriega's ouster. But Reagan's patience with the Panamanian dictator was exhausted. There was only so much screwing with the gringo a president could endure. After four months and rounds of fruitless negotiations, Ronald Reagan threw in the towel. Let his successor deal with the Noriega problem, he decided. If the election returned a Republican to the White House, it would wind up in George Bush's lap.

There were too many hot spots—and too little time left.

Throughout the spring of 1988 the Reagan administration expended energy in the Middle East and Afghanistan to reduce the powderkeg tensions that were threatening to blow. Roadblocks, however, proved insurmountable at every turn. Peace in the Middle East seemed more remote than ever. There was no letup in the Iran–Iraq War, which had already claimed more than half a million lives. The PLO had intensified its uprisings. The Israelis were unwilling to trade territory for peace, and the Arab nations vowed never to compromise. And even though Mikhail Gorbachev issued orders drawing his troops down in Afghanistan, both the Soviet Union and the United States determined to continue supplying arms to the opposing factions as civil war raged between the Communists in the cities and the mujahideen in the mountains and valleys. The CIA had already invested more than $2 billion in weapons to support the Islamic militant Taliban, seemingly oblivious to the fact that they were establishing a fundamentalist regime.

Toward the end of the second term, the leadership from the Oval Office felt even more disengaged. The president seemed more distant than usual, often running out of steam early in the day. He relied more on jokes than jawboning, trotting out old stories as a smoke screen for his vulnerabilities. Conservatives especially felt the disconnect. Paul Weyrich, one of the founders of the Heritage Foundation and a leader of the New Right, concluded, "Reagan is a weakened president, weakened in spirit as well as in clout."

In the months that remained in his presidency, Ronald Reagan trained his foreign-policy focus on one opening where he felt he could have a real impact and produce lasting change. He believed Mikhail Gorbachev was making an earnest effort to reshape communism and transform the Soviet Union. "He was the first [of its leaders] not to push Soviet expansionism,"

Reagan explained, "the first to destroy nuclear weapons, the first to suggest a free market and to support open elections and freedom of expression." The president saw a strong opportunity to promote Soviet–American relations by resuming the dialogue he and Gorbachev began in Geneva in 1985 and continued in Washington, D.C.

Plans for a Moscow summit began taking shape in the spring of 1988, with the signing of START as its historic centerpiece. The issue of strategic arms, the backbone of the U.S. nuclear arsenal, presented a more complex negotiation than the intermediate-range missiles of the INF treaty—and carried greater implications for the country's long-term security. Eliminating five thousand land- and sea-based ballistic missiles would be an enormous achievement, but the many harmonious parts of such an ambitious treaty proved too hard to achieve in a few months' time. Reagan knew as early as February that a START agreement remained out of reach for the Moscow summit, but he resolved to meet with Gorbachev to legitimize their ongoing efforts to end the Cold War.

In any case, during his visit he intended to press Gorbachev on human rights issues. It had been a sticking point between them in past meetings. Reagan had no right poking his nose into the internal matters of the Soviet Union, Gorbachev had insisted. "We want to build contacts among people in all forums," he said, "but this should be done without interfering in domestic affairs, without sermonizing or imposing one's views or ways, without turning family or personal problems into a pretext for confrontation between states." But the plight of Jewish dissidents and the refuseniks gave the president a way to approach the subject from a different angle: religious freedom. Perhaps, he ventured, if people were permitted to worship as they wished, maybe they wouldn't be so intent on leaving the Soviet Union. Still, there were 1,200 Soviet Jews he knew of who sought to emigrate. He had given Gorbachev a list of their names in Reykjavik, to little effect, and he'd brought them up again during the Washington summit. This time, he decided more action was necessary.

He'd received a gut-wrenching letter from a precocious Russian twelve-year-old named Vera Zieman, whose parents were refuseniks. It described in plaintive detail the "excruciating legal and social limbo" her family had lived in since they'd applied for permission to leave the Soviet Union. To the president, Vera sounded almost like a model *American* teenager. She "reads John Updike, finds Nancy Drew too predictable, and recites T. S. Eliot," her letter said. Nevertheless, she was shunned by classmates and ostracized for her parents' beliefs. She reported that for weeks after being questioned by the KGB, she screamed in her sleep. "It's very hard for me here," she complained. "Sometimes I'm very frightened."

Here was an example the president could exploit in his bid to keep human rights at the forefront of the summit. In fact, he and Nancy determined to visit Vera and her parents just as soon as they arrived in Moscow. But the Soviet deputy foreign minister sent word to Colin Powell that "the Ziemans would never be allowed to emigrate if Reagan insisted on visiting them." Instead, the president prepared several speeches designed to address the issue vigorously without jeopardizing individuals still waiting to leave.

I never expected to be here," Ronald Reagan thought as he disembarked in Moscow on May 28, 1988. It seemed to him like he had been "dropped into a grand historical moment." For him, an anti-Soviet crusader, Moscow was never-never-land back in the day when so-called fellow travelers rattled the Hollywood movie industry. But this was a different time—and a very different set of circumstances. The Leader of the Free World had come to the Motherland, the cradle of Communism, evidence that "the ever whirling wheels of change," as the poet Edmund Spenser said, were spinning in an extraordinary new direction.

The president sought to navigate that route as soon as he joined Mikhail Gorbachev, after hiking up a grand staircase into the Kremlin's opulent St. George Hall. Without hesitating, he brought up the delicate subject of religious freedom, so delicate, in fact, "that if word got out that this was even being discussed, [he] would deny that he had said anything about it." Reagan suggested that Gorbachev announce that "religious freedom was part of the peoples' rights." If Gorbachev could see his way clear to do that, the president was convinced, it would be seen as heroic and any ill feeling people had toward the Soviet Union would be erased. "This isn't something I'm suggesting we negotiate," he said, "just an idea. I'm not trying to tell you how to run your country." It was being offered as friendly advice, nothing more. Reagan "did not want to kick anybody in the shins," he said. And nonchalantly, so as not to press his luck, he added, "Wouldn't it be a good idea to tear down the Berlin Wall?"

Then he did press his luck. He handed Gorbachev a list of fourteen human rights cases that were on the State Department's action list. "Will you act on these requests?" he inquired. Gorbachev pocketed it and bristled, saying, "There are too many lists."

Nothing else of real importance was accomplished during the summit. Seven obligatory agreements were consummated, but they were minor for the most part, concerning such matters as fishing rights and the exchange of students. The main outcome was what *Time* referenced as the Photo Opportunity Summit, a public-relations extravaganza for both countries. The Reagans were photographed visiting Red Square, Lenin's tomb, the Bolshoi Theater, and a renovated dacha where the Gorbachevs hosted a casual dinner. The only unscripted event was a spur-of-the-moment stroll along the Arbat, a refashioned pedestrian mall lined with quaint shops and cafés their son Ron had urged them to visit in order to meet "real" Russians. The Reagans jumped out of their limousine in order to greet the Sunday-evening strollers, who converged around the American couple in order to shake their outstretched hands. "It was amazing how quickly the street was jammed curb to curb with people," Reagan recorded that night in his diary. "They were generally indistinguishable from people I had seen all my life on countless streets in America." The outpouring of affection took him by surprise, but it turned dark and scary within minutes. KGB goons "appeared out of nowhere to form a flying wedge around the Reagans," punching and kicking the well-wishers, flinging them violently aside. "I've never seen so much brutal manhandling as they did on their own people who were in no way getting out of hand," the president observed. As he was pushed back into his car, he muttered, "It's still a police state."

Still, he managed to salvage unprecedented highlights from the visit—a speech promoting religious freedom at a monastery given back to the Russian Orthodox Church; another at Moscow State University to explain the beauty of the U.S. Constitution; and an address on democracy and free enterprise to ninety-eight human rights activists, dissidents, and refuseniks, including the Ziemans, in which he quoted from works of suppressed

Russian authors. "Political leadership in a democracy requires seeing past the abstractions and embracing the vast diversity of humanity, and doing it with humility—listening as best you can, not just to those with high positions, but to the cacophonous voices of ordinary people, and trusting those millions of people, keeping out of their way," he told them. "And the word we have for this is 'freedom.'"

Reagan returned to the United States in triumph, but the strain of the trip was evident in his appearance. He was exhausted. The leading-man face showed the crags and lines of his seventy-seven years; the life-guard physique bowed slightly; his gait was slower, less exuberant, his stamina a quart low. Gorbachev had introduced him to passersby in Red Square as "Grandfather Reagan," and the gibe was not entirely unwarranted.

Admirers spoke privately about an unprecedented third term, but such an option was out of the question—legally and physically. Reagan was tired, "tired of living in a fishbowl," as his wife described Washington, and tired from the constant problem-solving that consumed the President of the United States. He was looking forward to the end of his administration, retiring with elder-statesman status to his Santa Barbara ranch and to a $2.5 million house in Bel-Air that eighteen wealthy friends had chipped in to buy for him. Otherwise, he spent the summer and fall of 1988 campaigning for a favored successor. George Bush, his faithful vice president and a man he'd grown to esteem, was locked in a tight contest with Massachusetts governor Michael Dukakis, and Ronald Reagan took to the stump with renewed vigor. "It rejuvenated him," said White House press secretary Marlin Fitzwater. The crowds he encountered were wildly enthusiastic, not as much for the candidacy of Bush as for the presence of their beloved president. His public image continued to excite and inspire.

Campaigning for Bush went toward strengthening his own legacy, which had been bruised by all the political scandals that had roiled his second term. And there were many. Beyond Iran-Contra and Ed Meese's ethical lapses, an investigation by the House Government Operations Committee into the Department of Housing and Urban Development revealed a government agency "enveloped by influence peddling, favoritism, abuse, greed, fraud, embezzlement and theft." The head of the Environmental Protection Agency's waste-management program was convicted of lying to Congress and obstructing a congressional inquiry. And the administration turned a blind eye to the imminent collapse of the savings-and-loan institutions that would eventually precipitate an expensive government scandal.

But none of it stuck to Ronald Reagan. *Teflon man.* His popularity was too strong. When it came to this president, the American public chose to look beyond the headlines, beyond the impropriety and the failure of Reaganomics. People were more likely to credit him with the economy's returning to form after the inflation and malaise of the Carter years, the softening of relations with the Soviet Union, and the eventual fall of Communism in Eastern Europe. Things were really much better in many ways, especially the economy, the grounds on which most people judge a president. Over the course of Reagan's two terms, unemployment had fallen from 7.5 percent to 5.4 percent and the inflation rate dropped to 4.3 percent from 11.8 percent.

The country's hunger for Reagan's inspirational leadership and gentle mirth overwhelmed any specific bad news. He made people feel proud to be American. He embraced the handle Dr. Feelgood, which his critics hadn't intended as a compliment, and his prescription to his patients was: resilience, hope, and faith. While accepting the nomination for president in 1980, Reagan had said, "More than anything else I want my candidacy to unify our country, to renew the American spirit and sense of purpose." And to a majority of Americans he'd delivered on his promise. He made the country feel better about itself; he restored its morale, its self-respect. Those were the intangibles. The more concrete results were harder to assess.

"Are you better off today than you were four years ago?" Or eight years, for that matter? Were Reagan's famous question posed as his era ended, many people would answer yes. But it was an emotional answer. There were those who more fully considered the ledger of accomplishments versus trade-offs, the cold, hard columns of credits and debits, and they expressed skepticism. As a Republican banker told correspondent David Broder,

"There is a widespread sense that the prosperity some have gained in this decade has been purchased at a cost still to be reckoned." The final tally would depend on the weight assigned to facts as opposed to feelings.

One unassailable entry in the credit column was Ronald Reagan's heart. It was big and expansive. He never stopped believing in "the American miracle" and the good people responsible for its achievements. He clung to the image of a nation populated by citizens "grounded in thoughtfulness and knowledge" and governed by ordinary American "values and common sense." In his final address to the nation, on January 11, 1989, he looked into the camera like a benevolent father and reflected on his romantic view of America—the "shining city upon a hill"—a place with "people of all kinds living in harmony and peace . . . and if there had to be city walls, the walls had doors and the doors were open to anyone with the will and the heart to get here." That was Ronald Reagan's America, welcoming and inclusive.

In the few weeks that remained of his presidency some general housekeeping was required. Medals of Freedom were awarded to various worthy high achievers; token gifts were given to trusted staff members. Contrary to expectation, there would be no last-minute pardons for North, McFarlane, or Poindexter. "Reagan was very clear about that," says Ken Duberstein, who became his fourth chief of staff, serving during the final few months after Howard Baker's departure, "especially concerning Ollie North. That had been decided months before." Despite the president's insistence that North was an innocent, maybe even a hero, in service to his country, the First Lady put her foot down: a pardon would tarnish her husband's place in history. Reagan acquiesced, leaving North's fate in the hands of the courts.

Pardoning Lyn Nofziger and Mike Deaver would be easier for him to reconcile. Both men had been convicted of lobbying violations—Nofziger for illegal lobbying,* Deaver for perjury—but the crimes had been committed *after* they'd left his employ, which made them easier to forgive. Reagan's instinct was to grant clemency to the former aides who had served him faithfully and for whom he had an abiding fondness. The pardons were a

---

* Nofziger's conviction was overturned later that June.

toss-up right down to the wire. Both men, however, sent word to the president that they considered themselves innocent of wrongdoing and thus ineligible for pardons.

George Steinbrenner was a different matter. The blustery New York Yankees owner had pleaded guilty in 1974 to making an illegal corporate contribution to Richard Nixon's presidential campaign and obstructing justice, and he had petitioned the White House for a presidential pardon. Nancy Reagan firmly opposed it. "She thought he was a boor and had embarrassed her in front of her friends," recalls A. B. Culvahouse, whose job it was to review each request. "But Steinbrenner had gone through the process. He'd done everything that people hadn't done who swooped in at the last minute and wanted a pardon. He waited the requisite period, and he provided a lot of assistance to the FBI and intelligence agencies through his shipbuilding business, putting assets in place. So he'd earned it." And the president, an unapologetic baseball fan, signed off on it.

Aside from packing up the Oval Office and the residence, most of Reagan's remaining days were filled with affectionate tributes, gestures of thanks, and receptions. The Notre Dame football team showed up to pay its respects days after being voted the national champions, bearing a special gift: the faded blue-and-gold letter sweater that had belonged to George Gipp, the president's muse. Members of Congress came by for a last handshake, to bid Reagan farewell. White House staff and Secret Service traipsed in for autographs and pictures.

But the president was reflective as well—even a bit melancholy. He was ready to leave the fishbowl, "totally prepared to turn the page and begin a new chapter," according to Fred Ryan, who would become Reagan's chief of staff in the new phase of his private life. Still, he was determined to drink in what was left of an extraordinary experience. Living in the White House, being president, was beyond anything he had imagined for himself. The view from the window of his study just off the Truman Balcony imbued him with this wonder; its awe-inspiring vista often absorbed him in a trancelike reverie. There, as he gazed across the South Lawn and the Ellipse all the way to the Potomac River Valley, stood the Washington Monument and the Jefferson Memorial. He was mesmerized by them and by what they represented to him personally. Contemplating his past and his future, it was hard to look away. An aide once came upon Reagan, staring out the window, not a muscle moving, seemingly in a hypnotic state. "What are you thinking about?" the aide asked the president, breaking his attention. Reagan smiled and whispered, "Everything."

Everything. Eight years full of memories—decisions and dramatic crises, "virtually all of life's highs and lows," as he put it. It was an experience that Hollywood couldn't have dreamed up, an experience he never foresaw— that no one foresaw—for the kid from Dixon, the Midwest sportscaster, the movie matinee idol, the television host. It was almost over now, time to move on.

Ronald Reagan rose earlier than usual on January 20, 1989. He had breakfast, read the paper starting with the comics as always, and spent a few abstracted minutes puttering around his nearly vacant study. On his way to the Oval Office, he fed acorns, as always, to the swarm of friendly squirrels that scampered along the colonnade abutting the Rose Garden. Even the unique events of Inauguration Day entailed a measure of routine. They had been replayed at the White House thirty-eight times, ever since John Adams transferred the seat of power to Thomas Jefferson in 1801— peacefully, methodically, as always.

This morning, the Oval Office was bare, with the exception of the desk and rug. The artwork and photos had been removed from the walls; the gallery of mementos no longer lined the shelves and windowsills. The august desk crafted from the timber of the HMS *Resolute* had been swept clean of everything but the telephone, its drawers emptied of personal papers. Even the jar full of jelly beans was gone.

Colin Powell, the national security adviser, arrived at 9:30 a.m., as always, to deliver the daily intelligence briefing. This morning, only an abbreviated report was necessary. "Mr. President," he said, "today the world is calm." A final phone call was made to console Lyn Nofziger's wife, whose daughter, Sue, was in the hospital dying of cancer. Word was passed that Orrin Hatch had called in a last-ditch effort to press for an Oliver North pardon, but Reagan only nodded without further response. Instead, he sat down at the desk and signed a letter of appreciation to Margaret Thatcher before scratching out a note to George Bush on a Post-it pad imprinted with the legend "Don't let the turkeys get you down." It was a simple, heartfelt message: "George I treasure the memories we share and wish you all the very best. You'll be in my prayers. God bless you and Barbara. I'll miss our Thursday lunches." He slipped it into the top drawer of the desk, where he knew the next president would be sure to see it.

George Bush was on his way in to meet the president for the traditional ride together to the Capitol, for the swearing-in ceremony. "Here, boys," Reagan said, extracting a card of white laminate from his pocket. "I won't need this any more. Who do I give this to?" It contained the fail-safe code that, when inserted into the "football" carried by his military aide, ordered the launch of nuclear missiles. It had haunted him for the entire eight years he was in office, and he was eager to get it out of his hands. "You can't get rid of it yet," Powell explained. "It's active until noon. Please put it back in your pocket."

The president stood up, paused, and took a last look around, a "nostalgic moment," he said, "of wanting to take one more look at the place that every morning I've been walking in." Then he saluted and walked out the door.

A fter the inaugural ceremony, Ronald and Nancy Reagan made their way to the east side of the Capitol where *Marine One*, renamed *Nighthawk* for the day because it was not in service as the presidential helicopter, was idling, ready to lift off. President and Mrs. Bush walked the Reagans to the chopper. "I was trying to keep the tears from flooding down my cheeks," Bush admitted. At the beginning of his inaugural address, he had paid tribute to his predecessor, saying, "There is a man here who earned a lasting place in our hearts and in our history," and he thanked Reagan for all "the wonderful things he had done" for America. Even for those listening who disagreed with him, it was impossible not to summon affection for a man who'd demonstrated such a deep-rooted love of country. Still, it irked Reagan's most devoted admirers—and no one more devoted than his wife—when Bush made an appeal for "a kinder and gentler nation." But that became water under the bridge when Reagan paused at the door to the helicopter and threw a crisp, respectful salute to President Bush.

Air Force One—renamed *Special Air Mission 27000* for the day—was parked on the tarmac of Andrews Air Force Base, waiting to carry the former president and First Lady home to California. As a surprise to Ronald and Nancy Reagan, the pilot of *Nighthawk* decided to make an unscheduled detour and swung the helicopter in a loop around the Capitol for a stunning view of the grounds and the monuments. Then he dipped it lower for a lap around the White House, where a line of moving vans was already unloading furniture for the new occupants. "Look, honey, there's our little cottage," citizen Reagan remarked as they hovered overhead. The helicopter then circled back over the Capitol one more time before heading out to Andrews.

Struggling out of his formal morning coat, Reagan slipped on a midnight-blue Air Force jacket with his name stitched above the left pocket. The plane ride was slated to be a casual, festive affair, and the guests of honor intended to partake of it in style. The cabins were crammed with friends and longtime aides, practically family now that the business of governing was behind them. The Reagans were unusually relaxed in their midst—even with the fourteen journalists aboard. Handshakes and hugs were meted out liberally. And champagne—bottles that ran the gamut from Korbel to Cristal—were poured to wash down slices of a cake inscribed "The Reagan Years 1981–89."

"It was very much a sentimental flight," recalled Fred Ryan. The former president shared personal stories with aides and their families, crouching in the aisle to exchange a few words. There was festivity, but also business. A lot of fund-raising had been done in advance for a presidential library, under rigorous terms that were set by the White House counsel. One of the strictest, to avoid any conflict of interest, stated that neither of the Reagans could know the name of anyone who had made a pledge or payment to the library. Now that they were private citizens, however, the list of major donors was produced, and they went through it with the delight of children opening gifts on Christmas morning. "Oh, Ronnie—just *look* what Walter Annenberg gave! And the Bloomingdales!" They were touched by the generosity. There were also speaking requests to sift through, many of which involved considerable honorariums, and contracts for book deals.

Even at seventy-eight, Reagan was keen to remain active. Foreign travel seemed attractive, as well as several offers to return to radio, although Reagan conceded that movies and TV were probably out of the question. What he looked forward to more than anything was having his privacy back, being able to spend time at the ranch, oblivious to politics, or even just taking a walk by himself. He was under the impression that no one would recognize him, and for today, but only today, his aides were content to let him believe that was true.

During the last half hour of the flight, Ronald Reagan slipped quietly away from the celebration and rode the remainder of the trip in the cockpit, next to the pilot. He wanted a little peace and quiet, but more than that he wanted to gaze at the terrain of his beloved California as it loomed into view. He'd told journalists earlier in the day, "California isn't a place in my mind—it's a way of life," and he'd meant it. He couldn't wait to touch down.

Peace and quiet—but not quite yet. As he and Nancy emerged from the plane at LAX, a homecoming rally organized by the White House staff swarmed toward them, seven hundred strong, chanting *"Four more years! Four more years!"* The Salvation Army Tournament of Roses Band, with help from the brass and woodwind sections of the USC marching band, struck up a thunderous fanfare: "California, Here I Come."

Here I come, indeed. To a new house in Bel-Air he'd never set foot in, a new office in Century City that he'd never seen. He listened to tributes from an assortment of local dignitaries: Los Angeles mayor Tom Bradley, comedian Rich Little, William French Smith, and actor Robert Stack. Following a stirring rendition of "America the Beautiful," Ronald Reagan grinned broadly, waved, and threw his arms into a familiar V above his shoulders. Stepping to a microphone, he quieted the cheering crowd and told them that there "aren't enough words to express" what was in his heart. Flush-faced, he admitted he'd been away from California for too long. "When you have to stay eight years away from California, you live in a perpetual state of homesickness." The crowd roared approval and resumed its chant.

"Four more years! Four more years!"

Ronald Reagan soaked it in, before slipping into the backseat of an unmarked Town Car. He could still hear the melodious incantation as the car rolled slowly across the tarmac toward the welcome anonymity of the L.A. streets.

"Then home," he recorded, "& the start of our new life."

CHAPTER FORTY-FIVE

AN ORDINARY CITIZEN

"I'm out to pasture now."

—RONALD REAGAN

Ronald Reagan had first gone west to California, like countless others before him, to stake his claim. He often quoted a popular vaudeville comic who said that "California was the only place where you could fall asleep under a rosebush in full bloom and freeze to death." And, brother, wasn't that the truth. In his journey from its southern palms to its northern vineyards, Reagan had encountered many hope-filled prospectors much like himself, shivering in the Golden State's hothouse milieu. But he had prospered in each stage of his life there, thriving as actor, company spokesman, and governor, and launching himself from there for his eight-year reign as the most powerful person in the world, with, as he put it, "temporary custody of the United States."

"If I could do this," he thought, "then truly any child in America had an opportunity to do it." But could he reverse that path up the mountaintop? Could he find satisfaction as an ordinary citizen again? Could he feel comfortable in his own skin, not as a movie star or celebrated politician, but simply as a plain American citizen again? For all his surface humility, Reagan had been driven at each stage of his career by a desire to stand out, from the plays he'd appeared in with Nelle to his broadcasting and movie endeavors and on into politics.

Making it harder, he was not returning home. The family house in Pacific Palisades had been emptied and sold in the months after the Reagans moved into the White House. In the intervening years, they'd either stayed at the ranch or bunked with the Annenbergs in Palm Springs. But they'd needed a place to put down roots in Los Angeles. It would be the nerve center of Ronald Reagan's post-presidency, close to transportation, to their friends' lavish homes, to their old restaurant hangouts, and to the Holly-wood movie studios, to which he still felt a powerful connection. And close enough to the ranch so he could get there easily.

The new house was a 7,192-square-foot, three-bedroom ranch all on one level at 668 St. Cloud Road.* A Norman Rockwell painting, *The Five Faces of Ronald Reagan*, hung just inside the front entrance, which opened onto an oversized living room paneled lavishly in the kind of dark wood that graced the old movie moguls' offices. A room had been set aside in the back, near the master suite, for Reagan's study. The three-car garage had been converted into a command post for his Secret Service detail. There were a lot of lovely touches that Nancy's decorator had installed, not the least of which was the transformation of a former pantry into a gorgeous breakfast room all in white accented with light greens, but Reagan's favor-ite feature was the heated swimming pool in the backyard, where he planned to resume his lifelong passion.

The spectacular skyline views were just as diverting on days when the smog rolled out to sea. From the knoll atop the sloping lawn, he could look out over greater Los Angeles, all the way to where his new office stood, in the penthouse of the tallest building in Century City.

The office had been in the works for some time. Federal buildings had been ruled out early in the process. Aides felt that it wouldn't be dignified for Ronald Reagan to be sandwiched in between, say, the EPA and a visa office. Instead, they found space in the Fox Tower, one of the most dazzling buildings in Los Angeles, next door to the Century Plaza Hotel, the scene of Reagan's presidential election celebrations. Even the street name dripped with glamour—*The Avenue of the Stars*. Fred Ryan, who had led the search team, was told that only one floor was available, the top one, the thirty-fourth floor, though it was in terrible shape at the time. It had served as the set for *Die Hard* and was riddled with fake bullet holes; shell casings littered

---

* The original address was 666, which Nancy Reagan had changed because of the number's reference to the anti-Christ in the Book of Revelation. (Kitty Kelley, *Nancy Reagan*, p. 449.)

the floor. "But it had incredible views," Ryan recalls. The windows offered up a 180-degree panorama of the Pacific Ocean, all the way out to the Channel Islands. "The moment I laid eyes on it, I said, 'We'll take it.'" Only the Secret Service registered an objection. "This is terrific," an agent told Ryan. "You're putting the president in a building where a movie has instructed people how to blow it up."

Reagan loved the location. Twentieth Century Fox was two blocks away. The studio's owner, Marvin Davis, was an old Reagan pal. "Any time you want to drop by and have lunch at the commissary, feel free," he offered. The president put it on his calendar as a weekly event.

Ronald Reagan planned the office as the focal point of his postpresidency. He had no intention of slowing down. There were political loose ends he vowed to tackle—the line-item veto was a particular pet project, along with a balanced budget amendment and the elimination of term limits, which he abhorred. He remained furious at the 1984 gerrymandering (a word he pronounced, correctly, with a hard g) engineered by Democratic congressman Philip Burton, which he pledged to remedy. He even expressed interest in delving more actively into the AIDS issue. There were also what he called "the normal people things"—paying a visit to a child in a hospital, shaking hands with ordinary Americans, "real people," or even stopping in at McDonald's for a shake. "I want to see all those people I haven't been able to see while I was chained to the Oval Office," he instructed his staff. A policy he put in place at the outset dictated that any person who'd ever worked for him at any time while he was a public servant was entitled to come and see him. That invitation extended to the years he was president of the Screen Actors Guild. And to old acquaintances. Once that news got around, requests poured in.

"Hi, my name is So-and-So and we were schoolmates in Dixon, Illinois."

"Sure, I remember you. C'mon in!"

He had planned to take a couple of weeks off to settle in and acclimate himself to the new house. He wanted to decompress, but that changed within a day of returning to Los Angeles. "We were preparing the office," recalls Joanne Drake, the president's scheduling director, "and Mrs. Reagan called and said, 'Okay, we're done with retirement now.'" She had her hands full unpacking the boxes at home. He was driving her nuts. "'This is not a good place for him. He has too much energy. I can't get anything done. You must find something for him to do in the office. I'm sending him to you.'"

Panic spread among the office staff—"*The President's coming in!*" They weren't nearly ready to receive him. Cardboard boxes were strewn around the floor. Everyone was in jeans and T-shirts. They scrambled to pull things together, racing around to make a room habitable. As soon as Reagan arrived he pitched in, helping with the unpacking process. "What can I do? Where do these go?" To keep him occupied, they took him to lunch in a public place. He wanted to eat ordinary food, a hamburger and a milk shake. Café Fifties, a diner across the street in the Century City Mall, suited his purposes nicely. He was besieged, of course, mobbed—surrounded by people who wanted to shake his hand, slap him on the back, tell him how much they'd appreciated his leadership. "He was a little frightened the first time it happened," recalls Drake, who was in charge of his advance team. "It had been so long since he'd felt such freedom." For his Secret Service detail, the situation was a nightmare. Access to the president had always been tightly restricted and controlled. At the White House, the agents always knew what was happening, where the rope lines were. They'd post a man on either side of Reagan and behind him. Here, people were walking right up and throwing things at him to autograph—a napkin, a menu, a dollar bill, a football, a baseball, even a bare arm. He signed each item graciously.

Back at the office, Drake had to lay down the law. "Mr. President, you can't sign everything people put in front of you. I've been told by the Secret Service you may not sign your name on a piece of currency. It's against the law."

"Welllll, they . . ."

"No, sir, I'm going to put my foot down on that. You cannot sign currency and you cannot sign anything that looks official. So from now on we will pass you the things to sign."

The whole money concept was new to him. He'd never had to worry about carrying cash as governor or president. Payment was taken care of by one of his aides. But now he carried a wallet, and he was quick on the draw. "Every day on the way to the office we passed a homeless guy on Beverley Glen," says Jon Hall, the Reagans' personal assistant. "The president would always roll down his window and give the guy five dollars, until an agent told him it was too risky."

"We didn't know what to do with him those first few days," says Mark Weinberg, who'd joined the staff as the president's press secretary. "He was so good natured. And he craved contact—human contact. He'd wander out of his office and talk to people. We had to come up with things for him to do."

They made sure there were plenty of newspapers for him to read, including the Hollywood trades—*Daily Variety* and the *Hollywood Reporter*. He was intent on staying current and connected to the movie business. A desk was set up for him with a working phone, and after he read something that hit him in a certain way he'd call the reporter or columnist to chat. He was on the phone incessantly, delighted to be able to make his own calls for a change.

"Hi, this is Ronald Reagan."

"Uh-huh. Sure it is."

On day two, he handed Fred Ryan a piece of paper and said, "These are people I'd like to meet with."

Ryan had worked with Reagan for a number of years and could usually look at a name and detect who they were or where they came from. But this list left him cold. "Just out of curiosity," he said, "what is the connection to these people?"

"They've been calling," the president answered.

It did not take long to discover that the new phone system had been set up inadvertently so that all outside calls were coming in to Reagan's private extension. The former President of the United States was serving as office receptionist.

"Hello," he'd answer each time it rang.

"I'd like to speak to Ronald Reagan."

"Well, this is Ronald Reagan."

"People were requesting private meetings with him, and he was saying yes to everybody," Ryan recalls. Needless to say, the phone was immediately disconnected and the wiring rejiggered, but by that time Reagan had a full schedule of appointments on the books. "We honored every one of them," Ryan says, but there were areas where he had to draw the line. "A couple of them said, 'I really liked meeting you. I'm going to send my neighbor in. He likes you, too.' I had to pull him aside afterward and say, 'Look, that's not going to happen.' But it was touch-and-go there for a while."

Eventually, a secure transmission phone was installed. George Bush intended to keep Reagan in the loop so that the former president could be briefed on a daily basis. But until that time, he got his news like everybody else, watching TV, reading newspapers, and chatting with friends, albeit in his case many of his friends were still Washington insiders.

There was plenty of downtime to contend with, but fairly soon the exigencies of business took over. "We had a roomful of sacks containing thousands and thousands of envelopes and letters that required Reagan's attention," says Joanne Drake. Six months of correspondence had piled up. Requests for speeches to business groups and trade associations poured in by the hundreds, offers for him to present awards, to keynote fund-raisers and charitable functions—everybody wanted him. He loved the idea of speaking to business groups. And he made it clear—"I want to hit the rubber-chicken circuit again," which he described as an arena where he could do his unfinished work. That meant scheduling events, many of which were gratis, while others promised to pay him a decent fee.

He and Nancy had both expressed an interest in making some money. They weren't poor by any stretch of the imagination. Income tax disclosures put their net worth at over $4 million. And the president's pension was $99,500 annually, which, combined with his governor's pension of $29,711, provided a steady income. A speaker's bureau told him that he and Nancy could expect upward of $40,000 for a speech. It had been some time since they'd worked for anything but scale, and in Hollywood, you had to keep up with the Joneses—the Jennifer Joneses. Elizabeth Taylor and Zsa Zsa Gabor lived right down the street, and God knows what they were raking in! The Reagans were the poor-relative members of their social circle, not exactly destitute but nowhere in the vicinity of the Annenbergs or Bloomingdales. Contracts sat on Reagan's desk for a two-book deal—a memoir and a volume of his speeches—that would net him nearly $8 million, and there was another book deal for Nancy, for $2 million. Still, he was not overly keen to sign his contract. Telling jokes and Hollywood stories was one thing. But when it came to opening up, expressing his innermost feelings, he struggled mightily; it was like pulling teeth. "A book is the last thing I want to think about now," he groaned, waffling, when the agent Mort Janklow and Richard Snyder, the publisher of Simon & Schuster, turned up to finalize the deal. But Nancy insisted, handing her husband a pen and double-checking to make sure he initialed the contract in the requisite places.

Nancy began work on her book right away. She was still sensitive to the criticism she'd received while in Washington and looked forward to settling scores. But Reagan hedged. For him, the book was more obligation than ambition. It was so time-consuming. He preferred to forget all about it. The office staff carved out a few hours a day for him to devote attention to organizing the memoir, but it wasn't until they brought in a cowriter, Robert Lindsey, the author of *The Falcon and the Snowman*, that a manuscript began to take shape. Work on it frustrated them both—for Reagan, who loathed going over the details, and for Lindsey, who was thwarted by the president's reluctance. It was a challenge for Lindsey to get him to reminisce. Going deep wasn't one of Ronald Reagan's virtues. He was not introspective. His memory was imprecise; he had trouble concentrating. He referred to the writing experience as "getting the monkey off my back." He cooperated, but grudgingly.

The man who had spent the past eight years keeping banker's hours in the Oval Office now settled again into the old pattern. He arrived in the office around ten o'clock every morning, spent a couple of hours working, then broke for lunch. "He was of that generation of men for whom lunch was a ritual at the same hour every day," says Joanne Drake. "God help you if anything interfered with that. Then at two or three he'd leave and go home."

Reagan got back on the golf course, playing once a week at the L.A. Country Club with old Hollywood pals. He loved their company, loved to hear what deals they had in the works, what was going on behind the scenes. It was important for him to stay plugged-in with the movie business, to reengage with Hollywood. Fortunately, there were many ways to do that in Los Angeles. Virginia Mayo and Eddie Bracken came in to see him. Lew Wasserman was a regular lunch date at Universal, where Reagan never failed to take a studio tour. He'd visit his friend, producer A. C. Lyles, at Paramount. Peter Guber stopped by the office to fill him in on what was happening at Columbia Pictures. And Ronald and Nancy huddled often with chummy Merv Griffin, who beguiled them with the latest gossip, as did Nancy's newest confidant, Warren Beatty.

They had missed the social scene. For dinner, they returned regularly to Matteo's or Chasen's, the favorite restaurant of A-list celebrities on Beverly Boulevard, where they sat in the Ronald Reagan Booth, the same booth in which he'd proposed to Nancy in 1952. Otherwise, they dined at their friends' houses, delighted at being able to see people on a casual basis, especially the Wicks, Charlie and Mary Jane, at whose home they spent every Christmas and whose son, Doug, and his wife, Lucy Fisher, were important Hollywood producers. Reagan never failed to pump Doug and Lucy for the latest show-business scuttlebutt. "I once saw him in an incredibly animated conversation with Lucy," Wick recalls, "and when I went over he was saying, 'Are you kidding? Robert Redford makes *five million dollars* a picture?!'"

Reagan said yes to two local speeches right away, at USC and Pepperdine, as warm-ups. Colleges were traditionally viewed as hostile territory. As governor, Reagan had been booed and heckled by liberal students. But his presidency had engaged many of those audiences and now, "he wanted to hear what was on the students' minds," says Mark Weinberg. "He wanted to do Q&As with them." During the presidency, Q&As were strictly a no-no, a policy that disconcerted Reagan. "There are an awful lot of people around here who are afraid for me to open my mouth," he'd grumble. He longed to have "a dialogue, not a monologue," as he was fond of saying. At USC and Pepperdine he fulfilled that urge and found it deeply satisfying. The students he spoke to were extremely well informed, their questions incisive, challenging, *respectful.* "He felt as if he had found his voice," recalls Joanne Drake.

It gave him a new sense of freedom. In New York City, shortly after the college speeches, Reagan pushed the boundaries to new limits. Standing at the window of his suite in the Carlyle Hotel, looking west at the leafy expanse of Central Park, the old feeling tugged at him of being confined, isolated from the public, restricted to antiseptic situations. "Boy, if I could only go for a walk," he said aloud, dreamily. Fred Ryan discussed it with the Secret Service detail. They had no trouble with a spontaneous excursion. It was the scheduled appearances, when details were announced in advance, that were concerning. So, minutes later, the former president found himself at liberty on the busy city streets, an experience he hadn't had in . . . he couldn't remember how long. "Where do you want to go?" "Central Park," the president responded without hesitation.

It was a gorgeous, picture-postcard spring day. The park was crowded with people who had been cooped up in apartments all winter, testing Mother Nature in shirtsleeves and shorts. And along came the president, taking a stroll, somewhat anonymously. No one really noticed the limousine following him a couple of hundred yards behind. Only the grin on his famous face might have given him away. Not two minutes passed when a nanny sitting on a park bench beside a baby stroller did a comical double take.

"*Ronald Reagan!*" she cried, jumping up. "Can I shake your hand?"

A few minutes later an orthodox Jew in a yarmulke with *payot** rushed over to thank Reagan for his service to Israel.

His chest puffed out as he walked farther into the park. The pure joy of being on his own, smelling the fresh air, seeing *real people*, was an intoxicating experience. It felt like he had his old life back, the life before he was president, before he was governor, before he was a movie star. When he was just Dutch. If Frank Capra were writing this scene, even he might have rejected as too corny what happened next. The president walked past a group of boys throwing a football. One of them missed a catch and the ball landed not far from Reagan's feet. Jogging over to it, he picked it up, cocked his arm, and threw a perfect bullet pass that the boy pulled in like a pro. The old Gipper still had the juice.

When Reagan got back to the hotel, he felt exhilarated. Nancy had been out shopping, but upon her return it was all he could talk about—how much fun he had had just going for that walk.

Not everything, however, was a walk in the park. Both Oliver North and John Poindexter faced upcoming trials for their indictments in the Iran-Contra affair, and Reagan's name appeared prominently on both of their witness lists. In fact, North based his defense on Reagan's role in the scandal. Reagan planned to resist any invitation to testify, citing

---

* Long sidelocks.

"serious constitutional issues." It wasn't dignified for a former president to be publicly cross-examined in court as an ordinary citizen. There were precedents that shielded him—immunity from disclosing national security issues. Nevertheless, he did not want to engage in an unnecessary skirmish or to be perceived as ducking the issue.

The president eventually agreed to be deposed, but in the federal courthouse in Los Angeles—and in private. It had been almost forty years since he'd participated in such a process, during his appearance before the House Un-American Activities Committee. Some pretrial guidance was necessary. Lawyers told him, "Just answer 'yes' or 'no.' Don't say anything [else]. Don't offer information." But Ronald Reagan couldn't help himself. He wanted to be informative, to come up with answers to the questions North's lawyers fired at him. Bud McFarlane had already testified that the president had called the Honduran president, asking him to intervene with his military officials who were holding up the transfer of military supplies to the Contras, and that Reagan had signed off on an airdrop of rifles at a time when Congress prohibited such assistance. But Reagan had no memory of either occurrence. North's defense suggested the president personally approved Security Council efforts to aid the Contras. "I don't remember," Reagan repeated over and over. Names were mentioned to him. "I don't remember." Top-secret documents were produced. He couldn't recall ever seeing them. He got confused over intricately detailed questions about the Contras. Dates, places, events drew vacant stares. A second deposition conducted in Reagan's office produced similar results. "I don't remember"— the phrase echoed throughout both proceedings.

On getaways to the ranch, the trials of public life melted away. The Santa Barbara ranch was perfectly remote, away from everything, a secluded mountaintop retreat of 688 acres, seven miles up a series of switchbacks from the nearest paved road. "This is where I restore myself," Reagan explained to anyone who visited. He liked "the wildness of the place," the rugged, undeveloped landscape bisected by groves of oak and madrone and bushy clumps of greasewood. Deer, bobcats, and bears stalked the property. Hawks and bats flew overhead, rattlesnakes occasionally got underfoot. In contrast to the surrounding natural splendor, the simplicity of the house pleased him; he found it honest and humbling. It had begun life as nothing more than an 1872 adobe shack with a corrugated metal roof. Assisted by two ranch hands, he had knocked out walls, torn down a screen porch, added a veranda, replaced the roof with fiberglass tiles, and converted the structure into a modest Spanish-style cottage. The patio he built by hand, dragging flat rocks into place and cementing them together. The fence-work surrounding the property was constructed out of old telephone poles that he'd split himself.

The ranch was Ronald Reagan's utopia. He transformed himself there. As soon as he arrived, the suit came off, contact lenses jettisoned for avia-tor sunglasses, and he pulled on a pair of jeans, a denim workshirt, western boots, and a cowboy hat. El Alamein, his trusty thoroughbred, a gift from Mexican president José López Portillo, was saddled and waiting. All in all, a formidable image, not quite John Wayne, but not Slim Pickens, either.

Now that he was no longer president, the goal was to be at the ranch at least once a month. The routine there was always the same. Ronald and Nancy took a trail ride each morning from nine to nine-thirty. Afterward, he'd load chain saws, handsaws, and pruning shears into his 1951 Willys Jeep, a big, clunky beast of a vehicle with a GIPPER license plate, and head out to clear brush, cut firewood, and mend fences. "Reagan loved to drive," says John Barletta, a longtime aide. "It was the only time in twenty years that anyone ever let him get behind the wheel of a car." And he loved the work, swinging those unwieldy saws as if they were no heavier than base-ball bats, whistling a jaunty tune that could be heard above the work.

The ranch was less of an undertaking now that the presidency was over. The helicopter pads and hangar that had housed *Marine One* were gone, as were the Secret Service outbuildings. Foundations were all that was left of the guardhouse and the lookout bunker where an agent had been staked out twenty-four hours a day shouldering a long-range rifle. In fact, the re-maining support staff could be counted on two hands, down from the force of 175 that normally serviced a presidential visit. The Navy Seabees detail that oversaw the wells and sewage system was no longer in residence, nor were the dog teams and countersnipers.

It was a blessing for the Reagans to have the ranch to themselves. They cherished the peace and quiet, the splendid isolation. Critics of "Queen Nancy" would have been shocked to see the modest interior—only fifteen hundred square feet, linoleum floors, a 1960s GE galley kitchen with harvest-gold Formica counters. Two fireplaces provided the only heat in the house, allowing them to spend the warm days outside on the patio and the cool evenings snuggled in their twin beds that had been pushed together and lashed with plastic cable ties.

But more often than not, responsibilities intruded. In May, it was announced that Reagan would visit Japan in the fall, sponsored by the Fujisankei Corporation, whose "attractive honorarium" was rumored to edge into the $2 million range. And in mid-June, he made his first trip to Europe since leaving the White House.

London was the first stop, where Margaret Thatcher threw him a lavish dinner at Number 10 Downing Street accompanied by bottomless glasses of Château Petrus. His engagement the next day at Buckingham Palace featured an even more spectacular reward. The queen and Prince Philip entertained the Reagans at a royal lunch in their private dining room. Following dessert, as a surprise to the president, the queen bestowed on him an honorary knighthood, the Order of Bath, one of the highest orders of chivalry, draping a neck piece in the form of a knight along with a crimson sash over his shoulders. And in Paris, while celebrating the hundredth anniversary of the Eiffel Tower with Jacques Chirac, Reagan was inducted into the French Institute's Academy of Moral and Political Sciences.

On July 4, 1989, he and Nancy accepted an invitation to celebrate Independence Day on a ranch belonging to his friend William Wilson, in Sonora, Mexico, just across the border from Arizona. Horseback riding had become second nature to the Reagans, and when Wilson, the former ambassador to the Vatican, suggested they go for a spin, his guests jumped at the chance. The terrain was bleak, they discovered, nothing like Rancho del Cielo, where the trails were sunbaked, lined with brush, and clearly marked at all intersections by numbers drilled into rocks. The rustic Mexican range was a soft, loamy mix of dirt, pebbles, and sand. As the trio climbed a hill, the president's horse stumbled, then reared up and "bucked wildly several times." Reagan hung on for a while before he was thrown. "He landed quite hard," says Carl Janisch, a Secret Service agent following a hundred yards behind in a blue Suburban. "The right side of the hill dropped off into a deep gulley, and Reagan rolled about fifteen feet to the bottom." He was "barely conscious" when the agent got to him. Fortunately, they came prepared with a FAT (First Aid Treatment) kit. They administered oxygen, strapped him to a stretcher, and drove him to a landing vehicle idling nearby. A Black Hawk choppered him to a hospital at Fort Huachuca, an Army base near Tucson, where doctors determined that he had suffered "minor abrasions" and bruises to his ego. "The one thing he made very clear was that he had not *fallen* off his horse; he was *thrown*," says Fred Ryan. An official statement upgraded the action to being *bucked from a wild horse*, a distinction that meant a great deal to a proud horseman. In any case, the president was given a clean bill of health, and he rebounded nicely a couple of days later.

Even so, aides described him as "a little moody," so unlike his unfailingly upbeat nature. Mark Weinberg recalls, "There was a bit of irritability after the horseback incident. We would have meetings with him and his eyes would get heavy. I remember thinking, 'He's out of sorts.'" He would forget names or hesitate to speak. During Major League Baseball's All-Star game in Anaheim a week later, Reagan joined Bob Costas and Vin Scully at the microphone, and according to people in the booth, "he was not quite himself." When Scully greeted him, saying, "How good it is to have you in the ballpark," Reagan grimaced, glanced around, and otherwise remained silent. He later chalked it up to being "a little uptight," but there was something else affecting his disposition. "There is something wrong," Nancy told an aide.

Six weeks later, during Reagan's annual checkup at the Mayo Clinic, a CT scan revealed a subdural hematoma—hemorrhaging resulting from torn veins in traumatic brain injury. There were two liquefied blood clots that required immediate attention. To remedy it, surgeons drilled "one burr hole roughly the size of a nickel" into the president's skull and drained the blood. The operation sounded dire, though in practice it was a routine affair. "Nothing is without risk, but this is straightforward," a doctor assured Nancy. "Your husband is in great shape." Nevertheless, for a seventy-eight-year-old man there were always concerns.

Reagan's recovery from the surgery was remarkably swift. Within two days, he was doing paperwork in his room at St. Mary's Hospital, up on his feet for a stroll through the halls. The only noticeable effect was his hair, which had to be shaved down to stubble for the operation. Nancy had scooped up the shorn locks into a plastic bag, which she stashed in her handbag. "I want to be able to prove that he doesn't dye it," she said glibly. Otherwise, she wasn't fond of the new look. "Reagan liked it, though,"

Mark Weinberg recalls. "He thought it made him look like a Marine." He covered his head with a baseball cap on his release from the hospital, mindful of Nancy's instructions not to remove it. But as he boarded a plane back to Los Angeles, waving to a throng of well-wishers, he paused on the steps, grinned, and swept the cap off his head to a fanfare of shouts and whistles.

The trips took their toll. The visit to Japan at the end of October 1989 was especially strenuous. The physical effort was punishing, but the criticism he faced for going was worse. The American public was incredibly sensitive with regard to Japan. Trade issues had inflicted serious damage on the U.S. economy, prompting a backlash against anything Japanese. The auto industry was particularly defensive. Objections were raised about buying Hondas or Toyotas. Real-estate developers who had been squeezed out of deals accused the Japanese of buying up New York. In September 1989, Sony bought Columbia Pictures (Reagan welcomed the takeover, saying it might "bring back decency and good taste" to American audiences) and Matsushita was negotiating for a major stake in Universal. Japanese investors were outbidding museums for masterpieces at Sotheby's and Christie's. Reagan's visit made him seem tone-deaf to America's anxiety.

The $2 million speaking fee didn't help. It was an astounding figure in 1989. "Former Presidents haven't always comported themselves with dignity after leaving the Oval Office," a *New York Times* editorial observed. "But none have plunged so blatantly into pure commercialism." The furor only intensified when it became known that Fujisankei put an entire 747 jet at his disposal for the flight to Japan. His staff performed damage control by engaging the USO to fill the empty seats with family members of military personnel serving in Japan, but it had little effect. A great hue and cry arose. *Ronald Reagan was greedy. He was cashing in on the presidency.* Aides attempted to explain that the money was earmarked for fund-raising for the Reagan Presidential Library, but the public wasn't buying it. It also wasn't entirely true. A large portion of the fee was allocated to pay back friends who had bought the Bel-Air house. In any case, the trip was a public-relations nightmare.

Great pains were taken not to repeat the mistakes a year later, when Reagan traveled to Europe. The eleven-day trip was dubbed the Victory

Lap—to Berlin, Russia, Poland, and the Vatican—where photo ops dominated the busy schedule. In Berlin, the press took one of Reagan standing on the *other side* of the Wall. It had "fallen" in November 1989, not as a result of Reagan's plea, as some believe. Triggered by the resignation of German Democratic Republic leader Erich Honecker in October and a chain of events that swept Eastern Europe, the East German government announced that GDR citizens could visit West Germany, effectively making the Wall pointless. It was the German people themselves who took up sledgehammers and pickaxes to demolish the ugly scar, and Reagan came prepared to participate. "We furnished him with a chisel," Fred Ryan recalls, "and did a photo op with him hacking away at the wall." A hammer was also produced, and the president took a few aggressive swings while the local press, fifty or seventy strong, screamed encouragement in German. Another op depicted Reagan addressing Solidarity workers at a shipyard in Gdansk, an awe-struck Lech Walesa at his side.

In Moscow, Reagan was advised to embrace Mikhail Gorbachev as soon as the two men saw each other. Reagan balked, fearing it might look as though he was doing it for the camera, but Nancy insisted. "No, as soon as you see him is the right time," she said. The encounter occurred in front of the Kremlin. As Gorbachev appeared in the doorway, Reagan reached to wrap him in a bear hug. Gorbachev jumped back, a look of panic across his face. Unbeknownst to the American contingent, an old Russian wives' tale prophesies that an embrace in a doorway signifies an end to a relationship.

The Victory Lap was a welcome diversion, but back home politics intervened. In March 1991, the Brady Handgun Violence Protection Act, named for Jim Brady, Ronald Reagan's press secretary who'd been paralyzed and brain-damaged as a result of the 1981 assassination attempt, was making its way through Congress. The Brady Bill, as it was called, established a seven-day waiting period and required law enforcement to conduct background checks before a firearm could be purchased. The National Rifle Association pumped millions of dollars into defeating the legislation and counted on the former president, a lifetime NRA member, to join its opposition. In his eight years in office, Reagan repeatedly expressed his objection to national gun control laws. But despite being an enthusiastic hunter with a lavish collection of guns in his house, there were indications that he intended to endorse the bill. During the speech at USC, he'd answered a student's question about gun control by very firmly stating that he viewed AK-47s as assault weapons and did not think they belonged in private hands. As governor, he'd expressed approval for a fifteen-day waiting period in California. "It's just plain common sense that there be a waiting period to allow local law enforcement officials to conduct background checks," he emphasized in an address at George Washington University.

"He had given Jim and Sarah Brady his word that he would support the bill," Mark Weinberg says. "He felt it was perfectly reasonable." Reagan echoed his support during a visit to the White House. The NRA had contributed a small fortune to George Bush's reelection campaign, as well as to Republicans running for Congress, and Reagan's remarks during an event in the Rose Garden were intended to give them political cover.* And just in case anyone remained unclear about where he stood, he wrote an editorial for the New York Times on March 29, 1991, entitled "Why I'm for the Brady Bill."

It wasn't the only time he found himself standing on the other side of the Republican Party line. Conservatives had never been comfortable talking about AIDS, and Reagan had adroitly sidestepped the issue for most of his administration while the epidemic ravaged the gay community. It wasn't until he read an article in the Los Angeles Times that the disease took on a human aspect for him. It was a story about Elizabeth Glaser, the wife of actor Paul Michael Glaser of Starsky and Hutch fame, who contracted AIDS after receiving a contaminated blood transfusion while pregnant with her son. The HIV virus was passed on through breastfeeding to her daughter, Ariel, who died of AIDS in 1988. Her son had also contracted HIV in utero, inspiring her to launch the Pediatric AIDS Foundation.

Reagan had ripped the article out of the paper and called the journalist who wrote it. He wanted to speak with Elizabeth Glaser. As it happened, she was friendly with Lucy Fisher, Doug Wick's wife, who arranged for Elizabeth to tell her story to the president. "He was very moved," Wick recalls, "really emotional—and angry. It was clear to him that his staff had intentionally kept him in the dark about AIDS, that they'd done him a

---

* In May 1995, George Bush ripped up his NRA membership card in response to an NRA fund-raising letter describing federal agents as "jack-booted government thugs."

disservice. He misunderstood the disease, thinking it occurred in far-off places, when the hospital where Elizabeth had gotten her blood transfusion was in L.A., at Cedars [Sinai Medical Center]," where he'd often been a patient during his Hollywood career.

Reagan told Glaser he wanted to get involved with whatever it was she was doing for AIDS awareness. Naturally, she was wary. So many AIDS activists were angry with Reagan for not acting while he was president. Glaser didn't want to be involved in something that played as an apology. "I'm not interested in going backward," she told him. "Only forward." Both of the Reagans promised they were fully on board. They agreed to make a public-service commercial that Paul Glaser would direct, as well as a six-figure donation to the Pediatric AIDS Foundation, which they joined as honorary chairmen. The commercial was particularly poignant. "Maybe it's time we all learned something new," the president said, looking earnestly into the camera. "I'm not asking you to send money. I'm asking for something much more important—your understanding." It acknowledged his own shortcomings. Reagan also relied on his friendship with Elizabeth Taylor, who helped to educate him on the AIDS crisis and to defend against the political fallout.

Politics took a backseat on November 4, 1991, at the dedication of the Ronald Reagan Presidential Library. The project had been in the works for more than six years, when the Kitchen Cabinet and close advisers, including Walter Annenberg and Lew Wasserman, began sketching blueprints for the building designed to seal the president's legacy. They began actively raising money and discussing architectural plans, consulting Jacqueline Kennedy Onassis on her experience launching the Kennedy Library. Originally, the Reagan edifice was to be housed on the Stanford University campus as part of the Hoover Institution, where Martin Anderson and George Shultz held chairs—that is, until the faculty and students fought it. To avoid smothering the project in controversy, it was decided to look for another location, perhaps closer to the Reagan Ranch.

Farmers volunteered their spreads. A woman who owned an enormous piece of beachfront property called Gull's Way in Malibu offered to donate it. But a developer in the Simi Valley, about thirty miles northwest of Los

Angeles, had a parcel of land that appealed most to Reagan. It was a hundred acres of rocky, scrub-covered hills that the movie studios had used as a location for countless westerns. A visitor could imagine Roy Rogers, Gene Autry, or even Ronald Reagan riding up over a crested butte. It had natural beauty; it made a statement about the mythic power of the American West.

The 153,000-square-foot Spanish-style library, enough to hold 55 million documents and paid for with private funds, opened to great fanfare, with four thousand mostly Republican guests thronging the manicured grounds. It was the first time in history that five living presidents appeared on the same dais. In addition, there were Kennedys, Trumans, Roosevelts, and Eisenhowers mingling in the crowd. "It was surreal," says Joanne Drake, who would eventually head the Reagan Foundation in a quadrant of the library. Minutes before the dedication began, she entered a holding room where all five leaders were sitting in a circle. Her mission was to fetch Reagan to the ceremony. "I leaned down and whispered, 'Mr. President,'" she recalls, "but I was on his bad-hearing side, so there was no reaction." She said more loudly, "Mr. President . . ." All five of them looked at her and, in unison, answered, "Yes?"

Each of the presidents contributed brief salutes. The last to speak, the current head of state, George Bush, called Ronald Reagan "a political prophet, leading the tide toward conservatism." The remark, however opportune, was tinged with ambivalence. Bush was engaged in a reelection campaign that effectively tied him to the Reagan legacy. But there were qualifications. Word had reached Bush that Reagan wasn't overly enthusiastic about his successor's record or the way that Bush had distanced himself once he won the White House. He'd vowed to reverse the feckless trends of the Reagan administration, insisting on an ethical, kinder and gentler government, and promising to be a "hands-on" president, in contrast to his predecessor. He'd also terminated research for the Star Wars program. Reagan had endorsed Bush as "our best hope to build a strong America," but Reagan's support for his former vice president was considered underwhelming by Bush strategists. The *Washington Post* reported that Reagan told friends, "[Bush] doesn't seem to stand for anything." Reagan categorically denied making that comment, but questions about his commitment persisted when he skipped a Bush fund-raiser.

In the months preceding the 1992 election, Ronald Reagan returned to the stump on George Bush's behalf. The race was tight. Bush's opponent, a political dynamo named Bill Clinton, had come seemingly out of nowhere to mount a serious challenge for the presidency. And Bush was damaged goods, plagued by a weak economy, a huge and growing deficit, a substantial tax increase, the emergence of the United States as a debtor nation, and his obsession with Saddam Hussein. His foreign policy accomplishments—presiding over the fall of Communism and defeating Saddam Hussein's Iraq—seemed distant to the concerns of most Americans.

It wasn't morning again in America; it was the morning *after*. Voters held George Bush up against their nostalgic recollections of Ronald Reagan, and they didn't appreciate the contrast. Bush's patrician DNA kept people from thinking, *He's one of us*, as they'd done with Reagan.

Reagan's rousing oratory at the Republican Convention in Houston, Texas, came too late to rescue Bush. The Grand Old Party was taking the low road. There was too much polarization, too much negativity in the boisterous Astrodome—talk about culture wars and family values, recognizing "good Christians" and casting antiwar activists as traitors—bumping Reagan's speech to a time slot so late that Eastern audiences had already gone to bed. The American public wanted intimacy from their president, and optimism. If anyone possessed Reagan's magnetism it was the Democrat, Bill Clinton. He was camera-ready, expressive, and entertaining. And he could cry on cue.

Clinton sought out Reagan soon after winning the election. The new president made a courtesy call to Reagan's Century City office on a toasty California afternoon in December 1992. It was an awkward rendezvous. Reagan had taken Bush's loss "personally and very hard," but he was "intrigued, even fascinated" with Clinton's persona. The meeting was scheduled for four p.m., but Clinton was characteristically running late. Twenty, thirty, forty minutes ticked by. Reagan stood at his office window, watching, as the Clinton motorcade approached with lights flashing and helicopters circling overhead. It was an odd, almost out-of-body experience observing the operation from a new and unfamiliar perspective.

Reagan had an agenda. "I've thought about three things you could do," he told Clinton as the two got comfortable on adjacent chairs. The first piece of advice was that the new president should use Camp David on the weekends. It was essential to get away from the White House—the fishbowl—to get outdoors and rejuvenate the spirit. His next suggestion was to extend the Grace Commission, which Reagan had authorized in 1982 as a way to control waste and inefficiency in the government. Only a few of its proposals had been enacted over the years, and Reagan urged him to step up its activity.

The third point was more unconventional. "You should salute the military," Reagan advocated. Reagan had begun the practice in 1981, "throwing a snappy 'high ball' during White House photo opportunities." There was no protocol for a presidential salute. Senior military officers acknowledged that a president could salute merely by standing at attention. But Reagan recognized its dramatic and public-spirited potential. George Bush, an authentic war hero, had continued the practice, but not all the time, occasionally just waving instead. Clinton's position was more precarious. He had opposed the Vietnam War and avoided the draft while studying at Oxford. And his intention to lift the ban on homosexuals in the military put him at odds with the military establishment. Still, Reagan encouraged him to salute and even stood up to demonstrate how it should be done— "the hand had to come up slowly, like it was covered with honey, and then brought down sharply."

Afterward, he handed Clinton a souvenir jar of jelly beans.

One thing was certain: Bill Clinton's ascendency to the White House signaled a changing of the guard. The contrast was stark in the two men's physical appearances—the eighty-two-year-old retiree and his forty-six-year-old heir apparent. Why, the younger man could be mistaken for his son. They were a generation—or two—apart. Politics aside, they had different ideals, different philosophies, different dreams. It was Clinton's turn to lead the nation in a different direction.

The so-called Reagan Revolution had officially ended. Ronald Reagan gracefully stepped aside.

CHAPTER FORTY-SIX

"THE SUNSET"

*"And before you know me gone
Eternity and I are one."*

—WILLIAM DEAN HOWELLS

Dick Allen had noticed it first: something was wrong with Ronald Reagan.

In the summer of 1991, Allen was walking through the Bohemian Grove with Ed Meese and Marty Anderson when they spotted Reagan on the porch of a ramshackle cottage. They bounded right over to pay their respects.

"Hello, Mr. President," they chimed in unison.

"He was seated in the chair and he was startled," Allen recalled. "I could see he had no idea who we were."

Reagan had famously been fuzzy on names. But faces?—never. "He always knew when he had met you or seen you before," says Joanne Drake. Suddenly, he'd begun forgetting words. "I *cannot* come up with it. What is that *word?*" he'd complain, frustration mounting as he racked his brain. Or he'd forget a word in a speech once in a while, and his aides would cringe. "We knew there was something wrong," Drake says. "But he was eighty years old. We wrote it off to the fact he was finally showing his age."

The doctors at the Mayo Clinic suspected otherwise. In 1993, during the president's annual checkup, they began to surmise that more was awry. Perhaps he was in the early stages of Alzheimer's disease, the progressive mental and physical deterioration that affected the minds of more than four million elderly Americans. Physically, he was in tip-top shape. But mentally? They weren't so sure.

Reagan himself wondered whether he might have Alzheimer's. His mother, Nelle, had been senile "for a few years before she died," and as early as 1980 he'd confided to an associate that maybe he'd inherited Alzheimer's from her. His brother, Neil, certainly had the symptoms. In fact, Reagan had told his White House doctors that "he expected them to check him periodically for signs of a failing memory" or mental deterioration, and should they discover he was at risk he would resign.

There were lapses when he was absent-minded, even inattentive, but for eight years in the White House Ronald Reagan tried to maintain the picture of a focused and decisive executive, his moments of haziness or distraction easily explained by mental overload or fatigue. His judgment was sharp, if not always . . . *that sharp.* He was engaged. His cognitive function was strong. Now, however, during a celebration in honor of his eighty-second birthday at the Simi Valley library, he raised his glass in a lengthy toast to a favored attendee, Margaret Thatcher . . . then toasted her again, repeating himself word for word.

Evidence of Alzheimer's revealed itself early in 1994 on a trip to New York. "He couldn't acclimate to his longtime hotel room at the Carlyle," says Fred Ryan. "He wasn't comfortable in his surroundings. They weren't familiar to him." According to Ryan "something didn't seem quite right." A few days later, in Washington, Reagan became disoriented in his hotel room. "Which way are we leaving again?" he wondered aloud. He was scheduled to speak at a big-ticket Republican fund-raiser, a black-tie affair with Margaret Thatcher again in the audience. It was the kind of after-dinner monologue he could do in his sleep. Plus he had his trusty index cards fanned out on the lectern.

This time, however, instinct failed him. Following a stirring introduction, he looked down at his cards and *nothing made sense.* He began speaking slowly. One. Word. At. A. Time. The audience squirmed. *What's wrong? Something is not right here.* "We were dying because of the full press coverage," Fred Ryan recalls. Then . . . Reagan blinked. Something shifted in his eyes. He noticed the teleprompter, swept his cards aside, and regained his equilibrium.

Then, in May 1994, on a chilly afternoon in Yorba Linda, California,

Reagan stood somberly at the rain-soaked grave site where Richard Nixon, a beloved mentor, was being buried next to his wife, Pat, who had died ten months earlier. He related how Nixon pressed him not to convert to the Republican Party so that he could campaign for Nixon in 1960 as a Democrat. A familiar account. But his fellow presidents in attendance exchanged whispers about Reagan's fitness. As Hugh Sidey recounted in *Time*, "George Bush told friends he was profoundly worried about his old compatriot. Jimmy Carter confided to a companion that Reagan's responses were not right. And Jerry Ford thought Reagan seemed hollowed out."

Hollowed out. Aides blamed it on jet lag. They built in more rest during trips, cleared great swatches of time during the day so he could adjust his inner clock to the travel. But on a visit to the Mayo Clinic for a checkup that summer, doctors developed an alternative theory. "We're seeing memory loss that is more than just age-related," they reported.

A battery of tests was run over two days. First, general questions: "Do you know who the president is? Can you count backward from fifty?" Then a more complicated quiz: three numbers and three colors, followed by a story in a book. Afterward: "What were those numbers and colors?" He had trouble remembering. It wasn't the first time that memory had failed him in this way. Recently, it was reported, he "now forgets the punch lines to some of his favorite jokes."

"I have this condition," Reagan told his daughter Patti; "I keep forgetting things."

The doctors finally put a name to it. On November 4, 1994, a doctor from the Mayo Clinic informed Nancy Reagan that, having had an adequate chance to observe the president, the diagnosis was conclusive: he had Alzheimer's. "She was quite upset, emotional," recalls Fred Ryan, who spoke with her at length later that evening. "So we're going to tell him tomorrow," she said, "and I'd like you to be there."

The next morning, a Saturday, they gathered in the library, a small, comfortable room at the front of the house where the Reagans typically received guests. The president seemed puzzled when the doctor and Ryan arrived. "Honey, come over here and sit down," Nancy said, directing him to a couch opposite the two men. "The doctor has something he wants to talk about."

The doctor didn't beat around the bush. "We think you have Alzheimer's," he told Reagan.

"Okay," he responded faintly. "What should I expect?"

"We don't know much about it," the doctor admitted. "It's a degenerative disorder." He ran down a few of the effects that Alzheimer's patients experienced while Nancy Reagan struggled to control her emotions. She tried her utmost to be supportive, but was overcome hearing about the devastations of the disease. Noticing her unease, the doctor made a point about how difficult Alzheimer's can be on loved ones and, particularly, the caretaker. He acknowledged, quite bluntly, "There is no cure."

"Can I ask a few questions?" Ryan interjected.

While he and Nancy discussed how to handle the president's activities—his schedule, office hours, appointments, and appearances—Reagan wandered over to a small round table in a corner and sat down, staring hypnotically into the yard. After a few minutes, he picked up a pen and began to write. When he finished, he handed two sheets of paper filled with his cramped handwriting to Ryan. "Why don't we get this typed up and put it out," Reagan suggested.

It was a letter dated November 5, 1994. "My Fellow Americans," it began, "I have recently been told that I am one of the millions of Americans who will be afflicted with Alzheimer's disease." He admitted struggling with whether to keep the news private or make it known, but decided to share it in order to raise public awareness. "At the moment I feel just fine," he went on. "I intend to live the remainder of the years God gives me on the earth doing the things I have always done. . . . Unfortunately, as Alzheimer's Disease progresses, the family often bears a heavy burden. I only wish there was some way I could spare Nancy from this painful experience. When the time comes I am confident that with your help she will face it with faith and courage.

"In closing, let me thank you, the American people, for giving me the great honor of allowing me to serve as your President. When the Lord calls me home, whenever that may be, I will leave with the greatest love for this country of ours and eternal optimism for its future.

"I now begin the journey that will lead me into the sunset of my life. I know that for America there will always be a bright dawn ahead.

"Thank you, my friends. May God always bless you."

Ryan read it once, choking back emotion. "You don't need to have this typed," he said. "Let's just put it out in your own handwriting."

The letter was photocopied and released to news organizations later that day, after the Reagans had left Los Angeles for the seclusion of the ranch.

Nancy left explicit instructions for the office staff. She wanted her husband's life to be normal and active to the extent that was possible. She didn't want any dramatic changes, but she expected everyone to be sensitive. If late in the day he wasn't faring as well, she insisted, people should be mindful of that. Reagan was just as emphatic. "He made it clear right from the beginning that he wanted people to remember him as they had known him," Ryan recalled. He did not intend to remain in the public eye if his condition started to degenerate. Hollywood vanity encroached. He called up the image of Bette Davis, an actress he considered beautiful in her youth, who had refused to yield to old age and continued making appearances, "no longer looking like herself," when, of course, he meant her glamorous, youthful self.

Reagan realized that from that point on, the story was going to be him, as opposed to an issue or policy he wanted to promote. The letter made that clear right away. It got a huge amount of attention. For weeks, thousands of letters—*tens* of thousands—were delivered to the office expressing their support, extending best wishes, and applauding him for his courage. Tributes were delivered from all quarters by politicians and world leaders, no matter their political affiliation or previous interaction.

For several months, Ronald Reagan kept to his old schedule, coming into the office every day, getting briefings, meeting with people. Groups would come by to have photos taken with him or just to say hello and shake his hand. A few speeches were interspersed, but mostly his public appearances were restricted to photo ops in order to avoid embarrassing situations in which he'd repeat himself or forget where he was. As the months wore on, he began to cut back. He might go home after lunch or hit a few golf balls. Appointments were kept to a minimum and geared to uncomplicated conversations, nothing substantive such as rehashing SDI or discussing upcoming legislation. Visitors were limited to people he knew from his school days, friends, or those who had worked with him.

Unexpectedly, he took up playing the harmonica—"for my own self-amusement," he insisted. "He was really taken with it," says Joanne Drake. "He kept one in his desk drawer and would take it out regularly to play a tune." His repertoire was limited to songs like "Red River Valley," "Git Along Little Doggies," or "Streets of Laredo." On his birthday in February 1995, Edward Rowney, Reagan's old arms-control negotiator, stopped by the house and taught him how to play "Happy Birthday." Rowney found him "still fairly coherent" but "fading." "He didn't remember things and was vague and got things mixed up."

Nancy noticed that over the six months since the diagnosis, her husband's deterioration had been dramatic. The diagnosis and his heartfelt letter had precipitated a "final letting go," a sort of surrender to the disease. Reagan slowed down—*slooooooowed* down—and his hair got a little grayer. He lost the pleasure of going to the ranch, an aversion to long car rides being one of the symptoms of Alzheimer's. In any case, John Barletta, his able ranch hand and riding partner, was recruited and, through a cascade of tears, told him that his horseback-riding days were over. At a certain point, Nancy made the decision that it was best for him not to be in public. People blamed her for overprotecting him, but her instincts prevailed. She was his loving wife but also his caretaker, and if anyone thought she was strong-willed in the former role, her tenacity in the latter was not to be misjudged. Overprotective?—not by a long shot. She gave up everything that had once taken precedence in her life—the lunches with friends, the shopping excursions, the parties, the invitations, the trips to Europe. None of that mattered anymore. She devoted herself exclusively to her husband's welfare, making sure he was never in jeopardy.

"She ached for him," Doug Wick explains. "She talked to me about the romance she had for him, how once, during his battle with Alzheimer's, he had gotten up at four in the morning and dressed, as if to go out, and how it had broken her heart to coax him back to bed."

He was failing, gradually and steadily. Long stretches went by during which he was stuck deep in a reverie. Ron Reagan recalled how throughout his childhood his father "was often wandering somewhere in his own head," but that referred to abstraction, concentration, when he tunneled into the complexities of his job. This was different. Now he was . . . *somewhere else*, somewhere unreachable. Occasionally, he'd lapse into a dissociative fugue that transported him to an earlier time and place in his life. If he had been watching football on TV, he might awaken in the middle of the night intent on suiting up for the home team. "There's a game. They're waiting for me," he'd insist to Nancy, who did everything in her power to restrain him.

Socializing was out of the question. Friends were no longer invited to the Reagan home, because he did not recognize them. If they went out at all it was to a local restaurant that would accommodate them with a private room or to visit the Wicks, who were like family. "It was too difficult for Reagan to communicate," Wick recalls. "He couldn't really follow a conversation. And he'd grow uncomfortable, but not be able to express it. It was clear to all of us that he was no longer fully inhabiting his body."

His eyes no longer showed signs of engagement. "He was sort of there, but not there," Ron recalled. Somewhere in the interim, he'd drifted away. "Ronnie's long journey has finally taken him to a distant place where I can no longer reach him," Nancy acknowledged.

Doctors had predicted that a man of Ronald Reagan's sturdy constitution might live another five to eight years. He'd surprised them, as he'd surprised all the pundits who predicted he'd never overcome the liabilities of his B-actor status, never survive the Justice Department's inquiries into MCA's monopolistic grip on the entertainment industry, never beat Pat Brown or Jerry Ford or Jimmy Carter or Walter Mondale, never stand up to the demands of the presidency or live down the detritus of the Iran-Contra scandal. Ten years after his initial diagnosis of Alzheimer's disease, he continued to hold on to life. But in the spring of 2004, Nancy could tell he was slipping away. Reagan had fallen and broken his hip three years before, and recurrence of its agonizing spasms had pretty much confined him to bed, leaving him unable to sit up. In early June, he stopped eating and taking fluids. His kidneys had begun to fail. Family members were summoned to say their goodbyes. Michael came and went while Ron and Patti maintained a bedside vigil.* Nancy, who hadn't budged from the room in weeks, reached a point of near exhaustion. "He hadn't opened his eyes for three days at all," Ron recalled. His breathing was irregular, ragged, he gulped for air. Ron felt that his father looked almost youthful in repose—his face "free

---

* Maureen Reagan had died in 2001.

of care . . . had lost many of its worry lines and wrinkles," his hair, neatly combed, "remained full and soft." Still, it was clear this was the end.

On June 5, 2004, shortly before one p.m., Ronald Reagan's breathing grew shallower, and he began to struggle. With his last breath, he angled his head to one side, opened his eyes wide, *wider*, until they found Nancy's face. He looked right at her, then he closed his eyes and was gone.

A great American life has come to an end," President George W. Bush told reporters hours after learning of Reagan's death. "Ronald Reagan won America's respect with his greatness, and won its love with his goodness. He had the confidence that comes with conviction, the strength that comes with character, the grace that comes with humility and the humor that comes with wisdom."

Bush's homage touched off an outpouring of tributes in print and over the airwaves, in the halls of Congress, and throughout the world, extolling Reagan's leadership and his indomitable spirit. Even Democrats who had fought him throughout the eight years of his administration esteemed him now as one of the important figures of the twentieth century. Massachusetts senator John Kerry, in the throes of challenging George W. Bush for the presidency, put Reagan's political integrity in perspective, saying, "Even when he was breaking Democrats' hearts, he did so with a smile and in the spirit of honest and open debate. Despite the disagreements, he lived by that noble ideal that at 5 p.m., we weren't Democrats or Republicans, we were Americans and friends."

The American public expressed its own extravagance of gratitude to the person considered by many as a man of the people. For days after Reagan's death, folks thronged to sites associated with his presidency, paying their personal respects to the man and to the concept of democracy he cherished. Crowds gathered outside his home in Bel-Air, at the foot of the Washington Monument, in front of the White House, on the steps of the Capitol, along the National Mall, and many points in between. "Makeshift shrines of flags, balloons, and flowers sprang up" in communities across the United States.

Thousands—hundreds of thousands—planned to observe some aspect of his funeral. Four public ceremonies were planned to mark his death. A committee of loyalists had met periodically to discuss the details, outlined in a 300-page document on file with the Military District of Washington. Originally, Reagan's body lay in state at the Reagan Presidential Library in Simi Valley, where more than 100,000 mourners came to pay their respects. From there, he was transferred via *Air Force One*—making an unscheduled low dip over Tampico, Illinois—to Washington, D.C., for the formal rites. At the Capitol, he lay in state in the Rotunda, below the Dome, on a velvet-draped catafalque first used at Abraham Lincoln's funeral, in 1865. Afterward, the casket continued its procession down Constitution Avenue on a horse-drawn caisson, accompanied by a riderless horse with the president's own English riding boots, expressly left unpolished for the occasion, reversed in the stirrups. A squadron of twenty-one F-15 Eagle fighters roared overhead as three howitzers thudded out a twenty-one-gun salute. A state funeral service was held at the Washington National Cathedral on June 11, 2004, followed by a private burial, timed to coincide with the sunset, on the grounds of the presidential library in California.

Afterward, at the grave site, several members of the library staff peered out the windows. In the distance, they recalled, they could make out the stooped figure of Nancy Reagan—not in her trademark red, but in black, mourner's black—standing small against the majestic natural backdrop and looking forlornly out across the sun-splashed hills, as though half expecting Reagan to come galloping over the rise at the end of the last reel.

He hardly ever played the hero on-screen, he rarely got the girl, seldom came across as the figure of authority. As Jack Warner enjoyed pointing out: "Bob Cummings for President, Ronald Reagan for Best Friend." Somehow in real life he managed to fold both roles into one and played it to perfection. In the eyes of his audience he was statesman extraordinaire *and* benevolent friend, someone to look to for reassurance, who wouldn't steer them wrong. The composite character—the Ronald Reagan who appeared at times distinguished and tough-minded, at times intimate and paternal—would have made Jack Warner reconsider.

Reagan's legacy as president was more spectacular and larger-than-life than anything he encountered as a movie star. Several highlights of his political career unspooled as only Hollywood would script it. He survived an assassin's bullet, struck back against the Evil Empire, and conducted a clandestine hostage caper whose props included high-tech weaponry, a bogus airline, and bags of unmarked cash. He delivered memorable lines: "There must be a pony in here somewhere." "Honey, I forgot to duck." "Mr. Gorbachev, tear down this wall." And he knew how to play to the crowd. Reviews didn't come any sweeter than the one scrawled on a sign held high on Constitution Avenue as his casket rolled by: "*Now there was a president.*"

Fate had cast him in the role of a lifetime, and he played the part for all it was worth. As the president he rebuilt the American military, beat back inflation, appointed the first woman to the Supreme Court, cut the top personal tax rate from 70 percent to 28 percent, encouraged free trade, oversaw the creation of 16 million new jobs, and eventually produced a nuclear arms agreement with the Soviet Union and effectively ended the Cold War.

His lack of empathy for those in desperate financial straits and for AIDS victims, the supply-side Reaganomics, the punitive "war on drugs," the reckless spending on the military, stratospheric budget deficits, the implausibility of the Strategic Defense Initiative, Bitburg, even Iran-Contra faded from memory as admirers eulogized Reagan in the weeks immediately following his death. His presidency had taken on an almost mythical revisionism. It represented something more than the sum of his accomplishments—or failures. It restored the power of the presidency in a way that rose above politics and deeds to a time when the country looked to the office for a sense of national identity.

"What I'd really like to do," Reagan declared six months into his first term, "is go down in history as the president who made Americans believe in themselves again." In that sense, he reached out to a segment of the populace whose everyday problems he understood so well, people much like those he'd grown up with in Dixon, like those who listened to him in Davenport and Des Moines, people proud of their country who worked hard pursuing the American dream but often felt thwarted by the vague and faraway concept of Big Government.

People much like himself. Reagan's humble beginnings in Illinois laid the foundation of his own humility. As a poor boy of the heartland whose first job paid him thirty-five cents an hour (most of which he contributed to the family's weekly budget), he had had to make many of the same difficult choices that working-class Americans faced every day. As president, he sought to apply the lessons he learned from personal hardship to a modern world that craved common sense and decency, and whether he succeeded or not, he never lost sight of where he came from, his mother's iron conviction of right and wrong. This was the root of his great communication. As *Time* impressed in a moving obituary, "He had a moral clarity that framed political choices in terms of core beliefs."

In all of Reagan's pursuits, he held to the persona of Everyman. As the most powerful leader of the free world, he played the leading man with the modesty of a stalwart supporting player, drawing inspiration from people who weren't stars in their own right. Nothing moved Reagan more than the letters he received from ordinary citizens. They reinforced all that he shared with them, mainstream values and a familiar dialect, a simple view of a complex world. In that mutual embrace, he often lost sight of those who didn't share his white-picket-fence, morning-in-America outlook.

Schooled in the ABC's of Hollywood fantasy, Reagan aspired to upbeat expectations and happy endings. His gospel of optimism restored the country's spirit, lifted it out of the malaise he inherited from Jimmy Carter. He ascribed to FDR's belief that "there is a better life, a better world, beyond the horizon," and he set out toward that destination from the day he entered office attuned to his inner compass. "His most endearing aspect was his fundamental decency," George Shultz reflected—his simple faith in people and in himself. "He appealed to people's best hopes, not their fears, to their confidence rather than their doubts."

The qualities Reagan held dear were woven into the time-honored American social fabric: honor your country, cherish your family, give thanks to a higher being, stand up for what you believe in, and refuse to be bullied by tyrants. He placed these values above the conventional dictates of the office. He had a firm idea of what America stood for, and he never doubted that the country's integrity would win out.

Reagan's priority was never iron-fisted rule. His White House was a collaborative effort, drawing on deputies whose expertise outmatched his own. Taking his cue, perhaps, from the latter-day British monarchy, he conducted himself more as a figurehead, a benevolent head of state with a view of the big picture and a strong sense of the country's ideals. He was the kind of president, with a genial face and sunny disposition, that Louis B. Mayer (not Jack Warner) might have projected in Technicolor.

From the 1970s on, the movies had turned away from the old white hats–black hats, good guys–bad guys studio era that Reagan knew so well. By the time he took office the Hollywood dream factory had turned its gaze to stories of anti-heroes, moral ambiguity, cruelty, and violence. Ronald Reagan never liked those movies. The sex scenes embarrassed him, too. On the national stage, he tried to hold the line and project the old-style moral certainty of the classics he loved. In later years, as people decried the ugliness of politics, the public viewed Reagan even more through a veil of nostalgia.

People felt about him the same way they felt nostalgia for old movies starring Gary Cooper and Jimmy Stewart, even the Gipper. He became beloved, even as many forgot the details of what he actually did. On the road to the funeral, Ron Reagan recalls driving from his parents' home to the Simi Valley library: "every single overpass on the 405 [Freeway] was jammed with people" standing ten deep, often in tears, along the route. Fire trucks and ambulances emblazoned with banners sounded their horns in salute. Several days afterward, as the coffin left for the trip to the Capitol, Ron noticed "people standing all alone out in farm fields . . . saluting, hands over their hearts."

It was the final ovation for an epic American life.

ACKNOWLEDGMENTS

Many people and institutions contributed to the vast research that shaped this account of Ronald Reagan's life, and I am profoundly grateful to their enormous efforts on my behalf. In particular, I must thank the late Nancy Reagan, whose health rendered her unavailable but who granted me extraordinary access to the president's restricted private papers and family scrapbooks, and instructed her husband's friends and colleagues to cooperate in the lengthy and demanding interview process. Mrs. Reagan's guidance throughout was overseen by her longtime associate Joanne Drake, the chief administrative officer (and self-described "chief of chaos") of the Reagan Presidential Foundation. The foundation's archives, which are separate from the public records contained in the Ronald Reagan Presidential Library, were invaluable in chronicling many personal details of the Reagan story. They also included access to the transcripts of the twenty-three interviews Edmund Morris conducted with President Reagan between June 1986 and January 1990. Joanne's proximity to the president in his post-presidency also contributed immeasurably to this book.

My gratitude goes to the many staff members who assisted my research at the Ronald Reagan Presidential Library in Simi Valley, California, an invaluable facility. In addition to the library's director, Duke Blackwood, I am indebted primarily to archivist extraordinaire Jenny Mandel, who guided me through the miles (literally) of documents in the library's collection. Her advice and expertise are evident throughout this book. My thanks also to Steve Branch, the library's audiovisual archivist, who condensed the sixty-thousand-plus photos on file to a manageable reserve that suited my purposes, and to his counterpart, Romeo Legaspi, at the Reagan Foundation.

I also want to express my appreciation to the libraries and institutions whose resources contributed to a thorough historical record of Ronald Reagan's life. They include Davidson Library at the University of California-Santa Barbara and its exceptionally fertile Lou Cannon Archive (particularly special collections director, Ed Fields); Charles E. Young Research Library's Special Collections at UCLA; Center for Oral History Research at UCLA; Galesburg Public Library (Patty Mosher, Special Collections); Margaret Herrick Library of the Academy of Motion Picture Arts and Sciences (Stacey Behlmer); Warner Bros. archive at the University of Southern California School of Cinematic Arts (Jonathan Auxier, Brett Service); Screen Actors Guild archive (Valerie Yaris); Clark County Library, Las Vegas, Nevada; Fulton Historical Society, Fulton, Illinois (Barbara Mask, Bill Blecha);

Ronald Reagan Birthplace Museum, Tampico, Illinois (Joan Johnson); Monmouth College, Monmouth, Illinois (Jeff Rankin); Ronald Reagan Boyhood Home, Dixon, Illinois (Brandi Lagner); Dixon Public Library, Dixon, Illinois (Lynn Roe); Lee County Genealogical Society, Dixon, Illinois; Eureka College archives, Eureka, Illinois (Anthony Glass); Dixon Historic Center, Dixon, Illinois; Dixon Chamber of Commerce, Dixon, Illinois (John Thompson); Ronald W. Reagan Society at Eureka College (John Morris); Dixon Geological Society, Dixon, Illinois (Jim Higby); Illinois State Historical Library; University of Illinois Urbana-Champaign archives (Scott Krinninger); Huntington Library, San Marino, California (Sue Hodson); the Reagan Ranch and its director, Andrew Coffin; Reagan Center, Santa Barbara, California; National Archives and Records Administration (NARA); National Archives II at College Park, Maryland (David Paynter); Hoover Institution at Stanford University; California State Library (Greg Lucas); and Miller Center for Presidential Oral History at University of Virginia.

I am especially grateful to the men and women who shared their recollections and insights. A few deserve special mention, in particular Robert (Bud) McFarlane, Ed Meese, and Jim Kuhn, all of whom endured repeated, long sessions with me going over—and over—the intricacies of a president's endeavors, patiently answering every question. They were joined in their efforts by these eyewitnesses to history: Leith Adams, Richard V. Allen, Annelise Anderson, Steven Avilla, Bill Bagley, Will Ball, John Barletta, the late Anthony Beilenson, the late Jeffrey Bell, Joanne Bell, Brian Bernardoni, Craig Biddle, Steve Bingen, Charlie Black, Mayor James Burke, David Chew, Steve Clow (*Los Angeles Times*), David Conrad, A. B. Culvahouse, Elliot Curson, Carolyn Deaver, Olivia de Havilland, Ken Duberstein (my former camp counselor), Rob Ehrgott, Dirk Eldridge, Fred Fielding, Esther Haack, Paul Haerle, Fawn Hall, Jon Hall, Ken Hall, Pete Hannaford, John Humenik, Carl Janisch, Jennifer Jo Janisch, David Keene, Ken Khachigian, Ed Kolk, Nancy Kolk, Jim Lake, Greg Langan, James Leach, John Lehman, William Lytton, Ned Martin, Suzanne Massie, Nathan Masters, Bonnie Parker McClosky, Peter McCoy, Burnett Miller, Theodore Olson, Kathleen Osborne, the late Robert Osborne, Duane Paulson, Richard Perle, John Poindexter, David Prosperi, Vickie Palmer Pruter, Richard (Sandy) Quinn, Tom Reed, Junius Rodriguez, Robert Roubik, Fred Ryan, Betty Schermer, Lloyd Schermer, John Sears, Stuart Shea, Stuart Spencer, George Steffes, Edward J. Stephens, Sheila Tate, Darrell Trent, Robert Tuttle, Mark K. Updegrove, Helene Van Damm, Marc Wanamaker, Mark Weinberg, Kirk West, Doug Wick, and Tom Wilson. Special mention must go to the gatekeepers—the assistants, who were besieged by my exhortations for interviews and graciously penciled my name into busy schedules. Most notable: Gay Gill (Richard Perle), Leslie McClellen (Ed Meese), Jennifer Nicholson (A. B. Culvahouse), Jennifer Peacock (Ken Duberstein), Stefanie Prelesnik (Fred Ryan), and Kathy Sanzaro (Charlie Black). My work is done; you won't have Bob Spitz to kick around anymore.

A number of scholars pitched in unselfishly to help shape my manuscript and to make the biographer's work eminently easier. Most notably, Anne Edwards, author of two excellent books on the early life of Ronald Reagan, opened her archives and allowed me to poach freely from her extensive research. Richard Reeves's *President Reagan* and Lou Cannon's superb Reagan trilogy provided a detailed road map from which to explore. Doug Cunningham shared his manuscript-in-progress on Hollywood's first motion picture unit, and James R. Walker, a noted Chicago Cubs authority, provided an understanding of the birth of baseball's broadcasting empire and the rites of spring training. My dear friends Neal Gabler and Allan Spiegel, historians and cinephiles alike, offered sage perspectives on the vagaries of Hollywood and Reagan's screen career. Marc Eliot donated a box of valuable artifacts from his *Reagan: The Hollywood Years.*

David Nasaw, a biographer whom I greatly admire, sent me two crackerjack research assistants, Ean Osterle and David Campmier, scholars in their own right. Their assistance and dedication throughout the research and writing stages were significant. Jonathan Eig, celebrated biographer (and friend), read and critiqued portions of the manuscript, and Rob Harris, whose longtime friendship is cherished, read every word and weighed in extensively at a crucial time in the editing process. Friends were essential to locating sources and general input. The work was greatly enriched by Jillian Manus, Tina Susman, Frazier Moore, Robert Hofler, John Scheinfeld, Yak Lubowsky, and Julie Bain. As always, Lindsay Maracotta and Peter Graves provided shelter from the storm.

The folks at Penguin Press offered support throughout the publishing process. First and foremost: Scott Moyers, a gentleman and an extraordinary editor, who stood behind this book from the beginning while offering encouragement and perceptive criticism at every turn. Editing is an art; in addition to the mechanics involved, it requires vision, judgment, and respect for the work. Scott brings all those qualities as well as brilliance—and style. Despite his grinding responsibilities as publisher of Penguin Press, he lavished time and energy on the manuscript for which I will be forever grateful. My hat goes off to Mia Council, his uncommonly efficient, long-suffering assistant, who no doubt dreads getting another "Urgent!" email from me. My sincere thanks to Mark Birkey for his heroic job of copyediting (How many ways can you misspell the name Meiklejohn?) and to production editor Eric Wechter who, in the tradition of Don Regan, was part of the shovel brigade that followed me from page to page, cleaning up. Darren Hagger and Gretchen Achilles and Claire Vaccaro produced a lovely book jacket and gorgeous art decoration.

My agent, Sloan Harris, has stood behind me through five books and countless crises. His canny advice and belief in my work somehow conspire to keep everything on an even keel. Heather Karpas, his former assistant and now colleague, pulled strings and oiled the gears.

Lastly, but most important, my wife, Becky Aikman, the Omniscient, the Queen of Context. Her insight, wisdom, and love guided me through every page of this book. She inspires me. She is the most remarkable person I know.

NOTES

ABBREVIATIONS

AAL: Ronald Reagan, *An American Life* (New York: Simon & Schuster, 1980)

AE: Anne Edwards, *Early Reagan: The Rise to Power* (New York: William Morrow, 1987)

DET: *Dixon [IL] Evening Telegraph*

FOIA: Freedom of Information Act

KK/NR: Kitty Kelley, *Nancy Reagan* (New York: Simon & Schuster, 1991)

LCA: Lou Cannon Archives (Davidson Library, University of California-Santa Barbara, Special Collections)

MCPA: Miller Center of Public Affairs, University of Virginia, Ronald Reagan Oral History

MI: Edmund Morris interviews for *Dutch* (New York: Random House, 1999)

NR/MT: Nancy Reagan with William Novak, *My Turn: The Memoirs of Nancy Reagan* (New York: Random House, 1989)

PP/HW: Personal Papers/Handwriting Files, part of the RRPL's public archives

PPP: Pre-Presidential Papers file

RRPL: Ronald Reagan Presidential Library

WTROM: Ronald Reagan and Richard Hubler, *Where's the Rest of Me* (New York: Deull, Sloan, and Pearce, 1965)

PROLOGUE

1 **"some rough sledding":** WTROM, p. 241.

1 **"a couple of turkeys":** Ibid., p. 245.

2 **$15,000 in new pumps . . . veterinary care:** Edmund Morris, *Dutch* (New York: Random House, 1999), p. 294.

3 **"I'm living from guest shot to guest shot":** Murphy James, "When the Gipper Played Vegas," *San Antonio Express-News*, 1984, Murphyjames.com /gipper. The friend is WB publicist Barney Oldfield.

3 **"of a Hollywood couple":** *Yearling Row* manuscript, RRPL, private papers.

4 **Billed as "Ronald Reagan Presents":** RR, letter to Murphy James, Mar. 9, 1983, RRPL, PHF Series 2, Box 18, Original Legal.

4 **"as sort of an impresario":** WTROM, p. 249.

4 **The El Rancho was the obvious:** Las Vegas Strip Historical Site, lvstriphistory.com.

4 **The deal was negotiated:** "In twenty minutes Beldon Katleman at the El Rancho was on the dotted line." WTROM, p. 249.

4 **"who left almost nothing to the imagination":** Obituary of Lili St. Cyr, *New York Times*, Feb. 6, 1999.

4 **The Last Frontier held more promise:** Las Vegas Strip Historical Site.

5 **"stick her toe in the water":** Ibid.

5 **Evelyn Ward, a glamorous:** Mike Barnes, "Actress Evelyn Ward Dies at 89," *Hollywood Reporter*, Jan. 11, 2013.

5 **the Adorabelles:** "A chorus of semi-nude girls." Robert Metzger, *Reagan: American Icon*, Phildelphia, PA: University of Pennsylvania Press, 1989, p. 144.

5 **"no singer or dancer":** Bob Thomas, "Reagan in Night Club; But Not from Choice," *Associated Press*, Feb. 15, 1954.

6 **"She was a great audience for him":** John Bradford, quoted in KK/NR, p. 91.

6 **"was rough as a cob":** James, "When the Gipper Played Vegas."

6 **"By the end of the first week":** Terry Mulgannon, "When Ronnie Played Vegas," *Los Angeles*, Apr. 1983, p. 179.

6 **the Four Aces were appearing:** Les Devor, "Vegas Vagaries," *Las Vegas Review-Journal*, Feb. 17, 1954, p. 6.

6 **"in a flimsy, see-through dress":** James, "When the Gipper Played Vegas."

6 **"This business was built":** Thomas, "Reagan in Night Club; But Not from Choice."

7 **"If you didn't sing or dance":** Ronald Reagan, "Remarks at the Kiwanis International Convention," in *Speaking My Mind* (New York: Simon & Schuster, 1989), p. 19.

7 **"Russian aggression aimed at world conquest"**: Ronald Reagan, "How Do You Fight Communism?" *Fortnight*, Jan. 22, 1951.

8 **another MCA agent, Taft Schreiber**: "It was Revue through Taft Schreiber who approached me." RR, testimony before federal grand jury, Feb. 2, 1962, pp. 95, 100.

8 **"everyone of stature"**: *WTROM*, p. 231.

8 **"personal interest in television"**: Ibid., p. 230.

9 **Reagan's only nod to fashion**: "If the debut doesn't work out, I'll be ready for mourning." Reba and Bonnie Churchill, "Ronald Reagan Launches Night Club Debut Soon," *News Life*, Oct. 11, 1953.

9 **Reagan turned up the heat**: "Nitery Reviews: Last Frontier," *Variety*, Feb. 17, 1954, p. 10.

10 **Once, when he was in high school**: "Mrs. J. E. Reagan Is Hostess to Society," *Dixon Telegraph*, Sept. 9, 1927, p. 3.

10 **The nightclub act did relatively**: Ralph Pearl, who covered the engagement, reported that the act did only "fair biz." *Las Vegas Sun*, Feb. 20, 1954.

10 **was well received by the critics**: "The question of what can Ronald Reagan do in a night club act has been answered. . . . He can entertain." Devore, "Vegas Vagaries."

10 **He only made $5,500 a week**: This figure was reported in an interview that Edmund Morris did with the Last Frontier's Herman Hover in *Dutch*, p. 754.

11 **After the shows, when most performers**: "They returned to their hotel room after each show and spent their days reading . . . and visiting Lake Mead." Murphy, "When the Gipper Played Vegas."

11 **"The nightclub life"**: NR/MT, p. 127.

11 **As a lifetime Roosevelt Democrat**: "I began my citizenship as a New Deal Democrat." Letter to Ms. Jamie Harrison, Spring 1977, RRPL, PPP Box 20, Folders G-H.

11 **"encroaching government control"**: *WTROM*, p. 267.

12 **And he'd gone for Ike in 1952**: "My first Republican vote was for Eisenhower." RR, letter to Lucinda Williford, c. 1980, RRPL, PPP Box 20, Folder W.

ONE: AN IDEAL PLACE

15 **Even well into his eighties**: The scenes of RR's Midwest upbringing are culled from MI, Sept. 17, 1986, p. 18, and Dec. 22, 1986, p. 47.

15 **"My hometown was a small town"**: MI, Mar. 24, 1987, p. 82.

15 **"one of those rare Huck Finn"**: *WTROM*, p. 18.

16 **"I've never known anything"**: RR, letter to Jo and Phil Regan, Apr. 22, 1987, PP/HW, RRPL.

16 **the cargo ship *Joseph Gilchrist***: Passenger list, emigrant ships, from Liverpool to US East Coast Ports, 1857, theshiplist.com.

16 **just twelve sod-and-stone huts**: "Reagan Genealogy," *New Yorker*, Nov. 9, 1981, p. 12; "The Irish

Ancestry of President Ronald Reagan," Debrett Ancestry Service, p. 4.

16 **"bright and ambitious"**: AE, p. 24.

16 **a boardinghouse with twelve**: London census, 1851.

16 **"gardener's laborer"**: 1851 census of Peckham, Parish of Camberwell, County of Surrey, District 8, Household #81.

16 **Her three uncles were notorious**: "Patrick Mulcahy's three brothers had all been imprisoned for long periods of their lives." AE, p. 24.

16 **"barbarity and atrocity"**: *National Enquirer*, Aug. 5, 1980.

17 **marrying at St. George the Martyr**: Marriage record of St. George the Martyr, Southwark, Surrey, England, Oct. 31, 1852.

17 **Michael signed the marriage certificate**: Alma Imhoff Lauritsen, "Michael Reagan Puts Down Roots in Illinois," essay in Patricia Meade White, *The Invincible Irish: Ronald Wilson Reagan: Irish Ancestry and Immigration to America* (Santa Barbara: Pertola Press, 1981), p. 79.

17 **"the Golden Doorway"**: "Rise of Industrial America: Immigration in the United States 1851–1900," U.S. Library of Congress report.

17 **"For richness of soil"**: Albert M. Lea, *Notes on the Wisconsin Territory* (Philadelphia: H. S. Tanner, 1836), pp. 13–14.

18 **As the early settlers discovered**: "There were no trees. It was all just prairie for as far as you could see." Ed Kolk, interview with author, May 5, 2015.

18 **You could gaze off**: "One of the early settlers built his 'house' eight or ten feet up a tree to escape the company of snakes." Lauritsen, "Michael Reagan Puts Down Roots in Illinois," p. 83.

18 **And game was plentiful**: Fay Freed Christian, "Early Carroll County," posted on genealogytrails .com.

19 **By the time the 1860 census**: 1860 census of Fair Haven township, Carroll County, Illinois.

19 **In nearby Savanna, the so-called**: "Preston's History," ch. 10, cited in AE.

20 **and sending them to school**: Ron Reagan, *My Father at 100* (New York: Viking, 2011), p. 35.

20 **died from tuberculosis**: Obituary of William Reagan, *Fulton [IL] Journal News*, Oct. 9, 1883.

20 **Thomas, the eldest son**: Obituary of Thomas Reagan, *Fulton [IL] Journal News*, July 5, 1889.

20 **"millinery and fancy dry goods"**: *Fulton [IL] Journal News*, Mar. 12, 1886.

20 **"the party began skylarking"**: "Reagan and others protested, all in vain." *Fulton [IL] Journal News*, July 9, 1889.

21 **"setting fire to a pile of velvet"**: "She returned in a few minutes, and on opening the door was driven back by the smoke." *Fulton [IL] Journal News*, Oct. 10, 1890.

21 **to avoid such a fate**: *Fulton [IL] Journal News*, Mar. 20, 1885.

21 **so that Jennie would be:** Barbara Mask, interview with author, May 6, 2015.

21 **Her symptoms took "an unfavorable":** "Mrs. John Reagan is very low with consumption and the disease has taken an unfavorable change." *Fulton* [IL] *Journal News*, Nov. 30, 1886.

22 **Soon after Jennie passed:** "At the time of Mrs. [Jennie] Reagan's death, Anna was afflicted with whooping cough." Obituary of Anna May Reagan, *Fulton* [IL] *Journal News*, Aug. 4, 1903.

22 **By mid-1888, reports:** "He has been failing in health for some time." *Fulton* [IL] *Journal News*, Dec. 28, 1888; "Johnny Reagan is very low and daily grows weaker." *Fulton* [IL] *Journal News*, Jan. 1, 1889.

22 **"John Reagan, aged thirty-four":** *Fulton* [IL] *Journal News*, Jan. 11, 1889.

22 **little Annie was placed:** *Fulton* [IL] *Journal News*, Oct. 14, 1892.

22 **Situated on a channel:** "This area, one of the narrowest spots on the Mississippi, is called The Narrows." Ed Kolk, interview with author, May 5, 2015.

23 **"Those riverboat crews were tough":** Ibid.

23 **In 1896, Orson G. Baldwin:** "Mr. Baldwin was one of the best merchants in Fulton . . . a member of the city council and prominent in society and politics." *Fulton* [IL] *Journal News*, Mar. 16, 1901.

23 **Bennett had no river:** "We think saloons are coming in a little too thick." *Bennett Buzzings*, 1898.

23 **He soon made it clear:** "Jack, a poor student, quit school at age twelve after completing the sixth grade." AE, p. 27; "Baldwin . . . continued to employ Jack, whose formal education had ended at the elementary level." Ron Reagan, *My Father at 100*, p. 39.

23 **Since the end of the Civil War:** Jules Tygiel, *Past Time: Baseball as History* (New York: Oxford University Press, 2000), p. 6.

24 **Jack found his footing:** "The Bennett boys have organized a ball nine." "J. Reagan" is mentioned as a member. *Tipton* [IA] *Advertiser*, Apr. 15, 1897, p. 8.

24 **Jaunty and gangly:** Verl L. Lekwa, *Bennett, Iowa and Inland Township* (Marceline, MO, privately printed, 1983), p. 96.

24 **Jack's job clerking at Baldwin's:** AE, p. 27.

24 **the Baldwins decided to close:** "Word comes from O. G. Baldwin in Bennett, Iowa, that he has sold out this department store for spot cash." *Fulton* [IL] *Journal News*, Mar. 16, 1901.

24 **He opened a lunch counter:** "John Reagan is in business for himself in Bennett, Iowa. He is proprietor of a lunch counter." *Fulton* [IL] *Journal News*, Mar. 29, 1901.

24 **taking a clerk's job:** "John Reagan is now a member of J. W. Broadhead's clerical force having entered upon his duties today." *Fulton* [IL] *Journal News*, Apr. 19, 1901.

24 **"quite well respected":** Nancy Kolk, interview with author, May 5, 2015.

24 **"tall, swarthy, muscular, and handsome":** Gordon P. Gardiner, "Nelle Reagan," *Bread of Life*, May 1981, p. 3.

25 **winding up in North Clyde:** Charles Bent and Robert L. Wilson, *History of Whiteside County, IL* (Morrison, IL, 1877), p. 145.

25 **Daniel, Alexander, and Charles:** Their tragic adventure is narrated in Daniel Blue, "The Thrilling Narrative of the Adventures, Suffering and Starvation of Pike's Peak Gold Seekers" (Whiteside County, IL, 1860, original typescript), p. 2.

26 **"in the teachings of the Christ life":** Obituary of Jane Blue Wilson, *Fulton* [IL] *Journal News*, May 7, 1894.

26 **"The Bible became":** "It was her chief book." Ibid.

26 **"with a flamboyant mustache":** Ron Reagan, *My Father at 100*, p. 37.

26 **"How those people survived":** Ed Kolk, interview with author, May 5, 2015.

26 **Dickson's *New Indexed Bible*:** The family Bible, passed from Jane Wilson to Nelle Reagan, appears on the cover of *Bread of Life*, May 1981, battered and held together by tape.

27 **"deep-seated yearning":** Obituary of Jane Blue Wilson.

27 **found Thomas living in La Crosse:** "Nearly twenty-five years ago he left here and went to Lacrosse [sic]." "The Death of Thomas Wilson," *Fulton* [IL] *Journal News*, Dec. 14, 1909.

28 **"A lot of capable people":** Ed Kolk, interview with author, May 5, 2015.

28 **And roughnecks passing through:** "They'd fight and steal; there was so much thievery." Nancy Kolk, interview with author, May 5, 2015.

28 **"she was a natural":** WTROM, p. 9.

28 **Mississippi Valley Stove Company:** The announcement of Nelle's reappointment appears in *Fulton* [IL] *Journal News*, Apr. 5, 1901, when she was eighteen; the announcement of her original appointment at sixteen has been lost.

28 **Thomas and Mary's marriage:** "Something went very wrong in the Wilson marriage." Ron Reagan, *My Father at 100*, p. 37.

28 **Mary, "toothless and wizened":** Ibid.

29 **"known for his copious blarney":** Edmund Morris, *Dutch* (New York: Random House, 1999), p. 17.

29 **"an attack of lung fever":** *Fulton* [IL] *Journal News*, Apr. 2, 1901; *Fulton* [IL] *Journal News*, Apr. 9, 1901.

29 **Annie Reagan, who had been sickly:** Obituary of Annie Reagan, *Fulton* [IL] *Journal News*, Aug. 4, 1903.

29 **"disapproved of Jack Reagan":** AE, p. 38.

30 **it was Nelle's uncle:** "My grandfather, Alex, Nelle's uncle, gave the bride in marriage to John Reagan." Anne Edwards, written questionnaire of Dwight Wilson, Mar. 25, 1986.

30 **Immaculate Conception, the Catholic facility:** "John Reagan and Miss Nelle Wilson, both of Fulton, will be married this evening at 7:30 in the Catholic Parsonage in this city." *Fulton [IL] Journal News*, Nov. 8, 1904.

30 **In Fulton, it was rare:** "In fact, even in the 1950s, you didn't intermarry between the two." Nancy Kolk, interview with author, May 5, 2015.

30 **"a mixed marriage":** "You weren't good enough to be married in the church if you didn't marry another Catholic." Ibid.

30 **"He was a restless man":** *WTROM*, p. 9.

TWO: A LITTLE BIT OF A DUTCHMAN

31 **The stores were limited:** William W. Davis, *History of Whiteside County, Illinois: From Its Earliest Settlement to 1908* (Chicago: Pioneer Publishing, 1908), p. 202.

32 **empty since the local:** Betsy Burkhard, "Tampico: Birthplace of a President," *DET*, Feb. 4, 1984.

32 **"a treacherous-looking stairway":** Ibid.

32 **Jack started work at a salary:** Myron S. Waldman, "Ronald Reagan's America," *Newsday*, Jan. 18, 1981.

32 **"an extremely popular man":** Morris, *Dutch*, p. 14.

32 **"Everybody liked Jack":** Joan Johnson, interview with author, Oct. 10, 2013.

33 **were earnest drinkers:** "The O'Regans of Ballyporeen had been famous for their liquor consumption." Morris, *Dutch*, p. 17.

33 **"the whole family drank":** Nancy Kolk, interview with author, May 5, 2015.

33 **"a two-fisted drinker":** "He was fast gaining a reputation as a two-fisted drinker when he married . . . Jennie Cusick in 1878." Jerry Oppenheimer and Ken Potter, "Ronald Reagan's Roots," *National Enquirer*, Aug. 5, 1980.

33 **There is strong evidence:** "There has been much said about Jack's drinking, but Elsey can't remember a time when Uncle Jack was drunk." Karen Putman, "Reagan Remembered by Cousin," *Coleta [IL] Daily Gazette*, undated, p. 1.

33 **But Jack Reagan was:** Nelle "never understood Jack's weekend benders." Paul Nicely, "Remembering Reagan," *Tampico [IL] Tornado*, Feb. 4, 1981.

33 **In April 1907:** *Tampico [IL] Tornado*, April 19, 1907; *Tampico [IL] Tornado*, April 26, 1907.

33 **In Jack's case:** "He then had to drink secretly, or go to Chicago on 'buying trips' as often as possible." Morris, *Dutch*, p. 17.

33 **she could smell it:** Ibid.

34 **she encouraged the move:** "Nelle persuaded Jack to leave Fulton and William's influence." AE, p. 32.

34 **"the Lunt-Fontanne":** "Jack, a ham, more in the raconteur mode, supported his wife's acting." Ron Reagan, *My Father at 100* (New York: Viking, 2011), p. 57.

34 **He opposed dancing:** "Three-fourths of all the fallen women fell as a result of the dance." William G. McLoughlin, *Billy Sunday Was His Real Name* (Chicago: University of Chicago Press, 1955), p. 132.

35 **Dr. L. W. Munhall's tabernacle:** *Tampico [IL] Tornado*, July 13, 1906.

35 **"It is an interesting sight":** William H. Lamon, letter published in "As Others See Us" column, *Tampico [IL] Tornado*, Aug. 23, 1907.

35 **"it was often after midnight":** Ibid.

35 **"My first appearance":** Neil Reagan, interview, UCLA Center for Oral History Research, June 25, 1981, p. 11.

35 **"Nelle would count":** "Nelle loved the apartment in the spring." Nicely, "Remembering Reagan."

36 **believed that a true:** Dr. Junius Rodriguez, interview with author, May 4, 2015.

36 **"tried very hard":** Gordon P. Gardiner, "Nelle Reagan," *Bread of Life*, May 1981, p. 3.

36 **As a prerequisite:** There is a story that after Neil's birth a priest, Father Defore, reminded Nelle of her promise to baptize the baby. She responded that such a promise was never made. As Neil recounts it: "And the priest turned to my dad and said, 'Jack, Nelle says nothing was told to her about bringing the children up Catholic. Why is that?' Jack snapped his fingers and said, 'Father, I completely forgot.'" Ibid.

36 **On Easter Sunday in 1910:** Ibid., p. 6.

36 **"one of the worst blizzards":** *Tampico [IL] Tornado*, Feb. 6, 1911.

37 **"Jack feared for her life":** AE, p. 34.

37 **"midwives with a hardiness":** Nicely, "Remembering Reagan."

37 **When the baby finally:** RR birth certificate, RRPL, PP/HF.

37 **Dr. Terry informed Nelle:** She suffered a prolapsed uterus during childbirth. Morris, *Dutch*, p. 688.

37 **All along, she had planned:** Ron Reagan, *My Father at 100*, pp. 42–43.

37 **"For such a little bit":** *WTROM*, p. 7.

37 **Dutch—he would be Dutch:** "We never used [Ronald] until he came out [to Sacramento]. We always called him Dutch—I still do." Neil Reagan, interview with Lou Cannon, 1968, LCA, p. 4.

37 **"evidently came about because":** "The letter in your recent issue regarding my 'name change . . .'" RRPL, PP/H, Box 47.

37 **"Now you can go home":** Neil Reagan, interview, UCLA Center for Oral History Research, June 25, 1981, p. 38.

38 **that Ronald was destined:** "I always say that Ronald is my mother's boy." Ibid., p. 43.

38 **Yes, Jack "loved shoes":** "He sold them as a clerk, managed shoe departments and his own stores." *WTROM*, p. 7.

38 **Jack won a 160-acre farm:** Myron S. Waldman, "Ronald Reagan's America," *Newsday*, Jan. 18, 1981.

38 **He immediately jumped:** "John Reagan . . . was a passenger over the Burlington Tuesday night, going to Aberdeen." *Tampico [IL] Tornado*, Oct. 8, 1909.

39 **"looking forward to God's plan":** Nicely, "Remembering Reagan."

39 **she would pass her son:** "They used to pass the president through there when Mrs. Reagan wanted to do some shopping." Burkhard, "Tampico: Birthplace of a President."

39 **"Upstairs flats were not":** Ibid.

39 **"a nice, white bungalow":** Nicely, "Remembering Reagan."

39 **the old Burden House:** "Jack Reagan has moved from the flat in the Graham building to the Burden House south of the depot." *Tampico [IL] Tornado*, May 5, 1911.

39 **"We spent a few minutes":** Neil Reagan, interview, UCLA Center for Oral History Research, June 25, 1981, p. 10.

39 **"They'd give you a piece":** MI, Sept. 17, 1986, p. 18.

40 **"with a hissing burst":** AAL, p. 23.

40 **In the spring of 1912:** "He really went off the track with his drinking over a girl . . . he had hoped to marry, but she jilted him." AE, p. 35.

40 **"seriously ill . . . unable to leave":** *Fulton [IL] Journal News*, Apr. 23, 1912.

40 **"he has not appeared":** *Fulton [IL] Journal News*, Apr. 3, 1914.

40 **Jack eventually committed:** "The commission declared that [Will Reagan] was mentally deranged and ordered him taken to Watertown [sanitarium] for treatment." *Fulton [IL] Journal News*, May 10, 1919.

41 **a Ford Model T:** *Tampico [IL] Tornado*, May 17, 1913.

41 **"It was an old touring car":** MI, Dec. 22, 1986, p. 44.

41 **"steering gear . . . failed to work":** *Fulton [IL] Journal News*, Dec. 16, 1913.

41 **lifelong struggle with claustrophobia:** "I've always wondered if that's the time it came about." MI, Dec. 22, 1986, p. 44.

42 **"intense dramatic action":** *Playbill for A Woman's Honor*, Jan. 13, 1906.

42 **"A pin dropped":** *Sterling [IL] Gazette*, April 21, 1913.

42 **"Well, yo' see, missus":** Lizzie May Elwyn, *Millie the Quadroon* (Clyde, OH: Ames Publishing, 1981).

THREE: "THE HAPPIEST TIMES OF MY LIFE"

43 **"We moved to wherever":** AAL, p. 23.

44 **"a city that was to forge":** Nelson Algren, *Chicago: City on the Make* (New York: Doubleday, 1951).

44 **"a congested urban world":** AAL, p. 24.

44 **"I got a larruping":** MI, Sept. 17, 1986, p. 25.

44 **"accepted a good position":** *Tampico [IL] Tornado*, July 31, 1914.

44 **"the store of the people":** Booklet published by the Fair Store, Chicago, 1915.

45 **"We were poor":** Neil Reagan, UCLA Center for Oral History Research, May 25, 1981, p. 43; "We were never anything but poor." RR, interview, Feb. 10, 1989, LCA, Box 23, Folder 77, p. 10.

45 **"We didn't have a cat":** Neil Reagan, interview, undated, 1968, LCA, Box 23, Folder 67.

45 **of "backdoor beer":** "Neil remembers bringing Jack butter-greased pails slopping over." Edmund Morris, *Dutch* (New York: Random House, 1999), p. 25.

45 **"There were times":** Neil Reagan, interview, May 19, 1988, LCA, Box 23, Folder 67, p. 2.

45 **"I can remember overhearing":** RR interview, Feb. 10, 1989, LCA, Box 23, Folder 77, p. 10.

45 **"She always tried to protect us":** Neil Reagan, interview, May 19, 1988, LCA.

45 **"She told us that we must not turn":** RR, interview, Feb. 10, 1989, LCA.

46 **Marx Brothers were given:** Tom Wilson, *Remembering Galesburg* (Charleston, SC: History Press, 2009), p. 125.

46 **town boss Omer N. Custer:** "He owned the bank, the radio, the newspaper, everything." Tom Wilson, interview with author, May 5, 2015; "Custer didn't want any more factories. He felt the town was just right as it was." Patty Mosher, interview with author, May 5, 2015.

47 **like grass snakes:** WTROM, p. 12.

48 **"Well, read me something":** Ibid.

49 **Nelle would walk the boys:** Tom Wilson, interview with author, May 5, 2015.

49 **"I could pick up something":** AAL, p. 25.

49 **"booby-trapped for adults":** Neil Reagan, interview, LCA, undated 1968, p. 2.

50 **Occasionally, when things boiled over:** "Sometimes . . . my mother bundled us up and took us to visit one of her sisters." AAL, p. 25.

50 **She even petitioned:** Patty Mosher, archivist, Galesburg Public Library, interview with author, May 5, 2015.

50 **Dutch remembered hearing:** "My brother and I often heard him telling Nelle that he would soon be doing better." AAL, p. 25.

50 **under cover of night:** "Jack Reagan, literally overnight, moved the family to Monmouth." Tom Wilson, interview with author, May 5, 2015. Confirmed by Patty Mosher, May 5, 2015.

50 **a booming wartime economy:** "Monmouth was a town on-the-grow. . . . The economy was soaring." Jeff Rankin, director of communications, Monmouth College, interview with author, May 5, 2015.

51 **"with his jaw set":** questionnaire of Gertrude Romine to Anne Edwards, Feb. 11, 1986.

51 **rescue a nest of birds:** Jeff Rankin, interview with author, May 5, 2015.

51 **the Knot Hole Gang:** Ibid.

51 **The city ordered its schools:** *Monmouth [IL] Daily Review*, Oct. 13, 1918.

51 **"The house grew so quiet":** "I sat watching for the [doctor] with the black bag." *Modern Screen*, March 1943.

52 **"keep [Nelle] stuffed":** *WTROM*, p. 13.

52 **moved back to Tampico:** *Fulton [IL] Journal-News*, Sept. 29, 1919.

52 **"a graduate of the American School":** *Tampico [FL] Tornado*, Sept. 29, 1919.

53 **"the most fortunate shift":** *WTROM*, p. 13.

53 **they played tag across:** Betty Burkhard, "Boyhood Chum Recalls," *DET*, Feb. 4, 1984.

53 **"The Sermon on the Mount":** RR radio address, undated 1976, courtesy of Peter Hannaford.

53 **"photographic memory for dates":** "President's 'Roots' Deep in Tampico," *DET*, Feb. 4, 1984, p. 38.

54 **"Nelle ran the . . . church":** Paul Kengor, "Jack and Nelle," May 5, 2008. education.org/articles /catholic_stories/cs0124.html.

54 **"in tragic tones":** *WTROM*, p. 15.

54 **"horsehair-stuffed gargoyles":** Ibid.

55 **"Immediately they tried to sell":** Paul Nicely, quoted in "President's Roots Deep . . . "

55 **"the happiest times of my life":** *WTROM*, p. 13.

FOUR: READY TO SHINE

58 **John Dixon bought it from him:** Dixon took over Ogee's property on April 11, 1830, but the deed wasn't recorded until 1832 in Galena. The deed is filed in Book A, pp. 163 and 164, March 1, 1832.

58 **In fact, a young Captain Lincoln:** Greg Langan, interview with author, Oct. 7, 2013.

59 **the O. B. Dodge Library:** Lynn Roe, interview with author, May 7, 2015.

59 **the general admission of one dollar:** George Lamb, *Dixon: A Pictorial History* (St. Louis: G. Bradley Publishing, undated), p. 121.

60 **"for special occasions only":** "Typically, Mrs. Reagan would . . . tell the boys, 'Don't set foot in the room. It's not for everyday use.'" Brandi Lagner, RR Homestead, Dixon, IL, interview with author, Oct. 7, 2013.

60 **"She'd never had a guest room":** Ibid.

60 **"He went through this period":** Neil Reagan, interview, LCA, undated 1968, p. 3.

60 **"The teachers didn't allow":** Esther Haack, interview with author, Jan. 28, 2014.

61 **"I simply thought that":** *WTROM*, p. 18.

61 **"a lot of heartache":** *AAL*, p. 35.

61 **Ed O'Malley recalled how:** Dan Miller, "Friends Take Pride in 'Dutch' Reagan," *DET*, Feb. 4, 1984; Myron S. Waldman, "Ronald Reagan's America," *Newsday*, Jan. 18, 1981.

61 **"something of a goody-goody":** W. L. Stitzel, quoted in James M. Perry, "Reagan's Roots," *Wall Street Journal*, Oct. 8, 1980; John Crabtree quoted

in same article: "Young Reagan came pretty close to being a goody-goody."

62 **"[Dutch] was the slowest one":** Waldman, "Ronald Reagan's America."

62 **a handful of torpedoes:** "'Torpedoes' my father would later call them." Ron Regan, *My Father at 100* (New York: Viking, 2011), p. 94.

62 **from atop a stoplight:** "Dutch just climbed up on one of those stop lights and sat there." Perry, "Reagan's Roots."

62 **the police chief, J. D. Van Bibber:** "Miscellaneous Information: Police Dept.," *Polk's Dixon City Directory, 1921–22.*

62 **"If you neglect to do that":** Brandi Lagner, interview with author, Oct. 7, 2013.

62 **He and Ed O'Malley joined:** "We were in Boy Scouts and the YMCA band." *"Remembering Ronald Reagan,"* pamphlet (Dixon, IL: Loveland Museum, 2001), p. 11.

63 **"The library was really":** RR, letter to Helen P. Miller, Sept. 3, 1981, RRPL, PPL.

63 **What's more, he could check:** Lynn Roe, interview with author, May 7, 2015.

63 **he called it "undisciplined":** "My reading I suppose was undisciplined and undirected and went through phases." RR, letter to O. Dallas Baillio, undated, RRPL, PPP Series II: Handwriting Files, Box 45.

63 **"read over and over":** *AAL*, p. 31.

63 **"Then I discovered Edgar":** RR, letter to Baillio, RRPL.

64 **"spread out as if he were crucified":** *WTROM*, p. 8.

64 **truth *happens* to an idea:** "It becomes true, is made true by events." William James, *Pragmatism*, "Lecture 1," 1907.

64 **"people follow the church":** Harold Bell Wright, *That Printer of Udell's* (New York: A. L. Burt Co., 1902), p. 114.

64 **into "two classes":** Ibid., p. 122.

65 **"I found a role model":** RR, letter to Jean B. Wright, daughter-in-law of Harold Bell Wright, Mar. 13, 1984, RRPL, PP/HW.

65 **"I'd like to be like him":** MI, Feb. 9, 1988, p. 178.

65 **"I want to declare my faith":** RR, letter to Jean B. Wright, RRPL.

65 **"you had to be ready":** "She made sure that I really meant it." MI, Sept. 17, 1986, p. 22.

65 **refused to baptize children:** The pastor was Ben Cleaver, Margaret Cleaver's father. Garry Wills, *Reagan's America: Innocents at Home* (Garden City, NY: Doubleday, 1985), p. 21.

65 **"Shh, we're going to get baptized":** Edmund Morris, *Dutch* (New York: Random House, 1999), p. 42.

65 **She was immediately elected:** "C. C. Elects Officers," *DET*, Jan. 24, 1921.

65 **She even became president:** "Christian Church Notes," *DET*, Dec. 11, 1922.

65 **often as the soloist:** MI, Sept. 17, 1986, p. 24.

65–66 **"she sandbagged merchants"**: Neil Reagan, interview, undated 1968, p. 5, LCA.

66 **"She would take her Bible"**: "Remembering Ronald Reagan," p. 4; "When I was a kid, she went down once a week to the county jail . . . and she would talk to them, to the men." MI, Feb. 9, 1988, p. 176.

66 **"So she would often invite"**: Brandi Lagner, interview with author, Oct. 7, 2013.

66 **On Thursdays, she took**: Helen Lawton, quoted in "Remembering Ronald Reagan," p. 17.

66 **"I love you, Daddy"**: Wills, *Reagan's America*, p. 25.

66 **"George Had a Grouch"**: DET, Jan. 21, 1922.

66 **"Pageant of Abraham Lincoln"**: "Pageant One of Greatest Productions," DET, Jan. 11, 1924, p. 1.

66 **"How the Artist Forgot"**: DET, June 3, 1920.

66 **"On the Other Train"**: DET, Nov. 24, 1923.

67 **"My mother inveigled me"**: MI, Sept. 17, 1986, p. 17; "Ronald would help her." Lynn Roe, interview with author, May 7, 2015.

67 **called "About Mother"**: DET, May 6, 1920.

67 **"The Sad Dollar and the Glad Dollar"**: DET, June 3, 1920.

67 **"Lavinsky at the Wedding"**: Parts I, II, III, IV, Columbia Graphophone Co., 1910.

67 **"I think that's where"**: MI, Sept. 17, 1986, p. 17.

67 **"practipedist," as the store's ads**: "Mr. Reagan . . . is an experienced shoe man and also a graduate practipedist, and understands all foot troubles and the correct methods of relief for all foot discomforts." DET, Feb. 22, 1921.

67 **"I remember my father"**: MI, date, p. 19.

67 **"Mrs. Wallace, it just isn't"**: Jean Wallace Rorer, quoted in "Remembering Ronald Reagan," p. 5.

68 **"Jesus walked barefoot"**: AE, p. 57.

68 **"the first salesman in Dixon"**: Wills, *Reagan's America*, p. 100.

68 **"oatmeal meat"**: "It was moist and meaty, the most wonderful thing I'd ever eaten." Ibid., pp. 28–29.

68 **insisted on tithing**: "Nelle had raised us to believe the Lord's share was a tenth." WTROM, p. 55.

68 **Dutch offered to contribute**: "I have 12 rabbits. . . . And I am going to kill three and eat them." RR letter to Gladys Shippert, undated 1922, RRPL, Pre-Presidential files.

68 **Moon went door-to-door**: "Come Friday night . . . I'd get the squabs . . . and I'd snap their heads off and clean them . . . and I never failed to sell all the squabs and rabbits." Neil Reagan, interview, UCLA Center for Oral History Research, June 25, 1981, p. 9.

68 **Jack took a lease**: "Mr. and Mrs. J. E. Reagan and sons are moving their household goods from 816 Hennepin Avenue to the new house built by John Huffman on West Everett Street." DET, Mar. 12, 1923.

68 **"No need to put up curtains"**: AE, p. 62.

69 **Saturday nights everyone headed**: "The businesses were open. People came downtown. They did shopping, but more than that. They came to visit and talk with each other." Greg Langan, interview with author, Oct. 7, 2013; "Saturday night was always busy in Dixon." Esther Haack, interview with author, Jan. 28, 2014.

69 **"The whole street was up"**: MI, Dec. 22, 1986, p. 43.

69 **Red Vaile's pool hall**: "Moon was always around Red Vail's [sic]." Ed O'Malley quoted in Waldman, "Ronald Reagan's America"; "I would go down to the one pool hall in town that was downstairs under a store, where your folks couldn't see you if they happened to walk by." Neil Reagan, interview, UCLA Center for Oral History Research, p. 9.

69 **an element of cruelty**: "Moon is . . . a young man who used humor to belittle, whose teasing was not good-natured"; also "Moon's 'needling manner' . . . could bring Dutch to tears." Ron Reagan, *My Father at 100*, pp. 94–95.

69 **viewed as "quiet"**: Neil Reagan, interview, UCLA Center for Oral History Research, p. 8.

69 **"down moments"**: "There was no such thought of, you know, putting my arm around his shoulder and saying, 'Let's talk this over.'" Ibid.

69 **"as a scared kid burying"**: Ron Reagan, *My Father at 100*, p. 95.

69 **"We didn't have what"**: Neil Reagan, interview, UCLA Center for Oral History Research, p. 8.

70 **"Nelle had left her eye-glasses"**: AAL, p. 37.

FIVE: "EVERYONE'S HERO"

71 **Klean Kids Klub**: RR is elected a lieutenant in "B Company." "Klean Kids of Y Organize at Sunday's Meet," DET, Sept. 17, 1923, p. 2.

71 **"hippodrome strut" along**: "William Rossiter remembers the flashy 'hippodrome strut' with which Reagan led the band." DET, Special Presidential Edition, Feb. 28, 1981.

71 **During a memorable Memorial Day**: RR relates this story often, including in AAL, p. 37.

72 **standard set of patriotic anthems**: Special Pres. Edition, Op. Cit., Sec. A, p. 12, DET.

72 **Dutch, ever the standard-bearer**: "Our drum major continued going straight down the street while the band followed the rest of the parade and made a turn." G. Warren Buckaloo, quoted in "Remembering Ronald Reagan," pamphlet (Dixon, IL: Loveland Museum, 2001), p. 6.

72 **Ed Worley's brother Bill**: Myron S. Waldman, "Ronald Reagan's America," *Newsday*, Jan. 18, 1981.

72 **"They'd changed the movies often"**: Esther Haack, interview with author, Jan. 28, 2014.

72 **L. G. Rorer, the procrustean**: Greg Langan, interview with author, Oct. 7, 2013.

72 **"It deals with the Ku Klux Klan"**: WTROM, p. 8.

73 **"There was no more grievous":** AAL, p. 30.
73 **While barnstorming as a traveling:** Jack is reputed to have said, "I'm a Catholic, and if it's come to the point where you won't take Jews, you won't take me, either." *WTROM*, p. 9; *AAL*, p. 30.
73 **"ultra-*ultra*-conservative":** Greg Langan, interview with author, Oct. 7, 2013.
73 *Let us not be weary:* II Corinthians 6:9.
73–74 *Be kindly affectioned:* Romans 12:10.
74 *God loveth a cheerful giver:* I Corinthians 9:7.
74 **"for the benefit of the American Public":** After-hours Inspirational Stories (inspirationalstories .com).
74 **started for the Whiffle Poofs:** "Haymakers Manage to Change Luck and Win," *DET*, Dec. 15, 1924, p. 7.
74 **"he was very slow of foot":** "Remembering Ronald Reagan," p. 11.
74 **and played outfield:** Dutch had a hit and scored a run. "North Central Team Is Winner of Tournament," *DET*, May 7, 1924, p. 2.
74 **"worshipped football more":** AAL, p. 38.
74 **He was good at it:** "Or maybe my father was simply blessed by genetics." Ron Reagan, *My Father at 100* (New York: Viking, 2011), p. 129.
74 **he would spring high:** Waldman, "Ronald Reagan's America."
75 **"a better than ordinary student":** "Remembering Ronald Reagan," p. 11.
75 **"just an average student":** "His real interest was in dramatics and sport." Freya Lazier quoted in Ibid., p. 10.
75 **"She was very pretty":** Esther Haack, interview with author, Jan. 28, 2014.
75 **Her name first started:** "Prosperous Year Christian Church Shows in Reports," *DET*, Jan. 17, 1924.
75 **often opposite Nelle Reagan:** They first appeared together in "The Pill Bottle" (May 6, 1924), during a recital (June 10, 1925), and in a church program (May 3, 1926).
75 **"The King's Birthday":** *DET*, Dec. 22, 1924.
75 **"They'd walk along the street":** Esther Haack, interview with author, Jan. 28, 2014.
76 **Chautauquas were the most popular:** Ibid.
76 **"for money is power":** Smith Zimmerman Heritage Museum, Dakota State University, Madison, South Dakota, Chautauqua files.
77 **"in the 1920s":** AAL, p. 44.
77 **"Dutch and his brother":** In a Mar. 2, 1985, interview with Anne Edwards, Bill Thompson says: "Dutch and Moon used to get their bits by carrying water to the elephants . . . and following the parade path." Original transcript provided to the author by John Thompson.
77 **paying eighteen dollars:** RR remembers it as $15 in his memoir, *WTROM*, p. 27; but in many interviews Ruth Graybill insists that $18 is accurate (for example Wills, *Reagan's America*, p. 32); and insists $16 in "Remembering Ronald Reagan," p. 7.

77 **Charles Russell Lowell:** A plaque at the beach says "Charles Russell Lowell, Colonel of Second Massachusetts Cavalry, Brigadier General United States Volunteers, Killed at Cedar Creek, Virginia, October 19, 1864."
77 **"Lowell Park was a great":** Greg Langan, interview with author, Oct. 7, 2013.
78 **And he'd even been invited:** Brandi Lagner, interview with author, Oct. 7, 2013.
78 **"You're pretty young":** Ruth Graybill, quoted in "Remembering Ronald Reagan," p. 7; Dan Miller, "Reagan Legend at Lowell Park," *DET*, Feb. 4, 1984.
78 **their old Dodge truck:** James M. Perry, "Reagan's Roots: Illinois Boyhood Meant Football, Swimming and Falling in Love," *Wall Street Journal*, Oct. 8, 1980; Wills, *Reagan's America*, p. 31; Beier's Bakery and Hartzell & Hartzell, Polk's Dixon City Directory, 1926–1927.
78 **"Dutch was no-nonsense":** Esther Haack, interview with author, Jan. 28, 2014.
78–79 **"a mob of water-seeking humans":** Ronald Reagan, "Meditations of a Lifeguard," *The Dixonian*, 1928.
79 **"He was the perfect specimen":** Dan Miller, "Friends Take Pride in Dutch Reagan," *DET*, Feb. 4, 1984, p. 4.
79 **"I had a friend":** Anonymous source, quoted in "Remembering Ronald Reagan," p. 8.
79 **"At the first hint":** "Superman Reagan Saved Our Lives," *National Enquirer*, June 25, 1985.
79 **"look over his glasses":** Bill Thompson, interview with Anne Edwards, Mar. 2, 1985, original transcript.
79 **"The drowning person invariably":** "You Saved My Life," *DET*, undated, Sept. 1941.
79 **"I sank under the water":** "Superman Reagan Saved Our Lives."
80 **"One second he was on a raft":** Ibid.
80 **"He was unconscious":** "Bert Whitcombe Was Near Death Saturday," *DET*, undated.
80 **"He started for a float":** "The one time I was really scared was about a blind man." "Superman Reagan Saved Our Lives."
80 **"a right cross to the jaw":** Ron Reagan, *My Father at 100*, p. 124.
80 **"I had to be pulled out":** *The Unfinished Oral History of District Judge James Benton Parsons*, p. 127, lb7.uscourts.gov/oralHistories/parsonsJames.pdf.
81 **"Dutch Reagan Has Made":** *DET*, July 23, 1932.
81 **"When the beach was not busy":** Ruth Graybill, quoted in "Remembering Ronald Reagan," p. 7.
81 **Dutch would perform graceful:** "He was a beautiful diver." Miller, "Reagan Legend at Lowell Park."
81 **Dutch set a record:** "Water Carnival Monday Proved Great Success," *DET*, Sept. 4, 1928.
81 **"He was everyone's hero":** "Remembering Ronald Reagan," p. 11.
81 **"All the young teacher":** Ibid.

81 **"every girl talked about"**: Esther Haack, interview with author, Jan. 28, 2014.

81 **"Me—I was in love!"**: *WTROM*, p. 22.

82 **"Somebody," Dutch said**: *AAL*, p. 41.

82 **"I thought I was going"**: Ibid.

82 **Helen Cleaver, Margaret's sister**: "Reagan was in our house all the time." Wills, *Reagan's America*, p. 18.

83 **He even taught Dutch**: Ibid.

83 **More than likely, he counseled**: Records of the First Christian Church, Dixon, IL.

83 **For the Indian Ritual**: Original program, Jr. and Sr. Powwow, June 2, 1927.

83 **"Everybody was a little scared"**: Esther Haack, interview with author, Jan. 28, 2014.

84 **Nov. 11, 1918**: RRPL, PPP 1918–80, Series II, Handwriting File, Box 49, date.

84 **Yale Comes Through**: Ibid., Nov. 17, 1927.

84 **heading "School Spirit"**: Ibid., Nov. 4, 1927.

85 **"to get under the skin"**: *AAL*, p. 42.

85 **"He fit into almost any"**: Bernard Frazer, quoted in "Reagan's Dixon," pamphlet (Dixon, IL: Official Dixon Press, 1980).

85 **"He never forgot his lines"**: Bernard J. Frazer, quoted in Waldman, "Ronald Reagan's America."

85 **Dutch talked incessantly**: "He was always talking about being in plays. I remember he said he'd love to be an actor when we grew up. When the talkies came in, he'd do imitations." Esther Haack, interview with author, Jan. 28, 2014.

85 **Radio came to Dixon**: Greg Langan, interview with author, Jan. 6, 2016.

85 **KDKA—the country's first**: "I remember sitting with a dozen others in a little room with breathless attention, a pair of earphones attached tightly to my head, scratching a crystal with a wire." *WTROM*, p. 17.

85 **The Reagans didn't have**: Brandi Lagner, interview with author, Oct. 7, 2013.

86 **"To hear the chimes"**: Gladys Shippert, quoted in Waldman, "Ronald Reagan's America."

86 **"severed his connection"**: *DET*, April 3, 1928, p. 7.

86 **Going to college was**: *AAL*, p. 44.

87 **"an almost mystical allure"**: Ibid., p. 45.

87 **"It was even lovelier"**: Ibid.

SIX: "LIVING THE GOSPEL"

88 **The Bible was the essential**: "The Bible is a regular textbook and every student may prepare and recite a lesson in it at least once a week." From an 1871 catalog, in Harold Adams, *The History of Eureka College, 1885–1982* (Eureka, IL: Eureka College, 1982).

89 **Alva Wilmot Taylor**: Dr. Junius Rodriguez, interview with May 4, 2015.

89 **Irwin St. John Tucker**: Ibid.

89 **Samuel Glen Harrod**: "He was an imposing bear of a man." Anthony Glass, interview with author, May 4, 2015.

90 **Dutch's "inflated tales"**: Ron Reagan, *My Father at 100* (New York: Viking, 2011), p. 147; "Coach didn't like the way Reagan claimed to be the star of Dixon High." Unnamed source, quoted in Edmund Morris, *Dutch* (New York: Random House, 1999), p. 67.

90 **"Dutch Reagan took care"**: *The Dixonian*, 1928.

90 **"created on the fly"**: Anthony Glass, interview with author, May 4, 2015.

90 **The $270 board would**: "In 1928 Ronald Reagan Embarked for College," *DET*, Presidential Edition, Feb. 28, 1981.

91 **Dutch made it a point**: "Ben Radford was one of the first people that Reagan met at Eureka." Dr. Junius Rodriguez, interview with author, May 4, 2015.

92 **Social reform . . . social justice**: "His lectures . . . were calculated to social justice." And: "His viewpoint was that what was needed was social reform." Burrus Dickenson, quoted in Myron S. Waldman, "Ronald Reagan's America," *Newsday*, Jan. 18, 1981.

92 **"He couldn't stand the rampant"**: Sam Harrod Jr., quoted in "In 1928 Ronald Reagan Embarked for College."

92 **Even so, Dutch got C's**: RR's Eureka transcript provided by a confidential source.

92 **"The practice might be compared"**: Raymond Holmes, *Raymond Holmes: His Family and Research with a Bang* (Richmond, VA, 1998), p. 78.

93 **"a sizable pool of shadow"**: *WTROM*, p. 33.

93 **one of the TKE fraters**: "In 1928 Ronald Reagan Embarked for College"; "It was wonderful to hear the response from all parts of the cemetery." *WTROM*, p. 34.

93 **There was a dress code**: AE, p. 84.

93 **"took a head count"**: Sam Harrod Jr., quoted in "In 1928 Ronald Reagan Embarked for College."

93 **"slow afoot, average"**: Ralph McKinzie, quoted in Dennis L. Breo, "Eureka! At 90, Reagan's Coach Still Calling Signals," *Chicago Tribune*, Sept. 7, 1985.

93 **"an austere, flinty"**: Morris, *Dutch*, p. 67.

93 **"revered and loved"**: AE, p. 86.

94 **"Dutch—I put him"**: Ibid., p. 87.

94 **"You played offense"**: Edwin Wilson, quoted in "In 1928 Ronald Reagan Embarked for College."

94 **"I told everyone"**: *WTROM*, p. 25.

94 **"was already known"**: Burrus Dickenson, quoted in "In 1928 Ronald Reagan Embarked for College."

95 **"Domineering" and "driven"**: Thomas F. Driscoll, "Memories of a Student Rebel," *Peoria [IL] Evening Star*, Mar. 8, 1981.

95 **He was so dead-set**: *Peoria [IL] Evening Star*, Mar. 8, 1981.

95 **Committee of 21**: Dr. Junius Rodriguez, interview with author, May 4, 2015.

95 **It took less than a week**: "Students Ask Resignation of Eureka Prexy," *Champaign [IL] News-Gazette*, Nov. 20, 1928.

95 "cutting out the heart": WTROM, p. 26.

96 "The board was outgunned": Dr. Junius Rodriguez, interview with author, May 4, 2015.

96 On November 23, The Pegasus: The Pegasus, Nov. 23, 1928.

96 Dutch recalled looking: "Everyone was hidden by a newspaper." WTROM, p. 27.

97 doubled as a common room: Anthony Glass, interview with author, May 4, 2015.

97 "I'd been told that I": WTROM, p. 28.

98 "We the students of Eureka": Daily Pantagraph (Bloomington, IL), Nov. 29, 1928.

98 "they came to their feet": WTROM, p. 28.

98 "heady wine": Ibid., p. 29.

98 "We put Reagan on": Garry Wills, Reagan's America: Innocents at Home (Garden City, NY: Doubleday, 1987), p. 48.

98 He was exhilarated: "For the first time in my life, I felt my words reach out and grab an audience, and it was exhilarating." AAL, p. 48.

98 "Neighbors and relatives": Mildred Neer, quoted in AE, p. 92.

99 "In some strange way": WTROM, p. 29.

100 Dutch for the Brat: Jean George Nathan, The Popular Theater (New York: Alfred A. Knopf, 1918), p. 187.

100 "I'd tolerated Mac": AAL, p. 48.

101 a "strong Republican": "My husband was a strong Republican. Reagan was only a kid, so he thought the Democrats were the best ones." Ruth Graybill, quoted in Myron S. Waldman, "Ronald Reagan's America," Newsday, Jan. 18, 1981.

101 "an offer too good": AAL, p. 49.

102 "Mr. Kennedy says if": Neil Reagan, interview, UCLA Center for Oral History Research, June 25, 1981, p. 7.

102 "It was about three-quarters": Dr. Junius Rodriguez, interview with author, May 4, 2015.

102 "If it was twenty below": Samuel Harrod Jr., quoted in "In 1928 Ronald Reagan Embarked for College."

102 "Ronald very seldom cracked": "Ronald actually has a photographic memory that's pretty phenomenal." Neil Reagan, interview, LCA, undated 1968, p. 6.

102 "And yet I have": Ibid.

103 "a good plugger": Ralph McKinzie, quoted in "In 1928 Ronald Reagan Embarked for College."

103 "He'd sit in front of a radio": Neil Reagan, interview, LCA, undated 1968, p. 6.

103 "O, we'll whoop 'em up": "Eureka College Songs" handbook, Eureka College, courtesy of Anthony Glass.

103 "They ran down the floor": Samuel Harrod Jr., quoted in "In 1928 Ronald Reagan Embarked for College."

104 he was the swim team: "In the beginning, Reagan was the swim team." Anthony Glass, interview with author, May 4, 2015; "If we had other swimmers, OK. If not, Dutch was it." Samuel Harrod Jr., quoted in "In 1928 Ronald Reagan Embarked for College."

104 He wasn't a giant-killer: "At Saint Victor on March 22 [1930], he . . . got two fourths." Ron Reagan, My Father at 100, p. 126.

104 evident the following year: "His 51 seconds for the 100-yard free-style was a state time." Samuel Harrod Jr., quoted in "In 1928 Ronald Reagan Embarked for College."

104 The Dover Road: "Dutch and Mugs: College Sweethearts," Peoria [IL] Journal Star, Mar. 8, 1981.

105 "In those days": Mark Shields, "A Sporting Interview with the President," Washington Post, Mar. 2, 1981.

SEVEN: "THE DISAPPEARANCE OF MARGARET"

106 In March, they were inducted: "The pledges included Margaret Cleaver and Ronald Reagan." The Pegasus, Jan. 8, 1929.

106 a profusion of social: The Pegasus, May 28, 1929; story headlineas before, The Pegasus, Nov. 9, 1929; The Pegasus, Nov. 23, 1929; AE, p. 107.

107 He'd never considered: "I discovered that in addition to athletics, the other thing that had gotten under my skin was show business." Mark Shields, "A Sporting Interview with the President," Washington Post, Mar. 2, 1981.

107 especially after Dutch's: WTROM, p. 44.

107 "He was an indifferent student": "Dutch and Mugs: College Sweethearts," Peoria [IL] Journal Star, Mar. 8, 1981.

107 "wanted more than he had": Motion Picture, November 1939.

108 Rumors persisted of another woman: "There were rumors of another woman, perhaps a professional." Ron Reagan, My Father at 100 (New York: Viking, 2011), p. 182.

108 "near starvation stalked": "City Wages War on Hard Times," DET, clip found in Anne Edwards's research files, undated 1932, p. 158.

109 "always well dressed": Mary Emmert, quoted in Garry Wills, Reagan's America: Innocents at Home (Garden City, NY: Doubleday, 1987), p. 58.

109 During 1931, foreclosures hit: Time, Jan. 4, 1932.

109 The John Deere Company: Greg Langan, interview with Oct. 7, 2013.

109 The Reynolds Wire factory: Ibid.

110 Like Dutch, Margaret required: From artifacts provided to the author by Eureka College.

110 There is a transcript: Anthony Glass, email to Junius Rodriguez, May 1, 2015, provided to author.

110 The University of Illinois: Scott Krinninger, University of Illinois, interview with author, May 29, 2015. "There is no matriculation record that [Margaret Cleaver] ever enrolled at the University of Illinois." When the author inquired if her record might be elsewhere or misplaced, he responded, "Not a chance." The university's morgue [obit] files, student files, and microfilm collection

of transcripts were all examined by the university archivist.

110 **"she could have gone away":** Dr. Junius Rodriguez, interview with author, May 4, 2015.

110 **the Baby Fold:** Greg Langan, interview with author, Oct. 7, 2013.

111 **taken this "for fun":** Anthony Glass, email to Junius Rodriguez, May 1, 2015, provided to author.

111 **with "absurdly handsome":** "He was, granted, absurdly, handsome—though in a boyish, wholesome sort of way." Ron Reagan, *My Father at 100*, p. 180.

111 **Dutch's grades junior year:** RR's college transcript, Eureka College archives.

111 **"This Younger Generation":** Written Oct. 27, 1931. RRPL, Pre-Presidential Papers 1918–80, Series II Handwriting File, Box 49.

112 **"Sweet Young Things":** Written Dec. 6, 1927, Ibid.

112 **"He was *no* star":** Ralph McKinzie quoted in "In 1928 Ronald Reagan Embarked for College," *DET*, Presidential Edition, Feb. 28, 1981.

112 **"Elmhurst hadn't lost a game":** Henry Allen, "The Saga of Burgie and Dutch," *Washington Post*, Mar. 7, 1981.

112 **"There were many towns":** Raymond Holmes, *Raymond Holmes: His Family and Research with a Bang* (Richmond, VA, 1998), p. 36.

112 **"Klansmen, Klanswomen, Kiddies":** From a 1924 Labor Day advertisement in the *Kewanee Daily Star*, Eureka College archives.

113 **"your two colored boys":** "I can take everybody but your two colored boys." *AAL*, p. 52.

113 **"Mac, if you do that":** Shields, "A Sporting Interview with the President."

113 **"'We can't serve you here'":** "I'm telling you how difficult it was in the Midwest." Allen, "The Saga of Burgie and Dutch."

113 **"took an awful lot":** "In those days if you had a black playing on your team. . . ." Shields, "A Sporting Interview with the President."

113 **a tuba player in the college:** "Neil was playing the tuba in the band." Griff Lathrop quoted in Harold Adams, "Reagan's College Years Recalled by Fellow Students," *Woodford [IL] County Journal*, Oct. 16, 1980.

113 **"On campus, he was":** Mary Eleanor Harrod, quoted in Myron S. Waldman, "Ronald Reagan's America," *Newsday*, Jan. 18, 1981.

114 **"hole-in-the-wall":** *WTROM*, p. 41.

114 **"A gifted storyteller":** Ralph McKinzie, quoted in *AE*, p. 110.

114 **In a pinch, Nelle had arranged:** "My mother, she just took kind of a table that was there and decorated it with some things like a tree." MI, Dec. 22, 1986, p. 46.

114 **"Moon and I were headed":** *WTROM*, p. 41.

114 **"Well, that's a hell":** *AAL*, p. 55; MI, Dec. 22, 1986, p. 46; *WTROM*, p. 41.

116 **"If I'm not making $5000":** "In 1928 Ronald Reagan Embarked for College," *DET*, Presidential Edition, Feb. 28, 1981.

116 **"We cannot squander":** Herbert Hoover, quoted in *Time*, May 30, 1932.

117 **"new deal for the American":** FDR's promise on accepting the Democratic nomination, June 1932. "FDR: Address Accepting the Presidential Nomination, July 2, 1932," The American Presidency Project, presidency.ucsb.edu.

117 **"Well, you've picked a line":** *WTROM*, p. 44.

117 **"take your chances":** MI, Feb. 9, 1988, p.176.

117 **"Believe you me":** "Classmates Recall President's Life," *DET*, Presidential Edition, Feb. 28, 1981.

117 **"Aren't you going to have":** "B.J. Frazier remembers that R.R. was dejected." Ibid.

117 **"By a stroke of luck":** "He didn't know what he missed. It was "$12.50 a week. We worked six days a week and Saturday nights and we worked a couple of extra nights a week, too." George Joyce quoted in "Lifetime Practice Paid Off at WOC," *DET*, Presidential Edition, Feb. 28, 1981.

117 **"quite a blow":** MI, Feb. 9, 1988, p. 176.

118 **"You'll find someone":** *AAL*, p. 61; "Come back and see me after you have some experience." *WTROM*, p. 46.

119 **"Hollywood was never":** Margaret Cleaver, quoted in Stephen Vaughn, *Ronald Reagan in Hollywood: Movies and Politics* (New York: Cambridge University Press, 1994), p. 20.

119 **"This is the one time":** Shields, "Reagan on Athletics."

119 **Phil Adler, the *Star*:** "What RR did was to take the AP sports scores, walk out on the balcony. . . ." Lloyd Schermer, Phil Adler's son-in-law, interview with author, April 4, 2014, and May 29, 2014.

119 **show, *Dave's Barn*:** Bonnie Palmer McCloskey, interview with author, Apr. 2, 2014.

120 **"I have this young guy":** Lloyd Schermer interview with author, April 4, 2014, and May 29, 2014.

120 **"It was about as strong":** James Leach, interview with author, May 15, 2013.

120 **"Where the West begins":** The sign-off for WOC, Palmer School Yearbook, 1929.

120 **"held the world's record":** Vaughn, *Ronald Reagan in Hollywood*, p. 23.

120 **a "scientific cult":** "Chiropractic and Public Health," *Journal of Manipulative Physical Therapy*, July 2008.

121 **Allegedly, D. D. Palmer:** James Leach, interview with author, May 15, 2013.

121 **"internal natural intelligence":** B. J. Palmer, *History in the Making* (Davenport, IA, 1957), p. 22.

121 **"Innate" directed him:** Garry Wills, *Reagan's America: Innocents at Home* (Garden City, NY: Doubleday, 1987), p. 98.

121 **By 1924, there were:** Steven C. Martin, "Chiropractic and the Social Context of Medical Technology: 1895–1925," *Technology and Culture*, Oct. 1993, pp. 808–34.

122 **"Scottish burr you could cut":** Neil Reagan, interview, UCLA Center for Oral History Research, May 25, 1981, p. 14.

122 **"How the hell do you":** *WTROM*, p. 48; *AAL*, p. 64; MI, Feb. 9, 1988, p. 177.

122 **"Make me *see* it":** *AAL*, p. 64.

123 **"a grand footballer":** Reprinted in *DET*, Oct. 28, 1932, p. 12.

124 **At the time of FDR's:** Adam Cohen, "The First 100 Days," *Time*, May 24, 2009; Kenneth T. Walsh, "The First 100 Days," *U.S. News & World Report*, Feb. 12, 2009.

124 **Charles Walgreen, the drugstore:** Greg Langan, interview with author, Oct. 7, 2013.

124 **"That place was always":** Esther Haack, interview with author, Jan. 28, 2014.

125 **He "was afraid to say":** MI, Nov. 8, 1988, p. 232.

125 **"His ambitions sort of crystallized":** Edmund Morris, *Dutch* (New York: Random House, 1999), p. 707.

125 **"He had an inability":** Ibid., p. 121.

126 **"unabashedly swiped from *The Register*":** Walter E. Shotwell, "Dutch Reagan's D.M. Days," *Chicago Tribune*, June 6, 1980, p. 1.

126 **"All day long, I'd been":** RR, on-air interview with Vin Scully, Jan. 24, 1980, transcript.

126 **"from coast to coast":** WHO's station ID from Jeff Stein, *Iowa's WHO Radio: The Voice of the Midwest* (Charleston, SC: Arcadia, 2011), back cover.

126 **mispronounced words like "rut beer":** Wills, *Reagan's America*, p. 133.

126 **"I stumbled over my words":** *AAL*, p. 70.

127 **"[Peter would] sit at home":** Shotwell, "Dutch Reagan's D.M. Days."

127 **Teaberry *Sports Review*:** *Des Moines Dispatch*, Aug. 3, 1934.

127 **It fell to Dutch:** "I had never seen a major league game." *WTROM*, p. 77.

127 **Western Union's Paragraph One:** James Walker, *Crack of the Bat: A History of Baseball on the Radio* (Lincoln: University of Nebraska Press, 2015), p. 176.

127 **"through a slit":** Transcript of questionnaire of Jack Shelley, Anne Edwards archives, p. 4.

127 **"Close to him was":** "Tg's Donohoo Remembers Dutch," by H. W. Van Donohoo, *Triangle*, July/August 1979, p. 7.

127 **The Yankees, Dodgers, and Giants:** James R. Walker, interview with author, Mar. 16, 2015.

127 **Pat Flanagan, a former:** Curt Smith, *Voices of Summer* (New York: Carroll & Graf, 2005), p. 13.

128 **"far better than":** Walker, *Crack of the Bat*, p. 173.

128 **with some early coaching:** "I went to Chicago where he generously instructed me in the technique and the problems." *WTROM*, p. 66.

128 **"This Tiger fielder, Fothergill":** Quin A. Ryan, "Inside the Loud Speaker," *Chicago Tribune*, May 1, 1927.

128 **As much as he enjoyed:** RR called it a "think-out-loud technique." *WTROM*, p. 77.

128 **"He had to ad-lib enormously":** Transcript of questionnaire of Jack Shelley, Anne Edwards archives, p. 4.

128 **Pat Flanagan claimed:** Edward Burns, "You Have to Be Air Minded to Try It, but Mr. M'Evoy Can't Complain That He's Lonely," *Chicago Tribune*, Feb. 21, 1937.

129 **"It'd almost blow":** MI, Sept. 23, 1987, p. 137.

129 **"We sang midwestern fight songs":** Wills, *Reagan's America*, p. 113.

129 **"what we called harmony":** "Everybody would gather out around the horse tank and sing what we called harmony." Neil Reagan, UCLA Center for Oral History Research, May 25, 1981, p. 14.

129 **1934 Nash Lafayette convertible:** RR, memo to his personal secretary, Kathy Osborne, RRPL, PP/HW, April 17, 1984.

129 **"Plan to spend two":** Ibid., p. 13.

130 **Dutch had been on a horse:** *AAL*, pp. 74–75.

130 **not "old plugs":** Myrtle Williams Moon, quoted in Wills, *Reagan's America*, p. 111.

130 **he rode with Dave Palmer:** "Dad and Ronald rode together." Bonnie Palmer McCloskey, interview with author, Mar. 31, 2014.

130 **"All he ever wanted":** Rich Kennelley, quoted in Shotwell, "Dutch Reagan's D.M. Days."

130 **"I began to dream":** *AAL*, p. 75.

130 **"a huge pool":** Richard Ulrich, quoted in AE, p. 141.

131 **"Right there in the light":** MI, Dec. 22, 1986, p. 50.

131 **a Walther PPK .30 pistol:** Morris, *Dutch*, p. 709.

131 **"Leave her alone":** Melba Lohmann King, quoted in Gene Raffensperger, "Reagan Saved Woman in '33 from Robber," *Des Moines Register*, Jan. 28, 1984; transcript of conversation between Melba Lohmann King and Anne Edwards, Feb. 19, 1983, AE files in author's possession;

131 **"in a fine old home":** Shotwell, "Dutch Reagan's D.M. Days."

131 **"heavy dark varnished woodwork":** *Des Moines Register*, Feb. 5, 1982.

132 **"quite the most glamorous-looking":** AE, p. 134.

132 **Dutch liked her family:** "Dutch would clear the dining-room table and with cards and markers recreate the football game he had just announced that day for her father's benefit." AE, p. 134.

132 **Max Baer who accidentally:** *WTROM*, p. 59.

133 **Jesse Owens, who set:** "Drake Relay Review," p. 7, www.drake.edu, "Indeed, I was broadcasting the day that the late Jesse Owens broke three American records at the Drake relays." RR, on-air interview with Vin Scully, Jan. 24, 1980, transcript.

133 **the batter was Augie Galan:** *WTROM*, p. 66; in *AAL*, p. 73 the batter was Billy Jurges.

133 **Harold Norem, Reagan's:** RR, letter to Harold A. Norem, RRPL, PP/H, Reagan's, Oct. 3, 1981; Norem, letter to RR, Aug. 14, 1981.

134 **"To millions of sports fans":** "Dutch Reagan Gives Sports Fans Daily Baseball Games," *Des Moines Dispatch*, Aug. 3, 1934, from Nelle Reagan's scrapbook, provided to the author, RRPL.

134 **"He is over six feet":** Adam Street, "Never Call Him Ronald," Nelle Reagan's scrapbook, RRPL, undated.

134 **he dated Lou Mauget:** Bonnie Palmer McCloskey, interview with author, Mar. 31, 2014.

134 **"one of the best-looking":** Paul McGinn, quoted in Myron S. Waldman, "Ronald Reagan's America," *Newsday*, Jan. 18, 1981.

134 **"I always had the feeling":** AE, p. 142.

134 **"a people pleaser":** Morris, *Dutch*, p. 128.

135 **"bittersweet" relationship:** "She remembers it as a 'bittersweet' episode." Shotwell, "Dutch Reagan's D.M. Days."

135 **"way too fast":** Jean Kinney, quoted in AE, p. 143.

135 **the "practical joker":** "He was Irish and loved to laugh and was always telling stories and gags." Neil Reagan, interview, undated 1968, LCA, p. 4.

135 **"We used to have":** Ibid., p. 7.

135 **"with his cigarette":** Myrtle Williams, quoted in Waldman, "Ronald Reagan's America"; "Myrtle Williams remembers Reagan's excitement as they rushed to the window and watched Roosevelt drive by the station." Wills, *Reagan's America*, p. 108.

136 ***Tomorrow's News Tonight:*** Stein, *Iowa's WHO Radio*, p. 26.

136 **"classic small-picture conservative":** James Leach, interview with author, May 15, 2013.

NINE: "ANOTHER ROBERT TAYLOR"

137 **pick up Charlie Grimm:** "Each year, Charlie Grimm, banjo in hand, hopped aboard at Kansas City." Roberts Ehrgott, *Mr. Wrigley's Ball Club* (Lincoln: University of Nebraska Press, 2013), p. 142.

137 **Shortstop Woody English:** "Charlie Grimm called Woody English 'a genius for pranks.'" Jim Vitti, *Chicago Cubs: Baseball on Catalina Island* (Charleston, SC: Arcadia, 2010), p. 21.

137 **"His escape is made":** *Des Moines Dispatch*, April 1937.

138 **Dutch stepped off:** "It was a record-breaking eighty-two degrees in February." *WTROM*, p. 70.

138 **Hall of Famer Gabby Hartnett:** "Hartnett liked to put on a brave front, although he was usually one of the first to break down." Ehrgott, *Mr. Wrigley's Ball Club*, p. 149.

139 **Jimmy Corcoran of the:** "There were words, and Jimmy went into action." Charlie Grimm with Ed Prell, *Jolly Cholly's Story: Baseball, I Love You!*, (Chicago: Regnery, 1968).

139 **Charlie Grimm allowed Dutch:** Vitti, *Chicago Cubs*, p. 76.

139 **A Des Moines theater owner:** "One of the studios was sending a crew around the country, testing people in various towns." *WTROM*, p. 71.

140 **"You know, just from watching":** Gene Autry, quoted in "The Greatest Bet Since Taylor Without Glasses," *The Reagan Times*, undated, p. 5.

141 **"Well, Miss Hodges":** Joy Hodges Schiess, interview with Anne Edwards, original transcript in author's possession.

141 **"He admitted he wanted":** Academy of Motion Pictures Arts and Sciences, letter to Anne Edwards, re: Joy Hodges film c.v., Apr. 18, 1986, in author's possession.

141–142 **Dutch inflated his acting:** "I decided a little lying in a good cause wouldn't hurt." *WTROM*, p. 72.

142 **Julius Epstein would suggest:** Steve Bingen, interview with author, Feb. 12, 2015.

142 **"rural and charming":** Olivia de Havilland, interview with author, Oct. 4, 2015.

142 **"It was the quickest decision":** Max Arnow, quoted in Marilyn Goldstein, "Reagan's America: The California Years," *Newsday*, Jan. 18, 1981.

143 **All day Sunday:** "I rehearsed with Dutch . . . all day Sunday. I was vitally interested." Joy Hodges Schiess, interview with Anne Edwards.

143 **Charlie Grimm let him know:** "Charlie Grimm . . . bawled me out for not even showing up at the practice field." *WTROM*, p. 71.

143 **"Warner Brothers sent Anita Louise":** Olivia de Havilland, interview with author, Sept. 3, 2015.

143 **players June Travis:** *Richmond [VA] News Leader*, Feb. 7, 1939; *Sunday Mirror*, May 20, 1937.

144 **"He didn't refer":** Goldstein, "Reagan's America: The California Years."

144 **Still, on the train ride:** "I said to myself: *What a damn fool you were*." *AAL*, p. 80.

145 **He treated himself:** Ronald Reagan, "The Making of a Movie Star," *Des Moines Sunday Register*, May 30, 1937.

145 **He also performed a personal:** "Reagan Alters Hairdress for a Leading Movie Role," *Des Moines Sunday Register*, May 30, 1937.

145 **"Somehow I can't see":** RR, letter to Dick Crane, May 15, 1937, Anne Edwards research, in possession of author.

145 **threw him a farewell party:** "Farewell Party for Reagan on Air Last Night," *DET*, May 20, 1937.

145 **Two days later, on Saturday:** "Reagan Alters Hairdress for a Leading Movie Role."

TEN: LETTING DUTCH GO

149 **"with every intention":** Ronald Reagan, "The Making of a Movie Star," *Des Moines Sunday Register*, May 13, 1937.

149 **"one awful ride":** Ibid.

150 **In fact, Birth of a Nation:** E. J. Stephens, interview with author, Feb. 4, 2015.

151 **picture called Don Juan:** E. J. Stephens and Marc Wanamaker, *Early Warner Bros. Studios* (Charleston, SC: Arcadia, 2010), pp. 25–27.

151 **The Warners pumped everything:** "They invested everything; they put all their chips in." E. J. Stephens, interview with author, Feb. 4, 2015.

151 **"without a doubt the biggest":** *Souvenir Programs of Twelve Classic Movies, 192–1941*, ed. Miles Krueger (New York, 1977), p. 9.

152 **Everything was wrong:** "The screen test . . . was terrible." Reagan, "The Making of a Movie Star."

152 **"The shoulders are too big":** Ibid.

152 **Even June Travis:** "She changed her name from Dorothea Grabiner, her real moniker. Her present name was selected from a telephone book." *Sunday Mirror*, May 20, 1937.

153 **"How about Ronald . . .":** *AAL*, p. 83.

153 **"The pace was incredible":** James Cagney, *Cagney by Cagney* (New York: Doubleday, 1976), p. 55.

153 **Hi, Nellie:** "Reagan's debut film . . . was a rehash of the 1934 Paul Muni picture *Hi, Nellie*." Tony Thomas, *The Films of Ronald Reagan* (Secaucus, NJ: Citadel, 1980), p. 32.

154 **had already made forty-five films:** Bryan Senn, *Golden Horrors* (Jefferson, NC: McFarland, 1996), p. 430.

154 **His job was to produce:** Rudy Behlmer, *Inside Warner Bros. (1935–1951)* (New York: Viking, 1985), p. 62.

154 **Warner fired Foy dozens of times:** E. J. Stephens, interview with author, Feb. 4, 2015.

154 **The Lights of New York:** Leith Adams, interview with author, Feb. 20, 2015; "Foy got fired for this." Marc Wanamaker, interview with author, Feb. 4, 2015.

154 **"an undemanding broth":** Anthony Lane, "The Method President," *The New Yorker*, Oct. 18, 2004.

154 **"a natural, giving one":** *Hollywood Reporter*, Aug. 19, 1937.

154 **"makes no pretensions to class":** Bosley Crowther, *New York Times*, Nov. 13, 1937.

156 **He spotted the Lane sisters:** *Des Moines Sunday Register*, May 27, 1937.

156 **"Dick Powell . . . wished":** Ibid.

156 **"a hotel for film people":** Marc Wanamaker, interview with author, Feb. 4, 2015; Steve Vaught, "The Hollywood Plaza—Hollywood's Forgotten Luxury Hotel," from "Paradise Leased" website, paradiseleased.wordpress.com/2012/10/24.

157 **"an architectural crazy house":** AE, p. 179.

157 **"Lights, millions of them":** *Des Moines Sunday Register*, Sept, 5, 1937.

157 **"I was in a new world":** *WTROM*, p. 77.

157 **"the manager introduced us":** "We had several dances and went home about midnight": *Des Moines Sunday Register*, May 20, 1937.

158 **"When the newspapers announce":** *Des Moines Sunday Register*, Oct. 3, 1937.

158 **"The studio had the option":** Olivia de Havilland, email to author, Sept. 3, 2015.

158 **"It was like a fiefdom":** Alan Spiegel, interview with author, Aug. 17, 2014.

158 **"has poise, a voice":** *New York Daily News*, Oct. 14, 1937.

158 **"crude, vulgar, shallow":** Neal Gabler, *An Empire of Their Own* (New York: Crown, 1988), p. 121.

159 **"He disliked actors":** Olivia de Havilland, interview with author, Oct. 4, 2015.

159 **"MY OPTION'S BEEN TAKEN UP":** *Des Moines Sunday Register*, 10/3/1937, p. 8

159 **He was also getting a raise:** Reagan contract, Warner Bros. Archives, USC.

159 **The gang of Iowa friends:** Garry Wills, *Reagan's America: Innocents at Home* (Garden City, NY: Doubleday, 1985), p. 145.

159 **"a dependable guy":** AE, p. 185.

160 **"Their actors portrayed the lowlifes":** Neal Gabler, interview with author, Aug. 18, 2014.

161 **referred to them as "uninspired":** Bosley Crowther, Review of *Secret Service of the Air*, *New York Times*, Mar. 2, 1939.

161 **"obvious . . . cheap action":** Bosley Crowther, Review of *Smashing the Money Ring*, *New York Times*, Nov. 17, 1939.

161 **"I learned that progress":** *WTROM*, p. 85.

161 **"Press agents were constantly":** *AAL*, p. 88.

161 **spurred "lunch-break trysts":** "Ex-Actress Talks About Reagan, *Lodi [CA] News-Sentinel*, Dec. 18, 1980.

162 **Rhodes assumed the studio:** "She blamed "movie moguls [who] decided romance between their stars was bad for box-office business." Ibid.

ELEVEN: "BUTTON NOSE"

163 **been known as Jane Durrell:** "For a while she was Jane Durrell." Sidney Skolsky, "Hollywood Is My Beat," *New York Post*, Nov. 8, 1953.

163 **French chanteuse LaJerne Pechelle:** Joe Morella and Edward Z. Epstein, *Jane Wyman: A Biography* (New York: Delacorte, 1985), p. 5.

163 **the self-described cocky:** "I covered up by becoming the cockiest of all, by talking the loudest, laughing the longest, and wearing the curliest, most blatantly false eyelashes in Hollywood." Lawrence J. Quirk, *Jane Wyman: The Actress and the Woman* (New York: Dembner Books, 1986), p. 17.

163 **in a scenic river town:** St. Joseph is on the Missouri River.

164 **"crippled" by shyness:** Quirk, *Jane Wyman*, p. 14.

164 **Richard Fulks, an unsparing disciplinarian:** "I was reared under such strict discipline." Jane Wyman quoted in Morella and Epstein, *Jane Wyman*, p. 6.

164 **Early in adolescence:** Gary Chilcote, "Jane Wyman, Reagan's First Wife, Grew Up Here," *St. Joseph's News-Press*, Nov. 7, 1980.

164 **When her husband died:** "My mother and I were bored to death with that town." Jane Wyman quoted in Quirk, *Jane Wyman*, p. 16.

164 **separated from him:** "Still in her teens she impulsively entered marriage . . . but in less than a month she knew it was a terrible mistake and the marriage was dissolved." Nell Blythe, "Jane Wyman," *Movie Life*, March 1957.

164 **Eugene Wyman was the name:** Edmund Morris, *Dutch* (New York: Random House, 1999), p. 717.

164 **It took another two years:** "Jane Wyman Divorced from Ernest F. [sic] Wyman," *Los Angeles Examiner* (morgue file), 1935, Warner Bros. Archives, USC.

164 **She later boasted:** "Star Began Her Career on a Hunch," *DET*, July 12, 1941.

164 **"Before I became a blonde":** "Jane Wyman's Hair Brings Luck," studio-written article in press book for *An Angel from Texas*, Warner Bros. Archives, USC.

165 **fraught with the kind:** "During this period, she made the casting rounds, rebuffing dozens of men who sought to exploit her sexually." Quirk, *Jane Wyman*, p. 18.

165 **"I had had enough":** "Jane Wyman's Hair Brings Luck."

165 **"a girl on the make":** Louella Parsons, quoted in Quirk, *Jane Wyman*, p. 43.

165 **In May 1936:** Jane Wyman's Warner Bros. contract, May 6, 1936, Warner Bros. Archives, USC.

165 **"wise-cracking chorus girl":** Referring to her role in *The King and the Chorus Girl*. Morella and Epstein, *Jane Wyman*, p. 14.

165 **"dumb bunny . . . floozie":** Referring to her roles in *Ready, Willing and Able* and *The King and the Chorus Girl*. Quirk, *Jane Wyman*, p. 23.

166 **"Ronnie was the dream":** Ibid., p. 30.

167 **Jane, impatient and high-strung:** "My first impulse, as always, was to resent it . . . to feel that someone was pushing us around." Jane Wyman quoted in untitled and undated article, *Photoplay*, from Anne Edwards's research in author's possession.

167 **he called "leadingladyitis":** "Leadingladyitis is an infatuation that won't hold up, once the play is over and you each go back to playing yourselves." *WTROM*, pp. 38–39.

167 **It hit him again:** Ibid., p. 79.

167 **"Everyone could see that Janie":** Quirk, *Jane Wyman*, p. 37.

167 **"I just couldn't see [Jane]":** Alex Gottlieb, interview with Anne Edwards, original transcript in author's possession.

168 **"She had real fire":** Olivia de Havilland, interview with author, Oct. 4, 2015.

168 **to "good scout":** Cynthia Miller, undated article, *Modern Screen*, from Anne Edwards's research in author's possession.

168 **"Ronnie always had a cause":** Leon Ames, quoted in Marilyn Goldstein, "Reagan's America: The California Years," *Newsday*, Jan, 18, 1981.

168 **"This time appeared to represent":** Lawrence Williams, "The Disordered Memories of a Movie Actor," *Westport News*, Oct. 31, 1980, p. 21.

169 **"Arguing politics drew them together":** June Allyson with Frances Spatz Leighton, *June Allyson* (New York: G. P. Putnam's Sons, 1982), p. 95.

169 **"I was a loyal":** MI, June 30, 1987, p. 110; "I always believed that all this left-wing talk": MI, Oct. 23, 1987, p.140; the party's platform against high tariffs: MI, June 30, 1987, p. 118.

170 **he created a job:** "After talking it over with my mother, I came up with a plan that worked like a charm." *AAL*, p. 93; *WTROM*, p. 84.

170 **"Ronnie had this wonderful":** Untitled article from Anne Edwards's research in author's possession, *Photoplay*.

170 **"She was so experienced":** Jerry Asher, quoted in Quirk, *Jane Wyman*, p. 42.

170 **"so nervous and tense":** Louella Parsons, quoted in Quirk, *Jane Wyman*, p. 45.

170 **Jane claimed he eventually:** "Ronnie simply turned to me as if the idea were brand new and said, 'Jane, why don't we get married?'" Quirk, *Jane Wyman*, p. 43.

170 **an old "stomach disorder":** A. Alleborn, memo to T. C. Wright, Oct. 4, 1939, Warner Bros. Archives, USC.

170 **Years later, Nancy Reagan disclosed:** Morris, *Dutch*, p. 162.

171 **"two of Hollywood's very nicest":** Louella Parsons, *Los Angeles Examiner*, Nov. 1, 1939.

171 **"wooing the blonde Miss Wyman":** Press book for *Brother Rat and a Baby*, Warner Bros. Archives, USC.

171 **Jane's sonar picked up:** "Jane was . . . making jokes constantly, [and was] terribly jealous." Louella Parsons, *The Gay Illiterate* (Garden City, NY: Doubleday, 1944), p. 161.

171 **The discord didn't help:** "[The show] may go big, but as it looked at its opening stand, it's nothing to stand in line for—and nobody did." Paul Spiegle, *San Francisco Chronicle*, Nov. 16, 1939.

172 **his Eureka College songs:** Joy Hodges, letter to Anne Edwards, May 4, 1986, in author's possession.

172 **Ronnie found his footing:** "Ronald Reagan [is] very personable, deft and obviously at home on a stage." *Variety*, Nov. 22, 1939.

172 **As 1939 drew to close:** *Los Angeles Examiner*, Dec. 31, 1939; Finland's Note *New York Journal and American*, Dec. 30, 1939.

172 **Finland's "stout resistance":** "Allies Pledge to Sweden Expected," *New York Times*, Dec. 28, 1939.

172 **"and join your Russian friends":** "Incidents in European Conflict," *New York Times*, Dec. 28, 1939.

172 **During interviews with the Washington:** "Flashbulbs popped as he engaged Casey Jones, managing editor of the *Post*, in a long discussion of the situation in Finland." Morris, *Dutch*, p. 165.

172 **"He did not always pick":** Joy Hodges, letter to Anne Edwards, May 4, 1986.

173 **"He was eager to absorb":** Ibid.

173 **"they'll be husband and wife":** Los Angeles Examiner, Jan. 26, 1940.

173 **"beautiful beyond dreams":** Leonora Hornblow, quoted in Morris, Dutch, p. 166; Los Angeles Examiner, Jan. 27, 1940.

174 **"I hope my Ronald":** Nelle Reagan, letter to Myrtle Kennedy, quoted in Morris, Dutch, p. 164.

TWELVE: "WHERE'S . . . WHERE'S THE
REST OF ME?"

175 **"was not an actor":** Garry Wills, Reagan's America: Innocents at Home (Garden City, NY: Doubleday, 1985), p. 177; Pat O'Brien said that Wallis saw RR as "a hick radio announcer from the Middle West." Pat O'Brien, The Wind at My Back: The Life and Times of Pat O'Brien (Garden City, NY: Doubleday, 1964), p. 240.

175 **"When you were struggling":** Olivia de Havilland, interview with author, Oct. 4, 2015.

175 **"generated so much good will":** Ruth Waterbury, quoted in Lawrence J. Quirk, Jane Wyman: The Actress and the Woman (New York: Dembner Books, 1986), p. 47.

176 **Ronnie spotted an announcement:** Variety, Jan. 17, 1940.

176 **George Gipp was a reprobate:** Sports Illustrated, Sept. 10, 1979.

176 **Wallis always envisioned Spencer Tracy:** "We should like nothing better than to have him play Rockne." Hal B. Wallis, letter to J. Arthur Haley (University of Notre Dame), Sept. 11, 1939, Warner Bros. Archives, USC.

176 **Cagney had been the studio's:** "Cagney would insure the picture's success. O'Brien would not." Robert Bruckner, letter to Rev. Hugh O'Donnell (University of Notre Dame), July 26, 1939, Warner Bros. Archives, USC.

176 **"the gangster type":** J. Arthur Haley, letter to Bryan Foy, Sept. 2, 1939, Warner Bros. Archives, USC.

176 **"the Loyalist Cause":** "The university, knowing this fact, do not feel that they can jeopardize their reputation because of the publicity thus received." Ibid.

176 **"get those double chins":** memo, Bob Fellows to Hal Wallis, 1/23/1940, Warner Archives, USC.

176 **Wallis had already rejected:** Memo from Hal Wallison personal note paper, Knute Rockne production file, Warner Bros. Archives, USC.

177 **he came prepared with props:** "I barged into his office and slapped the pictures down on his desk." WTROM, p. 92.

177 **Ronnie got him work:** Joe Morella and Edward Z. Epstein, Jane Wyman: A Biography (New York: Delacorte, 1985), p. 40.

177 **It already represented:** Dan E. Moldea, Dark Victory: Ronald Reagan, MCA, and the Mob (New York: Viking, 1986), p. 17.

177 **A pact with the American:** Ibid., pp. 17–18.

178 **Within eight years:** AE, p. 211, footnote sourced from a periodical cited as Reader, Nov. 2, 1984.

178 **"a magnificent piece of machinery":** RR, quoted in AE, p. 291.

178 **He refused to eat lunch:** Olivia de Havilland, interview with author, Oct. 4, 2015.

179 **"On Saturday, let's go out":** Lew Wasserman, quoted in Leith Adams interview with author, Feb. 20, 2015.

179 **"He loved motion and exciting":** Alan Spiegel, interview with author, Oct. 9, 2015.

179 **"Who cares about character?":** Aljean Harmetz, Round Up the Usual Suspects (New York: Orion Publishing, 1993), pp. 183–84.

179 **"He was a bully":** Olivia de Havilland, interview with author, Oct. 4, 2015.

180 **but he backed out:** "I MUST REFUSE THE ROLE OF CUSTER IS NO MORE THAN A FOIL TO JEB STUART." John Wayne, telegram to Bryan Foy, undated, Warner Bros. Archives, USC.

180 **She describes a publicity:** RR describes this event somewhat differently in WTROM, p. 96.

180 **"Flynn repeatedly showed up hours":** Olivia de Havilland, email to author, Sept. 4, 2015.

181 **"a damned noble organization":** WTROM, p. 132.

181 **"There was a caste system":** Olivia de Havilland, interview with author, Oct. 4, 2015; "They were largely people of lesser standing." Jack Dales, interview, "Pragmatic Leadership," Ronald Reagan as President of the Screen Actors Guild," UCLA Center for Oral History Research, May 2, 1981, p. 2.

181 **"You know we had a war":** B. P. Schulberg, quoted in Nancy Lynn Schwartz and Sheila Schwartz, The Hollywood Writers' Wars (New York: Alfred A. Knopf, 1982), p. 29.

182 **He resented being forced:** "I thought it was an infringement on my rights." AAL, p. 89.

182 **paying its quarterly dues:** RR's "Application for Senior Membership," SAG Archives, April 8, 1937; "He paid a $25 admission fee and $7.50 in quarterly dues." Valerie Yaros, SAG historian, quoted in "SAG Notes," SAG Archives, Aug. 12, 2002.

182 **"She nailed me in a corner":** WTROM, p. 133.

182 **His father was a flag bearer:** "Jack never bristled more than when he thought working people were being exploited." AAL, p. 90.

182 **"a good, solid board member":** Jack Dales, interview, UCLA Center for Oral History Research, May 2, 1981, p. 7.

182 **she "knew a guy":** Ibid., p. 5.

182 **"I want you to meet":** Jack Dales, interview with Anne Edwards, undated, original transcript in author's possession.

182 **"Jane Wyman wasn't wrong":** Ibid.

183 **"He seemed to enjoy":** Olivia de Havilland, interview with author, Oct. 4, 2015.

183 **Variety named him:** *Daily Variety*, Dec. 18, 1940.

183 **"the whole country is getting":** *Los Angeles Examiner*, Dec. 12, 1940.

183 **"I wanted one, too":** RR, quoted in Morella and Epstein, *Jane Wyman*, p. 42.

183 **"General Ronald Reagan Jr.":** Edmund Morris, *Dutch* (New York: Random House, 1999), p. 172.

183 **"I wanted a boy":** *DET*, undated; AE, p. 230.

184 **"We don't want to go":** *Los Angeles Times*, Sept. 24, 1944.

184 **"Next morning, we dashed":** Jane Wyman quoted in Morella and Epstein, *Jane Wyman*, p. 45.

184 **With a twenty-year:** Ibid., p. 52.

184 **"putting wifehood and motherhood first":** "She really worked at the marriage." Ruth Waterbury, *Photoplay*, quoted in Quirk, *Jane Wyman*, p. 53.

185 **"I was twenty-seven":** Ibid., p. 54.

185 **"I don't think Hollywood":** Adolph Zukor, quoted in *The Argus* (Melbourne, Australia), Aug. 12, 1939.

185 **"people whose daily morals":** David Denby, "From Hitler to Hollywood," *The New Yorker*, Sept. 16, 1913.

186 **"to combine entertainment":** Edward G. Robinson, letter to Prof. D. R. Taft, Dec. 22, 1938, quoted in Steven J. Ross, *Hollywood Left and Right* (New York: Oxford University Press, 2011), p. 103.

186 **seven times what it:** AE, p. 237.

187 **"As far as the plot":** Wolfgang Reinhardt, memo to Hal Wallis, July 3, 1940, Warner Bros. Archives, USC.

187 **Even before a script:** Joseph Breen, memo to Jack Warner, Apr. 22, 1941, Warner Bros. Archives, USC.

188 **"It got to the end":** RR, interview with Lou Cannon, May 5, 1989, LCA, p. 6.

188 **"All of a sudden a wave":** Ibid.

189 **"long, hard schedule":** *WTROM*, p. 103.

189 **"In our special field":** "Statement of Principles," Motion Picture Alliance for the Preservation of American Ideals, 1944, Society of Independent Motion Picture Producers Archive.

189 **"Most of the leading characters":** *Daily Variety*, Dec. 23, 1941.

190 **"I felt I had neither":** *WTROM*, p. 4.

190 **"Gradually, the affair began":** Ibid., p. 5.

190 **In the earlier version:** "Fine director that he was, he just turned to the crew and said, 'Let's make it.' Ibid.

190 **"No rehearsal—just shoot it."** AAL, p. 96.

191 **"I began to feel":** *WTROM*, p. 6.

THIRTEEN: IN THE ARMY NOW

193 **The stark reality of it:** "This easily is the greatest thrill I've ever had." "Squadron Debuts During 1941 Visit," *DET*, Presidential Edition, Feb. 28, 1981.

193 **The City of Los Angeles:** "Hollywood Moves to Dixon," *DET*, Oct. 12, 1941.

193 **a starring role in Casablanca:** *Hollywood Reporter*, Jan. 5, 1942.

193 **"We shot night exteriors":** *WTROM*, p. 103.

194 **"an action melodrama":** Bosley Crowther, "'Desperate Journey,' a Futile Chase Through Germany, with Errol Flynn and Ronald Reagan," *New York Times*, Sept. 26, 1942.

194 **"he did more or less":** Marilyn Goldstein, "Ronald Reagan's America: The California Years," *Newsday*, Jan. 18, 1981.

194 **Jack Warner had secured:** Draft of letter from Warner Bros. Pictures to Asst. Sec. of War, Sept. 1941, Warner Archives, USC; RR deferment: Jack Warner, memo, Jan. 1, 1942, Warner Bros. Archives, USC; RR's final orders, Mar. 24, 1942, Warner Bros. Archives, USC.

194 **studios "tremendous investment":** Letter from Roy Obringer to Commanding General, Ninth Corps Area, Mar. 28, 1942, Warner Bros. Archives, USC.

194 **"due to a shortage":** U.S. Army, telegram to Jack Warner, April 2, 1942, Warner Bros. Archives, USC.

195 **"She was furious with him":** Edmund Morris, *Dutch* (New York: Random House, 1999), p. 727.

195 **a strict policy to suspend:** RR's contract suspended Apr. 20, 1942. "History of RR's Contracts," Warner Bros. Archives, USC.

195 **His Army pay amounted:** Tony Thomas, *The Films of Ronald Reagan* (Secaucus, NJ: Citadel, 1980), p. 143.

195 **Ronnie dashed off a memo:** RR, memo to Steve Trilling, Apr. 5, 1942, Warner Bros. Archives, USC.

195 **"Long shots and shots":** "A lot of rescheduling took place to get my final scenes on film." AAL, p. 97.

196 **In the eighty years since:** In 1863, the government seized the property belonging to John C. Frémont on that ground that it was needed for the Civil War effort. Sally Denton, *Passion and Principle, John and Jessie Frémont, the Couple Whose Power, Politics, and Love Shaped Nineteenth-Century America* (New York: Bloomsbury, 2007).

196 **"tired of being used":** Morris, *Dutch*, p. 191.

196 **In late May 1942:** "I received word today that Reagan's agent has notified Trilling that Reagan's commanding general has approved his transfer to the Air Force." Hal Wallis, memo to Jack Warner, May 29, 1942, Warner Bros. Archives, USC.

197 **places like Kearney:** "U.S. Military Airfields, Camps, Forts and Stations," Wartime Press, war timepress.com.

197 **Disney had made a number:** Owen Crump, UCLA Center for Oral History Research, Margaret Herrick Library, Oct. 22, 1991, p. 7.

197 **March on Marines:** List of short films from Warner Bros. Archives, USC.

197 **By coincidence, in 1941:** Jack Warner, letter to Henry H. Arnold, Dec. 23, 1941, Warner Bros. Archives, USC.

197 **Warner, toting a sheaf:** Jack Warner consulted with director Howard Hawks on ideas for aviation films, including the recruitment and training of fighter pilots. Jack Warner, memo "Notes for Washington Talk," undated, Warner Bros. Archives, USC; Jack Warner, memo "Suggested Plan of Operations for the Motion Picture Activities Division, Army Air Forces," Apr. 24, 1942, Warner Bros. Archives, USC.

198 **"After the war is won":** Ibid.

198 **"people will know we really":** Ibid.

198 **"virtually in shambles":** Owen Crump, UCLA Center for Oral History Research, Oct. 22, 1991, p. 28.

198 **On June 8, 1942:** "Ronnie Reagan (2/Lt.) arrived June 8 to help out." Owen Crump, quoted in Morris, *Dutch*, p. 192.

198 **"I looked up":** Owen Crump, UCLA Center for Oral History Research, Oct. 22, 1991, p. 29.

198 **"My first assignment":** AAL, p. 98.

199 **was officially activated:** Doug Cunningham, *Hap Arnold, Warner Bros. and the Formation of the USAAF First Motion Picture Unit*, undated, typescript provided to the author, p. 1.

199 **The Rear Gunner:** The National Archives Motion Picture Collection, Record Group 18, Accession 2351.

199 **Recognition of the Japanese Zero Fighter:** Ibid., Group 208, Accession 3276.

199 **"prepared to lose ten million":** Quotes attributed to *Westward Bataan* are from Stephen Vaughn, *Ronald Reagan in Hollywood: Movies and Politics* (New York: Cambridge University Press, 1994), p. 115.

200 **"is morale in capital letters":** Review for *This Is the Army*, *Variety*, Aug. 4, 1943.

200 **He loved the magazine's:** An entry in Edmund Morris's War Diary, Feb. 19, 1943, says: "[RR] reveres [*Reader's Digest*] as the sum of All human wisdom." Morris, *Dutch*, p. 202.

201 **"a lovable scatterbrain":** Jessica Mitford, review of WTROM, *Ramparts*, Nov. 1965; *Los Angeles Times*, Aug. 17, 1980.

201 **"All he talks about":** Robert Cummings, quoted in Joe Morella and Edward Z. Epstein, *Jane Wyman: A Biography* (New York: Delacorte, 1985), p. 62.

201 **"was such a talker":** Ibid., p. 71.

201 **"the perfect American officer":** Lawrence J. Quirk, *Jane Wyman: The Actress and the Woman* (New York: Dembner Books, 1986), p. 63.

202 **"My Soldier, by Jane Wyman":** *Modern Screen*, January 1943.

202 **"I always felt":** Edward G. Robinson, quoted in Quirk, *Jane Wyman*, p. 63.

202 **"asking why, why":** Louella Parsons, quoted in Morella and Epstein, *Jane Wyman*, p. 69.

203 **"that drunk film":** Jack Warner, quoted in Quirk, *Jane Wyman*, p. 79.

203 **He knew the liquor industry:** Cameron Crowe, *Conversations with Wilder* (New York: Alfred A. Knopf, 1999), p. 115 (photo caption).

203 **"The Lost Weekend":** Bosley Crowther, *New York Times*, Dec. 3, 1945.

203 **"It changed my whole life":** Jane Wyman, quoted in Quirk, *Jane Wyman*, p. 80.

204 **"Above this they rigged":** WTROM, p. 118.

204 **"No twentieth-century president":** Vaughn, *Ronald Reagan in Hollywood*, p. 118.

FOURTEEN: "A DANGEROUS MAN"

205 **When he was discharged:** RR's Army Separation Qualification Record, RRPL, ORR: Pre-Presidential Papers 1918–80, Box 52.

205 **"coming back with new thoughts":** Mel Gussow, *Don't Say Yes Until I Finish Talking: A Biography of Darryl F. Zanuck* (Garden City, NY: Doubleday, 1971), pp. 200–201.

206 **"the sprightly little movies":** Otto Friedrich, *City of Nets: A Portrait of Hollywood in the 1940s* (New York: Harper & Row, 1986), p. 179.

207 **"Just relax until we find":** Jack Warner, quoted in *Los Angeles Examiner*, Dec. 3, 1945.

207 **ranked sixth among male:** Edmund Morris, *Dutch* (New York: Random House, 1999), p. 734.

207 **$3,500 a week:** For contract commencing Sept. 12, 1945, "History of RR's Contracts," Warner Bros. Archives, USC.

207 **who was twelve hours old:** "Michael was only twelve hours old when Ronnie and I got him." Joe Morella and Edward Z. Epstein, *Jane Wyman: A Biography* (New York: Delacorte, 1985), p. 78.

207 **his birth mother, Irene Flaugher:** "I was born . . . the result of a romantic liaison between a twenty-eight-year-old Kentucky farm girl . . . and a married Army Air Force cadet." Michael Reagan, *On the Outside Looking In* (New York: Zebra Books, 1988), p. 7; information about Irene Flaugher in NR/MT, p. 156.

207 **"to add from the outside":** Morella and Epstein, *Jane Wyman*, p. 78.

207 **"laze around and take time":** WTROM, p. 139.

208 **"she would come through":** Morris, *Dutch*, p. 220.

208 **The American Federation of Labor:** Friedrich, *City of Nets*, p. 247.

209 **By 1945, it had enrolled:** Larry Ceplair and Steven Englund, *The Inquisition in Hollywood: Politics in the Film Community, 1930–60* (Champaign: University of Illinois Press, 2003), p. 217.

209 **"What I heard and read":** WTROM, p. 138.

210 **"bring up the names":** Neil Reagan, interview, undated 1968, LCA, p. 8.

210 **"hemophiliac liberal":** *WTROM*, p. 103.

210 **According to FBI files:** Steven J. Ross, *Hollywood Left and Right: How Movie Stars Shaped American Politics* (New York: Oxford University Press, 2011), p. 442.

210 **"home-grown fascists":** Ronald Reagan, "Fascist Ideas Are Still Alive in U.S.," *AVC Bulletin*, Feb. 15, 1946, RRPL.

210 **He joined with internationalists:** Ibid., p. 142.

210 **"I was not sharp about Communism":** *WTROM*, p. 141.

210 **"helping the dispossessed":** Howard Fast, quoted in Morris, *Dutch*, p. 158.

211 **an astounding 4,600 strikes:** Ceplair and Englund, The *Inquisition in Hollywood*, p. 215.

211 **"then that person was *ipso facto*":** Ibid., p. 219.

211 **"3,300 professional exhibitionists":** "Political Notes: Glamour Pusses," *Time*, Sept. 9, 1946.

212 **"everybody who was anybody":** Joan LaCoeur, recording secretary of HICCASP, quoted in Nancy Lynn Schwartz, *The Hollywood Writers' Wars* (New York: Alfred A. Knopf, 1982), p. 241.

212 **"Many actors were caught up":** Olivia de Havilland, interview with author, Oct. 4, 2015.

212 **"an institution he [thought]":** "Mr. Reagan Airs His Views," *Chicago Tribune*, May 18, 1947.

212 **"controlled by the left":** Executive Council Meeting, July 3, 1946, minutes, provided to author by Olivia de Havilland.

212 **"fascist" . . . "capitalist scum":** *WTROM*, p. 167.

213 **"Whenever a motion was proposed":** Olivia de Havilland, interview with author, Oct. 4, 2015.

213 **"Ronnie got up and volunteered":** Ibid.

213 **"That's funny," he shot back:** Olivia de Havilland, interview with author, Oct. 4, 2015; *WTROM*, pp. 167–68; *AAL*, 111–13.

213 **In February 1946, Ronnie:** "SAG Timeline," SAG-AFTRA files.

214 **"It's a war to the finish":** Roy Brewer, quoted in George H. Dunne, "Christian Advocacy and Labor Strife in Hollywood," UCLA Center for Oral History Research, 1981.

214 **"open at all costs":** SAG Special Meeting, Feb. 18, 1946, minutes, SAG Archives.

214 **"We'll have to use":** Jack Warner, quoted in Alex Gottlieb, interview with Anne Edwards, undated, original typescript in author's possession.

214 **"a blow" to Ronnie:** *WTROM*, p. 186.

215 **Neil Reagan badgered him:** "I talked to him and talked to him about this organization." Neil Reagan, interview, UCLA Center for Oral History Research, June 25, 1981, p. 31.

215 **"Get out of that thing":** Ibid., p. 30.

215 **"this little rump group":** MI, Nov. 4, 1987, p. 153.

215 **"has no affiliation":** HICCASP executive council meeting, July 30, 1946, minutes, provided to author.

215 **"thought it didn't go":** Olivia de Havilland, interview with author, Oct. 4, 2015.

215 **"Ronnie hung in for":** RR maintained he resigned from HICCASP immediately after the statement was approved, by telegram, *WTROM*, p.169. In fact, records show he was still actively involved until Nov. 1946. Council minutes provided to author.

215 **"Very shortly, as he":** *WTROM*, p. 169.

215–216 **"shared the orthodox liberal view":** AAL, p. 115.

216 **"attempted takeover of Hollywood":** Ibid., p. 114.

216 **"There may be men hurt":** Herb Sorrell, quoted in Stephen Vaughn, *Ronald Reagan in Hollywood: Movies and Politics* (New York: Cambridge University Press, 1994), p. 139.

216 **"Warner Bros. turned high-pressure":** CSU circular inserted into *Hollywood Sun*, Dec. 8, 1946, original provided to author by SAG.

217 **Ronnie later claimed:** "Threatened in '46 Strike, Ronald Reagan Testifies," *Los Angeles Times*, Jan. 14, 1954; also: "Reagan Tells Scar Threat," *Los Angeles Examiner*, Jan. 14, 1954, p. 10.

217 **In any case, each day:** "I couldn't do that. So instead they made me sit by myself." *Los Angeles Examiner*, Sept. 6, 1958.

217 **On September 24, while shooting:** *Night Unto Night* production file, Warner Bros. Archives, USC.

217 **"A squad was ready":** "Threatened in '46 Strike," *Los Angeles Times*.

217 **That could only mean:** "I found out later . . . they weren't kidding. The plot was they were going to throw acid in my face." Ibid.

217 **"take Reagan home":** Viveca Lindfors, *Viveka-Viveca* (New York: Everest House, 1981), p.151.

217 **She was naturally "high-strung":** Hedda Hopper, "A Good Man Is Hard to Find," *Modern Screen*, Mar. 1948.

217 **"Politics!" she hissed:** Robert Cummings, quoted in Martin Kent, Ray Loynd, and David Robb, "Hollywood Remembers Ronald Reagan," unpublished, manuscript provided to the author, p. 35.

218 **"Ronnie lectured everybody":** Jane Wyman, quoted in Morris, *Dutch*, p. 237.

218 **On October 18, Reagan:** "The contents of his speech convinced the film technicians to reverse their decision." AE, p. 314.

218 **"pitch to the membership":** MI, Jan. 30, 1987, p. 65.

219 **"the liberal opposition":** Nancy Lynn Schwartz and Sheila Schwartz, *The Hollywood Writers' Wars* (New York: Alfred A. Knopf, 1982), p 249.

219 **"down the aisle slapping":** Ibid., p. 250.

219 **"If the actors and actresses":** Father George H. Dunne, "Christian Advocacy and Labor Strife in Hollywood," UCLA Center for Oral History Research, 1981, p. 23.

219 **"I am no longer neutral":** *Los Angeles Examiner*, Nov. 18, 1946.

219 **He continued to refer:** "At the end of World War II, I was a New Dealer to the core." *AAL*, p. 105.

219 **"thought government, not private companies":** Ibid.

219 **He believed that "America":** Ibid., p. 115.

220 **"Joseph Stalin," he said:** Ibid., p. 110.

220 **"well-meaning liberals (like me)":** Ibid., p. 114.

220 **"protect the people":** Ibid., p. 115.

220 **"interpreting everything in terms":** "I had the very definite impression, this was a dangerous man." Father George H. Dunne, UCLA Center for Oral History Research, 1981, p. 28.

FIFTEEN: TROUBLE IN PARADISE

222 **Dana Andrews, too:** "If I couldn't get Dana, then I wanted Bob Cummings." Irving Rapper, quoted in Martin Kent, Ray Loynd, and David Robb, "Hollywood Remembers Ronald Reagan" (unpublished manuscript), p. 41, provided to the author.

222 **"fussed around trying":** *WTROM*, p. 192.

222 **Warner had just seen:** "In February [1947], Jack Warner saw the first finished print of *Night Unto Night* and decided to shelve it." AE, p. 320.

223 **"marriage mourners are wondering":** *Screen Album*, 1947, quoted in Doug McClelland, *Hollywood on Ronald Reagan*, (Winchester, MA: Faber and Faber, 1983), p. 62.

223 **George Murphy and Gene Kelly:** "Minutes of the Regular Meeting of the Board of Directors," Mar. 10, 1947, SAG Archives.

223 **was conspicuously absent:** Notes of Valerie Yaros, SAG historian, Aug. 12, 2002, and Aug. 19, 2002, transcript in SAG Archives, Box 50, Folder 12.

224 **"not the two-fisted fighter":** Hedda Hopper, "Mr. Reagan Airs His Views," *Chicago Tribune*, May 18, 1947.

224 **"He's as green as grass!":** Hedda Hopper, quoted in Joe Morella and Edward Z. Epstein, *Jane Wyman: A Biography* (New York: Delacorte, 1985), p. 104.

224 **"I was never more wrong":** Hopper, "Mr. Reagan Airs His Views."

224 **"Let's face it":** Jerry Asher, quoted in Lawrence J. Quirk, *Jane Wyman: The Actress and the Woman* (New York: Dembner Books, 1986), p. 109.

224 **"glamorous little cookie":** "It is almost impossible to believe that this weary creature and the glamorous little cookie of *Night and Day* came from the repertoire of the same actress." Dorothy Kilgallen, review of *The Yearling*, *New York Journal American*, Dec. 18, 1946.

225 **"I was sure someone":** *WTROM*, p. 194.

225 **Production began on June 4:** *That Hagen Girl* production book, Warner Bros. Archives, USC.

225 **Ronnie insisted on doing:** AE, p. 325.

226 **Humphrey Bogart in a supporting:** "We played an interminable scene, exchanging and wearing innumerable trenchcoats." *WTROM*, p. 95.

226 **"given a good chance":** Hedda Hopper, "Stork Visits Jane Wyman," *Los Angeles Times*, June 27, 1947.

226 **"He tossed and fretted":** Louella Parsons, quoted in Morella and Epstein, *Jane Wyman*, p. 110.

226 **"When they were together":** Hedda Hopper, quoted in Quirk, *Jane Wyman*, p. 111.

226 **"tried to coax Jane out":** Hedda Hopper, quoted in Morella and Epstein, *Jane Wyman*, p. 111; "He tried to rekindle memories of the first days of their courtship by taking her to intimate supper clubs." Ibid., p. 110.

226 **"Work is the only answer":** Jerry Wald, quoted in Ibid.

226 **"It was hi":** Quirk, *Jane Wyman*, p. 111.

227 **"They just seemed to pass":** June Allyson with Frances Spatz Leighton, *June Allyson* (New York: G. P. Putnam's Sons, 1982), p. 74.

227 **"the greatest hotbed":** John Rankin, quoted in Otto Friedrich, *City of Nets: A Portrait of Hollywood in the 1940s* (New York: Harper & Row, 1986), p. 299.

227 **"I'm not in favor":** Hopper, "Mr. Reagan Airs His Views."

227 **"In our special field":** *Variety*, Feb. 7, 1944.

228 **"inasmuch as there would":** SAG board meeting, Sept. 12, 1947, minutes, SAG Archives.

228 **refused "for principle":** "I stand ready to go to jail for the Guild whenever her welfare so requires, but then let it be for principle, not for perjury." Anne Revere, resignation letter, Sept. 15, 1947, SAG Archives.

228 **"You know, anybody that's got":** *Los Angeles Times*, Aug. 17, 1980.

228 **"Commie sons-of-bitches":** Neal Gabler, *Walt Disney: The Triumph of the American Imagination* (New York: Alfred A. Knopf, 2006), p. 366.

229 **"at least six SAG members":** "On April 10, 1947, Ronald Reagan and Jane Wyman were 'at home' with an agent." Edmund Morris, *Dutch* (New York: Random House, 1999), p. 288; Morris cites "FBI report, 'Screen Actors Guild,' ca. April 10, 1947," p. 751.

229 **"hundreds of very prominent":** *Hollywood Reporter*, May 19, 1947.

229 **"had openly worked for causes":** Larry Ceplair and Steven Englund, *The Inquisition in Hollywood: Politics in the Film Community, 1930–60* (Champaign: University of Illinois Press, 2003), p. 256.

229 **"the conservative eminences":** Friedrich, *City of Nets*, p. 298.

230 **"When she would come in":** MI, June 27, 1989, p. 267.

230 **After a day spent bumping:** "Reagan drove up with Wyman and remained for a day before returning." AE, p. 327.

230 **"We felt so isolated":** Morella and Epstein, *Jane Wyman*, p. 117.

231 **"hey-hey blonde ingénue":** Quirk, *Wyman*, p. 111.

231 **He was a quiet:** "I pray every day." Pat H. Boeske, "Ayres Backs His Project Religiously," *Los Angeles Times*, Apr. 6, 1991.

231 **"platonic—yes, but":** Jim Reid, quoted in Quirk, *Wyman*, p. 112.

232 **"was spending five nights":** *WTROM*, p. 196.

232 **"All Out Fight on Commies":** *Hollywood Reporter*, Apr. 21, 1947.

232 **"injecting Communist stuff":** Warner's testimony is cited blindly in AE, p. 340, from an unnamed FOIA file.

232 **"unfriendly witnesses," as:** "*The Hollywood Reporter* was apparently the first to call them the 'unfriendly witnesses.'" Friedrich, *City of Nets*, p. 304.

232 **"Scratch a do-gooder":** Adolphe Menjou, quoted by Leonard Maltin, introduction to *State of the Union* on Turner Classic Movies.

232 **"sauntered jauntily up":** *Time*, Nov. 3, 1949.

233 **"send them back to Russia":** Robert Taylor, testimony, Hearings of the House Committee on Un-American Activities, Eightieth Congress, Oct. 22, 1947.

233 **a "small group within":** RR, testimony, Hearings of the House Committee on Un-American Activities, Oct. 25, 1947.

233 **"strange creatures crawling":** *WTROM*, p. 179.

233 **He met with committee counsel:** Garry Wills, *Reagan's America: Innocents at Home* (Garden City, NY: Doubleday, 1987), p. 255.

233 **"fight against the inroads":** "I happen to be very proud of the industry in which I work." RR, testimony, Hearings of the House Committee on Un-American Activities, Oct. 25, 1947.

233 **"deplor[ed] the action":** The Waldorf Statement, issued by the Association of Motion Picture Producers, quoted in Ceplair and Englund, *The Inquisition in Hollywood*, p. 455.

234 **"The purging of suspected":** Wills, *Reagan's America*, p. 255.

234 **"that he is not a member":** SAG board meeting, Nov. 10, 1947, minutes, SAG Archives.

234 **"so offended public opinion":** Walter Goodman, *The Committee* (New York: Farrar, Straus & Giroux, 1964), p. 300.

234 **When Ronnie returned:** "I arrived home from the Washington hearing to be told I was leaving." *WTROM*, p. 201.

234 **And they'd agreed to star:** Louella Parsons, "Reagan, Wyman Set to Star in 'John Loves Mary,'" *Los Angeles Herald-Examiner*, Dec. 5, 1947.

235 **"Hey, 'diarrhea of the mouth'":** Don Siegel, *A Siegel Film: An Autobiography by Don Siegel* (New York: Faber and Faber, 1993); Anthony Lane, "The Method President," *The New Yorker*, Oct. 18, 2004.

235 **"Ronnie talked all the time":** Leonora Hornblow, quoted in Bob Colacello, *Ronnie and Nancy* (New York: Warner Bros., 2004), p. 179.

235 **"Don't ask Ronnie what time":** Allyson, *June Allyson*, p. 96.

235 **"They weren't laughing at all":** Janet Franklin, "Winner Take All!?" *Modern Screen*, June 1949.

235 **"I got along without you":** "Onlookers who overheard it shrugged it off. 'A spat.'" Hedda Hopper, "A Good Man Is Hard to Find," *Modern Screen*, Mar. 1948.

235 **After the last scene wrapped:** "'With Ronnie and the kids?' someone asked. 'No,' she replied. 'Just me.'" *Modern Screen*, February 1948.

235 **"There's no use in lying":** *New York Herald-Express*, Dec. 17, 1947.

235 **"We're through," she confessed:** Gladys Hall, "Those Fightin' Reagans," *Photoplay*, Feb. 1948.

236 **He was back in Eureka:** "Reagan at Eureka Festival Tomorrow," *DET*, Sept. 25, 1947.

236 **"like a ton of bricks":** Quirk, *Wyman*, p. 113.

236 **"Right now, Jane needs":** *Los Angeles Examiner*, Dec. 15, 1947.

236 **Hedda Hopper piled on:** Hopper, "A Good Man Is Hard to Find."

236 **Pat Neal, who was brought:** Patricia Neal, *As I Am* (New York: Simon & Schuster, 1988), p. 90;

236 **"I'm in a situation":** Ruth Waterbury, "This Is a Love Story," *Photoplay*, Mar. 1949.

237 **In early February:** Louella O. Parsons, "Jane Wyman to Sue Reagan for Divorce," *Los Angeles Herald-Examiner*, Feb. 9, 1948.

237 **"[He] started talking and talking":** Dana Andrews, quoted in Kent et al., "Hollywood Remembers Ronald Reagan," p. 63.

237 **"too much time in film":** Louella O. Parsons, "Jane Wyman Divorces Reagan, Blames 'Politics,'" *Los Angeles Herald-Examiner*, July 29, 1948; *Los Angeles Times*, July 29, 1948.

237 **"Such a thing was":** *WTROM*, p. 201.

SIXTEEN: THE BLUE PERIOD

238 **"Be happy, old sport":** Errol Flynn quoted in Doris Lilly, "All for the Love of Ronnie," *Quest*, Oct. 1988.

238 **"one of Hollywood's most eligible":** Unsigned article, *Modern Screen*, Apr. 1949.

238 **"a lonely guy":** Eddie Bracken, quoted in Rogers Worthington, "Non-Political Science: When Ronnie Was Running as a Bachelor," *Chicago Tribune*, Sept. 11, 1980.

238 **"often in its bar":** Sheila Graham, *The Garden of Allah* (New York: Crown, 1970); Doug McClelland, *Hollywood on Ronald Reagan* (Winchester, MA: Faber and Faber, 1983), p. 124.

238 **"Hollywood for Harry Truman":** *Variety*, Oct. 6, 1948.

239 **this reeked of socialism:** "Our federal bureaucracy . . . began leading America along the path to a silent form of socialism." *AAL*, p. 120.

239 **an FBI informant whose conversations:** "T-10 stated it is his firm conviction that Congress should declare . . . that the Communist Party is not a legal Party, but is a foreign inspired conspiracy." Reagan FBI File #LA 100-15732.

239 **"rabid union man":** *WTROM*, p. 154.

240 **"The actors feel they should":** RR was guest writer for Victor Riesel's eponymous syndicated column, *Los Angeles Daily News*, July 3, 1948.

240 **"[the studios would] be crazy":** *WTROM*, p. 198.

240 **another "breezy, amiable":** Review of *The Girl from Jones Beach*, *Variety*, June 21, 1949.

241 **"when our blue-eyed cavalry":** *WTROM*, p. 205.

241 **"on the verge of emotional":** Sam Marx, quoted in Edmund Morris, *Dutch* (New York: Random House, 1999), p. 262.

241 **"We've bought it":** Steve Trilling, quoted in *WTROM*, p. 206.

242 **co-star "What's rationing?":** *Daily Mail*, Nov. 29, 1948.

242 **a "dismal wilderness":** RR, memo to Jack Warner, Dec. 1948, Warner Bros. Archives, USC.

242 **it as "overgenerous":** *Daily Express*, Nov. 29, 1948; Morris, *Dutch*, p. 266.

242 **they dined on pheasant:** "Now life couldn't be too fraught with hardship if a fellow could get pheasant under glass." *WTROM*, p. 209.

242 **a dozen steaks:** NR/MT, p. 95.

243 **"Although I was a young":** *People*, Aug. 10, 1981.

243 **"in a depressed state":** Jack Warner Jr., quoted in Stephen Vaughn, *Ronald Reagan in Hollywood: Movies and Politics* (New York: Cambridge University Press, 1994), p. 229.

243 **"a walking encyclopedia":** "It was kind of a joke around the lot that he could expound on almost anything." Vincent Sherman, quoted in McClelland, *Hollywood on Ronald Reagan*, p. 158.

243 **"while we have the atomic bomb":** Bertrand Russell, quoted in *New York Times*, Nov. 29, 1948.

243 **"I saw firsthand how":** *AAL*, p. 119.

243 **"a liberal, left-wing Democrat":** Vincent Sherman, quoted in McClelland, *Hollywood on Ronald Reagan*, p. 160.

243 **"I have never met":** Richard Todd, *Caught in the Act: The Story of My Life* (London: Hutchinson & Co., 1986), pp. 235–36.

244 **"President of the United States":** Patricia Neal, *As I Am* (New York: Simon & Schuster, 1988), p. 113.

244 **"when I've always been good":** RR, telegram to Jack Warner, Mar. 31, 1949, Warner Bros. Archives, USC.

244 **"He was not clicking":** Steve Trilling, quoted in Roy Orbinger, memo to Jack Warner, Jan. 17, 1950, Warner Bros. Archives, USC.

245 **"Lew added a five-year":** *WTROM*, p. 213.

245 **"I didn't exactly know":** Ibid., 203.

246 **"He loved to go out":** Doris Lilly, quoted in KK/NR, p. 78.

246 **his frisky "cocker spaniels":** Morris, *Dutch*, p. 282.

246 **"the best figure in Hollywood":** Rogers Worthington, "When Ronnie Was Running," *Chicago Tribune*, Sept. 11, 1980.

246 **Monica Lewis, an MGM starlet:** "The hottest spot proved to be Ronnie's apartment at the Sherry-Netherland, where we made love on our third date." Monica Lewis, *Hollywood Through My Eyes*, (Brule,WI: Cable Publishing, 2011), p. 70.

246 **"There was a little place":** Doris Day and A. E. Hotchner, *Doris Day: Her Own Story* (New York: William Morrow, 1975), p. 143.

246 **"sleeping with so many girls":** Morris, *Dutch*, p. 282.

246 **"We put him up":** William A. Raidy, "Bracken Recalls Run-in with Ronnie," *Newark Star-Ledger*, June 28, 1981.

247 **it seemed he had strained:** *Los Angeles Daily News*, June 21, 1949.

SEVENTEEN: "NANCY (WITH THE LAUGHING FACE)"

248 **her mother, a rabid:** "Mother always said that I was supposed to be born on the Fourth of July, but the Yankees were playing a doubleheader that day." NR/MT, p. 67.

248 **watch the Bombers whip:** Baseball Almanac website, 1921 NY Yankees season.

248 **By 1905, Luckett was appearing:** A box containing clips from Edith Luckett's career, dating from July 18, 1900. Edith Luckett's scrapbook, RRPL, RR's and NR's personal papers, Box 20A.

249 **"beauty, wit, and talent":** Ibid., untitled profile of Edith Luckett, Sept. 22, 1900.

249 **"Edie had the foulest":** Lester Weinrott, quoted in KK/NR, p. 21.

249 **unfiltered "exuberantly unshockable":** Gavin Lambert, *Nazimova: A Biography* (New York: Alfred A. Knopf, 1997), p. 189.

249 **a production of *Drifting*:** *New York Times*, Dec. 18, 1910.

250 **"kind of a mama's boy":** "Nancy Reagan's Early Years: A Matter of Relativity," *Los Angeles Times*, Jan. 20, 1981.

250 **Anne "Nanee" Ayres Robbins:** Nathalie A. Naylor, *Women in Long Island's Past* (Charleston, SC: Arcadia Publishing, 2012), unpaginated.

250 **play, *'Ception Shoals*:** Edith was billed as Edith Speare. "Nazimova Appears in 'Ception Shoals,'" *New York Times*, Jan. 11, 1917, p. 13; *Playbill*, "'Ception Shoals." undated.

251 **When she gave birth:** Birth certificate of Anne Francis Robbins, New York City Dept. of Health, Bureau of Vital Records.

251 **"their relationship was so tenuous":** NR/MT, p. 67.

252 **"carrying a tiny baby":** Ibid., p. 69.

252 **"It was hard, brain-tormenting":** Pat O'Brien, *The Wind at My Back: The Life and Times of Pat O'Brien* (Garden City, NY: Doubleday, 1964), p. 62.

253 **when the Galbraiths took:** "When [Edith] was in a play in New York, my mother took us up to see her." Charlotte Galbraith Ramage, quoted in KK/NR, p. 30.

253 **Nancy would stay:** Bob Colacello, *Ronnie and Nancy* (New York: Warner Books, 2004), p. 39.

253 **"with great love":** NR/MT, p. 70.

254 **"doctor she wanted to marry":** "Years later I came across the journal of Mother's trip." NR quoted in Nancy Reagan with Bill Libby, *Nancy* (New York, William Morrow, 1980), p. 26.

254 **"Uncle Walter stood up":** Lawrence Grobel, *The Hustons* (New York: Charles Scribner's Sons, 1989), p. 122.

254 **Both the bride:** *Chicago Tribune*, May 22, 1929.

254 **"My professional and personal life":** Loyal Davis, *A Surgeon's Odyssey* (Garden City, NY: Doubleday, 1973), p. 228.

254 **"He seemed formal and distant":** NR/MT, p. 74.

254 **"He was an austere":** KK/NR, p. 33.

254 **"rock-hard disciplinarian":** Chris Wallace, *First Lady* (New York: St. Martin's Press, 1986), p. 6.

255 **"men were to be":** AE, p. 387.

255 **"gruff on the outside":** ". . . but warm and tenderhearted underneath." NR/MT, p. 75.

255 **sometimes even into surgery:** "Usually she watched from a glassed-in balcony, but sometimes the doctor actually took her into the operating room to stand near him as he was operating." Jody Jacobs, quoted in KK/NR, p. 38.

255 **"that he practically became":** NR/MT, p. 78.

255 **"Jimmy Cagney was always there":** Edith Luckett, quoted in "Around About" interview, AE, p. 387.

256 **"She liked Bing Crosby":** Jane Wescott Marshall, quoted in KK/NR, p. 40.

257 **"they agreed reluctantly":** NR/MT, p. 78.

257 **The adoption was granted:** Petition of Anne Frances Robbins, Cook County Circuit Court, Chicago, IL, Apr. 19, 1938.

257 **"I don't recall much":** NR/MT, p. 82.

257 **she dated a Princeton student:** Frank O. Birney committed suicide on Dec. 15, 1941, during his courtship of Nancy Davis, KK/NR, p. 52; Colacello, *Ronnie and Nancy*, p. 135.

257 **she became engaged:** "Jim was devastated when she called it off." Bill Whorf, quoted in KK/NR, pp. 59–60.

257 **interned with summer-stock outfits:** Clippings from Nancy Reagan's scrapbook, RRPL, personal papers, Box 20.

258 **"awkward and amateurish":** John Houseman, *Run-Through* (New York: Simon & Schuster, 1972).

258 **"I suggested to the producer":** John Houseman, quoted in AE, p. 392.

259 **"I also had dinner a lot":** NR, quoted in Colacello, *Ronnie and Nancy*, p. 181.

259 **"I had no serious romances":** Nancy Reagan, *Nancy*, p. 69, p. 379

259 **"feature roles on":** *Mademoiselle*, Nov. 1948, clipping from Nancy Reagan's scrapbook, RRPL, personal papers, Box 20.

259 **"I wasn't setting show business":** Nancy Reagan, *Nancy*, p. 89.

259 **"someone from Metro":** Ibid., p. 91.

260 **practice of the casting couch:** "Thau's casting couch was the busiest in Hollywood." Charles Higham, *Merchant of Dreams: Louis B. Mayer, M.G.M., and the Secret Hollywood* (New York: Donald I. Fine, 1993), p. 132.

260 **"The girl knows how":** Spencer Tracy, quoted in Dore Schary, interview with Anne Edwards, AE, p. 393.

260 **"he told the studio":** Emanuel Levy, *George Cukor, Master of Elegance* (New York: William Morrow, 1994), p. 325.

EIGHTEEN: "RONNIE'S FINEST HOUR"

261 **In an early draft:** "Nancy mentioned to Dore Schary that she would like to meet Reagan." KK/NR, p. 71.

261 **In a later version:** "According to Miriam Schary . . . Nancy told her that she would like to meet RR." Bob Colacello, *Ronnie and Nancy* (New York: Warner Bros., 2004), p. 241.

261 **The Scharys' daughter, Jill:** "There was a lot of political talk." AE, p. 394; Edmund Morris, *Dutch* (New York: Random House, 1999), p. 280.

261 **triggered by an article:** "Signers of Appeal to High Court for Lawson, Trumbo," *Hollywood Reporter*, Oct. 28, 1949.

261 **"I knew my name":** NR/MT, p. 93.

262 **"100 percent American":** Louella Parsons, *Los Angeles Herald-Examiner*, Nov. 7, 1949, clipping in Nancy Reagan's scrapbook, RRPL, personal papers, Box 20.

262 **"not exactly love":** Ibid., p. 96.

262 **"She was sitting opposite him":** Jill Schary Robinson, quoted in AE, p. 394.

262 **"I don't recall his saying":** Miriam Schary, quoted in Colacello, *Ronnie and Nancy*, p. 241.

262 **"Phyllis told me they invited":** Olivia de Havilland, interview with author, Oct. 4, 2015.

262 **"indicated her willingness":** Memorandum, file 3957, SAG Archives.

263 **Loyal Davis had voiced:** "Richard Davis [Nancy's step-brother] said that his father had taken an instant dislike to Benny Thau." Colacello, *Ronnie and Nancy*, p. 226.

263 **"attractive," in Benny:** Benny Thau, quoted in KK/NR, p. 68.

263 **"Maybe it was because":** Ann Sothern, quoted in Ibid., p. 67.

264 **"bells didn't ring":** WTROM, p. 235.

264 **"He looks as good":** NR/MT, p. 94.

264 **"If I had my life to live over":** Morris, *Dutch*, p. 749.

264 **"I loved to listen":** Nancy Reagan, *I Love You Ronnie: The Letters of Ronald Reagan to Nancy Reagan* (New York: Random House, 2000), p. 11.

264 **"Never thought we'd come":** Editorial, *Silver Screen*, May 1950.

265 **Piper Laurie:** Piper Laurie, *Learning to Live Out Loud* (New York: Crown Archetype, 2011) p.173; Daniel Bates, "Virgin Starlet Claims Ronald Reagan Was a Show-Off in Bed," *Daily Mail.com*, posted Nov. 14, 2011, dailymail.co.uk/news/article-2061105 /Piper-Laurie-claims-Ronald-Reagan-bed.html.

265 **ingénue Jacqueline Park:** KK/NR, p. 80.

265 **joined the board:** "President Reagan welcomed Nancy Davis to her first Board meeting." SAG board meeting, Oct. 9, 1950, minutes, SAG Archives.

265 **Photos of them together:** There is a folder of clippings from local LA papers, as well as *Silver Screen* and *Photoplay* in Nancy Reagan's scrapbook, RRPL, private papers, Box 20.

265 **"Ronnie Reagan is a happy":** *New York Daily News*, undated clipping, Nancy Reagan's scrapbook, RRPL, private papers, Box 20.

265 **"Looks like this one's":** Neil Reagan, quoted in AE, p. 402.

265 **He'd given Christine:** KK/NR, p. 82.

266 **"Davis Reagan Nuptials Set":** *Los Angeles Herald-Examiner*, Feb. 21, 1952.

266 **"some small church":** MGM, press release, issued Feb. 21, 1952, Nancy Reagan's scrapbook, RRPL, private papers, Box 20.

266 **"Carroll was helpful":** Arlene Dahl, quoted in Colacello, *Ronnie and Nancy*, p. 256.

266 **Reagan-Wyman divorce date:** Ed Helin, quoted in Ibid.

266 **Shortly after their first date:** Invitation to "Aquarius Party" from Carroll Righter, Jan 20, 1950, Nancy Reagan's scrapbook, RRPL, private papers, Box 20.

266 **"Aquarians are capable of love":** NR/MT, pp. 104–5.

267 **gray wool suit:** Colacello, *Ronnie and Nancy*, p. 261.

267 **"We didn't invite anybody":** NR/MT, p. 101.

267 **Nancy had been notified:** "I think we'll drop the option." Al Corfino, memo, Jan. 31, 1952, MGM files, cited in KK/NR, p. 89.

267 **"I could telephone my lines":** *Los Angeles Mirror*, Jan. 6, 1950.

267 **"I would greatly appreciate":** Jack Warner, memo, Jan. 6, 1950, Warner Bros. Archives, USC.

267 **"he was being double-crossed":** "Reagan went into some more alleged abuses." Ray Orbinger, memo to Jack Warner, Feb. 17, 1950, Warner Bros. Archives, USC.

268 **"pat and pedestrian":** Bosley Crowther, "'Storm Warning' New Warners Film on Klan Violence Opens at Strand," *New York Times*, Mar. 3, 1951.

268 **killed in a fire:** RR, letter to C. C. Cantwell, Oct. 23, 1973, RRPL, private papers, : handwriting files.

268 **On January 15, Universal decided:** "We have exercised our right to terminate the third and fourth employment periods by reason of his refusal to render services in 'Fine Day' and 'Just Across the Street.'" Memo, "Matters to Review—Ronald Reagan," reproduced in AE, pp. 432–33.

268 **"I knew the script was hopeless":** WTROM, p. 241.

269 **"It was almost like living":** NR, quoted in Colacello, *Ronnie and Nancy*, p. 263.

269 **he couldn't afford to buy:** "It was a year and a half before we could afford to furnish our living room." NR/MT, p. 125; Laurence Leamer, *Make Believe: The Story of Nancy and Ronald Reagan* (New York: Harper & Row, 1983), p. 171.

269 **five million U.S. homes:** James Trager, *The People's Chronology* (New York: Henry Holt, 1994), pp. 924–25.

269 **"everyone of stature in Hollywood":** WTROM, p. 231.

270 **Lucille Ball starred:** *I Love Lucy* made its debut on CBS on Oct. 15, 1951, Ibid., p. 931.

270 **"for seven months":** RR, federal grand jury testimony, Feb. 5, 1962, FOIA.

271 **"The same group":** WTROM, p. 223.

271 **"It was a victory":** Ibid., p. 230.

271 **nickname "the Octopus":** Edward T. Thompson, "There's No Business Like MCA Business," *Fortune*, July 1960.

272 **"Well, of course that was":** Jack Dales, interview with Mitch Tuchman, UCLA Center for Oral History Research, June 2, 1981, p. 45; Ellen Farley and William K. Knoedelseder Jr., "Ronald Reagan in Hollywood," *Los Angeles Times*, Aug. 17, 1980.

272 **the proposal made good sense:** "I personally never saw any particular harm in it." RR, federal grand jury testimony, Feb. 5, 1962, FOIA.

272 **"they could not charge":** Jack Dales, interview with Mitch Tuchman, UCLA Center for Oral History Research, June 2, 1981, p. 45.

273 **"not take part in any":** Laurence Beilenson, quoted in Dan E. Moldea, *Dark Victory: Ronald Reagan, MCA, and the Mob* (New York: Viking, 1986), p. 99.

273 **"an agreement was reached":** SAG board meeting, July 14, 1952, minutes, SAG Archives.

273 **"The deal vaulted MCA":** Justice Dept. memo, quoted in AE, p. 439.

273 **"agency regulations in the future":** George Chandler, letter, quoted in Moldea, *Dark Victory*, p. 102.

273 **"I felt a little self-conscious":** RR, federal grand jury testimony, Feb. 5, 1962, FOIA.

274 **"I was all for anyone":** Ibid.

274 **"Ronnie's finest hour":** Jack Dales, interview with Mitch Tuchman, UCLA Center for Oral History Research, June 2, 1981, pp. 31–32.

274 **"What am I doing here?":** Ibid., p. 34.

NINETEEN: MOVING FROM LEFT TO RIGHT

275 **"His movie career was at a standstill":** NR/MT, p. 125.

275 She was "headstrong,": "Patti always, always wanted attention twenty-four hours a day from the day she was born." NR, quoted in Bob Colacello, *Ronnie and Nancy* (New York: Warner Bros., 2004), p. 266.

275 "I felt rejected": Michael Reagan with Joe Hyams, *On the Outside Looking In* (New York: Zebra Books, 1988), pp. 37–39.

276 "they painted in the cigarette": RR, interview with Lou Cannon, Oct. 26, 1968, LCA, p. 23.

276 "MCA promised us": Earl B. Dunckel, interview, "Ronald Reagan and the General Electric Theater, 1954–1955," UCLA Center for Oral History Research, Apr. 27, 1982, p. 2.

277 "I was always gun-shy": RR, interview with Lou Cannon, Oct. 26, 1968, LCA, p. 2.

277 "some personal appearance tours": WTROM, p. 231.

277 "Not only would MCA": Art Park, quoted in Dan E. Moldea, *Dark Victory: Ronald Reagan, MCA, and the Mob* (New York: Viking, 1986), p. 109.

277 "Few corporations were as obsessed": Rick Perlstein, *The Invisible Bridge* (New York: Simon & Schuster, 2014), p. 387.

278 "We had been very, very": Dunckel, interview, "Ronald Reagan and the General Electric Theater," pp. 2–3.

278 Edward Arnold and Walter Pidgeon: AE, p. 453.

278 "as natural as anyone": Ibid., p. 6.

278 Long-established movie stars: tv.com, show index for *General Electric Theater*, Season 3, 1954–55.

279 "hand-tailored for him": "Ron was going to star in a certain number of vehicles that . . . he particularly liked." Dunckel, interview, "Ronald Reagan and the General Electric Theater," p. 7.

279 It was a huge plant: "Schenectady Works Welcomes You!" (tourist booklet published by GE, 1949, 1953, 1956).

280 "the divorce level": "Seventy percent of our people are married, more than seventy percent of those to their first husband or wife." RR, speech, RRPL, audio-visual collection.

280 "a real black mark": Dunckel, interview, "Ronald Reagan and the General Electric Theater," p. 14.

281 "I was scared stiff": Ibid.

282 "I'll bet he's a fag": Ibid., p. 10.

282 "That's the way, Ron!": "He would not leave a department with the men over there scowling and snarling." Ibid.

283 "He was the most inventive": Thomas W. Evans, *The Education of Ronald Reagan* (New York: Columbia University Press, 2006), p. 64.

283 "the Communists had pretty much": Dunckel, interview, "Ronald Reagan and the General Electric Theater," p. 16.

283 "There can be no moral justification": RR, quoted in Kim Phillips-Fein, *Invisible Hands: The Businessman's Crusade Against the New Deal* (New York: W. W. Norton, 2010), p. 114.

284 *The ninety-first percentile!*: "True, I'd been making handsome money, but that handsome money lost a lot of its beauty going through the 91 percent bracket." WTROM, p. 245; "I was in the ninety-four percent tax bracket." AAL, p. 117.

284 "I was seeing the same people": Lou Cannon, *Reagan* (New York: G. P. Putnam's Sons, 1982), p. 94.

284 "spreading its influence": "The Powerhouse," *Time*, May 12, 1959, pp. 76–85.

285 "the importance of recognizing": Evans, *The Education of Ronald Reagan*, p. 89.

285 "out there, beating the bushes": AAL, p. 129.

285 "one of the most recognized": Edmund Morris, *Dutch* (New York: Random House, 1999), p. 305.

285 "His speech was always the same": Paul Gavaghan, quoted in Harry Levinson and Stuart Rosenthal, CEO: *Corporate Leadership in Action* (New York: Basic Books, 1984), p. 20.

285 "Thirty-four percent of your phone bill": GE *Schenectady News*, Jan. 30, 1959, p. 3.

286 were "absolutely uncanny": "It's an absolutely uncanny, extrasensory ability the man has." Dunckel, interview, "Ronald Reagan and the General Electric Theater," p. 20.

286 Ronald Reagan refused to believe: "A star doesn't slip. He's ruined by bad stories and worse casting." RR quoted in Hedda Hopper, *Los Angeles Herald-Examiner*, undated clipping, c. March 1950.

286 "the kind that are addicted": RR, address at the *Photoplay* awards dinner, quoted in *Variety*, Mar. 12, 1951.

287 "a slow invisible tide of socialism": Garry Wills, *Reagan's America: Innocents at Home* (Garden City, NY: Doubleday, 1987), p. 283.

287 he floated the idea: "Insurance executives loved it when he told them social security could be voluntary." Ibid.

287 "It was the GE managers": Dana Andrews, quoted in *Hollywood Remembers*, Martin Kent, Ray Loynd, and David Robb, "Hollywood Remembers Ronald Reagan" (unpublished manuscript provided to the author), p. 59.

287 "I was drumbeating": "I was, am, and always will be an arch conservative." Dunckel, interview, "Ronald Reagan and the General Electric Theater," pp. 15–16.

288 "intelligent, honest and smacked": RR, handwritten letter to Samuel Harrod II, c. summer 1952, Eureka College archives.

288 "a hand-picked errand boy": Ibid.

288 "Pink right down to her underwear": Rick Perlstein, *Nixonland* (New York: Scribner, 2008), p. 34.

289 135 GE plants: "Hey, Ronnie—Did the Guy Get the Girl?" *TV Guide*, Nov. 22, 1958.

289 "We drove him": Edward Langley, quoted in Cannon, *Reagan*, p. 93.

289 "I had television work down": RR, interview, "On Becoming Governor," UCLA Center for Oral History Research, Jan. 19, 1979, p. 5.

289 **low-budget "jingoistic potboiler":** *Halliwell's Film Guide*, 1986 ed., p. 589; AE, p. 589.

TWENTY: AN "APPRENTICESHIP FOR PUBLIC LIFE"

290 **A litany of grievances:** RR, speech, "Encroaching Control," Phoenix Chamber of Commerce, Mar. 30, 1961, Hoover Institution Archives, pp. 4–11.

290 **"Social Security is coming":** RR, interview with Lou Cannon, Oct. 26, 1968, LCA, p. 5.

290 **"He had them in the palm":** Paul Wassmansdorf, interview with Lou Cannon, Jan. 30, 1988, LCA, p. 7.

290 **"Those people just loved him":** William Frye, quoted in Bob Colacello, *Ronnie and Nancy* (New York: Warner Bros., 2004), pp. 279–80.

291 **It was a nonstarter:** "I didn't want to be mayor." MI, Jan. 30, 1987, p. 68.

291 **Not to be outdone:** Robert Tuttle, interview with author, Oct. 17, 2015.

291 **"I did not want to leave":** MI, June 27, 1989, p. 256.

291 **"Someday, I'm going to vote":** Bob Cummings quoted in AAL, p. 96; MI, Nov. 4, 1987, p. 155.

291 **"You know, you really should":** Robert Stack, quoted in MI, Nov. 4, 1987, p. 155.

291 **He loved having Jack Benny:** "Benny, for some reason, tabbed Reagan with the nickname 'the governor.'" Rick Perlstein, *The Invisible Bridge* (New York: Simon & Schuster, 2014), p. 398.

292 **"Never in my wildest dreams":** Ibid.

292 **"everybody would look better":** "We have a letter from GE to Reagan saying that he should have this lighting system so that everybody would look better." Norman Switzer, quoted in Colacello, *Ronnie and Nancy*, p. 275.

292 **as "electrical servants":** Jacob Weisberg, "The Road to Reagandom," *Slate*, Jan. 8, 2016.

292 **"We found ourselves with more":** Nancy Reagan, *I Love You, Ronnie: The Letters of Ronald Reagan to Nancy Reagan* (New York: Random House, 2000), p. 63.

292 **Ronnie sent the company:** Paul Wassmansdorf, interview with Lou Cannon, Jan. 30, 1988, LCA, p. 9.

293 **"when you live better electrically":** Weisberg, "The Road to Reagandom."

293 **Ronnie was panicked:** "I grew frightened every time I remembered that long night when Patti was born and didn't want to take chances." WTROM, p. 274.

293 **Nancy was determined:** "She was hoping and praying that her second child would be a boy." Arlene Dahl, quoted in Colacello, *Ronnie and Nancy*, p. 284.

293 **"I have hardening of the arteries":** Nelle Reagan, quoted in Bonnie Angelo, *First Mothers: The Women Who Shaped the Presidents* (New York: William Morrow, 2000), p. 329.

293 **"I am a shut in":** Anne Edwards, *The Reagans* (New York: St. Martin's, 2003), p. 370.

294 **"a three-pack":** AAL, p. 93.

294 **"worshipped at the altar":** Unidentified source, quoted in Colacello, *Ronnie and Nancy*, p. 304.

294 **"I was a little jealous":** Michael Reagan with Joe Hyams, *On the Outside Looking In* (New York: Zebra Books, 1988), p. 74.

294 **a "sullen" child:** Betsy Bloomingdale, quoted in Colacello, *Ronnie and Nancy*, p. 307.

295 **"a lifelong roller coaster":** Michael Reagan, *On the Outside Looking In*, p. 103.

295 **"couldn't seem to do":** Ibid., p. 64.

295 **"Although GE kept me":** AAL, p. 131.

296 **"so everybody's mind":** Jack Dales, interview with Mitch Tuchman, UCLA Center for Oral History Research, June 2, 1981, p. 36.

296 **Ronnie was convinced that serving:** "Convinced as I was that my previous service had hurt career-wise." WTROM, p. 276.

297 **"He has no ownership interest":** "Members are being told that Ronald Reagan, president of the Guild, produces and has an ownership interest in the television series, *General Electric Theater*." *Screen Actor*, December 1959, SAG Archives.

297 **To hasten things along:** "Between soup and salad I laid out exactly just what the guild would settle for." WTROM, p. 282; "It was Ron's judgment and mine that we should take the deal." Jack Dales, quoted in *Wall Street Journal*, Oct. 29, 1980.

297 **"thousands and thousands":** Bob Hope, quoted in Kent et al., "Hollywood Remembers Ronald Reagan," p. 20.

298 **"eighty million times":** "They can take Johnny Weissmuller and show *Tarzan* 80 million times and give him nothing." Mickey Rooney, quoted in Kent et al., "Hollywood Remembers Ronald Reagan," p. 29.

298 **"sold down the river":** Bob Hope, quoted in Kent et al., "Hollywood Remembers Ronald Reagan," p. 19.

298 **"crime showing our pictures":** Mickey Rooney, quoted in Kent et al., "Hollywood Remembers Ronald Reagan," p. 28.

298 **"I plan to change":** RR, resignation letter to Screen Actors Guild, July 3, 1960, SAG Archives.

299 **"the unwashed public":** AE, p. 461.

299 **"the American dangers":** "A series of hard-nosed happenings began to change my whole view on the American dangers." WTROM, p. 142.

299 **"a customer relations problem":** David W. Burke, letter to twelve regional GE vice presidents, Sept. 5, 1960, p. 1.

299 **"unfairly competitive with private business":** Ibid.

299 **They wanted him muzzled:** "It was made pretty plain that I was to be fired." WTROM, pp. 268–69.

299 **"I am never going to have":** Earl B. Dunckel, interview, "Ronald Reagan and the General Electric Theater, 1954–1955," UCLA Center for Oral History Research, Apr. 27, 1982, p. 23.

300 "delete all references to TVA": David W. Burke, letter to twelve regional GE vice presidents, p. 1.

300 "lambasting venal big business": Ibid., p. 2.

300 "On future speaking engagements": Ibid., p. 3.

300 "The biggest problem we had": Dunckel, interview, "Ronald Reagan and the General Electric Theater," p. 26.

300 "had one of the most recognized": Timothy Raphael, The President Electric (Ann Arbor: University of Michigan Press, 2009); Perlstein, The Invisible Bridge, p. 397.

301 "postgraduate education": Thomas W. Evans, The Education of Ronald Reagan (New York: Columbia University Press, 2006), p. 38.

301 Ronald Reagan had been courted: "He received a call from Joseph Kennedy." Ibid., p. 158.

301 "the foot in the door": KK/NR, p. 114.

301 "less than honest": RR, handwritten letter to Samuel Harrod II, c. 1949, Eureka College archives.

301 "I think you may be wrong": AAL, p. 133.

301 "He wasn't the villain": Ibid.

302 "a frightening call to arms": RR, letter to Richard Nixon, July 15, 1960, on file at the Richard M. Nixon Presidential Library; Edmund Morris, Dutch (New York: Random House, 1999), p. 315.

302 "the difference between creeping socialism": Bob Gaston, quoted in Rick Perlstein, Before the Storm (New York: Hill and Wang, 2001), pp. 165–66.

302 "a pleasant young man": "Opinion: Too Many People," Time, Apr. 21, 1961.

302 "outrageous that he went over": Olivia de Havilland, interview with author, Oct. 14, 2015.

303 the "rich Republicans": Dana Andrews, quoted in Kent et al., "Hollywood Remembers Ronald Reagan," p. 59.

303 Kennedy's approval rating: Gallup poll cited in Richard Reeves, "Saved by the Cold War," New York Times, Apr. 25, 2009.

303 lead to social "slavery": RR, address at Huntington Memorial Hospital, Pasadena, CA, Jan. 4, 1962, quoted in Colacello, Ronnie and Nancy, p. 320.

303 "infiltrating all phases": RR, speech, quoted in Senator Frank Church, letter to J. Edgar Hoover, Oct. 26, 1961, Seth Rosenfelt, Subversives (New York: Farrar, Straus & Giroux, 2012), p. 293.

304 "a complete slave of MCA": Leonard Posner, quoted in Dan E. Moldea, Dark Victory: Ronald Reagan, MCA, and the Mob (New York: Viking, 1986), p. 160.

304 "My memory would be": RR, testimony, Justice Dept., Feb. 5, 1962 transcript; Moldea, Dark Victory, p. 173; "New Info on Reagan, MCA Waiver Probe," Variety, Apr. 18, 1984, p. 35.

304 "selective amnesia," a strategy: Morris, Dutch, p. 321.

304 "likely that Reagan": Justice Dept., memo, Mar. 7, 1962, quoted in Moldea, Dark Victory, p. 203.

305 "an orthodox and patriotic": Lou Cannon, Reagan (New York: G. P. Putnam's Sons, 1982), p. 97.

305 for Loyd Wright: Perlstein, Before the Storm, p. 166.

305 "a right-wing zealot": Evans, The Education of Ronald Reagan, p. 163.

305 "was deeply and justifiably disturbed": Paul Wassmansdorf, letter to Garry Wills, Sept. 21, 1987, p. 1.

305 "The time had come": Paul Wassmansdorf, interview, Jan. 30, 1988, LCA.

306 "would be sales pitches": MI, May 30, 1987, p. 120.

306 "the new 1963 coffee pot": WTROM, p. 273.

306 to "peddle toasters": AAL, p. 137.

306 Someone high-placed: Maureen Reagan, First Father/First Daughter (New York: Little, Brown, 1989), p. 110; MI, Mar. 29, 1988, p. 183.

306 "Like any actor": RR, quoted in Sunset, Oct. 1961.

306 "You told me to wait": MI, Mar. 24, 1987, p. 75.

307 "I felt that I had": Ibid.; Morris, Dutch, p. 323.

TWENTY-ONE: THE FRIENDS OF RONALD REAGAN

309 "We didn't have anybody": Lou Cannon, Ronnie and Jesse (Garden City, NY: Doubleday, 1969), p. 72.

309 It cast a pall: "It was a very, very tough time." Angie Dickinson, quoted in Bob Colacello, Ronnie and Nancy (New York: Warner Bros., 2004), p. 322.

309 "he hated doing": Ibid.

309 "film noir masterpiece": Paul Brenner, "All Movie Guide," review of The Killers, New York, July 7, 1964.

310 "It kept him in": Neil Reagan, interview, UCLA Center for Oral History Research, June 25, 1981, p. 22.

310 "I sold him a Model A Ford": Holmes Tuttle, interview, LCA, Dec. 17, 1987, p. 1.

310 who "hated Roosevelt": Robert Tuttle, interview with author, Oct. 3, 2014.

310 debonair "an oracle": Betsy Bloomingdale, quoted in Colacello, Ronnie and Nancy, p. 326.

310 "a tremendous underdog": Jeffrey Bell, interview with author, Dec. 19, 2013.

311 "I remind you, that extremism": Barry Goldwater, Republican Convention acceptance speech, San Francisco, July 17, 1964. Washington Post, online, washingtonpost.com/wp-srv/politics/daily/may98/goldwaterspeech.

311 "lob one into the men's room": Lou Cannon, Governor Reagan (New York: Public Affairs, 2003), p. 133.

311 he called on the administration: Niall Ferguson, Kissinger: 1923–1968, The Idealist (New York: Penguin Press, 2015), p. 598.

311 "abrasive Götterdämmerung approach": Thomas C. Reed, The Reagan Enigma, (Los Angeles: Figueroa Press, 2014), p. 65.

311 "You're going to hold": Colacello, Ronnie and Nancy, p. 325.

311 "not Wall Street": Henry Salvatori, interview, Jan. 22, 1988, LCA.

312 **(Henry Salvatori put up seed):** "There was [sic] about ten of us and we'd all put up a couple of thousand dollars." Ibid.

312 **"stand athwart history":** William F. Buckley, "Publisher's Statement," *National Review*, Nov. 19, 1955.

312 **considered "a fiasco":** "Our convention in San Francisco was a fiasco." Cannon, *Ronnie and Jesse*, p. 72.

312 **"was more important than all":** AAL, p. 139.

313 **He'd make the president's plan:** "The President tells us he is now going to start building public housing units in the thousands." From "A Time for Choosing," Oct. 27, 1964, transcript, RRPL.

314 **"It was the best speech":** Henry Salvatori interview, Jan. 22, 1988, LCA.

314 **Holmes Tuttle recalled:** Colacello, *Ronnie and Nancy*, p. 332; "After the speech we were swamped with requests from people who said these are the things Goldwater's been missing." Cannon, *Ronnie and Jesse*, p. 72.

314 **"His philosophy was sound":** Henry Salvatori to Doris Klein, Associated Press, quoted in Bill Boyarsky, *The Rise of Ronald Reagan* (New York: Random House, 1968), p. 158.

314 **"We've got to get that speech":** NR/MT, p. 130.

315 **"it had always gotten":** AAL, p. 141.

315 **"I remember my father molding":** Patti Davis, *The Way I See It* (New York: Putnam, 1992), p. 97.

315 **"The delegation was at":** "Evolution of the Kitchen Cabinet, 1965–1973," UCLA Center for Oral History Research, Mar. 16, 1988, p. 114.

316 **"We were defeated":** Henry Salvatori, interview, Jan. 22, 1988, LCA.

316 **"Gentlemen," he said, "I think":** "Reagan's Inner Circle of Self-Made Men," *New York Times*, May 31, 1980.

316 **"Reagan is the man":** Cannon, *Ronnie and Jesse*, p. 72.

316 **"might be the only Republican":** AAL, p. 145.

316 **"I told him I knew it":** Holmes Tuttle, interview, Dec. 17, 1987, LCA, p. 5; Cannon, *Ronnie and Jesse*, p. 72.

317 **"I knew those people were going":** NR, quoted in Colacello, *Ronnie and Nancy*, p. 334.

318 **"a real right-winger":** Bill Roberts, quoted in Cannon, *Governor Reagan*, p. 135.

319 **"I don't think so":** Stuart Spencer, interview with author, July 21, 2014.

319 **"it was unfair to label":** Cannon, *Governor Reagan*, p. 153.

319 **"a person of great compassion":** William Roberts, interview, "Professional Campaign Management and the Candidate, 1960–1966," UCLA Center for Oral History Research, 1979, p. 15.

319 **"But he doesn't have a grasp":** Stuart Spencer, interview with author, July 21, 2014.

319 **Nancy's father, Loyal Davis:** "He said I would be crazy to run for office." AAL, p. 145.

319 **"I kept saying no":** Ibid., p. 146.

320 **"They kept insisting":** RR, interview, "On Becoming Governor," UCLA Center for Oral History Research, Jan. 19, 1979, p.?

320 **"I'll make the decision":** Ibid.

320 **"he had done his homework":** Leo E. Litwak, "The Ronald Reagan Story; Or, Tom Sawyer Enters Politics," *New York Times*, Nov. 14, 1964.

320 **"They're right," he told Nancy:** "About a month before December 31, I knew that I was going to say yes." RR, interview, "On Becoming Governor," p. 5.

TWENTY-TWO: THE CITIZEN POLITICIAN

321 **"Wait a minute!":** MI, Nov. 4, 1987, p. 156; Edmund Morris, *Dutch* (New York: Random House, 1999), p. 340.

321 **campaign's "sawdust trail":** RR, interview, "On Becoming Governor," UCLA Center for Oral History Research, Jan. 19, 1979, p. 8.

321 **"anarchy, with attempts to destroy":** "Reagan Demands Inquiry," *New York Times*, May 14, 1966.

321 **"Orgies . . . so vile":** Tom Wicker, "Reagan Shuns Image of Goldwater in Coast Race," *New York Times*, June 8, 1966.

321 **American troops "are being denied":** Ibid.; Rick Perlstein, *Nixonland* (New York: Scribner, 2008), p. 91.

321 **He opposed as unconstitutional:** David S. Broder, "Reagan Victory Aids G.O.P. Right," *New York Times*, July 9, 1966.

321 **"Our city streets":** Lou Cannon, *Governor Reagan* (New York: Public Affairs, 2003), p. 144.

322 **From the beginning:** "It was a total Reagan staged kickoff." Tom Reed, interview with author, May 5, 2015.

322 **"tanned and meticulously groomed":** Peter Bart, "Reagan Enters Gubernatorial Race in California," *New York Times*, Jan. 5, 1966, p. 21.

322 **"He was overanswering":** Stanley Plog, "More Than Just an Actor: The Early Campaigns of Ronald Reagan," UCLA Center for Oral History Research, Jan. 5, 1981, p. 6.

322 **"On matters on which":** Cannon, *Governor Reagan*, p. 139.

323 **"He could read an audience":** Stuart Spencer, interview with author, July 21, 2014.

323 **"His short little one-liners":** Stuart Spencer, interview with author, July 21, 2014.

323 **"Joe Dokes running":** Bill Boyarsky, *The Rise of Ronald Reagan* (New York: Random House, 1968), p. 137.

323 **"[His] solutions to most problems":** Stuart Spencer, interview, Jan. 6, 1988, LCA.

323 **"the right-wing conservatives":** *San Francisco Chronicle*, Jan. 5, 1966.

324 **"some of it occasionally clean":** "[He] had a remarkable ability to make a pun out of almost anything." Paul Haerle, quoted in "Ronald Reagan and Republican Party Politics, 1965–1965," UCLA Center for Oral History Research, 1982, p. 5.

324 **Plus, he had no respect:** Georges Steffes, interview with author, July 17, 2014.

324 **I was not sober":** Lyn Nofziger, *Nofziger* (Washington, DC: Regnery, 1991), p. 33.

324 **"a glamorous curiosity":** William French Smith, quoted in "Evolution of the Kitchen Cabinet, 1965–1973," UCLA Center for Oral History Research, Mar. 16, 1988, p. 10.

324 **"political switch-hitter":** "Reagan and G.O.P. Rival Clash: Question Each Other's Integrity," Lawrence E. Davies, *New York Times*, Dec.6,/1965, p. 26.

325 **Reagan had never gotten:** Lyn Nofziger, MCI, Mar.6/2003, pp. 4–5

325 **"What are you going to do":** "We had not briefed him properly." Ibid., p. 6.

325 **"complete and utter lack":** "California: New Role," *Time*, Jan. 14, 1966.

325 **"it irritated Reagan":** Lyn Nofziger, interview, MCPA, Mar. 6, 2003, p. 6.

326 **Goldwater "fire-breathers":** Tom Reed, interview with author, May 5, 2015.

326 **It was actually conceived:** "That was done with our approval, with us involved in the creation of the Eleventh Commandment." William Roberts, interview, "Professional Campaign Management and the Candidate, 1960–1966," UCLA Center for Oral History Research, 1979, p. 20; "We came up with this mainly to keep the other candidates from attacking Reagan for being ignorant." Lyn Nofziger, interview, MCPA, Mar. 6, 2003, p. 4.

326 **"I will have no word":** "California: New Role," *Time.*

326 **"How are Negro Republicans":** Boyarsky, *The Rise of Ronald Reagan*, p. 148.

327 **"I resent the implication":** "Reagan's Exit Stirs Negro G.O.P. Parley," *New York Times*, Mar. 7, 1966, p. 16.

327 **tried shushing him:** "He's cussing under his breath, and I'm saying, 'Shut up!'" Lyn Nofziger, interview, MCPA, p. 8; "He was walking off the stage throwing profanities around at Christopher. 'That son of a bitch.'" Stuart Spencer, interview with author, July 21, 2014; Boyarsky, *The Rise of Ronald Reagan*, p. 149.

328 **"If it's a good line":** Tom Reed, interview with author, Oct. 11, 2014.

328 **"If I'm asking them":** RR, interview, "On Becoming Governor," UCLA Center for Oral History Research, Jan. 19, 1979, p. 21.

328 **"They were scared to death":** Lyn Nofziger, interview, MCPA, p. 6; "Many reporters found him monumentally ignorant on state issues." Lou Cannon, *Reagan* (New York: G. P. Putnam's Sons, 1982), p. 114.

328 **a "moral crusade":** Wicker, "Reagan Shuns Image of Goldwater."

328 **"small minority of beatniks":** Wallace Turner, "Reagan Demands Berkeley Inquiry," *New York Times*, April 14, 1966.

328 **"And if that means kicking":** Wicker, "Reagan Shuns Image of Goldwater."

328 **"Campus unrest isn't even":** Stuart Spencer, interview with author, July 21, 2014.

329 **By late spring, the national press:** "Straw polls during the fall, winter and spring have given Mr. Reagan the lead." Lawrence E. Davies, "Reagan Endorsed by G.O.P. Assembly," *New York Times*, Apr. 4, 1966; *San Francisco Chronicle*, May 24, 1966.

329 **"Ronald Reagan has an excellent chance":** Wicker, "Reagan Shuns Image of Goldwater."

329 **He flew to Eureka College:** Perlstein, *Nixonland*, p. 91.

329 **"Did he jointly sponsor protest":** Drew Pearson, "Fear Reagan May Veer Left Again," *Nevada Daily Mail*, Oct. 27, 1966.

330 **Ronald Reagan had 1,385,550 votes:** "California: Up from Death Valley," *Time*, June 17, 1966.

330 **"against all counsels":** "California Primaries," *New York Times*, June 9, 1996.

330 **"'Bring him on'":** Boyarsky, *The Rise of Ronald Reagan*, p. 113.

330 **"A sweet, nice, all-around":** Anthony Beilenson, interview with author, Aug. 28, 2014.

330 **"not only a good man":** Stuart Spencer, interview with author, July 21, 2014.

330 **"There was no ideological divide":** Kirk West, interview with author, July 17, 2014.

331 **"reasonable, rational and realistic":** Robert Reinhold, Obituary of Edmund G. Brown, *New York Times*, Feb. 18, 1996.

331 **"We respected him":** Stuart Spencer, interview with author, July 21, 2014.

331 **"probably have Pat Brown":** Kirk West, interview with author, July 17, 2014.

331 **a "political giant":** Lou Cannon, *Ronnie and Jesse* (Garden City, NY: Doubleday, 1969), p. 79.

332 **"a very difficult candidate":** Tom Reed, interview with author, May 5, 2015.

332 **"front man" who "collaborated":** State Democratic chairman Robert L. Coate, "Ronald Reagan, Extremist Collaborator—An Expose," Democratic State Central Committee of California typescript in author's possession, Aug. 11, 1966, p. 1.

332 **"I'm not going to condemn":** RR, interview, "On Becoming Governor," UCLA Center for Oral History Research, p. 16; Bill Roberts, interview, undated, LCA, pp. 1–2.

332 **"he was a *citizen politician*":** Roberts interview, "Professional Campaign Management," p. 14.

332 **"Nowhere in the state constitution":** "Reagan Handles His Role as a Political Amateur Like an Old Pro," Warren Weaver Jr., *New York Times*, Oct. 2, 1966, p. 54.

332 **"He was running against Reagan":** Tom Reed, interview with author, Oct. 11, 2014.

333 **"Our research showed us":** Stuart Spencer, interview with author, July 21, 2014.

333 **"Our battle cry":** Roberts, interview, "Professional Campaign Management," p. 21.

333 **"The minute it became obvious"**: William French Smith, "Evolution of the Kitchen Cabinet," p. 12; "We brought them right into the campaign." RR, interview, "On Becoming Governor," p. 14.

333 **"The Democrats did everything wrong"**: RR, interview, "On Becoming Governor," p. 15.

334 **"I couldn't believe the stupidity"**: Ibid., p. 24.

334 **"Ronald Reagan is your grandfather's"**: Tom Reed, *The Reagan Enigma: 1964–1980* (Los Angeles: Figueroa Press, 2014), p. 38.

334 **"It was amateur hour"**: Tom Reed, interview with author, Oct. 11, 2014. OK? "The first batch we got out of them was crap!" Stuart Spencer, interview with author, July 21, 2014.

334 **"I drew the short straw"**: Stuart Spencer, interview with author, July 21, 2014.

335 **was "running scared"**: Lawrence E. Davies, "Reagan Plays It Like a Pro," *New York Times*, Aug. 14, 1966.

335 **His popularity continued to increase**: "On the basis of the latest opinion surveys, Mr. Reagan appeared to have a commanding lead." Gladwyn Hill, "Brown Pressing to Catch Reagan," *New York Times*, Nov. 6, 1966.

335 **"We figured by the spring"**: Stuart Spencer, interview, Jan. 6, 1988, LCA.

TWENTY-THREE: "PRAIRIE FIRE"

339 **"We must, I think, take Reaganism"**: James Q. Wilson, "A Guide to Reagan Country," *Commentary*, May 1967.

339 **"existed as a cowtown"**: Greg Lucas, interview with author, California State Librarian, Mar. 24, 2015.

339 **"It was a very sleepy"**: Ken Hall, interview with author, July 17, 2014.

340 **"We were in shock"**: Burnett Miller, interview with author, Feb. 26, 2015; "We were underimpressed; we didn't take him seriously." Anthony Beilenson, interview with author, Aug. 28, 2014.

340 **"Ronald Reagan, on the other"**: Steven Avella, interview with author, Apr. 17, 2015.

340 **"Here we are—now what"**: Tom Reed, interview with author, Oct. 11, 2014; "What are we going to do if we win?" George Steffes, interview with author, July 17, 2014.

340 **"I guess I thought more"**: RR, interview, "On Becoming Governor," UCLA Center for Oral History Research, Jan. 19, 1979, pp. 29, 34.

340 **"We were not only amateurs"**: Lyn Nofziger, interview, undated, LCA; Lou Cannon, *Governor Reagan* (New York: Public Affairs, 2003), p. 184.

340 **"specifically wanted people"**: George Steffes, interview with author, July 17, 2014.

340 **"the fair-haired boy"**: Stuart Spencer, interview with author, July 21, 2014.

341 **"He was a charming"**: Sandy Quinn, interview with author, Oct. 30, 2014.

341 **"the most dreary, dismal"**: RR, interview, "On Becoming Governor," p. 33.

341 **"a wooden firetrap"**: "Nancy described it to me as a wooden firetrap." Tom Reed, interview with author, Oct. 17, 2014; Ken Hall, interview with author, July 17, 2014.

341 **and "a tinderbox"**: "Its wooden frame eaten through by dry rot." NR/MT, p. 135.

341 **"It backs up"**: KK/NR, p. 138.

341 **"Those damn trucks!"**: RR, quoted in Kathy Randall Davis, *But What's He REALLY Like?* (Menlo Park, CA: Pacific Coast Publishing, 1970), p. 69.

342 **"Gentlemen," Champion said**: Ken Hall, interview with author, July 17, 2014.

342 **a shortfall that might run**: "A prospective state budget the Governor-elect's aides told him might be as much as $700 million out of balance." Gladwyn Hill, "Reagan Starts Down a Long Road," *New York Times*, Dec. 4, 1966.

342 **"I didn't realize it would be"**: RR, quoted in Bill Boyarsky, *The Rise of Ronald Reagan* (New York: Random House, 1968), p. 165.

342 **"Here I was, the big conservative"**: RR, "On Becoming Governor," p. 34.

343 **"Any major business can tighten"**: RR, quoted in "Reagan Appears on Television," *New York Times*, Jan. 17, 1967.

343 **"Our state has been looted"**: Lawrence E. Davies, "Reagan Attacks California Debt; Charges Brown 'Drained' State," *New York Times*, Jan. 31, 1967.

343 **"We can close hospitals"**: "Sounds good to me!" he said. RR, quoted in Tom Reed, interview with author, Oct. 11, 2014.

343 **"The whole system came unglued"**: Ken Hall, interview with author, July 17, 2014.

343 **"The roof fell in"**: "We had no time to warn legislators." RR, interview, Oct. 26, 1968, LCA, p. 3.

343 **the ax fell**: "I had to fire sixteen women on Christmas Eve. We had a mandate coming in: ten percent cuts." George Steffes, interview with author, July 17, 2014.

344 **"took his big stick"**: Carolyn Anspacher, "Reagan Blasts Kerr Over UC Freeze," *San Francisco Chronicle*, Jan. 18, 1967.

344 **"We would like to welcome"**: Lee Fremstad, "Harmony of UC Regents, Reagan Ends," *Sacramento Bee*, Jan. 21, 1967.

344 **He was trimming**: William Trombley, "Governor and Academia Never Came to Terms," in a special supplement entitled "Reagan's Quixotic Reign, 1967–1977," *Los Angeles Times*, Sept. 29, 1974.

344 **Students at Berkeley planned**: Anspacher, "Reagan Blasts Kerr."

344 **"He was having horrific fights"**: Stuart Spencer, interview with author, July 21, 2014.

344 **The skirmish cost UC president**: Lee Fremstad, "UC President Kerr Is Fired by Regents," *Sacramento Bee*, Jan. 21, 1967; "Dismissal Angers Students at UC," *Sacramento Bee*, Jan. 21, 1967.

344 Protesters on the Berkeley campus: "Savio, Four Others Are Found Guilty," *Sacramento Bee*, Jan. 21, 1967.

344 "to harass students, faculty": Seth Rosenfeld, "Secret FBI Files Reveal Covert Activities at UC," *San Francisco Chronicle*, June 9, 2002.

344 "I want to come talk to you": Tom Reed, interview with author, Oct. 11, 2014; Reed, *The Reagan Enigma*, p. 57.

345 Reagan knew it was premature: He told Tom Reed, "I don't want to hear about this all day long, but if you want to go do it, it's fine." Tom Reed, interview with author, Oct. 11, 2014.

345 "Those guys talk too much": "Their allegiances run in a lot of different directions." Reed, *The Reagan Enigma*, p. 58.

345 "I was opposed to it": Edwin Meese, interview with author, Dec. 9, 2014.

346 "This is not being done right": Stuart Spencer, interview with author, July 21, 2014.

346 "Those first months were replete": Ken Hall, interview with author, July 17, 2014.

347 Reagan's relationship with: "There were a few months there in which, oh, yes, I was very uncomfortable." RR interview, "On Becoming Governor," p. 43.

347 "He wasn't interested": Cannon, *Governor Reagan*, p. 193.

347 "He convinced Reagan": George Steffes, interview with author, July 17, 2014.

347 There were several Republican: "Bob Monagan, Jack Veneman, Hugh Flournoy, and Bill Bagley were all lovely guys I got along with." Anthony Beilenson interview, Aug.28, 2014.

347 "Every piece of legislation": Paul Haerle, interview with author, July 16, 2014.

348 He issued official press releases: Author interview with Paul Haerle, July 26, 2014.

348 "I tried to run everything": Cannon, *Governor Reagan*, p. 239.

348 "I started setting up lunches": William Clark, interview, July 3, 1981, LCA, p. 9.

348 "should be played by ear": Cannon, *Governor Reagan*, p. 187.

349 "Finally," he recalled: RR, interview, "On Becoming Governor," p. 41.

349 "The word 'abortion'": Anthony Beilenson, interview with author, Aug. 28, 2014.

349 "archaic, barbarous and hypocritical": Arguments before the California Judiciary Committee, Apr. 28, 1967; Anthony C. Beilenson, *Looking Back: A Memoir* (Privately printed, 2012), p. 94.

349 George Danielson, a state assemblyman: Ibid.

350 "I had never given": MI, Mar. 24, 1987, p. 81.

350 "This is not in my mind": "I . . . I just can't give you a decision." Edmund Morris, *Dutch* (New York: Random House, 1999), p. 352.

350 "He was really torn": Edwin Meese, interview with author, Dec. 9, 2014.

350 Stu Spencer was to recall: Stuart Spencer, interview with author, July 21, 2014.

351 "very rarely has rape": MI, Mar. 24, 1987, p. 81.

351 "I cannot justify morally": RR, quoted in Boyarsky, *The Rise of Ronald Reagan*, p. 189.

351 "It just finally came": MI, Mar. 24, 1987, p. 81.

351 "he never would have signed": Cannon, *Governor Reagan*, p. 213.

351 "in all the years": Beilenson, *Looking Back*, p. 116.

352 "a stage set": Joan Didion, "Pretty Nancy," *Saturday Evening Post*, June 1, 1968.

352 "There was always a distance": Davis, *But What's He REALLY Like?*, p. 36.

352 more than two martinis: "He had a martini 'up.' I circulated back twenty minutes later and the martini glass was empty. The Governor has a second martini, which he drains. He eyed mine and said, 'Give it to me,' and this was *before* dinner." George Steffes, interviews with author, July 17, 2014, and Nov. 22, 2016.

352 "had total trust in Phil": William Clark, interview, July 3, 1981, LCA, p. 4.

352 "my strong right arm": Cannon, *Governor Reagan*, p. 239; "RR thought Phil was the greatest thing since sliced bread." Tom Reed, interview, Nov. 24, 1971, LCA, p. 1.

353 said, "had presidentialitis": Sandy Quinn, interview with author, Oct. 30, 2014.

353 "a self-promoting autocrat": Reed, *The Reagan Enigma*, p. 101.

353 "cutting out and annihilating those": Tom Reed, interview, May 27, 1981, LCA, p. 11.

353 "trying to ram things through": Robert Monagan, interview, "Increasing Republican Influence in the State Assembly," UCLA Center for Oral History Research, 1981, p. 39; Reed, *The Reagan Enigma*, pp. 100–101.

353 "power–mad". . . "clinically crazy": Tom Reed, interview, Mar. 25, 1981, LCA, p. 13.

353 "So we figured out": Tom Reed, interview with author, Oct. 11, 2014.

353 "It was *evil* to be homosexual": Stuart Spencer, interview with author, July 21, 2014; "Homosexuality was considered to be a sin." Paul Haerle, interview with author, July 16, 2014.

353 "fairly high paranoia": Leland L. Nichols, interview with Donald B. Seney, California State University, State Government Oral History Program, Nov. 14, 1991, p. 340.

353 "a case of sickness and disease": LBJ, quoted in "Johnson and the Jenkins Case," *Time*, Nov. 6, 1964.

353 Quinn and Jack Kemp: "Jack was bisexual. We eventually knew about him." Stuart Spencer, interview with author, July 21, 2014.

354 "Clark and I were the ringleaders": Tom Reed, interview with author, Oct. 11, 2014.

354 "We made the Keystone Cops": Lyn Nofziger, *Nofziger* (Washington, DC: Regnery, 1991), p. 77.

354 **"I don't think there was anything":** "I think that was a dead end," Tom Reed, interview with author, Oct. 11, 2014.

354 **"It was all circumstantial":** William Clark, interview, July 3, 1981, LCA, p. 5.

354 **"It was decided that":** Edwin Meese, interview with author, Dec. 9, 2014; "We decided to get on different flights because we didn't want to all go down there together." Paul Haerle, interview with author, July 16, 2014.

355 **"Golly, are you quitting":** Cannon, *Governor Reagan*, p. 244.

355 **Bill Clark recalled:** Clark interview, memo on Western Union stationery, LCA, undated except for the notation "11/6."

355 **"This is not a Monday problem":** Holmes Tuttle, quoted in Tom Reed, interview with author, Oct. 11, 2014.

355 **"She saw the potential vulnerability":** Edwin Meese, interview with author, Dec. 9, 2014.

355 **"Phil," Tuttle said:** Robert Tuttle, interview with author, Oct. 3, 2014.

355 **He was shell-shocked:** "It was a big shock to him, as it was to me." Sandy Quinn, interview with author, Oct. 30, 2014.

356 **"He was very different":** George Steffes, interview with author, July 17, 2014.

356 **"This citizen politician has determined":** Cannon, *Governor Reagan*, p. 246.

356 **"Besides," Tom Reed continues:** Tom Reed, interview with author, Oct. 11, 2014.

356 **At a reception:** Tom Wicker, "Reagan Rebutted on Aides' Ouster," *New York Times*, Nov. 5, 1967.

356 **"Gov. Ronald Reagan Faces":** Bell-McClure Syndicate press release, "Drew Pearson Special," LCA, undated; "Spots on Mr. Clean," *Newsweek*, Nov. 13, 1967.

356 **"had harbored a homosexual ring":** "Spots on Mr. Clean," *Newsweek*.

356 **"I'm prepared to say that nothing":** Wicker, "Reagan Rebutted on Aides' Ouster."

357 **"hurt our relationship with everyone":** William Clark interview, "11/6," LCA.

357 **"Mike's father had caught him":** Edwin Meese, interview with author, Dec. 9, 2014.

357 **"We ought to troll him":** Robert Finch, interview, undated, LCA, p. 7.

357 **"Ronald Reagan has a strong":** Wallace Turner, "Reagan's Chances Found Improving," *New York Times*, June 18, 1967.

TWENTY-FOUR: THE NON-CANDIDATE

359 **Considered large as these places:** "We trucked tons of booze up there, whole truckloads." Peter Graves, interview with author, July 19, 2014.

359 **Early on the afternoon:** "Nixon and Reagan Hold Conference in California," *New York Times*, July 23, 1967.

359 **"If I were to choose":** "It marked the first milestone on my road to the presidency." Richard M. Nixon, *Memoirs*, (New York: Grossett and Dunlop, 1978).

360 **"working every state committee meeting":** Ibid.

360 **"Romney was wooden":** Tom Reed, interview with author, Oct. 11, 2014.

361 **"close to genius":** "It was a brilliant speech." Peter Graves, interview with author, July 19, 2014.

361 **orange juice laced with vodka:** Thomas C. Reed, *The Reagan Enigma* (Los Angeles: Figueroa Press, 2014), p. 97.

361 **"Nixon had a way of converting":** Peter Graves, interview with author, July 19, 2014.

361 **Ronald Reagan didn't share:** "Governor Reagan was thoroughly committed to a more hawkish position than anyone else in the Presidential picture." Gladwyn Hill, "Reagan Backers Split on Outlook," *New York Times*, Apr. 2, 1968.

361 **"I'd step up the war":** RR, press conference, transcript, May 9, 1967, LCA.

362 **"Forget it. That draft dodger":** Jonathan Eig, *Ali* (New York: Houghton Mifflin Harcourt, 2017), p. 503.

362 **Reagan also advocated eliminating:** "We've gone down a bad and dangerous road with peacetime conscription, and I would turn to a professional army and eliminate the draft." RR speech, University of Colorado, Boulder, transcript, RRPL, Apr. 27, 1968.

362 **Reagan reportedly "destroyed":** David Halberstam quoted in Lou Cannon, *Governor Reagan* (New York: Public Affairs, 2003), p. 260 (footnote).

362 **"It's almost as if a big light":** Tom Reed, interview with author, Oct. 11, 2014.

363 **"Are you in this thing?":** Reed, *The Reagan Enigma*, p. 119.

364 **"crusading on behalf of":** Gladwyn Hill, "Reagan Tour Aids G.O.P. War Chest," *New York Times*, Oct. 27, 1967.

364 **"He reserved his best acting":** Gladwyn Hill, "As a Non-Candidate, Reagan Is a Non-Slouch," *New York Times*, Oct. 8, 1967.

364 **Reagan was shocked and concerned:** Edwin Meese, interview with author, Dec. 9, 2014.

364 **"The city's going up":** Lyn Nofziger, *Nofziger* (Washington, DC: Regnery, 1991), p. 70.

365 **"Can I have your autograph?":** Edwin Meese, interview with author, Dec. 9, 2014.

365 **He denounced militant black leaders:** Tom Wicker, "Reagan Questions Motive for Warren's Retirement," *New York Times*, June 24, 1968.

365 **"Conservatives believed that if Nixon":** Edwin Meese, interview with author, Dec. 9, 2014.

366 **"I want a Rockefeller-Reagan":** Lyn Nofziger quoted, MCI, Mar. 6, 2003, p. 11.

366 **He'd already rejected a Nixon-Reagan:** RR and Eisenhower discussed a Nixon-Reagan ticket at a

March 11, 1968, meeting between the two in Palm Springs. "Reagan Bars Race for Vice President," *New York Times*, Mar. 13, 1968, p. 34.

366 **"It is a great tragedy"**: RR, letter to Patti Davis, June 5, 1968, reprinted in Kathy Randall Davis, *But What's He REALLY Like?* (Menlo Park, CA: Pacific Coast Publishing, 1970), p. 80.

366 **"I saw him the day"**: Tom Reed, interview with author, Oct. 11, 2014.

366 **Barry Goldwater urged him:** "Ron and I went to see Barry in Phoenix and he said, 'You've got to support Nixon.'" Ibid.

366 **had already sunk $366,000:** "The actual 1968 spending was $366,000." Cannon, *Governor Reagan*, p. 265 (footnote).

367 **"raised bundles of money"**: Ibid., p. 267.

367 **"Not this year, Ron"**: Charlie Dent, quoted in Reed, *The Reagan Enigma*, p. 171.

367 **"He had their hearts"**: Stuart Spencer, interview with author, July 21, 2014.

367 **"It was the greatest relief"**: MI, Mar. 29, 1988, p. 185; "Nancy and I were the two most relieved people in the world." MI, Jan. 9, 1989, p. 249.

TWENTY-FIVE: THE CONSERVATION GOVERNOR

368 **"the Batman of politics"**: Gladwyn Hill, "Reagan Assessed as Being 'the Batman of Politics,'" *New York Times*, July 23, 1967.

368 **the "Teflon President"**: The nickname is credited to congresswoman Patricia Schroeder in 1983; "Nothing Stuck to Teflon President,'" *USA Today*, June 6, 2004.

368 **"programs that reward people"**: RR, inauguration speech, Jan. 4, 1971, transcript, "The Presidency Project," UC-Santa Barbara; Wallace Turner, "Reagan, Heckled, Pledges Welfare Reform," *New York Times*, Jan. 5, 1971.

368 **"the truly needy as opposed"**: Edwin Meese, confidential memo, Aug. 4, 1970 (Meese Papers, Hoover Institution, Stanford University).

368 **The "welfare monster"**: RR, interview, *California Journal*, Dec. 16, 1970.

368 **as "criminal anarchists"**: RR, State of the State message to a joint session of the CA legislature, Jan. 7, 1969.

369 **"We are called materialistic"**: RR quoted in Bob Colacello, *Ronnie and Nancy* (New York: Warner Bros., 2004), p. 401.

369 **"provide for the expulsion"**: RR, State of the State, Jan. 7, 1969.

369 **"Observe the Rules or Get Out"**: "He believed that students should obey the rules—or get out." Tom Reed, interview with author, Oct. 11, 2014.

369 **"In the sixties"**: Ibid.

370 **"cowardly little bums"**: RR, quoted in Lou Cannon, *Governor Reagan* (New York: Public Affairs, 2003), p. 293.

370 **"If it takes a bloodbath"**: RR, address to California Council of Growers, Yosemite National Park, Apr. 7, 1970.

370 **"determined to get something done"**: Edwin Meese, interview with author, Dec. 9, 2014.

370 **"our number one priority"**: RR, quoted in Anthony C. Beilenson, *Looking Back: A Memoir* (Privately printed, 2012), p. 145; "My most important priority was welfare reform." AAL, p. 188.

370 **"able-bodied people"**: AAL, p. 188.

370 **"Reagan wasn't interested"**: George Steffes, interview with author, July 17, 2014.

371 **"one couple . . . earned more"**: AAL, p. 189.

371 **"He was very hands-on"**: George Steffes, interview with author, July 17, 2014.

371 **"He knew when to back off"**: Stuart Spencer, interview with author, July 21, 2014.

372 **"Getting the governor together"**: Ken Hall, interview with author, July 17, 2014.

373 **"We thought we had a chance"**: Ibid.

374 **"a know-nothing"**: Cannon, *Governor Reagan*, p. 230.

374 **"The governor got plenty accomplished"**: William Bagley, interview with author, Aug. 12, 2014.

374 **"Conservationists were absolutely appalled"**: "When he came into office they were up in arms." Kirk West, interview with author, July 17, 2014.

374 **"He decided to see the Minarets"**: Ed Meese, interview with author, Dec. 9, 2014.

374 **"waving a white hat"**: George Skelton, "The Man Who Saved the Sierra," *Los Angeles Times*, July 28, 1997.

375 **"Because such a crossing"**: RR, speech, Minarets Summit, quoted in *Los Angeles Times*, June 28, 1972.

375 **"As a result, he'd only"**: "His greatest weakness was that he didn't seek out different opinions." George Steffes interview with author, July 17, 2014.

375 **"I am absolutely convinced"**: Bill Boyarsky, *Ronald Reagan: His Life and Times* (New York: Random House, 1981), p. 161.

376 **"once-in-a-lifetime opportunity"**: RR, speech, California Newspaper Publishers Association, Feb. 8, 1973.

376 **"an economic war"**: Robert Moretti, quoted in Cannon, *Governor Reagan*, p. 371.

376 **"No, and he shouldn't try"**: RR, interview, KTVU-TV, Oakland, CA, Oct. 26, 1973.

377 **"Let's work everything out"**: Nicole Woolsey Biggart, "Management Style as Strategic Interaction: The Case of Governor Ronald Reagan," *Journal of Applied Behavioral Sciences*, 1981, p. 305.

377 **"There is a definite sickness"**: George Skelton, "Reagan Setbacks: Is Political Grip Failing?" *Los Angeles Times*, Feb. 5, 1974.

377 **"It's a partisan witch hunt"**: "Gov. Reagan Urges Support of President," *Atlanta Daily World*, Apr. 3, 1972.

377 **That same week:** RR, speech to Young Republicans, Washington, DC, Mar. 30, 1973 ; "Chotiner

Says Nixon Aides Should Have Come Forward," *Washington Post*, Apr. 1, 1973.

377 **"I can't say publicly":** RR, letter to Rev. B. H. Cleaver, May 24, 1973, in *AAL*, p. 94.

378 **"a truthful man":** RR, press conference, Sacramento, in *Daily Review*, Mar. 28, 1973.

378 **"well-meaning individuals":** RR, quoted by John Chancellor, NBC News, May 2, 1973.

378 **"no worse than double parkers":** RR, quoted in Rick Perlstein, *The Invisible Bridge* (New York: Simon & Schuster, 2014), p. 160.

378 **Even when Nixon admitted:** Seymour Hersh, "President Linked to Taps on Aides," *New York Times*, May 16, 1973; "Nixon Concedes Wide Net," *New York Times*, May 23, 1973.

378 **"not criminal, just illegal":** RR, quoted in United Press International, June 5, 1973; "Reagan: Watergate Spies No Criminals," *Washington Post*, May 2, 1973.

378 **"About ninety percent of everything":** RR, quoted in Bill Anderson, "Governors Split—Just on Essentials," *Chicago Tribune*, June 6, 1973.

378 **"the cacophony of seditious drivel":** Spiro Agnew, quoted in John R. Coyne, *The Impudent Snobs: Agnew vs. the Intellectual Establishment* (New Rochelle, NY: Arlington House, 1972), p. 292.

378 **"They'd become friends":** Ed Meese, interview with author, Dec. 9, 2014.

378 **"I have known Ted Agnew":** RR, quoted in David Broder, "GOP Left Speechless by Agnew Headlines," *Washington Post*, Aug. 8, 1973.

379 **April 1973 Gallup poll:** "Remembering Spiro Agnew," *MacNeil-Lehrer Newshour*, PBS, Sept. 18, 1996.

379 **"Should Mr. Agnew somehow":** R. W. Apple Jr., "Watergate and 1976," *New York Times*, May 21, 1973.

379 **"To conservatives," says Jeffrey Bell:** Jeffrey Bell, interview with author, Dec. 19, 2013.

379 **Holmes Tuttle and Justin Dart:** "I did my best, and so did Mr. Dart, to convince Nixon." Holmes Tuttle, quoted in "The Kitchen Cabinet: Four California Citizen Advisors of Ronald Reagan," UCLA Center for Oral History Research, 1983, p. 146.

379 **being "pretty shallow":** Richard Nixon and Henry Kissinger, conversation, Oval Office, Nov. 17, 1971; David Corn, "Nixon on Tape: Reagan was 'Shallow' and of 'Limited Mental Capacity,' " *Mother Jones*, Nov. 15, 2007; Wallace Turner, "Choice of Reagan Called Unlikely," *New York Times*, Oct. 11, 1973.

380 **surrogate—"a caretaker":** RR, quoted in Peter Goldman, "Ready on the Right," *Newsweek*, Mar. 24, 1975, p. 20.

TWENTY-SIX: A HORSE OF A DIFFERENT COLOR

381 **"not criminals at heart":** Lou Cannon, *Governor Reagan* (New York: Public Affairs, 2003), p. 385.

381 **"Let's give him the benefit":** Peter Hannaford, interview with author, July 18, 2014.

381 **"The governor was firmly":** Edwin Meese, interview with author, Dec. 9, 2014.

382 **Ford promised him:** Craig Shirley, *Reagan's Revolution* (Nashville, TN: Thomas Nelson, 2005), p. 20.

382 **"One term may not be enough":** Peter Hannaford, interview with author, July 18, 2014.

383 **"he felt a sense of disappointment":** Peter Hannaford, *The Reagans: A Political Portrait* (New York: Coward-McCann, 1983), p. 50.

384 **was "fairly smashed":** Peter Hannaford, interview with author, July 18, 2014.

384 **"Reagan didn't say much":** John Sears, interview with author, Jan. 30, 2014.

384 **"Can you imagine Jerry Ford":** Attributed to Richard Nixon in a *Newsweek* article and reported blindly in Jules Witcover, *Marathon: The Pursuit of the Presidency, 1972–1976* (New York: Viking, 1977), p. 37.

385 **"Everybody was in a state":** Jeffrey Bell, interview with author, Dec. 19, 2013.

385 **"He didn't have any":** Peter Hannaford, interview with author, July 18, 2014.

385 **"I think we ought":** Walter Cronkite, quoted in Yanek Mieczkowski, *Gerald Ford and the Challenges of the 1970s* (Lexington: University of Kentucky Press, 2005), p. 21.

385 **Dutch Reagan had even broadcast:** "I'd once broadcast a University of Michigan football game in which he played." *AAL*, p. 200.

385 **"We've got to give":** Ibid.

385 **"It is a tragedy":** *Modesto Bee*, Aug. 9, 1974.

386 **"Ford isn't up to the job":** John Sears, interview with author, Jan. 30, 2014.

386 **He wasn't, but he told:** "He told Hartmann he would take it if Ford chose him, but he didn't want it." Jim Lake, interview with author, Feb. 25, 2014.

386 **a congressman from Maryland:** Robert Bauman, quoted in James Walcott, "Ronald Reagan: The Great Orange Hope," *Village Voice*, Feb. 24, 1975.

387 **Polls showed that most Americans:** "Gerald Ford: Domestic Affairs," Miller Center of Public Affairs, University of VA, http://millercenter.org/president/biography/ford-domestic-affairs.

387 **"I support [Ford]":** RR, quoted in Rick Perlstein, *The Invisible Bridge* (New York: Simon & Schuster, 2014), p. 285.

387 **"Rockefeller and Ford are not":** Minutes of the ACU conference, quoted in Shirley, *Reagan's Revolution*, p. 30.

387 **"Those who fought and served":** Peter Hannaford, interview with author, July 18, 2014.

387 **"The governor felt that the deficit":** Edwin Meese, interview with author, Dec. 9, 2014.

388 **"It would be ridiculous":** "Politicians: Citizen Reagan," *Newsweek*, Jan. 6, 1975.

388 **"I think he was tired":** Lyn Nofziger, *Nofziger* (Washington, DC: Regnery, 1991), p. 154.

388 **"dying to return to Los Angeles":** NR/MT, p. 179.

388 **"think something out":** "There's no better place to do it than Rancho del Cielo." *AAL*, p. 195.

389 **"Hell, I can't afford":** Pete Hannaford, interview with author, July 18, 2014.

389 **"You'd be joining a ship":** "I told him not to take it." John Sears, interview with author, Jan. 30, 2014.

389 **"the state of the Union":** Gerald R. Ford, State of the Union address, Jan. 15, 1975, transcript at infoplease.com.

389 **"The producer thinks":** Efrem Zimbalist Jr., quoted in Peter Hannaford, interview with author, July 18, 2014.

390 **"With radio, you don't outlive":** Peter Hannaford, interview with author, July 18, 2014; "People will tire of me on television. They won't tire of me on the radio." RR, quoted in Mike Deaver, interview, July 1, 2002, LCA.

390 **James S. Copley, and many:** Joseph Trento, *The Secret History of the CIA* (New York: Basic Books, 2005).

390 **The first few shows:** Hannaford, *The Reagans*, p. 59.

391 **"If you've had the experience":** RR, radio broadcasts, tape 75-01/track 4, recorded Jan. 8, 1975, Hoover Institution, Stanford University.

391 **"If you're not familiar":** Ibid., tape 75-01/track 3, Hoover Institution.

391 **"the lingering mysteries":** Bob Lancaster, "Great Polish Bisexual Frogs Mystery," *Boca Raton News*, July 15, 1974.

392 **"abandoned his pledge":** RR, radio broadcast, tape 75-03/ track 1, recorded Feb. 14, 1975, Hoover Institution.

392 **"a new and revitalized":** RR, address to the Conservative Political Action Conference, Associated Press, Feb. 15, 1975.

393 **"We're completely different":** R. W. Apple Jr., "Reagan on the Road: Easy Smile and Hard Rhetoric," *New York Times*, Feb. 20, 1975.

393 **"You're a Republican":** Cannon, *Governor Reagan*, p. 401; *Newsweek*, Mar. 24, 1975.

393 **"He'd come out and visit":** Peter Hannaford, interview with author, July 18, 2014.

393 **He even recruited Jesse Helms:** Charlie Black, interview with author, Feb. 25, 2014.

393 **"I thought the party":** Jeffrey Bell, interview with author, Dec. 19, 2013.

393 **"if voters saw Reagan":** John Sears, interview with author, Jan. 30, 2014.

393 **"would never stand for it":** "It wasn't her idea image-wise or what a hero would do." Ibid.

393 **"If I were to run for president":** Peter Hannaford, interview with author, July 18, 2014.

393 **"He's running," Mike Deaver:** Deaver quoted in Jim Lake, interview with author, Feb. 25, 2014.

394 **"signed by 113 of 145":** "Ready on the Right," *Newsweek*, Mar. 24, 1975.

394 **"Paul was a respected senator":** John Sears, interview with author, Jan. 30, 2014.

395 **a convoluted letter:** RR, to Paul Laxalt, letter, July 14, 1975, RRPL, personal papers.

395 **"The purpose of this committee":** Paul Laxalt, prepared speech, quoted in Shirley, *Reagan's Revolution*, p. 75.

396 **"truly alarming increase":** Gerald M. Ford, "Address Before a Joint Session of the California State Legislature," Sept. 5, 1975, transcript, the American Presidency Project, UC–Santa Barbara.

396 **"This country is a mess!":** Lynette Fromme, quoted in Perlstein, *Invisible Bridge*, p. 498.

396 **"The notion that Ronald Reagan":** James Reston, "Political Adventures," *New York Times*, Sept. 7, 1975.

397 **"a lovefest" packed:** "They treated him like a rock star." Peter Hannaford, interview with author, July 18, 2014.

397 **"who cheered themselves hoarse":** Witcover, *Marathon*, p. 73.

397 **"He is perceived as a man":** Mary McGrory, "Nixon Could Still Win in New Hampshire," *Washington Post*, Sept. 9, 1975.

397 **"He was a hard-right-wing guy":** Jim Lake interview with author, Feb. 25, 2014.

397 **"Once we got Gregg":** John Sears, interview with author, Jan. 30, 2014.

398 **"His heart is in the right place":** Sears, quoted in Jim Lake interview with author, Feb. 25, 2014.

398 **him as "a racist":** John Sears, interview with author, Jan. 30, 2014; also, Jim Lake interview, with author, Feb. 25, 2014.

398 **"Finally, I took him aside":** John Sears, interview with author, Jan. 30, 2014.

TWENTY-SEVEN: "MOMENTUM"

399 **"It's been said":** RR, from stump speeches, 1974–75, quoted in Craig Shirley, *Reagan's Revolution* (Nashville, TN: Thomas Nelson, 2005), p. 80.

399 **"a horse race":** Jules Witcover, *Marathon: The Pursuit of the Presidency, 1972–1976* (New York: Viking, 1977), p. 84.

399 **"stomped out of a strategy":** "He felt it was wrong for Ronald Reagan to be opposing an incumbent president." Edwin Meese, interview with author, Dec. 19, 2014.

399 **"his candidacy would lead":** Witcover, *Marathon*, p. 96.

400 **"Well, Governor, I'm very disappointed":** Gerald R. Ford, *A Time to Heal* (New York: Harper & Row, 1979), p. 333.

400 **"After much thought, I have decided":** Gerald M. Ford, press conference, Nov. 3, 1975, the American Presidency Project, UC–Santa Barbara.

400 **"his presence had become detrimental":** Philip Shabecoff, "Mutual Decision: Vice President's Letter Gives No Reason for Withdrawal," *New York Times*, Nov. 4, 1975, pp. 1, 27.

401 **"Unfortunately," Spencer says:** Stu Spencer, interview with author, July 21, 2014.

401 **"Mr. Nice Guy image"**: Peter Goldman, "Can Reagan Stop Ford?" *Newsweek*, Nov. 24, 1975.

401 **"he plays Presidential politics"**: Ibid.

401 **"Polls show the President"**: Tony Fuller, "The First Real Test," *Newsweek*, Oct. 20, 1975.

402 **"one of the most conservative"**: "Reagan Zeroes in on New Hampshire," *Boston Globe*, Jan. 4, 1976.

402 **"New Hampshire would establish"**: John Sears, interview with author, Jan. 30, 2014.

402 **"was his knockout strategy"**: Charlie Black, interview with author, Feb. 25, 2014.

402 Politics is motion: "The Campaign: A-a-a-a-n-d They're Off!!! *Time*, Jan. 19, 1976.

402 **"He was a natural"**: John Sears interview, Jan. 30, 2014; also Jim Lake interview, Feb. 25, 2014.

403 **"I was scared to death"**: Stu Spencer, interview, July 21, 2014.

403 **"He was still harping"**: John Sears, interview with author, Jan. 30, 2014.

403 **"a vision of the future"**: "Come up with a vision of the future and put it into a speech." John Sears, quoted in Jeffrey Bell, interview with author, Dec. 19, 2013.

403 **"The press treated the whole thing"**: Peter Hannaford, interview with Lou Cannon, Oct. 14, 1981, LCA.

404 **"Earlier that day, every reporter"**: "[RR] couldn't even remember the speech." Stu Spencer, interview, Jan. 30, 2014.

404 **"throwing elderly people out"**: "The Reagan Plan," *New York Times*, Jan. 12, 1975.

405 **"If you send these programs"**: Jeffrey Bell, interview with author, Dec. 19, 2013.

405 **"I guess I made a mistake"**: "Reagan Conceding 'Mistake' Attempts to Clarify Program," *New York Times*, Jan. 13, 1976.

405 **"We win New Hampshire"**: John Sears, quoted in Jim Lake interview with author, Feb. 25, 2014.

405 If Reagan polled between: Attributed to Hugh Gregg, in Peter Hannaford, *The Reagans: A Political Portrait* (New York: Coward-McCann, 1983), p. 96.

405 Toward the end of January: "The Campaign," *Time*, Jan. 19, 1976; Jim Lake interview with author, Feb. 25, 2014.

405 Abortion "on demand": "Reagan Affirms Anti-Abortion Stand," *New York Times*, Feb. 8, 1976.

405 **"if you are a slum dweller"**: "Welfare Queen Becomes Issue in Reagan Campaign," *New York Times*, Feb. 15, 1976; *Washington Star*, Feb. 15, 1976.

405 **"has 80 names"**: "Welfare Queen," *New York Times*.

406 **"He devoted hours to reading"**: John Sears, interview with author, Jan. 30, 2014.

406 **"Reagan wouldn't do the homework"**: Jeffrey Bell, interview with author, Dec. 19, 2013; Jeffrey Bell, "The Candidate and the Briefing Book," *The Weekly Standard*, Feb. 5, 2001.

407 Reagan looked it up: "That was all he needed to get very interested in it." Peter Hannaford, interview with author, July 18, 2014.

407 **"We bought it"**: RR, quoted in Hannaford, *The Reagans*, pp. 76–77.

407 **"it brought the house down"**: David Keene, interview with author, Oct. 23, 2014.

407 Subsequently, in one of his: RR, radio broadcasts, tape 75-10/track 6, recorded May 1975, Hoover Institution, Stanford University.

407 **"our government had maintained"**: RR, quoted in Witcover, *Marathon*, p. 402.

408 **"speak from the heart"**: Peter Hannaford, interview with author, July 18, 2014.

408 **"I worked Reagan hard"**: John Sears, interview with author, Jan. 30, 2014.

408 **"We'd create an event"**: Jim Lake, interview with author, Feb. 25, 2014.

409 **"a kind of soft-cell"**: Witcover, *Marathon*, p. 197.

410 **"There is power"**: Stu Spencer, interview, July 21, 2014.

411 **"I want Mel Thomson"**: RR, quoted in Jim Lake, interview with author, Feb. 25, 2014.

411 **"It was a complete disaster"**: Ibid.

411 A bucket of chilled bottles: "The Nation: How Ford Won and Reagan Lost," *Time*, Mar. 8, 1976.

411 **"We were still holding out hope"**: Charlie Black, interview with author, Feb. 25, 2014.

411–412 **"to *act* like we're ahead"**: Ibid.

412 **"We could never come back"**: David Keene, interview with author, Oct. 23, 2014.

412 Social Security might be: RR, quoted in David E. Rosenbaum, "Social Security a Major Issue in Florida as Primary Day Nears," *New York Times*, Mar. 5, 1975.

412 **"They made Reagan sound"**: Charlie Black, interview with author, Feb. 25, 2014.

412 **"the personality a President"**: "Florida's Elderly Raise Hopes of Ford and Jackson," David E. Rosenbaum, *New York Times*, Mar. 6, 1976, p. 11.

412 **"Florida is really the key"**: Gerald Ford, quoted in Witcover, *Marathon*, p. 403.

412 **"We came up like a skyrocket"**: Jon Nordheimer, "Reagan Will Stay in Race; Denies Ford Won Triumph," *New York Times*, Mar. 11, 1976.

412 The Ford people orchestrated: "Rogers Morton . . . began to put together announcements from prominent Republican members of Congress." Hannaford, *The Reagans*, p. 106; Peter Hannaford, interview with author, July 18, 2014.

413 Even Nancy Reagan considered: "We were in High Point, [NC], and Nancy started thinking, 'Maybe it's time to bow out. We're going to lose here.' " Peter Hannaford, interview with author, July 18, 2014.

413 **"I wanted to cut a deal"**: John Sears, interview with author, Jan. 30, 2014.

413 Some reports put: Shirley, *Reagan's Revolution*, p. 159.

413 it was closer to $2 million: Peter Hannaford, interview with author, July 18, 2014; John Sears, interview with author, Jan. 30, 2014; Hannaford, *The Reagans*, p. 107; "The campaign was $1,167,000 in

debt when I came in." Darrell Trent, interview with author, Aug. 26, 2014.

413 **"Why aren't we taking off?":** Peter Hannaford, interview with author, July 18, 2014; Paul Laxalt, *Nevada's Paul Laxalt: A Memoir* (Reno, NV: Jack Bacon & Co., 2000), pp. 291–92.

413 hadn't taken a paycheck: David Keene, quoted in Witcover, *Marathon*, p. 410.

413 **"It was hand-to-hand":** Charlie Black, interview with author, Feb. 25, 2014.

414 **"Pete, we have five hundred":** Peter Hannaford, interview with author, July 18, 2014.

414 **"It's fifty-five to forty-five":** Frank Reynolds, quoted in Ibid.; Martin Anderson, interview, MCPA, Dec. 12, 2001, p. 29.

414 **"Okay, I win":** Martin Anderson, interview, MCPA, Dec. 12, 2001, p. 29.

415 **"This is a turning point":** "We were in Indianapolis when he got the news about Texas." Darrell Trent, interview with author, Aug. 26, 2014.

415 **"We're way ahead":** Wayne King, "Reagan Predicts First-Ballot Victory," *New York Times*.

416 Five weeks before: "The situation is highly volatile." "Republicans: They're So Close," *Time*, July 19, 1976.

416 **"Acquire delegates, protect your delegates":** James A. Baker III, quoted in Jeremy W. Peters, "Potential G.O.P. Convention Fight Puts Older Hands in Sudden Demand," *New York Times*, April 18, 2016.

416 **"The Ford campaign":** Ibid.

416 John Sears needed: "I knew maybe a month and a half before we gathered in Kansas City that I was going to have to do something." John Sears, interview with author, Jan. 30, 2014.

416 **"was in danger":** Martin Anderson, "Schweiker," a chapter in an unpublished manuscript, p. 3.

417 **"was too much of a stretch":** John Sears, interview with author, Jan. 30, 2014.

417 **"a very liberal guy":** Charlie Black, interview with author, Feb. 25, 2014.

417 a 100 percent rating: David. M. Alpern, "Reagan's Last Gamble," *Newsweek*, Aug. 9, 1976.

417 **"dressed like a Cleveland":** David Keene, interview with author, Oct. 23, 2014.

417 **"easy to like":** Anderson, "Schweiker," p. 24.

417 **"I've made a decision":** RR, quoted in Witcover, *Marathon*, p. 461.

418 **"When I heard about it":** David Keene, interview with author, Oct. 23, 2014.

418 **"was so shaken":** Tom Wicker, "The Reagan Gamble," *New York Times*, Aug. 1, 1976.

418 **"were alter egos":** Author interview with Darrell Trent, Aug. 26, 2014.

418 **"were stunned and outraged":** Alpern, "Reagan's Last Gamble."

418 **"Reagan has scuttled":** John Connally, quoted in Ibid.

419 **"I'm not a lawyer":** Jimmy Carter, quoted in Richard Reeves, *Old Faces of '76* (New York: Harper & Row, 1976), p. 15.

419 **"to bind our people together":** Jimmy Carter, quoted in Elizabeth Drew, *American Journal: The Events of 1976* (New York: Random House, 1977), p. 38.

420 **"119 delegates remaining":** Margot Hornblower, "Reagan, Schweiker Pick Up 6 Delegates in Northeast," *Washington Post*, Aug. 6, 1976.

420 **"Mr. Reagan about 100":** Douglas E. Kneeland, "Reagan Wooing Delegates and Arguing Rules Change," *New York Times*, Aug. 17, 1976.

420 **"a desperate-hours attempt":** David M. Alpern, "How Ford Did It," *Newsweek*, Aug. 30, 1976.

420 **"We knew 16-C":** Charlie Black, interview with author, Feb. 25, 2014.

421 **"Nancy and I aren't going":** Jon Nordheimer, "Reagan, On Dais, Spurs Party On," *New York Times*, Aug. 20, 1976.

421 **"I'm sorry that you all":** RR, quoted in NR/MT, p. 193.

421 **"I feel at peace with myself":** Nordheimer, "Reagan, On Dais."

421 **"He almost certainly believed":** Hannaford, *The Reagans*, p. 137.

TWENTY-EIGHT: THE FRONT-RUNNER

422 **"I'm at peace with the world":** "Reagan Will Not Bar Another Try in 1980," *New York Times*, Nov. 3, 1976.

422 The country's military's dwindling preparedness: "He felt that with détente we were failing. . . . It was wrong, and as a result, our national security was endangered." Edwin Meese, interview with author, Dec. 9, 2014.

422 **"America's longing to draw inward":** RR, speech to Young Americans for Freedom, quoted in James Reston, "Reagan on Panama," *New York Times*, Aug. 28, 1977.

422 **"courting conservatives who now call":** RR, quoted in Jon Nordheimer, "Reagan Urges His Party to Save Itself by Declaring Its Conservative Beliefs," *New York Times*, Dec. 16, 1976.

423 **"the New Majority":** RR first used this term in an interview with a reporter days after Jimmy Carter's election in 1976. Jon Nordheimer, "Reagan Hints at Active Role in Shaping G.O.P. Future," *New York Times*, Nov. 5, 1976. He then began using it in speeches as well as in interviews with the press.

423 he'd scotched that option: "I will absolutely never take that job." "The Nation: Reagan 'I Don't Want Another 1964,'" *Time*, Aug. 2, 1976; "I just wasn't interested in being vice-president." *AAL*, p. 202.

423 the job was never offered: "They didn't want to offer it; it's the last thing in the world they would have done." John Sears, interview with author, Jan.

30, 2014; Ford's people "absolutely refused to discuss the possibility of picking Reagan." Lyn Nofziger, *Nofziger* (Washington, DC: Regnery, 1991), pp. 202–3.

423 **"He was turning blue"**: Darrell Trent interview, Aug. 26, 2014.

423 **"Heart attack! Give"**: Nancy Reagan, *My Turn*, p. 183.

424 **whose price tag for tuition**: "Tuition Costs Will Increase at Yale," Anne Barrett, Harvard Crimson, Jan. 26, 1977.

424 **"His income from these activities"**: Nordheimer, "Reagan Hints at Active Role."

424 **"Nobody planted the seeds"**: Stu Spencer, interview, July 21, 2014.

425 **"Folks came away with"**: "It was ingenious." Peter Hannaford, interview with author, July 18, 2014.

425 **"Lyn was someone, I suspect"**: Edwin Meese, interview with author, Dec. 9, 2014.

425 **"He was a loose cannon"**: Jim Lake interview with author, Feb. 25, 2014.

425 **"Oh, I wish he wouldn't"**: NR, quoted in Ibid.

425 **"Nancy thought of Lyn"**: Edwin Meese, interview with author, Dec. 9, 2014.; "Nancy Reagan didn't like him at all—the way he looked and acted." Sheila Tate, interview with author, Oct. 3, 2014.

425 **"He did not dress to impress"**: Carolyn Deaver, interview with author, Mar. 17, 2015.

425 **"From the very start"**: NR/MT, p. 238; "Nancy and I hit it off from the very beginning." Michael K. Deaver with Mickey Herskowitz, *Behind the Scenes* (New York: William Morrow & Co., 1987), p. 39.

425 **"In that respect, from the beginning"**: Deaver, *Behind the Scenes*, p. 47.

426 **"Mike was emotionally tied"**: Sheila Tate, interview with author, Oct. 3, 2014.

426 **"Mike had a great gift"**: Peter Hannaford, interview with author, July 18, 2014.

426 **"He babysat their son"**: George Steffes, interview with author, July 17, 2014.

426 **"I had never known anyone"**: Deaver, *Behind the Scenes*, p. 40.

426 **"He was the first priority"**: Michael Deaver, interview, MCPA, Sept. 12, 2002, p. 5.

426 **the fey, gossipy friend**: Carolyn Deaver, interview with author, Mar. 17, 2015.

427 **"had the personality"**: Nancy Clark Reynolds, quoted in Bob Colacello, *Ronnie and Nancy* (New York: Warner Bros., 2004), p. 370.

427 **"Deaver was a great piano player"**: George Steffes, interview with author, July 17, 2014.

427 **"He was her eyes and ears"**: John Sears, interview with author, Jan. 30, 2014.

427 **"One thing you learn"**: Nofziger, *Nofziger*, p. 300.

427 **"a tenacious opponent"**: Deaver, *Behind the Scenes*, p. 111.

427 **When appropriate, he gamely conspired**: "Some of it was sort of a conspiracy between the two of us." Deaver, interview, MCPA, Sept. 12, 2002, p. 16.

427 **"Deaver knew how to deal"**: James Kuhn, interview with author, Nov. 20, 2013.

427 **"she didn't trust that many"**: James Kuhn, interview with author, Oct. 1, 2014.

427 **Both men were convinced**: "By early 1978 we all thought he'd decided to run again." Nofziger, *Nofziger*, p. 221.

427 **"wouldn't rule out"**: RR, quoted in "Reagan Will Not Bar Another Try in 1980," *New York Times*, Nov. 3, 1976.

427 **"the reluctant candidate"**: AAL, pp. 203–4.

428 **"Reagan was less than"**: Richard Allen, interview with author, Aug. 14, 2014.

428 **"look-and-listen visits"**: Peter Hannaford, *The Reagans: A Political Portrait* (New York: Coward-McCann, 1983), p. 156.

428 **"We wanted to present Reagan"**: Peter Hannaford, interview with author, July 18, 2014.

428 **"And as far as I know"**: Ibid.

429 **"Those beyond this wall"**: RR, syndicated newspaper column, Dec. 18, 1978, Hoover Institution archives.

429 **"You know, Dick, we've got"**: Richard Allen, interview, MCPA, May 28, 2002, p. 32.

429 **"I liked her immediately"**: RR, quoted in AAL, p. 204.

429 **She was first and foremost**: "She was a policy wonk and, like Reagan, a political junkie." Richard Allen, interview with author, Aug. 14, 2014.

429 **"two peas in a pod"**: Peter Hannaford, interview with author, July 18, 2014; Peter Hannaford, interview, MCPA, Jan. 10, 2003, p. 60.

429 **"the challenge to diminish"**: Martin Anderson, *Revolution* (New York: Harcourt Brace Jovanovich, 1988), p. 72.

429 **"A nuclear war couldn't"**: AAL, p. 258.

430 **"I've always liked the idea"**: RR, quoted in Anderson, *Revolution*, p. 73; Peter Hannaford, interview, MCPA, Jan. 10, 2003, p. 65.

430 **closest advisers "just smiled"**: Ibid., p. 73.

430 **"whatever we may think"**: RR, address to Conservative Political Action Conference, Washington, DC, Mar. 17, 1978.

430 **"owners would have to foot"**: RR, syndicated newspaper column, October 1978, reprinted in Hannaford, *The Reagans*, p. 185.

430 **"ballot measures . . . that advanced"**: Hannaford, *The Reagans*, p. 184.

430 **"I believe interrupting a pregnancy"**: RR, interview with Lou Cannon, Oct. 15, 1979, LCA, p. 12.

430 **"There were other serious problems"**: AAL, p. 205.

431 **"Age should be the least"**: RR, quoted in Nordheimer, "Reagan Urges His Party to Save Itself."

431 **"People don't knock him"**: James Doyle, "Tales of a Reagan Field Organizer," *Newsweek*, Nov. 5, 1979, p. 53.

431 **"Love Ronald Reagan"**: Connie Steward, "Reagan Not Too Old to be President," *Los Angeles Herald-Examiner*, Aug. 30, 1979.

431 **"thirty-nine or younger"**: "I didn't feel any different or any older than I'd *always* felt." AAL, pp. 206–7.

431 **"Look, it's steady as a rock"**: Tom Mathews, "The Leading Man," *Newsweek*, Oct. 1, 1979.

431 **"The age issue is a cover"**: Hannaford, *The Reagans*, p. 194.

431 **"It was ammunition"**: John Sears, interview with author, Jan. 30, 2014.

432 **the price of gasoline**: "May the Best Man Win," *Time*, Nov. 12, 1979.

432 **"They were the essence"**: Richard Allen, interview with author, Aug. 14, 2014.

432 **"community of shared values"**: RR, speech during appearances in 1978 and 1979, quoted in Hannaford, *The Reagans*, p. 180.

432 **"the acknowledged front-runner"**: Robert Lindsay, "Reagan Urges Senate to Reject Arms Pact, But His Tone Is Softer," *New York Times*, Sept. 17, 1979, p. 39.

432 **"giving the matter serious consideration"**: RR, statement issued to press, Mar. 8, 1979, LCA.

432 **"the office seeks the man"**: "He never got off that kick." Stuart Spencer, interview, MCPA, Nov. 15, 2001, p. 34; Stuart Spencer, interview with author, July 21, 2014.

433 **"In 1980, I don't think"**: Peter Hannaford, interview, MCPA, Jan. 10, 2003, p. 69; "Most of the old '76 operation did not want him." Deaver, interview, MCPA, Sept. 12, 2002, p. 28.

433 **"And his judgment wasn't perfect"**: Peter Hannaford, interview with author, July 18, 2014.

433 **"The smartest guy"**: "He understood how to analyze people and figure out what motivates them." Charlie Black, interview with author, Feb. 25, 2014.

433 **"Sears gave Ronald Reagan"**: "I thought it was a good idea to bring Sears back." Edwin Meese, interview with author, Dec. 9, 2014; "The chief strategist had to be someone whose own base was Washington and had high credibility with the national press." Hannaford, *The Reagans*, p. 202.

433 **"the wonder boy of 1976"**: NR/MT, p. 205.

433 **"We couldn't get it together"**: Jim Lake interview with author, Feb. 25, 2014.

433 **"Sears had undisguised disdain"**: David Keene, interview with author, Oct. 23, 2014.

434 **"that fucking Sears is a disaster"**: "We heard it over and over again." Jim Lake, interview with author, Feb. 25, 2014.

434 **"Life was easier"**: John Sears, interview with author, Jan. 30, 2014.

434 **"Deaver was territorial"**: Charlie Black, interview with author, Feb. 25, 2014.

434 **"It's like an orchestra"**: "I just wanted Deaver to take a fucking seat." John Sears, interview with author, Jan. 30, 2014.

434 **"I can't put up with this"**: John Sears, quoted in Jim Lake, interview with author, Feb. 25, 2014.

435 **"Reagan didn't like it"**: Charlie Black, interview with author, Feb. 25, 2014.

435 **"I forgot that Carolyn"**: Mike Deaver, interview, July 1, 2002, LCA, p. 18.

435 **"Sears thought Meese was ineffectual"**: Jeffrey Bell, interview with author, Dec. 19, 2013.

436 **"If you are the front-runner"**: John Sears, interview with author, Jan. 30, 2014.

436 **Many of the key Reagan**: "Connally's name had been jumping at all of us for several weeks." Hannaford, *The Reagans*, p. 202; Mathews, "The Leading Man."

436 **"He's like a Chinese lunch"**: Lee Atwater, quoted in Charlie Black, interview with author, Feb. 25, 2014.

436 **His lifetime rating**: Charlie Black, interview with author, Feb. 25, 2014.

436 **"just out here waiting"**: Bob Dole, quoted in Mathews, "The Leading Man."

437 **"Reagan's impression was that Ford"**: Hannaford, *The Reagans*, p. 187.

437 **"We're the front-runner"**: John Sears, quoted in Hannaford, *The Reagans*, p. 54.

437 **"I didn't even bother"**: John Sears, interview with author, Jan. 30, 2014.

437 **"The President of the United States"**: Ibid.

438 **"There will be some kind"**: "May the Best Man Win," *Time*.

438 **Her parents had no idea**: "She had left home, and they didn't have any idea where she was." John Sears, interview with author, Jan. 30, 2014.

438 **"I disagreed with my father's politics"**: Patti Davis, *The Way I See It* (New York: G. P. Putnam's Sons, 1992), pp. 236–37.

439 **"I am here tonight"**: RR speech, Nov. 13, 1979, transcript, RRPL.

TWENTY-NINE "BIG MO"

440 **"There is a sea-change coming"**: John Connally, quoted in "May the Best Man Win," *Time*, Nov. 12, 1979.

440 **a New York Times/CBS poll**: Adam Clymer, "Reagan Off to a Fast Start Ahead of the Field," *New York Times*, Nov. 18, 1979.

440 **"I cannot doubt"**: RR, speech, Florence, SC, Jan. 24, 1980, quoted in Bernard Weinraub, "Reagan Blames Carter 'Failure' for Soviet Move," *New York Times*, Jan. 25, 1980.

441 **"We were going to win"**: Jim Lake, interview with author, Feb. 25, 2014.

441 **"He was awkward"**: James Leach, interview with author, May 15, 2013.

442 **"We could sense him"**: Charlie Black, interview with author, Feb. 25, 2014.

442 **"Why give those other guys"**: John Sears, interview with author, Jan. 30, 2014.

442 **"You've pissed off everybody":** James Kuhn, interview with author, Nov. 20, 2013.

442 **"This is not looking good":** Kenny Kling, quoted in Charlie Black, interview with author, Feb. 25, 2014.

442 **"You have just witnessed":** Tom Petit, quoted in Jim Lake, interview with author, Feb. 25, 2014; James Kuhn, interview with author, Nov. 20, 2013.

443 **"We were really shocked":** Charlie Black, interview with author, Feb. 25, 2014.

443 **"This time," he said:** Ibid.

443 **"It's in the more liberal":** Jim Lake, interview with author, Feb. 25, 2014.

445 **"He was dog tired":** Charlie Black interview, Feb. 25, 2014.

445 **The minute he hit:** "I put on the news and there was George Bush on the tarmac, snow blowing all over, press surrounding him, and all he could talk about was Big Mo! Big Mo! Big Mo!" James Kuhn, interview with author, Nov. 20, 2013.

445 **"fake pearls and real family":** Marjorie Williams, "Barbara's Backlash," *Vanity Fair*, Jan. 1, 2007.

445 **"I think women like me":** Barbara Bush, quoted in Ibid.

445 **"On the face of it":** Sheila Tate, interview with author, Oct. 3, 2014.

446 **"close to $12 million":** Wayne King, "Reagan Is Buoyed by His Victory as His Campaign Enters a Difficult Period," *New York Times*, Jan. 28, 1980.

446 **"Every night, when we returned":** NR/MT, p. 206.

446 **"He was never one":** Jim Lake, interview with author, Feb. 25, 2014.

446 **"Things started to unravel fast":** Edwin Meese, interview with author, Dec. 9, 2014.

446 **"It's like a Civil War":** Peter Hannaford, interview with author, July 18, 2014.

446 **"Sears became impatient":** Jeffrey Bell, interview with author, Dec. 19, 2013.

446 **"The chemistry between":** NR/MT, p. 205.

447 **"He's a smart guy":** Edwin Meese, interview with author, Dec. 9, 2014.

447 **"You got Lyn Nofziger":** Ibid.; Peter Hannaford, interview with author, July 18, 2014; NR/MT, p. 206.

447 **"I was sure he was going":** Ibid.

448 **"It's not a matter of whether":** Charlie Black, interview with author, Feb. 25, 2014; Jim Lake, interview with author, Feb. 25, 2014.

448 **"If Reagan lost":** Richard Allen, interview with author, Aug. 14, 2014.

449 **"We *have* to do that":** NR, quoted in Jim Lake, interview with author, Feb. 25, 2014.

449 **"You can't do this":** Bruce Rounds, quoted in Ibid.

449 **"No way you're taking":** "George Bush told me himself." Charlie Black, interview with author, Feb. 25, 2014.

450 **Bob Dole was livid:** "He was furious! Really irate." Edwin Meese, interview with author, Dec. 9, 2014; Charlie Black, interview with author, Feb. 25, 2014; Jim Lake, interview with author, Feb. 25, 2014.

450 **"Mr. Breen says that if":** Richard Allen, interview with author, Aug. 14, 2014; Peter Hannaford, interview, MCPA, Jan. 10, 2003, p. 71.

451 **"Just a minute here":** RR, quoted in Peter Goldman, "Reagan Is Back in the Saddle," *Newsweek*, Mar. 10, 1980.

451 **"Bring them chairs!":** Peter Hannaford, interview with author, July 18, 2014; Peter Hannaford, *The Reagans: A Political Portrait* (New York: Coward-McCann, 1983), p. 238.

451 **He'd heard Spencer Tracy:** Tracy shouted: "Don't you shut me off. I'm paying for this broadcast." *State of the Union*, Liberty Films—MGM, 1948.

451 **"thoroughly embarrassed himself":** Goldman, "Reagan Is Back in the Saddle."

451 **"Looking back on it":** Lou Cannon, "Bush Reagan Even as New Hampshire Finish Line Nears," *Washington Post*, Feb. 25, 1980.

452 **Reagan "handily defeated":** "At 7:09 p.m., CBS News said that Reagan had 'handily defeated' Bush." Lou Cannon, "Reagan Leading GOP Field in N.H. As Bush Stumbles," *Washington Post*, Feb. 27, 1980.

452 **"the engine of his revival":** Goldman, "Reagan Is Back in the Saddle."

452 **"We can't go on like this":** NR, quoted in Richard Allen, reading from his diary, interview with author, Aug. 14, 2014; "It was felt they were a package." Edwin Meese, interview with author, Dec. 9, 2014.

452 **"Don't bother—I quit!":** Charlie Black, interview with author, Feb. 25, 2014; Jim Lake, interview with author, Feb. 25, 2014; John Sears, interview with author, Jan. 30, 2014.

452 **When he didn't want:** "He did that on purpose." Ed Meese interview, Dec. 9, 2014.

452 **"They would ask him questions,":** Peter Hannaford, Miller Center interview, Jan. 10, 2003. p. 74.

453 **recent Gallup polls showed Ford:** "The GOP's Hamlet," *Newsweek*, Mar. 10, 1980.

453 **"Carter would lose to Ford":** Ernest Conine, "President Reagan: How Does That Sound?" *Los Angeles Times*, Mar. 17, 1980.

453 **"should pack his long johns":** RR, quoted in Hannaford, *The Reagans*, p. 244.

453 **"She was a nervous wreck":** James Kuhn, interview with author, Nov. 20, 2013.

453 **"Ford was dismissive of Reagan":** "He felt Reagan cost him the election in '76." Tom Reed, interview with author, Oct. 11, 2014.

454 **"Why Ronald Reagan Will Be":** Richard J. Whalen, "Why Ronald Reagan Will Be the Next President," *Washington Post*, Mar. 23, 1980.

454 **"Nancy and I were just":** Gary F. Schuster, "Reagan Is Quiet on His Choice for a Running Mate," *Detroit News*, Convention section, July 15, 1980.

454 **One of the contenders:** Edwin Meese, interview with author, Dec. 9, 2014.

455 **"Reagan's people have given him":** Lowell Caulfield, "Campaign Notebook," *Detroit News*, July 1, 1980.

455 **Laxalt wanted the job—badly:** "Paul *really* wanted it." Stuart Spencer, interview with author, July 21, 2014; "Laxalt really wanted it." Stuart Spencer, interview, MCPA, Nov. 15–16, 2001, p. 52.

455 **"was the governor of":** Stuart Spencer, interview, MCPA, Nov. 15–16, 2001, p. 52; "You're not a senator or a governor in that state unless you do business with Moe [Dalitz] and the boys." Spencer, interview, MCPA, Nov. 15–16, 2001, p. 53.

455 **"voodoo economics":** George Bush, speech, Carnegie Mellon University, April 10, 1980.

455 **"Doesn't matter," Stu Spencer advised:** "He spent twenty minutes dumping all over George H. W. Bush. He didn't like all those attacks, the voodoo economics." Stuart Spencer, interview with author, July 21, 2014.

455 **Ford attempted to nip:** Adam Clymer, "A State of Some Confusion: Reagan's Search for Vice-Presidential Candidate Is Vital, Crucial and Highly Important—Or Is It?" *New York Times*, July 14, 1980; "The former President (and vice president) is not interested in being the bottom half of the 1980 ticket." J. F. terHorst, "Reagan's Choice Sure to Be an Issue," *Detroit News*, July 4, 1980.

455 **"There were a sufficient number":** Edwin Meese, interview with author, Dec. 9, 2014.

456 **"Ron said that he":** Gerald Ford, quoted in Carl S. Anthony and Anna McCollister, "Ronald Reagan: The Role of a Lifetime," *George*, Feb. 1999.

456 **"was surprised when Ford":** Edwin Meese III, *With Reagan: The Inside Story* (Washington, DC: Regnery Gateway, 1992), p. 43.

456 **"The ideal Reagan running mate":** J. F. terHorst, "Reagan's Choice."

456 **"the President would be":** Theodore H. White, *America in Search of Itself* (New York: Warner Books, 1982), pp. 321–22.

456 **"It was a bad idea":** Edwin Meese, interview with author, Dec. 9, 2014.

456 **Deaver, Nofziger, and Allen:** "I vigorously opposed the Ford gesture." Michael K. Deaver with Mickey Herskowitz, *Behind the Scenes* (New York: William Morrow & Co., 1987), p. 93; Lyn Nofziger, *Nofziger* (Washington, DC: Regnery, 1991), p. 242; Richard Allen, interview with author, Aug. 14, 2014.

457 **"Ford wants Kissinger":** RR, quoted in Richard V. Allen, "George Herbert Walker Bush: The Accidental Vice President," *New York Times Magazine*, July 30, 2000.

457 **"I thought the whole thing":** "But he didn't see it that way." NR/MT, p. 211.

457 **"If I go to Washington":** Adam Clymer, "Reagan Says Bush Backs Platform; Ford Was Offered Major Authority," *New York Times*, July 17, 1980.

457 **"Get Kissinger on the phone":** RR, quoted in Deaver, *Behind the Scenes*, p. 96; Richard Allen, interview with author, Aug. 14, 2014.

457 **Meanwhile, the networks were reporting:** At 9:30 p.m., Sam Donaldson reported on ABC-TV that Reagan and Ford would appear together later that night; at 9:45, CBS's Walter Cronkite announced that Reagan and Ford were meeting to confirm; Chris Wallace reported the Reagan-Ford ticket from the floor of the convention for NBC.

457 **"realize there is no way":** RR, quoted in Allen, "George Herbert Walker Bush."

458 **"Governor," Meese reported back:** Edwin Meese, interview with author, Dec. 9, 2014.

458 **"The television was on":** James Kuhn, interview with author, Nov. 20, 2013.

458 **George Bush was in the bar:** James Leach, email to author, May 18, 2013.

459 **Ronald Reagan was on the phone:** "He said, 'I need to get George Bush on the phone,' and had Dick Wirthlin put the call through." Edwin Meese, interview with author, Dec. 9, 2014.

459 **"George," he said:** Allen, "George Herbert Walker Bush."

THIRTY: "A REFERENDUM ON UNHAPPINESS"

460 **"A Referendum on Unhappiness":** Patrick Cadell, quoted in James David Barber, "Reagan's Sheer Personal Likability Faces Its Sternest Test," *Washington Post*, Jan. 20, 1981.

460 **"Politics is just like show business":** RR to Stuart Spencer, quoted in Gerald C. Lubenow, et al., "Ronald Reagan Up Close; Off and Running," *Newsweek*, July 21, 1980.

460 **Coming out of the conventions:** "Reagan's own polls . . . show him with a 15-point lead over Carter." Frank B. Merrick, "The G.O.P. Gets Its Act Together," *Time*, July 28, 1980; Peter Goldman, "Now for the Hard Part," *Newsweek*, Aug. 25, 1980.

460 **"Carter is expected to portray":** Merrick, "The G.O.P. Gets Its Act Together."

460 **"men of narrow vision":** Jimmy Carter, speech in Miami, FL, July 1980, quoted in Ibid.

461 **Carter of "economic failures":** RR, speech to International Business Council, Chicago, Sept. 7, 1980.

461 **"I told him I didn't want":** RR, comments at Renaissance Center, July 14, 1980, quoted in Hedrick Smith, "Reagan Is Promising a Crusade to Make Nation 'Great Again,' " by *New York Times*, July 15, 1980.

461 **"intention to reestablish official government":** *Los Angeles Times*, Aug. 23, 1980.

461 **Chinese "hopping mad":** NBC *Nightly News*, transcript, Aug. 19, 1980.

461 **"retrogression . . . [that] would be detrimental":** Huang Hua, Chinese foreign minister, quoted in Howell Raines, "Reagan Abandons Plan on Taiwan Office," Sept. 26, 1980; "[The Chinese] are hopping mad." NBC *Nightly News*, Aug. 19, 1980.

461 **"a noble cause":** RR, speech to Veterans of Foreign Wars: "Peace: Restoring the Margin of Safety." "Reagan Defends Viet War," *Chicago Tribune*, Aug.

17, 1980; Lou Cannon requoted "noble cause" in Stu Spencer's interview with him, Nov. 18, 1980, LCA, p. 5.

461 **"a great many questions":** RR, speech in Dallas, Aug. 22, 1980, quoted in Robert G. Kaiser, "Reagan's First 10 Days," *Washington Post*, Aug. 28, 1980.

461 **plants and trees caused:** "He said some dumb things in speeches." Stuart Spencer, interview with author, July 21, 2014.

462 **"Now, I'm happy":** RR, speech at Michigan State Fair, Sept. 1, 1980, RRPL.

462 **"I blew it":** RR, quoted in Lou Cannon, *Reagan* (New York: G. P. Putnam's Sons, 1982), p. 274.

462 **"This was the first week":** Stu Spencer interview, July. 21, 2014.

462 **"The level of campaigning":** Stuart Spencer, interview with Lou Cannon, Nov. 18, 1980, LCA, p. 8.

463 **"If we have an uptight ship":** Ibid., p. 19.

463 **"From that day on":** Stuart Spencer, interview with author, July 21, 2014.

463 **"We may have a surprise":** Dick Wirthlin, quoted in Richard Allen, interview with author, Aug. 14, 2014.

464 **"We have heard that":** Richard Allen, interview with author, Aug. 14, 2014.

464 **For years afterward, rumors:** *Nightline*, ABC-TV, June 20, 1991, transcript (Chevy Chase, MD: Radio TV Reports, Inc., declassified May 11, 2012).

464–465 **"the only loser":** "For Many in Iowa, Carter Lost Debate," *New York Times*, Sept. 23, 1980.

465 **"an articulate fellow":** Al Pinder, publisher of *The Grinnell Herald Register*, quoted. Ibid.

465 **at the Waldorf-Astoria:** "We went around the room and everybody gave their opinion about whether he should debate [Carter] or not." Edwin Meese, interview with author, Dec. 9, 2014.

465 **"I can beat that guy":** NR/MT, p. 218.

465 **She thought not:** "She was against any kind of debate.... She's just afraid Ron was going to screw up." Cannon, Stuart Spencer, interview with Lou Cannon, Nov. 18, 1980, LCA, p. 25.

465 **"Hell, yes!" Spencer exclaimed:** Stuart Spencer, interview with author, July 21, 2014.

465 **Reagan's positions on social issues:** "All of these factors . . . have combined to produce a clear sense of uneasiness among women." Edward Walsh, "Reagan Is Still the Women's Second Choice," *Washington Post*, undated clipping, LCA.

466 **"Jimmy Carter has been":** Betty Heitman, quoted in Ibid.

466 **He was still going:** "He must have heard me 100 times say, 'Ladies?' Goddamn it, Governor!" Stuart Spencer, interview with Lou Cannon, Nov. 18, 1980, LCA, p. 31.

466 **"to one of the first":** RR, press conference in Los Angeles, Oct. 14, 1980, quoted in Cannon, *Reagan*, p. 290.

466 **"dangerous" and "scary":** "The President describes Reagan as 'dangerous' and 'scary.'" Peter

Goldman, "Two Candidates for Reform," *Newsweek*, Oct. 20, 1980.

467 **"first and foremost is":** RR, speech, CBS-TV, transcript, Oct. 18, 1980; Douglas E. Kneeland, "Reagan Calls Peace His First Objective in Address to Nation," *New York Times*, Oct. 19, 1980.

467 **But twelve days before:** A Harris poll gave Reagan a lead of 4 percent, a Roper poll only 1 percent; Goldman, "Two Candidates for Reform."

467 **"a narrowing lead":** "New Poll Says Reagan Holds Narrowing Lead," Associated Press, Oct. 30, 1980.

467 **"Let's see what the polls are":** Richard Bergholz and Eleanor Randolph, "Carter Challenges Reagan to Debate Him," *Los Angeles Times*, Oct. 16, 1980.

467 **In his hotel room:** "He was very loose in the hotel room. Mike and I brought him a big bottle of red wine." Ibid.

468 **"I've been on the same stage":** RR, quoted in Bill Stall, *Los Angeles Times* pool report #3, Oct. 28, 1980, LCA.

468 **"extremely dangerous" attitude:** "Debate Between President Jimmy Carter and Governor Ronald Reagan," Oct. 28, 1980, transcript (Cleveland: Fincun-Mancini Court Reporters).

468 **"We doubt that it swung":** Editorial, "A Good Look at the Candidates," *Los Angeles Times*, Oct. 30, 1980; "Initial polls rated their performance as close to even or gave a modest edge to Mr. Reagan." Hedrick Smith, "Carter and Reagan Express Confidence on Debate Showing," *New York Times*, Oct. 30, 1980.

468 **Reagan "genial, open":** Editorial, "A Good Look at the Candidates."

468 **at times "very reassuring":** Smith, "Carter and Reagan Express Confidence."

468 **"intense almost to the point":** Editorial, "A Good Look at the Candidates."

468 **but "more informed":** Smith, "Carter and Reagan Express Confidence."

468 **Twelve cities in three days:** Reagan & Bush Committee News Release, "Schedule of Governor Ronald Reagan: October 30–November 4, 1980," Oct. 29, 1980, LCA.

468 **"We were relatively confident":** Ed Meese interview, Dec. 9, 1980.

469 **"I don't talk like that!":** RR, quoted in Stuart Spencer, interview with author, July 21, 2014.

469 **wryly to "the Meesecase":** "There were piles and piles of material in Ed's garage." Richard Allen, interview with author, Aug. 14, 2014.

469 **"No, Mike's a number-two":** RR, quoted in Stuart Spencer, interview with author, July 21, 2014.

470 **When they landed, Nancy prodded:** "Ronnie! Jim is getting off the plane. Now is the time to talk to him." NR, quoted in Richard Allen, interview with author, Aug. 14, 2014.

470 **predicting "a landslide":** "It's a landslide, don't worry about it." Neil Reagan, interview, UCLA Center for Oral History Research, June 25, 1981, p. 55.

470 offered "Cautiously optimistic": NR, quoted in "Election Day Pool Report," Nov. 4, 1980, LCA.

471 Nancy recalled that: NR/MT, p. 221.

471 John Chancellor was calling: Theodore H. White, *America in Search of Itself* (New York: Warner Books, 1982), pp. 407–8.

471 He reassured Marion Jorgensen: "The minute Ronnie became president, I called him 'Mr. President.' And he said . . . 'Not with you, my friend.' " Bob Colacello, *Ronnie and Nancy* (New York: Warner Bros., 2004), p. 505.

THIRTY-ONE: "THE O AND W"

475 "The governor of a state": Tip O'Neill, quoted in Peter Goldman et al., "Hail the Conquering Hero," *Newsweek*, Dec. 1, 1980.

475 "nothing less than a miracle": RR, inaugural address, Jan. 20, 1981, reprinted in *New York Times*, Jan. 21, 1981.

475 Ronald Reagan had been looped: "Carter was pretty honorable, and we got briefings on a regular basis." Edwin Meese, interview with author, Dec. 9, 2014; Richard Allen, interview with author, Aug. 14, 2014.

476 "Shitheels!" he muttered: Ken Khachigian, notes, Jan. 18, 1981, Ken Khachigian Papers, 1981, Inaugural, Box 1, p. 2, RRPL.

476 word drifted in: Haynes Johnson, "Freed Americans Land in W. Germany; Reagan Sworn In as the 40th President," *Washington Post*, Jan. 21, 1981.

476 "[Carter] said hardly": "It must have been very hard on him." AAL, pp. 225–26.

477 Preston Hotchkis, a California land: Mary Lou Loper, "A Favorite Quote Becomes History," *Los Angeles Times*, Jan. 26, 1981.

477 "America must win": RR, inaugural address, Jan. 20, 1981, transcript, the American Presidency Project, University of California, Santa Barbara; "An Obscure Hero Gets Big Tribute," *Chicago Tribune*, Jan. 21, 1981.

477 "Since the last one": Ken Khachigian, interview with author, Nov. 19, 2013.

477 "It's too good a story": Ibid.; "He still wanted to use the name." "Meeting with Governor Reagan, 1/18/1981, Blair House," Ken Khachigian Papers, 1981, Inaugural, Box 1, RRPL.

478 "Ron might be softening": Ken Khachigian, interview with author, Nov. 19, 2013.

478 and not just any Bible: "The family Bible . . . bears Mrs. Reagan's notation for 'a thought for today,' reading: 'You can be too big for God to use, but you cannot be too small.' " "Oath on the Bible Used by Reagan's Mother," *New York Times*, Jan. 21, 1981.

479 Inauspiciously, Frank Sinatra's seat: Peter McCoy, interview with author, Oct. 23, 2014.

479 "Wheels up in Tehran": "I handed him the slip of paper that came from the Sit Room." Richard Allen, interview with author, Aug. 14, 2014.

479 "Some thirty minutes ago": Lee Lescaze, "Hostage Release Opens Presidency on a Dramatic High Note," *Washington Post*, Jan. 21, 1981.

479 "You tell those bastards": Richard Allen, interview with author, Aug. 14, 2014.

480 "I'm the President": Michael Reagan, *On the Outside Looking In* (New York: Zebra Books, 1988), p. 188.

480 Portraits of Thomas Jefferson: Ken Khachigian handwritten notes, first Cabinet meeting, Jan. 22, 1981, Ken Khachigian Papers, Box 1, RRPL.

481 "When you need some energy": Lee Lescaze, "The First Full Day in the Oval Office; Concern for the Economy," *Washington Post*, Jan. 22, 1981.

481 "He made no pretense": Robert McFarlane, interview with author, Sept. 30, 2014.

481 "had their own ideas": Edwin Meese, interview with author, Mar. 18, 2015.

481 He knew that Henry Kissinger: "I understand that Kissinger is not under consideration." Richard Nixon, memo to RR, Nov. 17, 1980, p. 3, RRPL; "Ronald Reagan knew Kissinger was really the architect of foreign policy of the Nixon administration and wanted to go in a different direction." Edwin Meese, interview with author, Mar. 18, 2015.

482 "That'd be a big mistake": Richard Nixon, quoted in Richard Allen, interview with author, Aug. 14, 2014.

482 "a very bright, energetic": "I didn't feel Haig was a good choice for State." Richard Allen, interview with author, Aug. 14, 2014.

482 "Before, Al was unflappable": John Lehman, interview with author, Sept. 16, 2014.

482 "Those who oppose him": "He is intelligent, strong, and generally shares your views on foreign policy." Nixon, memo to RR, Nov. 17, 1980, p. 3, RRPL.

482 "The guy came out": "When [Haig] left, Reagan said, 'I don't understand what that was all about.' " Richard Allen, interview with author, Aug. 14, 2014.

482 Reagan had been flirting: "The Kitchen Cabinet included a bunch of ignoramuses who said, 'What do you do—ask him to leave a Cabinet meeting when you're discussing domestic policy?' " Richard Perle, interview with author, Apr. 25, 2015.

483 shultz a "candy-ass": Richard Nixon, quoted in Theodore H. White, *Breach of Faith: The Fall of Richard Nixon* (New York: Atheneum, 1975), p. 316.

483 "I do not believe": Nixon, memo to RR, Nov. 17, 1980, RRPL, p. 5.

483 Nixon was "very persuasive": Edwin Meese, interview with author, Mar. 18, 2015.

483 "Why, this memorandum means": James Baker, quoted in Richard Allen, interview with author, Aug. 14, 2014.

483 From what he could tell: "He wanted, literally, control of everything." Baker, quoted in Allen.

483 The idea that one person: Edwin Meese, interview with author, Mar. 18, 2015.

484 **"A lot of fairly"**: Fred Fielding, interview with author, Sept. 30, 2014.

484 **his nomination "disastrous"**: Peter Goldman et al., "Reagan's Finishing Touches," *Newsweek*, Jan. 5, 1981.

485 **"Everyone was prepared"**: Richard Allen, interview with author, Aug. 14, 2014.

485 **"Reagan's genius was"**: Kenneth Duberstein, interview with author, June 16, 2014.

485 **"It was smooth"**: Edwin Meese, interview with author, Mar. 18, 2015.

485 **"Really, they were always"**: Fred Fielding, interview with author, Sept. 30, 2014.

485 **"got totally entranced by power"**: "Mike really changed when he came to Washington. Power was of primary importance to him." Edwin Meese, interview with author, Mar. 18, 2015.

486 **"The Roosevelt Room was a mess"**: Peter McCoy, interview with author, Oct. 23, 2014.

486 **"It's not like we left"**: Jody Powell, quoted in Sheila Tate, interview with author, Oct. 3, 2014.

486 **"This place needs *everything*"**: NR, quoted in Peter McCoy, interview with author, Oct. 23, 2014.

486 **the "O and W"** Phil McCombs, "Sunshine and Reign in Reagan Country," *Washington Post*, Dec. 30, 1980.

486 **"The country is in the worst"**: "Transcript of Reagan Address Reporting on the State of the Nation's Economy," *New York Times*, Feb. 6, 1981.

486 **In the past two years:** Leonard Silk, "A Look at Reagan Economics 'Lesson,' " *New York Times*, Feb. 7, 1981.

487 **"a quarter, a dime, and a penny"**: "Transcript of Reagan Address," *New York Times*.

487 **The prime bank rate:** George J. Church, "The Biggest Challenge," *Time*, Jan. 18, 1981.

487 **the Dow Jones Industrial Average:** Vartanig G. Vartan, "Dow Falls 15.10 Points to 932.17," *New York Times*, Feb. 3, 1981.

487 **"We've got to get control"**: Lee Lescaze, "The First Full Day in the Oval Office," *Washington Post*, Jan. 22, 1981.

487 **The deficit for fiscal 1981:** Peter Behr and Lee Lescaze, "Reagan Economists Urge Swift Spending, Tax Cuts," *Washington Post*, Jan. 8, 1981.

487 **He ordered a federal:** Church, "The Biggest Challenge."

487 **"let the people flourish"**: "Here we are, a country bursting with economic promise." Ronald Reagan, *Speaking My Mind* (New York: Simon & Schuster, 1989), p. 75.

487 **"A tax cut not only increases"**: Jude Wanniski, "It's Time to Cut Taxes," *Wall Street Journal*, Dec. 11, 1974.

488 **From Keynesian John:** Galbraith and Feldstein are both quoted in Charles Alexander and David Beckwith, "Making It Work," *Time*, Nov. 21, 1981.

488 **"This tax program is not"**: RR, Cabinet meeting, Feb. 10, 1981, transcript, p. 2, Speechwriting Papers, White House Office, 1981–89, Box 3, RRPL.

489 **All told, analysts projected:** Lou Cannon, *Reagan* (New York: G. P. Putnam's Sons, 1982), p. 337.

489 **"We were not headed toward"**: David Stockman, *The Triumph of Politics: How the Reagan Revolution Failed*(New York: Harper & Row, 1986), p. 396.

489 **"Virtually everything I did"**: NR/MT, p. 23.

490 **$25,000 beaded gowns:** KK/NR, p. 273.

490 **One of the hottest-selling:** Donnie Radcliffe, "Queen Nancy," *Washington Post*, Sept. 8, 1981.

490 **"We had a huge"**: Sheila Tate, interview with author, Oct. 3, 2014.

490 **"She was a target"**: Peter McCoy, interview with author, Oct. 23, 2014.

490 **"There are times when"**: Sheila Tate, interview with author, Oct. 3, 2014: NR/MT, p. 23.

490 **"a bum rap"**: AAL, p. 244.

490 **"Dammit," he fumed:** "I never understood or got used to the sniping at her." AAL, p. 389.

490 **"Helen von Damm, explained"**: Helene von Damm, *At Reagan's Side: Twenty Years in the Political Mainstream* (New York: Doubleday, 1989), p. 71.

491 **"she is tougher on people"**: Michael K. Deaver with Mickey Herskowitz, *Behind the Scenes* (New York: William Morrow & Co., 1987), p. 110.

491 **"as the Invisible Hand"**: Ibid., p. 113.

491 **In the Troika:** "In the White House, it was always Baker and Deaver against Meese." Richard Allen, interview with author, Aug. 14, 2014; "Unfortunately, I think that was the case. Jim's people would be leaking stuff negative to me during the first term." Edwin Meese, interview with author, Dec. 9, 2014.

491 **"Ronnie's biggest mistake"**: "If Ronnie had given him the green light, Haig would have bombed everybody and everything." NR/MT, p. 242.

492 **variously "the beasts"**: "He'd say 'the beasts' were keeping him from the president." Richard Allen, interview with author, Aug. 14, 2014.

492 **"second-rate hambones"**: Al Haig, quoted in Lou Cannon, *President Reagan: The Role of a Lifetime* (New York: Simon & Schuster, 1991), p. 195.

492 **"Al would come back"**: Robert McFarlane, interview with author, Sept. 30, 2014.

492 **"And he considered Reagan"**: Richard Allen, interview with author, Aug. 14, 2014; "Deep down inside, he always thought he was smarter than RR. That was his fatal conceit." Edwin Meese, interview with author, Mar. 18, 2015.

492 **He'd returned from a Cabinet:** Edwin Meese, interview with author, Mar. 18, 2015.

492 **"He was very upset"**: AAL, p. 254.

492 **was "utterly paranoid"**: Ibid., p. 361.

492 **"The man is dangerous"**: *Gainesville Sun*, blind-quoted in Richard Reeves, *President Reagan: The Triumph of Imagination* (New York: Simon & Schuster, 2005), p. 32.

493 **"Right after the inauguration"**: Robert McFarlane, interview with author, Nov. 11, 2014.

493 **Jim Baker and Ed Meese:** "He alienated Baker and Meese in the process." Robert McFarlane, interview with author, Oct. 15, 2014.

493 **"Give me the word":** Michael Deaver, interview with Lou Cannon, Nov. 15, 1988, LCA; NR/MT, p. 242.

493 **"We could pave":** RR, quoted in Ronnie Dugger, *On Reagan: The Man and His Presidency* (New York: McGraw-Hill, 1983), p. 344.

493 **"one is the smooth-talking":** Lou Cannon, "The Haig Problem," *Washington Post*, July 7, 1981.

494 **"not only once, but twice":** Al Haig, quoted in Cannon, *Reagan*, p. 395.

THIRTY-TWO: SURVIVAL OF THE FITTEST

495 **Those damn House Democrats:** Edward Cowan, "Split Grows in House on Tax Cuts," *New York Times*, Mar. 30, 1981.

495 **National business bankruptcies:** "The Economy," *New York Times*, Mar. 30, 1981.

495 **Leaders of the nation's colleges:** Edward B. Fiske, "College Officials Push for Alternatives to Student-Aid Cuts Asked by Reagan," *New York Times*, Mar. 20, 1981.

495 **And the Soviets:** Anthony Austin, "Soviet Accuses Union of Seeking Control of Poland," *New York Times*, Mar. 30, 1981.

496 **"This was going to be":** Edwin Meese, interview with author, Mar. 18, 2015.

496 **Even Jim Brady:** "Larry Speakes was supposed to go." David Prosperi, interview with author, Sept. 24, 2014.

496 **The weather was overcast:** Weather for Mar. 30, 1981, wunderground.com.

496 **"Look, buster, you lay":** RR, speech, Mar. 30, 1981, quoted in Richard Reeves, *President Reagan: The Triumph of Imagination* (New York: Simon & Schuster, 2005), p. 33.

496 **The crowd, about two hundred:** "Report on the Performance of the U.S. Dept. of the Treasury in Connection with the March 30, 1981, Assassination Attempt on President Ronald Reagan," July 2, 1981, p. 9, RRPA, Edwin Meese files, Box 1.

496 **"I grabbed Jim Brady":** Michael Deaver, interview, MCPA, Sept. 12, 2002, p. 51.

497 **Not to be upstaged:** "Judy Woodruff came up to me and said, 'Can you escort me up to talk to Jim?'" David Prosperi, interview with author, Sept. 24, 2014.

497 **"I sort of knew":** Liam Stack, "Jerry Parr, Secret Service Agent Who Helped Save Reagan, Dies at 85," *New York Times*, Oct. 10, 2015.

497 **"What the hell's that?":** RR, quoted by Jerry Parr, in Reeves, *President Reagan*, p. 34.

497 **"Jerry," he begged:** AAL, pp. 259–60.

497 **"No matter how hard":** Ronald Reagan, *The Reagan Diaries: January 1981–October 1985*, ed. Douglas Brinkley (New York: Harper, 2009), pp. 30–31.

498 **But when he saw:** "There was blood coming from his mouth and it was bright red." Jerry Parr, quoted in "Agent Says He Knew Reagan Had a Lung Wound," *New York Times*, Apr. 3, 1981.

498 **"Jim was in bad shape":** David Prosperi, interview with author, Sept. 24, 2014.

499 **"The presidential motorcade":** John Pekkanen, "The Saving of the President," *The Washingtonian*, Aug. 5, 2014.

499 **"I'll walk in":** Reeves, *President Reagan*, p. 35.

499 **"Reagan had a habit":** Michael Deaver, interview, MCPA, Sept. 12, 2002, p. 51.

499 **He cut a strapping figure:** "I put on a brand-new blue suit for my speech." AAL, p. 259.

499 **As he pushed through:** Susan Okie, "Reagan's Risk May Have Been Much Greater Than Believed," *Washington Post*, Apr. 2, 1981.

499 **"Trauma team to the emergency room":** Joanne Bell, interview with author, June 19, 2015.

499 **"I feel so bad":** Pekkanen, "The Saving of the President."

499 **"You're ruining my suit!":** RR, quoted in Lyn Nofziger, interview, MCPA, Mar. 6, 2003, p. 42.

499 **lying naked as a jaybird:** "By the time we got to the emergency room he didn't have a stitch of clothing on him." Michael Deaver, interview, MCPA, Sept. 12, 2002, p. 51.

499 **"It was an unforgettable sight":** Robert Roubik, interview with author, June 2, 2015.

500 **She left the affair early:** "Something had been bothering Mrs. Reagan—she didn't seem sick, just anxious and unsettled." Del Quentin Wilber, *Rawhide Down: The Near Assassination of Ronald Reagan* (New York: Henry Holt, 2011), p. 102.

500 **"The police radio is saying":** Sheila Tate, interview with author, Oct. 3, 2014.

500 **One of the Secret Service:** Peter McCoy, interview with author, Oct. 23, 2014.

500 **"I'm going to that hospital!":** NR/MT, p. 3; italics added based on Sheila Tate, interview with author, Oct. 23, 2014.

500 **"If you were to call":** Robert Roubik, interview with author, June 2, 2015.

501 **Neither of them was:** Joanne Bell, interview with author, June 19, 2015.

501 **"That day, everyone's blood pressure":** Joanne Bell, interview with author, June 19, 2015.

501 **"Can anybody tell me":** Wesley Price, quoted in Pekkanen, "The Saving of the President."

501 **"Look, Bill," Price said:** Robert Roubik, interview with author, June 2, 2015.

501 **"The amount of noise":** Ibid.

502 **"Am I dying?":** Wilber, *Rawhide Down*, pp. 109–10.

502 **After clearing the corridors:** "Young staffers were parading around crying, 'Oh my God, the President's been shot.' We didn't have all the information at the time." Richard Allen, interview with author, Aug. 14, 2014.

503 *"George, it's Al—turn around"*: Richard V. Allen, "The Day Reagan Was Shot," The *Atlantic Monthly*, April 2001.

503 **"sat against the wall"**: Richard Allen, interview with author, Aug. 14, 2014.

503 **"Nobody in the Sit Room"**: Fred Fielding, interview with author, Sept. 30, 2014.

503 **"two minutes closer"**: Caspar Weinberger, quoted in declassified top-secret transcript, Mar. 30, 1981, Richard V. Allen Papers, RRPL, p. 23.

503 **"We determined it was eight"**: Richard Allen, interview with author, Aug. 14, 2014.

504 **As a result, Weinberger increased:** "I then told General Jones that we should increase the alert for the Strategic Air Command forces." Caspar Weinberger, *Fighting for Peace* (New York: Warner Books, 1990), p. 87.

504 **The president, if he felt:** "It is being prepared right now." Caspar Weinberger, quoted in declassified top-secret transcript, Mar. 30, 1981, p. 16.

504 **But the president was currently:** David Gergen, quoted in declassified top-secret transcript, Mar. 30, 1981, p. 16.

504 **And at 3:25 p.m.:** Tom Mathews, "Reagan's Close Call," *Newsweek*, Apr. 13, 1981.

504 **"The helm is right here"**: Alexander Haig, quoted in declassified top-secret transcript, Mar. 30, 1981, p. 16.

504 **accordingly "Fuck you!"**: "We rolled our eyes and just went: 'Fuck you!'" Richard Allen, interview with author, Aug. 14, 2014.

504 **"blood in the pleural cavity"**: Herbert L. Abrams, *"The President Has Been Shot"* (New York: W. W. Norton, 1992), p. 61.

504 **"The President's blood pressure"**: Joseph Giordano, "How We Saved Reagan's Life," *Newsweek*, Mar. 13, 2011; Rachel Muir, "Saving the President," *GW Today* (website), gwtoday.gwu.edu.

504 **"'Where do we go'"**: "They were remarkably calm." Robert Roubik, interview with author, June 2, 2015.

505 **"Ronnie looked pale and gray"**: NR/MT, p. 6.

505 **CT scans of Brady's brain:** Pekkanen, "The Saving of the President."

505 **Known as a Devastator:** "Mr. Hinckley fired six shots with a .22-caliber revolver loaded with explosive bullets called Devastators." "'Six Shots': A Presidential Assassin Fails—Just Barely," *New York Times*, Apr. 5, 1981.

505 **"We are *not* going to"**: Arthur Kobrine, quoted in Robert Roubik, interview with author, June 2, 2015.

505 **"Who's minding the store?"**: RR, quoted in Lyn Nofziger, interview, MCPA, p. 42; Edwin Meese, interview with author, Mar. 18, 2015; James Baker, quoted in Weinberger, *Fighting for Peace*, p. 93.

505 **"He looked terrible, pale"**: Edwin Meese, interview with author, Mar. 18, 2015.

506 **Certainly the surgeon, Ben Aaron:** "He didn't want to be wheeling a 70-year-old patient who was in shock into the operating room for chest surgery." Pekkanen, "The Saving of the President."

506 **led by "extremely aggressive"**: Joanne Bell, interview with author, June 19, 2015.

506 **CBS was the first:** "Dan Rather reported on television that Jim Brady had died from his wounds." Weinberger, *Fighting for Peace*, p. 92.

506 **Bill Plante, the ABC News:** "He saw me nod my head affirmatively and took that as confirmation that Jim had died." David Prosperi, interview with author, Sept. 24, 2014.

506 **Howard Baker, the Senate:** "Here it is: Howard Baker announced that Jim Brady is dead." Declassified top-secret transcript, tape 3, Mar. 30, 1981, Richard V. Allen Papers, RRPL.

506 **Dick Allen was infuriated:** "Gergen would come into the Sit Room from time to time, and then he would leave. I knew he was leaking." Richard Allen, interview with author, Aug. 14, 2014.

507 **"He's making a mess"**: Al Haig, quoted in Ibid.

507 **"Who's running the government"**: Larry Speakes with Robert Pack, *Speaking Out* (New York: Chas. Scribner's Sons, 1988), p. 7; Alexander M. Haig, Jr., *Caveat: Realism, Reagan and Foreign Policy* (New York: Macmillan, 1984), p. 159.

507 **"This is very bad"**: Richard Allen and Alexander Haig, quoted in declassified top-secret transcript, Mar. 30, 1981, Richard V. Allen Papers, RRPL, p. 16.

507 **"We've got to get"**: Ibid., tape 2, p. 26.

507 **"He started to quiver"**: Richard Allen, interview with author, Aug. 14, 2014.

507 **"Constitutionally, gentlemen, you have"**: Alexander Haig, quoted in declassified top-secret transcript, tape 2, p. 14, Mar. 30, 1981, tape 2, p. 26, Richard V. Allen Papers, RRPL.

507 **"What's this all about?"**: Donald Regan, quoted in Richard V. Allen, "When Reagan Was Shot, Who Was 'In Control' at the White House?" *Washington Post*, Mar. 25, 2011.

508 **Cap Weinberger very calmly announced:** "He said that I should read the Constitution." Weinberger, *Fighting for Peace*, pp. 89–90; Richard Allen, interview with author, Aug. 14, 2014.

508 **"They were not getting"**: Edwin Meese, interview with author, Mar. 18, 2015.

509 **"Please tell me"**: Pekkanen, "The Saving of the President"; Giordano, "How We Saved Reagan's Life."

509 **"He didn't look much different"**: Robert Roubik, interview with author, June 2, 2015.

509 **"a physique like"**: Max Friedersdorf, interview, MCPA, Oct. 24, 2002, p. 61.

510 **"I've got it!"**: Wilber, *Rawhide Down*, p. 184.

510 **"We are not going"**: Arthur Kobrine, quoted in Robert Roubik, interview with author, June 2, 2015.

510 **Heartbroken, Allen picked up:** Richard Allen, interview with author, Aug. 14, 2014.

510 **he grew groggy:** "About 8 p.m. the President experienced pain and was given morphine." Pekkanen, "The Saving of the President."

511 **"Am I alive?" he wrote:** Ibid.

511 **"All in all, I'd rather":** "Seriously, Folks . . ." *Time,* Apr. 13, 1981.

511 **"I'd like to do this scene":** Michael K. Deaver with Mickey Herskowitz, *Behind the Scenes* (New York: William Morrow & Co., 1987), p. 23.

511 **Joanne Bell, the change nurse:** "The Secret Service had told me, 'Do not tell him anyone else was hurt.'" Joanne Bell, interview with author, June 19, 2015.

511 **"deranged loner," as far:** "The President's Close Call," *Newsweek,* Apr. 13, 1981.

511 **"a friend of mine":** John Hinckley, quoted in Wilber, *Rawhide Down,* p. 128.

512 **"Jodie," he had scrawled:** "John Hinckley's Last Love Letter to Jodie Foster," *Newsweek,* Apr. 13, 1981.

512 **"Let the machine breathe":** Joanne Bell, interview with author, June 19, 2015.

512 **"This is it . . .":** Pekkanen, "The Saving of the President."

512 **"What was that guy's beef?":** Wilber, *Rawhide Down,* p. 210.

513 **"Mr. President," she said:** Joanne Bell, interview with author, June 19, 2015.

513 **"What makes you think":** Reeves, *President Reagan,* p. 44.

513 **"It was the first:** Kenneth Duberstein, interview with author, June 16, 2014.

514 **"a great big burly bear":** "Tip O'Neill was pretty brusque." Max Friedersdorf, interview, MCPA, Oct. 24, 2002, p. 59.

THIRTY-THREE: CRACKS IN THE FOUNDATION

515 **Following the assassination attempt:** An NBC/Associated Press poll reported RR's favorable rating at 77 percent. White House News Survey, Apr. 18, 1981, RRPL.

515 **Even reluctant Democrats began edging:** Among Democrats his approval rating was 64 percent. Ibid.

515 **"That reception," he joked:** AAL, p. 285.

516 **"In order to win in the House":** Kenneth Duberstein, interview with author, June 16, 2014.

516 **"I'd been handed a steamin' turd":** Richard Allen, interview with author, Aug. 14, 2014; "AWACS was a stone that came down the Hill on top of us." Max Friedersdorf, interview, MCPA, Oct. 24, 2002, p. 66.

516 **"the Saudis, who were notoriously":** Max Friedersdorf, interview, MCPA, Oct. 24, 2002, p. 66.

516 **An early loose poll:** Ibid.

516 **"Totally hopeless" was how:** Ibid., p. 67.

516 **"We pulled out all the stops":** Edwin Meese, interview with author, Apr. 24, 2015.

516–517 **The president leveraged his support:** Kenneth Duberstein, interview with author, Oct. 1, 2014.

517 **"reminding Heflin that the Bible":** Richard Reeves, *President Reagan: The Triumph of Imagination* (New York: Simon & Schuster, 2005), pp. 94–95.

517 **"Now Ronnie, you remember":** Max Friedersdorf, interview, MCPA, Oct. 24, 2002, p. 67.

517 **Four rabbis appeared:** "AIPAC is making all sort of religious bigotry remarks up here." Warren Rudman, quoted in Ibid., p. 68.

517 **"It is not the business":** "Ron to Israel: Butt Out—Raps Jewish Anti-AWACS Lobby," *New York Daily News,* Oct. 2, 1981.

517 **"It was my job to bring":** Richard Allen, interview with author, Aug. 14, 2014.

517 **"His philosophical approach":** Jim Wright, quoted in Laurence Barrett, *Gambling with History: Reagan in the White House* (New York: Doubleday, 1983), p. 15.

518 **"The President has become a hero":** Tip O'Neill, quoted in John A. Farrell, *Tip O'Neill and the Democratic Century* (Boston: Little, Brown, 2001), p. 556.

518 **But in mid-May:** David E. Rosenbaum, "First Major Cuts in Social Security Proposed in Detailed Reagan Plan," *New York Times* date?

518 **He had been told:** Lou Cannon, *President Reagan: The Role of a Lifetime* (New York: Simon & Schuster, 1991), p. 804.

518 **"The president primarily wanted":** Edwin Meese, interview with author, Apr. 24, 2015.

519 **"A woman's so-called right":** Ibid.

519 **O'Connor was personally against:** Reeves, *President Reagan,* p. 74.

519 **"she was a woman of great":** AAL, p. 280.

520 **"Dammit," he fumed:** RR, quoted at Cabinet meeting, July 7, 1981, in handwritten notes taken by David Gergen, David Gergen Papers, Box 1, RRPL.

520 **"too few people working":** RR, letter to Robert E. Poli, Oct. 20, 1980, David Gergen Papers, Box 1, RRPL.

520 **But Drew Lewis reported:** "Drew says they're overstaffed now." Notations ascribed to Drew Lewis by David Gergen, written in the margins of the Poli letter, Ibid.

520 **the FAA proposed $50 million:** Craig Fuller, "Memorandum for the President," June 18, 1981, David Gergen Papers, Box 1, RRPL.

520 **"The foremost factor in the front":** Edwin Meese, interview with author, Apr. 24, 2015.

520–521 **"desertion in the face of duty":** RR, quoted at Cabinet meeting, July 7, 1981, Gergen notes.

521 **"her appointment would cause":** Memorandum, "Congressional Telephone Calls," July 7, 1981, Max Friedersdorf Papers, RRPL.

521 **In particular, they protested:** Phil Gailey, "Reagan Accused of Betraying Right," *Washington Star,* July 10, 1981.

521 **"the bête noire of pro-family":** Michael Uhlmann, White House memo to Edwin Meese, "Candidacy

of Judge O'Connor for the Supreme Court," July 6, 1981, Edwin Meese Papers, Box 57, RRPL.

521 **"the best thing he's done"**: Tip O'Neill, quoted in *Newsweek*, July 20, 1981.

521 **"Every good Christian ought"**: Barry Goldwater, quoted in Reeves, *President Reagan*, p. 75.

522 **But Reagan believed that**: "All we are asking is that the Constitution be interpreted, as I believe it really reads, to say that if someone wants to have prayer in school, they can have prayer in school." Thomas Plate, "Reagan on the American Family," *Family Weekly*, June 1984.

522 **"practiced and revered"**: RR, president's weekly radio address, Feb. 25, 1984, RRPL.

522 **"faith in a Creator"**: Howell Raines, "Reagan Endorses Voluntary Prayer," *New York Times*, May 7, 1982.

522 **"Our strategic forces were growing"**: AAL, p. 205.

522 **"There was a perception"**: John Lehman, interview with author, Oct. 16, 2014.

522 **The Air Force claimed**: Richard Perle, interview with author, Apr. 25, 2015.

523 **"a one-way street"**: RR, press conference, Jan. 29, 1981, transcript, RRPL.

523 **"would be of great benefit"**: Lou Cannon, "Arms Boost Seen as Strain on Soviets," *Washington Post*, June 19, 1980.

523 **"I wanted to let him know"**: AAL, p. 270.

523 **"Reagan had looked"**: Richard Allen, interview with author, Aug. 14, 2014.

524 **Al Haig called it "naïve"**: quoted in Cannon, *President Reagan*, p. 301.

524 **"it was crazy"**: Richard Allen, interview with author, Aug. 14, 2014.

524 **"This isn't what I had written"**: RR and Mike Deaver, quoted in Deborah Hart Strober and Gerald S. Strober, *Reagan: The Man and His Presidency* (Boston: Houghton Mifflin, 1998), p. 116.

524 **"Ronald Reagan loved it"**: Richard Perle, interview with author, Apr. 24, 2015.

524 **"a frivolous propaganda exercise"**: Alexander M. Haig, Jr., *Caveat: Realism, Reagan and Foreign Policy* (New York: Macmillan, 1984), p. 229.

524 **"still the greatest guarantor"**: Al Haig, interview with Lou Cannon, June 6, 1989, LCA, Box 23, Folder 2, p. 4.

525 **"I remember one meeting"**: Richard Perle, interview with author, Apr. 24, 2015.

525 **"They cannot fly"**: Robert Poli, quoted in *Los Angeles Times*, July 15, 1981.

525 **"If passengers are killed"**: Robert Poli, quoted in "Who Controls the Air?" *Newsweek*, Aug. 17, 1981.

525 **"I must tell those"**: Ronald Reagan, "Statement Before the Press," Aug. 3, 1981, transcript, David Gergen Papers, Box 1, RRPL; Howell Raines, "Reagan Warns Controllers to Return or Face Dismissal," *New York Times*, Aug. 4, 1981.

525 **A federal judge in Brooklyn**: Joseph B. Treaster, "Crowds and Confusion Are Easing as Delays at Airports Are Reduced," *New York Times*, Aug. 5, 1981.

525 **"The weekend before the strike"**: Edwin Meese, interview with author, Apr. 24, 2015.

525 **"I'm doing the right thing"**: Fred Fielding, interview with author, Sept. 30, 2014.

526 **A Gallup poll**: "Who Controls the Air?" *Newsweek*.

526 **"The message is getting around"**: David Broder column, *Washington Post*, Aug. 9, 1981.

526 **Qaddafi "a madman"**: "Qaddafi was an unpredictable fanatic." AAL, pp. 280–81.

526 **"You can follow them"**: RR, quoted in Edwin Meese, interview with author, Apr. 24, 2015.

527 **"Let's make sure we have"**: Ibid.

527 **"He made a serious mistake"**: NR/MT, p. 241.

527 **"Meese's decision not to notify"**: *Washington Post*, Aug. 18, 1981.

527 **"The balanced budget is long gone"**: William Greider, "The Education of David Stockman," *The Atlantic Monthly*, Dec. 1, 1981.

528 **"Federal interest rates soared"**: Nicole Lewis, "Did Ronald Reagan's Tax Cut Super-Charge the Economy?" "Fact-Checker" column, *Washington Post*, Nov. 8, 2017.

528 **"A slight one"**: *Washington Post*, Oct. 22, 1981.

528 **"your ass is in a sling"**: Jim Baker, quoted in David Stockman, *The Triumph of Politics: Why the Reagan Revolution Failed* (New York: Harper & Row, 1986), p. 4.

528 **"I urged the president"**: Edwin Meese, interview with author, Apr. 24, 2015.

528 **He regularly undercut Haig**: Lou Cannon, *Reagan* (New York: G. P. Putnam's Sons, 1982), p. 395.

528–529 **"had a lot of hostility"**: "Mike didn't like Dick, pure and simple." Edwin Meese, interview with author, Apr. 24, 2015.

529 **"I went across"**: Richard Allen, interview with author, Aug. 14, 2014.

529 **"Al hasn't steered me wrong"**: Cannon, *Reagan*, p. 396.

529 **"we had the Soviets"**: Alexander Haig, interview with Lou Cannon, June 6, 1989, LCA, Box 23, Folder 2, p. 17; "[The Soviets] are in very bad shape." AAL, p. 316.

529 **an "arch villain"**: "No sooner did the President approve something than he would sabotage it." Ibid., p. 16.

530 **"There was hardly an issue"**: Ibid., p. 12.

530 **"He isn't a mean man"**: Alexander Haig, quoted in Reeves, *President Reagan*, p. 111.

530 **"We'll see who has"**: "I couldn't *believe* he said that." Richard Allen, interview with author, Aug. 14, 2014.

530 **removed from a receiving line**: "In the protocol line, Al was gently asked, 'Mr. Secretary, would you take your place here on the floor?' And Al got really mad about that." Robert McFarlane, interview with author, Sept. 30, 2014.

530 **a scheme his own lieutenants:** "I disagreed, which may be why he got rid of me and sent me back to the White House." Ibid.

530 **Six months later:** "I wrote a memorandum to him at the end of February." Alexander Haig, interview with Lou Cannon, June 6, 1989, LCA, p. 20.

531 **"There was a clash":** Robert McFarlane, interview with author, Sept. 30, 2014.

531 **"This mustn't happen again":** RR, quoted in Haig, *Caveat*, p. 311.

531 **"guerrilla warfare by a bunch":** Alexander Haig, interview with Lou Cannon, June 6, 1989, LCA, p. 21.

532 **"the crucial give-and-take":** George P. Shultz, *Turmoil and Triumph: My Years as Secretary of State* (New York: Scribner, 1993), p. 33.

532 **Weinberger also believed that Shultz:** Caspar Weinberger, *Fighting for Peace* (New York: Warner Books, 1990), p. 159.

532 **"we should push very hard":** Cannon, President Reagan, p. 310.

533 **"The brutal fact is":** George Shultz to Lawrence Eagleburger, quoted in Shultz, *Turmoil and Triumph*, p. 105.

533 **"Ronald Reagan was just livid":** Robert McFarlane, interview with author, Sept. 30, 2014.

534 **"If we show ourselves unable":** RR, quoted in Shultz, *Turmoil and Triumph*, p. 106.

535 **"The nation," as Tip O'Neill:** Reeves, President Reagan, p. 121.

535 **Unemployment had risen:** Lewis, "Did Ronald Reagan's Tax Cut."

535 **"I had to swallow hard":** RR, national television address, Aug. 16, 1982, transcript, RRPL.

535 **"the largest tax increase":** M. Stanton Evans, "The Largest Tax Increase in History," *Human Events*, July 31, 1982.

535 **"rapid decline of support":** The poll is attributed to Richard Wirthlin. Cannon, *President Reagan*, p. 233.

535 **"The President's image as a leader":** Memo, Richard Beale to Edwin Meese III, White House Staff and Office files, OA 9449, Elections 1982, RRPL.

THIRTY-FOUR: WAR AND PEACE

536 **"Mr. President . . . Mike":** Robert McFarlane, interview with author, Sept. 30, 2014.

536 **"He doesn't know his ass":** Alexander Haig, quoted in Richard Reeves, *President Reagan: The Triumph of Imagination* (New York: Simon & Schuster, 2005), p. 111.

537 **Still, the Republican Party:** Steven V. Roberts, "Republicans Meet Setbacks in House," *New York Times*, Nov. 3, 1982.

538 **"Republicans sought to disassociate":** Martin Tolchin, "Incumbents Have the Edge in Winning Senate Contests," *New York Times*, Nov. 3, 1982.

538 **"What we are witnessing":** David Broder column, *Washington Post*, Jan. 12, 1983.

538 **"Mr. Reagan's loss of authority":** Editorial, "The Failing Presidency," *New York Times*, Jan. 9, 1983.

539 **"No other presidential speech":** Henry Steele Commager, quoted in *Washington Post*, Mar. 9, 1983.

539 **"It was pretty clear":** Robert McFarlane, interview with author, Nov. 11, 2014.

541 **"They didn't like all the money":** Richard Perle, interview with author, Apr. 24, 2015.

541 **"I knew Jim was":** John Poindexter, interview with author, Oct. 16, 2014; "Jim told us, 'It's simply immoral for us to continue down this road.'" Robert McFarlane, interview with author, Nov. 11, 2014.

541 **"Everything is in place":** Daniel Schorr, "REAGAN RECANTS: His Path from Armageddon to Détente," *Los Angeles Times*, Jan. 3, 1988.

541 **"We may be the generation":** Ibid.

542 **"Mr. President," he said:** James D. Watkins, quoted in Robert McFarlane, interview with author, Nov. 11, 2014.

542 **"Bill, is he *serious?*":** Robert McFarlane, interview with author, Nov. 11, 2014.

543 **"We are going to embark":** RR, diary entry, Feb. 11, 1983, RRPL.

543 **"He kept talking about":** John Poindexter, interview with author, Oct. 16, 2014.

543 **"Let me share with you":** RR, speech, "Defense and National Security," Mar. 23, 1983, *New York Times*, Mar. 24, 1983.

543 **"We kept everyone":** John Poindexter, interview with author, Oct. 16, 2014.

543 **"It was the first":** Richard Perle, interview with author, Apr. 24, 2015.

544 **"How much better":** RR, quoted in George P. Shultz, *Turmoil and Triumph: My Years as Secretary of State* (New York: Scribner, 1993), p. 246.

544 **"We don't have the technology":** Shultz, *Turmoil and Triumph*, p. 250.

544 **"Write the speech *right here*":** RR, quoted in Robert McFarlane, interview with author, Nov. 11, 2014.

544 **"strategic experts within the administration":** Leslie H. Gelb, "Aides Urged Reagan to Postpone Antimissile Ideas for More Study," *New York Times*, Mar. 25, 1983.

545 **Ted Kennedy immediately ridiculed:** *Washington Post*, Mar. 24, 1983.

545 **"Buck Rogers style":** "The President went a little too far [with] this kind of Buck Rogers style last night." White House News Summary files, Mar. 25, 1983, RRPL.

545 **"cosmic war technology":** Tass, Mar. 25, 1983, reported in the White House News Summary, Mar. 26, 1983, RRPL.

545 **staggering under a military budget:** Richard Perle, interview with author, Apr. 24, 2015.

546 **"could offer to give that same":** RR, interview with White House correspondents, Mar. 29, 1983, quoted in Bernard Gwertzman, "Reagan Sees

Hope of Soviet Sharing in Missile Defense," *New York Times*, Mar. 30, 1983.

546 **"uncritically—even wishfully"**: Shultz, *Turmoil and Triumph*, p. 263.

546 **Syria agreed to leave Lebanon**: David C. Martin and John Walcott, *Best Laid Plans: The Inside Story of America's War Against Terrorism* (New York: Touchstone, 1988), p. 111.

546 **"a Lebanese government"**: RR, press conference, June 30, 1982, transcript, RRPL.

546 **Then, on April 18**: Thomas L. Friedman, "U.S. Beirut Embassy Bombed: 33 Reported Killed, 80 Hurt," *New York Times*, Apr. 19, 1983.

547 **"It was intended as a show"**: Robert McFarlane, interview with author, Oct. 15, 2014.

547 **"the most important foreign policy"**: Bill Casey, quoted in Shultz, *Turmoil and Triumph*, p. 285.

547 **"Mr. President, we have"**: Bill Casey, quoted in Richard Reeves, *President Reagan: The Triumph of Imagination* (New York: Simon & Schuster, 2005), p. 151.

548 **"the moral equal"**: Lou Cannon, "Reagan Says U.S. Owes 'Contras' Help," *Washington Post*, Mar. 2, 1985; RR called them "a military fighting force . . . bringing democracy to Nicaragua in the same way that the freedom fighters who led the American Revolution brought democracy to our people." *AAL*, p. 477.

548 **"for the purpose of overthrowing"**: Dept. of Defense appropriations bill, HR 7355, Dec. 8, 1982, congress.gov.

548 **"at our doorstep"**: RR, address to nation on Central American policy, May 9, 1984, RRPL; Francis X. Clines, "The Reagan Speech," *New York Times*, May 10, 1984.

548 **"First we will take"**: Reeves, *President Reagan*, pp. 153–54.

549 **"Nicaragua is not yet Cuba"**: *Human Events*, Mar. 20, 1982, clipping from Ronald Reagan's private office files, RRPL.

549 **Reagan clipped the article**: The author was granted access to the president's private papers, among which this file was retrieved.

549 **"If the Soviet Union"**: RR, address to nation, May 9, 1984.

549 **"resisting attempted subjugation"**: President Harry S. Truman, address to joint session of Congress, Mar. 12, 1947.

549 **"The CIA's assessment"**: Robert McFarlane, interview with author, Nov. 11, 2014.

550 **It said that no federal funds**: "The way we read it was that private funds or funds from other sources were okay." Edwin Meese, interview with author, July 20, 2015.

550 **"support and conduct covert"**: Roy Gutman, *Banana Diplomacy* (New York: Touchstone, 1989), p. 95.

551 **"My assignment was to try"**: "I shuttled between Damascus and Tel-Aviv." Robert McFarlane, interview with author, Oct. 15, 2014.

552 **"the cease-fire in Lebanon"**: George Shultz, memo, "Our Strategy in Lebanon and the Middle East," Oct. 13, 1983, NSC Records, RRPL.

552 **"Clark Takes Charge"**: *Time*, Aug. 8, 1983.

552 **"The process of managing"**: Shultz, *Turmoil and Triumph*, p. 313.

552 **"I told him he had"**: RR, diary entry, July 25, 1983; Ronald Reagan, *The Reagan Diaries: January 1981–October 1985*, ed. Douglas Brinkley (New York: Harper, 2009), p. 169.

553 **"He struck me as a user"**: NR/MT, p. 243.

553 **"a tough negotiator"**: Ibid., p. 243.

553 **She called Shultz**: "Nancy Reagan called me. She was furious. She thought Clark ought to be fired." Shultz, *Turmoil and Triumph*, p. 317; "I spoke to Ronnie about him." NR/MT, p. 243.

553 **James Watt, the confrontational**: "Nancy Reagan felt he was divisive." Edwin Meese, interview with author, Apr. 24, 2015.

554 **"I've had a lot of opposition"**: Hedrick Smith, *The Power Game: How Washington Works* (New York: Ballantine Books, 1988), p. 324.

554 **"How can you make"**: Edwin Meese, interview with author, Apr. 24, 2015.

554 **"In the Reagan administration"**: Alexander M. Haig, Jr., *Caveat: Realism, Reagan and Foreign Policy* (New York: Macmillan, 1984), p. 17.

555 **On September 14, Reagan**: Lou Cannon and George Wilson, "Reagan Authorized Marines to Call in Beirut Air Strikes," *Washington Post*, Sept. 13, 1983.

555 **"I want you to consider"**: William Clark, quoted in Lou Cannon, *President Reagan: The Role of a Lifetime* (New York: Simon & Schuster, 1991), p. 424.

555 **"The problem was"**: Edwin Meese, interview with author, Apr. 24, 2015.

555 **"I'll take the test—once"**: George Shultz, quoted in Ibid.; Shultz recounts this policy almost word-for-word in Don Oberdorfer column, *Washington Post*, Dec. 19, 1985.

THIRTY-FIVE: URGENT FURY

557 **"October of '83"**: John Poindexter, interview with author, Oct. 16, 2014.

557 **"The shelling out"**: Leslie H. Gelb, "Lebanon Peacekeeping Sets Stage for War Powers Debate," *New York Times*, Sept. 11, 1983.

557 **"they were sitting ducks"**: Robert McFarlane, interview with author, Oct. 15, 2014.

558 **"ammunition and morale"**: Robert C. McFarlane with Sofia Smardz, *Special Trust* (New York: Cadell & Davies, 1994), p. 251.

558 **"fish or cut bait"**: "I wanted them to either better equip our forces and authorize them to defend themselves—or to get 'em out of there." Robert McFarlane, interview with author, Oct. 15, 2014.

558 **"to put the screws"**: Bud McFarlane, quoted in George P. Shultz, *Turmoil and Triumph: My Years as Secretary of State* (New York: Scribner, 1993), p. 223.

558 "until the U.S. and the Arabs": Ibid., p. 225.

558 "There is not a significant": Gen. P. X. Kelley, quoted in Eric Hammel, *The Root: The Marines in Beirut, August 1982–February 1984* (San Diego: Harcourt, Brace Jovanovich, 1985), p. 221.

558 "Are we going to let": RR, quoted in Shultz, *Turmoil and Triumph*, p. 227.

559 "We have to show": RR, diary entry, Sept. 7, 1983, private papers, RRPL.

559 "Our problem is do we": RR, diary entry, Sept. 11, 1983, quoted in *AAL*, p. 446.

559 "Are we in Lebanon": Ibid., p. 447.

559 "Something's got to be done": RR's diary entry, Sept. 11, 1983.

559 A strong American presence: "My reasoning is that this can be explained as a protection of our Marines hoping it might signal the Syrians to pull back." Ibid.

560 "think ahead about potential": John Poindexter, interview with author, Oct. 16, 2014.

560 "Grenada has no known natural": "Grenada IG" document, Roger W. Fontaine files, Box 8 (1981 file), RRPL.

560 "Grenada doesn't even have": RR, nationally televised speech, Mar. 23, 1983, transcript, "Speeches," RRPL.

560 Local teenagers patrolled: Joanne Omang, "Americans in Grenada, Calling Home, Say They Were Safe Before Invasion," *Washington Post*, Oct. 26, 1983.

560 Earlier in the month: National Security Defense Directive 105, Oct. 4, 1983, RRPL; William F. Clark, "Memorandum to the President," top secret, "Grenada," undated, Roger W. Fontaine files, Box 8, declassified Aug. 12, 2007, RRPL.

561 "Their being there was a lucky": Ed Meese interview with author, Apr. 24, 2015.

561 was "in chaos": "The island, McFarlane said, "was in chaos." Richard Reeves, *President Reagan: The Triumph of Imagination* (New York: Simon & Schuster, 2005), p. 179.

561 "Hey, fuck, let's dump": William Casey, quoted in Edmund Morris, *Dutch* (New York: Random House, 1999), p. 500.

561 So with some prompting: "We got her, with some prompting, to call for U.S. assistance taking action in Grenada to protect the people and restore stability. 'A call for help would be helpful,' we told her." John Poindexter, interview with author, Oct. 16, 2014.

561 "We certainly can't refuse": Robert McFarlane, interview with author, Oct. 15, 2014.

561 said, "Do it": *AAL*, p. 450.

561 Its driver, a local man: Francis X. Clines, "Reagan Unhurt as Armed Man Takes Hostages," *New York Times*, Oct. 23, 1983.

562 "I don't want anything to happen": Fred Fielding, interview with author, Sept. 30, 2014.

562 The truck exploded on impact: White House Situation Room, top-secret memo, Oct. 23, 1983, partly declassified May 6, 2010, Exec. Secretariat NSC "Country" file, Box 41, RRPL.

563 "The president was distraught": Robert McFarlane, interview with author, Oct. 15, 2014.

563 "We cannot let this stand": Ibid.

563 "Congress was in an uproar": Tip O'Neill with William Novak, *Man of the House* (New York: Random House, 1987), p. 436; "There is intense congressional interest, mixed with criticism." Situation Listing, "Marine Explosion," Dec. 14, 1983, declassified Sept. 27, 2010, p. 1, RRPL.

563 "a well-planned and professionally": Edward V. Hickey Jr., top-secret Situation Room memo to Robert McFarlane, Oct. 27, 1983, declassified Oct. 15, 2008, p. 2, RRPL.

563 The truck had been waved: Thomas L. Friedman, "Beirut Death Toll at 161 Americans," *New York Times*, Oct. 24, 1983.

563 "The sentry on guard": Lance Cpl. Robert Calhoun, quoted in Harry F. Rosenthal, Associated Press, Oct. 25, 1983.

564 "Remind me never to go": RR, quoted in Caspar Weinberger, *Fighting for Peace* (New York: Warner Books, 1990), p. 113.

564 as looking "haggard": White House News Summary, quoted as "Gannett Newspaper report," Oct. 25, 1983, RRPL.

564 a "grief-stricken": Francis X. Clines, "Days of Crisis for President: Golf, a Tragedy and Secrets," *New York Times*, Oct. 26, 1983.

564 Weinberger had been reluctant: "Weinberger said we didn't know enough to act." Shultz, *Turmoil and Triumph*, p. 329; Robert McFarlane, interview with author, Oct. 15, 2014.

564 "Grenada wasn't part of": Edwin Meese, interview with author, July 8, 2015; "We didn't have very good maps of the area. There was a lack of intelligence preparedness." John Poindexter, interview with author, Oct. 16, 2014.

564 "There are Soviet officers": Francois Mitterrand, quoted in Jacques Attali, *Verbatim I: Chronique des Années, 1981–1986* (Paris: Robert Laffont, 1993), pp. 528–29.

564 "I want you to be absolutely": Robert McFarlane, interview with author, Oct. 15, 2014.

565 "They're invading Grenada": O'Neill, *Man of the House*, p. 437.

565 "What does Mrs. Thatcher": Ibid., pp. 438–39.

565 "We had to, Margaret": Edwin Meese, interview with author, July 8, 2015.

565 "the United States has no": *AAL*, p. 454.

565 "The decision had been made": Cliff Haas, "Grenada Briefing," Associated Press, Oct. 25, 1983.

566 "I'm not confident": Edwin Meese, interview with author, July 8, 2015.

566 "fierce house-to-house": Valerie Strauss, UPI, Oct. 26, 1983.

566 "another Iran or another Beirut": RR, speech, quoted in *New York Times*, Oct. 26, 1983.

566 **declining to criticize:** White House News Summary update of Associated Press report by Mike Shanahan, Oct. 25, 1983, RRPL.

567 **"I have no intent to get":** Tip O'Neill, quoted in Hedrick Smith, "2 Americans Killed," *New York Times*, Oct. 26, 1983.

567 **"The price of freedom":** Caspar Weinberger, quoted in Valerie Strauss, "Americans Evacuated," UPI, Oct. 26, 1983.

567 **"We had imagery":** John Poindexter, interview with author, Oct. 16, 2014.

567 **"All right, I've heard":** RR, quoted in Robert McFarlane, interview with author, Oct. 15, 2014.

568 **French warplanes to attack:** "The Christian Phalangist radio said the casualties numbered in the 'hundreds.'" Thomas L. Friedman, "French Jets Raid Bases of Militia Linked to Attacks," *New York Times*, Nov. 18, 1983.

568 **"You approved this operation":** McFarlane, *Special Trust*, p. 271.

568 **"It was so poorly ordered":** John Poindexter, interview with author, Oct. 16, 2014.

568 **"turn tail and leave":** AAL, p. 462.

568 **as "pullout fever":** Shultz, *Turmoil and Triumph*, p. 230.

568 **"He may be ready":** *Wall Street Journal*, Feb. 3, 1984.

569 **Even leading Republican legislators:** Robert Michel of Illinois, Dick Cheney of Wyoming, and Trent Lott of Mississippi. James Baker III file, Box 8, RRPL.

569 **against "second guessing":** Steven R. Weisman, "President vs. Congress," *New York Times*, Apr. 7, 1984.

569 **"We have information right now":** "Reagan Says 1,000 Terrorists Are Being Trained in Lebanon," *New York Times*, Dec. 10, 1983.

569 **"Our policy wasn't working":** AAL, p. 465.

569 **"a more vigorous and demanding":** The Long Report, U.S. Dept. of Defense, 1984, RRPL.

570 **"We don't refuse to talk":** RR, televised speech, Jan. 16, 1984, PP/HW, "Speeches," Folder 241, RRPL.

570 **"Andropov," by George Shultz's assessment:** Shultz, *Turmoil and Triumph*, p. 126.

570 **He'd even shared *Time*'s:** "Men of the Year," *Time*, Jan. 2, 1984.

570 **"I don't want to honor":** RR, quoted in Jack F. Matlock Jr., *Autopsy on an Empire* (New York: Random House, 1995), p. 87.

570 **"to stress in public":** Robert McFarlane, memo to RR, White House Staff and Office files, James Baker III file, Political Affairs, Jan. 1984–July 1984, RRPL.

THIRTY-SIX: "TEFLON MAN"

571 **"No matter who we have":** Lee Atwater and Edward J. Rollins, memo to James Baker III, Nov. 11, 1982, Craig Fuller files, Box 11, "84 Election," RRPL, p. 11.

571 **"No matter what we do":** Ibid., p. 3.

571 **In early 1983:** Michael Beschloss, "How Reagan Sold Good Times to an Uncertain Nation," *New York Times*, May 8, 2016.

572 **"She was hesitant":** Stuart Spencer, interview with author, July 21, 2014.

573 **"Everybody does it differently":** "I am not Rosalynn Carter. I am not Pat Nixon or Jackie Kennedy." NR, quoted in Laurence I. Barrett, "A Talk with Nancy Reagan," *Time*, Jan. 14, 1985.

573 **"The staff didn't know":** Sheila Tate, interview with author, Oct. 3, 2014.

573 **Quigley became known:** "It was Mary Jane [Wick] who paid Quigley $3000 a month to read the Reagans' charts, and Nancy reimbursed her friend." KK/NR, p. 321.

573 **On Quigley's advice:** Joyce Wadler, "The President's Astrologer," *People*, May 23, 1988.

573 **"I yearned for more":** NR/MT, p. 264.

574 **"cutting the deficit":** AAL, p. 325.

574 **"polls showing the people":** RR, interview with *Newsweek*, requoted in Adam Clymer, "Reagan in Interview Says He Favors Idea of Having a Debate," Jan. 30, 1984.

574 **"We will finish our job":** State of the Union message, Jan. 25, 1984, PP/HW, "Speeches," RRPL.

574 **"he was a cinch to win":** Joan Quigley, quoted in KK/NR, p. 362.

574 **"It's been nearly three years":** "Text of Speech by President on Plan to Seek Reelection," *New York Times*, Oct. 30, 1984.

575 **"He made good sport":** Editorial, "The President and His Signs," *New York Times*, Jan. 30, 1984.

575 **"Don't screw up":** Stuart Spencer, interview with author, July 21, 2014.

575 *Washington Post*–ABC News poll: White House News Summary, May 1984, RRPL.

575 **"They don't have":** Stuart Spencer, quoted in Jane Mayer and Doyle McManus, *Landslide: The Unmaking of the President, 1984–1988* (Boston: Houghton Mifflin, 1988), p. 4.

575 **"There is nothing left":** Richard Darman, quoted in Stuart Spencer, interview with author, July 21, 2014.

576 **"This is America":** Tom Messner, "The Tuesday Team: The Inside Story of the Admen Who Got Reagan Reelected in 1984," *AdWeek*, Apr. 19, 2016.

576 **"Prouder, Stronger, Better":** William Grimes, "James D. Travis Dies at 83; His TV Ads Lifted Reagan," *New York Times*, May 15, 2016.

576 **"I am ready to defeat":** Walter Mondale, quoted in Howell Raines, "Mondale Wins Handily in Iowa; Close Race for 2nd as Glenn Trails," *New York Times*, Feb. 21, 1984.

576 **Gary Hart gave Nancy:** "The one guy who shook her up was Gary Hart." John Roberts, quoted in KK/NR, p. 365.

576 **"so broad and unspecific":** Howell Raines, "Hart Takes Massachusetts, Florida and Rhode Island," *New York Times*, Mar. 14, 1984.

577 **"the homeless, you might say":** White House News Summary, recap of *Good Morning America* appearance, Feb. 1, 1984, RRPL.

577 **"My fellow Americans":** "Just Kidding," *New York Times*, Aug. 14, 1984.

577 **"I appointed five members":** James Watt, quoted in White House News Summary, Sept. 22, 1983, RRPL.

577 **"whether or not they agree":** Steven Weisman, "Teflon Man," *New York Times Magazine*, Apr. 29, 1984.

578 **"I've always thought":** AAL, p. 472.

578 **Only a mere 18 percent:** White House, internal memo, cited in Mayer and McManus, *Landslide*, p. 15.

578 **Outrage over the mining:** "I am pissed off. . . . This is an act violating international law. It is an act of war." Sen. Barry Goldwater, letter to William Casey, quoted in Bob Woodward, *Veil: The Secret Wars of the CIA* (New York: Simon & Schuster, 1987), p. 322.

579 **"Bud, I want you to do":** Robert C. McFarlane with Sofia Smardz, *Special Trust* (New York: Cadell & Davies, 1994), p. 68.

579 **"That allowed Bud and Ollie":** John Poindexter, interview with author, Dec. 19, 2014.

580 **"Mum's the word":** McFarlane, *Special Trust*, p. 70.

580 **"champions who helped free":** RR, speech, quoted in Joseph Petro with Jeffrey Robinson, *Standing Next to History* 2308 (New York: Thomas Dunne Books, 2005), p. 173.

580 **"Going to third countries":** George P. Shultz, *Turmoil and Triumph: My Years as Secretary of State* (New York: Scribner, 1993), p. 415.

580 **"It is merely helping":** Caspar Weinberger, quoted in Richard Reeves, *President Reagan: The Triumph of Imagination* (New York: Simon & Schuster, 2005), p. 225.

581 **"Reagan only has himself":** Claibourne Darden, quoted in "Tackling the Teflon President, *Time*, June 25, 1984.

581 **"an exciting choice":** Walter Mondale, speech, Democratic National Convention, July 19, 1984.

581 **"Questions about Social Security":** Roger Rosenblatt, "Mondale: This Is an Exciting Choice," July 23, 1984.

581 **only 22 percent of women:** Andrew Glass, "Ferraro Joins Democratic Ticket," *Politico*, July 12, 2007.

581 **"Reagan is detached from reality":** Walter Mondale, quoted in Evan Thomas, "Tackling the Teflon President," *Time*, July 18, 1984.

582 **In March, William Buckley:** "The men apparently forced Buckley into a white Renault 12 with covered license plates and drove away." White House Situation Room, confidential teletype, Mar. 12, 1984, p. 2, declassified July 15, 2002, Exec. Secretariat Country file (Lebanon), Box 41, RRPL.

582 **a date chosen by:** Joan Quigley, *What Does Joan Say?: My Seven Years as White House Astrologer to Nancy and Ronald Reagan* (New York: Birch Lane Press, 1990), p. 92.

582 **"I flattened out":** AAL, p. 328.

582 **"We spent eight hours":** Stuart Spencer, interview, MCPA, Nov. 6, 2001, p. 54.

582 **"He was just plain lazy":** Lou Cannon, *President Reagan: The Role of a Lifetime* (New York: Simon & Schuster, 1991), p. 547.

582 **"God, I was awful":** RR, quoted in Ibid.; Stuart Spencer, interview with author, July 21, 2014.

582 **"that debate was a nightmare":** NR/MT, p. 266.

582 **"I was sitting in my room":** Stuart Spencer, interview, MCPA, Nov. 15–16, 2001, p. 93.

582 **"He was trying to combat":** Carolyn Deaver, interview with author, Mar. 17, 2015.

583 **"New Questions in Race":** *Wall Street Journal*, Oct. 9, 1984.

583 **"for the last ten days":** Roger Ailes, quoted in Peter Goldman and Tony Fuller, *The Quest for the Presidency* (New York: Bantam, 1985), p. 339.

583 **"I recall," Trewhitt said:** Commission on Presidential Debates, "October 21, 1984 Debate," transcript.

584 **"I knew he had gotten":** Walter Mondale, interview with Jim Lehrer, *PBS News Hour*, Dec. 12, 2000.

584 **"among probable voters":** Hedrick Smith, "Failure to Win Independents Hurting Mondale, Poll Finds," *New York Times*, Oct. 26, 1984.

584 **"taken enough and swallowed enough":** Mayer and McManus, *Landslide*, p. 18.

THIRTY-SEVEN: "LET REAGAN BE REAGAN"

585 **North's guest was an unnamed:** Oliver North, memo to Robert McFarlane, Nov. 7, 1984, U.S. Senate Select Committee on Secret Military Assistance to Iran and the Nicaraguan Opposition.

586 **"There is plenty of work":** RR, quoted in Edwin Meese, interview with author, July 8, 2015.

586 **"These were tough jobs":** Michael Deaver, interview, MCPA, Sept. 12, 2002, p. 44.

586 **"an ambitious man":** NR/MT, p. 241.

586 **A Cabinet post:** "Jimmy wanted a more prestigious job, a Cabinet job." Stuart Spencer, interview with author, July 21, 2014.

586 **called "Potomac fever":** Ibid., p. 240.

586 **"The power intoxicated him":** Edwin Meese, interview with author, Apr. 24, 2015.

587 **Adding insult to injury:** Meese, in his defense, says, "I thought it was costume jewelry." Edwin Meese, interview with author, July 8, 2015.

587 **"finding the same problems":** Donald Regan, interview with Lou Cannon, May 17, 1989, LCA, Box 23, Folder 87, p. 25.

587 **"You know what's wrong":** Donald T. Regan, *For the Record: From Wall Street to Washington* (San Diego: Harcourt Brace Jovanovich, 1988), p. 219.

587 **Deaver helped sell the plan:** Don Regan recognized, "We've got to get Mrs. Reagan aboard or this thing isn't going to fly." Regan, interview with Cannon, May 17, 1989, LCA.

588 **"a bright man":** NR/MT, p. 312; "Deaver had to do a sales job there." Stuart Spencer, interview with Lou Cannon, May 2, 1989, LCA, p. 24.

588 **"I don't get ulcers":** Donald Regan, quoted in Jane Mayer and Doyle McManus, *Landslide: The Unmaking of the President, 1984–1988* (Boston: Houghton Mifflin, 1988), p. 39.

588 **"an absolute dictator":** Chris Welles, "The Making of a Treasury Secretary," *Institutional Investor*, Mar. 1981.

588 **"Mr. President," Regan said:** Donald Regan, interview with Johanna Neuman and Owen Ullmann, Dec. 7, 1986.

588 **"More than anything":** Stuart Spencer, interview with author, July 21, 2014.

589 **"a trigger-happy cowboy":** AAL, p. 557.

589 **"Improving U.S.-Soviet relations":** Lou Cannon, *President Reagan: The Role of a Lifetime* (New York: Simon & Schuster, 1991), p. 509.

589 **"The President has already won":** Richard Nixon, memo, "A New Approach for the Second Term," Jan. 6, 1985, James A. Baker papers, White House Staff and Office files, OA 10514, RRPL.

589 **"We propose that the Soviet Union":** Konstantin Chernenko, letter to RR, Nov. 17, 1984, quoted in George P. Shultz, *Turmoil and Triumph: My Years as Secretary of State* (New York: Scribner, 1993), p. 500.

589 **"the elimination of all nuclear":** Konstantin Chernenko, letter to RR, Dec. 21, 1984, quoted in Shultz, *Turmoil and Triumph*, pp. 507–8.

590 **The odds-on favorite:** Robert McFarlane, interview with author, Apr. 17, 2015.

590 **"I like Mr. Gorbachev":** "Gorbachov [sic] Links Arms Curb to Star Wars Ban," *The Times* (London), Dec. 18, 1984; Shultz, *Turmoil and Triumph*, p. 507.

590 **"He knew what she":** Robert McFarlane, interview with author, Dec. 10, 2014.

592 **"This could happen now":** Robert McFarlane, interview with author, Nov. 11, 2014.

592 **"When he read something":** Donald T. Regan, interview with Lou Cannon, Feb. 2, 1990, LCA, p. 13.

592 **"horrified" the president's top men:** Ibid.

592 **Stu Spencer ordered Mike Deaver:** "I told Deaver to hide the damn thing." Stuart Spencer, interview with author, July 21, 2014.

592 **"once they were ingrained":** Donald T. Regan, interview with Lou Cannon, Feb. 2, 1990, LCA, p. 1.

593 **"stubborn determination and willingness":** Shultz, *Turmoil and Triumph*, p. 559.

593 **"a handclasp over the graves":** Ibid., p. 541.

593 **"You know, he's a cheerful":** *New York Times*, Apr. 18, 1985.

593 **"I had to get":** Michael Deaver, interview, MCPA, Sept. 12, 2002, p. 58.

594 **"It was very picturesque":** Hedrick Smith, *The Power Game: How Washington Works* (New York: Ballantine Books, 1988), p. 375.

594 **But he was assured:** "Was there anything there that might embarrass our President, our country? The answer was no." Michael K. Deaver with Mickey Herskowitz, *Behind the Scenes* (New York: William Morrow & Co., 1987), p. 180.

594 **"You can be assured":** AAL, p. 612.

595 **"has iron teeth":** Andrei Gromyko, speech to Politburo, transcript, Mar. 11, 1985; Doder Dusko and Louise Branson, *Gorbachev: Heretic in the Kremlin* (New York: Viking, 1990), p. 64.

595 **they were good bargaining chips:** "We needed the vote badly for the sake of our security interests and for our negotiations." Shultz, *Turmoil and Triumph*, p. 533.

595 **"The Contra funding is like":** National Security Planning Group meeting, minutes, May 25, 1984, p. 11, RRPL.

595 **third-party contributions:** "In mid-April 1985, Lt. Col. North advised McFarlane that the Resistance had received a total of $24.5 million." *United States of America v. Oliver North*, court document, "U.S. Government Stipulation on Quid Pro Quos with Other Governments as Part of Contra Operations," Apr. 6, 1989, p. 3.

596 **Oliver North, who was coordinating:** "Lt. North informed McFarlane that the funds remaining were insufficient to support these operations." Ibid.

596 **"We cannot have":** RR, quoted in Richard Reeves, *President Reagan: The Triumph of Imagination* (New York: Simon & Schuster, 2005), p. 247.

596 **"Who's buried in Bitburg?":** Myron Waldman, quoted in White House press conference, Apr. 11, 1985, transcript, White House Communications office files, RRPL.

596 **Elie Wiesel, the esteemed:** "I know the President. I know this is not his sentiment." David Hoffman, "President Defends Tour Plans," *Washington Post*, Apr. 13, 1985

596 **"Get off this—don't go":** Donald T. Regan, interview with Lou Cannon, May 17, 1989, LCA, p. 22.

596 **"We were hoping that Kohl":** James Kuhn, interview with author, Nov. 20, 2013.

597 **He laid it on thick:** The United States was allying itself with "past and present Nazis." *Izvestia*, Apr. 25, 1985.

597 **"That place, Mr. President":** Bernard Weintraub, "Wiesel Confronts Reagan on Trip," *New York Times*, Apr. 20, 1985.

597 **"The drumbeat of criticism":** Robert McFarlane, letter to Horst Teltschik, Apr. 18, 1985, copies in Edwin Meese papers and elsewhere, RRPL.

597 **"Bitburg is a disaster":** Shultz, *Turmoil and Triumph*, p. 548.

597 **"deeply offensive and insulting":** Margaret Thatcher, quoted in *The Times* (London), Apr. 27, 1985.

597 **In an ABC News poll:** George J. Church, "Scratches in the Teflon," *Time*, May 6, 1985.

597 **"really sucking blood":** RR, diary entry, Apr. 18, 1985. Private Papers, RRPL.

597 **"Well d—n their hides":** RR, diary entry, Apr. 24, 1985. Private Papers, RRPL.

598 **"It's a memorial":** Smith, *The Power Game*, p. 379.

598 **"He was just sitting there":** James Kuhn, interview with author, Nov. 20, 2013.

598 **"I'm trying to do my damnedest":** Deaver, *Behind the Scenes*, p. 183.

598 **Deaver was ordered to coordinate:** Joan Quigley, *What Does Joan Say?: My Seven Years as White House Astrologer to Nancy and Ronald Reagan* (New York: Birch Lane Press, 1990), p. 120.

598 **"We're talking about":** Reeves, *President Reagan*, p. 251.

598 **"She was really agitated":** James Kuhn, interview with author, Oct. 1, 2014.

600 **"loyalty up, and loyalty down":** Donald Regan, quoted in Mayer and McManus, *Landslide*, p. 41.

600 **"They were the court jesters":** Edwin Meese, interview with author, Apr. 24, 2014.

600 **As a result, McFarlane:** Shultz, *Turmoil and Triumph*, p. 536.

601 **"A President in his second":** Nixon, "A New Approach for the Second Term."

601 **"This of course means":** RR, diary entry, June 17, 1985, Private Papers, RRPL.

602 **First Blood Part II:** RR, diary entry, June 29, 1985, Private Papers, RRPL.

602 **"Let's get them out":** Robert McFarlane, interview with author, Dec. 10, 2014.

THIRTY-EIGHT: INTO THE ABYSS

603 **During the president's annual physical:** "During the colonoscopy, two very small (1–1½ mm. in size) polyps were discovered and removed." Dr. T. Burton Smith, statement, in Gerald M. Boyd, "Doctors Remove Two Small Polyps in Reagan's Colon," *New York Times*, June 21, 1986.

603 **designation was "precancerous":** "The polyp was described as precancerous." Larry Speakes, press conference, July 13, 1985.

603 **was "beside herself":** "She was just scared to death." James Kuhn, interview with author, Nov. 20, 2013.

603 **"a protective bubble":** Sheila Tate, interview with author, Oct. 3, 2014.

604 **"My Friend":** "The First Lady referred to the woman in San Francisco as 'My Friend.'" Donald T. Regan, *For the Record: From Wall Street to Washington* (San Diego: Harcourt Brace Jovanovich, 1988), p. 4.

604 **"He can't be seen this way":** NR, quoted by Terry Arthur, White House photographer, in KK/NR, p. 389.

604 **"no mention of the words":** Larry Speakes, quoted in KK/NR, p. 389.

605 **the Soviet Union had agreed:** Anatoly Dobrynin to George Shultz, July 1, 1985, in George P. Shultz, *Turmoil and Triumph: My Years as Secretary of State* (New York: Scribner, 1993), p. 571.

605 **"Any word on the hostages?":** Regan, *For the Record*, p. 10.

605 **"longer than I would":** Ibid., p. 11.

605 **"a moderate faction":** Robert McFarlane, interview with author, Dec. 10, 2014.

605 **Nancy Reagan refused to let:** "She kept Bud McFarlane out for three or four days." Donald Regan, interview with Lou Cannon, May 17, 1989, LCA, p. 12.

606 **"It could be a breakthrough":** RR, diary entry, July 17, 1985, Private Papers, RRPL.

606 **"Gosh, that would be great!":** "That is spot-on what he said." Robert McFarlane, interview with author, Dec. 10, 2014.

606 **"unwilling to allow the United States":** Robert McFarlane testimony, Congressional Hearings, pp. 100–102; Report of the Congressional Committees Investigating the Iran-Contra Affair, Nov. 17, 1987, p. 167.

606 **"it did not seem unreasonable":** AAL, p. 506.

606 **"was all for letting":** Robert McFarlane, PROF note to John Poindexter, Nov. 21, 1986, Iran-Contra Affair Report, p. 167.

607 **"I didn't have to think":** AAL, p. 506.

607 **"Yes, go ahead":** Report of the President's Special Review Board (Tower Commission), Nov. 26, 1987, p. B-16.

607 **"He was dealing with":** Donald Regan, interview with Lou Cannon, May 17, 1989, LCA, p. 12.

607 **"This is almost too absurd":** George Shultz, handwritten note on National Security Decision Directive, June 17, 1985, U.S. Senate Select Committee on Secret Military Assistance to Iran and the Nicaragua Opposition.

607 **"a very bad idea":** Iran-Contra Affair Report, p. 167.

608 **"You know that thing":** Robert McFarlane, interview with author, Dec. 10, 2014.

608 **His Portuguese passport:** Top-secret dossier on Manucher Ghorbanifar, declassified Mar. 27, 1987, in author's possession.

608 **a Fabricator Notice:** Dennis St. John, profile of Manucher Ghorbanifar, U.S. State Dept., declassified Dec. 19, 2013.

608 **"should be regarded":** James Risen, "How a Shady Iranian Deal Maker Kept the Pentagon's Ear," *New York Times*, Dec. 7, 2003.

608 **"Ghorbanifar is a con artist":** William Casey to Robert Gates, in John Poindexter, interview with author, Dec. 8, 2014.

608 **"contingency plans for extracting hostages":** Tower Commission Report, p. B-25.

609 **"You were never quite sure":** "I wasn't really happy going through the Israelis." John Poindexter interview with author, Dec. 8, 2014.

609 **"We had great respect":** AAL, p. 506.

609 **Meanwhile, David Kimche:** "So because David believed in this guy, I was willing to believe in him—almost entirely because of that." Robert McFarlane, quoted in Jane Mayer and Doyle McManus, *Landslide: The Unmaking of the President, 1984–1988* (Boston: Houghton Mifflin, 1988), p. 126.

609 **Apparently, the shipment:** Lou Cannon, *President Reagan: The Role of a Lifetime* (New York: Simon & Schuster, 1991), p. 617.

609 **Because the faction he represented:** Peter Kornbluth and Malcolm Byrne, eds., *The Iran-Contra Scandal: The Declassified History* (New York: New Press, 1993), p. 245.

609 **"Do you want the Iranians":** Manucher Ghorbanifar, quoted in *Los Angeles Times*, Dec. 28, 1986.

609 **"We might as well":** Michael Ledeen, deposition, U.S. Senate Select Committee on Secret Military Assistance to Iran and the Nicaragua Opposition, Sept. 10, 1987.

609 **"It looks as though":** David Kimche, quoted in Mayer and McManus, *Landslide*, p. 134.

610 **"Though they do not want":** Rev. Benjamin Weir, quoted in Robert C. McFarlane with Sofia Smardz, *Special Trust* (New York: Cadell & Davies, 1994), p. 39.

610 **At her insistence, hospital officials:** KK/NR, p. 391; Mark Weinberg, interview with author, July 8, 2014.

610 **"Don was already on":** Sheila Tate, interview with author, Oct. 3, 2014.

610 **"That seemed wrong to me":** NR/MT, p. 313.

611 **"It came directly from":** KK/NR, p. 391.

611 **"he intended to bring":** Sheila Tate, interview with author, Oct. 3, 2014.

611 **Pat Buchanan, a fierce defender:** "I was sure Buchanan was undermining the policy by sending Reagan right-wing clippings, which distorted his thinking." Robert McFarlane, interview with author, Dec. 10, 2014.

611 **"eliminated the segregation":** RR, quoted in *New York Times*, Aug. 25, 1985.

611 **"I couldn't care less":** Thomas Dawson, quoted in Mayer and McManus, *Landslide*, p. 131.

612 **"Fish or Cut Bait, Mr. President":** *Washington Times*, October 10, 1985.

612 **"We had the JSOC":** John Poindexter, interview with author, Oct. 16, 2014.

613 **"advised strongly against":** Larry Speakes, press conference, Oct. 10, 1985, transcript, RRPL; Judith Miller, "Hijackers Yield Ship in Egypt, Passenger Slain, 400 Are Safe; US Assails Deal with Captors," *New York Times*, Oct. 10, 1985.

613 **"They aren't here anymore":** Hosni Mubarak, quoted in John Poindexter, interview with author, Oct. 16, 2014.

613 **"We had a guy—a spy":** Robert McFarlane, interview with author, Dec. 10, 2014.

613 **Oliver North had similar intelligence:** "Ollie talked to Simhoni and told him we'd like as much help as possible locating the terrorists." John Poindexter, interview with author, Oct. 16, 2014.

613 **"You may be in a situation":** Robert McFarlane, interview with author, Dec. 10, 2014.

614 **"I don't want to give":** John Poindexter, interview with author, Oct. 16, 2014.

614 **"But we couldn't get through":** John Poindexter, interview with author, Dec. 8, 2014.

614 **"You are to follow us":** John Poindexter, interview with author, Oct. 16, 2014; *Time*, Oct. 21, 1985.

614 **"Can you get the terrorists":** Caspar Weinberger, quoted in John Poindexter interview with author, Oct. 16, 2014.

614 **"a God-sent opportunity":** Gerald M. Boyd, "A Setback to Terrorism," *New York Times*, Oct. 12, 1985.

615 **"a message to terrorists everywhere":** RR, press conference, Oct. 11, 1985, transcript, RRPL.

615 **Newspapers in France and Egypt:** Transcript of articles in *Libération* and *al-Akhbar*, White House News Service summary, Oct. 13, 1985, RRPL.

615 **Reagan's approval ratings:** Richard Reeves, *President Reagan: The Triumph of Imagination* (New York: Simon & Schuster, 2005), p. 277.

615 **"a major turning point":** Lee Attwater, quoted in Boyd, "A Setback to Terrorism."

615 **"That guy in Mubarak's office":** Robert McFarlane, interview with author, Dec. 10, 2014.

615 **Throughout the fall, Oliver North:** "The Israelis will deliver 80 Mod[ified] HAWKS at noon on Friday 22 Nov. . . . There is a requirement for 40 additional weap[on]s of the same nomenclature for a total requirement of 120." Oliver North, memo to John Poindexter, Nov. 20, 1985, NSC file, RRPL.

616 **"without grand expectations":** "We viewed the Geneva meeting realistically . . ." *Memoirs*, Mikhail Gorbachev (NY: Doubleday, 1996), p. 403.

616 **"When Mr. Gorbachev and I":** RR, quoted in "UN: 40," address to the United Nations General Assembly, Oct. 24, 1985.

616 **"from a distinctly different mold":** Shultz, *Turmoil and Triumph*, p. 586.

617 **"In Gorbachev, we were clearly":** Ibid., p. 577.

617 **"Was it science fiction":** Mikhail S. Gorbachev, *Memoirs* (New York: Doubleday, 1995), p. 407.

617 **"What is Gorbachev made of?":** Robert McFarlane, interview with author, Apr. 17, 2015.

617 **"I am familiar with":** Mikhail Gorbachev, quoted in Ibid.

617–618 **"The Soviet Union will only":** Mikhail Gorbachev, quoted in Shultz, *Turmoil and Triumph*, p. 593.

618 **"Gorbachev," he reported:** AAL, p. 631.

618 **"Thanks to what you've done":** NR, quoted in Robert McFarlane, interview with author, Apr. 17, 2015.

THIRTY-NINE: "A FRESH START"

619 **Ronald Reagan was noticeably edgy:** "The president was a little nervous—not intimidated, but nervous." Mark Weinberg, interview with author, July 8, 2014.

619 **"bounced around, joking":** "Mrs. Reagan was in the best mood I'd ever seen her in." James Kuhn, interview with author, Dec. 19, 2013.

620 **Insiders suspected the hand:** "No doubt it came from Bill Casey, who was eager to sabotage the summit." Ibid.; Robert McFarlane, quote in Lou Cannon, "Reagan Voices Summit Hopes," *Washington Post*, Nov. 17, 1985.

620 **"Goodwill without illusion":** Caspar Weinberger, *Fighting for Peace* (New York: Warner Books, 1990), p. 34

621 **"to make a fresh start":** RR, quoted in R. W. Apple Jr., "Reagan–Gorbachev Talks End," *New York Times*, Nov. 22, 1985.

621 **prepare Gorbachev's horoscope:** Don Regan revealed that Quigley was consulted to "choose auspicious moments for meetings between" Reagan and Gorbachev, "but also to draw up horoscopes." Donald T. Regan, *For the Record: From Wall Street to Washington* (San Diego: Harcourt Brace Jovanovich, 1988), p. 301.

621 **"Are you ready, Dad?":** Ron Reagan, quoted in Evan Thomas, "Fencing at the Fireside Summit," *Time*, Dec. 2, 1985.

621 **More than three thousand:** Jay Winik, *On the Brink* (New York: Simon & Schuster, 1996), p. 389.

622 **Nancy Reagan had signed off:** "Mrs. Reagan was very keen on it." William Henkel, quoted in Hedrick Smith, *The Power Game: How Washington Works* (New York: Ballantine Books, 1988), p. 422.

622 **"Eddie, can I have my coat":** James Kuhn, interview with author, Dec. 19, 2013.

623 **"Here we are":** Thomas, "Fencing at the Fireside Summit."

623 **"the No. 1 Communist":** Mikhail S. Gorbachev, *Memoirs* (New York: Doubleday, 1995), pp. 405–6.

623 **"an intelligent man":** *AAL*, p. 638.

623 **"was warmth in his face":** Ibid., p. 635.

623 **"was a man you could":** Gorbachev, *Memoirs*, p. 405.

623 **"I'm not walking into":** James Kuhn, interview with author, Dec. 19, 2013.

624 **"Are you crazy?":** Robert McFarlane, interview with author, Apr. 17, 2015.

624 **"This guy is different":** James Kuhn, interview with author, Dec. 19, 2013.

624 **"done good," and:** "Our gang told me I'd done good." RR diary entry, Nov. 19, 1985.

624 **described them as "bizarre":** Regan, *For the Record*, p. 320.

625 **"Well, let's see what happens":** Robert McFarlane, interview with author, Apr. 17, 2015; Jane Mayer and Doyle McManus, *Landslide: The Unmaking of*

the President, 1984–1988 (Boston: Houghton Mifflin, 1988), p. 166.

625 **"Make no mistake":** Mikhail Gorbachev, quoted in George P. Shultz, *Turmoil and Triumph: My Years as Secretary of State*, p. 600.

625 **"Mr. President, you cannot do this!":** Robert McFarlane, interview with author, Apr. 17, 2015.

625 **"We should ban introduction":** Thomas, "Fencing at the Fireside Summit."

625 **"Well, I disagree with everything":** Mikhail Gorbachev, quoted in Robert McFarlane, interview with author, Apr. 17, 2015.

625 **"How about taking a walk?":** Gorbachev, *Memoirs*, p. 407.

626 **The president had concocted it:** Smith, *The Power Game*, p. 422.

626 **"tell Mr. Arbitov":** Thomas, "Fencing at the Fireside Summit."

626 **Gorbachev later acknowledged:** "The walk, the change of scene, the crackling of burning wood—all these helped to alleviate the tension." Gorbachev, *Memoirs*, p. 407.

626 **A lifelong Edgar Rice Burroughs:** "It's true—it happened. The president told me about it later that day." Robert McFarlane, interview with author, Apr. 17, 2015.

626 **They'd decided that their attendance:** "The two of them decided they didn't need to attend the plenary session." James Kuhn, interview with author, Dec. 19, 2013.

627 **whose "eyes shone":** "When he got excited, you knew he was excited." Regan, *For the Record*, p. 313.

627 **"My fundamental impression":** NR/MT, p. 338.

627 **"We have things of substance":** Donnie Radcliffe, "First Ladies, Firsthand," *Washington Post*, Nov. 21, 1985.

627 **"She was very sharp-tongued":** Edward Rowny, interview, MCPA, May 17, 2006, p. 18.

627 **Nancy Reagan didn't want:** "Her conversational style made me bristle." Rowny, interview, p. 339.

627 **"Who does that dame think":** Regan, *For the Record*, p. 314.

628 **"He just couldn't resist":** James Kuhn, interview with author, Dec. 19, 2013; Robert McFarlane, interview with author, Apr. 17, 2015.

628 **"They're not going to understand":** Donnie Radcliffe, "Nancy Reagan's Peak Role," *Washington Post*, Nov. 18, 1985.

628 **"How dare he upstage":** James Kuhn, interview with author, Dec. 19, 2013.

628 **"keep a low profile":** Regan, *For the Record*, p. 20.

628 **"Both sides are going to have":** Mikhail Gorbachev, Nov. 22, 1985, quoted in Thomas, "Fencing at the Fireside Summit."

628 **"We remain far apart":** RR, address to joint session of Congress, Nov. 21, 1985, transcript, RRPL.

629 **An overnight CBS News poll:** White House News Summary, Nov. 22, 1985, RRPL.

629 **"There is much that divides us"**: Larry Speakes with Robert Pack, *Speaking Out* (New York: Chas. Scribner's Sons, 1988), p. 136.

629 **"Larry often made up quotes"**: James Kuhn, interview with author, Dec. 19, 2013.

629 **"If I could ever get"**: RR quoted, Edward Rowny transcript, Miller Center Interview, May 17, 2006, p. 14.

629 **Gorbachev let it be known**: RR "told Nixon that he thought the leader of atheistic world communism, on some level, believed in God." Richard Reeves, *President Reagan: The Triumph of Imagination* (New York: Simon & Schuster, 2005), p. 294.

630 **"The missiles arrived"**: Manucher Ghorbanifar, quoted in Michael Ledeen, deposition, U.S. Senate Select Committee on Secret Military Assistance to Iran and the Nicaragua Opposition, June 19, 1987.

630–631 **"This is criminal!"**: Attributed to John McMahon, in Oliver North's notebook, Nov. 25, 1985, U.S. Senate Select Committee, documents, 1987.

631 **"And I want it retroactive"**: John McMahon, to CIA general counsel Stanley Sporkin, deposition of CIA officer Edward Juchniewicz, quoted in Mayer and McManus, *Landslide*, p. 167.

631 **"We know of your distaste"**: David Jacobsen, Lawrence Martin Jenco, Terry Anderson, and Thomas Sutherland, undated letter, personal papers, RRPL.

631 **"This thing is really eating"**: Noel Koch, testimony, U.S. Senate Select Committee, documents, June 23, 1987.

631 **"I think the tension"**: Robert McFarlane, interview with author, Oct. 15, 2014.

632 **saying, "I'll go"**: Ibid.; Mayer and McManus, *Landslide*, p. 65.

632 **"You get it into"**: "It was clearly said in a tone that he was talking down to a subordinate." Robert McFarlane, interview with author, Apr. 18, 2015.

633 **Meg Greenfield, the editorial**: "She was a friend who came to lunch and told me Regan was putting out nasty stories about me." Ibid.

633 **Reports of McFarlane's alleged exploits**: "Bob Simms, the NSC's press spokesman, told me, 'Don Regan is still spreading these stories about you.'" Ibid.

633 **"He's the most complex man"**: Richard Perle, interview with author, Apr. 24, 2015.

633 **"he broke down and sobbed"**: Unnamed White House official, quoted in Mayer and McManus, *Landslide*, p. 165.

634 **"When Mondale said"**: RR, to Thomas P. "Tip" O'Neill, Jr., quoted in Smith, *The Power Game*, pp. 494–95.

635 **"I think we need to discuss"**: Mayer and McManus, *Landslide*, p. 163.

635 **"knew the president didn't understand"**: Robert McFarlane, interview with author, Apr. 18, 2015.

636 **"It's a big mistake"**: Michael Deaver, quoted in Mayer and McManus, *Landslide*, p. 171.

FORTY: "SO FAR DOWN THE ROAD"

637 **It clearly laid out**: "It clearly made it look like it was an arms-for-hostages deal." John Poindexter, interview with author, Dec. 9, 2014.

637 **instructed CIA Director**: Report of the President's Special Review Board (Tower Commission), Feb. 26, 1987, p. B-40.

637 **Rather than circulating**: "I didn't want it circulated." John Poindexter, interview with author, Dec. 9, 2014; Report of the Congressional Committees Investigating the Iran-Contra Affair, Nov. 1987, p. 197.

637 **"significant political embarrassment"**: Iran-Contra Affair Report, p. 197.

638 **"anyone who wanted"**: John Poindexter, interview with author, Dec. 9, 2014.

638 **"We all agree"**: Oliver North, PROF to John Poindexter, Dec. 4, 1985; Tower Commission Report, pp. B-40–42.

639 **Shultz and Weinberger**: "I argued that it was a betrayal of our policies. . . . Cap Weinberger expressed the same point of view." George P. Shultz, *Turmoil and Triumph: My Years as Secretary of State*, p. 799; Lou Cannon, *President Reagan: The Role of a Lifetime* (New York: Simon & Schuster, 1991), p. 629.

639 **"Look," he said**: Cannon, *President Reagan*, p. 631.

639 **"no stone be left unturned"**: "I want to leave no stone unturned." RR, quoted in John Poindexter, interview with author, Dec. 9, 2014; John Poindexter, testimony, July 15, 1987. U.S. Senate Select Committee on Secret Military Assistance to Iran and the Nicaraguan Opposition.

639 **"Israel selling some weapons"**: RR, diary entry, Dec. 7, 1985.

639 **"The American people will never"**: RR, quoted in Jane Mayer and Doyle McManus, *Landslide: The Unmaking of the President, 1984–1988* (Boston: Houghton Mifflin, 1988), p. 179.

639 **"It's a risky operation"**: RR, quoted in John Poindexter, interview with author, Dec. 9, 2014; Robert McFarlane, interview with author, Apr. 18, 2015.

639 **"He didn't know the difference"**: Confidential source, interview with author.

640 **"The baby has been strangled"**: Caspar Weinberger, *Fighting for Peace* (New York: Warner Books, 1990), p. 373.

640 **"If you had to cast"**: Robert McFarlane, interview with author, Apr. 18, 2015.

640 **"The hell with the hostages!"**: Robert C. McFarlane with Sofia Smardz, *Special Trust* (New York: Cadell & Davies, 1994), pp. 48–49.

640 **"Go pound sand!"**: Iran-Contra Affair Report, p. 199.

641 **"a borderline moron"**: Ibid.

641 **"Ollie's boys in Central America"**: Manucher Ghorbanifar, quoted in Ibid., p. 205.

641 **"other cooperative activities"**: Iran-Contra Affair Report, pp. 201–2.

642 **Ed Meese assured him:** Mayer and McManus, *Landslide*, p. 184.

642 **"Sometimes you have to deal":** John Poindexter, interview with author, Dec. 8, 2014.

642 **Bill Casey assured the president:** William Casey, "eyes only" letter to RR, Dec. 23, 1985, private papers, RRPL.

642 **"Casey believes that Cap":** Oliver North, PROF message to John Poindexter, Jan. 15, 1986, Iran-Contra Affair Report, p. 206.

642 **"his people have looked":** Ibid., p. 208.

642 **"Involves selling TOW anti-tank":** RR, diary entry, Jan. 17, 1986, Private Papers, RRPL.

642 **"We sit quietly by":** RR, diary entry, Jan. 7, 1986, Private Papers, RRPL.

643 **He'd juggled his schedule:** "We did everything we could to get Reagan to Cape Canaveral." James Kuhn, interview with author, Dec. 19, 2013.

643 **"Those people out there":** RR, quoted in Tip O'Neill with William Novak, *Man of the House* (New York: Random House, 1987), p. 434.

644 **as though "it was measles":** Warren King, "Reagan Regarded AIDS Like It Was Measles," *Seattle Times*, Aug. 31, 1989.

645 **"Sir," he cried:** Larry Speakes with Robert Pack, *Speaking Out* (New York: Chas. Scribner's Sons, 1988), p. 117; "Buchanan just came flying through the door, which you *never* do." James Kuhn, interview with author, Dec. 19, 2013.

645 **"We watched that footage":** James Kuhn, interview with author, Dec. 19, 2013.

645 **"added proximity to the tragedy":** AAL, p. 403.

645 **"Ladies and gentlemen," he began:** RR, televised speech, Jan. 28, 1986, transcript at history.nasa .gov/reagan12866.

646 **In some recollections, he said:** Justin Wm. Moyer, "Exactly the Right Words, Exactly the Right Way," *Washington Post*, Jan. 28, 2016.

646 **"As I listened to him":** O'Neill, *Man of the House*, p. 435.

646 **"He lacked most":** Ibid., p. 431.

647 **"One of our highest":** RR, address to employees of the Dept. of Health and Human Services, Feb. 5, 1986, transcript, RRPL.

647 **"The poor homosexuals":** Pat Buchanan, quoted in Randy Shilts, *And the Band Played On* (New York: St. Martin's Press, 1987), p. 311.

647 **"marked by considerable fraud":** Richard J. Kessler, "Reagan and Philippine Reality," *Chicago Tribune*, Feb. 7, 1986.

647 **a pillar "of great importance":** AAL, p. 362.

648 **she would put Marcos:** *New York Times*, Dec. 17, 1985.

648 **"a dazed, vacant woman":** A. M. Rosenthal, quoted in Shultz, *Turmoil and Triumph*, p. 617.

648 **"Marcos people were considering":** "I said to get word back that we . . . would not countenance any such action." Shultz, *Turmoil and Triumph*, p. 618.

648 **"The Philippine elections are looking":** Sara Fritz and Don Shannon, "Philippine Election Rigged,

Members of Senate Committee Charge," *Los Angeles Times*, Jan. 24, 1986.

649 **"a very disturbing pattern":** Richard Lugar, quoted in Seth Mydans, "Observers of Vote Cite Wide Fraud by Marcos Party," *New York Times*, Feb. 10, 1986.

649 **One Marcos critic was chased:** Richard Reeves, *President Reagan: The Triumph of Imagination* (New York: Simon & Schuster, 2005), p. 309.

649 **the bodies of ten opposition:** *New York Times*, Feb. 15, 1986.

649 **A day or two later:** "Lugar estimated that Aquino had won more than 70 percent of the vote." *New York Times*, Feb. 13, 1986.

649 **"I am the President":** "They are not going to drive me out because the people are behind me." Ferdinand Marcos, quoted in Seth Mydans, "Aquino Proposes Nonviolent Moves to Depose Marcos," *New York Times*, Jan. 17, 1986.

649 **Despite evidence to the contrary:** "It is not appropriate for the United States to make such a judgment at this time." Bernard Weinraub, "President to Send an Envoy to Seek Views of Filipinos," *New York Times*, Feb. 12, 1986.

649 **"the election has effectively cost":** Reeves, *President Reagan*, p. 309.

649 **"Ronald Reagan still had no intention":** Shultz, *Turmoil and Triumph*, p. 630.

649 **"if it's a duly elected government":** Donald Regan, quoted in Kessler, "Reagan and Philippine Reality."

649 **"The Marcos era has ended":** Philip Habib, quoted in Shultz, *Turmoil and Triumph*, p. 635.

650 **"What we have here":** James Leach, quoted in Dale Russakoff, "The Philippines: Anatomy of a Looting," *Washington Post*, Mar. 30, 1986.

650 **"having stashed $400 million":** "Tracking Down Millions for Haiti," *New York Times*, June 28, 1987.

650 **"The Reagan administration deserves":** *Newsday*, Feb. 26, 1986.

650 **Only hours after Marcos:** David K. Shipler, "Reagan Asks $100 Million for Contras," *New York Times*, Feb. 26, 1986.

650 **"If the Sandinistas are allowed":** RR, blind-quoted in Reeves, *President Reagan*, p. 313.

650 **Republican Henry Hyde led:** "History is going to assign to you folks the role of pallbearers to democracy in Central America." Evan Thomas, "Tough Tug of War," *Time*, Mar. 31, 1986.

651 **In response to the criticism:** "Asked directly if they were supporting Communists, he said, 'If so, inadvertently.'" Gerald M. Boyd, "Reagan Says the Choice Is Between Backing Him or Communists," *New York Times*, Mar. 7, 1986.

651 **"With the vote on Contra aid":** Editorial, *Washington Post*, Mar. 12, 1986.

651 **"Republicans and Democrats went":** Kenneth Duberstein, interview with author, June 16, 2014.

651 **"H—l of a way":** RR, diary entry, Mar. 20, 1986, Private Papers, RRPL.

652 **"an outlaw regime":** RR, quoted in Thomas, "Tough Tug of War."

652 **He often cited:** "Right and Left: Reagan Takes on Tyranny," *Time*, Mar. 24, 1986.

652 **In 1984 alone:** Shultz, *Turmoil and Triumph*, p. 677.

652 **"The next time we have":** John Poindexter, interview with author, Dec. 8, 2014.

652 **"We are ready to die":** Muammar Qaddafi, quoted in Rod Nordland et al., "Crossing the Line of Death," *Newsweek*, Mar. 31, 1986.

653 **Seventy-two Libyans were killed:** Mayer and McManus, *Landslide*, p. 222.

653 **The next day, Qaddafi sent:** Shultz, *Turmoil and Triumph*, p. 681; "That message . . . outlines operational plans for more than ten terrorist attacks." U.S. intelligence officer, quoted in George J. Church, "Targeting Gaddafi," *Time*, Apr. 21, 1986.

653 **"causing maximum casualties":** Muammar Qaddafi, quoted in Church, "Targeting Gaddafi."

653 **"the crackpot in Tripoli":** *AAL*, p. 518.

653 **He'd already sanctioned:** John Poindexter, memo to RR, Aug. 14, 1986, advocating a plan that "combines real and illusionary events—through a disinformation program—with the basic goal of making Qaddafi *think* that there is a high degree of internal opposition to him within Libya." Bob Woodward column, *Washington Post*, Oct. 2, 1986.

653 **"a little psychological warfare":** George Shultz, quoted in Hedrick Smith, *The Power Game: How Washington Works* (New York: Ballantine Books, 1988), p. 448.

653 **"We have unmistakable proof":** John Poindexter, interview with author, Dec. 8, 2014.

653 **Reagan ordered an immediate military:** "Reagan signed off on the bombing two weeks ahead of time." James Kuhn, interview with author, Dec. 19, 2013; James Kuhn, interview with author, Oct. 1, 2014.

653 **"We have five specific targets":** RR, diary entry, Apr. 9, 1986.

654 **"We let the White House":** James Kuhn, interview with author, Oct. 1, 2014.

654 **"the headquarters, terrorist facilities":** RR, televised speech, Apr. 14, 1986.

654 **Qaddafi himself had not been:** "He was not a direct target." George Shultz, quoted in George J. Church, "Hitting the Source U.S. Bombers Strike At," *Time*, Apr. 28, 1986.

654 **"If he had been killed":** John Poindexter, interview with author, Dec. 8, 2014.

654 **"The one that missed":** James Kuhn, interview with author, Dec. 19, 2013.

FORTY-ONE: BACK ON THE ROLLER COASTER

655 **The primary objective was:** "Following the meeting, he was told, the four surviving hostages . . . would be freed." *AAL*, p. 520.

656 **they noted a banner:** Jane Mayer and Doyle McManus, *Landslide: The Unmaking of the President, 1984–1988* (Boston: Houghton Mifflin, 1988), p. 231.

656 **"I was convinced that":** Robert McFarlane, interview with author, Apr. 18, 2015.

656 **"They're just stringing us along":** Minutes of Tehran mission, taken by Howard Teicher, *Report of the President's Special Review Board* (Tower Commission), Feb. 26, 1987, p. B-110; Robert McFarlane, interview with author, Apr. 18, 2015.

656 **"It was a heartbreaking disappointment":** RR, diary entry, May 28, 1986, Private Papers, RRPL.

657 **"It gives us hope":** RR, diary entry, July 27, 1986, Private Papers, RRPL.

657 **"Back on the roller coaster":** RR, quoted in Richard Reeves, *President Reagan: The Triumph of Imagination* (New York: Simon & Schuster, 2005), p. 331.

657 **"I've been passing blood":** RR, diary entry, July 28, 1986.

657 **he was "falling apart":** Edmund Morris, *Dutch* (New York: Random House, 1999), p. 589.

657 **"a kind of low-level":** George P. Shultz, *Turmoil and Triumph: My Years as Secretary of State*, p. 725.

657 **"mad as hell":** RR, diary entry, Sept. 7, 1986.

658 **"I can give you":** White House Staff and Office files, Executive Secretariat, NSC, Head of State file, Box 40, USSR, General Secretarial Gorbachev, Sept. 5, 1986, RRPL.

658 **Reagan was criticized:** Editorial, "A Humiliation for the President," *San Diego Union*, Sept. 30, 1986; "Justice is not served." *Washington Times*, Sept. 30, 1986.

658 **He consoled himself:** "We'll trade Zakharov but for Soviet dissidents." RR, diary entry, Sept. 26, 1986.

658 **"In the final analysis":** RR/AAl, p. 674.

658 **"treating them as less":** Shultz, *Turmoil and Triumph*, p. 742.

658 **"There has been no movement":** White House Staff and Office files, Executive Secretariat, NSC, Head of State file, Box 40, USSR, General Secretarial Gorbachev, Sept. 15, 1986, RRPL.

658 **"I opt for Iceland":** RR, diary entry, Sept. 19, 1986, Private Papers, RRPL.

659 **On Ed Meese's advice:** "I urged the president to nominate Rehnquist chief justice." Edwin Meese, interview with author, Apr. 24, 2015.

659 **"social judgments that ought better":** Antonin Scalia, quoted in Stuart Taylor Jr., "More Vigor for the Right," *New York Times*, June 18, 1986.

660 **He was more interested:** "He also liked negotiation and considered himself quite a master of it." Ken Adelman, *Reagan at Reykjavik: Forty-Eight Hours That Ended the Cold War* (New York: Broadside Books, 2014), p. 69; "He felt he had a great power of persuasion." John Poindexter, interview with author, Dec. 9, 2014.

660 **At a final meeting:** Lou Cannon, *President Reagan: The Role of a Lifetime* (New York: Simon & Schuster, 1991), p. 764.

660 **"He was awfully excited":** Adelman, *Reagan at Reykjavik*, p. 69.

661 **categorically "Absolutely none":** RR, quoted in "Nicaragua Downs Plane and Survivor Implicates C.I.A." *New York Times*, Oct. 12, 1986.

661 **"That would be illegal":** Elliot Abrams, exchange with Robert Novak, quoted in Mayer and McManus, *Landslide*, p. 275.

661 **"This whole thing":** Bill Casey, quoted in Mayer and McManus, *Landslide*, p. 287.

661 **Joan Quigley had signed off:** James Kuhn, interview with author, Nov. 20, 2013.

662 **Perhaps the rumors:** "We heard rumors that Gorbachev would come to Reykjavik with a blitz of proposals." Shultz, *Turmoil and Triumph*, p. 754.

662 **"When you stop trying":** RR, quoted in Reeves, *President Reagan*, p. 340.

662 **He consulted note cards:** Mikhail S. Gorbachev, *Memoirs* (New York: Doubleday, 1995), p. 416.

662 **"We believe the world wanted":** Mikhail Gorbachev, quoted in Adelman, *Reagan at Reykjavik*, p. 93.

662 **His approach was threefold:** The proposals were contained in "Directives for the Foreign Ministers of the USSR and the USA to Prepare Agreements on Nuclear Disarmament," a summary that Gorbachev had prepared for Reagan.

663 **"Gorbachev indicated that":** Jack Matlock, notes, White House News Summary, Oct. 11, 1986, RRPL.

663 **"This is the best Soviet":** Paul Nitze, quoted in Shultz, *Turmoil and Triumph*, p. 760.

663 **"He's got a lot of proposals":** Reeves, *President Reagan*, p. 344; "Reagan knew it would mean the end of SDI." Richard Perle, interview with author, Apr. 24, 2015; "He was upset that Gorbachev wanted him to do away with SDI." John Poindexter, interview with author, Dec. 9, 2014.

663 **"We didn't have a lot":** John Poindexter, interview with author, Dec. 9, 2014.

664 **The Russians were agreeable:** "Akhromeyev was agreeable and thought we could get something done." Richard Perle, interview with author, Apr. 24, 2015.

664 **"If you accept this proposal":** Richard Perle, interview with author, Apr. 24, 2015.

665 **"this is taking too long":** Donald T. Regan, *For the Record: From Wall Street to Washington* (San Diego: Harcourt Brace Jovanovich, 1988), p. 349.

665 **"Nancy would kill me":** Richard Perle, interview with author, Apr. 24, 2015; Adelman, *Reagan at Reykjavik*, p. 351; Jack Matlock, *Reagan and Gorbachev: How the Cold War Ended* (New York: Random House, 2004), p. 232.

665 **"Perhaps she has something else":** Raisa Gorbachev, quoted in NR/MT, p. 345.

665 **"Let's do it!":** George Shultz, quoted in Reeves, *President Reagan*, p. 351.

665 **"I have promised the American people":** RR, quoted in Adelman, *Reagan at Reykjavik*, p. 169.

666 **"No statement!" he bristled:** "I asked him if they'd be making a statement." James Kuhn, interview

with author, Nov. 20, 2013; Larry Speakes with Robert Pack, *Speaking Out* (New York: Chas. Scribner's Sons, 1988), p. 178.

666 **His face was grim:** "I was very disappointed—and very angry." AAL, p. 679.

666 **"We won't be seeing":** Mikhail Gorbachev, quoted in Shultz, *Turmoil and Triumph*, p. 774.

666 **"Goddammit!":** RR, quoted by George Shultz in Reeves, *President Reagan*, p 352.

666 **"When one side suddenly springs":** Henry Kissinger, quoted in White House News Summary, Oct. 15, 1986, RRPL.

666 **Wall Street Journal/NBC News poll:** White House News Summary, Oct. 16, 1986, RRPL.

667 **He attempted to convince:** Gerald M. Boyd, "Reagan Asserts 'Star Wars' Plan Will Create Jobs and Better Life," *New York Times*, Oct. 31, 1986.

FORTY-TWO: SNAKEBIT

668 **Reagan aides expected the story:** John Kifner, "American Is Freed After 19 Months as Beirut Captive," *New York Times*, Nov. 3, 1986.

668 **"this snake never died":** George P. Shultz, *Turmoil and Triumph: My Years as Secretary of State* (New York: Scribner, 1993), p. 784.

668 **Its venom had leached out:** William Drozdiak and Walter Pincus, "Americans Reportedly Detained, Then Ousted," *Washington Post*, Nov. 5, 1986.

668 **A follow-up report revealed:** Walter Pincus, "Secret Talks with Iran Described," *Washington Post*, Nov. 6, 1986.

669 **responded, "No comment":** RR, quoted in news pool report, en route from Los Angeles to Andrews AFB, Nov. 4, 1986, LCA.

669 **Rumors circulated that George Shultz:** Walter Pincus, "Shultz Protested Iran Deal," *Washington Post*, Nov. 7, 1986; Bernard Gwertzman, "Shultz Reaffirms His Opposition to Negotiations with Terrorists," *New York Times*, Nov. 8, 1986.

669 **"And Secretary Shultz supports":** RR, remarks in informal exchange with reporters, pool news report, Nov. 7, 1986, LCA.

669 **"This all has the feel of Watergate":** Shultz, *Turmoil and Triumph*, p. 790.

669 **"We were not in the loop":** George Bush, interview with David Broder, *Washington Post*, Sept. 6, 1987.

669 **"The hell he wasn't":** Robert McFarlane, interview with author, Apr. 18, 2015.

669 **"We must say something":** Oval Office meeting, Nov. 10, 1986, Alton Keel notes, Vol. 14, Appendix B, Testimony, U.S. Senate Select Committee on Secret Military Assistance to Iran and the Nicaraguan Opposition, 1987, RRPL; Select Committee documents.

670 **"We didn't sell them":** Edwin Meese, interview with author, July 20, 2015.

670 **an official statement:** "Our policy of not making . . . " *New York Times*, Nov. 11, 1986.

670 **"a major foreign relations blunder":** Senator Robert Byrd, quoted in David Hoffman, "Reagan Denies Paying Ransom for Hostages," *Washington Post*, Nov. 14, 1986.

670 **In any case, leaders:** Senator Patrick Leahy, quoted in David Hoffman, "Mission Meant to Aid Iran Factions, Reagan Says," *Washington Post*, Nov. 13, 1986.

670 **Subpoenas were already being discussed:** "House Democratic Leader Jim Wright advised Chairman Lee Hamilton to issue subpoenas where subpoenas are called for." George J. Church, "Unraveling Fiasco," *Time*, Nov. 24, 1986, p. 21.

670 **"There'd be heads on stakes":** Oliver North, quoted in Peter Wallison, interview, MCPA, Oct. 28, 2003, p. 85.

670 **"a completely made-up story":** Peter Wallison, interview, MCPA, Oct. 28, 2003, p. 89.

671 **John Poindexter subsequently advised:** "The president is accepting John's position on this, and he doesn't want to disclose more than they've already disclosed." Don Regan, quoted in Peter Wallison, interview, MCPA, Oct. 28, 2003, p. 85.

671 **"The charge has been made":** "Remarks by President Reagan Regarding U.S.–Iranian Relations," transcript, Nov. 13, 1986, Briefing ID: 17121, RRPL.

671 **"less than the full story":** Church, "Unraveling Fiasco."

671 **"the arms may have included":** Hoffman, "Reagan Denies Paying Ransom."

671 **"Get the message out":** Richard Nixon, quoted in Jane Mayer and Doyle McManus, *Landslide: The Unmaking of the President, 1984–1988* (Boston: Houghton Mifflin, 1988), p. 307.

671 **An ABC News poll:** Walter Pincus, "Reagan Ordered Casey to Keep Iran Mission from Congress," *Washington Post*, Nov. 15, 1986; White House News Summary, Nov. 13, 1986, RRPL.

672 **And George Shultz, under:** *Face the Nation*, Nov. 16, 1986, CBS News, transcript, pp. 7–12; Office of the Press Secretary, RRPL.

672 **"I don't know what's gotten":** Don Regan, quoted in Larry Speakes with Robert Pack, *Speaking Out* (New York: Chas. Scribner's Sons, 1988), p. 292.

672 **"Some of us are like":** Bernard Weinraub, "Criticism on Iran and Other Issues Put Reagan's Aides on Defensive," *New York Times*, Nov. 16, 1986.

673 **Shultz's "public pouting":** William Casey, memo to RR, Nov. 23, 1986, quoted in Shultz, *Turmoil and Triumph*, p. 837.

673 **"I'm not firing anybody":** RR, quoted in *New York Times*, Nov. 25, 1985.

673 **"for the first time":** AAL, p. 48.

674 **"was about as bad":** Peter Wallison, interview, MCPA, p. 87.

674 **Only a week earlier:** "The information provided by Mr. Reagan did not seem to mesh with that issued earlier." Bernard Gwertzman, "Confusion Over Iran," *New York Times*, Nov. 20, 1986.

674 **"The conflict of pretension":** Anthony Lewis, "Abroad at Home," *New York Times*, Nov. 20, 1986.

675 **"deceived and lied to":** Shultz, *Turmoil and Triumph*, p. 828.

675 **"a long, tough discussion":** George Shultz, quoted in Report of the Congressional Committees Investigating the Iran-Contra Affair, p. 298.

675 **"The President seemed puzzled":** Donald T. Regan, *For the Record: From Wall Street to Washington* (San Diego: Harcourt Brace Jovanovich, 1988), p. 37.

675 **"He refused to recognize":** Shultz, *Turmoil and Triumph*, p. 832.

675 **"The President is in the hands":** Abraham Sofaer, quoted in Ibid., p. 836.

676 **An agitated Don Regan:** When Poindexter told Regan that the written chronology was incorrect and he wanted it back, Regan said, "You mean you guys can't get the story straight?" Donald Regan, interview, May 17, 1989, LCA, p. 17.

676 **"getting his arms around":** Iran-Contra Affair Report, p. 305.

676 **"make sure we have a coherent":** Edwin Meese, interview with author, July 20, 2015.

676 **a "shredding party":** Oliver North to Robert McFarlane, Nov. 21, 1986, quoted in McFarlane testimony, Report of the Congressional Committees Investigating the Iran-Contra Affair, May 11, 1987.

676 **"R.R. directed operation to proceed":** Oliver North, quoted in Mayer and McManus, *Landslide*, p. 327.

676 **"Holy Jesus! Look at this":** William Bradford Reynolds, quoted in Mayer and McManus, *Landslide*, p. 333.

677 **"$2 million will be used":** Oliver North, memo to John Poindexter, "Release of American Hostages in Beirut," Apr. 4, 1986, Iran-Contra Affair Report, p. 225.

677 **"It was like putting gasoline":** Edwin Meese, interview with author, July 20, 2015.

677 **The "wily renegade":** Rochard Stengel, "Hard Fall for a Man of Action," *Time*, Dec. 8, 1986.

677 **"He said nothing about":** Ibid.

678 **The closest he came:** "Admiral Poindexter was the point of contact with the President." Mayer and McManus, *Landslide*, p. 338.

678 **"In theory, I knew the president":** John Poindexter, interview with author, Dec. 9, 2014.

678 **"sitting on a nuclear bomb":** William Bradford Reynolds, quoted in Mayer and McManus, *Landslide*, p. 340.

678 **"The phrase," he recounted:** Regan, *For the Record*, p. 37.

678 **"horror, horror, horror":** Donald Regan, deposition , July 15, 1987.

678 **"We're facing a problem here":** Donald Regan, quoted in Peter Wallison, interview, MCPA, Oct. 28, 2003, p. 86; Peter J. Wallison, *Ronald Reagan* (Boulder, CO: Westview, 2003), p. 196.

678 **"the headline version"**: Edwin Meese, interview with author, July 20, 2015.

678 **"Yes, I did"**: Meese described the confrontation using stronger language, which Poindexter disputes. The description here combines their accounts: Edwin Meese, interview with author, July 20, 2015, and John Poindexter, email to author, Sept. 9, 2017.

678 **"was in a steamy"**: Shultz, *Turmoil and Triumph*, p. 838.

679 **"North and Poindexter would"**: Ibid.

679 **"His fault was he"**: Donald Regan, interview, Feb. 2, 1990, LCA, p. 15.

679 **He suggested that the president:** Lou Cannon, *President Reagan: The Role of a Lifetime* (New York: Simon & Schuster, 1991), p. 701.

679 **"a smoking gun"**: RR, diary entry, Nov. 24, 1986.

680 **"In the old Navy tradition"**: RR, diary entry, Nov. 25, 1986.

680 **"He thought North had done"**: Peter Wallison, interview, MCPA, Oct. 29, 2003, p. 92.

680 **"a liar" and "a fantasist"**: "He doesn't know the difference between reality and fantasy." Ibid., p. 90.

680 **"He is a national hero"**: Hugh Sidey, "An Interview with President Ronald Reagan," *Time*, Dec. 8, 1986.

680 **He was still blaming:** "This whole thing boils down to a great irresponsibility on the part of the press." Ibid.; "We were right in what we were doing, and it was only the press that was to blame for calling it into question." RR to George Shultz, Nov. 24, 1986, quoted in Shultz, *Turmoil and Triumph*, p. 838.

680 **"They were like a circle"**: RR, diary entry, Nov. 25, 1986.

681 **New polls were published:** Richard J. Meislin, "Poll Rating Dives," *New York Times*, Dec. 2, 1986.

681 ***Wall Street Journal*/NBC News poll:** White House News Summary, Dec. 5, 1986, RRPL.

681 **And the president's private pollster:** RR, diary entry, Dec. 1, 1986.

681 **"The administration is in disarray"**: Richard Reeves, *President Reagan: The Triumph of Imagination* (New York: Simon & Schuster, 2005), p. 369.

681 **"Your Presidency, sir, is teetering"**: Daniel Patrick Moynihan, Nov. 29, 1986, quoted in Gerald M. Boyd, "Reagan Tells U.S. Not to Overlook Issues Beyond Iran," *New York Times*, Nov. 30, 1986.

681 **"Reagan has surrounded himself"**: Editorial, *Philadelphia Daily News*, Nov. 25, 1986.

681 **Bob Dole urged recalling:** "Dole Urges Recalling Congress for Inquiry," *Washington Post*, Dec. 1, 1986.

681 **"a furtive 43-year-old"**: George J. Church, "Who Was Betrayed?" *Time*, Dec. 8, 1986.

682 **The Israelis publicly denied:** Gerald F. Seib, "Israel's Role in the Arms Sale to Iran Puts It at Odds with Reagan, Congress," *Wall Street Journal*, Dec. 3, 1986.

682 **Covert payments to the Contras:** "Mr. Perot said in an interview yesterday that he gave $2 million in cash." John Walcott, "U.S. Is Said to Have Made Hostage Offer," *Wall Street Journal*, Dec. 3, 1986.

682 **"the first flight"**: James LeMoyne, "Secret El Salvador Flights: High Risk on a Low Budget," *New York Times*, Dec. 5, 1986.

682 **Failed ransom attempts were disclosed:** Walcott, "Hostage Offer."

682 **"Washington is awash"**: Daniel Patrick Moynihan quoted. "Reagan Tells U.S. Not to Overlook Issues Beyond Iran," Gerald M. Boyd, *New York Times*, Nov. 30, 1986.

683 **The "shovel brigade" comment:** "I was furious when I read that." NR/MT, p. 314.

683 **"I can't deal with that man"**: NR, quoted in KK/NR, p. 428.

683 **"He genuinely liked Don"**: James Kuhn, interview with author, Oct. 1, 2014; "Ronnie genuinely liked him, and they had a good rapport." NR/MT, p. 317.

683 **"privately polled large numbers"**: Wallison, *Ronald Reagan*, p. 207.

683 **"She was behind it all"**: James Kuhn, interview with author, Oct. 1, 2014.

683 **Orrin Hatch called:** "He did not protect the President. He did not inform the President." *Washington Post*, Dec. 6, 1986.

683 **George Bush tended to agree:** "I didn't want to say this on the phone, but I think Don should resign." George Bush to NR, quoted in NR/MT, p. 315.

683 **"You have a serious"**: Robert Strauss, quoted in Mayer and McManus, *Landslide*, p. 362.

684 **"Staff morale was very low"**: Peter Wallison, interview, MCPA, Oct. 29, 2003, p. 93.

684 **On December 1, Bud McFarlane:** Bernard Gwertzman, "'No Indication' to Doubt Reagan; Ex-Aide to Reagan is Said to Link Him to Early Iran Sale," *New York Times*, Dec. 5, 1986.

685 **"I don't think there is"**: Oliver North, quoted in Bernard Gwertzman, "2 Reagan Ex-Aides Maintain Silence in House Hearing," *New York Times*, Nov. 10, 1986.

685 **The Senate committee concluded:** Wallison, *Ronald Reagan*, p. 217.

685 **As late as three days:** George Shultz claims he revealed Casey's new negotiations to RR on Dec. 14, 1986, "and the president was astonished. . . . I have never seen him so mad." Shultz, *Turmoil and Triumph*, p. 851.

685 **"was deeply involved in"**: NR/MT, p. 323.

685 **"He's hurting Ronnie"**: NR, quoted in KK/NR, p. 430.

685 **"unwise as well as inhumane"**: Regan, *For the Record*, p. 66.

685 **"it was obvious that Casey"**: Ibid., p. 75.

686 **"Nancy made it clear"**: James Kuhn, interview with author, Dec. 19, 2013.

686 **"in a daze"**: "I had never seen him like that before." Shultz, *Turmoil and Triumph*, p. 863.

686 **In her memoir, Nancy Reagan:** "Ronnie and I just don't talk to each other that way." NR/MT, p. 324.

687 **"They should be court-martialed":** Shultz, *Turmoil and Triumph*, p. 863.

687 **"just didn't seem ready":** Ibid.

FORTY-THREE: RECLAIMING THE SPOTLIGHT

688 **"about what he knew":** "The purpose of the meeting was to explore these questions." Peter J. Wallison, *Ronald Reagan* (Boulder, CO: Westview, 2003), p. 226.

688 **"Put together some sequence":** RR, diary entry, Jan. 3, 1987.

689 **"Do you remember Bud":** Donald Regan, interview, May 17, 1989, LCA, Box 23, Folder 87, p. 15.

689 **"told her that January":** Donald T. Regan, *For the Record: From Wall Street to Washington* (San Diego: Harcourt Brace Jovanovich, 1988), p. 70.

689 **"an old man hiding behind":** Donald Regan, interview, May 17, 1989, LCA, p. 6.

690 **"She had CNN on":** James Kuhn, interview with author, Dec. 19, 2013; "The parts about abortion have got to come out." NR, quoted in Regan, *For the Record*, p. 77.

690 **"Look, this is wrong":** Donald Regan, interview, May 17, 1989, LCA, p. 6.

690 **And she had new targets:** "Don Regan had told me Nancy wanted to get Buchanan out of the White House." Lou Cannon, *President Reagan: The Role of a Lifetime* (New York: Simon & Schuster, 1991), p. 833.

691 **"I don't remember you talking":** NR, quoted in James Kuhn, interview with author, Dec. 19, 2013.

691 **"We were in the back":** Mark Weinberg, interview with author, July 8, 2014.

691 **"The President had completely buffaloed":** George P. Shultz, *Turmoil and Triumph: My Years as Secretary of State* (New York: Scribner, 1993), p. 868.

691 **Little did anyone know:** "I had put in his briefing book a copy of McFarlane's public testimony." Wallison, *Ronald Reagan*, p. 253.

692 **"surprised to learn":** Cannon, *President Reagan*, p. 709; Wallison, *Ronald Reagan*, p. 255.

692 **It reached a damning verdict:** David E. Rosenbaum, "Senators Charge a Web of Deceit in Iranian Affair," *New York Times*, Jan. 30, 1987.

693 **The night before he was:** Robert C. McFarlane with Sofia Smardz, *Special Trust* (New York: Cadell & Davies, 1994), pp. 14–16.

693 **"he had walked in the woods":** Peter Wallison, interview, MCPA, Oct. 29, 2003.

693 **"That's just bullshit":** RR, quoted in Ibid.

694 **"a chorus building up":** Donald Regan, interview, May 17, 1989, LCA, p. 6.

694 **"Whether Mr. Reagan leaves":** Gerald M. Boyd, "Reagan Is Facing Pivotal Week on Iran Scandal," *New York Times*, Feb. 23, 1987.

694 **"We can't have him talking":** Regan, *For the Record*, p. 90.

694 **"I've done a very bad thing":** Donald Regan, quoted in James Kuhn, interview with author, Dec. 19, 2013.

694 **her office leaked the details:** Jane Mayer, "Nancy Reagan's Behind-the-Scenes Maneuvering Stands Out in Circumstances of Regan's Ouster," *Wall Street Journal*, Mar. 2, 1987; "The First Lady Is No Longer Speaking to Regan." Lou Cannon, *Washington Post*, Feb. 18, 1987.

695 **"obsession with the release":** Report of the President's Special Review Board (Tower Commission), quoted in Steven V. Roberts, "Reagan Flustered, Tower Reports," *New York Times*, Feb. 28, 1987.

695 **"the President clearly did not":** John Tower, quoted in *New York Times*, Feb. 27, 1987.

695 **"detached style, in which considerable":** Roberts, "Reagan Flustered."

695 **"He especially should have ensured":** Tower Commission Report, part IV, p. 11.

695 **"I'm a delegator":** RR, quoted in Paul Laxalt, interview, May 22, 1989, LCA, p. 12.

696 **"over a million dollars":** Howard Baker, quoted in Jim Kuhn, *Ronald Reagan in Private* (New York: Sentinel, 2004), p. 209.

696 **During the flight, he grew:** "I'd been planning all the way up on the airplane to tell him I couldn't do it." Howard Baker, interview, May 22, 1989, LCA, Box 22, Folder 14, p. 13.

696 **"What am I doing here?":** Howard Baker, quoted in James Kuhn, interview with author, Oct. 1, 2014.

696 **"we've got a bad situation":** Cannon, *President Reagan*, p. 731.

696 **"No, George has got that":** RR, quoted in Paul Laxalt, interview, May 22, 1989, LCA, p. 15.

697 **"I deserve better treatment":** Reagan, *For the Record*, p. 97.

697 **president "badly shaken":** Howard Baker, interview, May 22, 1989, LCA, Box 22, Folder 14, p. 13; Landon Parvin, quoted in Cannon, *President Reagan*, p. 734.

697 **"can't delegate freely":** Paul Laxalt, quoted in Steven V. Roberts, "Reagan Is Asking Bipartisan Ideas to Help in Crisis," *New York Times*, Mar. 1, 1987.

697 **"that you are the President":** Howard Baker, interview, May 22, 1989, LCA, p. 14.

697 **"inattentive and inept":** James Cannon, quoted in Jane Mayer and Doyle McManus, *Landslide: The Unmaking of the President, 1984–1988* (Boston: Houghton Mifflin, 1988), p. ix.

697 **primarily to deal:** "Howard wanted Ken to come in to deal with Nancy Reagan so that he wouldn't have to deal with her." James Kuhn, interview with author, Oct. 1, 2014.

697 **"find out everything there is":** Howard Baker, interview, May 22, 1989, LCA, p. 16.

697 **"You don't want to be":** Howard Baker, quoted in A. B. Culvahouse, interview with author, Sept. 17, 2014.

697 **"He was still resisting":** A. B. Culvahouse, interview with author, Sept. 17, 2014.

698 "There wasn't supposed to be": RR, quoted in A. B. Culvahouse, interview with author, Sept. 17, 2014.

698 "He kept arguing that the arms": A. B. Culvahouse, interview with author, Sept. 17, 2014.

698 "We snuck Tower in": Stuart Spencer, interview with author, July 21, 2014.

699 "I think he privately": Paul Laxalt, quoted in Steven V. Roberts, "President Admits Error in Rejecting Warnings on Iran," *New York Times*, Mar. 15, 1987.

699 Overnight polls showed: CBS News showed a 9 percent improvement. White House News Summary, Mar. 4, 1987; Gerald M. Boyd, "President Asserts He Is Moving Away From Iran Affair," *New York Times*, Mar. 6, 1987.

699 "The President did": Editorial, *Washington Post*, Mar. 5, 1987.

699 *Newsweek*, however, reported: "Reagan's Day of Judgment," *Newsweek*, Mar. 9, 1987; "President Reagan's Speech Helped Him, But Only Slightly," *Newsweek*, Mar. 16, 1987.

699 "The most popular soap opera": NBC *Nightly News*, July 8, 1987.

699 how she stuffed incriminating: Fawn Hall, interview with author, Feb. 18, 2015.

700 And that Elliot Abrams: "North's $10 million mistake," *New York Times*, May 13, 1987.

700 two files on A.B. Culvahouse's: A. B. Culvahouse, interview with author, Sept. 17, 2014.

701 He didn't want a pardon: "A pardon implies guilt after the commission of a crime. I wasn't convicted of anything." Robert McFarlane, email to author, Sept. 19, 2017.

701 On March 18, 1987: "Deaver Charged with Perjury," *New York Times*, Mar. 22, 1987.

701 "went off track": NR/MT, p. 240.

701 "Mike, you've made": Ibid., p. 239.

701 It galled Deaver: Michael K. Deaver with Mickey Herskowitz, *Behind the Scenes* (New York: William Morrow & Co., 1987), p. 257.

702 "probably since the founding": Arthur Burns quoted. Cannon, *ROAL*, p. 801.

702 "I still have confidence": RR, quoted in A. B. Culvahouse, interview with author, Sept. 17, 2014.

702 "AIDS affects all of us": RR, speech, American Foundation for AIDS Research awards dinner, transcript, May 31, 1987, RRPL.

703 "I come here today": Gerald M. Boyd, "Raze Berlin Wall, Reagan Urges Soviets," *New York Times*, June 13, 1987.

704 "I think the spotlight": RR, quoted in Richard Reeves, *President Reagan: The Triumph of Imagination* (New York: Simon & Schuster, 2005), p. 402.

704 Polls showed that only: *New York Times*/CBS News poll, quoted in Bernard Weinraub with Gerald M. Boyd, "Reagan's Ability to Lead Nation at a Low, Critics and Friends Say," *New York Times*, June 28, 1987.

704 "More than ever": Weinraub, "Reagan's Ability to Lead Nation."

704 "General Secretary Shultz": RR, quoted in Thomas M. DeFrank, "Reagan: A Valedictory for an Old Soldier," *Newsweek*, Nov. 9, 1987.

704 "recent detachment and vagueness": Howard Baker, interview, May 22, 1989, LCA, p. 13.

704 was "failing—fast": "Cannon told Howard that the president wasn't in very good shape." Confidential source, interview with author.

704 "members of his staff": Douglas Martin, "James M. Cannon, an Adviser to Ford, Dies at 93," *New York Times*, Sept. 20, 2011.

704 "regardless of his own": Bill Clinton, quoted in Joan Biskupic and Fred Barbash, "Retired Justice Lewis Powell Dies at 90," *Washington Post*, Sept. 26, 1998.

704 Reagan intended to appoint: "We wanted to move the Court in the right direction—toward the Constitution." Edwin Meese, interview with author, Apr. 24, 2015.

705 "He is widely regarded": RR, quoted in *Washington Post*, July 1, 1987.

705 "Robert Bork's America": Senator Edward M. Kennedy, quoted in *Congressional Record*, U.S. Senate, 100th Congress, July 1, 1987, pp. 18518–18519.

705 "We will fight it": Benjamin Hooks, quoted in *Philadelphia Inquirer*, July 6, 1987.

705 "Robert Bork is a lawyer": "Judge Bork, the Senate and Politics," *New York Times*, July 2, 1987.

706 "I've passed over Bob Bork": RR, quoted in A. B. Culvahouse, interview with author, Sept. 17, 2014.

706 "What do you want to do": Kenneth Duberstein, interview with author, Oct. 1, 2014.

706 the roll-call vote: "Senate Roll-Call on the Bork Vote," *Associated Press*, Oct. 24, 1987.

706 more conservative than Bork: "The hard-core conservatives thought Ginsburg was one of their own." Howard Baker, interview, May 22, 1989, LCA, p. 12.

707 "I know him well": Edwin Meese, quoted in Kenneth Duberstein, interview with author, Oct. 1, 2014.

707 Right to Life supporters: Cannon, *President Reagan*, p. 810.

707 She'd also lied about winning: "Ginsburg's wife called me at the office. 'I said I won a beauty pageant, but in honesty I was runner-up.'" Kenneth Duberstein, interview with author, Oct. 1, 2014.

707 "on a few occasions": Douglas Ginsburg, quoted in Linda Greenhouse, "High Court Nominee Admits Using Marijuana and Calls It a Mistake," *New York Times*, Jan. 6, 1987.

707 "I don't see any reason": RR, diary entry, Nov. 5, 1987.

707 "he not only smoked": A. B. Culvahouse, interview with author, Sept. 17, 2014.

707 **"You're going to withdraw":** "I called Doug and he came in to see me." Kenneth Duberstein, interview with author, Oct. 1, 2014.

707 **"are in no mood":** Howard Baker, quoted in Ibid.

FORTY-FOUR: THE LONG GOODBYE

708 **"powered by consumer spending":** John M. Berry, "Underlying Flaws in Economy Mar Legacy of Reagan Years," *Washington Post*, Nov. 6, 1988.

708 **"a very, very nasty run":** John Kenneth Galbraith, quoted in Stephen Koepp, "How Ripe for a Crash," *Time*, Oct. 5, 1987.

708 **"the underlying economy remains":** RR, quoted by Marlin Fitzwater in George J. Church, "The Great Crash: Panic Grips the Globe," *Time*, Nov. 2, 1987.

708 **"just a correction":** RR, response to a reporter's question: "What do you think of the stock market, Mr. President?" Oct. 17, 1987, quoted in Richard Reeves, *President Reagan: The Triumph of Imagination* (New York: Simon & Schuster, 2005), p. 424.

709 **"His trust":** Lou Cannon, *President Reagan: The Role of a Lifetime* (New York: Simon & Schuster, 1991), p. 823.

709 **"I have great confidence":** "The Congress is responsible for the deficit." RR, quoted in *New York Times*, Oct. 22, 1987.

709 **"I will meet with":** RR, press conference, transcript, Oct. 22, 1987, RRPL; R. W. Apple Jr., *New York Times*, Oct. 23, 1987.

709 **"I promise you":** Thomas M. DeFrank, "Reagan: A Valedictory for an Old Soldier?" *Newsweek*, Nov. 9, 1987; "Stock market or no stock market, it was mainly Nancy, not Wall Street, I worried about." *AAL*, p. 695.

709 **"She went against all medical":** One of NR's physicians, quoted in KK/NR, p. 439.

709 **"I couldn't possibly lead":** NR, interview with Barbara Walters, *20/20*, ABC-TV, transcript, Mar. 4, 1988; Tamar Lewin, "Nancy Reagan Defends Her Decision to Have Mastectomy," *New York Times*, Mar. 5, 1985.

709 **"the best way":** NR/MT, p. 287.

710 **"Ronnie wept," she said:** Ibid., p. 294; "I just dropped my head and cried." *AAL*, p. 694.

710 **"making her prospects":** Michael Specter, "Mrs. Reagan Expected to Make Full Recovery," *Washington Post*, Oct. 19, 1987.

710 **"all but certain to leave":** DeFrank, "Reagan: A Valedictory."

710 **"Very soon after Howard":** Confidential source, interview with author, Oct. 2014.

710 **He also advocated:** Michael R. Gordon, "'Star Wars' Focus of Reagan Meeting," *New York Times*, Feb. 10, 1987.

710 **"The spirit of compromise":** Pat Buchanan, quoted in White House News Summary, Nov. 16, 1987, RRPL.

710 **George Shultz had a mandate:** "The President said he understood and agreed: we should go forward on START." George P. Shultz, *Turmoil and Triumph: My Years as Secretary of State* (New York: Scribner, 1993), p. 985.

711 **"a profound, historic shift":** Ibid., 1003.

711 **"Gorbachev just blinked":** Ibid., p. 1002; "The Soviets blinked": RR, diary entry, Oct. 27, 1987.

711 **"SDI was not realistic":** Soviet deputy foreign minister to George Shultz, quoted in Reeves, *President Reagan*, p. 440.

711 **"set the whole process":** Mikhail S. Gorbachev, *Memoirs* (New York: Doubleday, 1995), p. 443.

711 **A group of conservative senators:** Jacob V. Lamar Jr., "How to Wreck the Treaty," *Time*, Dec. 21, 1987.

711 **"nothing more than a useful":** Howard Phillips, quoted in unsigned editorial, *New York Times*, Dec. 11, 1987; Jacob V. Lamar Jr., "An Offer They Can Refuse," *Time*, Dec. 14, 1987.

712 **America's "intellectual disarmament":** George Will column, *Washington Post*, Dec. 11, 1987.

712 **a time set by Joan Quigley:** Selwa Roosevelt, *Keeper of the Gate* (New York: Simon & Schuster, 1990), p. 245.

712 **"perhaps with a second car":** *AAL*, p. 715.

712 **"These are the houses":** RR, quoted in Fred Ryan, interview, MCPA, May 25, 2004, p. 20.

712 **Reagan had always harbored:** "I wanted to take him up in a helicopter and show him how Americans lived." Ibid.; "President Reagan had repeatedly said that he wanted me to see different parts of the United States." Gorbachev, *Memoirs*, p. 446.

712 **"a proposal then current":** *AAL*, p. 698.

712 **"I'm not on trial here":** Mikhail Gorbachev, quoted in Thomas A. Sancton, "The Spirit of Washington," *Time*, Dec. 21, 1987; "Mr. President, you are not a prosecutor and I am not on trial here." Gorbachev, *Memoirs*, p. 447.

713 **A flush of embarrassment tided:** "Gorbachev colored." Shultz, *Turmoil and Triumph*, p. 1011.

713 **"We can't let this happen":** Howard Baker, quoted in Don Oberdorfer, *The Turn: The United States and the Soviet Union 1983–1988* (New York: Simon & Schuster, 1991), p. 263.

713 **"entering a new phase":** Mikhail Gorbachev, quoted Dec. 8, 1987, in White House Staff and Office Files, Executive Secretariat, NSC System files, 8791384, RRPL.

714 **"Mr. President, do what you":** Mikhail Gorbachev, quoted in Sancton, "Spirit of Washington"; Shultz, *Turmoil and Triumph*, p. 1014.

714 **"meet American people outside":** Gorbachev, *Memoirs*, p. 446.

714 **"sending out good vibes":** Sancton, "Spirit of Washington."

714 **"Stop the car!":** Mikhail Gorbachev, quoted in Oberdorfer, *The Turn*, p. 468.

714 **he said, "World peace"**: Maureen Dowd, "The Summit; as Gorby Works the Crowd, Backward Reels the K.G.B.," *New York Times*, Dec. 11, 1987.

714 **Reagan now had competition**: "The Soviet 'Great Communicator,'" *Christian Science Monitor*, Dec. 9, 1987.

714 *Time* **even named him**: "A symbol of hope for a new kind of Soviet Union." *Time*, Dec. 27, 1987.

714 **"In the art of deal making"**: Dowd, "The Summit."

715 **sooner if Reagan agreed**: "He feels that for them to withdraw, we've got to stop helping or arming the Mujahidin." RR, quoted in MI, Dec. 14, 1987, p. 168.

715 **"it was an evil empire"**: RR/AAL, p. 703.

715 **"This is not the time"**: RR, news conference, Feb. 24, 1988, quoted in Susan F. Rasky, "Reagan Supports Any Contra Help," *New York Times*, Feb. 25, 1988.

715 **"We are afraid"**: Stephen Kinzer, "Sandinistas and Rebels Discuss Cease-Fire Details," *New York Times*, Mar. 29, 1988.

716 **Only a week earlier**: Philip Shenson, "North, Poindexter and 2 Others Indicted in Iran Contra Fraud and Theft Charges," *New York Times*, Mar. 17, 1988.

716 **"I have no knowledge"**: George Lardner Jr. and Joe Pichirallo, "Poindexter, North 2 Others Indicted in Iran-Contra," *Washington Post*, Mar. 17, 1988.

716 **"He just pleaded guilty"**: "'Careless Remark' Begets Another in Reagan's Talk with Reporters," Associated Press, Mar. 17, 1988.

717 **"Panama had been helpful"**: John Poindexter, interview with author, Dec. 8, 2014.

717 **"screw[ing] around with the gringo"**: Shultz, *Turmoil and Triumph*, p. 1062.

717 **Reagan promised that**: "Reagan Asserts U.S. Won't Invade Panama," *New York Times*, Mar. 25, 1988.

717 **"we should sit back"**: George Bush, quoted in Shultz, *Turmoil and Triumph*, p. 1063.

717 **"If we back away"**: Shultz, *Turmoil and Triumph*, p. 1063.

718 **"Reagan is a weakened president"**: Paul Weyrich, quoted in Lou Cannon, "More Than Teflon and Tinsel," *Washington Post*, Dec. 7, 1987.

718 **"He was the first"**: AAL, p. 707.

719 **Reagan knew as early as**: "We wouldn't be able to sign the START treaty in Moscow." Ibid., p. 705; "He told me in a February 25 interview . . . 'the time is too limited.'" Cannon, *President Reagan*, p. 782.

719 **"We want to build contacts"**: Mikhail Gorbachev, quoted in George J. Church, "A Gentle Battle of Images," *Time*, June 13, 1988.

719 **"excruciating legal and social limbo"**: Jacob V. Lamar Jr., "The Lonely World of a Refusenik," *Time*, June 6, 1988.

720 **"the Ziemans would never"**: Cannon, *President Reagan*, p. 784.

720 **"I never expected to be here"**: RR, quoted in Hugh Sidey, "Ronald Reagan: Good Chemistry," *Time*, June 13, 1988.

720 **"dropped into a grand"**: RR, quoted in Lou Cannon and Don Oberdorfer, "The Scripting of the Moscow Summit," *Washington Post*, June 9, 1988.

720 **"that if word got out"**: Memocon 8890497, White House Staff and Office files, Executive Secretariat, National Security Council, May 29, 1988, p. 3, RRPL.

720 **"This isn't something"**: AAL, p. 706.

721 **"did not want to kick"**: Sidey, "Ronald Reagan."

721 **"There are too many lists"**: Mikhail Gorbachev, notes from press corps pool report, quoted in Cannon, *President Reagan*, p. 783.

721 **The only unscripted event**: "Before we left Washington, Ron had said to me, 'Try to get out, Mom. . . . See the Arbat and get a feel for the people.'" NR/MT, p. 359.

721 **"It was amazing how quickly"**: RR, diary entry, May 29, 1988.

721 **"They were generally indistinguishable"**: AAL, p. 709.

721 **"appeared out of nowhere"**: Church, "A Gentle Battle."

721 **"I've never seen"**: AAL, p. 709.

721 **"It's still a police state"**: RR, quoted in Church, "A Gentle Battle."

722 **"Political leadership in a democracy"**: RR, address quoted in Sidey, "Ronald Reagan."

722 **"tired of living in a fishbowl"**: NR, quoted KK/NR, p. 449.

722 **"It rejuvenated him"**: Marlin Fitzwater, quoted in KK/NR, p. 451.

723 **"enveloped by influence peddling"**: "Panel Charges Pierce Steered Funds to Friends," *Los Angeles Times*, Nov. 2, 1990.

723 **"More than anything else"**: RR, acceptance speech, Republican National Convention, Detroit, July 17, 1980.

724 **"There is a widespread sense"**: Charles Fisher, quoted in David S. Broder, "The Decade of Patchy Prosperity," *Washington Post*, Dec. 10, 1989.

724 **"the American miracle"**: RR, final address to nation, transcript, Jan. 11, 1989, RRPL.

724 **"Reagan was very clear"**: Kenneth Duberstein, interview with author, June 16, 2014.

724 **Despite the President's insistence**: "The First Lady opposes a pardon lest it tarnish her husband's place in history." "North: A Reprieve for Reagan's 'Hero'?" *Newsweek*, Dec. 5, 1988.

725 **George Steinbrenner was a different**: "Guilty Pleas in Campaign Gift Case," *San Francisco Chronicle*, Aug. 24, 1974.

725 **"She thought he was a boor"**: A. B. Culvahouse, interview with author, Sept. 17, 2014.

726 **"virtually all of life's"**: AAL, p. 722.

726 **"today the world is calm"**: Colin Powell, quoted in Fred Ryan, interview, MCPA, May 25, 2004, p. 14.

727 **"Here, boys," Reagan said:** Kenneth Duberstein, interview with author, June 16, 2014.

727 **a "nostalgic moment":** RR, quoted in Lee May and Laurie Becklund, "Citizen Reagans Are Home After Bittersweet Farewell," *Los Angeles Times*, Jan. 21, 1989.

727 **"I was trying to keep":** George Bush, quoted in Tom Shales, "The Gaffes, the Glories, and a Short Goodbye," *Washington Post*, Jan. 21, 1989.

727 **"There is a man here":** George Bush's inaugural address, Jan. 20, 1989, transcript, The American Presidency Project, UC–Santa Barbara.

728 **"Look, honey, there's our little":** Kenneth Duberstein, interview with author, June 16, 2014; Fred Ryan, interview with author, May 13, 2015; RR substitutes word "shack" for "cottage" in *AAL*, p. 724.

728 **"It was very much":** Fred Ryan, interview, MCPA, May 25, 2004, p. 15.

728 **"Oh, Ronnie—just *look*":** NR, quoted in Fred Ryan, interview with author, May 13, 2015.

728 **What he looked forward to:** Fred Ryan, interview with author, May 13, 2015.

729 **"*Four more years!*":** Shales, "The Gaffes, the Glories."

729 **"Then home," he recorded:** RR, diary entry, Jan. 20, 1989.

FORTY-FIVE: AN ORDINARY CITIZEN

730 **"I'm out to pasture now":** "He'd always say 'I'm out to pasture now' when asked about issues like the 22nd Amendment." Fred Ryan, interview with author, May 13, 2015.

730 **"California was the only place":** Joe Frisco, quoted in *WTROM*, p. 70.

730 **"temporary custody of the United States":** RR, speech at LAX, transcript, Jan. 20, 1989, RRPL.

730 **"If I could do this":** *AAL*, p. 119.

731 **There were a lot of lovely:** Joanne Drake, interview with author, Feb. 23, 2015.

732 **"But it had incredible views":** Fred Ryan, interview with author, May 13, 2015.

732 **"Any time you want":** Ibid.

732 **the line-item veto:** "He drove us nuts with the line-item veto." Joanne Drake, interview with author, Feb. 23, 2015.

732 **"I want to see":** RR, quoted in Ibid.

732 **"We were preparing the office":** Joanne Drake, interview with author, Mar. 30, 2015.

733 **"Every day on the way":** Jon Hall, interview with author, Feb. 8, 2016.

734 **"We didn't know what to do":** Mark Weinberg, interview with author, Apr. 28, 2015.

735 **"We had a roomful of sacks":** Joanne Drake, interview with author, Feb. 23, 2015.

736 **"A book is the last thing":** RR, quoted in KK/NR, p. 459.

736 **"getting the monkey off":** RR, quoted in Mark Weinberg, interview with author, July 8, 2014.

736 **"He was of that generation":** Joanne Drake, interview with author, Feb. 23, 2015.

736 **Virginia Mayo and Eddie Bracken:** Mark Weinberg, interview with author, July 8, 2014.

737 **"I once saw him":** Doug Wick, interview with author, Feb. 9, 2015.

737 **"There are an awful lot":** "More than once I heard him say in the Oval Office . . . " Mark Weinberg, interview with author, Apr. 28, 2015.

737 **"He felt as if":** Joanne Drake, interview with author, Feb. 23, 2015.

738 **Reagan planned to resist:** David Johnston, "Reagan Objects to Appearing as Witness for North," *New York Times*, Mar. 30, 1989.

739 **"Just answer 'yes' or 'no'":** Fred Ryan, interview, MCPA, May 25, 2004, p. 20.

739 **Bud McFarlane had already testified:** "Reagan made the call and the ammunition reached the rebels." Also, "The memo [for the air-drop], from North to McFarlane, was marked 'President approves.'" Both quotes in Ed Magnuson, "Did He Lie?" *Time*, Mar. 27, 1989.

739 **North's defense suggested the president:** David Johnston, "North Trial Challenges Image of Aloof Reagan," *New York Times*, Mar. 20, 1989.

739 **"This is where I restore":** Robert Ajemian, "Where the Skies Are Not Cloudy," *Time*, Jan. 5, 1981.

739 **"the wildness of the place":** Ibid.

740 **"Reagan loved to drive":** John Barletta, interview with author, Apr. 1, 2015.

741 **whose "attractive honorarium":** Charles Wick, quoted in Steven R. Weisman, "Japan Bids Welcome (in 7 Figures) to Reagan," *New York Times*, May 10, 1989, p. 7.

741 **"bucked wildly several times":** Mark Weinberg, quoted in "Reagan Is Injured in Fall Off Horse," Robert Pear, *New York Times*, July 5, 1989.

741 **"He landed quite hard":** Carl Janisch, interview with author, Oct. 13, 2014.

742 **"The one thing he made":** Fred Ryan, interview with author, May 13, 2015.

742 **"he was not quite himself":** "People who saw him there said he was not quite himself." Mark Weinberg, interview with author, July 8, 2014.

742 **"How good it is":** Vin Scully, quoted in Dave Anderson, "Reagan 'Uptight' in Booth," *New York Times*, July 12, 1989.

742 **"There is something wrong":** NR, quoted in Joanne Drake, interview with author, Mar. 30, 2015.

742 **"one burr hole roughly":** Lawrence K. Altman, "Reagan Faces Added Risk of Clot," *New York Times*, Sept. 12, 1989.

742 **"Nothing is without risk":** Mayo Clinic doctor, quoted in Mark Weinberg, interview with author, July 8, 2014.

742 **"I want to be able":** NR, quoted in Mark Weinberg, interview with author, July 8, 2014.

743 **"bring back decency"**: RR, quoted in Steven R. Weisman, "Reagan Sees Virtue in Sale of Studio to Sony," *New York Times*, Nov. 26, 1989.

743 **"Former Presidents haven't"**: "Ronald Reagan, Still Hiding," New York Times, Feb. 7, 1990, p. A24.

743 **the Victory Lap**: "That was the one we internally dubbed . . . " Fred Ryan, interview with author, May 13, 2015.

744 **"We furnished him with a chisel"**: Ibid.

745 **"It's just plain common sense"**: RR, address, George Washington University, Mar. 30, 1991.

745 **"He had given Jim"**: Mark Weinberg, interview with author, Apr. 28, 2015.

745 **"He was very moved"**: Doug Wick, interview with author, Feb. 9, 2015.

746 **"I'm not interested in"**: Elizabeth Glaser, quoted in Mark Weinberg, interview with author, Apr. 28, 2015.

747 **"It was surreal"**: Joanne Drake, interview with author, Mar. 30, 2015.

747 **"a political prophet"**: George Bush, Ronald Reagan Presidential Library dedication, Nov. 4, 1991, quoted in Robert Reinhold, "4 Presidents Join Reagan in Dedicating His Library," *New York Times*, Nov. 5, 1991; George Skelton and Bill Stall, "Nostalgic Ceremony Opens Reagan Library," *Los Angeles Times*, Nov. 5, 1991.

747 **"our best hope to build"**: RR, dinner address to New Hampshire Conservative Political Victory Fund, Feb. 8, 1992, quoted in Steven V. Holmes, "Reagan Endorses Bush as 'Best Hope' for Nation," *New York Times*, Feb. 9, 1992.

747 **"[Bush] doesn't seem to stand"**: "The former president later denied ever making the remark." RR, quoted, "Reagan and Bush: Call It a Snub," *Newsweek*, Mar. 9, 1992.

748 **"personally and very hard"**: Joanne Drake, interview with author, Mar. 30, 2015.

748 **"intrigued, even fascinated"**: Fred Ryan, interview with author, May 13, 2015; "President Reagan was actually a little bit fascinated, almost intrigued." Fred Ryan, interview, MCPA, May 25, 2004, p. 22.

749 **"throwing a snappy 'high ball'"**: Charles Doe, "After a Ragged Start, President Bill Clinton Has Finally . . . " UPI, Apr. 2, 1993.

749 **Still, Reagan encouraged him**: "He stood up and showed him how to salute. 'You'll never go wrong,' he told Clinton." Joanne Drake, interview with author, Mar. 30, 2015.

749 **"the hand had to come up"**: Nancy Gibbs and Michael Duffy, "Secrets of the Presidents' Club: How Bill Clinton Learned to Salute," *Time*, Apr. 17, 2012.

FORTY-SIX: "THE SUNSET"

750 **"He was seated in the chair"**: Richard V. Allen, interview, MCPA, May 28, 2002, p. 68.

750 **"He always knew when"**: Joanne Drake, interview with author, Mar. 30, 2015.

750 **the president's annual checkup**: "Five of his doctors said the diagnosis had become apparent from checkups during the last year." Lawrence K. Altman, "Reagan's Illness Afflicts Millions in Varying Ways," *New York Times*, Nov. 7, 1994.

751 **"for a few years before"**: RR, quoted in Ibid.

751 **"he expected them to check"**: Lawrence K. Altman, "While Known for Being Forgetful, Reagan Was Mentally Sound in Office, Doctors Say," *New York Times*, Oct. 5, 1997.

751 **he raised his glass**: Edmund Morris, *Dutch* (New York: Random House, 1999), p. 656.

751 **"He couldn't acclimate"**: Fred Ryan, interview with author, May 13, 2015.

751 **"something didn't seem quite right"**: Fred Ryan, interview, MCPA, May 25, 2004, p. 28.

751 **"Which way are we leaving"**: Ibid.

752 **He related how Nixon**: Hugh Sidey, "Richard Nixon: Fanfare for an Uncommon Man," *Time*, May 9, 1994.

752 **"George Bush told friends"**: Hugh Sidey, "Ronald Reagan: The Sunset of my Life," *Time*, Nov. 14, 1994.

752 **"We're seeing memory loss"**: Ibid.

752 **"now forgets the punch lines"**: Lawrence K. Altman, "Reagan Discloses His Alzheimer's," *New York Times*, Nov. 13, 1994.

752 **"I have this condition"**: RR, quoted in Patti Davis, "The Faces of Alzheimer's," *Time*, Sept. 26, 2002.

752 **"She was quite upset"**: Fred Ryan, interview with author, May 13, 2015.

754 **"He made it clear"**: Fred Ryan, interview, MCPA, May 25, 2004, p. 30.

754 **He called up the image**: Ibid.

755 **"for my own self amusement"**: Maureen Dowd, "Reagan Burnishes Image with Soulful Harmonica," *New York Times*, Apr. 3, 1994.

755 **"He was really taken"**: Joanne Drake, interview with author, Mar. 30, 2015.

755 **"still fairly coherent"**: Edward Rowney, interview, MCPA, May 17, 2006, p. 19.

755 **"final letting go"**: Morris, *Dutch*, p. 666; "Dad seemed to relinquish himself to the disease." Ron Reagan, *My Father at 100* (New York: Viking, 2011), p. 220.

755 **In any case, John Barletta**: John Barletta, interview with author, Apr. 1, 2015.

755 **"She ached for him"**: Doug Wick, interview with author, Feb. 9, 2015.

755 **"was often wandering somewhere"**: Reagan, *My Father at 100*, p. 8.

756 **"There's a game"**: Ibid., p. 141.

756 **Friends were no longer invited**: "Well, now we don't have visitors." NR, quoted in "Reagan's Condition Worsening, Wife Says," *New York Times*, Dec. 19, 1999.

756 **"He was sort of there"**: Ron Reagan, interview with Larry King, *Larry King Live*, June 23, 2004, transcript.

756 **"Ronnie's long journey":** NR, quoted in Johanna Neuman, "Former President Reagan Dies at 93," *Los Angeles Times*, June 6, 2004.

756 **In early June, he stopped:** Reagan, *My Father at 100*, p. 193.

756 **"He hadn't opened his eyes":** Ron Reagan, interview with Larry King; "My father's eyes have not opened for days." Patti Davis, *The Long Goodbye* (New York: Alfred A. Knopf, 2004), p. 185.

756 **"free of care":** Reagan, *My Father at 100*, p. 193.

757 **"Ronald Reagan won America's respect":** George W. Bush, quoted in John M. Broder, "Reagan Remembered for Leadership and Optimism," *New York Times*, June 6, 2004.

757 **"Even when he was breaking":** John Kerry, quoted in David Von Drehle, "Ronald Reagan Dies," *Washington Post*, June 6, 2004.

757 **"Makeshift shrines of flags":** Charlie LeDuff and John M. Broder, "Shrines Show Reagan's Reach," *New York Times*, June 7, 2004.

758 **committee of loyalists:** Elisabeth Bumiller and Elizabeth Becker, "Down to the Last Detail, a Reagan-Style Funeral," *New York Times*, June 8, 2004.

758 **From there, he was transferred:** "The streaking 747 was so far ahead of schedule that a swing over Tampico, IL, Reagan's birthplace, was wedged into the flight plan." Hugh Sidey, "The Gipper's Final Flight," *Time*, June 21, 2004.

758 **A squadron of twenty-one:** Todd S. Purdum, "The 40th President: A Return to Washington," *New York Times*, June 10, 2004.

759 **"Now there was a president":** "I looked out at the crowd and there was somebody holding a sign." Ron Reagan, interview with Larry King.

759 **"What I'd really like to do":** RR, quoted in Frank Pellegrini, "Reagan at 90: Still a Repository for Our American Dreams," *Time*, Feb. 6, 2001.

760 **"He had a moral clarity":** Tony Karon, "Ronald Reagan: 1911–2004," *Time*, June 5, 2004.

760 **"His most endearing aspect":** George P. Shultz, *Turmoil and Triumph: My Years as Secretary of State* (New York: Scribner, 1993), p. 1135.

761 **"every single overpass":** Ron Reagan, interview with Larry King.

BIBLIOGRAPHY

BOOKS

Abrams, Elliott. *Undue Process.* New York: Free Press, 1992.

Abrams, Herbert L. *The President Has Been Shot.* New York: W. W. Norton, 1992.

Ackerman, Frank. *Reaganomics: Rhetoric vs. Reality.* Boston: South End Press, 1982.

Adams, Harold. *History of Eureka College.* Henry, IL, 1982.

Adelman, Kenneth L. *The Great Universal Embrace, Arms Summitry—A Skeptic's Account.* New York: Simon & Schuster, 1989.

———. *Reagan at Reykjavik: The Weekend That Ended the Cold War.* New York: Broadside Books, 2014.

Aldous, Richard. *Reagan and Thatcher: The Difficult Relationship.* New York: W. W. Norton, 2012.

Armstrong, Scott, and Peter Grier. *Strategic Defense Initiative: Splendid Defense or Pipedream.* New York: Foreign Policy Association, 1986.

Armstrong, Scott, Malcolm Byrne, and Tom Blanton. *Secret Military Assistance to Iran and the Contras: A Chronology of Events and Individuals.* Washington, DC: National Security Archive, 1987.

Anderson, Janice. *The Screen Greats: Ronald Reagan.* New York: Exeter Books, 1982.

Anderson, Martin. *Revolution.* San Diego: Harcourt Brace Jovanovich, 1988.

Anderson, Martin, and Annelise Anderson. *Reagan's Secret War: The Untold Story of His Fight to Save the World from Nuclear Disaster.* New York: Three Rivers Press, 2009.

———. *Ronald Reagan: Decisions of Greatness.* Stanford, CA: Hoover Institution, 2015.

Attali, Jacques. *Verbatim I: Chronique des Années, 1981–1986.* Paris: Robert Laffont, 1993.

Bagley, William T. *California's Golden Years: When Government Worked and Why.* Berkeley, CA: Berkeley Public Policy Press, 2009.

Barbas, Samantha. *The First Lady of Hollywood: A Biography of Louella Parsons.* Oakland: University of California Press, 2005.

Bardwell, H. C. *History of Lee County.* Chicago: Munshell Publishing Co., 1881.

Barletta, John R., with Rochelle Schweitzer. *Riding with Reagan: The White House to the Ranch.* New York: Citadel Press, 2005.

Barone, Michael. *Our Country: The Shaping of America from Roosevelt to Reagan.* New York: Free Press, 1990.

Barrett, Laurence. *Gambling with History: Ronald Reagan in the White House.* New York: Doubleday, 1983.

Bartlett, Bruce R. *Reaganomics: Supply-Side Economics in Action.* New York: Quill, 1982.

Behlmer, Rudy. *Inside Warner Bros. (1935–1951).* New York: Viking, 1985.

Beilenson, Anthony C. *Looking Back: A Memoir, Vol. II: The California Years.* Privately published, 2012.

Benson, Harry. *The President and Mrs. Reagan: An American Love Story.* New York: Abrams, 2003.

Berman, Larry, ed. *Looking Back on the Reagan Presidency.* Baltimore: Johns Hopkins University Press, 1990.

Birdwell, Michael. *Celluloid Soldiers: Warner Bros.'s Campaign Against Nazism.* New York: NYU Press, 1999.

Bjork, Rebecca S. *The Strategic Defense Initiative.* New York: State University of New York Press, 1992.

Blumenthal, Sydney. *The Permanent Campaign.* New York: Simon & Schuster, 1980.

Blumenthal, Sidney, and Thomas Byrne Edsall. *The Reagan Legacy.* Pantheon Books, 1988.

Bohn, Michael. *The Achille Lauro Hijacking: Lessons in Politics and Prejudice of Terrorism.* Washington, DC: Brassey's, 2004.

Bonner, Raymond. *Weakness and Deceit.* New York: Times Books, 1984.

Bosch, Adriana. *Reagan: An American Story.* New York: TV Books, 2000.

Boyarsky, Bill. *The Rise of Ronald Reagan.* New York: Random House, 1968.

———. *Ronald Reagan: His Life and Times.* New York: Random House, 1981.

Boyer, Paul, ed. *Reagan as President.* Chicago: Ivan R. Dee, 1990.

Boykin, John. *Cursed Is the Peacemaker.* Belmont, CA: Applegate Press, 2002.

Bradlee, Ben Jr. *Guts and Glory: The Rise and Fall of Oliver North.* New York: Donald J. Fine, 1988.

Brands, H. W. *Reagan: The Life.* New York: Doubleday, 2015.

Brinkley, Douglas. *The Boys of Pointe du Hoc: Ronald Reagan, D-Day, and the U.S. Army 2nd Ranger Battalion.* New York: William Morrow, 2005.

Broder, David S., and Stephen Hess. *The Republican Establishment.* New York: Harper and Row, 1967.

Bronner, Ethan. *For Justice: How the Bork Nomination Shook America.* New York: W. W. Norton, 1989.

Brown, Warren. *The Chicago Cubs.* New York: G. P. Putnam's Sons, 1946.

Brownlee, W. Elliot, and Hugh Davis Graham, eds. *The Reagan Presidency*. Lawrence: University Press of Kansas, 2003.

Brownstein, Ronald, and Nina Easton. *Reagan's Ruling Class: Portraits of the President's Top 100 Officials*. Washington, DC: Presidential Accountability Group, 1982.

Bush, George, with Victor Gold. *Looking Forward*. New York: Doubleday, 1987.

Cagney, James. *Cagney by Cagney*. Garden City, NY: Doubleday, 1976.

Cannon, Lou. *Ronnie and Jesse: A Political Odyssey*. Garden City, NY: Doubleday, 1969.

———. *Governor Reagan: His Rise to Power*. New York: Public Affairs, 2003.

———. *President Reagan: The Role of a Lifetime*. New York: Simon & Schuster, 1991.

———. *Reagan*. New York: G. P. Putnam's Sons, 1982.

Carney, John P., and William M. Alexander, eds., *California and United States Governments*. Dubuque, IA: W. C. Brown, 1967.

Carter, Jimmy. *Keeping Faith: Memoirs of a President*. New York: Bantam, 1988.

Ceplair, Larry, and Steven Englund. *The Inquisition in Hollywood: Politics in the Film Community, 1930–60*. Urbana, IL: University of Chicago Press, 1979.

Cockburn, Andrew. *The Threat: Inside the Soviet Military Machine*. New York: Random House, 1983.

Cogley, John. *Report on Blacklisting, 1*. New York: Fund for the Republic, 1956.

Colacello, Bob. *Ronnie and Nancy: Their Path to the White House—1911 to 1980*. New York: Warner Books, 2004.

Cordiner, Ralph. *New Frontiers for Professional Managers*. New York: McGraw-Hill, 1956.

Coyne, John R., *The Impudent Snobs: Agnew vs. the Intellectual Establishment*. New Rochelle, NY: Arlington House, 1972.

Cunningham, Doug. *Hap Arnold, Warner Bros. and the Formation of the USAAF First Motion Picture Unit*. Typescript provided to the author.

Dalgleish, Major Charles. *Recon Marine: An Account of Beirut and Grenada*. Detroit: Harlo Press, 1995.

Dallek, Matthew. *The Right Moment: Ronald Reagan's First Victory and the Decisive Turning Point in American Politics*. New York: Free Press, 2000.

Dallek, Robert. *Ronald Reagan: The Politics of Symbolism*. Cambridge, MA: Harvard University Press, 1984.

Darman, Richard. *Who's in Control?: Polar Politics and the Sensible Center*. New York: Simon & Schuster, 1996.

Davis, Kathy Randall. *But What's He REALLY Like?* Menlo Park, CA: Pacific Coast Publishers, 1970.

Davis, Loyal. *A Surgeon's Odyssey*. Garden City, NY: Doubleday, 1973.

Davis, Patti. *The Long Goodbye*. New York: Alfred A. Knopf, 2004.

———, with Maureen Strange Foster. *Home Front*. New York: Crown, 1986.

Davis, William W. *History of Whiteside County, IL: From Its Earliest Settlement to 1908*. Chicago: Pioneer Publishing, 1908.

Deaver, Michael K. *A Different Drummer: My Thirty Years with Ronald Reagan*. New York: HarperCollins, 2001.

———. *Nancy: A Portrait of My Years with Nancy Reagan*. New York: William Morrow, 2004.

———, with Mickey Herskowitz. *Behind the Scenes*. New York: William Morrow, 1987.

Dickenson, Burrus. *History of Eureka, Illinois*. Eureka, IL: privately published, 1985.

Dickenson, Mollie. *Thumbs Up: The Life and Courageous Comeback of White House Press Secretary James Brady*. New York: William Morrow, 1987.

Dickey, Christopher. *With the Contras*. New York: Simon & Schuster, 1986.

Dobrynin, Anatoly. *In Confidence: Moscow's Ambassador to America's Six Cold War Presidents (1962–1986)*. New York: Crown, 1995.

Doder, Dusko, and Louise Branson. *Gorbachev: Heretic in the Kremlin*. New York: Viking, 1990.

Doherty, Thomas. *Projections of War: Hollywood, American Culture, and World War II*. New York: Columbia University Press, 1993.

Draper, Theodore. *A Very Thin Line: The Iran-Contra Affairs*. New York: Hill and Wang, 1991.

Drew, Elizabeth. *American Journal: The Events of 1976*. New York: Random House, 1977.

Dugger, Ronnie. *On Reagan: The Man and His Presidency*. New York: McGraw-Hill, 1983.

Dunne, Father George H. *Hollywood Labor Dispute: A Study in Immorality*. Los Angeles: Conference Publishing, undated.

Dunne, Philip. *Take Two*. New York: McGraw-Hill, 1980.

Edwards, Anne. *Early Reagan: The Rise to Power*. New York: William Morrow, 1987.

———. *The Reagans: Portrait of a Marriage*. New York: St. Martin's Press, 2003.

Edwards, Lee. *Reagan: A Political Biography*. Columbus, IN: Viewpoint Books, 1967.

Ehrgott, Roberts. *Mr. Wrigley's Ball Club: Chicago and the Cubs During the Jazz Age*. Lincoln: University of Nebraska Press, 2013.

Eig, Jonathan. *Ali*. New York: Houghton Mifflin Harcourt, 2017.

Eliot, Marc. *Reagan: The Hollywood Years*. New York: Harmony Books, 2008.

Erickson, Paul D. *Reagan Speaks: The Making of an American Myth*. New York: NYU Press, 1985.

Evans, Rowland, and Robert Novak. *The Reagan Revolution*. New York: Dutton, 1981.

Evans, Thomas W. *The Education of Ronald Reagan: The General Electric Years*. New York: Columbia University Press, 2006.

Farrell, John A. *Tip O'Neill and the Democratic Century*. Boston: Little, Brown, 2001.

Felber, Ron. *Presidential Lessons in Leadership*. Lanham, MD: Hamilton Books, 2011.

Ferguson, Thomas, and Joel Rogers, eds. *The Hidden Election: Politics and Economics in the 1980 Presidential Campaign.* New York: Pantheon, 1981.

Ferraro, Geraldine, with Linda Bird Francke. *My Story.* New York: Bantam, 1985.

FitzGerald, Frances. *Way Out There in the Blue: Reagan and Star Wars and the End of the Cold War.* New York: Simon & Schuster, 2000.

Flynn, Errol. *My Wicked, Wicked Ways: The Autobiography of Errol Flynn.* New York: G. P. Putnam's Sons, 1959.

Ford, Gerald R. *A Time to Heal.* New York: Harper & Row, 1979.

Gabler, Neal. *An Empire of Their Own: How the Jews Invented Hollywood.* New York: Crown, 1988.

———. *Winchell: Gossip, Power and the Culture of Celebrity.* New York: Alfred A. Knopf, 1994.

Garrison, Winfred Ernest, and Alfred T. DeGroot. *The Disciples of Christ: A History.* Bloomington, MN: Bethany Press, 1948.

Germond, Jack W., and Jules Witcover. *Blue Smoke and Mirrors: How Reagan Won and Why Carter Lost the Election of 1980.* New York: Viking, 1981.

———. *Wake Us When It's Over.* New York: Macmillan, 1985.

Goalstone, Jodi. *Holmes Tuttle: His Life and Legacy.* Self-published by Tuttle family, no date.

Goldman, Peter, and Tony Fuller. *The Quest for the Presidency.* New York: Bantam, 1985.

Goldwater, Barry. *With No Apologies.* New York: Berkley, 1981.

Goodman, Walter. *The Committee: The Extraordinary Career of the House Committee on Un-American Activities.* New York: Farrar, Straus & Giroux, 1968.

Gorbachev, Mikhail S. *Memoirs.* New York: Doubleday, 1995.

———. *Perestroika.* New York: HarperCollins, 1987.

———. *At the Summit.* New York: Richardson, Steirman & Black, 1988.

Grande, Peggy. *The President Will See You Now: My Stories and Lessons from Ronald Reagan's Final Years.* New York: Hachette Books, 2017.

Greider, William. *The Education of David Stockman and Other Americans.* New York: Signet, 1986.

Grimm, Charlie. *Jolly Cholly's Story: Baseball, I Love You!* Chicago: Regnery, 1968.

Gutman, Roy. *Banana Diplomacy: The Making of American Policy in Nicaragua 1981–1987.* New York: Simon & Schuster, 1988.

Haig, Alexander. *Caveat: Realism, Reagan, and Foreign Policy.* New York: Scribner, 1984.

Hamilton, Gary, and Nicole Woolsey Biggart. *Governor Reagan, Governor Brown: A Sociology of Executive Power.* New York: Columbia University Press, 1984.

Hammel, Eric. *The Root: The Marines in Beirut, August 1982–February 1984.* San Diego: Harcourt Brace Jovanovich, 1985.

Haney, Lewis. *How You Really Earn Your Living.* Englewood Cliffs, NJ: Prentice Hall, 1952.

Hannaford, Peter. *The Reagans: A Political Portrait.* New York: Coward-McCann, 1983.

———. *Reagan's Roots: The People and Places That Shaped His Character.* Bennington, VT: Images from the Past, 2012.

Harmetz, Aljean. *Round Up the Usual Suspects.* New York: Orion, 1993.

Haslam, Jonathan. *The Soviet Union and the Politics of Nuclear Weapons in Europe, 1969–1987.* Ithaca, NY: Cornell University Press, 1990.

———, Henry. *Economics in One Lesson.* New York: Pocket Books, 1948.

Hersh, Seymour. *The Target Is Destroyed.* New York: Random House, 1986.

Hertsgaard, Mark. *On Bended Knee: The Press and the Reagan Presidency.* New York: Farrar, Straus & Giroux, 1988.

Higham, Charles. *Hollywood at Sunset: The Decline and Fall of the Most Colorful Empire Since Rome.* New York: Saturday Review Press, 1972.

———. *Merchant of Dreams: Louis B. Mayer, M.G.M., and the Secret Hollywood.* New York: Donald I. Fine, 1993.

Hirschhorn, Clive. *The Warner Bros. Story.* New York: Crown, 1979.

Holmes, Raymond. *Raymond Holmes: His Family and Research with a Bang.* Richmond, VA: self-published, 1998.

Houseman, John. *Run-Through.* New York: Simon & Schuster, 1972.

Jamieson, Kathleen Hall. *Beyond the Double Bind: Women and Leadership.* New York: Oxford University Press, 1995.

Jones, Charles O., ed. *The Reagan Legacy: Promises and Performance.* Chatham, NJ: Chatham House Publishing, 1988.

Kelley, Kitty. *Nancy Reagan.* New York: Simon & Schuster, 1991.

Kengor, Paul. *God and Ronald Reagan.* New York: HarperCollins, 2004.

Kengor, Paul, and Patricia Clark Doerner. *The Judge: William P. Clark, Ronald Reagan's Top Hand.* San Francisco: Ignatius Press, 2007.

Kent, Zachary. *Ronald Reagan: Fortieth President of the United States.* Encyclopedia of Presidents Series. Chicago: Children's Press, 1989.

Kirk, Russell. *The Conservative Mind.* Washington, DC: Regnery, 2001.

Kolata, Gina. *Flu: The Story of the Great Influenza Pandemic of 1918 and the Search for the Virus That Caused It.* New York: Farrar, Straus & Giroux, 1999.

Kornbluth, Peter, and Malcolm Byrne, eds. *The Iran-Contra Scandal: The Declassified History.* New York: New Press, 1993.

Kotkin, Joel, and Paul Grabowicz. *California Inc.* New York: Rawson Wade, 1982.

Kuhn, Jim. *Ronald Reagan in Private.* New York: Sentinel, 2004.

La Feber, Walter. *Inevitable Revolutions.* New York: W. W. Norton, 1993.

Lamb, George. *Dixon: A Pictorial History*. St. Louis: G. Bradley Publishing, 1987.

Laxalt, Paul. *Nevada's Paul Laxalt: A Memoir*. Reno, NV: Jack Bacon & Co., 2000.

Leamer, Laurence. *Make Believe: The Story of Nancy and Ronald Reagan*. New York: Harper & Row, 1983.

Ledeen, Michael A. *Perilous Statecraft*. New York: Scribner, 1988.

Lekwa, Verl L. *Bennett, Iowa and Inland Township*. Marceline, MO, 1983.

Levy, Emanuel. *George Cukor, Master of Elegance: Hollywood's Legendary Director and His Stars*. New York: William Morrow, 1994.

Levy, Peter B. *Encyclopedia of the Reagan-Bush Years*. Westport, CT: Greenwood Press, 1996.

Lewis, Monica, with Dean Lamanna. *Hollywood Through My Eyes: The Lives & Loves of a Golden Age Siren*. Brule, WI: Cable Publishing, 2011.

Link, William A. *Righteous Warrior: Jesse Helms and the Rise of Modern Conservatism*. New York: St. Martin's Press, 2008.

Livingstone, Neil C., and Terrell E. Arnold, eds. *Beyond the Iran-Contra Crisis*. New York: Lexington Books, 1988.

Marshall, Jonathan, Peter Drake Scott, and Jane Hunter. *The Iran Contra Connection*. Cheektowaga, NY: Black Rose Books, 1987.

Martin, David C., and John Walcott. *Best Laid Plans: The Inside Story of America's War Against Terrorism*. New York: Touchstone Press, 1988.

Massie, Suzanne. *Trust but Verify: Reagan, Russia and Me*. Rockland, ME: Maine Authors Publishing, 2013.

Matlock, Jack F., Jr. *Autopsy on an Empire*. New York: Random House, 1995.

———. *Reagan and Gorbachev: How the Cold War Ended*. New York: Random House, 2004.

Matthews, Chris. *Tip and the Gipper: When Politics Worked*. New York: Simon & Schuster, 2013.

Matzen, Robert. *Errol and Olivia: Ego and Obsession in Golden Era Hollywood*. Pittsburgh: Paladin Communications, 2010.

May, Larry, ed. *Recasting America: Culture and Politics in the Age of Cold War*. Chicago: University of Chicago Press, 1989.

Mayer, Jane, and Doyle McManus. *Landslide: The Unmaking of the President, 1984–88*. Boston: Houghton Mifflin, 1988.

McClelland, Doug. *Hollywood on Ronald Reagan: Friends and Enemies Discuss Our President, the Actor*. Winchester, MA: Faber and Faber, 1983.

McFarlane, Robert C., with Sofia Smardz. *Special Trust*. New York: Cadell & Davies, 1994.

McGirr, Lisa. *Suburban Warriors: The Origins of the New American Right*. Princeton, NJ: Princeton University Press, 2001.

Meese, Edwin, III. *With Reagan: The Inside Story*. Washington, DC: Regnery, 1992.

Menges, Constantine C. *Inside the National Security Council: The Making and Unmasking of Reagan's Foreign Policy*. New York: Touchstone, 1989.

Micklethwait, John, and Adrian Wooldridge. *The Right Nation: Conservative Power in America*. New York: Penguin, 2004.

Middendorf, J. William, II. *A Glorious Disaster: Barry Goldwater's Presidential Campaign and the Origins of the Conservative Movement*. New York: Basic Books, 2008.

Mitchell, Greg. *Tricky Dick and the Pink Lady: Richard Nixon vs. Helen Gahagan Douglas—Sexual Politics and the Red Scare*. New York: Random House, 1950.

Moldea, Dan E. *Dark Victory: Ronald Reagan, MCA, and the Mob*. New York: Viking, 1986.

Morella, Joe, and Edward Z. Epstein. *Jane Wyman*. New York: Delacorte, 1985.

Morris, Edmund. *Dutch*. New York: Random House, 1999.

Moynihan, Daniel Patrick. *Came the Revolution*. San Diego: Harcourt Brace Jovanovich, 1988.

Navasky, Victor. *Naming Names*. New York: Viking, 1980.

Neustadt, Richard E. *Presidential Power: The Politics of Leadership from FDR to Carter*. New York: Macmillan, 1980.

Nitze, Paul H. *From Hiroshima to Glasnost*. New York: Grove, 1989.

Nofziger, Lyn. *Nofziger*. Washington, DC: Regnery, 1992.

Noonan, Peggy. *What I Saw at the Revolution: A Political Life in the Reagan Era*. New York: Random House, 1990.

———. *When Character Was King*. New York: Penguin, 2002.

North, Oliver L., with William Novak. *Under Fire: An American Story*. New York: HarperCollins, 1991.

Noskin, Michael J. *Reagan and the Economy: The Successes, Failures and Unfinished Agenda*. San Francisco: Institute for Contemporary Studies, 1988.

Oberdorfer, Don. *The Turn: The United States and the Soviet Union 1983–1988*. New York: Simon & Schuster, 1991.

O'Brien, Michael J. *Irish Settlers in America*. Baltimore: Genealogical Publishing, 1979.

O'Brien, Pat. *The Wind at My Back: The Life and Times of Pat O'Brien*. Garden City, NY: Doubleday, 1964.

Olsen, Henry. *The Working-Class Republican: Ronald Reagan and the Return of Blue-Collar Conservatism*. New York: Broadside Books, 2017.

Palmer, B. J. *History in the Making*. Davenport, IA: privately published, 1957.

Palmer, Dave. *The Palmers*. Des Moines, IA: Bawden Press, 1977.

Palmer, John L., and Isabel V. Sawhill. *The Reagan Experiment*. Washington, DC: Urban Institute Press, 1982.

———. *The Reagan Record*. Pensacola, FL: Ballinger Publishing, 1984.

Parsons, Louella. *Tell It to Louella*. New York: G. P. Putnam's Sons, 1961.

Patrick, Curtis. *Reagan: What Was He Really Like?* Vol. 2. New York: Morgan James Publishing, 2013.

Paulsen, Duane. *Dixon, Illinois, and the Great War, 1917–1919*. Dixon, IL: privately published, 2013.

———. *Dixon and the Rock River*. Dixon, IL: privately published, 2012.

———. *A People's Legacy: History of the Dixon Public Library 1895–2004*. Dixon, IL: privately published, 2004.

Perlstein, Rick. *Before the Storm: Barry Goldwater and the Unmaking of the American Consensus*. New York: Hill and Wang, 2001.

———. *The Invisible Bridge: The Fall of Nixon and the Rise of Reagan*. New York: Simon & Schuster, 2014.

Petro, Joseph, with Jeffrey Robinson. *Standing Next to History*. New York: Thomas Dunne Books, 2005.

Phillips-Fein, Kim. *Invisible Hands: The Businessman's Crusade Against the New Deal*. New York: W. W. Norton, 2010.

Powdermaker, Hortense. *Hollywood: The Dream Factory*. Boston: Little, Brown, 1950.

Pye, Michael. *Moguls: Inside the Business of Show Business*. New York: Holt, Rinehart, Winston, 1980.

Quigley, Joan. *What Does Joan Say?: My Seven Years as White House Astrologer to Nancy and Ronald Reagan*. New York: Birch Lane Press, 1990.

Quirk, Lawrence J. *Fasten Your Seatbelts: The Passionate Life of Bette Davis*. New York: Penguin, 1990.

———. *Jane Wyman: The Actress and the Woman*. New York: Dembner Books, 1986.

Ranny, Austin, ed. *The American Elections of 1984*. Durham, NC: Duke University Press, 1985.

Raphael, Timothy. *The President Electric: Ronald Reagan and the Politics of Performance*. Ann Arbor: University of Michigan Press, 2009.

Reagan, Maureen. *First Father, First Daughter: A Memoir*. Boston: Little, Brown, 1989.

Reagan, Michael, with Joe Hyams. *On the Outside Looking In*. New York: Zebra Books, 1988.

Reagan, Nancy. *I Love You, Ronnie: The Letters of Ronald Reagan to Nancy Reagan*. New York: Random House, 2000.

Reagan, Nancy, with Bill Libby. *Nancy*. New York: William Morrow, 1980.

Reagan, Nancy, with William Novak. *My Turn: The Memoirs of Nancy Reagan*. New York: Random House, 1989.

Reagan, Ron. *My Father at 100*. New York: Viking, 2011.

Reagan, Ronald. *Speaking My Mind*. New York: Simon & Schuster, 1989.

———. *An American Life*. New York: Simon & Schuster, 1990.

Reagan, Ronald, with Douglas Brinkley, ed. *The Reagan Diaries: January 1981–October 1985*. New York: Harper, 2009.

———. *The Reagan Diaries: November 1985–January 1989*. New York: Harper, 2009.

Reagan, Ronald, with Jim Denney. *The Common Sense of an Uncommon Man: The Wit, Wisdom, and Eternal Optimism of Ronald Reagan*. Nashville, TN: Thomas Nelson, 1998.

Reagan, Ronald, with D. Erik Felten. *A Shining City*. New York: Simon & Schuster, 1998.

Reagan, Ronald, with Richard Hubler. *Where's the Rest of Me?* New York: Karz-Segil, 1981.

Reagan, Ronald, with Kiron K. Skinner, Annelise Anderson, and Martin Anderson, eds. *Reagan in His Own Hand*. New York: Free Press, 2001.

Reed, Thomas C. *The Reagan Enigma, 1964–1980*. Los Angeles: Figueroa Press, 2014.

Reeves, Richard. *Old Faces of '76*. New York, Harper & Row, 1976.

———. *President Reagan: The Triumph of Imagination*. New York: Simon & Schuster, 2005.

———. *The Reagan Detour*. New York: Simon & Schuster, 1985.

Regan, Donald T. *For the Record: From Wall Street to Washington*. San Diego: Harcourt Brace Jovanovich, 1988.

Roberts, Paul Craig. *Supply-Side Revolution: An Insider's Account of Policy-Making in Washington*. Cambridge, MA: Harvard University Press, 1984.

Robertson, Gilbert. *Reagan Remembered*. McLean, VA: International Publishers, 2015.

Roepke, William. *Economics of the Free Society*. New York: Harper, 1946.

Rolfe, Deette. *The Rock River Country of Northern Illinois*. Urbana: State of Illinois, Dept. of Registration and Education, 1929.

Roosevelt, Selwa. *Keeper of the Gate*. New York: Simon & Schuster, 1990.

Rosenfeld, Seth. *Subversives: The FBI's War on Student Radicals and Reagan's Rise to Power*. New York: Farrar, Straus & Giroux, 2012.

Ross, Murray. *Stars and Strikes: Unionization of Hollywood*. New York: Columbia University Press, 1941.

Ross, Steven J. *Hollywood Left and Right: How Movie Stars Shaped American Politics*. New York: Oxford University Press, 2011.

Rossiter, Clinton. *The American Presidency*. New York: New American Library, 1960.

Rusher, William A. *The Rise of the Right*. New York: William Morrow, 1984.

Saltoun-Ebin, Jason, ed. *The Reagan Files: The Untold Story of Reagan's Top-Secret Efforts to Win the Cold War*. Self-published, 2010.

———. *The Reagan Files, Vol. 2: Inside the National Security Council*. Self-published, 2012.

Sanford, Gregory, and Richard Vigilante. *Grenada: The Untold Story*. Lanham, MD: Madison Books, 1984.

Savage, David G. *Turning Right: The Making of the Rehnquist Supreme Court*. New York: John Wiley & Sons, 1992.

Scheer, Robert. *With Enough Shovels: Reagan, Bush and Nuclear War*. New York: Random House, 1982.

Schieffer, Bob, and Gary Paul Gates. *The Acting Presidency*. New York: Dutton, 1989.

Schwartz, Nancy Lynn, and Sheila Schwartz. *The Hollywood Writers' Wars*. New York: Alfred A. Knopf, 1982.

Sebetsyen, Victor. *Revolution 1989: The Fall of the Soviet Empire*. New York: Pantheon, 2009.

Secord, Richard V., and Jay Wurts. *Honored and Betrayed*. New York: Wiley, 1992.

Shadegg, Stephen. *What Happened to Goldwater?: The Inside Story of the 1964 Republican Campaign*. New York: Henry Holt, 1965.

Shirley, Craig. *Reagan Rising: The Decisive Years, 1976–1980*. New York: Broadside, 2017.

———. *Reagan's Revolution*. Nashville, TN: Thomas Nelson, 2005.

Shultz, George P. *Turmoil and Triumph*. New York: Scribner, 1993.

Sick, Gary. *October Surprise: America's Hostages in Iran and the Election of Ronald Reagan*. New York: Times Books, 1991.

Siegel, Don. *A Siegel Film: An Autobiography*. New York: Faber and Faber, 1993.

Skinner, Kiron. *Reagan in His Own Hand*. New York: Free Press, 2001.

Slosser, Bob. *Reagan Inside Out*. Waco, TX: World Books, 1984.

Smith, Hedrick. *The Power Game: How Washington Works*. New York: Ballantine Books, 1988.

Smith, William French. *Law and Justice in the Reagan Administration*. Stanford, CA: Hoover Institution Press, 1991.

Speakes, Larry, with Robert Pack. *Speaking Out*. New York: Chas. Scribner's Sons, 1988.

Spencer, J. W. *The Early Days of Rock Island and Davenport*. Chicago: privately published, 1942.

Stahl, Lesley. *Reporting Live*. New York: Simon & Schuster, 1999.

Steffgen, Kent H. *Here's the Rest of Him*. Reno, NV: Foresight Books, 1968.

Stevens, Frank. *The History of Lee County, Illinois*. Chicago: S. J. Clarke Publishing, 1914.

Stockman, David A. *A Triumph of Politics: Why the Reagan Revolution Failed*. New York: Harper & Row, 1986.

Strober, Deborah Hart, and Gerald S. Strober. *Reagan: The Man and His Presidency*. Boston: Houghton Mifflin, 1998.

Stuckey, Mary E. *Playing the Game: The Presidential Rhetoric of Ronald Reagan*. New York: Praeger, 1990.

Sullivan, George. *Ronald Reagan*. New York: Julian Messner, 1985.

Talbott, Strobe. *Deadly Gambits: The Reagan Administration and the Stalemate in Nuclear Arms Control*. New York: Alfred A. Knopf, 1984.

———. *The Russians and Reagan*. New York: Vintage, 1984.

Thomas, Bob. *Clown Prince of Hollywood: The Antic Life and Times of Jack L. Warner*. New York: McGraw-Hill, 1990.

Thomas, Tony. *The Films of Ronald Reagan*. New York: Citadel, 1980.

Thompson, Kenneth W., ed. *Leadership in the Reagan Presidency*. Lanham, MD: Madison Books, 1992.

Thompson, Marilyn W. *How Wedtech Became the Most Corrupt Little Company in America*. New York: Scribner, 1990.

Thurow, Lester C. *The Zero-Sum Society: Distribution and the Possibilities for Economic Change*. New York: Basic Books, 1980.

Timberg, Robert. *The Nightingale's Song*. New York: Simon & Schuster, 1995.

Todd, Richard. *Caught in the Act: The Story of My Life*. London: Hutchinson & Co., 1986.

Treverton, Gregory F. *Covert Action*. New York: Basic Books, 1987.

Tygiel, Jules. *Past Time: Baseball as History*. Oxford University Press, 2000.

U.S. News & World Report, eds. *The Story of Lieutenant Colonel Oliver North*. Washington, DC: *U.S. News & World Report*, 1987.

Vaughn, Stephen. *Ronald Reagan in Hollywood: Movies and Politics*. New York: Cambridge University Press, 1994.

Von Damm, Helene. *At Reagan's Side: Twenty Years in the Political Mainstream*. New York: Doubleday, 1989.

Wallison, Peter. *Ronald Reagan: The Power of Conviction and the Success of His Presidency*. New York: Basic Books, 2004.

Walsh, Lawrence E. *Firewall: The Iran-Contra Conspiracy and Cover-up*. New York: W. W. Norton, 1997.

Wanniski, Jude. *The Way the World Works: How Economics Fail—And Succeed*. New York: Basic Books, 1978.

Warner, Jack. *My First Hundred Years in Hollywood*. New York: Random House, 1964.

Weinberger, Caspar. *Fighting for Peace: Seven Critical Years in the Pentagon*. New York: Warner Books, 1990.

Weisberg, Jacob. *Ronald Reagan: The American Presidents Series: The 40th President, 1981–1989*. New York: Times Books/Henry Holt, 2016.

White, Patricia Meade. *The Invincible Irish*. Los Angeles: Pertola Press, 1981.

White, Theodore H. *America in Search of Itself: The Making of the President, 1956–1980*. New York: Warner Books, 1982.

———. *Breach of Faith: The Fall of Richard Nixon*. New York: Atheneum, 1975.

———. *The Making of the President, 1964*. New York: Atheneum, 1965.

Wilber, Del Quentin. *Rawhide Down: The Near Assassination of Ronald Reagan*. New York: Henry Holt, 2011.

Wilentz, Sean. *The Age of Reagan: A History, 1974–2008*. New York: Harper, 2008.

Wills, Garry. *Reagan's America*. Garden City, NY: Doubleday, 1985.

Witcover, Jules. *Marathon: The Pursuit of the Presidency, 1972–1976*. New York: Viking, 1977.

Woodward, Bob. *Veil: The Secret Wars of the CIA*. New York: Simon & Schuster, 1987.

Wright, Harold Bell. *That Printer of Udell's*. New York: A. L. Burt Co., 1902.

Wymbs, Norman. *Ronald Reagan's Crusade*. Peoria, IL: Skyline Publishing, 1997.

——. *Ronald Reagan and the Holy Spirit*. Oakland, CA: Elderberry Press, 2005.

JOURNALS AND ARCHIVAL PAPERS

Aaron, Benjamin I., and S. David Rockoff. "The Attempted Assassination of President Reagan: Medical Implications and Historical Perspective." *Journal of the American Medical Association* 272, no. 21, December 7, 1994.

——. "The Shooting of President Reagan: A Radiologic Chronology of His Medical Care," *Radiographics* 15, no. 2, March 1995.

Anderson, Totton J., and Eugene C. Lee. "The 1966 Election in California." *Western Political Quarterly*, June 1969.

Bent, Charles, and Robert L. Wilson, *History of Whiteside County, IL*. Morrison, IL, 1877. Full text online at archive.org.

Blue, Daniel. "The Thrilling Narrative of the Adventures, Suffering, and Starvation of Pike's Peak Gold Seekers on the Plains of the West in the Winter and Spring of 1859." Whiteside County, IL: U.S. District Court for the Northern District of Illinois, 1860 (typescript).

Boogie Man: The Lee Atwater Story. Interpositive Media, 2008.

California Journal archives. California State Library, Sacramento.

Coate, Robert. L. "Ronald Reagan, Extremist Collaborator—An Expose" (pamphlet). Democratic State Central Committee of California, Aug. 11, 1966.

Coleville's Galesburg (IL) Directory, 1915 16.

"Debate Between President Jimmy Carter and Governor Ronald Reagan" (transcript), Oct. 28, 1980. Cleveland: Finrcun-Mancini Court Reporters.

"Dixon Illinois" (pamphlet). Dixon Area Chamber of Commerce and Industry, undated.

Eureka College, Catalogs, 1928–1930.

"Eureka College Songs" (trifold pamphlet), c. 1928. Courtesy of Eureka College, Melic Library, Anthony Glass, archivist.

Gardiner, Gordon, ed. *Bread of Life*, vol. 30, no. 3. Brooklyn, NY: Ridgewood Pentecostal Church, May 1981.

Hearings of the House Committee on Un-American Activities, Eightieth Congress, 1947.

History of Carroll County. Chicago: H. F. Kitt & Co., 1878.

History of Dixon and Palmyra. Dixon Telegraph, Limited Sesquicentennial Edition, 1880. Dixon, IL: The Print Shop, 1980.

History of South Central, Los Angeles. southcentral-history.com.

Hogan, Terry. "O. T. Johnson's—the Dream Machine." www.thezephyr.com.

"Irish Ancestry of President Ronald Reagan: Fortieth President of the United States, The." Debrette Ancestry Service, undated.

"Jurisdictional Disputes in the Motion-Picture Industry." Hearings Before the Education and Labor Subcommittee, Eightieth Congress, 1947.

Lanoue, David J. "The 'Teflon Factor': Ronald Reagan and Comparative Presidential Popularity." *Polity* 21, no. 3, Spring 1989. University of Chicago Press.

Libertas. Young America's Foundation. Fifteenth Reagan Ranch Anniversary Issue, no date.

Marlow, Ron. "The First Christian Church and the Reagan Family, Vol. 1 (1920–1928)." Unpublished typescript.

——. "The First Christian Church and the Reagan Family, Vol. 2 (1929–1932)." Unpublished typescript.

Meese, Edwin. Papers. Hoover Institution, Stanford University.

"Michael Deaver Testimony." Michael Deaver, interview by Richard Darman, March 31, 1981. Miller Center of Public Affairs, University of Virginia, Ronald Reagan Oral History.

Morris, Edmund. Interviews of President Ronald Reagan, June 12, 1986–January 31, 1990 (indexed transcript). Courtesy of the Reagan Foundation.

National Security Archive.

Palmer School yearbook, 1929.

Parkinson, Gaylord, "Issues and Innovations in the 1966 Republican Gubernatorial Campaign," Oral History Center, University of California, Berkeley, 1980.

Pegasus, The. Eureka College newspaper.

Polk's Dixon City Directory, 1925 26. Chicago: Leshnick Directory Co., 1926.

Prism, The. Eureka College yearbook.

Public Papers of the Presidents of the United States, The: Ronald Reagan, National Archives, 1983 (all volumes online at the Ronald Reagan Presidential Library website).

Reagan, Nancy. Personal scrapbook. Stamped March 4, 1952, Ronald Reagan Public Library.

Reagan, Ronald, FBI Files, LA 100-15732 and LA 100-138754-314 and LA 100-138754-472, 11/14/1947; also LA-100-138754-513, 3/3/1949.

"Reagan's Dixon" (pamphlet). Dixon, IL: The Official Dixon Press, 1980.

"Remembering Ronald Reagan" (pamphlet). Dixon, IL: Loveland Museum, 2001.

"Report of the City Council Committee on Crime of the City of Chicago." Chicago: H. G. Adair Press, March 22, 1915.

"Report on the Performance of the United States Department of the Treasury in Connection with the March 30, 1981, Assassination Attempt on President Ronald Reagan" (draft). Washington, DC: Congressional Quarterly, July 2, 1981.

Report of the President's Special Review Board (Tower Report). Washington, DC: U.S. Government Printing Office, Feb. 26, 1987.

Robinson, John K. "Early Times at Dixon's Ferry." In Dr. Oliver Everett, *History of Dixon and Lee County, Chronological Record*. Dixon Telegraph Print, 1880.

Sacramento Bee 150-year headline timeline: 150th .mcclatchy.com.

Screen Actors Guild archives.

Story of the Screen Actors Guild, The. Membership pamphlet. Information Department of the Screen Actors Guild, June 1980.

Testimony at Joint Hearings, House Select Committee to Investigate Covert Arms Transactions with Iran and Senate Select Committee on Secret Military Assistance to Iran and the Nicaraguan Opposition, 12 volumes; and Appendixes, 27 volumes, 1987.

UCLA Center for Oral History Research, Special Collections, 1981.

Vincent, H. Ross, Jr. *An Historical Study of the Army Air Force's First Motion Picture Unit in World War II.* Master's thesis, USC, 1959.

Weather Underground. wunderground.com.

Whiteside County Highway Map. *Maps of Illinois Counties.* Warner & Beers, 1876.

IMAGE CREDITS

6 (bottom): Michael Evans, Ronald Reagan Presidential Foundation and Institute

15 (top): Jim Mone, AP Photo

15 (bottom): Pete Souza, Ronald Reagan Presidential Library

INDEX